The Routledge Handbook of Responsible Investment

The UN-supported Principles for Responsible Investment initiative has led to around a third of the world's financial assets being managed with a commitment to invest in a way that considers environmental, social or governance (ESG) criteria. The responsible investment trend has increased dramatically since the global financial crisis yet understanding of this field remains at an early stage.

This handbook provides an atlas of current practice in the field of responsible investment. With a large global team of expert contributors, the book explores the impact of responsible investment on key financial actors ranging from mainstream asset managers to religious organizations.

Offering students and researchers a comprehensive introduction to current scholarship and international structures in the expanding discipline of responsible investment, this handbook is vital reading across the fields of finance, economics and accounting.

Tessa Hebb is Director of the Carleton Centre for Community Innovation and Adjunct Professor at Carleton University, Canada.

James P. Hawley is Professor and Senior Research Fellow at the Elfenworks Center for the Study of Responsible Business at Saint Mary's College of California, USA.

Andreas G. F. Hoepner is Associate Professor of Finance at the ICMA Centre of Henley Business School, UK and Senior Academic Fellow at the United Nations supported Principles for Responsible Investment.

Agnes L. Neher is a PhD candidate at the University of Hohenheim, Germany and a Visiting Scholar with the University of St Andrews School of Management, UK.

David Wood is Adjunct Lecturer in Public Policy and the Director of the Initiative for Responsible Investment (IRI) at the Hauser Institute for Civil Society at the John F. Kennedy School of Government, Harvard University, USA.

Routledge Companions in Business, Management and Accounting

Routledge Companions in Business, Management and Accounting are prestige reference works providing an overview of a whole subject area or sub-discipline. These books survey the state of the discipline, including emerging and cutting edge areas. Providing a comprehensive, up-to-date, definitive work of reference, *Routledge Companions* can be cited as an authoritative source on the subject.

A key aspect of these *Routledge Companions* is their international scope and relevance. Edited by an array of highly regarded scholars, these volumes also benefit from teams of contributors which reflect an international range of perspectives.

Individually, *Routledge Companions in Business, Management and Accounting* provide an impactful one-stop-shop resource for each theme covered. Collectively, they represent a comprehensive learning and research resource for researchers, postgraduate students and practitioners.

Published titles in this series include:

The Routledge Companion to Fair Value and Financial Reporting
Edited by Peter Walton

The Routledge Companion to Nonprofit Marketing
Edited by Adrian Sargeant and Walter Wymer Jr.

The Routledge Companion to Accounting History
Edited by John Richard Edwards and Stephen P. Walker

The Routledge Companion to Creativity
Edited by Tudor Rickards, Mark A. Runco and Susan Moger

The Routledge Companion to Strategic Human Resource Management
Edited by John Storey, Patrick M. Wright and David Ulrich

The Routledge Companion to International Business Coaching
Edited by Michel Moral and Geoffrey Abbott

The Routledge Companion to Organizational Change
Edited by David M. Boje, Bernard Burnes and John Hassard

The Routledge Companion to Cost Management
Edited by Falconer Mitchell, Hanne Nørreklit and Morten Jakobsen

The Routledge Companion to Digital Consumption
Edited by Russell W. Belk and Rosa Llamas

The Routledge Companion to Identity and Consumption
Edited by Ayalla A. Ruvio and Russell W. Belk

The Routledge Companion to Public-Private Partnerships
Edited by Piet de Vries and Etienne B. Yehoue

The Routledge Companion to Accounting, Reporting and Regulation
Edited by Carien van Mourik and Peter Walton

The Routledge Companion to International Management Education
Edited by Denise Tsang, Hamid H. Kazeroony and Guy Ellis

The Routledge Companion to Accounting Communication
Edited by Lisa Jack, Jane Davison and Russell Craig

The Routledge Companion to Visual Organization
Edited by Emma Bell, Samantha Warren and Jonathan Schroeder

The Routledge Companion to Arts Marketing
Edited by Daragh O'Reilly, Ruth Rentschler and Theresa Kirchner

The Routledge Companion to Alternative Organization
Edited by Martin Parker, George Cheney, Valerie Fournier and Chris Land

The Routledge Companion to the Future of Marketing
Edited by Luiz Moutinho, Enrique Bigne and Ajay K. Manrai

The Routledge Companion to Accounting Education
Edited by Richard M.S. Wilson

The Routledge Companion to Business in Africa
Edited by Sonny Nwankwo and Kevin Ibeh

The Routledge Companion to Human Resource Development
Edited by Rob F. Poell, Tonette S. Rocco and Gene L. Roth

The Routledge Companion to Auditing
Edited by David Hay, W. Robert Knechel and Marleen Willekens

The Routledge Companion to Entrepreneurship
Edited by Ted Baker and Friederike Welter

The Routledge Companion to International Human Resource Management
Edited by David G. Collings, Geoffrey T. Wood and Paula Caligiuri

The Routledge Companion to Financial Services Marketing
Edited by Tina Harrison and Hooman Estelami

The Routledge Companion to International Entrepreneurship
Edited by Stephanie A. Fernhaber and Shameen Prashantham

The Routledge Companion to Non-Market Strategy
Edited by Thomas C. Lawton and Tazeeb S. Rajwani

The Routledge Companion to Cross-Cultural Management
Edited by Nigel Holden, Snejina Michailova and Susanne Tietze

The Routledge Companion to Financial Accounting Theory
Edited by Stewart Jones

The Routledge Companion to Ethics, Politics and Organizations
Edited by Alison Pullen and Carl Rhodes

The Routledge Companion to Management and Organizational History
Edited by Patricia Genoe McLaren, Albert J. Mills and Terrance G. Weatherbee

The Routledge Companion to Mergers and Acquisitions
Edited by Annette Risberg, David R. King and Olimpia Meglio

The Routledge Companion to Ethnic Market
Edited by Ahmad Jamal, Lisa Peñaloza and Michel Laroche

The Routledge Companion to Critical Management Studies
Edited by Anshuman Prasad, Pushkala Prasad, Albert J. Mills and Jean Helms Mills

The Routledge Handbook of Responsible Investment
Edited by Tessa Hebb, James P. Hawley, Andreas G. F. Hoepner, Agnes L. Neher and David Wood

The Routledge Handbook of Responsible Investment

Edited by Tessa Hebb, James P. Hawley, Andreas G. F. Hoepner, Agnes L. Neher and David Wood

Routledge
Taylor & Francis Group
LONDON AND NEW YORK

First published 2016
by Routledge
2 Park Square, Milton Park, Abingdon, Oxon OX14 4RN

Simultaneously published in the USA and Canada
by Routledge
711 Third Avenue, New York, NY 10017

Routledge is an imprint of the Taylor & Francis Group, an informa business

British Library Cataloguing in Publication Data
A catalogue record for this book is available from the British Library

Library of Congress Cataloging-in-Publication Data
The Routledge handbook of responsible investment / edited by
Tessa Hebb, James P. Hawley, Andreas G. F. Hoepner, Agnes L. Neher
and David Wood.—1 Edition.
pages cm — (Routledge companions in business, management
and accounting)
Includes bibliographical references and indexes.
1. Financial institutions—Investments. 2. Investments—Moral and
ethical aspects. 3. Social responsibility of business. I. Hebb, Tessa, editor.
HG1616.I5R685 2015
332.6—dc23
2015002977

ISBN: 978-0-415-62451-0 (hbk)
ISBN: 978-0-203-10441-5 (ebk)

Typeset in Bembo
by Apex CoVantage, LLC

MIX
Paper from responsible sources
FSC www.fsc.org FSC® C013056

Printed and bound in Great Britain by
TJ International Ltd, Padstow, Cornwall

Contents

List of figures *xii*
List of tables *xiv*
About the editors *xvi*
Notes on Contributors *xviii*
Acknowledgements *xxiv*

PART I

1 Introduction to *The Routledge Handbook of Responsible Investment* 3
Tessa Hebb, James P. Hawley, Andreas G. F. Hoepner, Agnes L. Neher and David Wood

2 Setting the scene: the basics and basis of responsible investment 16
James P. Hawley

3 Is responsible investment proportionally under-researched? 34
Andreas G.F. Hoepner, David G. McMillan and Michael Fraser

PART II

4 The responsible investment atlas – an introduction 53
Agnes L. Neher and Tessa Hebb

5 Responsible investment in the United States 58
Meg Voorhes

6 Responsible investment in Canada 70
Olaf Weber

7 Responsible investment in Mexico 81
Luisa Montes

8 Responsible investment in South America 86
Camila Yamahaki and Cinthia S. Gaban

9 Responsible investment in South Africa 99
Nadia Mans-Kemp and Suzette Viviers

10 Responsible investment in Nigeria 115
Innocent Okwuosa und Kenneth Amaeshi

11 Responsible investment in Tunisia 125
Kais Bouslah

12 Responsible investment in Israel: a case of regulatory-based development 138
Noga Levtzion Nadan

13 Responsible investment in Australia 149
Anna Young-Ferris and Louise O'Halloran

14 Responsible investment in China 166
Qian Li

15 Responsible investment in Hong Kong 182
Christine Chow

16 Responsible investment in Japan: a tale of two narratives 207
Kyoko Sakuma-Keck

17 Responsible investment in Russia 225
Yulia Sofronova

18 Responsible investment in Eastern Europe 233
Geoffrey Mazullo

19 Corporate social responsibility and responsible investment in Italy: an overview 243
Rocco Ciciretti, Annalisa Fabretti and Marco Nicolosi

20 Responsible investment in Spain 254
Luiz Ferruz Agudo, Jesus Gomez Daza and Sara Segura Querol

21 Responsible investment in France 262
Stéphanie Giamporcaro

22 Responsible investment in Austria, Germany and Switzerland 276
Agnes L. Neher

23 Responsible investment in Belgium 287
Céline Louche, Luc Van Liedekerke and Herwig Peeters

24 Responsible investment in the Netherlands 300
Heather Hachigan

25 Introduction to Scandinavia 313
Ane Jensen

26 Responsible investment in Denmark: practices among institutional investors in a context of statutory CSR reporting requirements 317
Karin Buhmann

27 Responsible investment in Finland 327
Antti Savilaakso

28 Responsible investment in Sweden 336
Sabina Du Rietz

29 Responsible investment in Norway 345
Ane Jensen

30 Responsible investment in the United Kingdom 355
Christoph Biehl and Jill Atkins

31 Reflection: responsible investment around the world 364
Maria Laura Tinelli

PART III

32 The changing role of asset owners in responsible investment: reflections on the principles for responsible investment – the last decade and the next 435
James Gifford

33 The responsible investment practices of the world's largest government-sponsored investment funds 444
Hugues Létourneau

34 Determining how to invest more responsibly as an institution: a case study at the University of Edinburgh 462
Liz Cooper

35 Religious investors and responsible investment 474
Laura Berry

36 Stakeholders of responsible investment: retail investors 485
Jonas Nilsson

37 Measuring the impact of engagement: evidence from Canadian institutional investors 494
Tessa Hebb, Heather Hachigian and Rupert Allen

38 Asset manager stakeholders: at the heart of supply and demand in responsible investment 510
Jean-Philippe Desmartin

39 Stakeholder perspective – investment consultants: 'the need to collaborate to ensure supply meets demand' 520
Danyelle Guyatt

40 Responsible investment indexes: origins, nature and purpose 527
Steve Lydenberg and Alexi White

41 Challenges in responsible investment research 536
Matthew Haigh

42 The natural environment 543
Ralf Barkemeyer and Andrea Liesen

43 What do we mean by the S in ESG? Society as a stakeholder in responsible investment 553
David Wood

44 Corporate governance research and ratings firms 565
Kimberly Gladman

PART IV

45 Contemporary issues in responsible finance and investment 575
Bert Scholtens

46 Addressing the challenges of transformation through sustainable investment 593
Gordon L. Clark, Heather Hachigian, Sarah McGill, Claire Molinari and Dariusz Wójcik

47 Overcoming distractions on the road to increased levels of ESG integration 610
Cary Krosinsky

48 Reliable sustainability ratings: the influence of business models on information intermediaries 620
Robert G. Eccles, Jock Herron and George Serafeim

49 Reclaiming pension fund fiduciary duty fundamentals — 632
James P. Hawley, Keith Johnson and Ed Waitzer

50 Governing fiduciary finance — 650
Benjamin J. Richardson

51 Socially responsible screening in mutual funds — 667
Jacquelyn Humphrey

52 Beyond outreach: corporate social responsibility and the financial performance of microfinance institutions — 677
Andreas G.F. Hoepner, Guan Huang and Hong (Frank) Liu

53 Financial markets' inefficiencies and long-term investments — 689
Sébastien Pouget

54 What matters to SRI investors? — 705
Peer Osthoff

Index — *725*

Figures

1.1	Growth of the Principles for Responsible Investment (©PRI)	8
2.1	Total assets under management and allocated to public equity	17
3.1–3.10	Evolution of aggregated research output estimations over time (1970–2008)	41
4.1	Responsible investment around the world	54
6.1	Sector distribution of the Canadian TSX 60	71
6.2	Two responsible investment strategies in Canada	72
7.1	Sustainability Index compared to main market index in Mexico	85
13.1	Australia's projected superannuation assets, 2012–2033	152
15.1	Vital factors that enable responsible investment to flourish	195
21.1	Assets managed by investment managers in the French RI non-segregated investment funds market	263
21.2	Institutional versus retail investors in France	269
21.3	French RI market asset allocation	270
22.1	RI strategies in Austria in 2012	278
22.2	RI strategies in Germany in 2012	280
22.3	RI strategies in Switzerland in 2012	282
25.1	PRI signatories and RI assets under management in Scandinavia	314
27.1	Number of companies in Finland and the total market value	329
27.2	Market value concentration of the largest companies in Finland in each sector	329
28.1	Swedish RI funds according to investment strategy	337
28.2	Types of asset classes in Sweden	339
29.1	Norway's GDP by sector of origin	347
29.2	Norwegian market evolution by strategy	349
29.3	Norwegian SRI market asset allocation	350
33.1	Regional division of fund sample	452
33.2	Frequency of GSIF scores on RI index	453
33.3	Regional frequency of GSIF scores on RI index	454
34.1	Types of respondents	467
34.2	Agreement with proposed principles to inform investment decisions	468
34.3	Popularity of strategic investment options	469
34.4	Agreement levels with investment view approach	471
35.1	Hierarchy of company engagement	481
42.1	Trends in broadsheet newspaper coverage	548

42.2	Trends in US and UK broadsheet coverage	549
42.3	Survey of RI practitioners (n = 149)	550
45.1	Number of articles in Scopus journals on 'responsible investment' (1973–2011)	576
45.2	Number of articles on 'responsible investment' by subject area (1973–2011)	577
45.3	Number of publications on 'responsible investment' in Scopus journals (1973–2011)	578
45.4	Keywords in publications on 'responsible investment' (1973–2011)	580
45.5	Composition of SRI in market centres as of 2011 based on total of $13,568 billion in responsible investments	583
45.6	Development of SRI in US and Eur-8	584
45.7	Composition of responsible investment strategies in Europe	586
45.8	Composition of responsible investment strategies in the US over time (1995–2009)	586
45.9	Responsible investment asset allocation (by per cent) in Europe (2009)	587
47.1	The Value of Everything	614
49.1	Relative priority on conflict of main fiduciary duties	639
54.1	Development of the SRI mutual fund market	710
54.2	Performance flow relationship	714

Tables

3.1 Aggregated research output estimations (1970–2009) 38
3.2 Distribution of the aggregated research output estimations across research quality scores (1970–2009) 40
3.3 Average annual research output estimations 44
3.4 Average annual growth rates of aggregated research output estimations (2000–8) 45
5.1 Assets under management in the United States 60
6.1 RI funds and assets under management in Canada 73
6.2 Impact investment assets in Canada 74
7.1 Comparison between the IPC main market indexes and Sustentable (Sustainability Index) in Mexico 83
7.2 RI stakeholders in Mexico 84
9.1 2011 mid-year population estimates for South Africa by gender and population group 100
9.2 Names for the RI phenomenon in South African academic literature (1997–2011) 101
9.3 Types of RI funds in South Africa 102
9.4 RI strategy used by fund managers of South African RI funds 103
9.5 Estimates of professional sustainable investment assets under management in South Africa on 31 December 2010 104
9.6 Key players in the South African financial markets 105
9.7 Legal provisions regarding ESG considerations in South Africa 106
9.8 South African PRI signatories 107
9.9 Summary of the most prominent ESG considerations in South Africa 110
10.1 Value of collective assets under management in Nigeria as of May 2014 117
10.2 Growth of ethical funds in Nigeria, 2011–2014 117
10.3 Ethical funds and their managers as of 9 May 2014 118
10.4 Proportion of RI asset classes by RI funds in Nigeria 119
10.5 Assets classes and growth of pension fund assets in Nigeria, 2011–2013 120
11.1 Overview of the Tunisian stock market 127
11.2 Tunisian RI funds 128
11.3 Tunisian RI mutual funds 129
11.4 ESG-related articles in the Constitution of the Republic of Tunisia (2014) 133
14.1 List of RI funds and ESG-themed funds in China 168
14.2 Historical landmarks of RI activities in China 170
14.3 List of ESG-themed indices in China 171

14.4	Policies promoting RI in China	173
15.1	Key players in responsible investment in Hong Kong	196
16.1	SRI concept and SIF Japan's endorsement	209
16.2	Focus of selected long-term actors based on mission, goals and investment principles in Japan	211
16.3	Declaration of Retail Investors, launched by Club Investlife® members, 14 January 2007	215
16.4	Most relevant information for selected long-term asset managers by Business Policy Forum Japan	219
19.1	Descriptive statistics of the Asset4 Rates for the Italian companies	249
19.2	Cumulative returns of the high- and low-ranked value-weighted portfolios	250
21.1	Investment vehicles in the French RI market	263
23.1	The RI market profile in Belgium for each portfolio manager, expressed in number of RI UCIs products and market share as of December 2011	290
23.2	Responsible savings in Belgium, 1984–2012	291
23.3	RI methodologies and criteria used in Belgium	295
23.4	Belgian RI products	298
23.5	Belgian organizations providing credits, microcredits, seed capital or cheap loans	299
27.1	Herfindahl index (Finland)	330
27.2	RI strategies in Finland	331
28.1	Demographic statistics of Sweden	336
28.2	Swedish RI funds according to investment strategy, 2009 versus 2011	338
33.1	Descriptive statistics	454
33.2	Results of regression of RI scores	455
36.1	Causes/issues that retail SR investors care about	489
42.1	The natural environment as a stakeholder of the company	544
45.1	Relationships between subject areas	581
46.1	Non-physical factors driving resource scarcity	595
48.1	Representative information intermediaries	624
49.1	Reclaiming fiduciary duties: key governing fiduciary issues	643
51.1	Five most widely used screens by mutual funds in different regions	668
51.2	The impact of specific screens on mutual fund performance	674
52.1	Social responsibility ratings and ROE of MFIs	683
52.2	Social responsibility ratings of FSS and MFIs	685
54.1	Summary statistics	709
54.2	Impact of the performance on net-inflows	713
54.3	Impact of the performance on net-inflows for sub-samples	716
54.4	Impact of the positive and negative rating on net-inflows	717
54.5	Impact of the positive and negative rating on net-inflows for sub-samples	718
54.6	Impact of single qualitative and exclusionary criteria on net-inflows	719

About the editors

Tessa Hebb (Senior Editor) is the Director of the Carleton Centre for Community Innovation, Carleton University, Canada, where she researches and teaches on Responsible Investment and Impact Investment and is funded by the Social Sciences and Humanities Research Council, Government of Canada. She received her Doctorate from Oxford University. She has published many books and articles on responsible investing and impact investing policies, including the volumes *Working Capital: The Power of Labor's Pensions*; *No Small Change: Pension Fund Corporate Engagement*; *The Next Generation of Responsible Investing*; and *SRI in the 21st Century: Does It Make a Difference to Society*?

James P. Hawley (Editor) is the Professor of Management, Saint Mary's College of California. He is the author of two books, *The Rise of Fiduciary Capitalism: How Institutional Investors Can Make Corporations More Democratic* and *Corporate Governance Failures: The Role of Institutional Investors in the Global Financial Crisis*, as well as co-editor of *The Cambridge Handbook of Institutional Investment and Fiduciary Duty*. He is the author (or co-author) of well over forty scholarly articles on a variety of topics, including corporate governance, responsible investment, the international monetary and financial system and environmental issues. He is also Chief ESG Strategist of TruValue Labs, a San Francisco, California start up which automates ESG uses big data to analyze responsible business data automatically.

Andreas G. F. Hoepner (Editor) is an Associate Professor of Finance at the ICMA Centre of Henley Business School and is currently also serving as the Senior Academic Fellow to the United Nations-supported Principles for Responsible Investment. His research has won several awards, including a 2012 Academy of Management Best Paper Proceeding. He is co-editor of the *Cambridge Handbook of Institutional Investment and Fiduciary Duty.* He is founding co-director of a social enterprise (Sociovestix Labs) and founding president of a charity (ReFine Research) that gives social reporting awards to pension funds. He currently serves on advisory boards for Bank J. Safra Sarasin and Corporate Knights Capital.

Agnes L. Neher (Editor) is a PhD candidate at the University of Hohenheim in Stuttgart, Germany. Her research focus lies on Responsible Investment, especially on the financial materiality of environmental, social and governance risks. Agnes is a member of the Promotionskolleg 'Soziale Marktwirtschaft' at the German Konrad-Adenauer-Stiftung.

David Wood (Editor) is an Adjunct Lecturer in Public Policy and the Director of the Initiative for Responsible Investment (IRI) at the Hauser Institute for Civil Society. Recent work has included the publication of the *Handbook on Responsible Investment across Asset Classes*, the development of a Responsible Property Investing Center and research into the investor use of corporate reporting on non-financial information. He was elected in 2008 to the Board of the Social Investment Forum. Before he came to the IRI, he taught the history of ethics, including the history of economic thought at Boston University. He received his PhD in History from the Johns Hopkins University.

Contributors

Rupert Allen is an economist working for the Federal Government of Canada on issues related to competition and foreign investment. He has an MA in Contemporary Art Theory from the University of Essex and is an Associate with the Carleton Centre for Community Innovation.

Kenneth Amaeshi (PhD) is a Reader in Strategy and International Business and the Director of the Sustainable Business Initiative at the University of Edinburgh Business School. He is currently leading an international research project on Africapitalism.

Jesus Ancizar Gomez is a doctoral candidate in Accounting and Finance at the University of Zaragoza in Spain. He has over 10 years' experience in financial institutions working in the areas of Financial Risk, Treasury and Financial and Administrative Management.

Jill Atkins is Professor of Accounting and Financial Management at Henley Business School, University of Reading, having previously been Professor of Corporate Governance and Accountability at King's College London, University of London.

Ralf Barkemeyer is Associate Professor at Kedge Business School, Bordeaux. Before joining Kedge, Ralf had lectureship positions at the Sustainability Research Institute, University of Leeds, and Queen's University Management School Belfast.

Laura Berry is the Executive Director of the Interfaith Center for Corporate Responsibility (ICCR), where she is responsible for ICCR's strategic leadership and the lead external representative for the organization.

Christoph Biehl is a doctoral researcher at Henley Business School. Previously he was the Project Manager for Asia at the Centre for Responsible Banking and Finance at University of St Andrews.

Kais Bouslah is a Lecturer in Banking and Finance at the University of St Andrews (since 2012). He received his PhD from the Université du Québec à Montréal, Canada.

Karin Buhmann, Dr.scient.adm., PhD (law), is an Associate Professor (CSR, Sustainability and Public-Private Regulation) at Copenhagen Business School (CBS) and a member of the Danish National Contact Point (NCP) under the OECD's Guidelines for Multinational Enterprises.

Christine Chow (PhD) has 16 years of experience in the investment management, research and hedge fund industry. She founded Homage Consulting Ltd in 2011 to promote sustainable and impact investment in Asia through industry consulting projects and academic work.

Rocco Ciciretti is an Assistant Professor of Economic Policy at the Department of Economics and Finance, University of Rome Tor Vergata. He was a Visiting Professor at New York University and Fordham University.

Gordon L. Clark is Director of the Smith School of Enterprise and the Environment, University of Oxford, and the Sir Louis Matheson Distinguished Visiting Professor, Faculty of Business and Economics, Monash University, Australia.

Liz Cooper is Research and Policy Manager in the University of Edinburgh's Department for Social Responsibility and Sustainability. She previously worked on supply chains and workers' rights initiatives in Senegal and India. She holds an MSc in Business and Community.

Jean-Philippe Desmartin is Head of ESG research at Oddo Securities since 2005. He is also the co-author of two books on Responsible Investment.

Sabina Du Rietz is Assistant Professor at the Norwegian School of Economics. She teaches Social and Environmental Accounting and Responsible Investment.

Robert G. Eccles is a Professor of Management Practice at the Harvard Business School and the founding chairman of the Sustainability Accounting Standards Board.

Annalisa Fabretti is an Assistant Professor at the University of Rome Tor Vergata. She earned her doctoral degree in Mathematics for Financial and Economics Application from Sapienza University of Rome in 2006.

Luis Ferruz (PhD) is a Professor at University of Zaragoza. He has published a large number of papers in the most important Spanish financial reviews and journals.

Michael Fraser is the Director of Technical Services for the New Zealand Institute of Chartered Accountants. He is a Chartered Accountant and previously a Senior Lecturer at Victoria University of Wellington.

Cinthia S. Gaban is a Brazilian national and the founder and partner of the Brazilian start-up Professores de Plantão. Previously, she worked as an ESG analyst at HSBC Global Asset Management in Brazil.

Stephanie Giamporcaro is the Research Director and a Senior Lecturer at the University of Cape Town Graduate School of Business. From 2003 to 2007 she was the Head of Responsible Investment Research for the French research think tank, Novethic.

James Gifford (PhD) is a Senior Fellow at the Initiative for Responsible Investment at the Harvard Kennedy School and Senior Advisor to Tau Investment Management. He was the founding

Executive Director of the Principles for Responsible Investment (PRI) and led the organization from inception to 2013.

Kimberly Gladman (CFA, PhD) is the Managing Director for Research at the Just Capital Foundation. Before joining Just Capital in 2013, Kimberly served for nearly six years as Research Director at GMI Ratings (formerly The Corporate Library).

Danyelle Guyatt is an independent researcher and consultant on long-term sustainable investment. She holds a PhD from the University of Bath, a MSc in Finance, and has 20 years' experience working in the finance industry.

Heather Hachigian is a DPhil candidate at the School of Geography and the Environment (Smith School of Enterprise and the Environment), University of Oxford.

Matthew Haigh uses field data obtained directly from investors, and identifies the symbolic significance of sustainability in the capital markets. He founded the *Journal of Sustainable Finance & Investment* and teaches accounting at SOAS, University of London.

Jock Herron is a Senior Research Associate in the Responsive Environments and Artifacts Lab at the Harvard Graduate School of Design where his primary focus is on food systems and sustainability. Earlier in his career, he was a senior managing director at a global banking firm.

Guan Huang obtained a MLitt in Finance and Management at the University of St Andrews in 2012, with a distinction-awarded master's thesis.

Jacquelyn Humphrey is a Senior Lecturer in Finance at the University of Queensland Business School, where her research focuses on Responsible Investment.

Ane Jensen is a Knowledge Network Manager within the Academic Network of the Principles for Responsible Investment (PRI), where she primarily finds new and relevant research for signatories in the field of responsible investment.

Keith Johnson chairs the Institutional Investor Services Group at Reinhart Boerner Van Deuren s.c. and is a Director of the Network for Sustainable Financial Markets.

Cary Krosinsky is Executive Director of the Network for Sustainable Financial Markets and teaches Business, Sustainability, and Investing courses at Yale University, Columbia University's Earth Institute and the University of Maryland Smith School of Business. Previously, he was Senior Vice President for Trucost.

Hugues Létourneau is Program Officer with the Shareholder Association for Research and Education in Vancouver, Canada, and research associate with the Carleton Centre for Community Innovation. He has a master's degree in International Affairs from Carleton University.

Noga Levtzion Nadan is the founder and CEO of Greeneye, the RI consultancy company in Israel. Noga has over 10 years of experience consulting on environmental and economic issues to policy-makers, the Israeli government, and the financial and business sectors.

Qian Li is a PhD candidate at ICMA Centre, University of Reading. She holds a master's degree in Banking and Finance from University of Newcastle Upon Tyne.

Andrea Liesen is a fellow at the Institute for Ecological Economic Research (GER). Prior to working as a Lecturer at the Umeå School of Business and Economics (SE), she received her PhD from the School of Earth and Environment at the University of Leeds.

Hong (Frank) Liu is a senior lecturer in Banking and Finance at University of Glasgow. He previously worked in the Bank of Communications, China, as Senior Foreign Exchange Trader and Credit Analyst.

Céline Louche is an Associate Professor at the Audencia Nantes School of Management. She teaches and researches in sustainability and corporate responsibility. Books include *Dilemmas for Responsible Investment* and *SRI in the 21st century: Does It Make a Difference for Society?*

Steve Lydenberg serves as Partner, Strategic Vision, for Domini Social Investments and is a Founding Director of the Initiative for Responsible Investment. He has authored several books and articles on responsible investment, including *Dilemmas in Responsible Investment.*

Nadia Mans-Kemp is a lecturer at the Department of Business Management at Stellenbosch University, South Africa. Her doctoral research focused on corporate governance and the financial performance of listed South African companies.

Geoffrey Mazullo is Principal of Emerging Markets ESG, an independent consultancy engaged in the promotion of ESG reporting in and about emerging markets, and an Adjunct Professor at the School of American Law (SAL) in Gdansk and in Wroclaw, Poland.

Sarah McGill is a research fellow at the Smith School of Enterprise and the Environment, University of Oxford. She received her doctorate from School of Geography and the Environment in 2015.

David G. McMillan is a professor of Finance at the University of Stirling. He is a co-editor for the journal *Economics and Finance Research.*

Claire Molinari is a Responsible Investment Analyst at Sarasin and Partner and Visiting Research Associate at the School of Geography and the Environment (Smith School of Enterprise and the Environment), University of Oxford.

Luisa Montes founded EcoValores, an independent research organisation specializing in environmental economics and sustainability assessments of Mexican companies. She holds two master's degrees, one from ITAM and another from the London School of Economics.

Marco Nicolosi is an Assistant Professor at the Department of Economics of the University of Perugia. He holds a PhD from the University of Rome Tor Vergata in Theoretical Physics.

Jonas Nilsson is an Assistant Professor of Marketing, School of Business, Economics and Law, University of Gothenburg, Sweden.

Louise O'Halloran is an independent adviser on impact investment, responsible investment and philanthropy. She was the Group Executive Director of the Responsible Investment Association Australasia (RIAA) for 11 years until the end of 2012.

Innocent Okwuosa (FCA, ACIB) is an investment adviser and is currently a doctoral researcher in Accounting at Henley Business School, University of Reading UK. He holds a master's degree (Distinction) from University of Stirling, Scotland.

Peer Osthoff is currently working as a financial supervisor. During his time as a research assistant at the University of Cologne and at the Centre of Financial Research he investigated questions concerning socially responsible investing.

Herwig Peeters is Managing Director and Auditor at Forum ETHIBEL, a Belgian independent research association. He is President of ARISE, the Association for Responsible Investment Services. He was Founder of Stock@Stake, the precursor of Vigeo Belgium.

Sébastien Pouget is a Professor of Finance at the University of Toulouse and a co-director of a research center on Sustainable Finance and Responsible Investment (Chaire Finance Durable et Investissement Responsable).

Benjamin J. Richardson is Professor of Environmental Law at the University of Tasmania. Prior, he was at the University of British Columbia where he held the Canada Research Chair in Environmental Law and Sustainability and was Director of the Centre for Law and the Environment.

Kyoko Sakuma-Keck is an independent researcher and consultant on sustainable investment and public policy. She holds a PhD from Université Libre de Bruxelles, and has over 20 years' experience in ESG analysis and EU affairs combined.

Antti Savilaakso is Director of Responsible Investments at Nordea Asset Management. He has eight years of experience in Responsible Investment (RI). He has lectured widely on RI and has co-authored a book on RI for the Finnish market.

Bert Scholtens is a Professor at the University of Groningen (the Netherlands) and at the University of Saint Andrews (Scotland, UK). His research is directed at international financial intermediation and environmental finance and economics.

Sara Segura Querol is a PhD candidate at University of Zaragoza. Her research interests are environmental finance and socially responsible investment. She has already published the first results of her research in Spanish and international journals.

George Serafeim is Jakurski Family Associate Professor of Business Administration at the Harvard Business School where he focuses on how organizations integrate sustainability into strategy, reporting and investing.

Yulia Sofronova is Manager, Networks and Global Outreach at the UN-supported Principles for Responsible Investment (PRI). Yulia graduated from the Kingston University Business School with an MA in Corporate Communications in 2009.

María Laura Tinelli has worked for the past three years for the Principles for Responsible Investment (PRI), managing the PRI Regional Networks in eight countries, advising investors and regulators on ESG incorporation from Asia to South America. She holds an MSc from the University of London SOAS.

Luc Van Liedekerke holds the BASF-Deloitte Chair in Corporate Sustainability at the Antwerp Management School. He teaches business ethics at the universities of Antwerp and Leuven and published extensively on business ethics, corporate social responsibility (CSR) and financial ethics.

Suzette Viviers is a Professor in the Department of Business Management at Stellenbosch University. Her doctoral thesis mainly centered on the risk-adjusted performance of RI funds in South Africa.

Meg Voorhes is Director of Research and Operations of US SIF. She is the author or co-author of several US SIF Foundation publications, including its biennial *Report on Sustainable and Responsible Investing Trends in the United States.*

Ed Waitzer is a Professor, holder of the Jarislowsky Dimma Mooney Chair in Corporate Governance, and Director of the Hennick Centre for Business and Law at Osgoode Hall and the Schulich School of Business, York University, Toronto.

Olaf Weber is Associate Professor at the School for Environment, Enterprise and Development (SEED) at the University of Waterloo, Canada. Between 2010 and 2014 he held the Export Development Canada Chair in Environmental Finance and is the director of the master's program in Sustainability Management.

Alexi White is a senior policy advisor in the Government of Ontario. He previously served as a research assistant with the Initiative for Responsible Investment at the Harvard Kennedy School, where he earned his master's in public policy.

Dariusz Wójcik is Professor of Economic Geography, School of Geography and the Environment, University of Oxford, and Visiting Professor, Beijing Normal University, China.

Camila Yamahaki is an independent researcher and consultant in Brazil. She holds an MA in CSR from The University of Nottingham and a PhD from Middlesex University. Her doctoral research focused on the determinants of shareholder engagement in Brazil and South Africa.

Anna Young-Ferris holds a PhD in Institutional Investment that focused on responsible investment and ESG integration. She is a Lecturer at the University of Sydney Business School teaching in the areas of corporate sustainability and integrated reporting, responsible investment, carbon accounting, and management accounting.

Acknowledgements

All books, especially ones of this magnitude, require considerable time, thought and energy in their production. This volume is no exception. The editors would like to take this opportunity to thank all the contributors to *The Routledge Handbook of Responsible Investment.* This new field of responsible investment has long needed an in-depth examination of this work to serve as a reference guide for both academics and practitioners. The seventy-four authors in this volume draw on their knowledge and expertise to provide us with this far reaching exploration. They come from a range of backgrounds, and have all given generously of their time to provide us with leading-edge analysis of responsible investment.

We would also like to thank our publisher, Routledge, and editor Sinead Waldron who has so ably and patiently guided us through the publication process.

We wish to thank the Principles for Responsible Investment for their assistance throughout this period. In particular, we thank Natalie Beinisch who initially began this journey with us. We also want to recognize Katherine Ng, Helene Winch, Lorenzo Saa, Rob Lake and Robert Harding, all of whom have contributed to the success of this work.

The initial impetus for this volume came from Andreas Hoepner, who saw the need for a comprehensive volume and convinced the publisher and fellow editors to join him in this endeavor. In addition, a special thanks goes to Agnes L. Neher who edited the largest section of this volume providing us with an atlas of responsible investment around the world. With twenty-six countries and regions to manage this was an enormous task, without which we would not have the breadth of understanding of responsible investment this volume provides.

We would also like to recognize the team at the Carleton Centre for Community Innovation who helped with this volume: Nicole Bedford, Lesley MacKinnon, Hakan Mustafa, Roy Sengupta and Genevieve Harrison. Additionally we benefited from the able assistance of George Fraser in the preparation of this volume.

A final note goes to our families. For some of us this is the first time editing and contributing to such a work, for others the role is more familiar. But regardless, when in the midst of these herculean tasks our families probably hear more about the work then they might want to know. We draw our strength and support from you, and without that, it simply would not be possible. Thank you.

Part I

1

Introduction to *The Routledge Handbook of Responsible Investment*

Tessa Hebb, James P. Hawley, Andreas G. F. Hoepner, Agnes L. Neher and David Wood

Understanding responsible investment

We hear a lot about responsible investment these days. But what is it and how is it being implemented around the world? What are the impacts of responsible investment for investors, for the financial industry and for society as a whole? *The Routledge Handbook of Responsible Investment* provides a deep examination of responsible investment. It brings together over 60 authors to explore responsible investment practices around the globe. You can think of this volume as an atlas of current practice, one that spans six continents and profiles over 25 countries.

This *Routledge Handbook* also draws on top experts in the field to explore the impact of responsible investment on key financial actors ranging from mainstream asset managers to religious organizations. These authors examine current strategies used to implement responsible investment and the challenges they face going forward. The volume concludes with a series of chapters from top academics in the field as they reflect on the implications of responsible investment now and for the future.

What is responsible investment? Put simply, responsible investment (RI) takes environmental, social and governance (ESG) factors into consideration in investment decision-making. It is an investment approached increasingly adopted by institutional investors. In fact the UN-backed Principles for Responsible Investing (detailed below) now has over 1,300 signatories representing $45 trillion of assets under management. These signatories have pledged to bring ESG considerations into their investment decision-making. Add to this the fact that Bloomberg and MSCI now provide ESG data to the financial industry as a major component of their company reporting, and it is clear that responsible investing is increasingly moving to the mainstream of investment practices.

In the past, these three factors were considered to be non-financial (sometimes termed extra-financial) concerns. It was assumed that all known information about the firm was embedded in its stock price, and therefore additional attention to ESG information was not required. But over time the risks (and possible rewards) for taking ESG into account have become more evident. Regulatory bodies such as the U.S. Securities and Exchange Commission (SEC) suggest that ESG factors have 'material' impact on companies' future earnings and as a result require mandatory reporting on these issues in annual reports to shareholders.

Events such as the Global Financial Crisis of 2008 reinforced the understanding that these factors play a critical role, particularly for long-term institutional investors, as these factors can pose risks to company performance over time. Post the Global Financial Crisis, and with a growing awareness of sustainability issues, mainstream investors are increasingly taking on responsible investing practices (UNPRI, 2014).

RI's theoretical underpinning

The old mindset of RI as divergent and to some extent adversarial to company and shareholder goals (Friedman, 1970) is eroding (Donaldson & Preston, 1995; Jones & Wood, 1995; Freeman & Phillips, 2002). Instead responsible investing is being seen as a means of driving shareholder profit rather than a performance laggard (Porter & Kramer, 2006). This fundamental change in mindset is the result of the RI business case that seeks to develop and bind the notions of financial performance with ESG indicators. The business case contends that it is not simply a matter of ethics but rather that financial gains, management of risk and corporate responsibility converge in the long run (Louche & Lydenberg, 2006). The RI advantage is one of anticipating and mitigating long-term risks through raised ESG standards, not simply moral and ethical considerations (Scholtens, 2010; UNEP, 2008).

The theoretical underpinnings of responsible investment address problems associated with the efficient markets hypothesis (Fama, 1970; Samuelson, 1965) and modern portfolio theory (Markowitz, 1952) with their assumptions of a rational market. There is increased criticism of this theory in light of the Global Financial Crisis of 2008 (Bogle, 2005; Fox, 2009; Taleb, 2008, 2010), with behavioral finance (Lo, 2005; Schleifer, 2000; Shiller, 2000) coming to the fore. Rather than an efficient market, information asymmetries in financial markets are the norm (Akerlof, 1970; Stiglitz, 1976). Responsible investing builds on this theoretical framework, recognizing that ESG factors are a source of information asymmetry in financial markets.

Traditionally, ESG factors have been viewed as externalities of the firm and therefore not considered in its value (Hebb, 2008; Kiernan, 2009; Krosinsky & Robins, 2009; UNEP, 2008). Yet taking ESG into consideration can reduce risk for investors and add value over time (Gompers et al., 2003; Porter & van der Linde, 1995). This understanding is known as 'the business case' for responsible investing. Building on the critique of efficient markets, the 'universal ownership hypothesis' (Hawley & Williams, 2000) suggests that because large institutional owners own the whole market, what may be negative externalities for one company in the portfolio are direct and often costly impacts on another holding. As a result, today's institutional investors must be concerned about the ESG standards of the firms they hold in their investment portfolios.

Additionally, the principal–agent problem (Jensen & Meckling, 1976; Fama & Jensen, 1983; Schleifer & Vishny, 1997) plays a part in the market failures that drive the need for responsible investment. The struggle for corporate control between owners and managers has a long history in legal, financial and economic literature (Berle & Means, 1933; Roe 1994). Responsible investing represents a shift away from firm managers and toward owners of corporations. It suggests that share owners provide active and engaged oversight of today's corporations (Monks, 2001; Davis et al., 2006). Responsible investment encourages active share ownership, and increasingly such oversight is seen as critical to the health of our financial markets.

Implementing responsible investment

Large institutional investors have become the dominant players in our financial system, representing over 70 per cent of today's shareholders. Many of these institutional investors hold retirement savings, and as a result have liabilities to beneficiaries that can last over 30 years. These long-term obligations have given rise to an increased awareness of risk over time in their investment portfolios. Increasingly, institutional investors are recognizing the danger of short-termism in our financial markets (Kay, 2012; Barton & Wiseman, 2014). The Global Financial Crisis served to heighten those concerns. Such a recognition is critical to understanding the risks posed from ESG factors, as these often play out over time. While in the short-term it may cost more to put safety mechanisms in place, over time these investments pay off. The challenge for the investor is to move away from an obsession with short-term quarterly returns and begin to view an investment in the firm over the long-term. However, one of the challenges for responsible investors is that the incentive structure deeply embedded in the financial system remains linked to short-term rather than long-term financial results.

Responsible investment requires a shift in temporal understanding. Large institutional investors either implicitly or explicitly[1] have a set of investment beliefs that underpin their investment decision-making. Increasingly these beliefs include a shift to long-term investment and a valuing of ESG factors embedded in that shift (see CalPERS Investment Beliefs for more on this point). Additionally, our understanding of fiduciary duty, which so often restricted these funds' actions in the past, has become more sophisticated with regard to the important role ESG considerations can and should take (Freshfields Bruckhaus Deringer, 2005; Hawley et al., 2013).

Responsible investment can be implemented in a variety of ways. Most common is through integration in the investment portfolio (UNPRI, 2014). Often the asset owner requests ESG integration from the internal and external asset managers. Such integration in investment portfolios is handled through stock selection often referred to as 'best of class' or 'best of sector'. Here, the investor selects a portfolio based on companies (and even countries in the case of sovereign bonds) that have the highest ESG standards. The asset owners believe that high ESG standards can reduce risk over time and may lead to outperformance.[2] Third-party rating agencies (such as Bloomberg, MSCI, and Sustainalytics) provide readily available ESG information to the market that assists in such investment decision-making.

Conversely, the investor can stay away from companies that have poor ESG ratings. Most responsible investors do not exclude whole sectors from their investment portfolios, but rather look for the highest ESG standards across the whole economy. While some investors bring ethical considerations to bare (particularly socially responsible and religious investors), most do not, preferring instead to focus on 'the business case' for RI rather than broad-based exclusions.

However, responsible investors often adopt codes and norms within their investment policies that help them to identify the standards they will apply when integrating ESG into their investment portfolio. These are usually globally-based sets of principles such as the UN Declaration of Human Rights, the Global Compact, the Global Sullivan Principles of Corporate Social Responsibility, the environmental CERES Principles, the Carbon Disclosure Project, or the Extractive Industries Transparency Initiative (EITI). These codes provide a generally accepted framework of corporate behavior that informs the institutional investor and are often monitored by third-party non-governmental organizations (NGOs) that bring the increased corporate (or country) transparency that responsible investors require. Violation of these codes of conduct can lead to divestment from companies and even sectors. One prominent example is divestment from companies that produce cluster bombs in violation of the Convention on Cluster Munitions. Many responsible investors have adopted this policy.

The second primary strategy used by responsible investors is shareholder engagement. This is a positive strategy that uses shareholder rights and active ownership to exert pressure on companies to raise their ESG standards. It can be an active or a passive strategy. Proxy voting is an example of a passive RI engagement strategy. Shareholder engagement can also be private or public. Private active engagement usually consists of some form of dialogue with the company, such as personal communication, letter writing and face-to-face meetings, in order to raise issues of concern away from public scrutiny. In contrast, public active engagement includes publishing focus lists of underperforming companies and putting minority shareholder resolutions forward at company annual meetings. These actions often bring public and media attention and can damage a company's reputation.

Engagement requires the responsible investor to maintain an ownership position in the company rather than to divest. It is the preferred strategy of most responsible investors and is seen as being more effective than divestment campaigns, as it has a direct impact on company management. The process of divestment means that when the investor sells his/her position someone else buys the stock, and the seller then often loses any way to influence and raise company ESG standards. That said, responsible investors find themselves under increased pressure to respond to divestment requests by stakeholders and beneficiaries. The recent fossil fuels divestment campaign is one such example (see Cary Krosinsky, Chapter 47, on this issue). With the growing size and influence of institutional investors in our economy, we can expect more pressure in these areas going forward, creating a second challenge for RI in the future.

While this collection adopts the business case that focuses on engagement rather than divestment, especially for fiduciary investors, we clearly recognize that the actions of others (e.g. NGOs, campaigns, legislative actions, the media) impact directly and indirectly the perspectives of institutional investors, as well as the larger socioeconomic environment in which they operate. For example, the growing movement among universities for fossil fuel divestment (e.g. Stanford University's divestment from coal) and some philanthropic endowments divestment from oil may in fact create enhanced opportunities for engagement. It is not difficult to imagine that major oil companies may in the future feel compelled to engage with their institutional RI owners to seriously consider scenarios for stranded assets in a way they have not so far done. There is a complex 'dance of disinvestment' that takes place on an expanded political, social and economic stage involving a variety of stakeholders taking different roles, and indeed, to follow the dance metaphor, even dancing to different beats.

One of the results of the shift to shareholder engagement is the willingness of large institutional investors to work together in broad coalitions. In the past, such coalition building was shunned because the 'free-rider' potential meant larger investors often shouldered the costs of these campaigns while smaller investors reaped the benefits (O'Barr & Connolly, 1992). However, in recent years large institutional investors have realized that coming together in coalitions gives them greater strength when engaging with companies to raise their ESG standards. Organizations such as the Principles for Responsible Investment (PRI) and the U.S.-based Institutional Investors on Climate Risk have crafted specific platforms that encourage coalition building.

RI moves to the mainstream: the Principles for Responsible Investment (PRI)

In early 2005, the United Nations invited the world's largest institutional investors to develop a set of Principles for Responsible Investment (PRI). The invitation was well received, with 20 institutional investors across 12 countries responding. Under the coordination of the UN Global Compact and the UN Environmental Programme Finance Initiative (UNEP FI), a working group was created comprising 70 experts from the investment industry, academia, (inter)governmental organizations and civil society in April 2005. Nine months later this working group had created the six Principles for Responsible Investment (PRI) that were officially launched in April 2006. The six principles, including the crucial preamble and postscript, read as follows:

> As institutional investors, we have a duty to act in the best long-term interests of our beneficiaries. In this fiduciary role, we believe that environmental, social, and corporate governance (ESG) issues can affect the performance of investment portfolios (to varying degrees across companies, sectors, regions, asset classes and through time). We also recognise that applying these Principles may better align investors with broader objectives of society. Therefore, where consistent with our fiduciary responsibilities, we commit to the following:
>
> Principle 1: We will incorporate ESG issues into investment analysis and decision-making processes.
> Principle 2: We will be active owners and incorporate ESG issues into our ownership policies and practices.
> Principle 3: We will seek appropriate disclosure on ESG issues by the entities in which we invest.
> Principle 4: We will promote acceptance and implementation of the Principles within the investment industry.
> Principle 5: We will work together to enhance our effectiveness in implementing the Principles.
> Principle 6: We will each report on our activities and progress towards implementing the Principles.
>
> The Principles for Responsible Investment were developed by an international group of institutional investors reflecting the increasing relevance of environmental, social and corporate governance issues to investment practices. The process was convened by the United Nations Secretary-General. In signing the Principles, we as investors publicly commit to adopt and implement them, where consistent with our fiduciary responsibilities. We also commit to evaluate the effectiveness and improve the content of the Principles over time. We believe this will improve our ability to meet commitments to beneficiaries as well as better align our investment activities with the broader interests of society. We encourage other investors to adopt the Principles.
>
> *(UNPRI, 2014)*

The PRI aims to reflect the core values of large institutional investors with a clear fiduciary-duty focus and long-term investment horizons. The PRI's development is a strong indicator of responsible investment's substantially increasing relevance within financial markets. Within the first 28 months following its launch in April 2006 (MacDonald et al., 2007), the Principles were signed by institutions representing more than $15 trillion of assets under management (UNPRI, 2008; UNPRI, 2006).

Responsible investment's growing acceptance was demonstrated in the aftermath of the 2008 Global Financial Crisis with calls in the international mainstream investment press for responsible investment to be a relative beneficiary of and to play a considerable role in the solution to the 2008 credit crisis (Greenhalgh, 2008; Melander & Turner, 2008). For instance, the Financial Times suggests socially responsible investment (SRI) as "a new investment code, a collaborative effort from a number of investors sufficiently large to bring about the desired change," who "ought to view SRI as an insurance premium, an investment in the stability of our financial and economic system" (Butz & Ginguené, 2009).

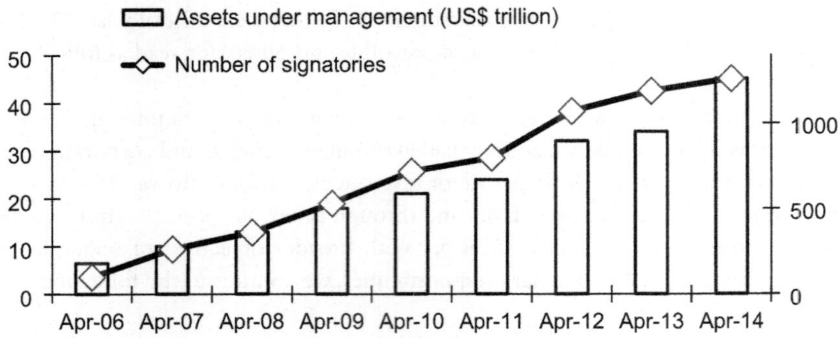

Figure 1.1 Growth of the Principles for Responsible Investment (© PRI)

By November of 2014, the PRI had more than 1,300 signatories with assets under management of $45 trillion (as shown in Figure 1.1) (UNPRI, 2014). While it is a matter of debate if responsible investment and the PRI are already mainstream or will be in 2015, it seems fair to conclude that after 8 years responsible investment has attracted strong interest from investors, investment professionals, policy makers and the general public.

RI challenges going forward

Responsible investment faces a host of challenges going forward, both external, driven by markets and the larger economy and society, as well as internal, such as how to interact with divestment campaigns, how to develop its own internal governance structures and how to create multi-tiered coalitions (e.g. not only with other investors, but with selected stakeholders as well).

Let us begin with some significant external challenges. It is an understatement to observe that as of this writing elites of all sorts (but especially political and economic elites) are under significant attack from across the political spectrum in numerous (democratic and not so democratic) countries. Corporations, in particular, can easily roll over on their so-called 'license to operate', as they are entirely creatures of the law, hence of the state. Chapter 2 of this volume takes up this issue in more detail.

RI faces perhaps its most formidable challenge in moving from a short-term to a long(er)-term investment system, with an accompanying set of expectations and values. Equity and many other asset markets have come to focus on the short-term (to the point of nanoseconds in the case of flash trading), where even the so-called long-term is 5 years or less. RI confronts the challenge of redefining risk and opportunity in terms far longer than half a decade, especially for resource- and climate change–related developments. From an RI perspective, the issue becomes how to redefine and align various incentive arrangements to reward performance for this longer time frame. A particular aspect of this is a search for alpha (above risk-adjusted market returns) in ESG areas. In our view, while alpha can sometimes be found in ESG arenas, and this may serve a legitimation function that ESG/RI factors matter and are material, it also has the potential to undermine what is critical: the change of the whole market (beta) to minimize and mitigate negative externalities. Such externalities, if left alone, undermine the ability to create sustainable long-term economic development. Thus, the search for ESG-based alpha is at best two sided: it may in the short-run legitimize ESG factors, but at the possible cost of clouding the long-term view of ESG as value added, and indeed as a value-creating essential.

Another external challenge for RI is financial market instability leading to systemic risk, as happened in 2008. The specifics of the challenge in this regard are to expand the pre-2008 scope of ESG/RI into the area of financial, and more generally economic, risks, and therefore opportunities as well. To some degree this is underway among some institutional investors (e.g. Hermes, CalPERs). Prior to the 2008 Global Financial Crisis, investment and investment side risk were left to those whose supposed expertise was to judge financial risk; that is, the investment side of institutional operations. But just as war is considered 'too important to be left to the generals', so, too, should financial risk be considered too important to be left to (only to) the investment side of institutional investment.[3] The expansion of RI to incorporate systemic risk monitoring and activity to mitigate such risk dovetails nicely with a long-term perspective on investment directly. Logically, this also implies a concern for macroeconomic issues and policies.

Another major challenge for RI is to incentivize and/or mandate ESG/RI analysis among private (corporate) pension funds and among (most) mutual/unit funds. While the latter have to some degree become more active on occasion than they were 10 years ago, most do not have an RI perspective for their major sub-funds. In the case of captive corporate pension funds, these funds have been and remain entirely inactive, even on governance issues. The unwritten rule among them is not to disturb their corporate neighbours (whatever the offensive circumstances might be) for fear that someday the funds of the egregious neighbours will bite back. In our view, both for mutual/unit funds and for corporate pension funds especially, legislative mandates of one sort or another are necessary. And in the case of corporate funds a more radical approach may be to hive them off from the parent corporation itself. Both are formidable challenges.

A final external challenge is that of the ongoing changing definition and practices related to fiduciary obligations. Without going into any detail, suffice it to say that fiduciary duties in common law countries (where they hold the most significant legal sway) may be at an inflection point in at least two significant dimensions. The first focuses on intergenerational equity; that is, the mandate to treat younger and older beneficiaries and investors equally. This means a long-term perspective must be incorporated into the fund's policies and procedures (approximately 50-plus years). The second dimension concerns the scope of what are the 'interests' of those to whom fiduciary obligation is owed. Is it their narrowly defined financial interests only? Or rather is it a broader set of interests that take account of the risk and opportunities in the future where those financial benefits will be expended? Thus, a pension cheque spent, for example, in an environment that lacks clean and/or adequate water is not a risk-adjusted benefit, as more of the beneficiary's or investor's funds will have to be expended to compensate for water problems. It is arguable that an ounce of prevention by a fiduciary is worth a pound of clean-up cure. Indeed, it may be a fiduciary obligation to take these issues into account from an intergenerational long-term perspective.

RI and its investors also face a number of internal challenges. One is that while there have been greater coordinated actions through forming coalitions (e.g. corporate governance engagement around a particular issue), the free-rider problem is endemic, and is likely to remain so. Only the largest investors (with some exceptions) undertake engagement, yet all investors benefit from a successful engagement that adds long-term value. We believe this should be accepted, as in the majority of ESG actions (e.g. engagement, proxy fights) the returns to the largest investors outweigh their costs over a 5-year period.

A second internal challenge in the ESG troika, concerns the S – the social. While equity markets since the turn of this century have tended to incorporate governance factors in the price of the share (at least in well-developed markets), thereby eliminating the premium that in the 1990s existed for good governance, this is not the case for S. (The E factor is a mid-point, as it is often incorporated into equity price, and more easily so, as environmental-contingent liabilities can be well quantified, although it is not evenly done so across market sectors.) The social factor is more complex for two reasons. The first is that it contains a host of (sometimes changing) elements that run, for example, from health and safety in the workplace, to wage and benefit levels, to the impact of an investment or operation on a local community, to various forms of discrimination on the job and so on. In turn, this leads to the second difficulty for the generic S. Some of these factors are quantifiable – health and safety, for example; others are less quantifiable, such as the impact on communities, where the details are often very specific and can be hard to come by.

A third internal challenge focuses on how far down the investment chain ESG is actively pursued in one manner or another. Even for large institutional investors committed to RI, at the individual investment portfolio manager level, far too often ESG fails to be taken into account. This, in part, is related to how investment managers are compensated and evaluated. Unless RI and ESG have metrics and measurements, they will likely not be managed but rather ignored. Thus, without metrics and some part of compensation attached to such metrics, commitment to RI too often remains a formality. The same dynamic applies to an institutional investor's external money managers, consultants and others linked to the investment chain.

And finally, a smaller but nonetheless significant challenge lies in the wide variety of names and labels within what is broadly termed RI. Terms such as responsible investment, ESG, socially responsible investment, sustainable and responsible investment, impact investment, micro-finance and ethical investment, to name only some, are increasingly interchangeable. Yet often those involved with RI have a specific and sometimes idiosyncratic meaning attached to a particular term. While this in some ways is a sign of what previously were often discrete investment philosophies and styles coming together, it does cause significant confusion among the general public.

Overview of the *Handbook*

This book is laid out in four parts. Our first part provides an overview of responsible investment. This part defines terms and issues in responsible investing. It develops an understanding of who uses responsible investment and why. This part tracks the growth and development of responsible investment over the past 10 years from niche activity to the mainstream. Chapter 2 addresses the major challenges facing responsible investment going forward. Hawley traces the partial convergence of socially responsible investment with emerging RI, in spite of the confusion of these and other terms. The chapter examines trends to mandate ESG reporting in various jurisdictions and briefly reviews the results of ESG-oriented investing and corporate governance. Chapter 2 concludes with some areas of future ESG investing and the reasons for them. This part of the volume concludes with an examination as to why responsible investment has been under-researched in the past. Hoepner, McMillan and Fraser suggest that responsible investment professionals need sufficiently reliable information on a large number of RI research questions. RI academics should generate research of proportional quantity and quality when compared to related research areas in finance. This chapter uses qualitative methods to explore the extent that RI is proportionally under-researched in comparison to other areas of finance.

In the second part of the volume, we examine the state of responsible investment in most countries and regions of the world. These profiles describe the unique characteristics of responsible investment in each country and/or region. An Appendix of Country Tables provides standardized tables, which display each country's characteristics, such as market size, major market participants, relevant legislation, investor preferences and prominent ESG issues.

Part II embraces 26 developed and emerging markets in the world. The status quo of the RI markets varies across countries and regions. The RI markets in North America are for the most part well developed. These markets have many PRI signatories. In the case of the U.S., there are 183 signatories, while Weber mentions 44 in the case of Canada. Voorhes highlights that the history of RI in the U.S. goes back to 1928 when the first RI investment fund was launched. In South America, according to Yamahaki and Gaban, the status of the RI market differs by country. Whereas Brazil has 61 PRI signatories, Argentina, Columbia and Ecuador have none. Australia, like the U.S. and Canada, also has a quite well-developed RI market with legislation regarding disclosure requirements for institutional investors in place. Moving to Asia, neither China, Hong Kong nor Japan have legislation in place focusing on RI. In Chapter 16, Sakuma-Keck suggests that Japan has the most developed RI market in this region.

Like South America, continental Africa has large variations in the RI market, with countries such as Nigeria and Tunisia being at an early stage of development and South Africa having a well-developed RI market. Whereas the latter has 36 PRI signatories and an RI infrastructure with the African Sustainable Investment Forum (AfricaSIF), RI in the former countries is in its infancy. Nevertheless, there are also some positive movements. In the case of Tunisia, for example, Bouslah points out that there are four RI funds and a portfolio of microfinance institutions. RI in Israel is also in its infancy, with no RI funds and no official RI organizations. In fact, Levtzion Nadan in Chapter 12 indicates that there is only one PRI signatory in Israel. Moving to Russia we get a similar picture. Sofronova talks about two PRI signatories and the lack of legislation in this regard.

The RI picture becomes brighter when looking at Europe, with the exception of Eastern Europe. In Estonia and Poland there are three PRI signatories and no national RI organizations. However, throughout most of Europe we see well-developed RI markets. Several countries have RI legislation and reporting requirements for institutional investors in place, and all have a national RI organization. Eurosif, the European RI umbrella organization, brings most of these national organizations together.

Tinelli, drawing on her own experience working in RI around the world (Chapter 31), comes to the conclusion that regulation is one of the key drivers for RI in all countries. Countries that have specific RI regulation in place, such as regulation regarding reporting requirements about ESG indicators, are more developed in regard to RI. The authors Louche, van Liedekerke and Peeters illustrate this type of regulation for the case of Belgium. Additionally, the structure of the pension system co-determines the development of RI. Countries with pay-as-you-go systems have fewer institutional investors with long-term investment horizons than we find in countries with defined-benefit pension plans. The latter are generally more developed with regard to RI. Such is the case in the United Kingdom, according to Biehl and Atkins in Chapter 30. Here we find a well-developed RI market characterized by defined-benefit pension plans in comparison to Germany with its pay-as-you-go pension system.

Overall, Part II of this volume demonstrates that RI is becoming a more relevant topic throughout the world. Some markets have already adapted to the challenges and opportunities; others are still at the beginning of this journey.

Part III analyses the views of relevant stakeholders on responsible investment. As these stakeholders collectively shape most of the responsible investment practice, understanding their views and especially the similarities and differences between them is of high value for readers. These stakeholders collectively shape RI, and it is from their practice that the theory of RI iterates. Together the chapters in this part of the volume help lay out both the networks in which the field has developed and the challenges that it faces in implementation.

Although RI is an investment strategy that spans across the agency chain of investors, consultants, managers and end users of capital, the various agents along this chain can approach the topic with different motives, goals and tools. Asset owners – in theory the drivers of the investment market – may adopt responsible investment for a variety of reasons. These include improving long-term performance through better fundamental analysis and active share ownership, to identifying risks and opportunities embedded in long-term social and environmental macro-trends, to better aligning their investments with their ideas of how investments are ethically implicated by their real-world effects. Laura Berry's chapter on the relationship of the faith-based investment community – a particularly active community in the development of both social and responsible investing, and a key stakeholder in shareholder activism – helps highlight the complex motives and roles that different kinds of asset owners can play in RI. Danyelle Guyatt's attention to the role that investment consultants play in RI and their delicate dance between being both guides for and respondents to their clients' needs illustrates several explorations in this section of the agency chain that allows for and constrains the growth of RI as a field. One key question for RI has always been how asset owners with notionally longer time horizons, whose beneficiaries need a world they can live in, can be empowered to act as first movers in the agency chain.

The concept of RI also implies a set of stakeholders outside the investor agency chain, those who are affected by investment. Part III has several chapters that look at RI from the perspective of stakeholders who are affected by RI in practice. Chapters in this part of the volume ask what the incorporation of ESG means to the environment, to society, and to corporations whose governance is a target for change by RI. Such questions call into relief the intricate interconnections between beliefs about how the investment markets work and beliefs about what makes the world a better place that shapes RI as a field. For instance, in their chapter on the environment as a stakeholder in RI, Ralf Barkemeyer and Andrea Liesen offer a compelling reflection on how the 'needs' of the environment can, via RI, enter into and impinge on investment decision-making. One way to read Kimberley Gladman's chapter on governance is as a way to understand how corporate governance opens a window for investors to see how the corporations they invest in set norms for social behaviour that have long-term value.

The authors of this collection are themselves stakeholders in the development of RI and its influence in investment markets and on the world. The field is built on reflective inquiry from motivated practitioners, advocates and researchers who draw on emerging strands of (often heterodox) financial theory and concern about major social and environmental issues with the goal of reshaping how investment relates to long-term sustainable financial and social performance. James Gifford's chapter on the formation of the PRI, and its focus on asset owners as potential change agents, exemplifies a theme that several chapters draw out – the role of information, network building and idea formation in the development of RI as a field of investment practice.

In sum, Part III addresses the way that stakeholders try to implement RI, how they see the impact of increasing uptake of RI and the mechanisms they see as shaping the field. The diversity of perspectives on how stakeholders shape RI is held together by the family resemblance we see from this diverse group as they define (and grow) the field.

The volume concludes with a final section of essays from well-known RI researchers and examines emerging issues in the field. Part IV highlights both the qualitative study of RI and the quantitative work necessary to underpin the business case for RI. Scholtens picks up the theme of RI research first explored in Chapter 3 by Hoepner, McMillan and Fraser. This chapter discusses the most important issues relating to the research and business practices of responsible finance and investing and focuses on theory and methods in the literature and on key issues in the practice of responsible investment.

Clark et al. set out to map the 'emerging realities' facing investors as a first step toward identifying strategies for navigating these new and complex relationships. Building on one of the major challenges facing RI detailed above, they suggest that the challenge confronting investors is to reconcile the short-term with the long-term perspective while maintaining efficient decision-making processes. They suggest that investors must "integrate mechanisms for learning from the past, anticipating future events and working against human predisposition to favour the short-term." Krosinsky is even more pointed in his advice to responsible investors, cautioning them to avoid current distractions in the field, such as the campaign to divest from fossil fuels, and instead equip themselves with data and information required to make the difficult decisions that RI demands. The need for both sustainability information and information intermediation is highlighted by Robert G. Eccles, Jock Herron and George Serafeim. They suggest that the need is even higher in sustainability reporting than it is in financial reporting because, in contrast to well-established financial measurements, similar standards do not yet exist in the area of sustainability. Fiduciary duty also remains a key challenge for responsible investment. Both Hawley, Johnson and Waitzer and Richardson explore the concept of fiduciary duty as it pertains to responsible investing. They find fiduciary duty to be an evolving concept.

Jacquelyn Humphrey turns her attention to the mutual fund industry, and in particular to the SRI screening of mutual funds and how such screening affects the risk and return profile of these funds. The final three chapters of Part IV provide qualitative analyses that underpin the business case for responsible investment. Hoepner, Huang and Lui provide the first analysis of the trade-off between financial return and social return in microloan funds aimed at poverty alleviation. Pouget looks at the sources and regulation of financial markets' short-termism in order to "show how an integrated multi-disciplinary framework might be useful to understand how inefficiencies arise in financial markets and how long-term investments, when they are desirable, may be promoted." Osthoff closes Part IV with an analysis of SRI mutual fund investors. He finds that in many ways they behave similarly to conventional fund holders and seek financial performance by buying SRI funds with top performance in the past. However, SRI fund holders also care about the ethical and social standards of the funds in which they invest.

Conclusion

Given the heightened interest in responsible investment and in environmental, social and governance factors in investment decision-making, *The Routledge Handbook of Responsible Investment* makes a substantial contribution to the RI literature. It represents leading-edge work on responsible investment across the multiple stakeholders and thought leaders involved in this work. The country profiles offer a snapshot of RI activity around the world. Bringing ESG factors into consideration in investment decision-making is becoming more critical with each passing day. We believe the *Routledge Handbook of Responsible Investing* will provide an invaluable guide to all those who wish to learn more on this important topic.

Notes

1 In 2013 the large U.S.-based pension fund CalPERS documented its investment beliefs, making explicit its view on long-term investment, its valuing of stakeholders and its belief that "long-term value creation requires effective management of three forms of capital: financial, physical and human".

2 Studies are unable to find causation in most cases between ESG standards and 'alpha', or performance above benchmark. However, it is evident that while corporate 'good news' may not have a significant impact on stock price, 'bad news' events are punished by the market with a drop in share price (Kruger, 2009). Witness BP and the 2010 Gulf of Mexico oil spill for example – BP's stock price has yet to recover its pre-spill value.

3 In part, this has been and is still too often the case that most financial risk analysts and managers have been schooled in the same set of theories and perspectives, based on modern portfolio theory and its various off shoots. Most teaching and learning (with some notable exceptions) deny that investments based on these theories are capable of creating financial risk.

References

Akerlof, G. (1970) 'The Market for 'Lemons': Quality Uncertainty and the Market Mechanism', *Quarterly Journal of Economics* (The MIT Press) 84 (3): 488–500.

Barton, D., and Wiseman, M. (2014) 'Focusing Capital on the Long Term', *Harvard Business Review* (Jan./Feb.).

Berle, A., and Means, G. (1933) *The Modern Corporation and Private Property.* Revised ed. 1967. New York: Harcourt, Brace and World, Inc.

Bogle, J. (2005) *The Battle for the Soul of Capitalism.* New Haven, CT: Yale University Press.

Butz, C., and Ginguené, O. (2009) Crisis calls for traditional ESG investing. Available: http://www.ft.com/cms/s/0/fe74da70–3685–11de-af40–00144feabdc0.html [Accessed May 24, 2009].

Davis, S., Lukomnik, J., and Pitt-Watson, D. (2006) *The New Capitalists: How Citizen Investors Are Reshaping the Corporate Agenda.* Boston: Harvard Business School Press.

Donaldson, T., and Preston, L. (1995) 'The Stakeholder Theory of the Modern Corporation: Concepts, Evidence and Implications', *Academy of Management Review* 20 (1): 65–91.

Fama, E. (1970) 'Efficient Capital Markets: A Review of Theory and Empirical Work', *Journal of Finance* 25 (2): 383–417.

Fama, E. F., and Jensen, M. C. (1983) 'Separation of Ownership and Control', *Journal of Law and Economics* 26: 301–325.

Fox, J. (2009) *Myth of the Rational Market: A History of Risk, Reward, and Delusion on Wall Street.* New York: HarperCollins.

Freeman, R. E., and Philips, R. A. (2002) 'Stakeholder Theory: A Libertarian Defence', *Business Ethics Quarterly* 12 (3): 331–349.

Freshfields Bruckhaus Deringer (2005) *A Legal Framework for the Integration of Environmental, Social and Governance Issues into Institutional Investment.* New York: UNEP FI.

Friedman, M. (1970) 'The Social Responsibility of Business Is to Increase Its Profits', *New York Times Magazine,* Sept. 13.

Gompers, P., Ishii, J., and Metrick, A. (2003) 'Corporate Governance and Equity Prices', *Quarterly Journal of Economics* 118 (1): 107–156.

Greenhalgh, H. (2008) Poor ethical standards causing financial crisis, Available: http://www.ftadviser.com/InvestmentAdviser/Regulation/Regulators/FSA/NewsAnalysis/article/20081013/ee5231fa-9523–11dd-8351–00144f2af8e8/Poor-ethical-standards-causing-financial-crisis.jsp [Accessed October 30, 2008].

Hawley, J., Hoepner, A., Johnson, K., et al. Eds. (2013) *Handbook of Institutional Investment and Fiduciary Duty.* Cambridge, UK: Cambridge University Press.

Hawley, J. P., and Williams, A. (2000) *The Rise of Fiduciary Capitalism.* Philadelphia: University of Pennsylvania Press.

Hebb, T. (2008) *No Small Change: Pension Fund Corporate Engagement.* Ithaca, NY: Cornell University Press.

Jensen, M., and Meckling, W. (1976) 'Theory of the Firm: Managerial Behavior, Agency Costs, and Ownership Structure', *Journal of Financial Economics* 3 (4): 305–360.

Jones, R., and Wood, D. (1995) 'Stakeholder Mismatching: A Theoretical Problem in Empirical Research on Corporate Social Performance', *International Journal of Organizational Analysis* 3: 229–267.

Kay, J. (2012) *The Kay Review of UK Equity Markets and Long-Term Decision Making,* Available: http://lawcommission.justice.gov.uk/docs/kay-review-of-equity-markets-final-report.pdf [Accessed November 15, 2014].

Kiernan, M. (2009) *Investing in a Sustainable World: Why GREEN Is the New Color of Money on Wall Street.* New York: AMACOM.

Krosinsky, C., and Robins, N. (2009) *Sustainable Investing: The Art of Long-Term Performance.* New York: Earthscan.

Kruger, P. (2009) 'Stakeholder Information and Shareholder Value', working paper, Available: http://www.idei.fr/fdir/wp-content/uploads/2011/02/GT1KRUEGERStakeholderInformationandShareholderValue.pdf [Accessed November 16, 2014].

Lo, A. (2005) 'Reconciling Efficient Markets with Behavioral Finance: The Adaptive Markets Hypothesis', *Journal of Investment Consulting* 7: 21–44.

Louche, C., and Lydenberg, S. (2006) 'Investissement Sociallement Responsible: Differences Entre Europe et Etats Unis', *Revue d'Economie Financiere* 85: 81–105.

Macdonald, D., Jeucken, M., Clemens-Hunt, P., and Power, G. (2007) 'Principles for Responsible Investment hit $8 trillion mark on first year anniversary', Available: http://www.unpri.org/media/PRI_media_release_29-04-07.php [Accessed November 8, 2007].

Markowitz, H. M. (1952) 'Portfolio Selection', *The Journal of Finance* 7 (1): 77–91.

Melander, I., and Turner, L. (2008) 'Not promising the earth, ethical banks win custom', Available: http://www.forbes.com/afxnewslimited/feeds/afx/2008/11/19/afx5717812.html [Accessed November 27, 2008].

Monks, R.A.G. (2001) *The New Global Investors.* Oxford: Capstone Publishing Ltd.

O'Barr, W. M., and Conley, J. M. (1992) *Fortune and Folly, the Wealth and Power of Institutional Investing.* Toronto: Irwin.

Porter, M., and Kramer, M. R. (2006) 'Strategy and Society: The Link Between Competitive Advantage and Corporate Social Responsibility', *Harvard Business Review* 84 (12): 78–92.

Porter, M., and van der Linde, C. (1995) 'Green and Competitive – Ending the Stalemate', *Harvard Business Review* 73 (5): 120–134.

Roe, M. (1994) *Strong Managers, Weak Owners: The Political Roots of American Corporate Finance.* Princeton: Princeton University Press.

Samuelson, P. (1965) 'Proof That Properly Anticipated Prices Fluctuate Randomly', *Industrial Management Review* 6: 41–49.

Scholtens, B. (2010) 'Sovereign Bonds and Socially Responsible Investment', *Journal of Business Ethics* 92 (suppl. 1): 131–145.

Shiller, R. J. (2000) *Irrational Exuberance.* Princeton: Princeton University Press.

Shleifer, A. (2000) *Inefficient Markets: An Introduction to Behavioral Finance.* Oxford, UK: Oxford University Press.

Shleifer, A., and Vishny, R. W. (1997) 'A Survey of Corporate Governance', *Journal of Finance* 52: 737–783.

Stiglitz J. (with M. Rothschild) (1976) 'Equilibrium in Competitive Insurance Markets: An Essay on the Economics of Imperfect Information', *Quarterly Journal of Economics* 90: 629–650.

Taleb, N. (2008) *Fooled by Randomness: The Hidden Role of Chance in Life and in the Markets*, 2nd ed. New York: Random House.

Taleb, N. (2010) *The Black Swan.* New York: Random House.

UNEP (2001) *Buried Treasure: Uncovering the Business Case for Corporate Sustainability.* London: UNEP.

UNEP FI (2008) 'Demystifying Responsible Investment Performance; A Review of Key Academic and Broker Research on ESG Factors', Asset Management Working Group (AMWG), the United Nations Environment Programme Finance Initiative and Mercer.

UNPRI (2006) 'Principles for Responsible Investment. An investor initiative in partnership with UNEP Finance Initiative and the UN Global Compact', Available: http://www.unpri.org/ [Accessed October 29, 2008].

UNPRI (2008) 'Signatories to the Principles for Responsible Investment', Available: http://www.unpri.org/signatories/ [Accessed August 31, 2008].

UNPRI (2014) 'Principles for Responsible Investment. An investor initiative in partnership with UNEP Finance Initiative and the UN Global Compact', Available: http://www.unpri.org/ [Accessed December 1, 2014].

2

Setting the scene

The basics and basis of responsible investment[1]

James P. Hawley

Introduction

Since the mid-1970s there has been a shareholder revolution that has transferred the ownership of corporate equities from individuals to institutional investors. Beginning first in the U.S., the UK and other common law jurisdictions, this transformation is increasingly global in scope. Even in countries that traditionally have not had significant individual investment in publicly traded equities (and in some cases, low equity ownership by any entity) we have witnessed the growth of institutional ownership. Not only in geographic scope have we witnessed institutional ownership growth, but there also has been a growth in investment in asset classes such as bonds, hedge funds, real estate, commodities of various types and private equity.

This chapter discusses a set of strategies that have been adopted over the last 10 or so years by a large number of institutional investors. Typically known as responsible investment (RI), these investment and corporate governance strategies focus on environmental and social issues, along with corporate governance ones. More recently, they also focus on financial stability concerns. A parallel has been made between what is known as the consumer revolution and responsible investment. The former suggests that 'you are what you own' (although perhaps not in a too literal sense), while the latter might be called 'you are what your investments do'. Here 'your' means not only the money management institutions (mutual/trust funds and pensions), but most importantly the individuals whose investment and retirement monies these institutions manage. If we think of the consumer revolution as a retail phenomenon, then we should think of these institutional money managers and owners as an ownership revolution.

The growth of institutional ownership began with mutual funds (unit trusts in the UK) and traditional defined benefit pension funds. In recent years there has been a diffusion of the types of institutional owners beyond these two types, including various hybrid retirements (partly mutual, partly defined benefit), sovereign wealth funds and sovereign pension funds. Why? Because these (and other institutions) have come to own the majority of investible assets in many, if not most, countries.

For example, Figure 2.1[2] lists the major institutions in OECD countries that are asset owners in U.S. dollars. While this figure appears clear, in fact there is much complexity behind the data. For example, investment funds may own equity in insurance funds, while insurance funds may

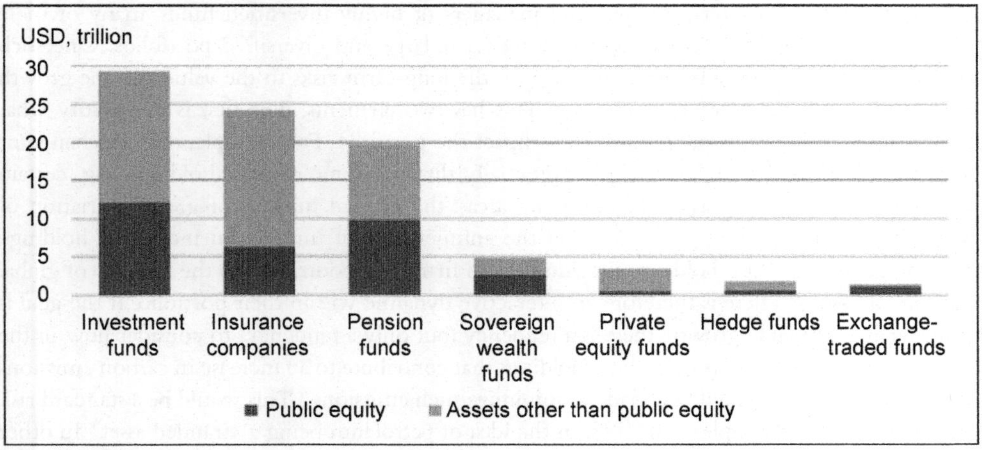

Figure 2.1 Total assets under management and allocated to public equity

Source: Çelik, S. and M. Isaksson (2013), 'Institutional Investors as Owners: Who Are They and What Do They Do?', OECD Corporate Governance Working Papers, No. 11, OECD Publishing; http://dx.doi.org/10.1787/5k3v1dvmfk42-en.

be investors in private equity or hedge funds, which, in turn, may invest in insurance companies. Yet, at bottom, the significance is that the majority of equity in OECD countries is owned by institutional investors. Additionally, these same institutions are significant (and in some cases majority) owners of other asset classes (e.g. bonds, commodities).

For example, U.S. mutual funds in 2014 held about $15 trillion in assets (about half of which was in equity holdings). U.S. funds accounted for half of all global mutual funds' assets. Mutual funds are highly concentrated, with the largest 25 funds accounting for 72 per cent of all assets.[3] U.S. defined-benefit pension funds accounted for just under $8 trillion in 2014.[4] Sovereign wealth funds' assets totalled $6.6 trillion in 2014, the main sources of which were in oil and gas, totalling just over $4 trillion.[5] In the U.S., historically the home of the largest direct individual ownership of equity, in 2014 only about 34 per cent of equity was individually held, with the remainder held by various types of institutional investors.

While the orientation, organization and missions of these various types of large institutional investors vary dramatically, they share a number of elements in common. First, most are very large, some huge. For example, the private-sector U.S. money manager BlackRock has assets under management (in 2014) of about $4.6 trillion. The Norwegian sovereign wealth fund (based on oil revenue) owns just under $900 billion (U.S.) in assets. Due to their sheer size these funds are very broadly diversified in the equities they own or manage, as well as increasingly in the other types of assets. Second, given their size, by necessity they have a global perspective and global reach. As well, there is a tendency to increase investment time horizons. This is aided significantly by their missions; in the Norwegian case explicitly intergenerational, and in the BlackRock case by its management of long-term funds, typically retirement funds of various sorts, either for individuals or for other institutions.[6]

The global growth of institutional ownership provides the structural basis for an interest in responsible investment along at least two dimensions. The first is that most large institutions have a long-term horizon, or at least claim that they do. The second is that they all have highly diversified investment portfolios.

As global and long-term owners and managers of highly diversified funds, many of these institutions consider the implications of long-term, large and diversified portfolios. One such implication is that they must account for both the long-term risks to the value and the growth potentials of what they own or manage. This has two elements. The first is to identify what macro, long-term events or trends could impact the portfolio. For example, climate change or water scarcity (partially related) could potentially threaten some of their holdings (e.g. certain agricultural investments, assets in low-lying areas, the myriad impacts of greater variation of weather generally). Going a step beyond the enumeration of impacts on individual holdings, these large investors also hold equities and debt in firms that contribute to the increase of global carbon emissions. There is therefore an interactive dynamic within their portfolio. If the goal is long-term, sustainable growth, there is a tendency (but only a tendency) to consider how, in the carbon instance, it might impact those holdings that contribute to an increase in carbon emissions and how the portfolio could be made to minimize such emissions.[7] This would be a standard risk perspective as, for example, is manifest in the idea of petroleum being a 'stranded asset'. In other words, an asset as valued today assumes certain price, supply and demand functions projected into the future explicitly or implicitly using current parameters of energy consumption. But change the assumptions (political, economic or ecological) of carbon, and those supply and demand assumptions collapse, leaving the asset value in the future 'stranded'.[8]

While the focus on climate change, volatile weather and water increasingly has been a global theme of responsible investment, the impact of the 2008 global financial crisis added a new dimension to such concerns. In both cases (along with other issues) a central concern of RI has been the so-called license to operate. The idea behind a license to operate (of a corporation) is that as a creature of law (and therefore of the state) depending on legal jurisdiction there is an implicit or explicit contract between the corporation and the government (representing, in theory, broad social interests). While the terms of the license has varied over time and place, common themes have been adherence to the law and operations that do not violate social norms and that do not harm either individuals or others' property. While often violated in practice, such transgressions bring social and political reactions in the long run, forcing greater conformance to such norms. What makes the situation dynamic is that social norms and values are a moving target. For example, while climate change has been understood in one form or another for many decades, only since the late 1980s has it become a major political, economic and social concern as the science has developed and scientific findings have been more widely diffused.

In addition to the social license to operate (meaning what society considers legitimate parameters of actions), the 2008 financial crisis brought financial risks to the fore. With exceptions few and far between, neither RI nor many others were focused on systemic financial risk prior to the financial crisis. Indeed, some institutional investors unwittingly contributed to the crisis through their investment activities (e.g. pouring funds into what turned out to be financial institutions that promoted risk). Besides these 'sins' of commission, 'sins' of omission occurred when institutional investors failed to use their influence and power to attempt to reign in the activities of the large systemically important financial institutions that these investors as a group owned.

Thus, systemic financial risk and climate change are two examples of areas that have had and continue to have grave social costs; that is, impacts on various sectors of society (and the economy) beyond the firm itself. Traditionally, many have viewed government as the entity that is responsible for adjudicating social costs through regulatory and tax policies. In many countries since the 1980s this role has declined or has been challenging to develop. Coincidentally, we have witnessed the rise of large institutional owners, which, as a group, own the majority of asset classes (including corporate debt and equity). These institutions own firms that create social costs (and benefits) – what economists call externalities – as a side effect of their 'normal' business operations. Negative externalities create long- and short-term risks. These take many forms and can impact highly specific sectors or geographic areas or demographic groups, or they can be extremely widespread.

The growth of RI has been partially in response to externalities and partially to the failure of (most) governmental and inter-governmental action to mitigate both externalities and, most recently, systemic financial risk. But this focus has not been primarily due to large institutional investors being 'do gooders'. Rather RI views these long- and short-term social costs as undermining both the social contract of corporations to operate (thus posing a long-term legitimation threat) and as costing these highly diversified owners directly as they internalize negative externalities as a direct result of corporate behaviour. For example, in the simplified case of a firm upstream on a river polluting the river so that downstream firms (and others) have a clean-up cost in order to use the river's water. The owners of the polluting firm thereby create a 'rent' (again using economic speak) for the downstream user, and benefit from this rent. But if both up- and downstream firms are owned by the same institutional entities, the upstream firm's benefit is the downstream firm's loss, and there is no net gain.[9]

This chapter outlines some of the most important developments that are driving the growth of RI and/or the use of RI to characterize investment activities. The most important of these has been in the last 30 or so years (varying by region and country) the massive growth of various types of investment institutions. Most important among these are mutual/unit trust funds, pension plans of various types and sovereign wealth funds (again of various types). What equity markets and other asset class markets (e.g. bonds, real estate, infrastructure) have seen during these last three or so decades has been their domination by these large institutional investors. In countries that traditionally have had large and deep equity markets (e.g. the U.S., UK, Canada), there has been a shift from individual to institutional ownership. The majority (and in some countries, the vast majority) of these markets are now institutionally dominated. The result is that an increasing number of markets are dominated by very large institutional investors of various types. As well, large institutions also dominate across various asset classes. It goes without saying that most markets themselves are increasingly global.

'Responsible investment' and terminology

The term 'responsible investment' (RI) came into existence more or less along with the global organization the Principles for Responsible Investment (PRI), which was founded in 2005. By 2014 the PRI, detailed below, had a membership of over 1,260, and its member organizations and institutions had approximately $45 trillion under management.[10] The idea behind the formation of the PRI was to 'mainstream' what had previously been called socially responsible investment (SRI) in the U.S., Canada and the UK.[11] In many European countries (and others) it was also called 'ethical investment', and sometimes 'green' (environmentally-friendly) investment. The underlying idea behind 'mainstreaming' SRI was what is known as environmental, social and governance (ESG) factors. ESG factors were argued to be material to a corporation's value in the short and/or long run. Yet they were typically not considered such by both owners and most corporations themselves. At the time some argued that ESG factors were 'extra-financial'; that is, they impacted the firm but were not accounted for by traditional financial analysis and accounting standards. Some claimed that in an efficient market such factors were already incorporated into the firm's stock price. Others suggested that, as in the case of corporate governance, they were or could be incorporated into an expanded financial analysis. Regardless of the point of view, the common factor was that ESG factors were material. This distinguished RI from earlier versions of ethical or SRI investing (of which more below).

The PRI defines RI in these words:

> Responsible investment is an approach in investment that explicitly acknowledges the relevance to the investor of [ESG] factors, and of the long-term health and stability of the market as a whole. It recognizes that the generation of long-term sustainable returns is dependent on sable, well-functioning and well-governed social, environmental and economic systems. . . . [and] correctly prices social environment and economic risk.[12]

In the almost 10 years since the founding of PRI, RI has indeed become 'mainstream' (at least in its usage). Yet in its widespread adoption it is used by various organizations and people to cover a range of meanings. To make matters more confusing, it is also used by some as synonymous with the terms 'SRI', 'ethical investment', 'sustainable investment', 'green investment' and 'impact investment' (which itself is often used in a variety of ways). For example, the largest global money manager, BlackRock, explicitly uses many of these terms without distinction.[13]

These often-interchangeable terms have to some degree come to lose meaning and specificity. The terms are also a moving target, in that not only do they sometimes have different meaning(s) in time, but also in various regions and countries. For example, in the 1990s SRI in the U.S. typically described boutique (smaller) investment firms that negatively screened out categories (e.g. nuclear power, adult entertainment, tobacco, alcohol), while at the same time in the UK it had come to mean either positive screening (e.g. alternative energy) and/or engagement (using corporate governance to attempt to change firms' behaviour). For example, the U.S. SRI 'trade group' was originally called the Forum for Socially Responsible Investment, but later changed its name to Forum for Sustainable and Responsible Investment.[14]

As of this writing, RI that prior to the 2007–8 global financial crisis did not concern itself with financial risk issues is coming to include this under what is considered responsible investment.[15] Yet some use the term 'sustainable finance' to incorporate financial risk, which RI ignored prior to 2008. And to make matters more confusing, the term 'sustainable investing', used to mean a focus on financial risk, but today it is also used to include a concern with environmental matters, as well as 'sustainable' social impacts. Some use the term 'double' or 'triple bottom line' ('people, planet, profits') to suggest a similar focus.[16]

In the U.S., ESG (RI) investment is estimated to have been $3.74 trillion in 2012. This includes investments that explicitly incorporate ESG factors ($3.3 trillion), plus investments that have had shareholder resolutions directed at them ($1.5 trillion), plus community investing ($66 billion).[17] While inherently difficult to estimate, $3.74 trillion in the U.S. is about one out of every nine dollars under professional management. In the European context, Eurosif (the 'trade group' of SRI in Europe) wrote that:

> There is no homogenous market for SRI in Europe . . . [it] is very much coloured by the cultural and historical diversity . . . At this stage, no consensus on a unified definition of SRI exists . . . regardless of whether that definition focuses on the processes used, societal outcomes sought or the depth and quality of ESG analysis applied.[18]

Eurosif estimated that in 2011 the SRI assets under management in 14 European countries were somewhat over €1.16 trillion.[19]

For the purposes of this book, we will use RI to mean (at a minimum) investment strategies and behaviours that incorporate, in any of a number of possible ways, environmental, social and governance factors (again, more of which is below). These factors are seen by most of those working in an RI framework as material. That is, using the standard of the U.S. Security and Exchange

Commission and the U.S. Supreme Court definition, it is information that a 'reasonable investor' thinks or would likely think could impact the value of an equity (or firm) positively or negatively. If value is affected, it is or may be material.

Additionally, RI also includes ethical/SRI investment that makes investment decisions not only, or even necessarily, based on materiality, but on various belief systems, be they moral, religious or political. To the degree that a particular belief comes to be widely held in a country, region or globally, it can be seen as a material factor. Thus, there is not necessarily a black-and-white partition between 'ethical' and ESG as material views. Indeed, oftentimes ethical/SRI investment foreshadows (sometimes by decades) what later becomes 'common knowledge' or common beliefs. The ethical and material approaches are often linked over time through looking at reputational risk (to individual firms or whole industries), market risk and political risk.[20] Ethical investment has often been called the 'canary in the coal mine', as it can be and often has provided early warnings and red flags of problems afoot.

Related to the dynamic between ethical and material emphasis is the growth of (and in some cases changing) role of fiduciary duty and obligation in law and practice. Most (but not all) of these institutional investors have fiduciary obligations. For example, mutual/unit funds and pension funds have fiduciary obligations; sovereign wealth funds do not. In common law countries (e.g. U.S., UK, Canada, India, Australia) fiduciary obligations are deeply rooted in common law itself, and all institutions (and trusts) that manage other people's monies and wealth are under fiduciary mandates. But as many of these institutional investors have emerged in non-common-law nations (those with either civil law or mixed common/civil law legal systems; e.g. France in the first case, and Thailand and Japan in the mixed case) fiduciary principles have been legislatively adopted. Thus, it is a reasonable generalization to say that the majority of global institutional investors have, or claim to have, fiduciary obligations.[21] We return to this theme below.

RI and ESG

Background in SRI/ethical investment

As suggested above, SRI/ethical investment has its origins (in the English-speaking world) in the eighteenth and nineteenth centuries (and in some ways going back to the sixteenth century) when the Quakers and later others (e.g. Methodists) tried to align investments with their religious beliefs, banning, for example, investments in tobacco, gambling and alcohol, and later, in the Quaker case, in the slave trade.[22] During the Vietnam War in the late 1960s and early 1970s disinvestment campaigns were waged against, for example, Dow Chemical for its production of napalm. SRI firms such as Pax World in the U.S. (formed during this period) developed portfolios that excluded weapons production. Late in the 1970s and 1980s the disinvestment movement focused on the South African apartheid regime. One result was the Sullivan Principles[23] as a global basis for investment. From these origins grew SRI and ethical funds (often but not always driven by religious convictions) as exclusionary funds (i.e. negative screening), either of classes of assets (e.g. weapons) or of specific firms for their behaviour and/or what they produced.

Parallel and partially related to these events developed the idea of 'corporate social responsibility' (CSR); that is, some form of 'good citizenship' principles and practices that were considered best practice to be adopted by individual firms. (This development also came from the 'lobbying of the corporation' by various groups.[24]) CSR content varied widely, and the term came to mean a variety of things to different people and to different firms. Oftentimes it was little more than window dressing, but in other cases it involved important changes in corporate behaviour.

During the 1980s and into the new century the spread of SRI/ethical investment firms and funds grew, especially post 2000. A number of strategies were developed to construct portfolios, first of equities, but later moving into bonds and various forms of so-called alternative investments (e.g. real estate, infrastructure). We mentioned negative screening above. Additionally, positive screening focuses on those firms whose products, processes and behaviours fit the investment firm's principles (e.g. a portfolio in which energy sector investment includes only clean alternative energy producers or disproportionately so). Similarly, a so-called best-in-class approach culls firms from all sectors (making a representative range of products across the whole economy), but selecting only the 'best' in each 'class' of firms, again based on the elaborated principles and standards of the investment firm. As well, so-called weighted portfolios would be representative of the whole economy (or some part of it) but underweight 'bad' firms while overweight 'good' ones. Most recently, the use of 'impact investing' has grown in the SRI/ethical investment world (as well as outside of it). Impact investing (also called in some cases 'targeted investment') is used to include investments that have a pre-defined desired social and/or environmental outcome, and may ask investors to accept below-market rates to achieve such outcomes. But it is also used to mean investments that generate acceptable market rates of risk-adjusted return while also creating positive impact. Key to impact investing is investors' intent to achieve both positive environmental and social returns in addition to financial returns.

One interesting development of some of these trends is that they have outgrown their clear demarcation definitions, crossing lines between SRI/ethical investment, RI investment and 'mainstream' investment. Again, we are witnessing the blurring of terms and categories and sometimes of behaviours.

Emergence of the ESG framework

The emergence of RI using the ESG rubric rather than using negative screening (or any other particular portfolio construction standard or method) based on moral, political and/or ethics views looked at E and S and G factors as actually or potentially material. 'Material' was defined much like the SEC's accounting standards define material: a factor or development that the 'reasonable investor' thinks could have a material impact on the firm's valuation in the long or short term. Thus, for example, potential environmental clean-up costs would be material, as would outstanding or contingent anti-discrimination litigation.

Since the extraordinary rapid adoption by both boutique and mainline investors of the ESG framework, various metrics and modes of measurement have been used by various rating firms, sell-side analysts, and in-house analysts of large investors in both the private sector (e.g. BlackRock. Goldman Sachs) and the quasi-public sector (e.g. CalPERs), as well as mutual type funds and money managers (e.g. TIAA-CREF, Wellington, State Street). In short, ESG factors are factors that a reasonable investor sees or could see as material or thinks could likely be material in the future under certain conditions. To a limited degree, U.S. regulatory authorities have accepted this – witness the SEC's decision that climate change is an E factor that a reasonable investor could see as material. To this end, it has allowed, for example, proxy material seeking to disclose a firm's carbon footprint. (In some cases, climate change also can have significant social, S, impacts as well).

For our purposes what is material can move markets. What moves markets (a long, hotly debated issue into which we will not enter) is what market participants think is important. It is not information per se (as the efficient market hypothesis suggests),[25] but rather what is taken to be actionable information (knowledge) and/or beliefs. It is not a question of what is right or wrong, but rather what is widely held and how market actors view such 'knowledge'.[26]

This formulation is closely related to Keynes' view of equity markets as similar to the 1920s British version of newspapers' beauty contests. What matters is not what an individual holds as beautiful (which woman is most 'beautiful') but rather what the crowd of beauty voters thinks. If each individual in the investor crowd plays a game of attempting to guess or 'know' what all others think, the process is entirely refractive.[27] While there is certainly more to market movement (e.g. fundamental factors, momentum factors), there can be little doubt that the investor beauty contest plays a critical role in multiple dimensions. It is a classic iterative game.[28] One of those dimensions is materiality. And, as such, refractive materiality is the stuff of crowd-sourced data (as in the wisdom of crowds in its optimistic version or the wisdom of lemmings in its pessimistic, herding version). But from our vantage it is the trend that counts, whatever its merits post hoc. This is not to deny the importance of expertise and 'true' knowledge, but rather to point to the importance of social subjectivity as a defining element in materiality. In this regard, it is performative. That is, it has the ability, based on the production of symbols, to create (or have significant input into creating) a reality.

For the purposes of this chapter we adopt a definition of materiality that was initially developed by Lydenberg, Rogers and Wood,[29] and elaborated by the Sustainability Accounting Standards Board (SASB).[30,31] As the more developed SASB version suggests in its 'materiality map' (developed in parallel to the SEC's view of materiality), the focus is on the 'reasonable investor' (as defined in a number of U.S. Supreme Court decisions). But what defines what is 'material' to the reasonable investor? The reasonable investor is a moving target. To cite only one example, in the early days of corporate governance activism (1990s in the U.S.) the G in ESG had little salience for the then 'reasonable' investor, yet by the turn of the century governance was well on its way to becoming a 'material' issue. For example, measures of governance were incorporated in Moody's and S&P's bond ratings. Why? Because the 'reasonable investor' thought it was a component that need be included in firm valuations, present and future. The parameters of reason had changed. Similar developments have in the last 15 years taken place with various components of E and S. SASB captures this trend in its materiality process called 'forward-looking adjustments', focusing on 'emerging interest' in elements of sustainability concepts among, for example, management or mismanagement that creates (or mitigates) negative externalities or fosters positive ones. It also tracks views among stakeholders.

A second element of materiality is more forward looking, concerned with risk assessment. Here the issue is not necessarily what is 'crowd accepted' (although it may include that), but rather what is likely and reasonable enough to be accepted in the future. While more amorphous than a more immediate 'wisdom-of-crowd' approach, it is an important (and indeed standard) element of risk analysis. Such analysis is often done in terms of scenario building, developing a number of likely (and sometimes overlapping) 'stories' or narratives of what is considered possible, probable or less likely but that has high potential impact.

In short, we suggest that materiality is that which is accepted among a critical mass of 'reasonable investors', which, in turn, is closely linked to broad (or specific) social, political, economic and other trends in the society as a whole (e.g. climate change, supply chain standards). SASB, unlike some other raters and rankers, formulate KPIs (key performance indicators) that attempt to track materiality 'that matters' or that is emerging as directly relevant to specific industrial sectors.[32]

These developments are hardly restricted to the U.S. Indeed, South Africa was the first jurisdiction to mandate ESG 'materiality' reporting. In 2011 regulations aimed at the country's pension funds went into effect that state that 'it is part of a fund's fiduciary duty to give appropriate consideration to any factor which may materially affect the sustainable long-term performance of the fund's assets, including factors of an environmental, social and governance (ESG) character'.[33]

The UK mandated ESG reporting beginning in 2013, while the EU as a whole passed a version of mandated reporting in 2014, to be instituted by 2017. The EU mandate is, as of this writing, quite vague. It states:

> Companies concerned will be required to disclose in their management report relevant and material information on policies, outcomes and risks, including due diligence that they implement, and relevant non-financial key performance indicators concerning environmental aspects, social and employee-related matters, respect for human rights, anti-corruption and bribery issues, and diversity on the boards of directors. Companies will retain significant flexibility to disclose relevant information in the way that they consider most useful, or in a separate report. They may use international, European or national guidelines according to their own characteristics or business environment (for instance, the UN Global Compact, ISO 26000, or the German Sustainability Code).[34]

Thus, there will be neither uniform reporting nor integrated ESG reporting. This is somewhat similar to the UK mandates as well as those of Sweden, Spain, Denmark and France, all of which introduced codes prior to the 2013 EU Directive.

These governmental mandates reflect that fact that ESG has become a permanent fixture of the global investment scene, albeit that ESG has not penetrated very deeply into the investment chain (i.e. at the actual investment level). Indeed, even within institutional investors who give lip service to it (and in some cases may use corporate governance techniques to raise ESG issues in corporate engagements) ESG is not often the stuff of core investment decisions or portfolio construction. This is a challenge yet to be significantly confronted.

It is difficult to measure the total assets under management (AUM), which have some form of ESG metrics. Very conservatively this would include the over 1,250 members of the global organization Principles for Responsible Investment (www.pri.org), with about $46 trillion managed by asset owner members and asset managers members in 2014. The total amount is likely higher, as many investment firms who are not PRI members factor in ESG in some form. In the coming few years it is likely this number of firms and their AUMs will grow markedly. ESG is also used by various rating agencies (e.g. Moody's, Fitch), as well as business media sources (e.g. Bloomberg, Thomson-Reuters).

In short, ESG is a prudent and holistic risk driver (risk being understood in its financial sense of risk/opportunity) when integrated with traditional financial analysis, often called 'integrated reporting'.[35] Because ESG and sustainability are seen by most as reflecting the recognition that they are material, mainstream investment professionals have adopted them, at least at the top management of many, if not most, investment organizations. ESG/sustainability parameters have yet to percolate down the investment hierarchy to impact the day-to-day trading and investment practices that most analysts and professional investors take into account. Nor has it deeply permeated the curricula of most business schools and industry certification bodies such as CFA (Certified Financial Analysts) in the U.S.

Why ESG?

Prior to the global financial crisis of 2007–8, there were two main reasons for the huge growth of ESG factors. The first is that, under significant pressure from a variety of sources, both corporations themselves and investment professionals have come to realize that traditional financial analysis (which does not take into account ESG) is simply too narrow to capture the costs and benefits from a broader, more realistic view of how the world works and how value can be either unlocked or destroyed if ESG is not taken into account. The second factor (in part related to traditional finance) is the widespread acknowledgment (but far less acted on) and widespread concern that current investment time horizons are far too short term, and are incentivized by the short-term compensation arrangements of financial managers and traders, as well as by some (but far from all) corporate executive compensation schemes. By its nature most (but not all) ESG factors are medium and long term, some very long term (e.g. climate risk/opportunity). Thus, a serious incorporation of ESG into investment analysis means, or should mean, a longer-term horizon. In short, the ESG-based criticism of traditional ('old school') financial analysis is that in its narrowness it becomes inaccurate and therefore imprudent.

Partially underlying ESG adoption is the increased pressure from some (but far from all) large institutional investors that are retirement funds (primarily non-corporate pension plans) and mutual funds (running U.S. 401-k type funds). Again, by definition these institutions are, or are coming to realize that they are, driven by fiduciary duty to secure long-term value for their investors and beneficiaries. As such, they are increasingly aware of the risk and uncertainties that weak ESG developments can pose.

In the years since the global financial crisis there has been the recognition that traditional ESG/RI lenses (with very few exceptions) simply ignored financial risk. The mostly unwitting assumption was that financial managers who were trained in risk management were handling financial risks. When this proved disastrously incorrect in 2008, there was a movement to include an analysis of how financial risk was being managed by systematically important financial institutions.[36]

However, two important caveats are in order. First, while there is, as noted, increasing use of ESG rhetoric and metrics, this has yet to penetrate, for example, sell-side analysts and risk departments. The second caveat is that there is significant regional variation both on the level of rhetorical ESG commitment and its complete implementation throughout the investment organization. Europe, for example, is significantly ahead of the U.S., though European firms and investment entities do not walk the walk anywhere near the level at which they talk the talk. ESG action has a long way to go (dare one say a long march?) in spite of remarkable advancement in the early 2000s.

What are the results of ESG (RI/SI) investing?

In a very comprehensive survey of academic (and some practitioner) studies of ESG, DB Climate Change Advisory (a Deutsche Bank Group) concluded that best-of-class ESG/RI/SI stock selection results in superior returns compared to non-ESG investment strategies. (We are not concerned here with funds that negatively screen out firms).[37] The survey focused especially on two dimensions: (1) cost of debt and equity capital and (2) accounting and market-based financial performance. Its findings are overwhelming: ESG-based investment, using a variety of styles of portfolio construction, along with one form or another of active engagement with management (governance), produces superior returns over the medium and long term (3–5 and 5–10 years, respectively).

Cost of equity

Studies examining the relation of CSP (corporate social performance, incorporating especially E and S factors, also known as 'corporate social responsibility') found (looking at a large sample of the largest U.S. firms) that firms with better CSP scores have cheaper equity financing, which augments valuation while reducing risk. One study, for example, looked at firms that after voluntary CSP disclosures were rewarded with cheaper equity capital.[38] Additionally, another study looks at 'capital constraints'; that is, frictions that prevent some firms from accessing capital due to poor CSP, resulting in higher costs, lower-than-desired capital raised, or, in the extreme, blocking access entirely. Firms with higher CSP faced statistically significant lower constraints.[39] A host of other studies focused on G (governance) have produced similar results.

Costs of debt (and regulatory risk)

A study by Gross and Roberts (2011) finds that firms that have better CSP pay between 7–18 basis points less than those that are considered less responsible. Thus, lenders are sensitive to ESG concerns, which result in both lower spreads and longer average maturity of loans of positive CSP/ESG borrowers.[40] Additionally, as the Deutsche Bank Group points out, the cost of both debt and equity is lower for firms particularly sensitive to regulatory risk (e.g. utilities).[41] However, a paper by Berg reports no negative or positive correlation between the cost of debt (as measured by credit spreads or cost of credit default swaps) except for the G factor. In this study, there is neither a positive return nor a loss when integrating ESG factors into portfolio ratings.[42]

Disaggregating E, S and G: a brief summary

As mentioned above, the G in ESG is the most widely studied in terms of what investors call generating 'alpha' (i.e. above risk-adjusted market-rate financial returns). Although not the only reason there is interest in G (as well as E and S), it has been and remains for some investors an important strategy. A host of academic studies have shown that in fact alpha has been (and may still be) achievable using a number of governance metrics.[43]

Studies focusing on G find that good governance reduced actual or potential conflicts between bond and equity holders, resulting in lower yields and high returns. As well, bond default risk is lower, while ratings are higher on new bond issues.[44] Again, as mentioned above, good governance (however measured) lowers the cost of equity, as does perceived good business ethics.[45]

A significant number of studies focused on environmental issues in ESG show similar results as the more numerous G studies. For example, Bauer and Hann find higher costs of debt for firms with environmental liabilities (or potential liabilities), as well as higher default rates.[46] Conversely, Derwall, Guenster, Bauer and Koelijk find an 'eco-premium' in well-managed environmental risk by firms.[47]

Margolis et al. in a meta-analysis of 44 studies found that corporate social performance (not quite the same as ESG, but overlapping) had a neutral or positive correlation with equity performance and accounting measures. A similar but earlier result was found by Orlitzky.[48]

While there are to date far fewer studies of S in ESG (S being very broad and in some cases difficult or impossible to quantify), the studies that have been done have similar conclusions to the E and G studies. For example, one study found a positive relation between credit risk and employee relations.[49]

Two cautionary notes should be addressed briefly about the tendency to have a composite rating or score using a variety of ESG metrics. For example, some energy companies have relatively strong scores on corporate governance and the management of environmental and social issues, while scoring low on a measurement of environmental impact (which is different from the management of environmental issues). Thus, in one ranking BP, Statoil and Total ranked high on social issues, yet by their nature could not rank equally high on climate-related environmental issues. How different responsible investors address these dilemmas varies widely and is obviously an important issue. In short, it is possible, and in some sectors likely, that E and S and

G may well diverge.[50] A second cautionary note is that in some ratings engagement (G) is used in particularly important cases, focusing on E, S and/or G itself. If the very act of engagement with a firm increases an ESG rating (regardless of outcome), what is being rated is process rather than outcome.

In sum

There is an increasingly large information and rating market for ESG factors, and the majority of academic studies of ESG factors suggest a positive correlation between 'good' ESG and lower debt costs (and more access to capital), fewer defaults and stronger equity pricing. In some cases and for limited time periods alpha seeking also contributes to higher equity prices. Different studies use a large variety of data to reach these conclusions and have looked at the data from both market-based views (e.g. bond/stock prices, fund returns and Tobin Q) and from accounting-based angles (e.g. ROA, ROE, firm value). To date, few studies have been able to establish causation in a robust manner, but rather have established correlation between performance and some element (and some definition) of ESG.

RI and fiduciary obligation

These topics, all related to materiality of ESG issues, lead us to a further consideration of fiduciary obligations and duties. There is an important link between fiduciary obligation and law, on the one hand, and RI on the other. Fiduciary obligations involve the duty of loyalty and the duty of prudence. Part of the duty of loyalty is the duty of impartiality. Loyalty means a single, non-conflicted focus on the beneficiary or investor (e.g. of a pension fund or mutual fund, respectively). These investors in their great majority are saving for retirement, a long-term prospect by definition. Pension funds and retirement investment institutions have a loyalty to a cross-generational population, from those in their early 20s to those who may have retired 20 or more years ago. As such, the duty of impartiality means that the older, for example, cannot be favoured at the (possible) expense of the younger. Thus, for example, ignoring climate change risk (which will disproportionately hurt the younger cohort) would violate standards of impartiality. Therefore, a core element of RI is investing for the longer term or, at minimum, not making short(er)-term investments that would put longer-term ones at risk. A balance must be struck to ensure that the obligation of loyalty is met.

The duty of prudence has been interpreted in a variety of ways: far too often it has meant doing what other professional investors in similar positions would do. This has been characterized as the lemming standard, and arguably contributed to the herding effect so clearly witnessed during the 2008 financial crisis and panic. Our view is that the duty of prudence means, in the traditional Latin meaning of the term ('prudentia'): foresight, wisdom and discretion.[51] The implication is that a multiplicity of investment strategies and philosophies would (and to a degree have) emerged, as no individual or entity can ever have a monopoly on wisdom or foresight.

In summary, the majority of global funds, and the great majority of RI funds, are bound by fiduciary law and tradition, with attendant obligations. RI therefore combines ESG and fiduciary obligations, although as indicated above excluding sovereign wealth funds and some other institutional investors.

That said, fiduciary duty in common law jurisdictions is far more constricting than in non-common-law regions. For example, in France it is possible (and commonplace) that institutional fiduciaries explicitly take into account stakeholders who are neither direct beneficiaries nor investors when making investment decisions. (Similarly, French corporations are mandated to consider stakeholder interests when conducting operations. Whether they in fact behave differently than their common law counterparts is another story.) This is in contrast to, for example, the U.S., where taking into account 'non-material' stakeholders in investment decisions is not permissible. Yet even in the U.S. (and other common law jurisdictions) there has recently been a tendency to somewhat blur or ease distinctions between stockowner/holder and stakeholder.

For example CalPERs, the giant California public pension fund in its 2013 'investment beliefs' (#3) states that its "investment decisions may reflect wider stakeholder views, provided they are consistent with its fiduciary duty to members and beneficiaries". This is the first time that CalPERs or any other public pension fund has (to our knowledge) brought any consideration of 'stakeholders' into its public statements in any form. Enumerating a number of considerations as to whether it will engage on 'issues raised by stakeholders' it stressed, among other factors, whether the issue was material; that is, "does the issue have the potential for an impact on portfolio risk or return?"[52]

Following logically from this belief is CalPERs' expansion of the very idea of what capital is composed of. Its investment belief #4 states that, 'Long-term value creation requires effective management of three forms of capital: financial, physical and human'.[53] Thus, financial capital focuses on alignment of interests between its managers, the 'investee' company and external managers. This is a governance issue and applies as well to environmental and human capital. The latter includes (but in CalPERs' view is not limited to) labour practices, health and safety, responsible contracting and diversity. Natural capital concerns environmental practices of various sorts.[54]

The CalPERs example reflects what Waitzer has suggested is the emergence of the 'public fiduciary'. The idea here is that:

> as societies become more complex, we are driven, in pursuing our self-interest, to cooperate and find nonzero-sum solutions to social problems – solutions that produce benefits for third parties as well as ourselves. This is the logic underlying . . . [Canada's] Supreme Court's promotion of the 'fiduciary society' concept and similar developments in other jurisdictions.[55]

Another way to put this idea is that fiduciaries have an obligation to their beneficiaries and investors to do due diligence in order to ensure their future 'risk-adjusted income'. That is, even if the narrow financial return to future retirees is superior, if it comes at the cost of, for example, increased climate risk, social disruption from potential massive inequality and the like, the income has not been risk adjusted. It will buy less. We might call this macro factor 'risk adjustment'.

These and similar trends and thinking tend to blur the once clear lines between ethical/SRI investing and fiduciary investing (based on finance theory) in common law countries. In sum, ethical investing, socially responsible investing, responsible investment and sustainable investment, while all originating in somewhat different venues and times, increasingly merge in many practices and sometimes in their meanings. In turn, ESG, RI and sustainability are increasingly terms and concepts used by mainstream investors that previously had avoided these issues. Added to this mix has been, since the global financial crisis of 2008, the inclusion of financial risk and stability as a core foci.[56] While (far too) much of mainstream investment is, rhetoric aside, short-term oriented, time frame should be a critical differentiator between what is RI and what is not. While RI can engage in tactical short-term actions, overwhelmingly it must be long-term oriented in rhetoric and reality; the latter is far more difficult than the former.[57]

Conclusion

Hebb and Louche write that they see three generally accepted arguments for what they call SRI (which for our purposes is the same as RI):

> (1) the business case or investment case where ESG factors are considered as valid components of investment decisions because of their materiality; (2) the reputation and license to operate case where SRI helps the financial institution to maintain or regain a good CSR reputation; and (3) the client case, where SRI is about delivering what the client wants in investment. In none of these three cases is instrumental social change part of the goal of SRI. As a result, we may want to add a fourth rational which would be the societal impact case where SRI is being considered because of the positive social and environmental change it (may) create in society. Ideally of course we would like SRI to integrate all four rationales.[58]

We might add that there is a link in some if not many instances where socioeconomic betterment may itself be a 'material' force. To the degree that such betterment focuses on economic development (e.g. better housing, infrastructure, less income inequality), it is demand stimulating and is not restricted to 'just' social issues. For example, reduction in income inequality is likely to stimulate consumer demand (for the lower two-thirds to three-quarters of the population), in turn, stimulating business and business investment in goods and services. Infrastructure improvement (e.g. roads, bridges, railroads) improves productivity that has the potential (but only the potential) to be passed on in better and/or less expensive goods. In short, the 'social' is almost always tightly integrated with the broader economic landscape. Indeed, economic landscapes are in fact socioeconomic ones. The same holds true for various environmental issues.

In the last decade RI has expanded beyond stocks and bonds into a variety of asset classes, such as infrastructure, emerging market assets of various sorts and private equity and some hedge funds. As well, RI has come to include a host of investment styles. The Investment Leaders Group lists eight major styles:[59]

- Green investment focusing on clean energy
- Best in class, which selects the most responsible investments across various sectors
- ESG integration, which goes more deeply than best in class into product strategy, innovation, research and development, human resources, etc.
- Thematic investment (e.g. agriculture, water, information technology)
- Impact investing, which seeks a focused investment objective (e.g. low carbon, homeless employment)
- Sustainable investing – can be similar to best in class, unless more specifically defined (e.g. promoting long-term financial stability)
- SRI private equity
- Shareholder engagement

Obviously these are not all-exclusive categories. What this list illustrates is the relatively rapid spread into many, if not all, asset classes of mainstream investment. Yet the weak point has been and continues to be in what is often called the 'investment chain', which is long and usually complex, involving investment advisers, fiduciary advisers and lawyers, investment consultants, brokers and the like. Each link in the chain is paid, and each has its own self-interests, often conflicting (even in a supposedly fiduciary context) with the ultimate investors or pension fund beneficiaries. This is the case regardless of portfolio styles. Aligning the agents in these chains remains a formidable yet crucial challenge. Here there is a crucial role for government policy in order to enforce fiduciary obligation throughout the investment chain and to minimize or eliminate conflicts of interests. The first step in investment chain reform is the need for total transparency, especially regarding fees and contract terms.

Assume this comes to pass; does all of this really matter? That is, is RI in all its forms actually having an impact on firms' behaviours? And if so, how much of an impact in a given area? Put another way, is RI affecting what is usually called corporate social responsibility (CSR)? From the point of view of mainstream business language, both RI and CSR are commonly used. Most large firms include a CSR section in their annual reports, while some issue separate (typically very glossy) CSR reports. But far too much of this is 'green wash', rather than clearly reflecting actual changed behaviour. We also need to know where there has been real improvement in CSR, how much can be attributed to RI, compared with, for example, social-civil society campaigns for corporate change, governmental regulation, media coverage and the like? There is precious little data to go on and few robust studies to guide us. Nevertheless, RI has the potential to infuse an element of accountability and standardization into CSR. This will be especially so if and when meaningful integrated reporting is mandated, as discussed above.

If we use a simple indicator of a move away from short-term behaviour of firms (and investors), we conclude that RI has yet a long road to travel. Short termism remains the overwhelming practice. Yet in other regards the last decade has made some progress, perhaps the most important is putting real CSR and RI on mainstream agendas. For example, Michael Porter and Mark Kramer in a widely read article suggest that most CSR is for public relations purposes and on the whole worthless. Alternatively, they put forward the idea of 'shared value'; that is, focusing on areas that can be profitable for the firm while having social value in one form or another, while coordinating with civil society organizations where possible.[60]

While Porter's ideas strike the author as somewhat abstract and naïve, the still limited growth in the U.S. of so-called 'B corporations' (benefit corporations) suggests an alternative paradigm. Facilitating public policies for such developments would strengthen both RI and the development of firms, such as 'B corps', that aim to incorporate social and environmental benefits into their core operations and business strategies.[61] While B corps will never replace dominant corporate forms, they may be able to set a standard for what is possible, and indeed necessary.

In sum, the growth of RI in the last decade has been remarkable and has achieved a degree of legitimacy that many did not expect. But as the saying goes, to have impact 'the rubber needs to meet the road'. But the rubber has barely begun to touch the road. RI, CSR (or call it what you will) and civil society organizations need to make sure that the tire lands fully on the road, and keeps rolling.

Notes

1 Many thanks to Tessa Hebb and David Wood for their helpful suggestions and comments.
2 Celik, S. and Iasksson, M. 'Institutional investors as owners: who are they and what do they do', OECD, *Corporate Governance Working Papers,* no. 11, OECD Publishing, 2013, p. 9.
3 Online. Available HTTP: <http://www.icifactbook.org/fb_ch2.html> (accessed 18 July 2014).
4 *Global Pension Funds Assets*, Towers Watson, 2014, pp. 6–7.
5 Online. Available HTTP: <http://www.swfinstitute.org/fund-rankings/> (accessed 18 July 2014).
6 Larry Fink, CEO of BlackRock, stated: "Many commentators lament the short-term demands of the capital markets. We share those concerns, and believe it is part of our collective role as actors in the global capital markets to challenge that trend". Online. Available HTTP: < http://blogs.marketwatch.com/thetell/2014/03/26/ceos-are-too-focused-on-the-short-term-larry-fink-head-of-biggest-money-manager-blackrock/>

(accessed 27 March 2014). However, it should be noted that while focusing on the long-term, many funds do not 'walk the walk', as many, if not most, of their fund managers are compensated on short(er)-term performance.

7 I have called these types of institutional portfolios universal owners, as they own a representative cross section of the investable universe. Such a portfolio internalizes what economists call (negative) externalities. As costs are, to one degree or another, internalized within portfolio holdings, there is a direct (long- or short-run) financial and economic consequence. See, Hawley, J. and Williams, A. (2000) *The Rise of Fiduciary Capitalism*, Philadelphia: University of Pennsylvania Press, and *Universal Ownership: Why Environmental Externalities Matter to Institutional Investors*, Principles for Responsible Investment and UNEP Financial Initiative, 2012. Online. Available HTTP: <http://d2m27378y09r06.cloudfront.net/viewer/?file=wp-content/uploads/UniversalOwner-Finallongreport.pdf> (accessed 20 January 2015).

8 Online. Available HTTP: <http://www.carbontracker.org/site/stranded-assets>, <http://blogs.worldbank.org/climatechange/carbon-bubbles-stranded-assets>, and <http://www.reuters.com/article/2014/05/19/shell-climatechange-idUSL6N0O54CB20140519> (accessed 21 July 2014). The latter (Shell) denies that carbon fuels will be stranded.

9 Indeed, there is typically a net loss as the clean-up costs over time outweigh, often by large amounts, the prevention costs. In some cases, the costs are so high as to entirely inhibit new business (or other) activities, what economists call an opportunity cost.

10 Online. Available HTTP: <http://www.unpri.org> (accessed 2 July 2014).

11 Hawley's discussion and consultation with the UN Environmental Project-Financial Initiative, Geneva, Switzerland, 2004–5, out of which the PRI developed.

12 As quoted in Investment Leaders Group (2014) *The Value of Responsible Investment*, University of Cambridge, Institute for Sustainability Leadership, May 2014. Online. Available HTTP: <http://www.cisl.cam.ac.uk/Business-Platforms/Investment-leaders-group.aspx> (accessed 20 January 2015).

13 Online. Available HTTP: <http://www2.blackrock.com/content/groups/global/documents/literature/1111157291.pdf>, p. 5 (accessed 20 January 2015). See also, for example, *The Emergence of Sustainable Investing*, Krosinsky, C. and Robins, N. (eds), London and Sterling, VA: Earthscan, 2008, pp. xxi–xxiii. See as well Robins, N., *The Emergence of Sustainable Investing*, op. cit., pp. 3–17. It has been suggested by some that the terms have always had more in common than being clearly distinct.

14 Online. Available HTTP: <http://www.ussif.org>.

15 For example, investment beliefs #9 ("Risk to CalPERS is multi-faceted and not fully captured through measures such as volatility or tracking error"), CALPERs. Online. Available HTTP: <http://www.calpers.ca.gov/eip-docs/about/press/news/invest-corp/board-offsite.pdf> (accessed 20 January 2015).

16 Online. Available HTTP: <http://www.sustainablefinancialmarkets.net>, for the former use; and, <http://www.unepfi.org>, for the later use (accessed 20 January 2015).

17 Online. Available HTTP: <http://www.ussif.org/photogallery/venn_diagram.jpg> (accessed 22 July 2014).

18 Eurosif (2012) *European SRI Study*, p. 9. Online. Available HTTP: <http://www.eurosif.org/publication/view/european-sri-study-2012/> (accessed 20 January 2015).

19 Ibid., p. 26. This includes six investment 'styles': sustainability, best in class/positively screened, norm based screening, exclusions, engagement/voting and integration.

20 Online. Available HTTP: <http://europe.nxtbook.com/nxteu/posthaste/actuarialpost18/#/16>, for a good discussion of these categories and how they interact.

21 Excluding sovereign wealth funds. I have previously characterized this as a new element in capitalism, 'fiduciary capitalism'. Hawley, op. cit.

22 Sparkes, R. (2006) 'A historical perspective on the growth of socially responsible investment', *Responsible Investment*, Sullivan, R. and MacKenzie, C. (eds), Sheffield, UK: Greenleaf.

23 As summarized by Rev. Sullivan, who created these standards, they "support economic, social and political justice by companies where they do business; to support human rights and to encourage equal opportunity at all levels of employment, including racial and gender diversity on decision making committees and boards; to train and advance disadvantaged workers for technical, supervisory and management opportunities; and to assist with greater tolerance and understanding among peoples; thereby, helping to improve the quality of life for communities, workers and children with dignity and equality". Online. Available HTTP: <http://www1.umn.edu/humanrts/links/sullivanprinciples.html> (accessed 25 August 2014).

24 Vogel, D. (1978) *Lobbying the Corporation*, New York: Basic Books.

25 Beyhaghi, M. and Hawley, J. P. (2006) 'Modern portfolio theory and risk management: assumptions and unintended consequences', *Journal of Sustainable Finance and Investment*, vol. 3, issue 1: 17–37.

26 This is not to suggest that we do not care about what is 'right', but rather we focus on the relation between state-of-the-art expertise and the 'wisdom of crowds' (investors), an always complex and changing dynamic.
27 Online. Available HTTP: <http://www.economicsnetwork.ac.uk/sites/default/files/Ashley/6%20References%20for%20KBC.pdf> (accessed 20 January 2015). Keith Ambachsteer has also written in his 'Newsletters' some very good material on this theme.
28 "We have reached the third degree where we devote our intelligences to anticipating what the average opinion expects the average opinion to be. And there are some, I believe, who practice the fourth, fifth and higher degrees". Keynes (1936) *General Theory of Employment Interest and Money*, Chapter 12.
29 'From Transparency to Performance', *Initiative for Responsible Investment*, Harvard University.
30 Hawley is on the Board of Advisors of SASB.
31 Lydenberg et al. write: "Our working definition of materiality is a modified version of the materiality test developed by AccountAbility and advocated by the Global Reporting Initiative. Our major substantive revision to the AccountAbility definition of materiality was to increase the emphasis on positive material opportunities for sustainability innovation (in business models or offerings) that might bring competitive advantage". Harvard University, p. 20.
32 SASB.org. Online. Available HTTP: <http://www.sasb.org/materiality/determining-materiality/>. See also: <http://www.sasb.org/materiality/sasb-materiality-map/> (accessed 5 June 2014). The prior four paragraphs are modified from a paper by Hawley, 'ESG/RI/Sustainability ratings, rankings and indexes: the potential of new technological frontiers – natural language processing, machine learning analytics and crowd sourced information', *PRI Academic Network conference*, Montréal, PQ, Canada, September 2014.
33 Pichardo-Allison, R., *ESG Takes Centre Stage with New Regulations*, South Africa. Online. Available HTTP: <http://www.professionalpensions.com/global-pensions/feature/2086032/esg-takes-centre-stage-regulations> (accessed 8 July 2014).
34 Online. Available HTTP: <http://europa.eu/rapid/press-release_MEMO-14–301_en.htm> (accessed 9 July 2014).
35 Online. Available HTTP: <http://blogs.hbr.org/2010/08/its-time-to-standardize-integr/>, <http://blogs.hbr.org/2013/04/corporate-reporting-needs-a-re/> (accessed 20 January 2015), <http://sloanreview.mit.edu/article/get-ready-mandated-integrated-reporting-is-the-future-of-corporate-reporting/; http://www.bwise.com/newsitems/ni002015> (accessed 20 January 2015).
36 See, Hawley, J. P., Kamath, S. and Williams, A. T. (2011) *Corporate Governance Failures: the Role of Institutional Investors in the Global Financial Crisis*, Philadelphia: University of Pennsylvania Press.
37 Online. Available HTTP: <institutional.deutscheawm.com/content/_media/Sustainable_Investing_2012.pdf> (accessed June 2012).
38 Dhaliwal, Li and Tsang, 'Voluntary nonfinancial disclosure and the cost of equity capital', *The Accounting Review*, 2011; Ghoul, Guedhimi, Kwok and Mishra, 'Does corporate social responsibility affect the cost of capital? (2011) *Journal of Banking and Finance*, as cited in Deutsche Bank study. It should be noted that the Dhaliwal et al. study is one of the few to have some statistically significant causality results. Most studies are correlational: it is not clear whether more successful firms can 'afford' ESG, or whether ESG contributes to/causes success. Whatever the causal issues, and the direction of causality is very important, ESG remains a critical factor in their behavior and business strategies.
39 Chen, Beiting, Loannou and Serafeim (2011) 'Corporate social responsibility and access to finance', *Harvard Business School Working Paper,* no. 11–130, June 2011. (forthcoming, *Strategic Management Journal*).
40 'The impact of corporate social responsibility on the cost of bank loans', *Journal and Banking and Finance*. See also, Cheng, B., Ioannou, I. and Serafeim, G. (2014) 'Corporate social responsibility and access to finance', *Strategic Management Journal*, January 2014, pp. 1–23. Online. Available HTTP: <http://onlinelibrary.wiley.com/doi/10.1002/smj.2131/full> (accessed 9 July 2014).
41 DB Climate Change study, p. 32.
42 Berg, F. (2014) *The Cost of Corporate Debt and Environmental, Social and Governance Performance across Europe, North America and Asia/Pacific*, Université Paris Dauphine, June 2014.
43 Alpha tends to revert to the mean (i.e. is no longer achievable) once the market widely recognizes its value. It is thereby incorporated into the equity price itself. G remains important under these conditions as a driver of equity price, but alpha itself cannot be found. A similar argument applies to debt ratings and bond pricing.
44 Cremers, Nair and Wei, 'Governance mechanism and bond prices', *Review of Financial Studies*, 20 (5); and Bhojrai and Sengupta, 'Effects of corporate governance on bond yields and ratings', *Journal of Business*, 2003; as quoted in Deutsche Bank study, op. cit., p. 34.

45 Deutsche Bank study, op. cit., p. 35.

46 Bauer and Hann (2010) 'Corporate environmental manager and credit risk', working paper, University of Maastricht, Department of Finance.

47 Derwall, J., Guenster, N., Bauer, R. and Koedijk, K. (2005) 'The eco-efficiency premium puzzle', *Financial Analysts Journal*, April 2005; same authors, 'The economic value of eco-efficiency', *European Financial Management*, Sept. 2011.

48 Margolis, Joshua, D. and Walsh, J. P. (2003) 'Misery loves companies: rethinking social initiatives by business', *Administrative Science Quarterly*, 48, June 2003, pp. 268–305; Orlitzky, M., Schmidt, F. and Rynes, S. (2003) 'Corporate social and financial performance: A meta-analysis', *Organization Studies*, 24, pp. 403–441.

49 Deutsche Bank, op. cit., p. 37.

50 Forrest, S., Ling, A. and Waghorn, A. (2006) 'The Goldman Sachs Energy ESG Index', *Responsible Investment,* Sullivan, R. and MacKenzie, C. (eds), Sheffield, UK: Greenleaf, pp. 110–121.

51 Online. Available HTTP: <http://www.latinwordlist.com/latin-words/prudentia-25559779.htm> (accessed 20 January 2015).

52 Online. Available HTTP: <http://www.calpers.ca.gov/eip-docs/about/pubs/board-offsite.pdf>, p. 3 (accessed 3 July 2014).

53 It can be argued that human and physical 'capital' are not capital at all. Physical (e.g. land, natural resources) have value only to the degree that they have investment or labor directed to them, while human 'capital' is in fact labor of all types. This formulation does not reduce their critical importance or the fact that both can be abused and/or devalued. See, for example, Piketty, T. (2014) *Capital in the Twenty-First Century,* Cambridge, MA: Belknap/Harvard University Press, pp. 46, 162–163.

54 Ibid., p. 6.

55 Waitzer, E. J. and Sarro, D. (2012) 'The public fiduciary: emerging themes in Canadian fiduciary law for pension trustees', *La Revue du Barreau Canadien*, p. 203. Online. Available HTTP: <http://irrcinstitute.org/pdf/2013-Practioner-Award-The-Public-Fiduciary_CBR.pdf> (accessed 8 July 2014).

56 Online. Available HTTP: <http://www.bis.gov.uk/assets/biscore/business-law/docs/e/12-1188-equity-markets-support-growth-response-to-kay-review> (accessed 20 January 2015).

57 An element of this is communication about the relation of sustainability to 'core' financial and corporate issues. See, Eccles, R.G. and Serafeim, G. (2013) 'A tale of two stories: sustainability and the quarterly earnings call', *Journal of Applied Corporate Finance, 25*(3): 8–19.

58 Hebb and Louche, 'SRI in the 21st century: Does it make a difference to society?', Louche, C. and. Hebb, T. (eds.), *Socially Responsible Investment in the 21st Century,* UK: Emerald, 2014, p. 282.

59 Investment Leaders Group, op. cit., pp. 55–57.

60 Porter, M. E. and Kramer, M. R. (2011) 'Creating shared value', *Harvard Business Review,* January/February 2011, pp. 152–167.

61 See, for example, online. Available HTTP: <http://www.bcorporation.net> and <http://benefitcorp.net> (accessed 20 January 2015).

3

Is responsible investment proportionally under-researched?

Andreas G. F. Hoepner, David G. McMillan and Michael Fraser

Introduction

We define responsible investment as investment in capital assets based on screening and selection processes or ownership policies, which are not exclusively developed and practiced on the basis of financial information, but are also developed and practiced on the basis of environmental, social or governance (ESG) criteria that account for the investment's current and future impacts on society and natural environment.[1]

If the vast majority of the European and Asian investment managers surveyed by Ambachtsheer (2005) are right, responsible investment[2] (RI) may become mainstream investment practice by 2015.[3] A strong indicator of responsible investment's increasing relevance within financial markets is demonstrated by the rapid growth of the UN-backed Principles for Responsible Investment (PRI) detailed in Chapter 1 of this volume.

If the responsible investment industry were able to utilize this current momentum and become mainstream investment practice, then many corporations can be expected to substantially react to responsible investors' joint force and adopt sustainable business practices and technologies (Heinkel et al. 2001). Similarly, governments, of which several (successfully) attempt to trigger such a development by passing legislation in support of responsible investment (Renneboog et al. 2008, Richardson 2008, Solomon et al. 2002), would very likely become increasingly reactive to pro responsible investment lobbying activities in such a scenario.

Therefore, responsible investment's development into mainstream investment practice, if realized, could significantly support global citizens in overcoming major current obstacles and eventually achieving an effectively ensured form of sustainable development. If this were to happen financial markets would be transformed from a suspected obstacle of (e.g. Haigh and Hazelton 2004, Murray et al. 2006) to a driving force towards sustainable development.[4]

However, the ability of the responsible investment industry to utilize the current momentum and become mainstream investment practice can be expected to depend substantially on responsible investment professionals' skill in developing and executing the best strategies for the optimization of the ratio of responsible investment's attractiveness to (conventional) mainstream investment's attractiveness for (especially institutional) investors. To allow responsible investment professionals to develop such strategies, sufficiently reliable information on a large number of responsible investment research questions needs to have been produced and communicated.[5]

Given the substantial growth and promising outlook of the responsible investment industry, it seems intuitive to assume that responsible investment has attracted considerable interest from academics as well as other researchers. Hence it should generate (academic) research output in at least proportional quantity and quality when compared to related research areas with similar structural conditions. However, 'anecdotal' evidence suggests the opposite. Skimming through the top finance journals, one hardly ever finds a study on responsible investment, while investigations of hedge funds or private equity appear rather regularly despite both industries being estimated to be only of about half the size of the responsible investment industry (Maslakovic 2008a, 2008b).

Three actions of the PRI support academic research in RI. First, they are the main driver behind the academic responsible investment conference (UNPRI 2008b). Second, they launched the Principles for Responsible Investment Academic Network (PRI AN), which "aims to stimulate interest in responsible investment research and provide multiple avenues for greater interaction between academia and practitioners" (PRI AN 2008: 1). Third, they agreed on a joint venture with the "Danish Government to promote academic research on responsible investment" (UNPRI 2009: 1). In 2008 the "first [academic] Responsible Investment Research Conference" was held (UNPRI 2008b: 1), while in the same year the responsible investment professionals met for the nineteenth time at the annual 'SRI in the Rockies Conference' (FAFN 2008) and academics in the sister research area of Social and Environmental Accounting held their twentieth annual 'International Congress on Social and Environmental Accounting Research' (CSEAR 2008). The substantial difference between these fields demonstrates a lack of interest in RI by the average researcher.

This chapter suggests that responsible investment is under-researched. As a result, reliable information on a number of responsible investment research questions is not readily available. This decreases the ability of the responsible investment industry to utilize its current momentum and become mainstream investment practice. This lack of research support is especially problematic in the case of responsible investment, whose development depends on its relative attractiveness to mainstream investment (Bauer and Smeets 2013, Lewis and Mackenzie 2000, Williams 2007).[6]

Such a problem of proportionally under-researched academic support on responsible investment is not only of concern for the direct supporters of responsible investment, such as the professional responsible investment organizations, the United Nations, and several developed country governments, but also for the indirect beneficiaries of the environmental, social and governance effects of responsible investment. These indirect beneficiaries can be thought of as any shareholder whose corporate governance efforts are supported by responsible investment (e.g. Barkemeyer et al. 2013, Clark and Hebb 2004, Hawley et al. 2013, Heinkel et al. 2001, Rivoli 2003, Sparkes 2002, Starr 2008).

This chapter investigates whether responsible investment is under-researched relative to its peers in the financial industry. We examine the research outputs of Scopus and Web of Science (WoS) to interrogate the absolute and relative outputs of five peer areas of financial research, responsible investment, hedge funds, private equity, social and environmental accounting and social marketing.

Research method

To address if responsible investment is proportionally under-researched, we contribute to the academic literature by pioneering the development of a generic benchmarking[7] approach for research subject area output. This chapter provides a high-level overview of this research, and the reader can find the precise development of this approach and the underlying literature described in more detail in the online appendix on the author's website.[8]

While the literature to date has made substantial contributions in the research output comparison of various primary subjects of investigation, including intuitive ones, such as academic institutions or individual researchers, as well as less intuitive ones, like central banks or conferences, we failed to locate a single study employing research specialisms (a term we define as research subjects, research categories or research areas[9]) as primary subject of analysis. Roughly a dozen studies have benchmarked research specialisms as their secondary subject of analysis, and their approaches include some fruitful components. But the secondary nature of their interest in research specialisms prohibits their approaches from being generally applicable or sufficiently unbiased. These studies either developed a case-specific benchmarking approach used only to research specialisms' development in a specific geographic region or they exposed their methods to substantial biases. For instance, they may employ research quality measures that ignore books and monographs and are based solely on citations, despite citations being highly problematic due to research specialisms' idiosyncratic and inconsistent citation behaviour (e.g. Agarwal and Hoetker 2007, Bensman 2008, Borokhovich et al. 1998, Huang and Chang 2008, Leydesdorff 2008, Nederhof 2006, Pieters and Baumgartner 2002).

However, a generally applicable and sufficiently unbiased approach to benchmark the output of a sample of research specialisms appears to be of substantial value for many stakeholder groups, including governments, research funding bodies, universities, R&D-focused corporations, individual researchers and organizations operating in the respective research specialism's market. Governments' interest in the impact of the research they fund has substantially increased over recent decades (e.g. Abramo et al. 2009, Geuna and Martin 2003). Furthermore, empirical studies have found results consistent with the hypotheses that government research funding policies affect research output (e.g. Butler 2003, Groot and García-Valderrama 2006) and that research output affects the knowledge base of organizations (especially those that are geographically close) (e.g. Arundel and Geuna 2004, Sorenson and Fleming 2004). Therefore, governments can be expected to have substantial interest in the ability to benchmark the research output of a sample of research specialisms matched on characteristics such as relevance for society and costs per research unit. This would support them in an attempt to align the annual or aggregated research output levels of similarly relevant research specialisms. Additionally, research funding bodies, universities or industrial corporation's R&D departments are likely interested in benchmarking the aggregated output of (potential) research specialisms with similar input requirements, market entry barriers and academic or commercial potential to gauge the competitiveness within the academic or commercial research specialism's market, respectively.

In our development of a generally applicable and sufficiently unbiased benchmarking approach (described in detail in our online appendix), we focus on research areas and research categories as opposed to research subjects. With respect to the former two, we overcome previous studies' biases to a degree, which is sufficient for us to consider the remaining limitations inconsequential for most applications of our benchmarking approach. For instance, we develop adjustments of research output quality-related measures for the influence of books and monographs. We also use the Australian Research Council's (ARC) rating of 19,537 research journals from any discipline, rather than simply the number of citations. The ARC rates each journal relative to its discipline and aims for an equal journal rating distribution across disciplines. This approach overcomes the bias resulting from different discipline behaviour found when only using citation-based measures of research output quality.

Aggregated research output

Our first and most important observation from our results on aggregated research output presented in Table 3.1 is that from 1970 to 2008 responsible investment had a lower research output quantity ($QUAN_a$) in any estimation specification than any of its peer research areas: hedge funds, private equity, social and environmental accounting and social marketing. Moreover, its lesser research output quantity is statistically significant with respect to all four peer research areas at least at the 5 per cent significance level. Hence, we find responsible investing proportionally under-researched. We do not consider this result to be biased by a potential seniority advantage of hedge fund research or private equity research, since both subject areas had less than 1/150 of their current aggregated research output accumulated at the end of 1969 when our sample period began.

Regarding quality-weighted research output quantity ($QLQN_a$), responsible investment, again, experiences a lower research output against all its peer research areas in any estimation specification. However, since WoS-based estimation specifications provide comparatively very low values for social and environmental accounting, responsible investment's underperformance is only statistically significant with respect to the other three peer research areas. Interestingly though, the significance picture changes after adjusting $QLQN_a$ for the influence of books and monographs published by each research area. Since we estimate that responsible investment research is least likely to be communicated through books and monographs, our estimation of the amount of responsible investment's aggregated quality-weighted research output quantity in any publication medium is significantly smaller than the equivalent of any of its peer research areas at a 10 per cent significance level. We carefully interpret this finding as some evidence that responsible investment does not only experience a substantial problem with its aggregated research output in terms of numbers, but also in terms general research strength, which we understand as aggregated quality-weighted research output in any publication medium.

In contrast, responsible investment's average research output quality ($QUAL_a$) is marginally higher than hedge funds' QUAL and, at least at a 10 per cent level, statistically significantly higher than the equivalent of all three of its peers. Given that hedge funds are least researched by (co-)authors who are affiliated with Australian institutions, and responsible investment is more researched by them than any of its peers except social and environmental accounting, this result, like the ones above, is unlikely to be biased by a potential favouritism of the ARC's journal rating for journals commonly used by scholars in Australia. In contrast, our adjustment for the influence of books and monographs suggests that bibliometric results based on conventional journal publication databases alone provide a biased account of research performance. For instance, social marketing's display of the lowest average QUAL appears strongly related to it being the only one of the five research areas whose publications through books and monographs are estimated to be on average of a higher quality than its journal publications, which leads it to have the best, as opposed to the worst, research output quality, if estimated based on any publication's source (JBMQUAL).

As social and environmental accounting similarly experiences a comparatively good quality in its books and monographs, responsible investment's JBMQUAL value is somewhat lower than that of its two socially responsible peer research areas. In contrast, RI research outperforms its two asset class peers (statistically significant at the 1 per cent level) in terms of average book and monograph influence on adjusted research output quality, especially since the hedge funds research area appears to comprise many low-quality publications in addition to its main journal articles.

But this information on average aggregated research output quality does not provide us with the opportunity to make valid inferences about a research area's ability to produce research output publishable in the world's very best journals, which is often considered to be the number one academic performance currency (e.g. Chan et al. 2002) and hence could be an important component of a research area's ability to stimulate individual researcher interest. Therefore, we investigate each benchmarked research area's distribution of research outputs over the five main research output quality scores in our analysis. We test significance of the differences in quality score exposure using the same process, which we apply to our aggregated $QUAL_a$ dataset. The results show that responsible investment's research output is roughly as often published in a first-tier journal as socially responsible research (for more see the online appendix). But both of its asset class peers' average ratio of publishing through first-tier journals is more than twice that of responsible investment's equivalent and is statistically significantly greater at the 1 per cent level.

In contrast, responsible investment, according to both the Scopus and WoS-based estimation, is especially good at producing mid-level research outputs, as its ratio of third-tier journal publications is more than 17 per cent higher than any equivalent of its peer research areas (with the differences being statistically significant at least at the 5 per cent level). Hence, we infer that responsible investment might experience difficulties in stimulating the interest of individual finance researchers, since its performance in terms of the important top-tier publications has been highly significantly worse than that of comparable capital asset class research areas, even though we estimate its average research output quality to be proportional. The average output quality appears to mainly result from responsible investment's substantially lower exposure to research outlets not rated by the ARC, such as many professional, as opposed to academic, journals.

Furthermore, two general observations from Tables 3.1 and 3.2 underline the necessity of multiple data sources and research area definitions, hence the value of our benchmarking approach. First, social and environmental accounting research appears strongly underrepresented

Table 3.1 Aggregated research output estimations (1970[1]–2009)

Research Output Measure	*Estimation Specification*[2]	*Research Area (a)*				
		Responsible Investment (RI)	*Hedge Funds*	*Private Equity*	*Social and Environmental Accounting*	*Social Marketing*
$QUAN_a$	Narrow (GS)	1,432	4,320	8,960	3,861	2,670
	Narrow (Sc.)	126	224	850	333	366
	Narrow (WoS)	126	187	946	163	321
	Medium (Sc.)	188	252	1,245	503	1,660
	Broad (Sc.)	313	378	2,389	731	2,068
	Broad (WoS)	227	311	1,542	325	702
Mean logged normalized ratio to RI[3]			+0.353**	+1.933***	+0.735**	+1.303**
$QLQN_a$	Narrow (Sc.)	68.85	122.10	422.83	173.38	151.28
	Narrow (WoS)	70.27	101.43	455.88	72.45	168.90
	Medium (Sc.)	106.58	141.13	565.85	253.28	596.20
	Broad (Sc.)	165.68	200.68	887.10	350.40	782.08
	Broad (WoS)	135.70	178.43	785.89	147.13	367.09

Mean logged normalized ratio to RI			+0.337**	+1.758***	+0.530	+1.187**
BMD_a		0.7082	0.5695	0.6501	0.6756	0.5827
$JBMQLQN_a$	Narrow (Sc.)	97.22	214.40	650.41	256.63	259.62
	Narrow (WoS)	99.22	178.10	701.25	107.24	289.86
	Medium (Sc.)	150.49	247.81	870.40	374.90	1023.17
	Broad (Sc.)	233.95	352.38	1364.56	518.65	1342.17
	Broad (WoS)	191.61	313.31	1208.88	217.78	629.98
Mean logged normalized ratio to RI			+0.555***	+1.843***	+0.577*	+1.382***
$QUAL_a$	Narrow (Sc.)	0.5464	0.5451	0.4974	0.5206	0.4133
	Narrow (WoS)	0.5577	0.5424	0.4819	0.4445	0.5262
	Medium (Sc.)	0.5669	0.5600	0.4545	0.5035	0.3591
	Broad (Sc.)	0.5293	0.5309	0.3713	0.4793	0.3782
	Broad (WoS)	0.5978	0.5737	0.5097	0.4527	0.5229
Mean difference to RI			−0.009	−0.097**	−0.080*	−0.120**
BMF_a		0.7371	0.5288	0.6250	0.9225	1.0719
$JBMQUAL_a$	Narrow (Sc.)	0.4028	0.2882	0.3109	0.4803	0.4430
	Narrow (WoS)	0.4111	0.2868	0.3012	0.4101	0.5640
	Medium (Sc.)	0.4179	0.2961	0.2841	0.4645	0.3849
	Broad (Sc.)	0.3901	0.2807	0.2321	0.4422	0.4054
	Broad (WoS)	0.4406	0.3034	0.3186	0.4176	0.5605
Mean difference to RI			−0.121***	−0.123***	+0.030	+0.059
% of research outputs of (co)author(s) from Australian institutions	Narrow (Sc.)	8.06%	1.83%	2.56%	10.03%	2.58%
	Narrow (WoS)	8.99%	0.80%	1.93%	9.90%	2.05%
	Medium (Sc.)	8.11%	2.03%	2.43%	10.48%	6.41%
	Broad (Sc.)	6.23%	1.93%	2.10%	10.86%	6.02%
	Broad (WoS)	7.82%	1.39%	2.95%	9.35%	5.42%

Notes: [1]If we had not restricted our dataset to research published after 1969 with respect to data sources providing reliable publication year information, it would have only covered 28 additional search hits in all 25 Scopus and WoS estimation specifications, of which all but 9 Private Equity hits were published between 1967 and 1969. [2]We abbreviate Scopus as Sc. [3]In our test of the relative difference between hedge funds' and responsible investment's aggregated research output based on equation (11), we excluded the GS-based estimation specification, as it represented an outlier even in its logged form, which is beneficial to Hedge Funds and threatens the robustness of our modified *t*-test.

Explanation: This table displays the aggregated research output estimations of responsible investment and its four peer research areas. The first column states our measures of research output quantity ($QUAN_a$), research output quality and quantity ($QLQN_a$), book and monograph influence adjusted research output quality and quantity ($JBMQLQN_a$), research output quality ($QUAL_a$) and book and monograph influence adjusted research output quality ($JBMQUAL_a$), which are defined in equations (1), (2), (5), (3) and (7), respectively. It also displays a description of the respective *t*-test of the relation between a peer research area's and responsible investment's research output for each measure. The logged normalized ratio and the difference-based *t*-test are defined in equations (12) and (11), respectively. Finally, column 1 shows our book and monograph influence divisor (BMD_a) and factor (BMF_a) defined in equation (4) and (6), respectively, and the percentage of research outputs of (co-)author(s) affiliated with Australian institutions. Column 2 displays the respectively estimation specification, while columns 3–7 display the results. ***, ** and * indicate the 1%, 5% and 10% statistical significance levels, respectively.

on WoS. This seems due to WoS's substantial lack of coverage of second- and third-tier accounting journals. Second, social marketing is proportionally under-researched because of the scope of its narrow research area definition, which implies a tendency for the social marketing literature to state its common descriptor in a study's keywords but not in its title.

Table 3.2 Distribution of the aggregated research output estimations across research quality scores[1] (1970–2009)

Research Quality Score based on ARC (2008) rating	*Estimation specification*[2]	*Research Area (a)*				
		Responsible Investment (RI)	*Hedge Funds*	*Private Equity*	*Social and Environmental Accounting*	*Social Marketing*
Not rated [$QUAL_a = 0$]	Narrow (Sc.)	16.67%	27.68%	31.53%	23.12%	28.42%
	Narrow (WoS)	17.46%	34.22%	33.40%	34.36%	15.89%
	Medium (Sc.)	14.89%	26.59%	35.74%	23.06%	34.88%
	Broad (Sc.)	21.73%	28.31%	44.83%	26.81%	31.19%
	Broad (WoS)	17.62%	30.55%	31.97%	30.15%	14.96%
Mean difference to RI			+11.80%***	+17.82%***	+9.83%**	+7.39%
C rated[3] [$QUAL_a = 0.25$]	Narrow (Sc.)	16.67%	16.12%	11.61%	19.52%	29.23%
	Narrow (WoS)	16.67%	18.50%	4.28%	19.02%	27.41%
	Medium (Sc.)	15.43%	16.55%	10.32%	21.87%	29.34%
	Broad (Sc.)	15.34%	17.20%	12.17%	20.93%	30.61%
	Broad (WoS)	11.01%	15.63%	4.82%	22.15%	28.35%
Mean difference to RI			+1.78%	–6.38%*	+5.67%*	+13.96%***
B rated [$QUAL_a = 0.675$]	Narrow (Sc.)	42.06%	13.88%	18.30%	20.72%	17.76%
	Narrow (WoS)	36.51%	7.29%	15.51%	12.88%	23.68%
	Medium (Sc.)	43.62%	13.73%	19.44%	21.07%	16.08%
	Broad (Sc.)	34.19%	10.84%	20.11%	19.70%	18.57%
	Broad (WoS)	34.80%	8.82%	15.76%	17.23%	25.36%
Mean difference to RI			–27.32%***	–20.41%***	–19.92%***	–17.95%**
A rated [$QUAL_a = 0.875$]	Narrow (Sc.)	19.05%	11.65%	20.98%	25.23%	19.40%
	Narrow (WoS)	16.67%	11.42%	21.39%	17.18%	23.68%
	Medium (Sc.)	20.21%	10.84%	22.62%	24.85%	14.82%
	Broad (Sc.)	20.13%	8.92%	19.58%	23.12%	14.75%
	Broad (WoS)	21.15%	13.62%	21.22%	14.46%	23.93%
Mean difference to RI			–8.15%***	+1.72%	+1.53%	–0.13%
A* rated [$QUAL_a = 0.975$]	Narrow (Sc.)	5.56%	26.82%	21.43%	11.41%	5.19%
	Narrow (WoS)	12.70%	29.39%	24.60%	15.34%	9.03%
	Medium (Sc.)	5.85%	23.13%	21.03%	9.15%	4.88%
	Broad (Sc.)	8.63%	18.08%	19.84%	9.30%	4.79%
	Broad (WoS)	15.42%	29.90%	27.65%	15.08%	7.12%
Mean difference to RI			+15.83%***	+13.28%***	+2.42%	–3.43%

Notes: [1]As ARC rates very few interdisciplinary journals differently in the respective disciplines and their $QUAL_a$ value therefore represents an average of multiple displayed values, the sum of the displayed percentages for each estimation specification does not always equal 100%. [2]We abbreviate Scopus as Sc. [3]Even though roughly 50% in ARC's journal rating are evaluated as C, the percentage of C-rated outputs of all five research areas is substantially lower due to the inclusion of not rated research outputs and especially due to a substantial mismatch between Scopus's or WoS's and ARC's journal coverage, in which the considerable smaller coverage of the former two tends to concentrate on journals rated highly by ARC, and hence causes our datasets retrieved from them to be substantially underexposed to journals rated C by ARC.

Explanation: This table displays the distribution of the aggregated research output estimations across research quality scores for responsible investment and its four peer research areas. The first column displays the five main research quality scores. Each of these is followed by a description of the *t*-test of a peer research area's relation to responsible investment regarding it, which is defined equivalently to equation (11). The second column states the respective estimation specifications, and the third to seventh column show the results per research area. ***, ** and * indicate the 1%, 5% and 10% statistical significance levels, respectively.

Annual research output

Aggregated research output informs us on the current state of overall research support in a research area, and even though it is limited, it remains one of the best possible approximations of knowledge production. However, it does not offer information on the evolution of and current trends in research support. Therefore, we analyzed responsible investment's annual research support in relation to its four peer research areas by means of observation and statistical analysis of absolute and marginal annual research output.

Initially, we plot the graphs of each research area's annual accumulation of $QUAN_a$ and $QLQN_a$ values to the end of 2008 (shown in Figures 3.1–3.10).[10] The graphs demonstrate that all research areas experienced a similar smooth and somewhat exponential growth pattern. In nearly all estimation specifications, in the 30 years leading up to 2000 a research area had not reached 50 per cent of its 2008 research support value. This result suggests a surge in global research output, as well as in WoS's and Scopus's coverage due to new information storage, analysis and communication techniques in the twenty-first century. However, the lack of early growth experienced by both responsible investment research and hedge fund research appears relevant. For instance, private equity and social marketing research achieved similar growth levels 10 years earlier than research in responsible investment. In contrast, responsible investment and hedge funds, whose average publication year is somewhat younger than the equivalent of the other three research areas, have experienced stronger growth in the period 2000 to 2008.

In summary, our observations suggests that responsible investment likely experienced under-proportional research support since its early years, which could represent a statistically significant relationship due to the smoothness of nearly all graphs. But responsible investment's recent research output growth suggests that responsible investment's annual research output might not be significantly lower than its peers.

Estimation specification	*Line shape in figures 1–10*	*Average publication year*				
		RI	HF	PE	SEA	SM
Narrow (Scopus)		2003.8	2005.2	2002.2	2000.7	1999.6
Narrow (WoS)		1999.5	2003.9	1999.4	1999.5	1998.4
Medium (Scopus)		2004.3	2005.3	2002.5	2001.4	2002.8
Broad (Scopus)		2004.1	2005.4	2002.5	2001.2	2002.0
Broad (WoS)		2001.6	2004.5	2000.9	1999.7	2000.6

Explanation: This table represents the legend to Figures 3.1–3.5, as well as 3.6–3.10 below, which display publication year on the x-axis and our measure of research output quantity ($QUAN_a$) as well as research output quantity and quality ($QUAN_a$) on the y-axis, scaled for the stated research area, respectively. The table above states an estimation specification, its representation in the figures and its average publication year per research area in columns 1–3, respectively. The abbreviations RI, HF, PE, SEA, and SM refer to responsible investment, hedge funds, private equity, social and environmental accounting and social marketing, respectively.

Figures 3.1–3.10 Evolution of aggregated research output estimations over time (1970–2008)

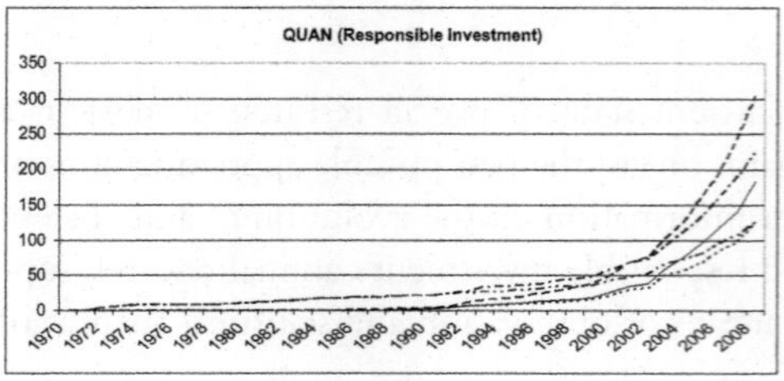

Figure 3.1

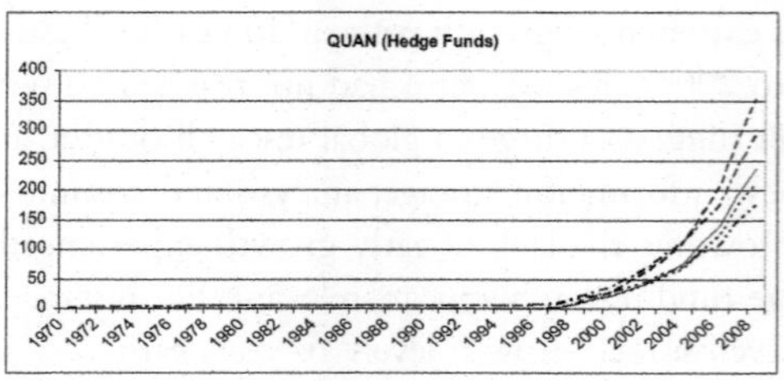

Figure 3.2

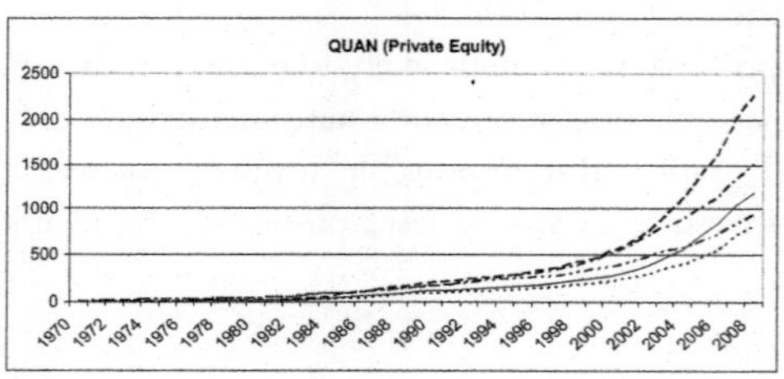

Figure 3.3

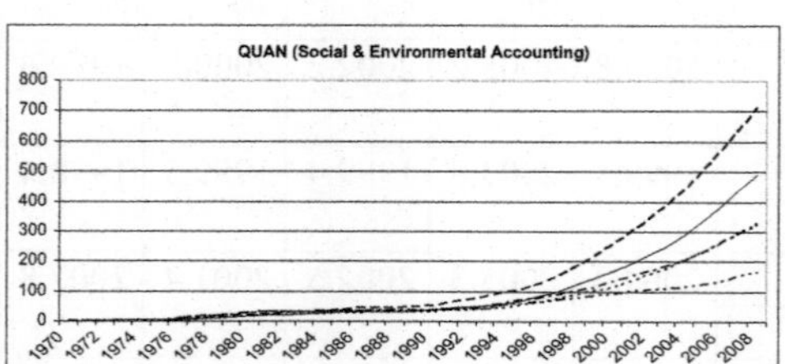

Figure 3.4

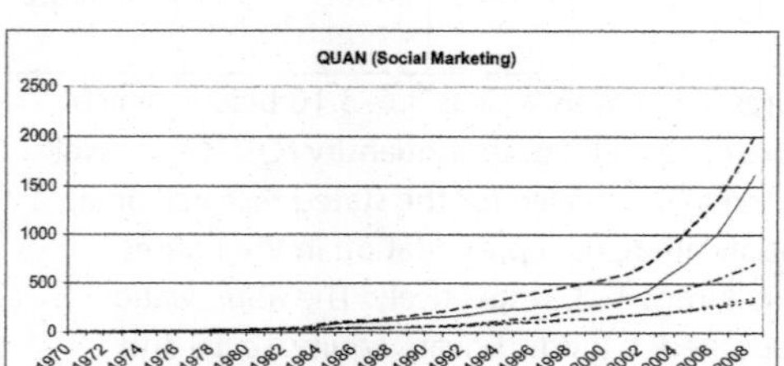

Figure 3.5

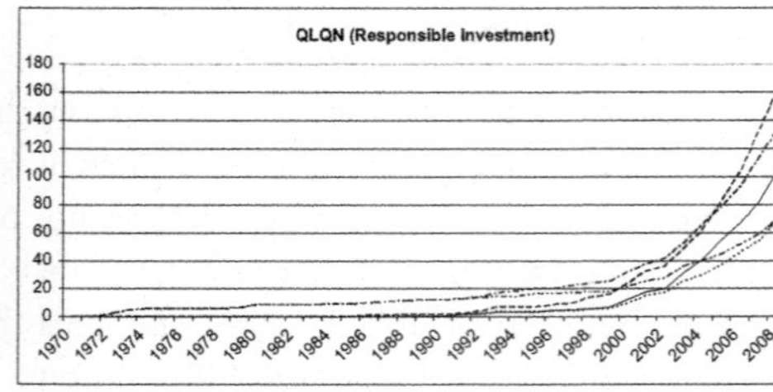

Figure 3.6

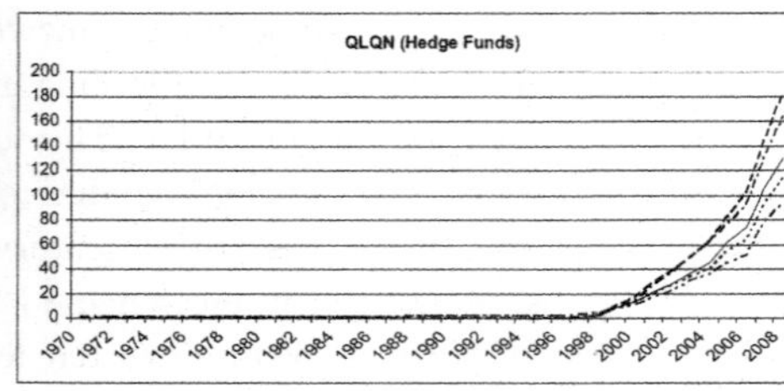

Figure 3.7

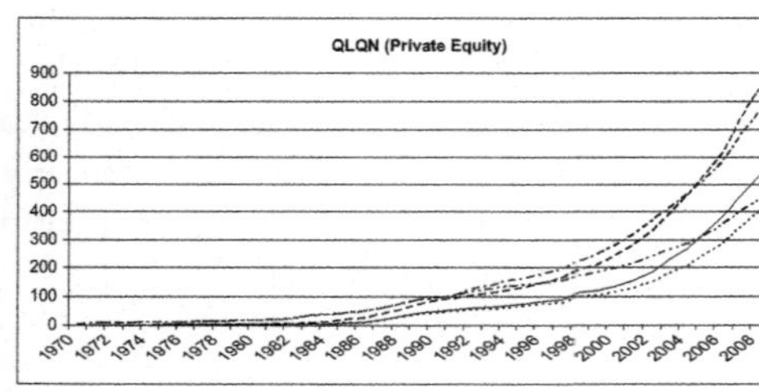

Figure 3.8

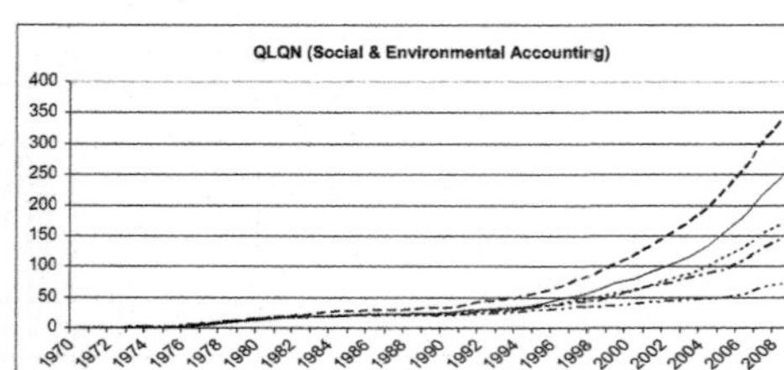

Figure 3.9

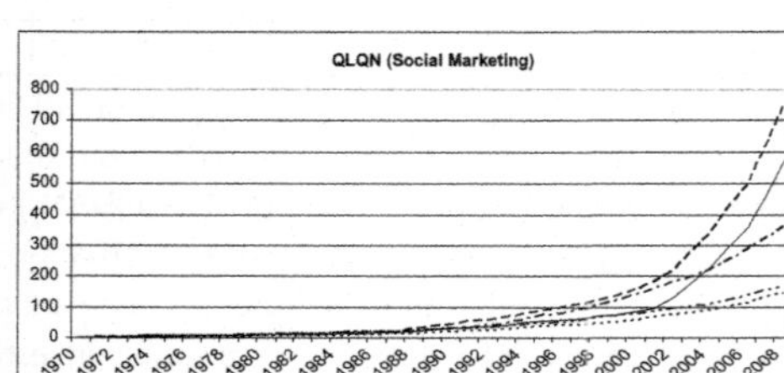

Figure 3.10

We analyze this suggestion by testing the statistical significance of the differences between responsible investment's and its four peers' mean research output quantity, quality-weighted quantity and quality for the full period of completed years (1970–2008) as well as for responsible investment's weaker years in the twentieth century (1970–99) and its stronger recent phase in the twenty-first century (2000–8). We assign a value of zero to each year without any research output in all three performance measures. The results reported in Table 3.3 confirm our hypothesis. While responsible investment's annual research output quantity is statistically significantly smaller than the equivalent of all its peers, except hedge funds, for the full period and in the twentieth century (all estimation specifications at the 1 per cent level), its twenty-first century performance is in all but one case similarly under-proportional but not consistently at the highest statistical significance level.

In contrast, responsible investment experiences an insignificantly higher research output quantity than hedge funds in the twentieth century and only underperforms them in one of five estimation specifications over the full period. But it significantly underperforms them in all but one estimation specification over the last 9 years. With respect to quality-weighed research output quantity, the results are overall very similar, albeit somewhat less statistically significant. Hence, committing to our synthetic statistical safety net against imprecision in our peer selection, we cannot conclude to have found evidence that responsible investment experiences under-proportional annual (quality-weighted) research output quantity. Instead, we carefully conclude that it appears as if responsible investment's annual (quality-weighted) research output quantity has been comparatively weak, especially in the period between 1970 and 1999.

Responsible investment's average annual research quality has been significantly higher than hedge funds' equivalent in some estimation specifications over the full period and in the twentieth century, while it has trailed its other three peers in some estimation specifications significantly over the same time periods. In stark contrast, responsible investment's average annual research output quality has been consistently higher than all of its peers but hedge funds in the twenty-first century. Especially since its annual average research output quality in the twenty-first century is also in any estimation specification higher than its aggregated average research output quality, these results imply that responsible investment research has improved substantially in recent years not only in terms of (quality-weighted) quantity but similarly in terms of quality. This implication is supported by our observation that in any estimation specification more than 17 per cent of responsible investment's A* rated papers[11] were published in 2008.[12]

Figures 3.1–3.10 suggest that responsible investment might have experienced a recent period with over-proportional growth rates and hence could potentially settle its (quality-weighted) aggregated research output quantity deficit sometime in the next two decades. This might imply that responsible investment has been able to make up some ground in its relative research support versus its main competitor for investor attention, mainstream investment, against which RI carries an immense research disadvantage.

We investigate these two suggestions by testing the statistical significance of the differences between responsible investment's average annual growth rate in aggregated (quality-weighted) research output quantity and the equivalent for its four peer research areas. We also test the research category 'investments', which comprises both responsible and mainstream investment during our 2000–8 sample period. As 'investments' is a very broad research category with a potentially high number of common descriptors, we employ a simple one-term definition and apply it only to our broad research area definition scope. Namely, we consider all research outputs to be part of the 'investments' category if they use the term 'investor(s)' in their title, abstract or keywords.[13] On this basis, we apply all procedures previously described for our five research areas to the research category 'investments'. Not surprisingly, we find the research category 'investments', using our

Table 3.3 Average annual research output estimations

Research Output Measure	*Estimation specification*	*Research Area (a)*														
		Responsible Investment			*Hedge Funds*			*Private Equity*			*Social and Environmental Accounting*			*Social Marketing*		
		1970–2008	*1970–1999*	*2000–2008*	*1970–2008*	*1970–1999*	*2000–2008*	*1970–2008*	*1970–1999*	*2000–2008*	*1970–2008*	*1970–1999*	*2000–2008*	*1970–2008*	*1970–1999*	*2000–2008*
$\overline{QUAN_{a,t}}$	Narrow (Sc.)	3.21	0.53	12.11	5.44>	*0.50*	21.89>>	20.72>>>	6.50>>>	68.11>>>	8.41>>>	3.40>>>	25.11>>>	9.03>>>	4.57>>>	23.89>>
	Narrow (WoS)	3.21	1.20	9.89	4.49	*0.73*	17.00>	23.79>>>	11.47>>>	64.89>>>	4.15>>>	2.80>>>	*8.67*	8.13>>>	4.60>>>	19.89>>>
	Medium (Sc.)	4.69	0.63	18.22	6.05	*0.53*	24.44	30.46>>>	8.23>>>	104.56>>>	12.59>>>	4.80>>>	38.56>>>	41.41>>>	10.30>>>	145.11>>>
	Broad (Sc.)	7.79	1.30	29.44	9.05	*0.67*	37.00>	57.97>>>	15.00>>>	201.22>>>	18.21>>>	7.13>>>	55.11>>>	51.59>>>	16.97>>>	167.00>>>
	Broad (WoS)	5.72	1.60	19.44	7.46	*0.90*	29.33>>	38.62>>>	14.80>>>	118.00>>>	8.26>>>	3.80>>>	23.11>	17.72>>>	7.97>>>	50.22>>>
$\overline{QLQN_{a,t}}$	Narrow (Sc.)	1.76	0.20	6.96	2.93>	0.25	11.89>	10.25>>>	3.44>>>	32.94>>>	4.37>>>	1.89>>>	12.67>>	3.63>>>	1.69>>>	10.08
	Narrow (WoS)	1.78	0.59	5.73	2.41	*0.24*	9.63	11.38>>>	6.13>>>	28.86>>>	1.84	1.20>>	*3.94*	4.27>>>	2.35>>>	10.66>>>
	Medium (Sc.)	2.66	0.22	10.78	3.34	0.28	13.53	13.62>>>	4.00>>>	45.70>>>	6.32>>>	2.43>>>	19.27>>>	14.63>>>	2.52>>>	54.99>>>
	Broad (Sc.)	4.14	0.53	16.18	4.72	*0.35*	19.30	21.64>>>	7.04>>>	70.31>>>	8.70>>>	3.44>>>	26.22>>>	19.32>>>	4.57>>>	68.49>>>
	Broad (WoS)	3.39	0.84	11.91	4.21	*0.29<<*	17.25>>	19.48>>>	8.23>>>	56.98>>>	3.71	1.74>>	*10.27*	9.22>>>	4.14>>>	26.13>>>
$\overline{QUAL_{a,t}}$	Narrow (Sc.)	0.262	0.156	0.615	*0.180*	*0.059<*	*0.582*	0.402>>>	0.371>>>	*0.505<<<*	0.494>>>	0.496>>>	*0.484<<*	0.402>>	0.393>>>	*0.434<<<*
	Narrow (WoS)	0.402	0.346	0.590	*0.205<<<*	*0.096<<<*	*0.567*	0.465	0.471	*0.445<<<*	*0.391*	0.381	*0.422<<*	0.504>	0.497>	*0.527<*
	Medium (Sc.)	0.253	0.141	0.628	*0.187*	*0.064*	*0.596*	0.370>>	0.346>>>	*0.450<<<*	0.483>>>	0.484>>>	*0.477<<*	0.321	0.298>>	*0.397<<*
	Broad (Sc.)	0.257	0.169	0.550	*0.174<*	*0.061<*	0.552	0.350>	0.347>>>	*0.361<<<*	0.473>>>	0.476>>>	*0.462<*	0.319	0.289>	*0.421<*
	Broad (WoS)	0.448	0.396	0.620	*0.204<<<*	*0.088<<<*	*0.591*	0.486	0.488	*0.483<<<*	*0.417*	0.412	*0.432<<<*	0.512	0.510	*0.518<<<*

Explanation: This table displays average annual research output estimations for responsible investment and its four peer research areas during our full sample period of completed years (1970–2008) as well as in a twentieth and twenty-first century sub period. The first column states the average of our measures of research output quantity ($QUAN_{at}$), research output quality and quantity ($QLQN_{at}$) and research output quality ($QUAL_{at}$) for each year (*t*), which are defined as annual versions of equations (1), (2) and (3), respectively. In case a year did not see a single publication of a research area, we assigned a value of zero to each performance measure. The second column lists our estimation specifications, while the third to seventh column provide the results for the respective research area and sample period. Average annual research output estimations of peer research areas displayed in italics in columns 4–7 are smaller than their responsible investment equivalent. >>>, >> and > as well as <<<, << and < indicate that a peer research area's average annual research output is significantly higher as well as lower than responsible investment's equivalent according to Fisher's (1925) *t*-test defined in equation 14 at a 1%, 5%, and 10% statistical significance level, respectively.

simple one-term definition, to be very large when compared to the five smaller research areas of responsible investment, hedge funds, private equity, social and environmental accounting and social marketing. The Scopus-estimated aggregated research output quantity for 'investments' is 17,534, and WoS estimates 11,006 outputs in this broad category, with an aggregated quality-weighted research output quantity of 7,414.12 or 6,628.78, respectively.

Our results displayed in Table 3.4 support the indication that responsible investment research is making up ground against mainstream investment research at least in terms of relative research support, since its (quality-weighted) aggregated research output quantity growth rates are statistically significantly higher than 'investment' growth rates in each estimation specification (at least at the 5 per cent level). The research category 'investments' comprises both responsible investment and mainstream investment in a categorization according to the variable responsibility of investment. We find that responsible investment's outperformance of mainstream investment in terms of twenty-first-century growth rates is somewhat stronger.

In contrast, our results do not support the assumption that responsible investment recently experienced a period with over-proportional growth rates, at least following our synthetic statistical safety net against imprecision in our peer selection. While responsible investment's recent growth rates in (quality-weighted) research output quantity are significantly larger than the equivalent of social and environmental accounting as well as private equity and social marketing in all but two estimation specifications, respectively, hedge fund research displayed (in half of the estimation specification) significantly stronger recent growth rates.

Interestingly, responsible investment is the only research area whose mean twenty-first-century growth rates in quality-weighted aggregated research output quantity is larger than its aggregated

Table 3.4 Average annual growth rates of aggregated research output estimations (2000–8)

Research Output Measure	*Estimation specification*	*Research Area (a)*					*Research Category: Investments*
		Responsible Investment	*Hedge Funds*	*Private Equity*	*Social and Environmental Accounting*	*Social Marketing*	
$\overline{\Delta QUAN_a}$	Narrow (Sc.)	26.36%	34.49%	17.19%	13.88%<<	11.09%<<	
	Narrow (WoS)	14.95%	26.14%>>	11.68%	7.60%<<	9.69%<<	
	Medium (Sc.)	29.28%	35.04%	19.14%<	14.61%<<	20.43%	
	Broad (Sc.)	25.81%	37.95%>>>	19.69%<<	14.27%<<<	16.60%<<	15.33%<<<
	Broad (WoS)	18.69%	30.45%>>>	14.56%<	12.25%<<<	12.53%<<<	13.33%<<
$\overline{\Delta QLQN_a}$	Narrow (Sc.)	32.28%	36.55%	16.26%<<	13.09%<<	12.10%<<	
	Narrow (WoS)	16.49%	33.78%>>	10.29%<<	8.01%<<	10.03%<<	
	Medium (Sc.)	37.36%	36.43%	18.04%<	14.51%<<	25.46%	
	Broad (Sc.)	29.95%	38.18%	16.66%<<	14.14%<<<	20.92%<	15.37%<<<
	Broad (WoS)	20.36%	39.74%>>	13.32%<<<	12.06%<<<	12.54%<<<	13.54%<<<

Explanation: This table displays the average annual growth rates of aggregated research output estimations for responsible investment, its four peer research areas and the research category investments. The first column states two terms, which represent the average annual growth rate in our measures of aggregated research output quantity ($QUAN_a$) and research output quality and quantity ($QLQN_a$), which are defined in equations (1) and (2), respectively. The second column lists the estimation specifications, the third to seventh column displays the results for the respective research areas, while the eighth column shows our computations for the research category investments. Average annual growth rates displayed in italics in columns 4–8 are smaller than their responsible investment equivalent. >>>, >> and > as well as <<<, << and < indicate that a peer research area's average annual growth rate is significantly higher as well as lower than responsible investment's equivalent according to Fisher's (1925) *t*-test at a 1%, 5% and 10% statistical significance level, respectively.

research output quantity growth rates. This suggests that sustainable research is making progress in both quality and quantity.

We conclude that responsible investment's recent research support growth rates appear to have been above average, especially in terms of quality-weighted research output quantity, but we find no evidence allowing us to label them over-proportional. However, we present evidence that responsible investment has caught up since the millennium in relative research support against its main competitor, mainstream investment, although the absolute research support disadvantage of responsible investment still widens every year.

Conclusions and implications

We find responsible investment to have experienced significantly lower aggregated research support quantity and aggregated research support strength in the period 1970 to 2008 than its peer research areas with similar research category parents, age and funding potential. We define quality-weighted research output as any publication regardless of medium. Furthermore, its annual research support quantity and strength appears substantially weaker than its peers' equivalent, especially in the twentieth but also in the twenty-first century, even though it has recently shown above-average growth rates not only against its peers but especially against mainstream investment. This proportionally under-researched support of responsible investment may be explained by its under-proportional extrinsic rewards offered to the average individual researcher and especially its over-proportional extrinsic costs required from the average individual researcher, which result from its below-average infrastructure (for more on this point see our online appendix). Regarding research output quality, responsible investment's aggregated average is comparatively competitive, which appears mainly due to its relatively low exposure to publications in the lowest-quality tier. However, RI research often appears in mid-level as opposed to top-tier publications. In this regard RI research significantly trails its finance peers.

Our empirical results have various implications for responsible investment's stakeholders. Many governments interested in realizing the potential of responsible investment as mainstream asset management practice (Ambachtsheer 2005) have established legislative frameworks that support RI (see Tenelli, Chapter 31 of this volume, on this point, also Renneboog et al. 2008, Richardson 2008, Richardson 2011). We suggest that these governments should also follow the example of the Danish government and provide research support in order for RI to succeed (UNPRI 2009). This is particularly important given our evidence that while the relative research support gap between responsible and mainstream investment is closing, responsible investment's absolute research deficit compared to mainstream investment research is immense. The UN-backed Principles for Responsible Investment (PRI) founded its academic network "to stimulate interest in responsible investment research" (PRI AN 2008: 1). One role it might play is to support research journals specializing in responsible investment in order to further improve RI's research infrastructure, as this appears to be a relevant driver of an average individual researcher's research area selection process. Professional responsible investment organizations and any interested indirect beneficiary of responsible investment could build a case to lobby for a proportional research support of responsible investment research based on our results summarized in this chapter.

Notes

1 Our definition of responsible investment is significantly different from but inspired by the definitions of Kreander, N. (2001) *An analysis of european ethical funds,* London: ACCA Occasional Research Paper no. 33, SIF (2006) '2005 report on socially responsible investing trends in the United States', online,

available HTTP: <http://www.socialinvest.org/areas/research/trends/SRI_Trends_Report_2005.pdf>, and Zadek, S., Merme, M. and Samans, R. (2005) 'Mainstreaming responsible investment', online, available HTTP: <http://www.weforum.org/pdf/mri.pdf>. We stress that investment in capital assets based on screening and selection processes or ownership policies, which are exclusively developed and practiced on the basis of financial market information and governance criteria, is only included in our definition of responsible investment if the governance criteria account for the investment's current and future impacts on society and the natural environment. This exclusion of purely governance criteria–based investment is directly in line with the responsible investment definitions of the biggest national and continental professional associations, which estimate their joint market size to be more than $7 trillion assets under management. SIF (2007), 'Report on socially responsible investing trends in the United States', online, available HTTP: <http://www.socialinvest.org/resources/pubs/documents/FINALExecSummary_2007_SIF_Trends_wlinks.pdf>, Eurosif (2008a) 'European SRI Study 2008', online, available HTTP: <http://www.eurosif.org/publications/sri_studies>, SIO (2007), 'Canadian Socially Responsible Investment Review (2006) 'A comprehensive survey of socially responsible investment in Canada', online, available HTTP: <http://www.socialinvestment.ca/publications.htm>. Eurosif (2008a) 'European SRI Study 2008', online, available HTTP: <http://www.eurosif.org/publications/sri_studies> for instance writes that "Corporate Governance risk should be limited [within responsible investment's ESG-risk integration strategy] to the interface between Governance and Social and Environmental issues." Furthermore, our definition of capital asset is based on Greer, R.J. (1997) 'What is an asset class, anyway?', *Journal of Portfolio Management,* Winter 1997: 86–91.

2 There are many other sequences of words, most predominantly 'socially responsible investing/-ment(s)' (SRI) or 'ethical investment/-ing', which are defined as a form of investment considering environmental, social, governance or ethical factors. In line with the overwhelming majority of the literature, Sparkes, R. and Cowton, C.J. (2004) 'The maturing of socially responsible investment: A review of the developing link with the corporate social responsibility', *Journal of Business Ethics,* 52(1): 45–57, Kurtz, L. (2005) 'Answers to four questions', *Journal of Investing,* 14(3): 125–139, Renneboog, L., ter Horst, J. and Zhang, C. (2008) 'Socially responsible investments: institutional aspects, performance, and investor behaviour', *Journal of Banking & Finance,* 32(9): 1723–1742, Bauer, R., Koedijk, K.G. and Otten, R. (2005) 'International evidence on ethical mutual fund performance and investment style', *Journal of Banking & Finance,* 29(7): 1751–1767, we consider this to be an issue of heterogeneity in the terminology of one single concept as opposed to an issue of heterogeneity between concepts. In fact, Sandberg, J., Juràvle, C., Hedesström, T.M. and Hamilton, I. (2008) 'The Heterogeneity of Socially Responsible Investment', *Forthcoming in Journal of Business Ethics* recently carried out a content analysis of websites, investment policy documents as well as quarterly and annual reports of 101 European and U.S. institutional investors that signed the UN Principles for Responsible Investment. They find 'that most investors generally define their SRI practice by emphasising the importance of environmental, social and corporate governance (ESG) issues (and to a lesser degree ethical issues) in their investment processes', which they carefully interpret 'as some agreement when it comes to general definitions of SRI'. For simplicity, we use responsible investment or equivalent terms throughout the text independent of the original wording used by referenced authors.

3 In fact, this prediction of responsible investment being mainstream by 2015 has recently been stated a second time independently of Ambachsheer, J. (2005) 'SRI: What do investment managers think?', online, available HTTP: <http://www.merceric.com/referencecontent.jhtml?idContent=1174905> in a responsible investment industry forecast of Radobank's asset management subsidiary Robeco and the management consultant Booz and Company, Robeco & Booz & Company (2008) 'Responsible Investing: a Paradigm Shift', online, available HTTP: <http://www.robeco.com/eng/press/period/pr/2008/10/responsible_investing.jsp>.

4 See, for example, Eurosif's (2008b) mission to 'address sustainability through financial markets'.

5 Reliable well-communicated information produced by (academic) research is inter alia needed on questions relating to (especially institutional) investor preferences, the financial performance of various responsible investment approaches, responsible investment's ability to receive (further) support from governments or its methods for supporting sustainable development. For instance, with respect to responsible investment's financial performance, Solomon, A., Solomon, J.F. and Suto, M. (2004) 'Can the UK experience provide lessons for the evolution of SRI in Japan?', *Corporate Governance: An International Review,* 12(4): 552–566, suggest that 'institutional investors are hungry for concrete evidence and, although they are actively pursuing SRI strategies at present, still require as much information on links with [financial] performance as possible'. For an extensive discussion of numerous obstacles, which potentially prevent

responsible investment from becoming mainstream and hence require to be researched, see Juravle, C. and Lewis, A. (2008) 'Identifying impediments to SRI in Europe: a review of the practitioner and academic literature', *Business Ethics: A European Review,* 17(3): 285–310.

6 To perceive the size of responsible investments' research support disadvantage burden in relation to (conventional) mainstream investment, consider that when Luther, Matatko and Corner in Luther, R.G., Matatko, J. and Corner, D.C. (1992) 'The investment performance of UK "ethical" unit trusts', *Accounting, Auditing & Accountability Journal,* 5(4): 57–70, published the first empirical study on responsible investment funds' financial performance in 1992, for instance Markowitz, H.M. (1952) 'Portfolio selection', *Journal of Finance,* 7(1): 77–91, ibid., Hamilton, S., Jo, H. and Statman, M. (1993) 'Doing well while doing good? The investment performance of socially responsible mutual funds', *Financial Analysts Journal,* 49(6): 62–66, portfolio selection without consideration of social, environmental or ethical criteria was known for 40 years.

7 Within our academic context, we understand benchmarking not as best-practice benchmarking with the aim to improve the performance of the benchmarking organisation, Camp, R. (1989) *Benchmarking: the search for industry best practices that lead to superior performance,* Milwaukee: Quality Press, but as closest-peer benchmarking with the aim to measure and explain performance differences of the benchmarked subjects.

8 Online, available HTTP: <http://www.icmacentre.ac.uk/person/dr-andreas-g-f-hoepner>.

9 Merging the terminology employed by Porter, A.L., Cohen, A.S., Roessner, D. and Perreault, M. (2007) 'Measuring researcher interdisciplinarity', *Scientometrics,* 72(1): 117–147, and Borokhovich, K.A., Bricker, R.J. and Simkins, B.J. (1994) 'Journal communication and influence in financial research', *Journal of Finance,* 49(1): 713–25, we define the term 'research subject' to describe concepts at the aggregation level of a Web of Knowledge subject category title such as Business Finance, Management or Economics. Research subjects consist in our terminology of many research categories like financial institutions or investment approaches, which themselves represent a group of research areas like hedge fund investment or responsible investment. Our terminological system allows overlaps between individual representations of the defined concepts at each aggregation level. Hence, one research area can belong to more than one research category, and one research category can be part of several research subjects. If we want to refer to research subjects, research categories and research areas, we use the term research specialisms, which we consider to be independent of an aggregation level.

10 We also draw the graphs of each research area's annual $QUAL_a$ values. However, as these do not display meaningful trends or other characteristics and are, especially in the twentieth century, considerably erratic, we do not consider them to provide any information value beyond the insights inferable from the $QUAN_a$ and $QLQN_a$ graphs.

11 These papers have been published in *Building Research Information, Environment and Planning A*, the *Journal of Banking and Finance* as well as the *Journal of Corporate Finance.*

12 Unfortunately, a too low absolute number of A*-rated research outputs, especially for responsible investment, prevents us from reliably analysing the research areas' annual top-tier journal publications.

13 We select 'investor(s)' as our one-term definition as opposed to 'investment(s)', since the latter is often used in ways unrelated to capital investments as simply an output or a unit, which is expected to lead to a higher future input (e.g. time investment). While we consider our simplistic one-word search term to be reliably applicable using our broad research area definition scope, as we expect the overwhelming majority of papers on investments to use the term 'investor(s)' at least in their abstract, we do not suggest a research category definition deliberately limited to one search term to be reliably applicable based on our medium or narrow research area definition scope.

References

Abramo, G., D'Angelo, C. A. and Caprasecca, A. (2009) 'Allocation efficiency in public research funding: Can bibliometrics help?', *Research Policy* 38(1): 206–215.

Agarwal, R. and Hoetker, G. (2007) 'A faustian bargain? The growth of management and its relationship with related disciplines', *Academy of Management Journal* 50(6): 1304–1322.

Ambachsheer, J. (2005) *SRI: What do investment managers think?.* Online. Available HTTP: <http://www.merceric.com/referencecontent.jhtml?idContent=1174905>.

ARC (2008) *Background.* Online. Available HTTP: <http://www.arc.gov.au/era/background_ranking.htm>.

Arundel, A. and Geuna, A. (2004) 'Proximity and the use of public science by innovative European firms', *Economics of Innovation and New Technology* 13(6): 559–580.

Barkemeyer, R., Figge, F., Hahn, T., Hoepner, A.G.F., Liesen, A. and Neher, A. L. (2013) 'Operationalizing socially responsible investment: a non-financial fiduciary duty problem', in Hawley, J. P., Hoepner, A.G.F, Johnson, K. L., Sandberg, J. and Waitzer E. J (eds.) *Handbook of institutional investment and fiduciary duty*, Cambridge: Cambridge University Press.

Bauer, R., Koedijk, K. G. and Otten, R. (2005) 'International evidence on ethical mutual fund performance and investment style', *Journal of Banking & Finance* 29(7): 1751–1767.

Bauer, R. and Smeets, P. (2013) 'Social identification and investment decisions'. Online. Available HTTP: <http://papers.ssrn.com/sol3/papers.cfm?abstract_id=2140856> (accessed 20 January 2015).

Bensman, S. J. (2008) 'Distributional differences of the impact factor in the sciences versus the social sciences: an analysis of the probabilistic structure of the 2005 journal citation reports', *Journal of the American Society for Information Science and Technology* 59(9): 1366–1382.

Borokhovich, K. A., Bricker, R. J., Brunarski, K. R. and Simkins, B. J. (1998) 'Finance research productivity and influence by topic area', *Journal of Financial Education* 24: 8–21.

Borokhovich, K. A., Bricker, R. J. and Simkins, B. J. (1994) 'Journal communication and influence in financial research', *Journal of Finance* 49(1): 713–725.

Butler, L. (2003) 'Explaining Australia's increased share of ISI publications – the effects of a funding formula based on publication counts', *Research Policy* 32(1): 143–155.

Camp, R. (1989) *Benchmarking: the search for industry best practices that lead to superior performance,* Milwaukee: Quality Press.

Chan, K. C., Chen, C. R. and Steiner, T. L. (2002) 'Production in the finance literature, institutional reputation, and labor mobility in academia: a global perspective', *Financial Management* 31(4): 131–156.

Clark, G. L. and Hebb, T. (2004) 'Pension fund corporate engagement. The fifth stage of capitalism', *Relations Industrielles/Industrial Relations* 59(1): 142–171.

CSEAR (2008) *20th International Congress on Social and Environmental Accounting Research.* Online. Available HTTP: <http://www.st-andrews.ac.uk/~csearweb/conferencesnews/comingsschool.html>.

Eurosif (2008a) *European SRI study 2008.* Online. Available: <http://www.eurosif.org/publications/sri_studies>.

Eurosif (2008b) *Mission.* Online. Available HTTP: <http://www.eurosif.org/about_eurosif/mission>. (accessed 20 January 2015).

FAFN (2008) *SRI in the Rockies. The premier conference for socially conscious investment professionals.* Online. Available HTTP: <http://www.sriintherockies.com/pressRoom.jsp>.

Fisher, R. A. (1925) 'Applications of "Student's" distribution', *Metron* 5: 90–104.

Geuna, A. and Martin, B. R. (2003) 'University research evaluation and funding: an international comparison', *Minerva* 41(4): 277–304.

Greer, R.J. (1997) 'What is an asset class, anyway?', *Journal of Portfolio Management,* Winter 1997: 86–91.

Groot, T. and Garc a-Valderrama, T. (2006) 'Research quality and efficiency. An analysis of assessments and management issues in Dutch economics and business research programms', *Research Policy* 35(9): 1362–1376.

Haigh, M. and Hazelton, J. (2004) 'Financial markets: a tool for social responsibility?', *Journal of Business Ethics* 52(1): 59–71.

Hamilton, S., Jo, H. and Statman, M. (1993) 'Doing well while doing good? The investment performance of socially responsible mutual funds', *Financial Analysts Journal* 49(6): 62–66.

Hawley, J. P., Hoepner, A.G.F., Johnson, K. L., Sandberg, J. and Waitzer, E. J. (2013) *Handbook of institutional investment and fiduciary duty,* Cambridge University Press: Cambridge.

Heinkel, R., Kraus, A. and Zechner, J. (2001) 'The effect of green investment on corporate behaviour', *Journal of Financial and Quantitative Analysis* 36(4): 431–449.

Huang, M. H. and Chang, Y. W. (2008) 'Characteristics of research output in social sciences and humanities: from a research evaluation perspective', *Journal of the American Society for Information Science and Technology* 59(11): 1819–1828.

Juravle, C. and Lewis, A. (2008) 'Identifying impedients to SRI in Europe: a review of the practitioner and academic literature', *Business Ethics: A European Review* 17(3): 285–310.

Kreander, N. (2001) *An analysis of european ethical funds.* London: ACCA Occasional Research Paper No. 33.

Kurtz, L. (2005) 'Answers to four questions', *Journal of Investing* 14(3): 125–139.

Lewis, A. and Mackenzie, C. (2000) 'Morals, money, ethical investing and economic psychology', *Human Relations* 53(2): 179–191.

Leydesdorff, L. (2008) 'Caveats for the use of citation indicators in research and journal evaluations', *Journal of the American Society for Information Science and Technology* 59(2): 278–287.

Luther, R. G., Matatko, J. and Corner, D. C. (1992) 'The investment performance of UK "ethical" unit trusts', *Accounting, Auditing & Accountability Journal* 5(4): 57–70.

Markowitz, H. M. (1952) 'Portfolio selection', *Journal of Finance* 7(1): 77–91.

Maslakovic, M. (2008a) *Fund management 2008*. Online. Available HTTP: <http://www.ifsl.org.uk/upload/CBS_Fund_Management_2008.pdf>.

Maslakovic, M. (2008b) *Hedge funds 2008*. Online. Available HTTP: <http://www.ifsl.org.uk/output/ReportItem.aspx?NewsID=73>.

Murray, A., Sinclair, D., Power, D. and Gray, R. H. (2006) 'Do financial markets care about social and environmental disclosure? Further evidence and exploration from the UK', *Accounting, Auditing & Accountability Journal* 19(2): 228–255.

Nederhof, A. J. (2006) 'Bibliometric monitoring of research performance in the social sciences and the humanties: A review', *Scientometrics* 66(1): 81–100.

Pieters, R. and Baumgartner, H. (2002) 'Who talks to whom? Intra- and interdisciplinary communication of economics journals', *Journal of Economic Literature* 40(2): 483–509.

Porter, A. L., Cohen, A. S., Roessner, D. and Perreault, M. (2007) 'Measuring researcher interdisciplinarity', *Scientometrics* 72(1): 117–147.

PRI AN (2008) *Welcome to PRI Academic Network*. Online. Available HTTP: <http://academic.unpri.org/> (accessed 20 January 2015).

Renneboog, L., ter Horst, J. and Zhang, C. (2008) 'Socially responsible investments: institutional aspects, performance, and investor behaviour', *Journal of Banking & Finance* 32(9): 1723–1742.

Richardson, B. J. (2008) *Socially responsible investment law: regulating the unseen polluters*, Oxford: Oxford University Press.

Richardson, B. J. (2011) 'From fiduciary duties to fiduciary relationships for socially responsible investing: responding to the will of beneficiaries', *Journal of Sustainable Finance & Investment* 1(1): 5–19.

Rivoli, P. (2003) 'Making a difference or making a statement? Finance research and socially responsible investment', *Business Ethics Quarterly* 13(3): 271–288.

Robeco & Booz & Company (2008) *Responsible investing: a paradigm shift*. Online. Available HTTP: <http://www.robeco.com/eng/press/period/pr/2008/10/responsible_investing.jsp>.

Sandberg, J., Juràvle, C., Hedesström, T.M. and Hamilton, I. (2009) 'The heterogeneity of socially responsible investment', *Journal of Business Ethics* 87(4): 519–533.

SIF (2006) *2005 Report on Socially Responsible Investing Trends in the United States*. Online. Available HTTP: <http://www.socialinvest.org/areas/research/trends/SRI_Trends_Report_2005.pdf>.

SIF (2007) *2007 Report on Socially Responsible Investing Trends in the United States*. Online. Available HTTP: <http://www.socialinvest.org/resources/pubs/documents/FINALExecSummary_2007_SIF_Trends_wlinks.pdf>.

SIO (2007) *Canadian Socially Responsible Investment Review 2006. A comprehensive survey of socially responsible investment in Canada*. Online. Available HTTP: <http://www.socialinvestment.ca/publications.htm> (accessed 20 January 2015).

Solomon, A., Solomon, J. F. and Suto, M. (2004) 'Can the UK experience provide lessons for the evolution of SRI in Japan?', *Corporate Governance: An International Review* 12(4): 552–566.

Solomon, J. F., Solomon, A. and Norton, S. D. (2002) 'Socially responsible investment in the UK: drivers and current issues', *Journal of General Management* 27(3): 1–13.

Sorenson, O. and Fleming, L. (2004) 'Science and the diffusion of knowledge', *Research Policy* 33(10): 1615–1634.

Sparkes, R. (2002) *Socially responsible investment: a global revolution*, Chicester: John Wiley & Sons.

Sparkes, R. and Cowton, C. J. (2004) 'The maturing of socially responsible investment: A review of the developing link with the corporate social responsibility', *Journal of Business Ethics* 52(1): 45–57.

Starr, M. A. (2008) 'Socially responsible investment and pro-social change', *Journal of Economic Issues* 42(1): 51–73.

UNPRI (2008b) *UNPRI & ECCE academic conference*. Online. Available HTTP: <http://www.unpri.org/academic08/>.

UNPRI (2009) *Agreement between PRI and Danish Government to promote academic research on responsible investment*. Online. Available HTTP: <http://www.unpri.org/files/20090514DanishJV.pdf>.

Williams, G. (2007) 'Some determinants of the socially responsible investment decision: a cross country study', *Journal of Behavioral Finance* 8(1): 43–57.

Zadek, S., Merme, M. and Samans, R. (2005) *Mainstreaming responsible investment*. Online. Available HTTP: <http://www.weforum.org/pdf/mri.pdf> (accessed 20 January 2015).

Part II

4

The responsible investment atlas – an introduction

Agnes L. Neher and Tessa Hebb

Responsible investing (RI) has grown significantly over the past 20 years to become a major force, bringing environmental, social, and governance (ESG) factors into consideration in investment decision-making. With total global assets of $45 trillion under management, signatories to the UN-backed Principles for Responsible Investment (PRI) have declared these factors to be an essential part of their investment process. The availability of ESG data through mainstream information providers such as Bloomberg and MSCI is further evidence of the growth of RI.

However, when we look closely at the development of RI around the world, we see a variety of different approaches and adoption rates across countries, and indeed across whole continents. To gain a deep understanding of responsible investment we need to examine RI at the country and regional level. This section of *The Routledge Handbook of Responsible Investment* provides a detailed exploration of the current state of responsible investment in 26 countries and regions around the world. It describes the drivers of RI growth and provides a guide to the future outlook for RI in each of the countries and regions where this approach is currently practiced.

This section of the volume provides the reader with a 'responsible investment atlas' as a guide to RI on a global basis. We examine RI in regions around the world, beginning with North America, South America, Africa, Australia, Asia, and concluding with Europe. Figure 4.1. shows all countries in the world that we consider in this handbook.

Three regions of the world dominate current responsible investment practice: Europe, North America, and Oceania. These regions not only encompass major global financial centres, but they also have the highest concentration of pension fund assets that are so closely tied to responsible investment practices. Based on PRI reporting in 2014, Europe accounted for 54 per cent of PRI's annual RI filings, while North America provided 19 per cent and Oceania 14 per cent of these annual reports. Europe has the largest number of asset owners and asset managers who are PRI signatories. European asset owners account for 77 per cent of the assets under management of the PRI, compared to 15 per cent in North America. However, when we look at individual countries in each region, the United States, with is large geographic size and population, has the highest number of PRI signatories at 212, followed by the UK (189), France (126), and Australia (119) as of 2014.

But RI has not developed at the same rate or in the same way around the world. This section of the *Handbook* provides insights not only on the current RI market in each country, but also on

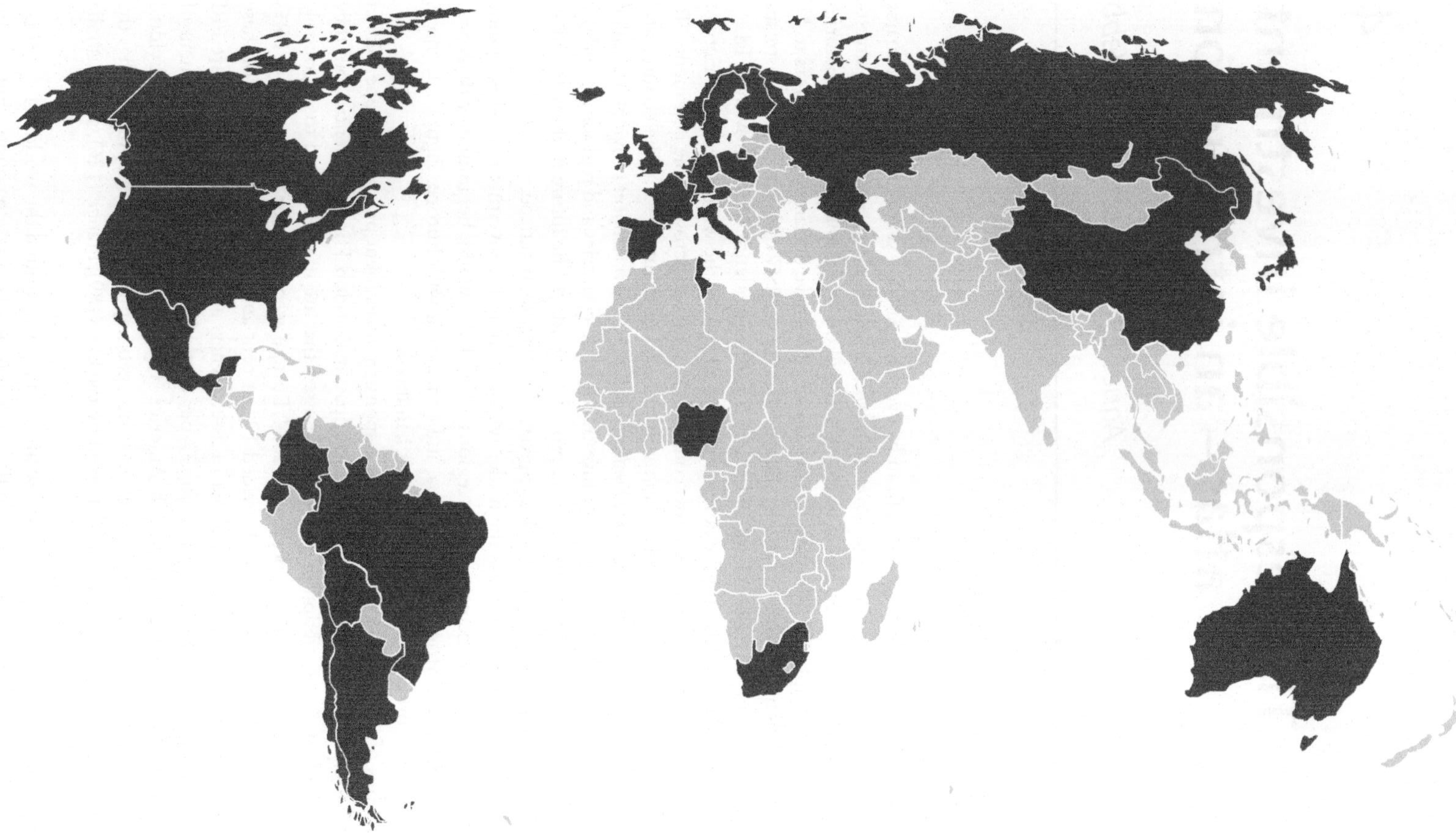

Figure 4.1 Responsible investment around the world

Source: Authors.

each country's pattern of RI growth, its challenges, and future directions. The drivers of RI are vastly different in South Africa, for example, than those in Sweden. Each chapter in Part II explores RI's rich history. We find that in most countries where RI is practiced adoption springs from one of two major forces. Either their earlier history created a path dependence that led the investment community toward RI or, where no such tradition exists, governments create regulatory regimes that incentivize or require ESG factors to be taken into consideration in investment decision-making. While both sets of drivers result in a country's adoption of responsible investment practice, each follows a different trajectory in its development.

The former case of path-dependent histories is found in countries such as the United States, Canada, Australia, and the UK. Voorhes, Weber, Young and O'Halloran, and Biehl and Atkins, respectively, detail the RI market in each of these four countries. All four countries draw on Anglo-Saxon roots, are common law countries, and have similar regulatory and legal systems. In these four countries RI sprang from an already existing socially responsible investment (SRI) community.

Often drawing on religious or ethical roots, this early movement aligned values with investment approaches. SRI was a comparatively small niche in contrast to mainstream financial markets in these early days. Through to the 1990s, divestment was a hallmark of this form of investment approach, with the South African anti-apartheid divestment campaign a symbol of success. However, in the 1990s, this ethical approach was replaced by what is often termed 'the business case' for responsible investment. The result was a reframing of ESG issues as potential risk factors in mainstream investment portfolios, as described by Jim Hawley in Chapter 2.

In these countries divestment strategies have been replaced with positive approaches such as integration that includes best-of-class stock selection and corporate engagement (described in more detail in Part III of this volume). These new strategies brought many new actors, such as pension funds and large asset management companies, to responsible investment, moving RI from a niche activity into the mainstream.

However, not all countries that adopt RI have long histories with this investment approach. In fact, for many countries RI is comparatively new. As Tenelli details in her reflections in Chapter 31 that close out this section of the volume, for many countries it is government regulation that has played a vital role in RI's development. In the 1990s, as continental Europe struggled to find solutions to its looming pension crisis, many governments moved from 'pay as you go' pension schemes, to more fully funded pension models. This shift included provision for these newly formed pools of capital to take environmental, social, governance, and in some cases ethical, considerations into account in investment selection. France, Germany, and the Scandinavian region as a whole all adopted more fully funded pension and savings schemes, and it was seen as important to acknowledge the role of multiple stakeholders in these new funds. The effect on the RI market in these countries was galvanizing and is detailed in Chapters 21 through 29. France, for example, has developed into one of the biggest RI markets in Europe. Giamporcaro explains that in addition to structural changes, there was a religious influence that fostered RI. Looking at Germany, we notice that the market is very distinct and different from the others, as there is a lack of institutional investors in this country. This can be partly explained by the structure of the German pension system, as Neher elaborates. Among the Scandinavian countries the status of RI is very similar. Jensen points out that it was among the first regions to introduce regulatory frameworks and standards regarding ESG integration. However, the countries in Southern Europe, Italy and Spain, have been slower in implementing RI and CSR practices, as Ciceretti et al. and Ferruz et al. write. Nevertheless, we observe a constant growth rate in these countries that is driven by increasing interest in the field of employment pension funds.

In many European countries RI has grown out of a concern for corporate social responsibility. For example, Sofronova details the development of RI in Russia, where it has not yet advanced as a major investment approach. Instead, it is issues of corporate governance and improved codes and standards of corporate behaviour that are fundamental to responsible investors' interests.

Government has also been instrumental in stimulating the RI market in South Africa, where asset owners and asset managers must take ESG considerations into account. In 2011, a Code for Responsible Investing in South Africa (CRISA) was introduced and the Pension Funds Act was amended to include ESG considerations, as Viviers and Mans-Kemp state.

In contrast, the Asian countries of China (including Hong Kong) and Japan have not taken a legislative approach to foster RI in their countries. Japan has the strongest RI in this region, and Sakuma-Keck explores its own trajectory in her chapter. While China and Hong Kong are both still in the primary stages of RI development, Li suggests that this is due to the limited available investment options to investors in China. While according to Chow, in Hong Kong, the RI focus is on improving the corporate governance and CSR of companies in this region.

We find that in most of the emerging market countries profiled in this 'atlas', legislation regarding RI is rare. While we may find legislation regarding human rights or labour protection, there are usually no specific regulations regarding RI as we find in more developed countries. Tunisia and Nigeria provide evidence that RI in these markets is in its infancy. Neither of these African countries have any RI regulation in place. Nevertheless, Okwuosa and Amaeshi point to movement in these countries where, for example, ESG consideration is encouraged by corporate governance codes.

Current challenges in responsible investment

RI faces different challenges around the world. In developed markets, RI must continue to demonstrate the link between raised ESG standards and reduced risk in portfolio management that underpins the business case behind this strategy. Evidence for these linkages is more forthcoming for environmental and corporate governance factors, while social factors continue to be harder to quantify. Additionally, responsible investment itself has to move beyond simply a box-ticking exercise toward a more fully integrated strategy for asset owners and asset managers in these developed markets, including aligning the incentive structure for asset managers to take ESG considerations seriously.

In contrast, in emerging markets it is a lack of general awareness of RI that poses a major challenge for RI going forward. This lack of knowledge results in a limited demand for RI in these countries. Additionally, in these markets ESG standards face issues that arise from corruption and bribery, poverty and inequality, labour conditions, deforestation, or waste.

Across all markets, whether developed or emerging, we continue to find that investors do not have enough information on ESG indicators to be able to fully integrate them into their financial analyses. Investors lack the capacity to disclose how they use ESG indicators in investment decision-making. Training and education will be required to overcome these obstacles.

A final challenge for RI is to move beyond its current focus on public equities and active management strategies and bring ESG considerations to a full range of investment options, including fixed income and alternative investments such as private equity, real estate, and infrastructure.

RI's future potential

The country profiles that follow provide a degree of optimism for the future of RI. Increasingly, ESG issues such as climate change, human rights abuses, or corporate malfeasance are gaining greater awareness in society. Investors are linking these ESG risks to the health of their investment portfolios. As RI moves to the mainstream, investors are able to find readily available information that allows them to more fully integrate ESG considerations into their investment portfolios. RI is also increasingly part of the legislative agenda in many countries. One example is the Proposal for Pension Fund Disclosure Directive recently put forward by the European Commission (2014). It requires disclosure of all relevant risks, including ESG risks, by pension funds in order for their beneficiaries to be fully informed about the pension plan and its specific investment approach. Europe is not the only region taking this approach, and such enabling legislation will stimulate RI around the world.

Nevertheless, we still have a long way to go before seeing RI fully integrated into mainstream financial markets. As you will find in the chapters that follow, some countries in the world are closer than others in achieving this goal.

5

Responsible investment in the United States

Meg Voorhes

Introduction

Responsible investing has gained ground in the United States in recent years.[1] The number of funds and other vehicles that take environmental, social and governance criteria into account in portfolio selection and investment analysis has surged as investment firms, including many of the largest in the United States, respond to client demand. Another sign is the increased support that investors now give to resolutions asking their portfolio companies to disclose their political spending and to strengthen their environmental and overall sustainability policies. Concerns about corporate governance, particularly in the wake of the 2007–2008 financial crisis, and the mounting risks of climate change are two factors driving interest in responsible investing strategies.

Country overview

The United States, with an ethnically diverse population of 316 million, has the largest economy in the world, with gross domestic product of nearly $16 trillion at the end of 2012. Demographically, the country exhibits the characteristics of a developed economy, with high rates of education, literacy and Internet use. While the United States is technically no longer in recession, economic growth has been slow since the 18-month contraction that began in December 2007 reached its nadir in June 2009, and the unemployment rate remains relatively high (7.0 per cent in November 2013).

Well over half of the total value of assets under professional financial management in the United States is maintained for the purpose of providing retirement income and security, and more than one out of every nine of the dollars under professional asset management is in funds or vehicles that employ responsible investment strategies. Responsible investing consists of investment analysis, portfolio selection or shareholder advocacy that considers environmental, social and corporate governance criteria to generate long-term competitive financial returns and positive societal impact.

Market environment

The US Securities and Exchange Commission (SEC) estimates the size of the investment management industry in the United States at $26 trillion,[2] but industry analysts estimated the total at more than $30 trillion by the start of 2012. Approximately half of this pool, at year-end 2012, was represented either by mutual funds ($13.0 trillion) or by other investment companies – closed-end funds, exchange-traded funds or unit investment trusts ($1.6 trillion).[3]

Most of the assets under professional management in the United States are managed in funds and accounts for the primary purpose of providing retirement income to their beneficiaries. Employer-sponsored retirement plans, individual retirement accounts (IRAs) and annuities amounted to $19.5 trillion at year-end 2012.[4] According to the Investment Company Institute,

> The largest components of retirement assets were IRAs and employer-sponsored defined contribution (DC) plans, holding $5.4 trillion and $5.1 trillion, respectively, at year-end 2012. Other employer-sponsored pensions include private-sector defined benefit (DB) pension funds ($2.6 trillion), state and local government employee retirement plans ($3.2 trillion), and federal government plans – which include both federal employees' DB plans and the Thrift Savings Plan ($1.6 trillion).[5]

Today, 60 per cent of US households report that they have employer-sponsored retirement plans, and 68 per cent report that they have either employer-sponsored retirement plans, individual retirement accounts or both.[6]

These private- and public-sector retirement funds and accounts supplement the basic retirement stipends provided by the US Social Security system, which are funded through a payroll tax equal to 12.4 per cent of covered workers' earnings up to a specified salary level ($110,100 in 2012), to which employees and their employers contribute jointly. The stipend, calculated against workers' average monthly pay, in inflation-adjusted terms, over their highest 35 years of earnings, is highly progressive. In 2007, a retiree at full retirement age "would have received 90 per cent of the first $680 of average monthly earnings, 32 per cent of earnings between $680 and $4,100, and 15 per cent of earnings above $4,100", according to a study by the Congressional Budget Office.[7]

Responsible investment market

According to surveys and research that the US SIF Foundation[8] commissioned in 2012, more than one out of every nine dollars under professional management in the United States[9] is invested according to strategies of sustainable and responsible investing (SRI). The SIF Foundation identified:

- $3.3 trillion in assets held by institutional investors or money managers to which various environmental, social, and governance (ESG) criteria are applied in investment analysis and portfolio selection, and
- $1.5 trillion in assets held by more than 200 institutional investors or money managers that filed or co-filed shareholder resolutions on ESG issues from 2010 through 2012.

These two segments of assets, after eliminating for double-counting, yielded the overall total of $3.74 trillion.[10] The assets involved were divided between institutional investors (asset owners)[11] and money managers, as shown in Table 5.1.

US SIF: The Forum for Sustainable and Responsible Investment, the US membership association for the responsible investment industry, defines sustainable and responsible investment as an investment discipline that considers environmental, social, and corporate governance criteria to generate long-term competitive financial returns and positive societal impact. In the United States, there is no single approach to or motivation for sustainable and responsible investing.

Table 5.1 Assets under management in the United States

Assets (in Billions US$) Represented by	*Considering ESG Factors in Investment Analysis*	*Filing Shareholder Resolutions*
U.S. Institutional Asset Owners	$2,484	$1,285
U.S. Money Managers	$1,412	$251
Total (after eliminating double-counting)	$3,314	$1,536

Source: US SIF Foundation (2012) *2012 Report on Sustainable and Responsible Investing Trends in the United States*, Washington, DC: US SIF Foundation, p. 14.

This multiplicity of motives was evidenced by the Foundation's 2010 survey results. A subset of 292 institutional asset owners, with $1.3 trillion in ESG assets, responded to questions about why they incorporate ESG criteria into their investments:

- More than half of these respondents – 52 per cent – reported regulation or legislation as a reason for incorporating ESG criteria.
- 44 per cent said they assessed ESG criteria in order to help fulfil their institution's mission.
- 32 per cent, with $598 billion in ESG assets, pointed to the desire to help bring about societal and environmental benefits.
- 23 per cent, with $651 billion in ESG assets, said they incorporate ESG criteria to fulfil fiduciary duty.

Similarly, a subset of 107 investment managers with more than $552 billion in ESG assets under management also responded to questions from US SIF Foundation in 2010 about their motivations for considering ESG criteria:

- 85 per cent cited client demand.
- 60 per cent pointed to the desire to help bring about societal and environmental benefits.
- 58 per cent said they assessed ESG criteria in order to help fulfil their institution's or clients' missions.
- 53 per cent said they consider ESG criteria in investment analysis in an effort to manage risk.
- 50 per cent said they review ESG issues in order to enhance financial returns.

In cumulative terms, assets engaged in SRI strategies grew 486 per cent from 1995 to 2012, while the broader universe of assets under professional management in the United States, according to estimates from Thomson Reuters Nelson, grew 376 per cent. The growth in the pool of assets engaged in SRI strategies reflects a number of factors, including net inflows into existing SRI products, the development of new SRI products and the adoption of SRI strategies by managers and institutions not previously involved in the field.

Many of these institutional investors and money managers participate in forums – both domestic and international – that provide information and networking opportunities to further the practice of sustainable and responsible investing across various issues, asset classes and investor types. These organizations include CERES, the Council of International Investors, the Interfaith Center for Corporate Responsibility, the Investor Network on Climate Risk, the Global Impact Investing Network and US SIF: The Forum for Sustainable and Responsible Investment.

Internationally, approximately 165 US asset owners and investment managers are signatories of the Principles for Responsible Investment.

Responsible investment institutions

Institutional asset owners

Institutional investors dominated the $3.7 trillion in assets in the US market in 2012 implementing sustainable and responsible investing strategies.

A wide range of institutions, including public employee retirement plans, government-sponsored college savings plans, philanthropic foundations, educational endowments, hospitals and healthcare plans and faith-based investors, are the primary owners of the nearly $2.5 trillion in assets to which they apply a wide spectrum of environmental, social and governance assessments. Many avoid or exclude companies that do not meet certain ESG standards, while others proactively seek investments that generate positive social or environmental impacts. Still others incorporate ESG factors to manage risk and pursue more sustainable investment outcomes. Increasing numbers of institutional plan sponsors are also making SRI options more commonly available to plan participants, particularly in defined-contribution retirement and college savings programmes. Public funds managed for federal, state, county and municipal governments, including public employee pension plans and other publicly pooled portfolios, account for more than two thirds of the institutional assets – $1.98 trillion – identified in the 2012 survey as considering ESG criteria.

In asset-weighted terms, concerns over corporate investment in the Sudan were the most prominent of the ESG factors incorporated into institutional investment policies. Sudan-related investment policies were driven primarily by student and civic campaigns for divestment that resulted in legislative mandates in states and cities and targeted divestment by dozens of educational endowments. To a lesser extent philanthropic foundations and faith-based investors concerned about the Khartoum government's genocidal policies also incorporated Sudan-related investing criteria into investment policy. In total, the US SIF Foundation identified $1.63 trillion in institutional assets that were subject to Sudan criteria at the start of 2012.

Concerns over corporate investment in Iran came second in asset-adjusted terms, affecting $1.24 trillion in assets. Concerns over executive pay, board issues, tobacco, climate change and labour issues were also prominent, with each of these issues affecting more than $500 billion in assets at the outset of 2012.

Additionally, many institutional investors are active shareholder advocates. The 176 institutional asset owners that filed or co-filed shareholder resolutions on ESG issues from 2010 to 2012 controlled more than $1.28 trillion in assets. The combined assets of institutions that incorporate ESG criteria or engage in shareholder advocacy in this way amounted to $2.7 trillion, or 73 per cent of the total sustainable and responsible investing assets identified by US SIF Foundation in its 2012 survey and research.

Money managers

US SIF Foundation's 2012 survey identified 720 funds with $1.01 trillion in assets at the start of 2012 that incorporated ESG criteria, up from 260 such funds with just $202 billion in assets 5 years earlier. The 2012 total includes 302 mutual funds with $456 billion in assets. In addition, the survey process identified 178 separate account vehicles with $338 billion in assets.

Across the spectrum of ESG investment vehicles, Sudan-related investment criteria were the predominant ESG factor, in asset-weighted terms, affecting $999 billion in assets. Governance issues were also important to money managers: 346 investment vehicles with $623 billion in assets in 2012 specified that they consider governance issues generally or focus on such specific areas as executive pay, the functioning of the board or corporate political activity.

US SIF Foundation found 301 alternative investment funds – private equity and venture capital funds, property funds and hedge funds – in 2012 that considered ESG criteria, and these vehicles collectively totalled $132 billion. The majority of the alternative fund managers considered several ESG criteria simultaneously, but environmental factors predominated, with 258 funds collectively managing $127 billion incorporating themes such as green building, climate change, clean technology, pollution reduction and sustainable agriculture.

Some money managers also filed shareholder resolutions on ESG issues. In 2012, US SIF Foundation identified 32 asset managers with $251 billion in assets under management that filed or co-filed resolutions from 2010 through 2012.

Policy environment

The shareholder proposal rule

The US policy environment is notable for the relative ease with which shareholders can introduce shareholder resolutions for inclusion in publicly traded companies' proxy statements and consideration by management and other shareholders at annual general meetings. The ground rules that control the process of filing shareholder resolutions are contained in the regulations and bulletins that the SEC has issued under Section 14a-8 of the Securities Exchange Act of 1934.

This shareholder proposal rule permits shareholders to file a proposal at a company if they own at least $2,000 or 1 per cent of the company's shares and have held the shares continuously for the past year. Proposals are limited to 500 words and cannot contain false or misleading information or be motivated by a personal grievance. Proposals generally need to address corporate environmental, social and governance policy questions considered significant public issues and cannot pertain to 'ordinary business' issues such as employee benefits, personnel changes or the sale of particular products. Finally, the shareholder proponent – or a designated representative – must attend the annual meeting in person to present the proposal formally.

Companies receiving proposals can challenge them at the SEC based on the proposal's content or length or the ability of the proponents to prove they meet share ownership requirements. The SEC acts as a referee in these cases by sending a letter to both corporate management and the filers of the resolution with its opinion on whether the company can omit the proposal from its meeting agenda and proxy statement – or must include it. In October 2009, the SEC issued a decision that clarified for companies that they could no longer omit shareholder proposals that request them to assess the risk they face from environmental and public health issues. In the past, the SEC had often allowed companies to omit these proposals, saying that risk assessment was an 'ordinary business' activity that was solely the province of management.

To resubmit resolutions in subsequent years after an initial filing, the proposal must win at least 3 per cent support in its first year, 6 per cent in its second and 10 per cent in its third year and all years after. The SEC calculates support levels by dividing the total votes cast for the proposal by the total votes cast for and against the proposal. (It does not count abstentions or non-votes.) If a proposal fails to meet the requisite resubmission thresholds, the filer must wait 3 years to resubmit it.

A wide array of individual and institutional investors, as noted earlier, now files or co-files shareholder resolutions at US companies, and hundreds of these proposals come to votes each year.

Proxy voting and disclosure

Regulatory developments over the last few decades have encouraged investors to take a thoughtful approach to proxy voting. In 1988, the US Department of Labor wrote a letter, in response to a query from the chair of Avon Products' Retirement Board, concluding that proxy voting should be considered a fiduciary duty and exercised solely in the interests of plan beneficiaries. Because the Department of Labor has the responsibility, under the 1974 Employee Retirement Income Security Act (ERISA), for ensuring that the administrators of private-sector pension plans fulfil their fiduciary duty to the beneficiaries of those plans, the "Avon Letter" was considered to apply to private-sector retirement plans in general. The Department of Labor elaborated further on the fiduciary duty of proxy voting in Interpretive Bulletin 94–2, saying that fiduciaries should maintain accurate records of their proxy voting and spell out their guidelines of proxy voting as part of their overall statements of investment policy.

Under rules issued by the SEC in January 2003, mutual funds and investment advisors began uniformly disclosing how they vote on a host of proxy issues in 2004. Investment advisors are also required to disclose voting guidelines and voting records to clients upon request. SRI mutual funds were leaders in disclosing their proxy votes and policies even before the SEC requirements.

Fiduciary duty

Over the past several years, private- and public-sector experts on fiduciary duty have supported the consideration of ESG factors within investment management practices provided that the investor expected competitive returns and completed and documented its due diligence process.

For private-sector retirement plans, the definition of fiduciary duty is codified in the 1974 ERISA law. Section 1104(a) of the law defines the 'prudent man standard of care' as follows:

> a fiduciary shall discharge his duties with respect to a plan solely in the interest of the participants and beneficiaries and-
>
> (A) for the exclusive purpose of:
> (i) providing benefits to participants and their beneficiaries; and
> (ii) defraying reasonable expenses of administering the plan;
>
> (B) with the care, skill, prudence, and diligence under the circumstances then prevailing that a prudent man acting in a like capacity and familiar with such matters would use in the conduct of an enterprise of a like character and with like aims;
>
> (C) by diversifying the investments of the plan so as to minimize the risk of large losses, unless under the circumstances it is clearly prudent not to do so; and
>
> (D) in accordance with the documents and instruments governing the plan insofar as such documents and instruments are consistent with the provisions of this subchapter and subchapter III of this chapter.

In 1998, Calvert, a US mutual fund company, sought an opinion from the Department of Labor on the application of ERISA to sustainable and responsible investing options as part of retirement plans. The response from the Office of Regulations and Interpretations expressed the view that ERISA's fiduciary standards "do not preclude consideration of collateral benefits, such as those offered by a 'socially- responsible' fund, in a fiduciary's evaluation of a particular investment opportunity".

> However, the existence of such collateral benefits may be decisive only if the fiduciary determines that the investment offering the collateral benefits is expected to provide an investment return commensurate to alternative investments having similar risks. . . . In other words, in deciding whether and to what extent to invest in a particular investment, or to make a particular fund available as a designated investment alternative, a fiduciary must ordinarily consider only factors relating to the interests of plan participants and beneficiaries in their retirement income. A decision to make an investment, or to designate an investment alternative, may not be influenced by non-economic factors unless the investment ultimately chosen for the plan, when judged solely on the basis of its economic value, would be equal to or superior to alternative available investments.[12]

In a paper for the California County Retirement System, the Baker & McKenzie law firm reached a similar conclusion for public funds: "If the social investment's rate of return is similar to the return on a similar type of investment sought, then it appears that public system retirement boards can make the social investment".[13]

A number of institutional investors also cite the conclusion of the 2005 'Freshfield' report. This analysis, by an international law firm, of fiduciary law in seven developed markets, including the United States, found that "The links between ESG factors and financial performance are increasingly being recognized. On that basis, integrating ESG considerations into an investment analysis is clearly permissible and is arguably required in all jurisdictions".[14]

Dodd-Frank financial reform law

In 2010, shareholder advocates in the United States were heartened when the Dodd-Frank Wall Street Reform and Consumer Protection Act was signed into law. It gave authority to the SEC to implement a rule to allow shareholders, within certain parameters, to nominate directors to the boards of their portfolio companies and to have access to the company's proxy statement to make the case for their nominees. The law specifies, too, that publicly traded companies must allow shareholders – at least once every 3 years – to hold an advisory vote on their executives' pay packages.

The Dodd-Frank Act, moreover, includes a requirement that publicly traded companies provide disclosure around four issues that have been of concern to sustainable investors:

- Pay disparity: Publicly traded companies must report the median of the annual total compensation of all employees, excluding the chief executive officer; the annual total compensation of the CEO; and the ratio of the median pay to the CEO's.
- Payments by extractive industries to host governments: Companies registered with the SEC must disclose the payments they make to foreign governments or the US government for the commercial development of oil, natural gas or minerals. Several human rights organizations and socially concerned investors have called for greater disclosure because the secrecy of extractive companies' payments to host governments can facilitate corruption and misappropriation of revenues, leading to social unrest and unstable operating environments for the companies.

- Mine safety: Companies that operate mines in the United States need to disclose in the quarterly and annual reports they file with the SEC the names of mines that have received citations or warnings under the Federal Mine Safety and Health Act of 1977, the number and type of citations and warning each mine has received and the number of mining-related fatalities at each mine.
- Mineral sourcing: Finally, publicly traded US companies that source minerals such as tantalum and tin must report the measures they use, which must include independent private-sector audits, to ensure that they are not sourcing minerals from mines and smelters controlled by armed factions in the Democratic Republic of the Congo. Humanitarian observers believe that these mines and smelters provide financing that fuels the conflict in the eastern part of the country. The conflict has inflicted severe suffering on the civilian population.

Decisions at the SEC

While the Dodd-Frank Act provided new authority to the SEC, the agency itself took steps in 2009 and 2010 under its existing authority to improve corporate disclosure:

- In January 2010, the SEC issued definitive guidance to companies on disclosing climate-change risks to investors.
- In December 2009, the SEC required companies to disclose their board diversity policies beginning with the proxy statements they issued in 2010.

Shareholder engagement

A broad range of US money managers and institutional investors pursue shareholder engagement to improve their portfolio companies' policies and management around environmental, social and governance issues and thereby help ensure the longer-term health of these companies and investments.

As TIAA-CREF noted in a 2010 policy brief,

> As providers of capital, long-term investors have among the most to lose if markets deteriorate and asset prices fall. Therefore, it is critical that such investors use their influence and leverage to promote good corporate governance and effectively functioning markets. This makes good economic sense in terms of our mission and is part of our job as fiduciaries representing our clients. Our participants and clients expect us to be stewards of their savings and to help provide for their financial security.[15]

In 2012, the California Public Employees Retirement System (CalPERS) released a report on the rationale and outcomes of its shareholder engagement programmes. The core of the engagement programme is its 'Focus List' in which it identifies US portfolio companies that it believes are poor performers both in terms of stock returns and in terms of governance factors or risk management of environmental and social issues. CalPERS follows up with those companies either directly or, where necessary, by filing shareholder proposals.[16] CalPERS says there is analytical evidence that its engagement activities have paid off.

> For example, a review of 155 companies that CalPERS had contacted as part of the Focus List Program between 1999–2008 found that, on average, all companies generated a total

cumulative excess return of 15.8 per cent above their respective benchmarks after three years.[17]

Based on the shareholder resolutions that institutional investors and money managers have filed at US companies in recent years on environmental and social issues, shareholders have focused particularly on improving disclosure or management of corporate political spending, environmental policy (especially with regard to climate change) and overall sustainability. The US Supreme Court's January 2010 decision in *Citizens United v. Federal Election Commission*, which removed legal restrictions on corporate political advertising, gave new impetus to a long-running shareholder campaign asking companies to disclose and curb their political spending and lobbying. Since 2010, shareholders have filed more than 100 resolutions each year at US companies concerning their political spending and lobbying.

The number and proportion of shareholder proposals on social and environmental issues that receive high levels of support has been trending upward. From 2007 through 2009, only about 17 per cent of the proposals that came of votes achieved the support of 30 per cent of the shares voted. From 2010 through 2013, that proportion has ranged from 23 to 30 per cent.

Responsible investors, including public pension funds, labour funds and sustainable investment firms, also seek to reform the governance of portfolio companies so that directors and executives consider and adopt policies in the long-term interests of the companies, their shareholders and other stakeholders. Too frequently, executives have little incentive – in their pay and bonus structures – to consider the company's share price and other indicators of corporate health beyond a 1- to 3-year horizon. Boards of directors can suffer from 'group think', especially when the chair of the board is the company's current or former chief executive officer or if the directors all come from similar backgrounds.

Accordingly, concerned shareholders have concentrated their efforts in recent years on shareholder resolutions to ensure that executive pay is properly aligned with shareholder interests and the company's long-term growth, to require a majority vote standard in director elections, to require the entire board of directors to submit to annual elections rather than staggered terms and to advocate that CEOs do not also chair their boards of directors.

Now that investors have won the right through the Dodd-Frank financial reform law to have an advisory vote on executive pay at their portfolio companies, they have occasionally rejected publicly held US companies' executive pay provisions through these votes.[18] A review by the *Wall Street Journal* found that the 'no' votes have consequences, with executive turnover at companies that failed say-on-pay votes about twice as high as at companies overall, and some companies have made changes that could improve performance issues.[19]

Outlook

In recent years, there have been a number of signals that interest in responsible investing practice is growing. To name just a few:

- In December 2011, Pimco, the multi-billion-dollar fixed-income specialist based in Newport Beach, California, announced that it had signed the Principles for Responsible Investment to underscore and further its research and investment analysis on ESG factors.[20]
- In April 2012, Morgan Stanley Smith Barney announced the launch of an "Investing with Impact" platform to help its four million clients – with $1.7 trillion in investable assets – align their financial goals and their personal values. The company said the decision was based on feedback from clients and financial advisors.[21]

- The millennial generation, encompassing individuals born between 1980 and around 2000, is adding to the demand for investments that consider environmental and societal impacts and corporate governance issues. According to a 2013 survey by Merrill Lynch Private Bank and Investment Group, 30 per cent of millennial investor respondents said that 'values-based investing' options were important in selecting a wealth management firm.[22]

These developments help to increase retail and institutional investor awareness of sustainable and responsible investing options. In the next few years, a challenge for proponents of sustainable and responsible investing will be to develop formal outreach and training for financial advisors, trustees and others who are potentially interested but lack the know-how or confidence to proceed further in this field. Until recently, there has been virtually no formal curriculum geared toward US financial professionals on sustainable investing strategies and ESG integration, but the US SIF Foundation established a Center for Sustainable Investment Education in 2013, and launched an introductory course to responsible investing, to begin to fill this gap.

Notes

1 This chapter went to press before updates could be included from the US SIF Foundation's *Report on US Sustainable, Responsible and Impact Investment Trends 2014.* To view the highlights of this report, see http://www.ussif.org/trends.

2 US Securities and Exchange Commission, *The Investor's Advocate: How the SEC Protects Investors, Maintains Market Integrity, and Facilitates Capital Formation,* online, available HTTP: <http://www.sec.gov/about/whatwedo.shtml> (accessed 30 December 2013).

3 Investment Company Institute, *2013 Investment Company Fact Book*, online, available HTTP: <http://www.ici.org/pdf/2013_factbook.pdf> (accessed 30 December 2013).

4 Investment Company Institute, *2013 Investment Company Fact Book*, online, available HTTP: <http://www.icifactbook.org/> (accessed 30 December 2013).

5 Investment Company Institute 2013.

6 Investment Company Institute 2013.

7 U.S. Congressional Budget Office, *The Earned Income Tax Credit and Expected Social Security Retirement Benefits Among Low-Income Women,* March 2012, online, available HTTP: <http://www.cbo.gov/sites/default/files/cbofiles/attachments/WorkingPaper2012–06-EITC_and_SS_Retirement_Benefits.pdf> (accessed 15 May 2012).

8 US SIF Foundation is a nonprofit organization. Its purpose is to support the activities of US SIF: The Forum for Sustainable and Responsible Investment Inc., its sole member, by undertaking certain educational and research activities.

9 Data provided by Thomson Reuters Nelson in 2012 suggested that as of December 31, 2011, $33.25 trillion was under professional asset management in the United States.

10 US SIF Foundation (2012) *2012 Report on Sustainable and Responsible Investing Trends in the United States*, Washington, DC: US SIF Foundation.

11 For the purposes of this chapter, an institutional investor is any asset-owning institution or investment plan sponsor, in contradistinction to individual investors and asset management firms. The main types of institutional investors are pools of investment assets sponsored by corporations, faith-based institutions, foundations, endowments, hospital and healthcare plans, labour unions and Taft-Hartley pension plans and public authorities, such as public employee retirement systems, as well as other nonprofit organizations. Institutions that did not respond to US SIF Foundation information requests or do not make their assets or ESG criteria publicly available are not captured in these figures.

12 Doyle, R.J., Office of Regulations and Interpretations Advisory Opinion (The 'Calvert Letter'), May 28 1998, online, available HTTP: <http://www.dol.gov/ebsa/programs/ori/advisory98/98–04a.htm> (accessed 15 May 2012).

13 Gibson, V., Levitt, B., and Cargo, K., Paper for California County Retirement System, Baker & McKenzie, 2000, Quoted from Baue, W., 'Baker & McKenzie Paper Concludes Social Investing Consistent with Fiduciary Duty', *Sustainability Investment News*, 21 May 2004, online, available HTTP: <http://www.socialfunds.com/news/article.cgi/1428.html> (accessed 15 May 2012).

14 Freshfields Bruckhaus Deringer, *A Legal Framework for the Integration of Environmental, Social and Governance Issues in Institutional Investment,* New York/Nairobi: UNEP FI, 2005, online, available HTTP: <http://www.unepfi.org/fileadmin/documents/freshfields_legal_resp_20051123.pdf> (accessed 15 May 2012).
15 TIAA-CREF (2010) *Responsible Investing & Corporate Governance: Lessons Learned for Shareholders from the Crises of the Last Decade,* New York: TIAA-CREF, online, available HTTP: <http://www.tiaa-cref.org/ucm/groups/content/@ap_ucm_p_tcp/documents/document/tiaa01012041.pdf> (accessed 15 May 2012).
16 California Public Employees Retirement System, *Toward Sustainable Investment: Taking Responsibility*. Sacramento: CalPERS, 2012, online, available HTTP: <http://www.calpers.ca.gov/index.jsp?bc=/about/press/news/invest-corp/towards-sustainable-investment.xml> (accessed 15 May 2012).
17 CalPERS, 2012.
18 Byrd, F., 'Citigroup Executive Pay Vote: Millstone or Milestone' *Byrd Watch*, 4 May 2012, online, available HTTP: <http://www.laurelhill.com/byrdwatch/byrdwatchi54.aspx>.
19 Chasen, E., '"Say on Pay" Changes Ways Companies Consult Investors, Stress Performance to Avoid Repeat of Negative Votes', *Wall Street Journal*, 22 February 2012.
20 Pimco (2011) *Pimco Becomes a UN PRI Signatory: Q&A 2011*, online, available HTTP: <http://www.wespath.com/assets/1/14/QA002–112911_ESG_Investing_GBL.pdf> (accessed 15 May 2012).
21 Morgan Stanley Smith Barney (2012) *Morgan Stanley Smith Barney Announces Launch of Investing with Impact Platform*, press release, 26 April , online, available HTTP: <http://www.morganstanley.com/about/press/articles/8d25155d-790c-4926-be23-dd559696b3b7.html> (accessed 15 May 2012).
22 Braswell, M. (2013) 'BofA Campaign Emphasizes Socially Responsible Investing', *On Wall Street*, 19 August, online, available HTTP: <http://www.onwallstreet.com/news/bofa-campaign-emphasizes-socially-responsible-investing-2686240–1.html> (accessed 30 December 2013).

References

Braswell, M. (2013) 'BofA Campaign Emphasizes Socially Responsible Investing' *On Wall Street*, 19 August 2013. Online. Available HTTP: <http://www.onwallstreet.com/news/bofa-campaign-emphasizes-socially-responsible-investing-2686240–1.html> (accessed 30 December 2013).

Byrd, F. (2012) 'Citigroup Executive Pay Vote: Millstone or Milestone' *Byrd Watch*, 4 May 2012. Online. Available HTTP: <http://www.laurelhill.com/byrdwatch/byrdwatchi54.aspx>.

California Public Employees Retirement System (2012) *Toward Sustainable Investment: Taking Responsibility*, Sacramento: CalPERS. Online. Available HTTP: <http://www.calpers.ca.gov/index.jsp?bc=/about/press/news/invest-corp/towards-sustainable-investment.xml> (accessed 15 May 2012).

Chasan, E. (2012) '"Say on Pay" Changes Ways Companies Consult Investors, Stress Performance to Avoid Repeat of Negative Votes' *Wall Street Journal*, 22 February, 2012.

Doyle, R. J. (1998) *Office of Regulations and Interpretations Advisory Opinion (The "Calvert Letter")*, 28 May 1998. Online. Available HTTP: <http://www.dol.gov/ebsa/programs/ori/advisory98/98–04a.htm> (accessed 15 May 2012).

Freshfields Bruckhaus Deringer (2005) *A Legal Framework for the Integration of Environmental, Social and Governance Issues in Institutional Investment,* New York/Nairobi: UNEP FI. Online. Available HTTP: <http://www.unepfi.org/fileadmin/documents/freshfields_legal_resp_20051123.pdf> (accessed 15 May 2012).

Gibson, V., Levitt, B. and Cargo, K. (2004) 'Paper for California County Retirement System', Backer & McKenzie, November 2000. Quoted from Baue, W. 'Baker & McKenzie Paper Concludes Social Investing Consistent with Fiduciary Duty' *Sustainability Investment News*, 21 May 2004. Online. Available HTTP: <http://www.socialfunds.com/news/article.cgi/1428.html> (accessed 15 May 2012).

Investment Company Institute (2013) *2013 Investment Company Fact Book*. Online. Available HTTP: <http://www.ici.org/pdf/2012_factbook.pdf> (accessed 30 December 2013).

Morgan Stanley Smith Barney (2012) 'Morgan Stanley Smith Barney Announces Launch of Investing with Impact Platform', press release, 26 April. Online. Available HTTP: <http://www.morganstanley.com/about/press/articles/8d25155d-790c-4926-be23-dd559696b3b7.html> (accessed 15 May 2012).

Pimco (2011) 'Pimco Becomes a UN PRI Signatory: Q&A 2011'. Online. Available HTTP: <http://www.wespath.com/assets/1/14/QA002–112911_ESG_Investing_GBL.pdf> (accessed 15 May 2012).

TIAA-CREF (2010) *Responsible Investing & Corporate Governance: Lessons Learned for Shareholders from the Crises of the Last Decade*, New York: TIAA-CREF. Online. Available HTTP: <http://www.tiaa-cref.org/ucm/groups/content/@ap_ucm_p_tcp/documents/document/tiaa01012041.pdf> (accessed 15 May 2012).

US Congressional Budget Office (2012) *The Earned Income Tax Credit and Expected Social Security Retirement Benefits Among Low-Income Women*. Online. Available HTTP: <http://www.cbo.gov/sites/default/files/cbofiles/attachments/WorkingPaper2012–06-EITC_and_SS_Retirement_Benefits.pdf> (accessed 15 May 2012).

US Securities and Exchange Commission (n.d.) *The Investor's Advocate: How the SEC Protects Investors, Maintains Market Integrity, and Facilitates Capital Formation*. Online. Available HTTP: <http://www.sec.gov/about/whatwedo.shtml> (accessed 15 May 2012).

US SIF Foundation (2010) *2010 Report on Socially Responsible Investing Trends in the United States*, Washington, DC: US SIF Foundation.

US SIF Foundation. (2012) *2012 Report on Sustainable and Responsible Investing Trends in the United States*, Washington, DC: US SIF Foundation.

6

Responsible investment in Canada

Olaf Weber

Introduction

The Canadian Social Investment Organization defines socially responsible investment as "the integration of environmental, social and governance (ESG) factors in the selection and management of investments" (Bragg and Smeh, 2013). The five major socially responsible investing (SRI) strategies they identified are screening, the integration of ESG factors, sustainability-themed investing, impact investing, and corporate engagement and shareholder action. This paper is structured as follows: the first section introduces basic facts about Canada; in the second section we will discuss what is considered responsible investing in Canada and how it is regulated. We will finish by reporting on specific Canadian issues with respect to responsible investing and some conclusions.

Country/region overview

Canada is geographically the second largest country in the world by area with a population in 2011 of approximately 34 million. The country is characterized by relatively expansive rural and unpopulated spaces and, with the exception of the large cities across the country, by a small population density. Canada usually scores very high in quality-of-life rankings, and much of its population growth is driven by immigration. About 1 per cent of the Canadian population is composed of permanent residents, with more than a third of them coming from the Asia-Pacific region. Furthermore, nearly 3 per cent are temporary residents. In 2006, 20 per cent of all Canadians were not born in Canada (see http://www4.hrsdc.gc.ca). The country has high life expectancy at 81 years and a 99 per cent literacy rate. Religious categorizations are representative of Canada's status as an immigrant country. In 2001, 42.6 per cent declared themselves as Catholic, 23.3 per cent as protestant, 1.9 per cent as Muslim, 11.9 per cent as other and 16 per cent as none. Approximately 30 per cent of the population attain some form of university or post-secondary schooling, while 88 per cent graduate from high school. The country has two official languages, English and French, with 23 per cent of the population having French as their mother language. With respect to internet use, Canada ranks second worldwide with respect to online hours per month (www.cira.ca).

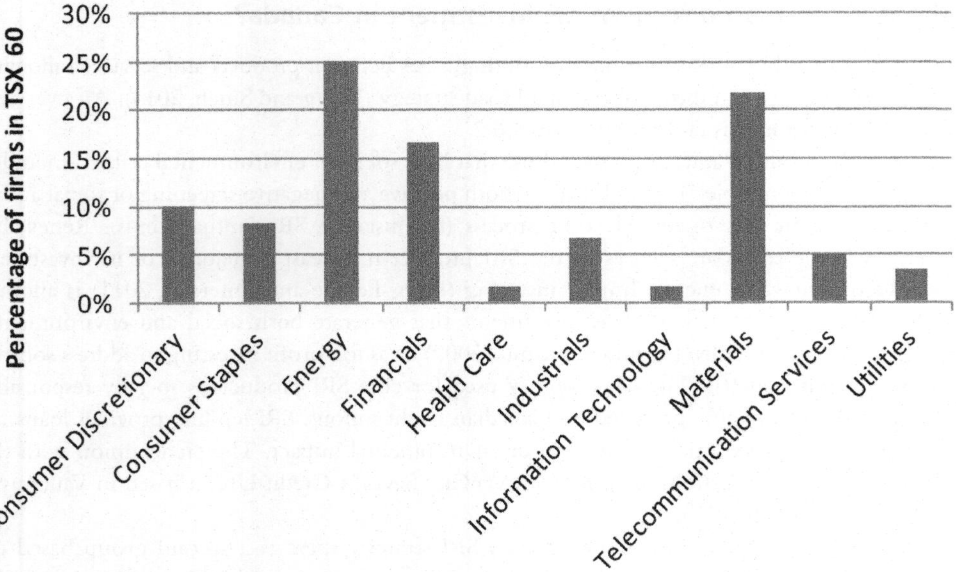

Figure 6.1 Sector distribution of the Canadian TSX 60

Source: www.tsx.ca.

Canada is a parliamentary democracy and a confederation with 10 provinces and three territories. It is a constitutional monarchy and a member of the Commonwealth. According to World Bank data, in 2013 its GDP per capita (PPP) was $51,964, ranking 16th globally.

The Canadian economy is characterized by natural resources. It is one of the few countries that is a net exporter of energy and mineral resources, which comprise more than 6 per cent of the GDP. In addition, Canada has a strong financial services sector, rated the world's soundest by *The Global Competitiveness Report 2011–2012* (Schwab and Sala-i-Martin, 2011). Other main industries are transportation equipment, and wood and paper products. The unemployment rate in Canada was 6.8 per cent as of May 2015 and the public debt in relation to GDP was 87 per cent end of 2014. The market value of Canadian publicly traded shares was $1.9 trillion at the end of December 2012, ranking Canada fifth in the world.

Regarding market capitalization, Canada has special characteristics with respect to sector distribution. More than 35 per cent of the market capitalization of the top 25 companies in Canada comes from the financial sector; a further 30 per cent comes from the oil and gas sectors and more than 15 per cent from the mining sector (see Figure 6.1). As of September 2011 the Toronto Stock Exchange (TSX 60), the large corporate Canadian stock index, consisted of 25 per cent of shares from the energy sector and nearly 22 per cent from the materials sector. As these two sectors have a significant impact on the environment, the sector influence on responsible investment in Canada is strong.

Special cultural aspects in Canada relate to the aboriginal groups (including First Nations, Metis and Inuit peoples), the two official languages, the country's proximity to and relationship with the United States, the strong influence of natural resources and embedded multiculturalism influenced by the high rates of immigration to the country. With regard to environmental issues and climate change, Canada plays a passive role. With a per capita CO_2 emission of nearly 15 tons per year, Canada ranks 17th globally on this index.

What is considered responsible investment in Canada?

Canada's Social Investment Organization distinguishes between products and services following a core SRI strategy and those following a broad strategy (Bragg and Smeh, 2013). An overview of the two categories is presented in Figure 6.2.

Core SRI products and services are those that have social or environmental criteria included in their investment objectives and that use both positive and negative screening or social auditing during their investment selection process (for instance, SRI mutual funds). Renewable energy income trusts are seen as a core SRI product if at least a majority of its investment consists of renewable energy. Impact investing (Bugg-Levine and Emerson, 2011) is another core SRI product. It is defined as investments that generate both social and environmental value and financial return (Monitor Institute, 2009) or as for-profit investing to address societal problems (Jones, 2010). The last category used for core SRI products is socially responsible lending, which is mainly provided by Canadian credit unions. SRI lending provides loans for borrowers that create a positive societal or environmental impact. The credit union with the biggest social loans portfolio in Canada is VanCity Savings Credit Union based in Vancouver (Geobey and Weber, 2013).

In addition to products based on a core SRI strategy there is a second group based on a broad SRI strategy. These products and services comprised nearly 88 per cent of all SRI products and services in Canada in 2010, and are mainly found in institutional finance. These products integrate environmental, social and governance factors into the portfolio analysis and management but do not exclude or include specific stocks because of their social or environmental performance only. The preferred strategy for this broad responsible investing is engagement that includes shareholder advocacy and proxy voting to mitigate risks in their investments.

The Canadian Social Investment Organization (European Comission) suggests that about 20 per cent of the assets under management in Canada are managed in a socially responsible way (2011). This makes $601 billion of investments under broad SRI-guided management

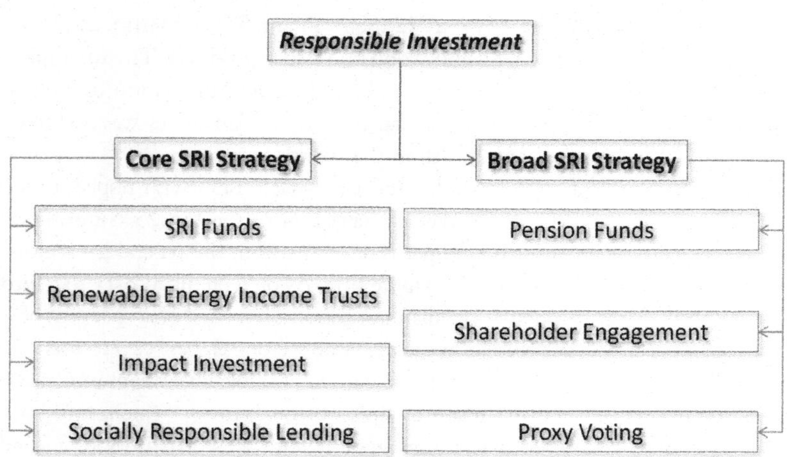

Figure 6.2 Two responsible investment strategies in Canada

Source: Author.

(Bragg and Smeh, 2013). Pension funds manage $533 billion according to this mandate, asset management firms direct approximately $48 billion using a broad RI mandate and $13.5 billion are managed by SRI retail funds. Impact investing reached $5.3 billion, and clean technology investments accounted for $1.3 billion. Overall the growth of SRI-guided investments was 68 per cent between the end of 2011 and the end of 2013. In the following sections we will describe the SRI retail funds market, the institutional sector and the impact investment sector in Canada.

Mutual retail funds

According to the Social Investment Organization (2010) there are a variety of suppliers offering retail mutual funds using the concept of socially responsible investment in Canada. Twelve of these firms are members of the Social Investment Organization. The types of funds that were created using social and environmental selection criteria are presented in Table 6.1 (all data for June 30, 2010 from Boshyk et al. [2011]).

RI in the institutional sector

Regarding institutional investors, and especially pension funds, Mercer, a pension fund consultant, in collaboration with the Canadian Social Investment Organization and Environment Canada, published a report in 2009 that analyzed the Canadian market (Social Investment Organization and Environment Canada, 2009). According to this report the adoption of responsible investment

Table 6.1 RI funds and assets under management in Canada

Fund Type	*Assets in $million*
Canadian Income and Income Equity	249.2
Canadian Equity	419.1
Canadian Equity Balanced	527.5
Canadian Fixed Income	614.9
Canadian Fixed Income Balanced	31.9
Canadian Focused Equity	1,443.4
Canadian Focused Small / Mid Cap Equity	77.9
Canadian Money Market	4.3
Canadian Neutral Balanced	103.3
Canadian Small or Mid Cap Equity	255.4
Global Equity	212.3
Global Small / Mid Cap Equity	8.2
Global Equity Balanced	61.5
Global Neutral Balanced	2.9
International Equity	44.9
Retail Venture Capital	8,371.8
Total	**12,428.5**

Source: Boshyk et al. (2011).

policies by many public and private pension funds caused a significant increase in responsible investment. Out of the largest 10 pension funds in Canada, 8 are signatories of the Principles for Responsible Investments (UNEP Finance Initiative and Global Footprint Network). While there are 1,100 registered pension funds in Canada, the largest of the funds manage approximately 90 per cent of all trusteed pension assets. For both broad and core responsible investment strategies, assets under management were estimated at $581 billion (Bragg and Smeh, 2013). SIO lists eight pension funds in Canada that use responsible investment approaches. All conduct both proxy voting and shareholder engagement, and seven apply ESG criteria for investment analyses (Bragg and Smeh, 2013).

Impact investment

Impact investment tries to solve social or environmental challenges while generating financial returns. The main goal of this RI strategy is to generate positive societal impacts. Impact investment asset categories are presented in Table 6.2; some, such as aboriginal funds, are very specific to the Canadian context. Aboriginal funds are used to support the development of aboriginal communities and invest in communities and business development. They are mainly capitalized by funds from the Canadian government.

Many impact investors arose from the financial cooperative movement (Quebec Development Capital and Quebec Solidarity Finance) and are located in Quebec, the French-speaking Canadian province. Community Futures Development Corporations, Community Loan Funds and Canadian credit unions also contribute directly to impact investment in Canada and are described later in this chapter. Overall $5.3 million was invested in impact investing assets in Canada in 2011, indicating an annual increase of 18 per cent over 2010.

In 2010 the Canadian Securities Administrators (CSA) published a staff notice on environmental reporting regarding the disclosure of environmental information that is pertinent to the value or risk of corporate securities (Canadian Securities Administrators, 2010, Chartered Accountants of Canada, 2010). In Canada, material ESG information has to be included in a range of tools, including financial statements, management's discussion and analysis, the annual information form, the information circular form, the executive compensation form and in the disclosure of corporate governance practices (Canadian Securities Administrators, 2010).

Table 6.2 Impact investment assets in Canada

Category	*Assets (millions)*
Aboriginal Funds	359.8
Community Futures Development Corporations	911.2
Community Loan Funds and Social Venture Capital	756.0
Credit Unions	1,348.3
Foundations	32.0
International Impact Investments	33.3
Quebec Development Capital and Solidarity Finance	1,899.6
Total	**5,340.2**

Source: Boshyk et al. (2011)

Canadian RI legislation and regulation

Based on the regulations regarding the disclosure of information responsible investors should be able to find information about the ESG performance of a corporation and the impact of some ESG criteria on the financial performance of a firm. However, the regulation deals with the disclosure of information that could describe potential risks and does not prescribe certain goals connected with environmental, social or governance issues. There is no information about the impact of these regulations because corporations decide on their own whether environmental risks are material for them.

There are no plans to integrate responsible investment aspects into other types of financial regulations in Canada as well. In contrast to many other countries that do not allow exclusion from investment because of extra-financial reasons, Canadian pension funds are allowed to exclude investments because of ethical reasons.

RI institutions

In this section we will describe ESG rating agencies and RI consultants, the Social Investment Organization (European Comission), called the Responsible Investment Association (RIA) as of 2013, credit unions and financial cooperatives, Community Futures Development Corporations and Community Loan Funds, the Social Finance Task Force and the Centre for Impact Investing as important players in responsible investing. These organizations are specific for Canada. In addition, banks, asset managers, retail investment funds and other institutions are involved in RI.

ESG rating agencies

Sustainalytics, the only independent Canadian-based global ESG rating agency that is not connected with a financial service provider, was founded in 1992 as Jantzi Research Inc. to monitor and report on environmental, social and governance performance of publicly traded Canadian and global corporations. In 2009 Jantzi merged with Sustainalytics, a European responsible investment services provider. Sustainalytics employs 27 professionals in Canada (2012). They provide products and services such as research, analysis and advice for investors, benchmarking and training for corporations and services for civil society that include donor and sponsorship risk assessments (see www.sustainalytics.com).

Another consultancy engaged in ESG in Canada is Mercer LLC. Mercer's Responsible Investing unit is global, working with institutional investors from the pension fund sector in integrating ESG considerations within the fiduciary framework (Mercer LLC, 2010). Mercer's RI business was established in 2004 and includes 14 professionals globally. Their areas of expertise include the integration of ESG factors into investment decision-making and identifying RI opportunities.

Responsible Investment Association (RIA)

Formerly the Social Investment Organization, the Responsible Investment Association (RIA) is a national membership-based organization that includes financial institutions, investment firms, financial advisors and various organizations and individuals interested in socially responsible investment (Social Investment Organization, 2012). Its mandate is to take a leadership role in furthering the use of ESG criteria in financial decision-making, to raise public awareness of SRI, to establish the SRI business case and to provide a forum for and information source on SRI (Social Investment Organization, 2012).

RIA consists of 31 members. They are credit unions, investment funds, asset management corporations, ESG rating agencies, and consulting firms connected with responsible investment. In addition to conducting research on responsible investing in Canada and publishing reports, RIA organizes an annual conference on responsible investing.

Credit unions and financial cooperatives

Forty-seven per cent of the economically active population are members of a Canadian credit union (World Council of Credit Unions, 2009). The Desjardins Group is Canada's largest association of credit unions. At the end of the third quarter in 2012 the group had $201 billion in total assets. VanCity, with $17.1 billion total assets in 2012, is Canada's second largest savings and credit union and is located in Vancouver, BC (Vancity, 2013). With respect to its balance sheet, VanCity is the second largest member of the Global Alliance for Banking on Values, the only global association of ethically driven financial institutions (Global Alliance for Banking on Values, 2012). In addition to VanCity, Assiniboine and Affinity Credit also are members of the alliance. Both Desjardins and VanCity have a strong focus on responsible investing and lending. This is also true for the Credit Union Central of Canada, the association of Canadian Credit Unions, which has a strong focus on social responsibility and community relations (Credit Union Central of Canada, 2010).

Desjardins has 5.8 million members and clients, and is the sixth largest financial cooperative in the world. The cooperative's main SRI products and services are as follows:

- Desjardins Mutual Assistance Funds are funds created to help those who have been excluded from traditional credit channels to regain confidence. These loans totalled $433.2 million in 2010.
- VISA Desjardins Affinity cards are credit cards that allow cardholders to support social and environmental organizations.
- Desjardins Energy-Efficiency Loans finance commercial projects that target a reduction in energy consumption and greenhouse gases.
- Solidarity products for business members that are excluded from the traditional credit channels.
- SRI funds, in which companies must go through a double-verification process, analyzing both financial and non-financial criteria.

Desjardins' mission is to improve economic and social well-being of individuals and communities.

Operating on Canada's west coast, VanCity describes its mission as seeking to redefine wealth in a way that surpasses profit alone to include social justice, environmental sustainability and community well-being that goes beyond the trade-offs assumed in a triple-bottom-line approach and uses the blended value proposition instead (VanCity, 2011). Amongst others, VanCity offers the following responsible investment products and services (VanCity, 2011): high-impact community investment loans, start-up finance for mission-based businesses, not-for-profit organizations, cooperatives, social enterprises, labor organizations and First Nations–owned entities, microlending for individuals and entrepreneurs, home renovation loans, loans for fuel-efficient vehicles, housing loans for First Nations' governments, mortgages for low-income families, loans for members of equity cooperatives to buy shares and deposit accounts to help rebuild credit histories.

Community Futures Development Corporations and Community Loan Funds

Community Loan Funds were founded in the 1990s by the Canadian government. They are rurally based community investment organizations providing loans and equity for businesses, housing, training, social enterprises and employment generation connected with community development. They include social community funds, peer lending circles, and community investment funds (Boshyk et al., 2011).

Community Futures Development Corporations (CFDCs) provide their rural communities with a variety of services, including business development loans, technical support, training and information. They are run by a board of local volunteers and are a form of responsible investing unique to Canada. The funding and the original capitalization stems from the Government of Canada. CFDCs invest in diversification of energy supply, community economic development and small businesses with a focus on job creation. In 2010 they provided over $200 million in loans across Canada.

Social Finance Task Force

The Canadian Task Force on Social Finance was conceived by Social Innovation Generation (SiG) to identify opportunities to mobilize private capital for public good within either non-profit or for-profit enterprises. In December 2010 they published a report that included seven recommendations to mobilize new sources of capital, to create an enabling tax and regulatory environment and to build a pipeline of investment-ready social enterprises in Canada (Canadian Task Force on Social Finance, 2010):

1 Canada's public and private foundations should invest at least 10 per cent of their capital in mission-related investments by 2020.
2 The federal government should partner with private, institutional and philanthropic investors to establish an Impact Investment Fund to mobilize new capital for impact investing.
3 Investors, intermediaries, social enterprises and policy makers should work together to develop new bonds and bond-like instruments for social and environmental interventions.
4 The opportunity of mobilizing the assets of pension funds in support of impact investing should be explored.
5 Charities and non-profits are positioned to undertake revenue generating activities in support of their missions.
6 Private investors are encouraged by a new tax regime to provide lower-cost and patient capital that social enterprises need to maximize their social and environmental impact.
7 The eligibility criteria of government sponsored business development programmes targeting small and medium enterprises should be expanded to explicitly include the range of social enterprises.

At the end of 2011 the Social Finance Task Force published a report about the progress made with regard to the seven recommendations, stating that some progress had already been made (Canadian Task Force on Social Finance, 2011). Amongst others, the amount of mission-related investment in Canada increased by $50 million, the amount of impact investing increased by $284 million and B corps increased their revenues by $230 million.

Centre for Impact Investing

Established in the fall of 2011, the Centre for Impact Investing is a national hub to increase the awareness and effectiveness of social finance that is seen as a means to tackle social and environmental problems. Its initiatives include:

- Socialfinance.ca, a platform providing analysis, community engagement, dialogue and information-sharing;
- A social venture exchange (SVX); and,
- A local hub for B corporations.

The Centre for Impact Investing is supported by The Rockefeller Foundation and the J.W. McConnell Family Foundation.

RI issues

Four key responsible investing issues in Canada highlighted in this report are:

1. The sector distribution in Canada, leading to the question of whether and how investments in the extractive sector can be called RI;
2. Investments in the oil-sand business;
3. Domestic and international impact investing and social finance; and
4. The strong market position of credit unions.

As mentioned above, the sector distribution in Canada is skewed with respect to the high ratio of extractive industries and the financial sector. As a result, RI striving to invest in a way that is representative of the industry distribution of the Canadian economy must invest in these two industries. While the Canadian financial service sector is relatively strong with respect to ESG performance (Weber, 2012), there is a discussion regarding how and whether RI should invest in the extractive industries. While one group rejects investments in the industry because of low environmental and sustainability performance, another group argues that socially responsible investors should be invested in the industry and engage through shareholder advocacy and proxy voting (Carbonnier, 2011, Fitzpatrick et al., 2011, Fonseca, 2010, Liebenthal et al., 2005, Peck and Sinding, 2003, Stern, 1995, Weber and Banks, 2012, Whitmore, 2006).

As a specific sector of the extractive industry, the Canadian oil-sands are a particular focus of RI (van Hasselt, 2010). Because of high CO_2 emissions (Charpentier et al., 2009) and other environmental and societal impacts, (for instance on the land of indigenous peoples in Canada), discussions regarding investments in oil-sands are highly polarized and controversial. On the one side, the oil-sands are a significant contributor to the Canadian economy. On the other hand, the price for this income is the negative impact on climate change and the environment. The controversial discussion has even motivated non-governmental organizations (NGOs) to put pressure on financial institutions because of their involvement in financing the oil-sands (van Hasselt, 2010). Recently, it has been discussed whether investments in the oil-sands industry could be stranded assets because it will not be possible to burn all the fossil energy resources without exceeding a global climate warming of 2 degrees Celsius and consequently causing high risks of climate change.

Impact finance has gained significant momentum in Canada over the last several years. There is a tradition of international impact investing by the Mennonite Economic Development Associates (MEDA) and its investment arm SARONA of trying to implement innovative and effective market-driven economic development programs that improve the livelihoods of millions of people living in poverty around the world (Mennonite Economic Development Associates, 2012). Domestically, the Canadian Task Force on Social Finance (Canadian Task Force on Social Finance, 2010) and the new Centre for Impact Investing (MaRS Discovery District, 2012, Perkins, 2011) push forward impact investing as a part of RI.

Credit unions and financial co-operatives are important players in Canadian RI as well. As their client and member bases are very high in Canada, they have a significant impact on RI. Desjardins, one of the biggest financial cooperatives in the world, has a strong orientation in direction to RI. This is valid for many other credit unions and savings banks, such as VanCity (2011) and Assiniboine Credit Union (2011). Together with the Canadian Affinity Credit Union, VanCity and Assiniboine Credit Union are members of the Global Alliance for Banking on Values, a 25-member association promoting the use of finance to deliver sustainable development for unserved people, communities and the environment (Global Alliance for Banking on Values, 2012, Weber, 2013).

Conclusion

Because of its resource-based economy and strong and stable financial sector, questions about RI in Canada center on the issue of whether or not RI should invest in these industries. Generally, as in many other countries, RI in Canada is increasing significantly but is far from being a core product in the financial sector. Broad RI approaches have gained strength in recent years in Canada, and it is anticipated that they will continue to grow.

References

Assiniboine Credit Union (2011) *2010 Annual Report*, Winnipeg, MB.

Boshyk, A., Bragg, I., Britto, N., Obaid, N. and Runnalls, J. (2011) *Canadian Socially Responsible Investment Review 2010,* Toronto: Social Investment Organization.

Bragg, I. & Smeh, D. T. (2013) *Canadian Socially Responsible Investment Review 2012*, Toronto: Social Investment Organization.

Bugg-Levine, A. and Emerson, J. (2011) *Impact Investing – Transforming How We Make Money While Making a Difference*, San Francisco: Jossey-Bass.

Canadian Securities Administrators (2010) *CSA Staff Notice 51–333: Environmental Reporting Guidance*, Montreal: Canadian Securities Administrators.

Canadian Task Force on Social Finance (2010) *Mobilizing Private Capital for Public Good*, Toronto: Canadian Task Force on Social Finance.

Canadian Task Force on Social Finance (2011) *Mobilizing Private Capital for Public Good – Measuring Progress During Year One*, Toronto: Canadian Task Force on Social Finance.

Carbonnier, G. (2011) 'Introduction: the global and local governance of extractive resources' *Global Governance: A Review of Multilateralism and International Organizations* 17: 135–147.

Charpentier, A. D., Bergerson, J. A. and Maclean, H. L. (2009) 'Understanding the Canadian oil sands industry's greenhouse gas emissions' *Environmental Research Letters* 4: 014005.

Chartered Accountants of Canada (2010) *Environmental, Social and Governance (ESG) Issues in Institutional Investor Decision Making*, Toronto: Chartered Accountants of Canada.

Credit Union Central of Canada (2010) *Social Responsibility and Canada's Credit Unions*, Ottawa: Credit Union Central of Canada.

Fitzpatrick, P., Fonseca, A. and Mcallister, M. L. (2011) 'From the Whitehorse Mining Initiative towards sustainable mining: lessons learned' *Journal of Cleaner Production* 19: 376–384.

Fonseca, A. (2010) 'How credible are mining corporations' sustainability reports? A critical analysis of external assurance under the requirements of the International Council on Mining and Metals' *Corporate Social Responsibility and Environmental Management* 17: 355–370.

Geobey, S. and Weber, O. (2013) 'Lessons in operationalizing social finance: the case of Vancouver City Savings Credit Union' *Journal of Sustainable Finance & Investment* 3(2): 124–137.

Global Alliance for Banking on Values (2012) *Global Alliance for Banking on Values*. Online. Available HTTP: <www.gabv.org> (accessed 6 December 2012).

Jones, J. F. (2010) 'Social finance: commerce and community in developing countries' *International Journal of Social Economics* 37: 415–428.

Liebenthal, A., Michelitsch, R. and Tarazona, E. (2005) *Extractive Industries and Sustainable Development,* in Bank, T. W. (ed.), Washington, D.C.: The World Bank.

Mars Discovery District (2012) *Centre for Impact Investing*, Toronto. Online. Available HTTP: <http://www.marsdd.com/aboutmars/partners/centre-for-impact-investing/> (accessed 2 March 2012).

Mennonite Economic Development Associates (2012) *MEDA*, Waterloo, ON. Online. Available HTTP: <www.meda.org> (accessed 5 March 2012).

Mercer LLC (2010) *Responsible Investment – Managing Risk for Long-Term Value*, Toronto.

Monitor Institute (2009) *Investing for Social and Environmental Impact*, Cambridge, MA.

Peck, P. and Sinding, K. (2003) 'Environmental and social disclosure and data richness in the mining industry' *Business Strategy and the Environment* 12: 131–146.

Perkins, T. (2011) 'MaRS to launch Centre for Impact Investing' *The Globe and Mail*, 28 September 2011.

Schwab, K. and Sala-I-Martin, X. (2011) *The Global Competitiveness Report 2011–2012*, Geneva, Switzerland: World Economic Forum.

Social Investment Organization (2010) *Your Guide to Socially Responsible Mutual Fund Companies in Canada*, Toronto.

Social Investment Organization (2012) *Social Investment Organization,* Toronto. Online. Available HTTP: <http://www.socialinvestment.ca/> (accessed 1 March 2012).

Social Investment Organization And Environment Canada (2009) *Best Practices in Responsible Investment for Canadian Pension Funds*, Toronto.

Stern, D. I. (1995) 'The contribution of the mining sector to sustainability in developing countries' *Ecological Economics* 13: 53–63.

Van Hasselt, C. (2010) 'Aboriginal groups chastise Royal Bank of Canada for oil-sands role' *Dow Jones Newswire*. Online. Available HTTP: <http://global.factiva.com> (accessed 3 March 2010).

Vancity (2011) *Vancity 2010 Annual Report*, Vancouver, BC: Vancouver City Savings Credit Union.

Vancity (2013) *The Vancity effect – 2012 annual report*, Vancouver, BC.

Weber, O. (2012) 'Environmental credit risk management in banks and financial service institutions' *Business Strategy and the Environment* 21(4): 248–263. doi: 10.1002/bse.737

Weber, O. and Banks, Y. (2012) 'Corporate sustainability assessment in financing the extractive sector' *Journal of Sustainable Finance & Investment* 2(1): 64–81. doi: 10.1080/20430795.2012.702501

Weber, O. (2013) 'Social banks and their profitability: is social banking in line with business success?' in San-Jose, L. and Retolaza, J. L. (eds.) *Prospective Innovation at Ethical Banking and Finance*, Sumy: Vinnychenko M.D.

Whitmore, A. (2006) 'The emperors new clothes: sustainable mining?' *Journal of Cleaner Production* 14: 309–314.

World Council Of Credit Unions (2009) *2009 Statistical Report*, Madison, WI.

7

Responsible investment in Mexico

Luisa Montes

Introduction

Responsible investment (RI), understood as that investment that not only takes into account financial criteria, but that also looks at the social and environmental impacts of the companies they are investing in, is not widely known in Mexico. Some very sophisticated investors, mainly individuals, have opened RI investment accounts abroad. The first fund addressing environmental, social and governance (ESG) factors in Mexico was the MSE Sustainability Index, which was launched in 2013.

Background on Mexico

Mexico is the 12th largest economy in the world as measured by GDP. Nevertheless, it has an unequal wealth distribution: according to the food-based definition, almost half of the population resides under the poverty line (47 per cent).

Mexico's economy is based on oil exports, remittances from Mexican workers aboard, tourism and industry. Oil is the main source of public income, as crude oil exports account for approximately 38 per cent of the government's revenue.

Among the most important industrial activities in Mexico are automobiles, cement, steel, textiles, chemicals and beverages. Mining is also very important, given that Mexico is the top silver producer in the world. The agricultural sector, which produces an array of agricultural products, including some organic produce, is also one of the main sources of export income. Interestingly, Mexico has the most free trade agreements in the world. In addition to NAFTA, Mexico has free trade agreements with almost all Latin American countries, as well as with many countries in Europe and Asia.

The Mexican pension fund and savings system

Savings of Mexican individuals, institutions and foreign savings in Mexico are mainly held by commercial banks operating in Mexico. According to the financial-sector regulator, the Comision Nacional Bancaria y de Valores (National Banking and Brokerage Commission, CNBV) includes 46 authorized and regulated financial institutions. At year-end 2013, commercial banks and credit unions held 18 per cent of national savings, 18 per cent was in foreign hands, 8 per cent was held by pension funds administrators, 7 per cent by investment funds, 11 per cent by companies and individuals and the rest by other financial institutions. Despite the local effects of the global financial crisis, national savings have continued to grow at a rate of 3.4 per cent per year in the last 11 years.

The retirement system was restructured in 1997 to allow commercial banks to administer retirement funds through a vehicle called Pension Fund Administrators (Administradoras de Fondos para el Retiro, AFORES) in which private-sector companies contribute to worker retirement benefits and housing savings that will provide beneficiaries with a guaranteed mandatory minimum pension. Years later the system was extended to government workers. Under the new pension fund system, workers are able to choose which fund managers manage their pension, rather than the employer. According to the National Pension Funds Regulator (CONSAR), the number of accounts managed by these administrators has grown from 11 million in 1997 to 50 million at the end of 2013. During the same period, the funds managed rose from US$5.7 million to US$154 million, representing almost 11 per cent of GDP.

Shareholder activism is not a common practice in Mexico. This is most likely for two reasons: the first is the relative small size of the market and the second is the fact that most public companies are family owned with a small percentage of stocks floating freely in the market.

Fiduciary laws in Mexico, as in most countries, oblige the fiduciary administrator to invest in the best alternative possible. If understood correctly, this legal stipulation would include the analysis of ESG risks.

Responsible investing in Mexico

Responsible investing in Mexico is something of a novelty. In 2006, the first 'green funds' were launched by Monex Financial Group; these were regular fixed-income investment funds where the fund's administrator donated 5 cents out of every peso invested for conservation projects in natural protected areas. These funds were unable to reach a breakeven point and were finally closed in 2010.

BBVA Bancomer, the Mexican arm of the Spanish-held BBVA, began another ethical fund called Fondo Educa in 2009. It is a fixed-income fund that provides scholarships for the education of sons left behind by Mexican migrant workers. The fund manages approximately US$385 million in assets for over 15,800 investors. Since its inception, the fund has granted US$5.7 million in scholarships, and this amount continues to grow steadily.

The most influential movement towards the development of a responsible investment market in Mexico was made by the Mexican Stock Exchange (MSE) when it announced the creation of a Sustainability Index in 2009 and launched it in December 2011. In the period before the launch, the announcement itself had the effect of increasing sustainability or social responsibility reporting by 20 per cent, according to a social responsibility reporting consultant based in Mexico City. Moreover, CONSAR published new investment rules for pension funds on 7 December 2011, just one day prior to the index's launch. Included were recommendations that pension fund administrators disclose if the companies in which they are investing have social responsibility certifications.

The MSE Sustainability Index was launched on 8 December 2011 and included 23 stocks. The stocks were chosen from the 70 most liquid stocks on the exchange and were researched by Ecovalores, EIRIS (Empowering Responsible Investment) Mexican partner and the Universidad Anahuac, which specializes in governance issues. The MSE selected the stocks by comparing

Table 7.1 Comparison between the IPC main market indexes and Sustentable (Sustainability Index) in Mexico

	2012	*2013*
IPC	17.88%	–2.24%
Composite	19.93%	0.15%
Large Cap	18.43%	–0.77%
Sustentable	30.41%	–0.26%

Source: Adapted from Bolsa Mexicana de Valores, public infomation.

them to EIRIS's global universe of more than 4,000 companies. Those whose sustainability records were in the top 50 per cent of this universe were included in the index. The MSE has announced that as the index evolves the requirements will become stricter.

The MSE Sustainability Index has had an impressive performance; during 2012 bull markets, it gained 30.41 per cent, versus 17.88 per cent of the main Mexican index, as shown in Table 7.1. During 2013 bear markets, the Sustainability Index lost only 0.26 per cent, compared to a 2.24 per cent loss by Mexico's largest index. This performance may show that sustainable companies have a better performance in bullish markets and are more resistant in bearish ones.

In May 2012, the first green bank was launched in Mexico. CIBanco – a bank created 25 years ago – decided to take advantage of the unexploited 'green bank' niche. It began by offering two innovative credit products to the market – special loans for the purchase of low-emission vehicles and for the purchase of solar panels. CIBanco is a relatively small financial institution; however, the main benefit derived from this initiative is the fact that its marketing campaign has nationwide reach, spreading the idea that a green financial institution is good business.

Growing awareness of corporate social responsibility in Mexico

While RI is not yet a market in the Mexican financial arena, social responsibility is starting to be recognized as an important topic. Nowadays, almost 1,000 companies apply every year to be awarded the Socially Responsible Company recognition from the Mexican Centre for Philanthropy (CEMEFI). Companies are aware that such distinctions or certification schemes represent a competitive edge commercially, since most consumers now recognize the ESR symbol on many products in Mexico. Consequently, the topic has gained importance.

Table 7.2 provides a summary of the organizations that are supporting the development of this market.

The future of RI in Mexico and Latin America

As stated before, the MSE Sustainability Index has demonstrated impressive performance compared to the main market index both locally and internationally (Figure 7.1). This positive correlation between ESG issues and financial performance is beginning to call the attention of significant investors, mainly international investors. As more investors realize the importance of this correlation, the market for RI will keep growing.

In addition to the strong performance of the MSE Sustainability Index, other initiatives will become important drivers of RI in the region, such as the Inter-American Development Bank,

Table 7.2 RI stakeholders in Mexico

Banks association	The National Banks Association has a Social Responsibility area in charge of coordinating the associated banks' social responsibility reports and actions; it has so far centered its activities on philanthropy and in measuring the sector's carbon footprint.
Banks	CIBanco is the first green bank in Mexico. It is actively seeking to develop new sustainability banking practices. Its goal is to finance only sustainable projects. It currently offers lower interest rates on loans for low-emission cars and sustainable housing. Banorte, a leading bank in Mexico with regard to considering ESG factors, is beginning to analyze the environmental and social impact of the projects it finances as well as to assess the climate-change risks of certain investments. Banorte is also co-financing several impact investment organizations, such as TONIC. The entrance of the Colombian financial group Suramericana, a member of the Dow Jones Sustainability Index, to the Mexican financial market will hopefully bring about changes in the responsible investment area, because it includes responsible investing as part of its strategy. Banamex's sustainable banking initiative includes the ESG screening of the projects it finances. It is also working towards an Earthcheck certification.
CONSAR	The national pension funds regulator requires pension funds to report if their investment decision-making considers sustainability. This requirement is not very strong, but it signals that regulators are beginning to consider the importance of integrating ESG issues into decision-making processes.
Global Compact (GC)	The GC was launched in Mexico in 2005; since then, 586 companies and NGOs have joined the network. In 2011, it was re-launched with a new organizational structure within UNIDO, which has allowed the network to develop new collaborative agreements to further advance GC principles among the corporate and social sectors and academia.
NGOs	The Mexican Centre for Philanthropy (CEMEFI) has awarded more than 773 recognitions to companies for corporate social responsibility. It periodically organizes SRI events for companies in Mexico and Latin America.
UN PRI	Currently, the Mexican branches of several PRI signatories have not yet signed the principles in the local offices. Several large and very influential banks are in this situation, such as Bancomer BBVA, which is owned by BBVA from Spain, which is a signatory internationally. Santander – the third-largest bank – and HSBC are other examples where head offices are signatories, but the Mexican banks have not yet signed.
Companies	Some large companies, such as Wal-Mart de Mexico y centroamerica, have been key drivers of ESG issues in Mexico by requesting their suppliers to have some form of certification on social corporate responsibility.
Research firms	Ecovalores is EIRIS (Empowering Responsible Investment) Mexican partner. Ecovalores began operations in Mexico in 2009 and is responsible for the ESG screening of the top 70 Mexican-listed companies for the MSE Sustainability Index. It has been working actively to promote RI in the region.

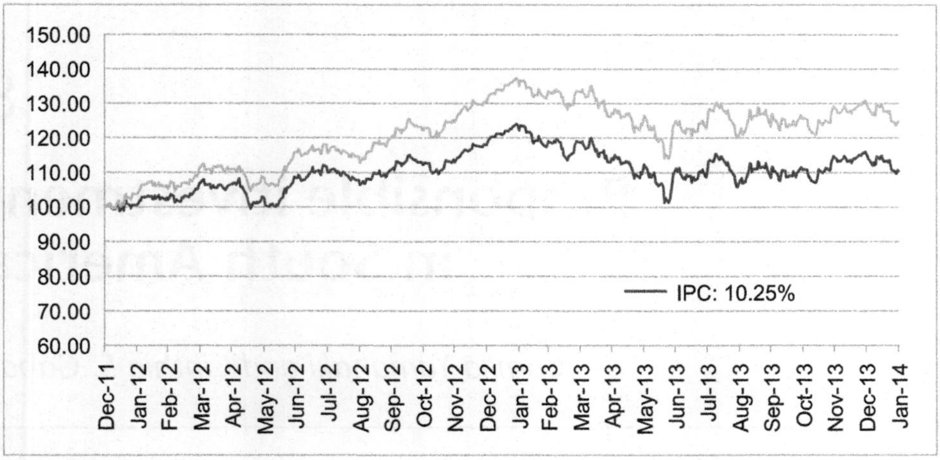

Figure 7.1 Sustainability Index compared to the main market index in Mexico

Source: Author.

which is supporting the creation of a Social Investment Forum in Latin America. Other drivers of RI will be the growth of pension funds and the region's growing population.

Conclusion

Internationally, the market potential is large if we consider that one of the main international RI funds diverted 20 per cent of its assets to emerging markets and, from that, 3 per cent was invested in Mexican stocks. According to Ecovalores, if we apply this same percentage to all potential investment funds, RI investments in Mexico from international investors are estimated to be between US$18 million and US$37 million. However, the challenge for Mexico is in developing its internal RI market in light of the recent international financial crisis. ESG risks have helped companies realize that having in place a strong social responsibility program is not only welcomed by its stakeholders, but is a smart way to manage and mitigate ESG risks.

8

Responsible investment in South America

Camila Yamahaki and Cinthia S. Gaban

Introduction

Responsible investment (RI) in most South American countries is fairly incipient. The majority of the RI initiatives in the region take place in Brazil, where a number of mainstream institutional investors have started incorporating environmental, social and corporate governance (ESG) issues into their investment policies and processes, largely encouraged by the Principles for Responsible Investment (PRI) local network and by local regulations. In other South American countries, the approach to responsible investment has been more focused on impact investing through the creation of high social impact funds to help tackle social inequalities in the region.

Overview of South America

Spread over 17.8 million square kilometres, South America is composed of 12 independent countries (Argentina, Bolivia, Brazil, Chile, Colombia, Ecuador, Guyana, Paraguay, Peru, Suriname, Uruguay and Venezuela) and the French Guyana, France's overseas region. Because the continent was predominantly colonised by the Iberics, 9 of the 12 countries speak Spanish and the majority of the South American population practice the same religion (81 per cent of the South American population is Roman Catholic) and the same legal tradition (11 countries feature the civil law system).

Brazil occupies half of the continent geographically and hosts half of the region's population. It is also responsible for the majority of the continent's economic power. In 2014, South America's GDP (Purchasing Power Parity) reached nearly US$ 6.4 trillion, 48 per cent of which was represented by the Brazilian economy. However, it is Chile, Argentina and Uruguay that house the best social indicators, featuring the highest literacy rates and the highest GDP per capita.

Brazil's BM&FBOVESPA is South America's largest stock exchange in absolute terms. As of December 2014, there were 363 companies listed on BM&FBOVESPA, accounting for US$ 844 billion in market capitalization, largely from the financial and consumer sectors. The Chilean Santiago Stock Exchange is the region's second largest stock exchange in absolute terms and the largest in market capitalization as percentage of GDP, representing US$ 233 billion, primarily from the financial and utilities sectors. The Colombia Stock Exchange is the third largest and accounts for US$ 147 billion, of which the financial sector dominates (WFE 2014). Moreover, Colombia has the largest bond market in South America and the fifth largest in the world, representing over US$ 675 billion in terms of bond trading (WFE 2014). To increase capital flow to and through the Latin countries, the Chilean, Colombian and Peruvian stock exchanges integrated their operations in 2011 through the Integrated Latin American Market (MILA) (Mapstone 2011). In December 2014, the entry of Mexico to MILA was made official with the inclusion of the Mexican Stock Exchange and Mexico's Central Securities Depository Indeval (MILA 2015). MILA now forms Latin American's largest stock exchange.

The markets of the other South American countries are of smaller size. In Argentina and Venezuela, this is explained by the lack of investor confidence in the economic and political stability of these two countries (Aguilera 2009). In Argentina, this is partly a result of the debt default in 2002 and the 2008 nationalization of local pension funds. The Argentinean high-risk political environment also led MSCI Barra to downgrade the country from the MSCI Emerging Markets Index to the MSCI Frontier Markets Index (MSCI 2009). In Venezuela, the stock exchange suffered a steep decline in mid-1990s when Hugo Chavez became president and increased Venezuela's risk perception by foreign investors.

Responsible investment in South America

While responsible investment in most South American countries is fairly new, the majority of RI initiatives are taking place in Brazil. To date, there is no record of responsible investment in South America. However, a study from the International Finance Corporation (IFC) and consultancy firm Mercer, 'Gaining Ground: Integrating Environmental, Social and Governance (ESG) Factors into Investment Processes in Emerging Markets', found that in 2008 there was approximately US$ 5 billion in assets under management invested in Latin America that have made some commitment to integrate ESG into their core investment process (IFC and Mercer 2009).

In Brazil, the inclusion of a special category for RI equity funds by Anbima, the Brazilian Association of Financial and Capital Markets, has facilitated the identification and performance tracking of these funds. As of April 2015, there were 31 funds under this category with assets under management equivalent to R$ 1.16 billion (or nearly US$ 364 million), or 0.05 per cent of total assets under management in Brazil. These funds follow local corporate governance or sustainability indices (as detailed below) or they employ their own ESG criteria (Anbima 2015).

Sustainability index and funds

In Brazil, the local stock exchange has been instrumental in encouraging more RI practices. In 2005, BM&FBOVESPA created the first sustainability index in Latin America, the Corporate Sustainability Index (ISE), selecting Brazilian companies according to ISE's own ESG criteria (BM&FBOVESPA 2015a). The questionnaire used to select the portfolio companies was developed by the Centre for Sustainability Studies (CES) – a research institute based at the business school Fundação Getúlio Vargas. The questionnaire requires companies interested in joining the index to self-evaluate their policies and practices related to ESG issues, including their governance structure and environmental management policies. This index caused an increase in the number of RI funds in Brazil (examples of funds include Banco do Brasil Ações ISE Jovem FIC FIA, Bradesco FIA Índice de Sustentabilidade Empresarial and Caixa FI Ações ISE). It also encouraged the launch of the ISE-indexed exchange-traded fund (ETF), allowing smaller investors to invest in companies with sustainability concerns (BM&FBOVESPA 2015b). Attention to the sustainability aspects of fixed income has also been increasing in Brazil: in 2011, HSBC launched the first Brazilian RI fixed income fund (HSBC FI Renda Fixa Crédito Privado Longo Prazo Performance SRI 20), selecting bond issuers according to HSBC's proprietary ESG methodology.

Corporate governance indices and funds

In 1997, the Brazilian government amended the Companies Law to facilitate the privatization of public companies that took place in the late 1990s. This amendment reduced the rights of minority shareholders, as its objective was to avoid the payment of premiums to minority investors and to maximize returns for the state. The temporary reduction of minority rights (deemed temporary, as Law 10303 restored some of the minority rights in 2001) caused a crisis in the capital markets: the volume of market capitalization represented on the exchange fell from US$ 190 billion in 1997 to US$ 65 billion in 2001 (Paschoarelli 2008; da Silva 2002).

To stimulate capital flows back into the market, in 2000 BM&FBOVESPA created special corporate governance listing segments (Level 1, Level 2 and Novo Mercado) to recognise companies abiding by corporate governance and transparency practices beyond the requirements of the Brazilian law and of the Brazilian Securities and Exchange Commission (Garcia 2005). A fourth listing segment was added in 2005 ('Bovespa Mais') for small and medium companies. The Novo Mercado level requires the most stringent standards of governance of all segments: listed companies must issue only common shares with voting rights, grant 100 per cent 'tag along' rights to all voting shareholders,[1] maintain a minimum of 20 per cent independent board members, and maintain a free float of at least 25 per cent of the shares representing their capital stock (CFA Institute 2009). As of 17 June 2015, 9 companies were listed at Bovespa Mais, 30 companies at Level 1, 20 companies at Level 2 and 133 companies at Novo Mercado (BM&FBOVESPA 2015c).

BM&FBOVESPA has also developed four corporate governance–related indices: the Special Corporate Governance Stock Index (IGC), the Special Corporate Governance Stock Index–Novo Mercado, the Special Tag Along Stock Index (ITAG) and the Corporate Governance Trade Index. The IGC Index includes all companies added to Novo Mercado, Level 1 and Level 2, while the Special Corporate Governance Stock Index–Novo Mercado includes only companies listed at Novo Mercado. Following the launch of the IGC Index, a number of RI funds tracking the index were launched, including BB Previdenciário Ações Governança FI and Bradesco FIC FIA Governança Corporativa. The ITAG Index selects companies offering tag-along rights above the legal requirements, while the IGCT Index consists of companies included in the IGC Index that comply with specific liquidity criteria.[2] An ETF tracking the IGCT index has also been created (BM&FBOVESPA 2015d).

Following the steps of BM&FBOVESPA, in 2008 the Lima Stock Exchange, created a corporate governance-themed index, the Índice de Buen Gobierno Corporativo (IBGC), to recognise companies that comply with voluntary corporate governance principles (as explained later in this chapter). The index's portfolio is composed of 10 Peruvian companies, 3 of which represent over 55 per cent of the index's participation (BVL 2014). The index has not yet generated RI indexed-tracking funds.

Other responsible investment funds

A few South American investors are adopting an impact investing approach by developing funds that invest in companies that promote positive social and environmental impact or by creating funds that donate parts of their revenues to fund community projects. This is especially important in a region where poverty and inequality are prevalent. One such fund is the Colombian Fondo de Capital Privado Inversor, a US$ 9 million private equity fund investing in small and medium companies whose activities aim to positively benefit vulnerable populations and to protect the environment (BVC 2014). This fund was launched in 2011 and is managed by La Corporación Inversor, a coalition of 14 institutions, including JPMorgan, Bolsa de Valores de Colombia and McKinsey & Co.

In Argentina, two funds were created by asset manager Equitas Ventures to finance high-impact projects and social enterprises: Equitas Funds I and II. Equitas Fund I was launched in 2009 as the first venture capital fund for social enterprises in Argentina, investing in five companies with social and environmental impact through a scheme of equity and debt. Equitas II, created in 2011 in partnership with Ashoka, is a US$ 10–15 million fund seeking to invest/finance projects with high social impact in the areas of affordable health, social housing, fair trade and base-of-the-pyramid initiatives in Argentina, Uruguay, Paraguay, Bolivia and Chile (Equitas Ventures 2014).

In Brazil, local asset managers adopt two approaches to promote social and environmental impact. First, asset managers like Itaú and Banco do Brasil donate a percentage of the management fees of some of their funds to finance community projects. Examples of these funds include Itaú's DI Ecomudança (it donates a share of its fees to environmental projects, which contribute to the reduction of carbon emissions), Itaú Unibanco's Social Excelence Fund and Banco do Brasil's DI Social 50 (both donate 50 per cent of their fees to social projects). Also, a handful of asset managers created private equity funds with environmental goals, largely focused on investing in companies that either develop (re)forestation projects (e.g. Investimentos Florestais Fund and Triscorp Ativos Florestais Fund), produce renewable energy (e.g. Votorantim Energia Sustentável Fund, Energia PCH Fund and Bioenergia Fund) and/or are committed to monitoring and reducing carbon emissions (e.g. Brasil Sustentabilidade) (CVM 2014). By investing in equity and/or debt, these funds have been investing towards promoting positive social and environmental impact in these countries.

Carbon markets

The Brazilian and Argentinean stock exchanges have launched a couple of initiatives to encourage investment in companies seeking to reduce their carbon emissions. In 2010, BM&FBOVESPA created the Carbon Efficient Index (ICO2), composed of companies listed in the IBrX-50 that are committed to reporting their carbon emissions inventory (BM&FBOVESPA 2015e). In the same year, BM&FBOVESPA prepared an action for carbon credits, offering 180,000 units of voluntary carbon units. However, no credits were purchased, which the stock exchange attributed to the early stage of development of this market in Brazil (BM&FBOVESPA 2011).

Similarly, the Buenos Aires Stock Exchange launched a carbon market where it supplies information about Carbon Development Mechanism (CDM), encourages the development of CDM projects and facilitates the link between the supply and demand of CDM projects through maintaining an updated list of projects seeking financial support (BCBA 2014). The initiatives of these two stock exchanges are a reflection of their recognition of climate change as an important sustainability issue to be dealt with by the financial sector.

ESG integration

In Brazil, a few pioneering institutional investors have initiated the process of integrating ESG issues into their investment processes. For instance, PREVI, the largest pension fund in Brazil and in Latin America, has a Social and Environmental Responsibility Policy and a Code of Corporate Governance Practices, committing the organization to consider ESG issues in the selection of investee companies and to promote good ESG practices among its investee companies. Itaú-Unibanco has developed a methodology to integrate ESG factors into its investment activities and to identify risks and opportunities that may cause an impact on the market value of the investee companies (Itaú Asset Management 2014). Although the process of ESG integration is in its early stages in the region, one can expect that these pioneers will contribute to the development and dissemination of RI practices and ESG integration across the investment industry.

Collaborative engagement

In Brazil, two collaborative engagement initiatives should be mentioned for highlighting the expectations of local investors regarding ESG performance of investee companies. The first one is the collaborative engagement promoted by the Latin American Sustainable Finance Forum (LASFF) in partnership with the PRI signatories (initiatives described in more detail below) and members of the UN Environment Programme Finance Initiative (UNEP FI). In 2009, LASFF's members engaged with Brazilian listed companies to encourage these organizations to eradicate slave labour in their supply chain and to investigate whether these companies conduct any type of monitoring to prevent slave labour. The coalition of investors sent letters to companies whose suppliers were spotted by the government for having used slave labour. The letter requested companies to answer to a short questionnaire, which asked companies to disclose their efforts to eradicate slave labour in the supply chain. In total, 64 of the 368 companies replied to the letter, and the aggregated results of the survey were later published by LASFF in the 'Engagement for Eradicating Slave Labour in Brazil' report. The survey found that 37 per cent of the surveyed companies were signatories to the National Pact for Eradication of Slave Labour, while 41 per cent of the non-signatories intended to sign the pact. Moreover, 83 per cent argued that they were aware of the risks related to being involved in slave labour, and 76 per cent claimed that they monitor the policies and practices of their partners. Although the initiative was met with a low response rate (83 per cent of the companies have not responded to the survey, which LASFF attributed to the fact that enquiry on this topic is a new demand on companies), the response rate is considered rather significant in terms of market capitalization, as the responding companies represented 52 per cent of the total value of tradable assets on BM&FBOVESPA. Hence, the initiative experienced a reasonable degree of success (LASFF 2010).

The second collaborative initiative that took place in Brazil was the engagement coordinated by the PRI Engagement Working Group in partnership with the Emerging Markets Disclosure Program (EMDP). From 2010 to 2012, the PRI group engaged with a number of Brazilian companies to encourage the adoption of the Global Reporting Initiative (GRI) framework in their sustainability reporting. The coalition tackled engagement in two stages. In the first phase, investors endorsed letters to companies in the IBrX-100 to congratulate those that had used the GRI framework to report in 2010 (45 in all) and to encourage the 50 companies that had not used it to produce a GRI-based report. In the second phase (coordinated by the authors), from 2011 to 2012, the investor signatories engaged with 22 companies through letter writing and meetings to encourage them to adopt the GRI framework. The investor group also promoted two workshops with the listed companies to discuss the importance of publishing ESG information. This engagement initiative was spearheaded by local signatories and was endorsed by a number of foreign PRI signatories who co-signed the letters to companies. In total, 36 PRI signatories participated in the initiative, the largest collaborative engagement to date in Brazil (US SIF 2012).

These initiatives demonstrate that Brazilian investors have been increasingly using collaborative engagement as part of their RI strategies to promote better ESG practices in the corporate sector.

Responsible investment institutions

The following South American institutions should be highlighted for promoting, or having promoted, RI in the region: the stock exchanges in Argentina, Brazil, Colombia and Peru; the Latin American Sustainable Finance Forum (LASFF); the Brazilian Association of Pension Funds (ABRAPP) and the UN-supported Principles for Responsible Investment (PRI).

Stock exchanges

Four stock exchanges should be mentioned for being active in sustainability issues in the region: BM&FBOVESPA, the Lima Stock Exchange, the Colombian Securities Exchange and the Buenos Aires Stock Exchange. As mentioned earlier, BM&FBOVESPA is one of the world's pioneering stock exchanges, having created a range of governance, carbon and sustainability indices; corporate governance listing segments and a carbon market (Responsible Research 2012). The Peruvian stock exchange has also been a pioneer in South America through the development of a corporate governance index. The Colombian Securities Exchange participated in the launch of Fondo Inversor and the LatinSIF, while the Argentinean stock exchange has created one of the only carbon markets in the region.

Latin American Sustainable Finance Forum (LASFF)

Despite the reference to Latin America in its name, the Latin American Sustainable Finance Forum (LASFF) was a Brazilian working group composed of local asset managers, banks and other financial institutions to promote sustainability practices in the financial sector. It was launched in 2008 and spearheaded by the business school Fundação Getúlio Vargas. As mentioned earlier, LASFF's members engaged with Brazilian listed companies to encourage these organizations to eradicate slave labour in their supply chain and to examine how these companies handle this issue (LASFF 2010). In another initiative, LASFF investigated the financial impacts of the sustainable practices of one particular listed company. LASFF was discontinued in late 2011 for losing momentum.

Brazilian Association of Pension Funds (ABRAPP)

Another important organization in the Brazilian RI environment is the Brazilian Association of Pension Funds (ABRAPP). ABRAPP has been actively promoting the concept of responsible investment and sustainability among pension funds through its Sustainability Committee and annual RI conferences, helping to build an enabling environment for responsible investment by keeping sustainability issues on the pension funds' agenda. Moreover, ABRAPP supports other RI initiatives, as a CDP (former Carbon Disclosure Project) sponsor, a PRI network supporter and it sits on ISE's Deliberative Council.

Principles for Responsible Investment (PRI)

The UN-supported Principles for Responsible Investment (PRI) was launched in 2006 and it has nearly 1,400 signatories worldwide. In South America, the PRI has 63 signatories: 60 in Brazil, 2 in Colombia and 1 in Chile (as of 17 June 2015) (PRI 2015a). The PRI Brazil Network (later expanding its focus in South America) was created in 2008 to coordinate the efforts of the growing number of signatories in the region. Current PRI working groups active in Brazil include the Engagement, Investment and Investment Policy Working Groups (PRI 2015b). The Engagement Group supports collaborative investor engagement efforts with local companies; the Investment Group assists signatories to identify the most material ESG issues in different sectors and the Investment Policy Group assists pension funds to develop their ESG investment policy. The latter has been created as a response to the launch of Resolution 3792 in 2009 by the National Monetary Council, which requires pension funds to report in their investment policies the extent to which they include social and environmental concerns into their investment decisions, as explained later in this chapter.

LatinSIF

The Latin American Sustainable Investment Forum (LatinSIF) was launched in 2013, driven by the Colombian Securities Exchange, Sustainalytics and Deloitte, with the goal of creating a network that encourages collaboration and the sharing of knowledge in the region. The LatinSIF plans to develop its activities on five work streams: institutional framework, capacity building, knowledge generation, market development and communications. In late 2013, the LatinSIF organised a roadshow to introduce the organization to the Latin American investment community and to discuss key concepts related to responsible investment. In partnership with the PRI, the LatinSIF organised events in Chile, Peru and Colombia, bringing the experiences of Brazilian Itaú Asset Management and pension fund Previ to the investment community (Sustainalytics 2013).

Policy environment

Responsible investment legislation in Brazil

Legislation encouraging investors to integrate ESG issues into their investment decisions is growing in South America. One piece of legislation that raises ESG criteria was issued by the Brazilian National Monetary Council, the highest deliberative body of the Brazilian financial system. As mentioned earlier in this chapter, in 2009, the Council issued resolution 3792 requiring all Brazilian pension funds to state in their investment policy whether they consider social and environmental issues in their investment decisions (BCB 2009). Although integrating ESG issues was not made mandatory, this piece of legislation brought the topics of responsible investment and sustainability to the forefront of the discussion in the pension fund industry. In 2010, 44 per cent of the 50 largest pension funds included social and environmental criteria in their investment policies (PREVI 2011).

Another piece of legislation on responsible finance is Resolution 4327, issued in April 2014 by the Brazilian Central Bank. This resolution requires that Brazilian financial institutions establish and implement a policy of social and environmental responsibility, and that the management of social and environmental risks of these institutions consider an early assessment of potential negative social and environmental impacts of new products and services (BCB 2014). Despite being fairly recent, one can expect that its requirements will create an additional driver for financial institutions to incorporate ESG issues in Brazil. More recently, in Peru, Superintendencia de Banca, Seguros y AFP (SBS) issued a new regulation (Resolution 1928/2015), requiring that financial institutions manage social and environmental risks of projects costing over US$10 million. Financial institutions must require that the borrowers fill a social and environmental questionnaire and, depending on the project's evaluation, that they develop a management plan seeking to reduce the project's social and environmental risk.

Voting guidelines

In terms of RI self-regulation that encourages investors to use their shareholder rights, the Brazilian investment association Anbima has established guidelines for the investment fund industry regarding the exercise of voting rights at annual general meetings (AGMs). According to these guidelines, all investors who own more than 5 per cent of a company's shares or who own funds in which the company's participation is over 10 per cent should have a proxy voting policy in place and should vote in this company's AGM. They should do so whenever the resolutions refer to issues that are considered 'relevant' by the guidelines (e.g. election of minority investor representatives to the board of directors and ownership changes) (Anbima 2008). Through these guidelines, Anbima incentivises investors to make use of their shareholder rights on corporate governance issues. Moreover, to improve voting levels, in 2011 Law 12431 amended the Companies Law to permit investors to vote electronically (previously, they could only vote in person at the AGM).

Corporate governance codes

As for self-regulation that encourages better corporate governance practices, Brazil, Argentina, Colombia and Peru have voluntary corporate governance codes in place. In Brazil, the Brazilian Institute of Corporate Governance (IBGC) launched its Code of Best Practices in 2001, and there have been four editions to date (IBGC 2014). In Argentina, Instituto Argentino para el Gobierno de las Organizaciones (IAGO) created a Code of Best Practices in 2003 aimed at listed and private companies (IAGO 2014). In Peru, the Principles of Good Corporate Governance was created in 2002 (and updated in 2012) and it works on a 'comply or explain' policy: companies that do not comply with certain principles must explain the reasons for non-compliance. For companies to be included in Lima Stock Exchange's Corporate Governance Index (as described earlier in the chapter), they must comply with these principles (BVL 2014). In Colombia, the Country Code (Código País) was launched in 2007, also adopting a 'comply or explain' model. However, the mechanism works differently from the Peruvian model: when the suggested measures are not adopted, it is at the discretion of the companies to decide whether they wish to report their reasons for not complying with the proposed practices (Superfinanciera 2007).

Effect of the 'comply or explain' approach on ESG disclosure

In terms of corporate ESG disclosure, BM&FBOVESPA adopted a 'comply or explain' approach in 2012 to encourage listed companies to report on ESG issues. By including a voluntary requirement for listed companies to report whether or not they publish a sustainability report, this initiative should drive improved ESG disclosure in Brazil (BM&FBOVESPA 2012).

Responsible investment issues

Corporate governance issues

Data on corporate governance in South America is relatively poor and of inconsistent quality among countries. Information on listed companies is also scarce as a result of different legal disclosure requirements. According to OECD's (2003) 'White Paper on Corporate Governance in Latin America', a high degree of concentration of ownership is one of the region's main characteristics. In Brazil, 74 per cent of publicly traded companies have a controlling shareholder (CFA Institute 2009). In Chile, the five largest shareholders of an average listed company hold 80 per cent of shares (Lefort and Walker 2000, cited in OECD 2003). In Latin America, families often hold controlling stakes, even among the largest traded companies, and board independence is low, as board members tend to be related to the controlling shareholders either through family ties, business relationships or friendship (OECD 2003). In addition, in Brazil, since legislation allows companies to issue shares without voting rights, it is common for insiders to retain voting shares and issue non-voting preferred shares to outsiders (Black et al. 2010), leaving non-voting shareholders in a weak position and vulnerable to the whims of controlling shareholders (Mallin 2013).

A few Brazilian institutional investors have been working towards promoting better corporate governance practices through seeking improved corporate disclosure. This is achieved by including corporate governance criteria in the selection of portfolio companies and appointing investor representatives to the companies' boards of directors. Large Brazilian pension funds such as PREVI, Petros and Funcef have significant shareholdings in many companies and, as allowed by the Companies Law, they have the ability to nominate representatives to boards of directors and fiscal councils of those companies. By appointing representatives, they participate and influence strategic discussions as insiders. PREVI is reported to train its board representatives on a range of sustainability themes through symposiums, presentations and online chats so that they can then raise not only corporate governance issues, but also social and environmental matters in board discussions. The Brazilian Companies Law also allows minority shareholders to collaborate to elect board members. Non-voting shareholders representing at least 10 per cent of the voting shares, and minority voting shareholders representing at least 15 per cent, may elect one board member each. As a result, a number of small Brazilian asset management firms who are activists in corporate governance issues (e.g. Rio Bravo, Polo) use this legal instrument to elect their representatives, and have their voices heard on boards (Yamahaki 2013).

Environmental issues

One of the most pressing environmental issues in South America relates to deforestation. In the Amazon, while agricultural expansion, infrastructure projects, energy exploration and illegal logging have been some of the contributors to deforestation, cattle pasture is the main culprit, occupying approximately 80 per cent of the deforested areas. Deforestation contributes to climate change, emitting significant amounts of carbon into the atmosphere annually. Although Brazil has low levels of carbon emissions in per capita terms (as 80 per cent of its electricity is supplied by hydropower), the country is the fifth largest carbon emitter when considering emissions from only deforestation (IHA 2013; UNDP 2007–2008; WWF 2014). To promote reforestation projects, the reduction of carbon emissions and the continuous adoption of renewable energy, a handful of Brazilian asset managers have developed funds investing in companies committed to these ends, as mentioned earlier in the chapter. However, the amount of assets under management of these funds is still modest.

Social issues

Poverty and social disparities represent a real concern in South America. It is estimated that 26 per cent of the South American population lives below the poverty line. In addition, Colombia, Brazil, Paraguay and Chile are among the 20 countries with the highest income disparity in the world. To overcome some of the social issues, a few asset managers have created investment funds with the purpose of making a positive social impact in the region. These are the cases of Colombian Fondo Inversor and the Argentinean Equitas I and II, as mentioned earlier. In Brazil, a recent study about the impact investing industry (Aspen Network, LGT and Quintessa 2014) found that the size of the Brazilian market is estimated to be US$ 177 million in assets under management (excluding assets managed by international investors), primarily concentrated in the areas of education, health and financial inclusion. The authors anticipate a steady but modest growth of the industry, as 19 of Brazil's largest impact investors, including fund managers, banks, foundations and family offices, expect to commit 40 to 50 per cent more capital to impact investments in 2014 compared to 2013.

Conclusion

As seen in this chapter, responsible investment in South America has two main approaches. The first is the integration of ESG issues by large Brazilian investors who have developed investment policies and proprietary methodologies incorporating ESG concerns, and who have been encouraging investee companies to consider ESG issues using strategies like collaborative engagements and the appointment of investor representatives onto Boards. Legislation on ESG disclosure has been an important driver for Brazilian pension funds to include ESG issues in their investment policies, and the newly issued Resolution 4327 should encourage further awareness on sustainability issues and ESG integration by Brazilian financial institutions.

The second approach has an impact investing component. Local organizations in Argentina, Brazil and Colombia have created funds investing in the promotion of high social and environmental impact. Although these funds represent a relatively limited amount of assets, they provide important funding for these organizations as they attempt to reach their social goals.

One can expect that the ESG integration efforts of the Brazilian investors will continue as they develop methodologies that incorporate ESG issues into their valuations. The membership of the large pension funds from Chile, Colombia and Peru (the Administradoras de Fondos de Pensiones – AFPs) to the PRI or to another responsible investment initiative would contribute to disseminating ESG integration to other countries. It is also expected that impact investment will continue growing in the region to support the activities of organizations interested in promoting positive social impact in South America.

Notes

1 Controlling shareholders are required to buy common shares at 100 per cent of the price paid for the shares rather than the 80 per cent that the legislation requires.
2 All stocks integrating the IGC that meet the following criteria are included in the index portfolio: (i) those included in a group of stocks whose combined negotiability indices represent 99 per cent of the total value of all individual indices and (ii) those with trading session participation that is equal to or greater than 95 per cent in the period.

References

Aguilera, R. V. (2009) 'A Comparative Analysis of Corporate Governance Systems in Latin America Argentina, Brazil, Chile, Colombia, and Venezuela', in McGee, R. W. (ed.) *Comparative Governance in Developing Economies*, New York: Springlink.

Anbima (Associação Brasileira das Entidades dos Mercados Financeiros e de Capitais) (2008) *Diretrizes do Conselho de Regulação e Melhores Práticas de Fundos De Investimento para Política de Exercício de Direito de Voto em Assembléias*. Online. Available HTTP: <http://www.anbima.com.br/mostra.aspx/?op=z&id=106> (accessed 13 April 2012).

Anbima (Associação Brasileira das Entidades dos Mercados Financeiros e de Capitais) (2015) *Indústria de Fundos*. Online. Available HTTP: <http://portal.anbima.com.br/informacoes-tecnicas/estatisticas/ind-de-fundos/Pages/default.aspx> (accessed 22 April 2015).

Aspen Network, LGV and Quintessa (2014) *Mapping the Impact Investing Sector in Brazil: Summary of Findings*. Online. Available HTTP: <http://www.aspeninstitute.org/publications/mapping-impact-investing-sector-brazil> (accessed 22 September 2014).

BCB (Banco Central do Brasil) (2009) *Resolução 003792*. Online. Available HTTP: <https://www3.bcb.gov.br/normativo/detalharNormativo.do?method=detalharNormativo&N=109082281> (accessed 13 April 2012).

BCB (Banco Central do Brasil) (2014) *Resolução 4.327*. Online. Available HTTP: <http://www.bcb.gov.br/pre/normativos/res/2014/pdf/res_4327_v1_O.pdf> (accessed 16 September 2014).

BCBA (Bolsa de Comercio de Buenos Aires) (2014) *El Mercado de Carbono en la Bolsa de Comercio de Buenos Aires*. Online. Available HTTP: <http://www.bcba.sba.com.ar/downloads/CARBONO_Resumen_general.pdf> (accessed 19 January 2014).

Black, B. S., De Carvalho, A. G. and Gorga, É. (2010) 'Corporate governance in Brazil' *Emerging Markets Review* 11(1): 21–38.

BM&FBOVESPA (Bolsa de Mercadorias & Futuros e Bolsa de Valores de São Paulo) (2011) *2010 Annual Report*. Online. Available HTTP: <http://ri.bmfbovespa.com.br//upload/portal_investidores/pt/informacoes_financeiras/relatorios_anuais/BM&F_Bovespa_RelatorioAnual2010_final_grafica.pdf> (accessed 19 January 2014).

BM&FBOVESPA (Bolsa de Mercadorias & Futuros e Bolsa de Valores de São Paulo) (2012) *BM&FBOVESPA recomenda que empresas publiquem Relatório de Sustentabilidade ou expliquem por que não o fazem*. Online. Available HTTP: <http://www.bmfbovespa.com.br/novo-valor/pt-br/noticias/2012/BMFBOVESPA-recomenda-que-empresas-publiquem-Relatorio-de-Sustentabilidade-20120104.asp> (accessed 13 April 2012).

BM&FBOVESPA (Bolsa de Mercadorias & Futuros e Bolsa de Valores de São Paulo) (2015a) *Índice de Sustentabilidade Empresarial*. Online. Available HTTP: <http://www.bmfbovespa.com.br/indices/ResumoIndice.aspx?Indice=ISE&idioma=pt-br> (accessed 22 April 2015).

BM&FBOVESPA (Bolsa de Mercadorias & Futuros e Bolsa de Valores de São Paulo) (2015b) *It Now ISE Fundo de Índice (ISUS11)*. Online. Available HTTP: <http://www.bmfbovespa.com.br/etf/ETFDetalhe.aspx?Codigo=ISUS11&idioma=pt-BR> (accessed 22 April 2015).

BM&FBOVESPA (Bolsa de Mercadorias & Futuros e Bolsa de Valores de São Paulo) (2015c) *Empresas Listadas – Segmento*. Online. Available HTTP: <http://www.bmfbovespa.com.br/cias-listadas/Empresas-Listadas/BuscaEmpresaListada.aspx?indiceAba=2&seg=BM&Idioma=pt-br> (accessed 17 June 2015).

BM&FBOVESPA (Bolsa de Mercadorias & Futuros e Bolsa de Valores de São Paulo) (2015d) *It Now IGCT Fundo de Índice (GOVE11)*. Online. Available HTTP: <http://www.bmfbovespa.com.br/etf/ETFDetalhe.aspx?Codigo=GOVE11&idioma=pt-BR> (accessed 22 April 2015).

BM&FBOVESPA (Bolsa de Mercadorias & Futuros e Bolsa de Valores de São Paulo) (2015e) *Índice Carbono Eficiente*. Online. Available HTTP: <http://www.bmfbovespa.com.br/indices/ResumoIndice.aspx?Indice=ICO2&Idioma=pt-br> (accessed 22 April 2015).

BVC (Bolsa de Valores de Colombia) (2014) *Private Capital Investing Fund*. Online. Available HTTP: <http://en.bvc.com.co/pps/tibco/portalbvc/Home/AcercaBVC/Responsabilidad_Social/Inversor?action=dummy> (accessed 19 January 2014).

BVL (Bolsa de Valores de Lima) (2014) *Índice de Buen Gobierno Corporativo*. Online. Available HTTP: < http://www.bvl.com.pe/acercabuengobierno.html> (accessed 16 September 2014).

CFA Institute (2009) *Shareowner Rights across the Markets: a Manual for Investors*, London: CFA.

CVM (Comissão de Valores Mobiliários) (2014) *Consulta Consolidada de Fundo*. Online. Available HTTP: <http://cvmweb.cvm.gov.br/SWB/defaultCPublica.asp> (accessed 19 January 2014).

Da Silva, A.L.C. (2002) *A influência da estrutura de controle e propriedade no valor, estrutura de capital e política de dividendos das empresas brasileiras*, Universidade Federal do Rio de Janeiro.

Equitas Ventures (2014) *Equitas II*. Online. Available HTTP: <http://equitasventures.com/equitasii.html> (accessed 19 January 2014).

Garcia, F. A. (2005) *Governança Corporativa*, Universidade Federal do Rio de Janeiro.

IAGO (Instituto Argentino para el Gobierno de las Organizaciones) (2014) *Código de Mejores Prácticas*. Online. Available HTTP: <http://www.iago.org.ar/iago/frameset.cfm?frame_contenido=codigo_mp> (accessed 20 January 2014).

IBGC (Instituto Brasileiro de Governança Corporativa (2014) *Código das Melhores Práticas*. Online. Available HTTP: <http://www.ibgc.org.br/CodigoMelhoresPraticas.aspx> (accessed 20 January 2014).

IFC and Mercer (2009) *Gaining Ground: Integrating Environmental, Social and Governance (ESG) Factors into Investment Processes in Emerging Markets*. Online. Available HTTP: <http://www1.ifc.org/wps/wcm/connect/topics_ext_content/ifc_external_corporate_site/ifc+sustainability/publications/publications_report_gainingground__wci__1319578881691> (accessed 13 April 2012).

IHA (International Hydropower Association) (2013) *2013 IHA Hydropower Report*. Online. Available HTTP: <http://www.hydropower.org/report> (accessed 20 January 2014).

Itaú Asset Management (2014). *Sustentabilidade*. Online. Available HTTP: <http://www.itauassetmanagement.com.br/asset/a-asset/sustentabilidade/index.html> (accessed 19 January 2014).

LASFF (Latin American Sustainable Finance Forum) (2010) *Engajamento para Erradicação do Trabalho Escravo no Brasil*. Online. Available HTTP: <http://intranet.gvces.com.br/cms/arquivos/trabalho_escravo.pdf> (accessed 13 April 2012).

Mallin, C. (2013) *Corporate Governance*, Oxford: Oxford University Press.

Mapstone, N. (2011) *Exchanges: Cross-Border Stocks Start Trading Slowly*. Online. Available HTTP: <http://www.ft.com/cms/s/0/882974d0-dace-11e0-a58b-00144feabdc0.html#axzz1rfns5fIe> (accessed 13 April 2012).

MILA (Mercado Integrado Latinoamericano) *About us*. Online. Available HTTP: <http://www.mercadomila.com/QuienesSomos> (accessed 22 April 2015).

MSCI (2009) *MSCI Barra Announcement on the Status of the MSCI Argentina and Pakistan Indices*. Online. Available HTTP: <http://www.msci.com/resources/pressreleases/20090218_2_pr.pdf> (accessed 13 April 2012).

OECD (Organization for Economic Co-operation and Development) (2003) *White Paper on Corporate Governance in Latin America*. Online. Available HTTP: <http://www.oecd.org/dataoecd/25/2/18976210.pdf> (accessed 13 April 2012).

Paschoarelli, R. (2008) *Como ganhar dinheiro no mercado financeiro*, 3 ed., Rio de Janeiro: Campus.

PREVI (2011) *Investimentos responsáveis: incorporação de práticas nas políticas de investimentos*. Study presented at ABRAPP's II Seminar on Sustainability and the Role of Pension Funds, Rio de Janeiro.

PRI (Principles for Responsible Investment) (2015a) *Signatories to the Principles for Responsible Investment*. Online. Available HTTP: <http://www.unpri.org/signatories> (accessed 17 June 2015).

PRI (Principles for Responsible Investment) (2015b) *Brazil and South America Network*. Online. Available HTTP: <http://www.unpri.org/areas-of-work/networks/?country=2> (accessed 22 April 2015).

Responsible Research (2012) *Sustainable Stock Exchanges: a Report on Progress*. Online. Available HTTP: <http://www.responsibleresearch.com/Sustainable_Stock_Exchanges_2012___Online.pdf> (accessed 13 April 2012).

Superfinanciera (Superintendencia Financeira de Colombia) (2007) *Código de Mejores Prácticas Corporativas*. Online. Available HTTP: <https://www.superfinanciera.gov.co/SFCant/Codigopais/textos/codigopias.pdf> (accessed 17 June 2015).

Sustainalytics (2013). *LatinSIF takes responsible investment on the road*. Online. Available HTTP: <http://www.sustainalytics.com/latinsif-takes-responsible-investment-road?utm_medium=email&utm_source=Act-On+Software&utm_content=email&utm_campaign=Sustainalytics%20Reporter%20%7C%20October%20%27013&utm_term=Read%20more%20about%20the%20roadshow> (accessed 01 February 2014).

UNDP (United Nations Development Programme) (2007–2008). 'Human Development Report 2007/2008: Fighting climate change – Human Solidarity in a Divided World'. Online. Available HTTP: <http://hdr.undp.org/en/reports/global/hdr2007–2008> (accessed 13 April 2012).

US SIF Foundation (2012) *Lessons Learned: the Emerging Markets Disclosure Project, 2008–2012*. Online. Available HTTP: <http://d2m27378y09r06.cloudfront.net/viewer/?file=wp-content/uploads/EMDP2012.pdf> (accessed 31 January 2014).

WFE (World Federation of Exchanges) (2014) *Monthly Reports*. Online. Available HTTP: <http://www.world-exchanges.org/statistics/monthly-reports> (accessed 22 April 2015).

WWF (2014) *Amazon*. Online. Available HTTP: <http://worldwildlife.org/places/amazon> (accessed 20 January 2014).

Yamahaki, C. (2013) 'Shareholder Engagement in Emerging Markets: Institutional and Organisational in Brazil and South Africa', PhD thesis, Middlesex University.

9

Responsible investment in South Africa

Nadia Mans-Kemp and Suzette Viviers

Introduction

This chapter deals with an overview of responsible investment (RI) in the South African context. South Africa is a developing country, located on the most southern tip of Africa. The country covers over 1 million square kilometres and is divided into nine provinces. There are 11 official languages, including Afrikaans, English and isiXhosa. The government is a multi-party constitutional democracy that operates at three distinct levels (national, provincial and local). South Africa has three capitals, namely Cape Town (legislative capital), Pretoria (administrative capital) and Bloemfontein (judicial capital) (South African Government Information 2011).

In South Africa, emphasis is mainly placed on voluntary compliance with the G component of environmental, social and corporate governance (ESG) criteria, namely corporate governance. This trend could be ascribed to the publication of three King Reports on corporate governance since 1994. These reports provide corporate governance guidelines to companies listed on the Johannesburg Stock Exchange (JSE). Interest in RI within the country is steadily growing, and positive ESG-related changes are occurring (Viviers, Bosch, Smit and Buijs 2009). Since 2011, a Code for Responsible Investing in South Africa (CRISA) was introduced and the Pension Funds Act was amended to pertinently include ESG considerations.

In the rest of this chapter, basic statistics on the country and its population will be provided, followed by a discussion on the South African RI market.

Basic statistics

Statistics South Africa (2011a) estimated the 2011 mid-year population as 50.59 million. Table 9.1 indicates the statistics according to gender and population group. Africans represent the largest population group (79.5 per cent), followed by Whites and people of color. Approximately 52 per cent of the total population is female (Statistics South Africa 2011a).

South Africa and Nigeria are the largest economies on the African continent (Sinclair and Yao 2011). The main economic sectors include mining, transport, energy, manufacturing, tourism and agriculture. According to the World Bank's country classification, South Africa is categorized as

Table 9.1 2011 mid-year population estimates for South Africa by gender and population group

Population group	*Male*		*Female*		*Total*	
	Number	*Percentage of male population*	*Number*	*Percentage of female population*	*Number*	*Percentage of total population*
African	19,472,038	79.4	20,734 237	79.5	40,206,275	79.5
Colored	2,188,782	8.9	2,351,008	9.0	4,539,790	9.0
Indian/Asian	626,690	2.6	648,177	2.5	1,274 867	2.5
White	2,227,526	9.1	2,338,299	9.0	4,565,825	9.0
Total	**24,515,036**	**100.0**	**26,071,721**	**100.0**	**50,586,757**	**100.0**

Source: Researchers' own construction based on information obtained from Statistics South Africa (2011a).

a developing country with an upper-middle income level. The official currency is the South African Rand (ZAR) (World Bank 2012).

The South African economy experienced robust growth between 2004 and 2007. Growth, however, began to slow down in the second half of 2007. The GDP equalled US $521.5 billion in 2009 and increased to $554.6 billion in 2011. The GDP real growth rate was −1.7 per cent in 2009 and improved to a positive growth rate of 3.4 per cent in 2011. Expressed in per capita terms, GDP also increased from $10,500 in 2009 to $11,000 in 2011. The country's economic policy is fiscally conservative, which implies that the focus is mainly on inflation control and the attainment of a budget surplus (Central Intelligence Agency World Factbook 2012). The average inflation rate was 7.1 per cent in 2009, decreasing to 5 per cent in 2011 (Statistics South Africa 2011b).

Southern Africa is one of the regions in the world that is the most affected by HIV/AIDS. South Africa has more people living with HIV/AIDS than any other country on the planet (Joint United Nations Programme on HIV/AIDS 2011). An estimated 16.6 per cent of the South African adult population (between the ages of 15 and 49) is HIV positive (Statistics South Africa 2011a). This pandemic provides both challenges and opportunities to long-term investors. HIV/AIDS has both direct costs for companies (e.g. higher health care and training costs) and indirect costs (e.g. lower revenue due to absenteeism and lower productivity). The disease also has a negative impact on social development and economic growth in South Africa (Seidl 2007). However, an opportunity exists for investors to promote dialogue between different stakeholders, including governments, companies and workers on HIV/AIDS issues and initiatives. Companies should be encouraged to adopt best practice responses to HIV/AIDS, such as policy development, counselling and training opportunities. Social change can thus be promoted and the spread of the disease can be limited (Robertson 2011).

Due to the apartheid regime, many North American and European investors divested from companies operating in South Africa in the 1980s (De Cleene and Sonnenberg 2004: 1). In the first couple of years after the democratic elections of 1994, South Africa received foreign capital averaging 1 per cent of GDP per annum (South African Reserve Bank 2001). The inflow of foreign direct investment (FDI) into the country is still disappointing, especially when compared to other developing countries (Gilroy, Gries and Naudé 2005; Sulaiman 2012). In terms of FDI inflow per country in the Southern African Development Community (SADC) region for 2009, South Africa received $5.696 million compared to the $13.101 million received by Angola (Van der Lugt and Hamblin 2011).

According to a report on sustainable investment in Sub-Saharan Africa (Sinclair and Yao 2011), global investors are becoming more interested in investment opportunities on the African continent. As South Africa is often seen as the gateway into Africa, considerable growth in foreign investment is expected over the next 5 years. Since JSE-listed companies are expected to provide integrated reports from 2011, it is anticipated that investors will increasingly integrate the published ESG aspects in the investment analysis process.

The responsible investment market

Defining RI in the South African context

As elsewhere in the world, the phenomenon of RI in South Africa is characterized by a lack of consensus regarding definitions and scope. A review of 15 academic articles published on the RI market in South Africa from 1997 to 2011 reveals that the phenomenon of integrating ethical and ESG considerations into investment analyses and decision-making is primarily referred to as 'socially responsible investing' (SRI). As shown in Table 9.2, increasing reference to 'responsible investing' (RI) has been made in academic articles in South Africa in the past 5 years. This is most likely due to the introduction of the UN-backed Principles for Responsible Investment (PRI).

Preference for the name RI is also evident in the definition used by one of the pioneers in the South African market, Futuregrowth Asset Management, which asserts that "RI encompasses a range of investment approaches including SRI, screening for ESG criteria, investor engagement and shareholder activism". Futuregrowth uses all of these approaches across a range of funds and asset classes. In contrast, Futuregrowth defines socially responsible investments (SRI) as "those investments that provide investors with both commercial returns and tangible social and developmental impact" (Responsible Investing 2011).

Table 9.2 Names for the RI phenomenon in South African academic literature (1997–2011)

	1997	*1998*	*2004*	*2005*	*2006*	*2008*	*2009*	*2011*	*Total*
Socially responsible investing	1	1	2	3	2		1		**10**
Responsible investing						3	1	3	**7**
Targeted investing				1		2			**3**
Green/environmental investing	2	1							**3**
Ethical investing	2								**2**
Social investing	2								**2**
Sustainable investing								1	**1**
Impact investing								1	**1**
Moral investing						1			**1**
Total	**7**	**2**	**2**	**4**	**2**	**6**	**2**	**5**	**30**

Source: Researchers' own construction based on De Vries and De Villiers (1997a); De Vries and De Villiers (1997b); Giamporcaro (2011); Heese (2005); Herringer, Firer and Viviers (2009); Rademeyer and Holtzhausen (2004); Sonnenberg and Hamman (2006); Van Niekerk and Vorster (1998); Visser (2005); Viviers (2005); Viviers, Bosch, Smit and Buijs (2008a); Viviers, Bosch, Smit and Buijs (2008b); Viviers, Eccles, De Jongh, Bosch, Smit and Buijs (2008); Viviers, Hand and Ractliffe (2011).

Types of RI products in the South African market

A wide range of unitized and non-unitized (pooled and segregated) funds with an RI mandate are available to institutional and retail investors in South Africa. Since the launch of the first two funds in June 1992, the Futuregrowth Albaraka Equity Fund (now called the Old Mutual Albaraka Equity Fund) and the Community Growth Equity Fund, 62 other RI funds have been established.[1] Over the year 2010, 10 new funds became available, the most RI funds launched in a single year. A total of 13 RI funds were discontinued over the research period; the most discontinuations occurred in 2002. A discontinued fund refers to a local RI fund that was established on or after 1 June 1992, but was either closed, merged with another fund or changed its investment mandate prior to the end of December 2011.

Table 9.3 provides a breakdown of the types of RI funds that are available in South Africa. As illustrated in Table 9.3, more than a third of active RI funds in South Africa on 31 December 2011 could be classified as equity funds. More details on the types of RI strategies used by fund managers of RI funds in South Africa are contained in Table 9.4.

As shown in Table 9.4, impact investing is by far the most important RI strategy in South Africa. It is employed either on its own or in combination with other strategies, most frequently positive screening. This is not surprising given the developmental opportunities and challenges facing South Africa, including investment opportunities in toll roads, electrification projects and the development of shopping centres in rural and suburban areas. Impact investing as an RI strategy is well suited to alternative funds, which primarily invest in unlisted securities and venture capital projects. More than a third of active RI funds in South Africa also employ ethical criteria, many of which are based on Shari'ah law,[2] to screen potential investments.

Although anti-South African sentiments sparked international interest in shareholder activism in the 1980s, this RI strategy is seldom employed among institutional investors in South Africa. Element Investment Managers is an exception in this regard. With the establishment of the Element Earth Equity Fund in October 2001, it became the first financial institution in South Africa to offer an investment fund with an embedded framework of constructive engagement.

Table 9.3 Types of RI funds in South Africa

Fund classification	*Active*	*Discontinued*	*Total N*	*Total %*
Equity[a]	18	5	23	35.9
Asset allocation[b]	12	6	18	28.1
Alternative[c]	14	2	16	25.0
Fixed interest[d]	6	0	6	9.4
Property[e]	1	0	1	1.6
Total	**51**	**13**	**64**	**100.0**

Source: Researchers' own construction based on their personal RI database and the classification system used by the Association of Savings and Investment SA's classification system (ASISA 2011).

[a] Equity funds are required to invest at least 75 per cent in equities. The remaining 25 per cent can be invested according to the fund manager's discretion.

[b] Asset allocation funds may invest in a spread of investments in the equity, capital, money and property markets. They generally hold a long-term view.

[c] Alternative funds generally invest in private equity initiatives by means of equity (including preference shares), debt or a combination thereof.

[d] Fixed-interest funds invest in the bond and money markets. No money market funds were, however, included in this database.

[e] Property funds invest in real estate through different channels.

Table 9.4 RI strategy used by fund managers of South African RI funds

RI Strategy	*Active*	*Discontinued*	*Total*	*%*
Impact investing[a]	11	5	16	25.0
Ethical exclusions[b]	14	0	14	21.9
Positive screening and impact investing	10	3	13	20.3
Positive screening[c]	6	5	11	17.2
Engagement[d]	3	0	3	4.7
Positive screening and engagement	3	0	3	4.7
Positive screening, engagement and impact investing	2	0	2	3.1
Positive screening, negative screening and impact investing	1	0	1	1.6
Ethical exclusions and engagement	1	0	1	1.6
Total	**51**	**13**	**64**	**100.0**

Source: Researchers' own construction based on their personal RI database and the investment mandate classification system used by the European Sustainable Investment Forum's guidelines (European SRI Study 2012).

[a] Refers to investments in a social and/or environmental purpose-driven company, organization or enterprise that addresses a social and/or environmental cause by applying market-based strategies in sustainable business models that can deploy and provide both financial returns and social and/or environmental impact.

[b] Refers to the application of negative screens to avoid investments in morally undesirable countries, industries and companies. This strategy is also referred to as 'exclusion of holdings from investment universe'.

[c] Positive screening refers to the selection of financial securities that meet a defined set of ESG criteria. This strategy is also referred to as 'norms-based screening'.

[d] Also called 'shareholder activism', refers to shareholders communicating with management boards on specific ESG issues. Investors can do so through dialogue, by filing resolutions, voting at annual general meetings and divesting from companies that fail to transform. This is a long-term process whereby investors seek to influence company behavior related to their ethical and ESG practices.

This approach was extended to all their funds under management shortly thereafter. Element Investment Managers was also the first local investment manager to sign the PRI and the first to publish its complete voting policy and record online (Element Investment Managers 2011).

A study by Winfield (2011) reveals that very few asset managers in South Africa are excited, passionate and serious about proxy voting (a potentially powerful tool in the hands of shareholder activists). This study also showed that asset managers are often unfamiliar with the documents and institutions that aim to help them develop and implement strong voting and other stewardship policies. In addition, there are very few sources of quality research relating to voting items and relatively little research is generated internally by asset managers. The author found that policy documents are typically weak and do not communicate effectively to clients, internal investment professionals or investee companies. Asset managers also prefer to engage with investee companies in private prior to the companies' annual general meetings.

One exception is Theo Botha, a legendary South African shareholder activist who regularly attends meetings of South Africa companies, often only holding one share in the specific company. He asks probing questions about issues such as corporate governance, environmental practices and Broad-Based Black Economic Empowerment (BBBEE). Botha often argues that South African corporate governance guidelines are too lenient (Sewing 2010; Steyn 2011). Botha's example indicates that public forms of shareholder activism are primarily employed as a strategy to promote organizational change in South Africa.

Table 9.5 Estimates of professional sustainable investment assets under management in South Africa on 31 December 2010 ($ billion)[a]

	Total assets under management	*ESG-integrated strategy*[b]	*% ESG-integrated/total assets under management*	*ESG-branded strategy*[c]	*% ESG-branded/ total assets under management*
General asset management	556.2	111.2	20.0%	4.2	0.8%
Private equity	14.2	6.3	44.0%	1.1	8%

Source: Adapted from Sinclair and Yao (2011).

[a] The authors of this report preferred the term 'sustainable investment' over RI and defined it as investments that integrate ESG factors into analysis, stock selection and active ownership practices in the belief that these factors can improve long-term risk management.

[b] Defined as approaches that include ESG factors, but that may or may not brand themselves as 'sustainable', 'responsible', 'impact-oriented', or 'green'.

[c] Defined as approaches that are explicitly ESG inclusive and marketed as such.

Market size

South Africa is Africa's biggest institutional investment market with assets under management (AUM) worth more than ZAR 4 trillion (approximately US$500 billion) (Pretorius, 2011). Research commissioned by the International Finance Corporation (Sinclair and Yao 2011) reveals that RI only represents a fraction of the total assets under management in South Africa (Table 9.5).

No statistics are available on the exact growth rate in responsible investments over the past 3 years (2009–2011). This is largely due to a lack of clarity on the definition of RI in the South African context. However, given changes in pension fund regulation in 2011, significant growth is expected in the market, particularly in the private equity space (refer to the policy environment section for more details).

Market environment

A breakdown of the key players in the South African financial markets is provided in Table 9.6. Retirement funds are major stakeholders in South African financial markets. It is estimated that they manage approximately half of all assets under management in the country (Pretorius 2011). The interests of organizations and individuals who are actively involved in the retirement industry are promoted by the Institute of Retirement Funds. This non-political body was established in March 1987 and consists of around 400 members (Institute of Retirement Funds 2011). The Principal Officers Association of South Africa is a trade association of pension fund members (425 principal officers and associate members) representing about $250 billion in assets under management. In November 2011, the International Finance Corporation signed an agreement with the association to work on a project to integrate ESG considerations into mainstream retirement industry investment practices regionally in Southern Africa. This project, called Sustainable Returns for Pensions and Society, aims at providing local retirement funds with a framework to improve compliance with the amended Pension Funds Act (International Finance Corporation 2011).

Other significant players in the financial markets in South Africa include insurance companies, medical schemes and collective investment schemes. Their collective interests are promoted by

Table 9.6 Key players in the South African financial markets

Category	*Stakeholders*	*Selected Industry Associations*
Retirement funds and insurers	• Pension and provident funds • Insurers (life and short-term) • Medical schemes	• Institute of Retirement Funds • Principal Officers Association of South Africa • Actuarial Society of South Africa • Life Offices' Association of South Africa • The South African Insurance Association • Association for Savings and Investment SA
Other financial intermediaries	• Collective investment schemes • Finance companies • Public sector financial intermediaries • Financial controlling companies	• Alternative Investment Management Association • Association of Black Securities and Investment South African • Africa Sustainable Investment Forum • South African Venture Capital and Private Equity Association
Banks	• Commercial and merchant banks • Mutual banks • Postbank • Landbank	• Banking Association of South Africa • Institute of Bankers in South Africa
Regulatory bodies	• South African Reserve Bank • Corporation for Public Deposits • Financial Services Board • National Treasury	

Source: Adapted from Van Zyl, Botha, Skerrit and Goodspeed (2009: 16).

the Association for Savings and Investment South Africa (ASISA), which was established in October 2008 (ASISA 2011). ASISA acts as the custodian of the majority of savings and investments in the country. Its strategic purpose is to proactively engage with stakeholders in the financial services industry on policy, regulatory and other issues of common concern (International Forum for Investment Education 2012). According to Pretorius (2011), the local investment industry in South Africa has gone a long way in promoting responsible self-regulation among key players in the country.

Although the venture capital market in South Africa is still young, several new finance companies have entered the market in recent years (Venture capital in South Africa 2010). The largest private equity industry body in Africa, the South African Venture Capital and Private Equity Association has more than 65 members and has started to actively explore ESG issues within the African context (Sinclair and Yao 2011).

The banking industry in South Africa also plays a significant role in mobilizing savings in the country and contributes about 5 per cent to GDP (Van Zyl et al. 2009: 84). The four largest banks (Absa Bank Limited, FirstRand Limited, Nedbank Limited and Standard Bank of South Africa Limited) have all adopted the Equator Principles for project financing. As a result, they are applying the IFC's social and environmental standards to all African deals (Pretorius 2011).

Policy environment

As shown in Table 9.6, a number of regulatory bodies are present in South African financial markets. The Minister of Finance and four underlying agencies (Financial Services Board, South African Reserve Bank, Financial Intelligence Centre and National Treasury) are mainly responsible for savings, pensions and investment regulatory bodies in the country. Capital markets are regulated by the Financial Services Board, whereas the National Treasury is responsible for efficient and sustainable public financial management. Sustainable public financial management is vital to the promotion of good governance, social progress and economic development in South Africa (Department: National Treasury Republic of South Africa 2012; Sinclair and Yao 2011).

A number of acts regulate the activities of investors and financial intermediaries in South Africa. The most pertinent acts include the Pension Funds Act (1956), Share Blocks Control Act (1980), the Financial Intelligence Centre Act (2001), Collective Investment Schemes Control Act (2002), Public Investment Corporation Act (2004), Financial Advisory and Intermediary Services Act (2002) and Securities Services Act (2004). Table 9.7 provides a list of selected legal provisions relevant to ESG considerations in South Africa.

For many years, RI in South Africa was stifled by the lack of enabling legislation. The situation, however, changed in March 2011 when Regulation 28 of the Pension Funds Act was amended. The act now explicitly states that prudent investing should take into account all factors that could materially affect an investment, including factors of an ESG character (Pension Funds Act, 1956: Amendment of Regulation 28 of the Regulations made under section 36 2011). According to experts in the field, the amendments to Regulation 28 represent a "fundamental shift in South Africa's investment landscape" and "Regulation 28 has finally put ESG into every Trustee Board Room as it ensures that Trustees must consider and apply their minds to sustainable investing" (Pretorius 2011).

ASISA was instrumental in amending Regulation 28 and developing the Code for Responsible Investing in South Africa (CRISA), launched in July 2011 (ASISA 2011). The code aims to provide the investor community with the guidance needed to give effect to the King Report III (a report on corporate governance principles for South African companies) as well as the PRI initiative. CRISA requires, inter alia, that institutional investors disclose the policies underpinning

Table 9.7 Legal provisions regarding ESG considerations in South Africa

Environmental	*Social*	*Governance*
• National Environmental Management Act (1998) • Environmental Conservation Act (1989) • National Water Act (1998) • National Environmental Management: Protected Areas Act (2003) • Air Quality Act (2004) • The Constitution: Section 24 • Polluter Pays Principle • National Energy Regulator of South Africa feed-in tariffs	• Broad-based Black Economic Empowerment Act (2003) • Labour Relations Act (1995) • Skills Development Act (1998) • Housing Protection Measures Act (1998) • Unemployment Insurance Act (2001) • Basic Conditions of Employment Act (1997) • Promotion of Equality and Prevention of Unfair Discrimination Act (2000) • Preferential Procurement Policy Framework Act (2000)	• Companies Act (2008) • National Credit Act (2005) • Insider Trading Act (1998) • Consumer Protection Act (2008)

Sources: Adapted from Sinclair and Yao (2011: 39) and ActsOnline (2012).

their investment decisions and actions. As with King III, CRISA is not legislation, but rather a set of principles and practices that should be adhered to on an 'apply or explain' basis (Girdwood 2011).

The South African investment community has slowly started to incorporate long-term sustainability objectives in their investment portfolios. However, the ability to apply ESG criteria is a skill that still needs to be refined in many investment management companies (Crotty 2013; MoneyMarketing 2013; Van der Merwe 2013).

RI institutions

A number of institutions actively participate in and promote RI in South Africa. One of the most important institutions is the Africa Sustainable Investment Forum, or AfricaSIF. The forum, launched in July 2009, is an independent, non-profit network of institutions and individuals that promote sustainable investment in Africa (Africa Sustainable Investment Forum 2012).

Since the launch of the PRI South Africa network in 2009, the number of signatories in South Africa has increased substantially (PRI 2010). The PRI signatories (as of 31 January 2012) (PRI 2012) are indicated in Table 9.8.

Table 9.8 South African PRI signatories

Asset Owner Signatories (n = 2)	*Investment Manager Signatories (n = 26)*	*Professional Service Partners (n = 8)*
• Eskom Pension and Provident Fund • Government Employees Pension Fund of South Africa	• 27 Four Investment Managers • Absa Capital Alternative Asset Management • Advantage Asset Managers • Afena Capital • Argon Asset Management • Atlantic Asset Management • Cadiz Holdings • Community Growth Management Company • Coronation Fund Managers • Element Investment Managers • Futuregrowth Asset Management • Investec Asset Management • Investment Solutions • Kagiso Asset Management • Mazi Visio Manco • Mergence Africa Investments • Oasis Group Holdings • Pan-African Asset Management • Prescient Investment Management • Prudential Portfolio Managers • Public Investment Corporation • RMB Asset Management • Royal Bafokeng Holdings • Sanlam Investment Management • STANLIB Asset Management • Vantage Capital	• Avior Research • Corporate Governance Accreditation • Empowerdex • Fiduciary Solutions • Johannesburg Stock Exchange • Malaczynski Burn • RisCura • Unity Incorporation

Source: Researchers' own construction based on information obtained from the PRI (2012).

In terms of asset owners, the Government Employees Pension Fund (GEPF) was the first South African signatory to the PRI (Republic of South Africa [RSA] GEPF 2012). The ultimate objective of investment decisions made by/on behalf of the GEPF is to include all financially material ESG issues. In 2009, the GEPF adopted its own RI policy, placing ESG factors at the heart of its investment strategy. Since the GEPF holds approximately 10 per cent of the FTSE/JSE All Share Index, its drive to invest in a more responsible manner can have a considerable impact on the South African investment industry as a whole (Pretorius 2011; RSA GEPF 2009).

The GEPF integrates ESG issues into its equity, private equity, property and infrastructure investments. The assumption is that better management of ESG issues by investee companies will lead to better long-run financial returns. Specialist external research, focusing on how well firms across different sectors of the South African economy manage ESG issues, is considered during investment decision-making. Regarding property investments, the GEPF focuses on energy efficiency in an attempt to mitigate climate change and unsustainable energy consumption in the country. A certain amount of the GEPF's assets are also dedicated to infrastructure development, linking investment returns with socioeconomic outcomes (RSA GEPF 2009).

As indicated in Table 9.8, 26 South African investment managers and eight service partners were signatories of the PRI in 2012. The Community Growth Management Company (COMANCO) and Unity Incorporation were the first to establish ESG practices. Unity Incorporation is a union-formed investment company that was established in 1992 to represent trade unions spanning several industries (including the largest trade union federations in the country, namely the Congress of South African Trade Unions and the National Council of Trade Unions). As an investment manager, the company aims to ensure that its members can have a say in the manner in which their money is invested. The company thus screens potential investments on a range of ESG issues that are deemed material in the South African context. It also focuses on ESG research, training of retirement fund trustees (such as training on changes in legislation) and engagement on social issues (Community Growth Funds 2012).

COMANCO is a jointly owned company between Unity Incorporation and Old Mutual Group South Africa. Funds are invested in companies that are expected to balance profit generation whilst meeting social and environmental obligations. COMANCO manages the Community Growth Funds, a range of RI funds that integrate ESG factors into the investment process. The Community Growth Equity Fund, for example, invests in JSE-listed companies that are deemed socially responsible. The Community Growth Gilt Fund aims to maximize total returns by investing in listed bonds with a particular emphasis on reconstruction and development. The Community Growth Fund of Funds likewise provides investors with financial and social returns by integrating ESG factors into investment analyses (Old Mutual 2012).

Another important investment manager in the South African context is the Public Investment Corporation Limited (PIC). The PIC is an asset management company that is fully owned by the South African government, with the Minister of Finance as its representative. The PIC was established in April 2005 and manages assets valued at R1,032 trillion (approximately US $150 billion) as of March 2011. The PIC's clients consist of 35 public sector entities, such as pension, provident, development, social security and guardian funds. The PIC is also the asset manager of most of the GEPF's assets (PIC 2012a; Pretorius 2011). The PIC invests primarily in equities (shares of JSE-listed companies), fixed-income investments (in domestic capital and money markets), properties (industrial, corporate, retail and specialized South African properties) and the Isibaya Fund when making investments on behalf of the GEPF. The Isibaya Fund provides finance for projects able to generate good financial returns while also supporting positive long-term economic growth, social infrastructure development, transformation and environmental sustainability outcomes (PIC 2012b).

Another important service provider listed in Table 9.8 is RisCura, an independent investment and risk consultant established in 1999. RisCura is often contracted to conduct surveys and analyses on sustainable investment in Africa (RisCura 2012). The company provides specialized investment advice and solutions to institutional investors (including medical schemes and retirement funds), stock exchanges, banks, custodians and investment managers.

The Johannesburg Stock Exchange (JSE) is the eighteenth largest stock exchange worldwide (Central Intelligence Agency World Factbook 2012) and became a signatory of the PRI in 2009. The JSE (2012a) joined forces with the FTSE to launch the FTSE/JSE SRI index in May 2004. It was the first index of its kind in emerging markets and encouraged greater focus on RI in South Africa. The FTSE/JSE SRI index acknowledges companies each year that incorporate sustainability into their business practices. The index had 74 constituents in 2011 (JSE 2012b), up from 51 constituents in 2004 (JSE 2012c). Various criteria are used to measure the triple bottom line performance of companies that are included in the FTSE/JSE All Share Index. Local and international investors can thus use this index as a tool to screen potential investments for ESG criteria (JSE 2012a).

RI issues in South Africa

The 2009 Emerging Markets Investor Survey (EMDP 2009) indicated that investors in major emerging markets require more disclosure on the management of ESG concerns. More than two thirds of respondents have been investing in emerging markets for over 6 years (Emerging Markets Disclosure Project 2009). Poor ESG disclosure by firms in emerging markets can potentially reduce investment allocations, as it greatly undermines investor confidence. The report recognized South Africa's progress on ESG disclosure among emerging countries (United States Forum for Sustainable and Responsible Investment 2012; EMDP 2009). There is, however, still room for improvement, especially in terms of environmental reporting.

According to the World Wildlife Foundation (2012), the most critical environmental issues in South Africa are a lack of water, destruction of natural habitats, overfishing, introduction of exotic species and pollution. These issues should thus feature prominently among the environmental criteria used by investors screening investment opportunities in South Africa. According to the FTSE/JSE SRI index, climate change and carbon emission disclosure are also important environmental factors to consider. Although environmental issues such as crude oil pollution attract attention worldwide (Brown 2002), there is still a lack of focus on these issues by South African companies and investors (JSE 2011).

The results of the 2010 South African Social Attitudes Survey indicated that the following were regarded as the four most important social problems facing citizens in the country (listed in order of importance according to the survey): unemployment, HIV/AIDS, crime and security and poverty (Roberts, Kivilu and Davids 2010). South Africa has a very high unemployment rate (about a quarter of all economically active persons), which contributed to the approximately 2.1 million serious crimes reported in South Africa during 2010/2011 (Central Intelligence Agency World Factbook 2012; South African Police Service 2011). In line with these findings, the FTSE/JSE SRI index focuses on the following social indicators: training and development, employee relations, equal opportunities, health and safety, community relations, stakeholder engagement, black economic empowerment (BEE) and HIV/AIDS (JSE 2011).

In terms of governance issues, South Africa pioneered the development of corporate governance guidelines and codes of best practices in 1994 with the publication of the first King Report on Corporate Governance (Armstrong, Segal and Davis 2005). Some of the King I recommendations on corporate governance were superseded by legislation, and the revised King II Report was published in 2002. Changes in international governance trends and the new Companies Act of South Africa (No. 71 of 2008) necessitated the issuance of the King Report III in 2009. The King III Report provides guidelines for corporate governance and follows an 'apply or explain' approach (Institute of Directors in Southern Africa 2009a). As mentioned, the King III Report makes it mandatory for JSE-listed companies to include ESG analysis in their corporate reporting as of 2011 (Pretorius 2011).

According to the King III Report (Institute of Directors in Southern Africa 2009b), the board of directors is the focal point of corporate governance. ESG reporting in South Africa is thus mainly focused on board-specific corporate governance factors, such as the composition of the board, director remuneration and attendance at board meetings. The Unit for Corporate Governance in Africa developed the PIC corporate governance rating matrix. The PIC is a major role player in the South African investment environment. The matrix is a developmental tool, aimed at assisting JSE-listed firms to improve their corporate governance performance and reporting (Centre for Corporate Governance in Africa 2010).

The relative importance of ESG criteria in South Africa

Two comprehensive studies on RI in South Africa by Eccles, Nicholls and de Jongh (2007) and Sinclair and Yao (2011) considered the opinions of investors and other stakeholders on the relative importance of ESG criteria. The results of these studies suggest that private equity investors viewed corporate governance, infrastructure development, employee relations, safety and worker rights, environmental management and water scarcity/sanitation as the most important ESG factors. Asset managers also regarded corporate governance, infrastructure development and water scarcity/sanitation as the most important ESG criteria in South Africa. Asset managers also prioritized HIV/AIDS, BBBEE and job creation issues. Local ESG issues thus gained considerable attention, with a key focus on development and empowerment. The high ranking of corporate governance could be due to a combination of the impact of the King Reports and high-profile corporate scandals on the South African business psyche.

Based on the preceding literature, Table 9.9 provides a summary of the most prominent ESG considerations in South Africa.

Table 9.9 Summary of the most prominent ESG considerations in South Africa

Environmental Issues[a]	*Social Issues*[b]	*Governance Issues*[c]
• Energy usage • Alternative energy • Water scarcity/sanitation • Clean technology • Climate change	• BBBEE • HIV/AIDS • Infrastructure development • Unemployment • Employee relations, safety and worker rights • Education	• Board composition • Meeting attendance • Board committees • Director remuneration

Source: Researchers' own construction.

[a] Based on the findings and predictions of Sinclair and Yao (2011) and Johannesburg Stock Exchange (2011).

[b] Based on the South African Social Attitudes Survey (Roberts et al. 2010), Sinclair and Yao (2011) and Eccles et al. (2007).

[c] Based on the King Report III (Institute of Directors in Southern Africa 2009b).

Some of the most prominent ESG criteria, notably HIV/AIDS, crime and unemployment, are not yet addressed by local investors. This is unfortunate when considering the power that investors, and in particular institutional investors, have to foster transformation and growth in the country. As indicated earlier, investors are currently focusing on corporate governance issues, followed by some social issues, such as social infrastructure development (Viviers, Hand and Ratcliffe 2011).

At present, environmental issues receive the least attention. This situation is, however, likely to change given the South African government's pledge to reduce the country's greenhouse gas emissions by 34 per cent by the 2020 and by 42 per cent by 2025 (Moholola 2011). Sinclair and Yao (2011) likewise predict that environmental concerns, such as alternative energy, water and clean technology, will become more important ESG considerations in South Africa in the next 10 years, specifically among private equity investors. In terms of social issues, they highlight education and health care as areas of increasing prominence.

Conclusion

Anti-South African sentiments in developed countries sparked global interest in RI in the 1980s. The RI market in South Africa, however, only came into existence later with the establishment of the first RI fund in June 1992. The South African RI market has not grown in line with its international counterparts in terms of the number of funds established or the size of assets under management. At present, RI is still very much a fringe activity in South Africa's financial markets.

The most important barrier to the uptake of RI relates to the belief among institutional investors that RI involves a financial sacrifice (Eccles et al. 2007). Studies have shown that this is not the case in the South African RI market (Viviers et al. 2009). Acknowledgment of this fact along with amendments to the Pension Funds Act, industry initiatives such as CRISA and growing pressure from stakeholders provide a strong opportunity for the expansion of the RI market in South Africa.

Notes

1 Finding based on researchers' own calculations based on a personal RI database.
2 The moral code and religious law of Islam.

References

ActsOnline. (2012) *Welcome to ActsOnline.* Online. Available HTTP: <http://www.acts.co.za> (accessed 17 February 2012).

Africa Sustainable Investment Forum. (2012) *AfricaSIF.org.* Online. Available HTTP: <http://www.africasif.org/> (accessed 29 January 2012).

Armstrong, P., Segal, N. and Davis, B. (2005) 'Corporate governance: South Africa, a pioneer in Africa', *The South African institute of International Affairs: Global Best Practice*, 1: 1–39.

Association for Savings and Investments SA (ASISA). (2011) *Responsible investment.* Online. Available HTTP: <http://www.asisa.co.za/> (accessed 4 December 2011).

Brown, C. E. (2002) *World energy resources: international geohydroscience and energy research institute*, Berlin: Springer.

Central Intelligence Agency World Factbook. (2012) *Africa: South Africa.* Online. Available HTTP: <https://www.cia.gov/library/publications/the-world-factbook/geos/sf.html> (accessed 7 February 2012).

Centre for Corporate Governance in Africa. (2010) *PIC corporate governance rating matrix.* Online. Available HTTP: <http://www.governance.usb.ac.za/current-projects/pic-corporate-governance-rating-matrix.aspx> (accessed 1 February 2012).

Community Growth Funds. (2012) *Unity profile*. Online. Available HTTP: <http://www.community growthfunds.co.za/about-us/unity-profile/> (accessed 29 January 2012).

Crotty, A. (2013) 'Few investors take CRISA principles seriously'. *Business Report*, 8 October. Online. Available HTTP: <http://www.iol.co.za/business/news/few-investors-take-crisa-principles-seriously-1.1588475> (accessed 4 November 2013).

De Vries, I. and De Villiers, C. J. (1997a) 'Ethical investing: background and criteria which can be applied to the South African environment', *Meditari Accountancy Research*, 1: 17–29.

De Vries, I. and De Villiers, C. J. (1997b) 'Ethical investing by South African unit trust managers', *Meditari Accountancy Research*, 1: 31–43.

De Cleene, S. and Sonnenberg, D. (2004) *Socially responsible investment in South Africa*, 2nd ed., Johannesburg: African Institute of Corporate Citizenship.

Department: National Treasury Republic of South Africa. (2012) *Welcome to the National Treasury website*. Online. Available HTTP: <http://www.treasury.gov.za/> (accessed 29 January 2012).

Eccles, N., Nicholls, S. and de Jongh, D. (2007) *The state of responsible investment in South Africa*. Online. Available HTTP: <http://www.unepfi.org/publications/africa/index.html> (accessed 27 January 2012).

Element Investment Managers. (2011) *Responsible investment*. Online. Available HTTP: <http://www.elementim.co.za/responsible-investment/overview/> (accessed 4 December 2011).

EMDP Emerging Markets Disclosure Project. (2009) *Emerging Markets Investor Survey Report: an analysis of responsible investment in emerging markets*. Online. Available HTTP: <http://www.eiris.org/files/research%20publications/emdpinvestorsurveyjune09.pdf> (accessed 24 January 2012).

European SRI Study. (2012) Online. Available HTTP: <http://eurosif.org/images/stories/pdf/1/eurosif%20 sri%20study_lowres%20v1.1.pdf> (accessed 4 November 2013).

Giamporcaro, S. (2011) 'Sustainable and responsible investment in emerging markets: integrating environmental risks in the South African investment industry', *Journal of Sustainable Finance and Investment,* 1(2): 121–137.

Gilroy, B. M., Gries, T. and Naudé, D. A. (2005) *Multi-national enterprises, foreign direct investment and growth in Africa: South African Perspectives*, Heidelberg: Physica-Verlag.

Girdwood, A. (2011) 'The regulatory context for responsible investing in South Africa', *World Wildlife Foundation*, August. Online. Available HTTP: <http://www.girdwood.co.za/responsible_investing_article_august_2011.pdf > (accessed 1 September 2011).

Heese, K. (2005) 'The development of socially responsible investment in South Africa: experience and evolution of SRI in global markets', *Development Southern Africa,* (22)5: 729–739.

Herringer, A., Firer, C. and Viviers, S. (2009) 'Key challenges facing the socially responsible investment (SRI) sector in South Africa', *Investment Analysts Journal*, 70(Nov): 11–26.

Institute of Directors in Southern Africa (2009a) *King's Council King III at a glance: steering point*. Online. Available HTTP: <http://www.iodsa.co.za/PRODUCTSSERVICES/KingIIIReportPapersGuidelines/KingReportonCorporateGovernanceinSA/KingIII.aspx> (accessed 29 January 2012).

Institute of Directors in Southern Africa. (2009b) *The King Report III on Corporate Governance*, Johannesburg: Institute of Directors in Southern Africa.

Institute of Retirement Funds. (2011) Online. Available HTTP: <http://www.irf.org.za/> (accessed 3 December 2011).

International Finance Corporation. (2011) *IFC and South African retirement industry to advance groundbreaking sustainability legislation*. Online. Available HTTP: <http://www.ifc.org/IFCExt/pressroom/IFCPressRoom.nsf/0/37B46A7E73BB249D42257958003C8657> (accessed 29 January 2012).

International Forum for Investor Education (IFIE). (2012) *About the Association for Savings and Investment SA (ASISA)*. Online. Available HTTP: <http://www.ifie.org/index.php/member-directory/86-association-for-savings-and-investment-south-africa-asisa> (accessed 29 January 2012).

Johannesburg Stock Exchange (JSE). (2011) *SRI index background and selection criteria 2011*. Online. Available HTTP: <http://www.jse.co.za/Libraries/SRI_Criteria_Documents/01_Background_and_Criteria_2011.sflb.ashx> (accessed 7 February 2012).

Johannesburg Stock Exchange (JSE). (2012a) *Introduction to SRI index*. Online. Available HTTP: <http://www.jse.co.za/About-Us/SRI/Introduction_to_SRI_Index.aspx> (accessed 5 February 2012).

Johannesburg Stock Exchange (JSE). (2012b) *SRI index constituents for 2011*. Online. Available HTTP: <http://www.jse.co.za/AboutUs/SRI/Constituents/SRIIndexConstituentsFor2011.asp> (accessed 7 February 2012).

Johannesburg Stock Exchange (JSE). (2012c) *SRI index constituents for 2004*. Online. Available HTTP: <http://www.jse.co.za/AboutUs/SRI/Constituents/SRIIndexConstituentsfor200 4.aspx> (accessed 7 February 2012).

Joint United Nations Programme on HIV/AIDS. (2011) *World AIDS Day report*. Online. Available HTTP: <http://www.unaids.org/en/media/unaids/contentassets/documents/unaidspublication/2011/JC2216_WorldAIDSday_report_2011_en.pdf > (accessed 1 February 2012).

Moholola, E. (2011) 'Urgent need for low carbon SA', *Parliament of the Republic of South Africa – News*, December. Online. Available HTTP: <http://www.parliament.gov.za/live/content.php?Item_ID=1870> (accessed 16 January 2012).

MoneyMarketing. (2013) *CRISA not getting full support*. Online. Available HTTP: <http://www.moneymarketing.co.za/crisa-not-getting-full-support/> (accessed 4 November 2013).

Old Mutual. (2012) *Investing responsibly*. Online. Available HTTP: <http://www.oldmutual.co.za/aboutus/sustainabilityreport/investingresponsibly/community-growth-fund.aspx> (accessed 29 January 2012).

Pension Funds Act, 1956: Amendment of Regulation 28 of the Regulations made under section 36. (2011) *Compliance SA*. Online. Available HTTP: <http://www.compliancesa.com/library/lib_doc_0068.pdf> (accessed 4 January 2012).

Pretorius, L. (2011) 'Growing African roots', *Financial Mail*, 18 August. Online. Available HTTP: <http://www.fm.co.za/Article.aspx?id=151080> (accessed 25 January 2012).

Principles for Responsible Investment (PRI). (2010) *Annual Report of the PRI initiative 2010*. Online. Available HTTP: <http://www.unpri.org/files/annual_report2010.pdf> (accessed 21 February 2012).

Principles for Responsible Investment (PRI). (2012) *Signatories to the Principles of Responsible Investment*. Online. Available HTTP: <http://www.unpri.org/signatories/> (accessed 29 January 2012).

Public Investment Corporation (PIC). (2012a) *The leading South African Investor*. Online. Available HTTP: <http://www.pic.gov.za/Inveloper.asp?iP=7&iVctg=360&iS={FD7CDAC2–47C4–4C7C-AECF-11C56EDD99CA}&iSL=:2083:;:2168:;:2315:;:> (accessed 29 January 2012).

Public Investment Corporation (PIC). (2012b) *Isibaya Fund*. Online. Available HTTP: <http://www.pic.gov.za/Inveloper.asp?iS=%7B8C717574-E406–47A5–90D3 01A901474679%7D&iP=7&iVctg=290> (accessed 24 January 2012).

Rademeyer, C. and Holtzhausen, J. (2004) 'King II, corporate governance and shareholder activism', *South African Law Journal*, 120(4): 767–775.

Republic of South Africa Government Employees Pension Fund (RSA GEPF). (2009) *Responsible Investment implementation: integrating ESG issues in investments*. Online. Available HTTP: <http://www.gepf.gov.za/Investments/Documents/ESG%20Issues%20in%20Investment.pdf> (accessed 24 January 2012).

Republic of South Africa Government Employees Pension Fund (RSA GEPF). (2012) *Investments*. Online. Available HTTP: <http://www.gepf.gov.za/Investments/Pages/default.aspx> (accessed 29 January 2012).

Responsible Investing. (2011) *Futuregrowth Asset Management*. Online. Available HTTP: <http://www.futuregrowth.co.za/page/responsible-investing> (accessed 1 December 2011).

RisCura. (2012) *What we do*. Online. Available HTTP: <http://www.riscura.com/sa/our_bus.htm> (accessed 29 January 2012).

Roberts, B., Kivilu, M. W. and Davids, Y. D. (2010) *South African Social Attitudes. 2nd report: reflections on the age of hope*. Online. Available HTTP: <http://www.hsrcpress.ac.za/product.php?productid=2280> (accessed 24 January 2012).

Robertson, M. (2011) *HIV/AIDS: an issue for responsible investors?* Online. Available HTTP: <http://www.eiris.org/blog/hivaids-an-issue-for-responsible-investors/> (accessed 21 February 2012).

Seidl, F. (2007) *Impact of the AIDS crisis on South Africa's prospects for development*, Norderstedt: GRIN Verlag.

Sewing, J. (2010) *Corporate divestiture management organizational techniques for proactive divestiture decision-making*, Heidelberg: Springer.

Sinclair, G. and Yao, R. (2011) *Sustainable Investment in Sub-Saharan Africa – investment practitioner views on sustainable investment in private equity and asset management in South Africa, Nigeria and Kenya*. Online. Available HTTP: <http://www.ifc.org/ifcext/sustainability.nsf/Content/Publications_Report_SISubSaharanAfrica> (accessed 29 January 2012).

Sonnenberg, D. and Hamman, R. (2006) 'The JSE Socially Responsible Investment Index and the state of sustainability reporting in South Africa', *Development Southern Africa*, 23(2): 305–320.

South African Government Information. (2011) *South Africa at a glance*. Online. Available HTTP: <http://www.info.gov.za/aboutsa/glance.htm> (accessed 29 January 2012).

South African Police Service. (2011) *Crime Report 2010/2011*. Online. Available HTTP: <http://www.saps.gov.za/statistics/reports/crimestats/2011/crime_stats.htm> (accessed 8 February 2012).

South African Reserve Bank. (2001) *Quarterly Bulletin*, 219–222, Pretoria: SARB.

Statistics South Africa. (2011a) *Mid-year population estimates 2011*. Online. Available HTTP: <http://www.statssa.gov.za/publications/P0302/P03022011.pdf> (accessed 18 November 2011).

Statistics South Africa. (2011b) *Statistical release Consumer Price Index*, December. Online. Available HTTP: <http://www.statssa.gov.za/publications/P0141/P0141December2011.pdf> (accessed 24 January 2012).

Steyn, L. (2011) 'Theo Botha – the shareholder activist', *Mail and Guardian online*, 13 May. Online. Available HTTP: <http://mg.co.za/article/2011–05–13-theo-botha – the-shareholder-activist> (accessed 29 January 2012).

Sulaiman, T. (2012) 'South Africa takes a knock in foreign direct investment', *Mail and Guardian online*, 24 October. Online. Available HTTP: <http://mg.co.za/article/2012–10–24-sas-foreign-direct-investment-drops> (accessed 22 October 2013).

United States Forum for Sustainable and Responsible Investment. (2012) *Press release: major emerging market investors want more disclosure on ESG issues, global survey finds*. Online. Available HTTP: <http://ussif.org/news/releases/pressrelease.cfm?id=142> (accessed 24 January 2012).

Van der Lugt, S. and Hamblin, V. (2011) *Addressing China's role in foreign direct investment in Southern Africa*. Online. Available HTTP: <http://www.ccs.org.za/wp-content/uploads/2011/03/Final-report-CCS-March-2011-CCS.pdf> (accessed 22 October 2013).

Van der Merwe, P. (2013) 'ESG thinking now a business imperative' *InvestSA Magazine*, 20 June. Online. Available HTTP: <http://www.investsa.co.za/esg-thinking-now-a-business-imperative/> (accessed 22 October 2013).

Van Niekerk, M. C. and Vorster, Q. (1998) 'The influence of environmental information contained in the annual financial reports of South African listed companies on the investment decisions taken by unit trust managers', *Meditari Accountancy Research*, 6: 319–336.

Van Zyl, C., Botha, Z., Skerrit, P. and Goodspeed, I. (eds). (2009) *Understanding South African financial markets*, 3rd ed, Pretoria: Van Schaik.

Venture capital in South Africa. (2010) *TradeInvest South Africa*, 20 May. Online. Available HTTP: <http://www.tradeinvestsa.co.za/feature_articles/516314.htm> (accessed 5 February 2012).

Visser, W. (2005) 'Corporate citizenship in South Africa – a review of progress since democracy', *Journal of Corporate Governance*, 18: 29–38.

Viviers, S. (2005) 'Socially responsible (ethical) investing in South Africa', *African Journal of Business Ethics*, 1(1): 21–30.

Viviers, S., Bosch, J. K., Smit, E.vd M. and Buijs, A. (2008a) 'The risk-adjusted performance of responsible investment funds in South Africa', *Investment Analysts Journal*, 68(November): 1–17.

Viviers, S., Bosch, J. K., Smit, E.vd M. and Buijs, A. (2008b) 'Is responsible investing ethical?', *South African Journal of Business Management*, 39(1): 15–25.

Viviers, S., Bosch, J. K., Smit, E.vd M. and Buijs, A. (2009) 'Responsible investing in South Africa', *Investment Analysts Journal*, 69(May): 1–14.

Viviers, S., Eccles, N. S., De Jongh, D., Bosch, J. K., Smit, E.vd M. and Buijs, A. (2008) 'Responsible investing in South Africa – drivers, barriers and enablers', *South African Journal of Business Management*, 39(4): 15–28.

Viviers, S., Hand, D. and Ractliffe, T. (2011) 'From philanthropy to impact investing: shifting mindsets in South Africa', *Corporate Ownership and Control*, 8: 25–43.Winfield, J. (2011) 'The landscape of proxy voting at South African asset managers', *RisCura*, July. Online. Available HTTP: <http://www.riscura.com/docs/research/SpoiltVotesHigh_Aug2011.pdf> (accessed 1 December 2011).

World Bank. (2012) *South Africa*. Online. Available HTTP: <http://web.worldbank.org/WBSITE/EXTERNAL/COUNTRIES/AFRICAEXT/SOUTHAFRICAEXTN/0,,menuPK:368082~pagePK:141159~piPK:141110~theSitePK:368057,00.html> (accessed 29 January 2012).

World Wildlife Foundation. (2012) *Environmental problems in South Africa*. Online. Available HTTP: <http://wwf.panda.org/who_we_are/wwf_offices/south_africa/environmental_problems__in_south_africa/> (accessed 5 February 2012).

10

Responsible investment in Nigeria

Innocent Okwuosa and Kenneth Amaeshi

Introduction

With the rebasing of Nigeria's 2014 Gross Domestic Product (GDP) (Bloomberg, 2014), the Nigerian economy is now the biggest economy in Africa, having overtaken that of South Africa But compared to South Africa, responsible investment (RI) practice is not well developed, as evidenced by the small number of Principles of Responsible Investment (PRI) signatories among asset owners, asset managers and service providers that are based in Nigeria. But given that RI has had an overall growth rate of 68 per cent over the last 3 years (see Table 10.3 later in this chapter) and that there has been a concerted effort on the part of financial market regulators (e.g. the Central Bank of Nigeria) to enthrone RI principles in bank lending, we are of the opinion that RI has enormous potential in the Nigerian market. We are also of the opinion that this regulatory policy will ultimately be a game changer in the development of RI in Nigeria, as it will not only prompt demand from market forces, but it will also engender regulatory push and an added impetus to market forces.

Country/region overview

Basic statistics

Nigeria has an estimated population of 177,155,754 (July 2014 est.) and an average life expectancy of 53 years (World Bank 2013). Nigeria is classified as a mixed economy and an emerging market It is Africa's biggest oil exporter, has the largest natural gas reserves on the continent, and accounts for 47 per cent of West Africa's population (World Bank, 2013). According to the World Bank (2013) the country has carried out an ambitious reform agenda over last 10 years, which has included, among other things, comprehensive power sector reform aimed at expanding supply by opening the door to private investment and addressing some of the chronic sector issues that hamper service delivery. It was among the first countries that adopted and implemented the Extractive Industries Transparency Initiative (EITI) aimed at improving governance and oil sector management. It passed the NEITI Act into law in 2007, and became EITI compliant in 2011. Overall the economy witnessed strong annual growth of 7.6 per cent, on average, between 2003 and 2010 (World Bank, 2013), and it is projected to grow by 6.9 per cent (inflation adjusted) between 2014 and 2016 (National Bureau of Statistics, 2013). This economic growth is broad based and driven by strong performance in the telecommunications, agricultural, manufacturing and trade sectors (World Bank, 2013). Portfolio capital inflow targeting the government bond market surpassed $17 billion in 2012 and has been short-term in nature. The country has witnessed stability in its macro-economic environment with a stable exchange rate to USD. The inflation rate is projected to average 9.73 per cent over the next 2 years (National Bureau of Statistics, 2013).

These strong fiscal and external buffers, coupled with ongoing strong economic growth, have resulted in improvement of Nigeria's long-term foreign and local currency sovereign credit ratings by Standard and Poor's (S&P), Fitch and Moody's, with Barclays and JP Morgan adding Nigeria's emerging market local currency bonds to their indices (World Bank, 2013).

RI market

Gauging the RI market in Nigeria is predicated on an understanding of RI itself. RI has been defined by Renneboog et al. (2008) as the investment that involves the integration of environmental, social and ethical considerations in investment decision-making. Whereas this definition includes ethical considerations, it is governance issues that are now generally accepted as being a point of concern within the investment community. Hence, Eurosif (2012) views RI products from the investment process perspective, which involves a combination of the primary investors' financial objectives and environmental, social and governance (ESG) considerations. Investment screenings to meet this consideration, according to Eurosif (2012), involve seven process-oriented categories that include (1) integration of ESG factors into financial analysis, (2) exclusion of holdings from the investment universe, (3) engagement and voting on sustainability matters, (4) best-in-class investment selection, (5) sustainability-themed investment, (6) norm-based screening and (7) impact investment. A closer look at the names of RI funds in Nigeria (see Table 10.2 later in the chapter) shows that RI in Nigeria is understood to be moral investments with an emphasis on ethics.

The RI market in Nigeria could be described as being in its infancy. The practice is not yet widespread, and there is no asset owner among the PRI signatories as at 30 May 2014 (see PRI, 2014). This is the general trend in most African countries, with the exception of South Africa, which has a number of PRI signatories that are asset owners (see PRI, 2014). An examination of PRI signatories published on PRI's website as at 30 May 2014 shows that there is only one PRI investment manager signatory and one PRI professional service provider partner in Nigeria. This trend provides an insight into the level of awareness of RI in Nigeria. With no asset owners and only one investment manager and one professional service provider as PRI signatories, it is doubtful that RI could be considered as being embedded in the Nigerian financial market. Preliminary interviews conducted with asset owners and managers in Nigeria for this chapter shows a lack of general awareness of the existence of the PRI as an organization and what its objectives are.

Data collected from the Securities and Exchange Commission (SEC), the body charged with regulating individual and collective investments in Nigeria, including registration of collective investment instruments (IMF, 2013), shows that the overall size of the Nigerian RI market is estimated at less than $50 million as of 9 May 2014. The small size of this market becomes glaring when it is compared to the entire net asset value of collective funds under management in a market estimated at US$1.1 billion as at May 2014, as shown in Table 10.1. Table 10.1 shows that RI constitutes less than 5 per cent of collective funds under management.

Table 10.1 Value of collective assets under management in Nigeria as of May 2014

	Mutual Fund Class	*Value 9 May 2014 (Nigeria Naira)*	*Value 9 May 2014 (US$)*	*Per cent (%) of Total Holdings*
1	Equity-based funds	42,242,263,389	264,014,146	24
2	Money market funds	51,753,167,032	323,457,294	29
3	Bond funds	16,171,543,295	101,072,146	9
4	Real estate funds	44,143,552,204	275,897,201	25
5	Balanced funds	10,125,044,740	63,281,530	6
6	Ethical funds	6,368,931,284	39,805,821	4
7	Umbrella funds	2,414,875,961	15,092,975	1
8	Exchange-traded funds	3,093,966,691	19,337,292	2
Total		**176,313,344,596**	**1,101,958,404**	**100**

Notes: Exchange rate US Dollar 1 = Nigerian Naira 160, May 2014.

Source: Author's compilation from SEC Report of NAV of Mutual Funds as at May 2014.

Table 10.2 Growth of ethical funds in Nigeria, 2011–2014

	Ethical Fund	*9 May 2014*	*4 November 2011*	*% Growth*
		Value in Nigerian Naira Value	Value in Nigerian Naira Value	
1	Stanbic IBTC Ethical Fund	2,950,828,265.74	na	
2	Stanbic IBTC Iman Fund	186,543,465.78	na	
3	Total Stanbic IBTC Ethical Fund	3,137,371,731.52	2,979,243,760.00	
4	ARM Ethical Fund	301,942,445.27	63,902,105.00	
5	Zenith Ethical Fund	813,650,073.25	733,170,662.00	
6	Lotus Halal Inv. Fund	2,115,967,034.31	0.00	
Total		**6,368,931,284.35**	**3,776,316,527.00**	**68.65%**

Note: Lotus reads nil in 2011 as it started its business afterwards.

Source: Author's compilation from SEC Report of NAV of Mutual Funds as at May 2014.

This does not compare well with the developed markets of the United States and Europe, where RI constitutes about 10 per cent of collective assets under management (see Renneboog et al., 2008). However, a better picture of the potential that lies in the market may be obtained by looking at RI market growth over the last 3 years broken down by individual RI fund.

The first RI fund, Stanbic IBTC Ethical Fund, was launched in 2005, an indication of the short history of RI market in Nigeria. A breakdown of the growth of RI funds under management between 2011 and 2014 is shown in Table 10.2. As can be inferred from Table 10.1, RI constitutes less than 5 per cent of total assets under management at present, but its growth rate, as shown in Table 10.2, has been approximately 69 per cent over the last 3 years. This growth rate can be considered phenomenal in terms of the absolute value of funds involved, as shown in the table.

This growth will be further boosted and enhanced by the recent introduction of sustainability banking principles (discussed later in this chapter) by the Central Bank of Nigeria (CBN).

RI strategy in Nigeria

RI strategies in investment selection generally can be classified as falling within the seven process-oriented categories found in the RI field (see Eurosif, 2012), such as:

- Sustainability themed investment;
- Best-in-class investment selection;
- Norm-based screening;
- Exclusion of holdings from investment universe;
- Integration of ESG factors in financial analysis;
- Engagement and voting on sustainability matters; and,
- Impact investment.

Jones et al. (2008) list five screening methods: (1) positive screening (inclusion), (2) negative screening (exclusion), (3) best of sector, (4) engagement (holding an asset and making effort to influence management through dialogue) and (5) an individualized hybrid of some of these methods. In Nigeria, however, the RI investment selection strategy widely adopted by all managers is predominately one of negative screening, which Renneboog et al. (2008) refer to as "the oldest and most basic RI strategy" (1728). This can be seen from our analysis below.

Negative screening strategy entails the exclusion of holdings from the investment universe (see Jones et al., 2008; Renneboog et al., 2008). Table 10.3 shows all the ethical funds managed by asset managers in Nigeria.

Analysis of funds' issue documents and mission statements and interviews of investment managers in Nigeria revealed the following:

Lotus Capital adopts a screening strategy that involves the exclusion of investments that fall under what it describes as prohibited sectors, based on sharia law. Such prohibited sectors are listed as alcoholic beverages, tobacco, conventional financial services (banks and insurance companies), gambling and adult entertainment.

The Stanbic IBTC Ethical Fund, which was the first ethical fund in Nigeria and is currently the largest such fund (see Table 10.2), also follows a screening process in which stocks are selected to exclude investments in breweries and tobacco sectors of the Nigerian Stock Exchange as well as companies whose activities are considered harmful to the society. It is not clear what basis is adopted by the fund managers in determining what is considered 'harmful'. For example the activities of oil and gas companies have been controversial in the Niger-Delta region of Nigeria; it will be interesting to know whether this ethical fund excludes such stocks. This is a topic for further research.

Table 10.3 Ethical funds and their managers as of 9 May 2014

Fund Manager	*Name of Fund*
Asset & Resources Management Ltd	ARM Ethical Fund
Lotus Capital Limited	Lotus Halal Investment Fund
Stanbic IBTC Asset Management Limited	Stanbic IBTC Ethical Fund
Stanbic IBTC Asset Management Limited	Stanbic IBTC Iman Fund
Zenith Capital Limited	Zenith Ethical Fund

Source: Author's compilation from SEC Report of NAV of Mutual Funds as at May 2014.

The investment strategy of fund managers at Zenith Ethical Fund is to maximize both investment return and social good. The managers therefore adopt a social screening process that excludes corporations whose revenues are derived from alcohol, tobacco, gaming and defense/weapons production, as well as banking and insurance.

From this analysis, one can infer that RI screening strategies such as sustainability-themed investment, best in class, norm-based screening, integration of ESG factors, impact investment and engagement are not common in the market. Employing exclusion as a dominant screening strategy points to the low level sophistication of the players in the market, and by extension the state of development of the RI market in Nigeria. One interesting further research question that should be addressed is why RI screening strategy in Nigeria has remained stagnant with negative screening, which has been described by Renneboog et al. (2008) as "the oldest and most basic RI strategy" (1728). Why has it not progressed to the second-generation screening method referred to as positive screening (Renneboog et al. 2008), which focuses attention on corporate governance, the environment, social and labour practices, sustainability of investments and cultural diversity? Can it not progress further to the use of best-in-class, sustainability-themed, ESG integration in financial analysis and engagement? There is the possibility of the emergence of these strategies with the introduction of sustainability banking principles by the CBN, as explained later in this chapter.

RI asset classes

Table 10.1 lists eight groups of mutual funds under collective management and the asset classes as approved by the SEC. The table shows that the asset classes in the Nigerian financial market range from money market instruments to capital market equities and fixed-income securities, including real estate. An examination of asset classes that RI fund managers invest in shows only two classes that include listed equities and fixed-income securities. Listed equity constitutes the bulk of the asset class and is present in almost all the RI funds. Fixed-income securities are also present in all the RI funds, except in the one that leans towards sharia law and that forbids the charging of interest. For example, the asset class of Lotus Capital, the second largest RI managed fund, and Zenith Ethical Fund, the third largest RI managed fund, do not invest in fixed-income securities because the income is in the form of interest. In addition, Lotus Capital fund does not invest in preferred stocks; it is not clear whether Zenith Ethical fund does. In contrast, Stanbic IBTC Ethical Fund, the largest managed RI fund, invests in 75 per cent of its fund in equity and 25 per cent in fixed-income securities. Table 10.4 shows the asset classes held by these three funds.

Unlike developed RI markets, venture capital, hedge funds, private equity, and commodities are not common among RI asset classes in Nigeria. The mangers of real estate investment funds do not profess responsible investment, and these funds are not included in RI funds despite their existence in the market.

Table 10.4 Proportion of RI asset classes by RI funds in Nigeria

RI Fund	*Asset Class*			*Total*
	Equity (%)	*Fixed Income (%)*	*Other*	
Stanbic IBTC Ethical Fund	75	75	0	100%
Zenith Ethical Fund	100	0	0	100%
Lotus Capital	100	0	0	100%

Source: Compiled from various SEC Statutory returns, issue documents, and websites.

Market environment

The impact of pension funds in the Nigerian financial market, which ultimately underpins the RI market, cannot be overemphasized. The government carried out a comprehensive reform of the pension policy system resulting in the enactment of Pension Reform Act of 2004. Under this act, a contributory pension scheme that requires both the employee and employer to contribute 7.5 per cent of the employee's qualifying remuneration is made compulsory for all employers. The new scheme stipulates that pension funds must be managed privately by Pension Fund Administrators (PFAs), who must be licensed and approved by the Pension Commission (PenCom). Licensed PFAs open individual Retirement Savings Accounts (RSAs), into which an employee's pension (made up of both the employee's and employer's contributions) is paid. The PFAs, in turn, invest and manage the pension funds in a manner prescribed by PenCom. Under current practice, the bulk of the country's pension fund contribution comes from this source. The transition arrangement allows the continuation of approved existing scheme (AESs), in which already the established defined benefits schemes of some organizations are allowed to continue. The PFAs appoint the Pension Fund Custodians (PFCs). Among the PFA's duties are maintaining accurate records of accounts of the pension funds it manages, providing employees or beneficiaries with regular information and paying the employees' retirement benefits in accordance with the act. Under the above arrangements, the employees or beneficiaries who own the RSA are the asset owners, who, in turn, entrust them to the PFAs for management. Given the long-term nature of pension funds, it could be hoped that both the RSA holders and the PFAs should be inclined towards RI, but that is not the case at the moment, as none of the PFAs emphasize an RI strategy yet, judging by PenCom's quarterly review report.

Analysis of asset classes where the pension funds have been invested, together with the size and 2-year growth of the funds, is shown in Table 10.5.

Table 10.5 Assets classes and growth of pension fund assets in Nigeria, 2011–2013

Asset Class	*September 2011*			*September 2013*		
	Billion Naira	*Change (%)*	*Billion US$*	*Billion Naira*	*Change (%)*	*Billion US$*
Ordinary Shares	344.69	15.36		501.14	13.44	
FGN Securities	1,124.68	50.12				
Bonds				1,625.18	43.59	
Bills				599.94	16.08	
State Government Bonds	81.29	3.62		164.38	4.41	
Corporate Debt Securities	69.32	3.09		77.43	2.08	
Supranational Bonds				1.72	0.05	
Local Money Market Inst.	398.52	17.76		416.73	11.18	
Open-/Closed-End Funds				20.84	0.56	
Real Estate Property	178.08	7.94		95.63	5.25	
Private Equity Fund				8.02	0.22	
Foreign Investment Equities				48.98	1.31	
Money Market Securities				2.04	0.05	
Cash and other assets	47.30	2.11		66.79	1.79	
Total	2,243.88	100	14.96	3,728.43	100.00	23.30

Note: Exchange rate US $1 = Naira 160 as of September 2013 and Naira 150 as of September 2011.

Source: Author's compilation from PenCom Quarterly Review Report.

In USD and Nigerian naira terms, pension fund assets have grown over 56 per cent and 66 per cent, respectively, between 2011 and 2013. This astronomical growth in pension fund assets ought to have impacted the RI market in Nigeria. According to Renneboog et al. (2008), pension funds in the United States and Europe are at the forefront of engagement with companies to promote responsible behaviour or integration of environmental, social and ethical considerations in their investment process. They cite the California Public Employees' Retirement System (CalPERS), the largest pension fund in the world, and the Dutch Pension Fund for Public Employees (APB), the largest pension fund in Europe, as examples. But, to date, this has not been the case in Nigeria, demonstrating the potential for RI growth that exists in the market.

The investments of the insurance industry ought to play an active role in the financial market of a country, too. In Nigeria, all insurance companies are regulated by the National Insurance Commission (NAICOM), which was brought into existence by the NAICOM Act of 1997. The Insurance Act of 2003 stipulates that insurance companies should hold investments in Nigerian assets equivalent to the amount of policyholders' funds. Such policyholder funds can be invested in shares of limited liability companies and other securities of a registered co-operative society. It could also be in the form of loans to building societies approved by the commission or invested in real property, machinery and plants in Nigeria. Finally, it could take the form of cash deposit in or bills of exchange accepted by licensed banks, and such investments as may be prescribed by the commission. Unfortunately, NAICOM does not publish data on investment portfolios or asset classes held by insurance companies in Nigeria. It is obvious, however, that no insurance company exists at the moment that professes to ESG issues in its investment decision policy according to information gathered from regulatory authority staff at NAICOM.

Apart from funds held by pensions and insurance companies, another type of fund in Nigeria that could have an immense impact on the financial market, and hence the RI market, is the $1 billion seed fund of the Nigerian Sovereign Investment Authority (NSIA). The entire fund, together with subsequent additions to it in the form of excess crude oil revenue accruing to the Nigerian federation account, is expected to be invested through three special funds. These are the Nigerian infrastructure fund, stabilization fund and future generation fund. Although the infrastructure fund ought to have a potential impact on the RI market, more impact might come from the future generation fund, whose asset classes, according to NSIA's CEO, is expected to include equities and fixed-income securities, private equity and unlisted securities, real estate, hedge funds and commodities. At present, NSIA is not known to be inclined towards ESG integration or engagement in its infrastructural finance, a huge potential for the RI market.

One of the avenues available for influencing corporate practices, and hence RI, is the annual general meeting (AGM). Amao and Amaeshi (2008) opine that shareholder participation at AGMs should be encouraged because "the AGM is the most viable avenue for shareholders to exert their influence" (126) on a company's policies. In Nigeria, it is expected that retail investors will utilize the avenue provided by the AGM to voice their individual concerns about ESG issues. To this end, the SEC encourages the formation of shareholders associations made up of retail investors and issues a code of corporate governance for them. This code of corporate governance encourages members to maintain high ethical standards and contribute positively to ensure that the affairs of the public company are run in an ethical and transparent manner and in accordance with the code of corporate governance for public companies. It is expected that this should provide retail investors with an avenue to voice their concerns on ESG issues at these AGMs or to engage with top management to improve on these issues. This, however, has not been the case, due in part to impediments to effective shareholder activism and participation at AGMs (see Amao and Amaeshi, 2008). This potential is therefore lost to the market at present.

Finally, unlike most developed RI markets, there is a clear absence of consumer and/or civil society groups that are interested in pushing for socially responsible investments in the country.

RI policy environment in Nigeria

The RI policy environment in Nigeria ought to be driven by investment regulatory authorities such as the SEC, CBN, NSE, PenCom, NAICOM and professional bodies. The best of what comes close to RI policy is the ethical considerations advocated by the corporate governance code for public companies issued by the SEC. Interactions with SEC officials in charge of regulating collective investment show that there is no specific policy that emphasizes RI. It can therefore be said that, as of now, there is no regulation on the part of the SEC that is aimed at institutionalizing RI practices in the Nigerian financial market. Was it market demand that led to the emergence of the first ethical fund, which was launched by Stanbic IBTC? Again, interactions with the fund managers at Stanbic IBTC does not suggest so. Rather, we saw the introduction of a product that was derived from international best practices with the goal of creating a special niche for a market that does not exist. In the words of one of the managers, "Stanbic – IBTC is at the fore-front of cut-edge innovation in the Nigerian financial market". Consequently, the first ethical fund in Nigeria may have been driven by innovation as opposed to yielding to a genuine demand induced by customers. Others that have followed may have simply copied this innovation. Lotus Capital brought a religious angle to RI practices. But going through the documents that brought the fund into the financial market, we saw innovation again in which a product is first created and then customers are marketed or convinced to buy into the philosophy underlying the product.

Renneboog et al. (2008) attribute the growth of the RI industry partly to regulations requiring pension funds and listed companies to incorporate environmental, social and ethical considerations into their operations and to disclose such information. Typical examples of such regulations abound in the United States and Europe (see Renneboog et al. 2008, 1727, for a comprehensive list). If these regulations help in the growth of the RI industry, then the RI industry in Nigeria is set to experience astronomical growth. This is because regulatory RI practices will emerge through the approval by the Bankers Committee in 2012 of the adoption of sustainable banking principles by banks, discount houses and development banks in Nigeria. Sustainable banking principles now require all banks, discount houses and development finance institutions to balance environmental and social risks while exploiting the opportunities presented by their business activities. This has the potential to make all the investment by these financial institutions to fall within RI investment. During the first phase, the Central Bank of Nigeria issued the following:

- Nigeria Sustainable Banking Principle Power Sector Guidelines,
- Nigeria Sustainable Banking Principle Agriculture Sector Guidelines and
- Nigeria Sustainable Banking Principle Oil and Gas Sector Guidelines.

These are expected to enthrone sustainability considerations in all financial institutions lending to the above sectors, and subsequently to all lending by all financial institutions. By implication it will, over time, engender impact investment in the Nigerian market.

A template of sustainability reporting has already been circulated to all banks, discount houses and development finance institutions which is expected to commence effective July 2014. The reporting template will enable the regulatory authority to monitor implementation at individual banks and various industry levels and provide an objective and equitable basis for possible incentives (CBN, 2014). This incentive, if properly handled, will be the catalyst for institutionalizing RI in the Nigerian financial market. An analysis of total bank lending by these institutions provides us with a fair idea of the huge amount of investment that will qualify as RI in the country. Given the co-operation that exists between the Financial Services Regulation Co-ordinating Committee (FSRCC), a committee established by CBN to coordinate common issues of regulation in the financial industry, and the financial industry, it will not be long before sustainability practices and reporting are introduced by NSE, PenCom and NAICOM. Consequently, pension funds and insurance companies will profess adherence to ESG principles, resulting in a change in the Nigerian RI industry.

RI institutions in Nigeria

In developed RI markets, RI institutions include asset owners (e.g. pension funds and insurance companies), asset managers and professional service providers (see PRI, 2014, for RI groups). An underdeveloped RI market is unlikely to have all the participants in an RI market, and this may explain the non-existence of asset owners that are PRI signatories in Nigeria. The bulk of activities in the RI market are carried out by about five asset managers, who incidentally are not signatories but manage ethical funds. The only PRI signatory, Access Bank, has no managed RI fund that is registered by the SEC. However, its RI may be linked to its professed banking philosophy, as it is amid the few indigenous banks that prepare sustainability reports in line with the Global Reporting Initiative (GRI). Although sustainable banking principles have just been introduced (as discussed earlier in the chapter), Guaranty Trust Bank already applies the Equator Principles in its lending, and we are of the opinion that in this context it can be considered an RI institution.

Apart from the above, there is one PRI professional service provider signatory, RegCharles Finance and Capital Ltd., who ought to be providing professional services relating to RI. A cursory look at its profile and services listed on its website (May 2014) did not show any peculiar RI service that it provides. It is therefore unclear how its operations and services contribute to the RI industry in Nigeria and why it registered with PRI as a service provider.

In addition to RI institutions in Nigeria, many non-governmental organizations (NGOs) also put pressure on corporations to be responsible in their operations, bringing to the forefront environmental, social and governance issues. One such organization is CSR-in Action, whose publication *The Collective Social Investment Report* acts as a torchlight that shines on the sustainability initiatives of companies operating in Nigeria, including financial institutions. It highlights the sustainability issue focus of each corporation, the sustainability activity reach, whether the organization has a foundation of sustainability issues and whether it reports on sustainability. Preliminary interviews of some corporate affairs officers of corporations included in the report emphasize the reputational assets gained by their corporations. This may lie at the root of innovation at introducing ethical funds in the country. One other observation highlighted by the publication is that most corporations that prepare sustainability reports are multinationals, highlighting the role that mimic isomorphism of institutional theory (DiMaggio and Powell, 1983) may be playing. With time, the publication from CSR-in Action may lead to the real emergence of RI service providers in the financial market and deepen the RI market.

Salient ESG issues

At present, salient ESG issues considered by RI fund managers are biased towards moral or ethical considerations, as can be seen from their screening which places emphasis on exclusion based on moral or ethical grounds. This is usually the case with the development of RI that originated with religious organizations (Renneboog et al., 2008). It can also be seen that social responsibility is of concern to the NGOs acting as pressure group to the corporations.

Whereas a regulatory authority like the SEC does not appear to have any ESG concerns, the CBN has pioneered a pull-driven ESG concern by requiring banks, discount houses and development finance institutions to adopt sustainable banking principles in their lending and to prepare sustainability reports. This regulatory requirement has the danger of engendering a box-ticking approach among these institutions since it has not arisen from genuine demand of Nigerian investors to institutionalize sustainability practices in banks. So, overall, it is difficult to determine the ESG issues that are of current concern to investors in the Nigerian financial market today. Further research may shed more light on that.

Conclusion

RI practice is an evolutionary concept in the Nigerian financial market. The overall market size is still small, but it has recorded tremendous growth since its inception. The major operators are asset managers who are not signatories to PRI and who employ negative screening as a dominant RI strategy. Other modern RI strategies such as engagement, integration of ESG in financial analysis, sustainability themed investment and best-in-class investment selection are absent, showing the unsophisticated nature of the market. There are no asset owners who are PRI signatories and profess concern for ESG issues. The RI market has developed out of innovation to offer a unique product that will appeal to the sentiment of a segment of the citizens religiously inclined to Christianity or Islam. Financial regulation by CBN has arisen to add impetus to the RI market in Nigeria, and it is only a matter of time before the industry blossoms forth.

References

Amao, O. and Amaeshi, K. (2008) 'Galvanising shareholder activism: a prerequisite for effective corporate governance and accountability in Nigeria', *Journal of Business Ethics,* Vol. 82:119–130.

Bloomberg (2014) 'Nigerian Economy Overtakes South Africa's on Rebased GDP.' Online. Available HTTP: <http://www.bloomberg.com/news/2014-04-06/nigerian-economy-overtakes-south-africa-s-on-rebased-gdp.html> (accessed 30 June 2014).

Central Bank of Nigeria (2014) 'Circular to All Banks, Discount Houses and Development Finance Institutions on *Reporting Template for the Nigeria Sustainable Banking Principles*', Abuja, Nigeria.

DiMaggio, P. J. and Powell, W. W. (1983) 'The iron cage revisited: institutional isomorphism and collective rationality in organizational fields', *American Sociological Review*, Vol. 48:147–160.

Eurosif. (2012) *European SRI Study 2012*, Brussels.

International Monetary Fund IMF (2013) 'Nigeria: Financial Sector Stability Assessment', *IMF Country Report,* May, No. 13/140.

Jones, S., van der Laan, S., Frost, G. and Loftus, J. (2008) 'The investment performance of socially responsible investment funds in Australia', *Journal of Business Ethics,* Vol. 80: 181–203.

National Bureau of Statistics (2013) *Economic Outlook for the Nigerian Economy, 2013–2016.* Online. Available HTTP: <http://www.google.ch/url?sa=t&rct=j&q=&esrc=s&source=web&cd=1&ved=0CB8QFjAA&url=http%3A%2F%2Fwww.nigerianstat.gov.ng%2Fpages%2Fdownload%2F95&ei=nJ1hVZqAFcStUYW8gJgP&usg=AFQjCNFq53sSn3s4plYADywEr8t2aBeYng&bvm=bv.93990622,d.d24> (accessed 12 June 2014).

PRI (2014) *Signatories to the Principles for Responsible Investment*. Online. Available HTTP: <http://www.unpri.org/signatories/signatories/#asset_owners> (accessed 12 June 2014).

Renneboog, L., Horst, J. and Zhang, C. (2008) 'Socially responsible investments: institutional aspects, performance, and investor behaviour', *Journal of Banking & Finance,* Vol. 32:1723–1742.

Securities and Exchange Commission (2014) 'Net Asset Value (NAV) of Collective Investment Schemes'. Online. Available HTTP: <http://www.sec.gov.ng/net-asset-value-(nav)-of-collective-investment-schemes.html> (accessed 10 June 2014).

World Bank (2013) 'Nigeria Overview: Economic Overview and Performance'. Online. Available HTTP: <http://www.worldbank.org/en/country/nigeria/overview#1> (accessed 13 June 2014).

11 Responsible investment in Tunisia

Kais Bouslah

Introduction

The recent Tunisian revolution in 2010 marked the beginning of a new historic era for Tunisia. It has not only shed doubts on the previous regime's development model, but has also increased the attention on the environmental, social and governance (ESG) challenges. The state-centred development model implemented in Tunisia since its independence was characterized by extensive state intervention in the economy and led to substantial challenges that were at the root of the revolution (IMF, 2012). For example, economic gains were not fairly shared among the population: economic and social disparities were high across regions and unemployment was high (13 per cent in 2010), especially among youth (30 per cent in 2010). Weak governance and favouritism also fuelled a sense of denied opportunities and depressed economic potential.

Firms, policy makers, civil society associations, international organizations and academics point to the advantages of responsible investment (RI) and corporate social responsibility (CSR) in mitigating such problems and in helping to shape a new development model. In addition, RI financial products, such as ethical or sustainability funds, that integrate ESG criteria are very attractive for investors who demand financial services that are consistent with their ethical or religious beliefs. However, little evidence exists on the functioning of the RI market in Tunisia.

The Tunisian RI assets under management (AUM) was estimated at \$0.2 billion in 2009, representing 1.5 per cent of total AUM (IFC, 2009). However, this figure should be interpreted carefully, as it originated from foreign private equity investors (\$0.13 billion) and foreign direct investments[1] (\$0.07 billion).[2]

The aim of this chapter is to provide an overview on the state of the Tunisian RI market. Specifically, I discuss the Tunisian RI market with regard to the three main RI strategies: ESG screening,[3] shareholder engagement and impact investing. I also discuss Tunisia's regulatory framework, RI institutions, and RI issues. For example, it is useful to examine whether and how the new Tunisian constitution, ratified in January 2014, integrates ESG issues. This will be a clear indication of the importance of ESG issues for Tunisian society.

Overview of Tunisia[4]

Tunisia is a North African country bordering the Mediterranean Sea to the north and east, Libya to the south and Algeria to the west. It covers an area of 162,155 square kilometers and has a population of around 11 million (2014).[5] Perhaps the two most well-known facts about Tunisia are the city of Carthage, founded in the ninth century B.C. by Elyssa-Dido, and the Tunisian revolution of 2010, commonly known as the starting point of the 'Arab Spring'. Carthage was the major city of the Punic civilization in Africa and the capital of the province of Africa in Roman times.[6] It played a central role in antiquity as a great commercial empire and was home to different civilizations and cultures (e.g., Phoenician, Roman, Berber, Paleo-Christian, Ottoman and Arab). The Arab conquest goes back to 647 A.D., and many Arab dynasties ruled the country for more than 10 centuries. In the sixteenth century, Tunisia became a province of the Ottoman Empire and in 1881 a French protectorate. It gained independence from France in March 1956.

Tunisia experienced two political regimes between its independence and the 2010 revolution. Both regimes were dictatorships, although to different degrees. The country's first president, Habib Bourguiba, established a one-party state for 31 years. In November 1987, Zine El Abidine Ben Ali took office and continued the one-party state for an additional 23 years. Ben Ali fled the country on 14 January 2011 after street protests and civil disobedience that led to hundreds of deaths. Freedom, dignity and employment were the main claims of the Tunisian people. The new Constituent Assembly, elected in October 2011, appointed the human rights activist Moncef Marzouki as interim president in December 2011 and ratified a new constitution in January 2014. The parliamentary and presidential elections for a permanent government were held on 26 October and 23 November 2014, respectively. Since its independence, Tunisia has been a republic with a mixed legal system of civil law, based on the French civil code, and Islamic law.

As of 2013, Tunisia had a per capita GDP of US$ 9,900 and a public debt to GDP ratio of 51.1 per cent. Services constitute the main GDP source (61 per cent), followed by industry (30.4 per cent) and agriculture (8.6 per cent). Main industries include petroleum, mining (particularly phosphate and iron ore), tourism, textiles, footwear, agribusiness and beverages. While Tunisia's economy has long been cited as a success story in Africa and the Middle East (4–5 per cent annual GDP growth during the 2000s), the revolution of 2010 has challenged this view and has highlighted the inability of the Tunisian development model to reduce the high unemployment rate, in particular among the university graduates. The unemployment rate was 17.2 per cent in 2013. This is a direct consequence of the existing economic model characterized by significant economic disparities between the more developed coastal region and the impoverished interior (Zekri, 2013). In fact, the revolution started in this impoverished interior, and then spread throughout the whole country. During 2012 and 2013, the government's focus on the political transition led to a neglect of the economy (e.g., tourism and investment declined sharply), resulting in several downgrades of Tunisia's credit rating. The transition from a dictatorship to a democratic regime has turned out to be longer and more difficult than expected. In 2014, the economy started to recover, but (current and future) governments face several challenges, such as ensuring the political stability necessary to reassure businesses and investors, restructuring of the financial system and reducing the high unemployment.

RI in Tunisia

Overview of the Tunisian RI market

To better understand the Tunisian RI market, this chapter provides a brief overview of the Tunisian stock market. Table 11.1 shows that the number of publicly listed firms in the Tunisian stock

Table 11.1 Overview of the Tunisian stock market

Year	*Number of Listed Companies*	*Market Capitalization (in TMD*)*	*TUNINDEX Base 1,000 as of 31/12/97*	*TUNINDEX Returns*	*Number of Mutual funds*	*Assets managed (in TMD*)*	*Variation of Assets managed*
1995	26	3,967					
1996	30	3,892					
1997	34	2,632	1,000		19	680	
1998	38	2,452	917	-8.3%	20	874	28.5%
1999	44	3,326	1,193	30.1%	23	1,102	26.1%
2000	44	3,889	1,443	20.9%	28	1,398	26.9%
2001	45	3,275	1,267	−12.2%	34	1,452	3.9%
2002	46	2,842	1,119	−11.7%	34	1,511	4.1%
2003	45	2,976	1,250	11.7%	35	1,672	10.7%
2004	44	3,085	1,331.82	6%	34	1,999	20%
2005	45	3,840	1,615.12	21%	39	2,353	18%
2006	48	5,491	2,331.05	44.33%	45	2,662	13%
2007	51	6,527	2,614.07	12.14%	57	3,025	14%
2008	50	8,301	2,892.40	10.65%	76	3,629	20%
2009	52	12,227	4,291.72	48.38%	88	4,383	21%
2010	56	15,282	5,112.52	19.00%	98	5,107	17%
2011	57	14,452	4,722.25	−7.63%	106	5,228	2%
2012	59	13,780	4,579.85	−3.02%	111	4,921	−6%

Source: Tunisian Security and Exchange Commission (Conseil du Marché Financier, or CMF), Tunisian Stock Exchange (Bourse des Valeurs Mobilières de Tunis, or BVMT).

*TMD: Tunisian million dinars.

Mutual funds include the Sociétés d'Investissement à Capital Variable (SICAV) and Fonds Communs de Placement (FCP).

market has increased over time (from 26 firms in 1995 to 59 firms in 2012). As of December 2012, Tunisian stock market capitalization was 13.78 billion dinars, accounting for 19.3 per cent of GDP. Financial industry, consumer goods and consumer services represent, respectively, 53 per cent, 17.8 per cent and 14 per cent of stock market capitalization. Foreign investors held 20.51 per cent of stock market capitalization as of the end of 2012.[7]

The Tunisian stock market index (TUNINDEX), which reflects the risk-return characteristics of the Tunisian stock market, experienced positive double-digit returns during the period 1998–2010, except in 1998, 2001 and 2002, when returns were negative. The TUNINDEX returns were negative in 2011 and 2012 as a result of the difficult economic, political and social conditions (i.e. social and political unrest, higher debt due to an increase in the budget deficit and the current balance).

Table 11.1 also shows that the number of mutual funds has increased significantly over time (from 19 funds in 1997 to 111 funds in 2012). AUM increased from 680 million dinars in 1997 to 4.92 billion dinars in 2012. As of June 2014, there are 115 mutual funds with total AUM of 4.71 billion dinars (CMF, 2014). Thirty-two of the 115 mutual funds are bond funds, representing 89 per cent of total AUM. The remaining 83 mutual funds are mixed funds (bond and equity), representing 11 per cent of total AUM. Examining the prospectuses of these 83 mutual funds, 4 RI mutual funds are identified: AL AMANAH ETHICAL FCP, FCP VALEURS AL

Table 11.2 Tunisian RI funds

Fund Name	*Launch Date*	*Category (Equity/ Bond)*	*Type*	*Portfolio Manager*	*AUM (TMD)*
Mutual funds (*fonds commun de placement*, or FCP)					
AL AMANAH ETHICAL FCP	25/05/2009	Mixed	Distribution	CGF	0.235
FCP VALEURS AL KAOUTHER	06/09/2010	Mixed	Capitalization	TUNISIE VALEURS	2.583
MAC AL HOUDA FCP	04/10/2010	Mixed	Distribution	MAC SA	1.779
FCP AL BARAKA	30/09/2013	Mixed	Distribution	CGI	0.087
Private equity (VC) investment fund (*fonds commun de placement à risque*, or *FCPR*)					
Fond de Développement Régional	03/06/2014	Equity	Distribution	CDC Gestion	100
FCPR MAX-JASMIN	21/06/ 2012	Equity	Distribution	MAXULA GESTION	100.2

TMD: Tunisian million dinars.
AUM: Assets under management.

KAOUTHER, MAC AL HOUDA FCP and FCP AL BARAKA. The AUM of these four mutual funds (4.684 million dinars) is very small (0.1 per cent of total AUM).

In addition to the four RI mutual funds, I identified two private equity (venture capital) funds (Fond de Développement Régional and FCPR MAX-JASMIN), each with 100 million dinars of AUM. Table 11.2 provides basic characteristics of the six Tunisian RI funds (launch date, category, type, portfolio manager and AUM). Table 11.3 provides additional information about these funds regarding the RI type, the screening criteria used, fund composition and investment horizon. Tunisian RI funds use two RI strategies: ethical- or values-based exclusions and sustainability-themed investment. The first strategy could be explained by the Tunisian Islamic culture (99 per cent of Tunisians are Muslim). The second strategy could be explained by the increased interest of the government, the political class and civil society in ESG values and principles (Ennaceur et al., 2012).[8]

Shareholder engagement and activism

Amico (2014) reviewed corporate governance in the Middle East and North Africa (MENA) region and found that developments in corporate governance in the MENA region are driven almost entirely by regulation. She argues that concentrated ownership and group structures (e.g., family-controlled companies) are extremely common in the MENA region; however, there is virtually no shareholder engagement due to regulatory barriers and to passive investor behaviour.[9] Shareholders in the region are not known to 'vote with their feet' or to take on large blockholders by launching proxy fights. The absence of the relevant precedents, the lack of a litigation culture and the lack of institutions such as shareholder associations all act as barriers to effective exercise of shareholder rights (Amico, 2014). She argues that corporate governance cannot be imposed through regulatory requirements only. Shareholders, especially large institutional shareholders, also need to be part of the ongoing debate on the role of corporations.

Table 11.3 Tunisian RI mutual funds (*fonds commun de placement*, or FCP)

Fund Name	*RI Type*	*Screening Criteria*	*Composition*	*Investment Horizon*
AL AMANAH ETHICAL FCP	Sustainability-themed investment	***Exclusion*** of firms selling or distributing alcoholic beverages, polluting firms and those causing environmental damages. ***Best-in-class*** approach: best-performing firms with high ESG scores will be selected (more weighted).	30–70% in listed stocks,10–50% in bonds, and a minimum of 20% in Treasury bills.	5 years
FCP VALEURS AL KAOUTHER	Ethical- or values-based exclusions	***Industry screening*** based on Islamic Shariah. ***Financial screening*** based on Islamic Shariah. Shariah scholar: Cheikh Mohamed Mokhtar Sellami Income purification (up to 5%)	Minimum of 50% in listed stocks, maximum of 30% in Treasury bills and 20% in cash.	3 years
MAC AL HOUDA FCP	Ethical- or values based exclusions	***Industry screening*** based on Islamic Shariah: exclusion of conventional financial services (banking, insurance, leasing), alcohol, tobacco, pork products. ***Financial screening*** based on Islamic Shariah:bond interest income/net income ≤ 5%; income from investing in securities/total revenue ≤ 5%;Debt/MVE 30%;Current assets/MVE ≤ 49%.(Non-current assets + Inventory)/TA ≥ 30%. MVE is the market value of equity and TA is total assets. ***Ethical screening*** based on Islamic Shariah: defined by a compliance committee (only one Shariah scholar: Cheikh Mohamed Mokhtar Sellami).	Minimum of 50% in listed stocks, maximum of 30% in stocks accepted by the compliance committee, and 20% in cash and cash equivalent accepted by the compliance committee.	3 years
FCP AL BARAKA	Ethical- or values based exclusions	***Industry screening*** based on Islamic Shariah: exclusion of weapons, defense, pork products, alcohol, tobacco, gambling, conventional financial services (banking, insurance). ***Financial screening*** based on Islamic Shariah: debt/MVE ≤ 33%, cash and interest-bearing securities/MVE ≤ 33%, accounts receivable/MVE ≤ 33%. MVE is the 12 months trailing market value of equity. Shariah scholar: Cheikh Mohamed Mokhtar Sellami	50–80% in listed stocks, 0–30% in Shariah-compliant securities other than stocks, and 20% in Shariah-compliant cash or cash equivalent products.	5 years

(*Continued*)

Table 11.3 (Continued)

Fund Name	*RI Type*	*Screening Criteria*	*Composition*	*Investment Horizon*
Fond de Développement Régional	Sustainability-themed investment	***Exclusion*** of activities involving forced labour and child labour, illegal activity/product, weapons, defence, alcohol, tobacco, pornography, gambling. ***Ethical criteria***: Manager shall respect the following ethical rules regarding: industry, anti-money laundering, respect the law and regulation to combat terrorism financing and money laundering, applying the procedures prescribed by national and international standards regarding anti-money laundering and combatting terrorism financing.	At least 80% of the assets are invested in non-listed firms, firms listed in the alternative market (i.e. listed SMEs), and no more than 20% of listed firms and/or financial products.	10 years
FCPR MAX-JASMIN	Ethical- or values based exclusions	***Industry screening*** based on Islamic Shariah: exclusion of alcohol, conventional financial services (banking, insurance), any non-Shariah-compliant stocks (e.g., pork products, gambling). ***Financial screening*** based on Islamic Shariah: debt/TA $\leq$ 30%, cash and short term investments/TA $\leq$ 30%,(non-current assets + inventory)/TA $\geq$ 30%,income from investing in securities/total revenue $\leq$ 5%. Shariah scholar: Cheikh Mohamed Mokhtar Sellami	At least 80% of the assets are invested in non-listed firms, and the reminder in Islamic financial products. 65% of the assets are invested in regional development projects.	10 years

To address some of these shortcomings, in 2008 the Arab Institute of Business Managers (IACE) and the Center of International Private Enterprise (CIPE) published the *Tunisian Code of Best Practice of Corporate Governance.*[10] The main corporate governance issues addressed in this code are internal audits, external audits, fiscal transparency, ethics and societal responsibility, managers' roles, employer–employee relationships, the board of directors, shareholder rights and managerial compensation. Several stakeholders have participated in the elaboration of this code, including representatives of the Tunisian security and exchange commission (Conseil du Marché Financier or CMF), the Tunisian central bank (Banque Centrale de Tunisie, or BCT), the Tunisian Stock Exchange (Bourse des Valeurs Mobilières de Tunis, or BVMT), and the Ministry of Finance.

Impact (community) investing: microfinance

Up to 2013, the Tunisian microfinance market consisted essentially of two players (one public and one private): Tunisian Solidarity Bank (Banque Tunisienne de Solidarité, or BTS) and the Microfinance Institution (MFI) 'enda inter-arabe' (Laroussi, 2009; Zekri, 2013).

Tunisian Solidarity Bank (Banque Tunisienne de Solidarité)

Tunisian Solidarity Bank (BTS) was established by the Tunisian government in 1997 as a state-owned commercial bank (the Tunisian government is the major shareholder). BTS specializes in financing small projects through direct funding or indirect funding through a network of more than 280 microcredit associations (MCAs) throughout the country. BTS provides both credits and microcredits. The maximum amount of credit is 100,000 dinars (80,000 dinars before 2008) for university graduates and 20,000 dinars for non-graduates. The maximum microcredit was 5,000 dinars, but has recently been increased to 20,000 dinars (Zekri, 2013). BTS activity is restricted to the provision of microcredit and, following a 1999 regulation, charges a fixed interest rate of 5 per cent. This low interest rate coupled with the low recovery rate (50 per cent) leads to an unprofitable business model (Laroussi, 2009).

Microfinance institutions (MFIs)

The unique Tunisian microfinance institution (MFI) 'enda inter-arabe' was founded in 1990 as an international non-profit non-governmental organization (NGO) and launched its microcredit programme in 1995.[11] As of 2012, enda inter-arabe had a gross loan portfolio of US$ 86.8 million and 209,861 active borrowers (of which 71 per cent are women) served through a network of 66 branches throughout the country. The average loan balance per borrower is US$ 413.7. The business model of enda inter-arabe is different from that of BTS (Laroussi, 2009). It is not restricted to providing microcredit only; it also provides other services, such as training, support and advice. Moreover, enda inter-arabe charges higher interest rates (25 per cent)[12] and has a very high recovery rate.

It is also important to note that in 1992 the Tunisian government established a national solidarity fund (fond de solidarité nationale 26–26) in order to improve the living conditions of people living in 'the shadow regions'. This fund takes the form of a current account 2626 to which Tunisian citizens and businesses can donate. It is used primarily to improve access to drinking water, electricity and finance infrastructure or to create jobs in the impoverished interior regions.

Market and legal environment

Tunisia has adopted the international conventions on human rights, has a fairly advanced labour code, features a developed a legal framework for environmental protection and has encouraged the implementation of the UN Global Compact since 2005 (Ennaceur et al., 2012).[13] For example, environmental concerns have been integrated into the country's political agenda for several years through a variety of programs that have allowed the Tunisian government to restrict the costs of environmental degradation to 2 per cent of GDP, similar to the rate of developed countries (Luçon and Lapujade, 2011). The Tunisian investment incentives code provides financial and fiscal incentives for investment in environmental protection and pollution reduction (e.g., reduced tax rate at 10 per cent, a premium of 20 per cent of the investment value). Tunisia's engagement toward sustainable development has materialized through the creation of a Ministry for the Environment in 1991, which has been strengthened by the establishment of a national sustainable development strategy. The first public institution in charge of environmental protection in Tunisia (the National Agency for Environment Protection, or ANPE) was created in 1988.

The Tunisian government has also established an environmental certification program 'Ecolabel Tunisien' (Decree No. 2007–1355 of 4 June 2007). Conformance with Tunisian Ecolabel's technical and ecological criteria is verified by an independent organization (third-party certification). The Tunisian Ecolabel is a Type 1 (i.e. performance-based) national certification, which is applied in three industries: textile, tourism accommodation services and agro-food products. Foreign environmental certifications are also used in Tunisia (Gana-Oueslati, 2011), such as those applied to the textile industry (Oeko-Tex Standard 100 and Oeko-Tex Standard 1000) and tourism accommodation services (pavillon bleu and clef verte).

In short, several laws and regulations have been put in place regarding labour relations, protection of employees' health, promotion of human rights, environment protection and combatting corruption (Ennaceur et al., 2012). Tunisia has adapted its social and environmental legislation based on the ratified relevant international conventions.[14] This provides a conducive regulatory framework for ESG implementation.

Table 11.4 shows that the new Tunisian constitution includes six articles that directly address ESG issues. In particular, there are three independent commissions: the Human Rights Commission, the Commission for Sustainable Development and the Rights of Future Generations and the Commission for Good Governance and Anti-Corruption. The commissions created based on Articles 128, 129 and 130 shall enjoy legal personality as well as financial and administrative independence (Article 125, Chapter 6).

Market and regulatory framework for microfinance

The Tunisian microfinance market is estimated at 1 million potential applicants for microcredits (Zekri, 2013). In December 2012, the Delegation of the European Union to Tunisia and the microfinance NGO enda inter-arabe signed a grant contract worth €1.2 million to support the development of 'branchless banking' (e.g., mobile applications), with the goal of enabling an additional 400,000 people to benefit from access to microcredit in the next 4 years.[15] The amount of €1.2 million represents more than 40 per cent of the total microfinance industry in Tunisia. The Tunisian microfinance market still requires additional MFIs, but not so many in order to avoid flooding the market.

The MFIs are primarily constrained by two regulations (Zekri, 2013). The first regulation, enacted in 1999 (the Organic Law No. 99–67 of 15 July 1999), fixes the maximum amount of the microcredit, the conditions of its grant and its reimbursement. The maximum amount of

Table 11.4 ESG-related articles in the Constitution of the Republic of Tunisia (2014)

Article	*Description*
Article 12, Chapter 1	The State shall seek to achieve social justice, sustainable development, balance between regions and rational exploitation of national wealth with reference to development indicators and based on the principle of positive discrimination.
Article 45, Chapter 2	The State guarantees the right to a sound and balanced environment and contribution to a sound climate. The State must provide the necessary means for combatting pollution.
Article 46, Chapter 2	The State shall commit to protecting women's achieved rights and seek to support and develop them.
	The State shall guarantee equal opportunities between men and women in the bearing of all the various responsibilities in all fields.
	The State shall seek to achieve equal representation for women and men in elected councils.
	The State shall take the necessary measures to eliminate violence against women.
Article 128, Chapter 6	The Human Rights Commission shall oversee (monitor) the extent to which human rights and freedoms are respected, and promote human rights and freedoms (e.g., propose reforms, conduct investigations into violations of human rights).
Article 129, Chapter 6	The Commission for Sustainable Development and the Rights of Future Generations shall be consulted on draft laws related to economic, social and environmental issues and on development planning. The Commission shall give its opinion on issues related to its specialisation.
Article 130, Chapter 6	The Commission for Good Governance and Anti-Corruption contributes to policies of good governance, preventing and fighting corruption and following up their implementation and dissemination of their culture, and strengthens the principles of transparency, integrity and accountability.
	The Commission shall be in charge of monitoring cases of corruption within the public and private sectors, investigating and confirming them, and submitting them to the relevant authorities. The Commission must be consulted on draft laws related to its specialisation and can give its opinion on general regulatory texts related to its mandate.

microcredit was 5,000 dinars in 2010, and the maximum annual interest rate is fixed at 5 per cent. The MFI may also collect from the beneficiary of the microcredit a commission of 2.5 per cent of the credit amount in addition to the fixed interest rate of 5 per cent (e.g. for application processing fees and administration costs). In September 2010, the above conditions of credit were limited to microcredits granted on budgetary resources mobilized within the framework of conventions concluded with the Tunisian Solidarity Bank. In other words, the interest rate is no longer capped for microcredits granted on other resources.

The second regulation, enacted in 2011 (Decree-law no. 2011–117),[16] is a more complete regulatory framework for the Tunisian microfinance industry, including the creation of a supervisory authority and a clarification of the accreditation process (Zekri, 2013). The new regulation specified the MFI legal forms (limited company or association); defined governance and internal control, consumer protection, reporting and sanctions in case of non-compliance; created a supervisory institution; increased the maximum amount of microcredit from 5,000 to 20,000 dinars and permitted the microfinance institutions to operate as agents for the insurance companies.

RI institutions

The main CSR players in Tunisia are firms, governmental institutions, civil society associations, international organizations and academics (Ennaceur et al., 2012). Civil society associations include primarily the Tunisian General Labour Union (UGTT), the main industry association (Tunisian Union for Industry, Commerce and Handicrafts, or UTICA), the Arab Institute of Business Managers (IACE), and the Confederation of Tunisian Citizen Entreprises (CONECT), which is a new trade union for small to medium enterprises (SMEs) launched in 2011. International organizations for cooperation include the United Nations Industrial Development Organization (UNIDO), *Agence Française de Développement* (France), and *Deutsche Gesellschaft für Internationale Zusammenarbeit* (Germany).

It seems that institutional investors (e.g., asset managers, pension funds) have limited involvement in the RI market. There are six RI funds (four mutual funds and two private equity funds) with about 205 million dinars of AUM. In particular, the AUM of RI mutual funds is very small (0.1 per cent of total AUM). Moreover, little is known regarding the investment policy of Tunisian pension funds. The two main pension funds in Tunisia, the CNRPS (the pension fund for the public sector) and CNSS (the pension fund for the private sector), do not provide any information related to their investments and whether those investments integrate ESG issues.[17] Clearly, institutional investors are not the main drivers of RI market in Tunisia.

It is useful to note that only two signatories to the PRI are from the Pan Arab region; both are from the United Arab Emirates (UAE): one professional service partner (Hawkamah) and one investment manager (The Abraaj Group). Hawkamah (the Institute for Corporate Governance for the MENA region) has created an ESG index for the Pan Arab region (the S&P/Hawkamah ESG Pan Arab Index).[18] The index is composed of the 50 highest-scoring stocks with respect to ESG issues (out of an investment universe of firms operating in the Pan Arab region), subject to a maximum individual country representation of 15 stocks. As of December 2012, no Tunisian firms are included in this index.

The Tunisian government is one of the most important RI players due to its involvement in public spending. Tunisia is one of the seven pilot countries selected to test the Sustainable Public Procurement (SPP) project developed by the Marrakech Task Force (Gana-Oueslati, 2011). Launched in January 2009 by the United Nations Environment Programme (UNEP),[19] the Sustainable SPP is a tool that allows governments to leverage public spending (between 15 to 25 per cent of GDP) in order to promote the country's social, environmental and economic policies. The project promotes capacity building and provides support for the development of SPP in developing countries.

RI issues and outlook

IFC (2009) identified the main ESG issues in the MENA region. Key social issues include the challenge of youth development and employment, the contribution of women to economic and social development and opportunities for women in the workplace and labour conditions. Environmental issues include water scarcity and climate change, while governance issues centre on governance reform and the push for greater transparency.

The main environmental issues of concern to Tunisian society include toxic and hazardous waste, water pollution, limited natural freshwater resources, deforestation, soil erosion and desertification (CIA World Factbook, 2014). Main social issues of concern include the establishment of a 'new social contract' between the government and citizens in the wake of the revolution, improved employee welfare,[20] and improved living conditions in communities, in particular those in the impoverished interior region. Despite the *Tunisian Code of Best Practice of Corporate Governance*, governance issues need to be developed further.

The extension of CSR actions in the community and their institutionalization is the major challenge for Tunisian firms in the current context characterized by the diversification of CSR actors and the reconstruction of legitimacy of the state after the revolution (Kolevadu and Gherib, 2012). Another challenge is the limited stock market participation due to the lack of a stock market culture and financial education (BVMT, 2012). By far, the main challenge for RI market in Tunisia is to attract institutional investors to integrate ESG into their investment decision-making and ownership practices.[21] What is promising for the future RI market is the increased interest of the government, the political class and civil society in CSR values and principles (Ennaceur et al., 2012). Moreover, several ESG initiatives (e.g., the UN Global Compact and the new ISO 26000 standard for CSR) could have a multiplier effect for developing the Tunisian RI market in the future (Ennaceur et al., 2012).

Conclusion

In this chapter, I reviewed the status of the Tunisian RI market. I show that the Tunisian RI market is very small, in particular with regards to ESG screening and shareholder engagement. Impact investing (essentially microfinance) is more developed in Tunisia in terms of market development and regulatory framework relative to the two other RI strategies. It is expected to be developed further in the future.

Institutional investors (e.g., asset managers, pension funds) seem to have limited involvement in the RI market. In particular, the AUM of RI mutual funds is very small (0.1 per cent of total AUM). Moreover, little is known regarding the investment policy of Tunisian pension funds. Clearly, institutional investors are not the main drivers of RI market in Tunisia. Shareholder engagement is very limited in Tunisia, and this characteristic seems to be common in the MENA region. This could be directly related to cultural factors shared in the MENA region (Amico, 2014). Greater shareholder activism and collaboration is in the interest of existing local and foreign investors in MENA markets (Amico, 2014).

The main challenge for the RI market in Tunisia is to encourage more institutional investors (local and foreign) to become active investors by integrating ESG into their investment decision-making and ownership practices in Tunisian firms. Institutional investors can play an important role in the future development of the Tunisian RI market, much as they are in several developed countries (e.g., Europe).

Notes

1 Foreign investments that involve World Bank/International Finance Corporation support, investment by foreign sovereign wealth funds or foreign pension funds.

2 Except for South Africa, RI is relatively small and at an emerging or non-existent level in most of Africa (Global Sustainable Investment Review, 2012). As of 2012, the total AUM of the African RI market is US$ 228.7 billion, representing 1.7 per cent of the global RI market.

3 For example, *sustainability-themed investment* and *ethical- or values-based exclusions.*

4 This section draws heavily from the CIA World Factbook (https://www.cia.gov/library/publications/the-world-factbook/geos/ts.html).
5 Life expectancy is approximately 75 years with 15 years of schooling on average. The literacy rate is 79.1 per cent.
6 http://whc.unesco.org/en/list/37.
7 Local Tunisian investors (80 per cent of stock market capitalization) have generally stayed loyal to the Tunisian stock exchange. Beyond short periods of high volatility, capital flight from the Tunisian stock exchange has not occurred on a major scale as a result of political instability (Amico, 2014). This could be explained by the fact that the Tunisian stock exchange is characterized almost entirely by controlled companies, whose owners understand local circumstances, are less prone to panic and also have much at stake (Amico, 2014).
8 Several studies and surveys have shown the existence of ESG investment at the firm level (corporate social responsibility, or CSR) in Tunisia, particularly among exporting firms (Boubaker and Salaani, 2007; Belgasmi, 2009; Golli and Yahiaoui, 2009; Labaronne and Gana-Oueslati, 2011; Ennaceur, Marouki and Louati, 2012; Kolevadu and Gherib, 2012; Gherib and Ghozzi-Nékhili, 2012). For instance, Ennaceur et al. (2012) reviewed the current CSR market in Tunisia and concluded the following: firms exhibit a limited commitment regarding ESG issues, ESG activities are too fragmented and too dominated by governmental institutions, there is only partial perception of the CSR definition (values and principles), and there is limited ESG reporting. They argue that the concept of ESG (CSR) was originally introduced in Tunisia as a result of political choice made by the Tunisian government with the support of international cooperation. The aim was to improve the competitiveness of Tunisian companies in the context of globalization. Firms are encouraged to implement CSR (e.g., Global Compact, ISO14001).
9 This is a common characteristic in African countries. Except South Africa, shareholder activism is nascent in Africa and intra-country shareholder involvement is limited by the relatively small market capitalization and concentrated company ownership (Global Sustainable Investment Review, 2012).
10 http://www.ecgi.org/codes/code.php?code_id=241
11 http://www.endarabe.org.tn/
12 The MFI 'enda inter-arabe' obtained special permission in 2005 from the Ministry of Finance to charge higher interest rates (higher than the 5 per cent fixed by the regulation of 1999) so that it can cover its costs (Zekri, 2013).
13 Thirty-nine firms adopted the UN Global Compact between 2005 and 2010.
14 Examples of international agreements pertaining to the environment that have been ratified by Tunisia: Biodiversity, Climate Change, Climate Change-Kyoto Protocol, Desertification, Hazardous Wastes, Ozone Layer Protection, Ship Pollution (CIA World Factbook, 2014).
15 http://www.enpi-info.eu/medportal/news/latest/31538/Tunisia:-EU-funded-project-to-facilitate-access-to-micro-credits-to-disadvantaged-population
16 The new regulation includes the following four texts: Decree-law no. 2011–117 of 5 November 2011, Decree no. 2012–2128 of 28 September 2012, *Arrêté du ministre des finances* of 18 January 2012, *Arrêté du ministre des finances* of 22 January 2013 (see http://www.finances.gov.tn/index.php?option=com_content&view=article&id=45&Itemid=342&lang=fr).
17 The CNRPS and CNSS have recently started to record deficits while their reserves have decreased.
18 http://www.hawkamah.org/sectors/esg/
19 http://www.unep.fr/scp/procurement/
20 After the revolution, several negotiations have taken place between different stakeholders, in particular UGTT (trade union), UTICA (industry) and government, regarding minimum salary increases and improvement of working conditions.
21 The Global Sustainable Investment Review (2012) identified the barriers slowing the growth of RI in Africa. On the demand side, low levels of awareness among pension fund trustees about RI opportunities and the need for better standards and reporting are limiting growth. On the supply side, small illiquid markets and few listed equity investments reduce the market for investment. There is also a need for increased ESG expertise and services from asset consultants, analysts and advisors along the investment value chain.

References

Amico, A. (2014) 'Towards "Shareholder Spring" in the Middle East?', in Boubaker, S. and Nguyen, D.K. (eds.), *Corporate Governance in Emerging Markets, CSR, Sustainability, Ethics & Governance*, Berlin Heidelberg: Springer-Verlag.

Belgasmi, J. (2009), 'Etude exploratoire du marché de la Responsabilité Sociétale d'Entreprise en Tunisie', Rapport Intermédiaire no. 2, Deutsche Gesellschaft für Internationale Zusammenarbeit (GIZ) and Ministère de l'environnement et du développement durable.

Boubaker, S. and Salaani, T. (2007) 'Effet de la privatisation sur l'importance des Stakeholders: Fondements théoriques et étude monographique', *La Revue des Sciences de Gestion*, 228: 117–126.

CMF (2014) 'Physionomie des OPCVM (Juin 2014)', Conseil du Marché Financier. Online. Available HTTP: <http://www.cmf.org.tn/pdf/statistiques/opcvm.pdf>.

BVMT (2012) 'Rapport annuel 1999–2012', Bourse des Valeurs Mobilières de Tunis. Online. Available HTTP: <http://www.bvmt.com.tn/fr/rapports-activites>.

CIA World Factbook (2014). Online. Available HTTP: <https://www.cia.gov/library/publications/the-world-factbook/geos/ts.html>.

Ennaceur, M., Marouki, S., and Louati, I. (2012) 'La Responsabilité Sociétale des Entreprises (RSE) en Tunisie: Etat des lieux', Partenariat de Développement avec le Secteur privé (GIZ-DPP), Center for Cooperation with the Private Sector Africa (CCPS), Deutsche Gesellschaft für Internationale Zusammenarbeit (GIZ). Online. Available HTTP: <http://www.giz.de/en/downloads/giz2012-fr-responsabilite-societale-entreprises.pdf>.

Gana-Oueslati, E. (2011) 'Etat des lieux pour la mise en place d'un processus d'achats publics durables', Ministère de l'Agriculture & de l'Environnement de Tunisie. Online. Available HTTP: <http://www.unep.fr/scp/procurement/pilotcountries/files/TunisiaMRA.pdf>.

Gherib, J. and Ghozzi-Nékhili, C. (2012) 'Motivations et implications organisationnelles de la certification ISO 14001: cas de la Tunisie', *Recherches en Sciences de Gestion*, 5: 135–154.

Global Sustainable Investment Review (2012) *The Global Sustainable Investment Alliance*. Online. Available HTTP: <http://www.gsi-alliance.org>.

Golli, A. and Yahiaoui, D. (2009) 'Responsabilité sociale des entreprises: analyse du modèle de Carroll (1991) et application au cas tunisien', *Management & Avenir*, 3: 139–152.

International Finance Corporation (IFC) (2009) 'Sustainable Investment in the Middle East and North Africa Region Report', IFC Advisory Services in the Middle East and North Africa, World Bank Group. Online. Available HTTP: <http://www.ifc.org/wps/wcm/connect/52d36d80405cc4fb93d09382455ae521/p_SIinMENAReport.pdf?MOD=AJPERES>.

International Monetary Fund (IMF) (2012) 'Staff Report for the 2012 Article IV Consultation', *IMF Country Report No. 12/255*.

Labaronne, D., and Gana-Oueslati, E. (2011) 'Analyse comparative Maroc-Tunisie du cadre institutionnel de la RSE dans les PME', *Management & Avenir*, 3: 103–121.

Laroussi, H. (2009) 'Femme et Micro-Credit en Tunisie: Le Micro credit, outil de valorisation de la femme au sein de la famille?', *Revue Tiers Monde*, 199: 501–516.

Luçon, Z. and Lapujade, J. (2011) 'Investissement socialement responsable: quelle stratégie pour la méditerranée', *Anima Investment Network*, Etude no. 32.

Kolevadu, P. and Gherib, J. (2012) 'La responsabilité sociale des entreprises en Tunisie: une lecture institutionnaliste', *Revue Tiers Monde*, 212: 83–99.

Zekri, S. (2013) 'Toward an inclusive vision of microfinance in Tunisia', *Journal of Business Studies Quarterly*, 2: 160–175.

12

Responsible investment in Israel

A case of regulatory-based development

Noga Levtzion Nadan

Introduction

The Israeli financial market is currently in the preliminary stages of adopting responsible investment (RI). Israel's cleantech investment sector is well developed, and, mainly due to recent regulation, corporate governance issues are being implemented. However, environmental and social issues have not been widely adopted. While the unique structure of the Israeli financial market might constitute an obstacle to RI, recent changes in regulation and public awareness might be a good incentive for the growth of an Israeli RI sector.

This chapter opens with an overview of Israel's economy and continues with an introduction to the long-term investment market in general. This is followed by a brief discussion of the regulation that put the spotlight on corporate governance analysis. The fourth section looks at the first steps toward adopting the RI market in Israel. This chapter concludes with an exploration of the challenges involved in adopting RI in Israel and offers several recommendations concerning RI in Israel.

Overview of Israel

Israel is a young country established as a democracy in 1948. The population of the country, as reported by the Israeli Central Bureau of Statistics (ICBS 2012a), has seen significant growth from 330,000 in 1948 to 7.7 million in 2012 due to Jewish immigration and natural increase. Current growth rates in 2012 are 1.8 per cent among the Jewish population and 2.5 per cent among the Arab population. Life expectancy at birth in Israel is 82 years (ICBS 2012b).

In 2010, Israel formally joined the OECD. Israel's economy is small, with a GDP of USD 194.9 billion (ICBS 2011). Still, it is considered a developed economy with a per capita GDP of $26,042 ($27,433 in purchasing power parity [PPP] – all based on 2009 data) (ICBS 2011:1003). While the leading exports are high-technology equipment and agricultural products (CIA 2014), Israel depends on imports of crude oil, grains, and raw materials. The energy structure of Israel has changed in the last 10 years due to the finding of natural gas off the shores of the Mediterranean. Since April 2013, natural gas has been fuelling the growth of Israel's economy. Approximately 283 billion cubic metres (BCM) of natural gas were found;

these reserves are expected to provide for the needs of the Israeli economy over the next two decades (Israel Ministry of Energy 2013).

The RI field in Israel has grown somewhat in recent years, even if only a few investors relate to issues involving the environment, society, and corporate governance (ESG). The growth is reflected in a variety of activities that relate to these factors as they pertain to long-term and short-term investments (in mutual funds), extension of credit, and basket-linked indexes and certificates.

While still sporadic, there is increased public interest in corporate governance, mainly regarding issues of remuneration to top management and board independence, with increasing activism by corporate investors and more stringent oversight by the regulators. Various regulators also act for the promotion of increased environmental responsibility in the credit market.

Additionally, kosher funds were created for the Orthodox Jewish segment, mostly focusing on avoiding direct investment in companies that might violate religious rules through the use of exchange-traded funds (ETFs).

Still, as of mid-2012, no organizations analogous to Social Investment Forums (SIFs) in other countries have been established in Israel, and no institutional bodies are signatories to the Principles for Responsible Investment (PRI) initiative. The regulator remains the central agent of change, with financial and environmental regulation being a catalyst for a change.

Market environment: background on the long-term investment market

Before 1995, most pension funds were managed by the Histadrut Employees Union. Because of major actuarial deficits that accumulated in some of the funds, the Ministry of Finance mandated the closure of funds operating before 1995 to new members. It also imposed solvency improvement plans on funds with actuarial deficits. A number of steps were taken to reduce the amount of insolvent bonds[1] in fund portfolios, increase involvement of pension funds in the capital market, and reduce government involvement in pension savings. Another significant step was taken in 2003 when the government nationalized eight funds with actuarial deficits, reduced the rights of their members, and sold the funds to insurance companies in order to reduce centralization of power in the industry (Kfir, LevtzionNadan, and Banika 2009).

Before 2004, when the recommendations of the Bachar Committee were implemented, the Israeli capital market was characterized by extensive centralization of economic power and systemic conflicts of interest that were reflected in the control of two banks –Hapoalim and Leumi– over commercial banking, provident funds, mutual funds, and underwriting. The Bachar reforms required the banks to sell the provident and mutual funds they managed to insurance companies and investment houses.

Today, most long-term investments are managed by insurance companies and investment houses, with a substantial number of them investing in stocks and corporate bonds. Thus, government involvement in the management and financing of the funds has been considerably reduced.

The long-term savings market has grown considerably in recent years. In 2005, the size of the market was NIS 551 billion; by late 2011 it had grown to over NIS 900 billion (Bank of Israel 2012).

Sector-affiliated provident funds are part of the long-term savings market, but, unlike in other countries, most workers contribute both to such funds and to general provident and pension funds. As of 2012, sector-affiliated provident funds managed NIS 66 billion (Israel Ministry of Finance 2012a) (around 7 per cent of total pension fund assets). These provident funds are managed by the labour unions themselves, and are open only to employees through their workplaces.

The management fees of these funds are significantly lower than for general provident funds because of shorter management chains.

While in various locations around the globe funds similar in nature to sector-affiliated funds have taken the lead in responsible investment, in Israel they are managed without the benefit of clearly outlined policies regarding responsible investment. One exception is the Hebrew University provident fund that declared it would not invest in companies whose owners have asked for an unjustified debt forgiveness.

Regulation: the environment and corporate governance

Responsible investment in Israel is largely the result of the actions of financial regulators. Though the Bank of Israel's Supervisor of Banks was not the first financial regulator to give thought to integration of environmental risks in evaluation of proposed investment, he put forward the most meaningful changes, the results of which we are now beginning to see.

On 11 June 2009, the Supervisor of Banks outlined environmental risks to corporate banks through a published circular (Supervisor 2009). In the circular, the Supervisor defines such risks as exposure to loss as a result of directives regarding the environment and their enforcement; for example, a decline in the value of realized guarantees or deterioration in the financial condition of a bank's customers as a result of cost increases stemming from environmental legislation. The circular, which is a binding legal instruction, stated that corporate banks could be exposed to environmental risks through activities that may affect other risks they are exposed to, such as credit, market, operating, legal, and liquidity risks. Reputational risk should also be taken into consideration because a bank's image may suffer if linked to environmental damage.

The Supervisor of Banks stated that the board of directors of corporate banks must establish by 30 June 2010 criteria and schedules for identifying and evaluating environmental risks when giving loans that are also to be integrated into their conventional risk-assessment process. The Supervisor also states that corporate banks should implement this requirement in adhering to acceptable practices carried out in developed countries abroad by making use of the recommendations, directives, and standards published by foreign bank–supervising authorities regarding environmental risk management. Thus, the Supervisor of Banks (2009) in essence demanded change but left implementation of such change to the banks themselves.

By requiring involvement and reporting of investment policies (Commissioner 2009), the Ministry of Finance's Commissioner of Capital Markets, Insurance, and Savings also laid the initial groundwork for supervision of institutional investors regarding environmental risks. The commissioner published a circular regarding 'credit risk management in investment activity' (Commissioner 2007) that refers to assessment of environmental risks. Among other issues, the circular states that investment committees must identify exposure stemming from non-observance by debtors of laws and directives, including those involving environmental protection. The circular does not require assessment of risks sourced from the environmental practices of debtors beyond what conforms to existing legal demands. The June 2011 circular, 'The Guide to Integrating Environmental Risk Management into the Investment Decision-Making Process', was published by the Ministry for Environmental Protection and the Commissioner of the Capital Market (LevtzionNadan 2011). Its aim was to provide institutional bodies with implementation tools for the integration of environmental risks. However, the circular only contained recommendations – legal requirements have yet to be established.

Regarding corporate governance, regulation is better defined, and more binding. The Hemdani Committee, formed to evaluate which steps were required to increase involvement of institutional bodies in the local capital market, completed its work in January 2008. Consequently, the supervisors published a circular that required increased involvement of institutional bodies in the capital market (Hemdani 2008). This document covered stakeholder voting, assessment of investments according to corporate governance standards, as well as active engagement through monitoring. Following this committee, in January 2010, institutional investors were required to disclose their voting policies and how they voted in cases that included conflicts of interest involving interested parties. In their reports on their actual voting, institutional investors are required, among other things, to explain cases where there was deviation from declared voting policies.

Following the global financial crisis, in an effort to improve the safety of long-term financial savings, in May 2009 the Hodek Committee was formed to advance the investment decision-making process of institutional bodies regarding corporate bonds. Among the committee's recommendations adopted in April 2010 (Hodek 2009) were requirements that institutional investors expand their analysis of corporate bonds prior to investing in them. Among the subjects required to be analyzed is the issuer's corporate governance. In parallel, the Israel Securities Authority declared that within the framework of amendment no. 16 to the Company Law, proper corporate governance in public companies would be based, in part, on mechanisms for control and monitoring that would include special rules for transactions by controlling shareholders.

This was followed by a prominent change – amendment no. 20 to the Company Law. This amendment took effect in December 2012 and is intended to give minority shareholders greater influence on executive compensation at public companies. This amendment states, among other things, that remuneration policies require approval by a majority of minority shareholders at the general shareholders meeting (Habib-Valdhorn 2014).

Amendment no. 20 was based on a review of compensation reforms in various countries and of sources such as the OECD Principles of Corporate Governance and the EU Directive on Directors Remuneration – along with specific aspects suitable to the Israeli market (Licht, Talmore, and Sachs 2013).

Since the amendment took effect, every company that has faced opposition in the general shareholders meeting has not approved its compensation policy (Habib-Valdhorn 2014).

In December 2013 the Israeli Promotion of Competition and Centralization Reduction law was approved. This law was intended to increase competition and prevent corporate structures that enhance centralization – such as financial pyramids and diversified holding companies. The law also included sections that promoted corporate governance practices such as increasing the number of independent directors.

Parallel to this, the Ministry of Environmental Protection and the Israel Securities Authority have in recent years initiated requirements to report on environmental conduct. They have also developed an environmental performance index that publicizes the compliance levels of corporations. These two processes aim to supply investors with information on how corporations manage environmental risk. In March 2011, an amendment to the securities regulations came into effect that requires public companies to produce extensive and detailed reports regarding environmental risks and how they address them (Israel Securities Authority 2010). This amendment, which was initiated by the Securities Authority, requires corporations to furnish information on their environmental performance and provides investors with a tool for evaluating the environmental risks of these companies.

In February 2012, the Ministry of Environmental Protection rated the environmental compliance of Israeli industrial public companies, and in 2014 this became the integrated environmental rating for industrial companies; it includes the level of emission, their locality, as well as their compliance. This rating provides institutions and financial bodies an additional important tool for evaluating companies and the financial risks they are exposed to as a result of their activity and their non-compliance with environmental regulations. These two tools will provide the means to integrate the regulatory demands of the Supervisor of Banks and the Capital Market Commissioner.

The actions of the Israeli regulator might have been promoted by business practices that have come under scrutiny in recent years. These actions steadily promote better ESG practices, mainly in the field of corporate governance. However, until now, initiatives from the business sector were very marginal, with the regulator serving as the prominent effecter of change.

The RI market in Israel: first steps towards adopting RI

In recent years, various financial institutions have started initiating activities and creating products that can be considered RI related. These include the following:

Banks

In keeping with directives issued by the Supervisor of Banks, all Israeli banks commenced developing procedures for evaluating and managing environmental risks when extending credit to businesses. The process of assimilating the directives involved the board of directors of each bank passing measures requiring the bank to consider environmental risks when extending credit, examining the various divisions of the bank with the aim of identifying those that expose it to environmental risk through their activities, and developing tools for evaluating the environmental conduct of potential borrowers. The first stage of implementation of the directives refers to extending credit for real estate, industry, and gas stations – with emphasis on assessing polluted land taken as collateral.

In recent years, the banks have offered a number of financial products and loans to private and business customers for such purposes as erecting solar systems, purchasing hybrid vehicles, and securing 'green' mortgages (for properties that are certified to conform to the Israeli Sustainable Building Standard – for example, Bank HaPoalim 2012).

Institutional bodies

In light of regulatory demands, institutional bodies expanded their investment analyses to include corporate governance and began to attend stockholders meetings. In order to implement their voting rights, most institutions outsource management of voting to bodies that make recommendations on how to vote, and in some cases actually vote for them. In order to broaden their analysis of corporate governance of potential investments, some institutions purchase assessments from outside sources. There are also a number of consulting bodies that offer such evaluations. At this point in time (2012), the interest of institutional bodies remains limited to corporate governance.

Kosher funds

The largest ethical funds in Israel are the so-called kosher funds. They are not linked to any specific religious body, but are meant to respond to the needs of Israel's religious-observant population, especially the ultra-orthodox sector, which makes up about 8.8 per cent of the population (ICBS 2012c). Such funds commit themselves to investing in accordance to guidance received from rabbinical authorities in companies that comply with religious practices, such as Sabbath observance, and not keeping non-kosher-for-Passover food during the holiday.

The rabbinical authorities make the decisions and hand down their instructions for managing the kosher funds, where they also generate lists of companies eligible for investment. In Israel there are now approximately 30 such mutual funds that manage USD 500 million (Aminia 2011:104–105).For example, Metav Hilit Shoham and 22 other provident and pension funds manage almost USD 140 million. Such funds are offered by all the major institutional bodies, such as Clal, Harel, Pisgot, and Metav.

Green and ethical funds

During the first decade of this century, a number of funds that promote investment exclusively in environmental activities were established in Israel. They offered basket-linked investments in companies that deal with optimizing utilization of resources or developing various green technologies. Among the financial institutions offering these funds were Altshuler Shaham, Ramco, Meitav, Prisma, and Excellence. As of today, the only green mutual funds that continue to operate belong to Altshuler Shaham and Meitav Green Energy. Altshuler Shaham's green fund earned low and even negative yields from 2010–2012, but in 2013 and 2014 the yearly yields were positive (Funder 2014).

Cleantech venture capital funds

During the last few decades Israel has enjoyed a reputation as a global leader in start-up companies, some of which are involved in cleantech. This field includes small technological companies that are financed by venture capital funds, which are investment bodies that manage the assets of private investors, large companies, and various institutional bodies (pension funds, provident funds, banks, insurance companies, and others). By their very nature, the mandate of these funds is investment in technology companies, and a particular fund may focus on companies in a more focused field, such as cleantech. In 2011, encouraged by a governmental support program, institutional investors began investing in venture capital funds, including those specializing in cleantech. The *Cleantech Global Innovation Index* ranked Israel's capacity to produce new innovative cleantech companies second in the world (Cleantech Group & WWF 2012). A survey carried out among senior managers of Israeli cleantech companies (Deloitte 2011) discovered that venture capital funds are the main source of financing for 23 per cent of the companies. This is their third largest source of financing, after company founders' equity and private investor financing (i.e., angels, friends, and family).

Funds that contribute to the community

Some Israeli funds commit themselves to contributing some of their income to the community. These are regular funds that carry an added value and are branded as contributing to the community. One example is the Yalin (00) Lapidot Short-Term Shekel-Based Community Fund, established in late 2009, managing around NIS 43 million (Maya.TASE 2013), which is committed to, according to its prospectus, contributing 40 per cent of its management fees to non-profit organizations chosen by its board of directors. For example, in 2010 the fund contributed NIS 21,000 to Bet-Yossi, a centre for children and families suffering from unemployment, poverty, neglect, and violence in the Israeli city of Ashdod (Maimon 2011).

A group of funds prominent in this context are the three MORE funds. The largest, MORE Tithe Bonds (Stepek and After 2011), promises to contribute 10 per cent of its management fees to four charitable organizations. Stepek and After found that since the fund manages approximately NIS 270 million with a management fee of 1.6 per cent per year, its annual contribution is roughly NIS 430,000 (Udi 2011).

The Maala Index

The Maala CSR Index was launched in 2005 in cooperation with the Tel Aviv Stock Exchange. The Tel Aviv –Maala Index[2] is a share index for public companies with high social awareness (Tel Aviv Stock Exchange 2014). It consists of public companies ranked by the Maala Organization that meet the minimum requirements of the index. The index is voluntary, and only companies interested in joining and that complete a questionnaire are included. The Maala 2013 Index consists of 82 companies that produce 63 per cent of Israel's GDP, with an overall turnover of 331 billion NIS. Out of the 82 companies, 32 are listed in Maala's CSR Index and are traded on the Tel Aviv Stock Exchange. Inclusion in the index is based on five areas: business ethics, work environment (including employee rights), community involvement, corporate governance, and environmental concerns (Maala 2014). Currently, basket-linked certificates based on the Maala Index are offered by the fund Excellence.

The FTSE4Good Index

In June 2008, Israel was recognized by the FTSE Index (FTSE 2012) as a developed nation, and Israeli companies were added to the FTSE All World Index. Israel was also added to the MSCI All World Index (MSCI) in May 2010. In light of Israeli companies joining international indexes, institutional bodies from abroad began demanding ESG assessments. In March 2011 eight companies were added to the FTSE4Good Index (FTSE 2011). The inclusion of the companies to the index, and the interest of large foreign funds in Israeli companies, serves as an external incentive for responsible conduct by Israeli companies and to the development of strategies for responsible investment by Israeli financial bodies.

Challenges and a look to the future

Responsible investment in Israel is developing in ways unlike in other developed countries in the world, and it is consequently difficult to discover how much money is managed under the classification of responsible investment. Regardless, it is possible to see that in cases where appropriate regulation exists, or where there is a clear-cut demand, the market knows how to respond accordingly. The future of responsible investment in Israel depends on increased public awareness and on regulatory initiatives that will specifically require consideration of all parameters related to responsible investment.

As of now, it is not clear the extent to which the general public is aware of the issues and its right to demand that companies conduct themselves in a manner commensurate with its ethical value system. Notwithstanding, during the summer of 2011 the Israeli public underwent a significant change. That summer saw hundreds of thousands of Israelis fill the streets in protest over the cost of living and the enormous economic gaps that exist in the country. Though responsible investment was not on the agenda, there was a call for change in the behaviour of business entities in the country. This demand had immediate impact and is still being addressed by Israeli companies: research shows that the protests negatively affected the price of food-retailers' stocks and that the food-retailers who properly responded to the protests were able to protect the stocks from falling (Chernin and Lahav, 2013).

As a result of the increasing awareness that began during the summer of 2011, different social financial initiatives are emerging; one of the most prominent of these is Ofek – the Cooperative Bank. This bank is expected to start operations in 2016, and is garnering the support of both the Finance Minister and the Supervisor of Banks, each moderating different stages of its establishment (Bassok 2013).

We believe that both consumers and financial institutions in the Israeli economy are ripe for financial products that conduct themselves according to principles of socially responsible investment.

As a result of reforms carried out by the Israeli government regarding management of long-term investment, most is managed today by non-governmental bodies such as insurance companies and investment houses, which invest much of it in corporate bonds. In such a situation, the influence of institutional bodies and pension and provident fund managers on the market has become decisive. In light of the obligation to look out for the long-term interests of the saving public, adoption and internalization of responsible investment principles in this sector has acquired particular importance.

Several characteristics of the local capital market have the potential to constitute challenges to integration of RI principles:

- *Size of the economy*: The small and centralized Israeli economy makes it difficult for institutional investors who want to maintain diverse portfolios to avoid investing in large local companies whose activities are not commensurate with their RI strategies.
- *The pervasiveness of holding companies*: Unlike customary practice in the leading global economies, shares of most Israeli companies are concentrated in the hands of dominant shareholders who control the decisions made in shareholder meetings. Under such conditions, the ability of institutional investors to influence the behaviour of the companies is limited. The Hemdani Committee (2008), which expressed its opinion on this limitation, emphasized the importance of offering legal protection for minority shareholder rights and recommended removing barriers to cooperation between institutions during shareholder meetings.
- *Conflicts of interest*: The pervasiveness of holding companies and the size of the local economy produce conflicts of interest when the controlling shareholders in institutional bodies are also the controlling shareholders in companies they invest in or with which they have business ties. In December 2013, the 'Law for the advancement of competition and limiting unfair concentration' was approved. It aims to increase competition and decrease the excessive control of a small number of groups over Israel's economy. One of the parts of the law is the prohibition of financial bodies owning non-financial companies (Israeli law 2420, year 2013).
- *Concentration of provident and pension funds*: Even though long-term financial instruments were taken away from the banks, the sector is still characterized by significant concentration. Despite a lack of resolve and the routine difficulty of large entities to change, under certain conditions this could actually assist in integrating responsible investment principals. This is dependent on one of the players deciding to lead the process.

In light of the structural challenges that exist in the capital market, as mentioned above, promoting responsible investment requires being active in a number of clear-cut directions, especially:

- *Raising public awareness*: Public awareness about responsible investment and the choices that routinely exist around the globe has the potential to act as an important impetus for pension funds to adopt such investment policies. Social awareness has increased in recent years.

- *Promotion of relevant legislation for responsible investment*: Adopting legislation similar to that of Great Britain (UNEP FI 2005), which takes into account environmental and social risks in the investment policies of financial bodies, has the potential to motivate such bodies in Israel to develop RI strategies. Experience abroad makes it clear that when pension funds are obligated to disclose the social and environmental issues they take in account in their investment policies, the public is also given the opportunity to take such issues into account. As a result, the public can influence the actions of financial bodies.
- *Establishment of a forum for responsible investment in Israel*: Collective action of financial bodies for RI has the potential to be an important driving force in eliminating obstructions to adoption of RI strategies. European, Australian, and American models of forums for responsible investment (SIFs) led by financial bodies that spearhead responsible investment should be embraced. The objective of the forums is to raise awareness of responsible investment through publishing articles, advancing legislation, and organizing events.

Notes

1 Non-negotiable government bonds that pay interest rates higher than those available on the market.
2 Maala, Business for Social Responsibility. Online. Available HTTP: <http://www.Maala.org.il>.

References

Aminia, R. (2011) 'Investing according to religious law (halacha)' *The Accountant,* December: 104–105.

Bank of Israel Information and Statistics Department (2012) *Development of the public's asset portfolio managed by financial institutions: 2008 through 2012.* Online. Available HTTP: <http://www.boi.gov.il> (In Hebrew).

Bank Hapoalim (2012) *Green mortgage.* Online. Available HTTP: <https://www.bankhapoalim.co.il/wps/portal/mashkanta/article?WCM_GLOBAL_CONTEXT=/wps/wcm/connect/mlib/mashkanta/home/sa_choosemsknt/greenmashkanta&WCM_PORTLET=PC_7_IO9ASI420GL3602J91DR8N0007_WCM&proceed=1> (accessed 4 June 2012).

Bassok, M. (2013) 'Lappid support the establishment of cooperative banks in Israel' *The Marker.* Online. Available HTTP: <http://www.themarker.com/news/1.2179629>(accessed 12 February 2014) (In Hebrew).

Chernin, Y. and Lahav, Y. (2013), '"The people demand social justice" a case study on the impact of protests on financial markets' *Accounting, Economics and Law,* 4(2): 99–121.

Cleantech Group and WWF (2012) *Coming clean; the Global Cleantech Innovation Index 2012.*Online. Available HTTP: <http://awsassets.panda.org/downloads/coming_clean_2012.pdf> (accessed 13 February 2014).

CIA World Fact Book (2014) Online. Available HTTP: <https://www.cia.gov/library/publications/the-world-factbook/>.

Commissioner of the Capital Market, Insurance, and Savings, Ministry of Finance (2007) 'Credit risk management for investment activities' *Institutional Bodies Circular,*15 September 2007 – 27 August 2007. Online. Available HTTP: <ozar.mof.gov.il/hon/2001/mosdiym/memos/2007–9–15.doc> (accessed 13 February 2014).

Commissioner of the Capital Market, Insurance, and Savings, Ministry of Finance (2009) 'Reporting in advance of institutional body regarding its investment policies' *Institutional Bodies Circular,*13 September 2009 – 26 July 2009. Online. Available HTTP: <http://ozar.mof.gov.il/hon/2001/mosdiym/memos/2009–9–13a.pdf> (accessed 13 February 2014) (In Hebrew).

Deloitte (2011).Online. Available HTTP: <http://www.deloitte.com/assets/Dcom-Israel/Local%20Assets/Documents/cleantech2011_final.pdf> (accessed 28 May 2013).

FTSE (2011) *Semi-annual review of the FTSE4Good indices.* Online. Available HTTP: <http://www.ftse.com/Indices/FTSE4Good_Index_Series/Downloads/March_2011.pdf> (accessed 4 June 2013).

FTSE (2012) *FTSE Sizes Up the World.* Online. Available HTTP: <http://www.indexuniverse.com/sections/features/3153-ftse-sizes-up-the-world.html> (accessed 30 May 2013).

Funder (2014). *Altshuler Shaham Green Mutual Fund*. Online. Available HTTP: <http://www.funder.co.il/fund.aspx?id=5105218> (accessed 21 May 2015).

Habib-Valdhorn, S. (2014) *Entropy: New executive pay rules having positive effect*. Globes. Online. Available HTTP: <http://www.globes.co.il/en/article-entropy-new-executive-pay-rules-having-positive-effect-1000914516> (accessed 1 April 2014).

Hemdani, A. (2008) *Report of the committee for the evaluation of the steps required to increase involvement of institutional bodies in the capital market*, Jerusalem: Ministry of Finance, Commissioner of the Capital Market, Insurance, and Savings. Online. Available HTTP: <http://www.finance.gov.il/hon/2001/gemel/memos/hamdani2008.pdf> (accessed 4 June 2012).

Hodek, D. (2009) *Report of the committee for establishing parameters for institutional bodies' investments in non-governmental bonds*. Online. Available HTTP: <http://ozar.mof.gov.il/hon/2001/hon_dep/chodek.asp> (accessed 13 February2012) (In Hebrew).

ICBS (2011) *Statistical abstract of Israel 2011*. Online. Available HTTP: <http://www.cbs.gov.il/shnaton62/st28_15.pdf>.

ICBS (2012a) *On the Eve of Israel's 64th Independence Day*. Online. Available HTTP: <http://www1.cbs.gov.il/www/hodaot2012n/11_12_106e.pdf>.

ICBS (2012b) *Statistical abstract of Israel 2011*. Online. Available HTTP: <http://www.cbs.gov.il/shnaton62/st28_03.pdf>.

ICBS (2012c).Central Bureau of Statistics. Online. Available HTTP: <http://www.cbs.gov.il/reader/publications/head_sub_new.htm> (accessed 4 June 2012).

Israel Ministry of Energy (n.d.) *Israel Natural Gas Industry*. Online. Available HTTP: <http://energy.gov.il/Subjects/NG/Pages/GxmsMniNGEconomy.aspx>(accessed 13 February 2013) (In Hebrew).

Israel Ministry of Finance (2012) *Gemelnet*. Online. Available HTTP: <http://gemelnet.mof.gov.il/views/dafmakdim.aspx> (accessed 1 January 2013) (In Hebrew).

Israel Ministry of Justice (2013) 'Law for the advancement competition and limiting unfair concentration', *Law 242*. Online. Available HTTP: <http://knesset.gov.il/Laws/Data/law/2420/2420.pdf> (accessed 13 February 2014) (In Hebrew).

Israel Securities Authority (2010) *Securities regulations, details of the prospect and prospectus draft – structure and form*. Online. Available HTTP: <http://www.isa.gov.il/Download/IsaFile_5275.pdf> (accessed 13 February 2014) (In Hebrew).

Kfir, R., Levtzion Nadan, N. and Banika, A. (2009) *Responsible investment, integrating ESG issues in long term investment, a global view and the Israeli challenges*, written for the First Seminar on Responsible Investment of the Tel Aviv Stock Exchange. (In Hebrew).

Levtzion Nadan, N. (2011) *Handbook for integrating environmental risks in investment*, written for the Second Seminar on Responsible Investment of the Tel Aviv Stock Exchange. Ministry for Environmental Protection and the Commissioner of the Capital Market. Online. Available HTTP: <http://www.sviva.gov.il/InfoServices/ReservoirInfo/DocLib2/Publications/P0601-P0700/P0605.pdf> (accessed 12 February 2014) (In Hebrew).

Licht, A., Talmore, R. and Sachs, H. (2013) 'Israel's executive compensation reform', *Harvard Law School Forum on Corporate Governance and Financial Regulation*. Online. Available HTTP: <https://blogs.law.harvard.edu/corpgov/2013/01/07/israels-executive-compensation-reform/> (accessed 31 March 2014).

Maala (2014) *Maala's 2013 Index | How the index promotes norms in the business sector Maala*. Online. Available HTTP: <http://www.maala.org.il/warehouse/userUploadFiles/File/dirug/2013/maala%20csr%20index%202013%20pressrelease.pdf> (accessed 12 February 2014).

Maimon, M. (2011) *Fund in focus: Yelin Lapidot Short-Term Shekel-Base Community Fund*, Funder website. Online. Available HTTP: <http://www.funder.co.il/article.aspx?idx=16611> (accessed 13 February 2014.) (In Hebrew).

Maya.TASE–Tel-Aviv Stock exchange. *Yalin Lapidot mutual fund, for the community*. Online. Available HTTP: <.http://maya.tase.co.il/bursa/report.asp?report_cd=823019> (accessed 23 May 2015).

MSCI (n.d.) *MSCI Israel reclassification*. Online. Available HTTP: <http://www.mscibarra.com/products/indices/international_equity_indices/msci_israel_index_reclassification.html> (accessed 13 February 2012).

Stepek, Z. and After, R. (2011) 'Desecrated the Sabbath? You're out of the portfolio', *Calcalist*, 18 January. Online. Available HTTP: <http://www.calcalist.co.il/local/articles/0,7340,L-3486292,00.html> (accessed 13 February 2014) (In Hebrew).

Supervisor of Banks, Bank of Israel (2009) 'Increasing the involvement of institutional bodies in the capital market', *Circular to Institutional Bodies*, Ministry of Finance, Capital Market, Insurance, and Savings

Division. Online. Available HTTP: <http://ozar.mof.gov.il/hon/2001/mosdiym/memos/2009-9-11.pdf> (accessed 12 February 2014) (In Hebrew).

Tel Aviv Stock Exchange (2014) *Tel Aviv Maala Index*. Online. Available HTTP: <http://www.tase.co.il/TASE/MarketData/Indices/Additional/IndexAboutSRI.htm?Action=2&addTab=&IndexId=150> (accessed12 February 2014) (In Hebrew).

Udi, M. (2011) 'The green trend turns out to be a disappointing investment', *Calcalist*. Online. Available HTTP: <http://www.calcalist.co.il/markets/articles/0,7340,L-3525652,00.html> (accessed 13 February 2013) (In Hebrew).

UNEP FI (2005) 'A legal framework for the integration of environmental, social, and governance issues into institutional investment', produced for the Asset Management Working Group of the UNEP Finance Initiative, October: 117–50. Online. Available HTTP: <http://www.unepfi.org/fileadmin/documents/freshfields_legal_resp_20051123.pdf> (accessed 13 February 2014).

13

Responsible investment in Australia

Anna Young-Ferris and Louise O'Halloran

Introduction

In Australia, asset owners and asset managers representing more than 50 per cent of total funds under management (FUM) support responsible investment.[1] According to the Responsible Investment Association Australasia (2013), responsible investment has become a vibrant sub-sector of the finance industry across superannuation, funds management, banking and wealth advice. Testament to this is a broad range of specialist products and ESG services that actively take environmental, social and corporate governance risks into account in investment decision-making. Furthermore, Australia's specialist or core responsible investment funds have largely and consistently outperformed the broader market over the short, medium and long term, although bearing in mind they still only represent just above two per cent of total assets under management in Australia.

In the first part of this chapter we provide an overview of Australia in terms of basic statistics and the country's demographic characteristics. The next section explains the drivers, events and circumstances that have shaped the responsible investment landscape in Australia. The third section describes the institutions involved in responsible investment and the final section outlines the ESG issues, risks and opportunities that currently inform responsible investment practice in the country.

Country overview

Australia is the world's sixth largest country by total area – about the same size as the United States, not including Alaska. Relative to its vast expanse, Australia has a small population of approximately 23 million people. Seventy per cent of the Australian mainland is classified as semi-arid, arid or desert, making it the driest inhabited continent on Earth. Only Antarctica is drier. This makes it easy to understand why 85 per cent of Australians live within 50 kilometres of the coastline. The country is characterized by densely populated urban cities, the two largest being Sydney with 4.6 million people and Melbourne with 4.2 million people (2012 census).

Australia is also one of the most biodiverse countries in the world – 85 per cent of our plants and 70 per cent of our animals are to be found nowhere else in the world. It is home to a vast array of landscapes, from the wild temperate forests of Tasmania, the great desert icon of Uluru and the Kakadu escarpments to the alpine ranges and tropical savannah. Our oceans have the highest marine biodiversity in the world, featuring 33,000 different species, including 5,126 different fish. The Great Barrier Reef on Australia's far northeast coast is the largest single reef and the largest area of coral reefs on the planet.

In terms of demographics, life expectancy for females is 84 years and for males is 79 years. The literacy rate for the total population is very high at 99 per cent; however, it is much bleaker for the indigenous population, at just 20 per cent. In 2006, Christianity was the chosen religious group for 68 per cent of the population, Buddhism for 1.9 per cent, Hinduism for 0.5 per cent, Islam for 1.5 per cent, Judaism for 0.4 per cent, no religion identified for 11.7 per cent and no response for 15.5 per cent. Apart from the multi-cultural immigrant population, another special cultural aspect of Australia is its unique indigenous heritage.

Australia has a liberal democratic system of government that reflects British and North American models, whilst at the same time being uniquely Australian. It is a member of the Commonwealth with a multi-tiered legal system that involves cooperation of federal and state parliaments and local councils to make laws. In 2014, GDP was US$1.5 trillion, or US$65,217 per capita. Australia is rich with natural resources, so mining is one of the major industries. Agriculture; construction; innovation, science and technology; manufacturing; retail; service industries; tourism and transport are the other main industries, according to the Australian Bureau of Statistics. At December 2014 the unemployment rate was 6.1 per cent. As of 2013 public debt as a proportion of GDP was 28.6 per cent. At December 2012 the market value of publically traded shares was US$1.286 trillion. 83 per cent of households use the Internet.

The RI market

Australia is a small country by many standards, ranking twelfth in the world according to GDP. But in other ways Australia outperforms, and this is especially true in finance. Australia's pool of funds under management is the third largest in the world (behind only USA and Luxembourg) and the largest in Asia.[2] This is mainly because of Australia's mandatory superannuation contribution scheme outlined in the third section of this chapter. The size of Australia's finance sector reflects its global contribution to responsible investment – ranking third with respect to number of signatories to the UN-supported Principles for Responsible Investment (PRI) (behind only USA and UK)[3] – with 9 of the country's 10 largest fund managers supporting this initiative. Australian (and New Zealand) signatories to the UN-supported PRI grew 8 per cent from 126 in 2012 to 136 in 2013.

Responsible investment in Australia can be traced back to 1986 when fund manager Australian Ethical Investment came to the market. Since that time, ESG integration, with its focus on investment risk analysis (as distinct from screening based products) has come to dominate the responsible investment industry in Australia, in both size and annual growth.

How the market is defined

In practice, responsible investment products and services in Australia cover the full range of strategies. For benchmarking purposes, the peak industry body Responsible Investment Association Australasia (RIAA) defines core and broad types of responsible investment strategies.[4]

Core responsible investment strategies

Core responsible investment refers to specialized managed funds explicitly branded as ethical or socially responsible and transparent about the nature and range of responsible investment strategies used in stock selection and portfolio construction. Core responsible investment strategies include:

- Screening of investments including negative, positive and norms-based screening;
- Sustainability themed investing (e.g. clean technology or sustainable agriculture);
- Impact and community investing; and
- Corporate engagement and shareholder action (i.e. raising resolutions and voting).

Broad responsible investment strategies

Broad responsible investment includes strategies adopted by mainstream institutional investors to integrate ESG issues explicitly into their day-to-day financial analysis, stock selection, portfolio construction, company engagement and proxy voting processes. Broad responsible investment includes integration of ESG factors.

Market size and annual growth

At December 2013,[5] total assets under management in Australia was US$838 billion, a 15 per cent increase from 2012. Responsible investment funds and strategies accounted for approximately 16 per cent of this total, with core responsible investment strategies representing 2.34 per cent (compared to 1.63 per cent in 2012) and broad responsible investment strategies representing 14.3 per cent of the total (compared to 14.5 per cent in 2012).[6]

Despite the tiny proportion when compared to the total assets under management, core responsible investment approaches grew by a massive 51 per cent during 2013 from US$12.91 billion to US$19.61 billion – an increase of US$670 million. Very strong investment performance throughout the year was the main factor contributing to this growth.

Broad responsible investment assets, primarily made up of investment funds and investment strategies that employ ESG integration have grown from US$106 billion in 2012 to US$119.9 billion in 2013, up by 13 per cent.

The market environment

Australia's savings and retirement system

Growth

Australia's US$1.5 trillion superannuation system is the fourth largest in the world and is a major driver behind Australia's globally significant funds management industry mentioned in the previous section. This pool of assets is expected to grow to US$7.1 trillion, or 180 per cent of GDP, over the next two decades, as seen in the graph below. Compulsory employer superannuation contributions and the prospect of a return to more 'normal' investment performance after the Global Financial Crisis underpin this growth projection.[7]

Compulsory superannuation contribution

Superannuation in Australia is government supported and encouraged, and minimum provisions for employees are compulsory. For example, employers are required to pay a proportion of an employee's salary and wages (9.25 per cent at 1 July 2013) into a superannuation fund, and people

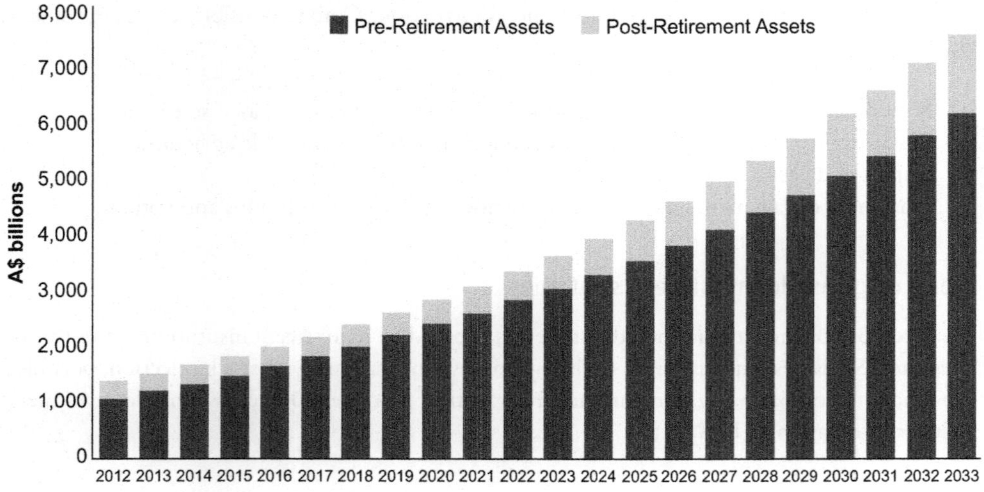

Figure 13.1 Australia's projected superannuation assets, 2012–2033

Source: Deloitte Actuaries and Consultants, Sept. 2013, Dynamics of the Australian Superannuation System, The next 20 years, 2013–2033, Figure 5, Page 12, Australia.

are also encouraged to put aside additional funds into superannuation. Australia's compulsory superannuation guarantee system was introduced by the Keating Labor Government in 1992, starting at 3 per cent and reaching 9 per cent by 2002. The minimum obligation required by employers is set to increase to 12 per cent by 2021, for which annual increases began in 2013.

Choice of superannuation funds

In 2005 legislation was introduced allowing Australian employees (except for some public servants) to select which fund their superannuation contributions are paid into. Prior to 2005, employers made this decision.

Types of superannuation funds

There are seven main types of superannuation funds in Australia:

1 Industry funds are not-for-profit, multi-employer funds run by employer associations or unions and are run solely for the benefit of members.
2 Wholesale master trusts are multi-employer funds run by financial institutions for groups of employees and classified as retail funds.
3 Retail master trusts or wrap platforms are funds run by financial institutions for individuals.
4 Employer stand-alone funds (or corporate super funds) are established by employers for their employees.
5 Self-managed superannuation funds (SMSFs, or do-it-yourself funds) are funds established for a small number of individuals (limited to four) and regulated by the Australian Taxation Office, with the fund members acting as the fund trustees. There are 534,000 SMSFs with total AUM of US$434 million in Australia representing just over 1 million people and 28 per cent of the US$1.55 trillion total superannuation assets (at 30 June 2014).

6 Small APRA funds (SAFs) are funds established for less than five individuals, but unlike SMSFs, the trustee is an approved trustee and the funds are regulated by APRA.
7 Public sector employee funds are funds established by governments for their employees.

Tax on superannuation

Most superannuation is concessionally taxed at a flat rate of 15 per cent on contributions and on earnings.

Who engages in shareholder activism and how?

The term 'shareholder activism' is rarely used in Australia, with a preference for terms such as 'active ownership', 'shareholder action', 'shareholder advocacy' or 'shareholder engagement'. This preferred terminology reflects a greater emphasis on engagement and voting, and less emphasis on raising resolutions.

Raising shareholder resolutions

The raising of shareholder resolutions is relatively undeveloped in Australia when compared to, for example, the USA. This is partly because of the different regulatory system in the USA that accommodates the resolution process and provides a structure featuring well-codified arrangements for the lodging of resolutions. The lack of such a regulatory process in Australia means that there is generally inactivity in formal environmental and social shareholder resolutions, with only a handful or so that have been filed in the past decade.

However, by contrast, institutional shareholder advocacy on corporate governance issues such as director and executive remuneration, board composition or failure to properly inform the market of material events has grown in Australia. This takes the form of organized institutional opposition to standard resolutions on board appointments and the remuneration report or class actions on behalf of an aggrieved group of shareholders. Although a challenge remains for Australian investors in that even if there is a voting outcome at an annual general meeting (AGM), for example in relation to executive remuneration, more often than not the outcome is non-binding. The company does not necessarily have to act, and it remains at the discretion of the board to decide the ultimate course of action, if any.

Despite the isolated nature of formal activity, there have been some interesting cases over the recent years. This is in contrast to the previous decade in Australia during which only one resolution that could be described as environmental or social was raised. During 2014 the Australasian Centre for Corporate Responsibility (ACCR) began actively engaging with the four big Australian retail banks (ANZ, CBA, NAB and WBC) urging disclosure of their carbon financing and investments. Associated resolutions were filed at the AGMs of ANZ and CBA and winning approximately three per cent of the vote. In the end, the four banks agreed to make additional disclosure about how much carbon they finance, although none of the disclosure was as detailed as requested.[8]

During 2010–11 there were four environmental resolutions raised, which was an isolated, yet historically significant, event. In 2010 the Climate Advocacy Fund was established by Australian Ethical Investment with the specific goal to raise resolutions on issues of materiality relating to climate change. Four resolutions were lodged with companies for consideration at the AGMs during this 2010–11 Australian corporate reporting season. The resolutions related to the disclosure of carbon emissions reduction plans and ensuring that investment decisions and balance sheet valuations were based on publically stated, reasonable assumptions about future carbon emission pricing and regulation.

Actively engaging with companies on ESG issues and proxy voting

The participation of institutional investors in active engagement and proxy voting as mechanisms to hold corporations accountable (as opposed to a sole reliance on regulation) has been on the rise in Australia. The objective of active engagement between investors and companies is to improve standards of ESG policy and practice, create long-term shareholder value and minimize investment risk. Active engagement can take some of the following forms: face-to-face meetings with individual companies participating in AGMs, writing letters and making submissions to regulatory reviews. The engagement issues of priority during 2013–14[9], [10] included:

- Board composition and diversity;
- Corporate governance practices;
- ESG disclosure and integrated reporting;
- Executive remuneration;
- Labour and human rights risks; and
- Stewardship for fossil fuels and fossil fuel divestment.

Increasingly, institutional investors in Australia will use firms to engage with listed companies on their behalf. As one of many examples, following the now infamous NewsCorp phone hacking scandal in 2011, the Australian Council of Superannuation Investors (ACSI) undertook extensive engagement with its superannuation fund members and recommended they vote against the re-election of six of its board members. ACSI and its members were amongst a number of global pension funds calling for change at NewsCorp. The result was a clear protest vote that sent the message to the board that unethical behaviour, poor quality governance and lack of director independence was unacceptable.[11] In 2012, once again ACSI undertook extensive engagement with its members and called upon them to vote against the NewsCorp remuneration report in the aftermath of the phone hacking scandal. ACSI acknowledged that bonuses had been reduced but that NewsCorp's board remuneration levels were still higher than most Australian companies, and it questioned how truly independent NewsCorp's board was.[12] In terms of proxy voting, best practice voting by responsible investors in Australia means to vote on all issues at company meetings, with all votes being made in the best interests of unit holders and clients to protect long-term shareholder value. Voting agency firms may also be employed to undertake proxy voting on behalf of the investor.

Policy environment: fiduciary law and other legislation that facilitate or create barriers for RI

Financial services reform

Financial System Inquiry

In November 2013 the incoming Abbott Federal Government announced the formation of the Financial System Inquiry. The Inquiry intends to "reduce the regulatory burden on the financial services sector wherever the benefits to competition, efficiency, market stability or consumer protection are questionable". As part of the Inquiry, some of the key legislative changes in Australia's financial services sector implemented as a result of the Global Financial Crisis of 2008–9, such as the Future of Financial Advice, are under review.

The Future of Financial Advice (FoFA)

Following a series of investment scheme collapses amounting to US$8.4 billion in losses to Australian retail investors, the former Labor Federal Government introduced the Future of Financial Advice (FoFA) reforms in July 2012. These were designed to tackle conflicts of interest affecting the quality of financial advice provided to Australian investors. These reforms reflected many of the concerns already addressed by the responsible investment sector.

The main reforms of FoFA include:

- A ban on commissions relating to the distribution of managed investments, superannuation and margin loans;
- The introduction of a fiduciary duty requirement on financial advisers to act in the best interests of their clients; and
- A requirement for advisers to gain an 'opt-in' services agreement from their client every 2 years.

At the time of writing the Federal Government has announced that some of the key FoFA reforms will be reviewed and debated as part of the Financial System Inquiry. It is as yet unknown how the review will impact recent positive developments in financial sector reform relating to conflicted advice and, by association, the responsible investment sector.

Carbon pricing and climate related legislation affecting responsible investment

The turbulent carbon policy regime in Australia

The recent history of carbon pricing policy in Australia is a tumultuous and frustrating one for proponents of responsible investment and investors more generally, especially those wanting to make long term investment decisions. Australia's first national carbon pricing scheme was introduced in July 2012 by the former Labor Federal Government. The scheme commenced with a carbon tax introduced at US$22 per tonne, and was to be followed by an emissions trading scheme in 2015. In September 2013 the Abbott Federal Government was elected, with a promise to abolish carbon pricing in Australia altogether. It's *Clean Energy Legislation (Carbon Tax Repeal) Act 2014* was successful and abolished the carbon pricing mechanism and came into effect on 1 July 2014. This has caused considerable uncertainty and risk for a wide cross section of investors and corporations, especially those investing in low carbon projects and strategies.

In addition to the carbon pricing repeal, under the auspices of the Abbott Federal Government, many other climate related policy settings and initiatives such as the Clean Energy Finance Corporation, the Australian Renewable Energy Agency and the Renewable Energy Target (designed by the previous Labor Government) to support Australia's transition to a low carbon economy, have been the subject of formal reviews in an attempt to wind them back or close them altogether. At the time of writing, the schemes, initiatives and related agencies aimed at climate change mitigation are summarised below.

Emissions Reduction Fund

The Emissions Reduction Fund (ERF) is the Abbott Government's flagship program to help Australia meet its target of reducing emissions by five per cent below 2000 levels by 2020. The fund conducts auctions to purchase the lowest cost abatements from businesses, households and landowners who have gained Australian Carbon Credit Units (ACCUs). The first auction was held in April 2015. 107 contracts were awarded, with a total value of US$528 million, delivering 470 million tonnes of abatement at an average price of US$11.16 per tonne. Most of the funded ACCUs related to methodologies around sequestration as well as landfill and alternative waste treatment.[13]

The Carbon Farming Initiative

The Carbon Farming Initiative (CFI) is a voluntary scheme that aims to reduce the amount of greenhouse gas entering the atmosphere from activities on the land. There are different types of activities that can be conducted under the CFI. These fall into two categories – emissions avoidance, where greenhouse gas emissions are prevented from entering the atmosphere, and sequestration, where carbon is stored on the land. It is important to note that as of 12 December 2014, the CFI has been integrated with the Emissions Reduction Fund.[14]

Carbon Pricing Mechanism

As previously noted, the Carbon Pricing Mechanism was an emissions trading scheme that put a price on Australia's carbon pollution. It was introduced by the former Labor Government as part of the *Clean Energy Act 2011* and related legislation and applied to Australia's biggest carbon emitters (called liable entities). The carbon pricing mechanism has been abolished and ceased operating in July 2014 with the repeal of the *Clean Energy Act 2011.*

National Greenhouse Energy Reporting Scheme

The *National Greenhouse Energy Reporting Act 2007*[15] (NGER) is an important source of financial, operational and environmental risk analysis information about companies for responsible investors. The NGER legislation requires certain companies meeting certain thresholds to report on their greenhouse gas emissions, energy production and energy consumption. Reporting obligations commenced in the 2009 financial year. The original intention behind this regulation was to provide a database of greenhouse gas and energy related emissions information to underpin the former Labor Government's carbon pricing schemes. Although the carbon pricing mechanism has been abolished since 1 July 2014, the repeal had no effect on reporting obligations for controlling corporations, reporting transfer certificate holders and responsible members under the NGER Act. As such, as far as the authors can determine at the time of writing, the Federal Government has no plans to dismantle NGERS.

Renewable Energy Target

In 2009 a new Renewable Energy Target (RET) was introduced, to ensure at least 20 per cent (or 41,000 GWh) of Australia's electricity supply would come from renewable sources by 2020. The future of the RET is currently and controversially under review by the Federal Government. Given the significant investment in the scheme, the proposed dismantling has caused outrage amongst responsible investors. On 30 September 2014, the members of the IGCC wrote an open letter urging Prime Minister Abbott to keep Australia an attractive investment destination by upholding its previous support for the RET. The letter cited that the savings of more than 10 million Australians in a clean energy future would be jeopardized if the RET was dismantled.[16] In line with these views, others argue that household electricity bills will increase, jobs and investment in an Australian industry will be lost, and pulling apart the scheme will cost more than it saves.[17] Despite these views, in May 2015 the RET was lowered from the established target of 41,000 GWh to 33,000 GWh.

Energy Efficiency Opportunities

The Energy Efficiency Opportunities[18] programme encourages large energy-using businesses to improve their energy efficiency. It does this by requiring businesses to identify, evaluate and report publicly on cost-effective energy-saving opportunities. With the change of government the *Energy Efficiency Opportunities (Repeal) Bill 2014* has been introduced which, if passed, will terminate the Energy Efficiency Opportunities Program.

Clean Energy Regulator

The Clean Energy Regulator is the regulatory body that administers the schemes to reduce emissions while encouraging business competiveness. The schemes include: Emissions Reduction Fund; National Greenhouse and Energy Reporting Scheme; Carbon Pricing Mechanism; Carbon Farming Initiative and the Renewable Energy Target.

Climate Change Authority

The independent Climate Change Authority plays an important role in the governance of Australia's climate change mitigation policies, and is tasked to undertake reviews and make recommendations on these schemes, such as emissions reduction targets and carbon budgets, the Renewable Energy Target, the Carbon Farming Initiative, and the National Greenhouse and Energy Reporting System.

Australian Renewable Energy Agency

The Australian Renewable Energy Agency (ARENA) was established under the former Labor Government and commenced in 2012 to manage approximately US$2 billion in existing government funding to support clean technology over a nine year period. ARENA has two major objectives: to improve the competitiveness of renewable energy technologies, and to increase the supply of renewable energy in Australia.[19]

Clean Energy Finance Corporation

As part of its Clean Energy Future[20] package, the former Labor Government committed US$9.37 billion over 5 years to the Clean Energy Finance Corporation (CEFC). The CEFC started operating in 2013 under the Clean Energy Finance Corporation Act 2012. The CEFC is independent from government, and its aim is to commercialize and deploy renewable energy and enabling technologies, energy efficiency and low-emissions technologies. Funding tools include loans on commercial or concessional terms and equity investments with any capital returned from investments to be reinvested. As at 30 June 2014, the CEFC had contracted investments of over US$707 million in projects with a total value of over US$2.36 billion.

Other types of legislation affecting responsible investment

The legislation covered below has been deemed important because it is used by responsible investors and analysts as part of their ESG integration processes, including risk assessment and analysis, comparative analysis and company benchmarking. In other words, the legislation and, more importantly, a company's response to it is used in formulating the analyst's views about company value and selection of stocks. In addition there is disclosure legislation directed at investors when designing and marketing investment products (e.g. Section 1013DA Disclosure Guidelines). That listed in this section is by no means exhaustive and, as previously acknowledged, given the change of federal government in Australia in September 2013, it is difficult to anticipate which policies and initiatives will remain in place, which will be abolished and if any new laws will be enacted over the coming years.

Section 299 of the Australian Corporations Act

To help inform a view on a listed company's operations and the board's capabilities the *Australian Corporations Act* – Section 299(1)(f)[21] identifies requirements regarding disclosure of general information about operations and activities in a company's directors' report. In particular, Section 299(1)(f) of the Act says that where an entity's operations are subject to any particular and significant environmental regulation under a law of the Commonwealth or of a state or territory, the entity must give details of the entity's performance in relation to that environmental regulation(s). Listed companies should also be aware of *Australian Corporations Act* – Section 299A,[22] which requires disclosure of information shareholders would reasonably require to make an informed assessment of the operations of the entity, the entity's financial position and the entity's business strategies and its prospects for future financial years. Relevant information could include a company's exposure to risk and its approach to managing those risks, including climate change risks.

CLERP 9

The *Australian Corporate Law Economic Reform Program (Audit Reform and Corporate Disclosure) Act 2004*[23] (CLERP 9) can be used by investment analysts to understand the corporate governance arrangements of a listed company in Australia. It amends a number of acts, including the *Corporations Act 2001*, to give effect to reforms aimed at restoring public confidence in corporate Australia. CLERP 9 requires disclosure by publically listed companies in relation to directors' remuneration, financial reporting, auditor independence and continuous disclosure with enhanced penalty provisions.

ASX Corporate Governance Principles and Recommendations

In accordance with Australian Securities Exchange (ASX) Listing Rule 4.10.3, listed entities are required to benchmark their corporate governance practices against the prescribed recommendations and, where they do not conform, to disclose that fact and the reasons.[24] During March 2014 the ASX released a third edition, and included a new recommendation under Principle 7: Recognize and Manage Risk. The new recommendation, Recommendation 7.4, now explicitly states "A listed entity should disclose whether it has any material exposure to economic, environmental and social sustainability risks and, if it does, how it manages those risks". In previous guidelines this requirement was not explicit and companies could chose to do so at their own discretion.

Section 1013DA Disclosure Guidelines

Unlike the legislations and guidelines listed above, Section 1013DA Disclosure Guidelines is aimed specifically at investors and not corporations. The Australian Securities and Investment Commission[25] (ASIC) provides guidelines on how product issuers can meet their obligations under s1013DA of the *Corporations Act 2001*. Product issuers are required to disclose in their Product Disclosure Statements (PDSs) how labour standards or environmental, social or ethical considerations are taken into account in selecting, retaining or realising an investment.

RI institutions in Australia

Responsible Investment Association Australasia

Responsible Investment Association Australasia[26] (RIAA) was established in 2000 and is the peak industry body for organisations and professionals who take ESG factors into account in their investment decisions. RIAA covers Australia and New Zealand. Membership consists of over 150 investment organisations and individuals, who manage over US$450 billion in funds under management, covering the investment spectrum – from advisers and dealer groups, to investment managers, superannuation funds, faith-based investors, research firms, asset consultants and insurance companies. RIAA's flagship programmes include a major annual report on the size and growth of responsible investment in Australasia, a biennial international conference, and an independently audited certification programme for responsible investment products and services.

The Australia Council of Superannuation Investors

The Australia Council of Superannuation Investors[27] (ACSI) is an independent organisation of Australian superannuation funds and overseas affiliates. ACSI provides independent research and advice on the ESG risks of companies in which its members invest both locally and internationally. Its vision is to achieve genuine, measurable and permanent improvements in the ESG performance of entities in which its members invest, and in the ESG investment practices of its members and their investment advisors and managers. Its mission is to enhance sustainable long-term value for the retirement savings that are entrusted to its members as fiduciary institutional investors. ACSI represents 33 Australian and international superannuation fund members who collectively manage over US$400 billion.

The Investor Group on Climate Change

The Investor Group on Climate Change[28] (IGCC) is a collaboration of Australian and New Zealand investors who focus on the impact that climate change has on the financial value of investments. It recognizes that the financial return of an investment is impacted by climate change. As such, IGCC aims to encourage government policies and investment practices that address the risks and opportunities of climate change, for the ultimate benefit of superannuants and unit holders. It aims to build a forum through which it will raise awareness of the potential impacts, both positive and negative, resulting from climate change to the investment industry, corporate, government and community sectors; encourage best practice approaches to facilitate the inclusion of the impacts of climate change in investment analysis by the investment industry and provide information to assist the investment industry to understand and incorporate climate change issues into the investment decision. Membership is open to institutional investors and current members of IGCC represent total funds under management of just over US$1 trillion.

ESG Research Australia

ESG Research Australia[29] (ESG RA) is an association of superannuation funds, fund managers and asset consultants. Members wish to encourage better investment research by increasing the amount and quality of mainstream stockbroker research that integrates consideration of ESG issues. By becoming a member of ESG RA an organisation publicly states the value of, and is committed to, raising the profile of ESG-inclusive research for better investment decision making. Superannuation fund members of ESG RA commit to requesting that their Australian equity fund managers to include ESG as a category in their panel structures, whilst fund manager members commit to including ESG considerations into their brokerage panel structures (or if they only 'tag' brokers for research they will 'tag' ESG research).

Business Reporting Leaders Forum (for integrated reporting)

Since its establishment in June 2010 the core purpose of the Business Reporting Leaders Forum[30] (BRLF) has been to collaborate with Australian stakeholders and work with global initiatives to promote the development and implementation of a strategy-aligned integrated reporting framework. This is largely a response to the work of the International Integrated Reporting Council (IIRC), whose aim is to create a globally accepted business reporting framework that brings together financial and ESG information in a clear, concise, consistent and comparable format – put briefly, an integrated report. The intention is to provide better insight about an organization's strategy, total performance and future prospects; to meet the needs of a more sustainable, global economic model; and ultimately to provide pertinent financial and ESG information for use in investment analysis. Membership is open to all stakeholders with an interest in integrated reporting for business.

Other institutions that participate in RI

There is a wide range of commercial institutions, civil society and political institutions in Australia that participate in the responsible investment debates, conduct research on ESG issues and the role of the investment sector and provide ESG issue–related services to clients, including, but not limited to:

Commercial institutions

- Accounting firms (e.g. Ernst & Young, PWC, KPMG, Deloitte, etc.)
- Legal firms (e.g. Baker and McKenzie, Clayton Utz, Henry Davis York, etc.)
- Specialised ESG research providers (e.g. Regnan, CAER, MSCI, Bloomberg, Sustainalytics, etc.)

Civil society institutions

- Non-government organisations (e.g. Amnesty International, Australian Conservation Foundation, Greenpeace, Wilderness Society, World Wide Fund for Nature, etc.)
- Not-for-profit organisations (e.g. 350.org, Market Forces, etc.)

- Research institutes (e.g. Australia Institute, Grattan Institute, etc.)
- Universities (e.g. The University of Sydney, University of NSW, Australian National University, etc.)

Political institutions

- The Australian Greens

RI issues in Australia

What are the salient ESG issues?

Reliance on coal

Australia is the world's largest coal exporter, the second largest exporter of thermal coal and is heavily reliant on coal for domestic energy use (75 per cent of total energy use). Research and analysis on the investment risks inherent in this situation escalated in 2013 and continue to grow. New factors driving this debate include plans for the massive expansion of export infrastructure and mining activity to meet demand for Australian coal from Asia, especially from China.

In December 2013, the Abbott Federal Government gave approval for extensive new coal mining and export facilities in Queensland. This includes new inland mines as well as nine new coal ports and terminals along the coast of the Great Barrier Reef World Heritage Area. One of these ports, at Abbott Point, will provide export facilities for coal mined from the Galilee Basin. If completed, Abbott Point will be the largest coal port in the world with the Galilee Basin being the largest new greenfield coal basin in the world. Two of the most advanced projects in the Galilee Basin face infrastructure costs, including mines, rail and ports of US$21 billion. In recent years international and local investment institutions have pulled out of funding for the projects citing various commercial risks related to the low quality of thermal coal involved, globally depressed seaborne coal prices, and no existing infrastructure.[31]

Investors in Australia and abroad continue to assess the degree of carbon asset risk in these prospective investments and whether future climate change regulation, and other factors, could result in stranded assets.[32]

In the public sphere, research has included *Stranded Down Under? Environment-related factors changing China's demand for coal and what this means for Australian coal assets* released by the Smith School of Enterprise and the Environment at Oxford University, as well as *Point of No Return* by Greenpeace International. The Oxford University report examines the potential for falling demand from China for Australia's coal owing to environmental regulation, developments in cleaner technologies, local pollution, improving energy efficiency, changing resource landscapes and political activism. The Greenpeace report analyses the impact that the planned coal asset expansion in Australia will have on global emission levels, citing that if the expansion is realised, coal exports in Australia will rise to 408 million tonnes per year above 2011 levels by 2025.[33] The report also states that if this quantity of coal is extracted, processed and burned, these projects will be responsible for an increase of 1.2 million tonnes of CO_2 emissions per year worldwide.[34] Other organisations at the forefront of this debate in Australia include 350.org, Carbon Tracker, Market Forces, the Australia Institute and the Institute for Energy Economics and Financial Analysis.

These campaigns have drawn on the global divestment community to encourage retail investors and some institutional investors to divest from fossil fuels. At the time of writing, whole or part divestment has been committed to by nine church groups (predominantly the Anglican Church and the Uniting Church), six local councils, four superannuation funds, seven foundations and, most notably and controversially, the Australian National University and the University of Sydney.

Other issues related to climate change and the environment of concern to responsible investors include:

- The lack of appropriate carbon pricing mechanisms in Australia (and abroad). However at the time of writing, responsible investors are looking towards the international negotiations set to take place in Paris in December 2015 at the 21st session of the Conference of the Parties to the United Nations Framework Convention on Climate Change (UNFCCC). The IGCC argue that Australia's post 2020 emissions reduction target should be consistent with the international community's commitment to limit the increase in global temperature below 2° Celsius this century. The IGCC argue the Australian Government should propose an Intended Nationally Determined Contribution (INDC) of approximately 30 per cent below 2000 levels in 2025 or in the order of 50 per cent below 2000 levels in 2030.[35]
- The impact of climate change on Australian rivers and water systems, already renowned for 'boom and bust' patterns of flood and drought.
- Investment and insurance risk exposure related to an increase in severe weather events.
- The planned massive expansion of Australia's coal seam gas reserves, most of which are earmarked for export, versus mounting backlash from communities over the potential negative impacts on water quality, farm lands, the environment, communities, residents' health, property values and tourism. In addition, protest against the projections that the price of gas in Australia will escalate dramatically in coming years to meet the price that international importers are willing to pay.[36]
- A relatively undeveloped marketplace for investment in renewable energy, energy efficiency, clean technology, as well as adaptation and low-carbon strategies and infrastructure.
- Conflicting demand for land use, primarily from mining companies, food producers and conservationists.

Other important ESG issues for Australia

The following issues also attract significant attention and research among Australian responsible investors, as current or potential investment risks or opportunities:

- Exposure to bribery and corruption, as Australian companies are expanding operations into countries that represent an increased likelihood of such risk.
- Supply chain working conditions and child labour, especially in Asia, and exemplified by the tragedy at the Rana Plaza clothing factory in Bangladesh in 2013.
- Diversity and inclusiveness, including gender diversity at the board level.
- Active ownership strategies related to board remuneration, composition and effectiveness and director elections.
- Workplace health and wellbeing, both physical safety and mental health.
- Obesity, diabetes and heart disease in relation to the food industry.
- Tobacco divestment.
- Financial markets functioning, long-termism and alignment of agents.
- Tax avoidance and transparency.
- Soft corruption, including regulatory capture by corporations, political donations, lobbying and the role of trade associations.
- Inadequate stakeholder management by corporations.

How ESG issues become important to investors

Strong ESG research tradition

Since the early 2000s, a strong field of ESG research providers has been a key feature in the development of Australia's responsible investment sector. Since then, the field has grown and now includes international providers and domestic buy-side, sell-side and institutional investment teams, resulting in a high standard of local research analytics.

Proximity to Asia

Australia's proximity to Asia has resulted in convincing research in relation to ESG issues in these markets, which are known for being relatively opaque and difficult to access.

Collaborative relationships with NGOs

Australian responsible investors have a long history of collaborating with NGOs in order to better understand the genesis of current ESG issues and the nature and drivers of emerging issues and to gain better insight into where and what kind of research and analysis might be needed.

Strong support for industry peak bodies

Industry collaboration has been a key driver in bringing many ESG issues to the fore. Australia is fortunate to have a number of strong industry bodies for responsible investment, as discussed earlier in this chapter. These organisations have played a key role in bringing industry together to collaborate on issues of concern, stage industry events and provide education and advocacy.

Australia as an outward-looking nation

Australia can be considered an outward-looking nation, despite its geographic isolation. As such, Australian responsible investment practitioners are well represented in international investment forums where ESG trends, issues and case studies are often explored. International forums often shed light on horizon issues and have provided an important catalyst for these issues to be better understood in an Australia context.

Conclusion

Three factors stand out when explaining the nature of Australia's responsible investment sector and the reasons for its growth over the last decade. These three factors are: Australia's contribution to responsible investment at the international level; the country's longstanding compulsory superannuation scheme; and the abundance of minerals, ores and fossil fuels. These three factors are explained, in turn, below.

The first factor to explain why Australia's responsible investment sector has developed the way it has is purely serendipitous, in that the founding executive director of the Principles for Responsible Investment, Dr James Gifford, is Australian, as indeed is his successor, Fiona Reynolds. Australians have also played a strong role on the board of the PRI since its inception in 2006. These close personal links with the global peak body has guided and accelerated Australia's participation in responsible investment.

The second factor is the dominance of Australia's finance sector (third largest in the world), largely owing to our country's compulsory superannuation scheme (which will reach 12 per cent by 2021), originally born out of the union movement. The sheer size of these investment flows combined with the role that unions play in the governance of our industry funds has resulted in significant alignment with responsible investment ideas by Australia's institutional investors.

Finally, Australia is home to significant reserves of minerals, ores and fossil fuels. This has resulted in a high reliance on coal and gas for our energy needs and on mining to boost our domestic economy and balance of trade. The economic, financial and human impacts have meant that Australia is now necessarily at the heart of the global climate change debate.

What is in store for the Australian responsible investment sector in the coming years? The authors predict: mounting community and international pressure in relation to coal mining, coal exports and coal seam gas exploration; continued political upheaval and resultant investor uncertainty around carbon pricing; gradual mainstream adoption of carbon asset risk analysis as planned coal infrastructure expansion rolls out; growing interest and market-making in alternative asset classes, such as impact investment, climate bonds and sustainable infrastructure; mounting investor concern over soft and hard corruption risk in Australia's corporate sector; greater efforts toward supply chain risk analysis, especially in neighbouring Asia; a rise in investor engagement on board diversity, especially in terms of gender and potentially other areas of diversity such as ethnicity and educational training; more attention on mental health and wellbeing, in addition to physical safety in the workplace; uncertainty in relation to the potential unwinding of financial market reforms and a rise in corporate integrated reporting in response to investor demand.

Notes

1 Responsible Investment Association Australasia (2013) *2013 Responsible Investment Benchmark Report*: 32.
2 Investment Company Institute (2014) *Worldwide Mutual Fund Assets and Flows Data.*
3 Principles for Responsible Investment (2014). Online. Available HTTP: <http://www.unpri.org> (accessed 10 February 2014).
4 Responsible Investment Association Australasia (2014) *2014 Responsible Investment Benchmark Report.*
5 All data in this section is for the year to December 2013, unless otherwise stated.
6 ibid.
7 Deloitte Actuaries and Consultants (2013) *Dynamics of the Australian Superannuation System, the Next 20 Years, 2013–2033*, September.
8 Australasian Centre for Corporate Social Responsibility (2015) *A Guide to Shareholder Advocacy in Australia*, Online. Available HTTP: <http://www.accr.org.au/advocacy> (accessed 4 May 2015).
9 Australian Council of Superannuation Investors (2014) *Annual Report for the financial year ended 30 June 2014.*
10 Regnan (2014) *Engagement and Advocacy Summary 2013–2014.*
11 Australian Council of Superannuation Investors (2011) *Major Vote against NewsCorp Directors*, media release. Online. Available HTTP: <http://www.acsi.org> (accessed 26 March 2014).
12 Australian Council of Superannuation Investors (2012) *Independence Still an Issue with the News Corporation Board*, media release. Online. Available HTTP: <http://www.acsi.org> (accessed 26 March 2014).
13 Carbon Market Institute (2015) *Emissions Reduction Fund.* Online. Available HTTP: <http://www.carbonmarketinstitute.org/knowledge/emissions_reduction_fund> (accessed 7 May 2015).
14 Clean Energy Regulator (2015) *Carbon Farming Initiative.* Online. Available HTTP: <http://www.cleanenergyregulator.gov.au/Carbon-Farming-Initiative/Pages/default.aspx> (accessed 7 May 2015).
15 Australian Government Department of Climate Change and Energy Efficiency (2007) *National Greenhouse Energy Reporting Act.* Online. Available HTTP: <http://www.climatechange.gov.au/reporting> (accessed 30 November 2011).
16 Investor Group on Climate Change (2014) *Open Letter to the Prime Minister from Institutional Investors.* Online. Available HTTP: <http://igcc.org.au/Resources/Documents/RETOpenLetter_Australian-540x372.pdf> (accessed 2 October 2014).

17 Australian Government (2012) *Australian Renewable Energy Agency*. Online. Available HTTP: <http://www.ret.gov.au/energy/clean/arena/Pages/arena.aspx> (accessed 24 August 2012 and 5 May 2015).
18 Australian Government Department of Resources, Energy and Tourism Energy (2006) *Efficiency Opportunities Act*. Online. Available HTTP: <http://www.ret.gov.au/energy/efficiency/eeo/> (accessed 30 November 2011).
19 Ibid.
20 Clean Energy Finance Corporation (2015) About. Online. Available HTTP: http://www.cleanenergyfinancecorp.com.au/about.aspx (accessed 5 May 2015).
21 Australian Securities and Investments Commission (2001) *Australian Corporations Act – Section 299(1)(f)*. Online. Available HTTP: <http://www.austlii.edu.au/au/legis/cth/consol_act/ca2001172/s299.html> (accessed 30 November 2011).
22 Ibid.
23 Australian Securities and Investments Commission (2004) *Australian Corporate Law Economic Reform Program (Audit Reform and Corporate Disclosure) Act 2004 (CLERP 9)*. Online. Available HTTP: <http://www.asic.gov.au/> (accessed 30 November 2011).
24 Australian Stock Exchange Corporate Governance Council (2014) *Corporate Governance Principles and Recommendations (Third edition)* . Online. Available HTTP: <http://www.asx.com.au/about/corporate_governance/> (accessed 8 May 2015).
25 Australian Securities and Investment Commission (2011) *Regulatory Guide 65 – Section 1013DA Disclosure Guidelines*. Online. Available HTTP: <http://www.asic.gov.au/> (accessed 24 August 2012).
26 Responsible Investment Association of Australia (2014) *2014 Responsible Investment Benchmark Report*.
27 Australia Council of Superannuation Investors (2014) *Annual Report for the financial year ended 30 June 2014*.
28 The Investor Group on Climate Change (2014). Online. Available HTTP: <http://www.igcc.org.au/> (accessed 10 February 2014).
29 ESG Research Australia (2012). Online. Available HTTP: <http://esgra.org.au/> (accessed 7 August 2012).
30 Business Reporting Leaders Forum (2010) *BRLF Background*. Online. Available HTTP: <http://www.ske.org.au/BRLF.php> (accessed 24 May 2012).
31 Tom Sanzillo (2014) *The Outlook for Financing Australia's Galilee Basin Coal Projects*, report undertaken for Institute for Energy Economics and Financial Analysis (IEEFA).
32 'Stranded asset' is a financial term that describes an asset that has become obsolete or non-performing, but must be recorded on the balance sheet as a loss of profit. The term has particular relevance to pricing long-term economic and environmental sustainability. Online. Available HTTP: <http://www.smithschool.ox.ac.uk/research/stranded-assets/>.
33 Greenpeace International (2013) *Point of No Return*, data supplied in 2012 by the International Energy Agency.
34 Ibid., data supplied on GHG emissions from the Department of Climate Change and Energy Efficiency, 2011, and National Greenhouse Accounts Factors, Australia.
35 The Investor Group on Climate Change (2015). Online. Available HTTP: <http://www.igcc.org.au/Resources/Documents/IGCC_INDC_150424.pdf> (accessed 14 May 2014).
36 In 2014, the first fine for aquifer contamination in Australia was issued to Santos, an oil and gas company.

14

Responsible investment in China

Qian Li

Introduction

China, officially the People's Republic of China, includes Mainland China and two special administrative regions, Hong Kong and Macao. The political, legal and economic systems of Mainland China are different from those of the special administrative regions. The development stage of responsible investment (RI) in Hong Kong is more advanced than that in Mainland China, while RI in Macau is still under-developed and has rarely been discussed. Therefore, this chapter uses data from Mainland China to avoid ambiguity and maintain clarity.

RI in China differs from the conventional definition that incorporates financial objectives with additional considerations of environmental, social and corporate governance (ESG) criteria into the investment process. In the Chinese context, RI signifies the adoption of four selection criteria – economic indicators, ethics, sustainability and legal issues; hence these criteria represent preferences towards government policy, tax and legal requirements in portfolio selection.[1] RI mutual funds in China can be ESG inclusive, fully integrating ESG criteria into investment, or ESG themed, such as environmentally-friendly funds, low-carbon funds and sustainable investment funds. Besides RI mutual funds, institutional and individual investors can also invest in ESG-themed pension funds, life and property insurance, renewable energies, green projects, etc. Compared with RI mutual funds, RI applied to other asset classes, such as venture capital, hedge fund and private equity, are relatively insignificant.

This chapter seeks to provide an overview of RI in China. It begins with a statistical overview of China's social and economic background in order to provide some thoughts on the driving forces of RI. It is followed by reporting the historical progress and state of the RI market in China and showing the rapid growth of the RI mutual funds industry. It then discusses the practices of RI institutions, aiming to provide a deeper understanding of support and engagement activities in China. It further briefly discusses the most urgent ESG risks, the most risk-exposed industries and the most controversial companies in China. In the end, it provides suggestions to promote the development of RI from both policy and investment perspectives.

Background

With a population of more than 1.3 billion, China has been placed on the top lists in the world, such as being the largest manufacturer, the largest holder of foreign exchange reserves, the second largest economy and the second largest destination of foreign direct investment (FDI) (Morrison, 2013). Since the economic reforms in 1978, China has shifted from a centrally planned economy to a market-based economy. Between 1991 and 2012, China's GDP growth has averaged 10.3 per cent per year and average income per capita has increased more than eightfold. Although the GDP growth rate in China has shown signs of slowing after the global financial crisis in 2008, it is still much higher than most of other major economies (World Bank).

The fast pace of economic growth reflects major improvements in the financial markets. The Shanghai Stock Exchange (SSE) and the Shenzhen Stock Exchange (SZSE) are the two domestic stock exchanges in China and were founded in the early 1990s. Both stock exchanges grew quickly in terms of market capitalization and trading volume. As of January 2014, their overall market capitalization reached US$3.837 trillion, with 2,489 firms listed on the market.[2] In addition to the stock market, the fund market is a driving force in enhancing the operational efficiency of the market and capital distribution. The first closed-end and open-end funds were established in 1997 and 2001, respectively. As of November 2013, there were 89 fund management firms managing 1,505 public funds, an increase from the 65 firms managing 551 funds in November 2009, with an average annual increase of approximately 238 funds.[3] China's economic growth over the past decades has posed many challenges to China, especially in the areas of domestic demand, inequality, urbanization, corruption and environmental pollution.[4] The ongoing concern that has been rising steadily is how to achieve a balance between economic growth and sustainable development in the long run. Reflecting its increasing awareness of this issue, the Chinese government adopted its 12th five-year plan in 2011, which has the goal of rebalancing development goals for sustainability. Additionally, both institutional and individual investors have been actively involved in seeking sustainable opportunities.

The potential benefits of integrating environment, social and governance (ESG) factors into investment processes are the driving force behind the growing interest in furthering the development of RI in China. Several studies claim that RI funds are superior to conventional funds (e.g. Kempf and Osthoff, 2007; Zheng, 2011). Thus, Chinese investors expect to gain a higher rate of return while exposing investments to less risk. Provided that companies with better ESG performance are likely to have easier access to bank loans and often raise more capital directly from investors (e.g. Goss and Roberts, 2011; Oikonomou, Brooks and Pavelin, 2014), the capital market can allocate financial resources more efficiently and fairly by applying ESG integration strategies. The Chinese government can also capitalize on these trends to maintain a stable society with a healthy cycle of economic development.

The state of the RI market

Compared to RI fund markets in developed countries, RI funds in China are in the primary stages, particularly given the limited investment options available to investors (Zheng, 2011). According to Table 14.1, there were only 14 RI funds available in China as of January 2014, including four ESG-inclusive RI funds, one RI fund of funds[5] and nine other ESG-themed funds. The four ESG-inclusive RI funds are the Industrial Social Responsibility Securities Investment Fund, the CCB Social Responsibility Open Index ETF, the China Universal Socially Responsible Investments Fund and the CCB Socially Responsible Investments Fund. The total assets of the four ESG-inclusive RI funds were about US$1.49 billion in January 2014, and the 14 funds

Table 14.1 List of RI funds and ESG-themed funds in China

Fund Name	*Bloomberg Ticker*	*Local Code*	*Category*	*Inception Date*	*Total Asset US$ (M)*	*Total Return 1Y*	*Rank*
BOC Investment Management Sustainable Growth Fund	BOCIGRO:CH	163803	ESG-themed fund	3/17/2006	1,209.79	12.13	775
Industrial Social Responsibility Securities Investment Fund	XYRESPS:CH	340007	RI Fund	4/30/2008	1,064.64	21.09	188
CCB SSE Social Responsibility Index ETF Linked Fund	CCBSSSR:CH	530010	RI fund of funds	5/28/2010	61.55	–9.77	1,138
CCB Social Responsibility Open Index ETF	510090:CH	510090	RI Fund	5/28/2010	57.03	–10.65	1,149
HSBC Low Carbon Pioneer Fund	HSBCLCP:CH	540008	ESG-themed fund	6/8/2010	247.84	43.43	34
Zhong Hai Green New Energy Flexible Allocation Fund	ZHGRNEA:CH	398051	ESG-themed fund	12/9/2010	57.89	–1.34	938
China Universal Socially Responsible Investments Fund	CHNUSRE:CH	470028	RI Fund	3/29/2011	295.39	19.95	204
Xingye Green Investment Fund	163409:CH	163409	ESG-themed fund	5/6/2011	221.18	41.79	39
Fullgoal Low Carbon Environmental Friendly Fund	FULLCEF:CH	100056	ESG-themed fund	8/12/2011	87.73	28.68	109
HFT CSI China Low Carbon Index Fund	HFTCHLC:CH	519034	ESG-themed fund	5/25/2012	12.16	26.78	127
CCB Socially Responsible Investments Fund	CCBSORE:CH	530019	RI Fund	8/14/2012	7.18	16.17	286
CSI Caitong ECPI ESG China 100 Index Fund	CTCECPI:CH	000042	ESG-themed fund	3/22/2013	12.35	N.A.	N.A.
Caitong Sustainable Development Theme Fund	CTSDVTH:CH	000017	ESG-themed fund	3/27/2013	13.1	N.A.	N.A.
Bank of China Beautiful China Fund	BOCBEAC:CH	000120	ESG-themed fund	6/7/2013	113.43	N.A.	N.A.

Source: Bloomberg LLC. Accessed 6 January 2014.

Notes: This table is an exhaustive list of all of the open and active RI funds and ESG-themed funds in China. Industrial Social Responsibility Securities Investment Fund is also named Xingye Responsible for Society Fund. Rank is based on rankings of total return in 2013 of 1,242 Chinese public funds with data available. Table is ranked by inception date.

together held approximately US$3.46 billion. All these funds consisted of only 0.7 per cent of the total assets of public funds.[6]

While the number of Chinese RI funds is relatively small, these funds have performed better than conventional funds. The first ESG-inclusive RI fund, which is the Industrial Social Responsibility Securities Investment Fund, was launched by Aegon-Industrial Fund Management Co., Ltd. in April 2008. This fund systematically applies RI concepts in the investment decision-making process and has raised 1.388 billion shares since its launch. The performance of this fund ranked 14th among 205 equity funds in 2008 and 5th among 152 funds in 2009 (Guo, 2012). By using Sharp Ratio and Jensen's Alpha to compare financial performance, Zheng (2011) also provides an empirical analysis of this fund based on the benchmark of CITIC-Standard & Poor's Index, which shows that this fund receives higher return with less volatility compared to conventional funds.

The success of the first RI fund was a key milestone in the progress of RI because investors began to recognize the potential benefits of early engagement in RI funds. As can be seen from Table 14.1, most of the ESG-inclusive RI funds and ESG-themed funds gained positive total returns in 2013. Based on the rankings of total return of 1,242 Chinese public funds in 2013, HSBC Low Carbon Pioneer Fund and Xingye Green Investment Fund both rank in the top 3 per cent of Chinese public funds. Three funds focused on low carbon are in the top 10 per cent of the market. In summary, seven out of 11 RI funds and ESG-themed funds are ranked in the first quartile of all the public funds.[7] Although most of the RI funds have performed very well in the market in 2013, the CCB Social Responsibility Open Index ETF and its linked fund, the CCB SSE Social Responsibility Index ETF Linked Fund, ranked poorly.

Besides the RI funds, other ESG-related products and activities have also made notable progress during the past decade (for a complete list of historical RI activities, see Table 14.2). One of the major achievements is that a number of ESG indices have been developed in the market. As of January 2014, there were 17 ESG-themed indices launched by SSE, SZSE, China Securities Index Co., Ltd (CSI) and Shenzhen Securities Information Co., Ltd (SSI) (see Table 14.3). These indices have served the purpose of stimulating listed companies to be concerned about ESG performance and provide valuable benchmarks for investors.

Last but not least, corporate social responsibility (CSR) reporting plays a significant role in improving ESG engagement, which suggests a positive trend for Chinese firms to disclose non-financial information (Weber, 2012). The State Grid Corporation of China, which is the largest state-owned electric utility company in the world, released its inaugural CSR report in 2006 to detail its CSR efforts. Subsequently, the number of CSR reports in China grew from 32 in 2006 to 817 in 2011 (Yue, 2012), and then dramatically increased to 1,705 CSR reports in 2012 (Syntao, 2013). These reports increase the awareness of Chinese companies with regard to the impact of their business activities on a range of stakeholders, and they are eliciting positive changes through this systematic approach to ESG integration. More important, these reports enable investors to evaluate the ESG risks of the companies in their portfolio based on the disclosed information.

RI institutions

This section reviews five types of major institutional supports that have been driving RI engagement in China: global initiatives, governments, stock exchanges, banks and non-governmental organizations (NGOs). This is not a comprehensive list given the influence of other forces on companies' ESG performance, such as, for example, social media, private regulation, community participation and stakeholder activism, etc.

Table 14.2 Historical landmarks of RI activities in China

Time	*Event*
2001	The concept of ethical investment was first introduced by Chen (2001).
2001	Tsing Capital became the first cleantech venture capital management firm in China. It has been one part of the venture investment branch of Tsinghua University Holdings company (Tsing Capital).
2002	Tsing Capital launched China's first cleantech and environment-themed closed-end fund, named China Environment Fund (Tsing Capital).
2002	Li and He (2002) mentioned the concept of socially responsible investment (SRI) in academic research in China (Zhou, 2010).
Oct. 2003	China Business Council for Sustainable Development (CBCSD) was founded though the Ministry of Civil Affairs, PRC. CBCSD aims to provide guidelines and policies for advocating CSR and facilitate the development of sustainable business (CBCSD).
Jan. 2006	Shenzhen Stock Exchange launched the first corporate governance index – SZSE CORP Governance Index – in China, composed of the stocks with good corporate governance (CNI).
Mar. 2006	The first ESG-themed fund, the Bank of China Sustainable Growth Equity Fund, was established. The fund was based on corporate governance and social values screening criteria, targeted at low risk and long-term growth companies (Bloomberg).
Jan. 2008	SZSE and TEDA Group jointly launched the first environmental index, the CNI TEDA EP Index. This index consists of 40 listed companies selected from 10 environment-relevant sectors (CNI).
April 2008	AEGON Industrial Fund Management Co. Ltd. established the first ESG-inclusive RI fund, the Industrial Social Responsibility Securities Investment Fund (Guo, 2012).
Aug. 2009	SSE launched the SSE Social Responsibility Index (SEE CGI), which built the foundation for the strategies of developing a socially responsible index in China. This index is the first index focused on social responsibility, with 100 SSE-listed stocks having strong social responsibility performance (CSI).
May 2010	CCB Principal Asset Management launched first SRI ETF in China, the CCB Social Responsibility Open Index Exchange Traded Fund. This fund is based on the SSE Social Responsibility Index (Bloomberg).
Sep. 2010	ECPI launched the first ESG index in China, the CSI ECPI China ESG 40 Equity Index. This index is based on collaboration between ECPI and CSI, with 40 listed companies in China (CSI).
Sep. 2010	CNI NANFANG Low-carbon 50 Index, jointly launched with NANFANG Media Group, is the first low-carbon index in China (CNI).
Aug. 2011	SSE launched the first sustainability index, the SSE Sustainable Development Industry Index (CSI).
May 2012	HFT investment management launched the first RI index fund in China, the HFT China Mainland Low Carbon Economy Index Fund. The fund follows the index of CSI China Mainland Low Carbon Economy Index (CSI).
Oct. 2012	ECPI jointly developed with CSI the second ESG index in China, the CSI CAITONG ECPI ESG China 100 Index. This index composed of 100 top ESG-rated companies in the CSI 300 Index (CSI).
Nov. 2012	China's first social investment forum, themed 'Creating Social Change Capital in China' was held by Avantage Ventures, an Asia-based social investment and advisory firm. This forum aims to focus on direct sustainable investment strategies and opportunities in China and Asia (Avantage Ventures, 2012).
Dec. 2013	The Chinese social investment forum (China SIF) released its first report – 'Survey on Chinese Socially Responsible Investment Funds in 2013' (China SIF, 2013).

Table 14.3 List of ESG-themed indices in China

Index Name	*Local Code*	*Launch Date*	*Index Provider*	*Index Composition*
SSE Corporate Governance Index	000019	02/01/2008	SSE	All stocks from the SSE Corporate Governance board.
SSE180 Corporate Governance Index	000021	10/09/2008	SSE	100 large and good liquidity stocks from the SSE180 index and the SSE Corporate Governance Index.
SSE Social Responsibility Index	000048	05/08/2009	SSE	Top 100 stocks ranked by social contribution value per share stocks from the SSE Corporate Governance Index.*
SSE Sustainable Development Industry Index	000114	22/08/2011	SSE	40 large and good liquidity sustainable development industry stocks listed in the SSE.
SSE Environmental Protection Industry Index	000158	25/09/2012	SSE	40 stocks from SEEA, SSE Environmental Protection Industry Index.
SZSE CORP Governance Index	399328	24/01/2006	SZSE	40 stocks have high management appraisal records in the CNINFO comprehensive evaluation system of governance structure.
SZSE CSR Price Index	399341	03/08/2009	SZSE	100 top stocks based on the rankings of the total contribution made to the country, employees, shareholders and creditors.
SZSE Environmental Protection Index	399638	15/11/2011	SZSE	40 stocks in environmental protection equipment manufacturing, environmental protection service industries.
SZSE SME CORP Governance Index	399650	20/08/2012	SZSE	50 stocks in SME board have high management appraisal records in the CNINFO comprehensive evaluation system of governance structure.
SZSE SME CSR Index	399651	20/08/2012	SZSE	50 top stocks in SME board based on the rankings of the total contribution made to the country, employees, shareholders and creditors.
CSI ECPI ESG China 40 Index	000970	17/09/2010	CSI	40 top stocks in the SSE180 Corporate Governance Index rated by ECPI ESG method.
China Low Carbon Index	H11113	16/02/2011	CSI	40 representative stocks active in the Chinese low-carbon economy.
CSI Environmental Protection Industry Index	000827	25/09/2012	CSI	100 stocks reflect the performance of the environmental protection industry.
CSI CAITONG ECPI ESG China 100 Index	000846	16/10/2012	CSI	Top 100 stocks in the CSI 300 Index rated by ECPI ESG method.
CSI Urbanization Green Cities Index	H30139	26/08/2013	CSI	100 stocks focus on the urbanization themes in an intensive, intelligent, green and low-carbon way.
CNI TEDA EP Index	399358	02/01/2008	SSI	40 stocks in environment-relevant sectors.
CNI Nangfang Low-carbon 50 Index	399378	20/09/2010	SSI	50 stocks in low-carbon industries.

Source: China Securities Index Co., Ltd. Accessed 14 January 2014.

Notes: Base value of all the indices is 1,000. Indices are ranked first by the importance of the index provider and then by the launch date.

* *The calculation method of social contribution rate*: Corporate social contribution per shares = (net profit + tax + salaries + net interest expense + community investment + environmental investment – environmental cost)/total number of shares. See R. Hu (2010) 'ESG Progress in China–Disclosure and the Shanghai Stock Exchange', Shanghai Stock Exchange. Online. Available HTTP: <http://www.responsibleinvestment.org/wp-content/uploads/2011/09/ProfessorHu-ShanghaiStockExchange.pdf> (accessed 21 September 2012).

Global initiatives

Many global initiatives are playing an important role in establishing principles and improving standards for the development of RI in China. The following organizations comprise those with which Chinese actors currently have the most engagement.

The UN-backed Principles for Responsible Investment (PRI) is an international network and has established six principles for RI practice. As of January 2014, the PRI had attracted 1,229 signatories worldwide. The three Chinese signatories include Jiuding Capital and Lunar Capital Management as investment managers and SynTao as a professional service partner.[8]

The UN Global Compact (UNGC), which is the world's largest corporate citizenship and sustainability initiative, has had long-term influences on RI in China. As of January 2014, 301 Chinese companies out of more than 10,000 participants around the world have embraced the UNGC's principals in the areas of human rights, labour, environment and anti-corruption practices.[9]

The Equator Principles provide international risk management standards for the financial industry that primarily assess, determine and manage environmental and social risks in project finance. In October 2008, Industrial Bank became the first Equator Principles Financial Institution (EPFI) in China, and thus committed not to provide loans to projects in which the borrowers were unable to comply with relevant social and environmental standards.[10]

The UN Environment Programme Finance Initiative (UNEP FI) works with partner organizations to contribute the perspectives of financial institutions on sustainable finance. Over 200 financial institutions are signatories to its statements. As of January 2014, four banks in China are signatories to the UNEP FI: China Development Bank, China Merchants Bank, Industrial Bank and Ping An Bank.[11] UNEP has also helped to bring the public and private sectors together to improve energy-efficiency implementation.

Government

One of the most important contributions of the Chinese government is to make efforts to raise the standards of ESG performance of listed firms (see Table 14.4 for detailed progress of historical policies). For instance, Article 5 of the Companies Law of the People's Republic of China, which took effect in January 2006, requires companies to observe social morals and commercial ethics and to be socially responsible (CSRC, 2006). Moreover, the revised version of the Guideline on the Annual Report of Listed Companies (January 2013) requires companies to disclose non-financial information to demonstrate corporate investment value for the first time. This guideline also encourages companies to include extra items in the report on a voluntary disclosure basis, such as social responsibility performance and the company's important suppliers and clients (CSRC, 2013a). These kinds of laws and guidelines are a positive contribution to CSR reporting and will help to increase transparency of listed firms in the market.

Another important contribution is that of the Ministry of Environmental Protection (MEP) of China, which has launched a series of green policies, including the 'Green Credit' policy in July 2007 and the 'Green Insurance' and 'Green Securities' policies enacted in February 2008. The 'Green Credit' policy aims to prevent credit risks, to reinforce the connections between environmental protection and financial management and to restrict lending to firms with high environmental risks. 'Green Insurance' encourages using environmental pollution liability insurance to require firms to minimize environmental pollution. Since some companies applying for initial public offering (IPO) may have potential ESG risks, the 'Green Securities Policy' requires companies in high-pollution industries to pass stringent environmental standards before being

Table 14.4 Policies promoting RI in China

Date	*Policy*
Jan. 2006	The Renewable Energy Law was issued as the principal framework for taking into account ESG development in China. The law promotes sustainable investment and provides discounted lending and tax preferences for renewable energy programs (UNEP).
Jan. 2006	Companies were required by the Article 5 of the Companies Law of the People's Republic of China to "observe social morals and commercial ethics" and "assume social responsibility" (CSRC, 2006).
Sep. 2006	The Shenzhen Stock Exchange issued the 'Social Responsibility Instructions to Listed Companies', which aimed to improve the quality of social responsibility reports (SZSE, 2006).
July 2007	The Ministry of Environment Protection, the People's Bank of China and the China Banking Regulatory issued the 'Green Credit' policy, which suggests that banks evaluate a company's environmental performance before lending and restrict loans to projects that are harmful to the environment. The Green Policy is considered to be an effective way to eliminate credit risks in the bank industry (Green Watershed, 2010).
Feb. 2008	The Ministry of Environmental Protection issued the policy of 'Green Security'. Listed companies in heavy polluting and high environmental risk industries were required to first conduct an environmental evaluation before launching an IPO. This policy was to make sure that financial institutions only finance green, energy-efficient and environment responsible companies (MEP, 2008).
May 2008	SSE released the 'Guide on Environmental Information Disclosure for Companies Listed on the Shanghai Stock Exchange'. It prompted the importance of disclosure of the contribution value of corporate social responsibility per share (Lin, 2010).
Jan. 2009	China Banking Association issued the guidelines on social responsibilities of financial institutions (Green Watershed, 2010).
April 2010	The Standing Committee of National's People's Congress passed amendments to the Renewable Energy Law, and the new law came into effect (Schaub, 2010).
May 2010	The People's Bank of China and the China Banking Regulatory Commission provided suggestions on improving the financial services of conserving energy, reducing emissions and phasing out of backward production capacity (CBRC, 2010).
June 2011	State-owned Assets Supervision and Administration Commission of the State Council (SASAC) published 'Guidelines to the State-owned Enterprises Directly under the Central Government on Fulfilling Corporate Social Responsibilities', in which state-owned enterprise (SOE) were required by a series of principals, guidelines and solutions to fulfil CSR and sustainable development at all levels (SASAC, 2011a).
Sep. 2011	SASAC issued the notice of harmonious development strategy for SOE in the twelfth 5-year plan. This notice encouraged 'Green SOE', which encourages SOE to implement the system for conserving energy and reducing emissions (SASAC, 2011b).
Feb. 2012	The China Banking Regulatory Commission (CBRC) issued the first guidelines for 'Green Credit', which encourage banks and financial institutions to evaluate environmental and social risks and to figure out the ratings that should be used as reference to access to credit (*China Daily*, 2012).
June 2012	Certification and Accreditation Administration of the People's Republic of China (CNCA) issued the 'Notice of Guidance for Certification Bodies to Fulfil Social Responsibilities'. This notice is focused on social responsibilities for certification bodies with specific requirements in building CSR awareness, CSR internal management systems and CSR reporting systems and encouraging supervision and examination of CSR activities (CNCA, 2012).

(*Continued*)

Table 14.4 (Continued)

Date	*Policy*
Jan. 2013	The revised version of the guideline on the annual report of listed companies took effect, whereby companies were required for the first time to disclose non-financial information to demonstrate corporate investment value. This guideline also encouraged companies to increase disclosure of items such as social responsibility performance and to reveal their important suppliers and clients on a voluntary disclosure basis (CBRC, 2013).
Jan. 2013	'The Rules for Corporate Governance of Securities Companies CSRC' published by CSRC came into effect, which aims to improve corporate governance and protect the rights and interests of stakeholders (CSRC, 2013b).

listed on the market (Shen et al., 2013). These policies are useful for reallocating more financial resources to firms with superior environmental performance and urge listed companies to improve their environmental performance.

Last but not least, the Chinese government has announced laws and regulations to improve sustainable development. For instance, the government launched China's Renewable Energy Law in 2006, with the goal of increasing the use of renewable energy sources. Moreover, the China State Environmental Protection Administration published the first legal regulation for environmental information disclosure in 2007 (Meng et al., 2013). In 2011, the Chinese government established sustainability development goals such as promoting a green and low-carbon society in the 12th five-year plan between 2011 and 2015 (Shen et al., 2013). Different from the policies related to CSR reporting and green policies, these policies are more likely to have positive effects on ESG performance in the long term, even though convincing evidence of such effects is lacking.

Stock exchanges

Stock exchanges are the key stakeholders in the Chinese financial markets, as they not only connect public companies and investors, but also play an important role in urging companies to release non-financial information. In China, the Shanghai Stock Exchange (SSE) and the Shenzhen Stock Exchange (SZSE) have contributed to raising awareness and improving transparency of ESG disclosure. Because of the requirements of the two stock exchanges, more than 25 per cent of all listed companies produce sustainability reports (BSR, 2012). In 2006, SZSE launched social responsibility instructions for listed companies in order to promote a commitment to social responsibilities and sustainable development. Some important requirements for public companies are: protecting environmental and community development, performing social responsibilities, improving corporate governance structures, improving occupational safety and health and regular voluntary disclosure on CSR performance (SZSE, 2006). Furthermore, SSE introduced a guideline on environmental information disclosure in 2008 in which companies were encouraged to disclose CSR in their annual reports. If companies had heavy pollution problems, they would be under the scrutiny of the Ministry of Environmental Protection (MEP, 2008). More recently, three types of companies must disclose CSR reports: companies included in the SSE Corporate Governance Index (240), companies that have issued shares both inside and outside China and financial companies (SSE, 2013).

SZSE and SSE have also launched a series of sustainability indices and specialized products and services in the market. In 2008, SZSE and TEDA Group jointly launched the first environmental index, the CNI TEDA EP Index, which consists of 40 listed companies selected from 10 environment-relevant sectors (see Table 14.3 for a list of ESG-themed indices). In addition to indices and products, SZSE also provides training opportunities for listed companies to become familiar with reporting processes and procedures.

Banks

The People's Bank of China (PBOC), the central bank of China, is the pioneer of incorporating 'green finance' and 'sustainable finance' into the Chinese banking system. Since December 2006, PBOC has collaborated with the State Environmental Protection Administration (SEPA) to add pollution records into its corporate credit database. PBOC also requires all commercial banks to follow more stringent environmental screens before lending, a policy that is known as 'green lending' (Guo, 2008).

In addition, commercial banks have made strides towards adopting international standards and principles, which are considered effective tools to enhance reputation and earn public trust and recognition. In 2010, 14 listed banks were selected as assessment projects in an annually published report, which aims to report the progress of green finance of Chinese banks. This report adopted the analytic hierarchy process (AHP) to rank the banks' performances on various indicators, including state policies and domestic and international best practices. Industrial Bank, as the first bank to adopt the UN Equator Principles and the first bank to release annual sustainability reports in China, ranked first among the 14 banks in this report. It should be mentioned that two other banks – China Merchants Bank and Industrial and Commercial Bank of China (ICBC) – have also adopted international environmental principles (Green Watershed, 2010).

NGOs

While NGOs have played a major role in encouraging RI engagement activities, monitoring ESG issues and providing analysis and expertise in RI at the international level, their ability to influence the development of RI in China remains limited.

Most of the active national NGOs focus on environmental issues and CSR, such as the China Dialogue,[12] Friends of Nature[13] and Business for Social Responsibility (BSR).[14] The Chinese Social Investment Forum (China SIF) is the first NGO to provide a platform to discuss RI research and opportunities in China.[15] In order to discover risks and opportunities of RI, China SIF conducted questionnaires based on 73 Chinese fund management firms and released its first report on Chinese RI funds in December 2013. The survey indicated that 70 per cent of the fund management firms are concerned about the CSR performance of listed firms in their portfolio, and more than half of the fund managers believed that CSR performance positively relates to long-term value (China SIF, 2013).

There are other regional NGOs that are also driving the growth of RI in China. For instance, the Association for Sustainable and Responsible Investment in Asia (ASrIA) is a non-profit association based in Hong Kong that is dedicated to supporting sustainable finance and RI in Asia. ASrIA provides research, training and services in the areas of RI, philanthropic investment and low-carbon investment across Asia.[16]

ESG issues in China

China has not established a comprehensive ESG disclosure framework; therefore, investors can practice responsible investment by evaluating corporate ESG behaviour and ESG risk-exposed industries. Several institutions, including Syntao, MSCI and China SIF, have produced reports of identifying key ESG issues in China. By combining the content of these institutional reports, it has been found that the key environmental risks are toxic emissions and waste, carbon emissions and financing environmental impact (MSCI, 2012) and environmental and industrial hazards (Syntao, 2011). The key corporate governance issues are fraud (Syntao, 2011; China SIF, 2013), corruption (Syntao, 2011; MSCI, 2012), instability (MSCI, 2012) and occupational health and safety (Syntao, 2011). The key social risks are product safety (Syntao, 2011; MSCI, 2012; China SIF, 2013), labour issues (MSCI, 2012) and business ethics (Syntao, 2011). It can be noted that issues related to product safety, corporate governance, corruption and fraud have been reported at least twice in these reports. Apart from the traditional risks, these are the additional risk factors investors should be concerned about in the broad market environment.

Industries exposed to higher ESG risks should also be considered in the investment process. In China, the industries most exposed to ESG risks are manufacturing, mining, transportation, financial services, construction (Syntao, 2011), extractive sectors, agriculture, forestry, animal husbandry and fishery and municipal public utilities (China SIF, 2013). Currently, most of the risky industries are heavy polluting industries, which is due to increasingly stringent pollution control standards and legal requirements, and these industries need to pay higher funding costs and loan rates than other industries.

To maximize benefits through ESG risk considerations, investors should also pay attention to the most risky companies. For instance, PetroChina, Sinopec and Foxconn have been identified as the most risky companies based on the number of ESG alerts (Syntao, 2011). Additionally, HEG Electronics (Huizhou), China National Petroleum Corporation (CNPC) and Ri-Teng Computer Accessory Co. have been reported as the most controversial companies based on scores of the highest peak RepRisk Index[17] within each country between October 2011 and October 2012 (RepRisk, 2012).

The potential risks of ESG issues are likely to impact shareholder value in both the short-term and the long-term. For instance, after the announcement of scandals such as melamine milk, fake vaccines and suicides, the share prices of these firms fell dramatically in just a few days. But even if the stock prices are able to recover after a certain period of time, the destroyed customer confidence and reputation are much harder to rebuild. Given the rapid economic development and the attractive equities return available in China, a deep understanding of ESG issues and risks will help both international and domestic investors to allocate their capital more wisely.

Suggestions for promoting RI in China

There is still a long way to go to fully develop RI in China. The following provides some suggestions and recommendations from both policy and investment perspectives.

Policy perspective

The Chinese government should take steps to publish more supportive laws and policies and formulate more appropriate standards to address ESG concerns. In order to deepen the understanding of RI, the government should foster a culture of CSR by providing more educational resources and encouraging the research and development of RI products. The government should also support professional RI service partners and guide NGOs to supervise the corporate social performance of listed companies. Most important, the government can draw lessons from other countries' successful experiences. For instance, the Chinese government could learn from the UK, which introduced a tax relief for investment in social enterprise to encourage social investment.[18]

While the 'ESG Reporting Guide' issued on 31 December 2012 by the Hong Kong Stock Exchange set out ESG subject areas, aspects, general disclosure requirements and key performance indicators (KPIs) on a level-by-level basis (HKEX, 2012), the ESG reporting guidelines published by SZSE and SSE are less comprehensive. Furthermore, all the guidelines and policies published by SZSE and SSE are voluntary, and companies have no mandatory reporting obligations. As such, both stock exchanges in China should set standardized and industry-specific reporting guidelines and encourage non-financial information disclosure. They should publish separate guidelines for listed and non-listed companies and separate voluntary and mandatory reporting contents. They should also take steps to increase the number of companies that produce mandatory CSR reports and to encourage more voluntary disclosure items. Last but not least, the stock exchanges should introduce more ESG-themed indices to provide better investment benchmarks for investors.

Since bank lending is the main financing channel of Chinese companies, setting up a comprehensive 'Green Credit' system is increasingly important. The ESG performance of companies should be carefully monitored and evaluated before loans are allocated. The relevant authorities, such as the People's Bank of China, the Ministry of Environmental Protection and the China Banking Regulatory Commission should work together to improve the efficiency of financial resource allocation, financial regulation and sustainable development.

Investment perspective

China is facing the demographic challenges of a shrinking workforce with the increased responsibility to support rising numbers of retirees, not to mention that the pension fund system is immature and lags behind the overall economic level. Reflecting the nature of long-term sustainable growth of RI, some developed countries, such as Belgium, the UK and the Netherlands, have encouraged pension funds to adopt ESG criteria in their investment process. Assuming that pension funds in China, especially China's largest pension fund, the National Social Security Fund of China (NSSF), act as the main asset owners of RI, the potential benefits could be obtaining a strong long-term growth rate of pension funds, mitigating the issue of an increasingly aging population and maintaining a stable and sustainable investment environment.

Another effective way to promote RI is to encourage state-owned enterprises (SOEs) to incorporate compliance with ESG strategies. SOEs dominate strategic sectors that are essential for China's economy, such as the oil, power and telecommunication industries. SOEs contribute a significant amount of business activity and profits in the economy, and often benefit from government policies and preferential market regulation (Li and Brodsgaard, 2013). Hence, encouraging SOEs to become champions of RI will help to speed up the RI investment process.

Last but not least, many investors in China are reluctant to invest in RI funds because they believe these investments are less profitable than conventional investments. RI is likely to represent a large percentage of the total market capitalization only if it can show the advantages. As such, investors should adjust their investment philosophy and realize the full potential by actively engaging in the RI industry.

Conclusion

Although the development of RI in China is still in the early stages, it is apparent that diverse investment opportunities will arise when ESG concepts and benefits are fully understood. RI has been attracting growing support from a wide range of stakeholders, including governmental and financial institutions, global and national organizations, institutional and individual investors and customers and communities, among others. In addition to risk considerations at the firm and industry levels,

RI guides investors to engage in monitoring ESG performance of Chinese companies and positively influencing companies' behaviour. With the conditions that companies are aware of ESG risks and take actions to consider them in operational and management goals, they are more likely to earn the confidence of current and prospective investors. For the next stage, it is believed that RI can fulfil investor's ethical goals to do good things in society while benefiting from higher financial returns.

Notes

1 For example, the Industrial Social Responsibility Securities Investment Fund considered these four criteria. Online. Available HTTP: <http://www.xyfunds.com.cn/column.do?mode=searchtopic&english=1&channelid=63&categoryid=1472> (accessed 8 January 2014).

2 Data calculated based on combined information from SSE. Online. Available HTTP: <http://edu.sse.com.cn/sseportal/en/home/home.shtml> and SZSE <http://www.szse.cn/main/en/> (accessed 14 January 2014). Calculation based on exchange rate: 1 USD = 6.0413 CNY.

3 Fund-related lists were collected from CSRC. Online. Available HTTP: <http://www.csrc.gov.cn/pub/csrc_en/participants/FundsRelatedList/> (accessed 11 January 2014).

4 A full list of issues can be found on website of Central Intelligence Agency World Factbook. Online. Available HTTP: <https://www.cia.gov/library/publications/the-world-factbook/geos/ch.html> (accessed 19 December 2013).

5 A fund of funds (FOF) is a portfolio of holdings of other investment funds. In this chapter, the CCB SSE Social Responsible Index ETF Linked Fund is a type of mutual fund FOF.

6 Data collected from Bloomberg LLC (accessed 6 January 2014). As of January 2014, the total net assets value of public funds in China was US$ 488.4 billion and all the 14 RI and ESG-themed funds together held US$3.46 billion: 3.46 divided by 488.4 equals approximately 0.7.

7 The calculations based on the ranking of each fund in Table 14.1 divided by 1,242.

8 See a full list of signatories from PRI. Online. Available HTTP: <http://www.unpri.org/signatories/> (accessed 6 January 2014).

9 See a full list of participants from China. United Nations Global Compact. Online. Available HTTP: <http://www.unglobalcompact.org/participants/search?business_type=all&commit=Search&cop_status=all&country%5B%5D=38&joined_after=&joined_before=&keyword=&listing_status_id=all&organization_type_id=&page=23&sector_id=all> (accessed 15 January 2014).

10 See China's Industrial Bank, Equator Principles Chronicle. Online. Available HTTP: <http://www.cib.com.cn/netbank/en/Sustainability/Sustainable_Finance_Chronicle/Equator_Principles_Chronicle.html> (accessed 4 September 2012).

11 See a full list of members of United Nations Environment Programme Finance Initiative. Online. Available HTTP: <http://www.unepfi.org/signatories/index.html?tx_phpadd_pi1%5bsortby%5d=country> (accessed 13 January 2014).

12 Online. Available HTTP: <https://www.chinadialogue.net/>.

13 Online. Available HTTP: <http://www.fon.org.cn/>.

14 Online. Available HTTP: <http://www.bsr.org/>.

15 Online. Available HTTP: <http://csr.stcn.com/zrtzltEN/>.

16 Online. Available HTTP: <http://www.asria.org/>.

17 The peak RRI is a risk indicator developed by RepRisk, which is a leading provider of dynamic ESG business intelligence on ESG risks for global companies. This indicator "addresses the harshness of the criticism or the gravity of the legal violations, combined with the influence of the source from which the news was taken as well as the newness of the accusation for the particular company. Companies with a peak of over 50 are considered in the high-risk category" (RepRisk, 2012: 2).

18 See the report: *Growing the Social Investment Market: 2013 Progress*. Online. Available HTTP: <https://www.gov.uk/government/uploads/system/uploads/attachment_data/file/205295/Social_Investment_Strategy_Update_2013.pdf> (accessed 21 December 2013).

References

Avantage Ventures. (2012) *China's First Social Investment Forum*. Online. Available HTTP: <http://www.avantageventures.com/chinas-first-social-investment-forum> (accessed 8 January 2014).

BSR. (2012) *Improving ESG Disclosure in China*. Online. Available HTTP: <https://www.bsr.org/en/our-insights/sustainable-investment-china-email/sustainable-investment-in-china-newsletter-q1–2012> (accessed 26 August 2012).

CBCSD. *About CBCSD*. Online. Available HTTP: <http://english.cbcsd.org.cn/aboutcbcsd/> (accessed 29 December 2013).

Chen, X. (2001) 'The definitions of ethical investment ("道德投资"的相关含义)'", *Reading (读书)*, 11: 135–183.

China Daily. (2012) *Green Credit Criteria Taking Shape*. Online. Available HTTP: <http://www.chinadaily.com.cn/business/2012–05/16/content_15311639.htm> (accessed 20 August 2012).

China SIF. (2013) *China SIF's First Survey on Socially Responsible Investment of Chinese Funds* (中国基金业责任投资调查报告). Online. Available HTTP: <http://upload.stcn.com/2013/1213/1386887779723.pdf> (accessed 29 December 2013).

CBRC. (2010) *Notice of Financial Services of Supporting Energy Saving, Emissions Reductions and Elimination of Backward Production Capacity* (关于进一步做好支持节能减排和淘汰落后产能金融服务工作的意见). Online. Available HTTP: <http://www.cbrc.gov.cn/chinese/home/docDOC_ReadView/201005310282238DB3FEF804FFE979FDCB907A00.html> (accessed 8 September 2012).

CNCA. (2012) *Notice of Guidance for Certification Bodies to Fulfil Social Responsibilities* (关于印发《认证机构履行社会责任指导意见》的通知). Online. Available HTTP: <http://www.cnca.gov.cn/cnca/zwxx/xwdt/zxtz/623383.shtml> (accessed 4 January 2014).

CNI. Online. Available HTTP: < http://www.cnindex.com.cn/en/> (accessed 4 January 2014).

CSI. Online. Available HTTP: <http://www.csindex.com.cn/sseportal_en/csiportal/indexquery.do> (accessed 10 January 2014).

CSRC. (2006) *Law of the People's Republic of China*. Online. Available HTTP: <http://www.csrc.gov.cn/pub/csrc_en/laws/rfdm/statelaws/200904/t20090428_102712.htm> (accessed 4 September 2012).

CSRC. (2013a) *CSRC Officially Promulgated the Revised Version of Guideline on The Annual Report of Listed Companies 2012*. Online. Available HTTP: < http://www.csrc.gov.cn/pub/csrc_en/newsfacts/release/201210/t20121012_215704.htm> (accessed 8 January 2014).

CSRC. (2013b) *The Rules for Corporate Governance of Securities Companies*. Online. Available HTTP: <http://www.csrc.gov.cn/pub/csrc_en/laws/overRule/Announcement/201301/t20130104_220053.htm> (accessed 8 January 2014).

Goss, A. and Roberts, G. (2011) 'The Impact of Corporate Social Responsibility on the Cost of Bank Loans', *Journal of Banking and Finance* 35: 1794–1810.

Green Watershed. (2010) *Environmental Record of Chinese Banks in 2010*. Online. Available HTTP: <http://www.banktrack.org/manage/ems_files/download/environmental_record_of_chinese_banks_2010/environmental_records_of_chinese_banks_2010_eng.pdf> (accessed 13 August 2012).

Guo, P. (2008) *Socially Responsible Investment Emerges in China*. Online. Available HTTP: <http://www.chinadialogue.net/article/show/single/en/2020-Socially-responsible-investment-emerges-in-China> (accessed 20 August 2012).

Guo, P. (2012) *The Growth of Responsible Investing in China*. Online. Available HTTP: <http://www.syntao.com/CSRNews/CSRNews_Show_EN.asp?ID=15531> (accessed 20 August 2012).

HKEX. (2012) *Environmental, Social and Governance Reporting Guide*. Online. Available HTTP: <https://www.hkex.com.hk/eng/rulesreg/listrules/mbrules/documents/appendix_27.pdf> (accessed 28 January 2014).

Kempf, A. and Osthoff, P. (2007) 'The Effect of Socially Responsible Investing on Portfolio Performance', *European Financial Management* 13, 5: 908–922.

Li, X. and Brodsgaard, K.E. (2013) 'SOE Reform in China: Past, Present And Future', *Copenhagen Journal of Asian Studies*. 31: 54–78.

Li, M. and He, J. (2002) 'Socially Responsible Investment: The Experiences of Other Countries And Its Inspirations for China (责任性投资－国外的做法及对我国的启示)', *Soft Science* (软科学) 16: 34–38.

Lin, L. (2010) 'Corporate Social Responsibility in China: Window Dressing or Structural Change', *Berkeley Journal of International Law* 28: 1–37.

Meng, X.H., Zeng, S.X. and Tam, C.M. (2013) 'From Voluntarism to Regulation: A Study on Ownership, Economic Performance and Corporate Environmental Information Disclosure in China', *Journal of Business Ethics* 116: 217–232.

MEP (2008) *The Guiding Suggestions for Listed Companies to Enhance Supervision and Management on Environment Protection* (关于加强上市公司环境保护监督管理工作的指导意见). Online. Available HTTP: <http://www.mep.gov.cn/info/gw/huanfa/200802/t20080225_118650.htm> (accessed 3 August 2012).

Morrison, W. M. (2013) *China's Economic Rise: History, Trends, Challenges, and Implications for the United States*. Online. Available HTTP: <http://www.fas.org/sgp/crs/row/RL33534.pdf> (accessed 20 December 2013).
MSCI (2012) *MSCI ESG IVA Country Report: China*. Online. Available HTTP: <http://www.msci.com/resources/pdfs/IVA_Country_Report_China_Extract.docx.pdf> (accessed 20 December 2013).
Oikonomou, I., Brooks, C. and Pavelin, S. (2014) 'The Effects of Corporate Social Performance on the Cost of Corporate Debt and Credit Ratings', *Financial Review* 49, 1: 49–75.
RepRisk (2012) *RepRisk Releases Report on Most Controversial Companies in BRIC countries*. Online. Available HTTP: <http://www.reprisk.com/downloads/specialreports/27/MCC%20BRIC%20Report%20FINAL.pdf> (accessed 20 January 2014).
SASAC (2011a) *Notice of Harmonious Development Strategy for State-Owned Enterprise (SOE) in the 12th Five-Year Plan* (关于印发《中央企业"十二五"和谐发展战略实施纲要》的通知). Online. Available HTTP: <http://www.sasac.gov.cn/n1180/n1566/n259760/n264836/14197866.html> (accessed 20 December 2013).
SASAC (2011b) *Guidelines to the State-owned Enterprises Directly under the Central Government on Fulfilling Corporate Social Responsibilities*. Online. Available HTTP: <http://www.sasac.gov.cn/n2963340/n13933222/14125651.html> (accessed 20 December 2013).
SSE (2013) *Notice on Doing Good Job in Listed Companies' Annual Reports of 2013*. Online. Available HTTP: <http://english.sse.com.cn/aboutsse/news/c/c_20140108_3762103.shtml> (accessed 20 December 2013).
Schaub, M. (2010) 'Renewable Energy Law in China', *China law insight*. Online. Available HTTP: <http://www.chinalawinsight.com/2010/06/articles/corporate/renewable-energy-law-in-china/> (accessed 27 August 2012).
Shen, B., Wang, J., Li, M., Li, J., Price, L. and Zeng, L. (2013) 'China's Approaches to Financing Sustainable Development: Policies, Practices, and Issues', *Wiley Interdisciplinary Review: Energy and Environment*, 2: 178–198.
Syntao (2011) *Revealing China's ESG Issues – 2011 – A Study of Chinese News about Companies in Connection to Environmental, Social and Governance (ESG) Issues*. Online. Available HTTP: <http://www.syntao.com/Uploads/%7B45646354-FEF3-4CD7-B3F2-91D7A4A1FB80%7D_SynTao%20ESG%20research%202011%20EN.pdf> (accessed 26 August 2012).
Syntao (2013) *A Journey to Discover Values 2012–2013: A Study of CSR Reporting in China*. Online. Available HTTP: <http://www.syntao.com/AboutUs/SyntaoNews_Show_EN.asp?ID=16579> (accessed 20 December 2013).
SZSE (2006) *Shenzhen Stock Exchange Social Responsibility Instructions to Listed Companies*. Online. Available HTTP: <http://www.szse.cn/main/en/rulseandregulations/sserules/2007060410636.shtml> (accessed 2 August 2012).
Tsing Capital. Online. Available HTTP: <http://www.cefund.com/tsingcapital_about_content.asp?pageid=3&pagename=China_Environment_Fund> (accessed 20 December 2013).
UNEP. *Renewable Energy in China*. Online. Available HTTP: <http://www.unep.org/greeneconomy/SuccessStories/RenewableEnergyinChina/tabid/29865/Default.aspx> (accessed 15 August 2012).
Weber, O. (2012) 'ESG Reporting of Chinese Companies and Responsible Investment'. working paper.
World Bank. Online. Available HTTP: <http://data.worldbank.org/indicator/NY.GDP.MKTP.KD.ZG/countries?display=default> (accessed 19 December 2013).
Yue, H. (2012) *Assuming Responsibility. Beijing Review*. Online. Available HTTP: <http://www.bjreview.com.cn/business/txt/2012-03/26/content_442022_2.htm> (accessed 2 August 2012).
Zheng, R. (2011) 'Does Social Responsible Investment Really Work? An Empirical Study on Chinese Case', working paper.
Zhou, C. (2010) 'The Development of Socially Responsible Investment and the Significance of Promoting SRI in China (社会责任投资的发展及在国内的倡导意义)' *Financial View (金融视线)*: 13–14.

Abbreviations

AHP	analytic hierarchy process
ASrIA	Association for Sustainable and Responsible Investment in Asia
BOC	Bank of China
BSR	Business for Social Responsibility

CBCSD	China Business Council for Sustainable Development
CBRC	China Banking Regulatory Commission
CIA	Central Intelligence Agency
CNCA	Certification and Accreditation Administration of the People's Republic of China
CNPC	China National Petroleum Corporation
CSI	China Securities Index Co., Ltd
CSR	corporate social responsibility
CSRC	China Securities Regulatory Commission
ESG	environmental, social and governance
EPFIs	Equator Principles Financial Institutions
ETF	exchange-traded fund
FDI	foreign direct investment
FOF	fund of funds
GDP	gross domestic product
ICBC	Industrial and Commercial Bank of China
IFC	International Finance Corporation
IPO	initial public offering
MEP	Ministry of Environmental Protection
NGOs	non-governmental organizations
NSSF	National Social Security Fund of China
PBOC	People's Bank of China
RI	responsible investment
SASAC	State-owned Assets Supervision and Administration Commission of the State Council
SEPA	State Environmental Protection Administration
SIF	Social Investment Forum
SOE	state-owned enterprises
SRI	socially responsible investment
SSE	Shanghai Stock Exchange
SSI	Shenzhen Securities Information Co., Ltd
SZSE	Shenzhen Stock Exchange
UN PRI	United Nations Principles for Responsible Investment
UNEP FI	United Nations Environment Programme Finance Initiative
UNGC	United Nations Global Compact

15

Responsible investment in Hong Kong

Christine Chow

Introduction

According to the World Federation of Exchanges, Hong Kong has the second largest stock exchange in Asia and the sixth largest stock exchange in the world (in terms of market capitalization in US$). As of August 2013, the Hong Kong Stock Exchange had 1,575 companies listed with a combined market capitalization of HK$22.66 trillion (US$2.80 trillion).

This chapter provides an overview of the current environment for responsible investment (RI) in Hong Kong,[1] followed by an analysis of the factors that have an impact on its progress, considering four selected segments of the investment industry: retail, retirement, private equity and impact investing. A number of industry experts were interviewed to gain an in depth understanding of sector specific initiatives (Appendix 15.4).

The conclusion of the chapter shows that with the support of committed stakeholders and a robust ecosystem for social innovation, impact investing is likely to lead to responsible investment in Hong Kong, with private equity managers becoming more active in taking the lead to integrate environmental, social and governance (ESG) considerations into their investments.

Overview of Hong Kong

Hong Kong is a former British colony, which became a Special Administrative Zone of the People's Republic of China in 1997. Hong Kong prides itself as Asia's World City and gateway to China. With an established history of an entrepôt, its significant role in the economic development in China has evolved over the decades and reached another milestone in September 2014 when the Hong Kong Exchanges and Clearing Limited (HKEx) signed an agreement with the Shanghai Stock Exchange (SSE) and China Securities Depository and Clearing Corporation (ChinaClear) for the establishment of Shanghai-Hong Kong Stock Connect. It is a long-waited 'through train' scheme that allows cross-border access to both markets, taking China one step closer to the liberalization of its capital account.

The regulatory environment

Companies Ordinance

The Companies Ordinance has been in an extensive public consultation process since 2006. The Companies Bill was submitted to the Legislative Council in January 2011. After 44 meetings lasting a total of 120 hours and consideration of over 200 papers or submissions, the bill was passed on 12 July 2012.[2] The many changes include strengthening the accountability of directors; clarifying directors' duties of care, skill and diligence; improving protection of minority investors' rights; improving disclosure of company information and creating a stronger audit team (OECD 2011a). Under the bill, the threshold requirement for shareholders to demand a vote at a company's general meeting would be reduced from 10 per cent to 5 per cent of the total voting rights and rules on directors' self-dealing and connected transactions would also be strengthened.[3]

The announcement that 'protected information' of directors is no longer available for public inspection under the new ordinance created public outcry in January 2013. The new rule helped to protect data privacy and personal security of individual directors; minority shareholders and creditors would have been required to assert extensive effort in order to obtain such information if they wished to have any remedy against the company or its directors. Under public pressure, the government decided to shelve this law in March 2013.

Listing rules

Related-party transactions (RPTs) are a significant corporate governance issue in Asia because the vast majority of publicly quoted companies are either family owned or state owned (Lee and De Ramos 2009) and often have diversified business interests that complement each other. RPTs often involve:

(i) Preferential terms for (a) sales of goods and services and (b) borrowing and lending;
(ii) Biased collateral valuations;
(iii) Securities issuances; and
(iv) Asset transfers, including intangibles such as trademarks and licenses.

Chapter 14A of the Hong Kong Main Board Listing Rules is dedicated to connected transactions of equity securities. The rules address governance issues arising from the aforementioned structural market constraints by empowering independent[4] shareholders through shareholder approvals on any new issue of securities and on asset transfers and continuous transactions at or above 5 per cent equity threshold (Lawrence and Smith 2011).

On environmental and social disclosure, Rule 18.05(6) requires the listing documents of mineral companies to disclose social and environmental matters, including risks arising from environmental, social and health and safety issues.

Between May and July 2011, the Hong Kong Stock Exchange organized a series of seminars and workshops on ESG reporting for listed companies.[5] The aim was to raise awareness and encourage listed companies to start ESG reporting, and to prepare them for future compliance with the *ESG Reporting Guideline*. Over 800 participants from 500 listed companies attended a total of 15 training sessions.

A consultation paper was subsequently published in December 2011 to seek comments on the proposed Guideline for issuers. The consultation process was completed in April 2012 and the associated conclusions published in August 2012. The general perception is that the Guideline[6] is a positive step towards creating data that will enable better ESG analysis over time. In terms of implementation, the Guideline is considered a recommended practice only. The exchange plans to raise the obligation level of some recommended disclosures to 'comply or explain' by 2015 for listed companies.

Codes on corporate governance

The current Code on Corporate Governance in Hong Kong was introduced in 2004. It was based on the 2003 UK Combined Code.[7]

Key recommendations of best practices include:

(i) The roles of chairman and chief executive officer should be separated;
(ii) One-third of board directors should be independent;
(iii) A majority of the members of the nomination committee should be independent non-executive directors;
(iv) Directors' remuneration should be linked to corporate and individual performance and the remuneration of senior management should be disclosed on a named basis; and,
(v) The division of responsibility between the board and management should be disclosed.

In March 2015, the Hong Kong Securities and Futures Commission (SFC) launched a three-month consultation on proposed Principles of Responsible Ownership that will provide guidance for how investors should fulfil their ownership responsibilities in relation to their investment in a listed company. Some believe that this is a timely effort to address extreme turbulence in the market, commonly known as the "A-shareisation" of the Hong Kong market.

The seven principles of responsible ownership ask investors:

- to establish and report to their stakeholders their policies for discharging their ownership responsibilities;
- to monitor and engage with their investee companies;
- to establish clear policies on when to escalate their engagement activities;
- to have clear policies on voting;
- to be willing to act collectively with other investors when appropriate;
- to report to their stakeholders on how they have discharged their ownership responsibilities; and
- when investing on behalf of clients, to have policies on managing conflicts of interests.

Different segments of the responsible investment market

The retail fund market

As of November 2013, there are 1,755 unit trusts and mutual funds registered with the Hong Kong securities regulator, the SFC. 45 funds, or 2.52 per cent of the total number of registered unit trusts, are deemed responsible investment (RI) funds.

RI funds are defined in this chapter as retail funds that:

(i) Include ESG criteria in their investment policy;
(ii) Invest according to Sharia principles; and/or
(iii) Invest in sustainability themes such as social infrastructure, resource scarcity (water, agriculture) and renewable energy.

RI funds do not include natural resources and healthcare funds unless a clear policy on investing according to ESG principles is in place.

The total assets under management (AUM) of the unit trusts and mutual funds amounted to US$1,237.62 billion as of 31 March 2013 (updated annually). The AUM of responsible investment RI funds available to retail investors amounted to US$12.03 billion. With an aggregate AUM of US$12.03 billion, RI retail funds contribute to approximately 1 per cent of the total mainstream retail fund market. International (non-Asian-origin) managers manage 38 out of 45 of these funds (see Appendix 15.1).

The first RI fund, the UBS Eco-Performance Fund, was launched in Hong Kong in 1997 (Park 2009: 209). This fund invests in large-cap global equities with good environmental and social performance records. Taifook Investment Managers, a local investment house, established the first local socially responsible investment (SRI) fund in October 2002, which invests in Asia.[8] The fund was rebranded as Haitong Socially Responsible Investment (SRI) Asia Fund in 2009 when Shanghai-based Haitong Securities took over the Hong Kong–based manager.

In July 2010, the Hang Seng Corporate Sustainability Index Series (HKCSI) was launched. The Corporate Sustainability Index Series[9] includes three indicators covering large and liquid listed companies in Hong Kong and Mainland China. The Hang Seng Corporate Sustainability Index Fund,[10] which tracks the HKCSI, was launched in 2011. It has US$20.08 million AUM as of December 2013. Asia-focused SRI funds are generally small, with less than US$20 million AUM. The general perception is that the local population is currently either unaware of, or uninterested in, RI funds.

A 2004 questionnaire targeted at specific groups within the Hong Kong population, such as the green segment, the caring segment, and women, found that religious orientation, advanced education and high income levels were positively associated with expressed interest in SRI funds in Hong Kong (Brown, Dering and Yeung 2004). Unfortunately, no comparable survey has since been conducted.

The results of this study show that those who are interested in RI funds claim they would invest based on values rather than on just the performance of the funds.[11] This suggests that there is interest in RI funds amongst the Hong Kong population based on their concerns over ESG issues, and that fund performance is not the only factor that affects investment decisions.

As the Hong Kong survey participants were biased towards intrinsic socially responsible investors, the above conclusions may suggest a sample bias and therefore not be representative of the investment attitude towards responsible investment funds for the wider population. Furthermore, the degrees of influence values and fund performance have, respectively, on investment decisions are not further assessed in this study.

One proposition would be as follows:

If (i) retail investors were obliged to make mandatory contributions to their investments, and therefore the choice of where to place their money was constrained to a selection of fund choices made available to them, and (ii) such investors would genuinely invest primarily based on values rather than performance, then there should be strong growth of SRI fund choices (supply-side mechanism) and contributions (demand-side mechanism), and possibly AUM under a mandatory savings scheme.

The retirement fund market

The Mandatory Provident Fund (MPF) system in Hong Kong was implemented in December 2000. Prior to that, only civil servants and employees of voluntary employer-sponsored retirement schemes (established under the Occupational Retirement Scheme Ordinance – ORSO) received pension benefits.

The Hong Kong retirement market is valued at HK$771 billion (US$99.49 billion) with 63.31 per cent and 36.69 per cent of assets coming from MPF and voluntary ORSO schemes, respectively (MPFA Sept. 2013).[12]

Amongst 301 pooled investment funds within 41 approved schemes, there is only one socially responsible fund option, offered by two AIA MPF schemes (Box 15.1) and managed by a third-party investment manager, Amundi. The Green Fund[13] represents 0.08 per cent of total AUM under the MPF system.

The small AUM of SRI funds in the MPF system could be explained by three factors:

(i) *Limited availability*:
Two product providers share 50 per cent of the MPF market (Appendix 15.2). SRI is not one of their fund options.

(ii) *Regional investor bias towards Hong Kong and China*:
Geographical biases of the local retirement population are reflected in the large contributions to, and AUM of, Hong Kong and China equity funds compared to other equity funds (MPFA 2011: 8 Chart III.4.2). The Green Fund, for example, invests in global equity and may therefore be less attractive to some investors.

(iii) *Risk-averse profiling bias*:
Although there are regular investment seminars by the MPFA and product providers, many members make their investment choices based on investor profiling questionnaires that come with their briefing packs or select the default choice based on age.

In a sample-profiling table, 2 out of 25 recommendations suggest investment in high-risk funds (Appendix 15.3). The Green Fund, given its 100 per cent equity and themed investment, is categorized as a high-risk fund. Five other recommendations fall into the 'medium to high' risk category. However, members are likely to follow the more conservative recommendation to invest in medium-risk funds because individual investors tend to be risk averse (Clark-Murphy and Soutar 2008) and are likely to be influenced by the risk-focused language used in the determination of their investment profile.[14] (See Box 15.1.)

Box 15.1 AIA MPF Green Fund

American International Assurance Trustee (AIA) ranks third amongst the five major MPF providers in Hong Kong, with 11 per cent market share. The top provider is HSBC with 32 per cent of the market, followed by Manulife with 17 per cent. In 1999, AIA formed an alliance with JF Asset Management (JF), one of the established "Big Three" pension fund managers in the ORSO era, to provide MPF services. Since 2005, the alliance has been broadening the investment choices of its schemes and started introducing other third-party investment managers to form a multi-manager platform.

The Green Fund option, introduced in March 2006, is provided under two of its three MPF schemes – the 'Basic' and 'Prime' Value Choice options. The underlying pooled investment fund is the Amundi HK Green Planet Fund, which is benchmarked against the MSCI World index.

There is also no concrete evidence that performance is one of the explanatory factors of lower interest in the MPF Green Fund as compared with other global equity funds because its *short- to long-term performance* is comparable to other global equity funds within the same scheme despite the fund consistently underperforming the benchmark (except in 2013),[15] and *performance is less volatile* than the country and regional specific equity funds, which falls within investor expectations with regard to risk/return profile.

Conversely, in the voluntary retirement scheme market, which is dominated by government and corporate retirement schemes, awareness of RI is high, but the adoption of ESG considerations in their investment policies has been slow. The Hong Kong Baptist University is one of the few institutional investors that have adopted a RI policy (see Box 15.2).

Box 15.2 Hong Kong Baptist University

In the past few years, Hong Kong Baptist University (HKBU) has been examining how their investment strategy can be better aligned with the values and beliefs of the institution. Sustainability is one of the values highlighted in the university's strategy plan, *Vision 2020*. In 2011, the university's investment committee decided to implement portfolio-wide screening criteria to exclude industries such as tobacco, alcohol and arms from its investments. In addition, it invested HK$18.7 million (US$2.4 million) in two RI funds as a pilot to awarding specialist RI mandates.

HKBU believes that the lack of awareness of ESG considerations and the limited number of RI fund options available have contributed to the slow adoption of responsible investment in Hong Kong. It is believed that as more universities offer courses on sustainability, social innovation, responsible banking and finance, and more case studies are provided through education and industry research, more investors will embrace responsible investment.

A number of factors explain the slow adoption of RI strategies amongst retirement funds:

Legitimized mandate

The mainstreaming of responsible investing is often prompted by government initiatives, such as regulations. In the UK,[16] proposed changes in pension regulations mandate the incorporation of ESG factors in the statement of investment policies of retirement funds.

The UK government has mandated retirement funds to disclose how ESG factors are addressed in their investment policies. There are implications to the way trustees consider their fiduciary responsibility, on two levels:

(i) *Definition*: Contrary to the traditional perception that RI would constrain the investible universe of an investment portfolio, the change in regulations legitimizes the ESG mandate, and therefore recognizes ESG considerations as part of trustees' duty to their members; and
(ii) *Practice*: By moving from opt-in to opt-out as the norm, trustees have to explain the reason for *not* including ESG considerations in their investments under the proposed regulations.

When there is no regulatory mandate and a lack of demand from institutional asset owners, established retirement fund consultants are relatively inactive in promoting RI in this market.

Lack of a concept of active ownership

There is no tradition of active ownership within the local Hong Kong institutional investor community. Where shareholder activism has become popular in Asian countries, this has been mainly due to local scandals. In India, shareholder activism grew as a reaction to stock manipulation scandals in the early 1990s. In South Korea, the People's Solidarity for Participatory Democracy (PSPD), a minority shareholder group and civil organization dedicated to promoting justice and human rights, criticized improper internal transactions at Samsung Electric in 1998, the company's board composition in 2000, and the bailout of the company's affiliated card business in 2005 (Chow 2010).

The major ESG-related scandals that have taken place in Hong Kong in recent years are related to governance (Cheung 1999, CFA 2010) and the mis-selling of financial products, such as the Lehman mini-bonds (Freshfields 2008). Mini-bonds are structured derivative products that were sold to approximately 43,700 investors, involving a total amount of US$1.8 billion. Customers complained that these products were sold to them as low-risk investments. Sixteen banks involved in the mini-bond sale eventually offered retail investors 80 per cent of the original investment from the underlying collateral.[17] (See Box 15.3.)

Box 15.3 What are the most pressing issues – E, S or G?

Based on interviews conducted for this study, corporate governance is widely recognised as the most pressing issue amongst ESG considerations by government and institutional investors. This is supported by academic literature with in-depth studies on: (a) how corporate governance can be put into practice within the constraints of family-owned shareholding structures and weak legal protection for minority shareholders that encourage connected transactions and discourage disclosure and transparency (Cheung 1999; Ho 2003) and (b) the correlation between corporate governance and market valuation for listed companies in Hong Kong and Greater China (Lei and Song 2008; Cheung et al. 2011).

Further academic studies on the correlation between environmental and social performance and financial performance using data relevant to the Hong Kong and China market will encourage a holistic approach to responsible investment.

An enquiry into the sale of mini-bonds prompted the Hong Kong Monetary Authority (HKMA), the local banking regulator, to propose that lenders physically separate deposit taking and investment businesses at their branches and record all conversations related to sales of investment products. The Securities and Futures Commission (SFC), the local securities regulator, has proposed improvements in the existing regulatory framework for unlisted investment products to safeguard investor interests.

There is little evidence to suggest that shareholders of mis-selling banks have sufficiently exercised their rights to put pressure on these banks to improve their risk management, internal control and disclosure. The concept of shareholder actions, such as class actions or derivative suits,[18] is not well developed in most Asian jurisdictions (Lee and de Ramos 2009). Foreign fund managers usually engage privately (OECD 2011a), as sanctions such as private reprimands and public censure are deemed inadequate to strengthen transparency and disclosure in Hong Kong (OECD 2011b). A shareholder association was established in 1999, namely the Hong Kong Institute of Investors;[19] however, visible activities such as collective shareholder proposals remain uncommon.

Market structure constraints

The family and cross-holdings share ownership model dominates the business landscape in Hong Kong, similar to some of its other Asian counterparts, such as South Korea. The National Pension Scheme (NPS) in South Korea, one of the PRI signatories, acknowledged that their shareholder influence is limited at times due to the circular ownership nature of domestic enterprises.[20] The same situation applies in Hong Kong.

Analysts find that if they ask too many difficult questions on ESG issues, especially in relation to governance, their access to management is cut off. However, there are also selective cases where companies actively engage in ESG discussions as they realize that their investor base is becoming more international, and that they need to meet best practices and expectations from the international investment community. There are also Chinese state-owned companies that advocate corporate social responsibility as a means of fulfilling their wider mission of maintaining social stability.

At the moment, commitment to RI by some of the biggest public pension funds outside of the region is most likely to create momentum as they seek to expand their portfolio exposure in Asia for yield enhancement and diversification. Some of these funds, including those in emerging markets such as Brazil and Thailand, have published information about how they put RI into practice (UNEP FI et al. 2007). They have become the 'champion' funds, significant shareholders with an interest in RI who are stepping forward as advocates of the practice.

Lack of local champions

In comparison to other markets in the region, Hong Kong *lacks local 'champion' asset owners* that are willing to take lead in promoting RI. As corporate pension funds are still in their infancy in China, the commitment to RI by one of the established retirement or endowment funds in Hong Kong, such as the Hospital Authority Provident Fund, or Prominent Government-Related Funds (GLFs), the National Social Security Fund (NSSF) or China Investment Corporation (CIC) would send a strong signal to the market to embrace RI.

Asset classes leading the adoption of RI in Hong Kong include private equity and impact investments (or 'impact alpha').

The private equity market

In 2013, the total private equity capital under management (CUM) in Asia totalled US$797 billion under 2,000 funds.[21] Together, Mainland China and Hong Kong manage just under half of the total private equity in Asia.[22] Hong Kong ranked second, accounting for 21.6 per cent of the Asian total, slightly behind Mainland China's 22.6 per cent and ahead of Japan's 14.2 per cent. The main investors in private equity projects include international insurance companies, development financing institutions (DFIs) such as the International Finance Corporations, GLFs such as the National Social Security Fund (NSSF), Temasek and private investors.

PRI signatories in Hong Kong are mostly service providers and private equity (PE) companies. Large PEs perform ESG audits in their investment processes for initial screening, interim evaluations and final due diligence, guided and encouraged by their Limited Partners (LPs). This applies particularly if the LP is a DFI. Key ESG risks are identified with corresponding improvement and mitigation procedures.

The argument for responsible investing in PE is strong because it:

(i) *Is legitimate*: Many PE managers have significant shareholder holdings and sit on company boards. They have the legitimacy and power to be engaged and active as investors. However, compared to their US or European counterparts, Asian PEs tend to take minority stakes in their deals, reducing the legitimate power they have on board decisions;
(ii) *Creates value*: Sustainable management of companies enhances exit premiums; and
(iii) *Manages risks*: Managing ESG risks can avoid high impact costs such as regulatory charges and lawsuits due to failures in corporate governance, labour disputes, and environmental penalties, amongst others. A key example was the milk power crisis of Sanlu Group. Fonterra, a New Zealand-based group that owned 43 per cent of Sanlu, was forced to take a 60 per cent write down of their investments (Rotherham and Russell 2009). After the milk scandal, Mainland Chinese who could afford to travel beyond the borders began purchasing milk products and other foodstuffs abroad, bringing them back to China for sale or personal use. This trend had since driven up local prices of food staples near the Shenzhen-Hong Kong border, and prompted community actions against cross-border traders who seek to profit from it.

Amongst PE projects, infrastructure investments comprise one sector with high potential for contributing to responsible investment. According to the Former US Secretary of State Madeleine Albright, these facilities are fundamental to the prosperity of a society,[23] especially in urbanized and urbanizing areas, such as growing cities and satellite towns in Asia, where rapidly expanding populations are putting a strain on local resources and infrastructure.

The state has traditionally been responsible for the provision of infrastructure, but increasingly the private sector is engaging in infrastructure activities. Infrastructure services mainly benefit the local population of the area in which they are built or based. The success of this investment is closely linked to the sustainability of the society that it serves. Furthermore, as noted by the Chairman of CIC, Lou Jiwei, "Investment opportunities lie in areas like infrastructure and industrial projects, as they can help economic recovery".[24]

Local governments want infrastructure investments to be built to last, with minimum negative environmental and social impact, and to be well-governed and well run by operators post-construction. Capacity estimates, planning scenarios and durability of physical assets involved in these projects cover a long-term period of no fewer than 20–30 years. As such, infrastructure presents a strong case for responsible investment through its function of creating a social good, provided the technologies used are sustainably developed, and implementation is managed prudently, for example by not displacing the local population without appropriate compensation and by adhering to the highest safety and environmental standards.

Infrastructure can be broadly categorized into three types:

(i) *Social infrastructure*:
Public facilities such as schools and hospitals to support the well-being of the local population;
(ii) *Utilities*:
Energy, water and waste management facilities to enable basic functioning of the society; and
(iii) *Transport*:
Mass transport systems, toll roads and railways to encourage trade and mobility of labour and resources.

In 2010, Robeco and the Tianjin government announced that they would jointly raise a US$500 million fund – the Robeco TEDA Sustainable Private Equity Fund. The fund intended to invest in energy, water, pollution and waste treatment projects that encourage the productive use of resources with reduced negative environmental impact.

In December 2013, Sustainable Development Capital (SDCL) teamed up with First Eastern Investment Group to launch a US$200 million fund that invests in energy-efficiency projects in the UK and China.[25]

Considerable investment opportunities are presented in different parts of the value-chain of green projects, from construction materials to the stable cash flow that completed infrastructure can offer (see Box 15.4).

Box 15.4 Baring Private Equity Asia

Baring Private Equity Asia is one of the largest and most established independent private equity firms in Asia, in operation since 1997. It has six funds with committed capital of close to US$10 billion. The firm runs a pan-Asian investment programme, specialising in mid-market companies needing capital for expansion, recapitalisation and acquisitions.

Baring has a strong interest in education investment opportunities in emerging markets, believing that it is one of the high-impact sectors that generate social and financial value for its stakeholders. Once it has passed initial screening, ESG considerations of a potential investment target are included in the investment recommendation paper for investment approval by the Investment Committee. After the investment is made, the ESG issues raised during the due diligence process are passed on to the operations and management team to implement and monitor.

Taking an integrated approach in evaluating ESG value add to the investment proposition presents new perspectives and investment opportunities, as compared with the traditional ESG audit approach.

The impact investing market

In 2006, the Hong Kong government earmarked a sum of HK$150 million for the following five years to provide grants for social enterprise projects and established the Enhanced Self-Reliance (ESR) Programme. The Central Policy Unit commissioned a conceptual model study to compare the different social enterprise models in the UK, US and Spain, in order to formulate policy recommendations on a suitable social enterprise model for Hong Kong (Tang et al. 2008).

By November 2012, the government had stepped up its support for social enterprises by setting up a HK$500 million Social Innovation and Entrepreneurship Development Fund. The exact mandate of this fund has yet to be finalized, but it is likely to be used for ecosystem building, possibly including a funding platform for social enterprises with opportunities for matching capital from the non-public sector.[26] It may also test the feasibility of new financial instruments, such as social impact bonds (SIBs), to harness the power of financial markets for positive social impact.

There are approximately 350 social enterprises in Hong Kong with 1,695 employees, 68 per cent, or 1,160, originating from socially disadvantaged populations.[27] The government offers a HK$3 million funding ceiling for a maximum of three years for each approved project to promote sustainable poverty prevention and alleviation, and a HK$2 million funding ceiling for a maximum of two years to enhance the employment of people with disabilities.[28] (See Box 15.5.)

Box 15.5 The University of Hong Kong (HKU) – 'EXCEL3' project

The University of Hong Kong launched a programme on the 'third sector' – the sector between businesses and non-governmental organisations. It soft launched the 'Excel3' project in June 2011 with support from the Hong Kong Jockey Club Foundation and the University of Hong Kong. Its objective is to provide a platform for research, training and education to encourage the growth of the 'third sector' and public governance.

Research focuses on establishing competency models, theory on philanthropic giving and practical assessment tools for measuring the impact of social enterprises at the project and organisational levels. Training covers two segments: (i) foundation/investor executives on investment opportunities, business assessment and impact monitoring criteria; and (ii) social entrepreneurs on capacity building, value creation and sector-based self-evaluation groups. Education focuses on creating a global case bank for innovative social enterprises working with other universities, such as Indiana University, and planning a degree course on the subject. The project was officially launched in May 2012.

Local foundations, the academic community, individual philanthropists and family offices from the high net worth (HNW) community have also been driving impact investing. The Hong Kong Social Enterprise Challenge[29] is a social venture business plan competition organized by The Chinese University of Hong Kong, which is open to the public and encourages the adoption of entrepreneurial approaches to solving social problems (see Box 15.6).

Box 15.6 First student-driven venture philanthropy fund

The Hong Kong University of Science and Technology (HKUST) launched an elective course targeted at its MBA students on Venture Philanthropy and Social Entrepreneurship in March 2013, with the financial support of the Yeh Family Philanthropy.

It is an experiential learning course with the objective of providing the students a unique opportunity to come face to face with leading impact investors in Hong Kong and China and to be part of a multidisciplinary team that helps to solve real-life social problems through business.

Students are asked to conduct due diligence on businesses that they wish to work with. Their deliverables include a funding pitch for an amount of HK$250,000 (US$32,000) to be awarded to the winning enterprise at the end of the course. The course currently runs every spring term.

An example of a successful social enterprise – defined as 'financially self-sustainable' – is the Senior Citizen Home Safety Association (SCHSA). It was established in 1996, and had annual turnover of HK$100 million (US$13 million) in 2013. Twenty per cent of its funding comes from charity fund raising and 80 per cent from service charges.[30]

SCHSA provides a 24-hour Personal Emergency Link (PE Link) service for the elderly and people in need of emergency support or emotional counselling services (HKSAR 2010). The elderly constitute 13 per cent of Hong Kong residents; 11.6 per cent of them live alone, and 21.2 per cent live with their elderly spouse.[31] The PE Link therefore serves a vulnerable and growing segment of the local population.

Dialogue in the Dark is a social franchise that employs visually impaired people. It offers experiences in the dark through events such as exhibitions, wine tastings, concerts, parties and corporate training and education activities. The enterprise became financially self-sustainable within two years in Hong Kong.[32]

The Hong Kong Social Enterprise Forum, a civil society initiative founded in 2008, conducts regular seminars to engage with potential investors, academics, young entrepreneurs and the general public.[33] The annual Social Enterprise Summit, founded in the same year, has attracted world-class speakers and increased awareness surrounding and the sophistication of impact investing.[34] Education for Good, a training institute for social entrepreneurs founded by the founder of the forum, Dr. KK Tse, was established in 2012.

Social Ventures Hong Kong (SVhk),[35] established in 2007, supports and nurtures successful social enterprises in Hong Kong. It supports enterprises such as 'Diamond Cabs', which operates as a management agent liaising between drivers and taxi license owners to provide a readily available fleet of wheelchair-friendly cabs. SVhk also launched the 'Light be' social enterprise to provide affordable housing to single-parent and disadvantaged families in Hong Kong where property and rental prices are extremely high.[36]

Other non-profit organizations such as Sow Asia,[37] Ventures in Development (ViD)[38] and the Asia Community Ventures,[39] networking organizations such as Asian Venture Philanthropy Network (AVPN),[40] and advisory firms such as Asia Value Advisors[41] also participate in efforts to promote social investment. There is considerable momentum within government, academia and civil society in support of social enterprises (Alto and Ming 2013).

The main challenges in encouraging impact investing are:

(a) *Few financially self-sustainable enterprises*: According to a Legislative Council paper released in January 2012,[42] only one-third of social enterprises achieve or exceed their target to become financially self-sustainable;
(b) *Market mismatch*: An increasing amount of investor capital has become available in recent years, but good and scalable projects are hard to find (SVhk 2011). Impact investors in Asia tend to be HNW individuals who have particular expectations and interests in terms of geographical locations and sectors. The primary aim of these enterprises is to create social capital, but different investors place varying degrees of importance on impact-first or sustainability-first value propositions. Finding the correct impact/sustainability profile to meet both the needs of the enterprise and of investors is challenging;
(c) *Lack of track record*: In order to attract more capital, such as capital from institutional investors, impact investing will have to fit into the asset allocation processes of these institutions. There is insufficient information on the risk and return characteristics of available impact investments as many of them are early stage enterprise investments, with an investment horizon of 5–10 years. As time goes by, more track record data will become available as business exits become more common, thereby providing further information for decision support; and
(d) *Measurement of success*: The impact of social enterprises cannot be totally captured by common financial metrics used in traditional financial analysis. Alternative measurement analysis tools, such as social return on investment (SROI)[43] exist, but the investment community continues to seek other methods of holistic assessment.

Recommendations that will encourage impact investing are:

(a) *More academic and industry research* to raise awareness and understanding, and to explore practical and cost-effective methods to measure the value-add of social impact. With improved quality of data metrics and tools, such as Impact Reporting and Investment Standards (IRIS) from the Global Impact Investment Network (GIIN)[44] and the Global Impact Investing Rating System (GIIRS),[45] more capital may enter the market (O'Donohoe 2010);

(b) *Private sector collaboration* with active participation of the private sector – through private capital and business talent – to add business acumen to social enterprises, helping to address issues such as scalability and replicability; and
(c) *Lead by example*, with government and government-related organizations taking a lead in purchasing the products and services of social enterprises, which is a growing trend; and
(d) *Build soft infrastructure for crowd funding* through guidelines on the legal framework that governs the rapidly growing crowd-funding platforms; they will build confidence and provide investor protection, encouraging more individuals to participate in the impact revolution.

Facilitators and key players

Unlike in Australia, the UK, the US and Continental Europe, where asset owners are the major drivers in the RI market, those who are driving RI awareness and practice in Hong Kong are foreign fund managers, professional services firms and non-governmental organizations (NGOs). Informal conversations with major insurance players in Hong Kong, such as AIA, SunLife, and Manulife, suggest that ESG factors have not been significant considerations in their investment processes.

Broker analysts such as CLSA and HSBC provide vital ESG research to the investor community. HSBC Global Asset Management has a global intranet research platform for its analysts around the world with access to third-party ESG ratings and back-testing datasets (HSBC 2013). Table 15.1 summarizes the key groups playing a role in the RI market in Hong Kong.

Conclusion

Four areas of the responsible investment industry in Hong Kong have been examined in this chapter, namely retail, institutional, private equity and impact investing.

Over the last 10 years, the Hong Kong government has been focusing on improving corporate governance and the corporate social responsibility of companies, seeking to lead disclosure and transparency standards in both Hong Kong and Mainland China. Company and investor interest in environmental, social and governance (ESG) issues may increase if and when ESG disclosure begins upon the formal introduction of the *ESG Reporting Guideline*, especially if the level of obligation is to 'comply or explain', similar to the Codes on Corporate Governance.

Academic research on governance by local universities has raised awareness of the importance of governance, and has encouraged the improvement of corporate governance standards. Expansion of the scope of RI research into social and environmental areas and impact investing will accelerate the mainstreaming of responsible investment.

This chapter has identified three factors that have contributed to the small fund size of retirement savings under the Mandatory Provident Fund (MPF) scheme:

(i) *Limited availability*, as products on offer are constrained by scheme participation;
(ii) *An asset allocation bias* towards Hong Kong and China, whilst the only RI fund on offer is in global equity; and
(iii) *The risk-averse nature of individual investors*, encouraged by risk-biased profiling assessments offered by providers.

The chapter has also identified four factors that have contributed to the sluggish growth in RI in the institutional market in Hong Kong, as follows:

(i) Lack of a legitimized mandate encouraged and validated by regulatory changes;
(ii) Lack of a concept of active ownership;
(iii) Structural market constraints due to shareholding structures, and;
(iv) Lack of local champions for RI. An influential champion can lead the creation of a critical mass to adopt RI, as evidenced in South Korea, Thailand and Malaysia.

Considerable momentum for RI is witnessed in:

(i) Private equity, especially in infrastructure and education projects capitalizing on urbanization trends in Mainland China; and
(ii) Impact investing, with noted government, academic and civil society support. It is generating a robust business ecosystem of its own that is rapidly integrating into the mainstream venture capital space.

There are some promising developments in the impact investment space. In order for an industry to flourish, a few factors have to work together (as demonstrated in Figure 15.1).

Clear government incubating policies, a proactive group of investors creating the critical mass including drivers from the HNW individuals, family offices, corporate philanthropy and endowments, a supportive civil society, high-profile and positive media exposure, sustainable 'showcase' enterprises and robust academic and research communities must be engaged in creating the environment for responsible investment. They are all key success factors for growth in this emerging asset class.

Impact investing is likely to continue in the form of specialized segments of the RI industry for some time, but the successful case studies produced that demonstrate the generation of financial return and social good will continue to inspire the wider investor community to invest responsibly.

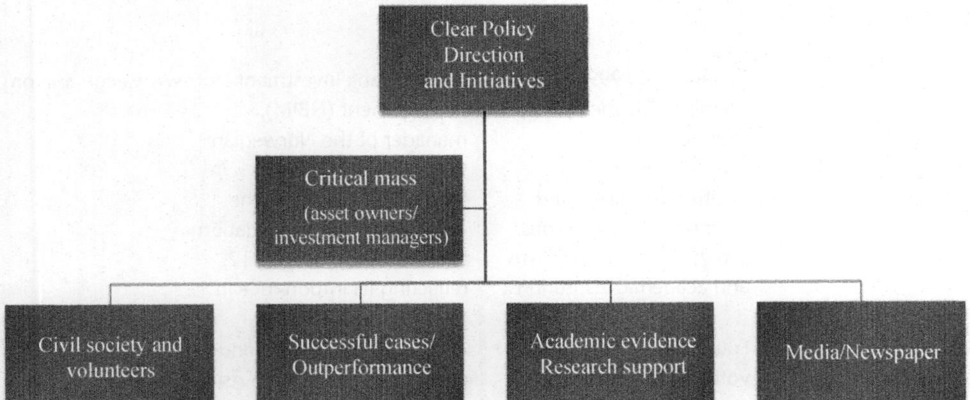

Figure 15.1 Vital factors that enable responsible investment to flourish

Table 15.1 Key players in responsible investment in Hong Kong

Institution	*Details (as of Dec. 2013)*	*Key Contributions*	*Website*
Fund managers			
BNP Paribas (Parvest unit trust funds)	A PRI signatory since 2006. Over 60 investment professionals on the sustainable investment team.	Established the first Asian environmental equity fund (Green Tiger) and the first Greater China Environmental Fund.	www.bnpparibas-ip.com.hk
Amundi	A PRI signatory since 2006. Launched and manages ethical funds, solidarity funds, social business funds and development aid funds.	Manages the only ESG fund in the mandatory savings MPF retirement market.	www.amundi.com/hkg/
BlackRock	A PRI signatory since 2008. Over 20 investment professionals on the corporate governance and responsible investment team.	Mainstream manager with significant assets in indexed funds. Engages on material ESG issues to fulfill fiduciary duty, consequently improving companies' ESG expectations.	www.blackrock.com
Professional services firms			
CSR Asia	Founded in 2004 to provide information, training and consultancy services on sustainable business practices in Asia.	A self-sustainable social enterprise demonstrates that there is established and growing demand for CSR services in Asia.	www.csr-asia.com
SustainAsia	Founded in 2004 to provide investment advisory on sustainability and clean technology, especially on environmental and energy infrastructure projects.	An independent advisory firm. Derives revenue from investors, corporations, other consulting forms and green technology companies.	www.responsibleresearch.com
Associations/NGOs			
Asia Corporate Governance Association (ACGA)	Founded in 1999 with 91 members. Its members include institutional investors, financial institutions (banks and insurance), corporations, professional services firms and academic institutions.	Norges Bank Investment Management (NBIM), manager of the Norwegian Government Pension Fund Global, became the association's first Foundation sponsor in February 2012, reflecting its importance in driving RI in Asia.	www.acga-asia.org
Association for Sustainable and Responsible Investment in Asia (ASrIA)	Founded in 2001 with 61 voting and supporting members. Its members include institutional investors, banks, professional services firms and NGOs.	ASrIA conducts events and provides RI research on Asia. It has been involved in the Carbon Disclosure Project (CDP) since 2005.	www.asria.org

Social Ventures Hong Kong (SVhk)	Established in 2007, a venture philanthropic organization aiming to provide financial and non-financial support to social purpose organizations or enterprises.	Major impact investor in Hong Kong with 14 companies in its portfolio.	www.sv-hk.org

Source: Homage Consulting.

Notes

1 Responsible investment in Hong Kong covers both sustainable investment philosophy and strategic sectors. Sustainable investment philosophy takes into consideration the non-financial information of companies, such as environmental, social and governance issues in valuation. Strategic sectors include infrastructure, clean energy, affordable housing, elderly care, education, waste management, agribusiness, green building and facilities and sustainable consumption, amongst others.

2 Online. Available HTTP: <http://www.cr.gov.hk/en/publications/docs/ec5–2012-annex-e.pdf>.

3 According to the paper LC Paper No. CB(1)1406/10–11(01) *Bills Committee on Companies Bill* by the Legislative Council. 24 February 2011.

4 HKEX Rule 14A.10(5): 'Independent shareholder' means any shareholder of the listed issuer that is not required to abstain from voting at a general meeting to approve a connected transaction.

5 Online. Available HTTP: <http://www.hkex.com.hk/eng/newsconsul/hkexnews/2011/110923news.htm>; <http://www.hkex.com.hk/eng/rulesreg/listrules/listsptop/esg/Documents/seminar_slides.pdf> and <http://www.hkex.com.hk/eng/rulesreg/listrules/listsptop/esg/Documents/ws_slides.pdf> (accessed 19 February 2012) (Source: Hong Kong Stock Exchange).

6 Online. Available HTTP: <https://www.hkex.com.hk/eng/rulesreg/listrules/mbrules/documents/appendix_27.pdf>.

7 Based on a presentation at the International Finance Corporation IO Training given by Mr. Patrick Convoy, the Chief Operating Officer of the HK Exchange and Clearing Limited on 30 April 2004.

8 Excluding Japanese equities.

9 Online. Available HTTP: <http://www.hsi.com.hk/HSI-Net/HSI-Net> (accessed 28 February 2012). The three indices include: (i) Hang Seng Corporate Sustainability Index ('HKCSI'), with 30 constituent holdings; (ii) Hang Seng (China A) Corporate Sustainability Index, with 15 constituent holdings and (iii) Hang Seng (Mainland and Hong Kong) Corporate Sustainability Index, with 40 constituent holdings.

10 Bloomberg stock code is HSCSUSI:KY (accessed 28 February 2012).

11 According to the 2004 survey, 47 to 79 per cent of the different income groups ranging from the bottom (under HK$10,000) to the top (over HK$60,000) would consider investing in SRI funds. The 2004 results are the latest available, as the study has not been repeated since.

12 ORSO was introduced in 1993 to govern voluntary occupational retirement schemes in Hong Kong, prior to the introduction of MPF.

13 The Green Fund aims to provide investors with long-term capital appreciation through well-diversified investments in global equities principally by investing in companies according to (i) their environmental ratings and (ii) financial performance expectations, with a view to outperforming the MSCI World Index over the medium to long term.

14 The investment profile table is translated as the 'investment risk table' in the Chinese version of the questionnaire.

15 Online. Available HTTP: <http://www.mpfratings.com.hk/media/FCRSdec11> (accessed 28 February 2012).

16 In 1999, the amendment of the UK Pensions Act require a pension fund's Statement of Investment Principles (SIP) to include "the extent (if at all) to which social, environmental, or ethical considerations are taken into account in the selection, retention and realisation of investments".

17 Master 2011 HK banks agree on resolution for Lehman mini bonds *Reuters* 27 March 2011.

18 Class actions take place when a group of shareholders sue board members directly for damages suffered by all shareholders. Derivative lawsuits take place when one or more shareholders file suit on behalf of the company against the board members to recover losses (OECD 2011a).
19 Online. Available HTTP: <www.hkii.org>.
20 Based on the materials presented by Mr. Jung Jae Young of Korea's National Pension Scheme at Asia Future Forum 2011 on 16 November 2011.
21 Asian Private Equity and Venture Capital Review 2013.
22 Speech by the Secretary for Financial Services and the Treasury in Hong Kong, Professor K C Chan at the 24th annual Asia Venture Capital Journal Hong Kong Forum: Investment Summit 2011 on 9 November 2011. Online. Available HTTP: <http://www.info.gov.hk/gia/general/201111/09/P201111090156.htm> (accessed 23 February 2012).
23 "Infrastructure by its nature is basic to the functioning of society" Madeleine Albright, former US Secretary of State and founder of Albright Stonebridge Group. McKinsey & Co. estimated that to keep pace with growth the world needs US$57 trillion investment in infrastructure through to 2030. Online. Available HTTP: <http://www.mckinsey.com/features/infrastructure>.
24 Qingden D (2012) 'New Capital for CIC to Acquire European Assets', *China Daily* 5 March.
25 Woodman A (2013) 'SDCL Launches $200m UK-China Energy Efficiency Fund', *Asian Venture Capital Journal* 4 December. Online. Available HTTP: <http://www.avcj.com/avcj/news/2316887/sdcl-launches-usd200m-uk-china-energy-efficiency-fund> (accessed 5 December 2013).
26 Based on various discussions that the author of this paper has had with the board members of the Social Innovation and Entrepreneurship Development Fund.
27 According to the Social Welfare Department, the 'disadvantaged population' includes the elderly, mentally and physically impaired, abused women, unemployed youths, offenders, new immigrants and ethnic minorities.
28 Online. Available HTTP: <www.social-enterprises.gov.hk>.
29 Online. Available HTTP: <http://entrepreneurship.baf.cuhk.edu.hk/content/hong-kong-social-enterprise-challenge-1>.
30 SCHSA is one of the right enterprises that won the 2011 Outstanding Social Enterprises Award. Online. Available HTTP: <http://www.se-award.hk/en/awardees_info.html>.
31 Data from the Hong Kong Council of Social Service.
32 Source: Hong Kong Social Enterprise Forum and Mr Patrick Cheung, Chairman of Dialogue in the Dark.
33 Online. Available HTTP: <http://www.hksef.org/>.
34 Online. Available HTTP: <http://www.social-enterprise.org.hk/>.
35 Online. Available HTTP: <http://www.sv-hk.org/index.php>.
36 Online. Available HTTP: <http://www.lightbe.hk/>.
37 Online. Available HTTP: <www.sowasia.org>.
38 Online. Available HTTP: <www.facebook.com/pages/Ventures-in-Development/79517264882>.
39 Online. Available HTTP: <www.asiacommunityventures.org>.
40 Online. Available HTTP: <http://www.avpn.asia/>.
41 Online. Available HTTP: <http://value.asia/home>.
42 According to the paper LC Paper No. CB(2)717/11–12(05) *Panel on Welfare Services: Background Brief Prepared by the Legislative Council Secretariat* for the meeting on 9 January 2012.
43 Online. Available HTTP: <http://www.thesroinetwork.org>.
44 Online. Available HTTP: <http://iris.thegiin.org/>.
45 Online. Available HTTP: <http://giirs.org/>.

References

Alto, P. and Ming Wong, P. (2013) *Mind the Gap: Lessons and Findings from EngageHK*, Asia Community Ventures and RS Group.

Brown, M., Dering, A. and Yeung, H. (2004) *The Case for SRI Funds: Hong Kong Investors Fit the Profile*, Association for Sustainable & Responsible Investment in Asia (ASrIA), Hong Kong.

CFA (2010) *Shareholder Rights in Asia: Are Shareholders Flexing their Muscles to Protect Themselves?* CFA Institute.

Cheung, Y. L., Connelly, J. T., Jiang, P. and Limpaphaayom, P. (2011) 'Does Corporate Governance Predict Future Performance? Evidence from Hong Kong', *Financial Management* Spring, 159–197.

Cheung, Y. L. (1999) 'Corporate Governance in Hong Kong, China: Rising to the Challenge of Globalization', *Rising to the Challenge in Asia: A Study of Financial Markets*, Volume 3 Sound Practices, Asian Development Bank, 1–19.

Chow, C. (2010) 'Cross Country Comparison of Shareholder Engagement for Responsible Investment' Ph.D. Thesis, University of Melbourne.

Clark-Murphy, M. and Soutar, G. N. (2008) 'Do Retail Stock Brokers Understand Clients' Investment Preferences?', *Journal of Financial Services Marketing* 13(2): 135–149.

O'Donohoe, N., Leijonhufvud, C. and Saltuk, Y. (2010) 'Impact Investments: An Emerging Asset Class', *JP Morgan Global Research*, 29 November.

Freshfields (2008) *Briefing: An Overview of the Lehman Brothers Minibonds Saga*, Freshfields Bruckhaus Deringer, 16 December. Online (accessed 2 March 2012).

HKSAR (2010) *20 Business Strategies for Social Enterprises*, Home Affairs Bureau, The Government of the Hong Kong Special Administrative Region. Online (accessed 1 March 2012).

Ho S. (2003) 'Corporate Governance in Hong Kong: Key Problems and Prospects', *CUHK Centre for Accounting Disclosure and Corporate Governance Research Paper No. 1*. Online (accessed 29 February 2012).

HSBC (2013) *How Does ESG Fit in our Investment Process*, September.

Lawrence, M. and Smith, D. (2011) *Around the World in 80 Trades: Approaches to Related-Party Transactions*, Institutional Shareholder Services.

Lee, K. L. and De Ramos, A. (2009) *Related-Party Transactions: Cautionary Tales for Investors in Asia*, Centre for Financial Market Integrity, CFA Institute.

Lei, A. and Song, F. (2008) *Corporate Governance, Family Ownership and Firm Valuations in Emerging Markets: Evidence from Hong Kong*. Online (accessed 29 February 2012).

MPFA (2011) *Mandatory Provident Fund Schemes Statistical Digest*, Mandatory Provident Fund Schemes Authority, December.

OECD (2011a) *Corporate Governance in Asia: Asia Roundtable on Corporate Governance*, OECD Publishing.

OECD (2011b) *Corporate Governance in Asia: Progress and Challenges Corporate Governance*, OECD Publishing.

Park, J. (2009) 'Sustainable Consumption and the Financial Sector: Analysing the Markets for Responsible Investment in Hong Kong and Japan', *International Journal of Consumer Studies* 33: 206–214.

Rotherham, T. and Russell, D. (2009) 'Trends in Responsible Investment in Private Equity', *UNPRI December 2009 Newsletter*, special feature. Online (accessed 23 February 2012).

SVhk (2011) *Money for Good: Global Trends and Local Potentials in Engaged Giving and Social Investing*, Social Ventures Hong Kong, November.

Tang, K. L., Fung, H. L., Au, K., Lee J. and Ko, L. (2008) *Social Enterprises in Hong Kong: Toward a Conceptual Model. Central Policy Unit*. Online (accessed 29 February 2012).

UNEP FI, AMWG, UKSIF and SPP (2007) *Responsible Investment in Focus: How Leading Public Pension Funds Are Meeting the Challenge*, United Nations Environment Programme Finance Initiative (UNEP FI). Online (accessed 1 March 2012).

Appendices

Appendix 15.1 Responsible investment funds registered in Hong Kong – retail unit trusts (in chronological order)

Fund name	Fund authorized in Hong Kong	Total fund size as of 30 Sep 2013 unless otherwise stated (AUM in US$ m)	Benchmark	1 year as of 4 Dec 2013 (%)	3 year as of 4 Dec 2013* (%)	5 year as of 4 Dec 2013* (%)
Benchmarks (as of 4 Dec 2013):						
MSCI World Index	*NA*	*NA*	*NA*	*21.87*	*27.45*	*97.09*
MSCI Asia Pacific ex Japan	*NA*	*NA*	*NA*	*4.03*	*3.05*	*114.12*
MSCI World Energy	*NA*	*NA*	*NA*	*–6.43*	*–19.19*	*42.26*
DAX Global Agribusiness	*NA*	*NA*	*NA*	*–8.24*	*–22.61*	*28.44*
1. Invesco Energy Fund	Mar 2001	192.68	MSCI World Energy	20.17	4.12	67.85
2. BlackRock (BGF) New Energy Fund (as of 31 Oct 2013)	Mar 2001	1,449.41	MSCI World	25.40	1.05	23.77
3. Haitong SRI Asia Fund (as of 31 Jul 2013)	Oct 2002	2.40	MSCI Far East ex Japan	7.15	–0.20	91.73
4. Invesco Asia Infrastructure Fund	Feb 2006	1,040.36	MSCI Asia Pacific ex Japan	–0.69	–9.95	69.34
5. Amundi Hong Kong Green Planet Fund	Mar 2006	46.66	MSCI World	26.50	33.79	94.95

Benchmarks (as of 4 Dec 2013):						
MSCI World Index	*NA*	*NA*	*NA*	*21.87*	*27.45*	*97.09*
MSCI Asia Pacific ex Japan	*NA*	*NA*	*NA*	*4.03*	*3.05*	*114.12*
MSCI World Energy	*NA*	*NA*	*NA*	*–6.43*	*–19.19*	*42.26*
DAX Global Agribusiness	*NA*	*NA*	*NA*	*–8.24*	*–22.61*	*28.44*

Fund name	**Fund authorized in Hong Kong**	**Total fund size as of 30 Sep 2013 unless otherwise stated (AUM in US$ m)**	**Benchmark**	**1 year as of 4 Dec 2013 (%)**	**3 year as of 4 Dec 2013* (%)**	**5 year as of 4 Dec 2013* (%)**
6. Schroder Alternative Solutions Agriculture Fund	Mar 2007	351.41	Rogers International Commodity Agriculture	–15.43	–23.07	6.84
7. Amundi Equity Global Aqua Fund	Mar 2007	49.97	MSCI World	19.97	29.29	86.19
8. Aberdeen Global Responsible World Equity Fund	Mar 2007	151.33	MSCI World	13.75	24.44	100.90
9. Lyxor Dynamic Water Fund (as of 25 Sep 2013)	Apr 2007	31.94	SG World Water	32.15	44.75	82.69
10. Lyxor Dynamic Alternative Energy Fund (as of 25 Sep 2013)	Apr 2007	6.16	SG World Alternative Energy	36.78	–21.31	–49.36
11. DWS Global Equity Agribusiness Fund	May 2007	472.88	MSCI World	1.45	3.55	137.07
12. Schroder Global Climate Change Equity	May 2007	223.07	MSCI World	28.07	27.43	102.93
13. Franklin Natural Resources Fund (as of 31 Oct 2013)	Sep 2007	255.95	S&P North American Natural Resources Sector Index	8.52	–10.10	94.25
14. Allianz RCM Global Sustainability Fund	Oct 2007	25.84	DJSI World	23.96	31.35	107.80
15. BoCHK NCB China Resources Opportunities Fund	Oct 2007	88.36	NA	0.11	–25.01	79.31
16. Allianz Global EcoTrends (as of 31 Oct 2013)	Oct 2007	196.56	FTSE ET50	29.73	14.71	48.13

(*Continued*)

(Continued)

Fund name	Fund authorized in Hong Kong	Total fund size as of 30 Sep 2013 unless otherwise stated (AUM in US$ m)	Benchmark	1 year as of 4 Dec 2013 (%)	3 year as of 4 Dec 2013* (%)	5 year as of 4 Dec 2013* (%)
Benchmarks (as of 4 Dec 2013):						
MSCI World Index	*NA*	*NA*	*NA*	*21.87*	*27.45*	*97.09*
MSCI Asia Pacific ex Japan	*NA*	*NA*	*NA*	*4.03*	*3.05*	*114.12*
MSCI World Energy	*NA*	*NA*	*NA*	*–6.43*	*–19.19*	*42.26*
DAX Global Agribusiness	*NA*	*NA*	*NA*	*–8.24*	*–22.61*	*28.44*
17. Hang Seng Islamic China Index Fund[1] (as of 4 Dec 2013)	Nov 2007	12.06	Dow Jones Islamic Market China/HK	0.43	2.75	13.46
18. HSBC Global Investment Funds – Climate Change	Jan 2008	27.26	HSBC Global Climate Change benchmark index	24.55	21.11	68.75
19. Pictet Clean Energy Fund (as of 2 Dec 2013)	Jan 2008	441.84	MSCI World	32.68	6.77	61.26
20. First State Global Listed Infrastructure Fund (as of 3 Dec 2013)	Jan 2008	39.23	S&P Global Infrastructure	16.01	31.93	94.66
21. BEA Union Investment Global Resources Fund	Jan 2008	4.10	50% MSCI World Materials, 25% MSCI World Energy, 25% MSCI World Industrials	14.70	3.49	79.17
22. Amundi Equity India Infrastructure	Feb 2008	22.47	MSCI India	–15.57	–44.93	41.28
23. Eastspring Investments Asia Infrastructure Equity Fund (as of 31 Oct 2013)	Mar 2008	39.11	MSCI AC Asia ex Japan customised index[2]	2.29	–5.12	71.56
24. Lyxor Agriculture Fund (as of 30 Sep 2013)	Mar 2008	11.26	SG Global Agriculture	–14.16	–14.60	33.97
25. JP Morgan Asia Resources Fund	Mar 2008	22.41	Euromoney Gold, Mining & Energy Net Index	–4.46	–20.78	88.58

Benchmarks (as of 4 Dec 2013):						
MSCI World Index	*NA*	*NA*	*NA*	*21.87*	*27.45*	*97.09*
MSCI Asia Pacific ex Japan	*NA*	*NA*	*NA*	*4.03*	*3.05*	*114.12*
MSCI World Energy	*NA*	*NA*	*NA*	*–6.43*	*–19.19*	*42.26*
DAX Global Agribusiness	*NA*	*NA*	*NA*	*–8.24*	*–22.61*	*28.44*
Fund name	**Fund authorized in Hong Kong**	**Total fund size as of 30 Sep 2013 unless otherwise stated (AUM in US$ m)**	**Benchmark**	**1 year as of 4 Dec 2013 (%)**	**3 year as of 4 Dec 2013* (%)**	**5 year as of 4 Dec 2013* (%)**
26. Allianz RCM Global Agricultural Trends Fund (as of 31 Oct 2013)	Apr 2008	179.26	Customised MSCI	3.42	6.05	108.73
27. Schroder Global Demographic Opportunities	May 2008	31.11	MSCI World	25.24	36.58	NA
28. UBS Emerging Markets Equity Infrastructure (as of 3 Dec 2013)	May 2008	84.41	NA	–4.61	–17.76	81.12
29. Amundi Equity Global Agriculture Fund	July 2008	136.93	S&P Global Agribusiness Equity	11.22	4.75	125.40
30. Pictet Water Fund (as of 2 Dec 2013)	Aug 2008	3,541.87	MSCI World	20.78	32.17	92.94
31. Pictet Timber Fund (as of 2 Dec 2013)	Sep 2008	607.11	MSCI World	15.30	23.53	130.85
32. First State Global Agribusiness Fund (as of 3 Dec 2013)	Sep 2008	32.45	75% DAX Global Agribusiness & 25% S&P Global Timber & Forestry	5.57	8.20	NA
33. BNP Paribas L1 Equity Sustainable Equity World (formerly Fortis Equity SRI)	Nov 2008	24.26	MSCI World	–14.80	15.07	NA
34. Blackrock World Agriculture Fund (as of 31 Oct 2013)	Apr 2009	202.60	DAX Global Agribusiness	7.30	6.78	NA
35. RobecoSAM Sustainable Agribusiness Equities (as of 10 Oct 2013)	Jun 2009	132.69	MSCI World	14.82	15.38	131.12

(Continued)

Benchmarks (as of 4 Dec 2013):						
MSCI World Index	*NA*	*NA*	*NA*	*21.87*	*27.45*	*97.09*
MSCI Asia Pacific ex Japan	*NA*	*NA*	*NA*	*4.03*	*3.05*	*114.12*
MSCI World Energy	*NA*	*NA*	*NA*	*–6.43*	*–19.19*	*42.26*
DAX Global Agribusiness	*NA*	*NA*	*NA*	*–8.24*	*–22.61*	*28.44*
Fund name	**Fund authorized in Hong Kong**	**Total fund size as of 30 Sep 2013 unless otherwise stated (AUM in US$ m)**	**Benchmark**	**1 year as of 4 Dec 2013 (%)**	**3 year as of 4 Dec 2013* (%)**	**5 year as of 4 Dec 2013* (%)**
36. ICBC Asia Infrastructure and Redevelopment Fund (as of 31 Oct 2013)	Jul 2009	2.07	MSCI AC Asia ex Japan	17.76	4.40	NA
37. UBS Equity Fund Infrastructure (as of 3 Dec 2013)	Aug 2009	38.30	UBS Global Infrastructure & Utilities 50–50 index	23.06	39.43	136.90
38. Pictet Agriculture Fund (as of 2 Dec 2013)	Apr 2010	260.00	MSCI World	8.64	2.27	NA
39. Aberdeen Global Emerging Markets Infrastructure Equity Fund (as of 31 Oct 2013)	Aug 2010	449.28	MSCI EM infrastructure	–2.65	3.52	NA
40. Morgan Stanley Investment Funds Global Infrastructure Fund	Sep 2010	372.62	DJ Brookfield Global Infrastructure Index	15.31	51.19	NA
41. Baring Global Agriculture Fund	Jan 2011	384.40	DAX Global Agribusiness	7.19	4.58	NA
42. Hang Seng Corporate Sustainability Index Fund[3]	Aug 2011	20.08	Hang Seng Corporate Sustainability Index	4.42	7.90	NA
43. Blackrock Natural Resources Growth & Income Growth (as of 31 Oct 2013)	Nov 2011	14.00	S&P Global Natural Resources	0.38	NA	NA

Fund name	Fund authorized in Hong Kong	Total fund size as of 30 Sep 2013 unless otherwise stated (AUM in US$ m)	Benchmark	1 year as of 4 Dec 2013 (%)	3 year as of 4 Dec 2013* (%)	5 year as of 4 Dec 2013* (%)
Benchmarks (as of 4 Dec 2013):						
MSCI World Index	*NA*	*NA*	*NA*	*21.87*	*27.45*	*97.09*
MSCI Asia Pacific ex Japan	*NA*	*NA*	*NA*	*4.03*	*3.05*	*114.12*
MSCI World Energy	*NA*	*NA*	*NA*	*–6.43*	*–19.19*	*42.26*
DAX Global Agribusiness	*NA*	*NA*	*NA*	*–8.24*	*–22.61*	*28.44*
44. Parvest Green Tigers[4]	Mar 2013	32.58	MSCI Asia Pacific ex Japan	15.13	–4.11	81.78
45. Parvest World Equity Energy (as of 31 Oct 2013)[5]	Mar 2013	282.17	MSCI World Energy 10/40	15.42	11.99	74.83

Source: Homage Consulting research.

** Cumulative performance. Note that the AUM of funds may be quoted on various dates and month end because different funds may have different reporting periods.*

[1] *Bloomberg stock code is HSISCIB*:HK. Accessed 4 December 2013.
[2] *Selected sectors*: Energy, industrials, materials, telecommunication services and utilities.
[3] *Bloomberg stock code is HSCSUSI*:KY. Accessed 4 December 2013.
[4] *Since June 2011, the fund has changed its benchmark index to a customized index calculated by S&P – the 'BNP Paribas Emerging Asia SRI ENV Index'. Formerly BNP Paribas Green Tiger Fund launched in July 2008.*
[5] *Formerly BNP Paribas L1 Equity World Energy Fund.*

Appendix 15.2 Mandatory Provident Fund market share

Top Six Providers by AUM	*As of September 2013*
HSBC/Hang Seng	31.3%
Manulife	17.7%
AIA	9.7%
BOCI – Prudential	7.9%
Bank Consortium	6.1%
Fidelity	4.6%
Market shares of top two providers	49.0%
Market shares of top six providers	77.3%

Source: Gadbury Group Reports. Private distribution to subscripted members of the MPF Reporting Services.

Appendix 15.3 Investor-profile table: results based on HSBC/Hang Seng investment profiling questionnaire

Total score	*Years to retirement (assumes retirement at age 65)*				
	Over 30	**Up to 30**	**Up to 20**	**Up to 10**	**Up to 5**
7 to 8	Medium	Low to medium	Low to medium	Low	Low
9 to 11	Medium	Medium	Low to medium	Low to medium	Low
12 to 16	Medium	Medium	Medium	Low to medium	Low to medium
17 to 19	Medium to high	Medium to High	Medium	Medium	Medium
20 to 21	High	High	Medium to high	Medium to high	Medium to high

Source: HSBC/Hang Seng Bank MPF service promotional materials.

Appendix 15.4: interview participants

Ms. Melissa Brown, Partner, **Daobridge Capital**
Ms. Vicki Chi, Asia Analyst, **Robeco Rotterdam**
Ms. Mabel Chu, Compliance Director, **Baring Private Equity Asia**
Ms. Cynthia Chua, Marketing Director, **Avantage Ventures**
Mr. Joseph Ferrigno, Managing Partner, **Asia Mezzanine Capital Group (AMCG)**
Professor Wai Fung Lam, **The University of Hong Kong**
Mr. Jonathan Maxwell, Founding Partner & CEO, **Sustainable Development Capital LLP (SDCL)**
Ms. Victoria Mio, CIO China, **Robeco Group**
Dr. Francois Perrin, Head of Greater China Equities, **BNP Paribas Investment Partners**
Dr. Stuart Rae, CIO Pacific Basin Value Equities, **Alliance Bernstein**
Mr. Yannick Rausis, Vice President, **Amundi**
Mr. Alex Shuen, Treasurer, **Hong Kong Baptist University**
Mr. Brian W. Tang, Director & Counsel, **Credit Suisse**
Dr. Christopher Wright, Asset Owner from Norway
Mr. Clarence Yang, Head of Corporate Governance & Responsible Investment, **BlackRock**
Mr. Charles Yonts, Head of Sustainable Research

16

Responsible investment in Japan

A tale of two narratives

Kyoko Sakuma-Keck

Introduction

A tale of responsible investment (RI) in Japan, which is more widely known as socially responsible investment (SRI), must incorporate two narratives. In the common narrative, Japan's SRI history begins with the launch of investment funds in the late 1990s when the financial 'big bang' swept Japan (Tanimoto, 2003; Sakuma and Louche, 2008).[1] A small number of SRI rating agencies and fund managers affiliated with large financial groups successfully channelled the money of environmentally conscious households into new financial products, called 'eco-funds' and, later, 'SRI funds' (Sakuma and Louche, 2008).[2]

At a glance, Japan's SRI differs from that of North American and European counterparts whose historical roots are founded in ethical beliefs (Sakuma and Louche, 2008). SRI in Japan, in contrast, has been driven by business incubation. Japan's new funds invested exclusively or predominantly in companies with high environmental performance.[3] An embryonic form of SRI in Japan can be traced to credit unions that emerged to support community development in the 1960s (JSIF, 2007).

Much less in the limelight is a narrative of independent 'long-term' asset managers. Unlike quickly institutionalized SRI, this handful of mainstream managers emerged in the late 1990s and 2000s and remained discrete. They were driven by a sole mission: to help ordinary people build assets by investing sustainably in value-creating companies. Japan's asset and fund management industry, which is still dominated by a small number of financial groups, shied away from redressing the sales commission and fund turnovers that impeded long-term performance (Iwai, 2007; Takehara and Yamada, 2007; Nomura Research Institute, 2013). It is the long-term investor group that harnessed a countrywide foundation of long-term and sustainable retail investors, rather than Japan's popularized SRI actors.

Fifteen years later, it remains still unknown if SRI has taken root in Japan. Although some institutional investors and pension funds entered into the SRI market, the amount of SRI assets under management (AUM) has declined in recent years. Meanwhile, a new kind of momentum is underway. The Japanese Trade Union Confederation published the *Guidelines on Responsible Investment of Workers' Capital* (Rengo, 2010), and Prime Minister Abe announced a corporate governance and pension reform policy in June 2013 to complement his monetary and fiscal policy.

As inflation risks rise, securing returns becomes an imminent issue. The launch of a new stock index focusing on return of equity (ROE), alongside Japan's first Stewardship Code, is said to facilitate more allocation to domestic equity away from dominant Japanese government bond holdings. At this juncture, it is worthwhile to explore the future of Japan's SRI, particularly if and how the long-term investment narratives may give substance to the SRI narrative.

This chapter is organized as follows. The first section gives an overview of Japan. The definition of the SRI market in the second section is followed by the description of the characteristics of SRI funds, long-term funds, pension funds, shareholder advocacy and engagement. The third section examines SRI practitioner discourse around salient environmental, social and governance (ESG) issues, and compares it with that of long-term investors. The fourth section looks at the main SRI actors in Japan and contrasts the characteristics of long-term investors. The fifth section reviews the regulatory and policy environment, including the most recent 'Abenomics'. The final section presents the argument that SRI must join forces with long-term investors to address underlying challenges if SRI is to have a fair chance for growth in Japan.

Overview of Japan

Japan still ranks among the richest developed countries in the world and remains a technology leader in many fields. Its GDP per capita in 2013 was USD 37,100. Having joined the OECD in 1965, the country established itself rapidly as one of major producers and exporters of technologically advanced products, including motor vehicles, electronic equipment, machine tools, and, more recently, high-tech components and advanced materials.

However, Japan's economic growth has been subdued in the last 25 years, accompanied by persistent deflation in consumer prices. This is partly due to the negative fallout of the bursting of the speculative economic bubble at the end of 1989. But perhaps more important, it reflects Japan's demographic trend, with a concomitant decrease in its workforce and sluggish consumption. The population in the world's third-largest economy dropped for the third consecutive year in 2013, to 127,103,388. This gives Japan the world's lowest ratio of children to the total population (12.8 per cent) compared with 19.5 per cent for the US and 16.4 per cent for China.[4] The government estimates that the proportion of people aged 65 or over will reach nearly 40 per cent of the population in 2060.

To revive economic growth, subsequent governments have resorted mostly to deficit-financing public spending. The current Japanese government under Prime Minister Abe has introduced a novel economic policy built on three policy pillars, so-called Abenomics: bold monetary policy, flexible fiscal policy and a growth strategy that encourages private investment and structural reform. While the quantitative easing has been effective in driving down the Yen and lifting the stock market and corporate sentiment, it has inevitably left the ever-climbing gross public debts untamed: 226 per cent to GDP (2013 estimate).

There is therefore a formidable challenge ahead to consolidate Japan's fiscal situation sooner rather than later. This is particularly true given that Japan's aging households – a major holder of Japan Government Bonds (JGBs) – will ultimately draw down their savings and that Japanese financial institutions and pension funds, another key holder of JGBs, might consider the re-allocation of assets.

The SRI market

The Japanese Social Investment Forum (JSIF, 2011) has adopted the European notion of 'broad SRI' but has adapted it to the Japanese reality. It defines SRI as 'conscious' investment activities undertaken by finance providers, including pension funds (Principle 1). Such activities encompass

Table 16.1 SRI concept and SIF Japan's endorsement (shaded)

Principle 2	*Principle 1*	
	Intention can be verified	
	Investment securities (stocks, fixed income, etc.)	Direct investment and others
Consider ESG in investment target-selection process	Eco-funds, SRI funds, etc.	Green building investment, etc.
Aim to provide solutions to ESG problems	Proxy voting, engagement, impact investment	Community investment
Do not consider ESG in investment processes	Financial products accompanying donation	

Source: http://japansif.com/2013review.pdf.

investments in stocks, fixed-income instruments and funds and the financing of community projects that are usually classified as share participation and loans (Principle 2). Table 16.1 illustrates the broad SRI concepts adapted by JSIF.

On the basis of the above definition, JSIF estimated the size of the SRI market in Japan at JPY 743.1 billion (USD 7.58 billion) as of September 2013.[5] Nearly all of this investment was in the retail market, with SRI funds accounting for 31 per cent (JPY 243.5 billion, or USD 2.48 billion) and social contribution bonds issued by international organizations accounting for 66 per cent (JPY 499.6 billion, or USD 5.096 billion). The institutional market is represented by social contribution bonds issued by international banks and sold to local banks, which totaled JPY 25.88 billion or USD 315 million (as of 31 March, 2013). Official statistics for pension fund–managed SRI are not available. Based on interviews with four pension funds, Kanai and Takezume (2011) estimated the size of Japan's SRI pension market at JPY 15 billion (USD 153 million) as of September 2011.[6] A recent JSIF survey (2013) confirms that SRI, including both retail and institutional markets, remains at 0.2 per cent of the total AUM in Japan.

The rise and fall of SRI funds

For historical reasons, including its business incubation motives, Japanese SRI is mostly found in retail funds and bond products created to follow 'trendy' themes. As a result, SRI AUM is particularly susceptible to changes in the size of the capital market. By March 2000, AUM in eco-funds had soared to JPY 220.7 billion (USD 2.25 billion), as first-time investors, primarily women and young adults, had rushed to buy SRI products (Sakuma and Louche, 2008). The bursting of the IT bubble in 2001 reversed this momentum. By September 2003, AUM in eco-funds plunged to JPY 71.8 billion (USD 730 million) despite an increase in the number of such funds from three to nine (Sompo Japan). The market then expanded again, peaking in October 2007 at JPY 1,243.9 billion (USD 12.7 billion) (JSIF, 2011), after which it was hit by the US subprime and Lehman shocks, and more recently by the European sovereign debt crisis.

Presently, the SRI retail market in Japan shows signs of decline in absolute terms and in comparison to mainstream investment funds.[7] As of June 2014, the market size was JPY 237.5 billion (USD 2.17 billion) with 72 funds, which was barely one-fifth of the value seen at the peak.[8] In contrast, conventional funds, which shrank by 45 per cent from their peak (JPY 6,968.1 trillion or USD 71.07 trillion) in October 2007 to January 2009, bounced back (Saotome and

Yamamoto, 2011). Notably, 74 per cent of these SRI funds were either global equity or global bonds funds that invested outside Japan (JSIF, 2011).[9]

One development that contradicted the market decline was the surge in impact investments, which was made available in the form of social contribution bonds. The first such bond was sold in March 2008. One of the most notable products is vaccine bonds.[10] Daiwa Securities provided Japanese retail investors with access to the government-guaranteed bonds issued by the International Finance Facility for Immunization (IFFim).[11] Since then, other financial group, notably HSBC, Nomura Securities and Mitsubishi UFJ, joined them. As of June 2014, there are 78 impact investment funds sold to retail investors, with a total size of JPY 652.8 billion (USD 5.97 billion). Daiwa Securities has since served as a catalyst for the development of an institutional market for similar bond products. Of 19 green bonds totaling JPY 25.8 billion issued by the World Bank and the Asian Development Bank to Japanese local banks between August 2010 and October 2012, 14 were arranged by Daiwa Securities Capital Markets and one by Daiwa Securities.[12]

Emergence of long-term funds

Compared to documented SRI funds, long-term investment funds are far less known. They emerged as an antithesis to the dominance of large financial institutions in the retail fund industry. Japanese households hold approximately half of their financial assets in cash and deposits. By the end of 2012, only JPY 16.8 trillion (USD 170 billion) was invested in investment funds out of JPY 1,446 trillion (USD 14.75 trillion) in financial assets (NRI, 2013).[13]

One important reason for this underdeveloped sector is an alleged vicious cycle. Fund turnover of open-ended investment funds in Japan is not only three times higher than that of the US and UK (Sugita, 1997), but it is also high compared to the turnover ratio of direct investment in its own equity market (Takehara and Yamada, 2007).[14] The high fund turnover, combined with high commissions, has created a short-term focus: fund managers engage in relatively short-term trading to adjust their portfolio positions in response to fund flows, negatively affecting the return (Takehara and Yamada, 2007; NRI, 2013).[15] There has been little change in this situation. Today, in fact, it may be even worse, given that the average sales commission for an open-ended fund increased to 2.6 per cent in 2012 from 1.75 per cent in 2003 (NRI, 2013).

The first long-term fund emerged in August 1999. Sawakami Fund, launched with a net asset of JPY 1.6 billion (USD 16.32 million) collected from 487 holders, is an open-ended, no load, active domestic equity fund. The founder of Sawakami Fund has his mission to create a new model of direct selling funds that use no benchmark index. In so doing, he aims to share the profit among fund participants, asset managers and the society without a conflict of interest.[16] The fund grew to a JPY 10 billion (USD 102 million) with 10,000 holders by March 2001 and continued its expansion in the 2000s. Today, Sawakami Fund is Japan's second biggest mutual fund in terms of net assets, with JPY 301,96 billion (USD 3.08 billion) held by nearly 120,000 holders at the end of December 2013.[17]

Several more funds with a similar remit of long-term value creation sprang up in the mid to late 2000s (Table 16.2). Although smaller in scale, these actively managed retail funds help to shape what has become known as a 'long-term investor group' (Choukitoshi no nakama, in Japanese). Unlike the institutionalized SRI, Japan's long-term investor group remains discrete and exists through a salon-like activity called the Club Investlife®.[18]

Table 16.2 Focus of selected long-term actors based on mission, goals and investment principles in Japan

	Date of Establishment	*Inception of Main Fund*	*AUMEnd 2013 (JPY billion)*	*Mission, Goals and Investment Principles*
Sawakami Asset Management	1996	1999	301,96	Create an exciting world through genuine, long-term investing. Make the Sawakami Fund No.1 in the world both in performance and customer trust. Share the profit from business growth with society in a broad perspective.
Arigato Asset Management*	2004	2004	10.59	Support investors' long-term asset building through investing in a diversity of funds. Pursue asset allocation that is suitable to the economic cycle. Select funds based on stringent criteria and allocate assets to capture market dynamism in advance. Pursue long-term asset growth without being allured by short-term market movement.
Saison Asset Management*	2006	2007	80.0**	Build assets of ordinary people in the long-term so that they will not be distracted by new theme funds and target distribution funds that have an average holding period of 2.3 years.***
Commons Asset Management	2007	2009	4.215	30 years: It is a symbolic number (not a holding period) to express that we invest in excellent companies creating value sustainably over generations. 30 stocks: We focus on excellent companies that continue to evolve, but not on average performance of average companies. Dialogue: As a truly long-term and stable shareholder, we build trust with management and participate in value creation.
Kamakura Asset Management	2008	2010	7.507	We aim to create a fund that has: A mechanism in which prospective good companies are able to get funding from investors. Is accessible to individual investors so that they feel our faith and philosophy. Individual investors can see how their money is invested and realize that they contribute to societal development. Build trust and share value among investors and asset managers, investors and investors, and investors and investee companies.

Source: Individual websites, accessed 6 January 2014. Translated from Japanese to English by the author.

*A total of two funds.

**Saison and Arigato manage a fund of funds. The latter invests in Sawakami Fund and Commons Fund, among others.

*** An excerpt from the CEO message dated 5 April 2013 on the website. Accessed 6 January 2014.

The pension market and SRI

By value, Japan's pension assets are the second largest after the US. As of end 2012, it had AUM of USD 3.721 billion (Towers Watson, 2013). The Government Pension Investment Fund (GPIF) is the world's largest public pension fund, with a reserve representing AUM of JPY 121 trillion (USD 1.23 trillion) as of end December 2012. GPIF continues to rely on the pay-as-you-go method, posing a significant threat to sustainable pension asset management against accelerating aging population demographics.[19]

Both public and corporate pension funds in Japan have faced serious financing problems for decades. The government had long shied away from necessary reforms, presuming that future generations would bear the pension deficit (Tajika, 2002; NRI, 2009).[20] The result is that Japanese workers' level of pensions relative to earnings is one of the lowest among OECD countries. Income provided by public pensions for an average worker is 33.9 per cent, compared to the OECD average of 59 per cent (Aronson, 2010). The prudent man principle of fiduciary duty was introduced in 1997, as well as a defined contribution (DC) scheme in October 2001 known as the 'Japanese 401k plan'. However, Japan's pension assets remain essentially all defined benefits (DB).[21]

Academics, companies, financial institutions and government officials have intensified the discussions regarding whether SRI can play a role in revitalizing and sustaining Japan's pension system (Jin et al., 2005). However, a decline of equity allocation of Japan's pension funds relative to bonds obscured several milestones in Japan's SRI history in 2003: introduction of the proxy voting principle by the Japanese Pension Fund Association, a launch of the first SRI index by Morningstar Japan and the adoption of SRI by first pension fund (Sakuma and Louche, 2008).[22] Indeed, no public pension funds had joined the UN Principles of Responsible Investment (PRI) as of December 2013, and only three Japanese corporate pension funds and two insurance companies were signatories of the UN PRI.[23]

Several surveys evidence the persistent lack of SRI popularity in Japan (Research Institute for Policies on Pension & Aging, 2008; JSIF 2013). The 2007 survey by Research Institute for Policies on Pension & Aging reveals that only 6.9 per cent (32 funds) of 465 respondents from corporate and public pension funds said that they had adopted an SRI approach, while 62.2 per cent had no plans to adopt such an approach. The proportion of pension funds that had adopted SRI had shrunk to 3.2 per cent (eight funds) in its 2011 survey, with 2 per cent responding that they no longer implemented SRI.[24] The more recent survey by JSIF (2013) shows that 46 per cent of pension funds had no plan to consider investing using ESG information, while only 7 per cent have already invested using ESG and non-financial information.[25]

One notable development has been the adoption of an SRI approach by non-PRI-signatory pension funds. The Pension Fund Association for Local Government Officials, known as Chikyouren, implemented SRI as part of its active management strategy in 2009. The corporate pension division of the National Association of Labour Banks, known as Roukin, announced a plan to invest up to 1 per cent in SRI products, when it published the 'Roukin principle on SRI' in April 2010 (Kanai and Takezume, 2011). An initiative by the National Federation of Mutual Aid Associations for Municipal Personnel, known as Shichousonren, is groundbreaking. In its request for proposals for its domestic equity passive funds, published on 30 January 2012, Shichousonren stipulated that the mandate is restricted to UN PRI signatory asset management companies. Moreover, it requests that the MSCI Japan ESG Index be used as a benchmark.[26]

Shareholder advocacy and engagement

Shareholder advocacy has traditionally been a taboo subject in Japan[27] and it remains a relatively foreign concept because of Japan's conflict-avoidance culture (Sakuma and Louche, 2008). One notable demonstration of the Japanese views on shareholder advocacy is found in the case of the California Public Employees' Retirement System (CalPERS). Throughout the 1990s, CalPERS pressured Japanese companies to remove takeover barriers and install an independent board of directors by submitting a 'wish list' for better corporate performance (Jacoby, 2007). However, this focus on public activism proved counterproductive and even adverse in Japan. Japanese companies continued to regard US-style activism as some kind of "foreign sōkaiya" (blackmailer) (Jacoby, 2006).[28] CalPERS finally shifted its strategy to relational investing by taking a minority stake in existing Japanese-owned and Japan-focused funds that targeted the restructuring of inefficient corporate operations (Jacoby, 2007).

Likewise, advocacy in the environmental, social and governance (ESG) areas remains under-developed (Takaba et al., 2011). Takaba et al. (2011) showed that the number of companies to which ESG-related shareholder resolutions were submitted declined from 32 in 2007 to 24 in 2011. They attributed this decline to a fall in governance-related resolutions. Steel Partners, the US-based activist investor, submitted 11 resolutions to six companies in 2007 but has submitted no such resolutions since (JSIF, 2009). Six environment-related cases, all of which were anti-nuclear resolutions, were filed against electric companies by individuals between 2007 and 2011 (JSIF, 2011). The Research Institute of Economy, Trade and Industry (RIETI) (2003) posits that shareholder resolutions submitted by individuals are considered odd and are seldom supported by institutional investors. Yamamoto (2011) and Takaba et al. (2011) hence argue that anti-nuclear resolutions have failed to become a countervailing power that induces companies to phase out the production or sale of nuclear energy.

Salient ESG issues

Environmental and 'trendy' concerns among SRI retail investors

In their analysis of the language used in SRI funds' prospectuses, Sakuma and Louche (2008) identify 'eco-efficiency/eco-friendly', followed by 'CSR/compliance', as the dominant concepts in Japan. Arguably, Japan's SRI community is lenient in the governance debate. Many funds with corporate social responsibility (CSR) criteria were established between 2003 and 2006 following corporate scandals involving accounting irregularities and unethical marketing (JSIF, 2009). Subsequently, nearly all new funds launched after 2007 were named eco- or environmental theme funds.

Indeed, the environment has become the most relevant issue in Japan in the aftermath of the financial crisis. As of September 2011, 74.5 per cent of SRI funds (in AUM terms) were invested in funds with environmental criteria or themes, while just 18.3 per cent were invested in funds with CSR criteria (Saotome and Yamamoto, 2011). Moreover, all social contribution funds sold to institutional investors were 'green' bonds.

Interestingly, Saotome and Yamamoto (2011) note that the sudden increase in AUM held by social contribution bonds was driven by retail investors' desire to shoot two birds with one stone: low risk fixed income and social responsibility. These bonds, which are denominated in an emerging country currency like the South African rand (ZAR) or Brazilian real (BRL), are inherently volatile and high risk.[29] Yet, the risk perception, together with emerging importance of global poverty and health issues in 2007–2008, as widely introduced by media and financial institutions, contributed to the rise in volume.[30]

Most recently, a number of local community funds focusing on renewable energy and solidarity sprang up in the aftermath of the nuclear disaster at Fukushima in March 2011.[31] In addition, many earthquake reconstruction funds were created by financial institutions around that time. These funds channeled retail investors' money into donations for reconstruction-related activities. Whether these initiatives become crucial over the long-term remains to be seen.

Corporate governance concerns among institutional investors

Corporate governance issues have been a prime concern for Japanese institutional investors since the 1980s (Jacoby, 2007). The Japanese model of corporate governance lost its foundation in the economic doldrums of the 1990s, which triggered a debate over a new model of governance (Sakuma, 2001). Foreign and domestic institutional investors have severely criticized the Japanese model of balancing the interests of various stakeholders, including those of the wider society (Kim, 2004). Indeed, corporate pension funds and trustee organizations in Japan have expressed concern about board independence and the absence of external directors (Omura et al., 2002).[32] The Commercial Code was revised in 2002 to allow Japanese companies to adopt an Anglo-Saxon style of management control in the form of auditing and remuneration committees. However, most companies' governance systems remain grounded on internalism (Buchernan, 2007; Gilson and Milhaupt, 2004).

Corporate governance remains the most salient ESG issue among institutional investors (JSIF, 2009; Securities Analysts Association of Japan, 2010). JSIF (2009) quotes a 2009 survey by Mercer stating that Japanese trust banks, investment advisory firms and life insurance companies placed more importance on governance than on environmental and social issues. Another survey undertaken by the Securities Analysts Association of Japan (SAAJ) also reports the salience of governance issues: in 2009, 74 per cent of security analysts believed that corporate governance would be a very important issue in the next three years, while only 66 per cent and 63 per cent felt the same was true for environment and social issues, respectively.[33] Of the governance issues, the financial sector's director remuneration, incentive systems and board composition were of particular concern (SAAJ, 2010). Similarly, JSIF's (2013) survey on pension funds unveils that governance is currently more prevalent than social and environmental issues.[34]

Social and societal concerns among long-term investors

Unlike the SRI investors' narrative, concerns of Japan's long-term investors are poorly documented. A survey by the Japan Securities Dealers Association (2013) suggests who the typical retail investors are: low- to middle-income earners.[35] Statistics show that 53.1 per cent of Japan's retail investors are over 60 year old, 47 per cent earn less than JPY 300,000 (USD 30,600 per year, and another 23 per cent earn between JPY 300 thousand and JPY 500,000 (USD 51,000).[36] This means that individuals' assets held in securities (stocks, mutual funds and fixed income) are relatively small.[37] Their primary concern therefore is to support their daily life and save for retirement.

Long-term investors aim to serve the very ordinary retail investors. The 'Declaration of Retail Investors', steered by the Club Investlife® and inaugurated among 500 supporters in January 2007, illuminates such concerns. In essence, long-term retail investors practice investment as part of daily life (Principle 1), aim for economic independence and giving a fair share back to the

Table 16.3 Declaration of Retail Investors, launched by Club Investlife® members, 14 January 2007

Preamble	Motivated to create happy, independent life as well as sustainable, better society, and steered by Investlife, we gather today in Tokyo to hold an in-depth discussion. As a result, we are convinced that independent-minded individuals' long-term investment be the ultimate mainstream investment we should pursue for Japan's and the world's future. With passionate mind and high ambition, we declare the following five principles.
Principle 1	We learn and practice long-term investment as part of our daily life.
Principle 2	We aim at economic independence and social contribution through long-term investment.
Principle 3	We support and invest in companies that would contribute to the creation of a better society.
Principle 4	We seek spiritual happiness from investment returns.
Principle 5	We take our time and are not hasty in making an investment.

Source: Club Investlife website, translated to English by the author.

society (Principles 2 and 4), and therefore invest in companies that would meet their goal for sustainability (Principles 3 and 5).

Key actors and regulatory environments

Key actors – SRI

SRI in Japan is essentially an initiative by specialized ESG rating agencies, companies, financial institutions and, more recently, western asset management companies to promote new products (Sakuma and Louche, 2008). Specialized ESG rating agencies, including Good Bankers, IntegreX and the Centre for Public Resource Development (CPRD) have acted as catalysts (Sakuma and Louche, 2008).[38] By 2005, research organizations affiliated with Japan's large financial groups and similar rating agencies of foreign origin had joined the market.

Asset management companies have sought to ensure that SRI is offered through dedicated partnerships with rating and research providers (Sakuma and Louche, 2008) in order to lock in specific methodological know-how and to deter its diffusion to competitors. Unlike their European counterparts, who promote knowledge diffusion, Japanese SRI actors tend to black-box their selection criteria, weightings and decision-making processes. The resulting competitive nature of the market may be one reason that there are still so few PRI signatories in asset management. As of December 2013, 18 asset management companies were PRI signatories, up from 11 as of December 2011.[39]

Today, the SRI community in Japan is led by non-profit associations promoting the merit of SRI. The Social Investment Forum Japan (JSIF), officially established in 2004, consists of 27 institutional members and many individual members. Eight of the institutional members are financial services institutions, seven are ESG information providers, and two are accounting firms.[40]

One important new SRI actor is the Japan Trade Union Confederation (JTUC-Rengo). When it published the Guidelines on Responsible Investment of Workers' Capital (Workers' Capital) in December 2010, JTUC-Rengo called on investment funds, GPIF and other pension funds to implement SRI. This initiative was launched in the same month as the release of an OECD working paper. The working paper, written by Stewart and Yermo (2010), called for

GPIF's integration of ESG factors,[41] by citing the 2009 OECD Guidelines for Pension Fund Governance that recommends pension funds' disclosure of ESG considerations in their investment policies (OECD, 2009). Stewart and Yermo (2010) recommended that "GPIF's investment policy should consider the fund's potential impact on the domestic economy and financial stability and it should integrate environmental, social and corporate governance (ESG) factors" (2010, p. 31).[42]

Key actors – long-term investment

Key actors in long-term investment are members of the Club Investlife®. The Club Investlife, which was started as a magazine edited by like-minded asset managers and financial advisors in early 2003, has 19 active members.[43] Atsushi Sawakami, founder of Sawakami Fund, played a pivotal role in growing a discrete, yet grassroots, movement. Founders of independent asset management companies, independent financial advisors and enlightened fund managers in large financial institutions assume responsibility for educating ordinary people free of charge and share their experience of long-term investment (Table 16.2).

Arigato Asset Management, which literally means 'thank you', was established in 2004 by five tax accountants and certified public accountants to assist the average Japanese with problems related to pensions, social securities and retirement plans. It offers a fund of funds that invests in long-term funds such as Sawakami Fund and Commons30 Fund, but also in an SRI fund (Asahi Life Asset Management's Asunohane Fund). In 2009, a former fund manager at Sawakami Fund assumed the chief investment officer of Arigato Asset.

Commons Asset Management's founder is fifth-generation descendent of Eiichi Shibusawa, one of Japan's first Meiji era venture capitalists, widely known today as the 'father of Japanese capitalism'. Kamakura Asset Management was launched by four former employees of Barclay Global Investors Japan (today Black Rock Japan). Saison Asset Management, which is 100 per cent owned by Credit Saison, is an exception to the independent asset manager group. Supported by Sawakami and Credit Saison's then CEO, its founder successfully created a new asset management company within the group.

Legal environment and policy initiatives

Disclosure laws: The ministries' competing initiatives

The Japanese government has focused on corporate disclosure and reporting as SRI enablers; however, this focus has not been adopted across the board. This is perhaps because financial institutions and pension funds, as well as environmental, governance and social issues, fall under the competencies of different ministries in Japan. Notably, the Ministry of Finance (MOF) holds sole authority for proposing revisions to statutory financial reporting requirements.

The disclosure initiative started with the Ministry of the Environment (MOE). Influenced by the European Union's environmental regulations on extended producer responsibility (e.g., WEEE and RoHS), the MOE issued an Environmental Reporting Guideline in 1997 (Solomon et al., 2004).[44] Subsequently, the Environmental Accounting Guideline and Environmental Performance Indicators were published in 2000 and 2001, respectively (Daiwa Research Institute, 2011).[45] In 2005, the Environmental Consideration Law was introduced, which called for the consideration of environment by businesses, organizations and citizens when making investment decisions.[46] In 2007, a new Environmental Reporting Guideline consolidated previous environmental guidelines.

More recently, a committee was set up within the MOE to discuss the finance industry's role in environmental issues. This led to the release of the Principles for Financial Action towards a Sustainable Society in October 2011 (MOE, 2011). The Principles, which consist of seven items, broadly sketch out the commitment of Japanese industry to collectively contributing to a sustainable society, but they impose neither monitoring instruments nor sanctions. As of August 2013, 185 financial institutions were signatories to the Principles, including 86 local banks and 40 local credit associations.[47]

For its part, the Ministry of Economic, Trade and Industry (METI) issued a set of Guidelines for Disclosure of Intellectual Asset-based Management in 2005. The ministry recommended processes for disclosing intangible assets, such as intellectual and human capital. This initiative later led to an intellectual asset project at the OECD (Sumita, 2008). Sakakibara et al. (2010) find that METI's guidelines have advanced private initiatives related to intangible value accounting and reporting.

The Ministry of Health, Labour and Welfare (MHLW) has promoted diversity and CSR at the workplace since 1999 through the Family Friendly Award and the Equal Opportunities Award.[48] These awards are granted to companies that have demonstrated best practices in work–life balance schemes and in the development of female employees' career paths. These awards have led to increased company disclosure on these issues, which, in turn, supported the launch of a few SRI funds focused on gender issues.

In 2006, the Tokyo Stock Exchange mandated reporting on corporate governance for listed companies in line with the 2003 disclosure decree, issued by the prime minister's Cabinet Office. The decree made the disclosure of business risks and corporate governance a mandatory part of statutory financial reporting.[49] In March 2010, Japan's Financial Services Agency (FSA) amended the ordinance to mandate the disclosure of director and auditor remuneration, as well as voting results and several other elements (FSA, 2010).

Abenomics and corporate governance reforms

Since becoming prime minister in December 2012, Shinzo Abe has introduced an aggressive set of monetary, fiscal and structural reform policies. While the Japanese economy shows signs of recovery, the structural reform, dubbed the 'third arrow' of Abenomics, is supposed to set Japan back onto a sustainable growth track. Unveiled in June 2013, the growth strategy contains some planned corporate governance revisions, such as amending the Company Act to promote 'truly independent' external directors, introducing a Japanese version of the UK Stewardship Code, encouraging private investment and improving the return of long-term investment.[50]

Currently, many preparatory measures are ongoing. In July 2013, METI launched a project entitled 'Competitiveness and Incentives for Sustainable Growth: Building Favorable Relationships between Companies and Investors'.[51] This multi-stakeholder project led to a call for evidence in October 2013 to collect the best dialogue in the value chain, the exercise of fiduciary duty and the effectiveness of independent directors. METI is analyzing the inputs at the time of writing, the results of which are expected to feed into a revision of the Company Act.

In August 2013, the FSA launched the Council of Experts Concerning the Japanese Version of the UK Stewardship Code in August 2013. This was followed by a public consultation for its draft Stewardship Code issued on 26 December 2013. The Code, consisting of seven principles, is an experiment for Japan to employ for the first time a 'comply or explain' method.[52] Meanwhile, the Nippon Individual Saving Accounts (NISA), a small lot, tax-free investment scheme, was launched on 1 January 2014. NISA, which grants up to a five-year tax-free period for the maximum investment of JPY 1 million (USD 10,200), is designed to encourage Japan's household savers to invest in stocks, bonds and other assets (FSA website).[53]

Finally, the Japanese government's pension reform is taking center stage at the time of writing. Released on 20 November 2013, an advisory panel to the Japanese government proposed that GIPF must reform its governance and investment strategy: reducing the domestic bond holdings to a lower limit of 52 per cent to diversify into overseas assets, private equity, commodities, infrastructure and real estate investment trusts. [54] A new index, JPX-Nikkei Index 400, launched jointly by the Japan Exchange Group, the Tokyo Stock Exchange and the Nikkei on 6 January 2014, is said to usher in both private investment and public pension reform. The index incorporates profitability criteria such as a minimum 40 per cent of three-year average ROE as well as three-year cumulative operating profit in its selection process.[55]

Prospects and challenges: will SRI and the long-term narratives integrate?

Today, the Japanese SRI community uses the Workers' Capital Guidelines, and disclosure pressure on gender diversity is seen as a universal remedy for the problems restricting the sustained take-off of Japanese SRI. The chief executive and secretary general of JSIF, in an interview by SRI-Connect, stated that "the government is starting to make connections between corporate values, women's empowerment and diversity strategy of companies. This is leading to better disclosure by companies".[56] In the same interview, GIPF reform, NISA and integrated reporting were also identified as positive factors that would increase SRI in Japan. In essence, the SRI community assumes that 'legitimate' external pressures will induce investors to dutifully consider ESG issues (Miyai, 2011; Kanai and Takezume, 2011; JSIF, 2011).

The Japanese government has not established substantial instruments to promote SRI. Policy makers remain unconvinced of the potential of SRI, referring to studies indicating that Japanese SRI funds perform worse than conventional funds (Jin et al., 2005) or on a similar level (Asano and Sasaki, 2011; Suto et al., 2006).[57] Moreover, pension funds have become more skeptical of SRI's credentials given the lack of an objective ESG evaluation standard (Kanai and Takezume, 2011). Highly regarded companies, such as TEPCO, Olympus and Oji Paper, have been embroiled in governance and business ethics scandals. Nuclear energy, supported by METI policy, was regarded as a vital clean energy solution among SRI practitioners up until the nuclear disaster of 11 March 2011.[58]

Furthermore, the FSA seems to regard SRI as part of financial institutions' CSR programs rather than as a strategic instrument for Japan's financial sector.[59] The FSA's 2009 survey revealed *inter alia* that most banks and insurance companies had already as part of their operation, implemented some CSR, while securities companies had been equally driven to implement CSR for image and reputation enhancement (FSA, 2009).[60]

In light of the perceived absence of legitimate pressures on ESG in Japan, one important question arises: will SRI take root in Japan without integrating into the long-term investment narratives? Kanai and Takezume (2011) present an argument, like most SRI supporters, that more pressures are needed to crystallize the most salient ESG criteria for meaningful SRI engagement in Japan.

This author takes another view: SRI is unlikely to take root in Japan before the SRI community addresses the fundamental concerns of retail investors and pension funds. Worse, exerting more pressures to adopt the ESG language may reinforce cyclical instability and artificial learning by pension and fund managers (Sakuma, 2012). The author suggests that Japan's SRI community needs to be integrated into the long-term investment movement. To reach that point, however,

Table 16.4 Most relevant information for selected long-term asset managers by Business Policy Forum Japan

Key Concept	*Nissay Asset Management(buy-side)*	*Commons Asset Management(buy-side)*	*Daiwa Capital Markets(sell-side)*
Mindset of managers	Top management's attitude or stance to society	Corporate attitude towards communication and disclosure	Management's view on competitor strategy/ vision of 10 years later
Consistency	Degrees of integration of corporate mission in employee behaviors	Consistency of corporate message	Management's passions ('omoi') and concrete plans to realize them
Internal integration	Link between CSR department and others	Link between a CSR department and investor relations	Link between investor relations and the top management
Ability to manage risks	Organizational ability to recover from disaster	Organizational ability to manage diversity	Organizational ability to manage regulatory and environmental risks

Source: Compiled by the author based on the interview text annexed to the Business Policy Forum Japan report, March 2012 (in Japanese).

it may require two conditions. First, the SRI actors need to speak out about uncomfortable issues related to Japanese management and governance. Without the profound engagement in discussions of the root causes of social and governance problems and in the creation of a logic for sustained performance, the government and the mainstream investment community is unlikely to be convinced.

Second, SRI leaders may need to broaden their perspectives of what ESG actually means in the Japanese societal context. The acronym ESG, like SRI, has been imported to Japan without profound contextualization. Sakakibara et al. (2010), for example, argue that experienced financial analysts in Japan already consider non-financial information such as management quality, human capital and relational capital in their investment decisions. Selected buy-side and sell-side interviews, conducted by Business Policy Forum Japan (2012), support this view: the most relevant information long-term investors look at are the mindset of corporate managers, consistency of messages, internal integration of CSR and organizational ability to manage risks (Table 16.4).

If this is the case, the SRI community should be bold enough to challenge the imported definition of SRI and develop its own notion of ESG integration with the help of grassroots long-term investors. This entails a shift from current demonstration of RI-SRI compliance to behavioral change.

Notes

1 As the acronym SRI more accurately represents the concept that has been embraced in Japan, SRI instead of RI is used throughout this chapter.
2 The first such eco-fund was the Nikko Eco Fund, which was launched in August 1999.
3 The Japanese government wished to turn Japan into a world-class financial center in the aftermath of the bursting of the financial bubble and the growing number of non-performing loans in the 1990s. Between 1997 and 2001, the government removed stock commission fees and facilitated new fund introductions with a view to shifting individual financial assets toward stocks and mutual funds (Gordon, 2003).
4 JiJi press news as quoted by Skynews.com.au, Monday, 5 May 2014.

5 The JPY-USD exchange rate at 1 JPY = 0.0102 USD as of 30 September 2013. The volume in USD is indicated based on this exchange rate, unless it is indicated otherwise.
6 This calculation was based on the PRI signatory Kikkoman Corporate Pension fund (8 per cent of all AUM), the Secom Corporate Pension Fund (less than 10 per cent of AUM) and the non-signatory Pension Fund Association for Local Government Officials (0.06 per cent of AUM).
7 Saotome and Yamamoto (2011) also show that outflow from eco and SRI funds has accelerated since 2008. Inflow into mainstream funds grew to JPY 15 trillion from September 2008 to September 2011, while eco and SRI funds experienced an outflow of JPY 280 billion during the same period.
8 JSIF website. Online. Available HTTP: <http://www.sifjapan.org/document/srimkt.pdf> (accessed 27 September 2014).
9 The extended period of sluggishness in the Japanese stock market and the low interest rate meant that most new retail funds were global equity, global fixed income or global hybrid funds.
10 Daiwa Securities launched the first vaccine bond, issued by IFFim, in March 2008 by bringing it to the Japanese uridashi market, which is a mechanism to raise money from individuals in markets less familiar with the direct purchase of bonds. Other popular impact investments are climate change bonds, anti-poverty bonds and water and education bonds (SIF Japan, 2011).
11 In effect, Japanese investors channeled JPY 111 billion as a donation to the Global Alliance on Vaccines and Immunization (GAVI Alliance) (IFFim press release, 20 May 2010).
12 In contrast to retail social contribution bonds denominated in emerging market currencies, the bonds sold to institutional investors are mostly denominated in USD.
13 The figure excludes ETF.
14 Takehara and Yamada (2007) find that the average turnover ratio for mutual funds is 18 per cent per annum and that of individual equity investment is 82 per cent from January 1981 to December 1999.
15 NRI (2013) explains that an increase in sales of products whose sales commission was particularly high contributes to an increasing trend of weighted average sales commission for open-ended funds in Japan.
16 Sawakami Asset Management website. Online. Available HTTP: <http://www.sawakami.co.jp/> (accessed 18 January 2014).
17 The biggest fund is Fidelity Japan Growth fund (JPY 361.87 billion, or USD 6.69 billion), according to the data generated by Ibbotson Associates Japan based on MorningstarDirect data.
18 The Club is managed by one member – I-O Wealth Advisor – specializing in organizing seminars and issuing magazines related to long-term investment. The founder is former CEO of Barclays Global Investors Japan (today Black Rock Japan).
19 There is a sign of improvement in Japan's pension sector. Japan's compound annual growth of the 5-year (2007–2012) and 10-year periods (2002–2012) was the lowest among the 13 largest pension markets (Towers and Watson, 2013), Nikkei (9 January 2014) reports that GPIF marked a record high return of 18 per cent in 2013. The total public funds' return was doubled to JPY 18 trillion from JPY 9 trillion in 2012.
20 Actuary calculations based on the decline in the fertility rate and the acceleration of the aging population have been presented on numerous occasions (Tajika, 2002). The 2004 pension reform introduced the most comprehensive trimming of benefits and increased the level of government support for the pension fund from one-third to one-half. Kage (2011) argues that the pension reform of 2004 made the public pension sustainable for the next 100 years.
21 According to Towers Watson (2013), 98 per cent of pension assets are of DB plans as of end 2012.
22 The Mutual Aid Association for Tokyo Metropolitan Teachers and Officials, which serves about 112,000 public school teachers and officials in the Tokyo metropolitan area, committed JPY 2 billion of its JPY 84 billion pension portfolio to SRI strategies. Online. Available HTTP: <http://www.socialfunds.com> (accessed 19 June 2003).
23 Both Kikkoman and Secom apply SRI to nearly 10 per cent of their respective corporate pension funds (Kanai and Takezume, 2011).
24 The 2011 survey's response rate was only 17 per cent (out of 1,430 target pension funds) in comparison with a rate of 32.5 per cent (out of 1,432 target pension funds), according to Kanai and Takezume (2011).
25 The JSIF survey should be read with prudence, as only 46 funds responded out of 2,000 pension funds surveyed (a response rate of 2 per cent) during the end of March 2013 to mid-May 2013. The remaining 42 per cent would like to consider and 5 per cent are considering or plan to consider.
26 Shichousonren press release, 30 January 2012.

27 Arisa Kishigami explains in her article on Responsible-Investors.com (21 July 2010) that companies have been weary of engaging with stakeholders because of Japan's history of dealing with the 'AGM people', or *Soukai-ya*, who used criminal extortion tactics that threatened to disrupt AGMs.
28 Jacoby (2006) quotes interview results by Learmount, S. (2002) Corporate governance: what can be learned from Japan? Oxford: Oxford University Press. P.24.
29 The other half is denominated in Australian dollars (AUD), New Zealand dollars (NZD), Turkish lira (TRL) and other currencies.
30 The Rockefeller Foundation developed the concept of impact investment in 2007–2008, and the Global Impact Investing Network was created in 2009.
31 Taga and Murakami (2011) find that 12 citizen funds focusing on autonomous renewable energy raised JPY 2.88 billion, while 28 solidarity funds for reconstruction organized by Music Securities only raised JPY 0.42 billion by the end of 2011.
32 Based on a survey of 1,143 corporate pension funds and their 87 trustee organizations (qualified response rates of 65 per cent and 63 per cent, respectively), Omura et al. (2002) find that 38 per cent of corporate pensions and 45.2 per cent of trustees believe that outside director systems and the independence of auditors are necessary for improving corporate management. These figures can be compared with those for the introduction of auditing committees (3.9 per cent, 4 per cent), the introduction of incentive rewards (4.4 per cent, 5.2 per cent) and the execution of shareholder oversight (3.45 per cent, 8.4 per cent).
33 The response rate is low for this survey (3.5 per cent). The questionnaire was distributed to 17,086 members of SAAJ and 599 responses were received, of which 39.4 per cent (236) came from professional analysts.
34 Based on JSIF's survey response of 19 funds out of 25 funds that have integrated or plan to integrate ESG into their active management, 84 per cent saw the governance the most important issue compared to 42 per cent for social and 58 per cent for environment.
35 The survey is based on a sample of 1,108 investors out of 2,300 (a response rate of 48 per cent). A questionnaire was sent by post and responses obtained during a period of 1 August 2013 to 12 August 2013.
36 OECD analyzes that Japan's average annual income in 2012 was JPY 400,300 (USD 4,080) on constant prices. Data extracted on 17 January 2014 06:02 UTC (GMT) from OECD.StatExtract.
37 26 per cent are holding less than JPY 3 million (USD 30,600).
38 CPRD's research was used by Morningstar Japan to create Japan's first SRI index in 2003.
39 Eight asset management companies of non-Japanese origin offered SRI funds: Amundi, Deutsch Asset Management, BNP Pariba Investment Partners, UBS Global, Fidelity, Invesco, Russell Investment and Pine Bridge.
40 Financial institutions included two banks from Mitsui Sumitomo group (trust and commercial) and Development Bank of Japan, two asset management companies, two insurance companies and one securities company. The information providers were: IntegreX, Carbon Disclosure Project, EIRIS, FTSE Group and Bloomberg LP, MSCI and Quick.
41 Kanai and Takezume (2011) suggest that the OECD recommendations have raised numerous concerns among the SRI community.
42 It also calls for GPIF to consider becoming a signatory of the UN PRI.
43 See more on the website. Online. Available HTTP: <http://www.investlife.jp/>.
44 After the introduction of the Kyoto Protocol (COP 3), the Japanese government enacted the Act on Promotion of Global Warming Countermeasures in 1998.
45 Both Guidelines were subsequently updated in 2002 and 2003. The Environmental Accounting Guideline was again updated in 2005.
46 This law, which is officially called the 'Law Concerning the Promotion of Business Activities with Environmental Consideration by Specified Corporations, etc., by Facilitating Access to Environmental Information, and Other Measures' (No. 77 of 2004), stipulates in Article 5 that "Citizens shall strive to include environmental information as a consideration in investing and other activities".
47 The Ministry of Environment's website shows the latest status on signatories. Online. Available HTTP: <http://www.env.go.jp/policy/keiei_portal/kinyu/shomeikikan.html>.
48 The MHLW merged the two awards in 2007.
49 This was followed by the Tokyo Stock Exchange's launch of Corporate Governance Principles for listed companies in 2004.

50 The Growth Strategy omits a labor reform and female empowerment in the board. Moreover, Abenomics' boosting of the employment rate of women (aged 25–44) to 73 per cent by 2020 (currently 68 per cent) will be done by building sufficient child care facilities to reduce the wait time.
51 METI was running a precursor project called Corporate Reporting Lab since July 2012 to provide companies and investors an opportunity to deepen dialogues and enhance corporate value. A progress report (August 2013) is available at <http://www.meti.go.jp/english/press/2013/0823_01.html>.
52 According to the *Financial Times* of 27 December 2013, the Japanese Code deviated from the UK Code in two scores: collective actions and disclosure items. The former is replaced with engagement with 'deep understanding' (brackets in the original text) and exchange of views, while the latter does not specify disclosure items as regards how investors vote.
53 Online. Available HTTP: <http://www.fsa.go.jp/policy/nisa/02.pdf> (accessed 20 January 2014).
54 An interview article with Mr. Ito, head of the advisory panel to GPIF, 'GPIF needs to sell bonds now, advisory panel chief says' by Bloomberg, December 6, 2013, originally published in Pension and Investment.
55 See more online. Available HTTP: <http://www.tse.or.jp/english/market/topix/jpx_nikkei.html> (accessed 20 January 2014).
56 An interview text is available online. Available HTTP: <http://www.sri-connect.com/index.php?option=com_content&view=article&id=368&Itemid=1022> (accessed 20 January 2014).
57 "ESG is not a big topic for discussion in the GIPF review" says the chief executive and secretary general of JSIF in the above interview.
58 Kawaguchi (2011) reported that 17 of 31 SRI funds had invested in nuclear energy generation companies; 11 of these had invested in TEPCO but sold their TEPCO investments following the nuclear disaster in Fukushima. Moreover, the Morningstar SRI Index included Olympus, FTSE4Good and Ethibel Index Oji Paper as of the latter half of 2010 (BERC, 2011). Kawauchi (2011) also asserts that the change by FTSE4good to include best-in-class nuclear energy generators as of the autumn of 2010 cemented the confidence in this industry conveyed by Japan's SRI community.
59 The Japanese FSA conducted surveys to assess the status of CSR among Japanese financial institutions in 2006 and 2009.
60 Banks and insurance companies pointed to their natural responsibilities in terms of their service of the local community as the main reason for CSR. This is in contrast with securities companies, for which CSR is driven by reputation and image improvement as much as by finance's role in local community development. A total of 1,343 banks, insurance companies and securities companies (response rate of 96 per cent) and 2,757 non-banks (59 per cent) were surveyed in early 2009 (FSA, 2009).

References

Aronson, B. E. (2010) 'A Japanese CalPERS or a new model for institutional investor activism? Japan's Pension Fund Association and the emergence of shareholder activism in Japan'. Online. Available HTTP: <http://works.bepress.com/bruce_aronson/1>.

Asano, R. and Sasaki, T. (2011) 'Empirical study on SRI funds performance', special report, Securities Analyst Association in Japan, May (in Japanese).

Buchanan, J. (2007) 'Japanese corporate governance and the principle for "internalism"', *Corporate Governance: An International Review*, Vol. 15, No. 1: 27–35.

Business Ethics Research Centre (2011) 'A list of Japanese companies included in major SRI indexes in latter half of 2010'. Online. Available HTTP: <http://www.berc.gr.jp/pdf/2010SRI_J.pdf>.

Business Policy Forum Japan (2012) *Non-financial reporting by companies (Kigyo no hizaimu johokaiji no arikata ni kansuru hokokusho)*, March. Online. Available HTTP: <http://www.bpfj.jp/act/download_file/8428429/95101661.pdf> (in Japanese).

Daiwa Research Institute (2011) 'CSR and sustainability (Kigyono shakaitekisekinin to jizokukanousei)', presentation by Mariko Kawaguchi, 24 August. Online. Available HTTP: http://www.fukuoka-realty.jp/pdf/study/csr20111017025724_a3f03e35b5ee73c2e176142493c14386.pdf.

Financial Services Agency (2009) 'A summary of surveys on financial institutions CSR', 31 March. Online. Available HTTP: <http://www.fsa.go.jp/news/20/ginkou/20090331-7.html> (in Japanese).

Financial Services Agency (2010) *Outline of disclosure items concerning corporate governance*, 26 March.

Gilson, R. J. and Milhaupt, C. J. (2004) 'Choice as regulatory reform: the case of Japanese corporate governance', ECGI – Law Working Paper No. 22/2004; Columbia Law and Economics Working Paper

No. 251; Stanford Law and Economics Olin Working Paper No. 282. Online. Available HTTP: <http://ssrn.com/abstract=537843>.

Gordon, B. (2003) *Effects of Japan's financial big bang on consumers*, October. Online. Available HTTP: <http://wgordon.web.wesleyan.edu/papers/bigbang.htm>.

Iwai, K. (2007) *The future of Japan's mutual fund industry*, Nomura Institute of Capital Markets Research, 18 October version. Online. Available HTTP: <http://www.nomurafoundation.or.jp/data/20071018_Koichi_Iwai.pdf>.

Jacoby, S. M. (2006) 'Principles and agents: CalPERS and corporate governance change in Japan', Institute for Technology, Enterprise and the Competitiveness, Doshisha University, ITEC Working Paper Series 06-03, March.

Jacoby, S. M. (2007) 'Principles and agents: CalPERS and corporate governance in Japan', *Corporate Governance: An International Review*, Vol. 15, No. 1: 5–15.

Japan Securities Dealers Association (2013) *The results of a opinion poll on retail investors' sentiment towards securities investment (Kojintoshika no shokentoshi nikansuru ishikichousa)* (in Japanese).

Jin, H. H., Mitchell, O. S. and Piggott, J. (2005) 'Socially responsible investment in Japanese pensions', NBER Working Paper Series, Working Paper 1174, National Bureau of Economic Research. Online. Available HTTP: <http://www.nber.org/papers/w11747>.

JSIF (former SIF Japan) (2007) *Review of socially responsible investment in Japan*. Online. Available HTTP: <http://www.sifjapan.org/document/sri2007_english.pdf>.

JSIF (former SIF Japan), (2009) *Review of socially responsible investment in Japan.*

JSIF (former SIF Japan) (2011) *Review of socially responsible investment in Japan.*

JSIF (former SIF Japan) (2013) *Pension funds in Japan and ESG investment* (in Japanese).

Kage, Y. (2011) 'Japan's reform of its pension system for sustainability', *Journal of Investment Consulting*, Vol. 12, No. 2: 59–66.

Kanai, T. and Takezume, H. (2011) 'Pension and SRI', *2011Review of Socially Responsible Investment in Japan*, chapter 2, Social Investment Forum Japan (in Japanese)

Kawaguchi, M. (2011) Nuclear energy and shareholder responsibility', *Kinyu ZaiseiJijo*, 25 July:16–19 (in Japanese).

Kim, K. B. (2004) 'Finding an entry point for the promotion of corporate social responsibility in small and medium-sized enterprises in Japan', preliminary draft.

Ministry of the Environment, Japan (2011) *Principles for financial action towards a sustainable society (principles for financial action for the 21st century).* Online. Available HTTP: <http://www.env.go.jp/press/file_view.php?serial=18559&hou_id=14289>.

Miyai, H. (2011) 'Pension assets investment in ESG towards sustainable economic growth', *Nikko Financial Intelligence Research Review*, December (in Japanese).

Nomura Research Institute (2009) *Demographic aging and Japan's public pension system*, Vol. 54, special edition, 10 April.

Nomura Research Institute (2013) *Japan's asset management business 2013/2014*. Online. Available HTTP: <http://fis.nri.co.jp/~/media/Files/publication/research/JAMB2013_2014.pdf>.

OECD (2009) *The guidelines for pension fund governance*, June 2009.

Omura, K., Suto, M. and Masuko, M. (2002) 'Corporate governance of Japanese institutional investors – major results of questionnaires concerning corporate governance by institutional investors', Ministry of Finance, Policy Research Institute, Discussion Paper Series (No.02A – 28), September.

Rengo (2010) *Guidelines on responsible investment of workers' capital.* Online. Available HTTP: <//www.jtuc-rengo.or.jp/kurashi/sekinin_toushi/data/20101216_workers_capital_en.pdf>.

Research Institute for Policies on Pension & Aging (2008) 'A research report related to SRI and PRI', January (in Japanese).

Research Institute of Economy, Trade and Industry (RIETI) (2003) *About CSR and new money flow – discussion points and policy directions*, 23 July (in Japanese).

Sakakibara, S., Hansson, B., Yosano, T. and Kozumi, H. (2010) 'Analysts' perceptions of intellectual capital information', *Australian Accounting Review*, No. 54, Vol. 20, Issue 3: 274–285.

Sakuma, K. (2001) 'Japan', in Gugler, K. (ed.) *Corporate Governance and Economic Performance*, chapter 12, Oxford University Press, 139–155.

Sakuma, K. (2012) 'Conformance and non conformance of asset managers to environment, social and governance pressures – sense making capacities and the use of external defined information', PhD thesis, Solvay Business School of Economics and Management, Universite Libre de Bruxelles, 18 June.

Sakuma, K. and Louche, C. (2008) 'Socially responsible investment in Japan: its mechanism and drivers', *Journal of Business Ethics*, Vol. 82: 425–448.

Saotome, T. and Yamamoto, S. (2011) 'Trends in retail SRI products', *2011 Review of Socially Responsible Investment in Japan*, chapter 1, Social Investment Forum Japan (in Japanese).

Securities Analysts Association of Japan (2010) 'ESG factors used in corporate valuations', Working Group on ESG Factors in Corporate Valuation, June. Online. Available HTTP: <http://www.saa.or.jp/account/account/pdf/report_esg_201006.pdf> (in Japanese).

Solomon, A., Solomon, J. F. and Suto, M. (2004) 'Can the UK experience provide lessons for the evolution of SRI in Japan?', *Corporate Governance: An International Review*, Vol. 12, No. 4: 552–566.

Stewart, F. and Yermo, J. (2010) 'Options to improve the governance and investment of Japan's government pension investment fund', OECD Working Papers on Finance, Insurance and Private Pensions, No. 6, OECD Publishing. Online. Available at: <doi:10.1787/5kgkmb9v0vhk-en>.

Sugita, K. (1997) 'How the Japanese investment trusts has changed since 1994', *Securities Analysis Journal*, Vol. 35: 2–12.

Sumita, T. (2008) 'Intellectual assets-based management for innovation: lessons from experiences in Japan', *Journal of Intellectual Capital*, Vol.9, No. 2: 206–227.

Suto, M., Masuko, M. and Wakazono, T. (2006) 'CSR activities and performance: return and risk (in Japanese)', Waseda University Institute of Finance Working Paper Series, WIF-06–002, September.

Taga, S. and Murakami, M. (2011) 'Community investment', *2011 Review of Socially Responsible Investment in Japan*, chapter 4, Social Investment Forum Japan (in Japanese).

Tajika, E. (2002) 'The public pension system in Japan the consequences of rapid expansion', World Bank Institute working paper, Stock No. 37203.

Takaba, M., Yamazaki, A. and Kishigami A. (2011) 'Shareholder advocacy', *2011 Review of Socially Responsible Investment in Japan*, chapter 3, Social Investment Forum Japan (in Japanese).

Takehara, H. and Yamada, T. (2007) *The impact of fund turnover on Japanese mutual fund performance*, NUS Business School. Online. Available HTTP: <http://bschool.nus.edu.sg/staffprofile/bizty/MFTover701.pdf>.

Tanimoto, K. (ed.) (2003) *Socially Responsible Investment*, Nihon Keizai Publisher (in Japanese).

Towers Watson (2013) *Global pension asset study 2013*, Executive Summary.

Yamamoto, T. (2011) 'Conclusions', *2011 Review of Socially Responsible Investment in Japan*, Social Investment Forum Japan (in Japanese).

17

Responsible investment in Russia

Yulia Sofronova

Introduction

The Principles for Responsible Investment (PRI) defines responsible investment as an approach of integrating environmental, social and corporate governance risks into investment decision-making processes. What are these risks for businesses and the investment community in Russia, and how are these issues being addressed?

Financial institutions in Russia have not always been in line with the highest standards and best international practices of their peers. The regulatory environment and the overall oversight of non-banking financial institutions have been weak, and the most significant problem has been insufficient transparency by financial market participants. The Investor Protection Association (2012) recommends that a key solution to these problems would be compliance of financial institutions with relevant industry standards and codes of practice, as happens in western practices.

Russia has seen a tremendous shift in its financial markets from 1991, and it has not always been able to keep up with establishing the necessary mechanisms, nor has it looked to best practices elsewhere in order to improve its own.

Overview of Russia

Russia is the largest country in the world by area, with its territory spreading over Eurasia from Eastern Europe all the way to Pacific Ocean. The country is a federal republic consisting of 21 republics (territories of resident ethnic groups), 46 provinces (regions), four autonomous okrugs, nine krays (territories), two federal cities and one autonomous oblast. Each constituent entity of the federation possesses its own charters, political institutions and local legislation (Baker & McKenzie, 2014). The president is the head of state, and the prime minister is the head of the government. The 'government' is composed of the premier, his deputies, and ministers (all appointed by the president). The premier is also confirmed by the Duma. The lowest governmental level is local self-government, which under current law can range from community-level government to the governments of towns and villages (Baker & McKenzie, 2014). Among its developed industries are mining and extractive industries; all forms of machine building; defence; shipbuilding; road and rail transportation equipment; communications equipment; agricultural machinery, electric power generating and transmitting equipment; medical and scientific instruments; consumer durables, textiles, foodstuffs, handicrafts, etc. Russia is one of the largest extractives producers in the world, and its wealth and economy is also largely dependent on these resources. According to CIA World Factbook, Russia's GDP per capita was $18,100 in 2013. Direct foreign investment reached $552.8 billion by end of 2013. Russia's population reached over 142 million (as of July 2014), with 99.7 per cent being literate. Average life expectancy is 64 years for men and 76 years for women. The judicial system of the Russian Federation includes the following highest courts: Supreme Court of the Russian Federation (consists of 23 members), Constitutional Court (consists of 19 members) and the Superior Court of Arbitration (consists of a chairman and four deputy chairmen). All members of Russia's three highest courts are nominated by the president and appointed by the Federation Council (the upper house of the legislature) and are appointed for life.

Russia has a goal of moving towards a market system based on private capital investment and enterprise. The government has set an ambitious goal of getting the country to 20th place by 2018 in the World Bank's 'Doing Business' survey (June 2013). Last year Russia rose by 20 places, from 112 to 92, out of 189 countries and appeared ahead of its BRIC counterparts Brazil, China and India. However, according to the World Economic Forum's Global Competitiveness Index 2012–2013, Russia's institutional investment ranks only 133 out of 144 countries. The Transparency International Corruption Index (2013) ranks Russia as 127th out of 177 countries with a score of 28 (where zero means that a country is perceived as highly corrupt and 100 means it is perceived as being free of corruption). These rankings demonstrate that the country is still viewed by the world as a difficult place to invest or do business in.

ESG challenges in Russia

According to Sustainalytics' report *Addressing ESG Risks in Emerging Markets* (2012), Russian companies are second to last with regard to the areas of business ethics–related practices and policies (bribery, corruption and whistleblowing) not because such practices and policies lack transparency, but in many cases because these have simply not been established.

Company ownership structure is another issue foreign investors face in Russia. In many cases the ownership structure is such that one person controls a majority stake in the company. State-owned corporations are common, and despite the first wave of privatization having taken place in the 1990s, the government still kept large stakes in companies in sectors of strategic importance, such as military, oil, aviation, manufacturing, utilities, media and finance. In October 2010 the government approved the plan for further privatization by 2016 of a wide range of state-controlled corporations, and the final privatization program was adopted in June 2013. The program foresees the Russian government fully divesting from such companies as VTB, Sovkomflot, Rosagroleasing, Sheremetyevo International Airport, etc. The government is also planning to reduce its stakes in Aeroflot – Russian Airlines, Alrosa and RusHydro. However, in many cases, such as the possible sale of shares in Aeroflot or Alrosa, the state may utilize its right to retain a 'golden share', a corporate governance mechanism allowing its representatives to stay on the board, and granting them the power to veto any significant transactions, changes in capital and corporate reorganization.

In addition to this, Russian law so far has made it legitimate for minority shareholders to be squeezed out by majority shareholders or avoid payment of dividends to shareholders. Last year the Federal Financial Markets Service (FFMS) banned Pakva and Novy Registrator (the registrar for Seventh Continent shares) from a mandatory buyout by minority shareholders – Pakva switched registrars to avoid the ban. In the TNK-BP story, Rosneft took away all the cash and left nothing for dividends to minority shareholders of TNK-BP when a takeover took place

(Gorst, 2013). There have been steps taken in the last few years to resolve these issues, and we will come back to the details of such initiatives later, but it can be said that until now Russia's business conditions – lack of transparency and involvement in corrupt practices, complicated governance practices discouraging influence from foreign investors and regulation not being able to protect minority shareholders' rights –set the precedent for a difficult investment environment for foreign investors.

When it comes to social issues, the challenges Russian companies face often relate to customers and employees. Customers have been greatly affected by the monopolistic nature of many companies and have concerns about antitrust practices and monopolistic approaches to pricing. Employee health and safety concerns are also significant due to the nature of Russia's primary industrial sectors (namely steel, mining, and oil and gas) and the lack of adequate oversight in this regard. However, it is worth highlighting that there is mixed feedback about company safety measures. While Sustainalytics (2012) reports that many of the controversies involving Russian companies have to do with incidents and fatalities on work sites, Nordea (2013) points out as key takeaways from their 2013 visit to companies that "many are implementing ESG risk management systems in line with those of their Western peers (environmental management systems being certified, other global certified systems, etc.), however, they lag behind on reporting and communicating how they work with ESG issues". Companies can and must be better at reporting and communicating ESG risks, something often heard from the investor side.

Last but not least, Russia's industrial infrastructure is underdeveloped and outdated, and this puts pressure on the environment. Strict environmental standards have yet to be imposed on companies, and thus this is not yet a matter of regulatory compliance, says Sustainalytics (2012) in its report. Of the Russian companies they analyzed, only 60 per cent have environmental policies or environmental management systems in place.

Today, awareness of ESG risks and what these may mean for investors and the business community is growing, driven by increased legislation and demand from both foreign investors and public opinion. There are some positive steps towards changes in the regulatory environment, legal frameworks and the enforcement of regulations relevant to corporate ESG performance. Of particular note are initiatives to address the country's regulatory and legislative issues, such as reviewing the Russian Corporate Governance Code, with an aim to increase disclosure and transparency, and strengthening the rights of minority shareholders.

Regulatory environment

The Russian government recognizes the challenge the country faces in attracting foreign investors, and the president has made the task of improving the country's investment attractiveness a top policy priority.

The Agency for Strategic Initiatives (ASI), formed in 2011 to support small and medium businesses (SMEs) in Russia, was also tasked to improve Russia's investment climate. Together with other business associations, the ASI has been working with federal and regional governments to create favourable conditions for SMEs and set the standards in the regions to help attract foreign investments. Regions have been given the opportunity to develop infrastructure, establish their own structures of cooperating with foreign investors and make use of public–private partnerships (PPPs). Regular assessment of progress towards set targets is carried out by ASI.

The Russian Direct Investment Fund (RDIF), a $10 billion fund established by the Russian government to make equity investments primarily in the Russian economy, was created in 2011 to co-finance foreign investments. A number of initiatives have been established by the RDIF to help achieve the set objectives, including the formation of the Investment Council, an advisory body that was created and mandated to produce legislation and improve existing rules in order to stimulate investment demand and supply in the country.

In 2010 the government launched an initiative to make Moscow one of the international financial centres, and partnered with 'TheCityUK' in 2011 to bring in the expertise of senior practitioners from both the Russian and UK financial services industries (TheCityUK, 2010). The Moscow International Finance Centre (MIFC) Taskforce set up by the group has focused its work on several areas, including, but not limited to, improving the regulatory and supervisory environment, putting an emphasis on education, training and professional qualifications and looking at funding options of available PPP models in Russia.

In the need for a unified approach to regulation of diverse financial groups, similar to the experience of the UK and other European countries, parts of the FFMS (and the non-banks supervisor) and the Central Bank of Russia (CBR) were integrated in early 2013 to create a so-called mega-regulator. Effective March 2014, financial market regulation, control and oversight functions were delegated to the new Bank of Russia (the mega-regulator). While the earlier regulator was responsible only for market control and oversight, the new mega-regulator has been designed to combine this responsibility with overall market development, and as such sets out three key tasks for the financial sector: regulation and oversight, financial market development and consumer rights protection. Although the Bank of Russia's new role may take time to bring positive change, many believe that the mega-regulator may standardize regulation and reporting by overseeing both commercial banks and other non-banking financial institutions. This, as quoted by Standard & Poor's (2014), may increase the country's institutional system transparency and improve today's weakness of some segments of non-banking regulation in the future. Currently, reporting forms of brokers and asset managers normally comply only with Russian Accounting Standards (RAS) (often lower in quality to International Financial Reporting Standards [IFRS]) and are not always published. Insurance companies have filed their annual reports according to IFRS since 2012, but continue to report quarterly on RAS and do not always publish full reports according to both standards.

New laws such as the federal law on the Central Depositary and amendments to the federal laws on the securities market and on joint stock companies were also adopted. These changes contributed to the improvement of protection of ownership rights, information disclosure and transparency and payment of dividends. According to the MIFC Roadmap Progress Report (Moscow International Finance Centre, 2014), the Ministry for Economic Development has been looking into the possibility of introducing amendments regulating affiliation and liability of controlling shareholders in the Joint-Stock Companies Act and Limited Liability Companies Act. For instance, the term 'affiliated' was proposed to refer to controlling and controlled companies, companies and individuals performing executive functions and companies owning or co-owning directly or indirectly over 25 per cent of the company. Affiliation should also cover an individual and his closest relations (spouse, parents, children, brothers/sisters and step-brothers/step-sisters, foster parents and adopted children, grandparents, grandchildren, cousins, uncles/aunts etc.)

On 1 July 2014 a new securitization law with rules regulating securitization of various types of assets came into force, which, according to Moody's Investors Service (2014), is a significant improvement to current practices and brings Russia in line with established structured finance markets.

The pension system in Russia

The current structure of the Russian pension system has been in place from 2002 and is the result of major changes to transform a single publicly managed distributive system into a multi-pillar system that consists of both pay-as-you-go funding elements and defined contributions (Pension

Funds Online, 2014). The structure includes obligatory pension insurance, non-state pension insurance and state pension support. Obligatory state pension insurance is a mandatory monthly contribution by employers towards their employees' pensions. Such pensions are paid out of the Pension Fund of the Russian Federation, and assets are managed by the state-owned asset manager Vnesheconombank by default. From 2004, non-state pension funds were allowed to participate in the state obligatory pension and citizens were given the option to outsource the management of their pension to a licensed non-state pension fund or to a third-party asset manager.

Non-state voluntary pension insurance are payments by non-state pension funds only, and to be eligible for such one needs to make voluntary contributions to one of the non-state pension funds via an individual voluntary pension plan or a voluntary corporate pension program.

State social security or state pension support is provided to those who for some reason are not entitled to labour-obligatory pension insurance payouts (e.g., disabled individuals, World War II veterans or those whose health was damaged due to military service, radiation or other technogenic disasters) (Pension Fund of the Russian Federation, 2014).

Russian Corporate Governance Code

Two milestones have been set to help achieve the bigger goal of creating a Moscow International Finance Centre. These are improvement of the Russian Corporate Governance Code and the non-state pension fund industry.

A responsible investment approach requires one to look at environmental, social and corporate governance issues. It is normal practice for investors to first start to look at corporate governance. The OECD initiated the project to review the Russian Corporate Governance Code (using the 2002 version), which led to creation of working groups comprising Russian government representatives and other key market players, including foreign stakeholders. The draft document was a joint effort by the Central Bank Financial Markets Service and the MIFC Taskforce. The new Code was approved by the Russian government in April 2014 and by the Central Bank of Russia board of directors in March 2014 (Moscow International Finance Centre, 2014). Although the Code is voluntary, and hence companies can implement the Code on a 'comply or explain' basis, the document is certainly a development of the corporate governance system in Russia. The Code promotes OECD corporate governance standards, and its recommendations include individual chapters on board of directors, including their composition and the more prominent role of independent directors, general shareholder meetings, information disclosure, etc. Key objectives of the Code are to protect the rights of minority shareholders, including their rights to receive dividends.

The Expert Panel on Corporate Governance under the Federal Service for Financial Markets of the Russian Federation, comprising a group of investors and other stakeholders, was established and tasked to work on the implementation of the Code by companies:

- A 30 June 2014 deadline was set for roadmaps on Corporate Governance Code (CGC) implementation in listed companies. Top implementation priority has been assigned to the articles on appointment and termination of appointment of a general director by the board, as well as board control over material transactions and corporate actions in subsidiaries.
- By 1 October 2014, the Ministry for Economic Development, the Central Bank and the MIFC Taskforce have been asked to draft amendments on access of board members to documents and information of controlled companies (on condition of non-disclosure of confidential information) and the general director's personal liability for failing to submit or disclose such information.

Critics say the challenges of implementing the Code may remain with state-owned companies, which are unlikely to comply with the Code. In order to address this, the Ministry for Economic Development, Federal State Property Management Agency, Open Government Minister Mikhail Abyzov and Alexander Voloshin's MIFC Taskforce are due to introduce a list of 50 per cent-plus state-owned companies to the government for priority CGC implementation (Moscow Financial Centre, 2014).

Stock exchange

A merger between the Moscow Interbank Currency Exchange (MICEX) and the Russian Trading System (RTS) reached completion in December 2011. The consolidated stock exchange has been designed as a universal platform for both Russian and international investors to trade in securities, bonds, derivatives and currencies. As of September 2013, Citigroup, Credit Suisse, Merrill Lynch and Morgan Stanley offer clients Direct Market Access to T+2 share trading on the Moscow Exchange. This has become possible due to the Russian stock market adopting the standard global practice of partial pre-deposit and T+2 settlement, centralized clearing and central depositary, making this a starting point for Moscow's integration into the international financial centres system. The united MICEX-RTS IPO took place in February 2013.

Amended listing rules by the Moscow Stock Exchange (MOEX) were released in February 2014. The new rules decrease a number of securities levels from six to three: Level 1, 2 and 3 (where Level 1 is the highest quotation level) and are in line with the revised CGC. Such requirements as at least 20 per cent and no fewer than three directors to be independent, requirement from the boards to form audit, remuneration and personnel committees, where majority of directors must be independent, are now mandatory for issuers to be included on the highest list – Level 1 (MOEX, 2014). For bond issuers, in addition to providing three year IFRS statements, the issuer must have a credit rating. These changes are set to improve corporate governance and boost transparency by companies.

The Bank of Russia website reported that in July 2014 the Central Bank sold off 267.3 million MOEX shares, or 11.7 per cent charter capital, following obligation by federal law for the government to exit MOEX by January 2016. The Central Bank's share was roughly split amongst investors: 15 per cent from Asia, 33 per cent from Europe, around 40 per cent from Russia and over 10 per cent from America. The Central Bank still holds a roughly 11.7 per cent stock in the exchange.

Conclusion and outlook

We have seen that in many countries corporate scandals related to environmental, social or corporate governance issues have caused both companies and investors to start looking into consideration of such risks more seriously. Russia is not an exception with a number of high-profile cases of corporate misbehaviour in the recent years. Some important regulatory changes have been introduced to address Russia's biggest challenges and concerns by institutional investors – legislative loopholes and abuse of minority shareholders' rights. Russia's revised Corporate Governance Code, which has been brought in line with OECD guidelines, and the new listing rules of the Moscow Stock Exchange reflecting new corporate governance recommendations, encouraging uptake of best practices by companies and promoting more transparency disclosure are all a big step forward. The government is continuing to work on the implementation of various related initiatives, and we look forward to seeing further development.

We must not forget that the Russian financial market is very young, and so are its participants, with much activity having started in the late 1990s or early 2000s. The Investor Protection Association (IPA) is an industry association that started in 1999 in this space as an investor coalition to influence change in companies' treatment of minority shareholders. As academic research (Solomon et al, 2004) suggests, there is a strong link between the development and use of corporate governance mechanisms such as engagement and dialogue with companies and the trend for development of social responsible investing, which prompts us to say that socially responsible or responsible investing in Russia is certainly in its infancy or growing stage. However, while progress and engagement around corporate governance issues of companies is obvious, there is yet little dialogue seen around environmental and social issues. This is something that investors in Russia will need to start looking at in order to reach the levels of their foreign counterparts. Perhaps an investor platform such as the IPA is a good place to learn from foreign investors, as IPA's membership comprises both Russian investors and their foreign peers investing in the Russian economy.

Both Sparkes and Cowton (2004) and Solomon et al (2004) draw an interesting parallel between development of socially responsible investment and corporate social responsibility. Vnesheconombank (the Russian national development bank) has been holding a number of conferences not just on the topic of CSR but also with focus on discussions of global practices, trends and opportunities in consideration of ESG in the process of investment decision-making, as well as challenges and advantages of implementing such practices in Russia. As we see in many other markets, there is confusion around the language and terminology of responsible investment, which makes us think that sometimes markets can be relatively advanced in responsible investing, they may just use a different terminology. 'No one size fits all approach' is indeed a good way to sum up the unique way ESG issues are gaining weight amongst the finance community in Russia. They are evolving as a result of extensive stakeholder interaction and consultation and necessary legislative changes and are being driven by investors on one side and the government on the other.

References

Baker and McKenzie (2014) *Doing Business in Russia*. Online. Available HTTP: <http://www.bakermckenzie.com/bkrussiadbi14/>.

CIA World Factbook. Online. Available HTTP: <https://www.cia.gov/library/publications/the-world-factbook/geos/rs.html>.

Gorst, I. (2013) 'Rosneft Rules out Dividend for TNK-BP Minority Shareholders', *Financial Times*, beyondbrics blog, June 6. Online. Available HTTP: http://blogs.ft.com/beyond-brics/2013/06/06/rosneft-rules-out-dividend-for-tnk-bp-minority-shareholders/.

Investor Protection Association (2012) *The Minority Squeeze-out Loophole in Russian Law (Case Studies of Seventh Continent and Power Machines)*. Online. Available HTTP: <http://ipa-moscow.com/content/resources>.

Moody's Investors Service. (2014) *New Russian Securitization Law Is Credit Positive for Russian Structured Finance*, June 17. Online. Available HTTP: https://www.moodys.com/research/Moodys-New-Russian-securitisation-law-is-credit-positive-for-Russian--PR_301943.

Moscow Exchange (2014) 'Moscow Exchange Implements New Listing Rules', press release 9 June. Online. Available HTTP: http://moex.com/n5676.

Moscow International Finance Centre (2013). Online. Available HTTP: <http://mfc-moscow.com/index.php?id=41>.

Nordea ESG annual report (2013). Online. Available HTTP: <http://esg.nordea.com/annualreport/articles/05_riginrussia.html>.

Pension Fund of the Russian Federation. Online. Available HTTP: <http://www.pfrf.ru/ot_en/system/>.

Pension Funds Online. Available HTTP: <http://www.pensionfundsonline.co.uk/content/country-profiles/russia/110>.

Russian Direct Investment Fund. Online. Available HTTP: <http://rdif.ru/Eng_Index/>.

Solomon, A., Solomon, J. F. and Suto, M. (2004) 'Can the UK Experience Provide Lessons for the Evolution of SRI in Japan?', *Corporate Governance 12*(4): 552–566.

Sparkes, R. and Cowton, C. J. (2004) 'The Maturing of Socially Responsible Investment: A Review of the Development Link with Corporate Social Responsibility', *Journal of Business Ethics 52*: 45–57.

Standard & Poor's. Online. Available HTTP: <http://www.mfc-moscow.com/index.php?id=73&_ktid=8&_publid=n1802#n1802>.

Sustainalytics (2012) *Bridging the Gaps: Effectively Addressing ESG Risks in Emerging Markets.* Online. Available HTTP: http://www.sustainalytics.com/node/874/lightbox2.

TheCityUK. Online. Available HTTP: <http://www.thecityuk.com/#&panel1–2>.

Transparency International Corruption Index (2013). Online. Available HTTP: <http://www.transparency.org/research/cpi/overview>.

World Bank's "Doing Business" survey. Online. Available HTTP: <http://www.doingbusiness.org/rankings>.

World Economic Forum's Global Competitiveness Index 2012–2013. Online. Available HTTP: <http://www.weforum.org/issues/global-competitiveness>.

18

Responsible investment in Eastern Europe

Geoffrey Mazullo

Introduction

In September 2012, there were only a few signatories to the UN-backed Principles for Responsible Investment (PRI) and other responsible investment (RI) institutions in Estonia and Poland. As of March 2014, there are three PRI signatories in Estonia and none in Poland. The departure of the Polish institutions demonstrates the fragility of RI in the region; nevertheless, RI is growing in Poland. These two countries will be analyzed in detail in this chapter. Outside of these two countries, as of March 2014 the author is aware of one RI service provider in Bulgaria, Copula Capital Advisors, which is not, however, a PRI signatory.[1]

Corporate governance is a widely known concept in Eastern Europe. In contrast, RI is neither widely known nor practiced. There is no generally accepted definition of RI in Eastern Europe. Only a very small group of financial institutions practice RI.

Prior to a more detailed analysis of the situation in Estonia and Poland, some general observations about the region are provided in order to explain why RI is still in its early stages, both in these two countries and across the region as a whole.

Region overview

Eastern Europe is generally viewed as comprising the following countries: Albania, Bosnia and Herzegovina, Bulgaria, Croatia, Czech Republic, Estonia, Hungary, Kosovo, Latvia, Lithuania, Macedonia, Montenegro, Moldova, Poland, Romania, Russia, Serbia, Slovakia, Slovenia and Ukraine.

Eastern Europe is heterogeneous ethnically, linguistically and in terms of religion. The structure of the economy also varies considerably from country to country, although a general distinction between the region as a whole and Western Europe can be discerned. Eastern Europe is (still) more agricultural, although this is changing in most countries. It industrialized later and is developing its service industries later than Western Europe. Also, a general financial distinction between Eastern Europe and Western Europe can be discerned. In each Eastern European country, GDP, GDP per capita, bank penetration, the size of the capital market, the size of the financial market and the amount of pension assets are, with the exception of Poland, smaller than in Western European peer countries.

The region shares a history of socialism, beginning somewhere between 1917 and 1945.

The financial sector in Eastern Europe transformed completely during the period 1991–2011. Following free elections, many socialist economies were dismantled. State-owned banks and insurance companies were privatized. Stock exchanges were reopened or established for the first time. Pension systems were privatized.

Globalization in general and European Union (EU) accession in particular in 10 countries led to the entry of Western European and global financial players into each Eastern European market. The majority of Eastern European financial institutions are now at least partially foreign owned. In many Eastern European countries one or two financial institutions remain predominately domestically/locally owned.

During the transformation of the financial sector, regulatory authorities and self-regulatory organizations[2] in each Eastern European country worked to adopt international standards and implement best practices in a number of areas. Each stock exchange adopted a corporate governance code. The Warsaw Stock Exchange was the pioneer; it was the first to adopt a 'comply or explain' corporate governance code (in 2002), followed by Budapest, Ljubljana and others. The Partners for Financial Stability (PFS) Program, working in partnership with local accounting and audit associations, conducted training on International Financial Reporting Standards (IFRS). The United Nations Development Program (UNDP) was active across the region, attracting members to its Global Compact, and therefore advocating corporate social responsibility (CSR). As of 2011, the following Eastern European countries have a CSR or sustainability award or index: Croatia, Estonia, Hungary and Latvia.[3]

In 2004, eight Central and Eastern European countries acceded to the EU: Czech Republic, Estonia, Hungary, Latvia, Lithuania, Poland and Slovenia. Bulgaria and Romania joined the EU in 2007. Croatia joined the EU in 2013.

Slovenia adopted the euro in 2007, Slovakia adopted the euro in 2009, Estonia adopted the euro in 2011 and Latvia adopted the euro on 1 January 2014.

EU accession and adoption of the Euro have decreased the risk premium for many Eastern European bonds and equities. Eastern European blue-chips are now found in the portfolios of large Western European institutional investors, including RI investors. Nevertheless, with the possible exceptions of Estonia, Slovakia and Slovenia, Eastern European countries remain emerging markets.

The relative newness of private financial institutions, relatively low GDP per capita, low income levels and relatively small pension assets are all challenges for the development of RI across Eastern Europe. Due to the size of its economy, capital market, financial market and stock exchange, Poland is one exception in the region. In 2009, the Warsaw Stock Exchange launched the first RI in the region – the RESPECT Index. However, in Poland the disproportionately large percentage of the labour force engaged in agriculture creates challenges for the pension system, and consequently for RI. Also, a large amount of remittances are sent to Poland each year. In 2011, the amount was estimated at $8 billion, or 1.5 per cent of GDP.[4] Remittances indicate that a certain percentage of the working population is working abroad and therefore not contributing to the Polish pension system. The Polish economy is still in a developing or emerging stage; thus, at this time many Poles do not have a large enough disposable income to invest a significant sum in pensions. However, this is changing, and therefore the amount of pension assets is predicted to increase.

RI in Estonia and Poland are described in greater detail below.

Estonia

Basic statistics

Estonia has population of 1.27 million (July 2014 estimate). According to the 2008 census, in 2011 the ethnic composition of the population was estimated as follows: Estonian 68.7 per cent, Russian 24.8 per cent, Ukrainian 1.7 per cent, Belarusian 1 per cent, Finn 0.6 per cent and other 1.6 per cent. Sixty-nine per cent of the population lives in urban areas.

By age, 15.6 per cent of the population is 0–14 years, 71.3 per cent is 15–64 years and 18.2 per cent are older than 65 years.

In 2013 GDP (PPP) was $29.94 billion, compared with $29.49 billion in 2012, $28.37 billion in 2011, $25.7 billion in 2010 and $25.13 billion in 2009. The GDP real growth rate was 1.5 per cent in 2013, 3.9 per cent in 2012, 9.6 per cent in 2011, 2.3 per cent in 2010 and 14.3 per cent in 2009. GDP per capital was $22,400 in 2013, compared with $22,200 in 2012, $21,200 in 2011, $19,200 in 2010 and $18,700 in 2009.

Two geographic realities influence the Estonian economy. On the one hand, Estonia's ethnic, linguistic and economic/financial ties with Finland have accelerated the process of integration with that country and more broadly with the EU, in particular the Nordic region. On the other hand, Estonia's economy is closely linked with its Baltic neighbours Latvia and Lithuania; for example, the stock exchanges in all three countries are part of the NASDAQ OMX group.

Like its Baltic neighbours Latvia and Lithuania, Estonia experienced dramatic growth in the years prior to and immediately following EU accession. This rapid growth in the three small countries, in large part caused by foreign investment – foreign direct investment (FDI), portfolio investment and real estate investment – contributed to a boom which ended in a bust, particularly in real estate. During the past two years the economy has recovered, although unemployment remains high – 12.1 per cent in 2011 compared with 16.9 per cent in 2010.

Estonia has an extremely low ratio of public debt to GDP – it was 5.9 per cent in 2011, compared with 6.6 per cent in 2010.

RI market

In 2010, the Baltic States (Estonia, Latvia and Lithuania) were included for the first time in Eurosif's European SRI Study. Eurosif estimated the size of the Baltic RI market at $19.5 million, representing the only RI fund (Limestone New Europe Socially Responsible Fund) in existence at that time.[5] In 2011 Limestone Investment Management and Northern Star Partners merged. The new company is now called Northern Star. Estonia was not included in the Eurosif European SRI Study 2012.

As of March 2014, there are three UN PRI signatories in Estonia, all investment managers: AS Avaron Asset Management, Baltcap (private equity) and Limestone.

At this time, no data is available about the size of the other two institutions' responsible investments.

At this time, no information is available about RI asset owners. Estonian pension funds are part of Scandinavian financial institutions. As noted in the above-mentioned Eurosif European SRI Study 2010, "it is not known to what extent (sustainable and responsible investment) principles are taken into account at their Baltic branches".[6]

At this time, no data is available about annual growth of the market.

Market environment

Following independence from the Soviet Union, Estonia embarked on reform of its pension system.

Estonia now has a three-pillar pension system, consisting of a mandatory basic pension (first pillar), mandatory participant contributions with matching government contributions (second pillar) and voluntary contributions (third pillar). In 1998 legislation was passed that established the third pillar. In 2001, legislation was passed that created the second pillar; it became operational in 2002.[7]

In 2010, the Estonian Parliament passed legislation that will raise the retirement age to 65 for women and men, up from 60 for women and 63 for men. The retirement age will increase three months per year until it reaches the new legally mandated age.[8]

Industry experts and multilateral financial institutions such as the World Bank view the Estonian model as a success story.

Funds in the second pillar are characterized as conservative, progressive or aggressive. The government pension's website does not include any information in English about RI.[9]

A 'comply or explain' corporate governance code was implemented in Estonia in 2006 by the Tallinn Stock Exchange, applying to companies listed on the exchange. The Estonian Financial Supervision Authority (*Finantsinspectioon*) conducts an analysis of the corporate governance reports published by listed companies.

Semi-annual surveys (Investor Relations Online [2001–2009; 2010] and Reporting on CSR [2003–2009]) conducted by the PFS Program document an improvement in the quality and quantity of governance disclosures by the 10 largest listed companies in Estonia following implementation of the Corporate Governance Code.[10]

Policy environment

The author is not aware of any specific legislation in Estonia related to RI.

RI institutions

As noted above, there are three PRI signatories in Estonia, all investment managers.

On its website, Avaron notes that it is a supporter of the following collaborative engagements: Carbon Disclosure Project (CDP), CDP Water Disclosure Program, Corporate Sustainability Reporting Coalition and Global Investor Statement of the Arms Treaty.[11]

At the end of 2011, Baltcap surveyed its portfolio companies about ESG issues. The survey covered the following topics: workplace, marketplace, community, environmental policies and company values. Baltcap described the survey results in its ESG Report 2011 published in February 2012.[12]

There is no national RI association or organization in Estonia.

There is no SRI index for Estonia on the Baltic Republics on the NASDAQ OMX stock exchange.

RI issues

As noted above, RI is not a widely known concept in Eastern Europe.

In November 2010, Emerging Markets ESG[13] launched a weekly expert interview series entitled, 'Five Questions about Socially Responsible Investment (SRI)'. 'Five Questions about

SRI' features a practitioner's insights about SRI in emerging markets and then Emerging Markets ESG shares this expertise with a wide global audience. The goals of the series are fourfold: (1) to collect a catalogue of examples of SRI in practice in emerging markets, (2) to raise awareness about SRI in emerging markets, (3) to reflect on what SRI in emerging markets means to practitioners and (4) to enable SRI practitioners in emerging markets to network with peers around the world.

Between November 2010 and January 2011 Emerging Markets ESG conducted interviews with two RI experts/practitioners in Estonia as part of the 'Five Questions about SRI' series. In response to the question "Which ESG issue is the most difficult for companies in Eastern Europe to manage?", the fund manager of Limestone Fund Management's New Europe Socially Responsible Fund noted that governance is a prerequisite, followed by environmental and social issues. The head of NASDAQ OMX Tallinn Stock Exchange stated that in Estonia the environment was an issue 15–20 years ago, and then governance was a priority, leaving the social component to be addressed now. In response to the question "Which ESG issue is the most difficult for investors in Estonian companies to analyze?", the former noted the broader/general problem of disclosure and transparency *per se*, whereas the latter noted the lack of "fully independent professional research".[14]

In response to the question "Which ESG issue is the most difficult for investors in Eastern Europe to analyze?", the fund manager of Limestone Fund Management's New Europe Socially Responsible Fund noted that ESG are equally important, "hence, it all boils down to disclosure and transparency, the prerequisites for a good corporate citizen". The head of NASDAQ OMX Tallinn Stock Exchange explained that Estonia is a small company, where on the one hand "it's rather difficult to hide any information about your company. At the same time, it's also difficult to have fully independent professional research".

The first year of the interview series ended in January 2012. The second year of the interview series ended in March 2013. On 22 March 2013, Emerging Markets ESG published an article entitled,'520 Insights about SRI' which analyzes the responses to the second year of the interview series, aggregating the responses by gender and geography and outlining some trends observed. The article also compares responses during the second year of the interview series with those during the first year.

The Estonian responses echo those of other emerging markets globally: In many emerging markets, experts and practitioners noted that corporate governance is a known concept, addressed through a corporate governance code. In comparison, environmental and social issues are not addressed systematically through a code, standardized disclosure or regulation. Several respondents noted that despite awareness about corporate governance, disclosure *per se* remains an issue. Also, many respondents noted that all three issues – E, S and G – were equally challenging for investors.

Those interested in comparing the Estonian responses with responses from other emerging markets as well as developed markets can analyze the above-mentioned publications that aggregate the responses to the questions by gender and geography.[15]

Poland

Basic statistics

Poland has a population of 38.35 million (July 2014 estimate). The population is primarily urban, with 60.9 per cent of the population living in urban areas. By age, 14.6 per cent of the population is 0–14 years, 70 per cent is 15–64 years, and 14.5 per cent is older than 65 years.

Whereas agriculture accounted for only 4 per cent of GDP in 2013, 12.9 per cent of the labour force was engaged in agriculture in 2011. The large percentage of the labour force engaged in agriculture presents a challenge for the pension system, and consequently for RI. Persons engaged in agriculture generally have low income, low disposable income, are financially under-educated and are less likely to invest significant amounts in private pension funds.

As noted earlier, remittances to Poland represented 1.5 per cent of GDP in 2011. Remittances indicate that a certain percentage of the working population is working abroad and therefore not contributing to the Polish pension system.

In 2013, GDP (PPP) was $814 billion, compared with $803.3 in 2012, $788.6 in 2011, $749 billion in 2010 and $720.6 billion in 2009. The GDP real growth rate was 1.3 per cent in 2013, 1.9 per cent in 2012, 4.5 per cent in 2011, 3.9 per cent in 2010 and 1.6 per cent 2009. GDP per capita was $21,100 in 2013, compared with $20,800 in 2012, $20.500 in 2011, $19,600 in 2010 and $18,900 in 2009.

RI market

In 2008 TFI SKOK SA launched the first RI investment fund in Poland, an ethical fund. It later launched an ecological fund.

In 2009 the Warsaw Stock Exchange established the RESPECT Index, the first RI index in Poland as well as in Central and Eastern Europe (CEE).

Also in 2009, the first online Internet portal *Odpowiedzialne Inwestowanie* (Responsible Investment) was established. It is a Polish-language resource about RI worldwide, including translations of articles into Polish from the mainstream financial press and specialized RI institutions (research institutions, service providers, etc.).

In 2010 Poland was included for the first time in Eurosif's European SRI Study. Eurosif estimated the size of the Polish RI market at $1.22 billion in 2010.[16]

Izabela (Kwiatkowska) Blazowska, editor of the above-mentioned online portal *Odpowiedzialne Inwestowanie* (Responsible Investment), conducted the analysis and research for Eurosif. She estimates that 90 per cent of the RI market consists of broad SRI, conducted by simple screening, and 10 per cent is core SRI, in which more detailed environmental, social and governance (ESG) analysis is conducted and ethical factors are considered.

Odpowiedzialne Inwestowanie (Responsible Investment) publishes a list, in Polish, of RI investment products.[17] The products are divided into the following asset classes: bank products (such as eco-loans), debt, equities, investment funds and real estate.

The above-mentioned Eurosif European SRI Study 2010 estimates that (S)RI accounts for 0.3 per cent of total financial assets under management in Poland.

According to the Eurosif European SRI Study 2012, "The Polish SRI market is still in an initial phase of development, and is driven by some pioneers. It is possible to indicate the presence of SRI funds, funds applying negative screening, and some companies practicing impact investment".[18]

The Eurosif European SRI Study 2012 documents that exclusions remain the overwhelmingly largest strategy of the Polish RI market, and that it grew 17 per cent from 2009 to 2011. In 2009, no institutions employed best-in-class, engagement and voting, integration, or sustainability-themed strategies. In 2011 the only two strategies not employed by a single Polish institution were engagement and voting and sustainability themed. Thus, the market is both diversifying and growing.

The author is not aware of any other pan-European RI survey that includes Poland.[19]

Market environment

During the socialist period, Poland had a monolithic pension system. Pensions were paid by the national social security system (*ZUS*).

The Polish pension system was reformed in 1999, creating private pension funds (*OFE*).

Depending upon their age, an employee (individual) could contribute to only the national social security system or the national social security system and a private pension fund. Older persons contributed only to the national social security system; the rationale being that due to their advanced age, investments in private pension funds would not reap financial benefits by the time of retirement. Younger persons contributed to both the national social security system (in order to keep it solvent) and into a private pension fund.[20]

The creation of private pension funds had an enormous impact on the Polish capital and financial market. Whereas prior to pension reform, the Polish capital market was dominated by foreign investors, after the reform Polish pension funds now own approximately 20–25 per cent of Polish equities. The dynamism and size of the Polish capital market also led companies from other Eastern European countries (including Czech Republic, Estonia, Hungary and Ukraine) to list on the Warsaw Stock Exchange instead of or in addition to their home exchange.

Some foreign and domestic (Polish) institutional investors – insurance companies, investment funds and pension funds – engage in shareholder activism, mostly on corporate governance issues. As noted above, the Warsaw Stock Exchange implemented a corporate governance code in 2002; it was the first stock exchange in the region to do so. The code was updated in 2008.

Policy environment

In 2009 the Polish Ministry of Economy established a Working Group on Responsible Investment, which brings together a range of RI institutions (asset owners, companies, institutional investors, regulatory authorities, self-regulatory organizations and service providers). The group makes recommendations to the government on proposed legislation.

RI institutions

Eurosif, the PFS Program and the Warsaw Institute of Banking organized the first event dedicated to SRI in Poland in November 2006. At the event a number of influential Polish capital market participants explained that the term 'socially' responsible investment was problematic in Poland due to the country's recent negative experience with socialism. The term 'responsible investment', focused on governance issues, was preferable.

When TFI SKOK SA launched the first RI investment fund in Poland in 2008, it cooperated with an Austrian ethical investment fund. In 2012, there are two RI service providers: Agencja Ratingu Spolecznego (which works in partnership with the Italian service provider ECPI) and GES Investment Services Poland, a subsidiary of the Swedish service provider GES Investment Services.

TFI SKOK SA describes its approach to RI on its website (in Polish only). It lists the negative and positive screens it employs for its two funds.[21]

The above-mentioned Internet portal dedicated to responsible investing is also an influential institution.

Within the financial community, awareness of ESG issues and RI has grown considerably during the past decade, beginning with corporate governance and later branching out to other ESG and (S)RI issues. It continues to grow.

Nevertheless, a number of commentators note that awareness of RI issues among the general public remains low.

There is no national RI association or organization in Poland.

RI issues

Corporate governance has been for a decade the most important RI issue in Poland.

Semi-annual surveys of reporting on CSR conducted by the PFS Program from 2003–2009 demonstrate that the largest Polish listed companies outperformed their CEE peers in disclosure of governance data. The same surveys also demonstrated significantly greater disclosure of governance data than data on environmental and social issues.[22]

Similar conclusions were made in a research survey conducted by GES Investment Services Poland in 2010.[23] In 2012, Accreo Taxand, GES and the Polish Association of Listed Companies undertook a national initiative, 'ESG Analysis of Polish Companies', in which 382 companies (listed and unlisted) ESG disclosures were analyzed. The methodology is based on disclosure of information related to international standards, such as International Labour Organization (ILO) conventions, ISO 14001, OECD Corporate Governance Principles and the UN Global Compact.[24]

Between May 2011 and January 2012, Emerging Markets ESG conducted interviews with six RI experts/practitioners in Poland about ESG issues and SRI as part of the above-mentioned series, 'Five Questions about SRI'. In response to the question "Which ESG issue is the most difficult for companies in Poland to manage?", two noted environment, two noted governance, one noted social and one noted environment as well as social. In response to the question "Which ESG issue is the most difficult for investors in Polish companies to analyze?", two noted environment and social, one noted environment, one noted governance, one noted all three and one noted the broader/general problem of ESG disclosure *per se.*[25]

As described above, these responses echo the responses from experts and practitioners across emerging markets globally.

Some of the experts/practitioners in Poland survey for the interview series and other RI experts/practitioners note that the current financial crisis and global interest in ESG risks may serve as drivers toward increased interest in RI in Poland. In order to move RI forward, however, they also note the need for legislation to require ESG disclosures, communication from investor relations officers of Polish companies about ESG issues and positive returns from the RESPECT index and other RI products.

In 2013 gender diversity on corporate boards/in corporate governance became a topic of public discussion in Poland. Several specialized media outlets (business, legal and financial) and professional associations conducted surveys of the role of women in Polish business and finance.

In June 2013, Emerging Markets ESG conducted an inaugural survey of gender composition of the management boards and supervisory boards of the constituent companies of the WIG 20, the main capitalization-weighted index of the Warsaw Stock Exchange. Emerging Markets ESG conducted a second survey in December 2013 and plans to conduct the survey semi-annually. As of the record date of 31 December 2013, women represent 9 per cent of management boards and 15 per cent of supervisory boards of WIG 20 companies.[26] Those percentages are roughly similar to June 2013 – 10 per cent of management boards and 14 per cent of supervisory boards. Developments in Norway, which led the way on gender diversity on corporate boards, neighbouring EU countries and EU legislation are watched closely in Poland.

Conclusion and outlook

The development of the RI market in Poland has been slow but progress is being made. Poland was a pioneer in Eastern Europe in corporate governance; as mentioned above, the Warsaw Stock Exchange was the first in the region to implement a corporate governance code. Disclosure by Polish companies about corporate governance continues to improve. However, disclosure about environmental issues lags behind. Gender diversity in corporate governance is a current topic. A small number of pioneer RI institutions have emerged and the market is growing and diversifying, albeit slowly. Conversely, the departure of Polish signatories from the PRI is perhaps a signal that some institutions are not quite ready to make the full commitment to RI. What would be useful would be ongoing data collection and analysis. A few specialized ESG consultancies cover Polish and other Eastern European blue-chips. If investor interest broadens and deepens, research converge may follow.

Notes

1 Online. Available HTTP: <http://www.copula.bg/>.
2 Self-regulatory organizations (SROs) include professional associations and stock exchanges.
3 Emerging Markets ESG, *Comparative Analysis of CSR Key Performance Indicators in 40 Emerging Markets*, September 2011. Online. Available HTTP: <http://www.emergingmarketsesg.net/esg/2011/09/01/comparative-analysis-of-corporate-social-responsibility-csr-key-performance-indicators-kpis-in-40-emerging-markets-%e2%80%93-september-1–2011/>.
4 Barbone, L., Pietka-Kosinska, K. and Topinska I., *The Impact of Remittances on Poland's Economy*, CASE Network E-brief, No. 12/2012, September 2012. Online. Available HTTP: <http://www.case-research.eu/sites/default/files/publications/2012–12_Barbone.pdf?goback=%2Egde_1579677_member_163454771>.
5 Eurosif, *European SRI Study*, 2010, p. 24. Online. Available HTTP: <http://www.eurosif.org/images/stories/pdf/Research/Eurosif_2010_SRI_Study.pdf>.
6 Ibid.
7 Social Science Research Network, *Estonia's Multi-Pillar Pension System: Solid First Miles of the Marathon*, 1 December 2011. Online. Available HTTP: <http://papers.ssrn.com/sol3/papers.cfm?abstract_id=2004647>.
8 'Estonian parliament passes pension reform', *The Baltic Times*, April 8, 2012. Online. Available HTTP: <http://www.baltictimes.com/news/articles/25504/>.
9 Online. Available HTTP: <http://www.pensionikeskus.ee/?index.php>.
10 *Partners for Financial Stability (PFS) Program*. Online. Available HTTP: <http://www.pfsprogram.org/archive/pfsorg/ovr0/capitalmarkets_research.php.htm>.
11 Online. Available HTTP: <http://www.avaron.com/?id=2250>.
12 Online. Available HTTP: <http://www.baltcap.com/content/files/BaltCap%20ESG%20Report%202011.pdf>.
13 Emerging Markets ESG is an independent consultancy engaged in the promotion of ESG reporting in and about emerging markets. The author is the principal of Emerging Markets ESG.
14 Emerging Markets ESG, *Five Questions about SRI*. Online. Available HTTP: <http://www.emergingmarketsesg.net/esg/category/five-questions-about-sri/>.
15 Emerging Markets ESG, *520 Insights about SRI*. Online. Available HTTP: <http://www.emerging-marketsesg.net/esg/2013/03/22/520-insights-about-sri-published-on-emerging-markets-esg-today-friday-march-22–2013/>.
16 Eurosif, *European SRI Study*, 2010, p. 46. Online. Available HTTP: <http://www.eurosif.org/images/stories/pdf/Research/Eurosif_2010_SRI_Study.pdf>.
17 Online. Available HTTP: <http://www.odpowiedzialne-inwestowanie.pl/index.php/wyszukaj-inwestycje.html>.
18 Eurosif, *European SRI Study*, 2012, p. 51. Online. Available HTTP: <http://www.eurosif.org/images/stories/pdf/1/eurosif%20sri%20study_low-res%20v1.1.pdf>.
19 Novethic's 2011 survey, 'European asset owners, ESG perceptions and integration practices' covers over 250 asset managers in 11 European countries, but does not include Poland.

20 Oudenampsen, I., *Polish Pension Reform*, European Pensions, 19 April 2011. Online. Available HTTP: <http://www.europeanpensions.net/ep/polish-pension-reform.php>.

21 Online. Available HTTP: <http://www.tfiskok.pl/etyczne-inwestowanie.html>.

22 Partners for Financial Stability (PFS) Program. Online. Available HTTP: <http://www.pfsprogram.org/archive/pfsorg/ovr0/capitalmarkets_research.php.htm>.

23 GES Newsletter, *Poland Leads New Europe to Responsible Investment*, 17 June 2010. Online. Available HTTP: <http://www.ges-invest.com/pages/?ID=193>.

24 Odpowiedzialne Inwestowanie, *Analiza ESG spolek w Polsce: Raport Stowarzyszenie Emitentów*, 31 August 2012. Online. Available HTTP: <http://www.odpowiedzialne-inwestowanie.pl/index.php/klasy-aktywow/przeglad/akcje-aktualnosci/581-analiza-esg-spolek-w-polsce-raport-stowarzyszenia-emitentow-gieldowych.html>.

25 Emerging Markets ESG, *Five Questions about SRI*. Online. Available HTTP: <http://www.emergingmarketsesg.net/esg/category/five-questions-about-sri/>.

26 Emerging Markets ESG, *Second Survey of Gender Composition of Management Boards and Supervisory Boards of Companies Listed on the Main Index of the Warsaw Stock Exchange, the WIG20 – Data as of December 31, 2013*. Online. Available HTTP: <http://www.emergingmarketsesg.net/esg/2014/01/20/emerging-markets-esg-second-survey-of-gender-composition-of-management-boards-and-supervisory-boards-of-companies-listed-on-the-main-index-of-the-warsaw-stock-exchange-the-wig20-d/>.

19

Corporate social responsibility and responsible investment in Italy

An overview

Rocco Ciciretti, Annalisa Fabretti and Marco Nicolosi

Introduction

The integration of products and financial markets has increased the interdependence of economic actions. Transnational corporations operate in an international scenario in which regulation is missing or inevitably weaker than in the domestic economic scenario. These factors may help to explain why individual and institutional investors are increasingly demanding corporations to act in a socially responsible way. Socially responsible investment (SRI) refers to investments through which investors combine financial objectives with their commitment to social concerns. In the absence of well-established and enforceable international regulatory frameworks, corporate social responsibility (CSR) can be a useful investment criterion to avoid potential negative externalities in the market (Siegel and Vitaliano 2007). Therefore, corporations are facing an increased demand not only to achieve robust economic growth, but to also pursue this goal in a more ethical and responsible manner.

Spurred by pressure from both consumers and investors, CSR is gradually becoming a relevant feature in industrial markets. Since the second half of the 20th century, there has been debate about the role of firms in society. The past 20 years in particular have seen lively debates and radical changes in the relationship between business and society. Several terms and concepts, including sustainability, CSR, and business ethics, have become commonplace, partially as a result of the presence of large multinational companies that are seen as more influential than some national governments with regard to their economic and social power. As a consequence, the business sector has come under pressure from politicians, non-governmental organizations (NGOs) and members of the business community to play an active role in the pursuit of a more sustainable and equitable future. For example, the Green Paper of the European Commission (2001) states that CSR is "a concept whereby companies integrate social and environmental concerns in their business operations and in their interaction with their stakeholders on a voluntary basis".

One of the fundamental issues in CSR is economic sustainability. In the short run, CSR activities may erode a corporation's short-term profit, but in the long run it may improve the firm's profits. CSR practices may find acceptance and further develop in the corporate environment only if they will not endanger firm survival in highly competitive markets. In this respect, an inspection of CSR criteria shows that CSR is not a 'free lunch', as it generally implies a change in the relative weight between the target of shareholders' value maximization and that of the welfare maximization of a wider set of stakeholders (incorporating shareholders, consumers, local communities, workers, subcontractors and other parties influenced by corporate actions). A consequence of this modified focus on social outcomes may seem to be a relatively lower performance in terms of shareholders' returns, which may endanger the survival of socially responsible firms when they operate in competitive financial markets in which they become potential takeover targets.

On the other hand, research has found evidence that companies complying with high CSR standards can be more financially stable compared to companies with poor CSR performance, which may incur significant financial losses. For example, Minor (2010) finds that companies with a strong reputation are less likely to face a bad event (such as a product recall). Becchetti and Ciciretti (2011) find that socially responsible companies are less affected by dramatic macro events such as the Lehman Brother default. Kruger (2009) finds substantial negative stock returns when third parties such as newspapers, CSR rating agencies or regulatory authorities report negative social responsibility on the part of companies.

Indeed one of the main concerns for socially responsible investors is whether and how a company's CSR levels may influence the financial performance of its stocks. In academic literature, the results are still inconclusive. For example Bauer et al. (2005) find no differences in risk-adjusted performances between ethical and conventional funds in different countries, after controlling for Fama-French risk factors, whilst Becchetti and Ciciretti (2009) find a positive one. Statman and Glushkov (2009) evidence that there is a competitive disadvantage when companies associated with controversial business are excluded from the investment strategy. However, this is largely offset when investors tilt their portfolios towards stocks with high CSR performance. Specifically, Herzel et al. (2012) analyze the effect of ethical screening on different mean-variance optimal portfolio strategies, finding that CSR screening has a small impact in terms of Sharpe Ratio even though it may have a big impact in terms of market capitalization. Finally, Barnett and Salomon (2006) find that the results depend on the intensity of screening and on the ethical criterion adopted.

In this international framework, Italy shows a slight delay in implementing SRI and CSR practices, even though in the last two years (2009–11) the SRI assets under management (AUM) has increased at a compound annual growth rate greater than the European one (19.7 per cent compared to 16.3 per cent, Eurosif [2012]). However, this increment was mainly due to the action of only two of the major domestic institutional investors, Pioneer and Assicurazioni Generali, which adopted some SRI criteria in their investment policies; despite this development, SRI still remains a niche practice in Italy. The contribution to SRI from retail investors is marginal. It is expected to enlarge thanks to changes in corporate pension funds' policies. In fact, the pension reform of 2005 obliges the disclosure of information on how ESG (environmental, social and governance) factors are taken into account in the investment process by pension funds. This reform is expected to push forward attitudes to adopt socially responsible investment practices. Corporate pension funds are also influenced to adopt SRI strategies by their own CSR policies. So far, looking at the Eurosif data (2012), this growth remains to be realized.

Recently, some institutional initiatives have been proposed to diffuse and promote CSR and SRI practices among investors, shareholders and entrepreneurs. Among these are an initiative proposed by the National Institute for Statistics (ISTAT), the CSR Manager Network Italy (CSRMNI) and two other minor institutions. Their project, presented at the Italian Bank Association (ABI) CSR Forum in 2012, consists of developing an indicator to merge corporate financial information with CSR information using the Global Reporting Initiative (GRI) standards as a benchmark.[1] Moreover, to help firms disclose information about their sustainable activities,

ABI, the Italian Insurance Association (ANIA) and the Bank and Insurance Federation (FeBAF) produced an Italian version of the Sustainability Reporting Guidelines and Financial Services Sector Supplement proposed by GRI (ABI, ANIA and FeBAF 2012). During the first 'Italian SRI Day' held in Rome on 6 June 2012, ABI, ANIA, the Italian Investment Management Association (ASSOGESTIONI) and FeBAF signed the 'Italian Sustainable and Responsible Investment Charter' to promote CSR and SRI.

The rest of the chapter is organized as follows: The second section provides a country overview. The third section describes the scenario of responsible investment and CSR practices in Italy. The fourth section shows an empirical analysis on returns of high- and low-ranked companies during the period 2002–8, based on the Asset4 dataset. The conclusion provided in the final section summarizes the analysis of this chapter.

Country overview

Italy is a republic with a civil law system. It has a population of roughly 61 million (almost half are Internet users). Life expectancy is almost 82 years, and the literacy rate is 99 per cent (average schooling is 16 years). The main religious group is Roman Catholic, at around 80 per cent. The GDP per capita (PPP) is $30,600, with a public debt over GDP ratio of around 127 per cent. The unemployment rate is close to 11 per cent.

The overall financial market is $1.2 trillion (in terms of AUM), of which the responsible investment (RI) segment accounts for $579 billion, with a three-year average growth rate of 19.7 per cent. The institutional side of the RI market is roughly $577 billion, while the retail is only $1.5 billion. In terms of asset classes, RI consists mainly of bonds (80 per cent); money market and equity account for 8 per cent and 6 per cent, respectively. The first RI fund (Eurizon Capital) was launched in 1997, while the first RI organization (Forum per la Finanza Sostenibile) was born in 2001. In the last decade, the main issues of concern to society are governance and community, while the current debate on ESG practices is mainly on transparency and lack of information.

From 2005 on, the legislature started to regulate aspects of ESG for institutional investors such as pension funds and insurance companies. In addition, parliament approved a law to oblige investment managers to report on products labelled as socially responsible. Also, regulations were implemented that required corporations to provide additional financial information on ESG in their reporting.

The SRI and CSR landscape in Italy

The state of SRI

Italy is not a leader with respect to the European average either quantitatively (e.g., SRI AUM) or in practice, such as implementing strategies. In Italy, the total value of SRI AUM as of December 2011 was around €447.6 billion, with a growth from €312.4 billion at the end of 2009, €243.4 billion in 2007 and €2.89 billion as of December 2005.[2] In the period 2005–7 the total value of AUM increased by 83 times. The outstanding growth over those two years is the result of the introduction by one of the larger institutional investors, Assicurazioni Generali, of a negative screening strategy that drove the Broad SRI[3] AUM from €2.89 billion to €240 billion. Core SRI[4] grew at a 10 per cent compound annual rate from €2.8 billion in 2005 to €3.4 billion in 2007.

Since core SRI is mainly characterized by the predominance of retail investors, it is worth noting that in the same period the Italian retail market was suffering a strong decrease. From 2007 to 2009 the compound annual growth rate was 14 per cent, mainly due to the Broad SRI that increased at a 12 per cent compound annual rate. In the same period, the core SRI experienced substantial growth, from €3.4 to €16.4 billion. From 2009–11 the total SRI AUM increased at a compound annual rate of 19.7 per cent. At the end of 2011, Italian SRI accounted for 47 per cent of the total national AUM (€940 billion) (Eurosif 2012), a figure in line with the European data. However, this increment cannot be seen as a market trend, but rather as a result of a small number of actors managing significant capital who adopted norm-based screening or exclusion[5] policies in their investment processes (Generali for norm-based screening in 2010 and Pioneer for exclusions in 2011).

Retail investors hold a minority share in the Italian SRI market, constituting about 1 per cent of investments in 2009 and 0.26 per cent in 2011. In terms of total portfolio composition in 2011, bonds represent the most popular asset class at 80 per cent, and equity represents 6 per cent of the SRI market (an incremental shift from 82 per cent and 9 per cent market share, respectively, in 2009). On the side of employed SRI strategies, while exclusion, best-in-class and norm-based screening lead as in 2009, at the end of 2011 engagement and voting[6] has largely increased, maybe due to a recent regulation issued by Bank of Italy and CONSOB encouraging investors to implement such voting policies.

SRI market growth is expected to be driven by pension fund and insurance companies. In fact, as a result of the 2005 pension system reform (law decree 252/05), pension funds are obliged to disclose information on whether and how ESG factors are taken into account in the selection and management of investments. This appears to be a relevant incentive for pension funds to implement their SRI strategy. Similarly, the Insurance Service Authority (Isvap) regulation 35/2010 imposes a disclosure of information for all insurance products labelled as ethically or socially responsible. Notwithstanding, the effect of such regulations has yet to be fully realized. In fact, the AUM of corporate pension funds at the end of 2009 was roughly $86 billion, which corresponds to 4.1 per cent of the Italian GDP.

According to the Eurosif Corporate Pension Fund Report (2011), SRI is not yet a common investment practice among corporate pension funds in Italy: six out of 18 respondents to the survey have adopted an SRI policy (33 per cent with respect to European average of 56 per cent), while 12 feel that ESG factors matter for the investment in the long term (around 67 per cent, compared to 60 per cent of the European sample); 16 out of 18 respond that SRI policy is a part of fiduciary duty (nearly 88 per cent, compared to 66 per cent of the European sample). The most important ESG factor for Italy is governance, in line with the majority of the other European countries. The meaningful sources for the implementation of SRI come both from pension fund boards (very common in all European countries, 9 countries out of 12), and the firm's CSR policy (not common in other European countries, 4 countries out of 12). Among the barriers to SRI implementation, the lack of information and concerns about performance dominate. Moreover, many pension funds "express the need to reach a common view on SRI among board members as an essential condition before adopting a formal instrument such as a SRI policy" (Eurosif 2011).

ESG indexes are fundamental instruments in the industry of responsible funds both for benchmarking purposes as well as for incorporating ESG criteria into the investment decision-making process. SRI index instruments are used by both institutional and retail investors who look to invest in the Italian financial market when they consider ESG performance as a constraint for their investment strategies. The ethical FTSE ECPI Italia SRI Indexes have been launched only recently. The Italian companies eligible to be included in the indexes are large and mid-cap stocks that are included in the FTSE Italia All-Share Index. ECPI, an Italian independent provider of sustainability rating and indexing solutions, regularly analyzes public documentation (such as websites and sustainability reports) to produce an ESG rating of the companies.[7] After defining nine levels of ranks, two different indexes have been created:

i) The FTSE ECPI Italia SRI Benchmark Index includes all the companies ranked in the first six levels. The index is value weighted with a maximum percentage allowed for each single constituent to avoid too large a concentration.
ii) The FTSE ECPI Italia SRI Leader Index is built on the best ESG-performing companies, including those in the first four levels. The index is equally weighted.[8]

According to the FTSE ECPI ITALIA SRI INDEX SERIES factsheet (2012), in the period 2006–11, both the Leader and Benchmark indexes performed better than the FTSE All Share in all years but 2008. Moreover, the Leader Index performed better than the Benchmark in all years, excluding 2008. This suggests that CSR investments can add to share value.

CSR attitudes and initiatives

When considering CSR attitudes and initiatives among Italian firms, we classify the firms according to size, specifically large and small and medium enterprises (SMEs). This distinction is necessary due to the peculiarity of the Italian industrial system. In fact, in Italy the average number of workers per company is 3.9, compared to the average of 6 in the 15 EU member states.[9] This defines a predominance of SMEs; in Italy, only 19.7 per cent of firms have over 250 employees, compared to the average of 34 per cent in the EU-15.[10]

Some recent studies based on a questionnaire of SMEs (Perrini et al. 2006) claim that Italy is at the forefront of CSR initiatives in Europe, as evidenced by the existence of numerous spontaneous CSR initiatives. However, as mentioned earlier, such initiatives carried out mostly by SMEs are not systematic, lacking consistent formalization of strategic processes. For this reason, CSR is a sort of 'sunken' phenomenon that is rarely visible beyond each individual company, thus limiting its usefulness as a competitive factor in the market. Italian SMEs are an embedded part of the local community, and their success is often related to their degree of legitimacy and approval from local stakeholders (such as employees, public authorities, financial organizations, suppliers and citizens). In this sense, Italian SMEs are highly aware of their stakeholder relationships.

According to a survey by Perrini et al. (2006) and to Perrini (2006), the most frequent CSR initiatives in Italian SMEs are training activities (89 per cent), employee involvement programs (83 per cent), safeguarding employees' health (82 per cent), sponsorships (75 per cent), support of the local community (72 per cent), support of cultural activities (70 per cent), control of product safety (67 per cent), environmental impact (62 per cent), donations (51 per cent), direct investments (47 per cent) and management systems (42 per cent).[11] However, only 45 per cent of the surveyed companies were familiar with the Green Paper on CSR promoted by the EU.

The two principal barriers to addressing CSR issues are a lack of time and lack of human resources. Listed companies appear to be less proactive in perceiving CSR standards, but at the same time they are more capable of organizing to manage CSR issues. The 2009 report issued by the Corporate Social Responsibility Manager Network (Molteni et al. 2009) analyzes the types of implementation of CSR, the existence of a CSR unit and its relations with the board of the firm, the communication of CSR policies and the effective integration of guidelines in productive enterprise. In 38.7 per cent of the respondent cases, the company had a dedicated unit for CSR that had well-defined tasks and a clear relationship to the company's board. According to the report, there is a positive trend of assigning CSR to a specific unit in the last decade (1998–2008), with an average annual growth of 3.71 per cent. Among the surveyed companies, in 1998 only

1.6 per cent had a specific CSR unit, increasing to 6.5 per cent in 2002, and increasing exponentially to 38.7 per cent in 2008. Twenty-nine per cent of companies surveyed in 2008 released a CSR policy, 46.8 per cent had specific guidelines, and 22 per cent had implemented a mechanism of incentives related to socially responsible practices.

An analogous picture emerges by studying Italian firms adhering to the United Nations Global Compact (UNGC) (Global Compact Network Italia 2009). From 2009 to 2013 the Italian firms and organizations participating in UNGC increased from 197 to 209. As of 2013, firms in general (SMEs and larger companies) represent around 55 per cent of all the Italian signatories to the GCNI. There are 36 NGOs, 26 business associations, 16 academic institutions, and 10 public sector signatories. Only seven Italian foundations and three cities are UNGC signatories (see www.unglobalcompact.org).

In 2009 the Global Compact Network Italy (GCNI) studied the state of corporate citizenship in Italy, looking at 112 firms associated with the UNGC. In the case of SMEs, the responsibility to manage the processes of corporate citizenship is entrusted to the CEO or the president in 60 per cent of the SMEs studied. Only 22 per cent of SMEs defined in advance their corporate citizenship targets, and a mere 28 per cent of the SMEs studied used indicators and/or standards to measure their performance. By contrast, in large corporations objectives are previously defined (59 per cent), and indicators are used to provide evidence of results in terms of performance (86 per cent). Ninety-two per cent of large companies chose indicators proposed by the Global Reporting Initiative (GRI), and 91 per cent produced documents of social accountability (such as social or sustainability reports). SMEs are less active in this respect, with only 33 per cent publically reporting their activities. Contrary to the common criticism of 'window dressing' that is generally associated to the companies linked to the Global Compact, only 58 per cent of the companies indicate on their website and/or other public documents their association to the Global Compact, and only 30 per cent of companies use the Global Compact logo (Global Compact Network Italia 2009).

Performance of firms in the Italian market

This section shows a straightforward comparison of the realized returns of stocks of Italian companies satisfying high CSR standards with the returns of companies with low CSR performance. One standard way to analyze the relationship between financial and CSR performance is to construct indexes of high- and low-ranked companies according to a set of CSR criteria and then compare them (see, for example, Kempf and Osthoff 2007, Statman and Glushkov 2009, and Nicolosi et al. 2011).

The rating system used in this analysis is the Asset4 ESG-Thomson Reuters (Asset4). Asset4 ranks more than 3,800 global companies, including MSCI World, MSCI Europe, STOXX600, NASDAQ100, Russell1000, FTSE250, ASX300 and MSCI Emerging Market. It considers four main pillars that measure economic, environmental, social, and corporate governance performance. The companies' rates in each pillar are given by the aggregation of category rates.[12] Asset4 also provides an 'integrated rate' (IR) that measures the overall ESG performance of the ranked companies from zero to one. The time period analyzed includes data from 2002 to 2008. The number of Italian companies rated has increased over time from 27 to 50, with an average of 40 companies per year. Financial data related to company performance is from Datastream-Thomson Reuters. The final dataset, resulting from the match, is described in Table 19.1.[13]

Table 19.1 reports descriptive statistics of the ESG rates and the IR of the companies in the dataset. First, it is possible to observe that the cross-sectional means and standard deviations of the rates are quite constant over time, except for the corporate governance case, for which a slight increase of the mean and standard deviation is observed. This trend is in line with the fact that

Table 19.1 Descriptive statistics of the Asset4 Rates for the Italian companies

Year	*2002*	*2003*	*2004*	*2005*	*2006*	*2007*	*2008*
N	26	26	35	40	41	42	46
Integrated rate (IR)							
Mean	0.42	0.43	0.50	0.49	0.46	0.53	0.51
SD	0.24	0.24	0.26	0.26	0.28	0.27	0.28
Skewness	0.45	0.08	0.07	0.07	0.27	0.13	0.14
Kurtosis	1.79	1.64	1.74	1.71	1.69	1.32	1.47
Environmental rate							
Mean	0.48	0.48	0.46	0.47	0.43	0.45	0.46
SD	0.31	0.32	0.31	0.31	0.31	0.33	0.33
Skewness	0.56	0.40	0.73	0.44	0.66	0.23	0.15
Kurtosis	1.44	1.16	1.68	1.41	1.64	1.24	1.23
Social rate							
Mean	0.51	0.53	0.59	0.58	0.56	0.58	0.59
SD	0.23	0.22	0.25	0.24	0.24	0.25	0.26
Skewness	0.45	−0.14	−0.26	−0.35	−0.04	−0.14	−0.18
Kurtosis	1.77	2.05	1.64	1.69	1.76	1.68	1.58
Corporate governance rate							
Mean	0.32	0.31	0.39	0.38	0.40	0.47	0.48
SD	0.14	0.15	0.17	0.18	0.19	0.18	0.23
Skewness	0.25	0.23	0.27	0.24	0.40	0.11	−0.06
Kurtosis	2.52	1.97	2.41	1.89	2.20	2.34	1.88

Note: The table shows the mean, standard deviation, skewness and kurtosis of the Asset4 rates for the Italian companies from 2002 to 2008. *N* is the size of the sample.

corporate governance is perceived by investors in Italy as the main ESG driver to account for (see also Gompers, Ishii and Metrick 2003).[14]

For each year and for each CSR dimension (ESG and IR), two groups of companies are formed. Industry effects are taken into account (see, among others, Benson et al. 2006). Therefore, companies are labelled as high or low ranked, depending on whether their rate is above or below the median value within each industry.[15] In most of the cases of the cross section of the high-ranked companies, it is observable that the mean (for each year and each criterion) of the realized returns is smaller than those of the low-ranked companies when returns are positive.

To analyze the financial performance of the high- and low-ranked companies, different portfolio strategies (or indexes) are considered. In particular, for each year t, portfolios are formed using the $t - 1$ information on ESG. Then, for each CSR dimension, as well as for IR, high- and low-ranked value-weighted portfolios are constructed. Portfolios are rebalanced quarterly.

Table 19.2 shows the portfolios' cumulative returns realized over different periods.[16] For convenience of the reader, the FTSE ITALIA ALL SHARE index's returns are also shown. In the second column, the market capitalization of the portfolios (as of June 2009) is shown. It is evident that high-rated companies account for the majority of the capitalization, with an amount that is on average almost four times that of the low-ranked companies. One possible interpretation can be that big companies must compete in an international environment that imposes a more proactive approach to CSR when compared to domestic Italian SMEs. Moreover, large firms are

Table 19.2 Cumulative returns of the high- and low-ranked value-weighted portfolios

	Mkt cap (EURm)	*Yearly*	*Yearly*	*Value-Weighted Portfolio Cumulative Returns (%)*						
	June 2009	*mean (%)*	*SD (%)*	*2009*	*2008–9*	*2007–9*	*2006–9*	*2005–9*	*2004–9*	*2003–9*
FTSE ITALIA ALL SHARE	26,3803	5.66	18.32	23.53	−33.44	−35.96	−21.58	−6.62	11.70	32.06
High IR	221,362	8.24	21.92	13.74	−26.24	−26.44	−12.41	2.68	26.31	49.66
Low IR	56,992	5.29	20.48	14.75	−30.00	−39.01	−27.09	−11.55	10.47	24.80
High En	222,162	7.62	22.50	13.66	−27.32	−27.99	−14.50	4.85	24.77	42.01
Low En	57,760	8.06	19.65	17.50	−27.23	−32.43	−16.85	1.17	28.64	53.28
High So	224,125	8.63	22.16	13.44	−25.97	−26.49	−12.47	4.70	28.80	53.22
Low So	56,674	4.92	21.29	18.58	−32.26	−40.38	−28.62	−13.59	7.37	19.89
High CG	219,822	8.26	23.07	13.61	−31.03	−31.51	−17.91	−3.35	14.05	47.16
Low CG	54,982	7.41	21.02	4.39	−36.72	−38.81	−22.17	0.12	25.71	43.29

Note: Market capitalization, annualized mean and standard deviation of the monthly returns and cumulative returns over different periods of the value-weighted portfolios that are high and low ranked according to the Asset4 rates. For each year *t* portfolios are formed using the $t-1$ Asset4 information. Portfolios are rebalanced quarterly. The FTSE ITALIA ALL SHARE index is shown for the convenience of the reader.

more organized and more transparent in reporting CSR, aligning with the resource constraints described in the previous section for SMEs.

Table 19.2 also indicates that portfolios that ranked high according to the integrated rate or the social rate performed better than low-ranked ones except for the period 2009. The behaviour of portfolios based on environmental or corporate governance criteria oscillates over time. Looking at the longest period, high-ranked portfolios performed better than low-ranked ones with the exception of the environment rate. It is notable to observe that the negative returns realized by all portfolios in 2007 and 2008 are less negative for the high-ranked than the low-ranked ones. This shows the better performance of socially responsible stocks with respect to those stocks not complying with CSR standards during the recession.

For completeness, the third and fourth columns show the annualized means and standard deviations, respectively, of the monthly realized returns of portfolios. High-ranked portfolios correspond to higher means and higher standard deviations, again with the exception of the environment rate.

Conclusion

When compared to Europe, Italian CSR implementation and SRI practice is lagging. One of the main barriers to the development of sustainability among shareholders, entrepreneurs and operators in financial markets is the lack of a consistent definition of the meaning and objectives of CSR and SRI, and insufficient information about standards and advantages.

At the corporate level, on the one hand, it is noteworthy that large Italian companies are better organized with an increased capacity for compliance with CSR standards due to their need to enhance international competitiveness. Moreover, these firms put in effort to report and disclose compliance with CSR according to European standards. On the other hand, Italian SMEs are strongly connected to their local communities and pay attention to the social impact of their activities. Nevertheless, they are not organized or systematic in their CSR activities or reporting. Due to the fact that Italian production is mostly composed of SMEs across a wide range of industries, this might present a strong incentive to invest in SRI even if there is not a stock market involved (i.e., through the indirect credit channel).

The main investor concern is whether the costs that companies absorb in order to be socially responsible are offset by better financial performance. There is no clear evidence in the literature addressing the relationship between stock returns and the level of compliance with CSR. In any case, it is safe to state that the stocks of companies highly ranked in CSR react better than stocks of low-ranked companies to bad events or to negative trends in the market. This fact is confirmed by the behaviour of the high- and low-ranked portfolios constructed on the basis of Asset4 ESG rates.

In this general framework, it is expected that the pension fund industry will play a central role in filling the gaps of SRI policy and practice in Italy. Several Italian institutions, including the Bank of Italy, ABI and ISTAT, are promoting initiatives to improve the general level of information concerning social responsibility among shareholders and entrepreneurs.

Notes

1 For more details on the indicator implementation, see CSR Manager Network Italy and ISTAT (2012) on GRI. Online. Available HTTP: <https://www.globalreporting.org/Pages/default.aspx>.
2 All data in this section refers to Eurosif (2006, 2008, 2010 and 2012).
3 According to Eurosif (2010), "Broad SRI consists of Simple screening (one or two exclusion criteria, norm-based or values/ethical based), Engagement, and Integration strategies".

4 According to Eurosif (2010), "Core SRI consists of multiple ethical exclusions (norms- and values-based) as well as different types of positive screens (Best-in-Class, thematic funds and others)".
5 According to Eurosif (2012), norm-based screening consists of "screening of investments according to their compliance with international standards and norms." Exclusion is "an approach that excludes specific investments or classes of investment from the investible universe such as companies, sectors, or countries".
6 According to Eurosif (2012), the best-in-class approach is an "approach where leading or best-performing investments within a universe, category, or class are selected or weighted based on ESG criteria". The engagement and voting policy consists of "engagement activities and active ownership through voting of shares and engagement with companies on ESG matters".
7 The considered areas include: environmental strategy and policy, environmental management, products (industry specific), production process (industry specific), community relations, employees and human capital, markets, corporate governance and shareholders.
8 These two indexes are reviewed quarterly.
9 Germany 8, France 7, United Kingdom 6, Spain 5, Netherlands 10, Belgium 6, Sweden 8 and Denmark 9.
10 The EU-15 area countries are: Austria, Belgium, Denmark, Finland, France, Germany, Greece, Ireland, Italy, Luxembourg, Netherlands, Portugal, Spain, Sweden and the United Kingdom. EU-19 area countries are the EU-15 countries as well as the Czech Republic, Hungary, Poland and Slovak Republic.
11 The survey is the result of a research project developed by Bocconi University on CSR on behalf of the Italian Ministry of Labour and Social Affairs.
12 The 'environmental' performance, for example, is obtained by integrating the information from three categories: 'resource reduction', 'emission reduction' and 'product innovation'. The 'social' score aggregates the performances relative to the categories: 'employment quality', 'health and safety', 'training and development', 'diversity', 'human rights', 'community' and 'product responsibility'. Finally, the 'corporate governance' score captures the company's behaviour related to the categories: 'board structure', 'compensation policy', 'board functions', 'shareholders rights' and 'vision and strategy'.
13 The investment set has been shrunken by getting rid of the not identified companies between the two datasets used. Moreover, for each year t only companies with financial data available at least at time t and $t + 1$ were considered.
14 Skewness and kurtosis are corrected to account for sample size bias. The score distributions are always platykurtic, as the kurtosis values are smaller than that of the normal distribution, with wider picks around the means and thinner tails. Moreover, the skewness values are slightly positive for all cases except the social rate; the distribution is negatively skewed, signifying a higher probability for low rates than high rates.
15 According to the Industrial Classification Benchmark (ICB), the following industries have been considered: basic materials, consumer goods, consumer services, financials, healthcare, industrials, oil and gas, technology, telecommunications and utilities. As for all the considered years, there is only one ranked company in technology; the two groups do not have any representative company belonging to that industry. The same is true for oil and gas in years 2002 and 2003.
16 We consider total return indexes.

References

Associazione Bancaria Italiana, Associazione Nazionale italiana Assicurazioni and Federazione Banche Assicurazioni Finanza (2012) *Linee guida per il reporting di sostenibilità & Supplemento per il settore dei servizi finanziari*. Online. Available HTTP: <http://www.abieventi.it/public/files/eventi/forum-csr-2012/Traduzione-in-italiano-del-Financial-Services-Sector-Supplement-GRI-.pdf> (accessed 4 April 2012).

Barnett, M. L. and Salomon, R. M. (2006) 'Beyond dichotomy: the curvilinear relationship between social responsibility and financial performance', *Strategic Management Journal* 27, no. 11: 1101–1122.

Bauer, R., Koedijk, K. and Otten, R. (2005) 'International evidence on ethical mutual fund performance and investment style', *Journal of Banking and Finance* 29, no. 7: 1751–1767.

Becchetti, L. and Ciciretti, R. (2009) 'Corporate social responsibility and stock market performance', *Applied Financial Economics* 19, no. 6: 1283–1293.

Becchetti, L. and Ciciretti, R. (2011) 'Stock market reaction to the Global Financial Crisis: testing for the Lehman Brothers' event', *Giornale degli Economisti e Annali di Economia* 70, no. 2: 3–58.

Benson, K. L., Brailsford, T. J. and Humphrey, J. E. (2006) 'Do socially responsible fund managers really invest differently?', *Journal of Business Ethics* 65, no. 4: 337–357.

CSR Manager Network Italy and ISTAT (2012) *Rendicontazione oltre il dato finanziario: dale imprese al sistema statistico nazionale*, presented at CSR Forum promoted by ABI, Rome, 26 January. Online. Available

HTTP: <http://www.csrmanagernetwork.it/wp-content/uploads/2012/01/120119-Presentazione_ISTAT.pdf> (accessed 6 February 2012).

European Commission (2001) *Promoting a European Framework for Corporate Social Responsibility*, Directorate-General for Employment and Social Affairs.COM 366.

Eurosif (2006) *European SRI Study 2006*. Online. Available HTTP: <http://www.eurosif.org/research/eurosif-sri-study/2006> (accessed 14 March 2012).

Eurosif (2008) *European SRI Study 2008*. Online. Available HTTP: <http://www.eurosif.org/research/eurosif-sri-study/2008> (accessed 14 March 2012).

Eurosif (2010) *European SRI Study 2010*. Online. Available HTTP: <http://www.eurosif.org/research/eurosif-sri-study/2010> (accessed 14 March 2012).

Eurosif (2011) *Corporate Pension Funds and Sustainable Investment Study 2011*. Online. Available HTTP: <http://www.eurosif.org/research/corporate-pension-funds> (accessed 7 February 2012).

Eurosif (2012) *European SRI Study 2012*. Online. Available HTTP: <http://www.eurosif.org/research/eurosif-sri-study/sri-study-2012> (accessed 31 October 2013).

FTSE ECPI ITALIA SRI INDEX SERIES factsheet 2012. Online. Available HTTP: <http://www.ftse.com>.

Global Compact Network Italia (2009) *L'orientamento alla responsabilità sociale delle imprese italiane. Una ricognizione sulle imprese aderenti al Global Compact*. Online. Available HTTP: <http://www.globalcompactnetwork.org/files/pubblicazioni_stampa/pubblicazioni_network_ialia/nota_ricognizione.pdf> (accessed 11 April 2012).

Gompers, P., Ishii, J. and Metrick, A. (2003) 'Corporate governance and equity prices', *Quarterly Journal of Economics* 118, no. 1: 107–155.

Herzel, S., Nicolosi, M. and Starica, C. (2012) 'The cost of sustainability in optimal portfolio decisions', *European Journal of Finance* 18, no. 3–4: 333–349.

Kempf, A. and Osthoff, P. (2007) 'The effect of socially responsible investing on portfolio performance', *European Financial Management* 13, no. 5: 908–922.

Kruger, P. (2009) 'Stakeholder information and shareholder value', *Mimeo*, Toulouse School of Economics.

Minor, D. B. (2010) 'Corporate social responsibility as reputation insurance: theory and evidence', *Mimeo*, UC Berkeley: Haas School of Business.

Molteni, M., Bertolini, S. and Pedrini, M. (2009) 'Il management della CSRnelle imprese quotate italiane Scelte strategiche e soluzioni organizzative', *CSR Manager Network Italy Report 090404*. Online. Available HTTP: <http://www.csrmanagernetwork.it/wp-content/uploads/2010/06/ReportDEFVideo.pdf> (accessed 11 April 2012).

Nicolosi, M., Grassi, S. and Stanghellini, E. (2011) 'Item response models to measure corporate social responsibility', SIRP working paper 11–04.

Perrini, F. (2006) 'SMEs and CSR theory: evidence and implications from an Italian perspective', *Journal of Business Ethics* 67: 305–316.

Perrini, F., Pogutz, S. and Tencati, A. (2006) 'Corporate social responsibility in Italy: state of the art', *Journal of Business Strategies* 23, no. 1: 65–91.

Siegel, D. S. and Vitaliano, D. F. (2007) 'An empirical analysis of the strategic use of corporate social responsibility', *Journal of Economics and Management Strategy* 16, no. 3: 773–792.

Statman, M., and Glushkov, D. (2009) 'The wages of social responsibility', *Financial Analysts Journal* 65, no. 4: 33–46.

UN Global Compact. Online. Available HTTP: <www.unglobalcompact.org>.

20

Responsible investment in Spain

Luiz Ferruz Agudo, Jesus Gomez Daza and Sara Segura Querol

Introduction

This chapter offers a chronological description of the developments in the field of corporate social responsibility (CSR) in Spain, with a special emphasis on the role played by retirement funds, both public and private. Therefore, CSR in this chapter focuses on socially responsible investment (SRI). According to Eurosif (2010), "SRI is an area often affiliated with the retail financial sector, which may incorporate environmental, social and governance (ESG) issues as well as criteria linked to values based approach. For example, it can involve the application of pre-determined social or environmental values to investment selection".

Basic statistics

Spain is a country situated in the Iberian Peninsula, located in southwest Europe, which it shares with Andorra and Portugal. The Canary Islands, the Balearic Islands and two small cities situated on the north coast of Africa (Ceuta and Melilla) are also Spanish territory. Spain is surrounded by the Mediterranean Sea, the North Atlantic Ocean, the Bay of Biscay, and the Pyrenees Mountains. It is bordered by France, Andorra, Portugal, Gibraltar and Morocco (Ceuta and Melilla). It is a member of the European Union (EU28) and the Euro Area (EA19).

Spain has national representation in major international organizations such as the United Nations (UN), the Organization for Security and Co-operation in Europe (OSCE), the Organisation for Economic Co-operation and Development (OECD), and the North Atlantic Treaty Organization (NATO).

Spain has a population of 47 million. It ranks 15th in the world for life expectancy, with an average life expectancy of 81.27 years. The considerably high life expectancy together with a significant and sustained decrease in the fertility rate are the main causes of the gradual ageing of the population.

Compulsory education is mandated until age 16, and the literacy rate is 97.9 per cent. Roman Catholicism is the predominant religion, accepted by almost the whole population.

After 36 years (1939–75) of Franco's dictatorship regime, the Spanish Constitution was approved by Spaniards in a referendum held on 6 December 1978. The constitution came into force on 29 December 1978 and defined Spain as a parliamentary monarchy. The constitution establishes that national sovereignty rests with the Spanish people, who are led by a king or queen. The king or queen serves as the head of state and is a symbol of the country's unity and permanence. The monarch's main role is to arbitrate and moderate the regular workings of the government institutions, as well as to assume the highest representation of the Spanish state in international relations.

As of 2011, Spain's GDP was $30,600 per capita, ranking it 43rd in the world. However, Spain has significant public debt – 68.2 per cent of GDP – and the government has taken several measures to reduce it that may have an effect on GDP per capita.

One of the main problems affecting the Spanish economy is its high unemployment rate of 20.8 per cent. The unemployment rate is even higher for young people (15–24 years), at approximately 40 per cent.

The SRI market

SRI appeared in Spain at the beginning of the last decade, considerably later than in the US and some countries in Europe, such as the UK, Germany, Switzerland and the Netherlands. Nevertheless, according to Eurosif (2010), the Spanish SRI market presents an upward trend. In 2005, the SRI market in Spain was €25.1 billion, and it grew to €30.8 billion in 2007 and €33.3 billion in 2009. Taking into account that the mutual fund sector has been drastically reduced due to the global financial crisis (falling from €238.7 billion in 2007 to €162.6 billion in 2009), SRI assets under management have doubled in percentage over the past two years (2007–9).

When focusing on SRI, traditionally the financial products taken into account are classified into three main groups: bonds, equity and 'other'. In 2012, 51 per cent of SRI assets under management in Europe were bonds, 33 per cent equity, and 16 per cent other, 7 per cent of which was in monetary assets (Eurosif, 2012). In Spain, there was a similar percentage of bonds, a significantly lower percentage of equity and a considerably higher percentage of other. In general, 58 per cent of assets were invested in fixed-income/monetary investments. Regarding impact investment, the microfinance market is the dominant sector, with a wide availability of funds. Eurosif (2012) shows that 55 per cent of resources were in this sector.

With regard to SRI strategies, Lozano et al. (2006) concluded that screening is the most popular strategy. In this respect, they studied the development of SRI in the Spanish financial market and found that Spanish fund managers have not adopted engagement with companies or shareholder activism as SRI strategies.

According to Spainsif (2011), Spanish companies are not leading in terms of shareholder activism, and most shareholder initiatives are linked to financial issues. Regarding ESG, governance factors are usually considered first, followed by environmental factors. In spite of the fact that institutional investors are more proactive than individual ones, generally speaking, they do not really seem to have a great interest in encouraging companies to take ESG issues into consideration. Labour unions play an essential role in establishing a dialogue between a company and its shareholders.

Demand for SRI takes place mainly at the institutional level, generally in the field of employment pension funds. Retail SRI mutual funds are scarce, with only €842 million in assets under management. Albareda et al. (2010) concluded that the Spanish SRI market is mainly composed of institutional investors, particularly pension funds. The retail market is irrelevant compared to the institutional market.

Market environment

As mentioned, Spanish SRI is led by institutional investors, particularly pension mutual funds. In this section we will focus on regulations regarding SRI in the institutional investment context. This section is divided into two parts: the first focuses on initiatives carried out by Spanish Association of Collective Investment Schemes and Pension Funds (INVERCO) in 1999; the second concentrates on fiduciary law concerning Spanish pension funds.

Spanish Association of Collective Investment Schemes and Pension Funds (INVERCO)

In 1999, the ethics committee of the Spanish Association of Collective Investment Schemes and Pension Funds (INVERCO, 2009a) issued a document[1] that established the requirements that a mutual fund must comply with in order to be considered 'ethical', 'ecological' or any other term related to social responsibility by collective investment institutions.

INVERCO requires that a mutual fund's brochure describe the fund's investment strategy with regard to social responsibility issues. In this regard, each mutual fund must establish an ethical commission. The main role of this commission is to determine which assets are susceptible to be included in the mutual fund's portfolio, according to both negative (assets that might not be 'ethical' are excluded) and positive screening (assets that are considered to be 'ethical' are included). However, the existence of this ethical commission is not compulsory for those mutual funds investing in ethical indexes which have already been defined as ethical by a rating agency. When disclosing mutual fund results, these funds must include relevant information about both the ethical commission and the ethical investment policy.

Finally, INVERCO has also stated that any advertisements of an ethical mutual fund must include the following statement: 'Check the ethical investment criteria in the brochure'.

Retirement system and fiduciary law

Article 41 of the 1978 Spanish Constitution specifies that "public authorities shall maintain a public social security system for all citizens guaranteeing adequate social assistance and benefits in situations of hardship, especially in case of unemployment. Supplementary assistance and benefits shall be optional".

The Spanish pension system is composed of two different categories of funds: public or private. The first category, public funds, includes two different kinds of pensions: contributory and non-contributory. Contributory pension beneficiaries include workers who have contributed to the system together with their employer during the period established by law. Non-contributory pensions include people who have a protected situation and do not have enough resources to earn their own living. This pension fund type does not require contributions from its beneficiaries.

The second category is contributory private pension funds. They are voluntary and private and are designed to complement the public pension system. Royal Legislative Decree 1/2002[2] (RD 1/2002) comprises all the regulations that are currently in force concerning private pension funds. RD 1/2002 has been modified by several laws and royal legislative decrees since coming into force in 2011.

Private pension plans are classified into three main groups: employment pension plans, associate pension plans and individual pension plans. Employment pension plans are those offered by an entity, society or firm for the benefit of its employees. Associate pension funds are those offered by any association, syndicate or firm for the benefit of its members. Finally, individual pension plans are those promoted by any financial entity. These pension schemes are open to everyone.

Private pension funds are divided into two main categories: employment pension funds and individual pension funds. The first group includes all pension funds that have an employment pension plan as its basis. The second group includes both employment and individual pension plans. According to INVERCO (2009b), "Contingencies that would cause a right to obtain benefits are the followings: retirement, permanent disability (total, absolute and severe disability), death affecting participant or beneficiary (widowhood, orphanage and pensions in favor of other heirs or other designated people), severe or high dependence affecting participant" (9). In order to guarantee beneficiary rights in the long run, RD 1/2002 Article 16 states that when making investment decisions the following must be taken into consideration: security, profitability, diversification and proper programming. This article also establishes that at least the 70 per cent of the pension fund capital has to be invested in financial assets traded in regulated markets, bank deposits, credits with mortgage guarantees or real estate.

Likewise, RD 1/2002 Article 22 requires pension fund management companies ('gestoras') and depositaries ('depositarias') to act in the best interest of the pension fund's beneficiaries when carrying out their tasks (managing and holding the assets, respectively).

In order to supervise management companies and depositaries, RD 1/2002 Article 14 specifies that each pension fund has to establish a supervisory commission ('Comisión de Control'). Furthermore, in the case of individual pension funds, there is also an Ombudsman ('Defensor del Partícipe'), who can be either an external entity or expert whose role is to receive claims from beneficiaries and make decisions about these claims.

With regard to the supervisory commission's duties, Law 27/2011[3] (the most recent amendment to RD 1/2002) states that the supervisory commission, together with the pension fund's management company, must disclose their investment policies in a written document. Additionally, in the case of employment pension funds, this document has to explain whether ESG governance practices are incorporated into the investment decision-making process. This initiative was put into practice in 2013.

Policy environment

As discussed earlier, SRI focuses on the responsibility of investment managers with respect to the ethical consequences of their investment decisions. Thus, this concept applies to financial institutions that manage the savings of the public, and, as such, they should be socially responsible when they make investment decisions. On the other side of the spectrum is the concept of CSR, which is a broader concept that includes both financial institutions and private companies. In this section we focus on CSR regulations at the company level. With this target in mind, we divide this section into three parts, each one corresponding to a specific governmental initiative. The first part analyzes Law 26/2003, whose objective is to improve the transparency of public limited companies. The second part describes the main role of the State Council on Corporate Social Responsibility. Finally, the third part concentrates on the study of major inclusions regarding SRI in Law 2/2011.

Law 26/2003[4]

The debate on financial reporting by Spanish companies emerged at the end of the last century with the publication of the 'Código Olivencia' in 1998 (CNMV, 1998). This document provided public limited companies with a wide range of recommendations associated with corporate governance. In this regard, the Código Olivencia gave great importance to business transparency, providing the market with relevant and reliable information about business activities and results.

Following these recommendations, Law 26/2003 came into force in 2004. This law established that all Spanish public limited companies are bound to disclose corporate governance information annually, explaining whether they have taken into consideration corporate governance recommendations. In this respect, the 'Comisión Nacional del Mercado de Valores' (CNMV), which is the agency in charge of supervising and inspecting the Spanish stock markets and the activities of all the participants in those markets, published the 'Código Unificado de Buen Gobierno' in 2006 (CNMV, 2006). This document includes all the corporate governance factors that are to be taken into consideration when creating the annual report on corporate governance.

In the context of the 2008 global financial crisis, the Spanish economy, which had experienced an upward trend for 15 years, saw a considerable decline in its national economy. This new scenario required a change in the drivers of economic growth. With this target in mind, in November 2009 the government designed the Strategy for a Sustainable Economy ('La Estrategia para una Economía Sostenible'), which is based on three main pillars: economic competitiveness linked to innovation and education, environmental responsibility in economic activity and, finally, social responsibility with the objective of guaranteeing equal opportunities not only in the workplace but also in society in general.

Based on the framework of the Strategy for a Sustainable Economy, the government has taken several measures. Among them, Law 2/2011 of Sustainable Economy ('Economía Sostenible') is one of the most important, as it establishes new rules to change current productive sector activity, creating a new model based on sustainable, well-balanced, lasting growth.

This law tackles, among other issues, the enhancement of social responsibility by companies (Article 39). It states that public agencies should encourage social responsibility practices among firms (giving special attention to SMEs), organizations and public/private institutions. In this regard, the government has provided firms with internationally approved social responsibility standards, with the objective of encouraging self-evaluation of their behaviour towards society. These standards focus mainly on the improvement of corporate transparency, attitudes toward the environment and workplace policies (e.g., equal opportunity).

Public limited companies have the option of disclosing information about the implementation of socially responsible policies regarding the issues mentioned above. Likewise, any company can apply to the State Council on Corporate Social Responsibility to achieve the status of 'socially responsible company'. However, if a company employs at least 1,000 workers, then it is required to disclose its CSR initiatives to the state council.

State Council of Corporate Social Responsibility

Corporate social responsibility (CSR) became popular within the Spanish government just a few years ago. The creation of the State Council on Corporate Social Responsibility in 2008 through Royal Decree 221/2008[5] is the most representative governmental initiative in this context.

This state council was created with the objective of being a forum to share knowledge about the field of CSR with institutions involved in its development, such as labour unions and public agencies.

One of its roles is to propose important CSR measures to the government, such as corporate governance codes, ethics committee recommendations and the periodic disclosure of information in annual reports. In addition, it is also to inform organizations that may be affected by these public measures and initiatives. It also governs the design and structure of reports on CSR and sustainability.

The State Council on Corporate Social Responsibility pays special attention to SMEs. Regarding the information about CSR, it concentrates mainly on Spain, but it also considers initiatives developed in the European Union.

Socially responsible investment institutions

The first socially responsible investment (SRI) institution in Spain appeared with the creation of 'Cajas de Ahorro'. The Spanish Confederation of Saving Banks (CECA) points out that Cajas de Ahorro are credit companies that invest a percentage of their benefits in initiatives ('Obra Social') linked to societal welfare.

Banco de España (2005) points out that Cajas de Ahorro activity has always been associated with the promotion of societal welfare. In this context, it highlights the importance of good governance and improving societal trust in financial institutions.

The first Caja de Ahorros in Spain was 'Caja Madrid', which has its origin at the Monte de Piedad de Madrid, founded on 3 December 1702. Another representative example is 'Caja de Pensiones para la Vejez y de Ahorros' (nowadays, 'CaixaBank'), which was set up by Francesc Moragas in 1905. When CaixaBank was established, Spain was an extremely poor country. Given that Spain's welfare state lagged behind that of other European countries, CaixaBank was not only concerned about its financial results, but also the promotion of societal welfare. Since its creation, it has maintained its ethical responsibility towards society (Argandoña et al., 2009).

In response to the 2008 global financial crisis and the collapse of the real estate bubble, a huge reform in the Spanish financial sector is being undertaken. In this context, the structural reform of savings banks not only raises questions about the future of their financial activity, but also that of their traditional fight against financial exclusion and support for culture and the welfare of society through their social work (Quesada, 2011. It is difficult to make an accurate long-term forecast of the situation.

The Spanish Social Investment Forum (–) is the most important Spanish SRI lobby. In fact, it promoted the change in RD 1/2002 that required pension fund supervisory commissions to disclose how they integrate ESG practices into their investment decision-making process. As we have already seen, this amendment was finally carried out through Law 27/2011.

Spainsif was launched in 2009 with the aim of promoting the UN-backed Principles for Responsible Investment (PRI; www.unpri.org.) in Spain. According to its website (www.spainsif.es), Spainsif is a non-profit association that was founded by organizations interested in promoting socially responsible investment in Spain and creating a platform that would integrate the SRI goals of financial institutions, management companies, service providers, non-profit organizations and unions.

Spainsif is composed of 41 Spanish entities that are interested in putting social responsibility into practice. These entities are divided by Spainsif into five main groups: financial institutions, investment managers, professional service partners, non-governmental organizations (NGOs) and trade unions.

CSR, ESG and SRI issues

Although the Spanish CSR discourse is considerably similar to the international approach, it has characteristics that are particular to Spain, as Canto-Mila and Lozano (2009) point out. In this section we will briefly analyze the salient Spanish ESG issues over the last decade.

Although business activity and societal welfare were first connected through the creation of Cajas de Ahorro centuries ago, SRI, as it is currently understood, appeared in Spain considerably later than in US and other countries in Europe (e.g. De la Cuesta-González et al., 2006; Ferruz and Marco, 2006).

Over the last decade, the CSR discourse focused mostly on governance rather than on sustainability and the environment. In this sense, as previously mentioned, in 2004 a law regarding the transparency of a public limited company's financial results came into force. However, political parties concerned about the transparency of collective investment institutions, especially employment pension funds, have incorporated ESG criteria into the management of the Social Security Reserve Fund.

Moreover, in recent years, the global economic and financial crisis has renewed the interest of governments and regulators of financial markets in the need to integrate ESG criteria and to the exercise of political rights of shareholders. This has been raised by authors such as Albareda et al. (2010). With this target in mind, transparency requirements for public limited companies have been increased over the last decade.

Furthermore, in the context of the financial crisis, the Spanish government has designed a 'Strategy for a Sustainable Economy' with the objective of creating a new economic model based on sustainable, well-balanced, lasting growth. In this context, this policy aims to enhance social responsibility, especially in the SME context.

Conclusion

It is clear that in Spain CSR has had an upward trajectory and has experienced high growth in recent years. The concept of SRI, which has also been increasing in acceptance over the past 20 years, applies directly to financial institutions that manage the long-term savings of workers for pension purposes. Suitable management of these assets will ensure a dignified and peaceful retirement for beneficiaries. For this reason, the concept of SRI is important. Nevertheless, it was the 2008 financial crisis that accelerated the development of SRI. After the 2008 crash, governments, regulators and supervisory bodies passed new laws and regulations with the purpose of increasing socially responsible investing. However, regulations were not solely responsible for this increase, pension funds – private and public – have also designed codes of ethics and corporate governance guidelines that will enable them to achieve the standards of management framed in CSR and SRI. Today, undeniable breakthroughs have been achieved in the areas of CSR and SRI in Spain. Consequently a smaller gap is evident in this type of financial regulation between Spain and countries such as the UK.

Notes

1 Circular sobre utilización por las instituciones de inversión colectiva de la denominación 'ético', 'ecológico' o cualquier otro que incida en aspectos de responsabilidad social.
2 ROYAL LEGISLATIVE DECREE 1/2002, 29 November, approving the revised wording of the act regulating pension plans and funds.
3 Law 27/2011, 1 August, on updating, amending and modernising the Social Security system.
4 Law 26/2003, 17 July, on reinforcing the transparency of listed public limited companies.
5 ROYAL DECREE 221/2008, 15 February, by which the State Council on Corporate Social Responsibility is created and regulated.

References

Albareda, L., Balaguer, M. and Murillo, D. (2010). *Observatorio 2010 de la Inversión Socialmente Responsable.* Online. Available HTTP: <http://itemsweb.esade.es/wi/research/iis/publicacions/OISR_2010.pdf> (accessed 30 February 2012).

Argandoña, A., Moreno, C. and Sola, J. (2009) 'Social Responsibility and Social Security: The Foundation of Caja de Pensiones para la Vejez y de Ahorros', *Journal of Business Ethics,* 89: 319–332.

Banco de España (2005) *Notas para la presentación del Gobernador. Foro estratégico de Cajas de Ahorro. Responsabilidad social corporativa. Confederación Española de Cajas de Ahorro (CECA).* Online. Available HTTP: <http://www.bde.es/webbde/es/secciones/prensa/intervenpub/archivo/caruana/090605.pdf> (accessed 28 March 2012).

Canto-Mila, N. and Lozano, J. (2009) 'The Spanish Discourse on Corporate Social Responsibility', *Journal of Business Ethics,* 87: 157–171.

CNMV (1998) El gobierno de las sociedades cotizadas (Código Olivencia) Online. Available HTTP: https://www.cnmv.es/DocPortal/Publicaciones/CodigoGov/govsocot.pdf (accessed 24 April 2015).

CNMV (2006) *Código unificado de buen gobierno de las sociedades cotizadas.* Online. Available HTTP: <http://objetivo15.net/doc/CNMV_CodigoBuenGobiernoDeLasSociedadesCotizadas.pdf> (accessed 25 February 2012).

De la Cuesta-González, M., Muñoz-Torres, Mª.J. and Fernández-Izquierdo, Mª.A. (2006) 'Analysis of Social Performance in the Spanish Financial Industry through Public Data. A Proposal', *Journal of Business Ethics*, 69: 289–304.

Eurosif (2010) *European SRI Study.* Online. Available HTTP: <http://www.eurosif.org/images/stories/pdf/Research/Eurosif_2010_SRI_Study.pdf> (accessed 24 February 2014).

Eurosif (2012) *European SRI Study.* Online. Available HTTP: <http://www.eurosif.org/research/eurosif-sri-study/2012> (accessed 6 February 2014).

Ferruz, L. and Marco, I. (2006) 'Algunas reflexiones sobre la inversión socialmente responsable', *Boletín económico de ICE, Información Comercial Española*, 2901: 35–44.

INVERCO (2009a) *Circular sobre utilización por las instituciones de inversión colectiva de la denominación "ético", "ecológico" o cualquier otro que incida en aspectos de responsabilidad social.* Online. Available HTTP: http://www.inverco.es/comisionEticaInverco.do (accessed 24 April 2015).

INVERCO (2009b). *Spanish Pension Funds System.* Online. Available HTTP: <http://www.inverco.es/documentos/publicaciones/documentos/0003_SPANISH%20PENSION%20FUNDS%20SYSTEM/C0_SPANISH%20PENSION%20FUNDS%20SYSTEM.pdf> (accessed 5 February 2012).

Law 26/2003, 17 July, on reinforcing the transparency of listed public limited companies.

Law 27/2011, 1 August, on updating, amending and modernising the Social Security System.

Lozano, J., Albareda, L. and Balaguer, Mª.R. (2006) 'Socially Responsible Investment in the Spanish Financial Market', *Journal of Business Ethics,* 69: 305–316.

Quesada, J. (2011) 'El futuro de la Obra Social de las Cajas', *Papeles de Economía Española,* 130: 307–319.

ROYAL LEGISLATIVE DECREE 1/2002, 29 November, on approving the revised wording of the act regulating pension plans and funds.

ROYAL DECREE 221/2008, 15 February, by which the State Council on Corporate Social Responsibility is created and regulated.

Spainsif (2011) *Diálogo activo accionarial en España.* Online. Available HTTP: <http://www.observatorio-rse.org.es/Publicaciones/spainsif_informe_2011_w3.pdf> (accessed 28 February 2012).

21 Responsible investment in France

Stéphanie Giamporcaro

Introduction

France, with its 66 million citizens located in metropolitan France and overseas departments, is a leader among European nations and one of the most modern countries in the world.[1] It plays an influential global role as a permanent member of the United Nations Security Council, the North Atlantic Treaty Organization (NATO), the G-8, the G-20, the European Union (EU) and other multilateral organizations. In recent decades, its reconciliation and cooperation with Germany have proven central to the economic integration of Europe. The French Republic remains committed to a form of capitalism in which social equity is maintained by means of laws, tax policies and social spending that mitigate economic inequality. The French economy is diversified across all sectors, such as machinery, chemicals and automobiles. Despite stagnant growth (France's real GDP per capita stagnated at around $35,000 in 2012 and 2013) and fiscal challenges, France's borrowing costs have declined in recent years because investors remain attracted to the liquidity of French bonds. Nevertheless, the public debt/GDP ratio was at 90.3 per cent in 2012, with an upward trend. Average life expectancy is 82 years, and France has a literacy rate of 99 per cent. Most of the French people are Christian (almost 90 per cent); 5–10 per cent are Muslim.

France is one of the biggest responsible investment (RI) players in Europe, together with the UK and the Netherlands. Historically, the concept of ethical investment appeared in France between 1995 and 2000, notably through the influence of religious congregations led by Sister Nicole Reilles (Giamporcaro 2006). Interestingly, at this stage ethical investment was not strictly defined as negative screening, but also allowed for the possibility of positive screening (Déjean et al. 2013). In 1999, ARESE, the French CSR rating agency financed by the public French bank Caisse des Depots, was created, enabling French fund managers to develop best-in-class screening practices (Crifo and Mottis 2013). In 2001, the French public bank launched the think tank and media platform Novethic to promote corporate social responsibility (CSR), sustainability and socially responsible investment (SRI). It sought to progressively impose the terminology of SRI funds over the terminology of ethical funds (Giamporcaro 2006). Today, as in many other countries worldwide (Giamporcaro and Viviers 2014), the vocabulary of responsible investment as defined by the UN-backed Principles for Responsible Investment (PRI) in 2006 is used to identify the broad and diversified integration of environmental, social and corporate governance factors (ESG) into investment decision-making and shareholder activities that are believed to have a positive impact on society as a whole. In contrast, from 2007 onwards the SRI vocabulary began to be used more often to identify niche investment funds applying systematic screening and engaging in shareholder activism strategies.

According to Novethic, as presented in the 2012 European SRI Study (Eurosif 2012: 34), at the end of 2011, on the demand side, the French RI market had reached 115 billion euros (see Table 21.1), and the following year (2012) it reached 149 billion euros. French clients' RI assets are managed by more than 40 investment managers, while 2 asset owners manage their RI funds internally (Novethic 2013).

In December 2012, the RI fund market on the supply side (excluding segregated mandates and including non-French clients' assets, as displayed in Figure 21.1) amounted to total assets of

Table 21.1 Investment vehicles in the French RI market (euros billions)

		2009	*2011*	*Trend*
Investment funds	Retail	€9	€21	133%
	Employee Savings Plans (ESPs)	€5.4	€11	104%
	Institutional	€14.5	€32.3	123%
	Sub-total	€28.9	€64.3	122%
Segregated mandates	Institutional Investors (delegated)	€10	€36.9	269%
	Institutional Investors (in-house)	€10.7	€11.9	12%
	Employee Savings Plans (ESPs)	€1.1	€2.1	95%
	Sub-total	€21.8	€51	134%
Total		**€50.7**	**€115.3**	**127%**

Source: Novethic/Eurosif Study 2012 (with permission).

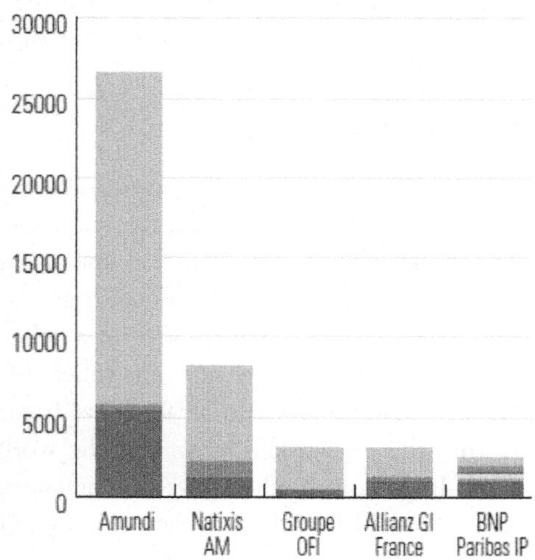

Figure 21.1 Assets managed by investment managers in the French RI non-segregated investment funds market

Source: Novethic Barometer, February 2012 (with permission).

76 billion euros and 304 RI funds (Novethic 2013). Fifty-nine investment management companies, local and foreign, operate on the open RI investment fund market. One French investment manager, Amundi, is dominant in the French market, with more than 32 billion euros under management; it is also one of the biggest European investment managers.

French investment managers, who are usually part of big retail banking groups, dedicate significant financial and human resources to their RI expertise. They host dedicated RI teams employing typically more than three people, and generally employ two to three ESG rating agencies in order to make investment and shareowner decisions (Giamporcaro and Gond 2013). In April 2013, the research think tank Novethic estimated that about 90 extra-financial analysts operated on the Paris Stock Exchange.

As of February 2014, 79 French investment managers had signed the PRI principles, compared to 107 in the UK and 40 in the Netherlands.[2] In the asset owner category, the UK and the Netherlands boast a larger number of RI signatories – 36 and 32, respectively – compared to 9 in France. This is primarily owing to the French 'pay as you go' retirement system, which limits retirement funds' exposure to financial markets. However, French public asset owners Caisse des Depots and Consignations and le Fond de Reserve des Retraites participated actively in the first drafting and launch of the PRI principles in April 2006 (Giamporcaro 2006). Vigeo Ratings, the local ESG rating agency, employs more than 55 RI analysts based in Paris, Brussels, Milan and Casablanca, and is characterized by multipartite share ownership (Novethic 2010). About 27 per cent of Vigeo Ratings' capital comes from companies (within a limit of 2 per cent of the capital per company), 26 per cent from trade unions and non-governmental organizations (NGOs) and slightly more than 46 per cent from investment managers and pension funds. The major international ESG rating agencies, such as EIRIS, MSCI, Oekom Research AG and Sustainalytics, have also set up offices in Paris.

In 1997, there were only a few ethical funds. They were managed by fewer than five investment managers, primarily on behalf of religious investors. There was no local ESG information provider (Giamporcaro and Gond 2013). So what happened between 1997 and 2012? This chapter proposes to show that through a successful blend of political framing and calculative framing (see Appendix 21.1 for a detailed chronology of political and calculative framing events), involving a wide range of public- and private-sector players, France became a stronghold for RI in the world. The chapter also details the latest trends and challenges for RI in France.

Political framing and calculative framing

Responsible investing (RI) can be characterized as an attempt to systematically integrate environmental, social, and governance concerns (ESG) into investment decision-making and the financial markets. Empirical qualitative studies in the organizational and management field (Cabantous and Gond 2009; Callon 2009; Giamporcaro 2011; Huault and Rainelli-Weiss 2011) demonstrate, however, that in order for risks such as climate change, adverse weather, and terrorism and, more important here, ESG risks to be considered as relevant to the sphere of financial markets, various interest groups have to build convincing political and calculative frames around such issues. On the one hand, one needs to stress that RI markets all around the world are embedded within a social and institutional context. Regulatory bodies, governmental agencies and other organized groups seek to shape the rules of local RI markets in their interest. The specific set of political activities led by the French state and trade unions that took place in France from 1997 to the present (referred to as 'political framing') to consolidate the French RI market will be analyzed later. On the other hand, integrating ESG concerns into investment decisions requires making calculable and quantifiable not only the ESG quality of stocks, and but also the ESG quality of RI investment products (Giamporcaro and Gond 2013). The French RI market went through a very active process of calculative framing during the period 1997–2013, led by investment managers, ESG service providers and asset owners.

Political framing through state regulation

After 2000, France launched a set of regulatory requirements that have boosted the development of RI among institutional investors, investment managers and corporations.

The perspective of managing employee savings according to RI standards attracted the attention of trade unions and state officials from 2000 (Déjean 2010; Déjean et al. 2013; Penalva-Icher 2012). Hence, the notion of RI became part of the debates about employee saving plans (ESPs) and the reform of the French pension scheme. The outcome of these debates was a set of laws from 2001: the 'Loi Fabius', passed on 19 February 2001 (Law 2001–152), which calls for investors managing employees' saving schemes to disclose how they take into account ethical, social and environmental information in their investment decisions and in the exercise of shareholder rights. For a decade now, RI has been promoted within ESPs through the involvement of the main French trade unions (Eurosif 2012: 34). Another direct leverage for RI since 2008 is for ESPs to include at least one 'fond solidaire' (Eurosif 2012; 34). These typical French funds include 10 per cent of unlisted assets targeting community investing and social entrepreneurship, while the other 90 per cent is allocated to listed assets, with some basic ESG screening.

Law 2001–624 created the 'FRR', an acronym that stands for 'Fonds de Réserve des Retraites', a public retirement buffer fund created to prevent a liquidity default of the 'pay as you go' retirement system through investment in financial markets, and whose promoters were committed to taking into account ESG issues in fund investment decisions (Giamporcaro 2006). Since its introduction in 2001 (Fabius Law), the FRR is consistently presented by government officials in the media as an opportunity to enhance 'responsible' types of investment (*Figaro Economie* 12/03/04). An RI call for tender for 600 million euros was launched in June 2005 by the FRR. More than 40 local and foreign investment managers replied.

At the end of 2005, the Etablissement de la Retraite Additionnelle pour la Fonction Publique (ERAFP) was the second state-owned fund to publicly 'convert' to RI (ERAFP press release 06/12/2005[3]). Created in 2001 by the French Retirement Law, the ERAFP can be considered to be the 'first' French state-owned pension fund. Its role is to capitalize the additional retirement contributions of 4.5 million French public servants through the financial markets. Criticized by some trade unions as a 'serious breach' of the French 'pay as you go' retirement system, the ERAFP executive directors stressed from the start that its full commitment to its inter-generational solidarity mission would be implemented through its RI strategy (*La Tribune* 04/07/2006).

In 2001, the Loi sur les Nouvelles Régulations Economiques (so-called Law NRE) was also voted in. This law makes the disclosure of information about social and environmental management mandatory in the financial statements of all stock-listed corporations from 2002. A second round of requirements were passed in 2012 (Article 225 of the Grenelle 2 de l'Environnement Law) to progressively extend the ESG reporting requirements to a wider scope of companies (SMEs and unlisted corporations). Another article in the Grenelle II de l'Environnement Law targets asset management firms and their communication about RI. Article 224 makes it compulsory for investment managers to describe on their websites (by July 2012 and later in their annual reports) how they take ESG issues into account in their investment policy, and which funds are concerned.

Calculative framing: measuring the ESG responsibility of stocks and RI funds

Before 1997, local investment managers could hardly evaluate whether a stock could be regarded as socially responsible or not. In this context, the first local ESG information provider, Arese, was established in 1997 as a joint venture between two French state-owned banks, the Caisses d'Epargne and the Caisse des Dépôts et Consignations (CDC). The mission of Arese was to provide investors with quantified information on French company stocks' social responsibility. The result of Arese's calculative activity was a set of quantified scores that could be easily manipulated and integrated by investment managers willing to engage in RI as they covered first the key French financial indices (CAC 40, and later SBF 120), and then corporations from key European indices (Crifo and Mottis 2013; Giamporcaro 2010).

Arese acted as a central piece in the calculative framing effort that supported the building of the RI market. From 1997 to 2002, the number of investment managers on the market increased from 7 to 35 (Giamporcaro and Gond, 2013). Arese was swallowed up in 2002 by a new ESG rating agency, Vigeo, launched by Nicole Notat, a political personality retiring from the presidency of one of the biggest French trade unions, CFDT (*Le Monde* 26/08/02; *Le Monde* 11/12/02). Although Vigeo inherited an important client base from the legacy of Arese (*Le Monde* 6/11/03), the competition for calculating ESG issues suddenly increased, creating a real "market for ESG information" (*La Tribune* 11/03/03). First, Arese's former CEO, Genevieve Ferone, created a competing agency, CoreRating. Next, attracted by the promises of the French RI market, European and American providers of ESG information stepped in. Innovest – an American-based ESG rating agency – decided to create a subsidiary in Paris to compete in this market with a new offer, which focused more on the environmental aspect. A UK-based agency, Eiris, soon after also offered its research services in France. In 2013, Vigeo still occupied a strong leading position on the French RI market, with a market share of more than 60 per cent, followed by Sustainalytics with 35 per cent and MSCI ESG Research with 22 per cent (Novethic 2012).

The multiplication of ESG rating agencies that provided sometimes contradictory ratings on the same stock led local French RI investment managers to develop in-house expertise in order to be able to integrate varied sources of ESG information. This internalization of ESG calculative capacities on the asset management side was accelerated by the creation of a label for ESPs by trade unions. In 2002, French trade unions got together to form CIES – an acronym that stands for 'inter-union committee for employee saving' – and created a label to guarantee, among other things, the social quality of investment products (Déjean 2010; Penalva-Icher 2012). Only those investment products that received the CIES label would be allowed to manage employees' savings (*La Tribune* 10/04/02). In practice, trade unions decided to grant their label to ESPs whose investment managers had internal RI capacities, and therefore did not rely solely on external ESG rating agencies (*Le Monde* 02/06/03).

However, in the growing and visible RI retail unit trusts and mutual fund market segments, no regulatory standard was available at this phase of market development to make visible the set of qualities that would define what an 'RI fund' was. The only valid convention among professionals and the French financial regulation authority (AMF) was that the public information notice had to specify which ESG criteria were taken into account. In the meantime, over this period the RI industry was often described by left-wing papers or watchdog organizations as 'opaque' (*Le Monde Diplomatique* 2002; Politis 2004; Que Choisir 2003).

In reaction to critique about the transparency of RI investment products, Novethic, a subsidiary created by the Caisse des Dépôts and Consignations at the end of 2001, proposed from

2002 a new online 'rating device' to assess in depth the extra-financial quality of RI investment funds. This calculative device was no longer focused on the assessment of the social responsibility of stocks, but on the social responsibility of RI funds. For each RI fund, a range of criteria scanning ESG screening and portfolio management approaches, including the degree of diversity and internalization of ESG information, were assessed according to a weighting system. Novethic followed the position defended by the CIES in attributing a better score to those investment management companies that diversified their ESG sources of information (*Le Monde Argent* 13/12/04). Despite an initial reluctance to be 'judged', investment managers eventually used the rating system for analyzing their competitive environment. A few started to use their Novethic rating in their advertising brochures or asked voluntarily to be evaluated. The 'Eurosif Code of Transparency' launched in 2003 was another strong call for disclosure by investment managers. In the same spirit as the Novethic rating, the Eurosif code detailed a range of information that needed to be made publicly available by investment managers about their ESG screening processes and portfolio management approaches. It also introduced the requirement to disclose an exhaustive list of portfolio holdings.

In 2009, Novethic transformed its rating system into a label, the first of its kind in Europe, in order to offer retail investors a better compass by which to find their way through the product offering (Eurosif 2010). It made compulsory the disclosure of an exhaustive list of the fund's portfolio holdings, a rare practice in the worldwide asset management industry (Hawken 2004) as a conditional sine qua non for being awarded the label. In the year after, 2010, the French asset management professional organization Association Francaise de Gestion (AFG) and the French Social Investment Forum (FIR) made compulsory the Eurosif Code of Transparency for all RI funds from 2010 onwards. In 2012, approximately half of RI funds (150 of the 300) available in France were awarded the Novethic SRI label (Eurosif 2012: 38). Eventually, these voluntary calculative framing efforts initiated by various RI market promoters in order to measure and judge the 'actual responsibility' of RI funds was framed politically in 2012 by Article 224 of the Grenelle II de l'Environnement law, which made it compulsory for investment managers to state how they take ESG criteria into account.

Latest market trends

ESG investment strategies

It is particularly striking that in the US, exclusion and shareholder activism can be traced to the origins of the RI movement (Alinsky 1971; Domini 1992; Giamporcaro 2006), whereas in France these two practices are to this day still largely under-developed. The traditional ESG exclusion screening on tobacco, alcohol, gambling and pornography found in the US, and to a certain extent in Scandinavian countries, does not really feature in the French context. With the exception of controversial weapons (anti-personnel mines and cluster bombs), which have been banned indirectly by French law since 2010, only one French asset owner excludes weapons from all its assets (Eurosif 2012). RI in France can hardly be described as a social movement led by political activists and civil society, despite the involvement of some religious groups and trade unions (Arjalies 2010; Déjean et al. 2013).

France is the country of the ESG best-in-class screening strategies (selecting or weighing leading or best-performing investments in an asset class), and today it is the European champion of the category (Eurosif 2012:14). Beginning in 1997, choosing the best-performing companies regarding ESG issues without ex-ante sector discrimination was selected by French market promoters as the preferred way to develop RI in France (Déjean et al. 2013). Neither investment managers nor public asset owners were convinced that ex-ante sector exclusions based on moral considerations should be used –the latter because it was hardly politically acceptable to exclude on moral grounds sectors in which French companies were good performers and employing French workers. Investment managers did not embrace this approach because of a technical reluctance to exclude ex-ante from their investment universe companies that could contribute to the overall performance of their portfolios (Giamporcaro 2006). However, beginning in 2010, and after some civil society criticism of the softness of French RI strategies (*Les Amis de la Terre* 2010; Husson 2010), ex-post exclusion of investment according to their compliance with international standards started to spread, affecting 73 per cent of the 149 billion euros managed for French investors at the end of 2012, compared to 21 per cent in 2010 (Eurosif 2012: 35; Novethic 2013).

In 2011, themed investment focusing on specific or multiple issues around ESG, such as climate change, eco-efficiency or health, represented a small fraction (1 per cent) of French RI assets (Eurosif 2012; 35) and featured negative growth (–56.4 per cent). In comparison, in the Netherlands and UK during the same period, according to a Eurosif survey (2012:14) sustainability-themed investments went through positive growth of 144 per cent in the case of the Netherlands and 40 per cent in the UK. This strong discrepancy could be explained by the mediocre local performance of RI-themed funds (Eurosif 2012; 14), a more stringent definition of RI themed funds in France and the necessity to demonstrate the adoption of clear RI screening strategies beyond the investment theme itself (Blanc and Hobeika 2008). Additionally, France's negative growth rate in themed funds could also be explained by institutional investors' lower appetite for private equity funds (Novethic 2011).

Historically, the rise of RI in France coincided with a willingness of asset owners and investment managers to exercise their voting rights, first on corporate governance matters, and progressively on social and environmental aspects (Giamporcaro 2006: 601). The FRR, for example, identified the release and implementation of its voting rights policy as a core aspect of its responsible investment commitment (Giamporcaro 2006: 516). In every dedicated RI team that was created after 2002 by investment managers, a voting right function was created, not only to vote on the RI portfolios, but often on all investment portfolios managed (Giamporcaro 2006: 516). Today, according to Novethic (Eurosif 2012: 35), 50 per cent of RI investors surveyed have declared voting for the majority of their shares and 69 per cent have published a voting report following general meetings. However, vocal shareholder activism to change corporate behaviour as understood and practiced in the US is not widespread, partly for cultural reasons and differences in corporate legislation (Giamporcaro 2006; Louche and Lydenberg 2006). A majority of French investors in 2012 listed the number of times they have engaged in dialogue with companies on ESG issues, but only 38 per cent declared having formal engagement policies and only 14 per cent made their policies public (Eurosif 2012: 35).

If France is not a historical stronghold of corporate engagement, it is the biggest player in terms of ESG integration, far ahead of the Netherlands and the UK (Eurosif 2012: 18). If the idea of integrating material ESG criteria into financial analysis as popularized by the preamble of the Principles for Responsible Investment is powerful, in practice ESG integration as a strategy is difficult to measure precisely (Eurosif 2010, 2012). In principle, an integration strategy will use ESG information to adjust the forecasting for companies upon which investment managers base their investment decisions (Eurosif 2012: 17). In practice, since ESG integration is at the discretion of the investment manager or the asset owner, it is almost impossible for external observers to measure its actual implementation. In France, ESG integration strategies are increasing at a fast pace, with the number of funds using this approach increasing from 47 per cent in 2009 to 59 per cent in 2011, as indicated in respective survey samples (Eurosif 2012: 36). Investment managers and asset owners state that they establish some crossover between financial and extra-financial analysis in their databases and internal structures (Eurosif 2012; 36). As documented by Novethic (Eurosif 2012; 36), these analyses apparently enable investment managers and asset owners occasionally or regularly to measure the ESG quality of portfolios ex-post, which are not subject to RI requirements, with a view to preparing for an eventual conversion of the fund and to identify any potential reputational risks.

In France, the best equivalent of 'impact investing', a term coined under the influence of the US foundation Rockefeller (Giamporcaro and Viviers 2014), is what is labelled '*finance solidaire*', amounting to the French variation of community investment in the US, for example. However, the latest form of impact investment, amounting to investing in unlisted equity and unlisted debt investment in emerging markets to boost positive social impact has yet to be adopted by private equity funds and developmental finance institutions in France.

Investors' profile

In December 2011, as displayed in Figure 21.2, institutional investors (mostly private insurance companies, pension funds and public institutions) represented 71 per cent of the RI market (Eurosif, 2012: 36), whereas individual investors represented 29 per cent. This trend remained steady in 2012 (Novethic 2013). On the individual investor side, the current rise of RI is mainly due to the growth of the Employee Savings Plan category (investment funds and segregated mandates).

Asset classes

When RI began in France, RI strategies focused almost exclusively on listed equity assets. The French CSR agency Arese, which became Vigeo, started by developing ESG calculative expertise on the stocks of the big French listed companies, before widening its geographical scope to Europe (Giamporcaro 2006: 195). However, because of the strong exposure of the majority of institutional investors to bonds and money market assets, the RI market asset allocation started

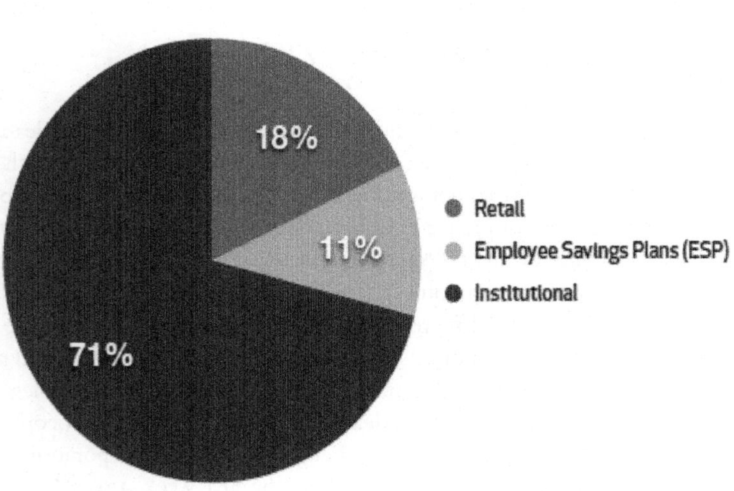

Figure 21.2 Institutional versus retail investors in France

Source: Novethic/Eurosif Survey 2012 (with permission).

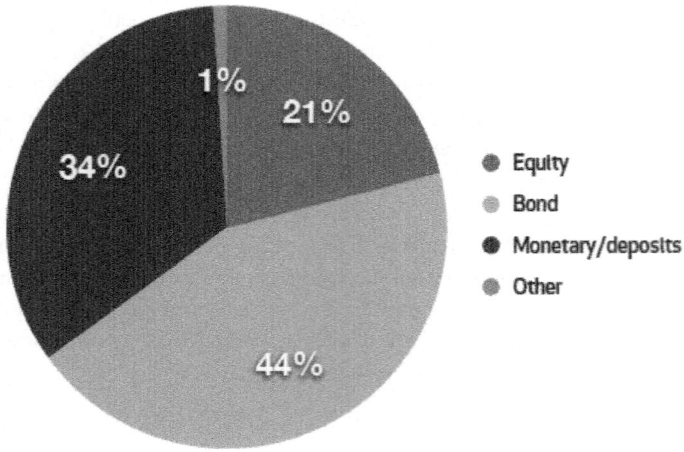

Figure 21.3 French RI market asset allocation

Source: Novethic/Eurosif Survey 2012 (with permission).

to shift quickly in about 2005 in favor of these categories (see Figure 21.3). The 2005 ERAFP call for tenders for sourcing the services of an ESG rating agency to assist the first French pension fund to internally manage its fixed income portfolios was a strong signal for RI investment managers and service providers to develop ESG calculative expertise with regards to bonds and money markets (Giamporcaro and Gond 2013; Novethic 2007).

In December 2011, bonds and money markets dominated equities (21 per cent), with 41 per cent and 21 per cent market share, respectively. This trend accelerated in 2012, with the bond market reaching 53 per cent, against 25 per cent for the money market and 20 per cent for equities.

Future challenges

Political framing: legislative impact, regulatory trends and raising individual investors' awareness

The 2012 political shift to the left by the French government and assembly may lead to increased support of RI. It will need to be monitored in the following years if the latest push through the Grenelle de l'Environment for further commitment and disclosure from French corporations and investment managers operating in France is to provide an actual boost to the RI market. Even though this trend could continue, the ESPs introduction of and the concomitant RI commitment requested by the trade unions has undoubtedly led to building RI awareness at the employee and employer representative levels. If there is still important awareness work to be done at the retail level, market promoters are supported by the state. For two years now the French Ministry of Sustainable Development has been organizing an 'SRI week' to raise awareness in the retail market. In 2012, an educational video was released that attempted to help people realize how investment in financial markets works and how their ESG views on corporations can be taken into consideration through RI products.[4] In 2013, for the SRI week, a social media campaign called 'Ask for SRI!' was launched. The idea behind the slogan was to stimulate retail investors to engage via emails with their bank advisers about RI (Novethic 2013).

Calculative framing: an RI market dynamic, but still in search of a more visible identity

The French RI market does not lack investment products, but until very recently investment managers were deploying marketing and sales efforts mostly towards the institutional segment. The institutional segment is still growing at a prudent pace, led by some very discreet private insurers and some more vocal state-owned funds. However, it is still to be seen if French asset owners will implement stronger and more visible RI strategies, such as engagement and norms-based exclusions (Eurosif 2012: 37). In the meantime, compared to British or Dutch investors, French institutional investors seem to have less appetite for alternative assets, such as responsible private equity.

The retail market has been considered by some investment managers as too complex, owing to the intrinsic difficulty of pleasing the aspirations of every type of client (Giamporcaro 2004). An in-depth qualitative survey that I led among retail investors (Giamporcaro 2004) holding some shares of one of the first SRI mutual funds (*Ecureuil 1,2,3 Futur*) indeed showed that clients' degree of expectations could vary greatly on ethical, environmental, social and corporate governance questions. What also varied was their trust in the banks' ability to respect their extra-financial expectations (Giamporcaro 2004). Interestingly, the quantitative survey that followed demonstrated that 60 per cent of the 200 clients surveyed were actually not aware of the extra-financial quality of the investment product in which they pooled money. When clients were told, their reaction varied from pleasant surprise to annoyance when realizing that they had been sold something they did not necessarily ask for, and which could be adverse to financial performance as well as to their ethical and political views.

Here significant questions can be asked: What is the best RI strategy that should be adopted in the retail market? Is invisible soft integration, which does not require the marketing of RI investment products on their extra-financial qualities, the strategic way to go for investment managers (Crifo and Mottis 2011)? Or, are proudly marketed stringent screening strategies the way to convince retail clients of the real societal value of RI? The latter clearly represents a bigger challenge and effort for the major retail banks since it means the development of specific marketing materials and the training of their network clients' advisers to adopt an alternative sales pitch not simply focused on financial performance arguments. Even though no retail banking network has yet launched a massive national public campaign on RI in France, it must be stressed that a growing number of insurers have started to adopt RI strategies in life insurance products, one of the most popular financial products in France (Eurosif 2012: 37). The latest increase of more visible ex-post norms-based exclusion screening and stricter best-in-universe screening strategies compared to best-in-class strategies (Eurosif 2012: 35) could be interpreted as an attempt from investment managers and market promoters to convince a wider civil society and sceptical audience (Friends of the Earth 2010; Husson 2010) that there is a genuine difference between RI and non-RI investment products.

The CIES label and the Novethic label play a valuable role in building transparency and trust in both the ESPs and the RI retail market space. However, in 2012 Amundi AM, the biggest RI investment manager in France, declined to comply with the assessment process to be awarded the Novethic RI label. Therefore, in 2013 the SRI Novethic label covered only 28 per cent of the RI funds available in France, while Amundi AM chose to get its RI funds certified by the French standardization authority AFNOR. There is also talk of the creation of a state-sponsored RI label. Could this development shake and reshape the calculative framing structure built progressively and cohesively by the various French RI market promoters? How will the multiple pieces of regulation around RI be further integrated in the future into the European regulation framework surrounding ESG issues and RI? Will French RI market players manage to boost the retail segment or more strongly occupy the newest RI asset class categories, such as private equity, and the rising impact investment space?

The French RI market is a stronghold of RI in Europe and in the world. In little more than a decade, RI, which in 2003, represented less than 1 per cent of assets under management in France, today represents around 5 per cent of these same assets (Novethic 2012). This increase is the result of a very active effort of political framing and calculative framing from a wide range of RI market promoters, from trade unions to investment managers and representatives of the French state (public servants, regulators, politicians). The future lies in seeing how the French RI market will continue to grow, and which paths it will take to do so.

Notes

1 All the facts about the political and economic state of France are available online. Available HTTP: <http://www.cia.gov/library/publications/the-world-factbook/geos/print/country/countrypdf_fr.pdf>.
2 As featured on the PRI website. Online, available HTTP: <http://www.unpri.org>.
3 Online, available HTTP: <http://www.rafp.fr>.
4 Online, available HTTP: <http://www.youtube.com/watch?v=_mkdzZhiDSE&feature=share>.

References

Alinsky, S. (1971) *Rules for radicals: A practical primer for realistic radicals*, New York: Random House.

Arjaliès, D. L. (2010) 'A social movement perspective on finance: How socially responsible investment mattered', *Journal of Business Ethics* 92: 57–78.

Blanc, D. and Hobeika, S. (2008) 'What role for environmental funds within SRI?'. Online. Available HTTP: <http://www.novethic.com/novethic/v3_uk/upload/What_Role_For_Environmental_Funds_Within_SRI.pdf> (accessed October 2012).

Cabantous, C. and Gond, J. P. (2009) 'Turning terrorism into markets: How calculability and power frame the genesis of markets', paper presented at the 2009 Academy of Management Meeting, Chicago, IL, USA, 7–11 August.

Callon, M. (2009) 'Civilizing market: Carbon trading between in vitro and in vivo experiments', *Accounting, Organization and Society* 34: 535–548.

Crifo, P. and Mottis, N. (2011) 'L'investissement socialement responsable en France: opportunite´ "de niche" ou placement "mainstream"?' *Gérer et Comprendre* 104: 14–25.

Crifo, P. and Mottis, N. (2013) 'Socially responsible investment in France', *Business & Society*, 0007650313500216.

Déjean, F. (2010) 'L'émergence de l'ISR en France: le rôle des Syndicats', *Economies et Societes* 1(K): 1827–1846.

Déjean, F., Giamporcaro, S., Gond, J. P., Leca, B. and Penalva, E. (2013) 'Mistaking an emerging market for a social movement? A comment on Arjaliès' social-movement perspective on socially responsible investment in France', *Journal of Business Ethics* 112(2): 205–212.

Domini, A. (1992) 'What is social investing? Who are social investors?', in Kinder, P., Lydenberg, S. and Domini, A. (eds), *The social investment almanac*, New York: Henry Holt.

Eurosif (2010) *Eurosif European survey 2010*. Online. Available HTTP: <http://eurosif.org> (accessed October 2010).

Eurosif (2012) *Eurosif European survey 2012*. Online. Available HTTP: <http://eurosif.org> (accessed October 2012).

Figaro Économie (2004) 'Les choix du Fond de Reserve des retraites', 12 March.

Giamporcaro, S. (2006) *L investissement socialement responsable entre l'offre et la demande: Analyse et enjeux de la construction sociale d'une épargne politique*, PhD dissertation in Sociology, University René Descartes-La Sorbonne, France. Online. Available HTTP: <https://tel.archives-ouvertes.fr/file/index/docid/357511/filename/TheseGiamporcaroISR.pdf>.

Giamporcaro, S. (2011) 'Sustainable and responsible investment in emerging markets: Integrating environmental risks in the South African investment industry', *Journal of Sustainable Finance and Investment* 1: 121–137.

Giamporcaro, S. and Gond, J. P. (2013) 'Organizing calculability for responsible investment: How calculative agencies interplay in market construction', PRI-CDC Academic Network Conference, session on Calculability and Investment, Paris, 13–15 November.

Giamporcaro, S. and Viviers, S. (2014) 'SRI in South Africa: A melting pot of local and global influences', in Hebb, T. and Louche, C. (eds.), *SRI in the 21st century: Does it make a difference for society?*, Series: Critical Studies on Corporate Responsibility, Governance and Sustainability, Volume 7, Bradford, UK: Emerald Group Publishing Limited.

Giamporcaro-Sauniere, S. (2004) 'L'investissement socialement responsable en France. Un outil au service d'une action politique par la consommation?', *Sciences de la Societe* 62: 168–187.

Hawken, P. (2004) *How the SRI industry has failed to answer to people who want to invest with a conscience and what can be done about it.* Online. Available HTTP: <http://www.naturalcapital.org/docs/SRIRepor2010–04_word.pdf>.

Huault, I. and Rainelli-Weiss, H. (2011) 'A market for weather risk? Conflicting metrics, attempts at compromise, and limits to commensuration', *Organization Studies* 32: 1395–1419.

Husson, A. C. (2010) *Quels sont les objectifs du label ISR Novethic?,* 23 September. Online. Available HTTP: <www.novethic.fr>.

La Tribune. (2003) 'La notation sociale cherche ses marques', 11 March.

La Tribune. (2006) 'La retraite des fonctionnaires choisit la responsabilité sociale', 4 July.

Le Monde. (2002a) 'Nicole Notat crée l'agence de notation sociale Vigeo', 26 August.

Le Monde. (2002b) 'Jacques Chirac en faveur des règles internationales', 11 December.

Le Monde Argent. (2004) 'Le lent essor des fonds socialement responsables', 13 December.

Le Monde Diplomatique (2002) 'La grande illusion des placements éthiques', 29 November.

Les Amis de la Terre (2010) 'Investissement socialement responsable: L'heure du tri.' Online. Available HTTP: http://www.amisdelaterre.org/Investissement-socialement.html.

Louche, C. and Lydenberg, S. (2006) 'Investissement socialement responsable: Différences entre Europe et États-Unis', *Revue d'Economie Financière* 85: 81–105.

Novethic (2007) *L'indicateur novethic* (Novethic Barometer). Online. Available HTTP: <http://www.novethic.fr>.

Novethic (2011) *L'indicateur novethic* (Novethic Barometer). Online. Available HTTP: <http://www.novethic.fr>.

Novethic (2012) *The French SRI market in 2011.* Online. Available HTTP: <http://www.novethic.fr>.

Novethic (2013) *The French SRI Market in 2012.* Online. Available HTTP: <http://www.novethic.fr>.

Novethic (2013) *L'indicateur Novethic.* Online. Available HTTP: <http://www.novethic.fr>.

Novethic (2013) *L'essentiel de l'ISR*, Novembre. Issue 38.

Penalva-Icher, E. (2012). 'How finance regulates trade union involvement in French SRI', in I. Huault and C. Richard (eds.), *Finance: The discreet regulator: How financial activities shape and transform the world*, Houndmills, UK: Palgrave Macmillan, 193.

Politis (2004) '*L'éthique touche le fonds'*, 1 December.

Que Choisir (2003). '*Vous avez dit éthique*?', 1 April.

US Social Investment Forum (2006). Online. Available HTTP: <http://ussif.org/pdf/research/Trends/2005TrendsReport.pdf> (accessed October 2012).

Appendix

Appendix 21.1 Political and calculative framing events, 1997–2012

Year	*Political Framing*	*Calculative Framing*
1997–98		Creation of ARESE as a joint venture by Caisses d'Epargne and Caisse des Depots.
1999		Launch of first RI funds using ARESE CSR ratings: ABF Eurosocietale, MACIF Sustainable Growth, Ecureuil 1,2,3 Futur. Creation of the French SIF (FIR).
2001	19 February: Law 2001–152 FCPEs are requested to disclose how they take into account ethical, social and environmental criteria in their investment decision/exercise of shareholder rights. May 2001: Law 2001–420 makes compulsory the obligation for French listed companies to publish CSR information in their annual reports. July 2001: Law 2001–624 creates the FRR; the first French public retirement fund requires that the investment policy general orientation disclose how ethical, social, environmental factors are taken into account. August 2003: French retirement Law ('Fillon Law') implements a legal framework to promote pension funds.	Sept 2001: Creation of Novethic, subsidiary of Caisse des Dépôts.
2002	January: In the framework of the Fabius Law, four French trade unions (CFDT, CFTC, CGC, CGT) create the Inter-unionist Committee for Employee Savings (CIES) and its label.	Creation of Eurosif. Vigeo is created by Nicole Notat, ex secretary of CFDT, a major French trade union movement.

Year	Political Framing	Calculative Framing
		Creation of CoreRatings by Genevieve Ferone, ex director of Arese. Launch of Novethic RI Ratings. First run of the CIES label.
2003	July: FRR calls for tender on active equities portfolios with some minor RI requirements.	US Innovest and British EIRIS enter the French RI market. Second run of the CIES label. Launch of the Eurosif Code of Transparency for RI funds. Launch of the Barometer Novethic (Indicateur Novethic).
2004	Following the Fillon Law, ERAFP, the first French state-owned pension fund, becomes functional.	First Eurosif measurement survey.
2005	FRR calls for tender for RI managers. ERAFP publicly converts to RI.	Vigeo buys the Belgian group Ethibel and becomes Vigeo Group. Innovest buys CoreRatings.
2006	April: FRR and ERAPF sign the PRI; ERAPF call for tender to hire a CSR rating agency for defining an internal RI strategy on fixed income. May: Unveiling of the successful asset manager for the FRR call for tender. June: ERAFP call for tender for RI asset managers on listed equities. October: ERAPF selects Oekom and Vigeo Group to work on RI fixed-income portfolios.	Group Vigeo buys Avanzi SRI Research and becomes Vigeo SAS. Broadening of the Novethic rating to RI fixed-income products.
2007	May: Unveiling of the list of the asset manager winner for the ERAFP call for tender.	Oekom German group signs an alliance with Vigeo in order to cater for ERAFP call on fixed income.
2008–2009		Transformation of the Novethic RI Ratings into a label.
2010–11		AFG makes the Eurosif Code of Transparency compulsory for its members. Creation of MSCI ESG Research.
2012	Article 225 of the Grenelle 2 de l'Environnement Law extends ESG reporting requirements to a wider scope of companies (SMEs and unlisted corporations). Article 224 Grenelle II de l'Environnement Law requires investment managers to describe how they take into account ESG criteria in their investment policy	Third round of the Novethic label: Novethic announces its willingness to make the label criteria more restrictive. Amundi AM, the RI leader in France, declined to be assessed by the Novethic RI label.

22

Responsible investment in Austria, Germany and Switzerland

Agnes L. Neher

Introduction

In recent years, the responsible investment (RI) market in German-speaking countries has experienced strong growth. Although it is still a niche market, it has the potential to move in the direction of more mainstream investment practices. In German-speaking countries, RI refers to investments that complement the usual indicators of profit, liquidity and risk with ecological, social and ethical (ESG) indicators. In German-speaking countries, RI is often called 'sustainable investment'. The RI markets in Germany, Austria and Switzerland together have a value of $164.9 billion (Forum Nachhaltige Geldanalge [FNG], 2013). From a research perspective, RI is still in its infancy in these three German-speaking countries.

This chapter is laid out in the following manner: the first section provides an overview of Austria, Germany and Switzerland. The following sections then examine each of the three RI markets individually, examining in detail the market and legal environment, RI institutions and RI issues. The chapter ends with a conclusion.

Overview of Austria, Germany and Switzerland

Austria, Germany and Switzerland are all German-speaking countries. In Switzerland, French, Italian and Romansch are also official languages. Germany, the largest economy in Europe, lies geographically in the middle of the continent. It is a member of the European Union (EU) and has used the euro since its introduction in 1999/2002. Austria and Switzerland are both Alpine countries, lying to the south of Germany. Austria is also a member of the EU and has adopted the euro. Switzerland is not a member of the EU and retains its strong commitment to neutrality with its own currency, the Swiss franc.

As of 2013, Germany was the largest of the three German-speaking countries, with a population of 81 million. Austria's population stood at 8 million people, while Switzerland's population was 7 million. As of 2012, Switzerland, the smallest of the three countries, had the highest GDP per capita ($46,200). Austria's GDP per capita was $43,100, and Germany had a GDP per capita of $39,700. Unemployment rates also differ among the three countries. In 2012, Switzerland's unemployment rate was only 2.9 per cent, whereas Germany had an unemployment rate of

5.5 per cent. Austria stood between the two with an unemployment rate of 4.4 per cent in 2012. Looking at the public debt ratio, as of 2012 Switzerland had the lowest ratio, at 52.4 per cent. Austria followed at 73.4 per cent, while Germany's ratio stood at 81.9 per cent.

The three countries are very similar in their development. Life expectancy is approximately 80 years, and most people receive at least 16 years of schooling. Austria and Germany are both federal republics. Switzerland is formally a confederation, but its structure is similar to a federal republic. All three countries have a civil law system.

Looking at the main industries in the three German-speaking countries, each focuses on different areas. In Austria, construction, machinery, vehicles and parts, food, metals, paper and tourism are the most relevant industries. Germany's industry is focused on production of iron, steel, coal, cement, chemicals, machinery, vehicles, machine tools, electronics, food and beverages, ships and textiles. Switzerland is famous for its watch industry, machinery and textiles, precision instruments and tourism. Banking and insurance are the main industries (CIA World Factbook, 2013).

It is important to point out two very distinct characteristics of Germany and Switzerland. First, the Green Party has played a conspicuous role in the German political party landscape since the 1980s. It has been represented in parliament for many years and was part of the German governing coalition from 1998–2005. The second point of distinction is that Switzerland has a grassroots/direct democracy. Swiss citizens have the right to vote on important decisions regarding taxes, education and infrastructure, and they have veto rights on resolutions and laws. This occurs on all three levels: city, canton and state.

All three countries have a three-tier banking system with public-owned banks, private banks and cooperative banks. Among these banks, there are sustainable banks that primarily engage in responsible investing (RI) (e.g. Steyler Bank, Pax Bank) and banks that have a range of investments, including those focusing on RI (e.g. Zurcher Kantonalbank, Union Investment).

RI in Austria

Overview of the Austrian RI market

In 2012, the RI market in Austria had assets under management of $7.66 billion and had a growth rate of 17 per cent over the prior year. The national RI organization, the Forum Nachhaltige Geldanlagen (FNG), was launched in 2001.

The RI market consists of both the institutional market and the retail market, with a value of $3.09 billion and $3.92 billion, respectively. RI is divided into different asset classes, with bonds dominating the market (83 per cent). Equities have a market share of 15 per cent, followed by other assets at 2.5 per cent. The major ESG issues of concern to Austrian society over the last decade have been the exclusion of controversial weapons, nuclear energy, the production and trade of weapons, pornography, tobacco and gambling. Figure 22.1 shows the RI strategies used by Austrian investors. Exclusion and norm-based screening are the most often applied strategies, followed by best in class and engagement. Impact investment and thematic funds are the least used RI strategies.

Market and legal environment

As with Germany and Switzerland, Austria has a three-tier banking system with public-owned banks, private banks and cooperative banks. The service sector is one of the largest sectors in the country, next to industry and agriculture. Austria, due to its geography, is strongly linked with

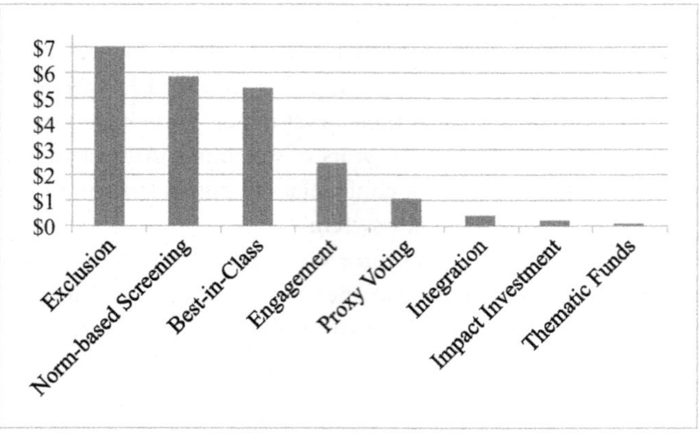

Figure 22.1 RI strategies in Austria in 2012 (in billion dollars)

Source: Forum Nachhaltige Geldanlagen (2013) (with permission).

Eastern European countries, particularly its financial sector, which has led to strong criticism, especially after 2007 and the Global Financial Crisis.[1]

Austria has both formal and informal regulation regarding RI. In 2005, Austria passed legislation that requires pension institutions to report ESG issues if they influence the assessment of the investment (Eurosif, 2011). Regarding the informal regulations, the Austrian Society for Environment and Technology (ÖGUT) has evaluated and certified the investment policy and practice of retirement funds and pension institutions regarding ESG issues since 2004. ÖGUT examines the 'principles and methodology', 'portfolio', and 'environment'. In 2013, 7 out of 10 institutions have asked for certification through ÖGUT (ÖGUT, 2013).

In addition, Austria has a very distinct 'eco-label' ('Umweltzeichen') that was initiated by the Federal Ministry of Environment in 1990. The label addresses issues that affect consumers and the economy. Currently, four sectors can seek independent certification through the 'eco-label': tourism institutions, educational institutions, and green marketing and events. The label aims to promote more environmentally-friendly products than those currently in the market. The ministry defines "[i]n this context environmentally-friendly [as] more environmentally-friendly than the current offer of other products fulfilling the same function" (Federal Ministry of Agriculture, 2013).

While the EU has several CSR reporting requirements, there has yet to be a directive that requires responsible investing or the reporting of ESG issues. In April 2013, the European Commission adopted a proposal for directives that would enhance the transparency of large companies and promote reporting on ESG matters (78/660/EEC and 83/349/EEC). The aim is to improve corporate transparency and performance on environmental and social matters, and, therefore, contribute effectively to long-term economic growth and employment (European Commission, 2013). The relevant companies have to publish information on policies, risks and results with regards to ESG matters. In 2003, the European Commission adopted Directive 2003/51/EEC, which states, "[t]o the extent necessary for an understanding of the company's development, performance or position, the analysis [in the annual review] shall include both financial and, where appropriate, non-financial key performance indicators relevant to the particular business, including information relating to environmental and employee matters". Additionally, in 2009 all EU member states adopted Modernisation Directive 2006/46 in their national laws. This directive states that European companies "must provide a Business Review including non-financial, environmental and social performance indicators, to the extent necessary for an understanding of a company's development, performance and position" (Wensen et al., 2011: 51). Although these directives focus on the company level, they raise awareness and interest of CSR and RI across the general population.

RI institutions

Forum Nachhaltige Geldanlagen (FNG), the largest RI network institution in the three countries, has nine Austrian members, including banks, rating agencies and fund managers. Further, there are five signatories of the Principles for Responsible Investment (PRI) in Austria (one asset owner and four managers).

Looking at the institutional investors in Austria in more detail, it becomes clear how underdeveloped this market is regarding RI. Three Austrian pension funds were included in the list of the 1,000 largest pension funds[2] worldwide in 2012. However, none of these funds mentioned any form of RI in their 2012 English-language annual reports.[3]

RI issues and outlook

A bright picture about the future of the RI market in Austria is painted in the recently published 'Sustainable Investment Market Report 2013' (Forum Nachhaltige Geldanlagen [FNG], 2013). Today, 3.6 per cent of all investments in the Austrian market are RI. Growth of between 5 per cent and 50 per cent is expected in future years, with the main driver being demand from institutional investors. Pressure from outside stakeholders, such as NGOs, the media or trade unions; international initiatives, such as the PRI; changes in the regulatory framework and demand from private investors are other drivers of growth. Opinions differ as to where the Austrian RI market will stand in 10 years. Some experts expect steady growth, but foresee that RI will still occupy a niche position; others expect RI to become mainstream within the next 10 years (Forum Nachhaltige Geldanlagen [FNG], 2013).

Responsible investment in Germany

Overview of the German RI market

In 2012, the RI market in Germany consisted of $100.21 billion with a 16.3 per cent growth over the previous year. The market consists of both the institutional market and the retail market. As of 2012, the former dominated, with a value of $60.79 billion, whereas the latter had a value of $39.40 billion. RI is divided into different asset classes: bonds dominate, with a market share of 57 per cent. Equities have a market share of 23 per cent, followed by the money market, at 10 per cent. In 2001, the national RI organization, Forum Nachhaltige Geldanlagen (FNG), was launched.

The major ESG issues of concern to German society over the last decade have been the exclusion of cluster munitions, trade of weapons, direct investment in food commodities, pornography, tobacco, gambling, nuclear energy and animal testing. Currently, one of the most debated ESG issues is the renewed abandonment of nuclear power stations by the government in 2011. Figure 22.2 shows RI strategies undertaken by German investors. Exclusion and best-in-class strategies dominate the market, followed by integration and proxy voting. The least popular strategies are thematic funds and impact investment (Forum Nachhaltige Geldanlagen [FNG], 2013).

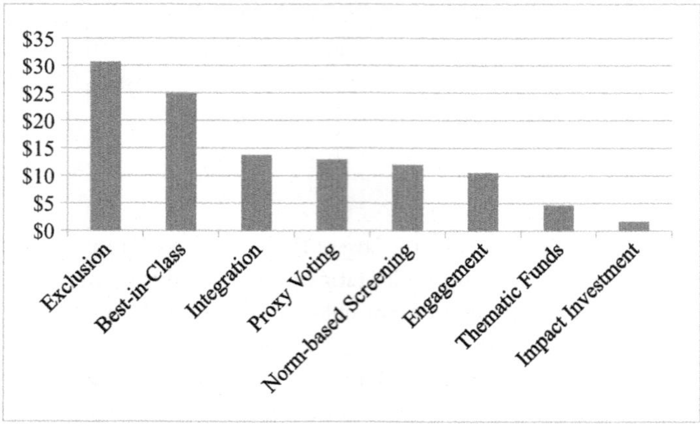

Figure 22.2 RI strategies in Germany in 2012 (in billion dollars)

Source: Forum Nachhaltige Geldanlagen (2013) (with permission).

Market and legal environment

The German investment market is very distinct as there is a reluctance by German investors to invest in equities. This is partly due to the attitudes of German investors, who are rather risk-averse (Preu & Richardson, 2011). It has been said that German investors "show a preference for interest-bearing low-risk investments like bank deposits or government bonds" (Schäfer, 2004: 270). Additionally, there is a lack of institutional investors in the German market. This phenomenon can be partly explained by the structure of the German pension system. The system consists of three pillars. The first and largest pillar is the mandatory public pension system. The money that is paid into the system is directly used to pay current retirees. This pay-as-you-go system does not provide a large amount of assets to be invested in the market, including the RI market. The second pillar is occupational and fully funded pension funds. The third pillar, also fully funded, is non-occupational and used by private investors. The last two pillars complement the first pillar (Boersch-Supan & Wilke, 2006). Although the second and third pillars are fully funded, and RI could be pursued through these channels, this does not occur in practice (Preu & Richardson, 2011).

Germany has made several regulatory efforts concerning CSR and SRI. The 'Renewable Energy Act' (Stromeinspeisungsgesetz) was passed in 1991. This act provided tax advantages to closed-end funds that invested in wind energy. In 2000, this act was replaced by the 'Act on Granting Priority to Renewable Energy Sources' (Erneuerbare-Energien-Gesetz [EEG]). In 2012, this law was reformed, such that

> The purpose of this Act is to facilitate a sustainable development of energy supply, particularly for: the sake of protecting our climate and the environment, to reduce the costs of energy supply to the national economy incorporating external long-term effects, to conserve fossil fuels and to promote the further development of technologies for the generation of electricity from renewable energy sources.
>
> *(Federal Ministry for the Environment, 2012)*[4]

In Germany, there is no law that either prohibits or mandates investment in RI. However, in 2003 the German 'Investment Modernization Act' (Investmentmodernisierungsgesetz) states that investment funds have to act not only "in the sole interest of its investors" but also for the "the integrity of the market". Although the latter focuses on the traditional forms of market abuse, it might "be interpreted more ambitiously to include goals of sustainable long-term investment, consistent with the objectives of [. . .] RI" (Preu & Richardson, 2011: 881).

Pension funds and insurance companies have specific legislation, the 'Law on the Supervision of Insurance Companies' (Versicherungsaufsichtsgesetz [VAG]). It directs funds "to seek the highest possible profitability and security for the fund, ensure diversification and liquidity of the portfolio, and manage investment professionally" (Preu & Richardson, 2011: 881). Insurance companies have an additional obligation in the 'Regulation on the Investment of Assets of Insurance Companies' (Anlagenverordnung), which limits investments in shares to 35 per cent of the fund's overall portfolio. Scharlau (2009) points out that RI is not prohibited by the VAG, but it is only allowed if it does not have adverse financial effects, does not reduce diversification of securities, or has a smaller risk spread.

German law requires disclosure of RI activities by some investors. For example, Paragraph 115.4 of the 'Amendment in Regulations Concerning Pensions Funds' (Versicherungsaufsichtsgesetz) states that pension funds must, in writing, inform their clients of how ESG issues are considered in the use of deposited funds. This is to be done annually, and also when a contract is signed. Pension funds have to report if they invest in RI or why they undertake certain activities. However, they are not obliged to invest in RI (SD-M et al., 2008). Investment managers have similar requirements, as they must also report on ESG issues in their annual reports. These "public disclosure duties were not only designed to protect beneficiaries by providing them with information about the investment chosen by their fund managers, but also to raise awareness about ethical, social and environmental issues in order to increase the demand for [. . .] RI" (Preu & Richardson, 2011: 882). In this regard, Germany requires more disclosure in comparison to other members of the EU.

RI institutions

FNG, the largest RI network institution in the three countries, has 114 German members, including banks (publicly owned as well as private and cooperative), insurance houses, rating agencies, fund managers, NGOs and charities. Additionally, there are 47 signatories of the PRI in Germany: 15 are asset owners, 21 are asset managers, and 11 are professional service providers.

Looking at institutional investors in more detail, it becomes clear how limited the RI market in Germany is. In 2012, 39 German pension funds were included in the list of the 1,000 largest pension funds[5] worldwide. However, only 2.6 per cent of these German funds discussed ESG issues in their annual reports.[6] As noted earlier, institutional investors in Germany are not obliged to invest responsibly, but they are required to disclose their ESG activities.

RI issues and outlook

One challenge in Germany in the development of RI is the structure of the German pension fund system. Another challenge is the high aversion to equity investments by German investors. This is why "RI retail funds should [. . .] offer a wide range of low-risk [. . .] RI vehicles such as interest-bearing assets or life insurance annuities" (Preu & Richardson, 2011: 899). Another challenge is the limited shareholder activism by German investors. A further challenge is the reflection of ESG issues in conventional market prices so that institutional investors do not come into conflict with the German 'Investment Modernization Act' (Investmentmodernisierungsgesetz).

Generally, the RI asset management industry in Germany is optimistic. The industry is expected to grow by 46 per cent over the next few years as more investors become aware of RI. ESG integration is thought to have promising future as well. According to Eurosif (2014), demand from institutional and retail investors might become the key driver for RI. Also, changes in the German legal framework and global initiatives might positively influence the development of RI. The recent abandonment of nuclear power stations and the strong awareness of the German population for the need to change the energy system might also be a strong force for RI in Germany. Further, the important role of specialized 'sustainable' banks in Germany, such as GLS Bank and the Bank im Bistum Essen, will play an important pioneering role for the whole RI market in the future.

Responsible investment in Switzerland

Overview of the Swiss RI market

In 2012, the RI market in Switzerland consisted of assets equal to $54.10 billion and had a growth rate of 14.7 per cent over the previous year. The Swiss RI market consists of institutional and retail markets, which are almost equal in size. This differs from the situation in Austria and Germany, where the institutional sector clearly dominates. In Switzerland, in 2012 the institutional RI market had a value of $28.98 billion and the private RI market had a value of $25.10 billion. The RI market is divided into different asset classes, and equity dominates the market (53 per cent). Bonds have a market share of 31 per cent, followed by other assets with 16 per cent. In 2001, the national RI organization, the Forum Nachhaltige Geldanalge (FNG), was launched.

The major ESG approaches over the last decade have been the exclusion of cluster munitions and the best-in-class-approach. Currently, one of the most debated ESG issues is proxy voting and the integration of ESG issues in financial analyses. Figures 22.3 shows the RI strategies utilized by Swiss investors. Exclusion and best-in-class dominate the market, followed by integration and thematic funds. The least popular RI strategies are norm-based screening and impact investment.

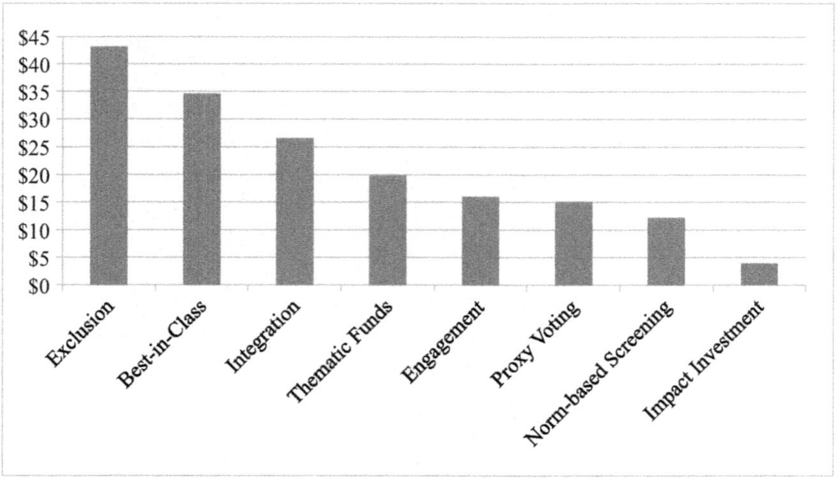

Figure 22.3 RI strategies in Switzerland in 2012 (in billion dollars)

Source: Forum Nachhaltige Geldanlagen (2013) (with permission).

Market and legal environment

Similar to Austria and Germany, Switzerland has a three-tier banking system with public-owned banks, private banks and cooperative banks. Among these banks, there are sustainable banks that primarily invest in RI and banks that have less of a focus on RI but will invest in RI if they find it suitable. In 2012, Auge et al. (2012) published a study on sustainability in Swiss banks. Approximately 300 Swiss bank customers were asked about their attitude toward sustainability in Swiss banks. The authors found that there is general interest for RI in Switzerland. Not only is RI of interest, but so is responsible bank lending. However, Swiss banking consumers expect a lower return from RI than from conventional investments. Swiss bank consumers consider fair working conditions and human rights as most relevant in the field of RI. The study demonstrates that there is a strong necessity for more information about RI in the Swiss financial market, with 70 per cent of the sample acknowledging these information needs.

Since 2000, important changes have been made that have had an impact on the shareholder environment. According to Theurillat et al. (2008) "[t]hese changes have strengthened the shareholders' position and made the Swiss model more transparent" (318). In 2002, legal changes[7] were made that require funds to establish rules on shareholder rights. Funds are not required to participate in proxy voting, but this regulation can be seen as a legal basis for shareholder engagement. It is sufficient to disclose whether the funds exercise their shareholder rights (Eurosif, 2011). Additionally, informal regulations have been implemented in Switzerland. For example, Economiesuisse (2013), the Swiss Business Federation, first published the 'Swiss Code of Best Practice of Corporate Governance' in 2002, and updated it in 2007. The Code includes rules regarding the role of shareholders, the function and composition of the board of directors and executive management, external auditing, and disclosure on corporate governance practices (Economiesuisse, 2007).

In March 2013, the referendum known as the 'Fat Cat Initiative' (Abzockerinitiative) was passed that will increase the use of voting rights by institutional investors (Forum Nachhaltige Geldanlagen & onValues, 2013), with 68 per cent of Swiss people voting in favour of institutional investors "exercising their voting rights at annual general meetings of Swiss companies, and of companies having to put their management remuneration to the vote" (Forum Nachhaltige Geldanlagen & onValues, 2013: 10). In January 2014, the decree ('Verordnung gegen übermässige Vergütungen bei börsenkotierten Aktiengesellschaften') will be put into force. As a result, annual shareholder meetings will vote annually on the remuneration for members of the board of administration, advisory board and management board.

Switzerland does not have further legislation in place that directly affects RI. However, RI currently benefits from encouraging regulation regarding different themes, such as renewable energy. Such regulations have a positive effect on RI assets (Belsif, 2015).

RI institutions

FNG, the largest RI network institution based in all the three countries (Austria, Germany, and Switzerland), has 36 Swiss members, including banks – publicly-owned as well as private and cooperative – insurance houses, rating agencies, fund managers, NGOs and charities. Additionally, there are 59 signatories of the PRI in Switzerland: 6 are asset owners, 40 are asset managers, and 13 are professional service providers.

Looking at institutional investors in Switzerland in more detail, it becomes clear how this market is developing with regard to RI. In 2012, 38 Swiss pension funds were included in the list of the 1,000 largest institutional investors[8] worldwide. However, only 2.6 per cent made mention of RI issues in their English-language annual reports.[9]

According to FNG and onValues (2013), the leading Swiss RI asset managers are Bank J. Safra-Sarasin, Ethos-Pictet, SAM, Credit Suisse, Vontobel-Raiffeisen, Swisscanto, Zurcher Kantonalbank and UBS.

RI issues and outlook

The 'Sustainable Investment Market Report 2013' paints a very bright picture about the future of the RI market in Switzerland. Today, 3.6 per cent of all investments in Switzerland are made in RI. In the following years, market growth of between 15 per cent and 50 per cent is expected. The main driver is demand from institutional investors. The changing legal framework, demand from private investors, and external pressure from the media and NGOs will also influence this growth. In general, the Swiss RI market is very dynamic, especially in regard to the traditional sustainable investment strategies, such as best in class or sustainable themes. As FNG points out, "[t]his is clearly demonstrated not only by the quantitative data, but also by the expectations of the market players and growing interest in the issue" (Forum Nachhaltige Geldanlagen & onValues, 2013: 10). In May 2013, the Sustainability Forum Zürich and Sustainable Finance Geneva published a white paper with the target of a 'Sustainable Financial Centre Switzerland'. The organization aims for Switzerland to become 'a financial centre that contributes to sustainable development and value creation in economic, environmental and social terms' (Sustainability Forum Zürich & Sustainable Finance Geneva, 2013: 4). How this target is to be achieved will be of interest.

Conclusion

Going forward, the RI markets of Austria, Germany and Switzerland look very promising. Strong growth is expected over the next 10 years. Demand from institutional investors is seen as the main driver of this growth, although the structure of the private and institutional markets in all three countries is very different. Given that "the national context is likely to be linked to the way phenomena like responsible investment [. . .] take place" (Sievänen et al., 2013: 139), it will be interesting to observe the rate and path of development in the three countries that, although similar, are also quite distinct.

Notes

1 Paul Krugman (2010), for example, claimed that Austria would go bankrupt after Ireland due to its strong linkage to the Eastern European countries.
2 According to the *IPE Top 1000* institutional investors list in 2012.
3 These results are based on the research taken by the author for the *RI Reporting Awards 2013* (Responsible Investor, 2013). For this work, an assessment framework was developed by the author to examine all annual reports of the 1,000 largest institutional investors and the PRI signatories that were published in English in 2012. The framework examined the quantity and the quality of social reporting activities. Overall, approximately 11 per cent of institutional investors reported some detail about RI.
4 In January 2014, the Minister for Energy presented a new proposal to reform the 'Renewable Energy Sources Act' again. The main changes will be in the subsidies provided for different renewable energy sources and compensation arrangements (Federal Ministry for Economic Affairs and Energy, 2014).
5 According to the *IPE Top 1000* institutional investors list in 2012.
6 Compare FN 3.
7 Compare BVV 1 regulation.
8 According to the *IPE Top 1000* institutional investors list in 2012.
9 Compare FN 3.

References

Auge, S., Baumast, A. und Fichter, C. (2012) 'Nachhaltigkeit bei Bankgeschäften in der Schweiz', SIF Schweizerisches Institut für Finanzausbildung. SIF Schweizerisches Institut für Finanzausbildung. Belsif. *EUROPE.* (2011). Online. Available HTTP: <http://www.belsif.be/default.aspx?page_id=715> (accessed 30 December 2013).

Belsif (2015). EUROPE. Online. Available http: <http://www.belsif.be/default.aspx?ref=AJADAA&lang=EN>

Boersch-Supan, A. und Wilke, C. (2006) *Reforming the German Public Pension System,* AEA Meetings, Boston.

CIA World Factbook (2013). Online. Available HTTP: <https://www.cia.gov/library/publications/the-world-factbook/> (accessed 11 December 2013).

Economiesuisse (2013). *Welcome.* Online. Available HTTP: <http://www.economiesuisse.ch/en/Pages/default.aspx> (accessed 31 December 2013).

Economiesuisse (2007) *Swiss Code of Best Practice for Corporate Governance.* Online. Available HTTP: <http://www.economiesuisse.ch/de/PDF%20Download%20Files/pospap_swiss-code_corp-govern_20080221_en.pdf> (accessed 1 December 2013).

European Commission (2013) *Non-Financial Reporting.* Online. Available HTTP: <http://ec.europa.eu/internal_market/accounting/non-financial_reporting/index_en.htm> (accessed 22 January, 2014).

Eurosif (2011) *Corporate Pension Funds and Sustainable Investment Study.* Online. Available HTTP: <http://www.eurosif.org/research/corporate-pension-funds, 2011>.

Eurosif (2014). SRI Study 2014. Online. Available HTTP: <http://www.eurosif.org/our-work/research/sri/european-sri-study-2014/>.

Federal Ministry for Economic Affairs and Energy (2014). Online. Available HTTP: <http://www.bmwi.de/DE/Themen/energie.html> (accessed 25 Janurary, 2014).

Federal Ministry for the Environment (2012) 'Act on Granting Priority to Renewable Energy Sources (Renewable Energy Sources Act – EEG)', *Federal Ministry for the Environment, Nature Conservation and Nuclear Safety.*

Federal Ministry of Agriculture, Forestry, Environment and Water Management (2013) *The Austrian Eco-label.* Online. Available HTTP: <http://www.umweltzeichen.at/cms/upload/20%20docs/2013/uz-fibel_englisch_jaenner_2013.pdf> (accessed 31 December, 2013).

Forum Nachhaltige Geldanalge (FNG) (2013). Online. Available HTTP: <http://www.forum-ng.org/de/nachhaltige-geldanlagen/nachhaltige-geldanlagen.html> (accessed 30 December 2013).

Forum Nachhaltige Geldanlagen (FNG) (2013) *Marktbericht Nachhaltige Geldanlagen 2013.* Online. Available HTTP: <http://www.forum-ng.org/images/stories/Publikationen/fng_marktbericht_2013_72dpi.pdf, 2013>.

Forum Nachhaltige Geldanlagen (FNG) and onValues (2013) *Sustainable Investments in Switzerland.* Online. Available HTTP: <http://www.forum-ng.org/images/stories/Publikationen/fng_sustainable_investments_in_switzerland-2013.pdf>.

Krugman, P. (2010) 'Wir müssten schon einen neuen Planeten finden', *Süddeutsche Zeitung,* 5.

ÖGUT (2013) *Awarded Sustainable Pension Fund.* Online. Available HTTP: <http://www.oegut.at/en/themen/nachhaltiger-finanzmarkt/nachhaltigkeitspruefung-mvk.php> (accessed 31 December 2013).

Preu, F. and Richardson, B. (2011) 'German socially responsible investment: barriers and opportunities', *German Law Journal,* 12(3): 866–900.

Responsible Investor (2013) *RI Reporting Awards.* Online. Available HTTP: <http://www.responsible-investor.com/events/events_page/ri_reporting_awards_2013_results/> (accessed 30. December 2013).

Schäfer, H. (2004) 'Ethical investment of German non-profit organizations – conceptual outline and empirical results', *Business Ethics: A European Review,* 13(4): 269–287.

Scharlau, J. (2009) *Socially responsible investment: die deutschen und europarechtlichen Rahmenbedingungen.* Bd. 30, Berlin: De Gruyter.

SD-M, BNP Paribas and Federal Ministry for the Environment (2008) *Occupational pensions and sustainable investments in Germany.* Online. Available HTTP: < http://www.sd-m.de/files/Hesse_Occupational_pensions_and_SRI_in_Germany.pdf>

Sievänen, R., Rita, H. und Scholtens, B. (2013) 'The drivers of responsible investment:the case of European pension funds', *Journal of Business Ethics,* 117(1): 137–151.

Sustainability Forum Zürich, and Sustainable Finance Geneva (2013) Sustainable Financial Centre Switzerland. Online. Available HTTP: <http://www.sfgeneva.org/doc/240613_TSF-SFG_White-Paper_Screen.pdf>.

Theurillat, T., Corpataux, J. and Crevoisier, O. (2008) 'The impact of institutional investors on corporate governance: a view of Swiss pension funds in a changing financial environment', *Competition and Change*, 12(4): 307–327.

Wensen, K, Broer, W., Klein, J. und Knopf, J. (2011) *The state of play in sustainability reporting in the European Union*, European Union.

23

Responsible investment in Belgium

Céline Louche, Luc Van Liedekerke and Herwig Peeters

Introduction

In Belgium, responsible investment (RI) has developed through active partnerships between grassroots movements and non-governmental organizations (NGOs) on the one hand and motivated financial institutions dedicated to a sustainable and solidarity economy on the other. Similar to most countries, RI in Belgium consists mostly of collective investment products such as investment or insurance funds (RI UCIs). However, the Belgian RI market is also characterized by an active involvement of saving products, what we call in this chapter 'responsible saving' (RS). The Federal Council for Sustainable Development defines RI as investment that "reconcile[s] traditional financial values with ethical, social and environmental considerations when purchasing, managing and selling investment titles and exercising related rights, including the right to vote" (Council of Ministers of Belgium, 2004).

The RI market in Belgium is supply-driven, with a limited number of banks promoting and contributing to the mainstreaming of RI. Nonetheless, its market share (in respect to traditional investing) is relatively high, and it remains one of the most active markets in Europe (Eurosif, 2010; Vigeo, 2011, 2013).

RI in Belgium is predominantly based on a positive and dynamic approach where positive screens are favoured and concepts of awarding improvements based on best-in-class methodologies are promoted. Moreover, Belgium has pioneered several innovations in the RI market, such as RI labels, laws, and a quality standard. 'Quality' has been an important discussion in Belgium, which has resulted in the active promotion of transparency and minimal norms.

Although the RI market has increased significantly since mid-2000, several challenges remain. The market showed some decline in 2012 because the RI regulatory environment is not yet mature and because RI has not spread to all asset classes.

Country overview

Belgium has a total area of 30,528 square kilometres, which makes it a rather small country. It is situated in the west of Europe and is bordered by the Netherlands, Germany, Luxembourg and France. As of March 2014 its population was 11.14 million people, with a population density of more than 360 people per square kilometre, the second highest population density in Europe.

Belgium scores well with regard to quality of life. It ranks among the top 10 countries in several topics in the Better Life Index. Life expectancy in the country as of 2012 was 79.65 years. It features a 99 per cent literacy rate, and the school life expectancy was 17 years as of 2011. In terms of employment, the level of unemployment was 8.5 per cent in 2013, compared to a rate of 21.2 per cent in the euro area (EU17). According to the World Bank, its GDP per capita was $43,413 in 2012, ranking 21st globally.

Roman Catholicism has traditionally been Belgium's majority religion. In 2010, 75 per cent of the population declared themselves as Roman Catholic. Despite the drop in church attendance over the last decade, the catholic identity nevertheless remains an important part of Belgium's culture.

The country is characterized by its multilingualism and multiculturalism and its culture of compromise. It has two cultural communities (Flemish and French) straddling the cultural boundary between Germanic and Latin Europe. The country has three linguistic groups Dutch-speakers, mostly Flemish (~ 60 per cent); French-speakers, mostly Walloons (~40 per cent); and a small group of German-speakers (less than 1 per cent).

With respect to Internet use, Belgium ranks 43rd worldwide, with 8.5 million users in 2011 (more than 81 per cent of the population).

Belgium is a federal parliamentary democracy under a constitutional monarchy whereby the king is the head of state and the prime minister is the head of government in a multi-party system. Its civil law system is based on the French Civil Code.

Belgium was the 18th largest trading nation in 2013, according to the CIA.[1] The country has capitalized on its central location in Europe through a highly developed transport network and a diversified industrial and commercial base. Belgium has few natural resources other than fertile soil. Nonetheless, most traditional industrial sectors are represented in the economy. Its main industries include engineering and metal products, motor vehicle assembly, transportation equipment, scientific instruments, processed food and beverages, chemicals, basic metals, textiles, glass and petroleum. However, Belgium is mainly a service-oriented economy, as services accounted for 74.9 per cent of its GDP in 2010.

RI market in Belgium

In Belgium, RI products can be divided in three main categories: (1) responsible investment UCIs (undertaking for collective investments), such as SICAVs, investment funds, insurance funds and structured products, including notes (RI UCIs); (2) responsible saving accounts (RS); and (3) other forms of RI. We will provide some insights into these three categories in the following sections, but first we would like to briefly discuss the data available on the Belgium RI market.

Sources of information about RI in Belgium

When looking for data on the Belgium RI market, several sources of information are available. However, the data provided varies greatly.

There are three main Belgian sources of information on the Belgian market: the Belgian Asset Managers Association (BEAMA), Mira & Forum Ethibel, and the Réseau Financité (RFA). In addition to these national sources are two European sources: Eurosif and Vigeo.

Each of these sources collects and calculates the data using their own methodology and with different assumptions. As a result, each source provides different figures (see Appendix 23.1). As such, we need to be careful when using and comparing RI data, and it is crucial to understand the way they have been collected. In this chapter, when available, we will use data from the Mira Report. The Mira Report has a long track record (since 1992) and provides data related to all asset classes. The Mira Report uses data from the Financial Services and Markets Authority (FSMA).[2] Although the FSMA listed 365 RI products in 2012, Mira selected only 315 of them based on transparency and the level of RI approach (Peeters & Raeymaekers, 2013). Among the 50 rejected funds, some did not have any explicit RI criteria and critically lacked transparency; others had only a very limited number of screens (one screen, for example), which was not enough to be considered a RI fund; and others were thematic funds – focusing for example on alternative energy – while not applying any RI method.

Responsible investing and undertakings for collective investments (RI UCIs)

Between 1995 and 2012, RI assets under management in Belgium increased from 8.9 million euro to 8 billion euro. As a result, the relative market share of RI compared to the market of traditional UCIs increased from 0.05 per cent to 9.6 per cent (Peeters, 2012). In 2012, 315 RI vehicles (investment funds, notes, insurance products, etc.) were offered on the Belgian market, of which 279 were specifically launched for the Belgian market (Peeters & Raeymaekers, 2013).

The market for RI UCIs started in Belgium in the early 1990s (Coeckelbergh, 2011). In 1991, KBC launched the first environmental technology fund, called KBC Ecofund. One year later, in 1992, Van Moer-Santerre & Co. initiated the first responsible investment fund, VMS Luxinter Ethifond. However, no other RI UCI initiatives were introduced until after 1996. The period 1996–2001 was a period of slow growth and ended with a stock market collapse in 2001. From 2002 and 2007, RI UCIs demonstrated impressive growth. This was due to the increased interest of large asset managers, notably Dexia, KBC and Fortis, that saw RI as a growth opportunity and a lasting market segment. The financial crisis in 2008 did not stop the growth of RI UCIs in Belgium. Although the assets under management decreased slightly in 2008, the relative market share of RI kept growing. This phenomenon was confirmed by Vigeo in its 2011 survey: "It was clear that the financial crisis that affected the asset management industry encouraged further sustainable investing, particularly in countries where [S]RI was already prevalent" (Vigeo, 2011). In 2011, the first signs of a slowdown were observed, a trend that was confirmed in 2012. Between 2010 and 2012, the number of RI products decreased by 21 per cent (Peeters & Raeymaekers, 2013).

Based on the Vigeo report, Belgium represented 6 per cent of the European market in 2012 in terms of number of funds, a decrease of 2 per cent compared to 2011 (Peeters & Raeymaekers, 2013).

Table 23.1 shows the number of RI UCIs per asset manager in Belgium, as well as their per cent market share. As of 2012, the market was led by three main players, namely KBC, BNP Paribas and Dexia. The same three asset managers have been dominating the Belgian market in terms of number of RI UCI products since 2008, although not always in the same order of importance.

Responsible saving and saving accounts (RS)

Responsible savings (RS), also called 'solidarity and sustainable savings', started in Belgium in 1984. By the end of 2012, it had 2.4 billion euro of assets under management and a market share of 0.95 per cent (Peeters & Raeymaekers, 2013). RS remains rather modest in terms of volume and market share. In 2012, RS represented 28 per cent of the volume of the total

Table 23.1 The RI market profile in Belgium for each portfolio manager, expressed in number of RI UCIs products and market share as of December 2011

Asset Manager Group	*Number of Products*			
	2009	*2010*	*2011*	*2012*
KBC AM	146	181	187	152
BNP Paribas	55	68	69	69
Dexia AM	21	23	25	23
Crédit Agricole	21	14	14	13
Ethias	5	6	6	5
Triodos	3	4	4	4
ING	2	4	3	4
Petercam	2	2	2	2
Degroof Fund MC	1	2	2	2
Axa	1	2	2	2
oikocredit	1	1	1	1
VLADUBEL	1	1	1	1
ARGENTA	1	1	1	1
Bank Delen	1	0	0	0
Dresdner Van Moer	1	1	1	0
TOTAL	**262**	**310**	**318**	**279**

Source: Peeters & Raeymaekers (2013).

responsible investment products (RI UCIs and RS) on the Belgian market. The RS market saw a growth of 1.93 billion euro between 2010 and 2011. One of the key explanations of the growth is the involvement of a newcomer in RS, namely Van Lanschot Bankiers, which in 2012 had the largest market share. However, a second important element of the growth has been a shift that is currently occurring in financial institutions. Banks are transitioning from including responsible principles in only a very limited number saving products (some very specific products) to their inclusion in all saving products. It started with Ethias, and it is expected that others will follow in the near future. Despite these initiatives the RS market saw a decline in 2012.

RS was introduced prior to RI UCIs; however, it was unable to gather the same interest, and today the RI UCI market is much larger than the RS market. The first RS product – 'Cricket saving' – was launched in 1984. This product was the outcome of a partnership between three organizations: BNP Paribas, a bank, and two NGOs, Netwerk Vlaanderen (now FairFin) and Réseau Financité. Partnerships remain an important characteristic of RS in Belgium. Five other RS initiatives have been launched in partnership between banks and NGOs (see Table 23.2).

As of December 2012, five RS products were on the market, namely Krekelsparen, Epargne Cigale, Hefboomsparen, Solidariteitsparen, Triodossparen and Spaarrekening Van Lanschot Bankiers. The activities of Ethias Bank have been stopped and partly taken over by Optima Bank. It is interesting to note that the financial institutions offering RS products are different from the institutions offering RI UCIs. Only two of the institutions active in RI UCIs also have RS products, namely BNP Paribas Fortis and Triodos Bank.

Table 23.2 Responsible savings in Belgium, 1984–2012

Initiation	*Saving Product*	*Partnerships*	*Per cent Market Share (as of December 2012)*
1984	Krekelsparen | Épargne Cigale | 'Cricket Savings'	BNP Paribas Fortis | Netwerk Vlaanderen + Réseau Financité	5.52
1995	World Savings	VDK Spaarbank | Trias + Wereldsolidariteit + CPP-Incofin + Broederlijk Delen	0.51
2000	Solidarity Savings	VDK Spaarbank | Hefboom + Welzijnszorg	
1993	North-South Savings	Triodos Bank | multiple partners until 2011	45.58
2006	Saving with Ethias Bank	Ethias Bank | no partner	0.00
2011	Saving Account VLB	Van Lanschot Bankiers | no partner	48.39

Source: Peeters & Raeymaekers (2013).

The approach adopted for RS varies greatly. It ranges from a solidarity approach, where investors directly invest a certain percentage of their assets in social projects, to using best-in-class criteria for positive or negative screening criteria. RS can also include impact investing, microfinance and engagement policies.

Other forms of RI

In addition to RI UCIs and RS products, other RI products are available in the Belgian market. This includes credits, microcredits and risk capital that provide capital efforts to stimulate sustainability-related projects.

Several organizations in Belgium provide some form of RI through seed capital, credits or warranties for specific social- or environment-related projects or economic activities. Depending on the size, the destination, the risk rate and the cost structure, they are classified as credits or microcredits, seed capital or interest-free loans. Appendix 23.2 provides a list of organizations (non-exhaustive) that were involved in such activities as of December 2012. Several of them specialize in microfinance, such as Alterfin, Incofin or Microstart. Others, like the Credal, Hefboom or Trividend, are active in the social economy, which is the third sector in economies.

Institutional versus retail RI market

Compared to other European countries, the retail RI market in Belgium is rather significant. According to the Eurosif 2012 report, retail investors represented 23 per cent of RI market (28 per cent in 2010; Eurosif, 2010) compared to the 6 per cent on average for Europe (Eurosif, 2012). The bulk of the market (77 per cent; Eurosif, 2010) remains, however, in the hands of institutional investors. In 2008, Belgian pension funds allocated only 15 per cent of their total pension assets – approximately €13 billion – in RI (Investments & Pensions Europe, 2008). Note that Belgian pension funds represent only one third of the total Belgian pension assets and that the remainder is managed by insurers (Peeters, 2009; Swaegers, 2010). However, very little is known about the RI activities of institutional investors, and the available data may not be fully reliable. Eurosif reports provide a very partial picture of what they do. Only four players reported for the 2012 Eurosif report (Eurosif, 2011).

Policy environment, regulations and fiduciary duties

Belgium is showing a real political will to stimulate and promote RI. In September 2004, the Federal Plan for Sustainable Development 2004–2008 was adopted. This plan recognized the importance of RI and encouraged 'ethically sound investment':

> §30801. Ethically sound investments reconcile traditional financial values with ethical, social and environmental considerations when purchasing, managing and selling investment titles and exercising related rights, including the right to vote. It is a sustainable development theme par excellence.
>
> *(Council of Ministers of Belgium, 2004)*

A number of laws have been adopted to support RI. Similar to many other countries, the emphasis is on transparency and disclosure (Steurer, Margula, & Martinuzzi, 2008). We enlist hereafter the main initiatives.

Disclosure laws

The Law of April 2003, also known as the Law on Supplementary Pensions or the 'Vandenbroucke' Law, requires pension funds to disclose in their annual report the degree to which social, environmental and ethical criteria are taken into account in the investment strategy (Article 42 of the law).

After the adoption of the Federal Plan in 2004, a new law of 20 July 2004 was enacted making transparency disclosures mandatory in both the prospectus and annual reports for Belgian Collective Investment Schemes (CIS) (Article 76 of the Law of 20 July 2004). Mutual funds and the SICAVs have to report in the prospectus and in the annual report the extent to which their investment policies take social, environmental, and ethical criteria into consideration. The way in which ESG criteria are used when exercising shareholder rights (voting rights, resolution submission) must also be disclosed in the annual report.

The objective of these two disclosure laws is to force trustees and fund managers to communicate to their clients or members their stance on ESG issues and, indirectly, to stimulate RI. However the regulations have had very limited impact, as the transparency improved only to a small degree and did not effectively stimulate RI (Bayot, Cayrol, & Marcelo, 2011; Peeters, 2009; Swaegers, 2010). As of June 2012, there are no transparency measures for the insurance sector.

Prohibition laws

In March 2007, and then in June 2009, the Belgium Parliament enacted two laws prohibiting Belgium investors from providing direct or indirect financing for the production, commercialization, use and possession of, respectively, anti-personnel mines, sub-munitions and depleted uranium weapons (European Commission, 2010). An amendment to the law regulating economic activities and individuals with weapons is currently under discussion. Its objective is to ban the financing of companies involved in the production or commercialization of incendiary weapons with white phosphorus (Belgian Parliament, 2009).

Code of conduct

In June 2009, the Belgian Asset Managers Association (BEAMA) adopted a code of conduct (as part of the Constitution of the Association) integrating elements of RI. The code takes 'fiduciary duty' as a starting point, which it defines as any entity and/or individual who assumes responsibility for any aspect of portfolio management in the broadest sense of the term, recognizes the principle of fiduciary duty and adheres to it when exercising their activities (BEAMA, 2009). The code of conduct deals specifically with the principles arising from the general principle of fiduciary duty, which covers all the others, and the practical interpretation of this principle.

Consumer protection

Discussions are also underway to create a Consumer Protection Agency on financial products that would have as a mission, among others, to promote and monitor ethical and solidarity-based finance aspects, and to prohibit the financing of certain products, as well as speculations harmful to public interest. A bill in a similar vein was been presented in the House of Representatives on 8 November 2010 (Bayot et al., 2011). As of December 2012, no decision had been taken yet.

RI institutions

In Belgium six main organizations are actively promoting and supporting responsible investment. They are described in the paragraphs below.

- Association for Responsible Investment Services (ARISE):
  ARISE is an international trade association, seated in Belgium, that owns and manages ARISTA®. ARISTA® is the Responsible Investment Research Standard, developed in response to the demands from global investors and companies for RI research groups to incorporate the key principles of quality, integrity, transparency and accountability into their research processes. (www.arista-standard.org)
- Belgian Asset Managers Association (BEAMA):
  Since 2001, BEAMA has been active in monitoring sustainable and socially responsible investment UCIs as well as in taking care of their quality control. (www.beama.be)
- Belgian Sustainable and Socially Responsible Investment Forum (BELSIF):
  BELSIF is a non-profit organization in which individual financial institutions participate along with social organizations and NGOs. BELSIF aims to stimulate, promote and support all types of sustainable and socially responsible investments, and to actively promote RI to public and private financial investors. BELSIF is the Belgian national member of Eurosif. (www.belsif.be)
- FairFin:
  FairFin promotes an environmentally and socially responsible approach to money, and strives for a just society. FairFin is a non-profit organization which campaigns against irresponsible and detrimental investments of banks. FairFin is active at the international level as part of BankTrack. (www.fairfin.be)
- Forum ETHIBEL:
  Ethibel, together with Van Moer-Santerre stood at the birthplace of RI in Belgium. After the merger of its research company 'Stock at Stake' with Vigeo, a new name was adopted. 'Forum ETHIBEL' promotes responsible investing, encourages dialogue between stakeholders, and provides specific instruments and labels to support investors. (www.forumethibel.org)
- le Réseau Financité (RFA)
  RFA is a non-profit organization consisting of a wide variety of social organizations. Its main aim is to develop and promote ethics and solidarity in dealing with money in order

to contribute to a more just and humane society. Its main activities are financial education, research in the field of responsible investment, as well as developing and labelling financial products/services that meet its standards for social responsibility and solidarity. (www.financite.be)

RI practices

In this section we will explore RI practices in the Belgian market. We will look at ESG criteria, shareholder engagement and RI quality. It is interesting to note that, so far, very few RI actors have signed the UN-backed Principles for Responsible Investment (PRI) (UNEP Finance Initiative and Global Footprint Network, 2012) in Belgium. In 2007–2008, five large Belgian financial institutions signed the PRI. By early 2012, all but one had withdrawn from the PRI. As of 2014, there are four signatories in Belgium, and contrary to the 2007 list, these are fairly small organizations.

In April 2010, BELSIF published the 'BELSIF Matrix', which is a comparison tool of various RI products in Belgium. The matrix details the methodologies and characteristics of 159 RI products available in Belgium. The following paragraphs are based on the information provided in the Matrix 2010.[3] Although the data is from 2010 and does not cover all existing RI products, it provides an accurate picture of the 2012 RI practices in Belgium.

RI methodologies and criteria used

Table 23.3 provides an overview of the practices of the 159 funds studied by BELSIF in 2010. We can see that most of the RI products use a combination of approaches. Almost 100 per cent have negative screening, which can be explained by the regulation requirement with regard to controversial weapons. Ninety-three per cent use a best-in-class approach, and more than 60 per cent have some form of engagement, mainly in terms of proxy voting. Thematic investment is also a popular approach, used by 31 per cent of the RI products. It is also interesting to note that the most important theme is the environment. Issues belonging to the social domain are less popular among RI actors in Belgium.

If we look more closely into the negative screens, divestment from weapons-producing companies is the most popular. This was already the case before the 2007 and 2009 legislation prohibiting the financing of weapons; however, since 2009 the use of this negative screen has been extended to almost 100 per cent of all investments in Belgium (RI and non-RI). Other popular negative screens include tobacco, gambling and nuclear power. Less common are those related to GMOs and oppressive regimes/countries.

With regard to engagement practices, some Belgian asset managers, like KBC AM, Dexia AM and BNP Paribas Investment Partners, have recently complemented their 'passive' RI policies with engagement initiatives, starting in the 2007–2008. They actively engage by exercising their voting rights through proxy voting resolutions concerning stocks in their portfolios or by participating in joint initiatives. Although the figures reported by the BELSIF study are quite high, engagement remains a recent and emerging activity in Belgium. There is also a relative lack of transparency in reporting on engagement processes. It is often very unclear to the investor how the engagement process was developed and how much energy was put into this process. This lack of transparency is often defended on efficiency grounds, claiming that this would harm the trust between the investor and the company.

Table 23.3 RI methodologies and criteria used in Belgium

Positive Screening	*Per cent of Products*
Positive methodologies used by SRI products	
Products using best-in-class method	93.08%
Products being thematic investments	31.45%
Products combining best-in-class and thematic investments	23.27%
Negative Screening/Exclusions	
Exclusions of specific issues and controversial activities	
Adult content	20.13%
Alcohol	39.62%
Animal testing	20.13%
Controversial weapons	99.37%
Gambling	54.72%
GMO	19.50%
Harmful substances for the environment	20.75%
Nuclear power	54.72%
Oppressive regimes/countries	19.50%
Tobacco	54.72%
Weapons	78.62%
Others	10.06%
Norms-based screening	
Anti-corruption	77.99%
Corporate governance	77.36%
Human rights	77.36%
Labour rights	78.62%
Environment	78.62%
Others	39.62%
Engagement	
Proxy voting	63.52%
Direct engagement conducted privately	62.26%
Collaborative engagement	27.67%
Filling shareholder resolutions	4.40%
Co-filling shareholder resolutions	4.40%
Others	4.40%

Source: BELSIF SRI Matrix, 2010.

RI quality and accountability

A strong characteristic of the Belgium RI market is its emphasis on quality and accountability. For this purpose, the Belgian members of the international trade association Arise (Association for Responsible Investment Services), Forum ETHIBEL and Vigeo have invested in the international quality standard ARISTA 3.0®.[4]

The objective of the standard is twofold: it aims to promote confidence in responsible investment, and it serves to answer the transparency criticism. RI institutions have been criticized for their lack of transparency and accountability by both companies and investors (Coeckelbergh, 2011). Methodologies and criteria used are not always clearly stated, and results are not always understandable. A number of reports such as 'Rate the Raters' published by SustAinability[5] and initiatives such as the Global Initiative for Sustainability Ratings (GISR)[6] were launched around 2010 to promote transparency and to work on solutions to overcome this problem. ARISTA is participating in this movement and provides key principles of quality, integrity, transparency and accountability to be incorporated into research processes.

Although the standard originated in Europe (seated in Belgium), ARISTA 3.0® is an open standard available to all RI research groups around the world that meet the certification criteria. As of December 2012, 14 RI research institutions were signatories.

Future challenges for RI in Belgium

Responsible investment in Belgium grew significantly between 1995 and 2011 with respect to market share, number and type of actors involved and the number of investment products. The changing landscape shows the dynamism of the RI market in Belgium; however, several challenges remain.

First, RI has yet to encompass all asset classes. It remains focused on equities, as is the case in many other countries. This limits its potential growth. Expansion into the insurance sector, credits and loans, saving products and treasury is a necessity in order to further mainstream RI. Expansion should also come in the type of clients. So far the market relies mainly on institutional investors. Retail investors, although reasonably well represented in Belgium compared to other European countries, still linger at the sideline, and RI is hardly present in private banking.

Second, despite the many initiatives with respect to the quality and accountability around RI screening and products, there is a clear need to extend the scope of the transparency and accountability requirements to the full supply chain of RI. Notably the process of engagement often remains unclear to RI investors.

Finally, we should mention a number of political initiatives that might have considerable influence on the future structure of the RI market in Belgium. There is an ongoing discussion to make RI the compulsory framework for all public investment and public saving pension schemes. Fiscal incentives to promote solidarity products are also on the table, as well as the introduction of a new regulation setting a minimum quality norm for RI products. This could be done by extending the principles of the Belgian law on controversial arms to other controversial or harmful activities. All these initiatives are characterized by a political battle between two groups: one pushing for legally binding regulations, the other insisting on stronger self-regulation. The first group mainly consists of NGOs and politicians, whereas the second group is driven by the Belgian financial sector federation, Febelfin (Peeters, 2011). Both groups meet in BELSIF and, despite tensions, they have managed so far to work together on a number of issues. Discussions around the legal initiatives mentioned above are not in a decisive stage yet, but they could determine the future growth prospects of the RI market in Belgium.

Notes

1 Online. Available HTTP: <www.cia.gov/index.html>.
2 FSMA, Financial Services and Markets Authority. Online. Available HTTP: <www.fsma.be>.
3 Online. Available HTTP: <www.belsif.be/default.aspx?ref=AJAG&lang=EN>.

4 Online. Available HTTP: <www.aristastandard.org>.
5 Online. Available HTTP: <www.sustainability.com/projects/rate-the-raters>.
6 Online. Available HTTP: <http://ratesustainability.org>.

References

Bayot, B., Cayrol, A. and Marcelo, C. (2011) *L'investissement socialement responsable en Belgiqu,* Rapport 2011, Réseau Financement Alternatif.

BEAMA (2009) *BEAMA Code of Conduct for the Asset Management Sector and Related Activities in Belgium,* Brussels, Belgium: Febelfin. Online. Available HTTP: <http://www.beama.be/en/organisatie-en/codeofconduct/code-of-conduct>.

Belgian Parliament (2009) *Loi réglant des activités économiques et individuelles avec des armes: Service Public Fédéral Justice.* Online. Available HTTP: <http://www.ejustice.just.fgov.be/cgi_loi/loi_a.pl?language=nl&caller=list&cn=2006060830&la=n&fromtab=wet&sql=dt='wet'&tri=dd+as+rank&rech=1&numero=1>.

BELSIF SRI Matrix (2010) *Belgian Sustainable and Socially Responsible Investment Forum,SRI Matrix* .Online. Avaiblable HTTP: <http://www.belsif.be/default.aspx?page_id=753>.

Coeckelbergh, D. (2011) *Ethisch en duurzaam beleggen in België. Historiek, stand van zaken en kritische visie: Garant.*

Council of Ministers of Belgium (2004) *Federal Plan for Sustainable Development 2004–2008.*

European Commission (2010) *Corporate Social Responsiblity, National Public Policies in the European Union,* Directorate-General for Employment, Social Affairs and Inclusion, Unit C.2.

Eurosif (2010) *European SRI Study 2010,* Paris. Online. Available HTTP: <http://www.eurosif.org/research/eurosif-sri-study/european-sri-study-2010> (accessed 15 October 2010).

Eurosif (2011) *Corporate Pension Funds and Sustainable Investment.* Online. Available HTTP: <http://www.eurosif.org/wp-content/uploads/2014/07/coporate-pensiosn-funds.pdf>.

Eurosif (2012) *European SRI Study 2012.* Online. Available HTTP: <http://eurosif.org/images/stories/pdf/1/eurosifsristudy_low-res v1.1.pdf: Eurosif>.

Investments & Pensions Europe (2008) *Cross-Border Intentions,* Vol. 12: 17: IPE International Publishers Ltd.

Peeters, H. (2009) *Onderzoek en evaluatie van de transparantieregeling in het kader van de aanvullende pensioenen en de instellingen voor collectieve belegging,* Forum ETHIBEL, POD DO.

Peeters, H. (2011) *Transparency, Audit and Control within a SRI Regulatory Framework,* Forum ETHIBEL for Febelfin. Online. Available HTTP: <http://www.febelfin.be/sites/default/files/files/PlatformSRBI_advice2_Ethibel.pdf>.

Peeters, H. (2012) *Duurzaam Sparen en Beleggen in België in 2011: Mira,* Forum Ethibel, Milieurapport Vlaanderen.

Peeters, H. and Raeymaekers, S. (2013) *Duurzaam Sparen en Beleggen in België: actualisatie tot 2012: Mira,* Forum Ethibel, Milieurapport Vlaanderen; Forum ETHIBEL vzw.

Steurer, R., Margula, S. and Martinuzzi, A. (2008) *Socially Responsible Investment in EU Member States: Overview of Government Initiatives and SRI Experts' Expectations Towards Governments,* commissioned by the European Commission (ed.), Vienna, Austria: Vienna University of Economics and Business Administration.

Swaegers, C. (2010) *SRI Disclosure : Evaluation of the Transparency Policy in Case of Belgian Pension Institutions and CIS,* Catholic University of Leuven.

UNEP Finance Initiative and Global Footprint Network. (2012) *A New Angle on Sovereign Credit Risk,* Geneva.

Vigeo. (2011) *Green, Social and Ethical Funds in Europe,* 2011 Review.

Vigeo. (2013) *Green, Social and Ethical Funds in Europe The Retail Market,* 2013 Review. Online. Available HTTP: <http://www.vigeo.com/csr-rating-agency/images/stories/formulaires/2013%20Green%20Social%20and%20Ethical%20Funds%20in%20Europe_Final%20version.pdf>.

Appendices

Appendix 23.1

RI market in Belgium

Table 23.4 provides an overview of the data provided on the Belgian RI market by five different sources. Note the large differences in absolute numbers as well as market share.

Table 23.4 Belgian RI products

Source	*Number of RI Products*		*Share*	*Source*
BEAMA	232 RI funds	€5.78 billion	5.42%	www.beama.be (2011 data)
Mira & Forum Ethibel	359 RI UCI vehicles 5 RS initiatives	• RI UCIs: €8.6 billion • RS: €2.4 billion	9.6%	Mira Report 2012 (2012 data)
RFA	340 RI funds 7 RS products	€15 billion, distributed as follows: • RI funds: €9.9 billion • RS: €1.05 billion	9.0%	2012 report (2011 data)
Vigeo	204 RI retail funds	RI funds: €6.4 billion	NA	Annual Survey 2013 (2012 data)
Eurosif	140 RI funds 20 other RI products	• (1) Sustainability themes assets + (2) best in class + (3) norms-based screening: €26.2 billion • 1 + 2 + 3 + (4) exclusions + (5) integration + (6) engagement: €129.3 billion		2012 report

Appendix 23.2

Table 23.5 Belgian Organizations providing credits, microcredits, seed capital or cheap loans

Organization	*Objective*
BIO	The mission of the Belgian Investment Company for Developing Countries is to support the private sector in developing countries by providing long-term financing for small-to-medium enterprises (SMEs) and microfinance institutions.
FHIC	The Federal Holding and Investment Company (FHIC) centrally manages the federal government's shareholdings, cooperates with the government on specific projects and pursues its own investment policy in the interests of the Belgian economy.
Alterfin cvba	Provides warranties for microcredit activities in developing countries and specific advice.
Crédal cvba	Support and investments in an economy of solidarity.
Hefboom cvba	Advice and investment in projects for a solidarity and sustainable society; promotion of RI products.
Incofin cvba	Management of microfinance funds.
Microstart	Microcredit institution focusing on the Belgian market.
Netwerk Rentevrij	A cooperative providing interest-free loans to projects with an added societal value.
Oikocredit-be	Oikocredit is one of the world's largest sources of private funding to the microfinance sector. Also provides credit to trade cooperatives, fair trade organizations and SMEs in the developing world.
Triodos	Triodos offers innovation funds to support companies active in clean energy, organic agriculture, fair trade, environmental technology and the care and services sector.
Trividend cvba	Advice and participation in social economy. Risk capital, subordinated loans.

Source: Peeters (2012).

24

Responsible investment in the Netherlands

Heather Hachigian

Introduction

The Netherlands boasts one of the most sophisticated markets for responsible investment (RI) in the world. In large part, this can be attributed to the high degree of cooperation between the public and private sectors. While exclusions make up a significant portion of the Dutch RI market, strategies such as engagement and positive selection are increasingly applied. The Netherlands is also home to one of the largest markets for impact investing. This chapter provides an overview of the Dutch market for RI. It is structured in the following way: the next section provides a country overview. This is followed by an explanation of how RI is understood in the Netherlands. The chapter proceeds with an account of RI. The penultimate section draws attention to the Dutch policy and regulatory environment. The chapter concludes with obstacles to the development of the Dutch RI market in the future.

Country overview

The Netherlands is the sixth largest economy in the European Union, with a gross domestic product (GDP) per capita of US $43,300. The constitutional monarchy, which borders Germany, Belgium and 451 kilometres of coastline, is an important European transportation hub. The Dutch economy has moderate unemployment and inflation, and a considerable trade surplus. Moreover, the Netherlands has one of the most mature financial markets in Europe. In particular, the financial sector is renowned for its exceptionally large pension funds. Proportionally, Dutch pension funds represent 170 per cent of the country's GDP, making the Netherlands the largest pension market in the world in relative terms (Towers Watson, 2014). In absolute terms, the Dutch pension sector is among the seven largest globally, with assets under management of over US $1 trillion (Towers Watson, 2014). This is remarkable given the country's modest population of 16.9 million. The size of the Dutch pension fund sector is explained by the government's power to mandate participation in industrywide schemes.[1] When the insurance and retail sectors are accounted for, the total Dutch investment management industry was estimated at US $2.3 trillion at the end of 2013.[2]

The 2007–9 global financial crisis hit the Dutch financial sector hard. The government injected billions of dollars into the financial sector to keep it afloat. This included the nationalization of two banks in 2008. The Dutch banking sector is still recovering six years later. This slow recovery has had negative consequences for domestic investment, particularly for small and medium enterprises (DNB, 2014a). Pension funds were also adversely affected by the financial crisis. As a percentage of Dutch pension commitments, the market value of pension funds declined from 130 per cent in 2007 to 95 per cent in 2008 (IMF, 2011).

Another notable feature of the Dutch financial sector is its high degree of consolidation. Since the 1990s, there have been several mergers among Dutch financial institutions, leading to increasing concentration in the market. In 2014, the Dutch Central Bank estimated that three banks (ING, Rabobank and ABN-Amro) account for 85 per cent of lending to Dutch households and 60 per cent to Dutch companies (DNB, 2014b). Pension funds are also becoming increasingly consolidated.[3] This consolidation provides a natural incentive for financial institutions to compete on the basis of their RI programs, as "responsible investment offering and a good reputation of handling ESG risks can create a competitive advantage" (Sustainalytics, 2013: 6).

With regards to unique cultural aspects of the Dutch financial sector, there is strong demand among pensioners and retail investors for the reflection of sustainability and international norms in their portfolios. One study finds the majority (86 per cent) of 518 Dutch pensioners surveyed want their funds to focus on long-term returns and 70 per cent want their pensions invested in a socially responsible manner (Responsible Investor, 2012). Non-governmental organizations have played a significant role in raising the specter of investment decision-making with respect to such issues. The Dutch documentary *Zembla*, which confronted pension funds on their investments in cluster munitions, spurred widespread interest among the public in RI when it first aired on Dutch television in 2007. Moreover, the unique geography of the low-lying country, which includes over a quarter of the land area and 60 per cent of the population below sea level and therefore in high-risk flooding areas, provides a strong impetus for taking into account climate change risks in investments.[4]

Another special cultural aspect is the importance placed on public participation in the investment decisions and practices of pension funds. Many Dutch pension funds have participant councils, which provide a mechanism for members to communicate their interests. In some instances, these councils provide a two-way dialogue with pension fund board members.

What is considered responsible investment in the Netherlands?

RI is relatively new in the Netherlands compared to the United States, where its historical roots can be traced back centuries. The first Dutch ethical fund, 'Het Aandere Beleggingsfonds', was established in 1991 by Triodos Bank. The fund combined a best-in-class approach with exclusion of sectors such as nuclear weapons and companies that violated international norms on human rights. Exclusions continue to make up the majority of the Dutch RI market (Eurosif, 2014). That said, the RI market has evolved over the past two decades to reflect a concern with long-term financial performance (Quak et al., 2014). RI now encompasses a broad range of strategies that are used in combination with each other and demonstrate investor concern for both social responsibility and risk-adjusted returns. For example, Dutch pension fund management giant APG claims: "We take account of environmental, social and governance factors as an integral part of the investment process in order to: (i) contribute to risk-adjusted financial returns (ii) demonstrate social responsibility and (iii) contribute to the integrity of financial markets."

RI is also understood in the Netherlands to extend across asset classes. In 2011, the Dutch Association of Investors for Sustainable Development (VBDO) adapted its annual survey methodology to include consideration for RI in asset classes such as sovereign bonds and real estate. In 2013 the survey extended consideration to private equity, hedge funds, commodities and infrastructure. With respect to the type of issues addressed by Dutch RI policies and practices, the UN Global Compact provides a standard for measuring commitment across environmental, social and governance issues.

Impact investing is increasingly considered alongside RI in the Dutch market. Impact investing has been included in the VBDO annual RI benchmarking survey since 2010. It is defined by the VBDO (2011b) as "active investments that are made in companies or projects that contribute to innovative technological development and create added value for society that can hardly be compared with mainstream solutions" (39). In contrast to the view that impact investing is an asset class in itself, there is a tendency among Dutch institutional investors to consider impact investing as an approach to be applied across its portfolio.

Responsible investment in the Netherlands

The Dutch market for RI has experienced considerable growth in a relatively short time span. In 2005, over US $62.9 billion was invested in a socially responsible manner.[5] By 2013, the Dutch RI market is estimated to represent over US $1.6 trillion.[6] While the majority of this market is captured by exclusions, in recent years there has been an increase in the application of other approaches, such as engagement, positive selection and ESG integration. Another important development is the growth of impact investing. This section explains what types of investors engage in RI in the Netherlands and accounts for the strategies these investors are using.

Who are responsible investors in the Netherlands?

Institutional investors

By 2012, almost all large pension funds in the Netherlands had an RI policy (VBDO, 2013a). This is a recent development. To illustrate, of the 30 pension funds in the 2007 VBDO survey, 8 indicated that they were working on an RI policy (Sustainalytics, 2013). In the 2013 survey, 49 of the 50 pension funds included in the survey claimed to have an RI policy. Moreover, pension funds surveyed by the VBDO are increasingly applying their RI strategies across the asset classes in which they invest. Dutch pension fund manager APG, for example, identifies itself as a leader in sustainable real estate. [7] In 2013, the VBDO began to analyze its scoring outcomes on the basis of investor size and confirmed that smaller pension funds are lagging larger funds.

Insurance companies are also found to be lagging pension funds with respect to the implementation and governance of their RI programs (VBDO, 2013a). For example, the 2013 VBDO insurance investor survey found that 9 of the 29 insurance companies that participated in the survey had no information publicly available on their sustainability policies. Similarly, smaller insurance companies lag their larger peers. That said, some recent progress has been made in the insurance sector. In 2011, the Dutch Association of Insurers created the Sustainable Investing Code, which seeks to commit its members to integrate ESG considerations into their investment decision-making and policies.

Foundations and charities

Since 2010, the VBDO has surveyed the charitable and foundation sector on their RI practices. The 2011 survey revealed that more than half of fundraising charities in the Netherlands have an

RI policy, while only a third of foundations have one. Of the funds that do have a policy, most are not transparent about its content. The most common strategy applied among these investors is exclusion, followed by positive screening. In general, the VBDO (2011a) concluded that most fundraising charities had an RI policy, but application is limited. One reason for this limitation posited by the VBDO is the (mis) perception among the charitable sector that sustainable and responsible investment is associated with increased risk.

Banking institutions

Triodos and ASN were among the first banks in Europe dedicated to ethical savings. ASN was founded in 1960 by a Dutch trade union. Triodos was founded in 1980 and now manages over 2.5 billion euro, largely representing Dutch household savings. As of 2014, the bank offers 18 investment funds that are considered impact investing or that apply socially responsible investment screens.

In more recent years, mainstream banking institutions in the Netherlands have begun to offer retail investors access to socially responsible investment opportunities. Indeed, every major bank in the Netherlands offers some version of a green or environmentally sustainable fund (PCV, 2011). More than taking advantage of a marketing opportunity, there is evidence that these banks are engaged in expanding the Dutch RI market. For example, ABN-Amro has promoted policy dialogue on social impact bonds in the Netherlands.[8] While there are some encouraging developments in the retail sector, growth has been slow. A review of the VBDO surveys of the Dutch retail saving and investments market reveals that since the first investment funds were established in the 1990s retail savings and investment funds have grown from 0.1 per cent to 4.2 per cent of the total retail market in 2011 (Quak et al., 2014). The 2013 VBDO survey found that investment and saving have grown to US $13 billion and US $20.6 billion, respectively, reflecting 5.9 per cent of total Dutch retail savings and investment.[9]

What are Dutch investors doing with respect to RI?

Exclusions

As stated earlier, exclusion is the most widely used RI strategy across the Netherlands. Dutch legislation introduced in 2013 requires all investors, including private equity funds, banks, pension funds and insurance companies, to exclude companies involved in the production, sale or distribution of cluster munitions. Prior to this legislation, however, a large number of Dutch pension funds had already excluded such companies from their portfolios. Indeed, many Dutch investors have taken steps to develop their own exclusion policies, taking the new legislation to be a minimum standard (Sustainalytics, 2013). For example, the Dutch healthcare pension fund PFZW divested from tobacco growers and producers of cigarettes in 2013. The fund cites failed attempts at engagement with the industry on child labour and poor working conditions as their reason for divestment. In a controversial move, the fund also divested from Israeli banks identified to be investing in settlements on the occupied West Bank of Palestine. PFZW has since reversed its position as other large Dutch funds announced their decisions not to divest, claiming, "banks do not breach international laws and as such do no merit their exclusion."[10] Other notable exclusions made by several Dutch institutional investors include Walmart and companies that sell, produce or distribute anti-personnel landmines.

ESG integration

The VBDO (2011b: 38) clarifies that ESG integration involves more than screening against exclusions criteria, but is not necessarily best in class or positive selection. In 2013, the VBDO pension fund survey found that 42 funds (84 per cent) have integrated ESG criteria into the investment process. Of these investors, 24 (48 per cent) have integrated ESG in a systematic manner. According to Eurosif (2014), ESG integration was applied to US $841 billion of Dutch investment in 2013.[11]

Engagement and voting

Dutch funds often discuss ESG issues at the board level with companies, and engagements tend to be consensus building and non-confrontational (De Graaf and Haigh 2011). In the 2013 VBDO pension fund survey, 88 per cent of the funds surveyed claimed to engage with companies on environmental, social and governance issues. Dutch funds surveyed also engage in their corporate bond portfolios. Breaking the engagement category down further reveals that corporate governance is the most frequent engagement topic raised with companies. For example, Ageon, one of the largest pension and insurance asset managers in the Netherlands, conducted over 200 engagements in 2013, 78 per cent of which were related to corporate governance matters.[12] There is increasing collaboration among investors through platforms such as Eumedion,[13] but again, the focus of engagement tends to be on corporate governance issues.

The majority of pension funds surveyed by the VBDO engage in proxy voting. The number of funds that initiate or publicly support shareholder resolutions has increased in recent years. In 2011, 8 of 49 funds surveyed by VBDO initiated and/or supported resolutions. By 2013, this number increased to 22 funds (VBDO 2014). Like engagement, voting is largely focused on corporate governance issues.

Positive selection

A small number of Dutch institutional investors use positive selection (including sustainability-themed investment and best-in-class strategies). The 2013 VBDO pension fund survey found that the majority of funds (88 per cent) do not engage in positive selection. Of the investors that do, they tend to apply this approach to less than 10 per cent of their total public equity portfolio. That said, there is reason to expect that positive selection will experience growth in the next few years. For example, the Dutch healthcare pension fund PFZW announced in 2014 its intentions to invest 16 billion euro over the next five years in "direct investments in green energy and clean technology, sustainable climate-related solutions and investments in food security and against water scarcity."[14]

Positive selection is more widely used among banking institutions and foundations, (VBDO, 2011b). Triodos and ASN were among the first banks to offer funds that included some form of positive selection in 1991 and 1993, respectively. Other banks did not begin offering such opportunities until the late 1990s (Louche, 2004).

Impact investing

Triodos offers a variety of impact investing funds to its retail clients. Another prominent financial institution in the Netherlands that offers clients exposure to impact investing opportunities is ASN Bank, which "provides loans to projects and organizations that match the bank's sustainable mission." The Dutch impact investing market is estimated at US $11.8 billion as of 2013.[15]

What is remarkable about the Dutch impact investing market is the participation of large institutional investors. In its 2014 survey, the VBDO found that 13 of 49 pension funds are using an impact investing strategy as part of their RI policy implementation. For example, Aegon, made its first investment in a green bond in 2013. Dutch pension manager PGGM has collaborated in a project with the University of Rotterdam to measure the social impact of its investments.[16] While some institutional investors are engaging in impact investing, there is room for growth. For example, the VBDO (2014) found that among the pension funds that engage in impact investing the majority (10) do not extend this strategy to more than 1 per cent of their total portfolio.

Policy environment, regulations and fiduciary duties

The Dutch government is a strong advocate for RI initiatives. Examples of government support for the sector include the provision of fiscal stimuli to encourage private retail investors to choose sustainable investment options, efforts to strengthen corporate governance and progressive regulations that seek to make pension fund RI programs more transparent and accountable. This section reviews some of the key policy and regulatory initiatives and considers how each has contributed to advancing RI in the Netherlands.

Fiscal incentives

One of the earliest forms of policy support for RI in the Netherlands is the Green Funds Scheme. This fiscal incentive was introduced in 1995 to promote private sector investment in environmental projects that are deemed to promote sustainability. The program provides investors with tax exemptions for investing in projects (not companies) that are designated by the government to be environmentally sustainable investments, both inside the Netherlands and abroad. Projects are supplied with low-interest rate loans. To offset the lower returns, investors are compensated with tax exemptions. Examples of certified projects include wind farms and organic agriculture. Between 1995 and 2008, 11 billion euro was invested in 5,761 environmental projects by 234,000 individual investors (Triodos, 2014).

Fiscal incentives have also been extended to social and cultural projects. For example, in 2004 the Dutch government created a Social-Ethical Fund program, which promoted investments in social enterprise in developing countries. It also established the Savings and Investment Plan for Cultural Organisations. The programs were not popular, which some attribute to concerns over political and economic risk (PCV, 2011). As of 2013, the Green Funds Scheme is the only remaining fiscal incentive program (Sustainalytics, 2013). While the Green Funds Scheme is regarded internationally as a success, changes to the Dutch fiscal framework, introduced in 2010, have led to a slowdown in the number of investors that take advantage of tax-exempt investment opportunities. The VBDO (2013b) estimates that the capital saved or invested in products offering tax exemptions has decreased by 9.5 per cent since 2012.

Corporate governance

The Dutch corporate governance regulatory framework is extensive with respect to corporate social responsibility. This section only highlights a few key aspects that have a bearing on responsible investors. First, while the rights of shareholders in the Netherlands have traditionally been weak, several changes have been made to shift toward the Anglo-American shareholder model of the firm. These changes were made in the 2003 Corporate Governance Code, following a set of 40 recommendations made by the first Dutch committee on corporate governance (the Peters Committee) in 1997. In particular, the Code allowed for any shareholder with at least 1 per cent of shares or 50 million euro market value to put an item on a company meeting agenda. Shareholders have the right to dismiss and appoint members of management and supervisory boards and have had a binding vote on executive compensation since 2004.

In more recent years, the government has gravitated back toward a more moderate position on the powers of shareholders in order to curb excessive shareholder activism. Measures include an increase in the threshold required for placing an item on a corporate general meeting agenda to 3 per cent under the 2013 Corporate Governance Act.

There is also a high regard for the rights of minority shareholders in the Netherlands. While Dutch law does not explicitly require controlling shareholders to demonstrate fiduciary duty with respect to minority shareholders, legal norms ensure some protection for minority holders (van Bekkum et al., 2010). The Dutch Corporate Governance Code (2003) states that "[t]he greater the interest which the shareholder has in a company, the greater is his responsibility to the company, the minority shareholders and other stakeholders" (cited in van Bekkum et al., 2010).

With respect to corporate disclosure, Dutch legislation introduced in 1997 and coming into force in 1999 requires publicly listed Dutch companies that are deemed to be conducting business activities with 'serious adverse effects on the environment' to report on their environmental performance. These companies must issue two reports annually: one to the government authorities and the second to the general public.

Strengthening pension fund governance

In recent years, legislative and regulatory initiatives have been introduced to increase the level of engagement in RI by investors and their asset managers. These frameworks have focused on the governance of institutional investors to promote the adoption of more substantive RI programs. New legislation coming into force in July 2013 has introduced several measures to strengthen statutory rules for governance and involvement of members in decision-making. Changes introduced in the new legislation to the Pension Fund Act of 2008 include the provision that "pension funds should report on their RI policies and implementation" (VBDO, 2013a: 23).

Also in 2013, a new Pension Governance Code was introduced. It is the first to address the responsibilities of a fund with respect to RI (Eurosif, 2014). Section 2.7 of the Code requires that pension funds publicly define their RI strategy. Moreover, the Code requires that the board of trustees publicly state considerations regarding sustainable investments. Further guidance suggests that funds acting in their capacity as investors promote good corporate governance of companies in which they invest. Stakeholders must be consulted and support the decisions made with respect to responsible (sustainable) investment.[17] The Code is embedded in the Pension Funds Act of 2008, and as such it applies to all Dutch pension funds.

In addition to specific initiatives aimed at strengthening governance of their RI programs, the Code seeks to enhance the overall governance of pension funds. For example, pension trustees are required to report on the costs of outsourcing, including remuneration policies of parties to which they delegate management and to take into account these policies in the process for selecting managers. Board diversity and expertise are also addressed. Compliance is supervised by the Dutch Central Bank and the Netherlands Authority for Financial Markets on a comply or explain basis.

Fiduciary duty

While fiduciary duty originates in Anglo-American common law systems, civil law countries like the Netherlands have equivalents (Richardson, 2013). Under the Dutch supervisory regulation, the equivalent of fiduciary duty is 'the prudent person rule' (Article 135, Dutch Pension Act 2008). Like several other civil law jurisdictions, the investment community in the Netherlands relies on the interpretation of fiduciary duty introduced by the *Freshfields Report, 2005.* The international law firm's interpretation suggests that "integrating ESG considerations into an investment analysis so as to more reliably predict financial performance is clearly permissible and is arguably required in all jurisdictions." The VBDO suggests that this principle

> implies that pension funds invest their capital with due regard to the interests of entitled and pensionable persons. . . . This restriction does not mean, however, that pension funds may not consider non-financial issues. They may do so, as long as non-financial interests do not dominate to the extent that the fund's investment policy no longer leads to an acceptable risk-return profile.
>
> *(VBDO, 2013b: 16)*

Similarly, the Dutch Fund and Asset Management Organization (DUFAS) defers to the Freshfields' interpretation in its Sustainable Investment Guide (2009) for asset managers.

Private sector–led initiatives

Notwithstanding the important achievements made by government-led initiatives in recent years, RI was largely initiated by the private sector in the Netherlands (Louche, 2004). That said, it is important to note that the division between private and public sector–led initiatives drawn in this chapter is somewhat artificial. Indeed, many initiatives are the result of collaboration and cooperation between the Dutch public and private sector.

Asset owners and managers

Trade unions were among the first advocates for ethical investment, beginning in the 1960s (Quak et al., 2014). More recently, industrywide and corporate pension funds have also begun to engage in efforts to promote the Dutch RI market. For example, in light of the strong public outcry in response to the documentary film *Zembla*, the pension fund umbrella organizations came together under the Practical Committee to develop a framework for establishing and implementing RI among Dutch pension funds. The Committee produced a report, called 'The Future Has Arrived' (2007), which responded to many of the challenges raised in the documentary and included suggestions for pension funds for designing and implementing their RI policy.

Dutch institutional investors have also been active in promoting more opportunities for impact investing in the Netherlands. In 2013, 13 Dutch institutional investors committed to the establishment of a privately owned company that would be mandated to facilitate much-needed investments in the Dutch economy. More specifically, "the aim of the NII [Netherlands Investment Institution] is to create a better match between the supply and demand of long-term financing in the Netherlands and by doing so remove bottlenecks in the financing of sectors such as the SME sector and sustainable energy."[18] It is expected that NII will act as an intermediary to facilitate investment in the local economy in projects that currently face barriers to capital, particularly in the face of the weak banking environment by providing investors with scalable investment opportunities and access to expertise. The initiative is the result of cooperation and collaboration with the Dutch government. It is anticipated that the NII will sustain itself through fees for its services and will not be funded on an ongoing basis with government guarantees or capital injections (OECD, 2014).

Globally, Dutch institutional investors are also actively engaged in promoting RI. For example, Dutch institutional investors were among the first signatories to the UN-backed Principles for Responsible Investment (PRI). Citing the investment organization's self-interest, the head of RI for Dutch asset manager PGGM explained the investor's reason for engaging in the PRI in an interview stating, "we want to mobilise other investors to get involved with responsible investing so that when we go to asset managers and demand integration of ESG (environmental, social and governance) factors, they can no longer say, 'you're the only one asking.'"[19] On the banking side, Triodos was involved in the creation of the impact investment measurement standards, the Global Impact Investing Rating System. The bank also works to promote impact investing among retail investors on a global scale (see Triodos, 2014).

Industry platforms and information providers

Industry organizations, consultants and information providers also play an important role in the market for RI in the Netherlands. The following section lists a few of the most prominent RI and impact investing organizations in the Netherlands.

Dutch Association of Investors for Sustainable Development (VBDO)

The VBDO is the Dutch version of Eurosif and was established in 1995. The VBDO has a mandate to contribute to the creation of a more sustainable capital market. It does so by engaging with corporations, financial institutions, government, the media and publicly listed companies. The organization also conducts research on sustainable investment in the Netherlands. The VBDO initially collected information on RI in the Dutch banking sector. Since 2007, the VBDO has extended this survey to include Dutch pension funds and, in 2009, to insurance companies. The surveys are highly regarded among the private and public sector.

Eumedion

Eumedion is a corporate governance lobby with 69 institutional investor members as of 2014, representing over 1 trillion euro in assets. It is legally structured as a foundation but it functions as a membership association, providing services and guidance to its members. Eumedion sends focus letters to Dutch companies on an annual basis to raise corporate governance issues. It then promotes collective dialogue between the company and its association members. Examples of corporate governance issues raised include improving the integrity of financial reporting and transparency on the selection of Dutch corporate board members.

Dutch Fund and Asset Management Association (DUFAS)

DUFAS promotes the collective interests of asset managers operating from the Dutch market and seeks to ensure a 'level playing field' for Dutch asset managers within the European Union. DUFAS represents over 90 per cent of Dutch asset managers. While the asset management organization does not have an explicit mandate to promote responsible or sustainable investment,

DUFAS has provided guidance to Dutch asset managers in its Sustainable Investment Guide (2009).

Sustainalytics

Sustainalytics is a global leader in sustainability research and analysis with headquarters in the Netherlands. The organization has offices in Canada, the United States, Germany, Spain and Singapore. It has 350 clients worldwide, including 50 Dutch investors. The Dutch pension manager PGGM owns one third of Sustainalytics. Other Dutch shareholders include Triodos and MeesPierson.

Dutch Platform for Inclusive Finance (NpM)

The NpM, established in 2003, is a platform that seeks to bring together developing organizations, social investors, private foundations and commercial banks to extend inclusive finance to underserved regions with a focus on international development. Inclusive finance, or microfinance, refers to loans, savings, insurance and other basic financial services that are not made available to individuals and small enterprises by traditional financial institutions. The platform is supported by the Dutch Ministry of Foreign Affairs and 13 Dutch investment organizations.

Future obstacles to responsible investment in the Netherlands

The cooperation between private financial institutions and the Dutch government has been instrumental to the rapid growth of the RI market. While the Netherlands is often invoked as a global exemplar, given its bold regulatory framework and strong investor commitment, several obstacles stand in the way of deepening RI practices among Dutch investors.

First, Dutch policy makers must continue to leverage the vast resources of Dutch institutional investors. For example, government guarantees could contribute to reducing the risks assumed by institutional investors seeking impact in domestic investments (Sustainalytics, 2013). Moreover, the fiscal stimuli to encourage investment in environmentally sustainable products is currently limited to retail investors, unnecessarily excluding other types of potential investors and projects (PCV, 2011). That said, there is also significant room for growth on the Dutch retail side, as highlighted by the VBDO surveys and Triodos (2014).

A second challenge relates to the potential perverse effects of strong financial sector regulatory initiatives in the Netherlands. For example, the Dutch government has recently passed legislation limiting the bonuses in financial sector, including pension and insurance fund managers, to 20 per cent of fixed compensation. This change is expected to come into force in January 2015. While a welcome move by many advocates of more sustainable compensation in the financial sector, it remains to be seen how this new rule will affect the global competitiveness of the Dutch asset management industry, including their RI programs. The European Union bonus cap only limits variable compensation to 100 per cent of fixed pay (and 200 per cent provided majority shareholder support) and does not apply to pension or insurance asset managers. Moreover, Dutch financial regulation has sought to make investing less complex. But this may undermine the ability of institutional investors to engage in impact investing strategies since such strategies often require investing in illiquid assets that are inherently complex.[20]

Third, while government support in the form of regulation and incentives is important, it is equally important to mitigate the potential for political interference. While the Dutch government has taken steps to promote transparent investment opportunities that inspire investor confidence through initiatives such as the NII, Dutch investors seeking sustainable investment opportunities abroad are often limited by political risks.[21]

A fourth obstacle relates to the governance of funds themselves. In 2010, only 10 per cent of pension funds surveyed by the VBDO had a mechanism for participants to provide input on their fund's RI policy (VBDO, 2011b). In 2013, the VBDO (2014) found that 28 per cent of pension funds consulted their participant councils, leaving significant room for improvement. It has also been suggested that pension funds need to take more initiative on formulating their own RI policies and rely less on their investment managers (VBDO, 2013). Moreover, smaller funds often lack the resources to engage in an effective RI program. While recent legislation and regulatory measures have set out to address pension fund governance, the challenge ahead is to ensure that funds have the capacity to implement these new governance standards.

Conclusion

Some predict that it will soon become incumbent upon Dutch investors to explain why they do not have an RI policy. Indeed, the Netherlands is revered around the world for its sophisticated RI market and, increasingly, its dynamic impact investment market. Strong collaboration and cooperation between the public and private sectors has been key to this success. Exclusions will continue to play a role with recent legislation introduced in 2013. That said, the Dutch market reflects significant diversity in its approach to RI. It is being rolled out across asset classes, and institutional investors are increasingly engaging in sustainable and impactful investment opportunities within the Netherlands. While Dutch investors have much to celebrate at home, the challenge going forward will be to expand opportunities for applying RI in their global portfolios. This will require continued engagement with European and international investors, organizations and governments.

Notes

1 The Dutch Pension System: An overview of the key aspects (2008) Available at: http://www.pensioenfederatie.nl/Document/Publicaties/English%20publications/Nederlandse_pensioensysteem_Engelstalige_versie.pdf [Accessed November 24, 2014].

2 DUFAS estimates the Dutch investment management industry to be 1.7 trillion euro at the end of 2013. US $ figure is calculated using European Central Bank annual average exchange rate (2014) between USD and euro of 1.3385.

3 In 2005 there were over 800 pension funds. By 2010, the number decreased to 545 pension plans, and most recent projections made in 2014 suggest pension funds may dip below 300. As of 2011 the 10 largest Dutch pensions represent over 78 per cent of the total market (IMF, 2011).

4 See PGGM speech, Lindeijer, E. (2014) 'Creating more room for green growth.' Speech for the Duisenberg School of Finance. Available at: https://www.pggm.nl/english/what-we-think/Pages/Creating-more-room-for-green-growth.aspx [Accessed November 27, 2014].

5 Eurosif (2006) estimated the Dutch RI market to be 47 billion euro. US $ figure is calculated using European Central Bank annual average exchange rate (2014) between USD and euro of 1.3385.

6 Eurosif (2014) estimated the Dutch RI market to be 1.2 trillion euro in 2013. US $ figure is calculated using European Central Bank annual average exchange rate (2014) between USD and euro of 1.3385.

7 APG is one of the largest Dutch pension fund managers, responsible for managing the assets of the Dutch civil service employees' pension fund, ABP.

8 ABN Amro is one of the largest full-service retail and commercial Dutch banks. The bank was nationalized in 2008, and at the time of writing this chapter the government was preparing to sell its shares back. See ABN Amro (2013) Social impact bonds: Opportunities and challenges for the Netherlands. Available at: https://insights.abnamro.nl/wp-content/uploads/2013/10/Social-Impacts-Bonds-rapport.pdf [Accessed November 28, 2014].

9 US $ figure is calculated using European Central Bank annual average exchange rate (2014) between USD and euro of 1.3385.

10 See *Financial Times* (2014) 'Dutch pension fund defends stance.' March 30. Available at: http://www.ft.com/cms/s/0/9fe2df4a-b680–11e3-b230–00144feabdc0.html [Accessed November 25, 2014]. Compare with: *Financial Times* (2014) 'Orchestrated boycott of Israeli companies falters.' June 15. Available at: http://www.ft.com/cms/s/0/075aa326-f22f-11e3-ac7a-00144feabdc0.html?siteedition=uk#axzz3L2WceBrh [Accessed November 25, 2014].

11 US $ figure is calculated using European Central Bank annual average exchange rate (2014) between USD and euro of 1.3385.

12 See Aegon (2013) 'Responsible investment report.' Available at: http://www.aegon.com/Documents/aegon-com/Sitewide/Reports-and-Other-Publications/RI-reports/Aegon-responsible-investment-report-2013b.pdf [Accessed December 1, 2014].

13 Eumedion is a lobby membership association for Dutch institutional investors on corporate governance.

14 See 'Dutch giant PFZW vows to quadruple sustainable investments.' Available at: http://www.ipe.com/news/esg/dutch-giant-pfzw-vows-to-quadruple-sustainable-investments/10003279.fullarticle [Accessed December 1, 2014].

15 Eurosif (2014) estimates Dutch impact investment at 8.8 billion euro. US $ figure is calculated using European Central Bank annual average exchange rate (2014) between USD and euro of 1.3385.

16 See 'PGGM builds tool to measure "social impact" of responsible investment.' Available at: http://www.workerscapital.org/images/uploads/IPE%20Article(1).pdf [Accessed December 3, 2014].

17 Code of Dutch Pension Funds (2013). Available at: http://www.pensioenfederatie.nl/Document/Publicaties/Servicedocumenten/Code_of_the_Dutch_Pension_Funds.pdf [Accessed: November 26, 2014].

18 See NII press release. Available at: https://www.nlii.nl/images/NII_launched-Press_release-20141001.pdf [Accessed November 24, 2014].

19 Responsible Investor Interview (2014) 'RI insight Netherlands: Dutch institutions engage for change.' May. Available at: https://www.responsible-investor.com/reports/ [Accessed November 24, 2014].

20 Responsible Investor Interview (2014) 'RI insight Netherlands: Dutch institutions engage for change.' May. Available at: https://www.responsible-investor.com/reports/ [Accessed November 24, 2014].

21 In an interview with Dutch pension manager APG, the CIO expressed concern over political decisions affecting deals in large infrastructure projects in renewable energy, including an offshore wind project in Mexico. See *Financial Times* (2014) 'Dutch pension chief believes in "controlled simplicity."' January 5. Available at: http://www.ft.com/cms/s/0/70e932fc-6739–11e3–8d3e-00144feabdc0.html#axzz3KsQGZMdL [Accessed December 1, 2014].

References

De Graaf, F. J. and Haigh, M. (2011) 'Activism in European pension funds', In Sun, W., Louche, C. and Pérez, R. (eds.), *Finance and sustainability: towards a new paradigm? A post-crisis agenda. Critical studies on corporate responsibility, governance and sustainability, Volume 2.* Bingkey UK: Emerald, pp. 118–143.

DeNederlandsche Bank (DNB) (2014a) 'New statistics show sharp contraction of small loans to SMEs.' Available at: http://www.dnb.nl/en/news/news-and-archive/dnbulletin-2014/dnb309784.jsp [Accessed November 29, 2014].

DeNederlandsche Bank (DNB) (2014b) 'Additional buffer requirement enhances resilience of Dutch systemic banks.' Available at: http://www.dnb.nl/en/news/news-and-archive/dnbulletin-2014/dnb306988.jsp April 29. [Accessed November 15 2014].

Dutch Association of Investors for Sustainable Development (VBDO) (2011a) *Benchmark responsible investment by fundraising charities and foundations in the Netherlands.* Available at: http://www.verenigingvanfondsen.nl/viewer/file.aspx?fileinfoID=290 [Accessed November 24, 2014].

Dutch Association of Investors for Sustainable Development (VBDO) (2011b) *Benchmark responsible investment by pension funds in the Netherlands.* In cooperation with Profundo. Available at: http://www.dnb.nl [Accessed November 25, 2014].

Dutch Association of Investors for Sustainable Development (VBDO) (2013a) *Benchmark responsible investment by pension funds in the Netherlands.* In cooperation with Profundo. Available at: http://www.vbdo.nl/files/media/Benchmark_Responsible_Investment_by_Pension_Funds_2013.pdf [Accessed November 25, 2014].

Dutch Association of Investors for Sustainable Development (VBDO). (2013b) *Duurzaam Sparen en Beleggen 2013 Keuze te over!* Available at: http://www.vbdo.nl/files/report/DuurzaamSparenenBeleggen2013.pdf [Accessed December 1, 2014].

Dutch Association of Investors for Sustainable Development (VBDO) (2014) *Benchmark responsible investment by pension funds in the Netherlands.* In cooperation with Profundo. Available at: http://www.vbdo.nl/files/media/VBDO_Benchmark_Pensioenfondsen.pdf [Accessed November 25, 2014].

Dutch Fund and Asset Management Association (DUFAS) (2009) *Sustainable investment guide.* Available at: http://www.dufas.nl/theme/dufas/uploadedFiles/Sustainable%20Investment%20Guide%20_final_.pdf.

EUROSIF (2006) European SRI Study. Available at: http://www.eurosif.org/publication/european-sri-study-2006/ [Accessed May 22, 2015].

EUROSIF (2014) *European SRI Study.* Available at: http://eurosif.org [Accessed November 27, 2014].

Freshfields Bruckhaus Deringer (2005) *A legal framework for the integration of environmental, social and governance issues into institutional investment – Report for UNEP-FI*, November.

International Monetary Fund (IMF) (2011) *Kingdom of the Netherlands-Netherlands: publication of financial sector assessment program documentation – technical note on pensions sector issues.* IMF Country Report No. 11/209. Available at: http://www.imf.org/external/pubs/ft/scr/2011/cr11209.pdf [Accessed November 29, 2014].

Louche, C. (2004) *Ethical investment processes and mechanisms of institutionalisation in the Netherlands.* PhD Thesis, Erasmus University Rotterdam.

Organization for Economic Co-operation and Development (OECD) (2014) *OECD economic surveys 2014: The Netherlands.* Available at: http://www.oecd.org/economy/surveys/economic-survey-netherlands.htm [Accessed November 24, 2014].

Pacific Community Ventures (PCV) (2011) *Green Funds Scheme, impact investing, a framework for policy design and analysis.* In partnership with the Initiative for Responsible Investment, Harvard.

Peters Committee. (1997) *Peters Report & Recommendations: Corporate governance in the Netherlands.* Available at: http://www.ecgi.org/codes/code.php?code_id=85 [Accessed November 25, 2014].

Practical Committee (2007) *The future has arrived: Dutch pension funds and the practice of responsible investment.* Dutch Association of Industry Wide Pension Funds.

Quak, S., Heilbron, J., & Meijer, J. (2014) 'The rise and spread of sustainable investing in the Netherlands', *Journal of Sustainable Finance & Investment*, *4*(3), pp. 249–265.

Responsible Investor (2012) 'Dutch pension saver survey finds 70% want socially responsible investment policies', September. Available at: https://www.responsible-investor.com/home/article/dutch_survey_nm/.

Responsible Investor (2014) 'RI Insight Netherlands: Dutch institutions engage for change.' May. Available at: https://www.responsible-investor.com/reports/ [Accessed November 24, 2014].

Richardson, B. (2013) *Fiduciary law and responsible investing: In nature's trust.* London: Routledge.

Sustainalytics. (2013) *Trends in responsible investment: The evolution of responsible investment in the Netherlands over the past 5 years.* Available at: http://www.sustainalytics.com [Accessed November 24, 2014].

Towers Watson (2014) *Global pensions assets survey.* Available at: http://www.towerswatson.com/en/Insights/IC-Types/Survey-Research-Results/2014/02/Global-Pensions-Asset-Study-2014 [Accessed November 24, 2014].

Triodos. (2014) *Impact investing for everyone. A blueprint for retail impact investing.* September. Available at: http://www.socialimpactinvestment.org/reports/Triodos-Bank-report-on-Impact-investing.pdf [Accessed December 1, 2014].

van Bekkum, J. Hijink, S., Schouten, M. and Winter, J. (2010) 'Corporate governance in the Netherlands.' International Congress on Comparative Law, Washington.

25
Introduction to Scandinavia

Ane Jensen

Responsible investment (RI) in Scandinavia, which comprises Denmark, Norway, and Sweden, has very strong similarities, both in definition and strategies practiced, across country borders. To understand these commonalities, evident in both socially responsible investing (SRI) and corporate social responsibility (CSR) in the region, it is necessary to understand the shared cultural heritage and history of the Scandinavian countries. Throughout history the Scandinavian countries have shared land, language, and rule: Denmark and Norway were one country from 1387 until 1814, and Sweden and Norway were united through a personal union of separate kingdoms from 1814 until 1905 (Morsing et al., 2007). The Scandinavian languages are easily understood across borders.

The Scandinavian-style welfare structure was developed through similar social movements in the three countries, being founded upon solid social democratic philosophies regarding the role of government and labour relations. Today, the social welfare models used across Scandinavia share a range of common characteristics: in the labour market, emphasis is on strong labour unions and corporate associations, which often meet in collective negotiations. The countries typically have low levels of corruption and a strong commitment to social mobility and trade, as well as low barriers to trade. Additionally, modern Scandinavian societies share a commitment to universal health care and strong educational systems, a high degree of state involvement, high taxes and small wage gaps. Companies often have flat hierarchies and a high degree of employee involvement (Morsing et al., 2007; Hofstede, 1980).

Due to the cultural homogeneity in the region, the Scandinavian countries have developed a common approach to CSR and SRI, as demonstrated in the macroeconomic and legal frameworks that guide each country's CSR and SRI activities. Emphasis is on power sharing, and strong participatory approaches to decision making are common across the region (Morsing et al., 2007).

The Scandinavian countries were among the first in the world to introduce regulatory frameworks and standards aimed at promoting environmental, social and governance (ESG) activities in financial management (Sandberg et al., 2009). Additionally, according to a study by Streuer et al. (2012) the Scandinavian governments are significantly more active in the promotion of CSR than their Central European counterparts. This regulatory promotion of CSR reflects the popularity of this topic at the management level across the continent, according to the authors, who conclude that public policy strengthens rather than reduces the European 'CSR gap'.

SRI in Scandinavia

Scandinavia has long been at the forefront of SRI, being consistently and disproportionally well represented in the top of international indices for sustainable performance, such as the Dow Jones Sustainability Index.

The region had an early focus on responsible investment. The SRI developments of the 1960s and 1970s took place on both sides of the Atlantic. AktieAnsvar Aktiefond, the first ethical investment fund open to the public, was established in Sweden in 1965 by the religiously motivated temperance movement (Bengtsson, 2007). The religious foundation of the fund was reflected in the chosen exclusions, which included alcohol and tobacco producers, as well as manufacturers of armaments and firearms.

The Church of Sweden has played a significant role in the establishment and expansion of the SRI market. Up through the 1980s, the Church of Sweden established several funds whose investment strategies were based on core Christian and humanitarian values. These funds used a negative screening strategy (Bengtsson, 2008).

Up through the 1980s and 1990s, a general shift in environmental awareness coupled with increased media attention was reflected in SRI across Scandinavia, which moved from being largely the domain of the Church of Sweden to becoming of interest to both public and private investors. Additionally, a shift in the type of investor appeared, and the small religiously based niche funds were soon replaced by broad-based SRI funds.

While the Church of Sweden is still active in the SRI marketplace, it is no longer the key player in the Scandinavian SRI market. It is a unique trait of the Scandinavian SRI market that almost all the key players are institutional investors.

Similarities and differences

While the SRI markets in Scandinavia are some of the most developed globally, there are significant differences between the individual markets, both in terms of the number of SRI funds and total assets under management (Figure 25.1, which uses PRI signatories as proxy; see also, e.g., Vigeo and Morningstar [2013]). The largest SRI market based on the number of SRI funds is Sweden, followed by Denmark; the largest SRI market in terms of assets under management is

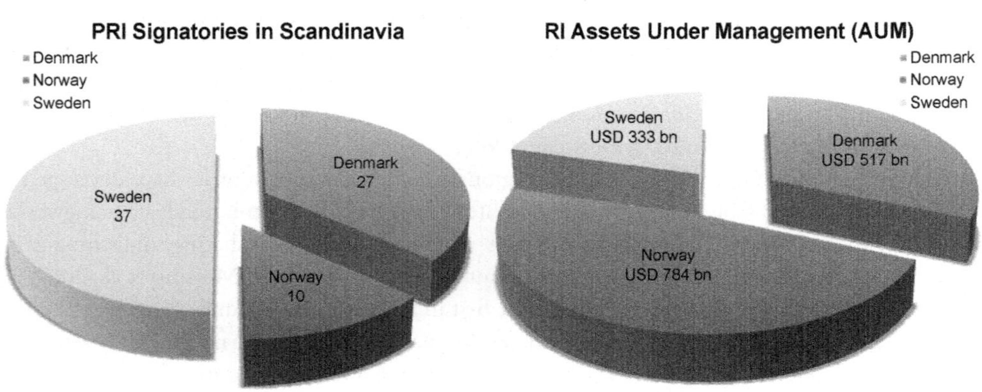

Figure 25.1 PRI signatories and RI assets under management in Scandinavia

Source: Adapted from www.unpri.org, Eurosif (2012) (with permission).

Norway. This is primarily due to the presence of the Norwegian Government Pension Fund – Global, the world's largest sovereign wealth fund, which manages revenue from Norway's oil ventures.

However, while there exist significant differences in terms of assets under management and number of investors engaged in SRI, the investment strategies employed follow much the same pattern across the region. This approach is commonly known as 'the Scandinavian model' for SRI.

The Scandinavian model

The Scandinavian model is a strategic approach to socially responsible investment, a term originally coined to describe the common Scandinavian approach to CSR. A version of this has since come to describe the common SRI strategies used across the Scandinavian region.

The Scandinavian model primarily employs negative norm-based screening and exclusion, usually with participation, in its management of assets. According to Dansif, this model dominates most management approaches to SRI across Scandinavia, and is used by 88 per cent of Danish institutional investors, who account for 97 per cent of all Danish assets under management in the SRI market (Dansif 2012).

Unlike in other market approaches, Scandinavian investors tend to include a large amount of shares of public and private institutions. SRI fund portfolios tend to be diversified, with relatively few thematic funds focusing on one particular form of responsible investment (e.g. green funds). Additionally, positive screenings and application of best-in-class approaches are rarely used.

The screening processes in the Scandinavian SRI markets tend to be well framed, with well defined, if not always strong, legal and regulatory frameworks, as well as detailed guidelines and emphasis on transparent procedures. It is, for example, common practice amongst a lot of the larger players to make the reasoning behind exclusions public in an effort to increase transparency.

Also common across Scandinavia is the size of the asset classes. Generally, fixed income is the largest asset class, as in the case in Sweden and Denmark, or very dominant, as in Norway, where fixed income is almost on par with equity.

The use of screening, which is part of the preferred strategy for responsible investments in Scandinavia, is seen as a way to minimize risk for a company's reputation and brand, a hypothesis backed by Norsif's research on incentives mentioned by Norwegian SRI asset owners and managers in 2011.

References

Bengtsson, E. (2007) 'A History of Scandinavian Socially Responsible Investing', *Journal of Business Ethics*, Vol. 82, Issue 4.

Bengtsson, E. (2008) 'Socially Responsible Investing in Scandinavia – A Comparative Analysis', *Sustainable Development*, Vol. 16.

Dansif (2012) *The Current State of Responsible Investment in Denmark*. Online. Available HTTP: <http://www.dansif.dk/>.

Eurosif (2012) *European SRI Study 2012*. Online. Available HTTP: <http://www.eurosif.org/>.

Hofstede, G. (1980) *Culture's Consequences: International Differences in Work-Related Values,* Sage Publications.

Morsing, M., Midttun, A. and Palmås, K. (2007) 'Corporate Social Responsibility in Scandinavia: A Turn Toward the Business Case?', in S. May, G. Cheney, and J. Roper (eds), *The Debate over Corporate Social Responsibility*, Oxford University Press.

PRI. Online. Available HTTP: <http://www.unpri.org/>.

Sandberg, J., Juravle, C., Hedesström, T. M. and Hamilton, I. (2009) 'The Heterogeneity of Socially Responsible Investment', *Journal of Business Ethics,* Vol. 87, Issue 4.
Streuer et al. (2012) 'Public Policies on CSR in Europe: Themes, Instruments, and Regional Differences', *Corporate Social Responsibility and Environmental Management*, Vol. 19, 206–227.
Vigeo and Morningstar (2013) 'Green, Social and Ethical Funds in Europe', *Review 2013.* Online. Available HTTP: <http://www.vigeo.com>.

26

Responsible investment in Denmark

Practices among institutional investors in a context of statutory CSR reporting requirements

Karin Buhmann

Introduction: the economic, political and legal context for SRI

The southernmost of the three Scandinavian and five Nordic countries, Denmark is a country of 5.55 million inhabitants in Northern Europe. Denmark joined the European Economic Community (now the European Union [EU]) in 1973. Denmark's per capita GDP ranks among the highest in Europe. Denmark is considered to be one of the most competitive economies in the world, with one of the most liberal capital and products markets globally. Denmark is a constitutional monarchy with a parliamentary system of government.

Denmark has a relatively high number of small and medium sized enterprises (SMEs) compared to many other countries, including other European countries. Approximately 30 per cent of Danish companies have 1–9 employees, 20 per cent have 10–49 employees, 15 per cent have 50–249 employees, and just 30 per cent employ more than 250. Denmark is home to several multinational companies, such as the Lego Group, Novo Nordisk, the Maersk Group, Dansk Supermarket, which supplies textiles and daily consumer goods primarily from low-wage countries, and Vestas, an energy windmill producer. On a global basis, however, most Danish multinational companies are not very large. A country bordered by international waters on most sides, Denmark has a long tradition of international shipping and international trade. This tradition includes imports of tropical and sub-tropical timbers for furniture production and other nationally based processes and overseas production and manufacturing of textiles and apparel for international export.

In Denmark, responsible investment (RI) is broadly understood to be socially responsible investment (SRI). In other words, RI/SRI is investment in accordance with the social expectations of investors (typically institutional investors and asset managers) to respond to environmental, social and governance (ESG) issues and that is in line with corporate social responsibility (CSR) expectations. Thus, RI/SRI expectations and actions may reflect the dynamic character of ESG and CSR from a global and regional perspective, as well Danish concerns. Since 2008 the handling of RI/SRI issues among Danish institutional investors and asset managers has been influenced by the political agenda set by the government's introduction of mandatory CSR reporting for institutional investors as well as large businesses.

According to the national SRI organization, the Danish Sustainable Investment Forum (Dansif), the SRI market in Denmark has grown in recent years after a slow start, due in part to a lack of investment alternatives and to a change in the understanding of the implications of requirements by financial regulators that institutional investors focus first and foremost on financial returns. Recent growth has been stimulated by the introduction of SRI fixed-income investment alternatives and the founding of Dansif, an umbrella group of Danish SRI funds, in November 2008, with the support of a number of Danish institutional investors and advisors.[1] The SRI market in Denmark is dominated by institutional investors. As of November 2012, Dansif had almost 30 members, approximately 80 per cent of which were institutional investors (i.e. banks, insurance companies, and pension funds). The remaining 20 per cent largely comprised consultants and advisors in the sector. The UN-backed Principles of Responsible Investment (UN PRI) is influential from a normative perspective, spurred by the introduction of mandatory CSR reporting in Denmark from 2009, which gives investors the option to report as a PRI signatory using the PRI Communication of Progress Report.

Apart from the reporting obligation, which corresponds to the CSR reporting obligation of large companies (see below), SRI is not regulated in Denmark. SRI had a slow start in Denmark because of initial uncertainty regarding whether SRI considerations in investment might conflict with the objective of institutional investors to generate the best possible returns for their customers, particularly given that the SRI market in Denmark is primarily composed of banks, pension funds and other institutional investors.

The cooperative bank Merkur, a relatively small financial institution by Danish standards, has been based on a social responsibility policy since its start in 1982. With the evolution of SRI, Merkur has developed an SRI policy.[2] After initial hesitation in the late 1990s and early 2000s, large institutional investors have picked up SRI. Among pension funds, the large Arbejdsmarkedets Tillægspensions (ATP), which by law obtains a small percentage of the salary of all Danish employees, has an overarching SRI policy, according to which SRI is seen to represent a "precondition for long-term, healthy earnings – and thus for the preservation of the real value of equity investments".[3] Indeed, ATP has declared that it perceives CSR reports as a solid risk indicator for business organizations in which ATP invests or considers investment.[4] With the evolution of SRI markets in neighbouring countries and social expectations among both individual and business clients, SRI policies have become common among Danish private institutional investors, although in most cases as one among other policies that investors may choose. The large bank Danske Bank introduced an SRI policy comprising ethical screening immediately before the 2008 financial crisis, and other large banks have similar policies.[5]

Several institutional investors cooperate with environmental, social and governance (ESG) specialists for the purposes of their SRI decisions. To promote SRI following the introduction of the government's first national action plan on CSR, the Danish government developed non-binding guidance on SRI, targeting asset managers, investment managers, professional service providers and SRI actors broadly.[6]

As noted below, CSR reporting is a major element of the SRI legislative framework. What follows is a brief introduction to the legal framework and techniques for legal analysis in order to understand the subsequent analysis of CSR reporting. Executive orders and other by-laws must have a legal basis in the statute from which they derive or they must have another recognized legal basis. Study of preparatory analyses forming part of the legislative history play a strong part not only for the courts' construction of legal provisions, but also as guidance for the public administration on the application of statutes, executive orders and specific provisions. The significance of preparatory works differs from that of many other jurisdictions, including EU law. In Danish law, elaborative documents and guidance developed by governmental agencies after the adoption of a law also play a part in the interpretation of a law and an understanding of it objectives. As will be noted below, analysis of preparatory research and guidance for application provide insight into the objectives of the statutory requirements on CSR reporting by institutional investors and other organizations. In addition, EU law is a source of law in Danish law, meaning that current or future EU regulations and directives, for example, such as those on ESG transparency, apply in Denmark.

In 2008 the Danish legislature introduced mandatory CSR reporting for institutional investors and large companies, including publicly owned companies (owned by shareholders). In 2012 an amendment strengthened the reporting requirement, introducing mandatory reporting on human rights and climate change mitigation action for organizations whose CSR policies refer to those issues. The Danish case complements other Nordic developments in which public authorities are engaging in directing CSR towards public policy implementation. Taking a point of departure in the government's regulation of business conduct towards socially responsible investment through the statutory requirements, this chapter provides an overview of the requirements and their objectives and effects so far.

RI practices among institutional investors in Denmark

According to 2011 and 2012 studies from Dansif, 88 per cent of Denmark's 50 largest banks, insurance companies, pension funds and other institutional investors (corresponding to 99 per cent of the total invested capital) have a formalized policy for responsible investment. As of early 2014, around 50 per cent of those had committed to invest according to the UN PRI.[7]

Practiced by approximately 70 per cent of institutional investors, engagement or exclusion are the most common RI strategies in Denmark. These strategies target companies that violate (or are reported to violate) environmental or social concerns. In addition to these general practices, around 50 per cent of institutional investors exclude investment in companies trading in goods such as weapons, alcohol, tobacco and pornography, and around 50 per cent exercise active ownership as an engagement method to affect the practices of companies seen to be controversial from an ESG/RI perspective. More than 50 per cent of institutional investors request standardized and systematic ESG reporting from companies in which they invest. Eighty per cent of institutional investors share information on their initiatives and results of RI practices with stakeholders or the general public. As of late 2011, 92 per cent reported considerations of ESG issues when selecting external investment managers and other business partners.[8]

Statutory requirements of CSR reporting

As noted, SRI in Denmark is largely unregulated, apart from the provision of transparency that is embodied in the CSR reporting requirement for large companies. As demonstrated in other chapters in this book, SRI assessment and reporting is often risk based when undertaken by individual organizations; in contrast, the Danish regulatory framework focuses on transparency. The implicit assumption is that transparency provides investors and other stakeholders with the opportunity to critically assess whether an organization constitutes a risk.

The reporting requirement

In December 2008, the Danish legislature introduced an obligation for what in this context is generally referred to as 'large Danish companies'[9] to submit an annual CSR report, effective for fiscal years beginning January 2009 or later. The reporting obligation was provided for through an amendment to the Danish Financial Statements Act, inserting a new section into the act (Section 99a).[10] A similar reporting requirement has been introduced for institutional investors, mutual funds and other listed financial enterprises (financial institutions and insurance companies, etc.) not covered by the Financial Statements Act. For these organizations, the requirement has been introduced in statutory orders issued by the Danish Financial Supervisory Authority.[11] The requirements for institutional investors are systematically structured to reflect the statutory requirement contained in Section 99a of the Act on Financial Statements. Thus, the requirement is often generally referred to as the 'Section 99a' requirement, and it essentially requires the same information regardless of whether an organization is an institutional investor or a business. The amendment introduced in 2012 on compulsory human rights and/or climate change reporting for organizations whose policies refer to one or both of those issues equally applies to both institutional investors and business organizations.[12] This requirement is discussed in more detail below.

The reporting provisions do not define CSR precisely but rather provide a guiding understanding according to which CSR is the voluntarily consideration of human rights and social, environmental and climate conditions, as well as anti-corruption strategies, amongst others factors.

Organizations to which the reporting requirements apply must provide the following information:

1 Policies on social responsibility, including any standards, guidelines or principles for social responsibility that the business employs.
2 Methods for the implementation of its social responsibility policies into practice, including any systems or procedures used.
3 An evaluation of what has been achieved through social responsibility initiatives during the financial year, and any expectations it has regarding future initiatives.

Reporting on CSR policies should include information on whether the company has a CSR policy and the main contents of such a policy. There is no obligation to publish a CSR policy *in extenso*, but the main contents must be provided.

The reporting requirements do not compel organizations to have a CSR policy. If an organization subjected to the reporting requirements does not have a CSR policy, the organization must provide that information. The reporting requirements do not establish an obligation to provide reasons for not having a CSR policy.

Reporting on what has been achieved as a result of the CSR policy does not have to be quantified. A company may therefore report on results using qualitative terms. For reports employing indicators, the Agency for Companies and Commerce recommends that internationally recognized indicators or indicator systems such as the Global Reporting Initiative (GRI) be employed rather than indicators developed by the reporting company itself. Use of internationally recognized indicators is assumed to better provide for transparency and to enable comparison with other companies.

If no specific results have materialized yet, the report must provide that information. If a company has expectations on future achievements as a result of its CSR policies, information on these must also be provided.

CSR reporting information applied in a marketing context must comply with guidance from the Consumer Ombudsman on ethical and environmental statements in marketing contexts.

Publication of CSR reports prepared according to the reporting requirement

The reporting requirements give organizations different options for the publication of CSR information. The CSR report must be provided in the general review section of the annual report, as a CSR report provided as a supplement to the annual report or on the organization's website. As a point of departure, the CSR report should form part of the management's report. However, the Act on Financial Statements and the Statutory Orders allows for the CSR report to instead be published on the reporting company's website or as a complementary report to the financial statement (typically a sustainability report). If these alternatives are employed for the publication of the CSR report, the management's report must provide a reference to where the CSR report can be accessed.[13]

Global Compact or PRI reporting

The provisions on mandatory CSR reporting provide for a special alternative reporting modality for companies, financial institutions and institutional investors that are participants in the UN Global Compact or the PRI. Companies, financial institutions or institutional investors that have acceded to the UN Global Compact or PRI may choose to honour the Danish statutory reporting obligation through the Communication of Progress (CoP) report, which they are expected to prepare under these international instruments. The provision on this in Section 99a of the Act on Financial Accounts is repeated in the executive orders that pertain to financial institutions and institutional investors. The CoP must contain reporting for the same period of time as the financial statement to which it relates.

The management's report must contain information stating that the company, financial institution or institutional investor has applied the special reporting modality provided for by the pertinent provision on mandatory CSR reporting. The management's report must also provide information on where the CoP is accessible. For example, the management's report may contain a reference to the company's website, which, in turn, provides a link to a CoP that is accessible via the website of the UN Global Compact.

CSR reporting for companies and other organizations not subject to the CSR reporting requirement

Companies and other organizations that are not subjected to the CSR reporting requirement may choose to prepare CSR reports according to the provisions in Section 99a of the Act on Annual Accounts. Such companies or organizations may also publish their report according to the methods stipulated in the act, should they choose to do so.

Enforcement of the reporting requirement

Non-compliance by the management with the reporting requirements on the publication of reports is subject to punishment by fine. In 2010, the first year of mandatory CSR reporting, the government agency responsible was flexible, announcing that the reporting process was considered a learning process and that it might take some time for some companies to report fully on all dimensions required by the reporting provision. An announcement of stricter monitoring from 2011 followed media reports that presented incomplete reporting as violations of environmental law.[14]

Auditing of CSR reports

As part of the management review, CSR reports are subject to auditing. Auditing, however, is limited to a consistency check. The audit must ensure consistency between the management report and other parts of the report subjected to audit requirements, but no audit of consistency between CSR policies and actual practice or performance is required.

The auditing process must ensure consistency among the reporting on policies, on practices for implementing the policies and on results and expectations. The consistency requirement means, for example, that if a CSR policy relates to environment and climate, reporting on practices, results and expectations must also be on environment and climate.

The auditor's statement on the company's mandatory report must cover the CSR report, regardless of whether the company's, financial institution's or investor's CSR report is published as part of the management's report, on the company website or in a separate report.

When CSR reports are published through the application of the alternatives to the management report, such as on the company website or through a Global Compact or PRI report, the auditor is required to verify that information in the general report on where the CSR report may be found is correct, and that the report is listed under the required title reference and contains the information required by the act. Thus, monitoring of consistency between CSR information and performance is left to others – generally civil society, investors, buyers and other interested stakeholders.

When the management's report declares that a company provides CSR reporting through a Global Compact or PRI report, auditing must include whether the company fulfils conditions for applying that particular reporting modality. The auditor must conduct a consistency check of whether a CoP has been prepared. For companies that declare to have made a Global Compact CoP, the auditor must check that the CoP is available to the public at the Global Compact website. For organizations declaring to have made a PRI CoP, auditing must include a check of whether the report is available to the public, for example, at the organization's website. The audit must also include a check of whether the information provided on where the CoP is available to the public is correct. For CSR reporting through Global Compact or PRI reporting, the auditor has no further obligations.

The auditor, therefore, is not required to conduct an audit of the CoP itself. A Global Compact or PRI Communication on Progress uploaded on the Global Compact website is not subject to formal auditing. These Communications on Progress are uploaded on the websites of the Global Compact and PRI. Partly for resource reasons due to limited staff with the relevant organizations, monitoring is effectively left to civil society. The effectiveness of this remains to be further explored. An auditor's non-compliance with the auditing requirements is subject to punishment by fine.

Mandatory CSR reporting – experience so far

At the time of writing (December 2013) only limited information has been collected on the impact of the reporting requirements. The studies that have been made have focused on business organizations. According to surveys[15] prepared for the Danish Agency for Commerce and Companies/Danish Business Authority on the basis of the initial reporting rounds of CSR reports submitted in 2010, 2011 and 2012 pertaining to financial years 2009, 2010 and 2011, a large proportion of companies have submitted the required CSR report, and compliance with the requested information increased between the first, second and third reporting years. According to the 2010 report, 97 per cent of companies subjected to the act's reporting requirement submitted a CSR report. Of these, 91 per cent stated having CSR policies, while 9 per cent stated that they did not. Among the 91 per cent of companies that reported having CSR policies, most informed on their policies and actions. Only 37 per cent provided information on what had been achieved through social responsibility initiatives during the financial year, and any expectations regarding future initiatives. Among reporting companies, the majority placed the CSR report within the management review section of the financial statement, meaning that only a minority elected to apply the alternative options (website report, Global Compact or PRI report). Twenty-eight per cent of companies drew on the UN Global Compact or other international standards as reporting inspiration. Only 9 per cent reported according to the Global Reporting Initiative (GRI). Limited resources to incorporate the Principles or limited relevance of the Principles in the Danish context were stated as the most common cause for companies not selecting to report according to Global Compact or other international CSR framework. Where applied, however, Global Compact was generally seen to lend structure to the reporting and to make implementation easier.

Among the CSR themes reported on, environment and climate were consistently the most frequent, likely mirroring the high engagement of Danish enterprise activities in those fields. Environment and climate were followed by reporting on social issues related to Danish workplaces. The latter finding probably reflects the fact that labour conditions are subjected to a high degree of regulation through Danish law, EU law and collective agreements, and that for these reasons many companies are attentive to these issues.[16] By contrast, fewer reports address qualitative human rights and supply chain labour issues.[17] These reporting patterns mirror those found in a recent analysis of UN Global Compact reports.[18]

When assessing the impact of the CSR reporting requirement in terms of quantitative studies, such as the one noted above, it should be kept in mind that the aim of the reporting requirement is qualitative. Indications on numbers of companies that report and the issues that they report on do not – or at best superficially – indicate to what extent companies change their conduct by internalizing externalities, as was the objective of the reporting requirement.[19] As with qualitative change in general, it is likely to take some years before the actual impact can be assessed.

Compulsory reporting on human rights and climate change

Based on recommendations from the government's advisory Council on Social Responsibility in 2011 to strengthen reporting on human rights and activities to reduce climate change,[20] the Danish government in late 2011 set in motion a proposal to make reporting on human rights and climate change issues compulsory for companies subjected to the general CSR reporting requirement. A bill based on the government's proposal was adopted by the Danish legislature in June 2012.[21] The strengthened reporting requirement makes it compulsory for companies whose policies refer to respecting human rights or reducing their climate change impact to include these issues in their CSR report submitted according to Section 99a of the Act on Financial Statements. The mandatory reporting requirement on human rights and climate change activities takes effect from financial years starting on or after 1 January 2013. Implemented through executive orders, similar reporting requirements apply to institutional investors.

Similar to the 2011 report from the Council on Social Responsibility, the explanatory comments to the bill referred to the UN Guiding Principles and the OECD's Guidelines.[22] Views expressed during the parliamentary debate and committee work[23] opposing the shift of CSR reporting from completely voluntary to subject to mandatory requirements were effectively overruled by the adoption of the strengthened reporting requirement.

Conclusion and outlook

It was noted in the introduction that in Denmark responsible investment (RI) is broadly understood to be socially responsible investment in accordance with social expectations of investors to respond to ESG issues and in line with CSR expectations. It was also noted that these expectations and actions may reflect the dynamic character of ESG and CSR from a global and regional perspective, as well as any particular Danish issues. As is apparent from the discussion in this chapter, the agenda set by the Danish government's introduction of mandatory CSR reporting for institutional investors as well as large businesses with effect from 2008 has been rather influential for the development of RI in Denmark over the past years. This is the case with regard to investors' investment priorities as well as particular activities, such as reporting. Investors have paid particular attention to their own policies and to reporting, as apparent from recent surveys of Dansif.

Not all Danish institutional investors pay the same level of attention to ESG or CSR issues as part of their business practices. Among those that pay significant attention, as the case of ATP shows, policies and reporting of actual or potentially invested companies are seen to reflect risk and risk management capacity indications. In the medium term, the expansion of SRI may grow among other institutional investors as well, but the strength of this growth will probably depend on the demonstrated economic effects of responsible investment as compared to other investment. This makes it difficult to predict the outlook for RI in Denmark.

Nevertheless, in the near future it is likely that RI and institutional investors in Denmark will pay more attention to human rights and climate change mitigation. This would be a logical reflection of the strengthened CSR reporting requirement, taking into account the influence of the original requirement on attention paid to CSR policies and reporting.

This chapter reflects the situation as of late 2013. The SRI field is highly dynamic due to economic, political and governance developments and the transnational character of investment. Because Denmark is a small but open economy, the outlook for SRI may generally be expected to reflect global trends. Danish leadership in terms of reporting obligations may have had an influence in the relatively short term, but in the longer term the legislative approach to influencing business and investors' practices may be overtaken by regional and global trends. Among these, EU policies and requirements, requirements and tendencies at key stock exchanges, as well as normative developments of a global or transnational character (such as PRI trends or World Bank or UN investment requirements that may reflect directly as well as indirectly on involved investors and their business partners) can be expected to be influential. Developments in the past few years in Denmark indicate that CSR issues for businesses and ESG issues for investors are becoming increasingly interconnected. If current globalization oriented financial trends continue, this development is also likely to continue.

Notes

1 Eurosif website. Online. Available HTTP: <http://www.eurosif.org/sri-resources/sri-country-resources/denmark> (accessed 19 December 2013).

2 Merkur Andelskasse website (in Danish). Online. Available HTTP: <https://www.merkur.dk/default.aspx>.

3 *ATP's Policy of Social Responsibility in Investments*. Online. Available HTTP: <http://www.atp.dk/X5/wps/wcm/connect/a8e493804dfa7ef19bb59f6fb281efbf/2_ATPs+policy+of+SRI.pdf?MOD=AJPERES>.

This policy sets requirements for the companies in which ATP invests. These include respecting the rule of law in the countries in which they operate and respecting the rules, norms and standards that ensue from conventions and other international agreements ratified by Denmark. The latter requirement applies irrespective of whether the country in which the company operates has ratified those agreements.

4 Ministry of Business and Growth (2013) *Samfundsansvar og rapportering i Danmark – effekten af 3. år med rapporteringskrav i Årsregnskabsloven*: 32–33.

5 For example, Danske Bank. Online. Available HTTP: <http://www.danskebank.com/en-uk/csr/business/sri/pages/sri.aspx>; Nordea. Online. Available HTTP: <http://www.nordea.com/About+Nordea/Corporate+Social+Responsibility/We+work+with+sustainability/Responsible+investments/1501902.html>; Sydbank. Online. Available HTTP: <http://www.sydbank.dk/omsydbank/samfundsengagement/csr/ansvarlige-investeringer>.

6 Samfundsansvar.dk/Ministry of Economy and Commerce (2011) *Guide to Responsible Investment.* Online. Available HTTP: <http://samfundsansvar.dk/file/319139/guide_to_responsible_investment.pdf>.

7 Danish Social Investment Forum (2011) *SRI undersøgelse – November 2011* [SRI assessment – November 2011]; Dansif (2012) *The Current State of Responsible Investment in Denmark: Dansif 2012 Study.*

8 Ibid.

9 The reporting obligation applies to large companies in accounting class C and listed companies and state-owned companies in accounting class D. Large companies in accounting class C comprise companies that exceed at least two of the following three size limits: total assets/liabilities of DKK 143 million, net revenue of DKK 286 million and an average of 250 full-time employees. Further details are available at the Danish Government's CSR website under 'Legislation'. Online. Available HTTP: <http://www.csrgov.dk/sw51190.asp>.

10 The reporting requirement was introduced through an amendment to the Act on Financial Statements (through Act 1403 27.12.2008). An unofficial translation of the reporting provision (Section 99a) and the explanatory comments is provided at the Danish Government's CSR website. Online. Available HTTP: <http://www.csrgov.dk/graphics/Samfundsansvar.dk/Dokumenter/Proposal_Report_On_Social_Resp.pdf>.

11 Statutory Order No. 1305 16/12/2008, Section 135, succeeded by Statutory Order No. 17 11/01/2011, Section 135, and Statutory Order No. 312 30/03/2012, Section 135; Statutory Order No 1043 05/11/2009, Section 62; Statutory Order No. 1310 16/12/2008, Section 132 succeeded by Statutory Order No 16 11/01/2011, Section 132, and Statutory Order No. 25 16/01/12, Section 132; and Statutory Order No. 1307 16/12/2008, Section 24, succeeded by Statutory Order No. 63 25/01/2012, Section 25.

12 For business organizations, the amendment making human rights and climate change reporting compulsory was introduced as part of another act, which introduced a statutory basis for the Danish National Contact Point under the OECD's Guidelines for Multinational Enterprises (Act No. 546, 18/06/2012); for amendments of statutory orders, see footnote above.

13 Executive Order No. 761 20/07/2009, on the publication of reports on corporate governance and CSR on the company's website etc. (Bekendtgørelse om offentliggørelse af redegørelse for virksomhedsledelse og redegørelse for samfundsansvar på virksomhedens hjemmeside mv).

14 Erhvervs- og Selskabsstyrelsen (2010) *Sådan skal lovkrav om rapportering af samfundsansvar efterleves.*

15 Ministry for Economics and Commerce (2010) *Corporate Social Responsibility and Reporting in Denmark,* Copenhagen; Ministry for Economic and Commerce (2011); *Corporate Social Responsibility and Reporting in Denmark,* report prepared by Peter Neergaard/CBS for the Centre for Social Reporting, Copenhagen; Ministry for Growth and Commerce (2013) *Samfundsansvar og rapportering i Danmark – effekten af 3.år med rapporteringskrav i Årsregnskabsloven,* Copenhagen; Danwatch (2011) *The Impact of the Danish Law on CSR Reporting,* report prepared for the European Coalition for Corporate Justice (ECCJ), Copenhagen/Brussels.

16 Compare also the reasoning for 'implicit CSR' in Europe, provided in Matten, Dirk and Moon (2008) '"Implicit" and "explicit" CSR: A conceptual framework for a comparative understanding of corporate social responsibility', *Academy of Management Review,* Vol. 33, No. 2: 404–424.

17 Ministry of Business and Growth (2011) *Corporate Social Responsibility and Reporting in Denmark,* report prepared by Peter Neergaard/CBS for the Centre for Social Reporting; Ministry for Economic and Commerce (2010) *Samfundsansvar og Rapportering i Danmark – Effekten af rapporteringskrav i årsregnskabsloven,* report prepared by Peter Neergaard/CBS for the Centre for Social Reporting; Danwatch (2011) *The Impact of the Danish Law on CSR Reporting,* report prepared for the European Coalition for Corporate Justice (ECCJ).

18 United Nations Global Compact (2011) *Annual Review 2010*, New York: Global Compact Office.

19 Buhmann, K. (2013) 'The Danish CSR reporting requirement as reflexive law: Employing CSR as a modality to promote public policy'. Accepted for publication in *European Business Law Review,* 2013, Issue 2: 187–216.

20 Rådet for Samfundsansvar (2011) *Anbefalinger til en ikke-retlig mæglings- og klage mekanisme* [Recommendations for a non-judicial mediation and complaints mechanism].
21 Technically, the strengthened reporting requirement was adopted as part of a bill to introduce a revised OECD National Contact Point, see Section 11, Subsection 2 of the Act on Mediation and Complaints Institution for Responsible Business Conduct, Act No. 546, 18 June 2012.
22 Explanatory Comments, Bill on Act on Mediation and Complaints Institution for Responsible Business Conduct, 28 March 2012
23 White Paper on Bill on Act on Mediation and Complaints Institution for Responsible Business Conduct, 29 May 2012.

27

Responsible investment in Finland

Antti Savilaakso

Introduction

Compared to the rest of the Nordic countries and Europe, responsible investment (RI) in Finland had a late start but has since spread widely and decisively to institutional asset owners and managers.

The Finland Sustainable Investment Forum (FINSIF) defines RI as "tak[ing] into account issues associated with the environment, society and good governance". The Finnish pension alliance, TELA, further defines RI as follows:

> Responsible investment takes into account issues associated with the environment, society and good governance [ESG]. These ESG issues are incorporated into the investment process and ownership practices with the view of promoting the return and risk profile of the portfolio.

FINSIF, TELA, and Hyrske et al.[1] make a clear distinction between ethical investment and RI. Ethical investors divest from securities and companies that are in conflict with their values, and financial factors are secondary in investment decision making. RI focuses on investments and potential investments and how they relate to various ESG issues. This is then taken into account when evaluating the overall risk and return expectation of a particular investment. The responsible investor's primary objective is to improve the return and risk profile of the investment within the aggregate of the investment portfolio.

Many Finnish investors further define their RI activities using categories established by Eurosif and the UN-backed Principles for Responsible Investment (PRI). These include exclusions, best-in-class strategies, thematic investments, norms-based screening, ESG integration and engagement and voting.

This chapter looks at RI activities in Finland. The first section describes Finnish society and the Finnish investment market in general, creating a relevant context for the following sections. The second section dives deeper into the Finnish RI industry. The third section describes the legal situation in Finland regarding RI and broader ESG issues, followed by a description of some Finland-specific phenomena in RI. The final section gives a brief outlook on RI in Finland.

About Finland

Finland is the smallest of the Nordic countries and is located between Russia and Sweden. It has almost 5.3 million inhabitants. The population has high life expectancy at 80 years and education levels of 17 years. The literacy rate is not officially followed, as it has been 100 per cent for several decades. Finland is predominantly Lutheran (78.4 per cent); however, a significant portion of the population (19.2 per cent) does not identify with a religion. Finland is a republic with a legal system based on civil law.

Finland joined the European Union (EU) in 1995 (Central Intelligence Agency 2013) and was one of the 11 countries joining the third phase of the Economic and Monetary Union of the EU, adopting the euro as the country's currency in 1999.

Strong growth, innovation, and economic structure prior to the 2008 economic and financial crises turned Finland into the third most competitive economy in the world, according to the World Economic Forum. This has ensured the maintenance of a welfare state that provides a high level of well-being for its citizens. According to OECD, competitiveness has deteriorated recently due to the collapse of traditional industries such as electronics and forestry.

Current economic challenges (and a lot of the political discussions) revolve around the economics of, and relationship to, the EU, and specifically regarding the use of the euro. The Finnish unemployment rate is at 8.1 per cent, and the ratio of public debt to GDP is at 56.6 per cent. The Finnish central bank (Bank of Finland (2014) Economic Outlook.) estimates the unemployment rate to remain stable with a structural general government deficit of more than 62 per cent by 2016.

Immigration is a relatively new but nowadays fast-growing phenomenon in Finland. In 2004, Finland only had 160,000 foreign-born members of its population. As of 2013, that number had grown to 300,000, representing 5.8 per cent of the population.

The traditionally low immigration numbers have been explained by Finland's less hospitable climate and the fact that the Finnish language shares roots with none of the major world languages, making it more challenging for most to learn. There is also anecdotal evidence in numerous polls that indicate that a large number of Finnish people want to limit immigration to the country in order to preserve the regional culture. This has been reflected in the political decision-making regarding immigration during past decades.

The total individual tax rate in Finland is 43.1 per cent. This rate is the highest among the Nordic countries, but less than that of many other EU countries, including large EU economies such as Germany, France and Italy, which all have tax rates of around 50 per cent (OECD).

The Finnish securities market is relatively small. The main stock market index lists only 125 companies with a combined market value of only €120 billion, representing around 0.3 per cent of the global equity market (World Bank). As Figure 27.1 demonstrates, the largest sectors are financials, with 31 per cent of the total market value and 12 per cent of the listed companies, and industrials, representing 20.1 per cent of the total market value and 36.8 per cent of the listed companies.

The Finnish equity market is also concentrated. Figure 27.2 illustrates how the largest 5 companies represent 54 per cent of the total market value, and the largest 10 companies represent 72 per cent of the total market value. This concentration is clearly visible in every sector, as the largest company represents a minimum 35.9 per cent of the total market value and the largest three combine to represent a minimum of 60.8 per cent of the total market value of each sector. The energy and utilities sectors each feature one company, both of which are government controlled. The telecommunication and healthcare sectors have two and five companies, respectively.

The Herfindahl index measuring market concentration using companies' market capitalization as an indicator of market share indicates that all but the industrial sector show either

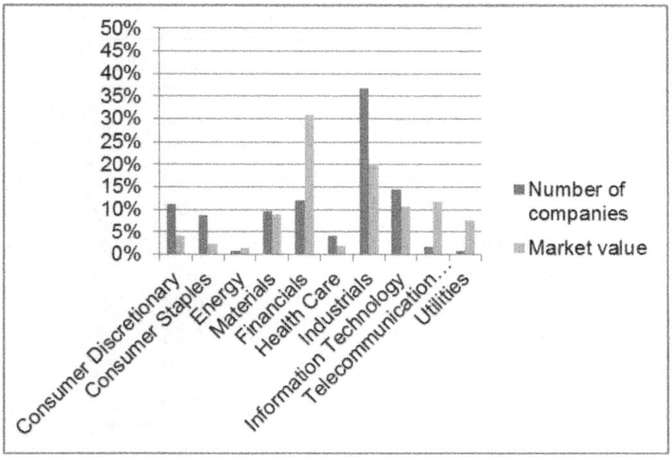

Figure 27.1 Number of companies in Finland and the total market value

Source: Author.

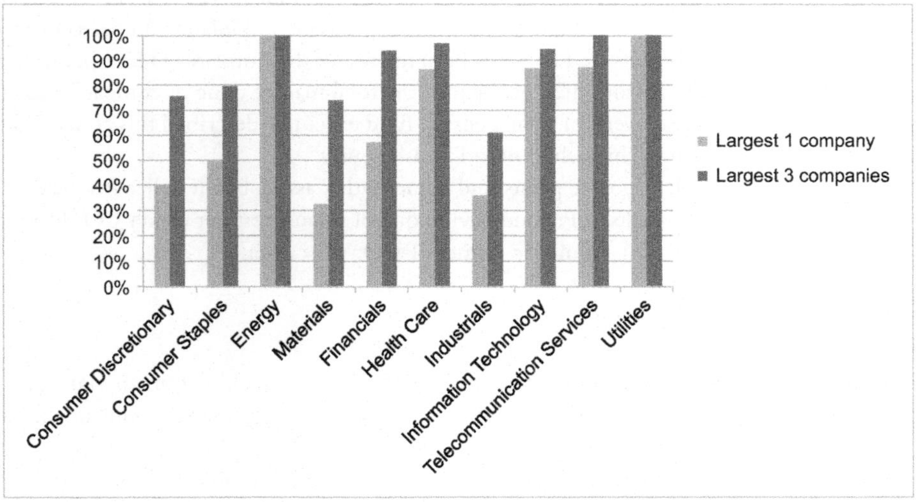

Figure 27.2 Market value concentration of the largest companies in Finland in each sector

Source: Author.

moderate concentration (index > 0.15) or high concentration (index > 0.25), as shown in Table 27.1.

Finnish employers choose pension funds for their employees from among the authorized pension managers in Finland. This means that, unlike many other countries, people in the pension system cannot directly decide on their pension investments. This results in a considerable amount of assets being managed outside of Finland, with authorized external pension managers overseeing approximately €165 billion (TELA). In comparison, asset managers domiciled in

Table 27.1 Herfindahl index (Finland)

Sector	*Index Value*
Consumer discretionary	0.23
Consumer staples	0.30
Energy	1.00
Materials	0.22
Financials	0.42
Health care	0.75
Industrials	0.04
Information technology	0.75
Telecommunication services	0.77
Utilities	1.00

Finland manage only €77 billion (FIVA), making these the largest institutional investors in the Finnish market. Other institutional investors, such as foundations, municipalities, trade unions, universities and religious institutions, manage considerably less funds. Households own around 15 per cent of the investable assets, according to the Bank of Finland.

Pension system portfolio ownership tends to be invested in Finland. At the end of 2013, the Finnish pension system invested around 30 per cent of its assets in Finland (30 per cent in real estate, 26 per cent in listed equity and 25 per cent in the rest of the Euro area [TELA]); this means that the pension sector owns around 25 per cent of the total market value of companies listed in Finland (based on a five-year average). One pension fund executive described this concentration: "We are like an elephant in a china shop with Finnish equity".

Finland has some nuclear power plants and some hydro assets, but it still relies heavily on imported fossil fuels. This results in Finland having one of the highest per capita CO_2 footprints in Europe and the OECD at 11.53 metric tonnes of CO_2 per capita.

RI in Finland

Many ESG issues that resonate globally within the RI industry, such as human rights, labour rights, environmental corruption and inequality, are already being addressed in Finland either by legislation or by social consciousness.

Finland scores high in several development and well-being indicators. Finland is one of the least corrupt countries in the world, currently ranking third in the Corruption Perceptions Index published by Transparency International. Finland has the most press freedom in the world, according to Reporters without Borders. The Finnish GINI index is 25.8, placing Finland among the 10 most equal countries in the world. Finland ranks ninth on the Democracy Index by the Economist Intelligence Unit. Women make up 42.5 per cent of Finnish parliament, placing the country as sixth in the world for diversity. Finland invests 3.9 per cent of its GDP in research and development (R&D). With the collapse of traditional industries, it has a strong focus on electronics and forestry and is increasingly directing its R&D into renewable energy.

As a result of Finland's high scores in development and well-being, RI practices have quickly gained wide acceptance within the Finnish investment industry, which has been marked by the growth of RI institutions, Finland's Sustainable Investment Forum (FINSIF), and the growth of signatories to the PRI. Most of the Finnish signatories joined FINSIF (established in 2010) and signed on to PRI relatively late (between 2012 and 2013).

FINSIF was founded in 2010 to serve as a forum for institutional investors interested in RI. The forum has close to 60 members and includes not only the largest pension funds and asset managers but also a wide variety of other types of sizeable investors, such as trade unions, universities, municipalities and foundations. The forum's purpose is to provide information and tools for adopting sustainable investment and RI in different member organizations, to inspire a national discussion on RI and an international discussion on sustainable development and corporate responsibility and to change attitudes towards RI.

Around 96 per cent of assets in investment funds registered in Finland are managed by investment managers that have signed on to the PRI (PRI; FIVA). 94 per cent of assets managed by pension funds are managed by funds signed to PRI (PRI; TELA). These in total can be estimated to represent more than 90 per cent of investable assets in Finland.

Finland currently has 33 PRI signatories: 10 are asset owners, 22 are asset managers and 1 is a service provider. Furthermore, a large portion of the Finnish asset management market is dominated by asset managers listed as PRI signatories in other countries, predominantly in Sweden. For example, the asset managers of Nordea, Danske Invest, SEB and Handelsbanken jointly have more than 50 per cent of the Finnish asset management market (FIVA; PRI).

One obvious question is: How did the FINSIF membership, together with PRI signatorship, penetrate the Finnish market so fast and decisively? One potential answer could be in the small and concentrated market where ideas spread quite quickly. Official endorsement from key organizations such as the Finnish Pension Alliance (TELA) probably also helped. On the other hand, Finland scores very high on a number of the indicators considered integral to sustainable development. It might well be that Finnish institutional investors found it easy to sign on to the principles and affiliate themselves with ESG integration if they felt they were doing so already.

The top three most popular strategies in Finland remain exclusion, norms-based screening and engagement and voting, according to European SRI Survey 2014 by Eurosif, as listed in Table 27.2. All of these strategies have exhibited some level of growth over the past year, while the growth rates of RI strategies in general have been quite modest. However, ESG integration is recording the fastest growth in Finland – more than doubling in assets under management. The high proportion of PRI signatories in relative terms to other markets and the commitment of some significant local or regional asset managers may explain part of this increase.

Exclusion criteria usually encompass illegal weapons and, in some cases, is extended to cover other weapons, manufacturers of alcohol and tobacco products, gambling or adult entertainment services (Nordea; Ilmarinen; Varma; Central Church Fund of Finland).

Norms-based screening is screening according to investment compliance with international norms that are loosely based on the UN Global Compact, the International Labour Organization

Table 27.2 RI strategies in Finland

Strategy	*2011 (in millions)*	*2013 (in millions)*	*Compound Annual Growth Rate (%)*
Integration	20,715	46,618	50.0%
Engagement and voting	44,870	50,785	6.4%
Exclusions	83,637	88,848	3.1%
Norms-based screening	62,336	64,667	1.9%
Thematic	322	220	–17.3%
Best-in-class	24,798	310	–88.8%

Source: Author.

(ILO), the OECD, and other internationally accepted principles. These principles are sometimes categorized as human rights, labour rights, environmental degradation and corruption. Norms-based screening often results in engagement processes rather than up-front exclusion.

Approaches vary considerably between domestic and foreign investments, the latter being that in which the majority of exclusion and norms-based screening takes place in Finland.

Engagement and voting strategies also vary between domestic and international investments. Due to the concentrated nature of the market (i.e. a small number of companies and a small number of investors), many large investors participate in Finnish companies' annual general meetings in person and engage quite informally and on an ad-hoc bases with companies. This is also quite practical since most of the investors and companies are located in a relatively small geographical area within the capital region. Engagement and voting in foreign investments tends to occur through proxy voting service providers and collaborative initiatives such as those facilitated by PRI.

There is very little thematic and best-in-class investment in Finland. This is understandable given that these approaches do not work well in a small and concentrated market. As a result, there are very few best-in-class funds that are managed in Finland, and most of those that are currently available in the market are managed outside Finland. According to the Eurosif, the large swings between asset classes reflect a concentrated market where the drop in best-in-class strategies can be explained by a few players changing their strategy.

Only one service provider – Earthrate – is among the PRI signatories in Finland. The relatively small number of service providers in Finland can be explained by the informal nature of the RI activities. Based on anecdotal evidence from the sizeable investor websites (Ilmarinen; Varma; Nordea; Danske Invest; SEB) exclusion and norms-based screening are mainly conducted by Swedish service providers, namely Ethix and GES, that, in turn, have a lot of expertise in these areas. At the same time, most of the global service providers have some clients in Finland. Some of the big four accountants also provide services related to corporate responsibility and responsible investing.

Legal situation of RI in Finland

In Finland, it is implicitly assumed that the state will take care of social issues. As a result, Finnish legislation has traditionally been thorough in the fields of labour law, labour protection law and environmental law. This also means that there is no actual legislation concerning ESG. Therefore, practices rest on organizations such as FINSIF and initiatives such as the PRI (Eurosif).

The Finnish government has announced that a climate change bill will be drafted (Ministry of Environment 2014). The bill will set a greenhouse gas emission reduction target of 80 per cent by the year 2050 compared to 1990. The planned bill will form a framework for setting climate policy, but it will not contain policies and measures intended to directly affect companies or individuals.

Listed companies have to provide a corporate governance statement annually. This is a legal requirement and is based on the relevant EU directive. The Finnish stock exchange refers to this regulation and gives out more detailed instructions in its listing requirements (Utter 2014).

Arvopaperimarkkinayhdistys (the securities market association, a co-operative organization established by a confederation of Finnish industries, Nasdaq omx Helsinki and the Finland Chamber of Commerce) published the Corporate Governance Code of Finland to complement statutory procedures (Securities Market Association). The Board of the Exchange has adopted this code as part of the exchange's self-regulation. The code helps to smooth corporate governance practices and reporting by providing an overall picture of the central principles of corporate governance. It is based on the 'comply or explain' approach and is self-regulatory by nature.

Since 2004, the Finnish Pension Alliance, TELA, has published principles and recommendations concerning RI for authorised pension providers, the most recent of which was published in June 2014 (Finnish Pension Alliance, Aspects on responsible investment by pension providers).

Characteristics of RI in Finland

The Finnish government is a substantial investor in the Finnish stock market. Currently the state owns €19.4 billion in publicly listed companies, representing around 12 per cent of the total market (VNK). The Finnish government directly owns more than 50 per cent of the country's largest airline (Finnair, 55.81 per cent), the largest utility company (Fortum, 50.76 per cent) and the largest energy company (Neste Oil, 50.1 per cent). Additionally, the government indirectly owns (via their wholly owned investment management company Solidium) €8.7 billion in 12 listed companies (Prime Minister's Office 2014). In 2011, the Finnish government adopted a resolution asking non-listed state-owned companies and state majority–owned companies to report their sustainability performance.

Government ownership is frequently debated in Finland. This is largely due to structural changes in companies in which the government owns a minority share, which has led to the downsizing of manufacturing capacity and the laying-off of thousands of people, especially in companies outside the capital region.

Finnish investors and companies, just as any other global players, are increasingly exposed to global sustainable development trends. The risks related to climate change and managing corporate responsibility are issues in complex global supply chains. Most of the ESG issues tend to be company specific, and the public discussion tends to revolve around separate companies that are facilitated by a few non-governmental organizations. A substantial part of these discussions tend to involve Finnish company operations outside Finland. Recent examples include Neste Oil operations based on palm oil (Greenpeace), Stora Enso operations outside Finland (Swedwatch) and TeliaSonera operations in the former Soviet Union (Finnwatch).

According to the Finland Chamber of Commerce, two-thirds of the listed companies in Finland (79 to be exact) follow the Corporate Governance Code without exception. In contrast, 41 companies deviate from one or more of the 55 recommendations. Most often, Finnish companies deviate from board gender diversity (10 of 41 deviating companies). At the same time, women represent 23 per cent of all board seats, putting Finland on top of the EU, but still well short of the EU commission 2012 proposal for a 40 per cent mandatory quota. All 757 board positions were divided among 652 people. According to the Finland Chamber of Commerce, the number of unique board members is quite widely distributed; only 78 people held more than one board position.

Conclusion with outlook

Finland continues to be a small and concentrated market, both in terms of investors and listed companies. This makes it relatively straightforward to conduct various different investment strategies. Exclusion, norms-based screening and integration of related RI strategies are likely to remain the dominant approaches to ESG integration by investment funds. Most of the perceived challenges will continue to come from international operations. This is true for companies expanding their operations outside Finland where, regardless of the target country, companies will face ESG challenges.

Investing globally outside Finland might also be the largest challenge for Finnish RI-minded investors. Conducting ESG analysis, engagement and corporate governance activities tends to be easier in a small, concentrated and homogenous market, whereas conducting these activities globally as a relatively small investor in a much more complex environment with almost non-existent support for domestic RI service providers might prove to be considerably more difficult.

Note

1 These authors have written the only volume on the RI market in Finland.

References

Bank of Finland (2013) *Investment Funds, Financial Statement Data.* Online. Available HTTP: <http://www.suomenpankki.fi/en/tilastot/sijoitusrahastot/Pages/index_siti_13_5_2014.aspx>.

Bank of Finland (2014) *Economic Outlook.* Online. Available HTTP: <http://www.suomenpankki.fi/en/julkaisut/bulletin/economic_outlook/Pages/default.aspx>.

The Central Church Fund of Finland, *Responsible Investment.* Online. Available HTTP: <http://sakasti.evl.fi/sakasti.nsf/sp?Open&cid=Content54FE91> (accessed 30 July 2014).

Central Intelligence Agency (2013) *The World Factbook, Finland.* Online. Available HTTP: <https://www.cia.gov/library/publications/the-world-factbook/geos/fi.html>.

Danske Invest, *Fund Profile – Sustainability Equity Fund D – Product Overview EN.* Online. Available HTTP: <http://www.danskeinvest.fi/web/show_fund.produkt?p_nId=1527&p_nFundgroup=61&p_nFund=2453> (accessed 24 July 2014).

Danske Invest, *Responsible Investment.* Online. Available HTTP: <http://www.danskebank.com/en-uk/CSR/business/SRI/Pages/SRI.aspx> (accessed 30 July 2014).

Economist Intelligence Unit, *Democracy Index 2013.* Online. Available HTTP: <http://www.eiu.com/public/topical_report.aspx?campaignid=Democracy0814> (accessed 23 July 2014).

European Union (2012) *Press Release – Women on Boards* (IP/12/1205). Online. Available HTTP: <http://europa.eu/rapid/press-release_IP-12–1205_en.htm>.

Eurosif (2012) *European SRI Survey.* Online. Available HTTP: <http://www.eurosif.org/publication/view/european-sri-study-2012/>.

Eurosif. (2014). *European SRI Survey.* Online. Available HTTP: <http://www.eurosif.org/publication/view/european-sri-study-2014/>.

Financial Supervisory Authority of Finland (FIVA) (2014) *Fund Management Companies' Market Shares.* Online. Available HTTP: <http://www.finanssivalvonta.fi/en/Statistics/Securities_market/Management_companies_ market_shares/Pages/Default.aspx>.

Finnish Chamber of Commerce (2014) *Corporate Governance Selvitys 2014.* Online. Available HTTP: <http://kauppakamari.fi/wp-content/uploads/2014/05/cg-selvitys-2014.pdf>.

Finnish Pension Alliance (TELA), *Summary of Investment Assets.* Online. Available HTTP: <http://www.tela.fi/en/economy/investment_statistics_and_analyses/summary_of_investment_assets>.

Finnish Pension Alliance (TELA) (2014) *Aspects Relating to Responsible Investment by Pension Providers.* Online. Available HTTP: <http://www.tela.fi/instancedata/prime_product_julkaisu/tela/embeds/telawwwstructure/17186_TELA_Aspects_relating_to_responsible_investment_by_pension_providers_2014.pdf>.

Finnwatch, *Reports.* Online. Available HTTP: <www.finnwatch.org/fi/julkaisut> (accessed 30 July 2014).

Finsif, *History.* Online. Available HTTP: <http://www.finsif.fi/22> (accessed 24 July 2014).

Greenpeace Finland. Online. Available HTTP: <http://www.greenpeace.org/finland/en/> (accessed 30 July 2014).

Hyrske, A., Lönnroth, M., Savilaakso, A. and Sievänen, R. (2012) *Vastuullinen Sijoittaminen.* Helsinki, Finland: Finva.

Ilmarinen, *Responsible Investment.* Online. Available HTTP: <http://www.ilmarinen.fi/Production/fi/ilmarinen/04_sijoitukset/04_vastuu_sijoitus/index.jsp> (accessed 30 July 2014).

Ministry of Environment (2014) *Government Proposal for Climate Change Act.* Online. Available HTTP: <http://www.ym.fi/en-US/Latest_news/Government_approves_proposal_for_a_clima(29845)>.

Nordea, *ESG at Nordea.* Online. Available HTTP: <http://esg.nordea.com> (accessed 30 July 2014).

OECD (2014) *Economic Survey Finland.* Online. Available HTTP: <http://www.oecd.org/economy/surveys/economic-survey-finland.htm>.

OECD (2014) *Taxing Wages 2014.* Online. Available HTTP: <http://www.keepeek.com/Digital-Asset-Management/oecd/taxation/taxing-wages-2014_tax_wages-2014-en#page1>.

Official Statistics Finland. Online. Available HTTP: <http://tilastokeskus.fi/>.

Prime Minister's Office (2014) *Value of State Direct Holdings in Listed Companies*. Online. Available HTTP: <http://valtionomistus.fi/suomi/tilastot/valtion-omistuksen-arvo-taulukkona/>.

Principles of Responsible Investment (PRI). Online. Available HTTP: <http://www.unpri.org> (accessed 24 July 2014).

Reporters without Borders, *World Press Freedom Index*. Online. Available HTTP: <http://rsf.org/index2014/en-index2014.php> (accessed 23 July 2014).

SEB, *Responsible Investment*. Online. Available HTTP: <http://sebgroup.com/en/About-SEB/Sustainability/Our-business-priorities/Responsible-investments/> (accessed 30 July 2014).

Securities Market Association Finland (2010) *The Finnish Corporate Governance Code*. Online. Available HTTP: <http://cgfinland.fi/en/recommendations/the-finnish-corporate-governance-code/>.

Solidium, *Portfolio*. Online. Available HTTP: <http://www.solidium.fi/investments/portfolio> (accessed 30 July 2014).

Swedwatch, *Reports*. Online. Available HTTP: <http://www.swedwatch.org/> (accessed 30 July 2014).

Transparency International, *Corruption Perceptions Index 2013 – Results*. Online. Available HTTP: <http://cpi.transparency.org/cpi2013/results/> (accessed 23 July 2014).

Utter, R. (2014) *A Climate Change Act, Comments from a Finnish Legal Perspective* (12), Legal Studies Research Paper, Law School, Finland: University of Eastern Finland.

Varma, *Responsible Investment*. Online. Available HTTP: <https://www.varma.fi/fi/tietoavarmasta/tulostiedot%20ja%20sijoitukset/vastuullinen-sijoittaminen/pages/default.aspx> (accessed 30 July 2014).

Vastuullinen sijoittaminen Suomessa. Online. Available HTTP: <http://www.finsif.fi>.

World Bank, *Market Capitalization of Listed Companies*. Online. Available HTTP: <http://data.worldbank.org/indicator/CM.MKT.LCAP.CD/countries?display=default> (accessed 31 July, 2014).

World Bank (2010) *World Development Indicators*. Online. Available HTTP: <http://data.worldbank.org/indicator/NY.GNP.PCAP.CD>.

World Economic Forum (2013) *The Global Competitiveness Index 2013–2014 Rankings*. Online. Available HTTP: <http://www.weforum.org/issues/global-competitiveness>.

28
Responsible investment in Sweden

Sabina Du Rietz

Introduction

Sweden has been described as a frontrunner in terms of responsible investment (RI)[1] (Eurosif, 2010). In the past, Swedish RI actors have pioneered RI strategies such as norm-based screening (Bengtsson, 2008; Eurosif, 2012) and have influenced the development of standards such as UN-backed Principles for Responsible Investment (PRI) (UN PRI, 2014). The Swedish RI market has continued to grow and is today considered to be quite mature. All of the largest asset managers adopt some form of RI strategy and have been active in this area more than 10 years (Eurosif, 2012).

Country/region overview

Basic statistics

Within a variety of capitalism frameworks, Sweden is usually considered a coordinated market economy. In a coordinated market economy, institutions reflect higher levels of reliance on non-market coordination in comparison to liberal market economies (Hall & Soskice, 2001). Sweden occupies, like the other Nordic countries, a top position when countries are ranked in terms of macroeconomic stability, international competitiveness and sustainable growth. The Nordic countries are among the OECD countries with the smallest income gaps (both before and after taxes), the largest public sectors, the highest labour-force participation rates and the strongest position for organized labour (Erixon, 2011). National indicators are regularly published by Statistics Sweden, see a selection in Table 28.1.

Table 28.1 Demographic statistics of Sweden

Population (October 2013)	9,633,490
Average age	41.1 years
GDP (in dollars, 2011)	~ 500 billion

Source: Adapted from Statistiska Centralbyrån (SCB).

RI market

Because of the international character of financial markets, drawing the line between the Swedish RI market and its surrounding markets is not easily done. For example, most Swedish asset managers have a cross-Nordic scope (Eurosif, 2010). Nevertheless, certain asset owners are clearly more Swedish than Nordic. Asset owners such as national pension funds, labour unions and the Swedish church belong foremost to the Swedish RI market.

Statistics on the Swedish RI market are still scarce. Eurosif, in collaboration with Swesif, produces the only available statistics of the Swedish RI market. Eurosif defines the Swedish market as assets managed by asset management teams located in Sweden (Eurosif, 2012). Hence, these figures, and the figures presented in the following discussion, reflect primarily the success of the Swedish asset management market rather than the origin of such funds or asset owners. According to this definition, the Swedish RI funds amounted to 305.5 billion EUR (389.66 billion USD) in 2009 (Eurosif, 2010) and 378.3 billion EUR (482.52 billion USD) in 2011 (Eurosif, 2012). Defined in this way, the Swedish market increased 24 per cent over a two-year period.

Eurosif also produces statistics on Swedish RI strategies. Eurosif (2012) sorts funds into seven RI categories: sustainability-themed investment, best-in-class investment selection, norm-based screening, exclusion of holdings from investment universe, integration of ESG factors in financial analysis, engagement and voting on sustainability matters and impact investment.[2]

According to the Eurosif figures presented in Figure 28.1, most Swedish RI funds employ an exclusion strategy, a strategy that holds a firm grip on the Swedish market. This is true both in terms of Eurosif's (2012) comparison in Table 28.2 as well as in a longer time perspective. Early Swedish RI attempts used negative screening and the subsequent exclusion of certain companies from the investment universe. The first ethical investment fund open to the public, AktieAnsvar Aktiefond, established in 1965 by the temperance and the dissenting Baptist movements, excluded certain companies based on values (Bengtsson, 2008). As in this case, the exclusion strategy is often combined with some form of negative screening. The result of a negative screening is a good basis for deciding which companies to exclude from the investment universe.

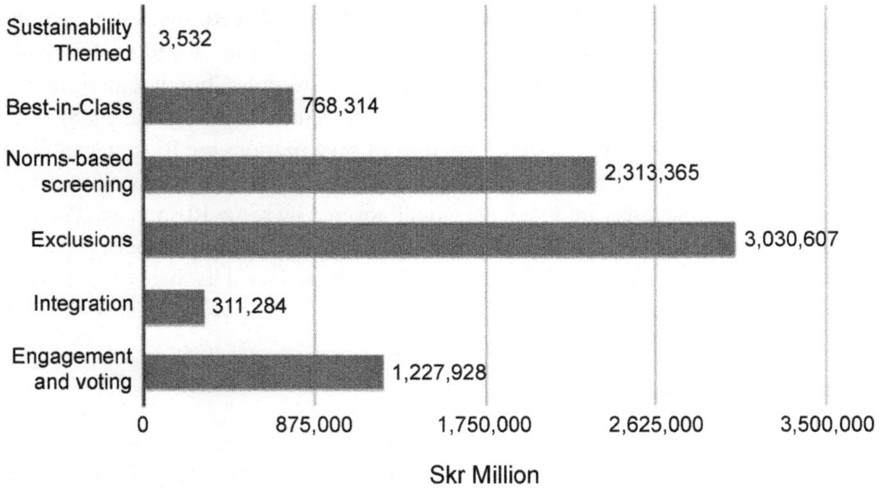

Figure 28.1 Swedish RI funds according to investment strategy

Source: Eurosif (2012) (with permission).

Table 28.2 Swedish RI funds according to investment strategy, 2009 versus 2011

Investment Strategy	*2009 (in Skr)*	*2011 (in Skr)*
Sustainability themed	0	3,532
Best in class	90,728	768,314
Norms-based screening	2,210,825	2,313,365
Exclusions	2,227,496	3,030,607
Integration	861,009	311,284
Engagement and voting	1,224,416	1,227,928

Source: Eurosif (2012) (with permission).

Norm-based screening, where investors identify companies that violate international principles, is a form of negative screening that is particularly popular among Swedish RI actors. In fact, norm-based screening is generally viewed as originating from the Nordic market and has since spread internationally (Eurosif, 2012). Norm-based screening emerged at a time of general RI mainstreaming in Scandinavia in the late 1990s. Negative screening as an RI approach spread and was adopted by mainstream actors. In the Scandinavian setting, this development coincided with the establishment of several national and international non-governmental (NGO) charters in Scandinavia. These NGOs focused on corporate conduct in relation to international conventions in general and CSR-issues in particular. For example, asset manager Banco initiated its negative screening–based funds after pressure from charitable organizations in its client base. As a result of these coinciding events, many of the new RI adopters based their negative screening on international conventions, norms believed to be shared with a wider society (Bengtsson, 2008).

Another significant event occurred in 2001 when the five largest public pension funds became obligated by law to include environment and ethics in their investment policies. In the consultation process leading up to the government bill, the largest federal trade union, Landsorganisationen (LO), emphasized the importance of considering international conventions in the investment process. Similarly, three NGOs questioned the appropriateness of public investors investing in tobacco companies. This resulted in the development of RI policies that emphasized international conventions. As a result, the previously common values-based exclusion strategy was replaced with norm-based screening. In 2002, even the Swedish Church reformed its ethical guidelines to include screening based on international conventions (Bengtsson, 2008).

In terms of specific asset classes, all of the Swedish RI organizations use RI strategies for public equities. Of the assets covered by RI strategy, equity represents the main type (Eurosif, 2012). In addition, fixed-income assets are to a large extent covered by some RI strategy. The category 'other' in Figure 28.2 represents assets such as hedge funds, structured products, private equity, venture capital and commodities. This category has slightly increased its share of RI capital since 2009 (Eurosif, 2012).

Market environment

As a result of the current pension system, introduced in 1999, 100 per cent of Swedes save in funds invested in the financial markets. One part of the pension system, the Premium Reserve System, allows individual pension savers to select from among 750 to 800 of funds with different levels of risk that are managed by accredited institutional investors. Less financially literate savers are guided through the investment process by being informed of the varying risk profiles of

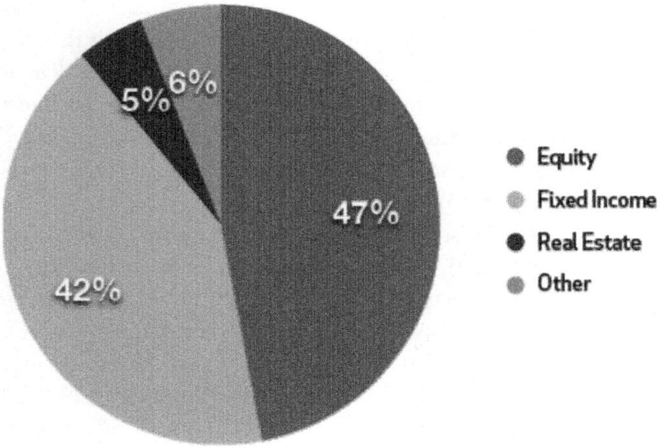

Figure 28.2 Types of asset classes in Sweden

Source: Eurosif (2012) (with permission).

funds, and are encouraged to reflect on their own levels of risk aversion (Belfrage & Ryner, 2009). Funds in the Premium Reserve System that take some form of sustainability consideration are marked with a green M/E symbol. In 2013, Swesif developed a sustainability profile for funds, available to savers of the Premium Reserve System. The sustainability profile is essentially a standardized fund fact sheet that specifically includes sustainability information. The sustainability profile aims to facilitate the choice making of savers with sustainability preferences by facilitating comparison of funds (Pensionsmyndigheten, 2013).

When Premium Reserve System savers do not make a choice, an index-tracking public pension fund, AP7, makes investments decisions for these passive or non-participatory pension savers (Belfrage & Ryner, 2009). The funds of the non-choosers are hence the responsibility of AP7 and covered by the four RI strategies that AP7 applies: exclusion, voting, engagement and legal processes. In terms of exclusion, AP7 conducts norm-based negative screening, which, in 2013, resulted in the exclusion of 47 companies. The norms AP7 relies on are the international conventions the Swedish state has signed. According to Swedish law, AP7 cannot vote for its Swedish holdings. AP7 votes in foreign holdings, however, and since 2013 also on sustainability issues. Some form of engagement is conducted with approximately 600 companies (AP7, 2013).

If one excludes the Premium Reserve System, approximately 76 per cent[3] of Swedes save in funds invested in the financial markets. Of these Swedes, 34 per cent considered ethical and environmental aspects in their investment choice in 2012, which is an increase from 31 per cent in 2010. Still, only 4 per cent save in funds with an explicit ethical or environmental profile (Fondbolagens Förening, 2012). More women than men consider sustainability issues when choosing funds (Fondbolagens Förening, 2014).

In terms of shareholder advocacy, shareholders may attend the annual general meeting (AGM) and thereby seek to influence corporate practices. An AGM in a Swedish setting offers the shareholders a chance to meet all the important representatives of the company and to pose any questions they may have. Shareholders have this right in addition to the right to introduce a formal proposal to an AGM as long as they own at least one share. The proposals should be presented in writing and reach the board in time, in which case it will be discussed during the AGM. In addition, the company's auditors have a right to be present at the AGM, and in practice generally exercise this right. At this occasion, shareholders vote on the discharge of liability of the board. However, the fundamental principle underlying the listing agreement is that no new information can be disclosed during the AGM, as this meeting only includes present shareholders (Catasús & Johed, 2007). Other common forms of investor–company interactions include private meetings between investor representatives and corporate managers and company visits (Hellman, 2005). There are also annual roundtable discussions specifically organized for investors concerned with sustainability issues (Du Rietz, 2013).

Apart from investors and the state, other Swedish actors that seek to influence corporate practices include trade unions and NGOs. Trade unions hold an exceptional position in the Swedish context, with a union density of 70 per cent in 2012 (Medlingsinstitutet, 2012). Instead of engaging with CSR policies and practices, trade unions attempt to form global framework agreements with Swedish multinationals. In addition, trade union funds are usually invested with a customized RI strategy (Du Rietz, 2013). In terms of NGO influence, NGO Amnesty Business Group previously used AGMs as a forum to promote their views (Sjöström, 2009). However, a more common form of NGO engagement with corporate practices is to disclose information. For example, NGO Swedwatch monitors Swedish companies' conduct and has produced more than 60 reports since its start in 2003 (Swedwatch, 2013).

Policy environment

RI practices in general are not governed by any explicit legal framework. However, the public pension funds are public authorities and are governed by Swedish law. Since 2001 the law suggests that the funds AP1, AP2, AP3 and AP4 take ethical, environmental and other sustainability considerations, but without compromising the overall objective of attaining high financial returns. The framework requires that they include environmental and ethics in their investment policies and annually report to the government with respect to how they adhere to these practices (Bengtsson, 2008).

Concurrently, Regulation 2000:192 prohibits an individual fund from acquiring too large a stake in any listed company (more than 10 per cent of the votes) or unlisted company (30 per cent), somewhat limiting the potential corporate governance influence. Likewise, the AP funds are supposed to compete with each other and not coordinate investments. Despite the general purpose of creating competition between the funds, in 2005 the funds created an Ethical Council, modelled on the Norwegian Governmental Pensions Fund (GPF). Through the Ethical Council, the funds cooperate when targeting environmental and ethical issues and addressing foreign-listed holdings (Bengtsson, 2008).

The public pension fund AP7, the default option for beneficiaries who do not choose a fund manager in the Premium Reserve System, can only vote for foreign holdings according to law. Like the first four public pension funds, it is currently required to take ethical, environmental and other sustainability considerations (Bengtsson, 2008). The fifth fund, AP6, is an evergreen fund that invests directly or through funds in unlisted assets and private equity. Although not explicitly required to take social and environmental issues into account, the fund hired service provider GES to review its sustainability work in May 2012 (Sjätte AP-fonden, 2012).

RI institutions

Eurosif (2012) describes the Swedish market as quite mature; the majority of participants have been active in RI more than 10 years. Today, almost all large asset managers and asset owners have some form of RI policy document. As of December 2013, 37 Swedish asset managers, asset owners and professional service partners have signed the PRI initiative.

To identify the institutions that in some respect participate in RI, one can look at the members of the Swedish RI network organization Swesif and the members of the Swedish version of the Sustainable Value Creation Initiative. In the latter, we find four of the pension funds, AP1–AP4; insurance and pension providers Skandia, Folksam and SPP; as well as the largest Swedish banks, SEB, Swedbank Robur, DNB, Handelsbanken and Nordea. Swesif, which has less stringent membership requirements, has a larger group of asset and fund managers. Swesif also includes asset owners such as the trade union LO and the research funding foundation KK-stiftelsen. Some, like the Swedish Church, are members of both the Sustainable Value Creation Initiative and Swesif. In addition, less formal collaborations among Swedish, Nordic and other foreign RI actors exist. Such collaborations, often limited in terms of time horizon and scope, are particularly common when addressing foreign companies through, for example, engagement (Du Rietz, 2013).

In terms of organization, asset managers generally have, since the early 2000s, specific departments providing RI analysis. An RI department may consist of 4 to 10 RI analysts, often with their own specialization (Du Rietz, 2013). Ethical councils, established to oversee and decide on the application of RI principles, became common among Scandinavian investors in the early 2000s (Bengtsson, 2008). Both of these features remain common, especially among asset managers. In addition, further investor organizations initiate their RI work while others expand and hire new RI staff. As a result, the number of employees working with RI in Sweden is currently growing (Du Rietz, 2013). A reflection of this development is, for example, the increasing number of members of Swesif.

According to Bengtsson (2008), a reason for the Scandinavian RI actors emerging sophistication in the early 2000s was the concurrent emergence and increase in the number and quality of RI service providers. Among the leading Scandinavian service providers today, there is GES Investment Services and Ethix SRI Advisors, both with offices in Stockholm. In 2000, Ethix took part in developing AP7's norm-based screening approach (Ethix SRI Advisors, 2014), whereas GES developed AP1's version of such screening (GES Investment Services, 2014). In addition to these two, the Swedish actors also employ large international RI service providers and asset managers (Du Rietz, 2013).

In the private equity and venture capital sphere, there are fewer actors with a history of responsible investment. However, RI approaches are recently becoming a mainstream phenomenon even in this industry. The state-founded Industrifonden, a venture capital actor investing in small and medium sized Swedish companies, has had a sustainability policy that includes environmental, social and economic aspects since 2013 (Industrifonden, 2013). Sustainability or CSR policy statements are increasingly common among private equity actors such as IK Investment Partners, Ratos, Altor Equity Partners and Nordic Capital, etc. These policies and signatories of PRI are a late addition to Swedish RI development. Private equity actor EQT, for example, signed onto PRI in December 2010 (EQT, 2012), and Nordic Capital published an RI policy as late as June 2013 (Nordic Capital, 2013).

RI issues

Salient 'ESG' issues

In 2009 and 2011, a questionnaire was sent to the 100 largest listed Swedish companies by the Swedish Sustainable Value Creation Initiative. The answers generated reflect the ESG issues that these very active Swedish RI institutions are concerned with. In the 2009 survey, six main environmental, social or sustainability areas were covered: human rights, labour rights, environment, anti-corruption, responsible business conduct and health, working environment and safety. These, in turn, had four governance aspects: accountability of the board, key policy documents, implementation and compliance and communication and reporting. In interviews, the actors emphasized that certain questions incorporated in the survey were not generally reported on by companies, and because the issues were important to the investors, there was a need for this particular survey to collect the information. Among the unique questions, there was, for example, one addressing the issue of accountability of the board and bonus systems linked to ESG indicators (Du Rietz, 2013).

The surveys, particularly the 2009 survey, are almost identical to the Norwegian Sustainable Value Creation Initiative, the forerunner to the Swedish one. Some of the members of the Swedish initiative are also members of the Norwegian initiative, such as Nordea and DnB Nor. Thus the view on ESG issues is not the main divider between the Nordic countries. Swedish Folksam, for example, cooperates in company engagements with Norwegian KLP and Finnish Ilmarinen in the Nordic Engagement Cooperation (NEC), which is partly managed by the service provider GES (Nordic Engagement Cooperation, 2013). Despite the mostly shared views, slightly different perspectives on ESG issues do exist among the actors, particularly among the asset owners. In particular, asset managers sometimes find it troublesome to handle customers' diverging ESG demands. Finding some common values, such as international conventions, is one way to solve this issue. Another is to run parallel analyses, incorporating the customer's specific demands into each fund (Du Rietz, 2013).

Among the venture capital and private equity actors, ESG concerns such as labour standards, human rights, environment, anti-corruption and ethics are emphasized in Nordic Capital's RI policy (Nordic Capital, 2013); Industrifonden emphasizes the environment, ethics and equality (Industrifonden, 2013) and EQT uses the terms environment, ethics and labour and human rights (EQT, 2012). Hence, these actors tend to specify fewer ESG issues and more often use the term 'ethics' than the more experienced equity RI actors.

Conclusion

Sweden occupies, like the other Nordic countries, a top position when countries are ranked in terms of macroeconomic stability, international competitiveness and sustainable growth. In terms of the RI market, the Nordic countries share further traits, such as generally being frontrunners in RI practices. Swedish investors pioneered norm-based screening, and it is still one of the most common RI strategies, together with the exclusion strategy. RI practices tend to spread easily between the Nordic countries, partly because most asset managers active in Sweden consider all of the Nordic markets as their home markets and because of cross-Nordic collaborations such as NEC. The existence of sophisticated Nordic service providers has also affected Swedish RI development.

As a result of the current pension system, all Swedes have invested in financial markets in some way. Sustainability profiles of funds to choose in the Premium Reserve System facilitates savers' decision-making in sustainability issues, and for the passive savers, who decline the right to choose, sustainability consideration is automatically taken by fund manager AP7. The state has hence supported Swedish RI development by requiring public pension funds to consider RI criteria. However, the current framework simultaneously limits the public pension funds possibility to pursue the engagement strategy. Despite this fact, a general trend among Swedish RI investors is to collaborate and conduct company engagements. There are also signs that voting on RI issues is increasing, particularly internationally, because of new available services. Another recent trend is the spreading of RI strategies to further types of asset classes, such as private equity and government bonds. Although a quite mature market, RI activity in the Swedish setting only seems to be increasing.

Notes

1 RI, in this chapter, is defined in line with Cowton (1999: 99) as "a set of approaches which include social or ethical goals in addition to more financial criteria".
2 There are currently no national Eurosif statistics for the impact investment category.
3 Excluding any pension saving through the employer, 66 per cent have private fund savings.

References

AP7 (2013) *Hållbarhetsredovisning 2012–2013,* Stockholm.

Belfrage, C. and Ryner, M. (2009) 'Renegotiating the Swedish Social Democratic settlement: from pension fund socialism to neoliberalization', *Politics & Society,* 37(2): 257–287. Online. Available doi: <10.1177/0032329209333994>

Bengtsson, E. (2008) 'A history of Scandinavian socially responsible investing', *Journal of Business Ethics,* 82(4): 969–983.

Catasús, B. and Johed, G. (2007) 'Annual general meetings – rituals of closure or ideal speech situations? A dual analysis', *Scandinavian Journal of Management,* 23(2): 168–190. Online. Available doi: <10.1016/j.scaman.2006.10.009>

Cowton, C. (1999) 'Accounting and financial ethics: from margin to mainstream?' *Business Ethics: A European Review,* 8(2): 99–107.

Du Rietz, S. (2013) *Accounting in the Field of Governance,* School of Business, Stockholm University, Stockholm. Online. Available HTTP: <http://urn.kb.se/resolve?urn=urn:nbn:se:su:diva-89126>.

EQT (2012) *Responsible Investment Policy for EQT,* p. 3. Online. Available HTTP: <http://www.eqt.se/globalassets/responsibility/responsible-investment-policy.pdf?id=9264>.

Erixon, L. (2011) 'Under the influence of traumatic events, new ideas, economic experts and the ICT Revolution – the economic policy and macroeconomic performance of Sweden in the 1990s and 2000s', in Mjøset, L. (ed.), *The Nordic Varieties of Capitalism,* UK: Emerald, p. xii, p. 420.

Ethix SRI Advisors (2014) *Conflict Minerals: Initiatives, Guidelines and Legal Requirements,* p. 18.

Eurosif (2010) *European SRI Study 2010.* Paris, p. 61

Eurosif (2012) *European SRI Study 2012,* Brussels, p. 68.

Fondbolagens Förening (2012) *Fondspararundersökning 2012,* Stockholm, p. 12.

Fondbolagens Förening (2014) *Fondspararundersökningen 2014,* Stockholm, p. 14.

GES (2014) *Investment Services Corporate History.* Online. Available HTTP: <http://www.ges-invest.com/pages/?ID=66> (accessed 15 September 2014).

Hall, P. A. and Soskice, D. (2001) *Varieties of Capitalism: The Institutional Foundations of Comparative Advantage,* Oxford; New York: Oxford University Press.

Hellman, N. (2005) 'Can we expect institutional investors to improve corporate governance?', *Scandinavian Journal of Management,* 21(3): 293–327. Online. Available HTTP: <http://dx.doi.org/10.1016/j.scaman.2004.06.005>

Industrifonden (2013) *Hållbarhetspolicy,* p. 3. Online. Available HTTP: <http://www.industrifonden.info/sites/default/files/hallbarhetspolicy.pdf>.

Medlingsinstitutet (2012) *Avtalsrörelsen och lönebildningen År 2011,* Stockholm.

Nordic Capital (2013) *Nordic Capital's Responsible Investment Policy ("RI Policy"),* p. 3. Online. Available HTTP: <http://www.nordiccapital.com/media/41598/nc_responsible_investment_policy__updated_version_sept_2014_final.pdf>.

Nordic Engagement Cooperation (2013) *Annual Engagement Report 2013,* p. 18. Online. Available HTTP: <https://www.klp.no/polopoly_fs/1.27009.1406028936!/menu/standard/file/NordicEngagementCooperationAnnualReport2013.pdf>.

Pensionsmyndigheten (2013) *Förbättrad information om hållbart premiepensionssparande,* p. 2. Online. Available HTTP: <https://secure.pensionsmyndigheten.se/download/18.70e56c27145a7fdc958313c3/1370961677180/130612+H%C3%A5llbarhetsprofil+premiepension.pdf>.

Sjätte AP-fonden (2012). *GES är hållbarhetskonsult för Sjätte AP-fonden*. Online. Available HTTP: <http://www.apfond6.se/sv/Kommunikation/GES-ar-hallbarhetskonsult-for-Sjatte-AP-fonden/> (accessed 19 November 2012).

Sjöström, E. (2009) *Shareholder Influence on Corporate Social Responsibility*, Stockholm: Economic Research Institute, Stockholm School of Economics EFI.

Statistiska Centralbyrån (2013). Online. Available HTTP: <http://www.scb.se/sv_/Hitta-statistik/Statistiknyheter/Nyckeltal-for-Sverige/>.

Swedwatch (2013). *Swedwatch tio år*, p. 42. Online. Available HTTP: <http://www.swedwatch.org/sites/default/files/_sw10_webb.pdf>.

UN-PRI. *History*. Online. Available HTTP: <http://www.unpri.org/about-pri/about-pri/history/> (accessed 15 September 2014).

29

Responsible investment in Norway

Ane Jensen

Introduction

As part of the Scandinavian push to promote responsible investment (RI), Norway is considered one of the countries at the very forefront these efforts (see, e.g., Bengtsson 2007, 2008; Eurosif 2012).

Despite a weaker representation in organizations promoting responsible investment, such as the Principles for Responsible Investments (PRI), the assets under management far exceed that of the other Scandinavian countries, primarily due to the strength of the responsible investment guidelines followed by investors for the sovereign wealth fund Norwegian Government Pension Fund – Global. This same fund has also played a key role in forming the guidelines and strategic approaches that define the way responsible investment is thought of by the majority of investors in Norway: a norms-based practice of investment consisting almost exclusively of engagement, norms-based screenings and exclusion, with only minor use of best in class and integration (please see the section on the fund for further detail).

This chapter provides a general introduction to Norway, followed by an overview of the historical and current development of responsible investment in Norway, as well as a description of the primary socially responsible investing (SRI) strategies employed. A few of the key Norwegian players in SRI are then introduced, and finally a few brief thoughts on the challenges ahead and trends for the future are presented.

About Norway

Norway is a small country of some 5.2 million people, making up the northwestern part of the Scandinavian Peninsula. Aside from the mainland, Norway's territory also includes the island Jan Mayen, the sub-Arctic Bouvet Island and the Arctic Archipelago Svalbard. The country spans a total of 148.7 square miles, making it the second least populated country in Europe (Statistics Norway 2014; CIA World Factbook 2014). Norway shares borders with Sweden, Finland and Russia, and Denmark is to the south across the Skagerrak Strait.

Norway is a highly developed country, consistently topping the Human Development Index (ranked first 2010–13), the Democracy Index (ranked first 2010–12) and the Legatum Prosperity

Index (ranked first 2009–13). The country is ranked in the top five for life expectancy according to OECD, and tops the European Union's statistics for healthy life years (HLY), at 72.1 years (OECD 2012; ECHI 2012). Its population is covered by universal health care, and it maintains a strong system for social welfare. Literacy is near 100 per cent, with the expected period of school attendance one of the highest in Europe at 18 years, topped only by Iceland (CIA World Factbook 2014).

Political system

Politically, Norway is a unitary constitutional monarchy, structured as a representative democracy, as in the other Scandinavian countries. Following Montesquieu's tripartite system, Norway has a parliamentary system of government, where both the government and the unicameral parliament, the Storting, hold legislative power. Elections for the Storting are held every four years, and the government must typically have the backing of the parliament to be able to govern. Judicial power is held by the Courts of Justice of Norway, a hierarchical judicial system with the Supreme Court at the apex, which is independent of the legislative and executive branches of power.

The Norwegian Constitution grants the king (currently King Harald V) the official executive power, but as is the case with most modern monarchies the executive power is in practice executed by the cabinet. The royal family stays out of day-to-day politics and fills a purely representative and ceremonial role.

In 2013, the centre-right politician Erna Solberg replaced Jens Stoltenberg as prime minister, replacing eight years of Social Democratic rule with a Conservative-Liberal platform. The new government was elected on promises of lower taxes, stricter immigration laws, increased spending on infrastructure and education and a higher service level.

Norway is divided into 19 first-level administrative counties called 'fylker'. Each county is run by county assemblies, which are elected directly from each county's inhabitants. Government is represented in each county through the appointment of a so-called 'fylkesmann', who effectively acts as a governor.

The counties are further divided into 428 second-level municipalities known as 'kommuner', which make up the smallest unit of local government in Norway. Each of the municipalities has a locally elected mayor, as well as an executive board, and is responsible for education up till grade 10, as well as other locally founded tasks, such as maintaining municipal roads, unemployment, senior citizen services and outpatient health services.

The economy

Norway has the fourth highest GDP income per capita in the world, according to The World Bank and IMF. The country has one of the lowest levels of unemployment in Europe, at just 3.6 per cent. Taxes amount to 43.2 per cent of the gross domestic income, and government spending amounts to 44 per cent of Norway's GDP, with about 9 per cent of public spending funded by revenues from Norway's oil and gas ventures. The country's public debt equals 34 per cent of the domestic economy.

As can be seen in Figure 29.1, Norway has a substantial service sector making up 59 per cent of the country's GDP in 2012, while 26 per cent of the GDP comes from petroleum and gas, and 8 per cent from manufacturing (Norwegian Ministry of Finance 2013).

Monetary policies in Norway are stable and generally follow free market principles, though with a number of state subsidizations, especially in projects meant to promote sustainability, such as renewable energy. The country has low average tariff rates of just 0.5 per cent, and

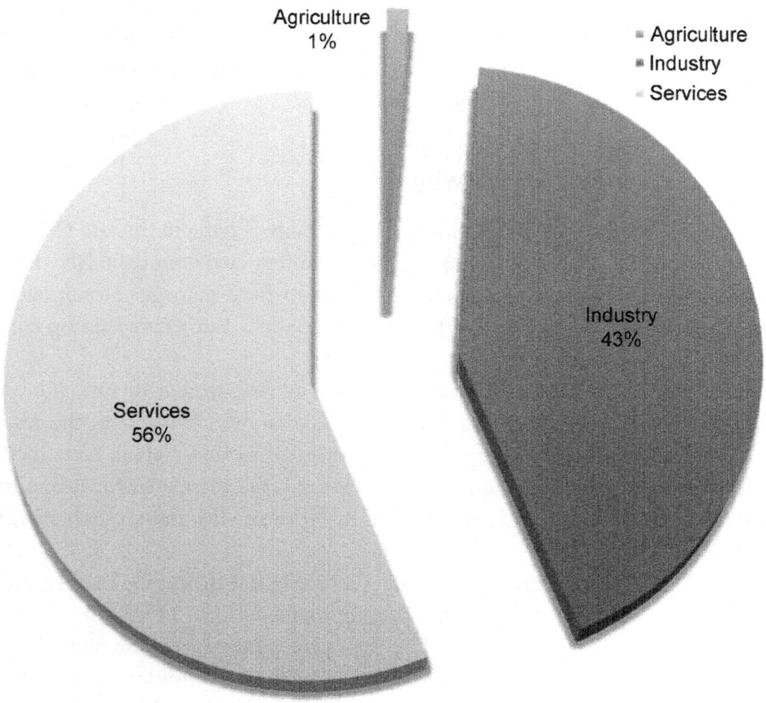

Figure 29.1 Norway's GDP by sector of origin

Source: Author from data from CIA World Fact Book (2013).

holds few barriers to international trade and investment, with the exception of selected screenings and exclusions, typically in areas considered at odds with the investment principles set forth by the Council of Ethics. Though the government holds ownership of the key financial player (the Norwegian Government Pension Fund – Global), the financial sector is generally market-driven.

Generally, the regulatory framework for businesses is transparent and competitive. Starting a business requires meeting minimum capital requirements, but the process is easy and straightforward. Labour costs are high, and bankruptcy procedures are simple and efficient. The regulatory framework generally follows international standards, and credit is allocated on market terms.

Oil and gas

Over the past 40 years, Norway's economic development has been boosted substantially by the country's petroleum and gas ventures. Norway is the largest producer of oil and gas outside the Middle East, though the country is not a member of OPEC. In 2012, the industry was responsible for 26 per cent of Norway's GDP and funded 9 per cent of the country's expenditures (Norwegian Ministry of Finance 2013).

Norway controls petroleum and gas activities in its territory through state ownership of stocks in the key operators of oil fields, as well as controlling licensing agreements for the exploration and production of oil fields. Additionally, the Norwegian state owns all of Petoro, a company that manages the State's Direct Financial Interest (SDFI) portfolio, and performs audits of Statoil's activities, on behalf of the Norwegian government.

Responsible investment in Norway

The development of the Norwegian RI market began taking shape in the late 1980s when Vesta formed Miljøinvest and Grønt Norge, the country's two first environmental BIC-funds (Bengtsson 2007). In 1995, the insurance company and pension fund manager Storebrand introduced the Storebrand Principle Global Fund, which soon became a European flagship for sustainable investment.

However, Norway's position at the very forefront of responsible investment was achieved when the Norwegian Government Pension Fund – Global, which manages the revenues made from oil and gas, implemented a range of detailed ethical guidelines, which were included in the Government Pension Act of 2005. Initiatives such as the UN's Principles for Responsible Investment (UN PRI) are still rather weakly represented in Norway, with just six asset owners and four asset managers as of 2014.

Today, Norway is still at the forefront of SRI. According to Eurosif, the market for responsible investment across the six main investment strategies totalled $US 784 billion in 2012, a growth of over 39 per cent since 2010 (Eurosif 2012). This places Norway as the largest SRI market of the Scandinavian countries, and in the top five markets for responsible investments in Europe. Additionally, the Norwegian Government Pension Fund – Global, which due to its size dominates most of the market for responsible investments in Norway, has come to serve as a form of benchmark for responsible investment, providing guiding principles for investors and asset managers alike, both within Norway and abroad.

The RI market is still evolving. A more recent focus in the public debate has been on how to increase the transparency of the exclusion process, which has led to a number of initiatives, including the publication of each decision made by the Norwegian Government Pension Fund – Global, and the reasoning behind it.

The legal framework

Aside from the Government Pension Act, which provides a framework for the investment activities of the Government Pension Fund – Global, the RI market in Norway is not governed by a legal framework as such. However, due to the size and influence of the Government Pension Fund – Global, which currently is the world's largest sovereign wealth fund, the RI market relies heavily on the guidelines put forth for the fund, as well as the recommendations made by the Council of Ethics.

RI strategies and asset classes

In the Nordic countries, the SRI markets are to a large extent characterized by what Eurosif defines as 'the Scandinavian model'. The investment model is largely based on a combination of ethical exclusions and engagement, and is applied in markets where institutional investors comprise the main players within the SRI market.

This is also true for Norway, where norm-based screening and exclusion make up the two main investment strategies by far, with engagement a distant second (Figure 29.2). Engagement

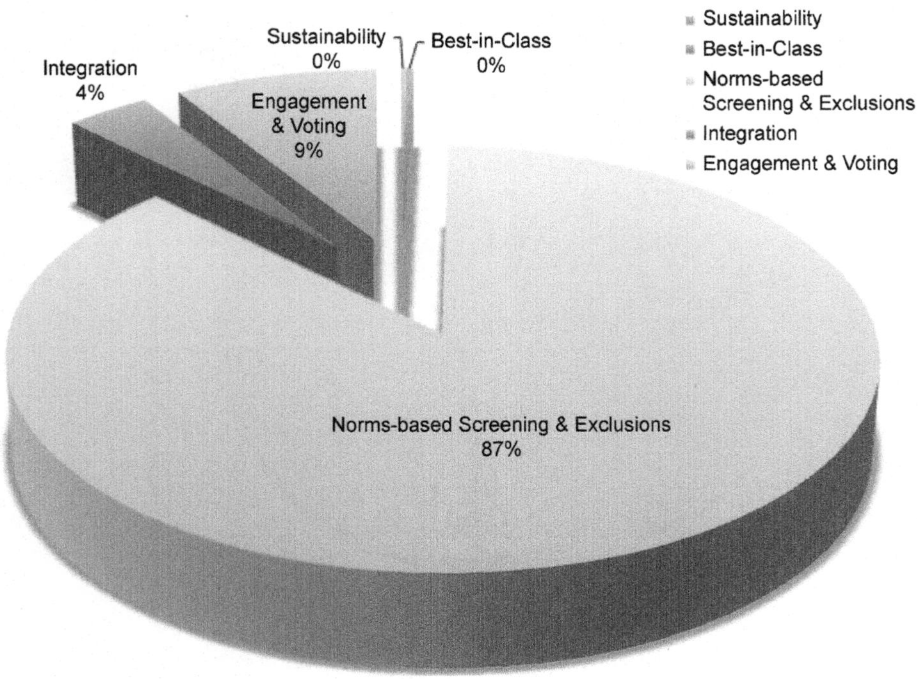

Figure 29.2 Norwegian market evolution by strategy

Source: Author with data from Eurosif (2012).

is here understood in the manner defined by Eurosif as "active ownership through voting of shares and engagement with companies on ESG matters" (Eurosif 2012: 10). And, like its Scandinavian counterparts, the Norwegian RI market is overwhelmingly dominated by institutional investors.

Similar to the rest of the Scandinavian market, the investments made are typically diversified, and funds are rarely limited to one specific category. Positive screenings are limited, and investments follow the best-in-class approach, and sustainability-themed funds only make a very small portion of the Norwegian RI market.

The exclusion criteria used by most investors have followed the guidelines set forth by Norges Bank Investment Management (NBIM) on behalf of the Ministry of Finance, and are formed with the advice of the Council of Ethics. A detailed list of the fund's exclusion criteria can be found under the section on exclusion criteria of the fund, and includes production of weapons, tobacco, companies using child labour and violating labour laws in general and environmental laws, as well as companies violating fundamental humanitarian principles (Ministry of Finance 2013).

Unlike the other Scandinavian countries, Norway's largest SRI asset class is equity, making up 54 per cent of the total Norwegian SRI asset allocation (Figure 29.3). Fixed assets make up 44 per cent; its share shrinking slightly compared to the fixed asset–equity allocation in 2010, where the two were just 0.9 per cent apart. The last 2 per cent encompasses hedge funds, real estate, commodities, PC/VC and structured products (Eurosif 2012).

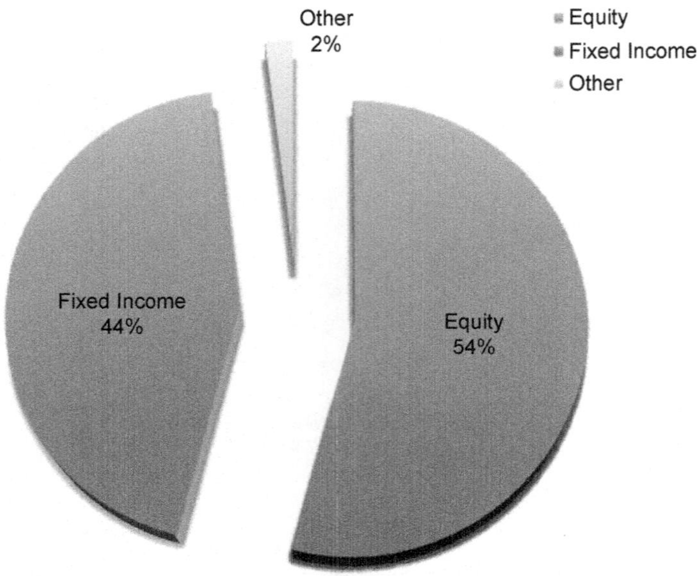

Figure 29.3 Norwegian SRI market asset allocation

Source: Author with data from Eurosif (2012).

The Norwegian Government Pension Fund – Global

By far the largest player and asset owner in the Norwegian RI market is the Norwegian Government Pension Fund – Global, the world's largest sovereign wealth fund.

In 1990, Norway established the fund to help manage the revenues from Norway's oil and gas activities. The fund is a fiscal tool to help reduce the risk of overheating the Norwegian economy with oil revenues, as well as to minimize the volatility of oil price fluctuations. Additionally, the pension fund is intended to help address potential macroeconomic issues associated with the aging of the Norwegian population, though the fund currently has no formal pension liabilities, despite its name (nbim.no).

The fund is managed by Norges Bank Investment Management (NBIM), on behalf of the Norwegian Ministry of Finance, and is owned by the Norwegian people. Policy guidelines and investment strategies are determined by the Ministry of Finance, informed by advice from Norges Bank and the Council of Ethics and discussions in the Storting (nbim.no).

The pension fund invests in financial markets outside of Norway, and fiscal policy states that the structural, non-oil budget deficit can be no greater than the real return of the fund, currently set at 4 per cent for 2013–14 (nbim.no). This is known as 'handlingsregelen', or the budgetary spending rule, first defined in 2001 (regjeringen.no).

As of June 2014, the Norwegian Government Pension Fund – Global is the largest sovereign wealth fund in the world, controlling assets worth NOK 5,434 billion, or $US 888 billion. The fund has an annual return of 6.4 per cent in USD and controls 2.5 per cent of all listed shares in Europe and 1.3 per cent of all listed shares in the world.

The investment strategy employed allows investments up to 60 per cent in capital shares, with the rest in bonds and real estate.

Exclusions and the role of the Council of Ethics

The pension fund practices responsible investment through exclusions of investment opportunities, which are deemed in conflict with the guidelines set forth by the Norwegian Parliament.

The guidelines, specified in the Government Pension Act of 2005 (which can be found at regjeringen.no), provide a framework for the Ministry of Finance, the Council of Ethics and NBIM regarding both the process and the choice of companies to exclude or to put under observation. The guidelines cover all of the fund's investment portfolios, be it equity, fixed income or real estate.[1]

Based on recommendations from the Council of Ethics, and in some cases additional assessment of NBIM on the positive or negative impact of active ownership by the fund, the Ministry of Finance determines the specific exclusion of companies, as well as which to put on a list for observation.

Both the final decision of the Ministry of Finance, as well as the recommendations of the Council of Ethics and reasoning behind it, is made public on government websites after securities in said companies are sold, in an effort to optimize transparency.

The Council of Ethics consists of five members, all appointed by the Ministry of Finance. The Council provides research on and evaluations of the social and ethical performance of specified companies and whether the behaviour of said company is in conflict with the established guidelines for the fund's investments. The Council may act on its own behalf or at the request of the Ministry of Finance.

Exclusion criteria of the fund

The guidelines defined in the Government Pension Act specifically instruct investment managers to avoid investing the fund's assets in companies and organizations that fulfil one of the following criteria. The list and guidelines set forth in the Government Pension Act also forms the basis of exclusion lists used by other investors and asset managers in the Norwegian RI market:

- Are owned or controlled by the fund itself;
- Produce tobacco;
- Produce weapons, which violate fundamental humanitarian principles through their use;
- Sell weapons or military material to countries, which have been restricted for investment by the fund;
- Serious or systematics human rights violations, such as murder, torture and forced labour;
- Use of child labour and other child exploitation;
- Gross violation of labour rights;
- Serious violations of individual rights during conflict or war;
- Severe environmental damage;
- Gross corruption; and,
- Other serious violations of fundamental ethical norms.

Companies considered for exclusion are given the chance to address the concerns raised by the Council of Ethics and are involved in the process early on. They are also given the opportunity to provide comments on the final decision.

Decisions to exclude specific companies are continuously and routinely revisited and can be revised and reversed if circumstances warrant such an action due to new information or altered behaviour by the company in question.

Other key players

While the Norwegian RI market is dominated by the presence of the Norwegian Government Pension Fund – Global, a number of other main investors and asset managers have had and continue to have significant influence on both the Norwegian and the international SRI scene. A few other key Norwegian investors and asset managers, all PRI signatories, are described below.

Storebrand

Storebrand is the largest insurance company and pension fund manager in Norway, as well as a leading company in the Nordic insurance market. The company can trace its beginning back to 1767, and has its current activities focused primarily in insurance, pension fund management and investment.

The company is one of the frontrunners in and early supporters of sustainable investment in Norway and Europe, funding the Storebrand Principle Global Fund, one of the first European environmental funds, in 1995. In 2005, Storebrand implemented minimum standards for responsible investment, which today encompasses all of Storebrand's investments.

The company's sustainable investment guidelines are based primarily on the 10 principles set forth by the United Nations Global Compact, the principles of the PRI as well as other core International Labour Organization (ILO) and UN conventions. The company uses a combination of exclusion and best in class as its RI investment strategy. Currently, 96 companies are excluded from investment, and 98 are deemed best in class.

In 2011, the company was named the Sustainable Asset Owner of the Year by *Financial Times*, and in 2012 the company announced the formation of its sustainability flagship, the global equity mutual fund Storebrand Trippel Smart.

KLP

Kommunal Landspensjonskasse Gjensidig Forsikringsselskap (KLP) is an insurance company managing municipal and county pension assets. The company holds assets exceeding $US 60 billion and serves over 2,600 public sector companies (klp.no).

The company's RI guidelines are inspired by the UN's Global Compact and follow the direction of the Norwegian Council of Ethics. Integration of CSR in all business processes is a stated requirement, and investments are long-term and use ISO 26000, an international standard for social responsibility, as a guide.

The company uses primarily exclusion and engagement in its investment approach and publicizes its reasoning behind each decision for exclusion on its website in an effort to increase transparency. Excluded companies include the French oil company Total in 2013, due to its involvement in Western Sahara, and the Japanese TEPCO, due to failure to eliminate risk of further emissions of radioactive material after an earthquake and subsequent tsunami destroyed TEPCO's Fukushima Dai-ichi nuclear power plant (klp.no).

In 2012, KLP joined forces with the Norwegian Investment Fund for Developing Countries (Norfund) to invest a total of $US 160 million in renewable energy projects, primarily in sub-Saharan Africa (NPRN Online, Sept. 2012).

ODIN

Established in 1990, ODIN Fund Management is the second largest fund manager in Norway, managing equity funds of $US 5.5 billion (PRI 2013). The fund is owned by the savings bank Sparebank 1 Gruppen AS.

ODIN promotes long-term investment and applies 'accepted guidelines' for social and environmental standards, obtained primarily through public sources such as the Council of Ethics and external specialists in SRI. The company uses ethical and risk-based exclusion to identify companies to avoid investing in, as well as engagement with the company following the exclusion.

Challenges and future trends

The Norwegian RI market has experienced significant growth the past few years, and Eurosif predicts that growth will continue in the coming years. Furthermore, the RI market is predicted to become increasingly more mainstream (Eurosif 2012).

While the Norwegian RI market is likely to be at the very forefront of SRI in the coming years, the asset size and nature may change over time. The current all-dominating figure within the Norwegian SRI scene is the Norwegian Government Pension Fund – Global, which is funded by oil revenues from sources that have peaked and will continue to decline in the future. While the Norwegian Government Pension Fund – Global is not the only Norwegian RI investor, it is by far the biggest, so the size of the Norwegian RI market is likely to directly reflect the activities of the fund. For that reason, the continued expansion of the market for responsible investments in Norway is very likely to be dependent on the continued growth of the fund, even as oil revenues continue to decline.

However, despite the decline in revenues of the Norwegian Government Pension Fund – Global, there is a strong belief reflected in both Eurosif and Norsif's research that the market for responsible investment will continue to grow. According to research done by Norsif and referenced by Eurosif, the key incentive for use of SRI criteria among Norwegian asset owners and managers was that SRI is used when there are strong ethical convictions internally. Other incentives listed were using SRI investments to reduce the risk of negative publicity, as well as external pressure to live up to a basic set of ethical guidelines.

The role of other investors in responsible investment is also likely to increase, and investment strategies will evolve. Negative screening, which historically has been the preferred investment approach in the region, is predicted by asset managers to decrease in favour of more prevalent use of positive screenings. Some asset managers predict that an increase in best-in-class strategies is also likely to happen in the next few years (Eurosif 2012).

Note

1 The full text of the Government Pension Act of 2005 can be found on the government website regjeringen.no. An unofficial English translation of the act is available on the website as well.

References

Bengtsson, E. (2007) 'A history of Scandinavian socially responsible investing', *Journal of Business Ethics*, Vol. 82, Issue 4.

Bengtsson, E. (2008) 'Socially responsible investing in Scandinavia – a comparative analysis', *Sustainable Development*, Vol. 16.

CIA World Factbook. Online. Available HTTP: <https://www.cia.gov/library/publications/the-world-factbook/>.

ECHI. Online. Available HTTP: <http://ec.europa.eu/health/indicators/echi/index_en.htm>.

Eurosif. (2012) *European SRI Study*. Online. Available HTTP: <http://www.eurosif.org/>.

KLP. Online. Available HTTP: <http://www.klp.no/>.

Nordic Region Pension and Investment News. Online. Available HTTP: < http://www.nprn-online.com>.
Norges Bank Investment Management. Online. Available HTTP: <http://www.nbim.no/>.
Norway Government. Online. Available HTTP: <http://www.regjeringen.no/>
Norway Ministry of Finance (2013) *The Management of the Government Pension Fund in 2012.*
OECD (2012). Online. Available HTTP: <http://www.oecd.org/>.
PRI. Online. Available HTTP: <http://www.unpri.org/>.
Statistics Norway. Online. Available HTTP: <http://www.ssb.no/en/>.

30

Responsible investment in the United Kingdom

Cristoph Biehl and Jill Atkins

Introduction

Responsible investment in the UK has a long history with early roots in ethical investment funds and other forms of dedicated portfolios managed on an ethical basis. In this chapter we trace the development of the UK's responsible investment landscape. We focus especially on the shift in investment strategy – screening to engagement and integration – which has encouraged the growth of socially responsible investment (SRI). We also emphasize the importance of institutional investor engagement and dialogue, driven by successive codes of corporate governance best practice (the Cadbury Code, the Combined Code and the Stewardship Code in particular).

Responsible investment in the UK has evolved differently from that in other countries, having a heavy emphasis on engagement. While the US has traditionally had a strong ethical investment movement, the style of responsible investment is different, with very little direct contact between companies and their core investors. A similar pattern is found in European countries, where voting is an important corporate governance issue but with relatively few one-on-one meetings taking place between institutional investors and companies. This situation appears to be changing in the European context as French investment institutions, for example, are beginning to use dialogue with investee companies far more frequently.

In this chapter we focus exclusively on the UK and suggest that in the area of engagement and dialogue UK responsible investment may be significantly more advanced than in other places around the world.

Country overview

The United Kingdom of Great Britain and Northern Ireland is a country within Europe and a member state of the European Union (joined in 1973). The United Kingdom consists, as the name suggests, of Great Britain and Northern Ireland. Great Britain consists of England, Wales and Scotland.

The UK is a constitutional monarchy and a Commonwealth Realm, with the queen as head of state and the prime minister as head of government. As the constitution is unwritten, these roles are defined by statutes, passed by the parliament, and conventions. The unwritten nature of the constitution provides a high degree of flexibility, which can be seen by the large number of changes made in the last two decades. The UK legal system consists primarily of legislation, common law and European law. In order for legislation to be passed it needs to be approved by parliament to become a bill, and by the queen to become a law. As the head of state the monarch is expected to act in a neutral manner at all times (i.e. it is expected that she does not interfere with the work of the parliament).

The Commonwealth of Nations can best be described as a voluntary association of 53 independent countries, all former British colonies. These countries are home to nearly 30 per cent of the world's population. Of these 53 countries, 16 are Commonwealth Realms (i.e. countries that have the queen as monarch). These countries include inter alia Australia, Canada and New Zealand.

Within the UK powers were devoluted from the central parliament in Westminster to local parliaments in Wales (Welsh National Assembly), Scotland (The Scottish Parliament) and Northern Ireland (Northern Ireland Assembly). This process started after referenda in 1997 in Wales and Scotland and 1998 in Northern Ireland. Following the referenda three devolution acts were passed by the government. Devolved matters include inter alia health care, education, environment and planning, agriculture and forestry. However, it is included in the acts that the parliament in Westminster remains sovereign and retains the power to amend the devolution acts and pass legislation covering matters included in the acts.

The GDP per capita of the UK as a whole was $37,300 in 2013, with the dominant driver of the economy being the service sector. In 2013 the service sector accounted for 78.9 per cent of total GPD.

Life expectancy in the UK is 80.42 years. Education levels are high; the literacy rate is 99 per cent, and school life expectancy is 16 years.

With 53.3 million people England is the home of 84 per cent of the population of the UK. London, the capital of the UK, is located in the southeast of England. It has 8.3 million inhabitants and is the largest city in the UK.

The strong financial sector within the city makes London one of the most important financial hubs of Europe, and indeed in the world. It is an important driver for the prosperous development of London, but the importance of the financial sector reaches further than London: With the main drivers of the British economy being banking, insurance and business services, London forms a cornerstone of the UK economy as a whole.

The growth and development of responsible investment

Ethical investment

Until the 1960s, ethical investment was practiced predominantly by religious organizations. The early roots of responsible investment involved the creation of dedicated portfolios invested on an ethical basis. These specialized funds were run according to a screening strategy whereby companies were screened in or out of the portfolios according to strict ethical rules. Clients selected portfolios which were most suited to their personal ethical profiles and preferences. Screening has been defined as,

> [a]voiding investments in companies that do not reflect an investor's values . . . The screening process is the inclusion or exclusion of corporate securities in investment portfolios, supporting companies with strong records in certain screens and avoiding investments in firms that fall short in these areas.
>
> *(Henningsen, 2002, p. 163)*

Screening was employed by the earliest forms of ethical investment and is still used by specialist ethical funds. In 1991 approximately £312 million was invested in UK green and ethical retail funds (UKSIF, 2011a). The UK Social Investment Forum (UKSIF) was officially launched in 1991, signifying the growth of ethical investment and the need for a common platform within the UK institutional investment community for collaborative discussion in this increasingly important area. By 1996 investment in UK green and ethical retail funds surpassed £1 billion (UKSIF, 2011b). In 2002, it was estimated that UK investment in ethical funds had grown over the previous 10 years from £318 million to almost £4 billion (Pensions Week, 2002b). These figures demonstrated an increase in traditional ethical investment but not an uptake of 'ethical' investment by the mainstream institutional investment community. It was only when the strategic approach towards ethical investment changed that the mainstream started to become interested.

Best-in-class investment

There is a clear distinction between 'ethical investment' and 'socially responsible investment' (SRI). Essentially, ethical investment refers to specialist investment which employs screening, whereas SRI implies a mainstream investment strategy of engagement and inclusivity (Clarke, 2002). Sparkes (2006) defines SRI as an investment philosophy which combines ethical or environmental goals with financial goals. Screening can have negative impacts on portfolio investment as modern portfolio theory emphasizes the enhanced risks associated with a restricted investment universe (Boatright, 1999, 2008; Solomon, 2013). It is this refocusing of this investment strategy which has effectively allowed ethical investment to evolve from a marginal into a mainstream form of institutional investment (Solomon, 2009d). Since the late 1990s the most significant change has been the shift from screening to a 'best-in-sector', or 'best-in-class', approach whereby investors do not screen out specific industries (such as oil and gas or those producing alcoholic beverages, for example) but select the 'best' companies in every sector according to a range of social, ethical and environmental (SEE) factors. In the investment industry the shift of terminology from 'ethical investment' to 'SRI' (socially responsible investment) and investment according to 'SEE' (social, ethical and environmental) issues signified this change in approach. This change in strategic approach involved a move from screening applied exclusively to dedicated ethical funds to a best-in-sector approach applied across mainstream investment portfolios. A best-in-sector approach is accompanied by tactics of active engagement and dialogue, as the strategy is based on active investors whose direct contact with their investee companies is assumed to improve corporate behaviour in the SEE domain.

Engagement

Engagement and dialogue involves voting by institutional investors and one-on-one meetings between the institutional fund manager and a manager from the investee company as well as shareholder resolutions. An engagement strategy began to be used increasingly in active corporate governance and was endorsed by recommendations of corporate governance codes of practice (Cadbury Report, 1992; Hampel Report, 1998) as a means of improving relationships between companies and their major shareholders. Around 2000, an example of an engagement approach involved an institutional investor engaging with 11 major clothing retailers asking them for information relating to the ethical standards they set for the factories they sourced from around the world. Initially only three of the companies had any code of conduct covering issues such as child labour and working conditions which were in line with the institution's standards. However, within a year the rest of the companies improved significantly their approach to these issues, introducing codes of conduct and/or performing ethical audits of the source factories (Litvack, 2002). This engagement within the clothing sector was carried out by Friends Ivory and Sime (as it was at the time). Another large institutional investor, Morley Fund Management, launched a socially responsible investment engagement programme in 2002 which aimed to monitor investee companies' social, ethical and environmental behaviour (Pensions Week, 2002c). Around the same time, many pension funds also started to advise their fund managers to adopt a socially responsible investment strategy of active engagement. For example, the trustees of the Church of Scotland pension fund were instructed to review the financial implications of the church pension fund's socially responsible investment policy. Baillie Gifford was the pension fund's investment manager at the time, and as an investment institution the church took a lead in active socially responsible investment engagement strategies. The Church of Scotland agreed to move away from a screening strategy and towards a strategy of engagement with investee companies on social, ethical and environmental issues. This shift was primarily due to fears that screening reduces investment return (Wadsworth, 2002).

Around the turn of the century, UK pension fund members (Targett, 2000) and social/environmental lobbyists (Solomon, Solomon and Norton, 2002) began to demand that pension fund managers develop SRI policies and participate in engagement. A best-in-sector approach appeared to be the only way of responding to this demand without reducing investment returns. Increasing awareness in society of social, ethical and environmental issues and a general increase in 'ethicality', a need to be ethical, linked to this heightened awareness, engendered a broader societal interest in SRI. For example, in a discussion of the historical development of SRI, Sparkes (2006) suggested that SRI may be a response to major geopolitical issues, including global warming and the impending climatic crisis. Sullivan and Mackenzie (2006) comment that "There is a growing belief that investors, in particular large institutional investors, have a responsibility to work proactively to address the environmental and social impacts of their investments" (p. 13).

Public resentment for poor business practices and unethical corporate activity was growing (Clarke, 2002). The individual investor (client of investment institutions) began to feel responsible for ensuring that the institutions invested in a way that was acceptable to the client. The potential power held by the financial institutions can be invested 'for the good of all' or can deny any social responsibility (Monks, 2001). Indeed, there has been a growing consciousness that the immense collectivized funds held by investment institutions can be 'used or abused' (Solomon, Solomon and Norton, 2002). Research showed that socially responsible investment by UK pension funds, and in the UK institutional investment community generally, had grown significantly in the decade preceding the new millennium. In the years from 1997 to 1999 a growth of 78.6 per cent in assets under management by UK SRI funds can be seen (Friedman and Miles, 2001). Furthermore, during the decade from 1990 till 2000 the number of SRI funds grew from 18 to 44 (Friedman and Miles, 2001).

The mainstream

Since this transition period around the turn of the century from ethical to SEE investment, SRI has become a mainstream issue in portfolio investment decision-making. Most large institutional investment houses now have a dedicated SRI manager and analysts specializing in SRI issues. Around 2005 there was another shift within the City of London to an approach where institutional investors began to consider ESG (environmental, social and governance) issues in their investment decision-making. Again, this shift to ESG investment signified a centralizing of SEE issues into the heart of investment as they became more firmly linked with corporate governance. The global financial crisis has highlighted the need for a greater ethical approach to business, especially in the banking sector (Biehl et al., 2012). Further, UK institutional investors were blamed to a large extent for an alleged lack of engagement with banks prior to the credit crunch. Indeed, the Walker Review (2009) highlighted the need for institutional investors to take a more active role in engaging with investees in order to proactively monitor, and effect change in, their behaviour. The outcome of this review was the Stewardship Code (FRC, 2010) which includes an allusion to the need for institutional investors to escalate their engagement activities where an issue of social or environmental concern is detected.

Shareholders have, over time, been concerned that SRI may restrict the investment universe and result in lower financial returns. Boatright (2008) explains that finance theory implies screened funds should have a lower return because of reduced diversification and higher transaction costs. However, evidence from around 2000 suggested that SRI benchmark indices were outperforming the market (Martin, 2002). Indeed, the change from SRI to ESG has been accompanied by a growing perception in the financial markets that SRI enhances rather than reduces investment returns (Mansley, 2000; Mayo, 2002; Solomon and Solomon, 2006). Recent empirical evidence from interviews with UK fund managers and pension fund directors indicates that although there is no strong statistical evidence, there is a growing belief that financial returns to investment are positively linked to SEE performance in companies and therefore to SRI (Solomon and Solomon, 2002; Solomon, 2013). Indeed, the risk-driven approach to SRI endorses SRI on the basis that improved corporate management of SEE risks through improved internal control leads to improved financial performance and better returns to investors (ACCA, 2000; Cowe, 2001; Montagnon, 2002). As explained in Louche and Lydenberg (2011), responsible investment can be motivated by a desire to identify social and environmental factors which may lead to financial risks which could affect the investment portfolio. The endorsement in 2006 by the United Nations of the Principles of Responsible Investment has highlighted the significant risks associated with 'irresponsible investment' and has illuminated the financial as well as societal benefits of responsible investment. It is largely the acknowledgment that ESG issues, especially climate change, present a significant and material financial risk, which has forced the responsible investment agenda into the mainstream (Solomon, 2010; Solomon et al., 2011).

The current state of UK responsible investment

The latest figures show substantial amounts of investment funds being managed on an ESG basis. The latest data show that nearly £940 billion in assets is managed responsibly in the UK. This is approximately 14 per cent of the over £6.5 trillion in responsibly managed assets tracked by sustainable investment and finance associations around the world (UKSIF, 2011a, p. 10). The UK currently ranks second in terms of the number of signatories to the UN-backed Principles for Responsible Investment, with 118 signatories. Only the US has more, and European countries have significantly fewer signatories (e.g. France, 70; Germany, 17) (UKSIF, 2011a). The latest evidence suggests that over half (54 per cent) of all British adults with investments want to "make money and make a difference" with their savings and investments (UKSIF, 2011a, p. 11).

Codes and legislation

In addition to voluntary codes of corporate governance best practice and shifts in societal attitude towards a more socially responsible approach to investment there have been some regulatory and legal developments which have influenced both the financial and corporate sectors. The change to pension fund law, which was operationalized in July 2000 and which forced pension fund trustees to disclose the extent to which (if at all) their funds consider social, environmental and ethical factors in their investment decisions, had a substantial impact on attitudes towards and practice of SRI in UK pension funds (ACCA, 2000; Cowe, 2001; Solomon and Solomon, 2002). As a result of the change in pension fund legislation, there was a significant increase in the value of UK equities held under SRI mandates (Brown, 2006). The Myners Report (2001) further highlighted the need for trustees to be more aware of their responsibilities, especially in terms of being aware of, and understanding, the risks involved in their portfolio investment. Ensuring that investee companies have a good track record in the SEE area is as important an issue for trustees as ensuring investee companies are managing currency effectively or avoiding bad debts. These moves, however, to improve the role and responsibilities of trustees were initially confined to the UK, as the European Commission decided not to apply the new trustees' SRI disclosure regulation across EU member states (Pensions Week, 2002a). Another important influence on SRI was the Modern Company Law Review which called for greater stakeholder accountability.

In recent years, the topic of responsible investment has built up momentum. This led inter alia to the passing of the Companies Act in 2006 which included the mandatory disclosure of voting records of institutional investors. However, this part of the Companies Act has not yet been brought in force (Eurosif, 2012).

The UK Stewardship Code in 2010 provided a set of good practice standards for engagement with companies. Whilst in general it is a voluntary code for asset managers, asset owners and service providers, it is mandatory for UK-regulated asset managers to report on a 'comply or explain' basis (Eurosif, 2012). Two years after the UK Stewardship Code, the latest UK Corporate Governance Code was published by the Financial Reporting Council in 2012. This report has been continuously developed since its introduction by the Cadbury Committee in 1992. It can be seen as a "guide to a number of key components of effective board practice" (FRC, 2012), including long termism and sustainable success. Similarly, the FRC updated the Stewardship Code in 2012. A report produced by the FRC in 2013 assessed the effectiveness of the Stewardship Code and asserted that in December 2013 there were 290 signatories to the Stewardship Code (FRC, 2013).

Private social and environmental reporting (SER)

A predominantly UK phenomenon?

As mentioned in the introduction to the chapter, one-on-one meetings between institutional investors and their investee companies have evolved more quickly and to a greater degree in the UK than in other countries, and "the UK is widely recognized as a global hub for sustainable and responsible financial services with about 14 per cent of that total managed by our world leading practitioners and firms" (UKSIF, 2011a, p. 4). The UK's advanced position in responsible investment is partly due to the investors being more proactive but also due to greater receptiveness and openness on the part of their investee companies. It seems that the UK institutional investment community has to some extent led the way in achieving detailed dialogue with their investee companies, and now other countries' investors are beginning to follow suit.

The shift from a screening strategy to a best-in-sector approach changed the ethical investment landscape to a new era of socially responsible investment which began to infiltrate the mainstream of UK institutional investment. ESG considerations have become the cornerstone of the new age of 'responsible investment' on the basis of material risks and opportunities arising from this approach. A substantial body of research has borne witness to this evolution, especially to the development of private social and environmental reporting, namely the one-on-one meetings between institutional investors and their investee companies devoted specifically to social and environmental issues.

One interview-based study found that the process of private social and environmental reporting (SER) had developed significantly since around 2000, with investors asking detailed questions of their investees in private meetings regarding their social and environmental impacts and policies (Solomon and Solomon, 2006). This study also uncovered an interchange of information between the two parties which was becoming increasingly 'dialogical' (i.e. two-way rather than unidirectional): companies were asking investors about social and environmental concerns, as well as investors asking investees. Further, the study found evidence that the private disclosure process was feeding into public sustainability reporting such that private SER was informing sustainability reports and helping to improve the quality and quantity of reporting. By 2006, assets managed responsibly in the UK had grown to about £540 billion in 'Broad SRI', mainly engagement and integration (UKSIF, 2011a, p. 9). There were concerns raised in the literature as to whether private SER represented a genuine exercise in enhanced stakeholder accountability, through the consideration of ESG issues in investment decision-making, or whether the meetings were more about a 'joint green myth' being created between the companies and their investors to enhance their public image (Solomon and Darby, 2005). A further study found that private SER was especially focusing on climate change issues and that private climate change reporting was accelerating in quality and quantity (Solomon et al., 2011). Climate change risks and opportunities were receiving increasing attention within meetings, and investors were asking detailed questions about the strategies their investees were developing to deal with these upside and downside issues. The research also suggested that private SER was increasingly dominated by a discourse of risk and opportunity in relation to climate change concerns.

Pension funds and ESG awareness

In the area of pension fund investment, a study commissioned by the Association of Chartered Certified Accountants (ACCA) found significant deficiencies among the pension fund trustee community in relation to their consideration and understanding of climate change issues. From a series of interviews with trustees from corporate pension funds, the researcher found that trustees had generally a very poor understanding of how climate change could represent a material issue for pension fund investment (Solomon, 2009a). Furthermore, the trustees were largely ignorant of their fund managers' programme of engagement and dialogue and often did not read the annual or biannual reports provided by their fund managers on their activities. A follow-up study found that there had been a sharp improvement in their attitudes and approach as the trustees interviewed had sought counsel on climate change risk by, in many cases, calling in their fund manager to give a presentation on climate change materiality and its implications for pension fund investment (Solomon, 2009b).

Work carried out by UKSIF mirrored these findings to some extent. The third biennial survey (2011) of the UK pension funds of companies seen as leaders in social responsibility showed early signs of a step change in the number of these corporate pension funds that were responding to the case for responsible ownership and investment. The findings suggested that once pension funds chose to adopt a responsible investment policy, they tended to deepen their practices over time (UKSIF, 2011b). The report ranked pension funds according to platinum, gold and silver, with three achieving platinum status (as opposed to only one in the two earlier surveys). These were the BT Pension Scheme, the Co-operative Pension Scheme (PACE) and the F&C Asset Management Ltd. Pension Plan. The report also found that responsible investment policies are increasingly being applied to a diverse range of assets, including private equity, bonds and property. Despite these improvements, the report suggested that the majority of corporate pension funds still need to accelerate their progress in implementing responsible investment practices to respond effectively to the risks and opportunities posed by ESG issues.

Conclusion

To summarize, there has been a significant and marked shift in UK attitudes to responsible investment, with the institutional investment industry shifting over approximately a 20-year period from individualistic, bespoke investment in ethical funds to an overarching, mainstream approach to responsible investment. The most significant UK feature in the responsible investment landscape has been the growth of engagement and dialogue, specifically in the form of private social and environmental reporting. Indeed, one-on-one meetings between UK institutional investors and their investees on ESG issues has become commonplace in recent years. Whether this trend continues to grow and whether it is taken up strongly by other countries remains to be seen. One study explored the possible future route for responsible investment and suggested that if responsible investment continues to become more embedded within mainstream institutional investment it will effectively disappear, with SRI specialists becoming superfluous as mainstream fund managers and analysts will be increasingly conversant with ESG issues (Atkins et al., 2015). A recent trend in corporate reporting is the development of integrated reporting, with integrated reports providing a more holistic view of companies, combining social, ethical and environmental issues with traditionally financial issues in one report. Atkins et al. (2015) suggest that private reporting is also becoming increasingly integrated, as ESG issues are becoming more integrated in corporate dialogue with core investors. This indicates a move towards integrated private reporting whereby separate SRI one-on-one meetings between institutional investors and investees gradually disappear, with ESG issues being discussed in mainstream financial meetings. In a way, the potential disappearance of SRI and SRI specialists would be the outcome of success, as it would show that responsible investment has become part of everyday mainstream investment behaviour and strategy.

References

Association of Chartered Certified Accountants (ACCA) (2000) *Turnbull, Internal Control and Wider Aspects of Risk*, commissioned by the ACCA Social and Environmental Committee, Certified Accountants Educational Trust, London.

Atkins, J. F., Solomon, A., Norton, S. D. and Joseph, N. L. (2015) 'The Emergence of Integrated Private Reporting', forthcoming in *Meditari Accountancy Research.*

Biehl, C. F., Hoepner, A.G.F. and Liu, J. (2012) 'Social, Environmental, and Trust Issues in Business and Finance', in Kent Baker, H. and Nofsinger, J. R. (eds), *Socially Responsible Finance and Investing*, New York: John Wiley & Sons.

Boatright, J. R. (1999) 'Ethics in Finance', *Foundations of Business Ethics*, Oxford, UK: Blackwell Publishers.

Boatright, J. (2008) *Ethics in Finance*, 2nd edn, Malden, USA: Blackwell Publishers.

Brown, M. (2006) 'Communicating Risks to Pension Fund Trustees: The UKSIF Sector Notes Project', in Sullivan, R. and MacKenzie, C. (eds), *Responsible Investment* (chapter 12), Sheffield, UK: Greenleaf Publishing.

Cadbury Report (1992) *The Financial Aspects of Corporate Governance*, London: The Committee on the Financial Aspects of Corporate Governance.

Clarke, M. (2002) 'The Checks and Balances of SRI', *Pensions Week*, 8 July: 22.

Cowe, R. (2001) 'Investing in Social Responsibility: Risks and Opportunities', *Association of British Insurers (ABI) Research Report*, London: ABI.

EuroSIF (2012) *European SRI Study*, Brussels: EuroSIF.

Financial Reporting Council (FRC) (2010) *The UK Stewardship Code,* London: FRC.

Financial Reporting Council (FRC) (2012) *The UK Corporate Governance Code,* London: FRC.

Financial Reporting Council (FRC) (2013) *Developments in Corporate Governance 2013: The Impact and Implementation of the UK Corporate Governance and Stewardship Codes,* London: FRC.

Friedman, A. L. and Miles, S. (2001) 'Socially Responsible Investment and Corporate Social and Environmental Reporting in the UK: An Exploratory Study', *British Accounting Review* Vol. 33: 523–548.

Hampel Report (1998) *Final Report*, London: Committee on Corporate Governance.
Henningsen, C. (2002) 'Investing as if the World Really Mattered', *Corporate Environmental Strategy*, Vol. 9, No. 2: 163–171.
Litvack, K. (2002) 'Using Index Funds to Meet the SRI Challenge', *Pensions Week*, 10 June: 26–27.
Louche, C. and Lydenberg, S. (2011) *Dilemmas in Responsible Investment*, Sheffield, UK: Greenleaf Publishing.
Mansley, M. (2000) *Socially Responsible Investment: A Guide for Pension Funds and Institutional Investors*, UK: Monitor Press.
Martin, I. (2002) 'SRI Winners and Losers Revealed as Returns Shine', *Pensions Week*, 9 September: 2.
Mayo, C. (2002) *Corporate Governance: Too Many Codes, Too Much Box-Ticking, Too Little Shareholder Value*, presentation at the Corporate Governance conference, London, 31 July – 1 August.
Monks, R.A.G. (2001) *The New Global Investors: How Shareholders Can Unlock Sustainable Prosperity Worldwide*, Oxford, UK: Capstone Publishing Limited.
Montagnon, P. (2002) *Defining the ABI's Position on Corporate Governance and Investor Guidelines*, presentation at the Corporate Governance conference, London, 31 July – 1 August.
Myners (2001) 'Institutional Investment in the United Kingdom: A Review', *The Myners Report*, London, UK.
Pensions Week (2002a) 'EC to Adopt Soft Touch on SRI', *Pensions Week*, 22 July: 6.
Pensions Week (2002b) 'Education Key to Selling SRI', *Pensions Week*, 12 August: 6.
Pensions Week (2002c) 'SRI Behaviour Monitor Launched', *Pensions Week*, 26 August: 8.
Solomon, J. F. (2013) *Corporate Governance and Accountability*, 4th edn, New York: John Wiley.
Solomon, J. F., Solomon, A., Joseph N. L. and Norton, S. D. (2011) 'Private Climate Change Reporting: A Discourse of Risk and Opportunity?', *Accounting, Auditing and Accountability Journal*, Vol. 24, No. 8: 1119–1148.
Solomon, J. F. (2010) *Corporate Governance and Accountability*, 3rd edn, New York: John Wiley.
Solomon, J. F. (2009a) 'Pension Funds and Climate Change: One Year On', *ACCA Discussion Paper*, September.
Solomon, J. F. (2009b) 'Pension Fund Trustees and Climate Change', *ACCA Research Report*, No. 106.
Solomon, J. F. (2009d) 'The Transformation of Socially Responsible Investment', in Young, S. (ed.), *Contemporary Issues in International Corporate Governance*, Australia: Tilde University Press.
Solomon, J. F. and Solomon, A. (2006) 'Private Social, Ethical and Environmental Disclosure', *Accounting, Auditing & Accountability Journal*, Vol. 19, No. 4: 564–591.
Solomon, J. F. and Darby L. (2005) 'Is Private Social, Ethical and Environmental Disclosure Mythicizing or Demythologizing Reality?', *Accounting Forum*, Vol. 29: 27–47.
Solomon, J. F., Solomon, A. and Norton, S. D. (2002) 'Socially Responsible Investment in the UK: Drivers and Current Issues', *Journal of General Management*, Vol. 27, No. 3, Spring: 1–13.
Solomon, A. and Solomon J. F. (2002) 'The SRI Dilemma for Pension Fund Trustees: Some Perceptions of their Evolving Role', Conference Paper presented at the *Multinational Finance Society Conference*, Paphos, Cyprus, July.
Sparkes, R. (2006) 'A historical perspective on the growth of socially responsible investment', in Sullivan, R. and MacKenzie, C. (eds), *Responsible Investment*, Sheffield, UK: Greenleaf Publishing.
Sullivan, R. and Mackenzie, C. (2006) 'Introduction', in Sullivan, R. and MacKenzie, C. (eds), *Responsible Investment*, Sheffield, UK: Greenleaf Publishing.
Targett, S. (2000) 'Friends Plans to Give Ethical Lead', *Financial Times*, Companies & Markets, 8 May.
UKSIF (2011a) *Taking Responsibility: Achieving Resilience*, London, UK.
UKSIF (2011b) *Responsible Business Sustainable Pension, The Third UKSIF Report on how the UK Pension Funds of Socially Responsible Leaders Are Approaching Responsible Investment*, London, UK.
Wadsworth, G. (2002) 'Holy Jocks Rock SRI Stocks', *Pensions Week*, 9 September: 3.
Walker Review (2009) *A Review of Corporate Governance in UK Banks and Other Financial Industry Entities*, London: HM Treasury.

31

Reflection

Responsible investment around the world

Maria Laura Tinelli

Introduction

How do you clock enough air miles in economy class to get all the perks that come with a Silver or Gold BA membership? This was never an intentional aim when I accepted the role of Head of Global Networks for the Principles for Responsible Investment (PRI), but after my first year in the role I received an exquisite envelope filled with leather bag tags and the little piece of plastic that would make my travel a nicer experience.

What follows is a recollection of my experiences, thoughts and views on responsible investment (RI) from the Regional Networks I had the honour to manage for the PRI. From Australia to Peru, I went around the world, hearing firsthand what investors, regulators, asset owners and other organizations were doing in terms of translating ESG into practice, their struggles. I met the leaders, the laggards and the fast learners who are leapfrogging and learning from best practice to fast-forward the process of becoming responsible investors.

My position gave me a unique opportunity to stand in the middle of it all and see, first of all, how fast this 'movement' for RI was growing (for good and bad) and where. It allowed me to see who the key actors were that prompted this to happen within different countries and the patterns that most countries seemed to follow in the path to RI. Government regulation is a key driver for the adoption of responsible investment, and this chapter provides some concluding thoughts on this topic. It draws on the country chapters detailed in this volume and on concrete examples of the countries I interacted with throughout my career.

A fast-growing momentum for responsible investment

The 2008 financial crisis exposed the failures of the financial system and the costly effects it has on the real economy and people's lives. The investment and financial sectors were targeted as the culprits of the unfairness of the burden then imposed over millions of taxpayers. Non-governmental organizations (NGOs) exposed how poverty levels have grown exponentially as a result, and how while the 1 per cent had managed to amass fortunes, the 99 per cent was less well off – their homes repossessed and their taxes diverted from health and education to resuscitating the financial system. Governments reacted the only way they could, with new measures, regulation and colossal fines that came into place before credit rate agencies could blink twice.

There are several drivers for the growth of RI in different markets, namely regulation, reputational risks and the advance of social media, mounting evidence of the financial materiality of ESG issues, RI-promoting organizations, and growing demands from asset owners and beneficiaries for more sustainable approaches to investment. Increasingly, investors concerned about the impact of short-termism within investment research, asset allocation and performance monitoring recognize that integrating ESG issues into both investment analysis and stewardship practices forms part of their fiduciary duty to clients and beneficiaries and want to see their portfolios managed in a way that systematically assesses drivers of risk and return over longer time frames.[1]

Regulation

In countries where there is not a long tradition of ethical or socially responsible investment, regulation has been one of the key drivers for the uptake of RI practices and the incorporation of ESG issues into investment analysis and corporate practices. Regulation can take the shape of an explicit requirement for pension funds to include ESG issues in their investments as part of their fiduciary duty (as is the case of South Africa). It can take the form of guidelines issued by the central bank that are applicable to all investors (as is the case of Brazil), stewardship codes (in the UK, Japan, and upcoming in Malaysia), stock exchange requirements or different versions of the 'comply or explain' approach present in various other countries in the world.

Countries with some form of regulation or guidelines in terms of RI and ESG incorporation are the ones most advanced in terms of the development of RI practices. What we also see is that some of these countries also have the highest uptake of different RI-related bodies or organizations, such as Social Investment Forums, the PRI, the Global Reporting Initiative, the UN Global Compact, and Sustainable Stock Exchanges, amongst others.

We can find the pioneers in RI regulation in Europe, Australia, South Africa and Brazil. Other countries are taking their first steps towards incorporating RI practices by picking examples of how regulation is developed in these regions and adapting it to local needs. Countries like Peru, Chile, Namibia, Botswana, Zambia and Japan, among others, are replicating what they find useful from leading countries in the field and adapting it to local regulation.

Multilateral bodies and regional economic areas also play a key role in the regulation and promotion of responsible investment. As an example, the European Union advocated for the importance of standardized reporting through the creation of the European Transparency Code in 2004 to harmonize the disclosure of extra financial data across Europe and to improve the clarity on principles and processes of SRI mutual funds.

The Scandinavian countries were among the first regions in the world to introduce regulatory frameworks and standards aimed at promoting ESG activities in financial management. The frameworks of Norway, Sweden and Denmark provide a good example of this approach.

As described by Ane Jensen in Chapter 29 of this volume, Norway's position at the very forefront of responsible investment was achieved when the Norwegian Government Pension Fund implemented a range of detailed ethical guidelines that were included in the Government Pension Act of 2005. Despite the fact that there is no other regulation in place, the size and influence of the pension fund means that the RI market relies heavily on the guidelines put forth for the fund, as well as the recommendations made by the Council of Ethics. Norway is the largest RI market of the Scandinavian countries, and one of the top five markets for responsible investments in Europe. As a result, the Norwegian Government Pension Act, and the ethical guidelines that accompany it, has become a benchmark for responsible investment good practice, providing guiding principles for investors and asset managers alike, both within Norway and worldwide.

In Sweden, as explained in the chapter by Du Rietz, the public pension funds are public authorities governed by Swedish law, which suggests that the funds take ethical, environmental and other sustainability considerations without compromising the overall objective of attaining high financial returns. The framework requires that they include environmental and ethical standards in their investment policies and annually report to the government with respect to how they adhere to these practices.

As a result of the exceptional welfare system in Finland, as explained by Antti Savilaakso, Finnish legislation has traditionally been thorough in the fields of labour and environmental law. Despite the fact that there is no actual legislation concerning ESG for investors, there exists a natural uptake of these issues by investors.

Karin Buhmann details the introduction of mandatory corporate social responsibility (CSR) reporting for institutional investors and large companies, including publicly owned companies, in Denmark in 2008. Denmark further amended this regulation in 2012 to strengthen the reporting requirement, introducing mandatory reporting on human rights and climate change mitigation action for organizations whose CSR policies refer to those issues. The Danish case complements other Nordic developments in which public authorities are directing CSR through public policy implementation.

Within Continental and Eastern Europe what we see is a clear distinction between the leaders and those taking their first steps in terms of responsible investment. Motivation for adopting RI practices and regulations varies from country to country.

The UK, with its enforcement of the Pensions Act in 2000, requires reporting from its pension funds on ESG issues. The issue of fiduciary duty lies at the centre of the debate in the UK. The Myners Inquiry in 2010 led to the establishment of a pensions regulatory body and the introduction of new codes guiding the responsibilities of pension fiduciaries, which expanded the scope of pension fund fiduciary duty and argued that corporate engagement should be a central component of an expanded definition of fiduciary duty, a view that eventually resulted in the UK's Stewardships Code in 2010 and the revision of the meaning of fiduciary duty in the Pensions Fund Act in 2014.[2]

In France, legislation on responsible investment refers to disclosure regulations on ESG issues for listed companies (2001) and the introduction of the Pension Reserve Fund and law relating SRI issues to Employee Savings Plans in 2001. The Grenelle 2 legislation passed in July 2010 introduced new obligations for asset managers to disclose how ESG factors are being incorporated into their investment strategies.

The Netherlands is one of the most advanced RI markets in the world and a leader in the field. Responsible investment has been steadily growing since the 1970s and is now deeply rooted in the way businesses operate. Although there is no RI-specific legislation, the Pension Federation has published a handbook regarding responsible investment followed by its subscribers. Furthermore, the umbrella organization for insurance companies introduced a Responsible Investment Code, effective beginning 2012, that requires its members to take a number of initiatives to make their investments more responsible.

The Belgian Law on Supplementary Pensions (2003) requires pension funds to disclose in their annual report the degree to which social, environmental and ethical criteria are taken into account in their investment strategy (Article 42 of the law). As explained by Louche, Van Liedekerke and Peeters in Chapter 23, the new Federal Plan Law from 2004 made transparency disclosures on environmental and ethical criteria and the way in which ESG criteria were used in the exercise of shareholder rights mandatory in both the prospectus and annual reports for Belgian

Collective Investment Schemes. In 2009, the Belgian Asset Managers Association adopted a Code of Conduct integrating elements of responsible investment.

As stated by Sofronova (Chapter 17, this volume), "The Russian government recognizes the challenge the country faces in attracting foreign investors, and the president has made the task of improving the country's investment attractiveness a top policy priority." Increased transparency and respect for the rule of law are two key drivers to achieve this.

> New laws, such as the federal law on the Central Depositary and amendments to federal laws on the securities markets and on joint stock companies were also adopted. These changes contributed to the improvement of ownership rights, information disclosure and transparency and payment of dividends. . . .[Moreover] the Ministry for Economic Development has been looking into the possibility of introducing amendments regulating affiliation and liability of controlling shareholders in the Joint-Stock Companies Act and Limited Liability Companies Act. . . . On 1 July 2014 a new securitization law with rules regulating securitization of various types of assets came into force, which . . . is a significant improvement to current practices and brings Russia in line with established structured finance markets.
>
> *(Sofronova, this volume)*

South Africa has the most developed financial system as well as regulatory frameworks for institutional investors amongst the countries of the region. Responsible investment has been top of mind in the South African retirement fund industry, following the amendment of Regulation 28 of the Pension Funds Act and the development of the Codes for Responsible Investing in South Africa (CRISA) in 2011. As explained by Mans-Kemp and Viviers in this volume, the Pension Funds Act

> explicitly states that prudent investing should take into account all factors that could materially affect an investment, including factors of an ESG character. . . . According to experts in the field, the amendments to Regulation 28 represent a "fundamental shift in South Africa's investment landscape" and "Regulation 28 has finally put ESG into every Trustee Board Room as it ensures that Trustees must consider and apply their minds to sustainable investing" (Pretorius, 2011).

Neighbouring countries are looking to South Africa in the development of regulations in retirement funds. Namibia, Botswana, Zambia and Swaziland have been referring to South Africa's Regulation 28 in the process of updating their own pension regulations. CRISA and the PRI have been influential in initiating discussions regarding the formulation of Code for Responsible and Sustainable Investing in Zimbabwe (CRESIZ).

Brazil is the leading the way in responsible investment in South America. As Yamahaki and Gaban explain in Chapter 8 of this volume, in terms of regulation in 2009, the Brazilian National Monetary Council issued a resolution "requiring all Brazilian pension funds to state in their investment policy whether they consider social and environmental issues in their investment decisions (BCB, 2009). Although integrating ESG issues was not made mandatory, this piece of legislation brought the topics of responsible investment and sustainability to the forefront of the discussion in the pension fund industry." In 2014, Resolution 4327 from the Central Bank established guidelines for financial institutions for the creation and implementation of social and environmental responsibility policies, and Resolution 3792 demands that pension funds explain and report on whether they observe ESG issues in their investment policies and practice.

The other countries in the region do not have clear regulation or policy on the matter. Public and private pension funds in different countries in South America are heavily regulated in terms of their investment options and the percentages they can invest in different asset classes. Most are restricted to investment in fixed-income assets. It is worth noting that Peruvian regulators have started exploring how countries in Europe, South Africa and Brazil have regulated on this matter, and are trying to select best practices and adapt them according to their local needs. On this note, the president of Chile, Mrs. Bachelett, has commissioned a review of the Chilean pension fund system by national and international experts in the field.

In Australia, RI-related legislation is primarily focused on environmental issues. As Young and O'Halloran point out, legislation, and more important a company's response to it, is used in formulating the analyst's views about company value and selection of stocks (e.g. National Greenhouse Energy Reporting Scheme, Energy Efficiency Opportunities, Section 299 of the Corporations Act, CLERP 9, Principles of Good Corporate Governance). In addition there is disclosure legislation directed at investors when designing and marketing investment products (e.g. Section 1013DA Disclosure Guidelines).

Sakuma-Keck provides a comprehensive analysis of the development of RI-related regulation in Japan. The Japanese government has focused on corporate disclosure and reporting as RI enablers. Sakuma-Keck points out that this focus has not been adopted across the board, perhaps because financial institutions and pension funds, as well as ESG issues, touch on the competencies of different ministries in Japan. In 2013 President Abe unveiled his government's sustainable growth strategy, including a planned amendment to the Company Act to promote 'truly independent' external directors, introducing a Japanese version of the UK Stewardship Code that seeks to encourage private investment and improve the return of long-term investment to the country.

In 2010, as Voorhes explains, US shareholder advocates won an important victory when the Dodd-Frank Wall Street Reform and Consumer Protection Act was signed into law. It gave authority to the Securities and Exchange Commission (SEC) to implement a rule to allow shareholders, within certain parameters, to nominate directors to the boards of their portfolio companies and to have access to the company's proxy statement to make the case for their nominees. The new law specifies, too, that publicly traded companies must allow shareholders – at least once every three years – to hold an advisory vote on their executives' pay packages.

In my meetings with investors and asset owners in the US, they all agreed on one fact: in a culture as litigious as the US, asset owners, investors and companies will seek regulation before acting, and unless compulsory ESG incorporation is clearly stated there, the chances are that they will continue with business as usual and not change their practices to incorporate ESG considerations.

Reputational risks

The material impact that ignoring or including ESG issues has over financial performance of investments has been widely demonstrated over the last 10 years, both by major events and a myriad of well-documented academic studies and research.

The World Economic Forum 2014 Global Risks report[3] presents the findings of a survey asking a multi-stakeholder group of leaders from business, government, academic and non-governmental and international organizations what the top risks facing the current economic system are. Respondents identified issues clustered into environmental, social, geopolitical or economic, and then plotted their likelihood of occurring in the next five years and their potential severity. Two patterns were revealed by these issues: the first has to do with how they exhibit classic 'tragedy of the commons' characteristics; that is, that the short-term advantage for one investor/group can mean long-term disadvantage for everyone. This point is particularly relevant to the large investors known as 'universal owners' – those who have a stake in every listed company within a particular jurisdiction. These investors, including most large pension funds with long-term investment horizons, suffer from these market failures. The second pattern revealed has to do with how these issues can be categorized as E, S or G issues which can and do affect investment performance.

The risk of reputational damage and the potential for financial damage through a high-profile ESG-related incident is also a driver for asset owners to expect their fund managers to effectively manage ESG risks and to prevent such outcomes. Examples from around the world, like BP and Tepco (on environmental issues); Lonmin and Foxconn (on social issues); and Barclays, UBS, Lehman Brothers, RBS and GlaxoSmithKline (on governance), clearly illustrate the material impact on loss of share value, reputation, and fines paid that result from ignoring ESG issues. Moreover, the increased demand for public accountability fuelled by the rise of instant global communication (i.e. social media) further exposes companies and investors to reputational and financial risks.

In my experience, reputational risks are paradoxically more damaging in countries where the environmental and social impact of companies and investors operating in a careless manner is not directly felt, but where societies are better educated and have the time and interest in holding them to account. These same societies and economies are the ones where RI is most developed both from an investor and regulation perspective. Investors and companies behave differently according to where they are in the world; regulation and civil society play a key role in this. These same societies are the ones that have the power to boycott companies, press for changes via annual general meetings or demonstrations and make investors nervous, thus affecting share prices, which is the ultimate lever to induce behavioural change in companies and financial institutions alike.

Mounting evidence of the financial materiality of ESG issues

On the positive side, appropriate consideration of ESG issues leads to opportunities for growth and better performance. In 2012, Deutsche Bank carried out a meta-study of the academic research to date. It found that all of these academic studies agree that companies with high CSR or ESG ratings have a lower cost of capital. In fact, nearly 90 per cent of these studies found that such companies outperformed the market to some degree.

These studies demonstrate that ESG can lead to opportunities or losses. Opportunities include operational efficiency, increased market share and revenues, improved access to capital, improved risk management and increased shareholder value. Losses range from penalties and fines to litigation, loss of social and regulatory license to operate, reputational costs, increased regulation, as well as higher costs for energy and increasingly scarce raw materials.

Well-performing companies also excel in their environmental credentials, they have high labour and social standards and they have clear and transparent governance structures that are conducive to better management and results. As a whole, what we see across the board is that countries that have a good levels of economic development are also the same countries where RI is most developed, and where companies and investors alike incorporate ESG as part and parcel of the way they operate, produce or function. For further evidence on this point see the Country Tables in Appendix 31.1 of this part of the volume.

Growing demands from asset owners and beneficiaries

What I could observe through my work at the PRI is that whenever economies are opening up to international investment or to private investors seeking funding, they are exposed to a growing number of demands and expectations related to responsible investment.

In the case of South America, for example, as countries such as Peru, Colombia, Bolivia, Chile, Argentina and Ecuador open up to foreign investment they face a range of requirements from investors. These have to do with the environmental credentials of the company or institution, disclosure and transparency on the governance structure and procedures within the invested companies, and information on employee welfare, working conditions and affected communities, to name a few. As a result, regulators in Peru and Chile, for example, are liaising with peers from Europe and other parts of the world to explore how to implement changes conducive to ESG integration within national law. Moreover, investors and companies from these countries are signing up to different multilateral global initiatives such as the PRI, the UN Global Compact, the Sustainable Stock Exchanges initiative, the Global Reporting Initiative (GRI), and the International Integrated Reporting Council (IIRC), to name a few, in order to satisfy the demands of international investors and asset owners.

In addition to this, multilateral RI and CSR reporting initiatives and principles-based organizations also demand a variety of indicators and information on the institutions' performance on ESG, further increasing the need for investors and companies to not only implement changes, but also to report on them.

With the advance of social media, and as a result of the increasing awareness of society at large of the negative effects that the misalignment between the financial sector and society have on their day-to-day lives, individuals, including beneficiaries, have reclaimed their voice and are demanding that their rights as the ultimate owners of the capital entrusted to pension funds are respected and taken into consideration. This pattern is particularly clear in universities, where students are pushing their university endowments to invest factoring ESG considerations into their analysis and decisions or demanding divestment from fossil fuels or other highly contentious sectors. Clear examples of this are the Harvard Endowment, which signed on to the PRI in 2014 after years of negotiation and pressure with their students, or the movement created within UK universities called 'push your parents' to systematically lobby pension funds to include ESG into their practices.

Lastly, the millennial generation, now reaching their twenties are adding to the demand for investments that consider environmental and societal impacts and corporate governance issues. According to a 2013 survey by Merrill Lynch Private Bank and Investment Group, 30 per cent of millennial investor respondents said that 'values-based investing' options were important in selecting a wealth management firm.

International ESG reference standards, principles, conventions, norms and collaborative initiatives

There are more than 60 internationally recognized standards and bodies that operate within the RI and sustainability field (see the Appendix 31.1 for a detailed listing) to which investors, companies and asset owners subscribe and are governed by.

Although the development of these different frameworks is positive in many different ways, in my experience, working with investors in different countries, there are three recurring issues. The first one is that there is a duplication of effort and work with some of the organizations operating in the RI field. A very clear example is the local and regional SIFs and the PRI. Many of these initiatives require a fee, and investors do not necessarily see the added value of signing up to two initiatives that in essence provide the same function.

The second is that the reporting burden both for investors and companies has exponentially increased after the last financial crisis, and with the incorporation of regulation specific to RI in many countries. This has been good news for consultancy firms and different service providers who are responding to this demand. It has been bad news for small and resource-constrained asset owners or companies who need to report but lack the capacity internally or the funds necessary to hire consultancy firms to report on their behalf. GRI has done a great job simplifying this reporting and could serve as a model for others.

The third issue is the 'green washing' and 'blue washing' exercises that many of these initiatives and fora lend themselves to. The lack of enforceability and transparency requirements of many of these initiatives means that investors and companies alike can subscribe and get the 'green' (environmental) or 'blue' (UN-related or social) stamp of approval, without much real change in practice. The impressive success of initiatives such as the PRI banked on the fact that the committed group of asset owners that created the organization demanded that their fund managers subscribe to the initiative. Fund managers subscribed in large numbers; the only requirement was to pay a minimal annual fee, and in return they got the PRI stamp of approval on their RI credentials. Since 2013, the PRI has wisely introduced the mandatory requirement that all signatories, with the exception of service providers and supporters, must report on their activities and efforts to progress in their path to becoming a responsible investor. Although the results reported by signatories do not carry any penalty with them, nor are they audited, they are a step in the right direction, as transparency will push investors to improve their practices.

On the positive side, newcomers to the RI market will start their journey being able to select the right organizations they need to sign up with and shop around for the ones that provide the best services and that allow them to be at the centre of the debate on RI issues internationally.

Conclusion

Today, the PRI represents more than USD $45 trillion of assets under management. My personal view and experience is that if those trillions of US dollars were being invested in a responsible manner the financial and economic paradigm would have already changed, and RI would not be a niche or a percentage of a fund's portfolio but rather business as usual. The fact that we are still taking, identifying and demonstrating the added value that being a responsible investor brings in terms of returns, and more important to society and the environment as a whole, means that there is still a long way to go.

There are some inspiring examples and countries that are leading the way, as demonstrated in this volume. In these places RI is becoming the norm and not the exception. But it is clear that many more need to follow if we are to shift the way the financial system defines business as usual.

Between the countries leading the way in terms of RI, the effects of the last financial crisis, pressure from civil society, access to global information in real time, the millennials entering the job market, regulation and multilateral institutions paving the way for RI to further develop, the road ahead looks promising. As I have mentioned many times when talking to students in different parts of the world, our job working in this field is to pave the way for the next generation so that by the time they enter the market responsible investment loses the word 'responsible' and is just referred to as investment. Our job is to put ourselves out of a job.

Appendix 31.1

International RI reference standards

Reference Standards

General

The IFC Performance Standards

The IFC Environmental, Health and Safety Guidelines

The IFC Environmental and Social Management Toolkit for Private Equity Funds

The Equator Principles

The UN Global Compact

The Global Reporting Initiative

The Principles for Responsible Investment

The US Private Equity Council Responsible Investment Guidelines

The EDFI Principles for Responsible Financing and Guidelines for Fund Investments

CERES Principles

Interfaith Centre on Corporate Responsibility

Global SIFs Association of Sustainable & Responsible Investment in Asia, RIAA, US SIF, EuroSIF, UKSIF, AfricaSIF

Australian Council of Superannuation Investors (ACSI)

CFA Institute of Financial Market Integrity

Global real Estate Sustainability Benchmark (GRESB)

Environment

The Montreal Protocol

The Rio Conventions: Convention on Biological Diversity; United Nations Convention to Combat Desertification; United Nations Framework Convention on Climate Change

The UN Framework Convention on Climate Change, the Kyoto Protocol & the Copenhagen Accord

The Stockholm Convention

The Rotterdam Convention

The Basel Convention

The Convention on International Trade in Endangered Species of Wild Flora and Fauna

The International Standards Organisation Standards, ISO 9000 & ISO 14000

Forestry Stewardship Council

Marine Stewardship Council

Roundtable on Sustainable Biofuels

Roundtable on Sustainable Palm Oil

UN Environment Programme Finance Initiative (UNEP FI)

Investor Group on Climate Change (Australia/New Zealand)

Institutional Investors Group on Climate Change

Climate Disclosure Project (Water, Forest, Climate Change)

Social Matters

The ILO Fundamental Conventions

The Universal Declaration of Human Rights

ILO Declaration on Fundamental Principles and Rights at Work

ISO 26000

The Occupational Health and Safety Assessment Series OHSAS 18000

Ethical Trading Initiative

Fair Labour Association

Voluntary Principles on Security and Human Rights

The UN Guiding Principles on Business and Human Rights (UNGPs)

Corporate Governance

The UN Convention against Corruption

OECD Guidelines for Multinational Enterprises

The UN Anti-Corruption Toolkit

The OECD Anti-Bribery Convention

Transparency International's Corruption Perceptions Index

Shareholder Association for Research and Educations (SHARE)

Asian Corporate Governance Association

Appendix 31.2
Country tables

(Alphabetical Austria through to the United States)

1. Austria, Germany, Switzerland

Agnes L. Neher

	AUSTRIA	*GERMANY*	*SWITZERLAND*
		COUNTRY OVERVIEW	
Population (2013)	8,221,646	81,147,265	7,996,026
Life expectancy (2011)	80.04 years	80.32 years	82.28 years
Literacy rate	98%	99%	99%
School life expectancy	16 years	16 years	16 years
Religious groups	Roman Catholic 73.6%, Protestant 4.7%, Muslim 4.2%, other 3.5%, unspecified 2%, none 12%	Protestant 34%, Roman Catholic 34%, Muslim 3.7%, unaffiliated or other 28.3%	Roman Catholic 41.8%, Protestant 35.3%, Muslim 4.3%, Orthodox 1.8%, other Christian 0.4%, other 1%, unspecified 4.3%, none 11.1%
Government type	Federal republic	Federal republic	Formally a confederation but similar in structure to a federal republic
Legal system	Civil law system; judicial review of legislative acts by the Constitutional Court	Civil law system	Civil law system; judicial review of legislative acts, except for federal decrees of a general obligatory character
GDP/capita (PPP) (2012)	$43,100	$39,700	$46,200

	AUSTRIA	*GERMANY*	*SWITZERLAND*
		COUNTRY OVERVIEW	
Main industries	Construction, machinery, vehicles and parts, food, metals, chemicals, lumber and wood processing, paper and paperboard, communications equipment, tourism	Among the world's largest and most technologically advanced producer of iron, steel, coal, cement, chemicals, machinery, vehicles, machine tools, electronics, food and beverages, shipbuilding, textiles	Machinery, chemicals, watches, textiles, precision instruments, tourism, banking, insurance
Unemployment rate (2012)	4.4%	5.5%	2.9%
Public debt/GDP (2012)	73.4%	81.9%	52.4%
Market value of publicly traded shares (2012)	$100.4 billion	$1.184 trillion	$932.2 billion
Internet users/ population	72.6%	80.3%	76.9%
Special cultural aspects		Strong green party	Grassroots democracy
		RESPONSIBLE INVESTMENT OVERVIEW	
Overall RI market without overlays	$7.66 billion* (€5.6 billion)	$100.21 billion* (€73.3 billion)	$54.10 billion** (CHF 48.5 billion)
Overall RI market growth rate	17%	16.3%	14.7%
Institutional RI market	$3.09 billion* (€2.26 billion)	$60.79 billion* (€44.471 billion)	$28.98 billion ** (CHF 26 billion)
Retail RI market	$3.92 billion* (€2.87 billion)	$39.40 billion* (€28.819 billion)	$25.10 billion ** (CHF 22.5 billion)
# of PRI signatories	5	47	59
# of PRI asset owner signatories	1	15	6
# of PRI investment manager signatories	4	21	40
# of PRI professional service provider partners	0	11	13
Asset classes used in RI	Bonds (83%), equity (15%), other (25%)	Bonds (57%), equity (23%), money market (10%), other (10%)	Equity (53%), bonds (31%), other (16%)
Overall financial market size	3.6%		3.6%
Launch year of first RI investment fund			
Launch year of national RI organization	Forum Nachhaltige Geldanlagen 2001	Forum Nachhaltige Geldanlagen 2001	Forum Nachhaltige Geldanlagen 2001
Largest three RI asset owners			

(Continued)

	AUSTRIA	*GERMANY*	*SWITZERLAND*
		RESPONSIBLE INVESTMENT OVERVIEW	
Largest three RI investment managers		Union Investment, KfW Bank	Bank Safra-Sarasin, Ethos-Pictet, Credit Suisse AG, Zürcher Kantonalbank
Important RI professional service partners		oekom research AG	robeccoSAM
Other relevant RI organizations	Forum Nachhaltige Geldanlagen	Forum Nachhaltige Geldanlagen, Association of Critical Shareholders (Kritische Aktionäre)	Forum Nachhaltige Geldanlagen
Major ESG issues of concern to society over the last decade	Exclusion of controversial weapons, nuclear energy, production and trade of weapons, pornography, tobacco and gambling.	Exclusion of cluster munitions, trade of weapons, direct investment in food commodities, pornography, tobacco, gambling nuclear energy and animal testing.	Exclusion of cluster munitions, best-in-class-approach
Currently debated ESG issues		Renewed abandonment of nuclear power stations	Proxy voting and integration ESG factors into financial analysis
		RESPONSIBLE INVESTMENT LEGISLATION	
Legislation on institutional investors and ESG issues	Obligation for pension funds integrating ESG criteria to report on the issues in 2005; Umweltzeichen.	Obligation to report on EES-criteria considered in the investment process for pension funds since 2001 and for direct insurers since 2005.	Since 2002, Swiss pension funds have to establish rules on exercising shareholder rights.
Legislation on investment managers and ESG issues		Since 2004, large asset management companies must report on non-financial/EES performance criteria in their annual reports; German Investment Modernization Act 2003.	
Legislation on corporations and ESG issues	Umweltzeichen	Renewable Energies Act since 2001	
		ADDITIONAL RELEVANT RESPONSIBLE INVESTMENT CRITERIA	
	'Umweltzeichen': A state-run environmental quality label for all kinds of products, including financial ones. Existence of 'ethical banks'	Existence of 'ethical banks'	Existence of 'ethical banks'

	AUSTRIA	GERMANY	SWITZERLAND
	Additional Relevant Responsible Investment Criteria		
Sources employed in the responsible investment section of tables	CIA World Factbook, accessed 11/12/2013. Eurosif SRI Study 2012http://www.eurosif.org/publication/european-sri-study-2012/, accessed 11/12/2013. FNG Marktbericht Nachhaltige Geldanlagen 2013, http://www.forum-ng.org/en/publications-and-literature/publications.html, accessed 11/12/2013. PRI, http://www.unpri.org/signatories/signatories/, accessed 11/12/2013.		

* Exchange EUR/USD 23/12/2013: 1.36707

** Exchange CHF/USD 23/12/2013: 1.12

2. Australia

Anna Young and Louise O'Halloran

	AUSTRALIA
	Country Overview
Population	23 million
Life expectancy	Female: 84 years Male: 79 years
Literacy rate	Total population: 99% Indigenous population: 20%
School life expectancy	12 years
Religious groups	Christian 68%, Buddhist 1.9%, Hindu 0.5%, Muslim 1.5%, Jewish 0.4%, other 0.5%, no religion 11.7%, N/A response 15.5%
Government type	Liberal democratic: reflects British and North American models. At the same time, uniquely Australian.
Legal system	Multi-tiered system involves cooperation between federal and state parliaments and local councils that make laws.
GDP/capita (PPP)	Total GDP: $1.5 trillion Per capita GDP: $65,217
Main industries	Agriculture; construction; innovation, science and technology; manufacturing; mining; retail; service industries; tourism; transport
Unemployment rate	5.8%
Public debt/GDP	29.30%
	Country Overview
Market value of publicly traded shares	$1.198 trillion
Internet users/population	82%
Special cultural aspects	Indigenous heritage Multi-cultural immigrant population
	Responsible Investment Overview
Overall RI market	$142 billion
Overall RI market growth rate (three-year average)	$142 billion represents approximately 16% of total assets under management (TAUM) in Australia, having grown from 13% of TAUM in 2011 and 8% in 2010.

(Continued)

AUSTRALIA	
	Responsible Investment Overview
Institutional RI market	The breakdown between wholesale and retail funds under management is unable to be reliably calculated.
Retail RI market	The breakdown between wholesale and retail funds under management is unable to be reliably calculated.
# of PRI signatories	126
# of PRI asset owner signatories	34
# of PRI investment manager signatories	79
# of PRI professional service provider partners	13
Asset classes used in RI	Cash, equities, fixed income, property, infrastructure, social bonds
Overall financial market size	$876 billion
Launch year of first RI investment fund	1986
Launch year of national RI organization	2000
Largest three RI asset owners	Local Government Super (LGS) VicSuper Unisuper
Largest three RI investment managers	AMP Capital Investors Hunter Hall International BT Investment Management
Important RI professional service partners	Bloomberg Corporate Analysis Enhanced Responsibility (CAER) CGI Glass Lewis FTSE MSCI Regnan Sustainalytics
	Responsible Investment Overview
Other relevant RI organizations	Australian Council of Superannuation Investors (ACSI) Business Leaders Reporting Forum ESG Research Australia Investor Group on Climate Change (IGCC) PRI Country Network PRI Regional Academic Network Responsible Investment Association Australasia (RIAA) GRI Australian Focal Point
Major ESG issues of concern to society over the last decade	Escalation of extreme weather events and changing weather patterns – especially flood, drought and fire Critical water flow issues related to the Murray-Darling River (Australia's 'food bowl') owing to over-extraction Controversy around the introduction of a price on carbon

	Responsible Investment Overview
Currently debated ESG issues	Competition for land among agriculturalists, conservationists and extractive industries Whether to extract and use Australia's massive uranium deposits A steady and significant rise in problem gambling following the legalization of poker machines in pubs in the 1990s Civil backlash against logging of native and old growth forests, especially in Tasmania Public uncertainty about and mistrust of the investment markets as a result of the Global Financial Crisis and associated local consequences Human rights in the Asian supply chain 'Brown labeling' of cigarettes Gender diversity at board and executive level in Australian corporations Investment risk in the food industry related to the rising rates of diabetes, heart disease and obesity Market uncertainty and confusion related to the winding back of climate change policy and initiatives by the Liberal Government, including the repeal of carbon pricing Expansion of coal mining and export facilities leading to greater carbon asset risk exposure Expansion of coal seam gas mining in prime agricultural areas Supply chain working conditions, especially in Asia Corporate governance especially related to executive and board remuneration, conflict of interest, short-termism and diversity
	Responsible Investment Legislation
Legislation on institutional investors and ESG issues	ASIC Section 1013DA disclosure guidelines
Legislation on investment managers and ESG issues	ASIC Section 1013DA disclosure guidelines
	Responsible Investment Legislation
Legislation on corporations and ESG issues	Direct Action Plan, Emissions Reduction Fund and related carbon policies CLERP 9 Corporations Act 2001 Section 299 Principles of Good Corporate Governance National Greenhouse Energy Reporting Scheme
Sources employed in responsible investment section of tables	Australian Bureau of Statistics, http://www.abs.gov.au/AUSSTATS/abs@.nsf/Lookup/4102.0Main+Features10Mar+2011. Central Intelligence Agency, The World Factbook, https://www.cia.gov/library/publications/the-world-factbook/rankorder/2200rank.html. PRI, http://www.unpri.org/signatories/signatories/?country=Australia (accessed 10 February 2014). Responsible Investment Association Australasia, '2013 Responsible Investment Benchmark Report', http://www.responsibleinvestment.org/wp-content/uploads/2013/07/2013-Benchmark-Report.pdf.

3. Belgium

Céline Louche, Luc Van Liedekerke and Herwig Peeters

BELGIUM	
	Country Overview
Population	11.14 million (March 2014 est.)
Life expectancy	79.65 years (2012 est.)
Literacy rate	99% (July 2011)
School life expectancy	17 years (2011)
Religious groups	Roman Catholic 75%, other (includes Protestant) 25%
Government type	Federal parliamentary democracy under a constitutional monarchy whereby the King of the Belgians is the head of state and the prime minister of Belgium is the head of government in a multi-party system.
Legal system	Civil law system based on the French Civil Code. Note that Belgian law continues to be modified in conformance with the legislative norms mandated by the European Union; judicial review of legislative acts.
GDP/capita (PPP)	$43,413 (2012 est.)
Main industries	Engineering and metal products, motor vehicle assembly, transportation equipment, scientific instruments, processed food and beverages, chemicals, basic metals, textiles, glass, petroleum
Unemployment rate	8.5% (2013 est.)
Public debt/GDP	99.6% of GDP (2012 est.)
Market value of publicly traded shares	$229.9 billion (31 December 2011)
Internet users/ population	81.3% (December 2011)
Special cultural aspects	Belgium is a multilingual and multicultural country characterized as a culture of compromise. It has two cultural communities (Flemish and French) straddling the cultural boundary between Germanic and Latin Europe. The country has three linguistic groups: Dutch-speakers, mostly Flemish (about 60%), French-speakers, mostly Walloons (about 40%), and a small group of German-speakers (less than 1%).
	Responsible Investment Overview
Overall RI market	$12 billion; 315 RI vehicles (investment funds, notes, insurance products, etc.) (as of December 2012)
Overall RI market growth rate (three-year average)	4% per year (average 2009 to 2012)
Institutional RI market	77% of RI AUM
Retail RI market	23% of RI AUM
# of PRI signatories	4
# of PRI asset owner signatories	0
# of PRI investment manager signatories	3
# of PRI professional service provider partners	1

BELGIUM	
	RESPONSIBLE INVESTMENT OVERVIEW
Asset classes used in RI	Equities (30%), bonds (66%), monetary/deposits (4%)
Overall financial market size	$135 billion AUM (collective investment funds)
Launch year of first RI investment fund	1984: First RI saving account, Krekelsparen 1992: First two investment funds, VMS Luxinter Ethifond and KBC Eco Fund
Launch year of national RI organization	1992, Ethibel, an independent consultancy agency for responsible investments
Largest three RI asset owners	Information not available.
Largest three RI investment managers	In terms of number of SRI products: KBC (53.02%) Dexia (17.62%) BNP Paribas (12.30%)
Important RI professional service partners	Forum Ethibel (www.ethibel.be) Vigeo (www.vigeogroup.com) Sustainalytics (www.sustainalytics.com)
Other relevant RI organizations	BELSIF (www.belsif.be) BEAMA (Belgian Asset Managers Association; www.beama.be) RFA (Reseau Financement Alternatif; www.rfa.be) FairFin (www.fairfin.be) ARISE (www.aristastandard.org)
Major ESG issues of concern to society over the last decade	Armament/cluster munitions GMOs Hazardous substances Layoffs and personal turnover
Currently debated ESG issues	Transparency Food speculation Land grabbing Coal finance Nuclear energy Regulation, norms
	RESPONSIBLE INVESTMENT LEGISLATION
Legislation on institutional investors and ESG issues	Vandenbroucke Law (2004): Pension funds are required to disclose in their annual report the degree to which social, environmental and ethical criteria are taken into account in the investment strategy.
Legislation on investment managers and ESG issues	2007 and 2009: Belgian parliament enacted two laws prohibiting Belgian investors from directly or indirectly financing of the production, commercialization, use or possession of anti-personnel mines, sub-munitions, and depleted uranium weapons.
Legislation on corporations and ESG issues	
Sources employed in the responsible investment section of tables	Eurosif, European SRI Study 2010 and 2012 Forum Ethibel, Duurzaam sparen en beleggen in Belgie, 2010 RFA, L'investissement socialement responsable en Belgique, Rapport 2011 Mira Report, 2013 PRI website as of 20/09/2012

4. Canada

Olaf Weber

CANADA	
	Country Overview
Population	34,030,589 (July 2011 est.)
Life expectancy	Total population: 81.38 years Male: 78.81 years Female: 84.1 years (2011 est.)
Literacy rate	Total population: 99% Male: 99% Female: 99% (2003 est.)
School life expectancy	Total: 17 years Male: 17 years Female: 17 years (2004)
Religious groups	Roman Catholic 42.6%, Protestant 23.3% (United Church 9.5%, Anglican 6.8%, Baptist 2.4%, Lutheran 2%), other Christian 4.4%, Muslim 1.9%, other and unspecified 11.8%, none 16% (2001 census)
Government type	A parliamentary democracy, a federation, and a constitutional monarchy
Legal system	Common law system except in Quebec, where civil law based on the French civil code prevails
GDP/capita (PPP)	$39,400 (2010 est.) Country comparison to the world: 22 $38,500 (2009 est.) $39,800 (2008 est.) Note: Data are in 2010 US dollars
Main industries	Transportation equipment, chemicals, processed and unprocessed minerals, food products, wood and paper products, fish products, petroleum and natural gas
Unemployment rate	8% (2010 est.) Country comparison to the world: 92 8.3% (2009 est.)
Public debt/GDP	84% of GDP (2010 est.) Country comparison to the world: 15 83.3% of GDP (2009 est.)
Market value of publicly traded shares	$2.16 trillion (31 December 2010) Country comparison to the world: 8 $1.681 trillion (31 December 2009) $1.002 trillion (31 December 2008)
Internet users/ population	26.96 million (2009) Country comparison to the world: 16
Special cultural aspects	French and English as official languages. Cultural differences in the financial sector between Quebec and other provinces. High percentage of immigrants and of Canadians not being born in Canada. Stronger public social system and public pension system compared to the US.

CANADA	
	Responsible Investment Overview
Overall RI market	$530.9 billion
Overall RI market growth rate (three-year average)	19%
Institutional RI market	$46.3 billion, or about 9% of the total
Retail RI market	$25.3 billion, or 5% of the total
# of PRI signatories	44
# of PRI asset owner signatories	17
# of PRI investment manager signatories	23
# of PRI professional service provider partners	4
Asset classes used in RI	Core SRI, broad SRI, renewable energy, impact investing
Overall financial market size	Total assets under management $2.747 billion (2010)
Launch year of first RI investment fund	1986, Ethical Growth Fund by VanCity
Launch year of national RI organization	1989, Social Investment Organization
Largest three RI asset owners	
Largest three RI investment managers	
Important RI professional service partners	Sustainalytics Mercer LLC
Other relevant RI organizations	Socialfinance.ca Mars Centre for Impact Investing
Major ESG issues of concern to society over the last decade	*Environmental concerns*: Climate Change, oil sands, extractive sector *Social concerns*: Diversity, human rights, consumer protection *Corporate governance*: Management structure, employee relations, executive compensation
Currently debated ESG issues	Sustainability, climate change, extractive sector, oil sands, First Nations, community development, impact investing
	Responsible Investment Legislation
Legislation on institutional investors and ESG issues	Canadian Securities Administrators (CSA) regulatory disclosure
Legislation on investment managers and ESG issues	No special legislation regarding RI
Legislation on corporations and ESG issues	OSC Notice 51-717 Corporate Governance and Environmental Disclosure (http://www.osc.gov.on.ca/en/SecuritiesLaw_sn_20091218_51-717_corp-gov-enviro-disclosure.htm)

(Continued)

CANADA	
	Additional Relevant Responsible Investment Criteria
	Strong extractive industry and controversies about oil sands First Nations concerns Social finance and impact investing
Sources employed in the responsible investment section of tables	Principles for Responsible Investment (2010). http://www.unpri.org/, accessed 25/05/2015.Chartered Accountants of Canada (2010). https://cpacanada.ca/en, accessed 25/05/2015.

5. China

Qian Li

CHINA	
	Country Overview
Population	1,349,585,838 (July 2013 est.)
Life expectancy	Total population: 74.84 years Country comparison to the world: 96 Male: 72.82 years Female: 77.11 years (2012 est.)
Literacy rate	Total population: 92.2% Male: 96% Female: 88.5% (2007)
School life expectancy	Total: 12 years Male: 11 years Female: 12 years (2009)
Religious groups	Daoist (Taoist), Buddhist, Christian 3–4%, Muslim 1–2% Note: Officially atheist (2002 est.)
Government type	Communist state
Legal system	Civil law influenced by Soviet and continental European civil law systems; legislature retains power to interpret statutes. Note that criminal procedure law was revised in early 2012.
GDP/capita (PPP)	$12.38 trillion (2012 est.) Country comparison to the world: 3 $11.48 trillion (2011 est.) $10.51 trillion (2010 est.) Note: Data are in 2012 US dollars.
Main industries	World leader in gross value of industrial output; mining and ore processing, iron, steel, aluminum, and other metals, coal; machine building; armaments; textiles and apparel; petroleum; cement; chemicals; fertilizers; consumer products, including footwear, toys, and electronics; food processing; transportation equipment, including automobiles, rail cars and locomotives, ships, and aircraft; telecommunications equipment, commercial space launch vehicles, satellites

CHINA	
Country Overview	
Unemployment rate	6.4% (2012 est.) Country comparison to the world: 66 6.5% (2011 est.) Note: Registered urban unemployment, which excludes private enterprises and migrants, was 4.1% in 2012.
Public debt/GDP	31.7% of GDP (2012 est.) Country comparison to the world: 110 38.5% of GDP (2011) Note: Official data; data cover both central government debt and local government debt, which China's National Audit Office estimated at RMB 10.72 trillion (approximately US$1.66 trillion) in 2011; data exclude policy bank bonds, Ministry of Railway debt, China Asset Management Company debt, and non-performing loans
Market value of publicly traded shares	$3.665 trillion (31 December 2012 est.) Country comparison to the world: 4 $3.408 trillion (31 December 2011) $4.763 trillion (31 December 2010 est.)
Internet users/population	389 million (2009) Country comparison to the world: 1 564 million (2012)
Special cultural aspects	'Three Represents', Confucianism, 'Green Credit' policy
Responsible Investment Overview	
Overall RI market	1901.31 US$ (M)
Overall RI market growth rate (three-year average)	
Institutional RI market	
Retail RI market	
# of PRI signatories	Mainland China: 3 Hong Kong: 12 Total: 15
# of PRI asset owner signatories	
# of PRI investment manager signatories	Mainland China: 2 Hong Kong: 9 Total: 11
# of PRI professional service provider partners	Mainland China: 1 Hong Kong: 3 Total: 4
Asset classes used in RI	Stock
Overall financial market size	$3.665 trillion (31 December 2012 est.) Country comparison to the world: 4 $3.408 trillion (31 December 2011) $4.763 trillion (31 December 2010 est.)

(*Continued*)

CHINA	
	RESPONSIBLE INVESTMENT OVERVIEW
Launch year of first RI investment fund	2006
Launch year of national RI organization	Mainland China: SynTao (2005) Hong Kong: ASrIA (2001)
Largest three RI asset owners	
Largest three RI investment managers	Liang Hong-Yun Hongjun Liang Ouyuang Qin-Chun
Important RI professional service partners	Syntao (www.syntao.com/index_CN.asp) Tsing Capital (www.tsingcapital.com)
Other relevant RI organizations	ASrIA (www.asria.org) CSR Asia (www.csr-asia.com) CSR China (www.csr-china.net/index.aspx) SICCSR (www.siccsr.org/index.aspx) China CSR (www.chinacsr.com/cn/) China CSR Map (www.chinacsrmap.org/index_EN.asp)
Major ESG issues of concern to society over the last decade	*Environmental risks*: Toxic emissions and waste, carbon emissions, financing environmental impact *Social risks:* Product safety and quality *Governance risks*: Corporate governance, corruption and instability
Currently debated ESG issues	Philanthropic investment Low-carbon investment
	RESPONSIBLE INVESTMENT LEGISLATION
Legislation on institutional investors and ESG issues	
Legislation on investment managers and ESG issues	
Legislation on corporations and ESG issues	April 2010: The Standing Committee of the National's People's Congress passed amendments to the Renewable Energy Law, and then the new law came into effect. July 2007: Ministry of Environment Protection, the People's Bank of China and the China Banking Regulatory issued the 'Green Credit' policy, which suggests that banks evaluate a company's environmental performance before lending and restrict loans to projects that are harmful to the environment. February 2008: Ministry of Environmental Protection issued the policy of 'Green Security'. Companies identified as heavy polluters or as having high environmental risks are required to conduct an environmental evaluation before an IPO application.

CHINA	
	Responsible Investment Legislation
Sources employed in the responsible investment section of tables	ASrIA. Online. Available HTTP: <http://portal.asria.org/sri_fund/database.php> (accessed 28 August 2012). Bloomberg (accessed on October 2012). Green Watershed. (2010) Environmental Record of Chinese Banks in 2010. Online. Available HTTP: <http://www.banktrack.org/manage/ems_files/download/environmental_record_of_chinese_banks_2010/environmental_records_of_chinese_banks_2010_eng.pdf> (accessed 13 August 2012). Industrial Efficiency Policy Database, Online. Available HTTP: <http://iepd.iipnetwork.org/policy/ee-financing-regulations-and-instruments#[1]> (accessed 15 August 2012). Ministry of Environmental Protection, (2008) The Guiding Suggestions for Listed Companies to enhance supervision and management on environment protection, Online. Available HTTP: <http://www.gov.cn/zwgk/2008-02/25/content_900324.htm> (accessed 3 August 2012). MSCI ESG Research, September 2012, Country Report: China. http://portal.asria.org/philanthropic_investment/about/index.html. Schaub, M. (2010). Renewable energy law in China. China law insight. Online. Available HTTP: <http://www.chinalawinsight.com/2010/06/articles/corporate/renewable-energy-law-in-china/> (accessed 27 August 2012). UN PRI. Online. Available <http://www.unpri.org/signatories/signatories/?country=China>.

6. Denmark

Karin Buhmann

DENMARK	
	Country Overview
Population	5,556,452 (July 2013 est.)
Life expectancy	Total population: 78.94 years Country comparison to the world: 48 Male: 76.54 years Female: 81.47 years (2013 est.)
Literacy rate	99%
School life expectancy	17 years
Religious groups	Evangelical Lutheran (official) 95%, other Christian (includes Protestant and Roman Catholic) 3%, Muslim 2%
Government type	Constitutional monarchy
Legal system	Civil law; judicial review of legislative acts
GDP/capita (PPP)	$213.6 billion (2012 est.) Country comparison to the world: 54 $214.8 billion (2011 est.) $212.5 billion (2010 est.) Note: Data are in 2012 US dollars.

(*Continued*)

DENMARK	
	Country Overview
Main industries	Agriculture, iron, steel, nonferrous metals, chemicals, food processing, machinery and transportation equipment, textiles and clothing, electronics, construction, furniture and other wood products, shipbuilding and refurbishment, windmills, pharmaceuticals, medical equipment
Unemployment rate	6%
Public debt/GDP	45.6% of GDP (2012 est.)
Market value of publicly traded shares	$179.5 billion (31 December 2011)
Internet users/ population	4.75 million (2009)
Special cultural aspects	
	Responsible Investment Overview
Overall RI market	$812 mio (50 largest institutional investors)
Overall RI market growth rate (three-year average)	
Institutional RI market	
Retail RI market	
# of PRI signatories	27
# of PRI asset owner signatories	
# of PRI investment manager signatories	
# of PRI professional service provider partners	
Asset classes used in RI	Listed equity, fixed-income corporate, fixed-income sovereign, fixed-income other, private equity, non-listed property, hedge funds
Overall financial market size	
Launch year of first RI investment fund	
Launch year of national RI organization	
Largest three RI asset owners	
Largest three RI investment managers	
Important RI professional service partners	
Other relevant RI organizations	Dansif
Major ESG issues of concern to society over the last decade	
Currently debated ESG issues	ESG policies, engagement

DENMARK	
	Responsible Investment Legislation
Legislation on institutional investors and ESG issues	Statutory Order No. 1305 16/12/2008, Section 135, succeeded by Statutory Order No. 17 11/01/2011, Section 135, and Statutory Order No. 312 30/03/2012, Section 135; Statutory Order No. 1043 05/11/2009, Section 62, Statutory Order No. 1310 16/12/2008, Section 132, succeeded by Statutory Order No. 16 11/01/2011, Section 132, and Statutory Order No. 25 16/01/12, Section 132; and Statutory Order No. 1307 16/12/2008, Section 24, succeeded by Statutory Order No. 63 25/01/2012, Section 25.
Legislation on investment managers and ESG issues	Statutory Order No. 1305 16/12/2008, Section 135, succeeded by Statutory Order No. 17 11/01/2011, Section 135 and Statutory Order No. 312 30/03/2012, Section 135; Statutory Order No. 1043 05/11/2009, Section 62, Statutory Order No. 1310 16/12/2008, Section 132, succeeded by Statutory Order No 16 11/01/2011, Section 132, and Statutory Order No. 25 16/01/12, Section 132; and Statutory Order No. 1307 16/12/2008, Section 24, succeeded by Statutory Order No. 63 25/01/2012, Section 25.
Legislation on corporations and ESG issues	General CSR reporting: Section 99a in the Act on Financial Statements (introduced through amendment to Act 1403 27.12.2008). Compulsory human rights and climate change reporting compulsory for companies with policies on those issues: Act 546, 18/06/2012, Section 11.
Sources employed in the responsible investment section of tables	ATP's Policy of Social Responsibility in investments, http://www.atp.dk/X5/wps/wcm/connect/a8e493804dfa7ef19bb59f6fb281efbf/2_ATPs+policy+of+SRI.pdf?MOD=AJPERES. Dansif 2012 study, available at http://www.dansif.dk/da-DK/Ressourcer/Dokumenter.aspx

7. Estonia and Poland

Geoffrey Mazullo

	ESTONIA	*POLAND*
	Country Overview	
Population	1,257,921 (July 2014 est.)	38,346,279 (July 2014 est.)
Life expectancy	74.07	76.65
Literacy rate	99.8%	99.7%
School life expectancy	17 years	16 years
Religious groups	Lutheran 9.9%, Orthodox 16.2%, other Christian (including Methodist, Seventh-Day Adventist, Roman Catholic, Pentecostal) 2.2%, unaffiliated 34.1%, other 0.9%, unspecified 16.7%, none 54.1% (2011 estimate)	Roman Catholic 89.8% (about 75% practicing), Eastern Orthodox 1.3%, Protestant 0.3%, other 0.3%, unspecified 8.3% (2002)
Government type	Parliamentary republic	Republic
Legal system	Civil law system	Civil law system
GDP/capita (PPP)	$22,400 (2013 estimate)	$21,100 (2013 estimate)

(Continued)

	ESTONIA	*POLAND*
	Country Overview	
Main industries	Engineering, electronics, wood and wood products, textiles, information technology, telecommunications	Machine building, iron and steel, coal mining, chemicals, shipbuilding, food processing, glass, beverages, textiles
Unemployment rate	10.9% (2013 estimate)	13.5% (2013 estimate)
Public debt/GDP	6% (2013 estimate)	48.2% (2013 estimate)
Market value of publicly traded shares	$2.332 billion (31 December 2012 estimate)	$177.7 billion (31 December 2012 estimate)
Internet users/ population	77.2% (2009)	58.5% (2009 estimate)
Special cultural aspects	Estonia's ethnic, linguistic and economic/financial ties with Finland have accelerated the process of integration with the European Union (EU) and Western Europe. However, Estonia's economy is strongly linked with its Baltic neighbors, Latvia and Lithuania. For example, the stock exchanges in all three countries are part of the NASDAQ OMX group.	A disproportionate percentage of the labour force engaged in agriculture creates a challenge for the pension system and consequently for RI. Many young Poles, highly educated, highly skilled and unskilled laborers emigrate to Western European countries to study or work.
	Responsible Investment Overview	
Overall RI Market	$19.5 million (2010)	$1.22 billion (2010)
Overall RI market growth rate (three-year average)		
Institutional RI market		
Retail RI market		
# of PRI signatories	3	1
# of PRI asset owner signatories	0	0
# of PRI investment manager signatories	3	0
# of PRI professional service provider partners	0	1
Asset classes used in RI	Investment funds, private equity	Bank products (eco-loans), debt, equity, investment funds, real estate
Overall financial market size	$147.8 billion (August 2012)	$1.9 billion (August 2012)
Launch year of first RI investment fund	2008	2008
Launch year of national RI organization	None	None
Largest three RI asset owners	Unknown	Pocztylion (pension fund)

	ESTONIA	*POLAND*
	Responsible Investment Overview	
Largest three RI investment managers	AS Avaron Asset Management Baltcap Limestone Investment Management	Centralny Dom Maklerski Pekao S.A. (CDM Pekao SA Securities) PZU (insurance company) TFI Skok SA (investment fund manager)
Important RI professional service partners	GES Investment Services (Sweden [headquarters] and Poland [subsidiary])	Agencja Ratingu Spolecznego (social rating agency) GES Investment Services (Sweden [headquarters] and Poland [subsidiary]) Investin
Other relevant RI organizations	Unknown	Ministry of Economy working group on RI, 'Odpowiedzialne Inwestowanie' (Responsible Investment internet portal)
Major ESG issues of concern to society over the last decade	Corporate governance Environment Disclosure	Corporate governance Corruption Disclosure
Currently debated ESG issues	Adoption and implementation of international standards	Corporate governance Gender diversity in management and boards (corporate governance)
	Responsible Investment Legislation	
Legislation on institutional investors and ESG issues	No specific legislation	No specific legislation
Legislation on investment managers and ESG issues	No specific legislation	No specific legislation
Legislation on corporations and ESG issues	Corporate Governance Code	Corporate Governance Code
Sources employed in the responsible investment section of tables	Avaron Baltcap The Baltic Times CIA World Factbook Emerging Markets ESG Eurosif Limestone Investment Management NASDAQ OMX PFS Program Social Science Research Network World Federation of Exchanges	Agencja Ratingu Spolecznego (social rating agency) CASE CIA World Factbook Emerging Markets ESG Eurosif European Pensions Investing GES Investment Services Poland Odpowiedzialne Inwestowanie PFS Program PZU Pocztylion TFI Skok SA World Federation of Exchanges

8. Finland

Antti Savilaakso

FINLAND	
	Country Overview
Population	5,268,799 (July 2014 est.)
Life expectancy	79.7 years (2014 est.)
Literacy rate	100% (No official statistics, 100% estimated since 2000 CIA World Factbook)
School life expectancy	17 years (2011 est.)
Religious groups	Lutheran 78.4%, Orthodox 1.1%, other Christian 1.1%, other 0.2%, none 19.2% (2010 est.)
Government type	Republic
Legal system	Civil law (based on Swedish model)
GDP/capita (PPP)	USD 35,900 (2013 est.)
Main industries	Metals and metal products, electronics, machinery and scientific instruments, shipbuilding, pulp and paper, foodstuffs, chemicals, textiles, clothing
Unemployment rate	8.1% (2013 est.)
Public debt/GDP	56.5% (2013 est.)
Market value of publicly traded shares	$158.7 billion (31 December 2013 est.)
Internet users/ population	83.3% (2009 est.), 92% (per cent of those 16–74 years who used Internet during last 3 months)
Special cultural aspects	
	Responsible Investment Overview
Overall RI market	Exclusions: $113.276 million Norms-based screening: $84.426 million Engagement and voting: $60.771 million Best-in-class: $33.586 million Integration: $28.056 million Sustainability themed: $436 million (Currency conversion at mid-market rates 31 December 2011) Due to overlap, above numbers cannot be summed. Around 96% of assets in investment funds registered in Finland are managed by investment managers that have signed to the PRI. 94% of assets managed by pension funds are managed by funds signed to PRI. These in total can be estimated to represent more than 90% of investable assets in Finland.
Overall RI market growth rate (three-year average)	9.8% (2008–2011, weighted average on different RI strategies)
Institutional RI market	Around 90% of total investable assets follow PRI Principles. Around 85% of the total AUM in Finland are institutional (Bank of Finland). The total investable assets in Finland are around $185 billion, which translates into an institutional RI market estimate at $157 billion.

FINLAND	
	Responsible Investment Overview
Retail RI market	Around 90% of total investable assets follow PRI Principles. Around 15% of the total AUM are retail. The total investable assets in Finland are around $185 billion, which translates into a retail RI market estimate of $28 billion.
# of PRI signatories	33
# of PRI asset owner signatories	10
# of PRI investment manager signatories	22
# of PRI professional service provider partners	1
Asset classes used in RI	Equity (41%), fixed income (44%), real estate (9%), other (6%)
Overall financial market size	Pension funds manage 165 billion EUR; investment managers registered in Finland 77 billion EUR; foundations, endowments, municipalities, trade unions etc. are an additional 20 billion EUR
Launch year of first RI investment fund	1999, Sampo Kestävä Arvo
Launch year of national RI organization	2010, Finland's Sustainable Investment Forum
Largest three RI asset owners	Varma Keva Ilmarinen
Largest three RI investment managers	Nordea Investment Management OP Investment Management Danske Invest
Important RI professional service partners	None of the large RI professional service partners have a structural presence in Finland. Ethix and GES in Sweden are at the closest proximity and, by the author's own estimate, have dominant market share.
Other relevant RI organizations	None
Major ESG issues of concern to society over the last decade	Climate change; Finnish companies investing abroad, especially in countries with high corruption rates; forestry-related issues, palm oil, mining in Northern Finland, labour conditions in developing countries
Currently debated ESG issues	
	Responsible Investment Legislation
Legislation on institutional investors and ESG issues	RI practices in Finland are not governed by any explicit legal framework; therefore, practices rest on organizations such as Finsif and initiatives such as UN-backed Principles for Responsible Investment.
Legislation on investment managers and ESG issues	RI practices in Finland are not governed by any explicit legal framework; therefore, practices rest on organizations such as Finsif and initiatives such as UN-backed Principles for Responsible Investment.

(Continued)

	Responsible Investment Legislation
Legislation on corporations and ESG issues	State is implicitly assumed to take care of social issues; as a result, Finnish legislation has traditionally been thorough in the fields of labour law, labour protection law and environmental law. This also means that there is no actual legislation concerning ESG. 2011: The Finnish government adopted a resolution asking non-listed state-owned companies and state majority–owned companies to report their sustainability performance. 2006: The Finnish accounting standards board published guidelines for environmental disclosure in annual reports.
Sources employed in the responsible investment section of tables	CIA World Factbook 2013–14. Washington, DC: Central Intelligence Agency, 2013. Finland Country profile [referred: 16.7.2014] retrieved from https://www.cia.gov/library/publications/the-world-factbook/geos/fi.html. European 2012 Study 2012, Eurosif, [referred: 16.7.2014] retrieved from http://www.eurosif.org/publication/view/european-sri-study-2012/. Fund Management companies' market shares, Financial Supervisory Authority of Finland (FIVA), [referred: 16.7.2014] retrieved from http://www.finanssivalvonta.fi/en/Statistics/Securities_market/Management_companies_market_shares/Pages/Default.aspx. History, Finland's Sustainable Investment Forum (FINSIF), [referred: 16.7.2014] retrieved from http://www.finsif.fi/22. Hyrske, Anna, Lönnroth, Magdalena, Savilaakso, Antti, Sievänen, Riikka, *Vastuullinen Sijoittaminen*, 2012, Finva. Print. Investment Funds, Financial Statement Data 2013, Bank of Finland, [referred: 16.7.2014] retrieved from http://www.suomenpankki.fi/en/tilastot/sijoitusrahastot/Pages/index_siti_13_5_2014.aspx. Official Statistics of Finland (OSF): Use of information and communications technology by individuals [e-publication]. ISSN=2341-8710. 2013. Helsinki: Statistics Finland [referred: 16.7.2014] retrieved from http://www.stat.fi/til/sutivi/2013/sutivi_2013_2013-11-07_tie_001_en.html. Signatories to the Principles for Responsible Investment, PRI, [referred: 16.7.2014] retrieved from http://www.unpri.org/signatories/signatories/?country=Finland. Summary of Investment Assets, The Finnish Pension Alliance (TELA), [referred: 16.7.2014] retrieved from http://www.tela.fi/en/economy/investment_statistics_and_analyses/summary_of_investment_assets. Sustainability Equity Fund, Basic Information, Danske Invest, [referred: 16.7.2014] retrieved from http://www.danskeinvest.fi/web/show_fund.produkt?p_nId=1527&p_nFundgroup=61&p_nFund=2453. All currency conversion EUR to USD mid-market rates 31 December 2011.

9. France

Stéphanie Giamporcaro

FRANCE	
	COUNTRY OVERVIEW
Population	65 million
Life expectancy	81.56 years
Literacy rate	99%
School life expectancy	16 years
Religious groups	Roman Catholic 83–88%, Protestant 2%, Jewish 1%, Muslim 5–10%, unaffiliated 4%
Government type	Republic
Legal system	Civil law; review of administrative but not legislative acts
GDP/capita (PPP)	$35,300 (2012 est.)
Main industries	Machinery, chemicals, automobiles, metallurgy, aircraft, electronics; textiles, food processing; tourism
Unemployment rate	9.8% (2012 est.)
Public debt/GDP	90.3% of GDP (2012 est.)
Market value of publicly traded shares	$1.569 trillion (31 December 2011)
Internet users/population	45.262 million; 44.625 million (metropolitan France) (2009)
Special cultural aspects	
	RESPONSIBLE INVESTMENT OVERVIEW
Overall RI Market	EUR 149 billion (2012) US$ 201.36 billion
Overall RI market growth rate (three-year average)	+44% (2010–2012)
Institutional RI market	EUR 107.2 billion (2012) US$ 145 billion
Retail RI Market	EUR 41.8 billion US$ 56.5 billion
# of PRI signatories	117 (February 2013)
# of PRI asset owner signatories	9
# of PRI investment manager signatories	97
# of PRI professional service provider partners	11
Asset classes used in RI	Equities, bonds, money market, cash, impact investing
Overall financial market size	US$ 1.569 trillion (31 December 2011)
Launch year of first RI investment fund	1997
Launch year of national RI organization	2000, FIR

(Continued)

FRANCE	
Responsible Investment Overview	
Largest three RI asset owners	ERAFP FRR CDC
Largest three RI investment managers	AMUNDI AM Allianz GI France BNP Paribas IP
Important RI professional service partners	Novethic Vigeo Ethifinance Proxinvest
Other relevant RI organizations	Eurosif AFG
Major ESG issues of concern to society over the last decade	Sourcing relevant ESG data Verifying the RI quality of RI funds
Currently debated ESG issues	RI retail investment market RI label
Responsible Investment Legislation	
Legislation on institutional investors and ESG issues	Fabius Law on ESPs (2001) Law 2001–624 creating the FRR
Legislation on investment managers and ESG issues	Article 224 Grenelle de l'Environnement Law on investment managers and ESG reporting
Legislation on corporations and ESG issues	2001: NRE Law (Nouvelle régulation économiques) 2012: Article 225 of the Grenelle 2 de l'Environnement Law
Sources employed in the responsible investment section of tables	Novethic

10. Hong Kong

Christine Chow

HONG KONG	
Country Overview	
Population	7.18 million (July 2013)
Life expectancy	Male: 79.47 years Female: 85.14 years
Literacy rate	93.50%
School life expectancy	16 years
Religious groups	Eclectic mixture of religions (Buddhism/Taoism/Islam/Hinduism) 90%, Christianity 10%
Government type	Limited democracy ('One country two systems')

HONG KONG	
	Country Overview
Legal system	Mixed legal system of common law based on English model and Chinese customary law (in matters of family and land tenure)
GDP/capita (PPP)	$52,300 (2012 est.)
Main industries	Financial services, tourism, retail, shipping, electronics
Unemployment rate	3.3%
Public debt/GDP	37.80% (2012 est.)
Market value of publicly traded shares	$2.81 trillion (as of 31 December 2012)
Internet users/ population	5.22 million (72.8% of the population) Broadband Internet access penetration rate: 85% 16.71 million mobile phone subscribers: 233% of the population
	Responsible Investment Overview
Overall RI Market	Over $12 billion
Overall RI market growth rate (three-year average)	
Institutional RI market	
Retail RI market	$12 billion
# of PRI signatories	9
# of PRI asset owner signatories	
# of PRI investment manager signatories	6
# of PRI professional service provider partners	3
Asset classes used in RI	Listed equity, debt/mezzanine financing, private equity, venture capital, angel investments, impact investment, venture philanthropy Sectors: Infrastructure, clean energy, affordable housing, elderly care, education, waste management, agribusiness, green building and facilities, sustainable consumption
Overall financial market size	Stock of broad money: $1.15 trillion Market value of publicly traded shares: $2.8 trillion (as of August 2013)
Launch year of first RI investment fund	1997
Launch year of national RI organization	1999
Largest three RI asset owners	
Largest three RI investment managers	BNP Paribas Amundi Blackrock

(*Continued*)

HONG KONG	
	Responsible Investment Overview
Important RI professional service partners	CSR Asia SustainAsia
Other relevant RI organizations	Asia Corporate Governance Association (ACGA) Association for Sustainable and Responsible Investment in Asia (ASrIA) Social Ventures Hong Kong (SVhk)
Major ESG issues of concern to society over the last decade	Corporate governance, corporate social responsibility, carbon emissions, labour, standards, supply chain management
Currently debated ESG issues	Resource scarcity, especially water risk; food safety; energy efficiency; environmental pollution and waste management; 'one share one vote' system (prompted by the planned listing of Alibaba in the US)
	Responsible Investment Legislation
Legislation on institutional investors and ESG issues	
Legislation on investment managers and ESG issues	
Legislation on corporations and ESG issues	Listing rules address independent shareholders concerns over related-party transactions (RPTs). The 'Environmental, Social and Governance Reporting Guide' (the 'ESG Guide') for issuers listed in Hong Kong. The Hong Kong Stock Exchange published consultation paper in December 2011 and consultation conclusions in August 2012. The Guide is divided into four areas: workplace quality, environmental protection, operating practices and community involvement. Each of the areas is divided into three sections: aspects, general disclosure recommendations and key performance indicators.
	Additional Relevant Responsible Investment Criteria
Impact of urbanization	Growing urban population and the laissez faire approach to urbanisation puts pressure on the environment, infrastructure, housing, education, medical facilities. etc.
Technology parks	Established in 2002 by the Hong Kong government, the Hong Kong Science and Technology Park uses solar energy and includes green building features in its master plan design (www.hkstp.org). The business incubation programme Incu-Tech provides administrative support and subsidised office space to technology start-up companies covering green technology.
Sources employed in the responsible investment section of tables	Homage Consulting research Gadbury Group HSBC/Hang Seng Bank World Bank Office of the Telecommunications Authority (OFTA), Hong Kong (2013)

11. Israel

Noga Levtzion Nadan

ISRAEL	
Country Overview	
Population	7,707,042 (July 2013 est.)
Life expectancy	81.17 years
Literacy rate	97.1%
School life expectancy	16 years
Religious groups	Jewish 75.1%, Muslim 17.4%, Christian 2%, Druze 1.6%, other 3.9% (2012 est.)
Government type	Parliamentary democracy
Legal system	Mixed legal system of English common law, British Mandate regulations and Jewish, Christian, and Muslim religious laws
GDP/capita (PPP)	$33,900 (2012 est.)
Main industries	High-technology products (including aviation, communications, computer-aided design and manufactures, medical electronics, fiber optics), wood and paper products, potash and phosphates, food, beverages, and tobacco, caustic soda, cement, construction, metals products, chemical products, plastics, diamond cutting, textiles, footwear
Unemployment rate	6.9% (2012 est.)
Public debt/GDP	66.9% of GDP (2012 est.)
Market value of publicly traded shares	$145 billion (31 December 2011)
Internet Users/Population	4.525 million (2009)
Special cultural aspects	
Responsible Investment Overview	
Overall RI Market	0 (kosher funds are not really RI)
Overall RI Market growth rate (three-year average)	
Institutional RI market	
Retail RI market	
# of PRI signatories	1
# of PRI asset owner signatories	0
# of PRI investment manager signatories	0
# of PRI professional service provider partners	1
Asset classes used in RI	
Overall financial market size	
Launch year of first RI investment fund	

(*Continued*)

ISRAEL	
	Responsible Investment Overview
Launch year of national RI organization	
Largest three RI asset owners	
Largest three RI investment managers	
Important RI professional service partners	Greeneye ESG Ltd, Partner of EIRIS Network Proxy Services Enthropy Emda
Other relevant RI organizations	
Major ESG issues of concern to society over the last decade	Corporate governance, customer and employee relations
Currently debated ESG issues	Remuneration to top management and board independence
	Responsible Investment Legislation
Legislation on institutional investors and ESG issues	The Hemdani Committee (2008), report for 'Increased Involvement of Institutional Bodies in the Capital Market' The Hodek Committee (2009), report for 'Establishing [CG] Parameters for Institutional Bodies' Investments in Nongovernmental Bonds' Ministry of Finance's Commissioner of Capital Markets' circulars: 'Credit Risk Management in Investment Activity' Bank of Israel's Supervisor of Banks' circular regarding 'Environmental Risks to Corporate Banks' (2011)
Legislation on investment managers and ESG issues	As above
Legislation on corporations and ESG issues	Israel Securities Authority, Amendment no. 16 to the Corporate Law, requiring proper corporate governance in public companies with disclosure requirements The report on environmental issues is included in the company annual report.
Sources employed in the responsible investment section of tables	CIA World Factbook (2014) Online. Available: <https://www.cia.gov/library/publications/the-world-factbook/geos/is.html> (accessed 9 February 2014).

12. Italy

Rocco Ciciretti, Annalisa Fabretti and Marco Nicolosi

ITALY	
	COUNTRY OVERVIEW
Population	61,482,297 (July 2013)
Life expectancy	81.95 (2013)
Literacy rate	99% (2011)
School life expectancy	16 years (2010)
Religious groups	Christian 80% (overwhelmingly Roman Catholic with very small groups of Jehovah Witnesses and Protestants), Muslims negligible (about 700,000 but growing), atheists and agnostics 20%
Government type	Republic
Legal system	Civil law system; judicial review under certain conditions in Constitutional Court
GDP/capita (PPP)	$30,600 (2012)
Main industries	Tourism, machinery, iron and steel, chemicals, food processing, textiles, motor vehicles, clothing, footwear, ceramics
Unemployment rate	10.6% (2012)
Public debt/GDP	127% (2012)
Market value of publicly traded shares	$431.5 billion (31 December 2011)
Internet users/ population	29.235 million (2009)
Special cultural aspects	
	RESPONSIBLE INVESTMENT OVERVIEW
Overall RI market	$579.14 billion*
Overall RI market growth rate (three-year average)	19.7% (compound annual rate)
Institutional RI market	$577.63 billion*
Retail RI market	$1.5 billion*
# of PRI signatories	10
# of PRI asset owner signatories	4
# of PRI investment manager signatories	6
# of PRI professional service provider partners	0
Asset classes used in RI	Bonds (80%), equities (6%), money market (8%)

(*Continued*)

ITALY	
	Responsible Investment Overview
Overall financial market size	$1216.27 billion*
Launch year of first RI investment fund	1997, Eurizon Capital
Launch year of national RI organization	2001, Forum Finanza Sostenibile
Largest three RI asset owners	Assicurazioni Generali
Largest three RI investment managers	Pioneer Investment Eurizon Capital Etica SGR
Important RI professional service partners	Avanzi (acquired by VIGEO) ECPI
Other relevant RI organizations	Banca Etica
Major ESG issues of concern to society over the last decade	Governance, community
Currently debated ESG issues	Transparency and lack in information
	Responsible Investment Legislation
Legislation on institutional investors and ESG issues	Decree 252/2005: Pension funds are obliged to provide information on whether and to what extent ESG criteria are adopted in asset management and in the voting exercise. ISVAP Regulation 35/2010: Insurances are obliged to provide a further disclosure for financial products labelled as 'socially responsible'.
Legislation on investment managers and ESG issues	The Parliament approved a law establishing an obligation to report on products labelled as 'socially responsible'. This principle has been implemented by CONSOB by Regulation 16190/2007.
Legislation on corporations and ESG issues	Decree 32/2007: Companies may integrate their reporting with extra financial indicators such as the ESG aspects related to their business. However, this choice is at the discretion of managers.
Sources employed in the responsible investment section of tables	Eurosif (2012), UN PRI, Morningstar.

* Exchange EUR/USD 30 December 2011: 1.2939.

13. JAPAN

Kyoko Sakuma-Keck

JAPAN	
	COUNTRY OVERVIEW
Population	127,103,388
Life expectancy	84.46 years (male: 81.13 years, female: 87.99 years)
Literacy rate	99%
School life expectancy	15 years
Religious groups	Shintoism 83.9%, Buddhism 71.4%, Christianity 2%, other 7.8%
Government type	Parliamentary government with a constitutional monarchy
Legal system	Civil law system based on the German model; system also reflects Anglo-American influence and Japanese traditions; judicial review of legislative acts occurs in the Supreme Court.
GDP/capita (PPP)	$37,100
Main industries	Among world's largest and most technologically advanced producers of motor vehicles, electronic equipment, machine tools, steel and nonferrous metals, ships, chemicals, textiles, processed foods
Unemployment rate	4.1%
Public debt/GDP	226.1%
Market value of publicly traded shares	$3.681 trillion
Internet users/population	99.182 million
Special cultural aspects	Strong tendency to avoid conflict; paternalistic society
	RESPONSIBLE INVESTMENT OVERVIEW
Overall RI market	$10.2 billion (1 JPY = 0.0123586 USD)
Overall RI market growth rate (three-year average)	
Institutional RI market	$0.48 billion (1 JPY = 0.0123586 USD)
Retail RI market	$9.74 billion (1 JPY = 0.0123586 USD)
# of PRI signatories	30
# of PRI asset owner signatories	5
# of PRI investment manager signatories	20
# of PRI professional service provider partners	5
Asset classes used in RI	Equity, fixed income, real estate
Overall financial market size	$25,017.1 trillion (2010)
Launch year of first RI investment fund	1999
Launch year of national RI organization	2004 (official date of the launch of Japan Sustainable Investment Forum)
Largest three RI asset owners	Retail investors Kikkoman Corporate pension fund Secom Corporate pension fund

(Continued)

JAPAN	
	RESPONSIBLE INVESTMENT OVERVIEW
Largest three RI investment managers	Daiwa Asset Management Mitsui Sumitomo Trust Bank Nikko Asset Management
Important RI professional service partners	Good Bankers IntegreX Japan Research Institute Daiwa Research Institute FTSE Group
Other relevant RI organizations	Japan Sustainable Investment Forum (JSIF) Japanese Trade Union Confederation (Rengo)
Major ESG issues of concern to society over the last decade	Environmental pollution, CSR, pension sustainability
Currently debated ESG issues	Radiation-contaminated food, nuclear energy, aging society, pension payments, global poverty (vaccines), water availability/quality, clean energy, food security, Fukushima reconstruction
	RESPONSIBLE INVESTMENT LEGISLATION
Legislation on institutional investors and ESG issues	None
Legislation on investment managers and ESG issues	None
Legislation on corporations and ESG issues	Information disclosure Law Concerning the Promotion of Business Activities with Environmental Consideration by Specified Corporations, etc., by Facilitating Access to Environmental Information, and Other Measures (2004) FSA amendments to Cabinet Office Ordinance on disclosure of the items concerning corporate governance of a company in its securities report (2010)
	ADDITIONAL RELEVANT RESPONSIBLE INVESTMENT CRITERIA
Sources employed in the responsible investment section of tables	Global poverty, vaccines, water, clean energy, food security, Fukushima reconstruction CIA UN PRI website JSIF website Socially Responsible Investment in Japan (2011) Sakuma and Louche (2008), 'Mechanisms and Drivers for SRI in Japan', *Journal of Business Ethics*, Vol. 82, pp. 425–448. McKinsey Global Institute (August 2011) Reuters (14 February 2011) Quick Business Research

14. Mexico

Luisa Montes Ecovalores

MEXICO	
Country Overview	
Population	118,397,000 (2013)
Life expectancy	75.43 years
Literacy rate	93.5%
School life expectancy	13 years
Religious groups	Catholic (76.5%), Protestant (5.2), Jehovah Witness (1.1%), unspecified (13.8%)
Government type	Federal republic
Legal system	Civil law system
GDP/capita (PPP)	$15,600 (2013)
Main industries	Food and beverages, tobacco, chemicals, iron and steel, petroleum, mining, textiles, clothing, motor vehicles, consumer durables, tourism
Unemployment rate	9.1%
Public debt/GDP	37.7% (2013 est.)
Market value of publicly traded shares	$525.1 billion (December 2012)
Internet users/population	31.02 million (2009)
Special cultural aspects	Increase in violence due to drug production and drug trafficking.
Responsible Investment Overview	
Overall RI market	
Overall RI market growth rate (three-year average)	
Institutional RI market	
Retail RI market	
# of PRI signatories	0
# of PRI asset owner signatories	
# of PRI investment manager signatories	
# of PRI professional service provider partners	1
Asset classes used in RI	
Overall financial market size	
Launch year of first RI investment fund	2007
Launch year of national RI organization	2011
Largest three RI asset owners	BBVA Santander Scotiabank

(Continued)

MEXICO	
Responsible Investment Overview	
Largest three RI investment managers	BBVA Santander Scotiabank
Important RI professional service partners	Ecovalores
Other relevant RI organizations	Ecovalores
Major ESG issues of concern to society over the last decade	Corruption, lack of water resources and environmental challenges
Currently debated ESG issues	REDD preparedness
Responsible Investment Legislation	
Legislation on institutional investors and ESG issues	Pension funds regulator CONSAR asked to declare if companies invested in it have SCR certification.
Legislation on investment managers and ESG issues	CONSAR requirement to disclose if companies invested in it are CSR certified.
Legislation on corporations and ESG issues	None
Additional Relevant Responsible Investment Criteria	
Sustainable index	Mexican Stock Exchange Sustainable Index
Sources employed in the responsible investment section of tables	Ecovalores

15. Netherlands

Heather Hachigan

NETHERLANDS	
Country Overview	
Population	16,877,351 (2014)
Life expectancy	81.12 years (women, 83.34 years; men, 81.12 years)
Literacy rate	99%
School life expectancy	18 years
Religious groups	Catholic (28%), Protestant (19%) other (11%), none (42%)
Government type	Constitutional monarchy
Legal system	Civil law (French)
GDP/capita (PPP)	43,300 (2012)
Main industries	Industrial (including agro-industries, metal and engineering products, electrical machinery and equipment, chemicals, petroleum) and services
Unemployment rate	8.3% (2013)

NETHERLANDS	
	COUNTRY OVERVIEW
Public debt/GDP	74.3%
Market value of publicly traded shares	$675 billion (2013)
Internet users/population	14.872 million
Special cultural aspects	Low-lying land area and population susceptible to climate change risk related to flooding. NGOs contribute to public dialogue on RI. In general, there is a high demand among Dutch population for RI and strong interest in participation in decision-making. For example, some Dutch pension funds have participant councils.
	RESPONSIBLE INVESTMENT OVERVIEW
Overall RI market	$1,665,864 (Eurosif, 2014) Note: The majority of this market is covered by exclusions. US dollar/euro exchange rate: 1.3385 (average annual rate for 2014, ECB).
Overall RI market growth rate (three-year average)	2005–2013 growth: $62.9 billion to $1.6 trillion 2011–2013 CAGR by activity: Exclusions: 27% (does not include cluster munitions) Engagement and voting: 27% Norms-based screening: 20% Best in class: 26.9% ESG integration: 8% Note: Figure calculated based on Eurosif 2006, 2012 and 2014 estimates of overall Dutch RI market. US dollar/euro exchange rate: 1.3385 (average annual rate for 2014, ECB).
Institutional RI market	$1,632,268 Note: Figure calculated subtracting VBDO estimate of Dutch retail RI savings and investments (25.1 billion euro) for 2013 from Eurosif 2014 estimate of overall Dutch RI. US dollar/euro exchange rate: 1.3385 (average annual rate for 2014, ECB).
Retail RI market	$33.6 billion (VBDO, 2013) Note: $13 billion (investments) and $20.6 billion (savings). US dollar/euro exchange rate: 1.3385 (average annual rate for 2014, ECB).
# of PRI signatories	89
# of PRI asset owner signatories	37
# of PRI investment manager signatories	45
# of PRI professional service provider partners	7
Asset classes used in RI	Public equity, corporate debt, real estate, infrastructure, commodities and private equity
Overall financial market size	$2.3 trillion (DUFAS) Note: DUFAS estimates at the end of 2013 that the total size of the Dutch asset management market was 1.7 trillion euro. US dollar/euro exchange rate: 1.3385 (average annual rate for 2014, ECB).
Launch year of first RI investment fund	1991 (Triodos)

(*Continued*)

NETHERLANDS

Responsible Investment Overview	
Launch year of national RI organization	1995
Largest three RI asset owners	Aegon Insurance Fund ING Group ABP
Largest 3 RI investment managers	APG Ageon Asset Management PGGM (IPE, 2014)
Important RI professional service partners	Sustainalytics Cardano AMA Partners Porfundo
Other relevant RI organizations	Eumedion Dutch Inclusive Finance Platform Dutch Association of Investors for Sustainable Development (VBDO)
Major ESG issues of concern to society over the last decade	Cluster munitions and anti-personnel land mines, tobacco, labour conditions, climate change (Sustainalytics, 2013)
Currently debated ESG issues	Divestment from Israeli banks investing in settlements on the occupied West Bank of Palestine has raised political tensions.
	Responsible Investment Legislation
Legislation on institutional investors and ESG issues	Bill "Wet Versterking Pensioenfondsbestuur", introduced on 13 July 2013, complements the Pension Fund Act 2008 to increase transparency, security and knowledge regarding pensions in the Netherlands. The new legislation includes provision for funds to report on their RI policies and implementation (VBDO, 2013).
Legislation on investment managers and ESG issues	In 2015, proposed legislation introduced a bonus cap on the financial sector: 20% of fixed compensation, which is the most stringent cap in the European Union, is expected to come into force. While it targets banks, the bonus caps will also apply to investment managers of Dutch pension and insurance funds.
Legislation on corporations and ESG issues	The Dutch Environmental Reporting Decree (1999) requires disclosure for companies deemed to be high risk with regards to the environment. Corporate Governance Code (2003) strengthened shareholder rights on issues, including remuneration. Corporate Governance Act (2013) increases the per cent of shares an investor must hold in order to place an item on the agenda from 1 per cent to 3 per cent, among other rules that affect shareholder rights.
	Public Policy and Regulation
Regulation	Pension Governance Code (2013): includes provisions for reporting on RI policy and implementation, board diversity and expertise, consultation and support of pension members for RI policy. "It is the first time a code explicitly mentions the responsibilities of a pension fund with regard to responsible investment" (VBDO, 2013: 22). The revised Governance Code applies to all Dutch pension funds and is supervised by the Dutch Central Bank and Financial Markets Supervisory body, AFM, on a comply or explain basis.

NETHERLANDS	
	PUBLIC POLICY AND REGULATION
Fiscal incentives	Green Funds Scheme, 1995–Present (2010 fiscal changes introduced to reduce tax exemptions). Social-Ethical Fund Program and Savings and Investment Plan for Cultural Organisations introduced in early 2000s. Both have been terminated as of January 2013.
New Developments	Netherlands Investment Institution (NII) announced in 2013 to encourage investments in Dutch economy in sustainable infrastructure, housing, SMEs, etc.
Consolidation	There is a high degree of consolidation in the Dutch financial sector (IMF, 2011).
Sources employed in the responsible investment section of tables	DUFAS (2014). http://www.dufas.nl/ (accessed 25/05/2015). Eurosif (2012). http://www.eurosif.org/publication/european-sri-study-2012/ (accessed 25/05/2015). Eurosif (2014). http://www.eurosif.org/our-work/research/sri/european-sri-study-2014/ (accessed 25/05/2015). IMF (2011). http://www.imf.org/external/data.htm (accessed 25/05/2015). IPE (2014). http://www.ipe.com (accessed 25/05/2015). NII Press Release (2013). https://www.nlii.nl (accessed 25/05/2015). OECD (2014). http://www.oecd.org (accessed 25/05/2015). Sustainalytics (2013). http://www.sustainalytics.com (accessed 25/05/2015). VBDO (2011/2013/2014). http://www.vbdo.nl (accessed 25/05/2015).

16. Nigeria

Innocent Okwuosa and Kenneth Amaeshi

NIGERIA	
	COUNTRY OVERVIEW
Population	177,155,754 (July 2014 est.)
Life expectancy	Total population: 52.62 years Male: 51.63 years Female: 53.66 years (2014 est.)
Literacy rate	Total population: 61.3% (2010 est.) Male: 72.1% Female: 50.4%
School life expectancy	Total population: 9 years (2005) Male: 10 years Female: 8 years
Religious groups	Muslim 50%, Christian 40%, indigenous beliefs 10%
Government type	Federal republic
Legal system	Mixed legal system of English common law, Islamic law (in 12 northern states) and traditional law.
GDP/capita (PPP)	$2,800 (2013 est.)

(Continued)

	NIGERIA
	Country Overview
Main industries	Crude oil, coal, tin, columbite, rubber products, wood, hides and skins, textiles, cement and other construction materials, food products, footwear, chemicals, fertilizer, printing, ceramics, steel
Unemployment rate	23.9% (2011 est.)
Public debt/GDP	19.3% of GDP (2013 est.)
Market value of publicly traded shares	$82.7 billion (31 December 2013 est.)
Internet Users/Population	28.4% (2012 est.)
Special cultural aspects	
	Responsible Investment Overview
Overall RI Market	$45,120,521.49
Overall RI market growth rate (three-year average)	26.85%
Institutional RI market	$45,120,521
Retail RI market	Nil
# of PRI signatories	2
# of PRI asset owner signatories	0
# of PRI investment manager signatories	1
# of PRI professional service provider partners	1
Asset classes used in RI	Equities and fixed-income securities
Overall financial market size	
Launch year of first RI investment fund	2005
Launch year of national RI organization	1 June 2004 (SEC)
Largest three RI asset owners	
Largest three RI investment managers	Zenith Assets Management Ltd. Stanbic IBTC Asset Management Ltd. Lotus Capital Ltd.
Important RI professional service partners	
Other relevant RI organizations	Access Bank Plc
Major ESG issues of concern to society over the last decade	Ethical issues relating to sin companies such as alcohol, tobacco, gambling and adult entertainment based on religious morality
Currently debated ESG issues	Corporate social responsibility
	Responsible Investment Legislation
	Sustainability banking principles agreed by Bankers Committee in July 2012. Another circular was issued to all banks, discount houses and development finance on March 6, 2014. Institutions by CBN specifying the uniform reporting template to be adopted by these institutions.

NIGERIA	
	Responsible Investment Legislation
Legislation on institutional investors and ESG issues	None, but ESG is encouraged through corporate governance code by SEC.
Legislation on investment managers and ESG issues	None, but ESG is encouraged through corporate governance code.
Legislation on corporations and ESG issues	The only regulatory ESG requirement is the sustainability banking principle that applies to all listed banks launched in 2012, but none to other industries except through corporate governance code.
Sources employed in the responsible investment section of tables	CIA World Factbook Central Bank of Nigeria (CBN) Securities and Exchange Commission (SEC) Researcher's interview with operators

17. Norway

Ane Jensen

NORWAY	
	Country Overview
Population	5,147,792 (July 2014 est.)
Life expectancy	81.6 years
Literacy rate	100%
School life expectancy	18 years
Religious groups	Church of Norway (Evangelical Lutheran – official) 82.1%, other Christian 3.9%, Muslim 2.3%, Roman Catholic 1.8%, other 2.4%, unspecified 7.5% (2011 est.)
Government type	Constitutional monarchy
Legal system	Mixed legal system of civil, common, and customary law; Supreme Court can advise on legislative acts.
GDP/capita (PPP)	$55,400 (2013 est.)
Main industries	Petroleum and gas, food processing, shipbuilding, pulp and paper products, metals, chemicals, timber, mining, textiles, fishing
Unemployment rate	3.6% (2013 est.)
Public debt/GDP	30.1% of GDP (2013 est.)
Market value of publicly traded shares	$252.9 billion (31 December 2012 est.)
Internet Users/Population	0.86/4.431 million (2009)
Special cultural aspects	
	Responsible Investment Overview
Overall RI Market (in US$)	$961.16 billion (2012)
Overall RI market growth rate (three-year average)	39.8% (based on Eurosif numbers 2010–2012), from $687.43 billion (€410.6 billion) in 2010 to $961.16 billion (€574.1 billion) in 2012.
Institutional RI market	
Retail RI market	
# of PRI signatories	10 (2014)

(Continued)

NORWAY	
Responsible Investment Overview	
# of PRI asset owner signatories	6 (2014)
# of PRI investment manager signatories	4 (2014)
# of PRI professional service provider partners	0 (2014)
Asset classes used in RI	Equity 54%, fixed income 44%, other 2% (2012)
Overall financial market size	Stock of broad money: $312.9 billion (31 December 2013 est.) Market value of publicly traded shares: $252.9 billion (31 December 2012 est.)
Launch year of first RI investment fund	1995 (Storebrand Asset Management launched Europe's first environmental fund)
Launch year of national RI organization	
Largest three RI asset owners	Norwegian Government Pension Fund Global (AUM 2014: $838 billion) Storebrand Asset Management (AUM 2013: $80 billion) KLP (AUM 2013: $60 billion)
Largest three RI investment managers	ODIN FSN Capital Partners Skagen AS
Important RI professional service partners	N/A
Other relevant RI organizations	Norsif.org Eurosif.org
Major ESG issues of concern to society over the last decade	Protection of fundamental human rights. Environmental and public health concerns Child welfare Labor rights (e.g. NGPF's sale of Walmart shares in 2006) Transparency
Currently debated ESG issues	
Responsible Investment Legislation	
	RI not explicitly governed by legislative framework, but is defined by the policy guidelines of the Norwegian Government Pension Fund.
Legislation on institutional investors and ESG issues	Introduction of ethical guidelines for the Norwegian Government Pension Fund in 2004 Government Pension Fund Act 2005
Legislation on investment managers and ESG issues	
Legislation on corporations and ESG issues	
Sources employed in the responsible investment section of tables	Eurosif.org Norsif.org Nortrade.com Regjeringen.no Yoursri.com Unpri.org

18. Russia

Yulia Sofronova

RUSSIA	
	Country Overview
Population	142,470,272
Life expectancy	70.16 years
Literacy rate	99.7%
School life expectancy	14 years
Religious groups	Russian Orthodox 15–20%, Muslim 10–15%, other Christian 2%. Russia has a large population of non-practicing believers and non-believers, a legacy of over seven decades of Soviet rule.
Government type	Federation
Legal system	Civil law system; judicial review of legislative acts
GDP/capita (PPP)	$18,100 (2013)
Main industries	Complete range of mining and extractives, all forms of machine building, defence, shipbuilding, road and rail transportation equipment, communications equipment, agricultural machinery, tractors, and construction equipment, electric power generating and transmitting equipment, medical and scientific instruments, consumer durables, textiles, foodstuffs, handicrafts
Unemployment rate	5.8% (2013)
Public debt/GDP	7.9% of GDP (2013)
Market value of publicly traded shares	$874.7 billion (2012)
Internet users/population	40.853 million (2009)
Special cultural aspects	
	Responsible Investment Overview
Overall RI market	
Overall RI market growth rate (three-year average)	
Institutional RI market	
Retail RI market	
# of PRI signatories	2
# of PRI asset owner signatories	0
# of PRI investment manager signatories	2
# of PRI professional service provider partners	0
Asset classes used in RI	
Overall financial market size	Banking system $31.5 billion
Launch year of first RI investment fund	
Launch year of national RI organization	2011
Largest three RI asset owners	Lukoil Garant Blagosostoyaniye Sberbank non-state pension fund

(Continued)

	RUSSIA
	Responsible Investment Overview
Largest three RI investment managers	Gazprombank Asset Management ($7.578 million) TransfinGroup Asset Management ($5.884 million) VTB Capital Investment Management ($5.205 million)
Important RI professional service partners	
Other relevant RI organizations	
Major ESG issues of concern to society over the last decade	Corruption and bribery
Currently debated ESG issues	Business transparency
	Responsible Investment Legislation
Legislation on institutional investors and ESG issues	None
Legislation on investment managers and ESG issues	None
Legislation on corporations and ESG issues	New Russian Corporate Governance Code
Sources employed in the responsible investment section of tables	Institutional Investor KPMG Doing Business in Russia (2014)

19. South Africa

Suzette Viviersand and Nadia Mans-Kemp

	SOUTH AFRICA
	Country Overview
Population	49,004,031
Life expectancy	Total population: 49.33 years Male: 50.24 years Female: 48.39 years
Literacy rate	Total population: 86.4% Male: 87% Female: 85.7%
School life expectancy	Total population: 13 years Male: 13 years Female: 13 years
Religious groups	Protestant 36.6%, Catholic 7.1%, Muslim 1.5%, other Christian 36%, other 2.3%, unspecified 1.4%, no religion 15.1%
Government type	Constitutional democracy
Legal system	Hybrid legal system (civil, common and customary law)
GDP/capita (PPP)	$11,000
Main industries	Mining, automobile assembly, metalworking, machinery, textiles, iron and steel, chemicals, fertilizers, foodstuffs, commercial ship repair
Unemployment rate	23.9%
Public debt/GDP	35.6%
Market value of publicly traded shares	$1.013 trillion

SOUTH AFRICA	
	Country Overview
Internet users/population	10.8%
Special cultural aspects	South Africa is an ethnic and culturally diverse country. The philosophy of humanism called Ubuntu refers to people's allegiances and relations with each other, more specifically: "I am what I am because of who we all are."
	Responsible Investment Overview
Overall RI market	Based on 2010 figures: General asset management: EGS-integrated plus ESG-branded products: $115 billion (20.7% of total assets under management) Private equity: EGS-integrated plus ESG-branded products: $7.4 billion (52.1% of total assets under management)
Overall RI market growth rate (three-year average)	No comparable statistics are available.
Institutional RI market	No statistics are available on the split between institutional and retail RI in South Africa. However, the institutional market dominates the market.
Retail RI market	No statistics are available on this market. It is, however, miniscule compared to the institutional market. Only a few RI funds are available for investors in this segment of the market.
# of PRI signatories	36
# of PRI asset owner signatories	2
# of PRI investment manager signatories	26
# of PRI professional service provider partners	8
Asset classes used in RI	Listed equities, private equity, economic and social infrastructure, fixed income, agriculture, commercial and residential property
Overall financial market size	$570.4 billion (2010)
Launch year of first RI investment fund	June 1992
Launch year of national RI organization	The Africa Sustainable Investment Forum (AfricaSIF) was launched in June 2010.
Largest three RI asset owners	Government Employees Pension Fund of South Africa Eskom Pension Provident Fund
Largest 3 RI investment managers	Old Mutual (including Futuregrowth Asset Management and Community Growth Management Company) Sanlam Investment Managers Oasis Asset Management
Important RI professional service partners	Johannesburg Stock Exchange RisCura Unity Incorporation
Other relevant RI organizations	Association for Savings and Investment SA Institute of Retirement Funds Principal Officers Association Institute of Directors in Southern Africa Financial Services Board

(Continued)

	SOUTH AFRICA
	Responsible Investment Overview
Major ESG issues of concern to society over the last decade	*Environmental*: Climate change, water supply and quality, energy supply *Social*: Broad-Based Black Economic Empowerment, HIV/AIDS, unemployment and education *Governance*: Board-specific issues
Currently debated ESG issues	Issues surrounding infrastructure development (e.g. funding of toll roads), water and energy (e.g. acid mine drainage, nuclear power)
	Responsible Investment Legislation
Legislation on institutional investors and ESG issues	Pension Funds Act (1956) Share Blocks Control Act (1980) Collective Investment Schemes Control Act (2002) Public Investment Corporation Act
Legislation on investment managers and ESG issues	Securities Services Act (2004) Financial Advisory and Intermediary Services Act (2002) Financial Intelligence Centre Act (2001)
Legislation on corporations and ESG issues	*Environmental:* National Environmental Management Act (1998) Environmental Conservation Act (1989) National Water Act (1998) National Environmental Management: Protected Areas Act (2003) Air Quality Act (2004) *Social:* Broad-based Black Economic Empowerment Act (2003) Labour Relations Act (1995) Skills Development Act (1998) Housing Protection Measures Act (1998) Unemployment Insurance Act (2001) Basic Conditions of Employment Act (1997) Promotion of Equality and Prevention of Unfair Discrimination Act (2000) Preferential Procurement Policy Framework Act (2000) *Governance:* Companies Act (2008) National Credit Act (2005) Insider Trading Act (1998) Consumer Protection Act (2008)
	Additional Relevant Responsible Investment criteria
	Labour issues (e.g. fair treatment of employees, employment equity, as well as health and safety considerations)
Sources employed in the responsible investment section of tables	ActsOnline (2012) Online. Available HPPT: <http://www.acts.co.za> (accessed 17 February 2012). Africa Sustainable Investment Forum (2012) AfricaSIF.org. Online. Available HTTP: <http://www.africasif.org/> (accessed 29 January 2012). CIA World Factbook (2012) Africa: South Africa. Online. Available HTTP: <http://www.cia.gov/library/publications/the-world-factbook/geos/sf.html> (assessed 7 February 2012). Du Toit, F. (2011) 'National report: The Republic of South Africa', *Journal of Gender, Social Policy & the Law*, 19(1): 277–288.

SOUTH AFRICA
Additional Relevant Responsible Investment criteria
Internet World Stats. (2009) South Africa internet usage and marketing report. Online. Available HTTP: <http://www.internetworldstats.com/af/za.htm> (assessed 7 February 2012). Ngcoya, M. (2009) Ubuntu: Globalization, accommodation, and contestation in South Africa, Doctoral thesis, American University. Michigan: Proquest. Parliament of the Republic of South Africa (2009) Our constitution. Online. Available HTTP: <http://www.parliament.gov.za/live/content.php?Category_ID=11> (assessed 7 February 2012). Principles for Responsible Investment (PRI). (2012) Signatories to the Principles of Responsible Investment. Online. Available HTTP: <http://www.unpri.org/signatories/> (accessed 29 January 2012). Sinclair, G. and Yao, R. (2011) 'Sustainable investment in Sub-Saharan Africa – investment practitioner views on sustainable investment in private equity and asset management in South Africa, Nigeria and Kenya. Online. Available HTTP: <http://www.ifc.org/ifcext/sustainability.nsf/Content/Publications_Report_SISubSaharanAfrica> (accessed 29 January 2012).

20. South America

Camila Yamahaki and Cinthia S. Gaban

	ARGENTINA	*BOLIVÍA*	*BRAZIL*	*CHILE*	*COLOMBIA*	*EQUADOR*
			Country Overview			
Population	42,610,981	10,461,053	201,009,622	17,216,945	45,745,783	15,439,429
Life expectancy	77.32 years	68.22 years	73.02 years	78.27 years	75.02 years	76.15 years
Literacy rate	97.9%	91.2%	90.4%	98.6%	93.6%	91.6%
School life expectancy	16 years	14 years	14 years	15 years	14 years	14 years
Religious groups	Nominally Roman Catholic 92% (less than 20% practicing), Protestant 2%, Jewish 2%, other 4%	Roman Catholic 95%, Protestant (Evangelical Methodist) 5%	Roman Catholic (nominal) 73.6%, Protestant 15.4%, spiritualist 1.3%, Bantu/voodoo 0.3%, other 1.8%, unspecified 0.2%, none 7.4%	Roman Catholic 70%, Evangelical 15.1%, Jehovah's Witnesses 1.1%, other Christian 1%, other 4.6%, none 8.3%	Roman Catholic 90%, other 10%	Roman Catholic 95%, other 5%

(*Continued*)

	ARGENTINA	BOLIVÍA	BRAZIL	CHILE	COLOMBIA	EQUADOR
			COUNTRY OVERVIEW			
Government type	Republic	Republic	Federal republic	Republic	Republic	Republic
Legal system	Civil law	Civil law	Civil law	Civil law	Civil law	Civil law
GDP/capita (PPP)	$17,900	$5,000	$11,700	$18,200	$10,700	$10,200
Main industries	Food processing, motor vehicles, consumer durables, textiles, chemicals and petrochemicals, printing, metallurgy, steel	Mining, smelting, petroleum, food and beverages, tobacco, handicrafts, clothing, jewelry	Textiles, shoes, chemicals, cement, lumber, iron ore, tin, steel, aircraft, motor vehicles and parts, other machinery and equipment	Copper, lithium, other minerals, foodstuffs, fish processing, iron and steel, wood and wood products, transport equipment, cement, textiles	Textiles, food processing, oil, clothing and footwear, beverages, chemicals, cement, gold, coal, emeralds	Petroleum, food processing, textiles, wood products, chemicals
Unemployment rate	7.2%	7.5%	5.5%	6.3%	10.4%	4.9%
Public debt/ GDP	44.8%	34%	58.8%	11.9%	40.5%	21%
Market value of publicly traded shares	$43.58 billion	$7.69 billion	$1.229 billion	$270.3 billion	$201.3 billion	$5.779 billion
Internet users/ population	32.1%	10.5%	37.8%	40.7%	49.3%	21.7%
Internet users	13,694,000	1,103,000	75,982,000	7,009,000	22,538,000	3,352,000
			RESPONSIBLE INVESTMENT OVERVIEW			
Overall RI market						
Overall RI market growth rate (three-year average)						
Institutional RI market						
Retail RI market						
# of PRI signatories	0	0	61	1	2	0

	ARGENTINA	BOLIVÍA	BRAZIL	CHILE	COLOMBIA	EQUADOR
			RESPONSIBLE INVESTMENT OVERVIEW			
# of PRI asset owner signatories	0	0	17	0	0	0
# of PRI investment manager signatories	0	0	31	0	2	0
# of PRI professional service provider partners	0	0	13	1	0	0
Asset classes used in RI	Private equity		Listed equities Fixed income Real estate Private equity		Private equity	
Overall financial market size (in US$ million)	$53,104.79		$1,020,455	$265,150.08	$202,693.25	
Launch year of first RI investment fund			2001 (Santander's Ethical Fund)			
Launch year of national RI organization			2008 – PRI Brazil Network 2008 – LASFF			
Largest three RI asset owners			Previ			
Largest three RI investment managers	Equitas Ventures		Itaú Asset Management Santander Brazil Asset Management HSBC Brazil Asset Management		La Corporación Inversor	
Important RI professional service partners	Buenos Aires Stock Exchange		BM& FBOVESPA			
Other relevant RI organizations	Buenos Aires Stock Exchange		PRI Brazil Network BM& FBOVESPA			

(Continued)

	ARGENTINA	BOLIVÍA	BRAZIL	CHILE	COLOMBIA	EQUADOR
			RESPONSIBLE INVESTMENT OVERVIEW			
Major ESG issues of concern to society over the last decade						
Currently debated ESG issues	Sustainable economic growth Building transparency Informal employment Quality education Desertification		Corruption Child labour Racial discrimination Deforestation		Poverty and inequality Conflict and human rights Cocaine production, conflict and environmental issues Corruption and transparency	
Responsible investment legislation						
Legislation on institutional investors and ESG issues			National Monetary Council's Resolution 2792			
Legislation on investment managers and ESG issues			Resolution 4327 ANBIMA's guidelines for exercising voting rights in annual general meetings (self-regulation)			
Legislation on corporations and ESG issues	Instituto Argentino para el Gobierno de las Organizaciones's Code of Best Practices (self-regulation)		BM&F Bovespa's 'comply or explain' approach (self-regulation) IBGC's Corporate Governance Code (self-regulation)		Country code (self-regulation)	

	ARGENTINA	*BOLIVÍA*	*BRAZIL*	*CHILE*	*COLOMBIA*	*EQUADOR*
			ADDITIONAL RELEVANT RESPONSIBLE INVESTMENT CRITERIA			
Other RI funds	Equitas I and II		HSBC FIC Referenciado DI Solidariedade Itaú DI Ecochange Itaú Unibanco Social Excelence Fund BB DI Social 50 Investimentos Florestais Fund Triscorp Ativos Florestais Fund Votorantim Energia Sustentável Fund Energia PCH Fund Bioenergia Fund Brasil Sustentabili-dade		Fondo de Capital Privado Inversor Bamboo Financial Inclusion Fund	
Sources employed in the responsible investment section of tables	CIA (2014) Equitas Ventures (2014) BCBA (2012) IAGO (2012) Irigoyen (2010) WFE (2013)	CIA (2014)	ANBIMA (2012) BM&F BOVESPA (2012) CIA (2014) IBGC (2014) BCB (2009) PRI (2014) WFE (2013) Yamahaki and Ursini (2010)	CIA (2014) WFE (2013)	Bancoldex (2013) CIA (2014) Urzola (2010) WFE (2013)	CIA (2014)

Maria Laura Tinelli

21. Spain

Luiz Ferruz Agudo, Jesus Gomez Daza and Sara Segura Querol

SPAIN	
	Country Overview
Population	47,042,984 (July 2012 est.)
Life expectancy	81.27 years
Literacy rate	97.9%
School life expectancy	16 years
Religious groups	Roman Catholic 94%, other 6%
Government type	Parliamentary monarchy
Legal system	Civil law system with regional variations
GDP/capita (PPP)	$30,600 (2011 est.)
Main industries	Textiles and apparel (including footwear), food and beverages, metals and metal manufactures, chemicals, shipbuilding, automobiles, machine tools, tourism, clay and refractory products, footwear, pharmaceuticals, medical equipment
Unemployment rate	20.8% (2011 est.)
Public debt/GDP	68.2% of GDP (2011 est.)
Market value of publicly traded shares	$1.172 trillion (31 December 2010)
Internet users/population	28.119 million (2009)
Special cultural aspects	The first example of an SRI institution in Spain appeared with the creation of 'Cajas de Ahorro'. These are credit companies that invest a percentage of their benefits in initiatives linked to societal welfare ('Obra Social'). Nevertheless, due to the global financial crisis and the burst of the real estate bubble, a huge reform in the Spanish financial sector is being carried out. In this context, these kinds of credit entities are a hot point of this financial reform and are likely to disappear.
	Responsible Investment Overview
Overall RI market	$43,313,129 million (€33,300,000 million) (2009)
Overall RI market growth rate (three-year average)	15.41%
Institutional RI market	$43,312,034 million (€33,299,158 million) (2009)
Retail RI market	$1095 million (€842 million) (2009)
# of PRI signatories	
# of PRI asset owner signatories	
# of PRI investment manager signatories	
# of PRI professional service provider partners	
Asset classes used in RI	
Overall financial market size	
Launch year of first RI investment fund	1999 (Morgan Stanley Fondo Ético)

SPAIN	
RESPONSIBLE INVESTMENT OVERVIEW	
Launch year of national RI organization	1702 (Caja Madrid, the first 'Caja de Ahorros')
Largest three RI asset owners	
Largest three RI investment managers	
Important RI professional service partners	Consultora de pensiones y previsión social, sociedad de asesores, S.L. ESADE Instituto de Empresa Novaster Oquendo Capital Sustainalytics UNED Vigeo
Other relevant RI organizations	AECA AERI CREAS FETS Forética Economistas sin Fronteras FIARE Fundación Ecología y Desarrollo Spainsif
Major ESG issues of concern to society over the last decade	Governance issues, especially transparency of public limited companies
Currently debated ESG issues	Transparency of public limited companies is becoming even more important than in the previous decade. In another vein, the Spanish government, through the 'Strategy for a Sustainable Economy', has designed a new economic model based on sustainable, well-balanced, lasting growth. In this context, this policy aims to enhance social responsibility, especially in the context.
RESPONSIBLE INVESTMENT LEGISLATION	
Legislation on institutional investors and ESG issues	Law 27/2011 Royal Decree 1/2002
Legislation on investment managers and ESG issues	Circular sobre utilización por las instituciones de inversión colectiva de la denominación 'ético', 'ecológico' o cualquier otro que incida en aspectos de responsabilidad social. (INVERCO)
Legislation on corporations and ESG issues	Law 26/2003 Law 2/2011 Royal Decree 221/2008
ADDITIONAL RELEVANT RESPONSIBLE INVESTMENT CRITERIA	
	Corporate transparency Equal opportunities at the workplace
Sources employed in the responsible investment section of tables	Eurosif (2010). https://cpacanada.ca/en. (accessed 25/05/2015) Spainsif (2011). http://www.spainsif.es/. (accessed 25/05/2015)

22. Sweden

Sabina Du Rietz

SWEDEN	
Country Overview	
Population	9,119,423
Life expectancy	81.28 years
Literacy rate	99%
School life expectancy	16 years
Religious groups	Lutheran 87%, other (includes Roman Catholic, Orthodox, Baptist, Muslim, Jewish, and Buddhist) 13%
Government type	Constitutional monarchy
Legal system	Civil law system influenced by Roman-Germanic law and customary law
GDP/capita (PPP)	41,900
Main industries	Iron and steel, precision equipment (bearings, radio and telephone parts, armaments), wood pulp and paper products, processed foods, motor vehicles
Unemployment rate	8 %
Public debt/GDP	38,2 %
Market value of publicly traded shares	$470.1 billion
Internet users/population	92%
Special cultural aspects	Strong influence of trade unions
Responsible Investment Overview	
Overall RI market	$482.52 billion
Overall RI market growth rate (three-year average)	24% during a two-year period
Institutional RI market	$482.52 billion
Retail RI market	Statistics not available
# of PRI signatories	37
# of PRI asset owner signatories	14
# of PRI investment manager signatories	20
# of PRI professional service provider partners	3
Asset classes used in RI	Equity, fixed income, real estate, hedge funds, structured products, private equity, venture capital and commodities
Overall financial market size	Statistics not available
Launch year of first RI investment fund	1965
Launch year of national RI organization	2003
Largest three RI asset owners	AMF Folksam AP2
Largest three RI investment managers	Handelsbanken Nordea SEB Swedbank Robur

SWEDEN	
RESPONSIBLE INVESTMENT OVERVIEW	
Important RI professional service partners	GES Global Engagement Services Ethix SRI Advisors
Other relevant RI organizations	Sustainable Value Creation initiative
Major ESG issues of concern to society over the last decade	Human rights and labour conditions in supply chains, environmental issues in general and specifically in the energy sector.
Currently debated ESG issues	Shale gas, gender equality and whatever ESG scandals appear in the news.
RESPONSIBLE INVESTMENT LEGISLATION	
Legislation on institutional investors and ESG issues	Law 2000:192, which governs public pension funds
Legislation on investment managers and ESG issues	None
Legislation on corporations and ESG issues	Since 2007, Swedish state–owned companies are required to report according to the Global Reporting Initiative (GRI) accounting guidelines.
Sources employed in the responsible investment section of tables	Bengtsson, E. (2008) 'A history of Scandinavian socially responsible investing', *Journal of Business Ethics*, 82(4), 969–983.CIA World Factbook: https://www.cia.gov/library/publications/the-world-factbook/geos/sw.html. Eurosif (2012) European SRI Study 2012 (pp. 68). Brussels: Eurosif. Ministry of Finance. (2012). Statens ägarpolicy och riktlinjer för företag med statligt ägande. Swesif, http://www.swesif.org/om-swesif/verksamhetsberattelse/. UN PRI website: http://www.unpri.org/signatories/signatories/?country=Sweden.

23. Tunisia

Kais Bouslah

TUNISIA	
COUNTRY OVERVIEW	
Population	10,937,521 (July 2014 est.)
Life expectancy	75.68 years
Literacy rates	79.1%
School life expectancy	15 years
Religious groups	Muslim (official; Sunni) 99.1%, other (includes Christian, Jewish, Shia Muslim, and Baha'i) 1%
Government type	Republic
Legal system	Mixed legal system of civil law, based on the French civil code, and Islamic law; some judicial review of legislative acts in the Supreme Court in joint session.

(*Continued*)

TUNISIA	
	COUNTRY OVERVIEW
GDP/capita (PPP)	$9,900 (2013 est.)
Main industries	Agriculture (8.6% of GDP); industry (30.4% of GDP) such as petroleum, mining, tourism, textiles, footwear, agribusiness, beverages; services (61% of GDP).
Unemployment rate	17.2% (2013 est.)
Public debt/GDP	51.1% (2013 est.)
Market value of publicly traded shares	$8.887 billion (31 December 2012 est.)
Internet users/population	3.5 million (2009)
Special cultural aspects	Tunisia was home to different civilizations and cultures (e.g., Phoenician, Roman, Berber, paleo-Christian, Ottoman and Arab). Society characterized by openness and welcoming people. Microfinance and ethical- or values-based exclusions: influence of the Tunisian Islamic culture (99% of Tunisian population is Muslim). Sustainability-themed investment: increased interest of government, political class and civil society in ESG values and principles.
	RESPONSIBLE INVESTMENT OVERVIEW
Overall RI market	RI funds (four mutual funds and two private equity funds): $124.66 million of AUM (2013, using an exchange rate of 1 TND = 0.6081 USD). Microfinance: as of 2012, the unique Tunisian MFI (enda inter-arabe) has a gross loan portfolio of $86.8 million. The Tunisian Solidarity Bank (BTS) has total assets of $422.13 million (2010, using an exchange rate of 1 TND = 0.6943 USD).
Overall RI market growth rate (three-year average)	
Institutional RI market	
Retail RI market	
# of PRI signatories	None
# of PRI asset owner signatories	
# of PRI investment manager signatories	
# of PRI professional service provider partners	
Asset classes used in RI	Mutual funds, private equity funds, microfinance institutions (MFIs)
Overall financial market size	$8.87 billion (2012, using an exchange rate of 1 TND = 0.6442 USD)
Launch year of first RI investment fund	2009
Launch year of national RI organization	
Largest three RI asset owners	
Largest three RI investment managers	MAXULA GESTION CDC Gestion TUNISIE VALEURS

TUNISIA	
	Responsible Investment Overview
Important RI professional service partners	None
Other relevant RI organizations	Tunisian General Labour Union (UGTT); Tunisian Union for Industry, Commerce and Handicrafts (UTICA); Arab Institute of Business Managers (IACE); Confederation of Tunisian Citizen Entreprises (CONECT) International organizations for cooperation: United Nations Industrial Development Organization (UNIDO), EU, France, Germany, Italy and Sweden.
Major ESG issues of concern to society over the last decade	*Social issues*: Improving living conditions of communities, in particular those in the impoverished interior region, challenge of youth development and employment, the contribution of women to economic and social development. *Environmental issues*: Toxic and hazardous waste disposal is ineffective and poses health risks; water pollution from raw sewage; limited natural freshwater resources; deforestation; overgrazing; soil erosion; desertification. *Governance issues*: Governance reform, greater transparency, combatting corruption.
Currently debated ESG issues	*Social issues*: Improving living conditions of communities, in particular those in the impoverished interior region, challenge of youth development and employment, opportunities for women in the workplace, labor conditions. *Environmental issues*: Toxic and hazardous waste disposal is ineffective and poses health risks, water pollution from raw sewage, limited natural freshwater resources, climate change. *Governance issues*: Governance reform, greater transparency, combatting corruption, anti-money-laundering, combatting terrorism financing.
	Responsible Investment Legislation
Legislation on institutional investors and ESG issues	Complete regulatory framework for the Tunisian microfinance industry, including the creation of a supervisory authority and a clarification of the accreditation process.
Legislation on investment managers and ESG issues	
Legislation on corporations and ESG issues	The Tunisian investment incentives code provides financial and fiscal incentives for investment in environmental protection and pollution reduction. Several laws and regulations have been put in place regarding labor relations, protection of employees' health, promotion of human rights, environmental protection and combating corruption.
	Additional Relevant Responsible Investment criteria
Constitution and ESG issues	The new Tunisian Constitution includes six articles that directly address ESG issues, in particular, the three created independent commissions: Human Rights Commission, Commission for Sustainable Development and the Rights of Future Generations, and the Commission for Good Governance and Anti-Corruption.

(*Continued*)

TUNISIA	
Additional Relevant Responsible Investment criteria	
Sources employed in the responsible investment section of tables	CMF (2014), Physionomie des OPCVM (2014), Conseil du Marché Financier, June. Available: <http://www.cmf.org.tn/pdf/statistiques/opcvm.pdf>. BVMT (2012), Rapport annuel 1999–2012, Bourse des Valeurs Mobilières de Tunis. Available: http://www.bvmt.com.tn/fr/rapports-activites. CIA World Factbook (2014), Tunisia. Available: <https://www.cia.gov/library/publications/the-world-factbook/geos/ts.html>.

24. United Kingdom

Christoph F. Biehl and Jill F. Atkins

UNITED KINGDOM	
Country Overview	
Population	63,742,977
Life expectancy	80.42 years
Literacy rate	99%
School life expectancy	16 years
Religious groups	Christian 59.5%, none 25.7%, Muslim 4.4%, Hindu 1.3%, other 2%, unspecified 7.2%
Government type	Constitutional monarchy and Commonwealth realm
Legal system	Common law
GDP/capita (PPP)	$37,300
Main industries	Services: banking, insurance, business services
Unemployment rate	7.2%
Public debt/GDP	91.1%
Market value of publicly traded shares	$3.019 trillion
Internet users/population	83.25% 51.444 million Internet users 61,792,000 million inhabitants in 2009
Special cultural aspects	England, Scotland, Wales and Northern Ireland Scotland independence referendum
Responsible Investment Overview	
Overall RI market	$2.89 trillion (£1.7 trillion)
Overall RI market growth rate (three-year average)	26.86% $1,699,185 (2011) $1,339,432 (2009)
Institutional RI market	$2.8 trillion
Retail RI market	$0.09 trillion
# of PRI signatories	181
# of PRI asset owner signatories	39
# of PRI investment manager signatories	113
# of PRI professional service provider partners	29

UNITED KINGDOM	
RESPONSIBLE INVESTMENT OVERVIEW	
Asset classes used in RI	Listed equity, fixed income, private equity, real estate, commodities, hedge funds, infrastructure
Overall financial market size	
Launch year of first RI investment fund	1984
Launch year of national RI organization	1991
Largest three RI asset owners	
Largest three RI investment managers	
Important RI professional service partners	
Other relevant RI organizations	UKSIF, EuroSIF
Major ESG issues of concern to society over the last decade	Executive remuneration Sustainable financial markets Lack of trust in financial institutions Climate change
Currently debated ESG issues	'Tax planning' Sustainable financial markets
RESPONSIBLE INVESTMENT LEGISLATION	
Legislation on institutional investors and ESG issues	Occupational Pension Schemes (Investment) Regulations (2005) – Regulation 2(3) (and equivalent for stakeholder pensions and charities) UK Stewardship Code Companies Act
Legislation on investment managers and ESG issues	UK Stewardship Code
Legislation on corporations and ESG issues	Companies Act UK Corporate Governance Code
ADDITIONAL RELEVANT RESPONSIBLE INVESTMENT CRITERIA	
	Institutional investors dominate the market (97%)
Sources employed in the responsible investment section of tables	CIA World Factbook Eurosif: European SRI Study 2012 PRI website, 2014/06/17 UKSIF: http://uksif.org/about-uksif/history/

25. USA

Meg Voorhes

UNITED STATES	
COUNTRY OVERVIEW	
Population	316 million (2012)
Life expectancy	78.7 years (2010)
Literacy rate	85.5% (2003)
School life expectancy	16 years
Religious groups	51% Protestant/other Christian, 23% Catholic, 14% none, 8% Mormon, Jewish, Muslim or other non-Christian, 3% no response

(Continued)

UNITED STATES	
Country Overview	
Government type	Democracy
Legal system	Federalist. US Constitution created federal court system but reserves some power for the 50 state court systems.
GDP/capita (PPP)	$49,800
Main industries	High-technology innovator, second largest industrial output in world; petroleum, steel, motor vehicles, aerospace, telecommunications, chemicals, electronics, food processing, consumer goods, lumber, mining
Unemployment rate	7.0% as of November 2013
Public debt/GDP	70% (2012 est.)
Market value of publicly traded shares	$15.64 trillion at year-end 2011 $17.14 trillion at year-end 2010
Internet users/population	71.7% (2011)
Special cultural aspects	
Responsible Investment Overview	
Overall RI market	$3.74 trillion
Overall RI market growth rate	22% over two-year period from year-end 2009 to year-end 2011
Institutional RI market	$2.5 trillion
Retail RI market	Not known definitively, but assets of mutual funds and other registered investment companies considering ESG criteria totaled $456 billion at year-end 2011.
# of PRI signatories	183
# of PRI asset owner signatories	21
# of PRI investment manager signatories	134
# of PRI professional service provider partners	28
Asset classes used in RI	Equity, fixed income, alternatives, loan funds, cash instruments
Overall financial market size	$33 trillion
Launch year of first RI investment fund	1928
Launch year of national RI organization	1984
Largest three RI asset owners	California Public Employees Retirement System (CalPERS), California State Teachers Retirement System, New York State Common Retirement Fund
Largest three RI investment managers	Among US SIF membership: Calvert, Parnassus, TIAA-CREF
Important RI professional service partners	See listings in US SIF Financial Services Directory, accessible at http://www.ussif.org/AF_MemberDirectory.asp.
Other relevant RI organizations	Ceres, the Council of International Investors, the Interfaith Center for Corporate Responsibility, the Investor Network on Climate Risk, the Global Impact Investing Network and US SIF

UNITED STATES	
Responsible Investment Overview	
Major ESG issues of concern to society over the last decade	Climate change and other environmental issues, corporate political spending and lobbying, advisory vote on executive pay, sustainability reporting, board independence and structure
Currently debated ESG issues	Climate change and other environmental issues, including environment health and safety of fossil fuel operations, clean technology and green building; corporate political spending and lobbying; advisory vote on executive pay; sustainability reporting; board independence and structure; majority voting; Sudan
Responsible Investment Legislation	
Legislation on institutional investors and ESG issues	
Legislation on investment managers and ESG issues	
Legislation on corporations and ESG issues	Wall Street Reform and Consumer Protection Act of 2010
Sources employed in the responsible investment section of tables	Bureau of Labor Statistics. Available HTTP: <http://data.bls.gov/timeseries/LNS14000000> (accessed 30 December 2013). Central Intelligence Agency. The World Factbook. Available HTTP: <https://www.cia.gov/library/publications/the-world-factbook/geos/us.html> (accessed 30 December 2013). Gallup. Available HTTP: <http://www.gallup.com/poll/1690/Religion.aspx> (accessed 30 December 2013). National Assessment of Adult Literacy. Available HTTP: http://nces.ed.gov/naal/estimates/overview.aspx (accessed 30 December 2013). PRI website. United States Courts website. Available HTTP: <http://www.uscourts.gov/EducationalResources/FederalCourtBasics/CourtStructure/UnderstandingFederalAndStateCourts.aspx> (accessed 27 March 2012). US Census. State and County Quick Facts. Available HTTP: <http://quickfacts.census.gov/qfd/states/00000.html> (accessed 30 December 2013). US Center for Disease Control. Deaths and Mortality. Available HTTP: <http://www.cdc.gov/nchs/fastats/deaths.htm> (accessed 30 December 2013). US SIF Foundation. (2012) 2012 Report on Sustainable and Responsible Investing Trends in the United States. Washington, DC: US SIF Foundation.

Notes

1 Introducing RI. Online, available HTTP: <http://www.unpri.org/introducing-responsible-investment/>.
2 Gordon L.C. (2014) 'Fiduciary duty and the search for a shared conception of sustainable development', *PRI RI Quarterly Report* Vol. 2, January.
3 World Economic Forum (2014) Global Risks report.

Part III

32

The changing role of asset owners in responsible investment

Reflections on the principles for responsible investment – the last decade and the next

James Gifford

Introduction

In this chapter I reflect on the last 10 years (2004–2014) of engaging asset owners in responsible investment. As the founding Executive Director of the Principles for Responsible Investment (PRI) (2006–2013), I look back at the origins of this initiative and how the PRI sought to define, for the first time, the role of asset owners in responsible investment. I explore whether the vision of asset owner mobilization around responsible investment is being achieved. I also look to the future of responsible investment, and the role asset owners might play going forward.

In November 2003, when working as an intern at the UN Environment Program Finance Initiative (UNEP FI) in Geneva, I floated the idea for a set of principles that would define best practice around shareholder engagement by pension funds. The working title was the 'Principles for Responsible Pension Fund Engagement', which would be a set of commitments that pension funds would sign around engaging with investee companies to abide by UN norms, translated for the corporate sector in the form of the UN Global Compact. This idea was merged with the existing work of UNEP FI around the materiality of environmental, social and governance (ESG) issues to equity pricing, and the project was renamed the 'Principles for Responsible Investment'. We were off and running to develop the first ever set of principles that would define the role of asset owners (and their agents) in responsible investment.[1]

My interest in engaging asset owners in responsible investment started a few years earlier when I was the first ever 'Internet campaigner' for the Wilderness Society, an Australian NGO. My job was to build the online applications that would allow members of the public to quickly and easily send customized emails to, for example, their local members of parliament. The particular company we were targeting at the time, Gunns Ltd., was a powerful forestry company with bipartisan political support at the state level. We started to think about levers beyond political lobbying that we could use to encourage the company to move out of old growth logging and into certified sustainable plantations. One strategy was to focus on those who owned and financed the company; that is, Australian superannuation (pension) funds, mutual fund managers and banks.

Millions of Australians supported the end of old growth logging in Tasmania, yet the banks and pension funds that held their savings and investments were directly or indirectly financing this company's activities. We felt that this was a market failure that needed to be addressed; an agency problem where the agents (in particular, the pension funds) were failing to act in the interests of their ultimate beneficiaries and clients.

To file a shareholder resolution in a public company in Australia at the time required 100 shareholders, regardless of the number of shares held. We put together a coalition of 100 small shareholders to force an extraordinary general meeting of the company. We also filed shareholder resolutions at the annual general meetings of the banks that were financing the company, either directly or through their fund management subsidiaries. Through our online campaigns, we generated thousands of emails from members of superannuation funds to the leadership of these organizations letting them know that their members care about how their money is invested. While the Gunns Ltd. resolution received only 0.4 per cent support, the resolution at the Commonwealth Bank on the same issue garnered support of 23 per cent of the voting shares, the largest percentage support for an environmental resolution in Australia's history.[2]

Over the 10 years of the campaign against Gunns Ltd.,[3] the loss of customers and financiers resulted in the share price going from over $4 to around $0.26. Finally, in 2010, the investors turned on the management, forced the exit of the long-time chairman and put in place a board and management team that was explicitly committed to a sustainable future for the forestry industry.

That experience at the Wilderness Society, together with a master's thesis I wrote on socially responsible investment strategies, solidified my view that asset owners, and pension funds in particular, had an incredibly powerful – and virtually unexplored – role in creating a more sustainable society.

It seemed obvious to me at the time that institutional asset owners like pension funds should be reflecting the interests of their members in investment decisions and should see themselves as key drivers of a more sustainable society. The reality was that most didn't – and still don't. However, back in 2004, there were a small number who did.

One member of the advisory group that I put together in the early days of the PRI was Raj Thamotheram,[4] the first head of responsible investment at the UK-based Universities Superannuation Scheme. I heard Raj speak in mid-2004, and he said something along the lines of: "It makes no sense to deliver strong investment returns for a person's retirement, if in doing so, we leave them without a decent world in which to retire". This remains quite a radical statement.

The lack of willingness of most asset owners to acknowledge they have any social responsibilities beyond financial returns is at odds with the stated views of many of the large companies in the portfolios of these same investors. Few leading corporations today would state publicly that they have no responsibilities to anyone beyond shareholder maximization.[5] Yet the majority of mainstream asset owners hold the view that it is not only appropriate, but required, to focus only on delivering financial returns to clients and beneficiaries. Only a small proportion acknowledge that they are societal institutions that can – and have a responsibility to – play a role in addressing some of society's challenges, in addition to their primary role of generating financial returns.[6]

In 2004, we concluded that if the PRI initiative was going to resonate within the mainstream asset owner community it needed to be framed in a way that would be compatible with how investors saw themselves and their role in society. It was clear that a radical attempt at reframing their responsibilities would likely fail.

As we began the process to develop the PRI, we needed a pathway for the asset owner organizations to feel safe in moving ahead. Given the all-pervasiveness of the paradigm of return maximization, we found two main avenues that appeared to have potential.

The first was shareholder engagement. With a focus on shareholder engagement, or 'active ownership', investors could invest in whatever they liked, based on traditional investment processes, and the shareholder engagement staff could use their influence as shareholders to seek improvements in corporate behaviour.[7] If this could be done in collaboration with other like-minded investors, it would form a powerful stakeholder coalition that would challenge the dominant signal coming from short-term investors who focused on a handful of short-term financial metrics. This was, in effect, the policy being implemented by most of the leading US pension funds, which had quite progressive shareholder engagement strategies around ESG issues, but were doing little on the investment side.

The second strategy was a focus on ESG integration. During this same period, UNEP FI and the UN Global Compact had started working on another angle – the idea that there is a lot of information about ESG performance of companies that is potentially material, yet because of market failures, such as short-termism, lack of decent metrics and lack of data around these issues, it is routinely ignored. Therefore, investors who integrate these issues in a systematic way into their investment processes should end up with a better understanding of risk and opportunity, and therefore should be able to be better investors and, ultimately, outperform their peers. These arguments became even stronger when taking a long-term, value-oriented investment approach, as many ESG issues are more evidently material and relevant to company success over the longer term.[8] This idea became known as 'ESG integration', and rather than seeing the incorporation of ESG issues into investment processes as something that might reduce returns, it was reframed as new and material information that can potentially enhance returns and reduce risk.

These two notions also avoided the divestment/screening approach, which was a nonstarter with most of these mainstream institutions, but was the basis of the more retail-oriented socially responsible investment industry.

Armed with these two concepts, as well as other ideas around transparency, investor engagement in public policy and pushing these concepts across asset classes, the UNEP FI and the UN Global Compact announced a process to develop the Principles for Responsible Investment.[9]

Asset owners in the articulation of the principles of responsible investment

'Asset owner' can be a confusing term.[10] It is commonly used to describe a subset of institutional investors such as pension funds, foundations, endowments and insurance companies that control investable assets.[11] These institutions are thought of as being at the 'top' of the investment chain and have the power to determine how their assets are invested. They often outsource the management of their assets to investment managers, and are advised on asset allocation and the selection of managers by investment consultants. However, many so-called asset owners are not, in reality, the ultimate owners of these assets. Rather, they are themselves agents for thousands and sometimes millions of beneficiaries whose savings they manage – a fact that lies at the heart of asset owners' role in responsible investment.

We made a very deliberate decision in the early days of the PRI development process to put these institutional asset owners in the driver's seat. Of all the arguments for being a responsible investor, the one that resonates most with investment managers is that this what clients want. Client demand is without doubt the biggest driver of investment managers' signing the PRI[12] and engaging in responsible investment activity.

We agreed from the very beginning that the asset owners needed to take the lead in developing the principles, and that we needed strong buy-in from the top of these institutions. We brought in Mercer, a leading pension consultant, to help facilitate the drafting sessions.[13] UN Secretary-General Kofi Annan sent personal invitations to the heads of 25 of the world's largest and most progressive pension funds to join the process. These included CalPERS, NYCERS, New York State Common, Canada Pension Plan Investment Board, British Telecom Pension Scheme, Universities Superannuation Scheme, Norwegian Government Pension Scheme, the French Fonds de Reserve, PGGM, ABP, Folksam and others. The drafting group of asset owners was supported by an 80-person expert group made up of socially responsible investment (SRI) and mainstream investment practitioners, academics, NGOs and consultants that met to provide input into the process and feedback on drafts.

After a year-long process, we had a set of agreed-upon principles. In April 2006, the Secretary-General launched the Principles for Responsible Investment at the New York Stock Exchange. The Principles were the first major effort to try to codify the responsibilities of asset owners around responsible investment.

Principle 1: We will incorporate ESG issues into investment analysis and decision-making processes.
Principle 2: We will be active owners and incorporate ESG issues into our ownership policies and practices.
Principle 3: We will seek appropriate disclosure on ESG issues by the entities in which we invest.
Principle 4: We will promote acceptance and implementation of the Principles within the investment industry.
Principle 5: We will work together to enhance our effectiveness in implementing the Principles.
Principle 6: We will each report on our activities and progress towards implementing the Principles.

On reading the Principles and the possible actions listed under each,[14] it is clear that the notion of incorporation of ESG issues into investment management processes (Principle 1) was core, being interpreted by most investors as the integration of these issues into mainstream investment decision-making for the purpose of delivering better risk-adjusted returns. However, 'incorporation' was left undefined by the PRI drafting group, allowing investors to incorporate these issues any way they choose, including various ethical screening approaches in addition to mainstream ESG integration approaches.

Active ownership, meaning voting at company meetings and dialogue with investee entities (Principle 2) around ESG issues, was clearly articulated and formed the second core commitment within the Principles. There was little disagreement that this activity was fundamental to being a responsible investor, and shareholder engagement with companies had been pushed for by various codes of corporate governance for some time. The PRI's contribution was to broaden the topics on which shareholders were expected to engage with companies beyond traditional corporate governance and strategy issues to include environmental and social issues.

Principle 3 was based on the notion that unless we have reliable and comprehensive ESG information at hand, it is not possible to implement the other Principles. Principle 3 called on signatories to seek out ESG information from the entities in which they invest.

Principle 4 acknowledged the role of agents within the chain, and encouraged asset owners to ensure that their investment managers and service providers also implement the Principles, or provide services to enable others to do so. It also acknowledged the role of investors in public policy.

Principle 5 recognized that many of the problems that responsible investment was seeking to remedy are collective action problems, and only by acting together could these issues be effectively addressed. The importance of collaboration emerged during the drafting process as something that was essential to the effectiveness of responsible investment, particularly with respect to collaborative shareholder engagement with companies and policy makers.

Principle 6 focused on investor transparency, and the necessity for clients and members of institutional investment funds to have regular reporting on how the asset owners and managers to whom their money is entrusted are implementing the principles.

These Principles, over the following years, formed the foundation for the largest investor initiative in responsible investment, and by 2014 more than 1,200 institutions had signed the PRI, representing more than $40 trillion in assets.

After seven years at the helm of the PRI, through its rapid growth and expansion, I am pleased with what has been achieved to date. That said, the remainder of this chapter will explore a number of additional areas that I believe constitute important roles and responsibilities for asset owners over the next decade, and, if the PRI were to have been drafted ten years on, would be on the agenda for inclusion.

The responsibility to reduce externalities

'Universal ownership' is a term that was coined by shareholder activist Robert Monks in 1995[15] and taken forward by James Haley and Andy Williams.[16] It is the idea that large, diversified investors end up owning a fairly representative slice of the capital stock of the global economy, and therefore their returns are driven more by the success of the economy as a whole than by their individual investments.

By way of example, picture 10 factories on a river, each of which needs clean water to operate. The factory at the top of the river saves some money by not treating its waste. This pollutes the river for the nine factories downstream, requiring them to put in place expensive treatment plants. A universal owner that owns shares in all the companies would see – as would any economist – that the economic output of the group of factories would be maximized through some mechanism that reduced the incentive to pollute. This concept is the merger of the theory of environmental externalities with the reality that large investors are incredibly diversified, and externalities generated by one company affect other companies in the portfolio, and the system as a whole.[17]

Because the world's asset owners have a stake in the prosperity of the economy as a whole, there is a strong argument that part of the role of an asset owner should be to push for policies and frameworks that reduce negative externalities. In practical terms, this would point to asset owners having a rationale to push investee companies to set minimum standards and certifications and to support sensible public policy (pollution control, emissions trading schemes, etc.) that would result in the most efficient allocation of environmental and social resources.

The responsibility to ensure time horizons are aligned

Many of the problems with the financial sector are caused by a misalignment of time horizons. Pension funds often have investment horizons of many decades. Most people who directly manage this pension capital are incentivized to 'outperform' in less than a year, and in many cases shorter periods. McKinsey and Company,[18] the Bank of England[19] and many others have identified a range of problems caused by this focus on short-termism, and how it results not only in lower returns and higher fees for investors, but can also send signals to companies to inflate short-term cash flows by under-investing in longer-term, yet more profitable, internal investments.

Shifting to an investment horizon that more closely matches the actual liabilities of long-term asset owners would allow greater investment in less liquid asset classes, particularly those that would help to build a low-carbon future. However, currently, short-term thinking is embedded in the financial system through compensation structures tied to short-term financial results.

The issue of long-termism was certainly on the table when the PRI was being drafted. It was debated by the investors involved, but the lack of a clear commitment to long-termism reflected investors' views at the time that their short-term investment strategies (in particular, hedge funds) were legitimate and shouldn't be seen as 'irresponsible'. Given the financial crisis and a much greater recognition of the problem of short-termism within policy and investment circles, a redrafted PRI would, it is to be hoped, have a much stronger commitment to long-term investing. Indeed, CalPERS' investment beliefs, published in 2014, state "A long time investment horizon is a responsibility and an advantage".[20]

The responsibility to select sustainable investment managers and monitor them

The majority of asset owners outsource most, if not all, of their investment management to external investment managers. Therefore, the most important role of a responsible asset owner is in the selection and monitoring of investment managers who manage their funds. While this was included in the possible actions of Principle 4 of the PRI, and progress has been made, particularly in Europe and Australia, there is still a long way to go.[21]

The first step is to put questions and expectations around responsible investment capability into requests for proposals that go out to the investment management community. These types of questions – and the implication that unless you are doing something on responsible investment you will miss out on investment mandates – have been pivotal in mobilizing the investment management community on responsible investment.

The next step is to ensure that these managers actually implement their own responsible investment policies and report on their achievements, goals and challenges in the same way they report on financial performance. Even for those asset owners that do set long-term, sustainable investment mandates, these intentions can quickly be undone by sending mixed signals in terms of what is important. If the first thing an asset owner asks when they sit down with an investment manager in a quarterly meeting is, 'run me through last quarter's performance', it is no surprise that a manager's investment horizon would shrink to fit what the client is indicating is really important. Manager meetings should be about how the ESG strategy is driving an investment strategy that will generate long-term, sustainable returns.

The responsibility to select an investment consultant with the right skills

Most asset owners use investment consultants to advise them on selection and monitoring of investment managers. While there are ESG specialists in most large investment consultancies, they are primarily servicing those clients who specifically ask for them. The great majority of mainstream investment consultants lack any understanding of responsible investment and don't see it as their role to show any leadership in this area.

One of the most important roles of an asset owner is to select an investment consultant who has a deep and holistic understanding of both responsible investment approaches and mainstream investment, and can be proactive in providing more sustainable investment solutions across asset classes.

The responsibility to seek positive impact

The last 10 years has seen a clear shift in thinking about responsible/sustainable investment, moving from a niche and mostly retail-oriented, values-based approach to the mainstream ESG 'movement' that contends that these issues are material and more relevant than ever and need to be integrated into investment processes. The public commitments made by PRI signatories when they sign the Principles are testament to that shift. Most large fund managers now claim (with varying degrees of validity) to integrate material ESG issues into their investment processes,[22] and many now have specialist staff to achieve this goal. Shareholder dialogue on ESG issues is happening more than ever before. Progress on the PRI's two core pillars of ESG incorporation and active ownership has been made. There is now a much greater recognition that ESG issues can be material to investment returns and should be incorporated as part of the normal investment process.

However, these two pillars are not enough. There was a third pillar that wasn't included in the PRI, and this, above all, would need to be addressed in any redrafting of the Principles – that is, the proactive allocation of capital to make a positive impact on society and the environment.

Capital needs to shift towards cleaner and more sustainable and impactful enterprises at scale, particularly to those that are solving major global challenges such as climate change, water scarcity, sustainable agriculture and fisheries, deforestation and poverty. Given the projected disruption to the global economy and uncertainly implicit in runaway climate change, no one could argue that it is the fiduciary duty of investors to support the 'business-as-usual' case for emissions growth.

I believe asset owners have a responsibility to be proactive in seeking out investments that deliver both market-rate, risk-adjusted returns and a positive contribution to this century's big challenges. They have the power to drive the market and the scale to have a tremendous positive impact. The most progressive pension funds have built expertise in many of these areas, such as renewable energy infrastructure, and are proactively seeking out opportunities in impact investing.[23] Some have also invested in microfinance, clean tech, low-income housing projects and many other impact investments.

Given the dominance of the return maximization paradigm, these investments need to deliver similar risk-adjusted returns as any other investment. However, with expertise and proactive approaches, asset owners can invest at least a proportion of their assets in high-impact enterprises that help to solve these big social and environmental challenges, and do so in commercial ways.[24]

One idea that was floated in the PRI drafting process was a commitment around 'all other things being equal, we will choose the most sustainable investment'. Given the proliferation of sustainable investment products and opportunities over recent years, and debates around divestment of fossil fuels, this commitment would certainly be an interesting area to explore if the PRI Principles were to be drafted today.

The responsibility to act in the best interests of your clients and members – broadly defined

The first era of responsible investment, pre-2004, was primarily around values-oriented and retail-focused SRI. The second era, 2004–2014, was the ESG era, where these issues went from being treated as irrelevant by investors to being treated as potentially material and incorporated into mainstream investment practices. This era also brought shareholder dialogue on ESG issues into the mainstream. I believe the next 10 years will see yet another transition where investors will be held accountable for their actual impact, positive or negative, on the world, in the same way that the largest corporations (sometimes) are.

Citizens are realizing that their savings are being invested in ways that are not representing their interests. They are realizing that the status quo of Wall Street and the City of London has failed them. The agency chain is broken, and it is becoming clear that the finance sector is primarily there to serve itself, and not the function for which it exists; that is, to efficiently allocate capital to productive enterprises.

Asset owners have been shielded from the types of campaigning that large corporations have faced for 25 years. Asset owners are often at least two steps removed from the actual negative impacts of corporate behaviour on the ground, and so it is easier to campaign directly against a company than with a group of investors who may only own a per cent or less of its shares. However, this is changing. NGOs such as ShareAction[25] and the continued shareholder activist work of groups such as The Wilderness Society will only increase.

The unprecedented transparency that is enabled by smartphone penetration in developing countries means that unethical or exploitative corporate practices have a greater chance of being exposed than ever before. The increasing use of big data also increases attention on corporate behaviour. This transparency will also shine sunlight on who owns what, and asset owners will be held to account more than ever for the actions of the companies in their portfolios. It will become clearer to their members and customers who is and who isn't investing their money in their best interests. Asset owners are actors in society, just like every other institution. Their actions, through their investment decisions, will increasingly be examined and judged.

Again, CalPERS' Investment Beliefs explicitly recognize stakeholder views in a way that very few others do, stating "CalPERS investment decisions may reflect wider stakeholder views, provided they are consistent with its fiduciary duty to members and beneficiaries".[26]

There is also a large upside in moving in this direction. Asset owners will have the opportunity to be proactive and demonstrate that their investments are actually supporting ethical and sustainable enterprises, while protecting the environment. They will be able to pick and choose among hundreds of commercially attractive sustainable investments. And they will be able to proudly tell their members and beneficiaries that they are helping to build the type of world their members want to retire into.

As this happens, asset owner institutions will recognize that they do indeed have responsibilities beyond maximizing returns, and that investing in ways that also enhance and protect human and environmental values is simply the way things will be done.

Notes

1 Online, available HTTP: <http://www.unepfi.org/events/2004/pensions/>.
2 Online, available HTTP: <http://www.maynereport.com/articles/2008/09/08–1751–3954.html>.
3 For a summary of the decade-long Gunns Ltd. campaign, see online, available HTTP: <http://www.theage.com.au/national/the-felling-of-gunns-20110311–1br9d.html>.
4 Raj Thamotheram's views are well captured online, available HTTP: <http://blueandgreentomorrow.com/features/the-long-term-matters-and-sustainable-investment-holds-the-key-to-prosperity/>.
5 That said, shareholder value maximization remains the dominant paradigm in business. The point is that most large corporations explicitly recognize the importance of stakeholders, corporate responsibility and the need to retain their 'licence to operate' within the communities in which they operate. Even the most progressive investors rarely acknowledge this, and rather describe their responsible investment in terms of risk mitigation or being a better investor.
6 PGGM is one large asset owner that believes that "that a sustainable world contributes to a valuable future for pension beneficiaries". Online, available HTTP: <https://www.pggm.nl/english/what-we-do/Documents/Responsible-Investment-Annual-Report_2013.pdf>.
7 This reflected the thinking of another veteran of responsible investment, Craig Mackenzie, who set up such a team at Friends, Ivory and Sime (now F&C) and then at Insight Investment. This 'shareholder engagement overlay' provided for direct dialogue with companies, without necessarily participating in the investment decision-making process. See Mackenzie, C. & Sullivan, R. (2008) 'Can investor activism play a meaningful role in correcting market failures', *Journal of Corporate Citizenship* 31: 77–88.
8 Online, available HTTP: <http://www.unepfi.org/fileadmin/documents/amwg_materiality_equity_pricing_report_2004.pdf>; <https://www.unglobalcompact.org/resources/218>.
9 Online, available HTTP: <http://www.unepfi.org/fileadmin/rii/20040715_unep_press_release.pdf>.

10 According to the FAQs of the Principles for Responsible Investment, they are those "Organisations that represent end-asset owners who hold long-term retirement savings, insurance and other assets". Online, available HTTP: <http://www.unpri.org/about-pri/faqs/>.

11 In theory, mutual funds that serve a retail clientele could also be considered asset owners. However, commercial retail mutual funds, with primarily contractual relationships rather than fiduciary relationships with clients, have tended to be considered in the PRI lexicon – not without controversy – as investment managers rather than asset owners. Online, available HTTP: <www.unpri.org/about-pri/faqs/>.

12 Significantly more investment managers have signed the PRI than asset owners: as of September 2014, 814 vs. 276, respectively. In addition, the assets managed by these investment managers far outweighed the assets controlled by these asset owners.

13 Mercer was the first asset consultant to build a substantial business in responsible investment, and remains the largest team today. Online, available HTTP: <http://www.mercer.com/services/investments/investment-opportunities/responsible-investment.html>.

14 For the full text and possible actions within each Principle see online. Available HTTP: <http://www.unpri.org/about-pri/the-six-principles>.

15 Monks, R.A.G. and Minnow, N. (1995) *Corporate Governance*, Cambridge, MA: Basil Blackwell.

16 Hawley, J. P. and Williams, A. T. (2000) *The Rise of Fiduciary Capitalism: How Institutional Investors Can Make Corporate America More Democratic*, Philadelphia: University of Pennsylvania Press.

17 See PRI publication *Universal Ownership: Why Environmental Externalities Matter to Institutional Investors.* Online, available HTTP: <http://www.unpri.org/publications/>.

18 For background, see the McKinsey and CPPIB initiative 'Focusing Capital on the Long Term'. Online, available HTTP: <http://www.fclt.org/>.

19 Online, available HTTP: <http://www.bankofengland.co.uk/publications/Pages/news/2011/043.aspx>.

20 Online, available HTTP: <http://www.calpers.ca.gov/eip-docs/about/pubs/board-offsite.pdf>.

21 See PRI publication *Aligning Expectations: Guidance for Asset Owners on Incorporating ESG Factors into Manager Selection, Appointment and Monitoring.* Online, available HTTP: <http://www.unpri.org/publications/>.

22 See PRI Report on Progress 2014. Online, available HTTP: <http://www.unpri.org/publications>.

23 See Christian Super. Online, available HTTP: <www.christiansuper.com.au>.

24 See Sonen Capital, *Evolution of an Impact Portfolio: From Implementation to Results.* Online, available HTTP: <http://www.sonencapital.com/evolution-of-impact.php>.

25 Online, available HTTP: <http://shareaction.org/>.

26 Online, available HTTP: <http://www.calpers.ca.gov/eip-docs/about/pubs/board-offsite.pdf>.

33

The responsible investment practices of the world's largest government-sponsored investment funds

Hugues Létourneau

Introduction

This chapter studies the factors that increase the propensity of government-sponsored investment funds (GSIFs) to integrate environmental, social and governance (ESG) considerations, into their investment decision-making process. Over the last 30 years, the increased utilization of financial markets as a repository of national and personal savings has led to a domination of the financial markets by large institutional investors (Gray, 2009). The most important class of institutional investors are public pension funds given their broad constituencies and their long-term investment horizon (Clark & Hebb, 2005). In recent years, another class of GSIF has also emerged in global finance: sovereign wealth funds (SWFs). Indeed, at the end of 2012 pension funds were the most important class of global investors with $33.9 trillion[1] in assets under management (AUM), whereas sovereign wealth funds cumulated $5.2 trillion in AUM (The City UK Research Centre, 2013).

Since the early 2000s, an increasing number of GSIFs, namely, public pension funds and sovereign wealth funds, have been taking an active ownership approach, through mechanisms such as shareholder engagement with corporate boards, proxy voting or divestment, towards corporate performance on environmental issues (e.g. increased carbon disclosure, sustainable use of resources such as water) and social issues (e.g. consultation with communities, labour rights, etc.) (Deutsche Bank, 2012). The term 'responsible investment' (RI) was coined around 2005 to describe an investment approach that considers ESG issues out of a belief that long-term risk-adjusted returns will be higher.[2] Among the public investors that have been at the fore of such an approach, we notably find the California Public Employees Retirement System's (CalPERS) ($220 billion AUM), Sweden's AP Funds ($137 billion AUM) and Norway's Government Pension Fund-Global (GPFG) ($656 billion AUM), a SWF investing surpluses from Norway's oil riches abroad.

This chapter seeks to understand the specific conditions that increase the likelihood that the international consensus on the merits of sustainable development can feed into the investment considerations of financial vehicles that are meant to serve collective needs (e.g. public pension funds and sovereign wealth funds). This work thus adheres to suggestions that government-sponsored investment vehicles can play a role in advancing values such as human rights

(Ghahramani, 2011), climate change protection (Reiche, 2010), environmental and social issues (Van Der Zee, 2012; Sethi, 2005) and international codes and conventions[3] (Ambachtsheer, 2011) that fall under the broad banner of sustainable development.[4]

I empirically test the importance of agency-related and structural factors in determining the likelihood that a GSIF will adopt an RI policy. The agent-centered arguments use the investor as the unit of analysis and stipulate that investors adopt RI out of rational motives as a mean of securing better risk-adjusted long-term returns. This interpretation rests mainly on the universal owner hypothesis, which stipulates that large, diversified portfolio owners own cross sections of the economy (Hawley & Williams, 2000; 2007). Their large equity positions, usually held in the form of minority ownership stakes across thousands of companies scattered across the globe notably means that their portfolios are exposed to costs linked to negative externalities like environmental damage. As a result, this hypothesis suggests that corporations should actively engage with corporations in order to minimize negative externalities. Structure-centered explanations account for the role of national political economic institutions in the adoption of RI policies for GSIFs. This theoretical stream factors the importance attributed by nations to environmental and social issues along with the ability of civil society to feed their values into the public policy process (Prakash & Potoski, 2006; Guillen, 1994; Cole, 1989; Baron et al., 1988).

Following a literature review that will provide theoretical grounds for the analysis, two research questions will be put to empirical scrutiny:

- Why have adoption rates of responsible investment policies by GSIFs varied across and within jurisdictions?
- What factors have shaped the perception of GSIFs about the legitimating value of such an initiative?

The hypothesized interplay between agency and structure will draw on the role of a logic of appropriateness relative to a logic of consequentiality in decision making (March & Olsen, 2008; 1989). Briefly stated, an agent acting under a logic of consequence assumes self-interested and rationally calculated decisions that maximize the actor's utility; a logic of appropriateness implies acting according to institutionalized practices that are thought to be good, desirable and appropriate. Under the logic of appropriateness, behaviour is directed by components of a society's structure (Finnemore & Sikkink, 1998). This framework recognizes the challenge associated to fitting both logics into a single framework but also stresses the importance of recognizing both logics in an actor's preference formation (March & Olsen, 2008). The hypothesized relationship between agency and structure for the case at play is the following: GSIFs will form the same preferences toward responsible investing based on a logic of appropriateness regardless of structural context. I stipulate that the structure – which shapes the appropriateness of GSIF consideration of RI – will outweigh the importance of the agent's rational preference for responsible investment in determining whether RI will be adopted. In other words, the more a fund displays agency features related to stronger preferences toward responsible investment – as hypothesized below – the more likely a favourable structural context to responsible investment (e.g. strong civil society, democratic institutions) will result in the adoption of responsible investment by a fund. Nonetheless, structural factors will tend to edge out agency factors in GSIF adoption of responsible investment; a universal owner evolving in an authoritarian regime is less likely to adopt responsible investment than a non-universal owner in a vibrant democratic regime where legitimacy, the 'social license to operate' of the fund toward the citizenry and beneficiaries, matters.

To investigate the research question, I will analyze a sample of the RI policies (or lack thereof), of 158 GSIFs: 48 sovereign wealth funds and 110 public pension funds spanning 47 countries across every continent. The methodology will borrow elements from comparative political analyses and yield inferences regarding the most important factors that have led to the adoption of RI policies by GSIFs. The statistical analysis is performed using the ordered probit regression function in Stata, the statistical software package. The dependent variable was developed through a qualitative evaluation of the largest public pension funds' and sovereign wealth funds' investment mandates and policies in order to grade their degree of commitment to RI principles.

This chapter will proceed as follows. The second section will give an overview of the importance of GSIFs in the global economy. The third section will define the concept of RI, locate it within a broader historical context and relate it to GSIFs. It also reviews the literature on RI in order to identify the factors that drive the adoption of RI policies. The fourth section derives hypotheses from the literature review. The fifth section explains the data and methodologies that are used to perform the analysis. The sixth section will report the findings of the statistical analysis of the six models tested. Finally, the conclusion will review the findings, their limitations along with their implications for the continued integration of sustainable development considerations into the global financial sphere.

Government-sponsored investment funds in the global economy

This section outlines the evolution, role and importance of GSIFs in the global economy. Investors, alongside corporations, are at the core of the capitalist system. GSIFs encompass publically mandated pension funds, along with an increasing number of sovereign wealth funds. Sovereign wealth funds are government-owned investment funds that "hold, manage, or administer assets to achieve financial objectives and employ a set of investment strategies which include investing in foreign financial assets" (Sovereign Investment Lab, 2012, p. 8). Public pension funds provide retirement income to the public (e.g. sovereign pension funds such as the Canada Pension Plan Investment Board) or to state employees (e.g. public-sector pension funds such as the Ontario Teacher's Pension Plan) and are generally funded through mandatory contributions.

Public pension funds and sovereign wealth funds are both asset owners that share a number of similarities. Having been set up through decisions by the legislative or executive branches, they are subject to the particular preferences, goals and objectives underlying decision making within their respective domestic authority structure, decision making which is not insulated from the public judgment (Dixon & Monk, 2012; Gray, 2009; Moravcsik, 1997). Furthermore, both SWFs and public pension funds tend to be long-term, conservative global investors. Also, they may have been set up at the national or sub-national levels.

Nonetheless, there are differences in their relation to government and their liability structure. First, the beneficiaries (directly or indirectly) of these pension funds are public workers, retirees or taxpayers, not the state, as is the case with SWFs (Chhaochharia & Laeven, 2009). This imposes a fiduciary duty for pension funds to act in the sole benefit of beneficiaries, unlike SWFs, which do not have fiduciary duties. Second, public pension funds, although government sponsored, tend to be at arm's length from the state, as reflected in the composition of the board of directors, which is generally independent. Third, unlike SWFs, whose funding comes from trade imbalances or resource earnings, public pension funds manage contributions from state employees, employers and/or contributions from taxpayers which may then provide a basic benefit to retired contributors.

The economic weight of these actors in global financial markets confers on them a key role if the paradigm of sustainable development is to be integrated into global finance. Indeed, pension funds are the largest class of global investors ($33.9 trillion AUM at the end of 2012) followed by insurance funds ($26.5 trillion), mutual funds ($26.1 trillion) and sovereign wealth funds ($5.2 trillion) (The City UK Research Centre, 2013). The recent growth of SWFs has been particularly important relative to other investor classes, and this growth is likely to further increase their weight in the global economy in years to come: in 2010 alone, nearly 20 governments considered or decided to establish such a fund (UNCTAD, 2011; Butt et al., 2007). Part of the growth in the number of funds can be attributed to macroeconomic developments such as the rise in commodity prices that occurred between 2002 and 2008, along with large trade surpluses generated by several Asian countries (Datz, 2009; Hawley et al., 2009). In addition, an increasing number of countries (e.g. Khazanah, Malaysia; Mudabala, UAE; Oman Investment Fund, Oman; Strategic Investment Fund, France) are setting up development funds to satisfy local development objectives.

Indeed, governments across the world have paid increasing attention to issues of environmental and social sustainability, notably since the 1992 Rio Summit (Deutsche Bank, 2012). The tie existing between governments and GSIFs could push the latter class of actors toward increased integration of environmental and social sustainability into the sphere of global finance. The literature review will help identify which, among agent- and structure-related factors, have driven a number of the aforementioned group of investors to become responsible investors.

Linking responsible investment to GSIFs

What is responsible investment?

Responsible investment emerged at the beginning of the twenty-first century in an attempt to reconcile sustainability considerations with profit maximization. Despite a lack of consensus over terms such as 'responsible' or 'ESG', in April 2006 partial agreement emerged and investors from every continent signed the UN-backed Principles for Responsible Investment (PRI), a framework that defines RI as an approach "that explicitly acknowledges the relevance to the investor of environmental, social and governance factors, and of the long-term health and stability of the market as a whole" (UNPRI, 2013). Large public pension funds such as CalPERS and Sweden's AP Funds were among the initial PRI signatories; as of October 2014, the signatories list – which includes asset owners, managers and service providers – now nears 1,300 institutions with $45 trillion assets under management, including 282 asset owners (UNPRI, 2014). The voluntary nature of the PRI along with the lack of a unique implementation framework has, however, resulted in a "varied and wide distribution of practical responses to the PRI" (UNCTAD, 2011).

Given the increasing buy-in from large institutional investors, such as GSIFs, into the tenets of RI, an analysis of the drivers and root causes behind the adoption of such policies becomes a compelling project. The literature review will provide the existing answers to the research questions by looking at two explanation nodes: first, the actor-centered rationalistic node, also known as 'the business case', which treats investors as utility-maximizing actors and which looks at investors as the fundamental unit of analysis, and second, a structural approach which ascribes particular behaviours to wider social structures in which the agent is located.

Agent-centered reasons for adopting responsible investment

The agent-centered explanations for adopting RI focus mainly on two elements on which I elaborate below: first, large investors such as GSIFs adopt RI because their size warrants it, and second, their liability structure affects the emphasis which they will put on risk management (including ESG risks) in their investment operations.

The agent-centered explanation for adopting RI ties in to risk minimization considerations by institutional investors who are particularly exposed to negative ESG externalities because of the large size of their portfolio. The universal owner theory suggests that large investors are diversified across and within all asset classes, thus owning a slice of the whole economy and market through their portfolios (Lydenberg, 2007; Hawley & Williams, 2000). The temporal structure of pension funds results in sensitivity toward the long-term value of holdings because they must be able to provide benefits for their members in the distant future (Hebb, 2008). Thus, it is in their interest to minimize risks tied to their long-term investment horizons (Mansley & Dlugolecki, 2001). In line with the 'universal owner' thesis, empirical studies have found the size of pension funds to be related to pension funds' responsible investments (Sievanen et al., 2012; Cox & Schneider, 2010; Bianchi et al., 2010).

The second element in the agent-centered view of investors which may have an impact on likelihood to adopt RI is the type of fund considered. A fundamental difference between pension funds and sovereign wealth funds is that the former have designated beneficiaries, are ruled by the principles of fiduciary duty and have well-defined time horizons (Clark, 2000). Debate remains as to whether fiduciary duty enables or inhibits the consideration of ESG factors in investment processes (Woods & Urwin, 2010). The Freshfields report (Deringer Freshfields Burckhaus, 2005) has somewhat dissipated the view that fiduciary duty is inconsistent with ESG consideration; it is even suggested that if the trustees of a pension fund ignore such issues, and thereby incur financial losses, they could be legally liable (Richardson, 2012). The view taken here is that pension funds, given the fiduciary duty of trustees to beneficiaries, will integrate ESG to maximize risk-adjusted returns and thereby act as universal owners; this imperative is less clear for SWFs, which lack a fiduciary duty toward designated beneficiaries. Indeed, sovereign pension funds scored higher than SWFs on Truman's (2010) assessment of structure, governance and accountability and transparency. Thus, we can explore whether a fund's liability type affects the likelihood that it will adopt an RI policy.

Few empirical studies have analyzed the drivers behind RI practices of sovereign wealth funds, with the exception of single case studies (Clark & Monk, 2010; Foldal, 2010; Reiche, 2010; Tranoy, 2009) or studies with a small sample of SWFs (Van Der Zee, 2012; IRRC, 2009). Hawley et al. (2009) argue that there has been a higher uptake of RI by sovereign pension funds (SPFs) than SWFs as a result of 'universal owner-like' portfolios, but they go on pointing to the importance of democracy in advancing RI, thus leaving the observer to ask if a democratic regime is not a more important determining factor than fund type with regards to responsible investing.

The sole consideration of instrumental motives as the rationale for being a responsible investor does not enable us to adequately capture the timing of the emergence of RI and the variation in scope and depth of RI policies across and within jurisdictions. Furthermore, GSIFs are carved in a variety of structural settings (e.g. political regimes) to act in the realm of financial markets where private agents are portrayed as utility maximizers. This underlines the importance of considering structural explanations to the adoption of RI by GSIFs.

Structural motives for the adoption of RI policies

According to the structural approach, investors are part of a wider social environment, and their behaviour can be influenced by the rules, norms, culture and institutions that prevail in that particular environment. Indeed, investors do not exist in a vacuum; rather, they operate in institutional contexts that create barriers and opportunities (Gjolberg, 2009). Institutional theory stipulates that firms are embedded in different institutional settings and that these firms' structures and actions will be shaped by conformity to normative standards established by institutions external to the firm such as governments, NGOs, incentives and rules (Wright & Rwabizambuga, 2006).

In Scandinavian countries, institutions were found to influence the emergence of RI (Sandberg et al., 2009; Bengtsson, 2008), although this has subsequently been questioned (Scholtens and Sievanen, 2012). Most studies (Sandberg et al., 2009; Bengtsson, 2008; Aguilera et al., 2006) fail to provide an empirical investigation of the impact of institutional factors with a structurally informed framework of analysis, with the exception of Scholtens and Sievanen (2012), who focus on European markets.

The adoption of RI among GSIFs also ties in to the role of these organizations as legitimacy seekers. Legitimacy usually refers to considering the actions of an entity as "desirable, proper or appropriate within some socially constructed system of norms, values, beliefs and definitions" (Suchman, 1995, p. 574). It is embedded in social systems that make the purposes and goals of an institution justifiable to relevant societal audiences (Weber, 1994). In democratic societies, the state owes its legitimacy to public participation in the decision-making process (Clark & Monk, 2010).

GSIFs are subject to the particular preferences, goals and objectives underlying decision making within their respective domestic authority structure, which is not insulated from the public judgment (Dixon & Monk, 2012; Moravcsik, 1997); this could explain why public pension funds have been pioneers and the most activist in pension fund RI (Cox & Schneider, 2010; Sievanen et al., 2012).

Thus, on the whole, there is a gap in the empirical literature assessing agent-centered motivations and structural context motivations to the likelihood of adopting RI. I draw on Olsen and March (2008) to evaluate the interplay between logic of consequence and logic of appropriateness in GSIF adoption or RI policies. Under a logic of consequence, the agent (i.e. the GSIF) would adopt responsible investment because it has calculated that its utility will be maximized (e.g. financial returns) by doing so. Under the logic of appropriateness, the GSIF will adopt RI – at least in part – as a result of the social structure that determines RI to be desirable, good and appropriate. I stipulate that the more a fund displays agency features related to stronger preferences toward responsible investment, as seen in the hypotheses developed below, the more likely a favourable structural context to responsible investment (e.g. strong civil society, democratic institutions) will result in the adoption of responsible investment by a fund. Nonetheless, structural factors will tend to edge out agency factors in GSIF adoption of responsible investment; a universal owner evolving in an authoritarian regime is less likely to adopt responsible investment than a non-universal owner in a vibrant democratic regime where the fund needs to remain legitimate toward its constituency. Again, one of the caveats of the 'logics of appropriateness' framework is the difficulty in determining how both logics interact and feed into each other, but it is recognized that both are important in preference formation. Furthermore, one of the shortcomings in the current analysis is the characterization of GSIFs as agents; this approach discounts the preference formation of the individuals that take decisions within GSIFs – the governance processes.

Development of the hypotheses

The hypotheses developed below draw on the literature review and are guided by the research questions. Below each hypothesis, I discuss the methods utilized in order to operationalize each dependent variables that will figure in the quantitative analysis.

Agent-centered hypothesis

The first proposition originates from the agent-centered view of GSIFs as rational agents who will adopt RI as a result of their universal owner status. Universal owners, categorized as such according to their size and diversified portfolios, own a representative sample of the market and thus have a rational interest in minimizing corporate behaviours that generate negative externalities (Hawley et al., 2009). Accordingly, I derive the following hypothesis linking investor size to the likelihood of being a responsible investor:

H1: The likelihood that a GSIF will adopt an RI policy is positively related to the size of its AUM.

The size of assets under management in billions of US dollars (*aum*) of each fund was taken from sources ranging from official websites, the SWF Institute, and the Pensions & Investments/Towers Watson index. A logarithmic variable for AUM (*logaum*) was created in order to assess whether the propensity of investors to engage in RI increases at a diminishing rate.

Second, the agent-centered explanations for the adoption of RI also enable us to formulate a hypothesis that differentiates among two large types of GSIFs: public pension funds and sovereign wealth funds. The liability structure of pension plans, conferring a fiduciary duty to trustees to act in the best interest of designated beneficiaries, establishes a clearer link between the fund and the ultimate beneficiaries than in the case of SWFs. In addition, risk management is more important at pension plans than SWFs, because pension entitlements, in the case of the former, are reliant upon fund performance (Clark & Knight, 2009). This factor could translate into increased consideration for a risk-based approach to ESG. Thus, I advance the following hypothesis:

H2: The liability structure of public pension funds makes them more likely to adopt RI policies than SWFs.

In order to test this proposition, I enter a dummy variable (*swf1*), 1 for sovereign wealth funds, 0 for public pension funds.

Structure-related hypothesis

Third, countries with high CSR scores are found to share several political-economic features, such as extensive social and environmental public policies (Gjolberg, 2009). Since GSIFs all share a more or less proximate rapport to the state, pressures for strong social and environmental public policies may also translate into pressures for the GSIF to consider sustainability aspects in its investments. Accordingly, I derive the following hypothesis:

H3: GSIFs are more likely to adopt RI policies in institutional contexts where extensive social and environmental public policies have been implemented.

This explanatory variable (*epi*) is constructed using the 2012 Environmental Performance Index that ranks countries "on performance indicators tracked across policy categories that cover both environmental public health and ecosystem vitality" (Yale University, 2012). In order to account for the large number of US Public Pension funds in the sample (see the section 'Methodology and Data'), I also use a US state–level index on environmental performance created by *Forbes* magazine (Wingfield & Marcus, 2007) to construct a US state–level performance indicator, thereby enabling weighting of US state performance relative to other countries.

Fourth, in institutional contexts where firms are highly exposed to public criticism, ranging from the media to NGOs, these movements have the power to affect corporate reputation (Dudok van Heel et al., 2001). Indeed, in societal contexts where there is strong exposure to media or NGO criticism, firms are found to make more effort with respect to corporate social responsibility (CSR) (Gjolberg, 2009). Societal structures that are tolerant of public criticism will favour the involvement of civil society in public debates. Therefore, I submit this structural context proposition to empirical scrutiny with the following hypothesis:

H4: GSIFs are more likely to adopt RI policies in institutional contexts where civil society has a strong involvement over public decision making.

I operationalize this proposition using the 2011 Voice and Accountability index from the World Bank Governance Indicators. The indicator (*voice&account*) "reflects perceptions of the extent to which a country's citizens are able to participate in selecting their government, as well as freedom of expression, freedom of association, and a free media" (Kaufmann et al., 2010, p. 4).

Fifth, a GSIF evolving in a structure where numerous other asset owners (public and/or private) are responsible investors may generate a reaction from the fund. It might be concerned about lagging behind these other asset owners, thereby losing legitimacy toward the citizenry given its embedded relation to the state. Therefore, I expect the following:

H5: GSIFs are more likely to adopt RI policies in institutional contexts where non-GSIF asset owners have already adopted such principles.

I operationalize this hypothesis by calculating the number of asset-owner PRI signatories (excluding the GSIF being observed) in the country where the fund is based (*PRI*).

The final structure-related hypothesis relates to country wealth. Richer countries generally have more means at their disposal to uphold strong environmental and social standards, which, in turn, may translate into a greater willingness to adopt an RI criterion. Therefore, the following hypothesis is formulated:

H6: GSIFs evolving in richer countries are more likely to adopt RI policies.

GDP per capita is considered both in its linear (*gdpcap*) and squared (*sqgdpcap*) forms. The GDP per capita data, gathered from the International Energy Agencies' database, is for the year 2009 and is measured in purchasing power parity–adjusted US dollars.

Residual explanations

Smaller populations may facilitate closer contacts between the citizenry and the government, and by extension, the GSIF. This proposition is derived from a theory formulated by Jean-Jacques Rousseau, who wrote:

> Almost all small states, republics and monarchies alike, prosper, simply because they are small, because all their citizens know each other and keep an eye on each other, and because their rulers can see for themselves the harm that is being done and the good that is theirs to do and can look on as their orders are being executed.
>
> *(Rousseau, 1976, p. 25)*

Based on this, I test the following hypothesis:

H7: GSIFs evolving in smaller countries are more likely to adopt RI policies.

Population is assessed in its linear (*pop*) and squared *(sqpop)* form. The population measurements are from 2009, and they are taken from the International Energy Agency's website database.

Finally, I add a dummy variable (*us1*) to determine the impact that US funds have on the model given that they make up 37 per cent of the sample observations (59 out of 158).

Methodology and data

To investigate the hypotheses developed in the last section, I compare the adoption rates of the RI policies of 158 GSIFs across 47 countries (see Figure 33.1). The concept of GSIF is a broadly encompassing definition of investors that were set up through legislative or executive government decisions. For the purposes of the chapter, GSIFs must invest a portion of their portfolio in public equities, as the current concept of RI has been primarily associated to this class of assets.[5] This sample includes countries at different levels of development, and in all continents.[6]

The dependent variable measures a fund's disclosed commitment to RI policies on a four-level grading scale (*RIscore*). I use disclosure as a proxy for assessing the strength of RI policies because it has been argued that investors who take a genuine interest in RI will likely ensure that their consideration of ESG would be accessible to the public at large (Bianchi et al., 2010).

I have developed a grading scale that considers the extent of RI internalization within investment activities. The grading scale was exclusively focused on the stance of GSIFs on the environment and social dimensions of ESG;[7] it did not consider a fund's position on matters of corporate governance. Social issues considered in the grading of a fund are those that can – when considered on their own, irrespective of wider geopolitical considerations – affect the performance of investment portfolios. For example, some funds will evaluate the performance of a company's human rights standards in the workplace and stipulate that high labour standards may have a

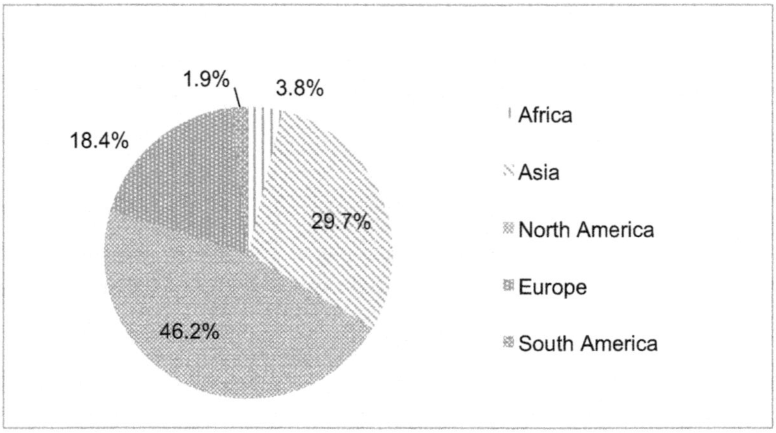

Figure 33.1 Regional division of fund sample

Source: Author's calculations.

positive impact on the performance of a company. On the other hand, some US funds are prohibited by law to invest in companies involved in proscribed activities in Sudan or Iran. These funds thus follow a government directive at the federal or state level that is primarily linked to the political environment in which a company is operating – not the social or environmental performance of that company.

The coding methodology is provided along with examples of funds associated to each score. A score of 0 means that investors do not disclose any consideration of environmental or social factors at all within their investments or that they explicitly mention that they do not consider ESG issues when developing their investment policy. A score of 1 indicates that a GSIF states a broad consideration for ESG issues in proxy voting without having a corporate engagement strategy on ESG matters. A score of 2 means that the GSIF has an explicit policy stating how ESG issues are considered in its investment portfolio and that it has proxy voting guidelines signaling an active stance on ESG issues. Furthermore, these funds either (a) have a corporate engagement policy whereby they may enter into dialogue with corporate management in order to signal concerns over ESG issues to management and demand action or (b) are signatories to the PRI. Finally, a score of 3 signifies that the GSIF has all the elements of a fund that has a score of 2 but that it also has an explicit policy of exclusion of companies based on unsatisfactory performance on environmental and/or social factors or relevant international conventions that the country subscribes to (see Figure 33.2 for scoring distribution on RI index).

The evidence for scoring individual funds was gathered through data that was compiled from publicly available sources such as legislative statutes, official websites and annual reports outlining investment mandates and policies. Every effort was made to carefully consider the investment policy of each fund given the time and resources constraints.

In the sample of GSIFs selected for this analysis, approximately 38 per cent of funds (60 funds) displayed a form of commitment to RI (score of 1, 2, or 3 on the RI index). Funds coming from North America and Europe are the most likely to have a RI policy (see Figure 33.3).

The regression model employed for my analysis is ordered probit regression. This enables me capture the impact of the four ordinal outcomes of the dependent variable. Probit models assume a cumulative standard distribution that is typically estimated using a maximum likelihood technique. The maximum likelihood estimation technique selects the set of values of the model

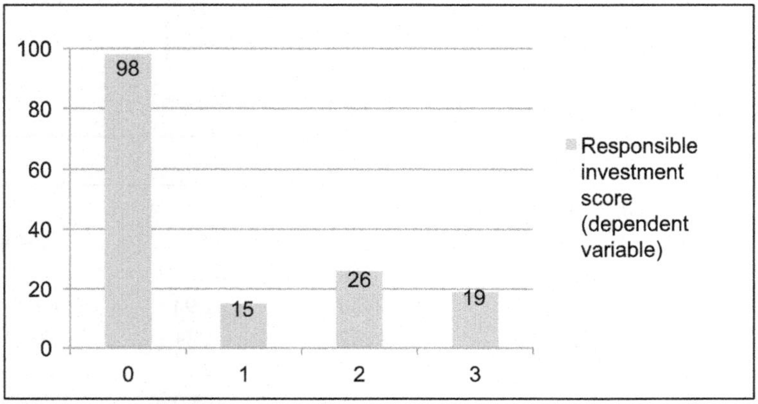

Figure 33.2 Frequency of GSIF scores on RI index

Source: Author's calculations.

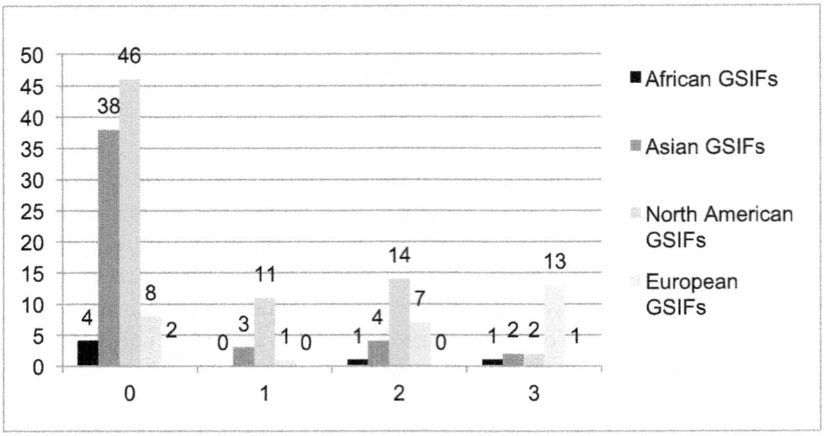

Figure 33.3 Regional frequency of GSIF scores on RI index

Source: Author's calculations.

parameters that maximizes the likelihood function. The general formulation of the ordered probit equation is as follows:

$$y_i^\star = x_i\beta + \varepsilon_i$$

where $y^\star$ is the latent variable, x_i is a matrix of explanatory variables and β is the vector of equation parameters to be estimated. The ε_i term represents the error term in the proposed equation. Table 33.1 presents the descriptive statistics.

There are several shortcomings associated with this research design. First, the data selected assesses all of the world's SWFs with assets over $1 billion, but time and resource constraints have limited the sample size for pension funds to 110. This results in an important domination of developed country pension funds in the data sample. A second shortcoming is the relatively small sample size to perform a large-*n* analysis. Third, a higher level of abstraction discounts the particularity of each fund's unique governance structure. Finally, the data gathered is a snapshot that reflects the RI policies in effect between June and November 2012; it does not offer a sense of the temporal evolution of fund adherence to RI.

Table 33.1 Descriptive statistics

Variable	*Obs*	*Mean*	*Std. Dev.*	*Min*	*Max*
RIscore	158	0.7848101	1.107828	0	3
Aum	158	78.91639	153.9806	1.2	1,394.87
swf1	158	0.3037975	0.4613586	0	1
epi	156	57.05718	10.42465	32.94	76.69
voice&account	158	0.6974683	0.9442821	–1.84	1.63
prisign	158	12.36709	9.600527	0	34
pop	158	1.89e+08	2.61e+08	398,920	1.34e+09
gdpcap	158	33,597.08	13,026.32	832.18	73,196.38
us1	158	0.3734177	0.4852497	0	1

Findings and implications

This section will report the most salient findings of the six models that test the hypotheses that were developed earlier (see Table 33.2 for regression results). Model 1 is the best fit model using all the sample observations.[8] Model 2 builds on Model 1 by assessing the impact of fund type on the likelihood of adopting an RI policy, thus testing hypothesis 2. Model 3 is equal to Model 1, but it removes population outliers China and India, host countries of 5 and 1 funds, respectively. Model 4 uses Model 1 as a foundation and removes the *prisign* variable originating from hypothesis 5, given the ambiguous causal link tied to the variable. Model 5 uses Model 1 as a foundation and controls for the role of US funds in the sample by inserting the *us1* dummy variable. Finally, Model 6 removes US funds and the population variable from Model 1 to see how the hypotheses fare without the population variable whose theoretical grounding is uncertain. US funds are removed from this model because of the variation of RI score within the sample of US funds.

The size of assets under management was tested both linearly (*aum*) and logarithmically (*logaum*), and it was in the latter case that statistical significance was found. The *logaum* variable's

Table 33.2 Results of regression of RI scores

Variable/ Model	*Model 1*[a]	*Model 2*	*Model 3*	*Model 4*	*Model 5*	*Model 6*
logaum	0.21882	0.25671	0.28127	0.21449	0.27275	0.13484
	(2.10)**	(2.35)**	(2.55)**	(2.10)**	(2.49)**	(1.13)
swf1		0.41893				
		(1.29)				
epi	0.01604	0.01925	0.0183	0.01304	0.0192	–0.00383
	(–1.24)	(1.45)	(–1.42)	(1.01)	(1.48)	(–0.2)
voice & account	0.97656	1.10438	1.11394	1.36485	1.09552	1.02187
	(3.64)***	(3.84)***	(4.05)***	(5.30)***	(3.97)***	(3.73)***
prisign	0.06877	0.07039	0.07019		0.06928	0.04554
	(3.29)***	(3.31)***	(3.21)***		(3.20)***	(2.31)**
gdpcap	–0.00013	–0.00014	–0.00016	–0.00011	–0.00017	–0.00007
	(–3.17)***	(–3.31)***	(–3.75)***	(–2.53)**	(–3.72)***	(–1.88)*
sqgdpcap	1.71E-09	1.77E-09	1.90E-09	1.47E-09	1.97E-09	1.15E-09
	(2.90)***	(3.01)***	(3.14)***	(2.28)**	(3.22)***	(1.98)**
pop	–8.46E-09	–8.12E-09	–2.61E-08	–5.15E-09	–1.79E-08	
	(–4.92)***	(–4.67)***	(–3.68)***	(–3.59)***	(–3.99)***	
sqpop	5.11E-18	4.86E-18	6.04E-17	2.40E-18	1.16E-17	
	(2.30)**	(2.21)**	(2.81)***	(1.02)	(2.57)**	
us1					2.28957	
					(2.32)**	
# of observations	156	156	150	156	156	97
Pseudo R^2	0.2851	0.2901	0.2941	0.2512	0.3024	0.2699

[a] The *z*-statistic appears in parentheses below the coefficient estimate.

* Significant at the 5% level, two-tailed test.

** Significant at the 2.5% level, two-tailed test.

*** Significant at the 1% level, two-tailed test.

significance (2.5 per cent level) along with its positive coefficient, as expected theoretically, suggests that as the AUM of GSIFs gets larger, the more likely they are to be responsible investors; however, this effect levels off as GSIFs grow in size, thus lending credence to the universal ownership hypothesis.

The second agent-related variable hypothesized to have an impact on the likelihood that a GSIF will adopt an RI policy was fund type. The resulting coefficient estimate for *swf1* cannot be accepted as statistically significant even at the 10 per cent significance level, thus pointing to the weakness of the variable in predicting whether a GSIF is more likely to implement RI.

We now turn to structure-related variables. It was found that the impact of a country's environmental performance on the likelihood of GSIFs adopting RI policies was not statistically significant, unlike what was expected under hypothesis 3.

The voice and accountability indicator, used as a proxy to measure institutional contexts where civil society has a strong involvement over public decision making, was found to be the most robust and most consistent variable across the different models (significant at the 1 per cent level across all models). As expected in hypothesis 4, GSIFs based in countries with higher *voice&account* scores are more likely to have a higher score in terms the strength of their commitment to RI.

The number of asset-owner PRI signatories in the GSIFs' jurisdiction variable *(prisign)* shows significance at the 1 per cent level, and the sign of the coefficient is positive, as expected. However, this variable needs to be interpreted cautiously given the unknown direction of causality between the independent variable (*prisign*) and the dependent variable (*RIscore*): non-GSIF asset-owner PRI signatories could increase the expectation that the GSIF should be at least as considerate of ESG issues as private funds given that it needs to legitimate itself in the eyes of a state's constituents. On the other hand, since the majority of the initial PRI signatories were GSIFs, it could be that GSIFs were the first to implement RI programs and that private funds followed suit.

The fifth variable to be tested, GDP per capita, relates to hypothesis 5, which stipulates that funds are more likely to be responsible investors as country wealth increases. A significant relationship between income and RI score emerges, a relationship that is significant at the 1 per cent level for both quadratic and linear terms in three out of six models, including the core model (Model 1). The quadratic relationship stipulates that as country wealth increases, GSIFs are less likely to adopt RI until reaching the $38,000 mark, after which adherence to RI increases.

In Model 4, we check for the effect of US funds by inserting a US fund dummy in the model. The US fund dummy variable is indeed significant at the 5 per cent significance level, and the coefficient is positive. Nonetheless, as stated earlier, it appears that US funds are skewed toward lower levels of RI scores.

The population variable displays an interesting pattern of significance across models. It is both in its linear and squared form. The negative coefficient of the *pop* variable (significant at the 1 per cent level in Model 1 to 5) suggests that GSIFs based out of smaller countries are more likely to enact RI policies. The population level associated with the minimum likelihood that a GSIF will be a responsible investor is 827 million.[9] Only China and India have larger populations than this figure, and none of the funds based in these countries have RI policies. When these two outliers are removed from the analysis (Model 3), the pseudo R^2 coefficient remains relatively constant (0.2941).

In addition to the insights provided by the analysis of individual variables, the pseudo R^2 levels yielded across the six models demonstrate the value of analyzing the chosen variables together. Model 1, the core model, produced a pseudo R^2 value of 0.2851 and this was fairly consistent across the different models. The chi-squared test statistic (0.000) demonstrates that the selected variables are indeed helpful in explaining at least part of the variation observed in the dependent variable. The multicollinearity and heteroskedasticity tests that were conducted revealed that the statistical results were not affected by these effects.

Conclusion

This chapter examines the factors that increase the likelihood that a GSIF will adopt an RI policy along with the factors that shape the legitimating value of such an initiative. The main findings are as follows. Among the agent-centered hypotheses, I found that GSIFs with more AUM are more likely to have stronger RI policies; no association was found between liability structure and RI policies. Second, among structure-centered explanations, the strongest association with the likelihood of adopting an RI policy revolved around civil society strength: countries where citizens and civil society have avenues to participate in the public policy process along with a free press are more likely to lead GSIFs to adopt RI policies. Indeed, the GSIFs of the highest-scoring countries on this index (Switzerland, Scandinavian countries, Australia, New Zealand, the Netherlands, along with Canada) tend to have strong RI policies. This result also suggests that these funds, which all share a degree of accountability to governments and, by extension, citizens, may be adopting RI policies as a way to legitimate themselves as institutions that are in tune with citizens' values and expectations. Nonetheless, the findings did not find a strong association between a country's environmental performance and the likelihood that the fund will adopt RI. One of the challenges with the environmental performance measurement used in this chapter is that it considers more than the simple stringency of environmental regulation because data which solely focused on this matter was patchy at best. An association was also found between the GSIF's likelihood of adopting RI and the number of PRI signatories present in the country, although the causality of this finding needs to be further explored. A U-shaped relationship was found between the strength of RI policies and country wealth and population size. As a result, the empirical findings presented in this paper would tend to validate the necessity to take into account both logic of appropriateness and logic of consequences; a larger fund is more likely to adopt responsible investment as a mean of maximizing its utility; structural characteristics also play a role in making RI adoption the appropriate decision for a fund to maintain legitimacy – its social license to operate toward its beneficiaries.

Some implications emanate from these observations. Given that large pools of money administered by GSIFs are emerging at a fast pace across the world, it is important to understand how this analysis can guide us in ensuring that the largest number of funds adopt RI policies in order to solidify the link between sustainable development and global finance. First, in the US, where an important pool of the world's largest pension funds are concentrated, RI has yet to make the headway it has in other Anglo-Saxon countries (e.g. Australia, Canada, UK) or in Scandinavian countries (e.g. Denmark, Norway, Sweden). Given the relatively high score of the US on the voice and accountability indicator – a variable that is associated to the logic of appropriateness – structured and sustained pressure by citizens, NGOs and public sector employee unions on policymakers and funds could lead to more widespread adoption of RI policies.

A second implication relates to the emerging wave of sovereign wealth funds across the world. Since many of the funds that are emerging are based in resource-rich developing countries (e.g. Papua New Guinea, Mongolia, Angola, Gabon) where the tradition of public participation in the policy process and the freedom of the press may not be as far-reaching as in more consolidated democratic societies, the driving justification for these funds to adopt RI may be by outlining that the size of their assets under management puts them in the category of universal owners and justifies a RI policy on grounds of the business case – a logic of consequences approach to RI adoption. For example, the Mudala Development Company, an SWF based in the United Arab

Emirates, a country with a low score on the voice and accountability indicator, joined the Abu Dhabi Sustainability Group, a forum made up of the government and private companies aiming to adopt and report on environmental and social sustainability management practices. A case like this suggests that funds may be convinced to consider RI in settings where public participation in the policy process is low. Furthermore, although new funds are principally emerging in developing countries with lower income levels, lower-income countries can still implement RI, as demonstrated by the likes of South Africa's and Brazil's GSIFs.

As mentioned earlier, there are certain limitations to the empirical analysis performed in this chapter: First, the findings focus on a sample of the largest funds across the world, thus resulting in a heavy bias toward US-based GSIFs. Second, the results provide a snapshot of RI adoption rates in 2012; they do not explain the dynamics that could help uncover the patterns of RI adoption over a 10-year period. Third, the large-*n* analysis discounted unique fund governance features. Fourth, the inclusion of a number of funds based in developing countries reduced the scope of data sources.

The empirical findings provided in this chapter identify further research avenues in order to better understand what affects the likelihood that a GSIF will adopt RI policies. First, the current analysis fails to adequately explain the significant variation in the rate of adherence to RI by US funds. Further research could also assess whether there has been a neighbourhood effect or a diffusion effect via participation in international or regional educational organizations (e.g. Pacific Pension Institute) in the spread of RI across time. The impact of the private versus public nature of a fund in the likelihood of adopting RI is also a relevant empirical question that has not been addressed by this chapter or in past research. Finally, a mixed approach linking quantitative evidence to case-study analysis could better uncover the relationship that exists between fund governance and the likelihood of adopting RI. It would also allow for a more refined assessment of the weights and balances in the interplay between logic of consequences and logic of appropriateness. Indeed, the findings presented above do not enable a clear validation of the hypothesized relationship between both logics.

In conclusion, this chapter's novel findings established a link between theory and empirical evidence on the factors that increase the likelihood that government-sponsored investment funds will enact policies that consider ESG issues within their investment portfolio. The findings provide some insights regarding the role of national political economic institutions, along with fund-specific factors that determine the likelihood that funds will be responsible investors. These novel findings were obtained through the development of a unique database of public pension funds and sovereign wealth funds across the world, along with a scoring methodology which enabled a finer degree of analysis than a dichotomous outcome. This chapter will thus serve in advancing the literature on the factors driving the adoption of RI by GSIFs, along with the larger topic of linking sustainable development to global finance.

Notes

1 All figures are in US dollars.
2 For empirical support on this position, see Deutsche Bank (2012).
3 For example, investors are embedded as stakeholders in the Extractive Industry Transparency Initiative.
4 Sustainable development is defined as "development that meets the needs of the present without compromising the ability of future generations to meet their own needs" (Brundtland Commission, 1987, p. 41).
5 There is an increasing integration of RI in other investment classes such as private equities, infrastructure and fixed income (see PRI.com for more information).
6 Annex with fund sample and RI information is available in the working chapter version of this article on the Carleton Centre for Community Innovation website.

7 The term 'ESG' is used because it is a widely accepted terminology when discussing RI. Nonetheless, the analysis presented in this chapter considers solely the E and S dimensions of ESG.
8 In total, 156 observations were maintained in the model because there was no data on the EPI for two observations (Bahrein and Timor Leste, which both scored 0 on the RI index).
9 Solved using $-b/2a$ equation where a is the coefficient on the squared term of the variable and b is the coefficient on the linear term.

References

Aguilera, R., Williams, C., Conley, J. and Rupp, D. (2006) 'Corporate governance and social responsibility: a comparative analysis of the UK and the US', *Corporate Governance* 14(3): 147–158.

Ambachtsheer, J. (2011) 'International codes and conventions: Are prension funds missing in action?', *Rotman International Journal of Pension Management* 4(2): 26–36.

Baron, J., Jennings, P. & Dobbin, F. (1988) 'Mission control? The development of personnel systems in U.S. industry', *American Sociological Review* 53(4): 497–514.

Bengtsson, E. (2008) 'A history of Scandinavian socially responsible investing', *Journal of Business Ethics* 82(4): 969–983.

Bianchi, R., Drew, M. and Walk, A. (2010) 'On the responsible investmen disclosure practices of the world's largest pension funds', *Accounting Research Journal* 23(3): 302–318.

Brundtland Commission (1987) *Report of the World Commission on Environment and Development: Our Common Future*, Oxford: Oxford University Press.

Butt, S., Shivdasani, A., Stendevad, C. and Wyman, A. (2007) 'Sovereign wealth funds: a growing global force in corporate finance', *Journal of Applied Corporate Finance* 19(1): 73–83.

Chhaochharia, V. and Laeven, L. (2009) *The Investment Allocation of Sovereign Wealth Funds*, Washington: IMF Working Paper Series.

Clark, G. (2000) *Pension Fund Capitalism*, New York: Oxford University Press.

Clark, G. and Hebb, T. (2005) 'Why should they care? The role of institutional investors in the market for corporate global responsibility', *Environment and Planning* 37(11): 2015–2031.

Clark, G. and Knight, E. (2009) 'Temptation and the virtues of long-term commitment: the governance of sovereign wealth funds investment', *Asian Journal of International Law* 1(1): 1–28.

Clark, G. and Monk, A. (2010) 'The legitimacy and governance of Norway's sovereign wealth fund: the ethics of global investment', *Environment and Planning* 42(7): 1723–1738.

Cole, R. (1989) *Strategies for learning*, Berkeley: University of California Press.

Cox, P. and Schneider, M. (2010) 'Is corporate social performance a criterion in the overseas investment strategy of US pension plans? An empirical examination', *Business and Society* 49(2): 252–289.

Datz, G. (2009) 'State of change: global turmoil and government reinvention', *Public Administration Review* 69(4): 660–667.

Deringer Freshfields Burckhaus (2005) *A Legal Framework for the Integration of Environmental, Social and Governance Issues into Institutional Investment*, Geneva: UNEP-FI.

Deutsche Bank (2012) *Sustainable Investing: Establishing Long-Term Value and Performance*, Frankfurt: Deutsche Bank Group.

Dixon, A. and Monk, A. (2012) 'Rethinking the sovereign in sovereign wealth funds', *Transactions of the Institute of British Geographers* 37(1): 104–117.

Dudok van Heel, O., Elkington, J. and Fennel, S. (2001) *Buried Treasure: Uncovering the Business Case for Corporate Sustainability*, London: SustainAbility.

Finnemore, M. and Sikkink, K. (1998) 'International norm dynamics and political change', *International Organization* 52(4): 887–917.

Foldal, O. (2010) 'Mitigating tensions between domestic politics and global finance – a study of the decision-making process of Norway's sovereign wealth fund', Unpublished thesis, University of Oslo. Online. Available HTTP: <http://ssrn.com/abstract=1664344> (accessed 28 November 2012).

Ghahramani, S. (2011) 'Governments, financial markets and international human rights: the state's role as shareholder', *Yale Journal of International Affairs* 6(1): 85–95.

Gjolberg, M. (2009) 'Measuring the immeasurable? Constructing an index of CSR practices and CSR performance in 20 countries', *Scandinavian Journal of Management* 25(1): 605–637.

Gray, T. (2009) 'Investing for the environment? The limits of the PRI', Working paper, Oxford University. Online. Available HTTP: <http://ssrn.com/abstract=1416123> (accessed 20 November 2012).

Guillen, M. (1994) *Models of Management*, New York: University of Chicago Press.

Hawley, J., Kamath, S. and Williams, A. (2009) 'Fonds souverains et fonds de pension: conceptualiser les implications pour l'investissement responsible', *Revue d'économie financière* 9(1): 395–415.

Hawley, J. and Williams, A. (2000) *The Rise of Fiduciary Capitalism: How Institutional Investors Can Make Corporate America More Democratic*, New York: University of Pennsylvania Press.

Hawley, J. and Williams, A. (2007) 'Universal owners: challenges and opportunities', *Corporate Governance* 15(3): 415–420.

Hebb, T. (2008) *No Small Change: Pension Funds and Corporate Engagement*, New York: Cornell University Press.

IRRC. (2009) *An Analysis of Proxy Voting and Engagement Policies and Practices of the Sovereign Wealth Funds*, New York: IRRC Institute.

Kaufmann, D., Kraay, A. and Mastruzzi, M. (2010) *The Worldwide Governance Indicators: A Summary of Methodology, Data and Analytical Issues*, Washington: World Bank Policy Research.

Lydenberg, S. (2007) 'Universal investors and socially responsible investors: a tale of emerging affinities', *Corporate Governance* 15(3): 467–477.

Mansley, M. and Dlugolecki, A. (2001) *Climate Change – A Risk Management Challenge for Institutional Investors*, London: Universities Superannuation Scheme.

March, J. and Olsen, J. (1989) *Rediscovering Institutions*, New York: Free Press.

March, J. and Olsen, J. (2008) 'The logic of appropriateness', *Handbook of Public Policy*, New York: Oxford University Press: 689–709.

Moravcsik, A. (1997) 'Taking preferences seriously: a liberal theory of international politics', *International Organization* 51(4): 513–553.

Prakash, A. and Potoski, M. (2006) *The Voluntary Environmentalists: Green Clubs, ISO 14001, and Voluntary Environmental Regulations*, Cambridge: Cambridge University Press.

Reiche, D. (2010) 'Sovereign wealth funds as a new instrument of climate protection policy? A study of Norway as a pioneer of ethical guidelines for investment policy', *Energy* 35(9): 3569–3577.

Richardson, B. (2012) 'Fiduciary and other legal duties', *Socially Responsible Finance and Investing: Financial Institutions, Corporations, Investors and Activists*, John Wiley & Sons.

Rousseau, J. J. (1976). *The Government of Poland*, Indianapolis: Hackett Publishing.

Sandberg, J., Juravle, C., Hedesstrom, T. and Hamilton, I. (2009) 'The heterogeneity of socially responsible investment', *Journal of Business Ethics* 87(4): 519–533.

Scholtens, B. and Sievanen, R. (2012) 'Drivers of socially responsible investing: a case study of four Nordic countries', *Journal of Business Ethics* 115(3): 1–12.

Sethi, S. (2005) 'Investing in socially responsible companies is a must for public pension funds – because there is no better alternative', *Journal of Business Ethics* 56(2): 99–129.

Sievanen, R., Rita, H. and Scholtens, B. (2012) 'The drivers of responsible investment: the case of European pension funds', *Journal of Business Ethics* 117(1): 1–15.

Sovereign Investment Lab (2012) *Follow the Money: SWF Annual Report 2011*, Milan: Sovereign Investment Lab.

Suchman, M. (1995) 'Managing legitimacy: strategic and institutional approaches', *Academy of Management Review* 20(3): 571–610.

The City UK Research Centre (2013) *Financial Market Series: Sovereign Wealth Funds,* London: The City UK Research Centre.

Tranoy, B. (2009) 'Flexible adjustment in the age of financialisation: the case of Norway', *Geopolitics* 14(2): 360–375.

Truman, E. (2010) *Sovereign Wealth Funds: Threat or Salvation?* Washington: Peterson Institute for International Economics.

UNCTAD (2011) *Investment and Enterprise Responsibility Review*, Geneva: United Nations.

PRI (2013) *What is responsible investment*. Online. Available HTTP: <http://www.PRI.org/introducing-responsible-investment/> (accessed 20 July 2013).

PRI (2014) *About*. Online. Available HTTP:<http://www.PRI.org/about-pri/about-pri/> (accessed 20 November 2014).

Van Der Zee, E. (2012) 'Sovereign wealth funds and socially responsible investment: dos and don'ts', *European Company Law* 9(2): 141–150.

Weber, S. (1994) 'Origins of the European Bank for Reconstruction and Development', *International Organization* 48(1): 1–38.

Wingfield, B. and Marcus, M. (2007) 'America's greenest states', *Forbes Magazine,* 17 October.
Woods, C. and Urwin, R. (2010) 'Putting sustainable investing into practice: a governance framework for pension funds', *Journal of Business Ethics* 92 (1): 1–19.
Wright, C. and Rwabizambuga, A. (2006) 'Institutional pressures, corporate reputation and voluntary codes of conduct: an examination of the Equator Principles', *Business and Society Review* 111(1): 89–117.
Yale University (2012) *Environmental Performance Index.* Online. Available HTTP: <http://epi.yale.edu/> (accessed 27 November 2012).

34

Determining how to invest more responsibly as an institution

A case study at the University of Edinburgh

Liz Cooper

Introduction

As of July 2013, the University of Edinburgh held endowment funds valued at over £280 million. This is one of the largest such funds in the UK, made up of numerous philanthropic donations which must be invested for a financial return, and these returns used for specified purposes. In January 2013, Edinburgh became the first higher education institution in Europe, and the second globally, to adopt the UN-supported Principles for Responsible Investment (PRI). Concurrently, students, in particular through the student organisation People & Planet, have been vocally campaigning for 'ethical' investment, with a particular focus on calling for divestment from fossil fuels industries, reflecting a growing global movement. In 2014, in light of our commitment to the PRI, and in order to respond to points raised by campaigners within and beyond the University community, we have been reviewing our principles, values, policy and practices related to the investment of our endowment funds. This includes taking into account the views of financial and ethical experts as well as students, staff and the local community. This case study first details the social responsibility and investment contexts at the University of Edinburgh, and then presents and discusses our investment consultation. This case study concludes that establishing agreed-upon values and principles for a large institution, and defining how these are to be interpreted into investment practices, is challenging. Nevertheless, consulting widely has been a worthwhile exercise in terms of demonstrating a commitment to engaging with and listening to stakeholders, gathering varied views to complement expert knowledge and highlighting the interest of our stakeholders in being involved in thinking through complex ethical issues.

Social responsibility context at the University of Edinburgh

The University's Strategic Plan outlines the creation, dissemination and curation of knowledge as its mission, aiming to enhance its position as one of the world's leading research and teaching universities, providing the highest quality learning and teaching environment, and producing graduates fully equipped to achieve the highest personal and professional standards. Social responsibility is included within the University Strategic Plan 2010–2020 as one of six strategic themes. The objectives within this theme commit the University to minimising its environmental impact and maximising its contribution to society. The Plan also puts forward other commitments, such as exhibiting high ethical standards, advocating strategies that demonstrate and report our main social, environmental and economic impacts and motivating members of the University community to demonstrate and share best practice in social responsibility and sustainability.

In 2013, a new Department for Social Responsibility and Sustainability was created within the University, bringing together and building on work done by an existing Sustainability Office, and by the Procurement Department on supply chain ethics. This new department is working to bring together, support and build on efforts of researchers, operations staff and students on social responsibility and sustainability issues. Over the past two years, the Department for Social Responsibility and Sustainability has engaged with nearly 3,000 members of the University community who are interested in the University's performance in this area. There is a particular focus on facilitating links between research and practice on issues such as energy, waste and recycling, socially responsible procurement, wellbeing and many others. The efforts of the University in these areas reflect increasing interest from students, with 80 per cent of undergraduate students surveyed in 2013 by the Higher Education Academy and National Union of Students stating that sustainable development should be actively promoted and incorporated by UK universities (Drayson et al., 2013).

Investment context at the University of Edinburgh

The University of Edinburgh is internationally renowned for its research and teaching, holding seventeenth place in the 2013–2014 QS World University rankings. The financial turnover of the University at the end of 2012–2013 exceeded £730 million, and the University maintains a strong record of continued growth each year, both financially and in terms of its physical estate (around 300 buildings across five campuses). Philanthropic donations enable the University to achieve its goals, with the most common uses being scholarships and bursaries, academic chairs and professorships and building works. Funds raised from philanthropic donations are passed through a separate charitable body called the University of Edinburgh Development Trust, which ensures that the interests of the donor are reflected in their use. Stringent due diligence is carried out on significant new donations to ensure that the source of the money is legitimate and would be something with which the University would wish to be associated.

As of 31 July 2013 the University held endowment investments valued at £284 million, of which 65 per cent were invested in equities, 20 per cent in fixed-interest stocks, 11 per cent in property and 4 per cent as cash and working capital. There were 778 individual endowments, and the expenditure distributed in 2012–2013 amounted to £8.5million.[1] Our review of our investment approach relates only to these endowment funds, not to how other money is spent by the University. Nor does it link to existing socially responsible investment efforts in university pension funds such as the University's superannuation scheme. However, ways to reflect the same principles adopted for investment in these other areas are being considered where appropriate. The investment of the University's individual endowments is pooled, with individual endowments holding units in the fund and receiving an income distribution on the units held. The capital value of the endowment fund is measured by the calculation of the unit price; detailed records of this calculation are available and show the capital growth of the fund over 50 years.

In terms of how investment decisions are made, the Investment Committee of the University is responsible for the oversight and strategic direction of endowment investments. The University Court appoints members to the Investment Committee drawn from both Court members and external investment professionals. The Investment Committee proposes and agrees with the

Court on an investment strategy, following any guidance from the Court on social responsibility issues. It also identifies fund managers and monitors fund performance.[2]

The concept of ethical investment has been on the agenda at the University since the late 1990s, when Edinburgh University Students Association began campaigning for an ethical investment policy to be put in place and implemented. In 2003, the University Court adopted proposals for a Socially Responsible Investment Policy, which was updated in 2006.[3] An engagement or shareholder activism approach is endorsed, allowing any group within the University to submit a case for engagement with a particular company based on ethical considerations, which is to be considered by the Investment Committee in terms of whether the investment reflects University values. The policy does recognize that there are cases where an engagement approach would not be appropriate, and so divestment would be considered. Divestment has been carried out in two instances to date. First, in 2004, the Court accepted a proposal to divest from the tobacco industry, due to the negative impacts of tobacco on health not being considered compatible with the University's status as a major centre of medical research. Second, in 2013, the University withdrew its £1.2 million investment in a manufacturer of parts for US drones.

In January 2013, the University publicly took a step to link its social responsibility and sustainability efforts with its investment strategy by becoming a signatory to the PRI. The PRI offers a framework for incorporating environmental, social and governance concerns into investment approaches, recognizing the need to address such factors to minimize risk and improve long-term performance of investments. The initiative suggests possible actions to be taken in order to meet the principles, including undertaking a peer review of investment approaches, developing a statement of investment beliefs and creating a plan to amend and review investment policy. Adopting the PRI has acted as a catalyst to the University for reviewing its approach to investment. While it is accepted that the University of Edinburgh's endowment fund is comparatively small in the investment world, the intention is to ensure that the investment approach reflects the University's growing commitment to social responsibility.

Definitions and values

In reviewing our investment approach, there is an issue of terminology to be resolved. As described above, student campaigners have typically used the term 'ethical investment', whereas the University has devised a Socially Responsible Investment Policy. The University has then adopted the PRI. Sandberg et al. (2009) highlight how the wide range of terms used reflect different values, norms and ideologies. Sparkes (2001) considers the term 'ethical investment' to more accurately describe the actions of values-based organizations, such as religious groups and charities, applying internal principles to an investment strategy, than funds that apply investors' ethical preferences (which Anderson et al., 1996, cited by Sparkes, 2001, consider should simply be called investment that reflects the investor's opinion, as the fund managers are not ethically motivated themselves). Reflecting this definition of ethical investment, through this review process the University is indeed attempting to apply agreed-upon principles based on institutional values, but can the University be defined as a values-based organization? On the same note, the University Chaplaincy has hosted a recent events series entitled 'What's the University for?' including a session discussing 'Can the University afford to have values?' in February 2014. The University's core purpose is to further knowledge through research and to educate. Values held by members of the vast University community are likely to vary much more than within a church or charity. Academics from different disciplinary backgrounds, such as finance, law, politics and religious studies, are researching and teaching on investment and on ethics in different ways. Student-led campaign groups have their own perspectives, informed by global campaign trends.

Views on socially responsible investment vary depending on levels of expertise in finance and ethics. While our consultation on investment aims to gain insights into what different members of this heterogeneous University community consider our common values to be, it is expected that views may be contradictory at times. The challenge is to pinpoint the values that reflect commonly held notions of what the University is for.

On the other hand, it may be appropriate to continue to use the term 'socially responsible investment', reflecting the University's choice of name for the new Social Responsibility and Sustainability Department. In this case, we have the task of defining more clearly what is meant by social responsibility in the context of the University. As Michelson et al. (2004) point out, the term 'socially responsible investment' can mean different things to different investors, in the absence of any single definition of social responsibility. Rather than simply selecting funds that describe themselves as socially responsible, investors are requesting personalized portfolios to reflect their own values (Sparkes and Cowton, 2004). Again, the need to agree on institutional values is the running theme, yet, in the case of the University, the value of academic freedom in research and teaching must be taken into account when defining social responsibility values. Once values are defined, there is the challenge of interpreting these into investment practice. For example, if arms industries are deemed to be incompatible with an investor's values, there are different ways to interpret this: some screen out any firms involved in the arms trade, while others only divest from arms manufacturers, and others focus on what percentage of turnover a firm gained from the arms trade (Cowton, 1993, cited by Sandberg et al., 2009).

Both ethical investment and socially responsible investment in many cases have tended to be more focused on this approach of negative screening, rather than actively selecting firms and funds due to their positive effects on society. Responsible investment is often more focused on performance, and defined, for example, by the PRI, as referred to above, as incorporating environmental, social and governance factors in order to minimize risk and improve long-term performance. Several additional terms are offered to describe investment approaches that go further than these – Krosinsky (2013) promotes the concept of sustainable investing, which is about considering future social and environmental trends and taking them into account in investment decision making, calling for trends to be anticipated ahead of market changes. The concept of impact investing is described as having a local community or environmental benefit (Krosinsky, 2013), often for below-market returns (Sparkes, 2001). For Sparkes (2001), these latter three are more accurately referred to as 'socially directed investing', rather than socially responsible investment. Whichever terminology is used at the University, we are proposing to move away from just negative screening, to an approach that also incorporates anticipating future trends and actively seeking community and environmental benefits.

Methodology

As part of our institutional assessment on our investment approach, a number of actions have been taken as part of a review process led by the Department for Social Responsibility and Sustainability. A University working group made up of staff and student representatives has been formed to discuss the PRI and how to follow the principles put forth. Academics with expertise in ethics and finance have been approached directly in order to encourage detailed reflection and input (e.g. Cook et al., 2014). A number of events with both internal and external speakers have been held in 2014 to inform students and staff on the investment context and issues, and to encourage feedback. A peer review is currently underway, looking at what other higher education institutions, in particular, are doing. Current donors of money are being consulted to ascertain if they have preferences on how donated money is to be invested.

The focus of this case study is the public consultation on our investment approach carried out between January and April 2014. There were various motivations behind undertaking such a consultation. As identified by Welp et al. (2006), when referring to public consultation on complex scientific issues with an ethical dimension, there is a need to respond to calls for accountability from stakeholders, a need to gain varied views as a 'reality check' for experts and decision makers and a need to generate discussion on ethics and values to complement experts' facts. The focus was on establishing a sense of the views of University stakeholders, which includes those who affect or are affected by the University and its investment activities (Freeman, 1984). While primarily the aim was to collect views of students, staff and alumni, in light of public funding of the University as a public good, the general public were also encouraged to participate. Our approach reflects Brickson's (2007) depiction of descriptive stakeholder theory, where views of participants are sought on the mission and actions of an organization, with a view to developing shared perceptions. Yet there is also an element of what is described as normative stakeholder theory, where an organization has moral obligations towards stakeholders and wishes to strengthen relationships with them (Brickson, 2007). This consultation sought to develop shared perceptions through informing and encouraging discussion, to identify broad consensus on principles and approach where possible and to strengthen relationships between stakeholders through an ongoing, iterative package of informing and consulting. Welp et al. (2006) identify such stakeholder dialogues as now being key to many companies' corporate social responsibility strategies. This is also reflected in the fact that the international standard for social responsibility, ISO 26000, defines identifying and engaging with stakeholders as a key requirement.

Due to the nature of the issue consulted on, with investment decisions needing to be informed by financial and legal expertise, and needing to generate returns so that money donated can continue to be used for its intended purpose on multiple occasions, it is recognized that the type of stakeholder participation remains lower on the scale than it could be with other issues. Looking at Arnstein's (1969) widely cited ladder of citizen participation, which portrays a scale from non-participation and manipulation at the bottom to citizen control at the top, consultation in itself is referred to as 'tokenism', with views being heard but citizens lacking power to know they will be taken into account. Similarly, Spitzeck and Hansen (2010) examined a large number of cases of companies consulting with stakeholders, but found that in the majority of cases stakeholder engagement had limited impact on decision making. The most common impact was on what Spitzeck and Hansen (2010) term an 'intermediary sphere of decision making', such as on reporting or establishing a materiality process. This highlights the need for University communications post-consultation to clearly identify how and where stakeholder views have been taken into account in decision making, as well as explaining why full 'citizen control' would not be appropriate for this issue.

The consultation process included a document, detailing a proposed approach and asking 12 questions (some with yes/no answers, but with space for text responses, too), which was made available on the University website and sent directly to key stakeholders. Focus groups were held with students and staff, and members of the University community were approached in public spaces on campus. A total of 218 responses were gathered, with the vast majority being via the online form, and analyzed with the help of qualitative analysis software Nvivo. As shown in Figure 34.1, students made up over a third of respondents, staff made up just under a quarter of respondents, and the remainder of responses came from alumni, external organizations, students at other institutions and the general public. There have been no significant findings in terms of different views coming from different stakeholder groups, with similar proportions expressing similar views in each group. A larger, more representative sample size may allow the identification of trends in views by stakeholder grouping. However, overall trends as well as specific comments

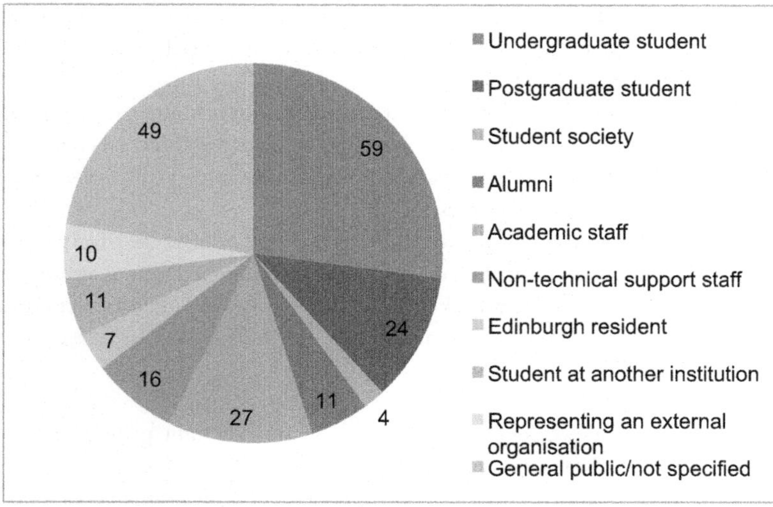

Figure 34.1 Types of respondents

gathered that do not reflect these trends have been useful to inform decision makers – these are presented and discussed below.

Consultation results and discussion

The consultation document asked questions in six areas: principles to inform decision making, strategic options, divestment, values, organizational and policy changes, and transparency and reporting.

Principles to inform decision making

A review of literature and of other organizations' approaches to responsible investment, plus discussion amongst University staff prior to the consultation, led to the formulation of seven principles to inform investment decision making. Academics, senior managers (including Finance and Investment Committee members), other staff members and student representatives discussed how the investment approach could reflect the type of organization they would like the University of Edinburgh to be, while taking into account the need for endowment funds to be preserved and enhanced. The principles proposed in the consultation document are as follows:

- Principle 1: The University will seek to maximize the opportunities to utilize its endowment funds to further its mission to advance human knowledge and benefit society, and to support its students.
- Principle 2: The University should take a long-term view of its investment approach, fully informed by the need for financial sustainability, wealth creation, ethical developments, environmental sustainability and public and social value.
- Principle 3: No investment choices will be made which threaten the long-term viability of the university as an ongoing institution or undermine its core academic freedom principle.

- Principle 4: In making, managing and reporting on its investment choices, the University should be open and transparent about the reasoning behind its choices, and the approaches it has adopted to inform its activities.
- Principle 5: The University will seek to maximize its opportunities to act as an agent for change, to encourage a wealthier and fairer, smarter and healthier, greener and safer, and stronger society, ensuring that it considers the potential impact of investment choices as drivers for positive change where possible.
- Principle 6: The University will seek to ensure it receives a wide range of advice and consults widely before it makes substantial changes to its responsible investment approach.
- Principle 7: The University reserves the right to avoid investing in particular types of activities which are fundamentally incompatible with the mission of the university to benefit society as a whole.

The vast majority[4] of respondents agreed that these are the right principles to inform the University's investment decisions, as shown in Figure 34.2, but a range of suggestions for improving them were made. A significant number of respondents felt the principles should be bolder, or more actively worded. A fairly large number called for less focus on financial sustainability and on wealth creation, and queries were raised about how wealth and wellbeing goals could be met simultaneously, as proposed in principle 5. On the other hand, a small number felt that maximum financial return should be a key goal, as they felt it is difficult to balance ethics with safe investment. Some of these stated that there is a responsibility to staff and students to raise as much money as possible, and that a relatively small group of campaigners' ideals should not influence the investment strategy.

A small number of respondents proposed that a principle should be added on ensuring there is no hypocrisy when divesting from a particular industry, for example, if the University relies on its products or funding in other areas. This issue of consistency also arose in responses to several other questions. Related to this, one respondent suggested that the same principles should also be applied to University pension funds, and another suggested the same for procurement activities.

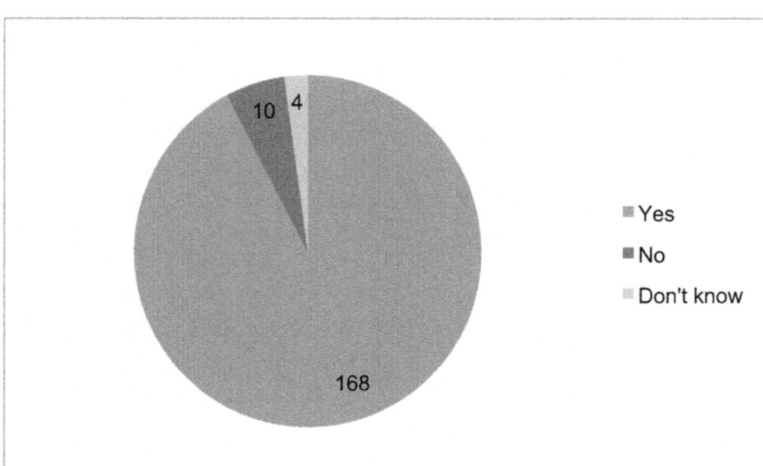

Figure 34.2 Agreement with proposed principles to inform investment decisions (number of respondents = 182)

Reflecting Arnstein's (1969) definitions of levels of participation, in relation to principle 6, a fairly large number proposed that rather than just consulting widely before making substantial changes to the investment approach, that there should be a democratic decision-making process involving students, staff and other stakeholders. Among these, there were suggestions of referenda and citizen juries. A small number of people questioned why the University needed to continue investing so much money for a return, and why it couldn't be spent on research, teaching and facilities now – indicating limited understanding of the endowment fund among the wider University community. This highlights a need for the University to better inform stakeholders on how decisions are made and why, and on how endowment funds work.

Strategic options

The following four strategic options to investment were proposed, and respondents were asked which ones they agreed with (they could select more than one option):

- Option 1: Investment in companies and funds which contribute to a wealthier and fairer, smarter and healthier, greener and safer and stronger global society
- Option 2: Direct investment in university activities and objectives e.g. renewable energy generation – on-site or off-site – climate emissions reduction, energy efficiency, etc.
- Option 3: Direct investment in a range of 'start-up' innovative companies or social investments linked to identified social responsibility themes, perhaps using concepts such as social impact bonds
- Option 4: Avoid investment in sectors or companies failing to reach recognised standards

In contrast to current campaigning, which focuses predominantly on calling for particular divestments, these options reflect a desire to move towards actively seeking investments with social and environmental benefits, while still carrying out negative screening at the same time. As shown in Figure 34.3, all of the four strategic investment options were popular among the majority of respondents, with options 1, 2 and 4 receiving very similar numbers of votes, and option 3 receiving slightly fewer. Comments were made on the different options. For option 1, as with

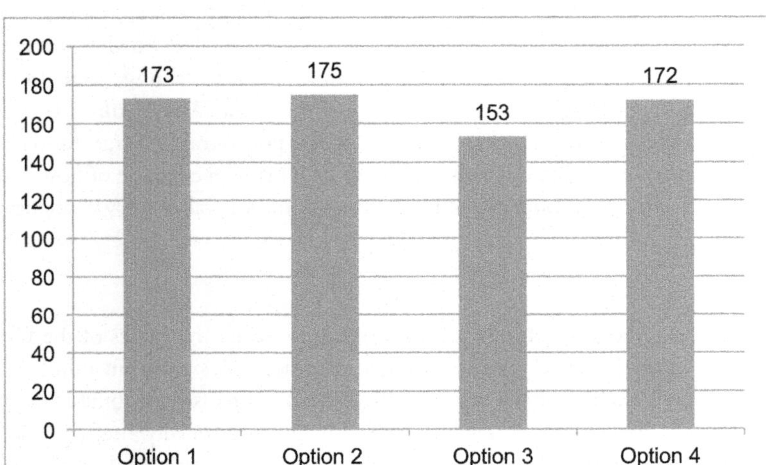

Figure 34.3 Popularity of strategic investment options (number of respondents = 199)

the principles discussed above, questions were raised about whether wealthier and fairer ambitions for society could be successfully married. There were mixed views in comments on option 3, regarding whether investing in start-ups would be a risky approach, how start-ups would be selected and whether this was appropriate for a university. A fairly large number of respondents were concerned about the use of the term 'recognized standards' in option 4, asking for greater clarity on which standards, recognized by whom.

Divestment

Respondents were asked what process should be followed to make any decisions about divestment from particular industries based on ethical considerations. The idea of a materiality test, to screen out companies with, for example, over five per cent of their core business in an area the University did not wish to invest in, was popular. There were varying views on who should make divestment decisions, with a small number proposing expert advice to inform decision making by high-level University committees, yet a large number of others calling for increased consultation, public discussion and even democratic decision making across the University community, reflecting some of the views expressed regarding levels of participation in decision making described above in relation to the principles to inform investment decisions.

A significant number of respondents specified particular industries or activities that should be divested from, with only one respondent stating that no divestment decisions should be made based on ethics, only on financial considerations. Reflecting current global campaigning, more than half of respondents called for divestment from fossil fuels – either immediately or to be planned over a longer period. A few of these specifically proposed divesting from coal only. These calls were backed up with statements about an engagement approach not being appropriate for industries whose core business did not fit with University values (assuming these are agreed on). Respondents calling for divestment from fossil fuels also highlighted the reputational risk of not divesting, and better long-term performance and lower risk through divesting, in reference to the concept of the carbon bubble. Small numbers proposed engagement with energy companies in favour of renewable energy development, rather than divestment. Again, the issue of consistency across University operations such as research funding and procurement, as well as investment activities, was raised here.

A significant number called for divestment from arms manufacture, yet small numbers engaged in discussion about cases where they consider arms to be acceptable. Small numbers called for divestment from a wide range of other areas, including factory farming, cosmetics testing on animals, companies supporting or involved in occupation of the West Bank or Gaza, gambling, mining or specifically conflict minerals, alcohol, drugs, pornography, large food and alcohol retailers, nuclear power, payday loans, banks and biofuel. This is an example of how diverse views are across the University community, making defining common values very challenging.

Values

The consultation document asked what people considered to be the values of the University of Edinburgh, which would be relevant to investment decisions. A significant number of respondents proposed values such as social responsibility, social equity, sustainability, contributing to society, health and wellbeing, universal human rights, putting socially useful knowledge into action, fairness, justice, collaboration for sustainability, a better world and public good. Large numbers proposed knowledge, the pursuit of truth, academic freedom, critical thinking and education. A large number made reference to the existing University mission, which includes the statement, "As a world-leading centre of academic excellence we aim to . . . make a significant, sustainable and socially responsible contribution to Scotland, the UK and the world, promoting health and economic and cultural wellbeing". There appears to be broad consensus on the University having a role in creating social and environmental benefits (the difficulty is defining what these should be), yet there are some concerns about whether a focus on social responsibility and sustainability could infringe on academic freedom (e.g. if funding for particular areas of research, such as fossil fuels extraction, is not welcomed for ethical reasons).

Organisational and policy changes

The consultation paper proposed the drafting of a public document which would explain the reasoning behind the University's investment stance, principles and strategic options, to replace the current Socially Responsible Investment Policy. This document would be updated every four years to reflect ongoing developments and emerging issues.

The majority of respondents, when asked if the investment view approach would be useful and would fulfil the Principles for Responsible Investing requirements, did not agree, as indicated in Figure 34.4. However, a large number of those who said they disagreed did go on to state that it would be useful, but that they had other concerns. A large number of respondents questioned as to whether updating every four years would be often enough, and called instead for open and transparent review annually. A significant number of respondents requested specific information in the documents on industries that should be avoided. In relation to the Principles for Responsible Investment commitment to providing guidance to investment managers, a separate, more detailed guidance document for investment managers was proposed in the consultation paper, but a large number of respondents felt that the publicly available document should be detailed enough on issues of principles, divestment and engagement approach to act as guidance for investment managers.

To go beyond the current approach, which waits until submissions of cases for divestment are made before considering them, the consultation document proposed the establishment of an advisory forum, representative of the University community, to actively investigate and consider

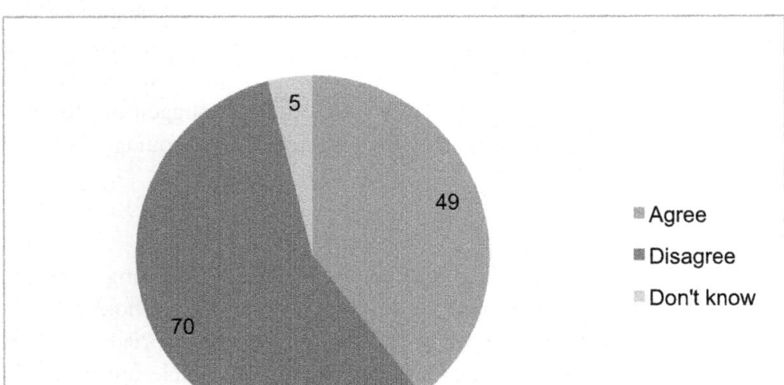

Figure 34.4 Agreement levels with investment view approach (number of respondents = 124)

investment issues related to ethics, and advise the University Court and the Investment Committee. Respondents were asked to comment on the potential remit and membership of such an advisory forum. In terms of remit, proposals were made about the advisory forum scrutinizing investment decisions, checking the expertise and commitment to the investment stance of investment managers and linking to University courses on social responsibility and sustainability issues, to allow students' research to inform the agenda. It was widely felt that an advisory forum should include a range of stakeholders, including students from different fields, student campaign groups, and different types of staff, alumni and external expertise. Such a forum would promote ongoing involvement of stakeholders in investment decision making, demonstrating that this is not a one-off, tokenistic consultation.

Transparency and reporting

The consultation document recognized that transparency and reporting on the investment process could be improved, and so proposed a transparency package to include:

- Publication and regular updating of the investment view document discussed above
- Publication of any specific guidance from University Court to the Investment Committee
- Publication of any specific guidance given to the University's Investment Managers under the UN PRI
- Publication of the annual report from the University to the UN PRI process
- Proactive publication of the University's investment portfolio on a quarterly or annual basis
- Publication of the active investor activities of the University's investment managers on behalf of the University

The vast majority of respondents (117 out of 120 who answered this question) felt this transparency package would be effective. A large number went on to specify further details about the amount of transparency they would like to see, such as including figures in the publishing of the investment portfolio (by company and by sector) and publishing minutes from meetings. A small number of respondents proposed ways in which information should be made accessible, including online through one distribution point, and at public events to encourage feedback on the investment approach. A large number requested information on investment to be made available in an easier to understand format, so that those without the relevant financial expertise could engage. Only two respondents expressed concerns about how much transparency was feasible, for reasons of business sensitivity. A large number also made the suggestion that the University should share its approach to investment with other institutions, to encourage them to follow suit.

Conclusion and next steps

This consultation experience has highlighted the complexities of defining agreed-upon values and principles for a large institution made up of a wide variety of stakeholders. The University of Edinburgh has the challenges of selecting and defining the appropriate terminology for its investment approach – be it ethical, socially responsible or sustainable investment, pinpointing values that reflect the core purpose of the University today, and further refining principles and approach to investment, taking into account consultation outcomes. While it is not possible to incorporate all views in an investment strategy, trends in views will be taken into account, as well as thoughtful comments that go against majority-held views. Consulting widely on a complex, ethical issue has been a worthwhile exercise in terms of demonstrating listening to stakeholders, gathering varied views to complement expert knowledge, and highlighting the interest of stakeholders in being involved in thinking through complex ethical issues. In order to demonstrate that participating in such a consultation goes beyond tokenism on the part of the University, an iterative, ongoing process of reflection on investment is envisaged, with events, research and student projects informing and gathering expert and non-expert views to continually inform investment decisions in future. Accessible documentation detailing decisions made and how varied inputs are taken into account will be made available. The appetite for greater involvement in decision making on ethical issues related to University practices, shown in responses to this consultation, indicates that there is room for future consultations on a range of such issues, while learning from and building on this experience. The University's Department for Social Responsibility and Sustainability is now in the process of launching new channels to increase staff and student input into policy and practice, including an academic network and a student forum, both focusing on social responsibility and sustainability.

Notes

1 Online, available HTTP: <http://www.accounts.finance.ed.ac.uk/edinburgh-finanical>.
2 Online, available HTTP: <http://www.ed.ac.uk/schools-departments/finance/about/sections/financial-accounting/investment>.
3 Online, available HTTP: <http://www.docs.sasg.ed.ac.uk/GaSP/Governance/SociallyResponsibleInvestment.pdf>.
4 Numbers of people who made particular points are referred to in the text below using the following terms: 1 = one respondent, 2–9 = a small number, 10–49 = a fairly large number, 50–79 = a large number, 80–114 = a significant number, 114+ = more than half/the majority.

References

Arnstein, S. R. (1969) 'A ladder of citizen participation', *Journal of the American Institute of Planners*, 35(4): 216–224.

Brickson, S. L. (2007) 'Organizational identity orientation: the genesis of the role of the firm and distinct forms of social value', *Academy of Management Review* 32(3): 864–888.

Cook, P., Crips, E., Dineen, C., Hayward, T., Oberman, K. and Thaler, M. (2014) *Response to University of Edinburgh consultation paper on responsible investment*, Edinburgh: Just World Institute.

Drayson, R., Bone, E., Agombar, J. and Kemp, S. (2013) *Student attitudes towards skills for sustainable development*, York: Higher Education Academy.

Freeman, R. E. (1984) *Strategic management: a stakeholder approach*, Boston, MA: Pitman.

Krosinsky, C. (2013) *The short guide to sustainable investing*, Oxford: Do Sustainability.

Michelson, G., Wailes, N., van der Laan, S. and Frost, G. (2004) 'Ethical investment processes and outcomes', *Journal of Business Ethics* 52: 1–10.

Sandberg, J., Juravle, C., Hedesström, T. M. and Hamilton, I. (2009) 'The heterogeneity of socially responsible investment', *Journal of Business Ethics* 87(4): 519–533.

Sparkes, R. (2001) 'Ethical investment: whose ethics? Which investment?', *Business Ethics: A European Review* 10(3): 194–205.

Sparkes, R. and Cowton, C. J. (2004) 'The maturing of socially responsible investment: a review of the developing link with corporate social responsibility', *Journal of Business Ethics* 52: 45–57.

Spitzeck, H. and Hansen, E. G. (2010) 'Stakeholder governance: how stakeholders influence corporate decision making', *Corporate Governance* 10(4): 378–391.

Welp, M., de la Vega-Leinert, A., Stoll-Kleemann, S. and Jaeger, C. C. (2006) 'Science-based stakeholder dialogues: theories and tools', *Global Environmental Change* 16(2): 170–181.

35

Religious investors and responsible investment

Laura Berry

Introduction

In the 400 years since the creation of the corporate entity, people of have consistently spoken out about the social impact of capital. Jewish, Christian and Muslim leaders have long recognized practices to encourage ethical investments while identifying investments to avoid. During colonial times in North America, both the Quakers and Methodists explicitly avoided investments that supported the slave trade. Muslims have had strict prohibitions against interest-bearing investments. Likewise, Judaism and Catholic teachings are clear on the responsibility to attend to the needs of the poor.

Religious investors have been shaping responsible investment (RI) practices before the language of 'responsible investment' was coined – indeed the current field of responsible investment is itself a legacy of faith-based efforts to link ethics and investment. This influence is particularly noteworthy in the early history of the United States and its Puritan founders. In fact, John Wesley often taught on money and materialism, developing his Trilateral Sermon, in which he challenged Christians to, "Gain all you can. Save all you can. Give all you can". Wesley preached from New Testament text, such as:

> (1 Timothy 6–9) 6Of course, there is great gain in godliness combined with contentment; 7for we brought nothing into the world, so that we can take nothing out of it; 8but if we have food and clothing, we will be content with these. 9But those who want to be rich fall into temptation and are trapped by many senseless and harmful desires that plunge people into ruin and destruction. 10For the love of money is a root of all kinds of evil, and in their eagerness to be rich some have wandered away from the faith and pierced themselves with many pains.

He drew from the Sermon on the Mount as well.

> (Matthew 19–24) 19Do not store up for yourselves treasures on earth, where moth and rust consume and where thieves break in and steal 20but store up for yourselves treasures in heaven, where neither moth nor rust consumes and where thieves do not break in and

> steal 21For where your treasure is, there your heart will be also. 22The eye is the lamp of the body. So, if your eye is healthy, your whole body will be full of light; 23but if your eye is unhealthy, your whole body will be full of darkness. If then the light in you is darkness, how great is the darkness! 24No one can serve two masters; for a slave will either hate the one and love the other, or be devoted to the one and despise the other. You cannot serve God and wealth.

In this chapter I look at how faith-based investors developed these ideas over time, and how they have come to play a role in the RI movement today. Much of what follows is drawn from reflection on the 40-year history of the Interfaith Center on Corporate Responsibility (ICCR), an organization whose experience and practices are representative of the broader stakeholder group of faith-based investors, of which I am the executive director.

ICCR is described in its 2012 annual report as follows:

> Currently celebrating our 41st year, the Interfaith Center on Corporate Responsibility is a pioneer and a leader in the corporate responsibility movement. . . . Today our membership is comprised of 300 institutional investors representing over $100 billion in assets. Representing faith-based communities with congregations all over the world, SRI asset management companies, unions, pension funds and a global network of allies; ICCR members are not only shareholders, but also trusted partners in corporate responsibility initiatives that promote a more just and sustainable world.

Although most religious investors continue to avoid investing in activities contrary to the tenets of their faith – the 'sin stocks' that have traditionally included alcohol and other intoxicants, tobacco, weapons manufacturers and gambling – the level of sophistication demonstrated by religious investors and their allies has grown beyond avoidance. The history of ICCR is the story behind the growing sophistication of religious investors, which in both approach and influence has been akin to broader changes in the RI industry.

This chapter looks at the field of shareholder advocacy, and how the faith-based investment community in general and ICCR in particular have participated in and shaped this practice. It looks at shareholder advocacy as a developing practice and tactical behavior pattern. As the chapter explores the issues addressed, and the challenges and barriers faced, the wide-ranging contributions of religious investors will be described through the lens of this particular interfaith organization. Over 40 years from its founding, shareholders around the world continue to use the engagement practices refined by practitioners over many years of faithful, persistent action.

A short history of religious shareholder activism from the 1970s

Faith-based investment activity is closely linked to the rise of corporate power in the twentieth century. Corporations and the capital they wield exert an extraordinary influence on global economies, governments and policies, and hence people and the environment. Fast-forward to the present and there are many thought leaders and scholars asking the same question[1] once posed by an article in *Time* magazine, 'Are Companies More Powerful than Countries?' (Foroohar, 2012[2]).

But the emergence of religious investors' influence reflects the fundamental role that one issue in particular had in shaping shareholder advocacy work in the United States. ICCR was originally founded to coordinate religious investor action in response to the emergence of a galvanizing issue – South African apartheid. In the early 1970s, the abhorrent policy of apartheid (the legislated segregation of races in South Africa) became a rallying point for faith communities and their investment activity. In 1971 the Episcopal Church in the U.S.A. filed the first ever religious-sponsored shareholder resolution with General Motors, requesting that the company withdraw its operations until apartheid was abolished. Other faith organizations soon joined the campaign and organized themselves as the ad hoc Inter-Faith Committee on Social Responsibility in Investment, which later became the ICCR.

Shareholder activism from the faith-based community led to a new dynamic between large corporations and their investors. Accustomed to more compliant investors, corporations bristled at this check on their power and pushed back by tightening the rules around the filing of resolutions. Those that were the targets of activity[3] took to waiting until the last minute to disclose the dates of their annual general meetings and began holding them in out-of-the-way locations to limit shareholder participation. One beleaguered corporate secretary addressed the audience gathered at the 1971 annual meeting of Gulf Oil, summing up the feelings of many in saying, "Before now our shareholders have always been loyal".

Religious investors quickly added to the list of issues they took on via shareholder advocacy, growing from the anti-apartheid efforts. Religious investors reported 478 individual actions involving over 200 companies in 2013.[4] Many of the issues that ICCR members began addressing during the 1970s foretold coming cultural shifts such as equal employment opportunity and corporate diversity initiatives, concerns about military profiteering, excessive drug pricing, access to adequate nutrition and infant formula marketing practices, political contributions, equal access to capital and the environmental impact of the extractive industries.

As the anti-apartheid campaign became a broader social movement in the late 1970s, ICCR members pressured companies to adopt the Sullivan Principles – a code of corporate conduct developed in 1977 calling for political justice through fair employment in South Africa.

The Sullivan Principles

1. Non-segregation of the races in all eating, comfort, and work facilities.
2. Equal and fair employment practices for all employees.
3. Equal pay for all employees doing equal or comparable work for the same period of time.
4. Initiation of and development of training programs that will prepare, in substantial numbers, blacks and other nonwhites for supervisory, administrative, clerical, and technical jobs.
5. Increasing the number of blacks and other nonwhites in management and supervisory positions.
6. Improving the quality of life for blacks and other nonwhites outside the work environment in such areas as housing, transportation, school, recreation, and health facilities.
7. Working to eliminate laws and customs that impede social, economic, and political justice. (added in 1984)

The Sullivan Principles became a model for other issue-based engagements, including the MacBride Principles, which were developed in 1984 to address unequal labor practices in Northern Ireland.

Led by ICCR, churches and a growing coalition of institutional investors, such as pension plans and others, filed 185 shareholder resolutions on apartheid during the culminating summer of 1986. On 20 October 1986 General Motors announced it was selling its South African investments, followed the next day by IBM declaring its intention to withdraw – both historic victories. The trickle of U.S. corporations withdrawing from South Africa became a flood, with 50 U.S. corporations leaving South Africa in 1986 alone.

In the 1980s, new issues emerged. ICCR members also focused on the negative portrayal of women and minorities in advertising campaigns. An example was their work with Colgate Palmolive on its 'Darkie' brand of toothpaste, which featured a minstrel character in blackface, which resulted in the elimination of the brand and a renewed focus on the use of stereotypes in marketing practices around the globe.[5]

As ICCR members expanded their activism, corporate secretaries' frustration grew. In 1983, A. Joseph Dowd, the corporate secretary for American Electric Power complained:

> For the past few years, we have watched helplessly as 'well-intentioned' shareholders have bombarded and overloaded the proxy statements of issuers with proposals which are at best occasionally constructive and at worst absurd and often times more appropriate for the platform of a politician.[6]

In the same year, SEC Commissioner Bevis Longworth spoke more admiringly of the active religious investors, saying, "The magic of this process is that the proxy lands on the desk of every important institutional investor. It can't be thrown in the wastebasket without being opened. The trustees actual have to look at it".[7]

With their renewed interest in the connection between invested capital and social change, the 1980s also saw religious investors develop an interest in improving equitable access to capital. Due to their traditional roles in schools, hospitals and social service agencies in vulnerable communities, 'women religious' were well positioned to observe and respond to the needs for the poor. A critical mass of various forces was accelerating the pace of demographic changes taking place in central cities around the United States. And less developed rural communities continued to struggle. With the emergence of micro lending and other innovative approaches to addressing community development, religious investors were poised to contribute to the developing field of community investment. Seeing another opportunity to leverage their investment for the common good, ICCR members launched a Clearinghouse on Alternative Investment to encourage faith community participation in community economic development. Hundreds of millions of dollars were earmarked for projects such as affordable housing, enterprise development and worker-owned businesses, while community loan funds and banks were urged to broaden their credit offerings to women, minorities and inner-city communities. By 1995, these faith-based 'impact investments' would exceed $300 million.

These new markets and products caught the attention of financial super-markets that were expanding rapidly after the Glass-Steagall Act of 1934 was struck down by Congress in the Gramm-Leach-Bliley Act of 1999 (GLBA). With a public policy environment that encouraged home ownership and growing home prices, commercial banks developed newly profitable lines of business in the domestic sub-prime lending market. At the same time, these global enterprises were exploring ways to take global micro lending to profitable commercial scale.[8]

The activism related to equitable access to capital was a precursor to investigations and inquiry that would lead religious investors to be among the first voices raising concerns about underwriting practices in the later decades. This issue work led to over 400 investor actions in the mid-1990s and beyond, expressing concerns regarding financial innovations related to sub-prime debt and transparency regarding collateral and risk assessment. These early warnings were later well documented in the media, with an article published in the *Christian Science Monitor* (Francis, 2008)[9] describing ICCR members as an 'early warning system' for mainstream investors and policy makers. It was clear that the global economic crisis that was gaining momentum in the fall of 2008 was the result of catastrophic defaults that began in the very neighborhoods where ICCR began its efforts in the 1980s. By observing the impact on consumers through a community lens, the religious investors had access to a different form of insight, creating opportunities with a sort of justice arbitrage that could have guided policy and investor action.

Religious investors broaden the issue base

The issues related in the previous section focused largely on social justice, and provide insight not merely on the work, but also on the organizing principle of shareholder advocacy used to address apartheid. But, beginning in the 1980s, religious investors increasingly joined forces with others to address a broad array of social and environmental corporate practices. It was also in the 1980s that ICCR began reaching out beyond religious organizations for members. Recognizing that many secular institutional investors share common goals of building a more just and sustainable corporate world, ICCR invited like-minded investors to join. In 1982 the Calvert Group joined ICCR as its first associate (secular) member. Throughout the 1980s, labor unions and some of the country's largest pension funds, including TIAA-CREF and public plans from New York, California, Wisconsin and Minnesota, began collaborating with faith-based investors in challenging the companies they held in their portfolios to improve their social and environmental practices.

The 1990s led religious investors to focus significantly more attention on the environment. The attention of shareholders on environmental issues was driven in part by highly publicized events in the United States in the recent past, including in particular the health disaster of Love Canal, the environmental disaster surrounding the Exxon Valdez and the Three Mile Island nuclear disaster. It was also closely linked to the implications for corporate performance represented by a changing regulatory environment, such as the Environment Protection Agency's Superfund Act of 1980. Religious investors appreciated the hand-in-glove relationship as regulatory reform allowed them to apply new pressures, urging companies to adopt voluntary initiatives for waste reduction, energy conservation and a more rigorous commitment to public safety.

Globalization also became a topic for religious investors as it emerged in public debate in the United States. For instance, as a result of debates of trade-related policy in the United States, in particular the North American Free Trade Agreement Act of 1993, ICCR members developed a growing awareness of sweatshop conditions in Mexico's maquiladoras – the approximately 2,100 mostly U.S.-owned factories situated along the southern border of the United States. This began a new series of efforts to develop guidelines to transform the way corporations related to communities and the environment, beginning with the 1995 publication of the ICCR's 'Principles for Global Corporate Responsibility'.[10]

The 1990s were the years when questions about marketing and product-related corporate practices began being raised in the battle with 'Big Tobacco'. Throughout the decade, ICCR members used their power as shareholders to help limit public health risks by asking tobacco companies to include warning labels on their products and advertising. Foreshadowing battles to come, activist shareholders began requesting that the companies refrain from lobbying against legislation aimed at regulating tobacco and smoking. Once again religious investors identified concerns that soon became part of the broader public discourse. They used the tools they developed to identify and connect corporate practices to social justice issues. Two decades after corporate marketing practices were identified as contributing to smoking-related risks, the corporate influence on the latest public health crisis – obesity – follows a similar path. Through tools developed during years of shareholder activism, religious investors are addressing the corporate role in this growing concern. The recently published *New York Times Sunday Magazine* article[11] 'The Extraordinary Science of Addictive Junk Food' (Moss, 2013) recognizes the parallels.

Time and time again, religious investors made note of effective approaches to addressing corporations through their ownership interests; often adapting tactics that had been successfully deployed in one arena to gain traction in another. The long history of the 'Troubles' in Northern Ireland was another example of this approach. As an interfaith organization, ICCR had a unique perspective and role in Northern Ireland, working across faith lines toward equality of opportunity and an end to religious discrimination in the workplace. ICCR members filed scores of shareholder resolutions asking companies to implement the MacBride Principles on Fair Employment in Northern Ireland. As described earlier, these 'principles-based' efforts clearly had their roots in the earlier apartheid work. ICCR has also called on companies to cut their ties to the notoriously repressive military government of Burma (Myanmar).[12]

Religious investors and the emergence of corporate social responsibility

Religious investors have played a role in broader efforts in the 2000s to take the shareholder advocacy and investment themes that emerged from several of the strains of investment described above and to link them more directly to the financial consequences of corporate social and environmental policy. Today, most Fortune 500 companies have corporate responsibility departments and are formally disclosing their environmental and social impacts. A growing group of investors has campaigned for transparency on corporate social responsibility (CSR) issues where it does not exist. And corporate CSR activity has been directly tied to engagement with responsible investors, including those from the faith-based community.

Typical of the growing support for corporate social responsibility (CSR) initiatives, in honor of ICCR's fortieth anniversary in 2011, a number of representatives from leading corporations weighed in on the influence of the religious stakeholders over the years.

Mark Presinger, The Coca-Cola Company's Director of Corporate Governance said:

> Over the years, The Coca-Cola Company built a relationship of trust and respect with ICCR as we worked together to address many challenges facing our company. This collaboration on a range of issues from workplace rights to water stewardship has truly led to improvement in our policies and practices.

Similarly, William Clay Ford, Ford Motor Company's Executive Chairman, offered:

> When I began speaking out on environmental and social issues more than 30 years ago, the Interfaith Center on Corporate Responsibility was a welcome voice of encouragement among many that were doubtful. They cheered us on when we made progress, and challenged us to move faster and do better when we didn't. Thanks in large part to the work done by ICCR, today the idea that businesses can do well by doing good is widely acknowledged.

And Mark Spears, Director of Disney Consumer Products Sustainable Business Practices added:

> Today's increasingly complex social and environmental issues require a broad stakeholder approach which is collaborative, informative and mutually supportive. ICCR has routinely provided experience, insight and a results-orientation to a relationship with The Walt Disney Company, which began in the mid-1990s. If people and organizations are in fact known by the relationship they keep, we are truly honored to be considered a member of the ICCR community.[13]

In the course of over 40 years, the CSR movement has developed into a serious field of inquiry and practice as evidenced by the explosion of 'social' investment firms and the burgeoning CSR staff at most large companies. Helping to drive this growth is investor and consumer demand, with brand identity increasingly linked to 'green' or 'fair trade' and 'ethically sourced' products. Consumer buying guides feature products of companies that are held to increasingly stringent environmental, social and governance (ESG) standards. Both investors and consumers are empowered in their choices by a proliferation of organizations dedicated to promoting shareholder advocacy.

The emerging generation of religious shareholder activism

The field of shareholder advocacy is now an established practice in the United States and internationally – how has it come to scale? And what role do religious investors in particular play in the practice now?

Ferraro and Beunza (2014) describe how the field itself has emerged over the past few decades:

> [U]ntil the 1970s the SEC rejected all proposals focused on 'general economic, political, racial, religious, social or similar causes' (Regulation X-14a-8(c)(2)). But in 1970 a Federal Court allowed a shareholder proposal on the sale of Napalm to appear on the proxy statement of Dow Chemical, and eventually led the SEC to allow shareholder proposals on social issues. Since then, activists such as Ralph Nader and Saul Alinsky, but also religious investors and eventually public pension funds, have been filing shareholder proposals on a host of environmental, social and governance issues. In the mid-1980s, large institutional investors leveraged their ownership positions to exert more influence in the governance of public corporations and the shareholder proposals was one of the tools they used. These investors were more focused on re-establishing the primacy of shareholder value than on promoting social causes through their shareholding. . . . Despite the different motives, the confluence of institutional investors and activist shareholders led to the growth in shareholder proposals filed. From the 597 proposals filed in the period 1973–1978, by the period 1989–1993 investors were filing 1,365 proposals. Since 2005, at least 1,000 proposals were filed each year.

Clearly an expanding pool of shareholders, including those with widely divergent interests, now understands the tactical utility of the shareholder resolution. The view that shareholder activism was an essential activity for responsible investors was enhanced by the increasing awareness of efficacy. Religious investors recognized undeniable change as a result of their efforts including improved environmental disclosure (Reid and Toffel, 2009) and performance. Shareholder engagement was proving to be both strategic and effective in encouraging desirable changes in corporate practice.

Long-time ICCR member representative and University of New Mexico business professor, Harry Van Buren, noted in a 2007 study (Van Buren, 2007) that

> Resolutions are not generally ends in themselves, but a means to an end. Shareholder activists seek to use the access to other shareholders and to management afforded by a shareholder resolution (or the threat of one) to engage in dialogue with corporate management and to attempt to affect social change.

Van Buren's comments anticipated the fundamental shift in religious investor practices.

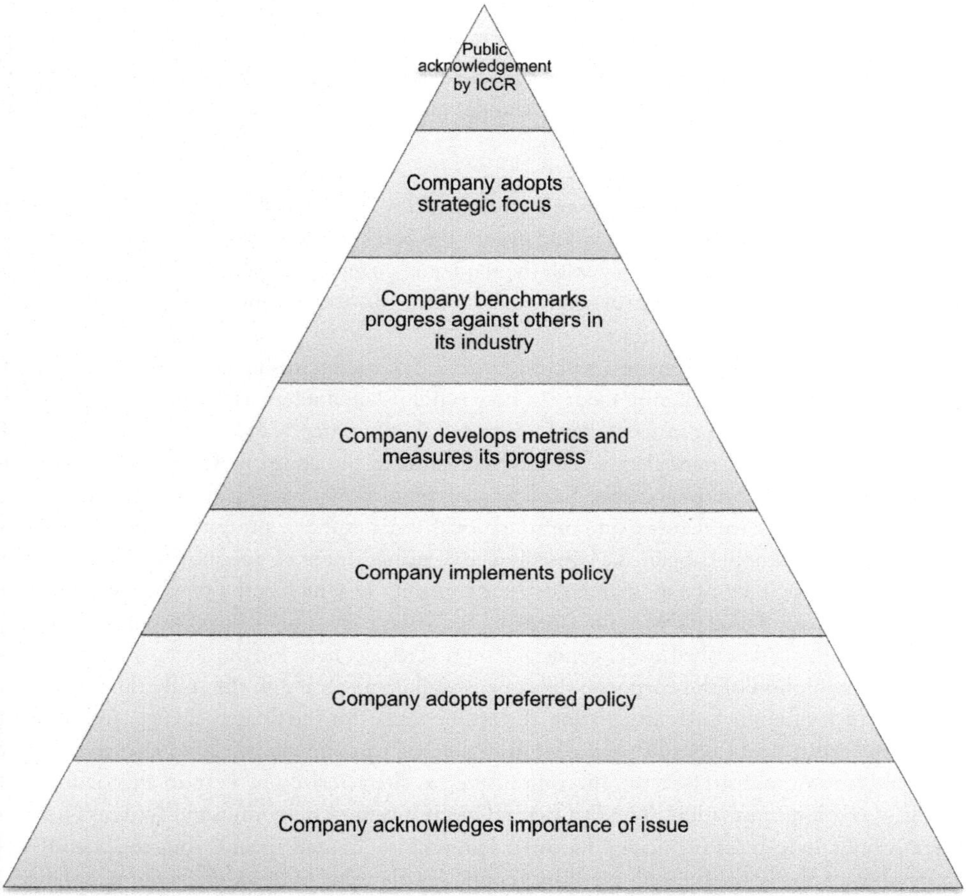

Figure 35.1 Hierarchy of company engagement

Source: ICCR (with permission).

The 2011–2012 corporate proxy season was the first year where the number of corporate engagements outstripped the number of shareholder proposals filed, with 2012–2013 following the same pattern. As the history suggests, religious investors are increasingly serving consultative roles, moving companies and their operations through a 'hierarchy of change' detailed in Figure 35.1. ICCR members regularly use this hierarchy in assessing where a company's transformation falls on a scale that begins with the company acknowledging the importance of the issue and ends with a public acknowledgement of the company's progress, as in the adoption of fleet emissions reduction targets by Ford Motor Company[14] in 2008.

In some ways this hierarchy is an activist complement to the Zadek (2004) model on how companies change.[15]

In the current state of play, resolutions are frequently seen as a last resort, with religious investors choosing to file when private negotiation fails. In addition, once filed, if continuing negotiations between investors and management lead are successful, resolutions can be withdrawn.

One ICCR leader described the early years this way,

> For the most part, we really filed the shareholder resolution and then had no contact with the company until we went to the stockholder meeting. And in many cases it was just giving your speech and waiting for the results.

The results the member awaited were to meet the SEC-required thresholds of 3, 6 or 10 per cent of the vote tally. These results would ensure the issue could be raised again the following year, if the company did not comply with the requested change. Today's activist investors expect double-digit votes and are not surprised by tallies in the 30–40 per cent range – by all measures, a significant change in expectations.

There is considerable fascination with both the fact of the increasing efficacy of the religious shareholder and in the developing theory of how activist shareholders wield their influence. Ferraro and Beunza (2012), for instance, have conducted an ethnography of ICCR members and staff to study how activist shareholders voice their concerns to the companies they invest in, influencing them to act more responsibly. Existing analyses of how social movements try to change corporate behavior have focused on confrontational tactics such as protest and boycotts. They assume change will only happen as a consequence of management caving in. This study explores a different approach, known as 'shareholder engagement', in which activists who own shares in a corporation have dialogues with management, requesting them to change corporate policies.

With sensitizing described as "engendering mutual respect between the activists and the executives", the evolution of the corporate dialogue is well documented in the study. The reframing process, which often includes articulating 'the business case' for the desired change, describes the more transformational cases of shareholder dialogue, and can ultimately lead to change across an entire industry or industrial sector. In 'committing', as characterized by Ferraro and Beunza, the length of relationship matters. The fact that religious investors are committed activists and represent serious, long-term financial fiduciaries demonstrates commitment throughout decades of dialogue. And finally, the breaching process requires participants to break through organizational inertia by "defying the dominant interaction order in these face-to-face meetings (dialogues)".

Of course there are challenges to this approach, which can test the patience of more externally focused activism, including religious investors being used by the very corporations they are work to change, a sort of 'corporate co-option'.

As the approach of religious investors is taken up by a new generation of responsible investors, the 2006 book *The New Capitalists: How Citizen Investors Are Reshaping the Corporate Agenda* (Davis, Lukomnik and Pitt-Watson, 2006) comes to mind. In the chapter describing the role of NGOs and civil society as part of a "new capitalist ecosystem", the authors describe the "Ten Rules for Sustainable Engagement" this way:

> In truth, though, religious investors have had their most profound influence in establishing what amounts to a prototype of a civil society organization using capital markets to influence corporate behavior. The building blocks they fashioned would later be used by trade unions, environmental activists, antipoverty lobbies, and other nongovernmental groups electing to pursue their missions through capital. Lessons we can extract boil down to ten basic principles, what we might describe as the genetic code for a new-capitalist organization in a civil economy.
>
> 1 Convert the values mission to a business mission.
> 2 Assert rights of ownership.

3. Break out of the ghetto.
4. The more capital, the louder the voice.
5. Build investor coalitions.
6. Become a utility.
7. Multitask campaign issues.
8. Watch the gatekeepers.
9. Believe companies could be on your side.
10. Go global.

As some activists encourage investors to return to the days of exclusionary 'sin stocks', redefining 'sin' to address a wide-range of issues that invoke outrage and concern, religious investors continue their steady, faithful committed approach, once again redefining responsible investment practice through the wide aperture of the lens of faith. For nearly 5,000 years the world's great faith traditions have had a lot to say about wealth and justice, and it is clear they intend to continue to use their collective voice as investors.

Notes

1. Online, available HTTP: <http://business.time.com/2012/01/27/are-companies-more-powerful-than-countries/>.
2. Foroohar, R. (2012) Are Companies more Powerful than Countries? *Time Magazine*, Jan. 27, 2012, online, available HTTP: <http://business.time.com/2012/01/27/are-companies-more-powerful-than-countries/>.
3. Meeting notes from ICCR archives, online, available HTTP: <http://findingaids.cul.columbia.edu/ead//nnc-rb/ldpd_8429461>.
4. Shareholder Action Database, online, available HTTP: <www.iccr.org>.
5. Online, available HTTP: <http://articles.latimes.com/1987–02–28/local/me-6477_1_colgate-palmolive>.
6. ICCR archives, op. cit.
7. Ibid.
8. *The Corporate Examiner*, Vol. 36, No. 1, July 25, 2008, 'The buck stops here: how securitization changed the rules for ordinary Americans'.
9. Francis, D. (2008) Economic slump: Ethics loom large Christian Science Monitor, Sept. 15, 2008, online, available HTTP: <http://www.csmonitor.com/Business/2008/0915/p16s03-wmgn.html>.
10. ECCR, ICCR, TCCR. *Principles for global corporate responsibility: benchmarks for measuring business performance*. New York: The Corporate Examiner (Volume 24 Issues 2–4), 1995.
11. Online, available HTTP: <http://www.nytimes.com/2013/02/24/magazine/the-extraordinary-science-of-junk-food.html?pagewanted=all&_r=0>.
12. ICCR Shareholder Action Database.
13. Online, available HTTP: <http://www.iccr.org/about/quotes.php>.
14. Online, available HTTP: <http://www.iccr.org/news/press_releases/2008/pr_gm05.27.08.htm>.
15. Online, available HTTP: <http://hbr.org/2004/12/the-path-to-corporate-responsibility/ar/1>.

References

Davis, S., Lukomnik, J. and Pitt-Watson, D. (2006) *The new capitalists: how citizen investors are reshaping the corporate agenda*, Boston: Harvard Business Review Press.

Ferraro, F. and Beunza, D. (2014) 'Why talk? A process model of dialogue in shareholder engagement', Working paper series, London, UK: Social Science Research Network (SSRN).

Foroohar, R. (2012) 'Are companies more powerful than countries?' *Time*, January 27. Online. Available HTTP: <http://business.time.com/2012/01/27/are-companies-more-powerful-than-countries/> (accessed May 2015).

Francis, D. (2008) 'Economic slump: ethics loom large', *Christian Science Monitor*, September 15. Online. Available HTTP: <http://www.csmonitor.com/Business/2008/0915/p16s03-wmgn.html> (accessed May 2015).

Moss, M. (2013) 'The extraordinary science of addictive junk food' *New York Times Sunday Magazine*, February 20. Online. Available HTTP: <http://www.nytimes.com/2013/02/24/magazine/the-extraordinary-science-of-junk-food.html?pagewanted=all&_r=1> (accessed May 2015).

Reid, E. M. and Toffel, M. W. (2009) 'Responding to public and private politics: corporate disclosure of climate change strategies', *Strategic Management Journal* 30(11): 1157–1178.

Van Buren, H. (2007) 'Speaking truth to power: religious institutions as both dissident organizational stakeholders and organizational partners', *Business and Society Review*, 112: 55–72.

Zadek, S. (2004) 'Paths to corporate responsibility', *Harvard Business Review*, December.

36

Stakeholders of responsible investment

Retail investors

Jonas Nilsson

Introduction

The market for retail responsible investment products has gone through a tremendous change in the last few decades. These days, the phenomenon most often known in the marketplace, as well as in this chapter, as 'socially responsible investment' (SRI) mutual funds, has grown to become a recognized segment in many countries. While the retail market will always have difficulties matching the sheer size of institutional SRI investment, the fact is that retail investors increasingly seem to opt to put at least part of their investments in funds that incorporate some sort of social or environmental concern. For example, in Europe, EuroSIF (2010) reports that the retail SRI segment has grown in almost all European markets. Meanwhile, in the United States, there now are around 250 SRI investment funds to choose from, compared to only 55 in 1995 (USSIF, 2010). The fact that this growth is taking place despite being impeded by factors such as a limited set of SRI investment options and conventional theories of portfolio diversification that disfavour SRI is a testament to the strength of this trend.

In light of the aforementioned trend, socially responsible (SR) retail investors have become important actors in shaping the future of responsible investment. This chapter provides a starting point for understanding the phenomenon of retail socially responsible investment. It highlights socially responsible mutual fund investors by addressing such issues as their socio-demographic characteristics, the preferences that drive them, as well as the environment in which they make their decisions. It begins by looking at the macro-level trends that serve as underlying drivers of responsible retail investment.

Setting the scene: the context that drives development

In 1997, Barbara Krumsiek of Calvert Investments published an insightful article in the *Journal of Investing* that focused on the development of socially responsible mutual fund investment. In it, she argued that two societal trends drive the growth of retail SR investment: (1) a gradual increase in social and environmental concern and (2) a higher level of involvement and familiarity with investments and investment products. The fundamental argument was that when these two trends come together, and the socially concerned consumer starts making more investment decisions, the socially responsible investor emerges. As these two trends continue to develop, Krumsiek (1997) argued, it is only natural that people will increasingly look to SRI mutual funds as part of their portfolio.

Now, some 15 years later, it is easy to see that the article accurately described the ongoing trends. In fact, since then, these two trends have developed even further. Taking the examples of America and Sweden, industry sources report that considerably more households invest in mutual funds today as compared to the mid-1990s when the article was written. While 28 per cent of the American population and 50 per cent of the Swedish population invested in mutual funds in 1995, the figures in 2009 were 43 per cent and 74 per cent (Pettersson et al. 2009, ICI 2010), representing considerable growth in both markets. Furthermore, many countries have introduced privately managed pension plans where citizens are responsible for investing at least part of their own pension, making investments an even more natural part of the everyday life of many people.

Although no such hard numbers can be reported for social and environmental concerns, several factors indicate that these values have also continued to spread since the 1990s. One anecdotal example: the environment came into public view as Al Gore's movie *An Inconvenient Truth* managed to gain mainstream success and win two Academy awards in 2007. More broadly, ethics in the corporate world have been continuously debated, with the scandals of the early 2000s, such as the accounting fraud and collapse of Enron in 2001, and the financial scandals associated with the subprime crisis in 2007–9, prominent in news headlines. These scandals act as lead signals of public concern – and there is little reason to believe that people are now less concerned with environmental and social issues than they were in the past.

In all, it is safe to say that the trends that drive retail investors towards SRI funds, originally highlighted in Krumsiek's 1997 article, are still highly relevant. For the mutual fund industry, a likely prediction is that socially responsible investment will continue to be relevant for a socially conscious segment of the private investor population.

A difficult decision

However, while there seems to be a desire to invest in a responsible manner, this desire needs to be separated from retail investors' actual investment behaviour. To begin with, it is often very difficult for a non-expert investor to make educated investment decisions. Considering the decision-making environment retail investors face, this is not surprising. For example, when retail investors make decisions, they have to navigate through obstacles such as a large amount of information that is often highly complex, an uncertain future, and potentially large (negative) consequences of poor decisions (e.g. Ennew and McKechnie 1998, Lichtenstein et al. 1999, Kozup and Hogarth 2008, Kozup et al. 2008, Morrin et al. 2008). Given these issues, and the fact that retail investors often have inadequate levels of financial knowledge (e.g. Capon et al. 1996, Devlin 2003), it is not surprising that consumers often make poor financial decisions.

However, for investors who want to focus on responsible investment, making a good financial decision is only one part of an appropriate decision. On top of the already difficult task of evaluating the financial characteristics of various funds, they must also attempt to evaluate the socially responsible characteristics of the funds. A look at the state of the market for SRI funds indicates that this also involves numerous challenges for investors who want to make educated responsible investment decisions. For example, one of the more important factors that complicate the decision-making process for retail investors is that there is little agreement as to what SRI actually entails in the retail sector (Sandberg et al. 2009). Thus, while most products and services that claim to take some sort of social or environmental responsibility are objectively evaluated and labelled by independent organizations, responsible investors have to evaluate all the characteristics of the particular SRI fund themselves. Moreover, as funds that market themselves as 'socially responsible' differ widely in their choice of issues, as well as in the application of these issues, it is an absolute necessity for investors that want to make an educated decision to do so.

Take the example of screening – understood here as the tolerance for certain types of activities in publicly traded corporations. For a given issue – say the manufacturing of weapons – some funds might choose to avoid any company engaged in these activities; others might choose to avoid only those companies who receive less than 10 per cent of their revenues from this activity; still others might choose to engage corporations they own on particular issues related to the activity. All might market themselves to socially responsible investors as funds that discourage certain forms of arms manufacture.

Although it could be argued that this is positive for consumers, as they have more freedom to choose an investment alternative that matches their own values and preferences, the fact is that consumers have to sort through a large number of funds in order to choose the fund that is best suited to their preferences. Given the fact that there are numerous funds, and as a result of complex terminology it is not always clear how each fund actually practices social responsibility, there is a clear risk that consumers may choose a fund that is not in line with their preferences. Moreover, as there is limited transparency in the marketplace (Schwartz 2003, Michelson et al. 2004), it may actually be close to impossible to compare some of the characteristics relating to the social responsibility of different funds.

In all, socially responsible investors face a tough task. Not only must they deal with the challenges involved in making regular investment decisions. They must also attempt to evaluate the funds' socially responsible characteristics in a marketplace that is fragmented and lacks transparency.

Profiling the socially responsible retail investor

One of the more fundamental questions when focusing on retail investors is whether there are any general characteristics of the people who want their fund to incorporate concern for social and environmental issues. Although this question may be new in the investment research context, it has been addressed in detail in much research on socially responsible consumer behaviour (for a thorough review, see, for example, Diamantopoulos et al. 2003 or Papaoikonomou et al. 2011). While socio-demographics seem to have a limited influence on socially responsible consumer behaviour (Straughan and Roberts 1999, Jansson et al. 2010), the question is still of interest as there is some evidence that certain groups are more prone to behave in a socially responsible manner in the marketplace.

Research into the socially responsible (SR) mutual fund investor largely parallels findings on the SR consumer. For example, a higher level of education usually is connected to responsible consumer behaviour (e.g. Jansson et al. 2011); several studies point to the fact that this also is relevant in predicting responsible investment behaviour (Nilsson 2008, Säve-Söderbergh 2010,

Pérez-Gladish et al. 2012). Moreover, female consumers are more likely to incorporate social and environmental factors into their consumer behaviour (Diamantopoulos et al. 2003); female investors also seem to be more willing to invest in SRI (Schueth 2003, Säve-Söderbergh 2010, Pérez-Gladish et al. 2012). This notion, that women are more dedicated to social goals in the investment context, is further displayed in a study by Cheah et al. (2011). Here, the authors show that there are gender-based differences even among SR investors. For example, in their study, female SR investors were more likely to believe that the financial and socially responsible performance was equally important, while male SR investors put more emphasis on the financial return of the investment.

In all, the picture that emerges is fairly consistent with the previous research in the consumer behaviour field. Gender, education, and, to some extent, income, all seem to be related to responsible investment. However, based on previous consumer behaviour studies, it may be unwise to place much emphasis on socio-demographic variables as determinants of SR investment behaviour. While these variables may be somewhat linked to investing in SRI, motivational factors such as preferences, attitudes, and values are likely to be more important in predicting who will invest in SRI.

The preferences of the retail SR investor

While the preceding section dealt with the characteristics of the SR investor, it is perhaps even more important to understand why investors choose SRI and what they want out of their investment. On this topic, the fact is that for many responsible investors social responsibility is a preference for their investments that is as natural as it is when they make regular purchasing decisions. Although research does not give us a complete picture, it does give insight into the motivations, goals, and preferences of the SR investor. Some of these insights are presented below.

The underlying motivations: values, attitudes, and preferences

Starting first with the motivations for investing in SRI, at least two different perspectives have been used. First, there are a number of studies that apply some measure of personal attitudes or values and relate these to socially responsible investment behaviour (e.g. Getzner and Grabner-Kräuter 2004, Nilsson 2008, Iyer and Kashyap 2009, Kashyap and Iyer 2009, Nilsson et al. 2010, Jansson 2011, Jansson and Biel 2011). A second group of studies has used more exploratory and open-ended methods in surveying the socially responsible preferences of SR investors (e.g. Rosen et al. 1991, Beal and Goyen 1998, McLachlan and Gardner 2004, Statman 2008). While somewhat different in methodology and perspective, both of these streams of research have generated valuable insight into the investment behaviour of retail SR investors.

Together, these studies suggest that socially responsible investors are guided by fundamental attitudes and values in their choice of SRI-profiled investment services. For example, Jansson and Biel (2011), as well as Jansson (2011), show that investors who hold an altruistic self-transcendent value orientation, as opposed to investors who hold the more egoistic self-enhancement value orientation, are more likely to choose SRI. Moreover, Getzner and Grabner-Kräuter (2004) found that pro-environmental attitudes increase willingness to invest in SRI. This is supported by Nilsson (2008), who finds that pro-social attitudes are significantly

Table 36.1 Causes/issues that retail SR investors care about

Study	*Method*	*Causes/Issues Investors Care About*
Qualitative studies		*Some issues mentioned*
Mackenzie and Lewis (1999)	20 semi-structured interviews	Third world debt, employee pay and conditions, pornography, arms manufacturing, executive salary, harm to animals, etc.
Statman (2008)	Conversations with eight responsible investors	Investors did not share the same concerns. Some issues mentioned include environment, employee rights, sin industries, fairness and civil rights, etc.
Quantitative surveys		*Top three causes/issues*
McLachlan and Gardner (2004)	Survey to 55 conventional and 54 responsible investors	(1) Nuclear weapons, (2) arms exporting, (3) pornography
Pérez-Gladish et al. (2012)	Survey to 145 SR investors	(1) Water pollution, (2) climate change, (3) pollution
Valor et al. (2009)	Questionnaire to 400 investors	(1) Human rights, (2) labor conditions, (3) transparency, labor policy, cooperation with social and cultural community-based activities

related to investment in SRI-profiled mutual funds. Against the background of these studies, there seems to be some consensus regarding the influence of attitudes and values on the decision to invest in SRI.

However, one area where there is less agreement is which issues or causes socially responsible investors care about. This becomes evident when considering Table 36.1, which is a summary of issues raised in a selection of the literature on retail socially responsible investors. While the table highlights some common themes, such as the environment, military activity, sin industries, and employee and civil rights, pinpointing exactly what issues and causes investors care about has proven to be difficult. This, however, may not be surprising given the multitude of possible causes and issues addressed in SRI. Moreover, as each study is performed in a specific cultural context and uses differing measurement instruments, different results are expected, to at least some extent.

The question of impact

While SR-investors often differ in the causes they support, many SR investors share one characteristic: they want their investment to have some form of non-financial impact. This desire to use investments as a positive influence is natural as it exists at the very centre of socially responsible investment. For example, in a survey to private fund investors, impact issues were on the top of the list both as an incentive to invest (to be able to influence corporate behaviour) and as a disincentive to invest (to lack control over investment choices) (Haigh 2008). However, while many investors want to have an impact through their investment behaviour, a common perception among individual investors is that their role in solving various social or environmental issues is a limited one.

There are many factors that cause the perception of having limited influence. For example, SRI mutual funds may not be able to fully communicate their impact even if they are successful. In any case, the role of the individual investor in the massive financial system is small, leaving the investor potentially sceptical of the value of investing in SRI. It is therefore not surprising that current research has shown that the perception of efficacy is one of the most important determinants of the decisions to invest in SRI (Nilsson 2008, Iyer 2009, Jansson 2011,). While many people may be socially or environmentally concerned, it is often those investors who perceive they can have an impact through their investment behaviour that choose to invest in SRI mutual funds.

Conclusion: challenges for the industry

The objective of this chapter has been to provide a short and general insight into the nature of retail socially responsible investment. Several issues, including the difficulty of making educated and responsible investment decisions, the importance of social impact, and the heterogeneous preferences of investors, have been discussed. Against the background of this discussion, it is possible to identify several factors that could improve the situation for retail responsible investors. Therefore, this chapter ends with the presentation of two challenges targeted to providers and regulators of SRI mutual funds that focus on improving the situation for retail responsible investors. However, as these factors are important for the general development of the phenomenon of responsible retail investment, it could also be of interest of any actor who wants to see the development of responsible investment to consider them.

Challenge 1: provide tools to aid retail investors in their decision making

The first challenge revolves around the notion that it is often very difficult for retail investors to make educated SR investment decisions. This chapter has presented a number of issues that are at the heart of this difficult situation. For example, while the standard in most other industries that sell goods and services positioned as socially responsible is to develop some sort of third-party labelling scheme (eco, organic, fair trade etc.), this has not yet been done in the case of responsible investment. Instead, this lack of objective labelling schemes, combined with the fact that there is no standardization in the market, means that investors have to evaluate the socially responsible characteristics of each fund they consider. This is in stark contrast to most other industries where consumers can make good decisions just by considering the labels on the packaging. Given that the terminology surrounding the investment industry is often complex and that there are serious issues with transparency, properly evaluating the funds may be a close to impossible task for investors.

Taking these issues in account, it seems clear that the industry is in need of easy-to-use tools that investors can utilize to make educated decisions. While risk charts and Morningstar grading systems represent shortcuts for evaluating the financial aspects of the fund, no such shortcuts exist to evaluate the socially responsible characteristics of the fund. If there is a desire to make it easier for investors to make appropriate financial and socially responsible decisions, developing similar decision-making tools for how different funds work with social responsibility is a necessity.

Challenge 2: show social impact and results

The second challenge revolves around the notion that social impact is important to responsible investors. Many responsible investors are driven by the fact that they want to have a positive influence on certain social issues. Preferences regarding the best way to achieve social change and relevant issues to be addressed may differ between investors, but a common driver is the notion of using one's investments for good.

For investors, however, it is difficult to know whether their investment has had any impact. One of the fundamental reasons for this is that mutual funds often choose to communicate what they will do (i.e. their policies) rather than what they have actually done. Often, the investor is presented with a fund prospectus that describes the policies regarding controversial goods and engagement in general terms. This, however, gives little guidance on the impact that the fund will have (or has had in the past). While the financial history of the fund is tracked using all kinds of different statistics, the social or environmental performance seem to be less important. However, this history also holds crucial information that can be used by social investors in order to make an educated decision.

Against this background, there is a need to start communicating the impact and results that the mutual fund has had. While it may be unrealistic to have ESG indices that are similar to the financial indices, there are several things that can be done to improve the situation for investors. For example, if you have a 5 per cent cut-off point for including companies in a certain industry, what does that mean in practice? What companies have been excluded because of this? Another issue could be to address the manner in which the fund has engaged certain companies. What level of success have these had? A structured and understandable way of reporting this impact would help retail investors to make better decisions.

References

Beal, D. and Goyen, M. (1998) '"Putting your money where your mouth is" A profile of ethical investors', *Financial Services Review* 7(2): 129–143.

Capon, N., Fitzsimons, G. J. and Prince, R. A. (1996) 'An individual level analysis of the mutual fund investment decision', *Journal of Financial Services Research* 10(1): 59–82.

Cheah, E. T., Jamali, D., Johnson, J.E.V. and Sung, M. C. (2011) 'Drivers of corporate social responsibility attitudes: The demography of socially responsible investors', *British Journal of Management* 22(2): 305–323.

Devlin, J. F. (2003) 'Monitoring the success of policy initiatives to increase consumer understanding of financial services', *Journal of Financial Regulation & Compliance* 11(2): 151–163.

Diamantopoulos, A., Schlegelmilch, B. B., Sinkovics, R. R. and Bohlen, G. M. (2003) 'Can socio-demographics still play a role in profiling green consumers? A review of the evidence and an empirical investigation', *Journal of Business Research* 56(6): 465–480.

Ennew, C. T. and McKechnie, S. (1998) 'The financial services customer', in Gabbot, M. and Hogg, G. (eds) *Consumers and services*, New York: John Wiley & Sons, 185–207.

Eurosif (2010) *European SRI study*. Online. Available HTTP: <www.eurosif.org>.

Getzner, M. and Grabner-Kräuter, S. (2004) 'Consumer preferences and marketing strategies for "green shares": Specifics of the Austrian market', *International Journal of Bank Marketing* 22(4): 260–278.

Haigh, M. (2008) 'What counts in social managed investments: Evidence from an international survey', *Envisioning a New Accountability* 13: 35–62.
ICI (2010) *Investment Company Institute factbook,* Investment Company Institute. Online. Available HTTP: <www.ici.org>.
Iyer, E. S. and Kashyap, R. K. (2009) 'Noneconomic goals of investors', *Journal of Consumer Behaviour* 8(5): 225–237.
Jansson, J., Marell, A. and Nordlund, A. (2010) 'Green consumer behavior: Determinants of curtailment and eco-innovation adoption', *Journal of Consumer Marketing* 27(4): 358–370.
Jansson, J., Marell, A. and Nordlund, A. (2011) 'Exploring consumer adoption of a high involvement eco-innovation using value-belief-norm theory', *Journal of Consumer Behaviour* 10(1): 51–60.
Jansson, M. (2011) 'Moral and financial motives for socially responsible investment', in Psychological influences on adoption of socially responsible investment [Doctoral Dissertation], Department of Psychology, University of Gothenburg, Sweden.
Jansson, M. and Biel, A. (2011) 'Motives to engage in sustainable investment: A comparison between institutional and private investors', *Sustainable Development* 19(2): 135–142.
Kashyap, R. and Iyer, E. (2009) 'Not everybody wants to save the world', *Journal of Financial Services Marketing* 14(2): 118–134.
Kozup, J. and Hogarth, J. M. (2008) 'Financial literacy, public policy, and consumers' self-protection – More qustions, fewer answers', *Journal of Consumer Affairs* 42(2): 127–136.
Kozup, J., Howlett, E. and Pagano, M. (2008) 'The effects of summary information on consumer perceptions of mutual fund characteristics', *Journal of Consumer Affairs* 42(1): 37–59.
Krumsiek, B. J. (1997) 'The emergence of a new era in mutual fund investing: Socially responsible investing comes of age', *Journal of Investing* 6(4): 25–30.
Lichtenstein, D. R., Kaufmann, P. J. and Bhagat, S. (1999) 'Why consumers choose managed funds over index funds: Hypotheses from consumer behavior', *Journal of Consumer Affairs* 33(1): 187–205.
Mackenzie, C. and Lewis, A. (1999) 'Morals and markets: The case of ethical investing', *Business Ethics Quarterly* 9(3): 439–452.
McLachlan, J. and Gardner, J. (2004) 'A comparison of socially responsible and conventional investors', *Journal of Business Ethics* 52(1): 11–25.
Michelson, G., Wailes, N., van der Laan, S. and Frost, G. (2004) 'Ethical investment processes and outcomes', *Journal of Business Ethics* 52(1): 1–10.
Morrin, M., Broniarczyk, S., Inman, J. J. and Broussard, J. (2008) 'Saving for retirement: The effects of fund assortment size and investor knowledge on asset allocation strategies', *Journal of Consumer Affairs* 42(2): 206–222.
Nilsson, J. (2008) 'Investment with a conscience: Examining the impact of pro-social attitudes and perceived financial performance on socially responsible investment behavior', *Journal of Business Ethic,* 83(2): 307–325.
Nilsson, J., Nordvall, A. C. and Isberg, S. (2010) 'The information search process of socially responsible investors', *Journal of Financial Services Marketing* 15(1): 5–18.
Papaoikonomou, E., Ryan, G. and Valverde, M. (2011) 'Mapping ethical consumer behavior: Integrating the empirical research and identifying future directions', *Ethics & Behavior* 21(3): 197–221.
Pettersson, F., Helgesson, H. and Hård af Segerstad, F. (2009) *30 years of investment funds,* Swedish Investment Fund Association. Online. Available HTTP: <www.fondbolagen.se>.
Pérez-Gladish, B., Benson, K. and Faff, R. (2012) 'Profiling socially responsible investors: Australian evidence', *Australian Journal of Management.*
Rosen, B. N., Sandler, D. M. and Shani, D. (1991) 'Social issues and socially responsible investment behavior: A preliminary investigation', *The Journal of Consumer Affairs* 25(2): 221–234.
Sandberg, J., Juavle, C., Hedesström, T. M. and Hamilton, I. (2009) 'The heterogeneity of socially responsible investment', *Journal of Business Ethics* 87(4): 519–533.
Schueth, S. (2003) 'Socially responsible investing in the United States', *Journal of Business Ethics* 43(3): 189–194.
Schwartz, M. S. (2003) 'The "ethics" of ethical investing', *Journal of Business Ethics* 43(3): 195–213.
Statman, M. (2008) 'Quiet conversations: The expressive nature of socially responsible investors', *Journal of Financial Planning* 21(2): 40–46.
Straughan, R. D. and Roberts, J. A. (1999) 'Environmental segmentation alternatives: A look at green consumer behavior in the new millennium', *Journal of Consumer Marketing* 16(6): 558–575.

Säve-Söderbergh, J. (2010) 'Who lets ethics guide his economic decision-making? An empirical analysis of individual investments in ethical funds', *Economic Letters* 107(2): 270–272.

US SIF (2010) 'Report on socially responsible investing trends in the United States', Social Investment Forum Foundation. Online. Available HTTP: <www.ussif.org>.

Valor, C., de la Cuesta, M. and Fernandez, B. (2009) 'Understanding demand for retail socially responsible investments: A survey of individual investors and financial consultants', *Corporate Social Responsibility and Environmental Management* 16(1): 1–14.

37

Measuring the impact of engagement

Evidence from Canadian institutional investors

Tessa Hebb, Heather Hachigian and Rupert Allen

Introduction

Increasingly when institutional investors embrace responsible investing (RI), they declare that corporate engagement is their preferred strategy for raising environmental, social and governance (ESG) standards in the companies in which they invest (Principles for Responsible Investment, 2012). Such engagement is usually conducted privately, often through informal dialogue. The effectiveness of engagement, both in terms of enhancing shareholder value and improving corporate ESG standards, is often cited as a reason to maintain ownership of a company rather than to divest when ESG standards are below acceptable levels. However, even when companies respond to investor demands, they often are reluctant to acknowledge the role shareholders may have had in changing company policies. As a result, it remains difficult for those on the outside to judge the effectiveness of corporate engagement.

Our research suggests that corporate engagement is an effective responsible investing tool. This chapter draws on two case studies of engagements and sponsoring institutions, to provide both shareholder and company perspectives on engagement.[1] We ask what makes these stakeholders salient to the company. We examine the impact of power, urgency and legitimacy on stakeholder salience (Mitchell et al., 1997) and build on the sub-attributes of shareholder saliency (Gifford, 2010). We use third-party data to evaluate the success of these engagements.

Understanding corporate engagement

Corporate engagement utilizes the rights of shareholders to influence company management in order to protect or raise shareholder value. Increasingly, ESG factors are seen to be instrumental in reducing risk and generating positive returns for shareholders. In the past, the wide disbursement of shareholders, each with small individual holdings, meant that they lacked the ability to act as effective monitors of corporate management. However, with increased holdings by large institutional investors willing to act in coalition, we are seeing a shift toward active ownership of today's corporations.

Shareholders can use two fundamental mechanisms when dissatisfied with company performance: voice and exit (Hirschman, 1970). Voice can take many forms: private dialogue, proxy voting, public shaming, shareholder proposals and active monitoring. Exit, in contrast, has one simple option: divestiture. However, once divested, the investor no longer has the means to influence company behaviour. As a result the investor is no longer salient.

Full divestiture is a way of ridding shareholders of poor performing stocks (Alexandrou and Sudarsanam, 2001). Some studies have noted that incentives to divest may not be based solely on performance, but rather private and political views that may influence management strategies (Jensen and Murphy, 1990; Wright and Ferris, 1997). In theory, divestment is seen as a way to have a negative impact on firms that can result in raising the cost of capital for the firm. In reality, divestment does not often have an impact on the cost of capital but rather corporate reputation, which can effect stock prices and the ability to attract top talent.

Activist shareholders who choose to exercise voice in terms of influencing the direction of corporate strategy use a variety of methods to signify their displeasure with corporate policies and governance issues (Hebb, 2008). These include monitoring, dialogue, focus lists, shareholder resolutions and even taking seats on boards. Several studies point to the positive impact of shareholder activism by large institutional investors, which is known as the 'CalPERS effect' (Anson et al., 2003; Barber, 2006; Smith, 1996) and the 'Hermes effect' (Becht et al., 2008). However, for other academics, such monitoring remains a contested terrain. Many studies suggest that shareholder activism has limited positive effect on stock price or company strategy (Gillan and Starks, 2007; Karpoff et al., 1996; Romano, 2001).

Shareholders have a particular problem when it comes to interacting with firms in which they have an ownership stake; that is, ensuring that the firms, or rather firm-level managers, are pursuing and making decisions that are in the best interests of the shareholders, not simply representing their own opportunistic ends and needs. This is known as the 'principal/agent problem', and it arises when there is a separation of ownership and control (Jensen and Meckling, 1976). The separation occurs when the principals, the shareholders, delegate their decision-making responsibilities to managers, who then act in their own self-interest. As a result, managers' interests may diverge from those of the shareholders (Berle and Means, 1932; Galbraith, 1976; Koford and Penno, 1992), particularly when managers are incentivized to deliver short-term outcomes and shareholders are interested in longer-term value.

Theory suggests that principals delegate their decision-making authority to agents because agents have a greater knowledge and awareness of day-to-day company operations. As a result, managers are in a superior position to facilitate profit-maximizing decisions and choices, which coincides with the primary goal of shareholders (Friedman, 1970). This means that actions taken by the agents have the potential to create significant, and possibly beneficial, impacts not only for themselves, but also for the principals. However, as noted above, there are certain risks and conflicts of interest associated with this type of relationship (Jensen and Meckling, 1976; Koford and Penno, 1992; Luft, 1997).

Monitoring is one of the control mechanisms that owners are able to exert on firms as a method of realigning their interests and values with those of the managers and ensuring that their values are taken into consideration. However, monitoring is not something that can realistically be undertaken by a solitary investor because of the prohibitive costs and the propensity of the free-rider problem, which undermines the incentives of any one firm to initiate a monitoring program on its own (Coffee, 1991, 1997).

The active nature of voice-centred shareholder engagement can make it excessively expensive in terms of potential returns (Bainbridge, 1995). As such, it is often beyond the means of most mainstream small-scale investors who can rationalize leaving engagement to others rather than engaging themselves (O'Barr and Connely, 1992; Hendry, 2004). Generally, only large institutional investors are able to absorb the hefty costs of continuous monitoring and overcome the free-rider problem of small investors receiving the same benefit without the associated costs (Coffee, 1991; Gantchev, 2011).

However, the willingness of institutional investors to act in coalition is making it easier for smaller investors to pursue meaningful engagements (Hawley and Williams, 1997, 2000; Monks, 2000). While institutional investors acting alone may have some influence with company managers, it is when they act in coalition that their numbers shift the power dynamic between owners and managers (Clark and Hebb, 2004, Hebb, 2008). Such investor coalitions include the UN-backed Principles for Responsible Investment (PRI), with signatories representing $45 trillion of assets under management. The PRI coordinates activities through a clearinghouse for engagements that enables greater influence to be exerted on corporate managers. Similarly, the Carbon Disclosure Project, with 767 institutional members managing $92 trillion of assets, is able to bring considerable influence to bear when requesting greater transparency and progress on climate change issues from today's companies.

Recent studies of stakeholder theory reinforce the claim that shareholders play an increasingly important role in determining corporate strategy (Wood and Jones 1995; Hillman and Keim 2001; Moneva et al., 2007). But how do firms give priority to the rising number of stakeholder claims? How do they choose who to listen to? Not all stakeholders are treated equally. Some appear to have stronger voices than others (Henriques and Sadorsky, 1999). In the past, the importance of stakeholder claims was thought to rest solely on the shoulders of whether the particular claim or stakeholder was deemed to be legitimate or not (Clarkson, 1995). Mitchell et al. (1997) suggest that there are three key attributes that affect shareholder salience: power, urgency and legitimacy. Gifford (2010) builds on the descriptive framework established by Mitchell and further subdivides the categories into sub-attributes assigned to shareholder engagement practices.

Gifford (2010) suggests that the sub-attribute with greatest saliency is shared value between the manager and the stakeholder: "Within the engagement practitioner community, there is a strong preference for legitimacy-based engagement in the first instance, with an appropriate degree of intensity, and power being applied only after legitimacy-based options have been exhausted" (97). This would suggest a temporal element with factors drawn upon in a sequential pattern rather than all at once during shareholder engagement of ESG factors (Gifford, 2010). But how does the influence of shareholders work in practice? Do these attributes and sub-attributes hold explanatory power as to the saliency of shareholders? How does the company adjudicate between multiple competing claims? We test these assumptions using two case studies of shareholder engagement in Canada.

Corporate engagement in Canada

We examine two Canadian engagements: the first is the Shareholder Association for Research and Education (SHARE) and its corporate governance engagement with the Canadian financial sector on the advisory vote for executive compensation, commonly referred to as 'Say on Pay'. The second is Northwest & Ethical Investment (NEI) Funds' engagement with Barrick Gold on human rights issues. We use these case studies in order to gain a deeper understanding on the impact of engagement. Each of the case studies is separate and distinct; that is, each has different organizational structures, policy frameworks and mandates. As a result, each case study's engagement process should be viewed as a discreet set of practices.

The first case study we explore is the Shareholder Association for Research and Education (SHARE), a social enterprise established in 2000 with a mandate to coordinate and implement responsible investment practices in Canada. SHARE provides services mostly to smaller funds. SHARE's Say on Pay campaign promoted the establishment of an advisory vote on executive compensation. Meritas Mutual Funds, which has combined assets under management (with Qtrade Fund Management) of $350 million, commissioned SHARE to act on its behalf in the Say on Pay campaign. This campaign began with the banking sector in Canada and grew to include the energy and oil and gas sectors, among others.

The second case study draws on the engagement between NEI Funds and Barrick Gold. NEI Investments, a Canadian mutual fund company that has been active in socially responsible investing since the 1980s, established its Shareholder Action Program in 2000.[2] NEI Funds has $5 billion in assets under management (as of November 2014). We focus on NEI's engagement with Barrick Gold, a multi-national mining company headquartered in Canada that operates mines around the world. Areas of engagement with this company included human rights, environmental justice, biodiversity, climate change and HIV/AIDS.

SHARE's advisory vote on executive compensation

It is widely acknowledged that skewed executive compensation practices encouraged excessive risk taking by large financial institutions, contributing significantly to the 2008 global financial crisis. While the public has become preoccupied with CEO compensation levels, fuelled by the sensational statistics on the growing gap between the earnings of executives and the average employee,[3] shareholders are more concerned with misalignment between pay and performance. Misalignment leads to perverse incentives (Bebcuk and Fried, 2004), poor firm performance and ultimately to inefficiency in financial markets (Davis, 2007). In light of these concerns, the advisory vote on executive compensation, particularly with regard to financial institutions, known as Say on Pay (SoP) is gaining increasing recognition for providing shareholders with a critical monitoring and engagement tool (see Bebchuck et al., 2010, on the need to align long-term executive compensation incentives to reduce risky behaviour in the financial sector).

The SoP mechanism is praised by some for lowering the cost of coordinating shareholder monitoring of the firm, while also providing shareholders with a voice to pressure directors to better align executive pay with performance (Davis, 2007; Ertimur et al., 2008; Cotter et al., 2012). Some early empirical work investigating the impact of the vote on firm value has found that it has a positive impact,[4] but there are significant difficulties with separating the influence of the vote from other corporate governance reforms (Trottier, 2011; Cunat et al., 2012).

However, not everyone agrees that giving shareholders more power over management is the most efficient way to align pay with performance. SoP is viewed by some as a 'blunt instrument' that interferes with responsibilities of the board of directors, undermines the compensation committee, privileges some shareholders over others and fails to allow for sufficient communication between boards and shareholders (Slipp and Knieriem, 2009; Bainbridge, 2009). SoP has also met opposition from those who see the growth of executive compensation as commensurate with productivity, and therefore only a symptom of growing inequality rather than the cause. For example, Kaplan (2007) argues "the U.S. economy and, particularly, the U.S. corporate sector has performed extremely well in the last 15 years, the period in which corporate governance and CEO pay have been criticized" (p. 6). As a result, SoP can impose unnecessary costs on firms by attempting to fix a problem that does not require fixing (Mirvis et al., 2007). Some even suggest that SoP could result in negative implications for alignment between pay and performance, as the diffusion of responsibility for executive compensation would also mean the diffusion of scrutiny facing directors, thereby lowering their incentive to getting alignment right (Myers, 2011).

Recent empirical evidence drawn from event studies suggest such negative impacts of the SoP vote are only true of firms that already align their pay with performance (Cai and Walking, 2011; Ferri and Maber, 2012). For firms with weak pay for performance links and weak governance overall, these studies suggest that adopting an advisory vote on compensation packages enhances firm value. Allair (2010) and Gox et al. (2009) arrive at similar conclusions, with Allair suggesting that "the adoption of a SoP procedure should be reserved for companies where shareholders have reasons to be dissatisfied with their executive compensation programs" (p. 29).

Yet many jurisdictions, including the United Kingdom, the United States, Australia, the Netherlands, Norway, Spain, France and Sweden, have legislated binding or non-binding votes for all public companies. Canada remains outside this club, as it has not introduced legislation requiring managers to submit their executive compensation plans to a vote. In part, this can be explained by the fact that many larger companies in Canada often meet with investors before publishing proxy circulars (a practice not common in other jurisdictions), thereby providing greater opportunity for resolving issues with shareholders without the need for a vote. Further, executive compensation has not been as high profile an issue in Canada as in the United States. That said, some expect Canada's compensation levels to converge with U.S. levels, because many Canadian corporate CEOs are viable candidates in U.S. markets (Howell, 2007).

Despite the lack of regulatory impetus for the advisory vote on executive compensation, 97 Canadian issuers – that is, 38 per cent of companies listed on the Standard and Poor's Toronto Stock Exchange (S&P/TSX) Composite Index have adopted the vote as of 2012. SHARE has been at the forefront of engagement efforts with Canadian issuers since launching its executive compensation campaign in 2007. While not an investor in its own right, SHARE offers proxy voting and advisory services to individual and small investors in Canada, leveraging economies of scale through pooling investor resources. SHARE's SoP engagement campaign involves a combination of the submission of shareholder proposals, written correspondence and private dialogue with issuers.

Interviews were conducted with representatives at SHARE and with firms that have been engaged by SHARE to better understand the degree of influence that investors and their representatives bring to bear on companies in their portfolios. (See Appendix 37.1 for a complete list of those interviewed for these case studies.) Questions addressed factors that motivate investors to engage firms on ESG issues and those that motivate corporations to respond. The interviews also explored the factors that contribute to a successful engagement, with reference to Gifford's shareholder salience framework. In addition, the research reviewed shareholder proposals filed by SHARE and correspondence between SHARE and the issuers they engaged during the period of 2007–10. Finally, consideration of firm-specific factors offered additional insight into the motivation for engagement and the characteristics that lead to a successful outcome.

Interviews began by asking SHARE staff to describe what motivates their engagement on ESG issues. A SHARE staff member acknowledged that engagement is an integral part of SHARE's responsibility as a long-term investor: "Using the rights associated with share ownership, investors can influence companies to improve their management of environmental, social and governance risks and opportunities, helping to build accountability and long-term shareholder value".

A common restraint that investors face is the limited resources available for engagement, thereby requiring the development of focus areas. As a result, concern for the likelihood of success plays a role in determining the issues on which investors engage. According to a SHARE, "Some issues are harder to engage with than others. Corporate governance is easier because there are mechanisms and support to make this work". From the corporate perspective, respondents recognized engagement as part of their duty as a public corporation.

With respect to the corporations interviewed in this study, respondents attributed engagement as a factor of their visibility in the market. In general, corporate representatives interviewed suggested that the more visible a corporation is, the more likely it is to be a target for engagement. Also, from the investor's point of view, corporate respondents suggested that it is strategic to engage a more 'visible' company first, since this can help build momentum for other corporations to follow a leading company.[5]

A strong theme that emerged in response to questions regarding investors' approach to engagement is the importance of establishing legitimacy with the corporation. Legitimacy is not strictly dependent on relative size and reputation of the engager, but on the approach that the investor takes in the engagement. For example, SHARE suggests that "media attention gave SoP the profile it needed for support, but it is always and ultimately an issue of legitimacy. The size of stake is not as critical".

Corporate representatives we interviewed agreed that legitimacy is an important factor to successful engagement. Both respondents considered SHARE to be a legitimate representative of investors. However, their emphasis on this attribute of legitimacy differed from SHARE's. Legitimacy may be seen as a necessary condition, but corporate respondents also highlighted the importance of persistence (a sub-attribute of urgency). In one corporation's experience, "SHARE approached us three times before we came around to agreeing we would implement a vote" (Sun Life Financial). Another agrees, suggesting that "as long as the engager is viable and is articulate and reasonable in their requests, we are open to engagement" (Royal Bank of Canada). SHARE did recognize the value of persistence: "We attribute our success to hiring knowledgeable staff, good research, a professional approach and persistence".

The importance of persistence is also reflected in the proposal filings. In 2008, the first round of resolution filings by SHARE on SoP received average support of 40.5 per cent. In 2009, average support increased by 12 percentage points, to 52 per cent, and 14 resolutions out of 35 were withdrawn with agreement of the company to comply, compared to previous years, such as in 2008, when only 1 out of 42 was withdrawn. In 2010, 12 of 23 proposals filed on SoP were withdrawn because the corporation they were filed against had agreed to adopt the vote before the proxy voting season. This also reflects the importance of private dialogue as an effective engagement tool.

Corporate representatives did not see the time-sensitivity factor of urgency in Gifford's framework as a salient factor: "We did not feel a great deal of urgency; it was a growing trend and we were moving in that direction" (Sun Life Financial). "We are not looking to be the first to adopt a new trend, but we always keep up with trends; we like to be somewhere in the middle" (Sun Life Financial).

With respect to power, both SHARE and the corporate respondents agreed that it is not in the best interest of investors to move an engagement into the public light to generate momentum from negative public pressure, as this also risks generating negative pressure on share value. One corporate representative responded, "we believe that if investors perceive you are willing to engage on an issue and talk about it, then they will be respectful and engage in a constructive manner" (Sun Life Financial). The analysis of shareholder proposals and the correspondence between SHARE and issuers confirms that power was not used in the engagement campaign. There was no evidence of aggressive language, appeals to reputation or threats in any of the correspondence. The analysis also finds that the appeal to long-term share value has been present in almost all proposals filed since 2005, which confirms the importance of legitimacy that is highlighted in the interviews.

Impact of SHARE's engagement

SHARE's definition of success requires:

> a concrete balance of depth of dialogue with the companies and the breadth of the engagers willing to address the issue . . . Success is about attention to an issue where there was no attention before and bringing about change where issuer willingness and/or shareholder consensus is found.

SHARE's SoP campaign did raise awareness of the executive compensation issue in Canada. It was one of several pressure points that changed this corporate governance practice. While it is possible that adopting SoP causes companies to increase their corporate governance performance, it is also possible that adopters are more likely to have effective corporate governance frameworks in place prior to adoption and it is the corporations that do not have good practices that fail to adopt the vote (Allair, 2010).

To consider the presence and direction of causality, we examined corporate governance data from Sustainalytics from 2004 to 2007. This data range precedes SHARE's SoP engagement campaign. On average, we found the scores for corporations that adopted SoP in 2009 and 2010 to be higher (7.2) than those for non-adopters (6.5). Similar results are found using the CCBE Board Confidence Index. Using numerical weightings as a proxy for the letter grades given in the index, the average total corporate governance rating for adopters is 7.65 (out of 10), compared with the average rating for non-adopters, which was 6.84 in 2009. This finding is consistent with a study conducted by the CCBE in 2012, which finds, on average, that the 66 firms that had adopted the vote by 2011 had previously adopted more disclosure components rated in their index than non-adopters, suggesting that firms with better corporate governance are more likely to adopt SoP.

While size and governance performance may influence the likelihood of adopting the vote, interviews suggest that SHARE's engagement campaign was important. SHARE suggests that the campaign has brought more awareness to the issue of excessive executive compensation in Canada and that "implementation of the proposal is the ultimate measurement of success". With respect to the advisory vote, according to SHARE, "it is clear that say on pay would be nowhere in Canada without the engagement process and attention it has garnered to the issue". Although corporate representatives did not exclusively attribute the decision to adopt the advisory vote to the engagement efforts of investors, they did acknowledge that SHARE played a significant role in bringing attention to the issue: "SHARE and Meritas did a good job of keeping attention and awareness on the issue" (Sun Life Financial).

Increasingly, shareholders in Canada are beginning to voice their concerns through this new mechanism. For the first time since the vote was held by Canadian issuers (2009), a company failed to receive majority support for its compensation plan (QLT Media), and as of 2012 there has been an increase in the number of votes that have support levels falling below 70 per cent (SHARE 2012).

The SoP vote has garnered significant attention in Canada, despite the lack of regulatory impetus. The Canadian Coalition for Good Governance, once opposed to the vote, has now become one of its strongest advocates. While SHARE's engagement was not the only reason cited by issuers for adopting the vote, interviews suggest that SHARE played an important role in bringing attention to the issue. This attention was effective because of the knowledge and approach to dialogue that SHARE used, rather than appeals to power.

NEI's engagement with Barrick Gold

The second case study on the impact of engagement focuses on human rights issues at Barrick Gold. NEI Investments engaged Barrick on a number of different areas in mines around the world. NEI's focus in recent years has been on human and indigenous rights and community engagement. NEI's work in this area has focused on mines in Latin America (Chile), North America (Nevada, United States) and Southeast Asia (Papua New Guinea). This case study highlights these projects, and the human rights and community engagement issues between 2005 and 2010.

NEI's 2005 shareholder report stated that NEI was engaging with Barrick Gold on issues relating to human rights and management guidelines. Barrick responded to these engagements by informing NEI that it would be adopting the Global Compact as its new framework for human rights management. NEI was also prepared to engage with Barrick while it divested of another mining company, Placer Dome, in 2005, because of its use of riverine tailings disposal (RTD) in the Porgera Mine in Papua New Guinea. It should be noted that, subsequently, Placer Dome was acquired by Barrick Gold in 2006. Rather than divest of Barrick, as it had done with Placer Dome, NEI decided to increase its engagement with Barrick in an effort to get Barrick to raise its ESG standards.

NEI targeted Barrick in 2006 on the issues of public health and community engagement. NEI filed a shareholder proposal, which asked Barrick to commission a third party to evaluate the level of community involvement and support on the Pascua Lama project in Chile. After a further agreement by Barrick to develop and publicly release its community engagement guidelines, NEI withdrew the shareholder proposal.

In 2007, NEI focused on the Cortez Hills, Nevada, operations of Barrick Gold. The Cortez Hills dialogue included community engagement and human rights. By 2009, NEI filed a shareholder resolution with Barrick regarding its community engagement strategies and practices, which included earlier dialogues on the Pascua Lama, Porgera and Cortez Hills mines. The proposal was a result of a perceived lack of progress through dialogue.

NEI continued to use a combination of dialogue and shareholder proposals in its engagement with Barrick Gold. The following year NEI put forth a shareholder proposal requesting that Barrick nominate a new director to its board who had significant experience in corporate social responsibility, human rights or environmental issues. However, the resolution was not submitted for a vote, as Barrick responded favourably to the idea and agreed to start looking for a possible nominee. It should be noted that NEI was not the only stakeholder petitioning Barrick Gold for greater corporate responsibility and accountability during this period of time or relating to these issues.

The majority of the interviewees (see Appendix 37.1) felt that constructive dialogue and willingness for meetings were integral elements to shareholder engagement. While there was complete agreement that engagements between companies and shareholders can result in positive impacts, there was significant dissension in terms of the specifics.

The Barrick representative felt that engagements could be positive when they are open and constructive and when the shareholder has knowledge of and implicitly understands the issues. The representative also considered it important that investors acknowledge company restraints and that the proposals be realistic in terms of both scope and time. Barrick also noted that engagements are more suited towards long-run issues. However, only a minority of the other investor interviewees held this view.

Three respondents, including NEI, noted that engagements that promoted and recognized good practices and governance were more likely to yield positive results, as they were seen as more mainstream and less adversarial. Some of the financial professionals mentioned that reputational risk and social license to operate are important for extractive companies, because they have the potential to derail production chains and interrupt value growth and, ultimately, destroy value if not addressed. As such, issues around these areas are likely to gain acknowledgment and increase a company's willingness to start a dialogue.

Barrick suggested that its engagement with NEI over these past years has been constructive and tracked progress over time. Barrick mentioned that one of the main reasons that it continues to deal with NEI, over other stakeholders, is the credibility that NEI brings to the table. Barrick indicated that NEI's knowledge of the company and its situation played a key part in the credibility of its engagement.

Interviewees, including NEI and Barrick, point to the need for credibility in the engagement, particularly a high degree of knowledge about the issues and situation of the company. Both NEI and Barrick suggest that a high degree of knowledge (sound and solid research and a deep understanding of the issues) is the most important attribute in developing credibility with the company in the engagement. When the company faces numerous and sometimes conflicting demands from stakeholders, credibility is a key driver in establishing the engagement. Neither the attributes of power nor urgency as drivers of engagement saliency were raised with the same degree of frequency as legitimacy (credibility) with key informants. While the company did acknowledge that the size of shareholdings is used as one measure of saliency, size did not trump credibility as the primary engagement driver. Interestingly, all interviewees pointed to raised ESG standards within the company, with particular reference to issues of human rights and Human Rights Impact Assessments (HRIAs), as a result of stakeholder engagement.

Impact of engagement

When asked about success, NEI defined it in three ways: getting the issue on the agenda, affecting corporate policy and affecting the situation on the ground. NEI felt it had achieved a certain amount of success in its dealings with Barrick, although noting that there was still room for improvement and continued engagement. However, measuring success is a difficult task, especially on an annual basis. In many cases it may take a few years before changes are seen in a firm's behaviour. Additionally, there is difficulty when there is a disconnect between a corporations' policy and its performance. A third problem identified is determining whether a change in behaviour is a direct result of engagement actions, as "corporations are loath to admit that our engagement had an impact on them" (NEI).

NEI measures its success by setting objectives for engagement and tracking against these benchmarks. The results of its engagement are measured against key progress indicators that are reported annually. While the results of the Barrick engagement have been mixed, NEI is able to point to positive changes in many company policies through these years. As with the SoP case study, we tested these findings against those of an independent third-party ESG rating agency, Sustainalytics.

The Sustainalytics data demonstrates that between 2004 and 2007 Barrick generally showed an incremental improvement in overall ESG performance, with a progression between 2004 and 2006 and a slight dip in 2007. Out of an overall score of 10, Barrick hovered slightly below 5 in 2004 and 2005, whereas it was slightly above 5 between 2006 and 2007. This places Barrick as a mid-level ESG performer among its peers in the mining sector.

Barrick displayed its strongest ESG performance in the field of governance. The governance heading notably encompasses executive compensation, board accountability, shareholder rights and disclosure. Barrick performed strongly under the management systems and code of business conduct categories. However, among the indicators, Barrick's lowest performance was in the field of human rights, where it never reached a score of 5.

In the community and society indicator, Barrick made important improvements between 2005 and 2006 in the field of aboriginal relations and the mechanisms of engagement and consultation. This could be seen as correlating with the NEI engagement with Barrick on the publication of community engagement guidelines, an issue to which Barrick agreed to in 2006. Nevertheless, between 2006 and 2007 scores concerning the impacts of mining activities on local and aboriginal communities took a severe plunge, thus leaving Barrick very close to its 2005 ranking on community and society.

It must be noted that reliable longitudinal data comparison from 2004 to 2011 is not possible using the Sustainalytics data because the weight matrices and specific scoring criteria were redesigned, the tracking of new indicators was undertaken and the broad ESG categories were reduced from six to three when the firms Jantzi and Sustainalytics merged.

In general, the Sustainalytics scores on ESG demonstrate that Barrick Gold's strength lies in the field of corporate governance and its weakness has mainly been on the fronts of community and society, along with environment, as it relates to ESG factors. It is possible to relate some of NEI's engagements with changes in scores, but it would not be adequate to claim causality, since the engagement by NEI cannot be isolated among the different independent variables that could have affected Barrick's scores. These results suggest that in broad social areas of concern such as human rights, while investor engagement appears to raise attention with company managers, we cannot attribute direct causation or even correlation as a result of these engagements. Seeking positive changes through the adoption of concrete codes and norms by the company is often more successful, whether these codes are governance related, environmental or social. Once the code is adopted by the company, a range of stakeholders (including NGOs, governments, consumers and investors) are able to exert influence and hold the company to account.

Testing the saliency of shareholder engagement

The mantra of today's investors is one of active ownership. Shareholders are encouraged to act as corporate monitors, applying a level of oversight to their actions and decision making. However, it is fair to say that, to date, shareholder rights have been restricted to a narrow band of influence, focusing primarily on corporate governance issues. In the past, establishing ESG corporate practices was seen as the domain of managers. Such practices were deemed 'ordinary business', and therefore not subject to shareholder intervention. As a result, company managers were unwilling to acquiesce their day-to-day management authority on these issues to shareholders. They resisted external interference in setting corporate standards.

However, increasingly institutional investors are directly engaging companies in their investment portfolios in an effort to raise their ESG standards. They indicate that corporate engagement is their preferred method of responsible investing and active ownership. They see positive corporate engagement as a more effective method of influencing and raising corporate environmental, social and governance standards then using negative screens or divestment.

The question we ask in this chapter is whether such engagement does indeed have a measurable impact on companies' ESG standards. If so, to what extent can we attribute the saliency of these particular stakeholders? It has been suggested that power, legitimacy and urgency are the key attributes of stakeholder saliency (Mitchell et al., 1997; Gifford, 2009). Our findings suggest that the power of the shareholder appears to be the least important of the three attributes that contribute to shareholder saliency. In most cases, power strategies of divestment and leveraging media for negative campaigns have not been used. In fact, it was suggested that such campaigns are far less successful in achieving meaningful change with companies, as they result in entrenched positions and have a negative impact on the reputation of the engager. Further, this can have a negative impact on share value; therefore, it is not in the interest of the investor to appeal to power through such negative campaigns. It appears that legitimacy and urgency in corporate engagement are of greater significance in achieving actual change within companies than power.

While shareholders have legitimacy with the firms they hold in their portfolio, it could be argued that when it comes to raising ESG standards legal status is a necessary but not sufficient condition. Our case studies suggest that for shareholder influence on corporate ESG standards other sub-attributes of legitimacy and urgency are required. Here we draw on the work of Gifford (2010). Both SHARE and NEI undertake extensive research on the issues. They use research to establish a strong case for the ESG issue on which they engage.

Strategies to develop legitimacy on issues include white papers, reports, roundtables and presentations to company managers on the issue. SHARE and NEI look for allies, work in coalitions, and point to legislative and regulatory agendas as part of their engagement with companies. Both cases highlighted the critical importance of having a solid case to put before management, establishing a reputation, adding value in the discussion and coming with solution-oriented approaches. Both SHARE and NEI credit their success to the ability to engage management in a positive and constructive manner.

Legitimacy is further enhanced through attributes of knowledge, reputation and individual values. The status of the engager is also important. Development of the business case for the issue under engagement is critical to success in the engagement, as is presenting the societal case and the legal and regulatory framework. SHARE and NEI indicated that without building a substantive case on which to engage they doubted that they would have been successful.

Urgency is generated in the engagements but is not the essential driver. SHARE and NEI both benchmark their engagement outcomes. Several engagements took place over a number of years with successful conclusions. Neither of the cases under investigation pointed to the attribute of urgency as a driver of successful engagements, nor was the lack of urgency discussed as the cause of unsuccessful engagements. In most cases the ability to bring forward a strong business case to back the ESG concern, combined with a reputation for positive, solution-oriented outcomes, was given as the key driver in successful engagements. However, the companies interviewed suggested that persistence was a driver of success, an attribute not raised by the investors as a consideration.

As suggested by Gifford (2010), each case stressed that the moderating influence of individual values of company management played a role in ensuring successful results from the engagement. In many cases, engagers seek out company managers with shared values and a deep understanding of the issue under discussion.

We acknowledge the limitations of this research when making generalized statements about the impact of corporate engagement and the attributes of successful engagement based on case studies. While we can draw insight from these cases, it does not provide correlated evidence on which to assess these impacts. However, this research is among the first to examine the issues of corporate engagement and its use of private dialogue, as well as the attribution problems associated with it (for an examination of the financial impact of investor engagement, see Dimson et al., 2014).

To date, the evidence points to shareholder engagement as a driver in raising ESG standards within firms. Linking those raised standards with long-term value creation, risk reduction and companies' social license to operate is critical when aligning the interests of shareholders with those of management. Our research points to the ability of shareholder engagement to raise these standards and suggests that constructive corporate dialogue based on a deep knowledge and understanding of the company and its situation is critical to the success of these engagements.

While power and urgency are key attributes in shareholder saliency, our findings suggest that legitimacy (credibility) remains the dominant force in bringing about successful engagement.

Notes

1 This chapter is drawn from research work conducted at the Carleton Centre for Community Innovation from 2010 through 2012. We would like to acknowledge two previous publications from which excerpts have been taken in this chapter: Hebb, T., Hachigian, H. and Allen, R. (2012) 'Impact of corporate engagement in Canada', in Hebb T. (ed.), *The next generation of responsible investing*, Springer Publishing, Netherlands; and Allen, R., Letourneau, H. and Hebb, T. (2012) 'Shareholder engagement in the extractive sector', *Journal of Sustainable Finance and Investing* 1(4).
2 In 2007, Ethical Funds partnered with Northwest Funds, creating Northwest & Ethical Investments L.P. (NEI).
3 In 1991, the average CEO of a large corporation in the United States earned approximately 140 times the pay of an average worker, and by 2003 this ratio had increased to 500 to 1 (Bebchuk and Grinstein, 2005). Also see Mishel and Sabadish (2012): "From 1978 to 2011, CEO compensation increased more than 725 per cent, a rise substantially greater than stock market growth and the painfully slow 5.7 per cent growth in worker compensation over the same period".
4 Cunat et al. (2012) find firm value reacts positively to SoP vote in the United States (7.9–10.5 per cent).
5 Three years into the campaign, SHARE had filed only one proposal with a firm that had a market cap under $1 billion (Gennum Corporation). By 2011, the average market cap of adopters ($20.5 billion) far exceeded the average of non-adopters ($6.8 billion) (CCBE, 2012). This trend has continued through to 2012: 80 per cent of Canada's 60 biggest publicly traded companies (the TSX 60) have adopted SoP, compared with only 7 per cent of small cap issuers (Davies et al., 2012, p. 25). Online, available HTTP: <http://www.dwpv.com/~/media/Files/PDF/Governance-Insights-2012-v1.ashx>.

References

Alexandrou, G. and Sudarsanam, S. (2001) *Shareholder wealth experience of buyers in corporate divestitures: Impact of business strategy, growth opportunities and bargaining power.* Paper presented at the European Financial Management Annual Meeting, Lugano, Switzerland, June 27–30.

Allair, Y. (2010) *Giving shareholders a say on pay; A measure leading to better governance?*, Montreal: Institute for Governance of Private and Public Organizations (IGPPO).

Anson, M., White, T. and Ho, H. (2003) 'The shareholder wealth effects of CalPERS' focus list', *Journal of Applied Corporate Finance* 15: 102–111.

Bainbridge, S. (1995) 'The politics of corporate governance: Roe's strong managers, weak owners', *Harvard Journal of Law and Public Policy* 18: 671–734.

Bainbridge, S. (2009) 'Is say on pay justified?', UCLA School of Law, Law-Econ Research Paper No. 0919, *Regulation* 32(1): 42–47.

Barber, B. M. (2006) Monitoring the monitor: Evaluating CalPERS' activism. *Journal of Investing* 16(4): 66–88.

Bebchuk, L. and Fried (2004) *Pay without performance, the unfulfilled promise of executive compensation*, Cambridge, MA: Harvard University Press.

Bebchuk, L. and Grinstein (2005) 'The growth of executive pay', *Oxford Review of Economic Policy* 21(2): 21.

Bebchuk, L., Cohen, A. and Spamann, H. (2010) 'The wages of failure: Executive compensation at Bear Stearns and Lehman 2000–2008', Harvard Law School, Discussion Paper No. 657.

Becht, M., Franks, J. R., Mayer, C. and Rossi, S. (2008) *Returns to shareholder activism: Evidence from a clinical study of the Hermes U.K. Focus Fund.* ECGI Finance Working Paper, 138/2006.

Berle, A. A. and Means G. C. (1932 [1968]) *The modern corporation and private property*, New York: Brace and World.

Cai, J. and Walkling, R. (2011) 'Shareholders' Say-on-Pay: Does it create value?', *Journal of Financial and Quantitative Analysis* 46(2): 299–339.

Clark, G. L. and Hebb, T. (2004) 'Corporate engagement: The fifth stage of capitalism', *Relations Industrielles/Industrial Relations* 59: 142–170.

Clarkson, M.B.E. (1995) 'A stakeholder framework for analyzing and evaluating corporate social performance', *Academy of Management Review* 20(1): 92–116.

Coffee, J. C. Jr. (1991) 'Liquidity versus control: The institutional investor as corporate monitor', *Columbia Law Review* 91: 1277–1368.

Coffee, J. C. Jr. (1997) 'The folklore of investor capitalism', *Michigan Law Review* 95: 1970–1989. (Book review of Useem, M. [1996], *Investor capitalism: How money managers are changing the face of corporate America*, New York: Basic Books.)

Cotter, J. F., Palmiter, A. R. and Thomas, R. S. (2012) 'The first year of "Say on Pay" under Dodd-Frank: An empirical analysis and look forward', Vanderbilt Law and Economics Research Paper No. 12–32. Online. Available HTTP: <http://ssrn.com/abstract=2162957>, or, <http://dx.doi.org/10.2139/ssrn.2162957>.

Cunat, V., Gine, M. and Guadalupe, M. (2012) 'Say pays! Shareholder voice and firm performance', London School of Economics Working Paper, February. Online. Available HTTP: <http://www.hec.ca/finance/Fichier/SayonPaySept72012Complete.pdf>.

Davis, S. (2007) 'Does "Say on Pay' work? Lessons on making CEO compensation accountable', Policy Briefing Number 1, Millstein Center for Corporate Governance and Performance, Yale School of Management.

Dimson, E., Karakas, O. and Li, X. (2014) 'Active ownership', Working paper. Online. Available HTTP: <http://papers.ssrn.com/sol3/papers.cfm?abstract_id=2154724>.

Ertimur, Y., Ferri, F. and Stubben, S. (2008) 'Board of directors' responsiveness to shareholders: Evidence from shareholder proposals', Working paper, Durham, NC: Duke University.

Ferri, F. and Maber, D. (2012). 'Say on pay votes and CEO compensation: Evidence from the UK', *Review of Finance:* 1–37. Online. Available doi: <10.1093/rof/rfs003>.

Friedman, M. (1970) 'The social responsibility of business is to increase its profits', *New York Times Magazine*, 13 September: 122–126.

Galbraith, J. K. (1976) *Money: Whence it came, where it went*, England: Penguin Books.

Gantchev, N. (2011) *The costs of shareholder activism: Evidence from a sequential decision model*, University of Pennsylvania, Publicly accessible Penn Dissertations. Paper 442.

Gifford, J. (2010) 'Effective shareholder engagement: The factors that contribute to shareholder salience', *Journal of Business Ethics* 92(suppl. 1): 99–115.

Gillan, S. L. and Starks, L. T. (2007) 'The evolution of shareholder activism in the United States', *Journal of Applied Corporate Finance* 19(1): 55–73.

Göx, R., Imhof, F. and Kunz, A. (2009) 'Say on Pay' and its repercussion on CEO investment incentives, compensation, and firm profit. Online. Available HTTP: <http://ssrn.com/abstract=1588682>.

Hawley, J. P. and Williams, A. T. (1997) 'The emergence of fiduciary capitalism', *Corporate Governance* 5(4).

Hawley, J. P. and Williams, A. T. (2000) *The rise of fiduciary capitalism: How institutional investors can make corporate America more democratic*, Philadelphia, PA: University of Pennsylvania Press.

Hebb, T. (2008) *No small change: Pension funds and corporate engagement*, Ithaca, NY: Cornell University Press.

Hendry, J. (2004) 'Beyond self-interest: Agency theory and the board in a satisficing world', *British Journal of Management* 16(S1): S55–S63.

Henriques, I. and Sadorsky, P. (1999) 'The relationship between environmental commitment and managerial perceptions of stakeholder importance', *Academy of Management Journal* 42: 87–99.

Hillman, A. J. and Keim, G. D. (2001) 'Shareholder value, stakeholder management and social issues: what's the bottom line?', *Strategic Management Journal* 22: 125–139.

Hirschman, A. O. (1970) *Exit, voice, and loyalty: Responses to decline in firms, organizations, and states,* Cambridge, MA: Harvard University Press.

Howell, B. (2007) 'Executive fraud and Canada's regulation of executive Compensation', *The University of Miami Inter-American Law Review* 39(1): 111–143.

Jensen, M. C. and Meckling, W. H. (1976) 'Theory of the firm: Managerial behavior, agency costs, and ownership structure', *Journal of Financial Economics* 3: 305–360.

Jensen, M. C. and Murphy, K. J. (1990) 'Performance pay and top management incentives', *Journal of Political Economy* 98: 225–264.

Kaplan, S. (2007) 'Empowering shareholders on executive compensation', testimony on the Shareholder Vote on Executive Compensation Act (H.R. 1257), Committee on Financial Services, United States House of Representatives.

Karpoff, J. M., Malatesta, P. H. and Walkling, R. A. (1996) 'Corporate governance and shareholder initiatives: Empirical evidence', *Journal of Financial Economics* 42: 365–395.

Koford, K. and Penno, M. (1992) 'Accounting, principal-agent theory, and self-interested behaviour', in Bowie, N.E. and Freeman, R.E. (eds.), *Ethics and agency theory: An introduction*, New York: Oxford University Press, 127–142.

Luft, J. (1997) 'Fairness, ethics, and the effect of management accounting on transaction costs', *Journal of Management Accounting Research* 9: 199–216.
Mirvis, T., Rowe, N. and Savvit, W. (2007) 'Bebchuk's case for increasing shareholder power: An opposition (May 2007)', Harvard Law and Economics Discussion Paper No. 586.
Mitchell, R. K., Angle, B. R. and Wood, D. J. (1997) 'Toward a theory of stakeholder identification and salience: Defining the principle of who and what really counts', *Academy of Management Review* 22(4): 853–886.
Mishel, L. and Sabadish, N. (2012) 'CEO pay and the top 1%. How executive compensation and financial-sector pay have fueled income inequality', Issue Brief # 331, Economic Policy Institute, May.
Moneva, J., Riviera-Lirio, J. and Munoz-Torres, M. (2007) 'The corporate stakeholder commitment and social and financial performance', *Industrial Management & Data Systems* 107: 84–102.
Monks, J. (2000) 'The returns to individual and college characteristics: Evidence from the National Longitudinal Survey of Youth', *Economics of Education Review* 19(3): 279–289.
Myers, M. (2011) 'The perils of shareholder voting on executive compensation', *Delaware Journal of Corporate Law* 36(2): 417–461.
O'Barr, W. M. and Conley, J. M. (1992) *Fortune and folly: The wealth and power of institutional investing*, Homewood, IL: Business One Irwin.
Principles of Responsible Investment (2012) *PRI report on progress 2012*. Online. Available HTTP: <http://2xjmlj8428u1a2k5o34l1m71.wpengine.netdna-cdn.com/wp-content/uploads/Annualreport20121.pdf> (accessed May 2015).
Romano, R. (2001) 'Less is more: Making institutional investor activism a valuable mechanism of corporate governance', *Yale Journal on Regulation* 18: 174–252.
Shareholder Association for Research and Education (SHARE) (2012) Shareholder proposal database. Online. Available HTTP: <http://www.share.ca/shareholderdb/>.
Slipp, L. and Knieriem, A. (2009) 'Executive remuneration perspective: Is say on pay here to stay? What to do now?', *Mercer Report*.
Smith, M. P. (1996) 'Shareholder activism by institutional investors: Evidence from CalPERS', *Journal of Finance* 51(1).
Trottier, K. (2011) *What does the market say about say on pay? A look at the Canadian bank experience*. Online. Available HTTP: <http://ssrn.com/abstract=1840673> or <http://dx.doi.org/10.2139/ssrn.184067>.
Wood, D. J. (1991b) 'Social Issues in management: Theory and research in corporate social performance', *Journal of Management* 17(2): 383–406.
Wood, D. and Jones, R. (1995) 'Stakeholder mismatching: A theoretical problem in empirical research on corporate social performance', *International Journal of Organizational Analysis* 3: 229–267.
Wright, P. and Ferris, S. (1997) 'Agency conflict and corporate strategy: The effect of divestment on corporate value', *Strategic Management Journal* 18: 77.

Appendix

Appendix 37.1

List of interviewees

SHARE say on pay engagement

Shareholder Association for Research and Education, Laura O'Neil, Director of Law and Policy

Royal Bank of Canada, Carol McNamara, Corporate Secretary

Royal Bank of Canada, Bill Anderson, Director of Investor Relations

Sun Life Financial, Joan Wilson, Vice President and Corporate Secretary

NEI–Barrick Gold engagement

Primary

Barrick Gold, Anonymous Manager

NEI Investments, Bob Walker

NEI Investments, Michelle De Cordova

NEI Investments, Jennifer Coulson

NEI Investments, Jamie Bonham

Secondary

Mining Watch, Catherine Coumans

Bâtirente, François Meloche

Porgera Landowners Association, Spokesperson

Halifax Initiative, Karyn Keenan

CIMM Centre of Excellence, Jan Vavrek

Canadian Bank, Anonymous, Private Investment Manager

Canadian Bank, Anonymous, Private Investment Manager

Canadian Hedge Fund, Anonymous, Private Investment Advisor

Global Investment Bank, Anonymous, Buy-Side Analyst

Global Investment Bank, Anonymous, Buy-Side Analyst

Management Consulting Firm, Anonymous, Corporate CSR Advisor

Management Consulting Firm, Anonymous, Resource and Energy Analyst

38

Asset manager stakeholders

At the heart of supply and demand in responsible investment[1]

Jean-Philippe Desmartin

Stakeholder overview: asset managers, a key player overlooked by civil society

Asset managers: a long-term social purpose, savings and financing of the economy

The place of asset managers or management companies in the market-finance chain is that of supplier to asset owners, be they private clients or institutional investors (corporations, local authorities, governments, pension funds, etc.). Asset owners of whatever type rarely directly manage their own money, generally delegating this task to a specialist, the asset manager. Their main corporate purpose is therefore to manage these financial assets for external clients. This accounts for the particular care given to factoring in and honouring the contractual direction and constraints indicated by the client. This relationship can be a fiduciary responsibility (i.e. in its narrow sense), factoring in the interests of the asset owner as though the manager were its legal agent, with duties of loyalty and care to the client. Conventionally, asset managers have seen their role with their clients as optimizing the risk/yield curve of their assets ('the risk-adjusted financial returns') by safeguarding and increasing the financial value of the assets entrusted to them.

Asset managers are subject to multiple regulatory constraints at the local and the international levels. A key question for the field of responsible investment is that of fiduciary duty, and how responsible investing (RI) practices correspond to that duty. In 2005, Freshfields Bruckhaus Deringer, the global law firm headquartered in London, published a report entitled *A Legal Framework for the Integration of Environmental, Social and Governance Issues into Institutional Investment*, which marked a milestone by legally recognizing the integration of environment, social and governance (ESG) factors by the institutional investor without contradicting the investor's "legal responsibility to exercise reasonable care, skill, caution and loyalty". However, all aspects of this issue have not yet been resolved, nor has the question been settled in all regions of the world. This is clearly reflected in the obstacles to responsible investment raised by legal departments and law firms in the US in the name of fiduciary responsibility. Asset managers may be left uncertain as to the how their RI practice will be received in different legal regimes. As a major and direct consequence, asset owners and asset managers tend to develop their RI policy in the US at a slower pace.

In practice, asset managers, even as their choices are largely guided by their clients' demands, structurally determine capital allocation with a rationale of optimizing and, at least in theory, financing the real economy through financial instruments such as shares, bonds, private equity, real estate, etc. These financial assets, the fruit of longer-term savings, should play a key role for society. Like infrastructure financing, they contribute to society's economic and social development, and first and foremost to its real economy. Their role is therefore central even though largely overlooked by civil society.

Asset manager profiles are particularly diverse

There are many different kinds of asset managers, and it is difficult to fully review in a few short lines the considerable diversity of asset manager profiles engaged in responsible investment. The asset management industry has steadily grown more structured over the past 40 years, prompting fund managers to increasingly formalize their work methods. The investment strategy is based on three essential planks that bind asset managers to their clients: the management objective (investment time frame, performance target, level of risk aversion), the management style chosen and the investment process. Bear in mind that this diversity among asset managers is key. Using a single example, passive investors are naturally drawn more to implementing engagement than adopting a best-in-class approach in their RI investment processes. Here we can cite four key criteria to establish a typology.

First, shareholding structure: firms may be independent (so-called 'boutique') asset managers, for which the lion's share of the capital is held by the fund's founders and sometimes employees. Within the RI community – as signatories to the Principles for Responsible Investment – one can cite firms such as Generation Investment Management (UK) or Sycomore (France). Subsidiaries of major banks and insurers with PRI signatories such as AXA IM (AXA Group, France) or even Newton IM (UK, subsidiary of the US bank BNY Mellon) constitute another shareholding category. A number of players, listed and non-listed, for which the capital is not controlled, have a diluted shareholding structure like that of the leading asset management group worldwide, BlackRock (US), also a PRI signatory.

A second characteristic criterion is that of client guidance, with (i) private management specialists, such as Bank Sarasin in Switzerland, primarily dedicated to high net worth private clients, (ii) asset management groups particularly focused on retail clients of distribution networks also concentrated on the retail segment and (iii) specialists for institutional clients. The reality is clearly considerably more complex with multi-client and multi-distribution channel asset managers.

A third criterion is that of the investment strategy, with a key distinction being that of active asset management style, in which responsible investment criteria guide active selection of investment opportunities (e.g. a company such as Oddo AM [France]), and a passive management style that favours RI criteria shaping passive index construction, as practiced by State Street Global Advisors in the US. And of course within active and passive investment strategies there are numerous tactics.

Finally, the more or less long-term investor culture is the final criterion that characterizes asset managers. Thus we can make a distinction between management companies that, in principle, operate on a long-term basis (the subsidiaries of pension funds such as APG in the Netherlands) versus hedge funds that, in principle, operate on a short-term investment horizon (GLG, UK) with, for instance, long-short positions (M&As, special situations). All the aforementioned asset managers are PRI signatories and clearly reflect the diversity of these stakeholders, including in their relationship with responsible investment.

While various asset managers are positioned on responsible investment, the typical pioneering profile has historically been that of an independent boutique, with an active management process, a strong track record in equity management, a stock picker, long only, and with an institutional client base focused on long-term investments, such as pension funds or insurance groups. It is in these categories that the influence of ESG information is seen as most likely to be felt – as environmental and social issues favour long-term analysis and suggest active incorporation of information for superior investment outcomes. Pure RI players from inception, such as Generation IM (UK), Impax (UK), SAM (Switzerland), Triodos (the Netherlands) or even Walden AM (US), are exceptions. Until 2006 and the creation of the PRI, the vast majority of asset managers positioned on the RI segment proposed an RI business line in addition to a 'traditional' offer. But, as noted, all kinds of asset managers have found it opportune to join the PRI, suggesting that the influence of ESG integration as a mode of practice, or at least as something important to a significant number of clients, has spread beyond the smaller set of pioneer institutions.

Being 'in line with the market', a priority that leads to short-term and lemming-like behaviour?

The asset manager is required to prudently manage the funds entrusted to him. In the first instance, this typically means capital preservation: over the long term, the end-investor/client expects an absolute positive performance that at least covers inflation. But investors such as pension funds target returns that meet their obligations over time. European pension funds today often target an overall long-term (i.e. five years) yield of 5–6 per cent on the assumption of inflation of around 2 per cent. In contrast, US pension funds often seek returns of about 7.5 per cent.

The measurements used to evaluate whether managers achieve this goal often call for the asset manager to adopt the tactics of a marathon runner as opposed to those of the 100-metre sprinter. But reporting on progress against targets involves short-term steering of performance in relative terms. Asset managers often compare the performance that they deliver with a benchmark, that of indices for the various asset classes. Many active managers, in addition to passive managers who replicate the indices, aim to deliver a performance in line with the indices in terms of both performance and risk with an investment time frame often limited to one year or less. This situation is partly attributed to the remuneration mode of asset managers with, generally speaking, fees based on the total assets managed and additional remuneration linked to relative rather than absolute performance over a standard investment horizon that is one year. This remuneration format used by investors for asset managers is changing in light of the 2008 Global Financial Crisis, with some asset owners adopting performance targets measured over three- to five-year investment horizons.

Consequently, whilst by construction, the asset manager has a long-term focus and although via his rational choices he targets an optimized allocation of those assets entrusted to him, the reality is more complex. Much criticism has been levelled at the short-termist culture of asset managers and their tendency to follow each other – something called a 'lemming instinct' – that has sometimes fuelled financial bubbles. The subject is more complicated than it seems as asset managers often only replicate the short-termist pressure of institutional clients. A major issue partly responsible for short-termism in practice is fund managers' remuneration; this question was clearly posed in Danyelle Guyatt's 2006 work 'Identifying and Overcoming Behavioural Impediments to Long Term Responsible Investment: A Focus on UK Institutional Investors'. As a result, short-termism may make it harder to integrate ESG issues. This raises the issue that the system for asset manager evaluation may disfavour responsible investment even if an RI strategy improved long-term performance.

Recent evidence suggests that, despite structural bias towards short-termism, empirical evidence does not suggest RI underperformance. Standard measurements for asset managers' success – those used to measure the impact of responsible investment on the debate on optimizing the risk-adjusted performance on which asset managers are typically asked to deliver – suggest that responsible investment neither positively nor negatively affects the fundamental rules of the game for asset managers. In practice, RI funds statistically present, on average, a performance/risk profile neither more nor less favourable than that of the overall market. This 'in-line' performance was far from certain some 15 years ago in terms of both practitioners and academic research and is now providing a strong 'licence to operate' for the asset management industry before aiming for a 'licence to compete'. This detail is hardly anodyne as we have been able to observe since the start of the 1990s that the commitment and sectoral best-in-class funds offer less risky profiles than ethical funds that use exclusion criteria or theme funds such as cleantech and renewables.

Apart from near-term benchmarks, asset managers also face systemic risk in the context of their asset allocation with a question linked to sustainable development: how do sustainable development and corporate responsibility contribute (or fail to contribute) to reducing systemic risks at the micro- and macro-economic levels? Ultimately, management of all of these constraints is not easy. It is facilitated by the asset manager's independence, which is based on transparent governance, the absence of conflict of interest and a corporate culture based on the 'client-first' premise. Responsible investment as a strategy may help asset managers take into account sustainable development risks both by extending investment time horizons and by integrating new forms of information into investment decision making that take these risks into account.

Responsible investment overview

Five historic stages for asset management and responsible investment

It is useful to trace the historical relationship between asset management and responsible investment to better understand how the emerging field has developed through its use by managers. We suggest five key stages in the development of the relationship between asset management and responsible investment. As each new stage, quite rightly, builds on and complements the previous stage, they represent an accumulation of strategies and tactics rather than the replacement of one by the other. The five stages of this development are:

- the ethical funds of the 1920s,
- shareholder involvement as of the 1960s,
- the social and environmental themes of the 1980s,
- funds drawing on the concept of sustainable development and notably the best-in-class approach of the 1990s and, lastly,
- the emergence of the ongoing main-streaming of this approach with the integration of ESG processes as of 2006 and the creation of the Principles of Responsible Investment (PRI).

Driven by religious movements (Baptists, Methodists), in particular in the UK and US, ethical funds have been developing regularly since the 1920s. And the origins of these initiatives can be traced to the seventeenth and eighteenth centuries, when the Quakers refused to invest in the arms and slave trade. The choices are clear, with the recourse to exclusion criteria for identified activities and/or business practices. This type of investment was founded on the convictions of individuals and/or communities. These management companies, closely tied to the history of these religious movements, have for many years been positioned on this type of investment, such as CCLA (UK), Friends & Ivory (UK) and Meerschaert (France). These ethical funds are just as likely to develop in Christian environments as in the Islamic (Sharia funds) and Jewish cultures. In theory, the work for the asset manager is relatively simple since it involves excluding sectors of economic activity (tobacco, for example) and/or companies. The integration of ethical considerations via the exclusion of entire economic sectors could have a significant impact on the investment process of the asset manager. The asset manager may use external providers to supply lists of the stocks to exclude due to their activity or controversial practices (human and fundamental employment rights, for example) or may develop in-house research capacity to evaluate corporate behaviour.

The 1960–80s saw the emergence of shareholder activism, particularly in UK and US, spurred on by pivotal national events (the Vietnam war, the struggle against apartheid in South Africa, for example) and militant shareholders (religious congregations, non-governmental organizations, workers' unions, Council on Economic Priorities in the US) who challenged the corporate role in major social and political debates. These investors took direct action at annual general meetings to file resolutions and appealed to asset managers to join them in their campaigns. Activist practices and shareholders' resolve did not necessarily have any impact on the asset manager's investment process, although it did raise the need for new skills and tools for those managers who specialized in resolution filing and corporate engagement. It was also during this period that the first community, solidarity or shared funds, which represent around 10 per cent of responsible investment in its earliest form, began to appear.

In the 1980s, we saw the development of thematic funds taking a social and environmental positioning. The approach is solutions based, much like eco-funds. The current trend in the impact investing in Asia and North America can be associated with this theme, and suggests an expanding demand among asset owners for managers that target specific social benefits that also meet portfolio constraints. Funds tend to have a predominantly environmental theme (climate change funds, water funds, timber funds, etc.), although there are also funds with a bias towards social issues (job creation, education, business close to local communities, ageing population, etc.).

The formalization of the sustainable development concept in 1987 under the auspices of the United Nations (Brundtland Report) provided the first international overview of responsible investment. This stage was key, since it opened the way for asset managers to take an overall approach rather than one that was solely local or specific case-by-case with investments tailored to investors' requirements. This approach notably triggered the development of so-called best-in-class funds and a mainstream approach via the integration of ESG. This could have a significant impact on the investment process operated by the asset management firm.

The most recent stage, the creation of PRI in 2006, was a strong signal in the promotion of responsible investment for all asset manager signatories, and not only for a few categories or specialized socially responsible investment (SRI) niches. The asset management company commits over the long term to a gradual ESG integration not only for a number of specialist SRI funds, but for all asset categories and open funds. This ESG integration stage ultimately aims to impact all of the investment processes of the asset management company. The ongoing learning curve of these five complementary stages partially explains the wide diversity observed in the practice of responsible investment: shareholder activism in the US, shareholder dialogue in the UK and Scandinavia, ethical funds in Islamic countries, impact investing in Asia, sector-wide best-in-class in continental Europe, green funds in Brazil and Japan, etc. Asset managers are at the heart of managing the supply/demand curves for responsible investment across a full range of RI strategies.

Indirect ESG impacts and the concept of materiality at the centre of asset manager concerns

Whilst an asset management company has direct ESG impacts from its own firm practice to manage, these tend to be less fundamental than the impact of ESG via its investment policy. Direct environmental impacts are relatively limited (environmental impact of managers' business travel, for example), and the direct challenges tend to be focused on the social policy (human resources management, particularly with a view to attracting, training and retaining key personnel) and questions of governance (notably, conflicts of interest).

The heart of the ESG engine can be found in an asset manager's investment policy or policies on which, as we have already said, the asset manager is not the sole decision-maker, since he guides and is guided by his clients. Within the framework of asset management, the asset manager is faced with an imperative, that of materiality. In concrete terms, the asset manager will primarily look to identify ESG themes and criteria, as well as the risks and opportunities that are likely to have a favourable or unfavourable stock market impact in the short, medium and long term on the price of the assets under management (shares, bonds, etc.). ESG analysis covers a number of themes and has an innovation bias.

This analysis includes events (e.g. the Fukushima nuclear plant disaster), long-term social and environmental drivers (corruption, water, obesity, etc.), analysis grids and the evaluation of quantitative and qualitative cross-sector indicators (energy consumption, employee training), and criteria that are specific to different sectors, and even the question of controversial practices. These tools have multiple uses, from examining companies' business models to validating the quality of the management or evaluating the balance sheets and earnings prospects. Lastly, and outside the realms of materiality, responsible investment is a process that can strengthen the reputation of the asset manager much as it can for the client asset owner. A number of asset managers have thus decided to no longer invest in companies or in the sovereign debt of countries that continuously contravene major international laws and codes, such as the Universal Declaration of Human Rights (which is the case for Sudan, for instance).

Are asset managers beneficiaries of responsible investment? Yes, but not all of them!

In principle, the asset manager appears to be the natural beneficiary of responsible investment since the issue constitutes a growth driver for those positioned on this opportunity. In practical terms, the opportunity is less obvious since it often involves no more than a simple shift in direction or the redirection of investment and not necessarily the setting up of a new fund with new cash inflows. In effect, net inflow is guaranteed on a specialized savings fund, but in general this concerns only a small percentage of the assets managed by a management group. For the rest, we are essentially talking in terms of a reallocation. As such, not all managers necessarily benefit from the presumed windfall of responsible investment, only those who most effectively meet the requirements of responsible investment.

The theme therefore benefits the asset management industry as a whole, but not all of its managers. It is up to each asset manager, drawing on his culture, processes and strengths to develop an RI approach that meets some or all of the various criteria. Such criteria can include improved performance (alpha), emergence of new investment ideas (stock picking) and the more effective management of the volatility of the funds under management (beta). Note that for an aggressive view, responsible investment can be a growth driver for the asset manager, with the increase in requests for proposals that mention RI, whilst for a defensive view it can be seen as a barrier to entry.

The last, but not least, of the innovative opportunities is the implementation of non-financial analysis to round out the financial analysis, which can improve performance in the asset manager's core business by providing an insight into the yield/risk profile via a focus for the active investor on three growth levers: (i) a better understanding of the business models in the sector and businesses and their development, (ii) the validation, or not, of the quality of top management, with the first criterion 'go, no go' for the active asset manager, and (iii) lastly, a more in-depth examination of balance sheets (goodwill, R&D costs, social and environmental liabilities, stock options, etc.). In the first instance, asset managers see ESG analysis as an additional proxy to risk analysis and, as such, the subject of governance provides a natural bridge between financial and non-financial analysis. The integration of ESG thus rounds out the financial analysis and the asset manager's investment approach by enhancing their requirements and discipline.

ESG implementation, the biggest challenge for asset managers

Responsible investment constitutes a development opportunity, a future vector of growth for a number of asset management companies. It is therefore an attractive opportunity, albeit one which poses a number of challenges to asset managers.

The biggest challenge lies in the choice of the responsible investment niche and/or a more mainstream approach to the integration of ESG. These are not mutually exclusive, quite the contrary, with the historic performance of the niche sector constituting, in practical terms, a very valuable experience base and guideline for the entire ESG integration processes. The signing of the PRI implies the gradual integration of ESG, but deciding between a specialized SRI approach and/or overall ESG integration is the first obstacle to overcome. Behind this lies the question of not only the asset manager's capacity to fulfil the demands of specific clients via a well-targeted niche offering, but also his capacity to create a unique responsible investor profile.

The second challenge lies in analyzing how implementing ESG strategies impacts internal investment processes, and whether their implementation will occasion hostility from practitioners unfamiliar with or sceptical of the field. Responsible investment is still a new and experimental subject. It raises difficult questions such as how ESG methodologies should be adapted, what the related constraints are and how they impact performance, the relationship with portfolio theory, the identification of the most material ESG criteria for particular firms, sectors and portfolios and across which timeframes, how due account should be taken of behavioural finance, the analysis of intangible assets, etc. Note that hostility towards responsible investment can come from both outside the asset management company as well as from within. Outside the company, the client investor might see responsible investment as a waste of time and energy entailing extra constraints and additional costs which could come between the asset manager and his financial performance target or even lead to a poor track record. Within the company, responsible investment comes up against the habitual resistance to change that we can see whenever anything new is introduced. Adopting an ESG approach as part of the signing of the PRI therefore presents the challenge of how to drive change management within an asset manager's organization.

Successfully dealing with the hostility that can come from both outside and within an asset management company hinges on a number of factors, including the leadership qualities of the top management team and the efforts devoted to raising awareness, providing training and making ESG-related information and databases available. Other key factors are mobilizing operational teams, especially portfolio managers, and developing close ties with the academic world in order to make inroads in these new, exploratory subjects and grant them legitimacy. The development of the PRI Academic Network since 2009 is, in this respect, a source of support that asset managers that have signed the PRI initiative should not hesitate to draw on.

The last, and by no means easiest, challenge is to gain access to quality ESG-related information in order to be able to invest – that is, data that is pertinent, consolidated, comparable and durable. This is the challenge facing asset managers for the current decade, as indeed it was for the last one. The progress made by asset managers in terms of implementing an ESG strategy will also be informed by advances made in companies' ESG reporting. This will necessarily involve a standardization of reporting, even though the diversity of the present initiatives (AA1000, EFFAS, GRI, IIRC, ISO 26000, OECD, WICI, etc.) plays an indispensable role in ensuring that the best-possible standards eventually emerge.

Responsible investment is set to see growth at the institutional investor level provided that certain ground rules are respected

Responsible investment is set to continue developing over the next five years in both the specialist niche and mainstream investment channels. Asset managers are identifying the development of responsible investment with institutional investors as a priority. Development with retail investors is limited to a motivated client base that represents 1–10 per cent of clients, depending on the country. Based on our estimates, responsible investment for retail clients is likely to be capped at 5–10 per cent by 2020. The potential of institutional investors and their interest in responsible investment appears to be higher, with an estimated threshold of around 30 per cent in a 5–10 year timeframe versus approximately 10 per cent at present in some advanced markets, such as Europe and Australia.

Over the next five years, a key step, which is currently under way, is to disseminate this type of investment to all existing asset classes. Responsible investment is activist in origin and initially involved equities where the holder of the security was its owner and likely incorporated shareholder activism and corporate engagement. Over the past 10 years, asset managers have extended the scope of responsible investment to encompass other asset classes: corporate and sovereign bonds since the early 1990s, commodities strategies since 2005–6, real-estate assets since 2006–7 and private equity since 2010. APG in the Netherlands is an example of these recent moves.

Finally, over the next five years we are likely to see a degree of stabilization in the diversity of RI products available. This should facilitate the task of finding a common definition for responsible investment and formally delimiting its scope of intervention. The lasting success of this development over the next few years hinges on two prerequisites – transparency and stringency – while at the same time fulfilling the twin constraints of market needs (soft law) and regulatory requirements (hard law). Transparency is a prerequisite because asset managers need to follow the same standards that the responsible investor requires from companies on a daily basis. Stringency is another requirement because responsible investment needs to be more than a simple exercise in communication with only a marginal impact on day-to-day activity and the investment policy. Stringency is the only way to provide empirical evidence that the high standards and consistency required in the field of financial analysis are also present in ESG analysis.

What do RI asset managers hope to see from public authorities?

Asset managers hope to receive three forms of support from public authorities. First, they could play a part in standardizing regulations, at least at a regional level (Europe, for example) and perhaps even at a global level. This could, for example, include shareholders' rights, standards in corporate ESG reporting or reporting by asset managers about how they have integrated ESG into their investment policies.

Public authorities could also provide responsible investment with support in ultimately standardizing corporate non-financial reporting. The toolbox of non-financial reporting systems is currently full (AA1000, Balanced Scorecard, EFFAS, GRI, IIRC, ISO 26000, OECD, SASB, WICI, etc.). What will facilitate the task of asset managers is the gradual rollout of integrated reporting. It would be a definite advantage to them if, for their daily tasks, they could have a registration document including both financial and non-financial information that would be of material import to the investor. This is the principle informing the 'One Report', as defined by Robert Eccles and Michael Krzus in 2010 ahead of the creation of the IIRC (International Integrated Reporting Committee) initiative. Support from public authorities for the principle of an integrated report as recommended by the IIRC initiative would be a significant driver for progress. The company could also use its website to further its ESG communication towards other stakeholders such as consumer associations, clients, employees, media, NGOs or public authorities.

Finally, and even though this might seem obvious, asset managers look favourably on any fiscal arrangements that benefit long-term investment, and therefore, by its very nature, responsible investment fills this need.

Role of the PRI: high expectations for widening and deepening, with asset owners taking the lead

The development of the PRI has sped up since 2006, with over 1,200 signatories as of mid-2014, representing over USD 35 trillion in assets under management. Asset managers have played a large part in this increase. By 2012, asset managers accounted for the majority of the signatories, far ahead of asset owners and professional service partners. Overall, the majority of PRI signatories represent institutional investors with a natural long-term focus (insurers, pension funds, long-only funds, etc.).

Many asset managers want the PRI to continue playing a key role in institutionalizing responsible investment across the globe. While significant progress has already been made in certain areas (Brazil, Europe and Oceania, for example), extending responsible investment to emerging markets and Asia is still a challenge. Many asset managers therefore recommend that the PRI continue its global agenda in order to bring more and more asset owners on board, especially in North America, Japan and emerging markets. As a final point, there is a need for closer involvement from independent or captive distribution networks in the initiative, in addition to asset owners, asset managers and providers (agencies, brokers, consultants).

Another high expectation, which does not necessarily contradict this widening process, is for a deepening of the ESG approaches adopted by existing signatories. Many asset managers advocate the deepening of the PRI to avoid the pitfalls of green washing, which would undermine the initiative as a whole. They criticize the situation of asset managers where little progress is made in terms of adopting a genuine ESG approach, which is therefore at odds with their high-profile communication about their membership in the PRI. This deepening could involve tighter checks on the actual approach taken by the signatories, not just on what they disclose. In concrete terms, this might lead to certain signatories being excluded for reasons other than an absence of annual reporting. An example would be an exclusion due to a lack of progress in ESG integration by the signatory after three or four years.

Aside from these twin expectations of widening and deepening, most asset managers agree that the lead given to asset owners in the PRI is of key importance and should be maintained. Asset owners were at the origin of the PRI, which is one of the reasons it has succeeded. They are located upstream in the financial services industry and, as the end client, their contribution flows back to all players, asset managers and providers alike. As such, they are the trigger of a gradual domino effect.

Finally, asset managers welcome the work and coordination role of the PRI, particularly in its facilitation of the creation and ongoing existence of working groups and the global cooperation on concrete projects such as shareholder commitments or private equity, which is the latest major segment in the financial services industry to join the RI fold. Generally, any manner in which the PRI helps to restore a long-term time frame to asset managers' investment policies is welcome. There are two fields where the PRI is expected to play a part: identifying ESG factors, which are of the greatest materiality for the investor, and granting legitimacy to the adoption of ESG strategies with respect to fiduciary responsibility.

Note

1 I would like to thank all of the asset managers with whom I was able to regularly discuss the development of responsible investment over the past 14 years as a service provider (agency, broker and consultant), especially in Europe and North America. I would like to thank, in particular, the asset managers at Amundi, AXA IM, Newton IM and Sycomore for their contributions to the ideas expressed in this chapter.

References

Eccles, R. G. and Krzus M. P. (2010) *One Report: Integrated Reporting for a Sustainable Strategy*, New York: John Wiley.

Freshfields Bruckhaus Deringer (2005) *A Legal Framework for the Integration of Environmental, Social and Governance Issues into Institutional Investment*, London: UNEP Finance Initiative. Online. Available HTTP: <www.unepfi.org/fileadmin/documents/freshfields_legal_resp_20051123.pdf> (accessed 31 July 2012).

Guyatt, D. J. (2006) 'Identifying and overcoming behavioural impediments to long term responsible investment: A focus on UK institutional investors', PhD dissertation, UK: University of Bath.

39

Stakeholder perspective – investment consultants

'The need to collaborate to ensure supply meets demand'

Danyelle Guyatt

Overview

This chapter sets out the role of investment consultants in the proliferation of responsible investment (RI). Investment consultants represent a key part of the investment chain as advisors to trustees and investment committees of pension funds and other institutional asset owners. Consequently, their ability to provide advice to asset owners on RI issues is important not only for the legitimacy of RI at the investment committee level, but also to ensure that the skills and tools are available to implement policies in an effective manner.

It will be argued in this chapter that the challenge the industry faces is that the demand for, and indeed supply of, advice on RI issues is still sporadic and patchy. The investment consultants are faced with the need to balance their desire to be proactive and show leadership on RI issues against the reality of a lower willingness to pay for this advice, the frequent use of alternative sources for such advice and, in many instances, a lack of interest among asset owners.

This represents a challenge not only for the investment consultants but also for those asset owners that seek strong RI advice and want the industry to mature. There is a clear need and opportunity for the engaged asset owners and investment consultants to collaborate to find areas of common ground to ultimately deliver higher standards of RI-related advice at the industry level. A collaborative and organized approach would reduce the risk of a small number of asset owners bearing a disproportionate amount of the costs involved in receiving that advice, while at the same time ensuring that any one consultant does not risk too much in the way of unrealized demand for developing the expertise. In this sense it is a clear win/win collaborative opportunity (Guyatt, 2006).

Who are the investment consultants?

Depending on the nature of the asset owner and its level of internal resources and expertise, there is more often than not a need for asset owners to draw from investment consultant advice in making decisions on matters related to developing investment beliefs, investment policies, investment strategy and the selection of new investment mandates, as well as the review of existing mandates.

Investment consultants also provide bespoke advice to asset owners on a range of issues such as asset/liability management, responding to regulatory changes and, inter alia, responding to new industry developments such as the growing adoption and integration of RI amongst institutional investors.

There are two primary ways that asset owners engage investment consultants: on a retainer, contract basis or on a specific project basis.

The most common method is on a retainer basis where investment consultant agreements are in place for typically three years. At the end of the retainer period the contract is reviewed and possibly renewed depending on the asset owner's satisfaction with the relationship, the service provided and value for money. The nature of the services on a retainer contract can also vary depending on the needs of the asset owner. For small and medium-sized asset owners with relatively small internal resources, the dependence on investment consultant advice can be quite high, and hence the advice will cover all aspects of investment decision making, as specified above. Larger asset owners may employ the services of an investment consultant for a smaller range of services, such as manager research on niche asset classes.

The second way that asset owners employ consultants, less common but nonetheless prevalent across different sized funds and regions, is to hire a consultant to undertake bespoke projects. The consultant might be selected because it has particular internal expertise that the retainer consultant does not have, or indeed the asset owner wants to have more than one opinion on a particular issue. On the ESG area this bespoke project approach is still the most common avenue for interaction between asset owners and consultants, with retainer relationships that embed ESG being less common. As this article discusses later, this will ideally change as/when the level of engagement and interaction on ESG issues between consultants and asset owners strengthens. But for now, the bespoke project approach is the most pervasive delivery mechanism.

Investment consultant firms take various forms, ranging from small one- or two-person outfits that specialize in providing niche areas of investment advice through to large multi-national entities that might exist as part of a global listed corporation. While the degree of market penetration varies significantly by region, amongst the largest global investment consultants that have been active in responsible investment include Mercer, Towers Watson and Aon Hewitt.

There are other players in the industry, and in some countries, such as Australia, the local consultants dominate the advisory services more than the global players. Large pension funds and sovereign wealth funds are increasingly utilizing boutique specialist advisors as well as developing their own internal investment expertise.

Nevertheless, the focus of this chapter is on global consultants, as they provide advice to a substantial proportion of asset owners globally and consequently have a strong influence on the decision making of investment committees and trustees within these institutions, including their attitude and adoption of RI.

What are the investment consultants doing about RI?

A brief summary of the core activities with respect to RI for some of the global consultants is provided below. This list is not intended to be exhaustive and is constantly evolving, but it provides a snapshot of how the global investment consultant industry has participated and supported the evolution of RI to varying degrees.

As the following examples illustrate, the consultancies have responded to the industry growth and interest in RI in different ways – from building a large internal team of specialists that is a revenue-generating part of the business through to having one or two internal champions who advocate RI in their capacity as a core investment consultant. It is interesting to observe the different approaches and why they have emerged as they have, in part driven by the perceived client demand for the services still being on the fringe, but also a reflection of the business model of the consultant firm itself.

Some investment consultancies 'invest' more time and effort in research and what are considered to be ancillary activities to the core business, but that are nonetheless important enough to support with time and effort of staff members. Others may be more bottom-line (revenue) focused and will pursue the activities to the extent that clients demand the services and revenue can be generated to reflect the time/effort of staff. It is fair to say that with either approach RI is still considered to be a niche component of what an investment consultant firm offers its clients, and the divergence in approaches is more about responding to the perceived niche demand, rather than changing the core business model.

Three international consultant firms

Three international consultant firms that specialize in providing RI advice to asset owners and managers are Mercer, Towers Watson and Aon Hewitt. We will examine each one in turn.

Mercer

One of the 'first movers' amongst the global investment consultants in developing its advice on RI issues was Mercer.

In 2004 Mercer established a specialist business unit of RI consultants that is now 15+ people who undertake research and provide advice on issues related to voting, engagement and the integration of ESG issues into portfolio management.[1] The firm was involved in the early development of the UN-backed Principles for Responsible Investment (PRI), together with other industry stakeholders, and has been and remains a signatory to the PRI.

It has initiated and over the years led a number of collaborative projects that have set out to improve the industry's knowledge, awareness and ultimately the acceptance of ESG issues as material factors to consider as part of the investment process, ranging from white papers on specialist topics through to analyzing the asset allocation implications of climate change.

Mercer developed a process to rate fund managers across all asset classes according to their ability to integrate ESG into core processes, with a rating pool in excess of 5,000 strategies at the time of writing. These ESG ratings are offered to all clients as part of their selection and monitoring of fund managers.

Towers Watson

Towers has taken a slightly different approach to Mercer and has gradually built up internal expertise through a small team of champions, as opposed to treating it as a business unit. The RI topics cover a wide array of issues, from ESG integration through to sustainability and subjects related to long-term investing.

RI topics have been pursued via research papers in connection to Towers' Thinking Ahead group and other research teams across different groups. This has contributed to the industry's conceptual thinking on how ESG issues might be integrated into core investment processes.[2] Investment beliefs and how these are developed and where ESG fits has been one of the key topics advanced by Towers Watson working with its asset owner clients.

It participates and leads collaborative projects via networks such as the PRI, of which it became a signatory in 2008, as well as through academic groups such as University of Oxford with which is it is partnering on various topics related to long-term investing.

Aon Hewitt

Prior to the merger with Aon, Hewitt was developing some internal processes and tools to integrate ESG factors into fund manager selection and monitoring. Since the merger there has not been much information on the ongoing development of ESG services within the firm to report.

It utilized third-party ESG data to offer its clients an ESG assessment of their equity portfolios based on the underlying stock holdings.

This firm developed a sustainability multi-manager product that incorporated key sustainability themes.

Aon Hewitt participates in industry events and discussions on ESG and sustainability issues, mainly in the UK/Europe where the internal champion is based. It is a signatory to the PRI.

In summary, the nature of the work typically undertaken by a consultant on RI issues varies considerably. The questions and issues are not homogenous across asset owners, as they are at different stages of development in terms of their beliefs and what they want to achieve. The starting point for discussions is usually around education on what RI means, the different approaches to implementation, case studies on what other asset owners are doing, an assessment of the relative merit of participating in different collaborative initiatives and the development of a policy and set of beliefs around RI issues. For the more advanced asset owners, discussions may then move to considering what impact RI has on asset allocation decisions, the selection, review and compensation of fund managers, the development of a company engagement strategy and investment in new opportunities that have an RI component as part of its value added.

Supply and demand for RI advice

It is important to bear in mind that the investment consultants can go only as far as the overall marketplace will allow them to. As an industry insider previously in an investment consultant firm and now as an asset owner, I have observed that the demand for advice on RI matters from the asset owner community is sporadic and not as widespread as one might expect based on the number of signatories to initiatives such as the PRI, for example. Indeed, there is a wide dispersion of asset owners in terms of their openness and demand for RI advice that makes it challenging for investment consultants to respond to. Investment consultants are profit-seeking organizations and therefore need to be mindful of how they allocate their resources. As mentioned previously, the nature of RI advice is also more difficult to standardize as asset owners will approach the issue from a different perspective and stage of development, hence the costs incurred for the consultancy in providing the advice and the fees to cover the time spent may well be higher than the asset owners' willingness to pay.

On the supply side of RI advice, the examples provided above illustrate that the approach amongst the global consultants varies considerably and, as a result, the advice that asset owners receive will also vary depending on what investment consultant they use. The large global players mentioned above are on the more proactive end of the spectrum; in some of the smaller boutique consultancies there can be very little (sometimes no) internal expertise or effort put into RI issues. This could mean that an asset owner may find another consultant for bespoke advice on RI matters and/or they develop more internal capability to address the issues. There are few cases where an investment consultant has been replaced purely due to its lack of RI coverage; however, if a consultancy was falling short on delivery in other areas, no doubt that would also be a reasonable response.

On the demand side of the equation, the most engaged asset owner institutions on RI issues tend to be public pension funds, corporate pension funds whose stakeholders have a link to ESG issues, local authority schemes, union-backed funds, industry funds, as well as some faith-based endowments and charities. Of those that are engaged, some may seek advice from their core investment consultants on RI issues if it exists, while the more committed funds will also develop their own expertise in-house and/or obtain advice from other parties outside of the investment consultant relationship as a bespoke project.

The need to embed RI into core investment advice

As mentioned above, broadly speaking there are three avenues that an engaged asset owner might take in building up its knowledge on RI issues:

Outside specialist consultant

The specialist may be inside the same firm as the core consultant but is a different person to the one the investment committee normally interacts with.

Depending on the strength of the relationship between the outsider and the investment committee, there are a number of drawbacks with this approach that could undermine the wider adoption and integration of RI into core investment processes. This is because the obstacles to RI integration in investment decisions are not as simple as receiving a magic report or an essential tool that will suddenly open the doors to change. Overcoming the obstacles necessitates a gradual process of change: relationships, trust, and what investment committees perceive to be issues that are relevant to them as decision makers. If their trusted, core investment consultant provides advice on RI issues and sets out a pathway to achieve progress over time, then that will carry much more weight than advice received from an outside consultant, regardless of that person's credentials. The outside consultant will likely have a weaker relationship with the investment committee as it takes time to build such relationships. Therefore there will be less trust in place, and the advice may be at a level that makes it difficult to implement as the outsider does not have the inside knowledge on the ins and outs of the asset owner's portfolio structure. In short, while it is understandable that this approach prevails to some extent given the still early phase of the industry's development, over the long term there are a myriad of behavioural impediments that stand in the way of progress via outsourcing RI advice to an outside consultant.

In-house expertise

Refers to an ESG specialist that in the majority of cases does not have an investment background and is not part of the investment committee.

The in-house expertise model is another approach that has become increasingly popular amongst asset owners, large and small. While not always the case, invariably the specialist will come with a stronger background in ESG issues than investment expertise. The specialist will likely not be considered to be an 'investment' person by the majority of the internal staff, and the specialist's role will be viewed as one that is very specific to developing and implementing policies regarding ESG issues and, if the asset the owner is a signatory to the PRI and other initiatives, meeting those various obligations. The presence of the in-house specialist takes the pressure off the core consultant to provide advice, as it exists in-house, and hence there is unlikely to be much appetite to pay for advice on the issues. It also takes the pressure off the investment committee to take the issues onto their agenda and to learn new skills and challenge the status quo, as there is a specialist on the case. The in-house specialist then needs to ensure that the issues remain on the investment agenda and do not get relegated into a specialist and forgotten corner of the institution. Again, while it is perfectly understandable that internal champions are needed to advance the issues of ESG within organizations (Juravle and Lewis, 2009), their presence could have the undesired effect of taking the pressure off investment consultants to take the issues on to their agenda and become more learned on the issues. Similar obstacles could then stand between the in-house specialist and the investment committee's perception of investment legitimacy, as discussed in the case of the outside consultant above.

Core consultant

Refers to the investment consultant that the investment committee draws from for advice on a range of investment issues. There may be more than one core consultant depending on their expertise.

As mentioned above, there are some economic constraints on the core consultant that have the effect of either limiting how much they are able to offer to their clients on RI advice or necessitating the consultant to charge an additional fee for it. This economic imperative no doubt reflects the current state of the industry rather than a permanent structure, as the more that ESG issues become embedded into processes the more they will be considered a core part of consulting advice and hence the fee differentiation issues will disappear. But this has not yet occurred in the global investment consultant market. The result is that some global consultants are investing more than others in being proactive, which given the financial pressures that all companies have been under over recent years may be difficult to sustain. Without core consultants embedding ESG into their advice, the legitimacy of the issues will be weaker, the investment committees will retain their distance and continue to view it as a separate function from them and overall the pace of change at the industry level will be much slower than it otherwise would be.

Collaboration between consultants and their clients

No doubt there are a number of possible avenues to pursue to make progress from where we are today on the link between core consultant advice and RI integration. One possibility that stands out as an obvious avenue to pursue is collaboration between a collection of asset owner clients and their shared consultant(s) to find common ground and engage with them on the key areas where they seek more integrated ESG advice.

This idea has been discussed within an Australian-based collaborative network of asset owners, where there is a high concentration of industry funds that tend to utilize small, local consultants more than the global consultants mentioned in this chapter. Without going into the specifics of those discussions, as it is in the conceptual phase, the idea is simple. It is to sort the asset owners according to what consultant they rely on for their core investment advice. This group would then write a 'wish list' of their expectations for RI issues now and into the future. This sort of approach, if backed by chief investment officers of asset owner organizations and given sufficient internal support, could provide a clear win/win for all parties.

The need for collaboration of this kind is backed up by the observation made in the Ceres (2012: 8) survey of investment consultant practices that noted:

> If asset owners want to work with a consultant who understands how ESG factors might impact long-term financial risks and returns, they need to ask a range of questions including whether the consultant is a PRI signatory, whether they are serving global clients (who are more likely to integrate ESG factors into their investment decision-making) and some in-depth questions about how the consultant believes ESG factors impact investments.

Being more engaged and proactive in interacting with consultants on ESG issues would benefit the asset owners through improving the way investment consultants embed ESG issues into core investment advice. It would also help redress some of the behavioural impediments that prevail inside consulting firms where there is a risk of specialization and isolating the ESG issues from the core investment advice.

The investment consultant would also benefit from a more focused exchange on expectations around ESG with their clients, as they would no longer be guessing what some asset owners may/may not need and would be able to establish, in a more cost-effective way, a deliberate program of action to meet their client's growing need for advice on these issues.

Conclusion

This chapter has set out the important role that investment consultants play in mainstreaming RI into core investment practices. While some global consultants have made efforts to increase their knowledge, tools and advice on ESG issues, the demand for ESG advice from asset owners is variable. It is understandable that a hybrid approach to meeting asset owners' needs on ESG issues has developed, involving mainly a combination of outsourcing to specialist consultants and relying on in-house expertise, with far less utilization of advice from core consultants. For more robust consultant engagement on the topic, it will be vital to mobilize the integration of ESG issues into investment committee structures, and that asset owners convey to their core investment consultants the need to embed ESG into their advice. Collaboration between asset owner clusters and their consultants has been put forward as one possible way to accelerate this process of change. At least one network has started to think about these possibilities, and there will likely be substantial innovation and progress over the coming years.

Notes

1 Further information can be found online, available HTTP: <http://www.mercer.com/articles/ri-background>.
2 For an example, see online, available HTTP: <http://www.towerswatson.com/newsletters/emphasis/5469>.

References

Ceres (2012) *Incorporating environmental, social and governance factors into investing: A survey of investment consultant practices,* September 2012. Online. Available HTTP: <http://www.ceres.org/resources/reports/incorporating-environmental-social-and-governance-factors-into-investing-a-survey-of-investment-consultant-practices>.

Guyatt, D. (2006) *Institutional investor collaboration: enhancing effectiveness,* Rotman ICPM sponsored research. Online. Available HTTP: <http://www.rijpm.com/admin/article_files/collaboration_paper_(final).pdf>.

Juravle, C. and Lewis, L. (2009) 'The role of championship in the mainstreaming of sustainable investment (SI). What can we learn from SI pioneers in the United Kingdom?', *Organization & Environment,* 22: 75–98.

40

Responsible investment indexes

Origins, nature and purpose

Steve Lydenberg and Alexi White

Introduction

Responsible investment has followed the example of the mainstream financial community by developing an increasing number and variety of indexes in recent years. Like traditional financial indexes, responsible investment (RI) indexes can serve as definitions of markets available for investment, as the basis for investment products and as benchmarks for the measurement of investment performance. What are the different approaches to the creation of the RI indexes now being used? How are RI indexes different from, or similar to, conventional financial indexes? In what sense are they 'responsible'? What is their future likely to be? These are some of the questions this chapter seeks to answer.

Background on indexes and index-related investments

Prior to the mid-1970s, indexes were used primarily to track the performance of financial markets in the aggregate, not as the basis for investment vehicles. The first stock index was created by Charles Dow in 1884. The Dow Jones Transportation Average was established primarily to track the performance of railroad stocks, which dominated the stock markets at that time (Dow Jones 2014). In 1896, the Dow Jones launched its Industrial Average index to reflect the growing role of other large industrial companies in the economy (Dow Jones 2013). In 1923, Standard & Poor's created the first of its indexes with 233 U.S. stocks. Three years later it began daily publication of the capitalization-weighted 90 Stock Composite Price Index and then introduced its Standard & Poor's 500 Stock Index in 1957 (Standard & Poor's 2009).

In the late 1960s and early 1970s, publications such as Burton Malkiel's *A Random Walk Down Wall Street* (Malkiel 1973) popularized academic research showing that professional money managers charging substantial fees did not consistently outperform stock market benchmark indexes.[1] This academic research led to the creation of the first index mutual fund, launched by the Vanguard Group at the end of 1975 and modelled on the S&P 500 Index. John Bogle founded Vanguard, now one of the largest mutual fund companies in the United States, with the explicit goal of launching indexed stock products. 'The firm I had founded in 1974', he explains

> was focused on low cost, precisely the key to having an index fund that would emulate a cost-free index. It was the opportunity of a lifetime: to prove that the basic theory

> enunciated in these [academic research] articles could be put into practice and made to work in a real-world framework.
>
> *(Bogle 1999)*

Today index investing is one of the most popular investment strategies for institutional investors. Index providers now offer hundreds of thousands of different indexes. Financial products based on these indexes now have trillions of dollars under management. As of 2014, for example, MSCI alone offered over 100,000 indexes covering a broad range of asset classes, and the Vanguard Group alone had more than $1 trillion in indexed stock funds under management (Vanguard Group 2014).

Given the success of indexes in the investment marketplace, it is not surprising that the number of responsible investment indexes has also grown and that most of the major index providers have entered the market for RI indexes.

Definition and functions of RI indexes

Like traditional financial indexes, RI indexes serve three fundamental purposes. First, they define the markets available to responsible investors. These RI markets may be defined by region (e.g., North America, Europe or Asia), by size or style (e.g., large cap or small cap, growth or value), or by sector (e.g., clean technology, alternative energy, or water). Second, they provide tools for the creation of low-cost, passive RI vehicles (e.g., RI index funds or exchange-traded funds). Third, they provide asset-based benchmarks against which the performance of RI managers can be measured.

RI indexes have four additional characteristics that distinguish them from traditional indexes:

- They define standards for responsible policies and practices at corporations or other issuers of securities. The social and environmental criteria for inclusion on a RI index become de facto definitions of responsible behavior.
- They encourage companies to improve their social and environmental policies and practices. The reputational value of being included in these indexes motivates companies to make such improvements.
- They answer the question of whether the inclusion of these standards in stock selection helps or hurts performance. They make possible the apples-to-apples comparison of the performance of RI indexes with traditional indexes.
- They identify a universe of corporations that meet particular RI standards within given markets or for certain issues. They can therefore become the basis for the creation of a variety of RI investment products or services.

The use of RI equities indexes has grown substantially since the launch in 1990 of the first responsible equities index, the Domini 400 Social Index (now the MSCI KLD 400 Social Index). In addition, RI indexes for other asset classes are increasingly being developed. For example, in June 2013, MSCI and Barclays announced the creation of an extensive family of fixed-income indexes (MSCI 2013a).

Growth of RI stock indexes

RI stock indexes have grown in number and popularity over the past 25 years, from the launch of the first in 1990 to the more than 170 that have been created by index providers and stock exchanges around the world.

As of 2014, four of the dominant index providers worldwide had RI indexes on the market. The Dow Jones Sustainability Index family included 20 indexes representing a variety of markets around the world (RobecoSAM 2014a). The FTSE4Good family of responsible indexes included 16 responsible investment indexes (FTSE 2014). Standards & Poor's offered 13 environmental, social and governance (ESG) indexes (McGraw Hill Financial 2014a). And MSCI maintained a family of some 90 RI equity indexes (MSCI 2013).

In addition, according to research by the Sustainable Stock Exchanges initiative, some 40 per cent of the 55 stock exchanges around the world it reviewed maintained at least one index integrating social and/or environmental factors as of 2014, and seven required all their listed companies to report on various aspects of their social and/or environmental records (Principles for Responsible Investment 2014, p. v). One leader in the creation of socially responsible investment (SRI) stock exchange indexes has been the JSE (Johannesburg Stock Exchange), which launched its SRI Index in 2004 (JSE 2013).

Three methods for RI equities index construction

RI stock indexes are currently constructed using three different methods for selecting companies for inclusion. These are the best-in-class, values-based and themes-based approaches.

The 'best-in-class' approach is used, for example, by the Dow Jones Sustainability family of indexes. Its basic principle is to include in its various global and regional indexes the most sustainable companies in each industry. This research method was developed by RobecoSAM (formerly SAM Group),[2] which was based in Zurich in the late 1990s, and its first RI index was launched in 1999.

The best-in-class approach excludes no industries per se. This allows institutional investors to be diversified across all sectors of the economy. Because some investors concerned about sustainability require tobacco-free, nuclear-weapons-free or similar exclusionary indexes, Dow Jones will create customized indexes upon request. In answer to the question 'Why best in class?' RobecoSAM's answer is:

> Because sector-specific sustainability opportunities and risks can play a key role in companies' long-term success. Aside from the selection of the sustainability leaders on the basis of clearly defined criteria, the best-in-class approach also provides SAM with the opportunity to conduct a dialogue with companies from all sectors and thereby influence incremental improvements in companies' sustainability practices. Thanks to the best-in-class approach, a vibrant competition among companies for inclusion in the Dow Jones Sustainability Indexes has ensued. To be included or remain in the index, companies have to continually intensify their sustainability initiatives. SAM believes this approach will benefit all stakeholders: investors, employees, customers and, ultimately, society and the environment.
>
> *(RobecoSAM 2014a)*

The distinguishing elements of this approach are RobecoSAM's assertion that strong sustainability records can be equated with long-term success; the use of a scoring system across multiple issues relating to multiple stakeholders to rate and rank the strength of a company's sustainability initiatives; the ability of this scoring system to direct corporate managers' attention to specific ESG issues, including those that are sector specific and for which they can improve their scores by taking clearly defined steps; and the arousal of the natural competitive instincts of corporate managers to be considered best in their class.

To select the members of its indexes, RobecoSAM sends questionnaires to some 2,500 companies globally each year. The questionnaire poses 80–100 questions, about half of which are industry specific with a focus on "companies' long-term value creation". It then scores the companies on their responses to these questions. Giving equal weighting to the scores in the economic, environmental, and social sectors – and slightly more weight to industry-specific factors than general issues – RobecoSAM then aggregates these specific scores into an overall score for the company. Companies are then ranked on these aggregated scores relative to peers in their industry. At the same time RobecoSAM conducts media and stakeholder analyses of issues relating to company controversies and can adjust its rankings depending of the nature of this additional information. RobecoSAM then includes in these indexes those companies scoring in the top 10 per cent for each industry in its RI indexes (RobecoSAM 2014b).

The values-based approach begins from a different premise: companies must pass certain values-based thresholds to qualify for inclusion. This approach is used, for instance, by the FTSE-4Good family of RI indexes. The research methodology for these indexes was developed by FTSE in collaboration with the UK-based research firm EIRIS. The first of its indexes was launched in 2001.

In the values-based approach only companies that meet certain broadly agreed-upon social or environmental standards, no matter what their industry, are included. For a given industry, all, none or some of the companies might be included depending upon which meet threshold requirements for these values-based standards. In selecting firms for its indexes, FTSE4Good employs absolute thresholds. These thresholds include standards for environmental sustainability, human rights, supply chain labour rights, countering bribery and mitigating and adapting to climate change. EIRIS ranks each industry as high, medium or low in its impact in relation to each standard and sets higher thresholds for companies in the higher-impact industries. It originally excluded all tobacco, weapons, nuclear power, infant formula, and uranium mining, although it subsequently limited the excluded industries to tobacco and weapons (FTSE Group 2011, p. 9).

The key objectives of this approach to RI index creation are, according to FTSE4Good:

- To provide a tool for responsible investors to identify and invest in companies that meet globally recognized corporate responsibility standards
- To provide asset managers with a socially responsible investment benchmark and a tool for socially responsible investment products
- To contribute to the development of responsible business practice around the world

FTSE4Good employs two methods for encouraging responsible corporate behaviour. First, it gradually and deliberately raises the bar for inclusion in each of its five areas of focus. Its policy committee strengthened the environmental criteria in 2002, human and labour rights in 2003, supply chain labour rights in 2004, counter-bribery criteria in 2006 and climate change criteria in 2007.

In addition, it engages with companies to encourage them to meet its values-based criteria in each area.

> As new standards and requirements are introduced FTSE informs affected companies to help them understand the changes they need to make, and by when, in order to maintain inclusion in FTSE4Good. This takes the form of letters, emails, calls and meetings to provide guidance and support as they work towards meeting the tougher ESG standards. The result of a company not keeping pace with the new criteria – deletion from the FTSE4Good index – is also made clear.
>
> *(FTSE Group 2011, p. 11)*

A 2012 study by the University of Edinburgh Business School found that within three years of introducing more stringent environmental management criteria, of over 1,000 firms evaluated on FTSE4Good's criteria, 49 per cent of the subset engaged by FTSE4Good had reached the new standard, while only 23 per cent of the remaining firms did so (Mackenzie 2012).

In the theme-based approach an index is created around a single RI theme such as clean technology, alternative energy or water. Standard & Poor's, for example, offers a family of ESG indexes. Among these are seven green investment indexes, including two water indexes, two eco indexes, and three carbon-efficient indexes.

The criteria for inclusion in these indexes are related to the companies' core businesses and not to explicit or implicit environmental or social values or sustainability scores. These indexes in fact look much like traditional sector indexes that give investors overall exposure to certain sectors of the market that may or may not have financial appeal at any given time. The S&P Global Water Index, for example, is approximately 40 per cent water utilities and 50 per cent industrial companies involved in water-related businesses (McGraw Hill Financial 2014b). Some of these themes, however, might permit the inclusion of companies that some responsible investors find problematic. For example, carbon-efficiency funds could include large oil companies working to reduce their carbon footprint, eco-funds might include controversial waste management firms, and so on.

Because these theme-based indexes are similar to traditional sector-based index products, a substantial number of financial services firms and stock exchanges maintain them. Nasdaq/OMX, for example, offers a family of Green Economy Indexes and the Bombay Stock Exchange launched a carbon-themed index in 2012. A number of high-profile financial services companies have launched RI-themed index funds, including Merrill Lynch (Energy Efficiency Index) and Barclays Capital (Global Carbon Index).

While these RI index methods represent distinctly different approaches, the line between these approaches can also become blurred, and they may be employed in a variety of combinations and permutations. MSCI, for instance, maintains a family of approximately 90 RI indexes that, instead of employing a single standard for RI index construction, adapts all three of the above approaches in a variety of ways to serve the needs of varying RI investors. Thirty-one are maintained according to a best-in-class method, including 50 per cent of the market capitalization of all industries and regions while screening out companies that are rated poorly in their industry or have encountered major controversies. Twenty-six are described as socially responsible indexes. They completely eliminate companies in the nuclear power, alcohol, tobacco, gambling, weapons, firearms, adult entertainment and genetically modified organism (GMOs) industries, while simultaneously including the top-rated companies without major controversies that represent up to 25 per cent of the market capitalization of the remaining industries. Its Global Environmental Index is made up of five thematic indexes that include companies deriving at least 50 per cent of revenues from alternative energy, sustainable water, green building, pollution prevention or clean technology. Its Global Climate Index is an equal-weighted index of 100 companies that are leaders in mitigating climate change. Twenty-seven other indexes simply eliminate manufacturers of controversial weapons (e.g., cluster bombs, land mines). MSCI maintains its own in-house RI research staff, whose research is used in support of these indexes.

New RI indexes and index-maintenance methodologies continue to be introduced. In 2013, for example, the United Nations Global Compact launched its Global Compact 100 Index, which includes 100 large companies from around the world that have made notable efforts in the implementation of the Global Compacts core principles.[3] Also in 2013, STOXX, the European-based index development specialist, launched its EURO iSTOXX 50 SD-KPI Index, which includes all 50 stocks on the EURO-iSTOXX 50 Index, but overweights or underweights them by up to 30 per cent of their weighting in the traditional index depending on their sustainable development key performance indicator (SD-KPI) scores developed by SD-M, GmbH, in cooperation with the German Environment Ministry, accountants and global investors and analysts (SD-M no date).

Contributions and challenges of RI indexes

The fundamental contributions that RI indexes can be said to make lie in three primary areas:

- They call the attention of corporate management to ESG issues that might otherwise go unnoticed.
- They provide guidelines to best practice in the development and implementation of ESG policies and practices, particularly those that help align companies' actions with broadly recognized, long-term goals of society.
- They provide investors with tools to distinguish among companies on their relative ESG performance.

In addition, because the creators and maintainers of RI indexes must be transparent about their methods and practices, these indexes not only create definitions of the markets available to RI investors, but also create definitions of responsible investment itself. These de facto definitions of responsible investment, in turn, provide a forum for ongoing public debate on what constitutes a responsible corporation and, equally important, what constitutes a responsible investor.

Because RI indexes are part of the rapidly growing practice of index or 'passive' investment, they are subject to some of the criticisms that traditional indexing increasingly faces. Since the 2008–12 financial crisis, a number of market observers have pointed out some of the unintended consequences of the widespread use of indexing. "[I]ndex funds are a force for inefficiency", notes *Financial Times* columnist John Authers,

> as they make no attempt to spot which stocks are over- or under-valued, and instead accept the market's judgment. When bubbles start, index funds automatically buy more overpriced stocks, and sell stocks that are underpriced. If internet stocks are rising and displacing industries that generate real profits, then index funds must dumbly buy them and make the mispricing all the worse. If managers at a company misbehave, index funds do nothing to stop them, even though the capitalist system relies on shareholders, the companies' owners, to enforce good behavior.
>
> *(Authers 2010, p. 21)*

With something like 30 per cent of the equities market now indexed – for example, as of September 2010, of the $3.5 trillion in equity mutual fund assets, $1.2 trillion was passively managed in index or exchange-traded funds (Sullivan 2012, pp. 70–84) – such criticisms are worth serious consideration.

One of the implications of the argument of Authers and other critics of indexing is that indexers, who often consider themselves long-term investors because they employ buy-and-hold trading strategies, actually contribute to short-termism in the stock markets. Simon Zadek has described this counterintuitive situation as turning indexers into "perpetual investors making short-term investments forever" (World Economic Forum 2005, p. 19). That is to say, if the markets are short-term in their perspective – driven by investors who set prices based only on companies' short-term prospects – index investors in effect continually validate these short-term perspectives by purchasing and selling stocks at whatever today's prices may be.

In 2012, the *Financial Analysts Journal* published an analysis of the effects of the increased predominance of indexing in the stock market – research needed because the authors noted that "We know so little about the consequences of the growth in index investing – for example, how it affects underlying market liquidity, volatility, and price discovery. . . ." (Sullivan 2012, p. 71). The authors found certain adverse market effects that began in approximately 1996, about the time that institutional investors began allocating substantial portions of their equity portfolios to indexing:

> Whatever the drivers behind the observed rise in index-related investing [at that time], the result is higher systematic, common trading across a basket of many stocks simultaneously, which means increased overall market risk via higher pairwise stock price correlations and lower dispersion of changes in trading volume.
>
> *(Sullivan 2012, p. 75)*

In other words, because market baskets of stocks are all traded at the same time in the same direction (i.e., all sell or all buy), stock prices as a whole in these markets not surprisingly tend to move together in an undifferentiated manner (i.e., all up or down by the same amount). By 2005, the net effect of this trend was to eliminate much of the difference in the price movements between pairs of stocks, as well as the difference in trading characteristics between large and small capitalization companies and between value and growth stocks. This increased correlation produces what the authors termed "an undesirable effect on markets" (Sullivan 2012, p. 70). They concluded that because of these effects "the fragility of the U.S. equity market has risen over the decades" (Sullivan 2012, p. 83).

RI indexers can be said to avoid these criticisms to a certain extent. The number and variety of RI indexes, each holding different constituents even within the same markets, in and of itself provides some assurance that RI indexers, unlike conventional indexers, are not in effect buying (or selling) the same baskets of stocks simultaneously. In addition, although it is true that they do not attempt to value individual stocks within indexes as they make their indexed trades, they do in effect provide feedback to management in the use of ESG criteria to guide the selection of those stocks that are included in their indexes. The application of these criteria sends clear messages to corporate managers on which ESG policies and practices are valued by RI indexers and which are not.

Furthermore, RI indexers often use their role as stockowners to communicate actively with management on particular ESG issues. For example, the UN-backed Principles for Responsible stresses the importance of proxy voting and engagement as well as the use of indexes that "integrate ESG factors into index design and management" (Principles for Responsible Investment 2011, p. 4).

Communication can take place on three levels. First, if whole industries are excluded, companies understand that RI investors have concerns about the basic business model of those industries. Second, if companies are rated and ranked by ESG or sustainability factors, companies understand which factors are important to investors and to what degree. Third, if the creators/maintainers of RI indexes engage with companies on specific issues, managers are compelled to evaluate and articulate the specifics of their policies and practices on these issues. Over its first 10 years, for example, FTSE reports having made over 1,000 attempts to engage companies and influence their business or disclosure practices, with a success rate of 60 per cent.

One further criticism occasionally made of RI indexes is that RI practitioners cannot in fact agree upon, or indeed even identify, companies that are truly 'responsible'. For example, at the time of the BP Deepwater Horizon explosion and oil spill in the Gulf of Mexico, a number of RI indexes and money managers held BP, while others did not. It is in fact not unusual for one RI index to hold companies that another does not. Critics ask, how can this be so if the concept of corporate responsibility is to have any meaning?

One response to this criticism is that these differences of opinion form the basis for a much needed informed public debate on what are the responsibilities for corporations to society and its stakeholders beyond the narrow world of stock owners. The debate about what constitutes responsible behaviour for particular companies in particular industries at particular times should in fact be an ongoing one. A variety of RI indexes transparently discussing their selection methodologies provides a useful mechanism for provoking and conducting this ongoing debate.

A second response is that the ultimate goal of responsible investment is not to identify and promote responsible corporations as such, although that is certainly an important part of RI's practice. RI's ultimate goal is to identify and promote responsible investors as such. That is to say, to promote within the investment community the concept that investors have an obligation to understand that their investment decisions inevitably have social and environmental implications, and that at certain times and under certain circumstances these implications rise to a level of concern that action on their part is appropriate. That responsible investors understand and act upon that obligation, not that their actions are identical, is of primary importance.

Conclusion

RI indexes serve a valuable role in the investment marketplace as a means for encouraging debate about what constitutes responsible behaviour by corporations and by investors, as well as for setting ESG standards for their conduct. In addition, these indexes provide opportunities for the creation of a variety of financial vehicles for responsible investors. Given the importance of well-informed corporate policies and practices to the social, environmental and economic progress of the world today, not to mention the similar importance of responsible behaviour by the investment community itself, and at the same time the continuing success of conventional indexes, it is likely that the world of RI indexes and their related financial products will continue to grow in the coming decades.

Notes

1 In 1974 Fischer Black and Myron Scholes published an article in *The Journal of Finance* arguing that only gamblers or fools would try to beat the market and that both "would probably be better off holding at least some of their money in a market portfolio". The article went on to document some of the practical difficulties that money managers at Wells Fargo had in creating the first market-based index portfolios. They found that "The major problems . . . were the costs of dealing with government restrictions on investment companies in general and bank-affiliated investment companies in particular, and the costs of selling. The costs of management were important, too, because the increased the break-even size for the fund' (Black 1974, p. 404). Other early pioneers in the index fund markets were Batterymarch Financial Management and American National Bank in Chicago.

2 In 2013, ORIX Corporation, a Japanese financial services firm, acquired Robeco Asset Management.

3 See press release 'UN Global Company Launches Stock Index'. Online, available HTTP: <http://www.sustainalytics.com/un-global-compact-launches-stock-index> (accessed 29 October 2014).

References

Authers, J. (2010) *The Fearful Rise of Markets: Global Bubbles, Synchronized Meltdowns, and How to Prevent Them in the Future*, Upper Saddle River, NJ: FT Press.

Black, F. and Scholes, M. (1974) 'From theory to a new financial product', *Journal of Finance* 29(2): 404.

Bogle, J. (1999) *Common Sense on Mutual Funds*, Hoboken, NJ: John Wiley & Sons.

Dow Jones (2013) *Dow Jones History*. Online. Available HTTP: <http://www.dowjones.com/history.asp> (accessed 28 October 2014).

Dow Jones (2014) *Dow Jones Transportation Average*. Online. Available HTTP: <http://www.djaverages.com/?go=transportation-overview> (accessed 28 October 2014).

FTSE Group (2011) *Ten Years of Impact Investment*. Online. Available HTTP: <http://www.ftse.com/products/downloads/FTSE4Good_10_Year_Report.pdf> (accessed 29 October 2014).

FTSE Group (2014) *FTSE4Good Index Series*. Online. Available HTTP: <http://www.ftse.com/Analytics/FactSheets/temp/25b435e7-e154–4598-a232–3d6b873b8fa8.pdf> (accessed 28 October 2014).

JSE (2013) 'The JSE Socially Responsible Investment (SRI) Index promotes sustainable and transparent business practices'. Online. Available HTTP: <https://www.jse.co.za/services/market-data/indices/socially-responsible-investment-index> (accessed 29 October 2014).

Mackenzie, C., Rees, R. and Rodinova, T. (2012) 'The FTSE4Good effect: the impact of responsible investment indices on environmental management'. Online. Available HTTP: <http://papers.ssrn.com/sol3/papers.cfm?abstract_id=1966474> (accessed 29 October 2014).

Malkiel, B. G. (1973) *A Random Walk Down Main Street*, New York: W.W. Norton & Co.

McGraw Hill Financial (2014a) 'S&P Dow Jones indices: environmental, social and governance – all'. Online. Available HTTP: <http://us.spindices.com/additional-reports/all-returns/index.dot?parentIdentifier=52481e0f-3d70–4d5b-a6d6-468e51efe131&sourceIdentifier=index-family-specialization&additionalFilterCondition=> (accessed 28 October 2014).

McGraw Hill Financial (2014b) 'S&P Global Water Index'. Online. Available HTTP: <http://us.spindices.com/indices/equity/sp-global-water-index> (accessed 29 October 2014).

MSCI (2013a) 'Barclay's MSCI fixed income indices – product launch'. Online. Available HTTP: <http://www.msci.com/insights/responsible_investing/barclays_msci_esg_fixed_income_indices_-_product_launch.html> (accessed 28 October 2014).

Principles for Responsible Investment (2011) *Responsible Investment in Passive Management Strategies: Case Studies and Guidance*, London: United Nations Principles for Responsible Investment.

Principles for Responsible Investment. (2014) *Sustainable Stock Exchanges: A Report on Progress*, London: United Nations Principles for Responsible Investment.

RobecoSAM (2014a) 'DJSI family overview'. Online. Available HTTP: <http://www.sustainability-indices.com/index-family-overview/djsi-family-overview/index.jsp> (accessed 28 October 2014).

RobecoSAM (2014b) 'Corporate sustainability assessment'. Online. Available HTTP: <http://www.sustainability-indices.com/sustainability-assessment/corporate-sustainability-assessment.jsp> (accessed 29 October 2014).

SD-M GmbH, 'SD-KPIs'. Online. Available HTTP: <http://www.sd-m.de/en/sd-kpis.htm> (accessed 29 October 2014).

Standard & Poor's (2009) 'A history of Standard & Poor's'. Online. Available HTTP: <http://www.standardandpoors.com/about-sp/timeline/en/us/ > (accessed 28 October 2014).

Sullivan, R. N. and Xiong, J. X. (2012) 'How index trading increases market vulnerability', *Financial Analysts Journal* 68(2): 70–84.

Vanguard Group. (2014) 'Index equity: overview'. Online. Available HTTP: <https://institutional.vanguard.com/VGApp/iip/site/institutional/investments/equityoverview> (accessed 28 October 2014).

World Economic Forum (2005) *Mainstreaming Responsible Investment*, Geneva: World Economic Forum.

41

Challenges in responsible investment research

Matthew Haigh

Introducing the research challenges in responsible investment

As a field of practice, responsible investment has most often been designated as a niche investment style or labelled as corporate social responsibility (CSR). Neither is completely incorrect. What is responsible investment? The research has stumbled on a definition. Descriptors such as sustainable, responsible, social and environmental that may preface finance and investment can, it seems, sideline finance and investment into areas that are ill-defined (and which may seem unhelpful to the career paths of scholars interested in the area!). It seems fair to state that the research on responsible investment – and those that would participate in the research – face problems of aim, scope and nomenclature. Whatever the researcher's 'home' research field or teaching department, a researcher in responsible investment needs to recognize the existence of differing definitions of core concepts in the field, and differing relevancies accorded to those definitions.

As important are questions for the field, namely: questions of method, timing and the specific circumstances in which investing and financing activity can connect with sustainability and responsibility. Solutions to problems of social responsibility in the current era of globalized markets have, if unsurprisingly, sought refuge in market-based ideas. Shamir (2008) develops a concept of 'responsibilization' to describe contemporary tendencies to economize public domains and methods of government. This becomes a convenient working definition of responsible finance.

Examples of responsibilization are manifold in finance. The shifts of retirement provision from private provision in the first half of the twentieth century to a public governmentality in the post-war period to the current return to private arrangement is one.

Responsibilization has accompanied the rise of fiduciary capitalism in the latter half of the twentieth century. It is in this period that the recognizable form of responsible investment arrived. This is a version of fiduciary investment that widens its fiduciary scope to include notions of the public good and the public interest. Cochran (1974) characterizes the public interest along a spectrum of four types: normative, abolitionist, consensualist and process types. The normative view is necessarily consistent with the concept of the common good bound in the welfarist state. At the other end of the spectrum, the abolitionist views the public interest as an orientation toward the maximization of private interests. Responsible investment covers both spectrums, causing scholars and practitioners enormous problems as a result.

We turn now to consider the related multiaspect problem of sustainability. Costanza and Roberts (1995) use three questions to unravel sustainability:

- What system or subsystems or characteristics of systems persist?
- For how long?
- When do we assess whether the system or subsystem has persisted?

Sustainability and responsibility intersect when sustainability is treated as taking responsibility for preserving the stock of wealth a society might lay claim to, including facilitating networks or social capital, and ecological systems. The fields of responsible investment research become many: financial services, financial economics, corporate governance and social and environmental accounting are stalwarts. Contributions can also be counted from organizational change management, business innovation, organizational leadership, identity formation, business education, intercultural value theory, project management, entrepreneurship and social auditing.

New connections between these fields echo what Tim Cadman (2011) refers to as participatory governance structures: those that sustain activity and widen the parameters used as yardsticks for valid research. Success in interdisciplinary terms is hardly measurable in terms of a consensus on, for example, an ideal of the highest rate of financial return or an ideal of a heavily cited and therefore high-quality interdisciplinary research journal. When responsibility is treated as what is at stake rather than the mechanisms devised to deal with a paucity of responsibility, successful research on financing and investing activity is measurable in terms of social analysis.

As a place to start understanding how responsibility and sustainability might play out in the capital markets, and what that means to scholars working in these areas, Costanza and Roberts' questions above seem promising. These questions are likely to prove useful to considering the ways sustainability and responsibility articulate with investing and financing activity. This chapter applies these questions to the trajectories of at least three refereed journals that cater for researchers on responsible investment: the *Journal of Business Ethics*, the *Journal of Environmental Investing* and the *Journal of Sustainable Finance & Investment*. All three journals are interdisciplinary, recent and illustrate certain challenges that exist for editors and authors seeking to publish the results of responsible investment research. Those challenges are examined in what follows.

How publications have treated responsible investment

The *Journal of Environmental Investing*, financed by a Scandinavian energy company, is a biannual, open-access, online-only publication. The journal focuses on, as its title suggests, environmental aspects of responsible investing. The journal's objective is one of "creating, deploying, financing, structuring, and managing successful market-based solutions to the environmental challenges of today". Partiality more than impartiality describes a focus "to facilitate the flow of capital to solutions to problems arising from natural resource depletion, pollution, demographic changes, sustainability, and climate change". The journal's authors are practitioners rather than academic researchers, and have come from asset management, investment analysis, economics and policy. Recent issues have commented on carbon emissions permits trading schemes and the UN environmental programme. The journal's aims and scope dovetail with those of established scholarly journals such as *Ecological Economics*, *Climate Policy* and *Energy Policy*.

The print-based *Journal of Sustainable Finance & Investment* (published by Routledge) is a subscription-based, quarterly, scholarly journal. Its editorial board numbers scholars working in the disciplines of finance, geography, law, policy, accountancy, sociology, ethics and social entrepreneurship. Its express aims and scope are to critique the practices and theories of responsible investment. Responding to calls for new understandings on finance's hold on modern life (see, for example, Callon, 2009; Forslund and Bay, 2009; Baumol, 2005; Bernstein, 1996), the journal seeks to put together a new research project. The project is new in the sense that the coupling of sustainability and responsibility with investing and financing suggests a need for ontological interrogation.

Work in critical finance studies and the social studies of finance has produced occasional anthologies and conference proceedings. Responsible investment has also been the subject of special issues and thematic issues of investing, finance and business journals. Examples include:

- *Business & Society*
- *Competition & Change*
- *Journal of Applied Portfolio Management*
- *Journal of Investing*
- *Journal of Investment Consulting*
- *Journal of Portfolio Management*
- *Journal of Private Equity*
- *Journal of Wealth Management*

There are also suggestions that special book-length editions and edited collections of scholarly articles are increasing in frequency. Recent examples of edited collections include *Finance and Sustainability: Towards a New Paradigm: A Post-Crisis Agenda*, edited by Sun, Louche and Pérez (2011), and *The Cambridge Handbook of Institutional Investment and Fiduciary Duty*, edited by Hawley et al. (2013).

Ad hoc book-length editions tailored to professional education markets have been published by various research centres and are too numerous to list. An example is *The Handbook on Climate-Related Investing across Asset Classes*, edited by LaVoie and Wood (2009) and issued by Boston College's Institute for Responsible Investment.

Nonacademic markets offer, for example, *GreenMoney Journal* and, hailing from Australia, *Ethical Investor.*

Challenge one

It would seem that responsible investment research faces daunting problems of legitimacy. The idea of an expanded scope of social responsibility for intermediated finance challenges conventional finance and economic theory, leading some to discount the field as trivial, as seemingly out of place. Further, the notion of embedding moral, other-directed values inside the world of financial investment has aroused the derision of sociologists, ethicists and organizational theorists.

In response, the *Journal of Sustainable Finance & Investment* and work in critical finance studies and social studies of finance provide platforms for interdisciplinary approaches, such as found in economic sociology, and a spectrum of relevant applied research methods. The *Oxford English Dictionary* defines investment as "giving one's capital a new form" and "to endow with a quality or characteristic". Financial capital in Marxist terms is both an enabler and a destroyer of various forms of capital: social, cultural, financial and economic. Recognition of the unsustainability and irresponsibility of finance (in these terms) requires an impartial voice that seeks to strengthen debate and deepen the research.

Research on companies that have issued social responsibility 'reports' into the public domain has successfully transplanted to the responsible investment research field, and looks set to remain an important subfield of research. Transparency, for some academic accountants and financiers, is the name of the game (e.g., Dillenburg et al., 2003). For others, there is more interest in examining the lens through which investing and financing activity is understood. Scholars working on the frame through which financial activity is understood have directed attention to the institutional arrangements that dictate much of the activity of capital markets (e.g., McGoun, 2002).

Challenge two

A systemic perspective is useful to answer our three questions from above: What system or subsystems or characteristics of systems persist? For how long? When do we assess whether the system or subsystem has persisted? These questions do not automatically beget a need for more sophisticated portfolio analysis. "We do not need better financial tools; rather, we need to see these tools" (Forslund and Bay, 2009, p. 296) for their effects and the meanings that they create.

Rescher (1998) understands complex adaptive systems as composed of interconnected components, the interaction of components and their relation with an environment in which they operate. This becomes a useful addition to definitions of responsibility and sustainability in the capital markets. Schematic concepts of 'sustainability problems' and 'responsibility problems' suggest that a scholarly approach to these problems must be transdisciplinary. Understanding financing and investing activity as complex adaptive systems allows for the positive, creative aspects of dissensus, contradiction, multiplicity, plurality and interdisciplinarity. This will without doubt shock some scholars. A need for transdisciplinarity introduces a within-discipline challenge for researchers located in finance departments, accounting departments, political science, economics, and so on.

If the factors to be included in a responsible and sustainable investment framework are equitable distribution of resources (wealth), and the preservation and remediation wherever possible of ecological systems, then research on sustainable financing and investing activity means to address the cycle of resource appropriation and selective distribution which that activity engenders and on which it depends. This suggests an extremely broad research program, one that academics seeking to publish in top-ranked journals in any particular field might be loath to embrace.

Even so, scholars engaged in the responsible investment field must come to terms with its epistemological and career challenges. The difficult dialectic between other-directedness and wealth generation suggests there might be value in interrogating the concept of wealth. Aristotle recognized that money symbolizes wealth without being wealth (1992, Book I). Wealth is that which we lay common claim to; the wealth of the planet, the wealth of relationships and of a well-functioning group (*oikos*). The pursuit of monetary returns on financial investment for its own sake is something that Aristotle condemns. Money is a mere means to achieving a secure *oikos*.

Responsible investment in these lofty terms means to respond to a belief that legal, financial, trade and business practices pursue a common end, not individualized ends. And yet, in a competitive, globalized economy, fiduciary finance means to provide for select groups, not whole societies. Scholars grappling with the dialectic this poses may feel forced to choose between, for example, corporate social responsibility and the career trajectory that might promise, and, as another example, publishing in the *Journal of Finance* and the career trajectory that might promise.

The next section is used to consider possible, and desirable, interconnections between sustainability, responsibility, financing and investing, and between research and practice.

How scholars and publications might approach responsible investment

It would seem that an interdisciplinary mobilization of researchers is needed. Academics, practitioners and policy makers could be connecting more than they have been in the past. Research on responsible finance necessarily extends beyond traditional discipline-focused study. Ecological thinking in terms of the interconnected thinking advocated by Félix Guattari (2008) permits critique of institutional effects on the agency of responsible investment, its theoretical concepts and its analytic goals and practices. Critique (rather than the usual consensus in finance research) is permitted, and encouraged. This is because the concept of ecological-cum-interconnected thinking "foregrounds the institutional context, its constraints, organizations, practices, etc. – all those things and relations which normally exist in the background" (Genosko, 2008, p. 51). Foregrounding the social environment of the financial institution, be it midtown Manhattan or Dhaka, makes explicit the institutional features that characterize practiced responsibilities and their social ramifications, referring to the effects of an ethics of responsibility on practitioners and researchers, as well as investors' goals (e.g., to improve workplace conditions in companies and stem damage to natural ecological systems).

The aims and scope of responsible investment research necessarily direct attention to institutional and policy connections between a range of financing and investment activities – from regulation of securities exchanges and financial institutions to the behaviour of venture capitalists that finance social development projects. The inherent flexibility of the definition of responsible investment permit differing and shifting value systems. This will represent a challenge to practitioners and scholars alike; even so, flexibility of definition is a durable characteristic of the field and should be looked on for the opportunities it represents.

Traditional disciplinary problems of quantifying and predicting economic returns to investors are, particularly in the top-ranked finance journals, grounded in a neoliberal conception of social value that consists of (a) achieving maximal economic wealth generation, then (b) distributed that wealth through institutional arrangements (principally, taxation receipts and social welfare) to reach the furthest corners of society. Alternatives such as an expanded role of the state, and a flexible definition of fiduciary portfolio management, are given extremely short shrift. The transdisciplinary nature of responsible investment, however, requires that researchers and publication outlets value dissensus and accord legitimacy to varying value systems.

Conclusion

Outlets publishing the outcomes of research on responsible investment occupy an odd place in the research publication ecosystem. Their legitimacy is shaped by research departments' conceptions of responsible investment definitions, conceptions that depend on the definitions of responsible investment. Surely, the slipperiness of defining the field is related to the uncomfortable realization that much of financing activity is *un*sustainable and irresponsible. This leads to a further challenge shared by researchers and practitioners.

Challenge three

The fund manager with a niche product will not want other financial products to dilute its potential market share, and so will continue to identify a need for reform. The challenge this dialectic represents for the fund manager is that she or he now has a vested interest in financing activity that she or he considers as unsustainable and irresponsible. Ergo, the problem of legitimacy described above (Challenge One) comes to the fore. The popularity of the Principles for Responsible Investment and the CDP (formerly known as the Carbon Disclosure Project) bears witness to this dialectic. This is a dialectic, it is suggested, that has led to a common conception of responsible investment as finance in need of reform.

On the scholarly side, as academics develop a scholarly field, they become reluctant to abolish the state of affairs on which their publication plans depend. CSR scholars need the world to remain in need of CSR. Scholars aiming for top-ranked finance journals and researching in responsible investment may feel a need to relegate their interest in this field and concentrate on the rigorous, if narrow, field of financial economics.

So it can be seen that researching in responsible finance and investment requires that the researcher adopt a certain ethics of responsibility. If the researcher is to analyze and reflect on the transforming capacity of financial capital, it should not be impertinent to reflect on transformations of self "in relation to transcendent forces, whether they be higher values, moral codes, authoritarian knowledge, political correctness, academic manners, common sense, implicit presupposition" (Forslund and Bay, 2009, p. 285). Reflexivity renders the researcher as much as her or his research object vulnerable, open to charges of hypocrisy, of not 'walking the walk'.

This might account for the absence of considered ontological debate in the top-ranked finance journals. Questioning the ways of life imposed by investing and financing have never been posed by any of the leading finance journals, although tirelessly answered by all of them (Froud and Johal, 2008). Outlets that publish sustainable and responsible investment research should encourage authors to reflect on relevant contradictions and compromises, on the differences between the values that underlie a life that 'sustains' and that underlie financing and investing activity.

Commentators have noted that the leading finance journals have ignored the contractual and cultural aspects of sustainable and responsible financing activity, preferring to focus on the salience of environmental, social and governance issues for economic performance. Overt disconnects between finance and other disciplines, and also within the finance discipline, suggest relevant problematics for a new research program. The very oddness of a proposition that, for example, financial intermediation networks should contribute to societal responsibility might create spaces for imaginings that will be needed for criticism and transformation.

A new mobilization of researchers, it would seem, is called for. If bridging the meanings of responsibility, investment, sustainability and financing is at all important and desirable, then academics, practitioners and policy makers should be connecting more than they have been. Academics working in the multifarious fields that inform financing and investing activity should be connecting more than they have been. Researchers need to acknowledge a responsibility to accept the divergent approaches of others and to connect with other disciplines. Application of a multi- and interdisciplinary approach to responsible investment is the work of a new and invigorated research program.

References

Aristotle (1992) *The politics*, London: Penguin Books.

Baumol, W. J. (2005) 'Errors in economics and their consequences', *Social Research* 721: 169–194.

Bernstein, P. L. (1996) *Against the gods: The remarkable story of risk*, New York: John Wiley & Sons.

Cadman, T. (2011) 'Evaluating the governance of responsible investment institutions: An environmental and social perspective', *Journal of Sustainable Finance & Investment* 1(1): 20–29.

Callon, M. (2009) 'Civilising markets: Carbon trading between in vitro and in vivo experiments', *Accounting, Organizations and Society* 34(3–4): 535–548.

Cochran, C. E. (1974) 'Political science and 'the public interest'', *Journal of Politics* 36(2): 327–355.

Costanza, R. and Patten, B. C. (1995) 'Defining and predicting sustainability', *Ecological Economics* 15: 193–196.
Dillenburg, S., Greene, T. and Erekson, O. H. (2003) 'Approaching socially responsible investment with a comprehensive ratings scheme: Total social impact', *Journal of Business Ethics* 43(3): 167–177.
Forslund, D. and Bay, T. (2009) 'The eve of critical finance studies', *ephemera* 94: 285–299.
Froud, J. and Johal, S. (2008) 'Questioning finance': A special issue of *Competition & Change*. Editorial', *Competition & Change* 122: 107–109.
Genosko, G. (2008) 'The life and work of Félix Guattari: From transversality to ecosophy', In Guattari, F. *The three ecologies*: 46–78.
Guattari, F. (2008) *The three ecologies*, Trans. I. Pindar and P. Sutton, London and New York: Continuum.
Hawley, J. P., Hoepner, A.G.F., Johnson, K. L., Sandberg, J. and Waitzer, E. J. (eds.) (2013) *The Cambridge handbook of institutional investment and fiduciary duty*, Cambridge: Cambridge University Press.
LaVoie, V. and Wood, D. (2009) *Handbook on climate-related investing across asset classes*, Boston: Institute for Responsible Investment at the Boston College Center for Corporate Citizenship.
McGoun, E. (2002) 'Resistance is futile: The assimilation of behavioral finance', *Journal of Economic Behavior & Organization* 48(4): 375–389.
Rescher, N. (1998) *Complexity: A philosophical overview*, London: Transaction Publishing.
Shamir, R. (2008) 'The age of responsibilization: On market-embedded morality', *Economy and Society* 37(1): 1–19.
Sun, W., Louche, C. and Pérez, R. (eds.) (2011) *Finance and sustainability: Towards a new paradigm: A post-crisis agenda*, Bingley, UK: Emerald.

42

The natural environment

Ralf Barkemeyer and Andrea Liesen

Introduction

The vital role of the natural environment for the continued survival of mankind has been well documented in the popular media and epistemic communities: the natural environment provides the ecosystem services and the resource base to support any type of economic and social activity. The increasing threats the natural environment is exposed to are equally well documented. According to the Millennium Ecosystem Assessment (2005), approximately 60 per cent of global ecosystem services are degraded, with this degradation expected to continue at an accelerated rate. The loss of biodiversity, marine and air pollution, over-fishing, soil erosion, increasing water scarcity, deforestation, landfill waste and, most prominently, climate change all have to various degrees been recognized as vital problems which need to be addressed to ensure the life opportunities of current and future generations.

Against the backdrop of these mounting environmental pressures, the essential role of the natural environment for any type of economic activity has long been theorized in the management literature. It has also been captured by stakeholder theory, conceptualizing the natural environment as one stakeholder of the company (Table 42.1). However, very different views exist within the stakeholder literature as to whether and in what way the natural environment should be considered a stakeholder. As illustrated in Table 42.1, two dominant positions are the normative perspective, defining stakeholders as "any group or individual who can affect or is affected by the achievement of the firm's objectives" (Freeman, 1984: 25), and the instrumental perspective, defining stakeholders as those "on which the organization is dependent for its continued survival" (Freeman and Reed, 1983: 91; cf. Donaldson and Preston, 1995).

Using this debate as a starting point, the aim of this chapter is to illustrate how the natural environment differs from conventional stakeholders and to spell out the implications this dissimilarity has for the prospects of responsible investment to effectively address different environmental concerns. Following a brief overview of the academic debate of whether the natural environment should be considered as a stakeholder of the firm, its relevance in the context of responsible investment will be discussed. Subsequently, the impact of (a) inherent characteristics of environmental problems, (b) the social construction of their perceived importance and (c) their

Table 42.1 The natural environment as a stakeholder of the company

What is the purpose of this stakeholder group in society?	*Ecosystems support, resource base*
What are the three most relevant examples of this stakeholder group?	Climate change, water scarcity, pollution and degradation of ecosystems are commonly perceived as paramount environmental concerns.
What characterizes the behaviour of this stakeholder group?	Agency; the natural environment as a 'dependent' stakeholder

value-relevance will be analyzed. The chapter concludes with summarizing comments on the ability of responsible investment to effectively address different types of environmental concerns.

The natural environment as a stakeholder of the company

A number of authors have repeatedly argued that the non-human natural environment should be treated as a stakeholder of the firm (Driscoll and Starik, 2004; Haigh and Griffiths, 2009; Starik, 1993, 1995). This argument has commonly been made on the grounds that the firm cannot survive without its continued support. Hence, the natural environment bears some similarity with Clarkson's (1995) definition of primary stakeholders. Based on this characteristic, Driscoll and Starik (2004) go even further and argue that the natural environment should be recognized as a 'primordial'; that is, the most important of the firm's primary stakeholders. However, what these perspectives have in common is that they were published as reactions to the widespread perception that the natural environment should not be categorized as a stakeholder (cf. Phillips and Reichart, 2000; Starik, 1995).

Donaldson and Preston's (1995) distinction between normative and instrumental stakeholder perspectives serves well to illustrate this common perception that the natural environment is not a stakeholder of the firm: from a normative perspective, companies ought to integrate environmental concerns into their decision-making. Unfortunately, these normative insights do not necessarily translate into environmental responsibility. From an instrumental perspective companies will not be able – or even willing – to satisfy all demands of all of their stakeholders. Instead, they are likely to prioritize their most salient stakeholders; that is, they address the most powerful, urgent and legitimate claims (Mitchell et al., 1997).

Mitchell and colleagues (see Mitchell et al., 1997) develop a framework of stakeholder identification and salience based on these three attributes: power, legitimacy and urgency. They identify seven conceptually distinct stakeholder types that differ in terms of their salience and thus the extent to which they require the attention of managers of the firm. Curiously, the natural environment is categorized here as a "dependent" stakeholder: using the example of marine mammals, Mitchell and colleagues (1997, p. 877) argue that these are holding urgent and legitimate claims but are lacking the power to enforce these claims. In other words, whilst they grant stakeholder status to marine mammals, they acknowledge that these can never become salient stakeholders without the support of other, more powerful, stakeholders. In a similar vein, Hart and Sharma (2004: 7) categorize the natural environment as "fringe stakeholder", alongside "the poor, weak, isolated [and] non-legitimate"; that is, other stakeholders that lack salience.

Irrespective of the question of whether the natural environment – including our marine mammals – should be considered as a fringe stakeholder (Hart and Sharma, 2004), a dependent stakeholder (Mitchell et al., 1997), a primary stakeholder (Haigh and Griffiths, 2009; Starik, 1995) or even a primordial stakeholder (Driscoll and Starik, 2004), it is obvious that the natural environment differs significantly from conventional stakeholders such as employees, shareholders, governments, consumers or the media. In essence, the natural environment cannot interact or actively apply pressure on the firm. Rather, it has to rely on the agency of sufficiently salient stakeholders to make its claims heard.

The problem that the natural environment depends on the agency of other stakeholders does not necessarily represent a problem for environmental concerns per se. Increasing levels of environmental awareness have triggered the emergence of environmental consumers and rising numbers of environmental pressure groups (Rawcliffe, 1998) that have proven to be salient agents for the environment. Numerous campaigns, usually focusing on specific environmental issues or targeting particularly polluting companies, have successfully encouraged companies to align their actions with the interests of the natural environment that have been brought forward by other stakeholders. Partly as a result of pressure groups, and to move beyond this ad hoc character of the environmental movement, an increasing institutionalization of environmental concerns has taken place in most, if not all, nation-states over the last four decades. The creation of national ministries for the environment, the formation of green parties, tightening environmental legislation and the increasing integration of non-governmental organizations into legal procedures in many countries have institutionalized and formalized the integration of environmental concerns into national and international policy arenas.

One result of the actions of salient stakeholder may be that costs to the environment are internalized, as with, for example, the European Emissions Trading Scheme (European Commission, 2010), which has pushed the debate on how the internalization of costs to the environment impacts company and investment returns (Carbon Trust, 2006). In addition, beyond these predominantly regulatory mechanisms, and triggered by key events such as the Brundtland Report in 1987 or the Rio Summit and the launch of the World Business Council for Sustainable Development (WBCSD) in 1992, a new wave of primarily voluntary instruments and initiatives or 'governance beyond government' (Rosenau and Czempiel, 1992) has taken centre stage in the last two decades. Among these instruments, responsible investment has emerged as a potentially powerful mechanism to assemble investors that act as an agent for the natural environment.

Responsible investment and the natural environment

The natural environment only surfaced as a focal point of responsible investment beginning in the 1990s. Traditionally based in religious and political motivations, responsible investment (RI) has more recently been captured by investors concerned about the environment and/or seeking profit opportunities in green investing. The increasing emergence of thematic environmental funds, commonly focusing on clean technologies, renewable energy, water or climate change performance, is a good example in this context. In the academic literature the question of whether it is financially rewarding to invest in environmentally well-performing companies has been researched under the overarching question of whether it pays to be green. Overall, no consensus has been reached in this stream of literature with regard to the relation between corporate environmental and financial market performance. The discrepancy in existing findings is commonly argued to be rooted in major differences in the underlying research designs of respective studies (cf. Horváthová, 2010; Ullman, 1985).

Nevertheless, some interesting findings support the argument that the agency of other stakeholders has transformed information on a company's relation to the natural environment into information that is relevant to its financial market performance. For example, the effects of negative events such as oil spills and positive environmental events such as environmental awards on stock prices has been researched in an event study by Klassen and McLaughlin (1996). They found significant negative abnormal returns when firms experienced environmental crises and positive returns when firms received environmental awards. Similar findings were reported in an event study by Shane and Spicer (1983), who found that the release of rankings on corporate pollution control records resulted in more negative returns for companies with low pollution controls. Hamilton (1995) found significant negative abnormal returns on the day that the toxic release inventory was announced for the first time.

Especially with a view to the expenses for clean-up operations, fines, regulatory risk and reputational damage that may occur as a result of negative environmental effects, event study findings suggest that the financial market incorporates reduced profit expectation for poor environmental performers (cf. Ambec and Lanoie, 2008). In other words, the value-relevance of this respective information on corporate environmental performance aligns the interests of the natural environment as a stakeholder of the company with the interests of mainstream investors. There is also mounting evidence that investors in the long term are rewarded – or at least not punished (Olsson, 2007) – for investing in an environmentally responsible manner. For example, Derwall, Guenster, Bauer and Koedijk (2005) evidenced an annualized alpha of around 6 per cent for a strategy that buys a best-in-class environmental portfolio and sells a worst-in-class environmental portfolio.

These findings support the process of mainstreaming responsible investment in the context of the natural environment and give rise to an interesting argument of Heinkel, Kraus and Zechner (2001, p. 447). The authors showed that if a sufficiently large number of investors refuse to hold stocks of polluting firms, the cost of capital of the respective firms would rise, thus incentivizing polluting firms to change to more environmentally responsible business practices. The argument of Heinkel, Kraus and Zechner is, however, only applicable to those environmental concerns considered important by a sufficiently large number of investors.

The perceived importance of environmental concerns determines the salience of other stakeholders on which the natural environment relies and consequently the ability of RI to effectively address concerns of the natural environment. Investors, representing an important stakeholder group, can have a different motivation to act as an agent for the environment. In very general terms, their agency can be the result of ethical considerations or profit-seeking behaviour. Along these lines, two different types of responsible investors can thus be identified: value-driven and profit-seeking investors (cf. Derwall et al., 2011). For value-driven investors, ethics rather than financial considerations shape the perception of the importance of an environmental concern. For profit-seeking investors, the importance of an environmental concern is determined by its relevance to the intrinsic value of the firm. In the following, it is argued that the unequal representation of environmental concerns in RI is a result of the perceived importance of environmental concerns by different types of investors.

Unequal representation of environmental concerns

As pointed out above, the willingness of investors to represent environmental interests can be based on ethical or profit-seeking considerations. In order to act as an effective agent for the environment, a sufficient number of investors need to perceive an environmental concern as a worthwhile issue to address. Notwithstanding the continued mainstreaming of responsible investment in general, not every type of environmental concern is likely to be perceived as important by a sufficient number of investors. Instead, some environmental concerns can be expected to be prioritized at the expense of others, based on (a) their underlying characteristics, (b) context-specific perceptions of stakeholders and, ultimately, (c) their value-relevance in a responsible investment context. Whilst these three aspects are interrelated, the former two can be expected to be more relevant for value-driven ethical investors, whereas the latter aspect is of foremost importance to profit-seeking investors. In essence, they result in an unequal representation of environmental concerns in responsible investment and consequently limit the likelihood of responsible investment to integrate specific environmental concerns. This unequal representation is not necessarily specific to responsible investment, but also impacts, for example, public opinion or policy responses, which, in turn, also contribute to shaping the RI agenda. It does, however, also serve directly as a significant barrier to the extent to which responsible investment will be able to deliver environmental sustainability.

Characteristics of underlying problems

Previous studies in policy and media research have shown that different environmental issues attract public awareness in varying degrees (Enchloe, 1975; Neuman, 1990; Solesbury, 1976). Along these lines, some environmental issues are more likely to be perceived as important, and consequently incorporated into the responsible investment agenda, by responsible investors. Public pressure to act, which is likely to correspond to the perceived importance of an environmental concern in responsible investment, is to a certain extent determined by the degree to which a problem lends itself to 'politicization' (see, for example, Jänicke and Weidner, 1995; Weidner and Jänicke, 2002). Aspects such as the time frame and urgency of the problem or its visibility have proven to impact the prospects of a problem being placed on the political agenda (ibid). It did not come as a surprise that the Chernobyl catastrophe, as an immediate and urgent concern, triggered a response that was very different from respective policy responses to problems such as biodiversity or soil erosion. The pressure to act is also determined by the extent to which the problem can be 'generalized' and 'particularized' (Solesbury, 1976): a problem can be generalized if it can be linked to a broader context or problem and is potentially applicable to a wider audience. Particularization refers to the prospects of the problem appealing to specific actor groups that lobby or campaign for respective solutions.

Furthermore, problems that can be measured face improved prospects of being placed on the political agenda (Enchloe, 1975). For example, one difficulty climate change activists faced in recent years was that due to the complex interdependencies and multitude of influencing factors that cause climate change it has been very difficult to establish the extent to which specific activities contribute to global warming. Hence, it proves difficult to measure and assess both the problem and the extent to which specific activities are likely to contribute to it.

Unfavourable actor constellations can also serve as a barrier to effective solutions. If a powerful societal group expects to be negatively impacted by specific actions to solve a socioeconomic or environmental problem, this is likely to restrict the options for society to address the problem. The difficulty of cutting down transport-related environmental impacts can serve as a case in point. Environmental concerns involving a win-win situation are generally more likely to be solved successfully than situations that involve trade-offs between actors. A further restriction to the effective solution of an environmental problem is the lack of an affordable and standardized technical fix. It does not come as a surprise that most notable success stories in the field of environmental policy can be found in cases in which end-of-pipe technologies could be applied to minimize impacts (cf. Jänicke and Weidner, 1995; Weidner and Jänicke, 2002). For example, the successful phasing out of ozone-depleting substances in the 1990s has to a large extent been attributed to the availability of readily available substitutes (ibid).

Looking at broadsheet newspaper coverage between 1990 and 2010 can illustrate the varying degrees to which different environmental problems have managed to attract media attention. A range of models have been developed that theorize the relationship between public awareness and public policy (Baumgartner and Jones, 1991; Dearing and Rogers, 1996; Downs, 1972;

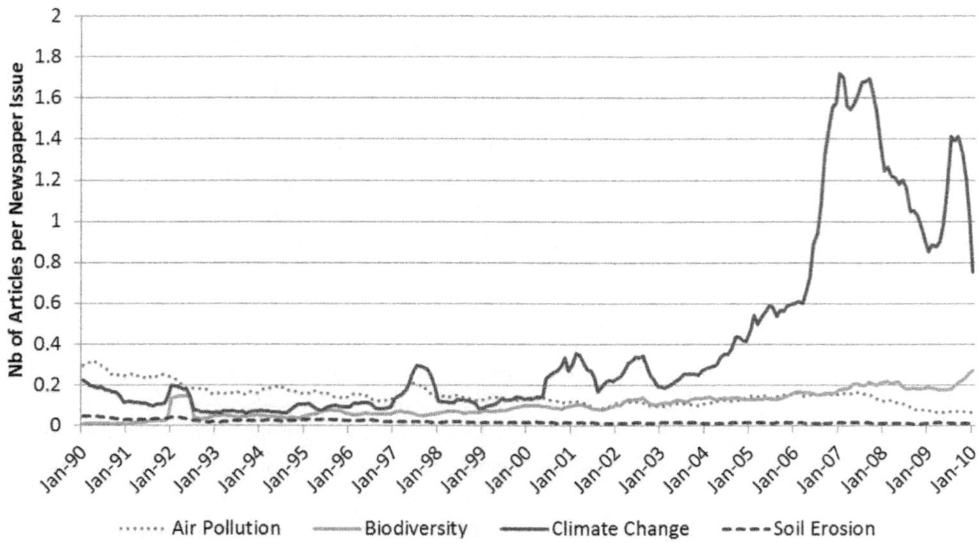

Figure 42.1 Trends in broadsheet newspaper coverage (January 1990–January 2010, 6-month moving averages; 115 leading international broadsheet newspapers)

Source: www.trendsinsustainability.com. Please see Barkemeyer et al. (2009, 2013) for information on the underlying methodology and sample.

Neuman, 1990; Yanovitzky, 2002). Here, it is commonly assumed that high levels of media coverage are indicative of high levels of public awareness: items that are high on the public agenda are more likely to be addressed by policy-makers. It is safe to assume that levels of public awareness and unequal representation of environmental concerns in the media have similar implications for the responsible investment agenda.

Figure 42.1 serves to illustrate that different environmental challenges are likely to receive different amounts of public attention based on their underlying characteristics. It shows the development of coverage of the four environmental concerns – air pollution, biodiversity, climate change and soil erosion – in 115 major international newspapers between the years 1990 and 2010. There is an unprecedented rise in coverage on climate change increasing from below 0.3 articles per issue on average in the 1990s to a maximum of 2.3 articles per newspaper issue in recent years. Air pollution emerged as the dominant of the four environmental issues in the early 1990s. In stark contrast to climate change, however, coverage on air pollution has steadily decreased throughout the period. Apart from increased coverage around the Rio Summit in 1992, biodiversity only slowly increased over the last two decades; at the far other end of the spectrum, soil erosion only rarely finds its way into international broadsheet newspapers. Environmental problems that fail to gain recognition in the public sphere are less likely to be addressed by public pressure groups and policy-makers. Consequently, they are also less likely to be incorporated into the responsible investment agenda.

Social construction of environmental problems

The perceived importance of an environmental issue is not solely linked to its underlying characteristics. Instead, it is important to note that levels of public attention are typically context specific, as the severity and urgency of specific environmental concern can differ dramatically in different countries and regions. In addition, the urgency and severity of a specific environmental

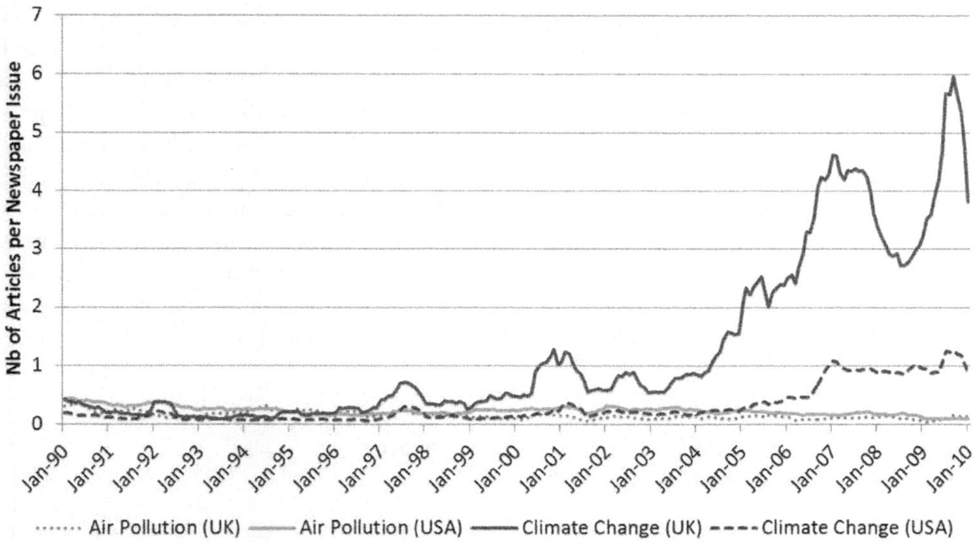

Figure 42.2 Trends in US and UK broadsheet coverage (January 1990–January 2010, 6-month moving averages; various newspapers, climate change and air pollution)

Source: www.trendsinsustainability.com.

concern is to a certain extent socially constructed: whether a problem is recognized as such is likely to be determined by a range of contextual factors such as levels of economic development, the existence of competing environmental and socioeconomic challenges, the existence of environmental policy institutions or of a politically independent middle-class or the strength of environmental NGOs (cf. Jänicke and Weidner, 1995; Weidner and Jänicke, 2002).

Figure 42.2 illustrates the socially constructed nature of different environmental challenges, resulting in different sustainability agendas in different contexts. Shown are the levels of coverage on climate change and air pollution in a sample of major UK and US broadsheet newspapers between 1990 and 2010.

In very general terms, similar patterns can be identified in the two countries with climate change–related coverage accelerating dramatically towards the end of the 20-year period and air pollution becoming an increasingly marginal issue over time. However, a number of marked differences can also be identified. Most notably, climate change–related coverage reached markedly higher levels in the UK in the 2000s and picked up at an earlier stage. In contrast, air pollution generally appeared to be a slightly more widespread topic in the US, albeit at a significantly lower level.

The socially constructed importance of climate change as an environmental concern is likely to have influenced the responsible investment agenda differently in the UK and the US. For example, Aguilera et al. (2006) hint at the fact that institutional investors in the UK emphasized issues such as climate change at an earlier stage than their US counterparts.

Value-relevance of environmental concerns

The level of public awareness and the prospects of an environmental concern to be placed on the political agenda are also likely to be indicative of the perceived importance of an environmental concern to the profit-seeking investor. Awareness determines the ability of an environmental concern to affect the intrinsic value of firms. For example, reputational and regulatory risks that might impact the financial performance of companies are more likely to exist in areas of high public and political awareness. For profit-seeking responsible investors, the existence of a business case linked to a specific environmental concern is also likely to impact its relevance to the responsible investment agenda. When there is an investment opportunity created by environmental concerns or on the basis of specific policy initiatives, in turn, changing the risk/return profiles of respective investments, profit-driven responsible investors are likely to act as an agent of the natural environment. The clean-tech sector can serve as one of the key examples in this context. In contrast, environmental concerns for which value-relevance is hard to establish are likely to have a low perceived importance to the profit-seeking responsible investor. The problem of soil erosion, which cannot be linked to regulatory or reputational risk nor to a clear business case, is a good example in this context.

Ability of responsible investment to integrate environmental concerns

In fact, RI practitioners seem to be well aware that responsible investment might lend itself to effectively address some types but not all types of environmental challenges. Figure 42.3 presents the results of a recent survey of 149 RI practitioners from various countries who were asked to rate the extent to which responsible investment lends itself to effectively addressing environmental challenges on a six-point Likert scale (cf. Barkemeyer et al., 2014). Cleaner technologies, climate change, as well as air and water pollution were scored comparatively high. These environmental challenges are altogether characterized by high levels of public awareness and high importance on the political agenda. In contrast, the comparatively imperceptible environmental challenges of marine ecosystems and soil erosion were found at the end of the scale. In other words, they were classified as environmental challenges that do not lend themselves to be effectively addressed by

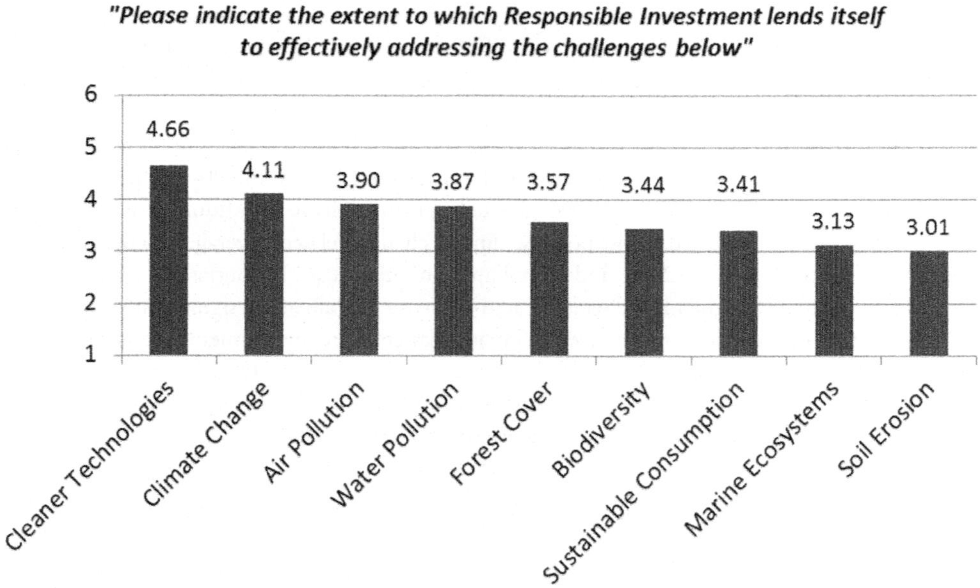

Figure 42.3 Survey of RI practitioners ($n = 149$)

responsible investment. Unless these latter challenges facing the natural environment are put on the public and political agenda through the agency of other stakeholders, responsible investment cannot be expected to effectively address them.

Conclusion

This chapter illustrated how the natural environment differs from 'conventional' stakeholders, as it depends on the agency of other stakeholders. Previous studies in the domain of policy and media research have been related to the perceived importance of environmental concerns that is likely to influence the responsible investment agenda. It has been argued that responsible investment practices are effective in addressing some environmental concerns, but are less likely to address environmental concerns that fail to attract the attention of both value-driven and profit-seeking investors. Ultimately, effective agency and the importance of an environmental concern to the responsible investment agenda depend on its value-relevance and the extent of stakeholder awareness.

References

Aguilera, R. V., Williams, C. A., Conley, J. M. and Rupp, D. E. (2006) 'Corporate governance and social responsibility: a comparative analysis of the UK and the US', *Corporate Governance: An International Review*, 14: 147–158.

Ambec, S. and Lanoie, P. (2008) 'Does it pay to be green? A systematic overview', *Academy Of Management Perspectives*, 22: 45–62.

Barkemeyer, R., Figge, F., Hahn, T., Hoepner, A.G.F., Liesen, A. and Neher, A. L. (2014) 'Operationalizing socially responsible investment: a non-financial fiduciary duty problem' in Hawley, J. P., Hoepner, A.G.F., Johnson, K. L., Sandberg, J. and Waitzer, E. J. (eds.), *Cambridge Handbook of Institutional Investment and Fiduciary Duty*, Cambridge: Cambridge University Press, 364–377.

Barkemeyer, R., Figge, F., Hahn, T. and Holt, D. (2009) 'What the papers say: trends in sustainability. A comparative analysis of 115 leading national newspapers worldwide', *Journal of Corporate Citizenship*, 33: 69–86.

Barkemeyer, R., Figge, F. and Holt, D. (2013) 'Sustainability-related media coverage and socioeconomic development – a regional and North/South perspective', *Environment and Planning C: Government and Policy*, 31: 716–740.

Baumgartner, F. R. and Jones, B. D. (1991) 'Agenda dynamics and policy subsystems', *Journal of Politics*, 53: 1044–1074.

Carbon Trust (2006) *Climate Change and Shareholder Value*, London: Carbon Trust.

Clarkson, M.B.E. (1995) 'A stakeholder framework for analyzing and evaluating corporate social performance', *Academy of Management. The Academy of Management Review*, 20: 92–117.

Dearing, J. W. and Rogers, E. M. (1996) *Agenda Setting*, Thousand Oaks, CA: Sage.

Derwall, J., Guenster, N., Bauer, R. and Koedijk, K. (2005) 'The eco-efficiency premium puzzle', *Financial Analysts Journal*, 61: 51–63.

Derwall, J., Koedijk, K. and Ter Horst, J. (2011) 'A tale of values-driven and profit-seeking social investors', *Journal of Banking and Finance*, 35: 2137–2147.

Donaldson, T. and Preston, L. E. (1995) 'The stakeholder theory of the corporation. Concepts, evidence and implications', *Academy of Management Review*, 20: 65–91.

Downs, A. (1972) 'Up and down with ecology – the issue attention cycle', *Public Interest*, 28: 38–50.

Driscoll, C. and Starik, M. (2004) 'The primordial stakeholder: advancing the conceptual consideration of stakeholder status for the natural environment', *Journal of Business Ethics*, 49: 55–73.

Enchloe, C. H. (1975) *The Politics of Pollution in a Comparative Perspective. Ecology and Power in Four Nations*, New York: David McKay.

European Commission. (2010) *Emissions Trading System (EU ETS)*. Online. Available HTTP: <http://ec.europa.eu/clima/policies/ets/index_en.htm> (accessed 3 April 2012).

Freeman, R. E. (1984) *Strategic Management. A Stakeholder Approach*, Boston: Pitman.

Freeman, R. E. and Reed, D. L. (1983) 'Stockholders and stakeholders: a new perspective in corporate governance', *California Management Review*, 25: 88–106.

Haigh, N. and Griffiths, A. (2009) 'The natural environment as a primary stakeholder: the case of climate change', *Business Strategy and the Environment*, 18: 347–359.

Hamilton, J. T. (1995) 'Pollution as news: media and stock market reactions to the toxics release inventory data', *Journal of Environmental Economics and Management*, 28: 98–113.

Hart, S. L. and Sharma, S. (2004) 'Engaging fringe stakeholders for competitive imagination', *Academy of Management Executive*, 18: 7–18.

Heinkel, R., Kraus, A. and Zechner, J. (2001) 'the effect of green investment on corporate behavior', *Journal of Financial and Quantitative Analysis*, 36: 431–449.

Horváthová, E. (2010) 'Does environmental performance affect financial performance? A meta-analysis', *Ecological Economics*, 70: 52–59.

Jänicke, M. and Weidner, H. (eds) (1995) *Successful Environmental Policy. A Critical Evaluation of 24 Cases*, Berlin: edition sigma.

Klassen, R. D. and McLaughlin, C. P. (1996) 'the impact of environmental management on firm performance', *Management Science*, 42: 1199–1214.

Millennium Ecosystem Assessment (2005) *Ecosystems and Human Well-being: Synthesis*, Washington, DC: Island Press.

Mitchell, R. K., Agle, B. R. and Wood, D. J. (1997) 'Toward a theory of stakeholder identification and salience: defining the principle of who and what really counts', *Academy of Management. The Academy of Management Review*, 22: 853.

Neuman, W. R. (1990) 'The threshold of public attention', *Public Opinion Quarterly*, 54: 159–176.

Olsson, R. (2007) *Portfolio Performance and Environmental Risk*, MISTRA Foundation.

Phillips, R. A. and Reichart, J. (2000) 'The environment as a stakeholder? A fairness-based approach', *Journal of Business Ethics*, 23: 185–197.

Rawcliffe, P. (1998) *Environmental Pressure Groups in Transition*, Manchester: Manchester University Press.

Rosenau, J. N. and Czempiel, E. O. (1992) *Governance without Government. Order and Change in World Politics*, Cambridge: Cambridge University Press.

Shane, P. B. and Spicer, B. H. (1983) 'Market response to environmental information produced outside the firm', *The Accounting Review*, 58: 521–538.

Solesbury, W. (1976) 'Issues and innovation in environmental policy in Britain, West Germany and California', *Policy Analysis*, 2: 1–38.

Starik, M. (1993) 'Is the environment an organizational stakeholder? Naturally!', in Pasquero, J. and Collins, D. (eds.) *Proceedings of the Fourth Annual Meeting of the International Association for Business and Society*, San Diego, 466–471.

Starik, M. (1995) 'Should trees have managerial standing? Toward stakeholder status for non-human nature', *Journal of Business Ethics*, 14: 207–217.

Ullman, A. A. (1985) 'Data in search of a theory: a critical examination of the relationships among social performance, social disclosure, and economic performance of U.S. firms', *Academy of Management Review*, 10: 540–557.

Weidner, H. and Jänicke, M. (2002) *Capacity Building in National Environmental Policy. A Comparative Study of 17 Countries*, Berlin, Heidelberg, New York: Springer.

Yanovitzky, I. (2002) 'Effects of news coverage on policy attention and actions: a closer look into the media-policy connection', *Communication Research*, 29: 422–451.

43

What do we mean by the S in ESG?

Society as a stakeholder in responsible investment

David Wood

Introduction

The conventional definition of responsible investment (RI) proposed by the UN-backed Principles for Responsible Investment (PRI) is the integration of environmental, social, and governance (ESG) information into investment decision-making. The motives for integrating ESG are typically presented by practitioners as an effort to improve long-term investment performance by better assessing the investment risks and opportunities posed by long-term environmental and social trends or highlighting indicators that better identify quality of management in corporations or investment intermediaries. Summed up in the words of one practitioner:

> Today's institutional approach to responsible investment starts from the observation that a range of environmental and social issues are increasingly significant in business and investment terms. Issues such as climate change, water stress, resource scarcity, ageing populations, and human rights in supply chains are shaping markets, consumer preferences and government regulation. Companies need the right governance to align their strategy with these trends and protect their investors' interests.
>
> *(Hayat 2014)*

ESG, in other words, is enhanced investment analysis.

But there also resides in the theory of responsible investment a belief that the field itself is a step towards a better world, in which the integration of ESG information into investment decision-making is tied to greater social utility from financial activity. We see this in the preamble to the PRI, which makes a direct, if somewhat tenuous, link between the incorporation of ESG information into investment decision-making and beneficial long-term social outcomes – famously (at least in this small neck of the financial woods) declaring, "We also recognize that applying these Principles may better align investors with broader objectives of society" (PRI 2014). We can take the development of the Principles themselves, and their subsequent uptake by a large global set of asset owners, managers, consultants, and others, as at least an implicit affirmation that adopting responsible investment as a goal, and ESG integration as a tool, has some broad social benefit that non-ESG-related investing is unlikely to provide. Otherwise, why would advocates take the time to develop and support the Principles – and engage the investment community on the topic – in the first place?

The actions that would tie ESG incorporation to social objectives are not immediately clear in the six Principles themselves, which are focused on the mechanisms for, rather than the outcomes of, responsible investment. The language of the preamble – the alignment between investors and society – suggests a distinction between broad social objectives and the particular use of social information in investment decision-making. Put another way: the social (the S) in ESG is not the same thing as society, though the two are inextricably linked.

This chapter examines the sometimes uneasy relationship between the 'society' that is the object of 'broader objectives' and the social that is incorporated into ESG information and investment decision-making. It argues that the complicated relationship between enhanced investment analysis and social good found in responsible investment is particularly brought into relief by the S in ESG. It takes on the following two related issues:

- How investors incorporate social information – the S in ESG – into their decisions, and
- How investors take into account the effects of their investments on society.

The first focuses more operationally on criteria related specifically to human relations embedded in financial and business activity, and how such relations are financed and how information about them can inform investment strategy and tactics. The second refers to the overall benefits for human society that would come from a financial system more in tune with human needs.[1] Together they shed light on how social issues, and society, become relevant to responsible investment.

What constitutes the S in ESG?

As with the E and G, efforts to define the S in ESG typically list a set of issues that investors take into account when they integrate responsible investment into their investment practice. A PRI (2013) publication entitled *Integrated Analysis: How Investors Are Addressing Environmental, Social, and Governance Factors in Fundamental Equity Analysis* includes in a list of six social factors to illustrate the S in ESG corporate analysis: "consumer rights, supply chain management, health and safety, product safety, labour relations, inc. relationships with unions, [and] community/stakeholder relations".

A similar list, drawn from Clark, Feiner, and Viehs' 2014 article 'From the Stockholder to the Stakeholder: How Sustainability Can Drive Corporate Performance', adds to the list with: "controversial business, diversity issues, and responsible marketing and R&D".

These issues become ways to evaluate corporate performance or to define investment strategies. Again, as with the issues of E and G, these factors are taken to represent sliding scales. Be it supply chain management or responsible marketing, companies can have poor to excellent performance, and investors can set standards for good performance as criteria for determining potential investments.

However, RI practitioners often single out the S as a different kind of category from its peers. There have been dozens, if not hundreds, of conference panels, blog posts, listserv chats, and other discussions that pose the S in ESG as a problem to be solved. The assumptions behind these discussions often imply that:

- The E invokes issues such as carbon intensity or energy and resource consumption that are easily quantifiable and with comparable units of measure;

- The G invokes industry standards of board structure, shareholder rights, or standards of business ethics on which there is relatively widespread agreement in principle; but
- The S invokes issues which are often hard to quantify, not so clearly linked to the risk/reward analysis in investment decision-making, and may touch on culturally specific norms that do not so easily translate into guidance for (often globally focused) investment decision-makers.

When posed as a problem, the S may be seen as, to use two adjectives that pop up from time to time, 'softer' or 'mushier' than its counterparts – practitioners may claim both that the unit of analysis for social issues may more often be qualitative than quantitative and that the relationship to better long-term investment outcomes (as opposed to better social outcomes) is less clear (on mushiness of environmental, social, and ethical information, especially the S, see Hummels and Wood 2005). There may also be some sense that social issues are more likely to invoke ethical issues that lie beyond the scope of proper investment strategy or to require cultural judgments about potential consumer, reputational, or political risks that are particularly difficult to gauge (for a useful reflection on the ties between ethics and RI in practice, see Joly 2014).

For instance, in a representative account of the S, the Deutsche Bank Climate Change Advisors' report on the academic literature of responsible investment argues that:

> The social factor (S), sometimes (and incorrectly) confused with the overall SRI sector, may be the most difficult to quantify and has been subjected to the least academic and investor attention. . . . We believe the S factor deserves increasing academic and investor interest as its material relevance to the final output of a firm is increasingly relevant (i.e. human capital, health and safety, license to operate in a community) and social considerations may well offer potential for generating alpha.
>
> *(Fulton, Kahn, and Sharples 2012)*

The "confusion with the overall SRI sector" is intended by the authors to be read as a confusion of ethical and material investment criteria in investment decision-making, the difficulties in quantification, and yet salience of the topics to long-term returns are often linked in RI statements about the S. (The authors also note the findings of Eccles, Krzus, and Serafeim [2011] that at "the aggregate market level, there is greater interest in environmental and governance information than in 'social' information".)

Part of the tension or 'softness' of social issues may be related to the multiple sets of stakeholders that are encompassed by the analytical category of the S. We can differentiate at least three different stakeholder types bound up in the social factors listed above:

1. End users of company products (and the effects that products have on them),
2. Company employees or employees in the company's supply chain (and their relationship with the company in question), and
3. Stakeholders affected by company decisions (including people who live in places where the company works or communities that are affected by the company's activities or the effects of its products).

This breakdown of stakeholder groups offers a window into the broad range of information that is meant to inform ESG analysis on the social. In order to integrate the S into the analysis that encompasses these different stakeholder groups, an analyst would need to know something about the particular products a company makes and their attraction to and effects on consumers; the company's employee and labour relations practices and employee satisfaction; and its productivity performance; as well as a sense of community relations and stakeholder management practices. While these all fall under the heading of human relationships with a corporate entity or investment practice, they are very different kinds of relationships, carrying very different sorts of potential impacts on corporate or investment performance.

In the context of responsible investment, the S is meant to better evaluate how well positioned a company is for the long term, the reputational value it or its products gain from goodwill, the stability and long-term efficiency of its workforce, potential costs of labour conflicts, the political risk of conflicts with communities, the legal and reputational risks that it runs from potential problems with supply chain employment practices or community protests, and so on. In theory, this web of human relationships with the company offers critical information on the ability to manage long-term risks and opportunities, and can serve as an important proxy for quality of management that may not be found in corporate quarterly or annual reporting. But to make the investment analysis effective, investors have to have a solid handle on the legal and cultural norms that are likely to turn egregious social practices into risk factors or make superior social performance translate into corporate or investment value.

In sum, we might think of the S in ESG as a way to evaluate a corporation's (or other investable entity's) relationships with the people who are attached to or are affected by its actions. But, to do so, investors must have some sense not only of the corporate actions but also the likely stakeholder understanding and reaction to those actions. The S calls into particular relief the ways that investment value and the values of stakeholders intertwine. This can perhaps be seen more clearly by looking at the actual practice of integrating the S into investor decision-making.

Integrating the S into investor practice

How do investors incorporate the S into their investment decision-making? As noted, the range of social issues that falls under the heading is quite wide, and will require very different types of analysis to be made relevant for investment decision-making. We also see in the S a complicated interplay between responsible investment as a way to mitigate risk and identify material issues that better anticipate long-term performance and ethical issues traditionally associated with socially responsible investment that may be motivated by broader social concerns. As a result, we naturally find a variety of different ways of incorporating social concerns into investment practice.

Here I offer a quick snapshot of four such ways of incorporating the S into investment practice. The point here is not to provide a comprehensive account of the myriad examples of how social issues inform investment decisions, but rather to highlight the complex ways in which the idea of the social and society enter into responsible investment practice.

Integrating social information into valuation

There are many social issues that fit clearly into the vision of responsible investment as a method for improving long-term investment performance. One key area for social evaluation is workforce relations. As investors have adopted the phrase 'human capital' to explain their interest in the S (e.g. CalPERS 2012), issues such as employee satisfaction have become proxies for good management of one's workforce – and oft-cited research in the RI space such as the links between corporate performance and employee measures found in the Forbes 100 Best Companies to Work For list have reinforced the idea that long-term performance can be linked to stronger worker relations (Edmans 2011). Diversity reflected in gender, ethnic, and sexual orientation on company boards and in company workforces is argued to be a sign of effective management and able corporate culture. It has also received significant attention from responsible investors (see Keefe and Krawcheck 2014).

Social issues also extend across corporate supply chains, with examples in the garment and electronics industries of prominent media coverage of poor working conditions in offshore manufacturing plants that has posed reputational risks to corporations who purchase from those plants. Similarly, measures of consumer satisfaction and community relations can be incorporated into investment research, with corporate reputation seen as an important, if potentially intangible, driver of corporate value. For instance, conflicts with local communities over human rights issues or with workers over labour rights issues may point to areas where corporations face significant reputational risk or where fundamental social and political concerns emerge around the corporate 'license to operate'.

Workforce issues around health and human safety are used in responsible investment as important indicators of exposure to catastrophic risk to corporate reputation and legal liability (CWC 2012). A prominent recent example was the BP oil spill in the Gulf of Mexico in 2010. RI advocates have argued that the oil spill was the sort of 'preventable surprise' that ESG information could have mitigated, with the BP employee safety record as one example of the sort of information that could identify potential areas of catastrophic risk (Thamotheram and Le Floc'h 2012). Effects on consumers may play a similar role in risk evaluation – products that harm consumers should pose risks to long-term performance. The reverse of course is also true, and social issues might be used to identify companies with socially valuable products or community relations strategies, improving their valuation for ESG investors.

Social issues are used to evaluate potential corporate performance in different ways. They may be seen as proxies for good management, signals of long-term value generated from positive stakeholder relations or as indicators of the risk companies face from consumer backlash, legal trouble, or changes in the regulatory and political environment which affect company performance. Investors may choose to use social issues to weight company valuations or to identify issues around which to engage companies as shareholders in order to improve corporate performance on social issues. That the potential risks or benefits on which social information can shed light cannot always be easily measured does not mean that they cannot influence investment decisions.

When used as a guide to evaluation, there is an underlying belief (often backed by evidence) that when applying the S positive social outcomes for some set of stakeholders – whether consumers, employees, or citizens – will be correlated with either reduced risk, superior long-term investment performance, or, at the worst, comparable investment returns compared to conventional strategies. In other words, there are no responsible investors who argue that the integration of social issues into investment decision-making might allow investors to better profit from, say, those companies who are best situated to benefit from the exploitation of labour or indigenous communities. This can lead to overlapping motives for different sorts of investors: those concerned with ethical performance may choose to invest in companies with better consumer relations alongside those who believe that good community relations are a proxy for good corporate management. But even for the latter investors, investing solely on the belief that good community relations are material to investment returns depends on some set of stakeholders making ethical judgments about corporate behaviour or the possibility of future regulation that restricts the exploitative activity. For RI social criteria, there is a necessary link between an evaluation of what is good for society and the theoretically cold-hearted judgment of the investor seeking returns.

Incorporating social issues into investment mandates

Asset owners may integrate social issues into their investment mandates, shaping the criteria by which they select asset managers. Asset managers may create investment funds based on social criteria that distinguish their products. Rather than focusing on using social information to evaluate individual corporations or investment opportunities, these mandates, and the funds which execute them, create frameworks that determine which sorts of corporations or investments meet the standards which define an investable universe for a given strategy.

The tradition of exclusionary screens, drawing from the history of social investment, offers one clear example of this strategy (on screening as standard-setting, see Domini 2001). Social investors have designed investment strategies and funds meant to remove what they see as particularly socially harmful activities from their portfolios – a tradition drawn in the United States from faith-based investors' avoidance of sectors such as alcohol, gambling, and tobacco. The screen is a standard-setting exercise that removes investments from a portfolio. The goal of such exclusionary screening may be to remove morally objectionable activity from investment portfolios – such screens have been developed over time by the faith-based community of investors in particular. But they may also be based on the idea that over time the externalized costs of socially pernicious activity may be internalized into fund performance, whether through increased costs imposed by political and legal challenges or collateral harm to investment portfolios created by the cost of the activity itself. In any case, responsible investors will point to return studies which suggest that the financial costs of skilfully managed screening practices are negligible (for a quick guide to return studies, see Kurtz 2013).

Exclusionary screens are often portrayed by responsible investors as focused exclusively on ethical principles that are more political and/or moral than simply investment strategies. The archetypal example of targeted disinvestment in South Africa under apartheid exemplifies the political use of exclusionary screening. Investors shaped mandates to exclude investment in activity seen to economically support the apartheid regime because of the moral imperative of human rights (Seidman 2003). Similar campaigns in recent years, notably against investing in the Sudan, have led to investor action on the basis that human rights violations in the Sudan 'shock the conscience', and require action from investors not for financial but for moral reasons (Investors against Genocide 2014). It should be noted that here, too, it would be possible to argue that political and legal risk from business activities in pariah states might also create long-term risk to investment performance – the language of long-termism allows for many social issues to enter the realm of materiality.

But the practice of standard-setting, of which exclusionary screens form a part, has become inextricably linked to responsible investment and ESG in practice. For example, one developing trend in responsible investment is that of identifying particular social goals that can drive the design of investment mandates or funds, a practice that may take the name of 'impact' or 'targeted' or 'thematic' investment (PRI 2012). The investment universe of such a strategy is defined by those opportunities that deliver on specific social goals. Among the most prominent international examples of impact investment has been the development of the microfinance industry in emerging markets, built on the idea that impoverished communities suffer from a lack of, and would benefit from, access to finance. Responsible investors have also developed strategies and funds that target impoverished areas in developed markets, often through investment in commercial real estate development and small business lending that is meant to create good jobs in underserved communities or affordable and workforce housing development meant to allow higher living standards for people with limited resources (Daniels et al., 2007; Hebb and Sharma, 2014). A similar tactic may be seen in the adoption of responsible contracting policies that specify labour standards, for example, in real estate investments, that set standards for employee compensation and benefits in investee companies (for an example, see OPERS 2014).

Strategies that target specific social benefits may be based on the idea that, thanks to cultural bias or information asymmetry, there are unexplored opportunities in underserved areas: microfinance, for instance, has drawn on the language of the 'base of the pyramid' and the potential commercial opportunities in developing unopened markets among the world's poor; while targeted investment in the United States has drawn heavily on theories such as Michael Porter's that investors have failed to properly evaluate the competitive advantages of American inner cities, creating arbitrage opportunities for those who can invest well in inner cities (the seminal works are Prahalad 2004; Porter 1995). In other words, social value is presented as a core driver of a strategy's investment proposition.

But funds that target specific social benefits also draw on the language of 'collateral benefits'. In other words, strategies that incorporate social goals can deliver on those goals in addition to offering (potentially) competitive returns (as in Hagerman, Clark, and Hebb 2005). The differentiating factor for the strategy is not a business case built on social value but the delivery of social value itself, through the medium of a competitive financial instrument. This is the language adopted, for instance, by many funds that differentiate themselves by adhering to high labour standards or that target job creation (Croft 2009; LAPFF 2012).

The point here is that the 'social' enters into RI mandates and strategies through different channels. In some cases, the social creates a moral claim that guides investor practice. In others it provides the business case for investment strategies. And in still others social benefits are the targets of investments that are meant to be financially indistinguishable from the peers. These multiple motivations create measurement issues when the targeting of social goals is not undertaken with the sole purpose of achieving financial returns or mitigating long-term risk. How does one identify and measure social benefits or be sure that products based on 'bottom of the pyramid' or 'targeted investment strategies' actually deliver social benefits, rather than exploit the populations they are meant to serve?

This complex interplay of investment and the ethical reasons for these strategies is closely tied to extended debate over the constraints and obligations of fiduciary duties of investors as they relate to responsible investment. In cartoon form: sceptics argue that the fiduciary duty of care, limits investors such as pension funds from taking into account issues other than financial return and, in particular, binds analysis to an evaluation of financial risk and return derived from modern portfolio theory; advocates, in turn, claim that the duties of loyalty and impartiality to beneficiaries supports ESG integration as a means to improve long-term performance and also the environment in which beneficiaries will enjoy their retirement benefits. This simplified vision presented here is meant to illustrate two things: (1) the notion of long-term performance is an idea often used to resolve the potential tension between investment returns and social benefit and (2) this sort of debate over fiduciary duty manifests the sorts of shifts that responsible investment implies for conventional investment decision-making, including the need to take the long-term real-world consequences of investment into account (for a sophisticated set of essays on this topic, see Hawley et al. 2013).

Social norms and standards of practice

Along with integrating social issues and information into their investment decision-making, investors also participate in identifying and codifying best practices and standards of behaviour around key social issues. This may be done by identifying sets of principles that corporations are meant to adopt or against which their behaviour may be measured. Investors may adopt such corporate social responsibility standards as part of their investment analysis as the means to incorporate the S into corporate valuation (on investor roles, see Ambachtsheer 2011).

Responsible investors, and social investors before them, have looked to collaborative identification of principles and best practices for corporate behaviour as a tool for evaluation and engagement, often targeted at specific issues that have risen to the level of public concern. For instance, the Sullivan Principles, created by Leon Sullivan in 1977 to outline principles for equal treatment of workers regardless of race, were used by investors to engage companies active in apartheid South Africa. To those that subscribed to them, the Sullivan Principles came to define corporate norms, or at least the minimum acceptable standards, around the issue of equal treatment. They also gained currency in wider public debate through their use by investors (Human Rights Library 2014).

This sort of setting of standards has become an important part of responsible investment in practice, and a core way in which the S in ESG is applied. Investors collaborate to subscribe to, or to help create, standards that then become rules of thumb they can integrate into their evaluation of individual corporations or use in their development of investment mandates. These standards are often sector specific in application. Investors and human rights activists concerned about relations with local and indigenous communities, for instance, have worked together to develop best practices for Free and Prior and Informed Consent (FPIC), in an effort to define standards of corporate behaviour around engagement with (and payment to) local communities by the extractive resource industries (UN-REDD 2013). More recently, the fallout from disasters related to unsafe working conditions in garment factories in Bangladesh has led some responsible investors to ask for new norms of conduct for garment industry supply chains (ICCR 2014).

There are clearly close links between these norms and codes of conduct and the elaboration of corporate social responsibility (CSR) norms in the business community. Thus the development of organizations such as the United Nations Global Compact, which lays out principles for ethical corporate behaviour drawn from the Universal Declaration of Human Rights and the International Labour Organization's Declaration on Fundamental Principles and Rights at Work, among other sources, creates a means for investors to express their concerns around social issues. Adoption of the Global Compact as a guide to corporate best practice may provide investors a rule of thumb for identifying companies that at least claim to integrate social issues into corporate practice. It can also reinforce the idea that investors find social issues important in their decision-making. Further, it can allow a framework for engaging corporations on social issues when evidence suggests that they have not lived up to recognized standards of conduct detailed in the Global Compact (UN Global Compact 2014).

More recently, the development of the UN Guiding Principles on Business and Human Rights has created a framework for evaluating the private sector's role in ensuring human rights protections. Responsible investors have explored how to integrate these Guiding Principles into their interaction with companies in which they invest (UN Guiding Principles 2014). The Guiding Principles themselves become a standard against which to judge any particular corporate human rights concern, setting the terms of debate for investors who wish to raise standards of corporate behaviour around human rights, whether for ethical reasons or through the belief that a poor human rights record creates long-term political and consumer risk. They become the vehicle for investor–corporate dialogue on the topic.

The value of different forms of standard-setting, obviously, is a subject of much debate, especially where standards are voluntary and penalties for violating standards are hard to administer or toothless. My point here is not to evaluate the effectiveness of standard-setting, but to note that in practice the sorts of standard-setting described here have become a core part of integrating social issues into responsible investment. Investors have played key roles in promoting and developing standards as a way to set social norms. This is different from (though frequently complementary to) using social information to evaluate future corporate performance. Rather, investors, when involved in standard-setting, become active agents in developing the criteria against which performance will be judged, not just by the investment community, but by the broader group of stakeholders, including public sector officials, community advocates, consumers, and others, who create the kinds of political and reputational risk that investors evaluate. In other words, by adopting these standards, investors do more than just evaluate the role that social issues and actors play in determining corporate performance. They become active agents in making social issues relevant to corporate performance. Waitzer and Sarro (2014) have argued, in part building on arguments developed by Henderson and Ramanna (2014) for the corporate realm, that standard-setting by investors is a natural response to inadequacies in the public governance of investment markets, and the likely role of the 'future fiduciary' in light of investors' power in society and the need for stable social and financial systems in which to generate long-term sustainable returns. Following along this line of reasoning, standard-setting becomes a fundamental part of the active role that shareholders take in defining market performance as consonant with social goals.

Society as the context for investment

The last way that the S in ESG enters into responsible investment that I will touch on in this chapter is through the lens of society broadly, as the context in which investment takes place and in which investment returns are generated and the fruits of investment enjoyed.

Among the more prominent theories used in support of responsible investment is that of Universal Ownership, proposed by Robert Monks and elaborated by James Hawley and Andrew Williams (2000). The theory suggests that investors at scale (and the investment market in aggregate) are so large that they are invested not just in a set of companies, but also in the interrelated network of social systems that make up society. Their portfolio performance depends on the economic growth and social value that their investments, and therefore society, create in aggregate. Costs externalized by one set of investments onto society are likely to weigh down performance in other parts of the portfolio. By extension, 'universal owners' will only benefit when investments have positive social value. The means of implementing this theory are, of course, complex and contested, as there are not always clear and agreed upon ways to define the social value of investments. Nevertheless, the theory of Universal Ownership naturally leads responsible investors to an idea of 'society' and social value against which they can evaluate their investment decisions. If externalities are necessarily internalized, an obligation like fiduciary duty will lead investors to integrate ESG performance into their investment practice.

The lens of society also enters responsible investment through the idea of social macro-trends that will condition investment returns over the long term. In the same way that issues around, say, climate change and resource scarcity are macro-trends that investors use to determine how the E in ESG is integrated into investment decision-making, demographic changes such as rapid global urbanization, population growth, or aging populations also become the context in which investment decisions are (or should) be made.

Over the last few years, one of the most prominent social issues publicly debated has been the growing inequality of wealth and income. This issue has highlighted an accelerating trend that raises fundamental questions of fairness and is a potential source of social instability. The macro-trend of growing inequality has begun to enter RI discourse in the wake of research that suggests that high and growing levels of inequality may have deleterious effects on economic growth. Such effects include reducing effective consumer demand, promoting regulatory capture and speculative financial activity at the expense of real economic growth, or creating socially unstable conditions that create risk and uncertainty in economic activity. For these reasons, inequality has become a more frequent topic at RI conferences, and more frequently cited as a core social issue that investors should take into account. Again, as with the theory of Universal Ownership, it is not entirely clear how this concern translates into investment practice (Wood and Youngdahl 2014).

Finally, there are occasional instances where responsible investors point to society as the context in which investors enjoy the fruits of their investments – and therefore these investors see an obligation to consider the social effects of their investments not only because of the effects on long-term investment returns, but because the ultimate beneficiaries will suffer if they must spend their returns in worse social circumstances. An example of this vision of society as context can be found in the RI report of the Dutch pension fund PGGM, which includes the statement, "We firmly believe that contributing to a sustainable world is part of building a valuable future for those beneficiaries" (PGGM 2013). The dual meaning of 'valuable' in this context, tied to investment returns and the world in which they are enjoyed, projects the slipperiness in which responsible investment, in practice, can move back and forth between investment and ethical justifications for integrating ESG in general, and the S in particular.

Conclusion: the social and society as stakeholders in responsible investment

To sum up, the social plays at least four different roles in responsible investment:

1 Social issues are a lens with which to view corporate value, by identifying places where corporations or investments improve their financial performance through more effective management of human relations with employees, communities, or other stakeholders.
2 Social factors can be used to define investment mandates and strategies, shaping the investment universe for responsible investors.
3 Social norms (held by particular stakeholder groups, or society at large) create risks and opportunities for investors, for instance by determining levels of consumer or political risk.
4 Social objectives are themselves goals that investors can try to achieve through financial instruments, for instance by targeting socially beneficial activity, avoiding socially harmful investments, or generally taking into account the social consequences as well as expected financial results when making their decisions.

From the perspective of the business case for responsible investment, social issues and norms become things that investors should evaluate for the sake of their long-term financial performance. But from the perspective of norm-setting and the achievement of social objectives, investors are agents that help set ethical guidelines and create social outcomes in society (Welker and Wood 2011).

Returning to the PRI, we see this tension embodied in the understanding that the broader interests of society will align with ESG. There is both an implicit assumption that social value and financial returns are necessarily linked over the long term, and a belief that investors wield influence that can yield positive social outcomes. In practice, the mechanisms that link financial returns and social objectives, and the role of investors in relation to other stakeholders in creating those outcomes, are not always obvious. It may be a clearer articulation of the ethical role of investors in promoting the broader interests of society, the role of ethical norms in shaping the financial systems in which investment returns are generated, and commonly held definitions of social value that investments do or do not create might help resolve the tensions between financial return and social value that underlie the S in ESG.

Note

1 I should note that the chapter focuses on how investors think about the S, and society, in responsible investment, rather than the equally important topic of who speaks for society in responsible investment, and how various stakeholder groups in society may or may not have a voice in how investment activity affects them or the issues they care about.

References

Ambachtsheer, J. (2011) 'International codes and conventions: Are pension funds missing in action?', *Rotman International Journal of Pension Management*, 4(2): 26–38.

CalPERS (2012) *Towards Sustainable Investment: Taking Responsibility*. Online. Available: <http://www.calpers.ca.gov/eip-docs/about/pubs/esg-report-2012.pdf> (accessed 2 December 2014).

Clark, G., Feiner, A. and Viehs, M. (2014) 'From the stockholder to the stakeholder: How sustainability can drive corporate performance', *Social Science Research Network*. Online. Available: <http://papers.ssrn.com/sol3/papers.cfm?abstract_id=2508281> (accessed 2 December 2014).

Committee for Worker's Capital (CWC) (2012) 'Investing in decent work: Leveraging workers' capital for healthy and safe workplaces', Capital Briefing Paper 3. Online. Available: <http://www.workerscapital.org/images/uploads/CWC-Investing%20in%20Decent%20Work%203%20Final%282%29.pdf> (accessed 2 December 2014).

Croft, T. (2009) *Up from Wall Street: The Responsible Investment Alternative*, Pittsburgh: Heartland Institute.

Daniels, B., Flynn, E., Gross, J., LaFranchi, D. and Nixon, J. (2007) *The Double Bottom Line Handbook: A Practitioner's Guide to Regional Double Bottom Line Investment Initiatives and Funds*, New York: Ford Foundation. Online. Available: <http://community-wealth.org/_pdfs/tools/pris/tool-ford-DBLHandbook.pdf> (accessed 2 December 2014).

Domini, A. (2001) *Socially Responsible Investing: Making a Difference and Making Money*, Chicago: Kaplan Business.

Eccles, B., Krzus, M. and Serafeim, G. (2011) 'Market interest in nonfinancial information', *Journal of Applied Corporate Finance*, 23: 113–127.

Edmans, A. (2011) 'Does the stock market fully value intangibles? Employee satisfaction and equity prices', *Journal of Financial Economics*, 101: 621–640.

Fulton, M., Kahn, B. and Sharples, C. (2012) 'Sustainable investing: Establishing long-term value and performance', *Social Science Research Network*. Online. Available: <http://papers.ssrn.com/sol3/papers.cfm?abstract_id=2222740> (accessed 2 December 2014).

Hagerman, L., Clark, G. and Hebb, T. (2005) *Pension Funds and Urban Revitalization New York Case Study: Competitive Returns and a Revitalized New York*. Cambridge: Labor and Worklife Program, Harvard Law School.

Hawley, J., Hoepner, A., Johnson, K., Sandberg, J. and Waizter, E. (eds.) (2013) *The Cambridge Handbook of Institutional Investing and Fiduciary Duty*, Cambridge: Cambridge University Press.

Hawley, J. P. and Williams, A. T. (2000) *The Rise of Fiduciary Capitalism: How Institutional Investors Can Make Corporate America More Democratic*, Philadelphia: University of Pennsylvania Press.

Hayat, U. (2014) 'The big picture of responsible investing: An interview with Rob Lake', Enterprising Investor Weblog, CFA Institute, April 23. Online. Available: <http://blogs.cfainstitute.org/investor/2014/04/23/the-big-picture-of-responsible-investing-by-large-asset-owners-an-interview-with-rob-lake/> (accessed 2 December, 2014).

Hebb, T. and Sharma, R. (2014) 'New finance for America's cities', *Regional Studies*, 48(3): 485–501.

Henderson, R. and Ramanna, K. (2014) 'Managers and market capitalism', Harvard Business School Working Paper No. 13–075. Online. Available: <http://papers.ssrn.com/sol3/papers.cfm? abstract_id=2231526> (accessed 2 December 2014).

Human Rights Library (2014) *Global Sullivan Principles*. University of Minnesota. Online. Available: <http://www1.umn.edu/humanrts/links/sullivanprinciples.html> (accessed 2 December 2014).

Hummels, H. and Wood, D. (2005) *Knowing the Price, but also the Value? Financial Analysts on Social, Environmental and Ethical Information*, Boston: Neyenrode Business Universiteit and Boston College. Online.

Available: <http://hausercenter.org/iri/wp-content/uploads/2010/05/Admin-PWC-Knowing-The-Price-and-Value-Sustainability.pdf> (accessed 2 December 2014).

Interfaith Center for Corporate Responsibility (2014) 'Investor statement on Bangladesh', May 13. Online. Available: <http://graphics8.nytimes.com/packages/pdf/business/Bangladesh-Investor-Statement.pdf>.

Investors against Genocide. (2014) 'About us'. Online. Available: <http://www.investorsagainstgenocide.org/about/about-us/> (accessed 2 December 2014).

Joly, C. (2014) 'The moral case: Why invest responsibly" in Investment Leaders Group (eds.) *The Value of Responsible Investment: the Moral, Financial, and Economic Case for Action*, Cambridge: University of Cambridge Institute for Sustainability Leadership. Online. Available: <http://www.cisl.cam.ac.uk/Business-Platforms/Investment-leaders-group.aspx> (accessed 2 December 2014).

Keefe, J. L. and Krawcheck, S. L. (2014) 'Why gender diversity should matter to investors', Pax World Ellevate Management. Online. Available: <http://www.paxworld.com/system/storage/14/8f/a/3853/why_gender_diversity_should_matter.pdf> (accessed 2 December 2014).

Kurtz, L. (2013) *Looking Forward, Looking Back: A Hitchhiker's Guide to Research on Social and Sustainable Investment*, Utrecht: Tillburg University.

Local Authority Pension Funds Forum (LAPFF) (2012) 'Investing for growth'. Online. Available: <http://www.lapfforum.org/Publications/latest-research/files/Investing_for_Growth_Oct_2012.pdf/view> (accessed 2 December 2014).

OPERS (2014) *Responsible Contractor Policy of the Ohio Public Employees Retirement Plan*. Online. Available: https://www.opers.org/pdf/investments/policies/Responsible-Contractor-Policy.pdf (accessed 2 December 2014).

PGGM (2013) *Responsible Investment Report 2013*. Online. Available: <https://www.pggm.nl/english/what-we-do/Documents/Responsible-Investment-Annual-Report_2013.pdf> (accessed 2 December 2014).

Prahalad, C. K. (2004) *The Fortune at the Bottom of the Pyramid: Eradicating Poverty through Profits*, Upper Saddle River, NJ: Pearson F.T. Press.

Porter, M. (1995) 'The competitive advantage of the inner city', *Harvard Business Review*, May: 282–295.

PRI (2012). *Environmental and Social-Themed Investments*. Online. Available: <http://intranet.unpri.org/resources/files/PRI__Environmental_and_social_themed_investing_October_2012.pdf> (accessed 2 December 2014).

PRI (2013) *Integrated Analysis: How Investors are Addressing Environmental, Social, and Governance Factors in Fundamental Equity Analysis*. Online. Available: <http://2xjmlj8428u1a2k5o34l1m71.wpengine.netdna-cdn.com/wp-content/uploads/Integrated_Analysis_2013.pdf> (accessed 2 December, 2014).

PRI (2014) 'The six Principles'. Online. Available: <http://www.unpri.org/about-pri/the-six-principles/> (accessed 2 December 2014).

Seidman, G. W. (2003) 'Monitoring multinationals: Lessons from the anti-apartheid era', *Politics and Society*, 31(3): 381–406.

Thamotheram, R. and Le Floc'h, M. (2012) 'The BP Crisis as a "Preventable Surprise"', Rotman International Journal of Pension Management, 5(1): 68–78.

UN Global Compact (2014) 'The ten principles'. Online. Available: <https://www.unglobalcompact.org/AboutTheGC/TheTenPrinciples/index.html> (accessed 2 December 2014).

UN Guiding Principles on Human Rights (2014) 'The guiding principles'. Online. Available: <http://business-humanrights.org/en/un-guiding-principles> (accessed 2 December 2014).

UN-REDD Programme (2013) 'Guidelines on free, prior and informed consent'. Online. Available: http://www.un-redd.org/Launch_of_FPIC_Guidlines/tabid/105976/Default.aspx (accessed 2 December 2014).

Waitzer, E. and Sarro, D. (2014) 'Fiduciary society unleashed: The road ahead for the financial sector', *The Business Lawyer*, 69: 1081–1116.

Welker, M. and Wood, D. (2011) 'Shareholder activism and alienation', *Current Anthropology* 52(S3): 57–69.

Wood, D. and Youngdahl, J. (2014) 'How might responsible investors address income inequality?', Paper presented to the UN PRI Academic Network Conference, Montreal.

44

Corporate governance research and ratings firms[1]

Kimberly Gladman

What is corporate governance?

When newcomers to the field of responsible investment learn that it incorporates environmental, social, and governance (ESG) factors into investment decision-making, 'governance' is often the least well understood of the three terms. This may be because environmental and social issues were first raised in an investment context by retail investors and by activist movements familiar to the general public, such as the anti-apartheid movement of the 1970s and 1980s. While the ways that investors approach E and S issues have grown increasingly varied over the past several decades, the issues and language involved (e.g., climate change, human rights, or employee safety) are still fairly accessible to people without specialized knowledge. Corporate governance, in contrast, has been a focus of attention primarily for institutional investors, and discussions of it often dwell on features that may seem obscure or technical to a layperson (e.g., plurality voting, restricted stock, or poison pills).

In reality, however, corporate governance addresses problems fundamental to capitalist societies. In theory, publicly traded corporations should be vehicles of wealth creation for all investors, and by extension for society as a whole. But in practice, the executives who are managing the company may not work to maximize value for the entire investor base – either due to conflicts of interest or because of simple inability. When the neglect of investor interests is widespread, serious damage to an economy can result: the financial crisis of 2008 and the Enron-era accounting scandals of 2001–2 are only two recent examples. Governance analysis seeks to identify firms where there is a serious misalignment between the actions of management and the interests of the company's owners (what economists call an 'agency problem'), and to propose remedies for such situations.

The evolution of the field

While economists, political scientists, and financial analysts have long pondered agency problems and studied the quality of corporate management, the professionalization of governance research and ratings as a separate field of endeavour is a relatively recent phenomenon. Many of the best-known organizations in the industry had their origins in the US in the mid-1980s era of corporate takeovers. At that time, a number of long-term institutional investors – including many retirement funds of states, municipalities, and labour unions – were concerned about the often narrow and short-term agendas of the corporate raiders, which they felt did not align with their own. At the same time, these investors were also alarmed to observe many companies responding to the takeover climate by strengthening their defences – and to see a number of state law changes that also strengthened the ability of incumbent boards to resist unwanted takeovers. These developments, the investors feared, could entrench unproductive management teams and be equally at odds with broad shareholder interests. In 1985, a group of these investors came together to form the Council for Institutional Investors, which served a coordinating function for a number of shareholder proposals and corporate dialogues focused primarily on decreasing takeover defences or subjecting them to shareholder approval.

At about the same time, the U.S. Department of Labor (DOL) was beginning to develop an interpretation of the Employee Retirement Security Act of 1974 (ERISA) which would require trustees of private retirement plans to exercise active ownership of companies' securities. Initiated by governance activist Robert Monks, who was then serving in the DOL as a pension administrator, this interpretation was advanced by a number of regulations over the following decade, and became fully formalized in 1994.

In 1985, Monks, who had left the DOL, founded Institutional Shareholder Services (ISS) to advise institutional investors on how to fulfil their proxy voting responsibilities. (Proxy votes are cast by shareholders on ballot proposals presented in a company's proxy statement, which is released in advance of its annual general meeting.) The early clients of ISS included public pension funds and mutual funds interested in advice on how to vote on the period's many takeover transactions, as well as on the shareholder proposals being filed in response to them. The firm's business expanded rapidly after a 1988 statement by the DOL (known as the 'Avon Letter') which officially declared proxy voting to be part of trustees' fiduciary duty to their funds' beneficiaries. By 1990, when Monks left the firm, it had 80 institutional clients managing more than $1.3 trillion in assets.

More than 20 years later, after having been sold several times to other firms, ISS remains one of the most significant firms in the governance field. ISS offers a number of other data, ratings, and research services in addition to proxy voting – which remains, however, a major way that many investors engage with governance issues. Partly due to the technological complexities associated with executing proxy votes, ISS has been joined in the proxy voting business by a relatively small number of competitors, the most prominent being San Francisco-based Glass Lewis & Co.

Around the turn of the millennium, former ISS executives Robert Monks, Nell Minow, and Howard Sherman were instrumental in founding two separate governance research firms which did not provide proxy recommendations but offered in-depth data, analysis, and ratings of public companies. One of these firms, The Corporate Library, specialized in US companies, with particular attention to compensation and board issues. The other, GovernanceMetrics International, covered a universe of global large-capitalization firms and included some environmental and social data points as well as traditional governance information. In 2010, the two firms merged with each other and with Audit Integrity, a forensic accounting firm. The resulting company, GMI Ratings, where I served as Director of Research from 2008–13, was the largest provider of governance research outside the proxy advisory space in that period.

In 2014, ISS was sold by its parent, MSCI, to private equity firm Vestar Capital Partners; GMI Ratings was acquired by MSCI, and independent research firm Sustainalytics announced its intention to build its own internal team devoted to governance research. These developments suggest that all three firms' governance-related ratings and other offerings may evolve significantly in the near future.

Governance ratings methodologies

A number of the firms discussed above have devised governance ratings systems. Some other kinds of firms (such as credit ratings agencies) have at times also developed their own governance ratings, for internal or external use. These various ratings systems differ from each other in a number of ways. For instance, some have sought to rank companies relative to others (e.g., those in the same geographical region or industry), while others rate each firm against absolute standards. Some have tried to create ratings predictive of particular future outcomes (often investment returns), while others have aimed at a present-moment judgment of governance quality. Furthermore, data availability issues sometimes influence the character of ratings systems. For example, some seek to compare a large number of global companies to each other, and must therefore use relatively simple data points that can be obtained even in markets where information is scarce; other ratings specialize in a single region where more detailed information can be obtained. In addition, ratings can be expressed in many forms (e.g., letter grades, percentiles, concern levels), each of which suits the needs and purposes of different audiences.

Most important, all governance ratings systems grapple with the central fact that governance is a matter of human behaviour, and one that cannot be directly observed. Most discussions held in boardrooms and C-suites are not publicly disclosed, and it is difficult to know for sure whether a CEO is inclined to be selfish, whether a board is deferential to executives, or whether directors ask good questions about the information they receive. Anyone designing a rating system must decide which broadly attainable data points to use as indicators of governance quality, bearing in mind that any indicators that are consistently and publicly available – and thus, practical to use – will by definition be imperfect. Each governance ratings system that has been developed makes somewhat different choices about which data points to include, and how to weight them relative to each other.

Because of these many methodological differences, various ratings systems have sometimes produced divergent – even contradictory – ratings on the same company. Critics of the governance research and ratings industry have sometimes seized on this lack of alignment in an attempt to argue that there is no consensus about what constitutes good, or bad, governance. In fact, however, there is broad agreement among governance research specialists about how companies should best be organized to benefit all investors. The professional disagreements that exist centre much more on which methodology does the best job of discerning governance quality, given the various goals and constraints described above. The following section describes the main ideas shared by nearly all governance ratings systems, and outlines some of the different ways they have been put into practice.

Governance ratings subject areas

Board

The central focus of governance research and analysis is the company's board of directors. In well-governed firms, directors oversee the design of a company's strategic plan, and engage competent chief executives to carry it out. They monitor the performance of those executives carefully, and replace them when necessary. In addition, directors are responsible for oversight of financial reporting. To perform these tasks well, most researchers believe that a majority of directors should be independent of company management and free of relationships with the firm that could create conflicts of interest. At the same time, directors should be also well-informed about the company's business, have experience with the kind of issues it is facing, and be able to help managers craft strategies to address both risks and opportunities.

To glean a sense of board quality, research firms may examine some of the following questions.

What relationships exist between the directors and the company or its management, and how do these relationships affect the way directors carry out their duties? In general, it is assumed that directors who are independent of the firm – meaning that they have no significant relationship to the firm other than their board service – are most likely to be objective and effective overseers of management. Assessments of independence are complex, however. Many directors who meet the technical independence requirements of listing exchanges may still have relationships to the company or its executives that could compromise their objectivity (e.g., consulting contracts, familial or social relationships, or previous work relationships at other firms). As a consequence, each governance research firm has elaborated its own slightly different methodology for assessing director independence. A particularly subtle area of this research concerns directors who represent particular large shareholders or shareholder groups: for these individuals, the question is whether they seem likely to protect the interests of all shareholders equally or to prioritize the rights of those who have nominated them.

What range of backgrounds and perspectives do the directors bring to the board, and how does this affect the board's functioning? It has long been accepted that boards should be made up of directors with a range of experience and knowledge relevant to the company's business (e.g., in finance, marketing, or operations; in various regions of the world where the company operates; in the company's industry; and in legislative and political matters related to its work). Recently, a view has developed that certain overarching skill sets should also be represented: for example, expertise in risk management or awareness of sustainability issues. Finally, recent academic research suggests that people with differing personal characteristics – including gender and race – may bring different viewpoints and communication styles to a director group, preventing too-rapid agreement, enhancing the quality of discussion, and improving board monitoring of management.

What relationships exist among directors, and how do they affect board effectiveness? While this is not considered by all governance research firms, it is a significant focus at some. The purpose of assessing intra-board relationships is to assess whether any of them are so friendly – or antagonistic – that they could impair directors' oversight abilities. For example, researchers may look to see whether a group of long-tenured directors all came on the board at the same time or all previously worked together at a predecessor firm; whether some directors serve together on other companies' boards or on the boards of nonprofits; or whether the company's related party transactions disclosure suggests other connections (e.g., joint ownership by several directors of a vendor to the company). All of these relationships would raise concerns that for these directors collegiality might take precedence over individual critical thinking and that they might function as a bloc. In contrast, there are also relationships that offer potential for discord, such as that between a current CEO and former CEO who is serving as chair but potentially unwilling to relinquish control.

Is the structure of the board conducive to effective oversight of management? Most governance research firms take the position that boards should have independent chairs. This is in large part for the simple reason that one of the board's main responsibilities is to hire, compensate, and if necessary fire the chief executive; it is more difficult for it to do this well if it is led by the CEO or another person aligned with management. Some researchers also believe that even in the absence of an independent chair, board oversight can be strengthened by the presence of a lead independent director, as well as by the practice of independent directors meeting regularly as a group. Other structural issues include whether the board has committees with particular functions (such as sustainability oversight or risk management); whether any key committee, or the board itself, appears too large or too small to function well; whether key committees are independent; and whether those committees are all dominated by the same directors.

What do the board's past decisions suggest about its oversight abilities? Regardless of its qualifications or structural features, the most important source of information about a board's quality is its track record. If a board has appointed a series of failed CEOs or overseen a major scandal or bankruptcy, it is probably not functioning well, even if its individual members appear distinguished. Conversely, a board might look just average on paper, but have shown itself adept in navigating challenges or crises. Most governance research and ratings firms ground their work in an understanding of recent board performance.

CEO pay

Remuneration – or compensation, as it is called in a US context – is another main focus area for governance research, for two principal reasons. First, incentivizing the CEO through pay is arguably among the board's most important responsibilities. Second, in the US, where many governance research firms are based, disclosure requirements set by the Securities and Exchange Commission (SEC) have made available a wealth of data about the decisions boards make on pay. Remuneration can therefore serve as a window into the relationship between the board and CEO, as well as the board's overall capacity for independent oversight. The key questions many researchers seek to answer when studying pay packages include the following.

Is the CEO being given appropriate performance goals? Ideally, CEO performance goals would focus on multiple important aspects of the company's business, would encourage behaviour that benefits the company over the long term, and could not be achieved easily. Governance analysts often critique one-dimensional targets (such as earnings per share, which can be subject to manipulation), insufficient performance periods (e.g., 'long-term' incentives based on one- or three-year results), and payouts made for underperformance relative to the company's peers. There is also growing interest in the integration of sustainability metrics into CEO performance plans, particularly at companies facing significant environmental or social risks.

Does the board ensure that the CEO's pay moves in parallel with investors' fortunes? Pay packages should be designed to align the CEO's interests with those of investors. In addition to plan design, however, it is important to consider actual behaviour by remuneration committees, which may include out-of-plan payments. In some cases, CEOs are effectively insulated from downturns affecting other investors (e.g., when options are exchanged when significantly underwater, or when discretionary bonuses are given despite failure to reach targets).

Do the levels and elements of CEO pay raise any concerns? If the overall level of executive pay is excessive, the company may be diverting resources to CEO remuneration that could be more profitably invested in future growth. At the same time, certain elements of compensation – such as lavish perquisites – may suggest that boards are too inclined to defer to CEO wishes and requests. Furthermore, a wide disparity between pay levels for the CEO and other top executives suggests several potential problems. On the one hand, if the CEO truly warrants much higher remuneration than the other named executive officers (NEOs), they may not be capable of succeeding him or her should that become necessary. Alternatively, if all NEOs are strong performers but the CEO receives a disproportionate pay package, shareholders are overpaying for his or her services.

Ownership and control

As explained earlier, corporate control issues were central to the origins of specialist governance firms in the 1980s takeover era, and they remain important today. Research in this area focuses on two main (and interrelated) questions.

If directors are performing poorly, how difficult will it be for shareholders to replace them? Boards may adopt a number of governance features to protect their control over the company. One well-known example of what are often called 'takeover defences' is a poison pill (or 'shareholder rights agreement') which gives shareholders the right to buy a new issue of shares at a discount if one shareholder acquires more than a threshold percentage of the company's stock. Because such an agreement would greatly dilute the acquirer's interest, it functions as a powerful deterrent to anyone seeking to gain a controlling interest in the company. Another simple example is a prohibition on investors' calling a special meeting, at which new directors could be elected. There are many other takeover defences, which vary by legal jurisdiction, evolve over time, and may interact with each other in complex ways.

Some governance ratings systems assume that strong takeover defences are bad for shareholders, and some academic research has supported this claim, at least for certain historical periods and regions. In this view, strong defences may harm investors in two ways. First, because they prevent acquisitions, they deprive shareholders in a target company of the profits they would otherwise receive (since deals are typically made at a premium above the current stock price). Second, strong defences may allow poor managers and directors to continue underperforming, since they are insulated from shareholder disapproval.

Other ratings systems, although sharing this generally negative view of takeover defence, evaluate each company's particular defences in conjunction with the quality of its board and overall governance. If the latter are positive, these systems will not penalize the company heavily for strong defences, on the theory that investors may be content to have well-run companies remain protected from takeover.

Does the company's ownership structure raise concerns that the interests of some particular shareholder(s) may take priority over others? The ownership profile of a company is one of its most salient governance features. A controlling or dominant shareholder may have the ability to influence decisions by the board in ways that benefit that shareholder at the expense of other investors. In some governance ratings methodologies, the mere fact that this could occur is viewed as a serious risk, and controlled companies and others with large blockholders are therefore rated poorly with regard to their ownership. Depending on other aspects of the ratings methodology, this may exert downward pressure on ratings in countries where family firms or cross-shareholdings among public companies are common.

In other ratings systems, concentrated ownership is viewed as a potential concern warranting further investigation, but companies are only downgraded if there is evidence of abuse of power by the dominant owner. Nearly all ratings systems, however, raise concerns about situations where investors' voting control is out of proportion to their economic interests in the company, as can occur when there are multiple classes of common stock with disparate voting rights (e.g., if the publicly traded shares have 1 vote per share and the shares held by the founding family have 10 votes each).

Financial reporting

At least since the turn-of-the-millennium scandals at Enron, WorldCom, etc., it has been widely understood that financial reporting is a key issue in governance, and that the integrity of a company's financial statements is a key indicator of management quality. However, it has proved difficult to fully integrate the insights of forensic accounting into most corporate governance research and ratings models. A key obstacle to this integration is professional specialization: relatively few people who are capable of rigorous financial statement analysis are also experienced in qualitative research related to board structure or remuneration, and vice versa.

As a result, research and ratings on financial reporting has developed on two parallel tracks. On the one hand, specialist firms like the Center for Financial Research and Accounting (CFRA), Audit Analytics, and Audit Integrity (AI, later part of GMI Ratings and then MSCI) have focused on financial statements, identifying items suggestive of manipulation. For example, a company may record revenue too early or delay recording expenses in order to boost its apparent earnings. On the other hand, in a time where business is already bad, the company may accelerate expenses or delay recording earnings in order to show a single bad period followed by a marked improvement. Assets and liabilities may be similarly misrepresented. These assessments of a company's accounting practices may be presented to clients in narrative form or via quantitative models that produce statistically driven ratings.

At the same time, more generalist governance firms like ISS, GovernanceMetrics, and The Corporate Library (the latter two of which became part of GMI Ratings and later MSCI) stressed the quality of accounting oversight rather than that of the financial statements themselves. Their research and ratings systems considered such indicators as the qualifications and independence of audit committee members, as well as the company's record of accounting-related violations (e.g., financial restatements; fraud prosecutions; or, in the US, management reports of inadequate internal control over financial reporting, which are made in response to the requirements of the Sarbanes-Oxley Act).

What does the future hold? Governance and ESG

In the course of the last decade or so, the field of ESG research has been both created and consolidated. Specialists in environmental, accounting, governance, or social research did not necessarily consider themselves peers or competitors in the early years of the millennium, but are now often working together in the same firm. The reasons for this development are both economic and philosophical. On the one hand, the market for what has often been understood as 'extra-financial' research has not expanded as rapidly as many practitioners had hoped, particularly in the US, and especially following the financial crisis of 2008. This has made it difficult for many specialist firms to survive, and has led many clients to demand a 'one-stop' vendor for all of what is now called 'ESG research'. At the same time, all of these branches of research were originally motivated by concern about the ways that the activities of corporations may lead to harm – either to investors, the environment, or other groups affected by companies' actions (e.g., employees, communities, or governments). Despite their varying methodologies and subject matter, all have sought to understand how and why these negative impacts occur, and what can be done to mitigate them. There is thus a great potential for synergy in the combination of these various fields of inquiry.

However, ratings and evaluation systems that seek to combine these different approaches must confront a central theoretical difficulty. The work of governance and forensic accounting firms has always focused on the interests of investors – often primarily shareholders. More socially and environmentally focused firms, however, have embraced a stakeholder model of the corporation, which considers the interests of many groups and entities that enable the corporation to exist, and which therefore have the right to benefit from its operations or at the very least not to be harmed by them. As they seek to integrate the various facets of ESG into their models, therefore, firms need to decide which model to adopt. Since investors are often already one of the parties whose interests are considered by stakeholder models, firms using the latter may simply strengthen them with the addition of more data and metrics related to governance and/or accounting. For firms using the shareholder or investor model, however, the situation is more complex, since many social and environmental indicators do not have proven short-term impact on investment performance. As a result, these firms may limit the number of E and S metrics they add to their models, focusing only on those deemed most relevant to market perception of the rated company.

Finally, even as they make these modelling decisions, researchers throughout the field of ESG research are aware that the investor versus stakeholder model dilemma exists in large part because corporate operations impose many costs on society that the company is not required to reimburse (e.g., the treatment expense of pollution-related illnesses). In economic parlance, these are 'externalities', costs external to the company's financial accounts. If our financial reporting system required companies to internalize these costs, harm to non-investor stakeholders would also negatively impact the bottom line. As a result, many ESG research professionals and firms are strongly supportive of efforts to integrate corporate financial and non-financial reporting and, when possible, to develop an accounting vocabulary that can translate social and environmental impacts into financial terms. If integrated reporting is more widely adopted in the near future, it will reshape the practice of governance research and ratings.

Note

1 I would like to thank the following people for their insightful discussions and comments on drafts of this chapter, which was written while I served as Director of Research and Risk Analytics at GMI Ratings (now part of MSCI): Agnes Grunfeld, Laurence Hazell, Michelle Lamb, Bob Monks, Howard Sherman, and Beth Young.

Part IV

45

Contemporary issues in responsible finance and investment

Bert Scholtens

Introduction

Taking account of moral issues in finance is nothing new. As written in the Old Testament:

> You shall not charge interest to your countrymen: interest on money, food, or anything that may be loaned at interest. You may charge interest to a foreigner, but to your countrymen you shall not charge interest, so that the Lord your God may bless you in all that you undertake in the land which you are about to enter to possess.
>
> *(Deuteronomy 23:19–20)*

> Wealth obtained by fraud dwindles, but the one who gathers by labor increases it.
>
> *(Proverbs 13:11)*

In fact, in all world religions there are instructions on how to include moral issues in financial and economic matters. This notion also was at the basis of the faith-based investment decisions of the Methodists and Quakers in the eighteenth century (Domini, 2001). Faith has been, and still is, an important screening device for many investors and relates to all kinds of economic activities. However, increasingly, other motives and ideologies are providing a basis for considering non-financial and moral issues when making decisions about finance and investing. These range from social and labour concerns to environmental issues, political conflicts and governance of the firm, to name but a few. In fact, the number of issues that connect to the notion of responsibility and that can be a factor in the exclusion or inclusion of particular firms, industries or countries in an investment portfolio has risen enormously and is unlikely to stop. For example, screening and rating agencies like ASSET4, EIRIS, Innovest, MSCI KLD, Sustainalytics and Vigeo include an increasing number of items in their checklists almost every year, and the Global Reporting Initiative (GRI) proposals on what a firm should account for show a continuous increase in the items to be covered.

At the same time, academic interest in responsible finance and investment has increased. This is evidenced by the number of articles published in this area. For example, in March 2012, according to Scopus, 2,064 articles on 'responsible investment' were produced. Figure 45.1 shows the

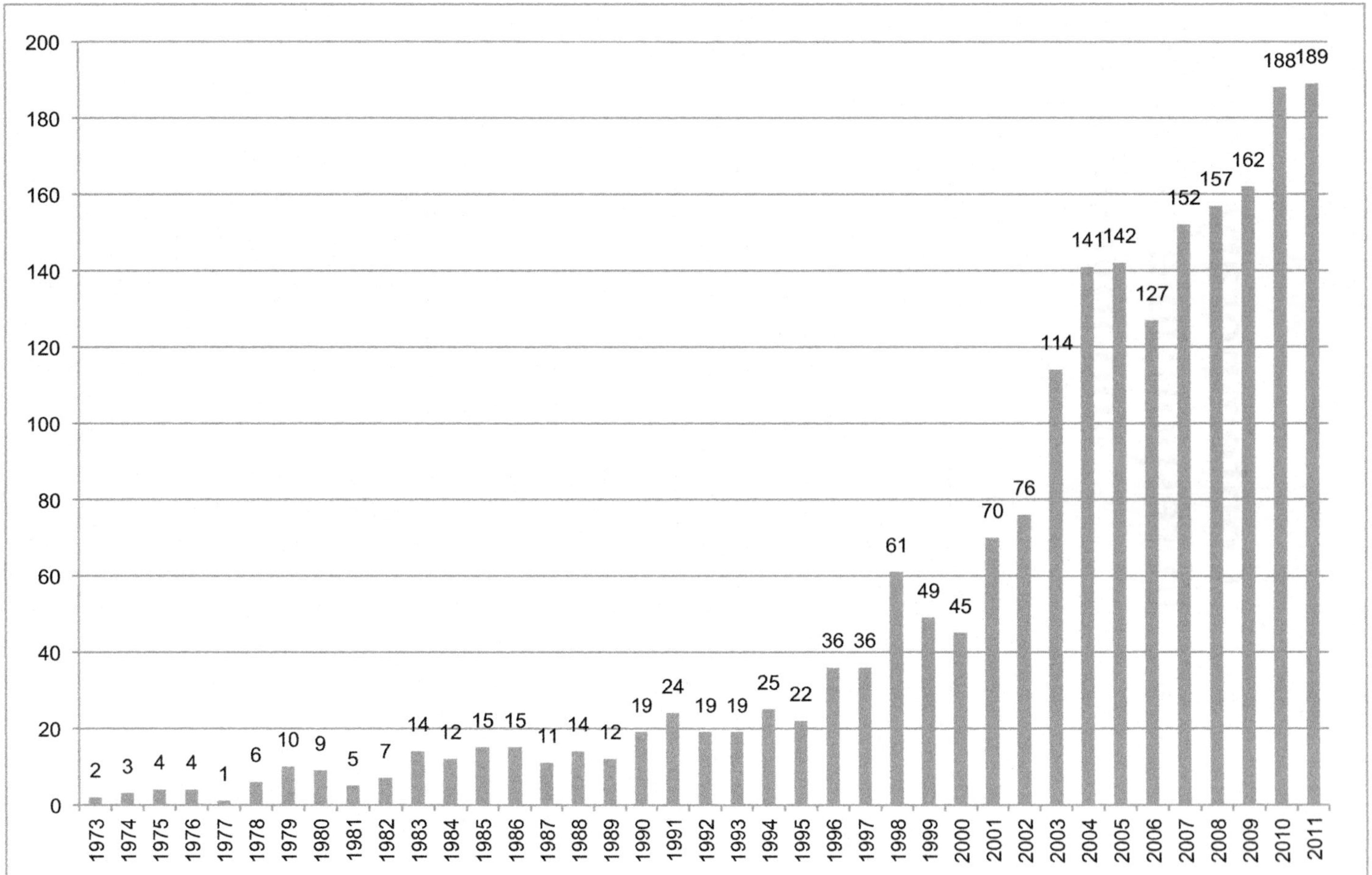

Figure 45.1 Number of articles in Scopus journals on 'responsible investment' (1973–2011)

Source: Scopus.

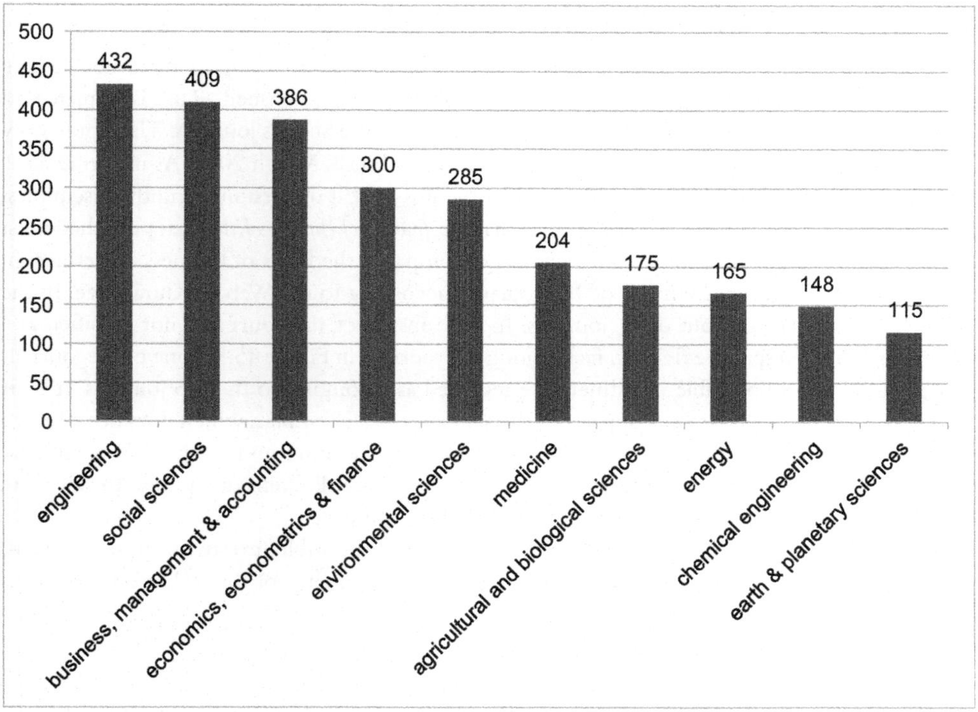

Figure 45.2 Number of articles on 'responsible investment' by subject area (>100; 1973–2011)

Source: Scopus.

increase in the number of these publications over the past 40 years. Research since the turn of the millennium has contributed significantly to our understanding of responsible investment, with, on average, 130 publications per year since 2000. In the 1970s, this number was 4, in the 1980s it was 11, and in the 1990s it stood at 31. Figure 45.2 shows the distribution of the articles by subject area. It shows that research on responsible investment is undertaken in a variety of disciplines. About one quarter are in (chemical) engineering; one fifth are in the social sciences, and another fifth are in business, management and accounting. About one seventh of the responsible investment research has appeared in economic, econometrics, and finance journals, as well as in environmental science journals. Medical papers make up one tenth of the overall article production in 1973–2011 on responsible investment. The remainder appeared in a larger number of subject areas. The focal point of this chapter is to discuss the most important issues relating to the research and business practices of responsible finance and investing. As such, this certainly is not a review of the literature. Instead, we focus on theory and methods in the literature and on key issues in the practice of responsible investment.

The structure of this chapter is as follows. We first highlight the main issues of theoretical, methodological and data development in the field of responsible finance and investment. Then, we look into the main issues in business practices. We conclude by discussing how the two arenas may be connected and what could be on the responsible finance and investment agenda.

Theory, methodology and data

Here, we discuss responsible investment research. To this extent, it is important to note where most research about responsible investment is actually being published. This is depicted in Figure 45.3, which shows the distribution of articles among the Scopus journals. This figure only includes journals for which Scopus reported at least seven hits in March 2012. As in Figure 45.2, Figure 45.3 and the underlying data suggest that there is a great dispersion along the disciplines. The research also is quite skewed, as it appears that the *Journal of Business Ethics* has published most articles on responsible investment. This journal encompasses the fields of business and ethics. In the business field, it ranks 59th out of 103 journals, according to the Web of Knowledge. In the ethics field, it ranks 10th out of 31 journals. In both instances, this journal is not classified as a top journal in the respective field. In fact, among the journals in Figure 45.3, none of the journals that published on responsible investment are regarded as belonging to the top journals in their field. The fact that most research appears in the *Journal of Business Ethics*, which does not advance the most rigorous theoretical or methodological analyses, is writing on the wall; it suggests that research on responsible investment is not at the frontier of the different disciplines. In our view, this results from a lack of rigorous theory, methodology and data.

Two interesting reviews of the academic literature on responsible investment have appeared. One, by Hoepner, McMillan and Fraser, is at the basis of Chapter 3 of this volume, the other is

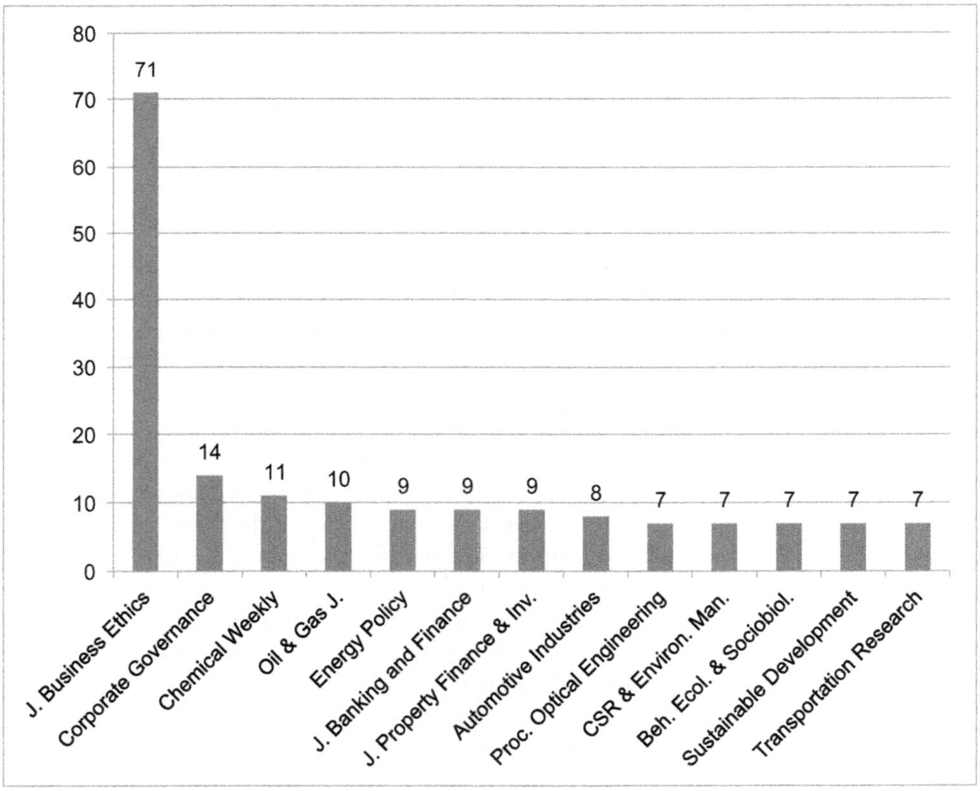

Figure 45.3 Number of publications on 'responsible investment' in Scopus journals (>6; 1973–2011)

Source: Scopus.

a paper by Capelle-Blancard and Monjon (2012) from the University Paris and the University Paris Dauphine in Business Ethics: A European Review, respectively. Hoepner, McMillan and Fraser engage in a so-called influential literature analysis (ILA) of 51 studies. They arrive at the following conclusions. First, influential research on responsible investment is dominated by institutions from the US, the UK and the Netherlands. Second, influential authors from the US rarely collaborate with scholars from non-US institutions. This suggests that the links within the international responsible investment research community are not very strong.

Hoepner and McMillan (2009) find that the influence of responsible investment studies is significantly driven by research awards, recommendations and journal quality. They observe a strong effect of the amendment to the 1995 British Pension Act, which required occupational pension funds to disclose the consolidation of their environmental, ethical and social criteria in their statement of investment principles as of July 2000. In particular, post-amendment studies document a much more sophisticated understanding of the responsible investment sector. Furthermore, they observe that financial market culture is an obstacle to progress in responsible investment. The case that responsible funds – but not comparable conventional funds – underperform their benchmark does not seem to favour the case of responsible investment.

Capelle-Blancard and Monjon (2012) review the literature on responsible investment as well, but they take a completely different approach. They use online search engines and archive collections to detect the popularity of responsible investing in newspapers and academic journals. Capelle-Blancard and Monjon (2012) engage in a content analysis of the literature, finding that most of the papers on responsible investment focus on financial performance; that is, 'Does it pay to be good?' Furthermore, these papers generally rely on the same class of models and arrive at similar results. Most use the capital asset pricing model (CAPM) or a multifactor model to assess the risk-adjusted returns of socially responsible investment (SRI) funds. In general, they observe that financial performance of responsible investment (funds) is not significantly different in relation to their peers. Capelle-Blancard and Monjon (2012) observe that despite this general result newspaper articles almost persistently present contradictory evidence based on specific case studies. They also point out that it is the availability of the data and the ease of access, together with the opportunity to use econometric tests, that play a major role in the choice of questions dealt with. They explain the high number of papers on financial performance of responsible investment on the basis of data availability. In their view, this has resulted in a general tendency to over-analyze the data and that research on responsible investment is the victim of the 'looking for the keys under the lamppost' syndrome (the lamppost being the most likely place to find anything in the dark, but not being the most likely place to lose items). In addition, Capelle-Blancard and Monjon (2012) establish that words connected with personal value are used less frequently over time. Instead, there is growing use of terms such as 'best in class', 'filter' and 'screen' in newspapers. The term 'stakeholder' also has gradually become more popular in academic articles. Last, responsible investment papers mention less frequently the boycott of South Africa and apartheid, but do cite human rights, climate change, sustainable development, and corporate governance with increased frequency.

Both Hoepner and McMillan (2009) and Capelle-Blancard and Monjon (2012) conclude that the responsible investment literature is quite 'under-theorized'. Both papers mention that the question of the financial performance of responsible investment is important. However, they also conclude that too much attention is being paid to this issue. As a result, other issues in responsible investment have been left unexamined. For example, the impact of responsible investment on environmental, ethical, governance and social performance of the firm, the motivations of financial institutions to support or hamper responsible investment, the role of regulators and supervisors and the marketing of responsible investment remain under-studied.

Regarding the methodology of research on responsible investment, the different disciplines (as depicted in Figure 45.2) so far rely on the conventional models and techniques of their specialties. In most research, the field of responsible investment is a niche, a new field of application. Chegut et al. (2011) investigated research in performance measurement in responsible investment. They describe how financial performance research of responsible investment funds is conducted and what can be regarded as best practice. They examine 41 studies (encompassing a study period of 45 years, 21 countries and the use of more than 20 different data sources). Chegut et al. (2011) consider five research themes based on their relationship with eliminating bias and estimation error in performance estimates: data quality, social responsibility verification, survivorship bias, benchmarking and sensitivity and robustness checks. They find that this literature uses exactly the same models and methodologies as a conventional investment analysis, and their recommendations for best practices are in line with those evident in the general performance measurement literature. In fact, only in the case of benchmarking and social responsibility verification do Chegut et al. (2011) find that very specific methods for performance measurement of responsible investment funds are addressed.

Very little multidisciplinary research appears to be going on in this field, which by definition would seem to call for a joining of forces from different disciplines. This cannot directly be derived from the Scopus analysis though, but results from an analysis of the papers from this database. In particular, we analyze the keywords of the Scopus articles. Figure 45.4 identifies keywords that were used at least 50 times. By far, as expected, 'investment' is the most often

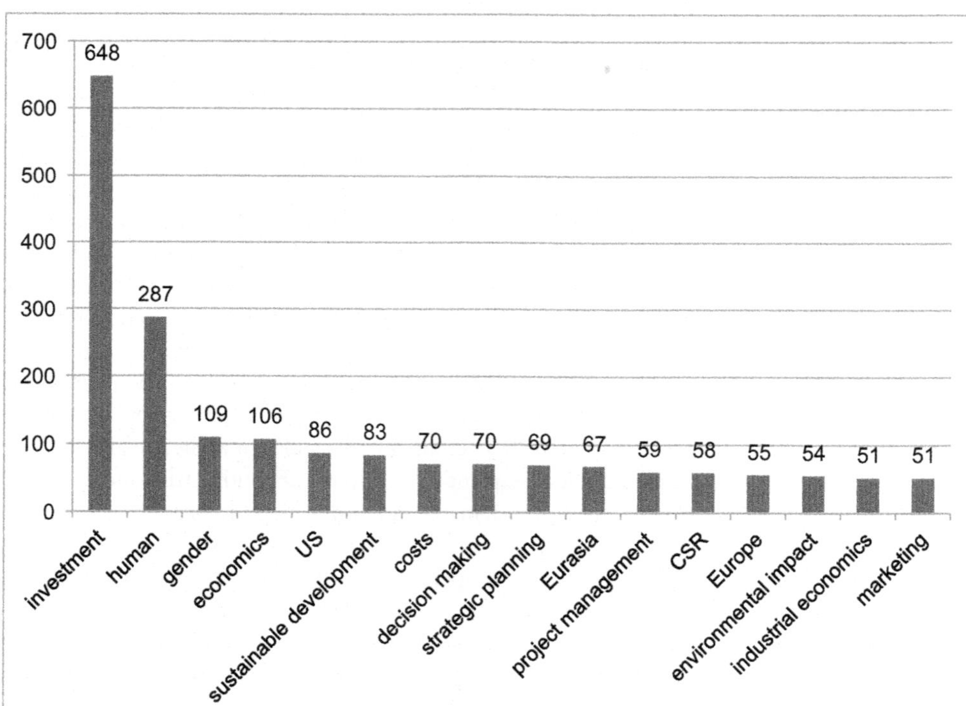

Figure 45.4 Keywords in publications on 'responsible investment' (>50; 1973–2011)

Source: Scopus.

used keyword. 'Human', 'gender', and 'economics' are also used in many studies. As expected, the different disciplines use a large number of different keywords, demonstrating the diversity of the topic. Interestingly, methodological issues or specific techniques were not among the keywords; the general term 'methodology' is used as a keyword in 41 instances, but no particular methodological approach appears among the keywords. Furthermore, we infer the degree of cross-disciplinary research on the basis of the congruence among subject areas. To this extent, Table 45.1 shows how often other subject areas are listed in a particular field. We selected the top five fields related to the research on responsible investment from Figure 45.2: (1) Engineering; (2) Social Science; (3) Business, Management & Accounting; (4) Economics; Econometrics & Finance and (5) Environmental Science. For example, of the 432 publications in Engineering that relate to responsible investment, 30 also connect with the Social Science (7 per cent); 35 with Business, Management & Accounting (8 per cent); 1 with Economics, Econometrics & Finance (0 per cent); and 30 with Environmental Science (7 per cent). Thus, for Engineering, the interaction between disciplines is very low. We apply this approach to all five fields and find that the linkages are slightly higher in Environmental Science and Social Science. With Business, Management & Accounting, we see substantial congruence with Economics, Econometrics and Finance and less with Social Science. In Business, Management & Accounting and Economics, Econometrics & Finance, there is very limited congruence with publications in Engineering and Environmental Science. There appears to be a concentration of responsible investment research in Business, Economics and Social Science, but there is no well-established link with Engineering and Environmental Science.

The data we find in Engineering and Environmental Sciences suggests that the researchers have primarily focused on specific emissions and efficiency performance indicators. Often, they investigate health, energy or pollutants. In contrast, in Business, Management & Accounting; Economics, Econometrics & Finance and Social Sciences most of the research is conceptual and directed at the policy level. Here, the empirical research is either case based or relies on ratings information. There is little focus on performance in empirical research, given the heavy emphasis on policy.

Using responsibility ratings appears to be the primary vehicle through which academics in social sciences, business and economics assess responsibility. This is probably due to the fact that

Table 45.1 Relationships between subject areas (as % of total number of publications in the subject area; total number of publications in parentheses)

	Engineering	*Social Science*	*Business, Management & Accounting*	*Economics, Econometrics & Finance*	*Environmental Science*
Engineering	100 (432)	7 (30)	9 (35)	0 (1)	11 (30)
Social Science	7 (30)	100 (409)	24 (90)	27 (81)	24 (69)
Business, Management & Accounting	8 (35)	22 (90)	100 (380)	52 (155)	11 (30)
Economics, Econometrics & Finance	0 (1)	20 (81)	41 (155)	100 (300)	5 (15)
Environmental Science	7 (30)	17 (69)	8 (30)	5 (15)	100 (285)

Source: Scopus.

responsibility is a complex concept, consisting of several dimensions, and one can question if every dimension is even quantifiable, let alone suitable for aggregation (Wood, 2010). However, the issue of selecting dimensions and variables and of giving weights remains, to date, unaddressed in the literature.

The MSCI KLD ratings are among the oldest and most influential and are the most widely analyzed by academics. In 2010, the US investment analysis and index company MSCI formally adopted the environmental, social and governance (ESG) indexes developed by KLD Research & Analytics, after it acquired the business earlier that year. Sharfman (1996) discusses the validity of these ratings and concludes that the KLD ratings correlate sufficiently with other measures of corporate social performance. Sharfman (1996) concludes that researchers interested in studying corporate social performance can have confidence in the KLD measures and feel secure in the idea that this data does tap into the core of the social performance construct. Other researchers have used KLD data when investigating the relationship between social and financial performance (e.g. Graves and Waddock, 1994; Berman et al., 1999; Hillman and Keim, 2001; Becchetti et al., 2005). Waddock (2003) concludes that the KLD data can be referred to as the de facto research standard at the moment.

However, Chatterji et al. (2009) find little evidence that responsibility ratings predict outcomes. Ratings do a reasonably good job of aggregating past performance, but they do not optimally aggregate the historical data. More specifically, KLD 'concern' ratings seem to be fairly good summaries of past environmental performance. Firms with more KLD concerns have slightly, but statistically significant, more pollution and regulatory compliance violations in later years. In contrast, Chatterji et al. (2009) find that KLD environmental strengths do not accurately predict pollution levels or compliance violations. Moreover, they find evidence that KLD's ratings are not optimally using publicly available data. To a large extent the responsibility metrics measure policies, not actual ESG performance (Chatterji et al., 2009). Furthermore, the assessment of firms' responsibility is not size or industry adjusted. The result is that the KLD measure may be biased and censored. The censoring results because very small firms are unlikely to be rated. In addition, Mattingley and Berman (2006) show that there is a positive correlation between KLD strengths and concerns regarding the various CSR dimensions. Given the fact that the other ratings metrics (e.g. EIRIS, Innovest, Oekom, Sustainalytics, Vigeo) are very much tailored along the same lines as those of KLD, we suspect that they are subject to these weaknesses as well. Wood (2010) finds that actual and valuable data about responsibility are inaccessible. She argues that some companies are non-transparent, whereas others are outright manipulative or deceptive in the provision of relevant information.

That responsible investment research is very much data driven is also evidenced by our finding that research on niche markets is much more developed than that of core markets. For example, there only are a couple of papers on responsible investing in bonds (e.g. Derwall and Koedijk, 2009; Scholtens, 2010) and even less so in credits (e.g. Goss and Roberts, 2011). However, there are a large number of papers on responsibility issues in real estate and on microfinance (see Bauer et al., 2011; Galema et al., 2011). Real estate research to a large extent relies on labelling data of occupational housing and offices. Microfinance research mainly concentrates on the number and type of households reached.

In all, we conclude that despite the enormous increase in the number of publications, research on responsible investment is still in its infancy. This conclusion is based on the fact that the number of cross-disciplinary connections in the literature produced remains limited. Given the fact that responsibility relates to many different dimensions, this is a matter of serious concern. It also suggests that the field is under-theorized as, in addition to the previous remark, most research is case and data driven (Chapter 3 of this volume has this as its focal point). These data, especially in the fields of economics and business, are subject to very serious flaws. Furthermore, there is no specific methodology to assess responsible investment, and the studies in the different subject areas subsequently rely on conventional approaches.

Business practices

This section aims to delineate business practices in responsible investment. We first give an overview of the market for responsible investment and then detail how responsible investment is actually undertaken and what the current main issues and challenges are.

In order to provide a comprehensive overview of the current size and composition of SRI, we rely on data that is compiled by Eurosif and the US Social Investment Forum (US SIF). Eurosif is a partnership of European national sustainable investment forums. The member affiliates include institutional investors, financial service providers, academic institutes, trade unions and non-governmental organizations (NGOs). The data we use are produced by the national SIFs. National SRI markets are defined by the country where the SRI assets are being managed. As such, Eurosif data reflect the size of the SRI asset management markets. The data is based on self-reporting by asset managers and self-managed asset owners and includes both institutional and retail assets (Eurosif 2010). This way of calculating SRI faces methodological problems (see Scholtens, 2014). In particular, we doubt the validity and consistency of their approach between different countries. Furthermore, we have concerns about the reliability of the size of responsible assets relating to integration, activism and exclusion strategies. However, it is the only dataset that is freely available for these markets. Given the uncertain quality of the data, the results have to be interpreted with great care (Scholtens, 2014).

Figure 45.5 details the composition of responsible investment of the main market centres. It shows that responsible investment in the main centres was about $13.5 trillion at year-end

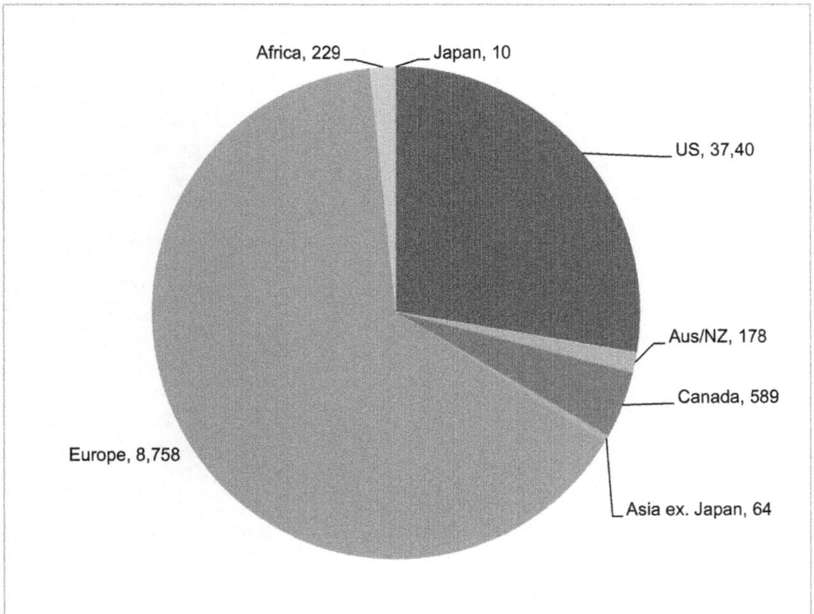

Figure 45.5 Composition of SRI in market centres as of 2011 based on total of $13,568 billion in responsible investments

Source: 2012 Global Sustainable Investment Review.

2011. Figure 45.5 demonstrates that Europe dominates responsible investment and that the US ranks second. Responsible investment in Canada is also well developed, whereas the sector clearly lags in Australia, New Zealand and especially Japan. Figure 45.6 shows the development of responsible investment over time. The longest time series is available for the US. It suggests that responsible investment grew very fast in the 1990s and then tapered off in the period 1999–2005. Since then, growth has resumed. For the eight European countries for which we have data, which covers a time span of about seven years, we find that growth was very impressive in the period 2003–7. The growth rate of responsible investment in the eight countries in 2007–9 was slightly above that in the US, but Figure 45.6 clearly indicates that growth rates have converged.

Eurosif distinguishes between different types of SRI. First, it determines 'core' and 'broad' SRI. Core SRI consists of multiple ethical exclusions and positive screening and a combination of these two. More specifically, Eurosif defines core SRI as including investments which take into account at least three negative criteria (i.e. norms and values-based investing) and positive screening (i.e. best in class and SRI-themed funds). The exclusions typically are based on international legal, ethical, social and environmental standards. A problem, however, is that it is not clear how to account for exclusions. For example, if an investor is to exclude investments in particular firms, it seems appropriate to take the amount of investments that are liquidated because of the exclusion in that year as a measure of exclusion. However, it does seem to be the case that asset managers report the amount of funds they screen for the eligibility regarding the exclusion criteria as exclusion. As such, this figure will be highly inflated. With best-in-class investing, investment managers choose the top-performing companies in an industry based on how they meet selected

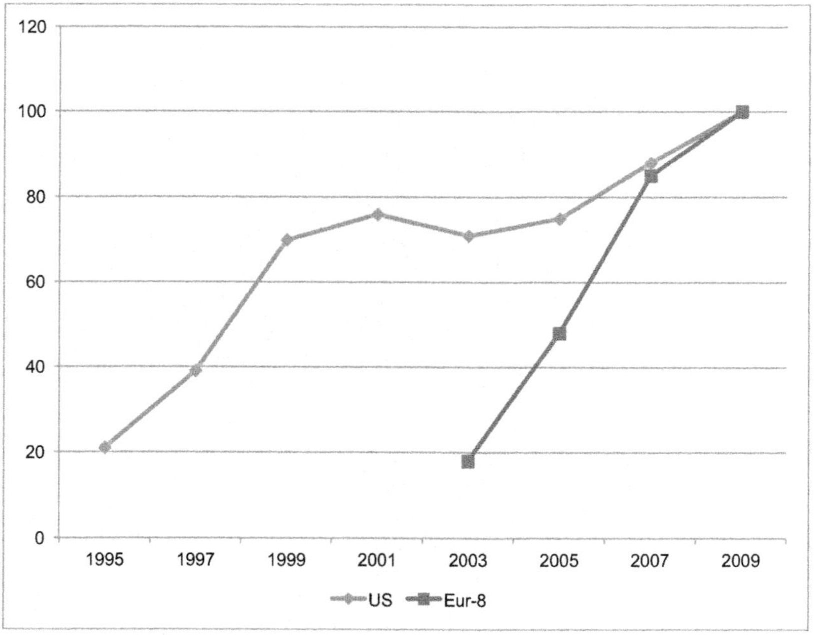

Figure 45.6 Development of SRI in US and Eur-8

Notes: Index number, 2009 = 100. Eur-8 is Austria, France, Germany, Italy, the Netherlands, Spain, Switzerland and the United Kingdom.

Source: US SIF (2010), Eurosif (2010).

ESG issues. The thematic funds are invested with a very specific focus. Examples are clean energy, clean water and microfinance.

Broad SRI includes three forms of SRI. The first is simple exclusions, which means restricting the scope of investment with one or two norms-, values- or ethically-based criteria. Here, the same caveat holds that is mentioned above. The second form of broad SRI is active dialogue with the management of investee companies. This is labelled 'engagement'. Engagement activities mostly concern governance issues, and such engagement is primarily private and direct. Public engagement and filing of shareholder resolutions are seldom used in Europe. Again, it is not clear what the reported numbers actually relate to, although it seems as if they relate to the asset base from which these engagements are being made. Eurosif does not report data regarding actual engagements. The third form of broad SRI is integration, which refers to the integration of ESG risk into traditional financial analysis (Eurosif, 2010). It is the explicit inclusion by asset managers of ESG risk factors into the traditional financial analysis. Again, the reported numbers seem to inflate what actually is going on; instead of solely relying on monetary units, other indicators are likely to be helpful, too. As can be derived from these descriptions, there is a thin line between core and broad responsible investment strategies, and different strategies can be used at the same time.

For the US, the data is compiled in a somewhat different manner. US SIF deviates from the classification used by the European forums. It distinguishes between three types of responsible investment. The first is ESG investing, which can be related to positive and negative screening in Eurosif's approach (best in class and norms- and values-based investing). The second type of responsible investment is shareholder advocacy, which resembles engagement and integration, and the third is community investments, which relates to direct investments in ESG projects.

Figure 45.7 shows the composition of responsible investment strategies in Europe in 2011. (Note, however, that this figure does not correct for double counting.) The figure shows that broad strategies relate to more than three times as many funds as core strategies do. Within core strategies, norms- and values-based investing makes up more than 80 per cent of the total. Other positive screens and best-in-class investing each constitute about 10 per cent of the total. Thematic funds make up less than 2 per cent of core responsible investments. With the broad responsible investment strategies in Europe, Figure 45.7 shows that exclusion is primarily undertaken and accounts for more than 40 per cent of broad strategies. As such, it also is the largest category of responsible investment. Engagement makes up about 20 per cent and integration about two thirds of the broad responsible investment strategies. Figure 45.8 gives the composition of the different strategies in the US over the period 1995–2009. In 2009, more than 60 per cent of US responsible investment relates to ESG investing and almost 40 per cent to shareholder advocacy. In the US, investors engage more via public engagement and by filing shareholder resolutions than is the case in Europe. Community investing makes up 1 per cent of total responsible investment in the US. Figure 45.8 shows that ESG investing gradually became more popular in the US but has lost ground since 2003. The complement is that shareholder advocacy as community investing always makes up at most 1 per cent of total responsible investments.

Responsible investment is driven by institutional investors, especially in countries with a well-developed pension system. Public pension funds, reserve funds, insurance companies, mutual funds and universities and other academic institutions, in particular, invest in a responsible manner (Eurosif, 2010). Retail investors are important in countries like Austria, Germany, Belgium and France, and they have become more important in the last couple of years. Institutional investors represented more than two thirds of the total market in Europe in 2011. According to Eurosif (2012), demand for responsible investment is driven by demand from both institutional and retail investors, rules and legislation, international initiatives and external pressure. For

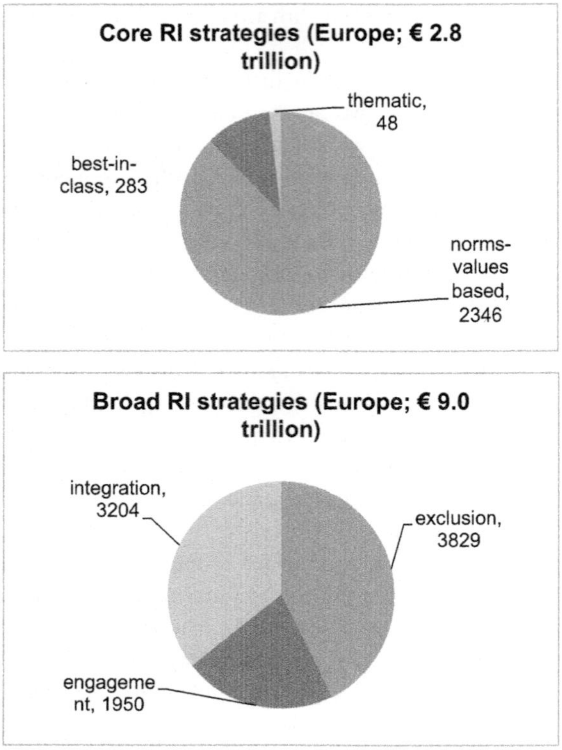

Figure 45.7 Composition of responsible investment strategies in Europe

Note: € billion; includes overlapping strategies.

Source: Eurosif (2012).

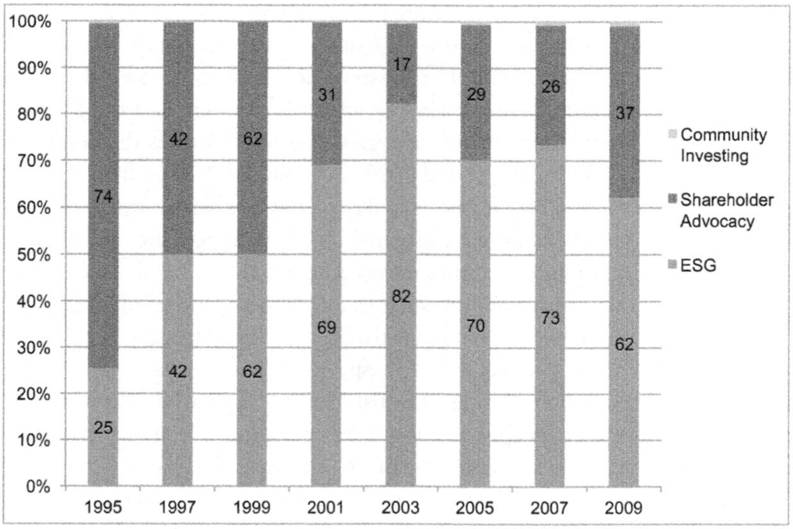

Figure 45.8 Composition of responsible investment strategies in the US over time (1995–2009)

Note: By per cent; includes overlapping strategies.

Source: US SIF (2010).

institutional investors, responsible investment increasingly seems to be a matter of risk management and of complying with (expected) regulation. Demand from retail investors is driven by growing mistrust of conventional financial products. External pressure is especially strong from media and NGOs and is often incident (accident) driven. International initiatives such as the UN-backed Principles for Responsible Investment (PRI), EU position papers on the transparency of corporations and the labelling of responsible investment funds may all serve as factors 'institutionalizing' the market for responsible investment.

In Europe, discretionary mandates are the main investment vehicle (84 per cent of total investments), and investment funds make up one seventh of the market. In the US, investment funds incorporating ESG factors made up 18 per cent of all responsible investing in 2009. This is a remarkable increase, as previously it stood at about 7 per cent. This suggests that responsible retail investments are gaining ground in the US.

Regarding the asset allocation of responsible investment, it appears that bonds are currently the most favoured asset class. In Europe, they represent more than half of all assets under management. Equity investments make up one third of the total, and this share has dropped in past couple of years. As to the remaining one seventh, alternative or hedge fund assets make up almost 50 per cent. This especially results from the substantial investments in these vehicles from Finland, Denmark and Sweden. Property investment accounts for about 3 per cent of total responsible assets under management. Private equity and venture capital as well as liquid assets and money market funds make up about 1.5 per cent. Responsible investment in commodities is about 0.5 per cent. The asset allocation of responsible investment in Europe in 2009 is depicted in Figure 45.9. Eurosif (2010) reports that there is a geographical bias in the allocation of the European responsible investments, as about 75 per cent is allocated in Europe and 10 per cent in the home country. Only 15 per cent of the responsible investments are allocated outside Europe.

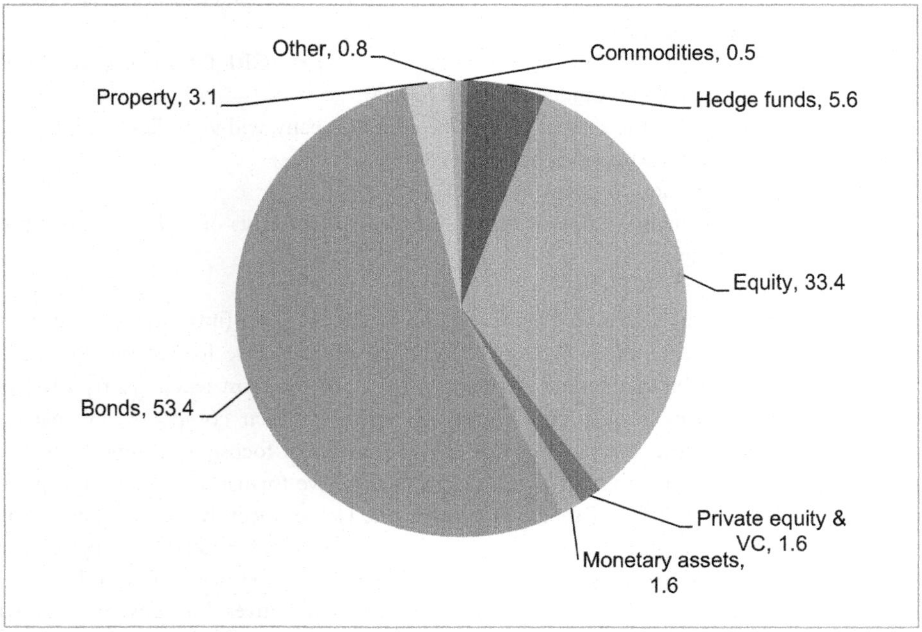

Figure 45.9 Responsible investment asset allocation (by per cent) in Europe (2009)

Source: Eurosif (2010).

In addition to these data by the national social investment forums, we discuss business practices in responsible investment on the basis of a recent survey of the private equity industry by PricewaterhouseCoopers (PwC, 2012). PwC interviewed 17 private equity houses in the period November 2011 to January 2012. Ten were headquartered in Europe and seven in the US. The interviews were conducted with members of senior management or with individuals from other functions and roles who have responsibility for the ESG agenda. PwC complemented the interviews with desk research on each private equity (PE) house.

The PwC survey shows that risk management and investor concern are the main drivers of responsible investment in private equity. ESG issues can have the potential to materially impact the valuation of investments over the longer term. However, the PE houses are not yet in the right position to address ESG issues themselves. An important unsolved issue remains: it is very difficult to quantify the value of ESG programmes of companies and of responsible investment strategies. PwC suggests improving upon external reporting on responsible investment to measure the financial value created by responsible investment, to develop expertise and to adopt best practices. Measuring value is an especially prominent concern. In this respect, PwC suggests it is important to collect ESG relevant financial data and use this in conventional analyses. To measure the direct value of ESG initiatives, it is important to have data on eco-efficiency measures and the corresponding savings in terms of energy, water and waste. In addition, it is important to quantify the indirect value arising from responsible investment, such as the contribution to customer loyalty, brand value and stakeholder relations. There are several approaches to ascribe value to ESG activities. The following suggestions are based on a report by WWF and Doughty Hanson (WWF, 2011):

- Identify a corporate sustainability metric or index that is closely correlated with shareholder value.
- Identify value drivers; try to find out how responsibility activities relate to the key financial metrics that drive corporate earnings or cash flows.
- Rely on existing global reporting frameworks for ESG, like the GRI (Global Reporting Initiative) sustainability reporting guidelines or ISO26000.
- Focus on consistency as the material issues for each company will vary depending on location and industry. Uniformity might be problematic.
- Focus on quality and not on quantity.
- Take account of qualitative approaches, too, especially if the costs of gathering quantitative data appear prohibitive.

It appears that these suggestions are yet to be implemented by the (investment) industry and that many corporations are still struggling to prove the business case for responsible conduct of firms and for responsible investment (McKinsey, 2011). In the most recent yearly McKinsey survey of 3,203 executives in July 2011, more executives say their companies are managing sustainability to improve processes and pursue growth instead of focusing on reputation alone. They assume that those firms that prioritize the issue and have formal structures are capturing the most value (McKinsey, 2011). Executives mention the lack of incentives tied to performance on these initiatives, the pressure of short-term earnings performance, a lack of key performance indicators, and insufficient resources for sustainability initiatives as the main barriers that prevent companies from capturing potential value from sustainability initiatives. For most executives, the relationship between sustainability and quantifiable value is still unclear; about one third of the respondents say they do not know how much sustainability initiatives add to shareholder value at their companies. About half assume there is a positive contribution to short-term value. The executives cite several levers connected with value creation, namely managing corporate reputation, capturing sustainability trends in the business portfolio and committing R&D resources to sustainable products. Their interaction with growth, return on capital and risk (management) should relate to value creation. Across industries, the relative importance of each effort varies (McKinsey, 2011).

In all, we can observe that responsible investment is growing fast and is becoming a substantial part of conventional financing. This seems to be due to risk management and investor concern. We also establish that responsibility and sustainability is on the corporate agenda. At the same time, we find that for many market participants it is not clear whether and how responsibility impacts on the value of the firm. This seems to result in part from the lack of a proper metrics, and in part from a lack of information. This implies the conclusion that for many firms the business case for responsibility is not very clear.

Reflection

The overview of the literature on responsible investment and business practices suggests that there are some discrepancies, but also that there are important similarities.

The main similarity is the lack of an appropriate theoretical background, the lack of a valid metric to quantify or qualify responsible investment activity and the lack of a solid business case for responsible investment. The academic literature on responsible investment is to a large extent (rating) data driven and has not succeeded in attaining a solid and robust position within the top academic journals. The data on responsible investment activity is not consistent and not validated and appears to hugely exaggerate what is really going on in investment portfolios. The business case for responsible investment is still weak. Corporate executives mainly engage with responsibility to guard their reputation and to manage risks. As such, they take a rather defensive position. This attitude is also found in finance, where the move towards responsible finance and investment meets a lot of resistance and lessons from the credit crisis have still not been not learned.

The main discrepancies are the dominance of the research on the impact of responsible investment on stock returns, whereas executives are interested in how responsibility interacts with firm value and risk. Furthermore, most responsible investment is in bonds, whereas there is very little research on responsible investing in the bond and credit markets. In contrast, there is a lot of research on responsible investing in real estate and in microfinance. In addition, the research after the impact of responsibility issues on credit markets is almost non-existent. The lack of sound and validated information about responsible investment activities and performance is especially pressing.

This suggests that there is a need for theorizing about responsible finance and investing, especially regarding its impact, its performance and the responsible investment process. We feel that it is important to address the shareholder value–maximization view, the motives for acting responsibly and the interaction between social and financial performance. Tirole (2001) shows how shareholders and stakeholders connect with corporate governance and how the 'shareholder society' is a second-best solution. He suggests that modern incentive theory provides some foundations for the narrow and a priori peculiar concept of shareholder value. Shareholder value in certain environments is a second-best optimum once incentive considerations have been considered. Shareholder value makes up for the dearth of pledgeable income, it provides more focus and sharper incentives to managers and the undivided control prevents foot-dragging and deadlock in decision-making (Tirole, 2001). However, shareholder value may generate choices that are biased.

Despite substantial attention paid to the protection (in the form of covenants, exit options and flat claims) granted to non-controlling stakeholders, shareholder value still leaves scope for important externalities and has some distasteful implications. Besides, we observe other types of governance structures such as associations, joint ventures or partnerships that seem to work well in the specific environments to which they are applied.

Bénabou and Tirole (2010) try to account for behavioural characteristics in decision-making and in theorizing about corporate social responsibility (CSR) and SRI. They argue that there are three possible understandings of CSR: the adoption of a more long-term perspective, the delegated exercise of philanthropy on behalf of stakeholders and insider-initiated corporate philanthropy. Prosocial behaviour by investors, consumers and workers is driven by a complex set of motives: intrinsic altruism, material incentives (defined by law and taxes) and social or self-esteem concerns. These three motives are mutually interdependent, and both policymakers and social activists must have a good understanding of these interactions in order to properly harness people's desire to behave pro-socially (Bénabou and Tirole, 2010). The importance of social and self-signalling concerns provides a powerful and cheap lever for certain types of interventions up to a point, but makes others counterproductive. The pursuit of social and self-esteem per se is a zero-sum game distorting actions towards the more visible.

Dam and Scholtens (2015) try to build a coherent framework from which they logically derive propositions about the relationship between social and financial performance. Their key assumptions are that socially responsible investors value taking account of external effects of production and accept a lower financial return on responsible stock compared to irresponsible stock. Furthermore, regarding the supply side of the economy, socially responsible entrepreneurs internalize the external effects of their production. This results in less input of capital and a higher return on assets because of decreasing marginal returns to production. The implication from the demand-side assumption is that responsible firms are characterized by higher market-to-book ratios than irresponsible firms. The implication from the supply-side assumption is that more responsible firms are characterized by a higher return on assets. Combining the two in the equilibrium situation regarding stock market returns gives an ambiguous result; it is not clear beforehand whether stock market returns are higher for responsible than for irresponsible firms. This ultimately depends upon the relative strength of how investors and firms respectively value the internalization of external effects (Dam and Scholtens, 2015). It is important to distinguish between the different dimensions of financial and social performance (Chatterji et al., 2009). Using KLD data, Scholtens (2008) shows that the relationship between financial and social performance is complicated indeed. He finds that financial returns precede firms' social, community, diversity, environmental and product strengths. However, social, product and environmental concerns precede financial risk.

Accounting for the role of value, for different motives and for the complex interaction between social and financial performance, is key in reconciling the gap between the responsible investment literature and business practices as well in addressing the under-theorizing in the literature and the lack of a proper framework at the level of the firm. However, they do not provide an answer to the multidisciplinary character of responsibility issues. To this extent, scholars and practitioners from different backgrounds (especially those from the beta and the gamma sciences) will have to work together to help improve our understanding of responsible finance and investment. Issues to be addressed would be the social and environmental impact of (responsible) finance and investment, actions and motivations towards responsible investment by the financial community, regulators and society, and the impact of finance and investment on ESG issues.

Conclusion

This chapter addresses contemporary issues in responsible finance and investment. It argues that the academic literature on this topic is still in its infancy as, so far, it has not reached the top journals in any primary discipline where responsible finance is currently being researched. It remains under-theorized, and a specific methodology that integrates the key ingredients, namely physical, natural, social and economic aspects, has yet to evolve. It appears that most academic studies are data driven. In practice, responsible investment has grown enormously in the past decade, despite the fact that statistics on which these claims are based seem to be inadequate in several respects. However, many executives have no proper idea of how sustainability and responsibility relate to the value of the firm. They engage with sustainability and responsibility because of risk management and investor concern. In the financial industry, it appears that especially the traditional culture is a factor that blocks innovation towards responsible finance and investment.

As a way forward, we suggest that researchers do influential research on theoretical foundations of responsible finance and investment. This requires a cross-disciplinary approach, combining theories and methodologies from both the natural and social sciences. Especially combinations between engineering, environmental sciences, on the one hand, and business, management, economics, finance and social sciences, on the other hand, might prove fruitful. The result could be a theory that is able to explain the connections between ESG issues and the value of the firm, as well as the interaction between ESG issues and finance and investment and the role of regulators, supervisors and stakeholders in responsible finance and investment. Furthermore, it is essential that the industry can use and report well-defined responsible investment activities and that reliable metrics and statistics become available.

References

Bauer, R., Eichholtz, P., Kok, N. and Quigley, J. M. (2011) 'How green is your property portfolio? The Global Real Estate Sustainability Benchmark', *Journal of Pension Management* (Rotman International) 4: 34–43.

Becchetti, L., Giacomo, S. di and Pinnachio, D. (2005) 'Corporate Social Responsibility and Corporate Performance: Evidence from a Panel of US Listed Companies', CEIS Research Paper Series: 26–78.

Bénabou, R. and Tirole, J. (2010) 'Individual and corporate social responsibility'. *Economica* 77: 1–19.

Berman, S. L., Wicks, A. C., Kotha, S. and Jones, T. M. (1999) 'Does stakeholder orientation matter? The relationship between stakeholder management models and firm financial performance', *Academy of Management Journal* 42: 488–506.

Capelle-Blancard, G. and Monjon, S. (2012) 'Trends in the literature on socially responsible investment: Looking for the keys under the lamppost', *Business Ethics: A European Review* 21 (3): 239–250.

Chatterji, A. K., Levine, D. I. and Toeffel, M. W. (2009) 'How well do social ratings actually measure corporate social responsibility?', *Journal of Economics & Management Strategy* 18: 125–169.

Chegut, A., Schenk, H. and Scholtens, B. (2011) 'Assessing SRI fund performance research: Best practices in empirical analysis', *Sustainable Development*, 19 (2): 77–94.

Dam, L., and Scholtens, B. (2015) 'Towards a Theory of Corporate Social Responsibility', *Resource and Energy Economics* 41, 103–121

Derwall, J. and Koedijk, K. (2009) 'Socially responsible fixed-income funds', *Journal of Business Finance and Accounting* 36: 210–229.

Domini, A. (2001) *Socially Responsible Investing*, Chicago: Dearborn.

Eurosif. (2010) *European SRI Study 2010*, Brussels.

Eurosif. (2012) *European SRI Study 2012*, Brussels.

Galema, R. J., Lensink, B. W. and Spierdijk, L. (2011) 'International diversification and microfinance', *Journal of International Money and Finance* 30: 507–515.

Goss, A. and Roberts, G. (2011) 'The impact of corporate social responsibility on the cost of bank loans', *Journal of Banking and Finance* 35: 1794–1810.

Graves, S. B. and Waddock, S. A. (1994) 'Institutional owners and corporate social performance', *Academy of Management Journal* 37: 1034–1046.
Hillman, A. and Keim, G. (2001) 'Shareholder value, stakeholder management, and social issues: What's the bottom line?', *Strategic Management Journal* 22: 125–139.
Hoepner, A.G.F. & McMillan D. G. (2009) 'Research on "Responsible Investment": An Influential Literature Analysis Comprising a Rating, Characterisation, Categorisation & Investigation', Working Paper, August.
Mattingly, J. E. & Berman, S. L. (2006) 'Measurement of corporate social action: Discovering taxonomy in the Kinder Lydenburg Domini ratings data', *Business and Society* 45: 20–26.
McKinsey (2011) *The Business of Sustainability*. McKinsey & Company. Online. Available HTTP: <http://www.mckinsey.com>.
PWC (2012) "Responsible Investment: Creating Value from Environmental, Social and Governance Issues', PricewaterhouseCoopers. Online. Available HTTP: <http://www.pwc.com/sustainability>.
Scholtens, B. (2008) 'A note on the interaction between corporate social responsibility and financial performance', *Ecological Economics* 68: 46–55.
Scholtens, B. (2010) 'The environmental performance of Dutch government bond funds', *Journal of Business Ethics* 92 (S1): 117–130.
Scholtens, B. (2014) 'Indicators of responsible investing'. *Ecological Indicators* 36: 382–385.
Sharfman, M. (1996) 'The construct validity of the Kinder, Lydenberg, and Domini social performance ratings data', *Journal of Business Ethics* 15: 287–296.
Social Investment Forum (2010) *Socially Responsible Investing Trends in the United States*, Washington D.C.: SIF.
Tirole, J. (2001) 'Corporate governance', *Econometrica* 69: 1–35.
Waddock, S. (2003) 'Myths and realities of social investing', *Organization & Environment* 16: 269–280.
Wood, D. J. (2010) 'Measuring corporate social performance: A review', *International Journal of Management Reviews* 12: 50–84.
WWF (2011) *Private Equity and Responsible Investment: An opportunity for Value Creation*, London: Doughty Hanson and WWF-UK.

46

Addressing the challenges of transformation through sustainable investment

Gordon L. Clark, Heather Hachigian, Sarah McGill, Claire Molinari and Dariusz Wójcik

Introduction

For much of the post-WWII era, financial crises flowed from the periphery of the global economy to core financial markets, disturbing equilibrium and challenging established practices (Barro, 2006). Over the last couple of decades we have witnessed a new phenomenon: systemic risk emanating from core financial markets of the global economy and propagating around the world. Settled expectations, the rules of investment management and the virtues of tried-and-true recipes for asset allocation have been turned upside down. Research linking financial uncertainties with social and environmental trends of the twenty-first century is attracting increasing attention among some investors. Macroeconomic imbalances, ageing Western societies leading to increasing dependency ratios, and a political impasse where rules and regulations 'solve' past problems but do little to address larger, structural issues such as degradation of the environment, resource scarcity and climate change all contribute to drastically changing the landscape of global financial markets.

Uncertainty derived from the complex linkages between financial, environmental and social factors cannot be reduced through traditional risk assessments that treat the long-term as simply an aggregate of short-term positions. The challenge confronting investors is to reconcile the short-term with the long-term perspective while maintaining efficient decision-making processes. Transitioning to sustainable investing on the scale that is necessary to meet the challenges of the twenty-first century requires investors of all stripes to challenge existing norms and social conventions that underlie investment rules and decision models and integrate mechanisms for learning from the past and anticipating future events. Governments also have a role to play in this transformation by providing new interpretations of rules that allow investors to incorporate innovate strategies for managing risks, while also supplying markets with sufficient information to price both short-term and long-term environmental, social and governance (ESG) risks.

These are not modest goals, as they require working against human predisposition to favour short-term payoffs (Kahneman, 2011) and the inertia that characterizes social and economic systems. Equally, new relationships are being forged between companies and their workers, consumers and society. Expectations are growing with regards to corporate social responsibility (CSR), responsible investment and sustainable investment (Woods and Urwin, 2010).

A generation ago, notions of CSR were caught up in geopolitics and much larger debates about capitalism versus socialism. As these issues have receded, a new generation has looked at CSR recognizing that the reputation of the corporation is an asset in its own right and that it can be 'priced' in consumer markets. So, for example, how companies manage their supply chains, carbon footprints and the relationships between suppliers, intermediaries and the final consumer have come to dominate the headlines. Business schools take these issues seriously; witness the recent papers on the concept of shared value by Michael Porter and colleagues at the Harvard Business School.[1] Financial markets have come to recognize that corporate reputation is a significant albeit intangible asset. Media campaigns by non-governmental organizations (NGOs), social activists and activist investors have transformed corporate reputation from 'name recognition' into a managed asset.

If once thought to be a minor issue found amongst public sector pension funds and related investment institutions, the concept of sustainable investment has been rewritten by those who contend that all kinds of institutional investors have the responsibilities of 'universal owners' (see Hawley and Williams, 2000). That is to say, universal owners recognize that through their portfolios they own a slice of the whole economy, and so should help the economy achieve a more prosperous future (Urwin, 2011). Given the significance of financial markets for Western societies, developing economies, and emerging markets, and given the importance of their investments for the long-term welfare of beneficiaries, a new generation of activists have argued that institutional investors and the investment management industry have responsibility for the integrity of the global financial system (at one level) and oversight and engagement with the companies that are included in their investment portfolios (at another level). Governments have been studiously quiet on these issues, preferring to emphasize the connections between fiduciary duty and long-term commitments.

The UN-backed Principles for Responsible Investment (UN PRI) boasts over 1,200 signatories as of 2014. We recognize that many are cautious about taking on these types of responsibilities, using these kinds of new institutions as listening posts for learning about the issues and the ways in which corporate social responsibility and sustainable investment are being recast. Even so, institutions have sought to re-conceptualize their goals and objectives and the means by which those will be realized. The UN PRI has encouraged reflection on these issues. Equally, financial risks and uncertainties combined with the structural issues associated with global economic and environmental transformation have challenged institutional investors to place themselves in this debate.

This chapter contributes to this debate in the following way. In the first instance, we map the emerging realities associated with environmental degradation, in particular resource scarcity and climate change. In order to do so we draw on the best available scientific information and judgment about these issues and place them in the much wider context of the emerging global macroeconomic, social, and geopolitical issues of the twenty-first century. We do so as part of a larger commitment to exploring the universal owners concept and its manifestation in practice in what Woods and Urwin previously have termed as 'sustainable investment'. By their account, this is a commitment to a disciplined approach to long-term investment that considers both immediate investment opportunities and their currently 'un-priced' externalities to guard against the prospect that these un-priced externalities will result in a discounted rate of return.[2] This is followed by consideration for how conceptions of fiduciary duty could change in the future. Just as important, we provide a governance perspective on integrating short-term with long-term investment emphasizing learning, adaptation, and integration. Both governance and the concept of fiduciary duty are crucial elements in taking forward an institutional commitment to sustainable investment.

Environmental degradation, emerging social realities, and investors

Conceptualizing the issues

Recent advancements in scientific research have brought into the open information that is required to move from uncertainty to risk in the evaluation of structural issues such as climate change and resource scarcity. Thus, there is no excuse for investors to ignore research on environmental degradation writ large. There is a goldmine of data and research on both issues, which allows investors to analyze each in terms of risk, its levels, dimensions, and sources. Some financial tools already exist, and more are emerging to transform resource scarcity–related risks into investment opportunities.

It has become conventional wisdom that the primary drivers of natural resource scarcity are social, economic, political, and cultural, rather than biophysical. At the same time, the temporal dimensions of scarcity have received less attention from investors. Too often, resource scarcity is caught up with short-term market movements, prompting confusion with long-term processes that may produce scarcity but, equally, discount scarcity as economies and societies adapt to the relative prices of complementary resources. Long-term resource scarcity is deeply implicated in structural transformation – a point that many perceptive investors are turning to their advantage.

In Table 46.1 we distinguish between three main groups of non-physical factors driving resource scarcity, again at the global level, and show how these differ between individual resources. Socio-economic factors refer to the issue of affordability and access of particular socioeconomic groups to resources, within and across nations and regions.[3] A good illustration is the case of the highly uneven socioeconomic distribution of water pollution. While 190 million water pollution–related illnesses are reported each year, in 2011 only 36 per cent of companies operating in China acknowledged water scarcity as a risk to their business operations[4]. However, as we will discuss shortly, overall this may be gradually changing.

Resource governance refers to the management and oversight of the production, distribution, and consumption of the resource by relevant authorities, from local through national to international levels, including governments, corporations, markets, and civil society. At least in principle, the best-known example at the global level is the infrastructure governing climate change mitigation and adaptation, the Kyoto Protocol, and associated institutions, including carbon markets,

Table 46.1 Non-physical factors driving resource scarcity

Resource	*Socio-economic*	*Resource governance*	*Geopolitical*
Atmospheric waste sink	XXX	XXX	XX
Water	XXX	XXX	XXX
Biodiversity	XX	XX	X
Food	XX	XX	XX
Agricultural land	XX	XX	XX
Rare earth elements	XX	X	XXX
Mineral fertilizers	XX	XXX	XXX
Oil and gas	X	XX	XXX
Metals	X	X	XX
Coal	X	XX	X
Terrestrial waste sinks	XXX	X	XX

X = low risk, XX = medium risk, XXX = high risk.

although over time these frameworks have proven highly flawed in their design and execution. A more successful example from the relatively recent past may be the Montreal Protocol. Ratified in 1987 and overseen by a number of UN agencies and the World Bank, this treaty has proven highly successful at coordinating international efforts to halt the depletion of the ozone layer. By contrast, governance of mineral fertilizers is lacking: the product life cycle is spread across the extractive and chemical industries, agricultural markets, and wastewater treatment. Since no single transnational entity has oversight, few relevant organizations (e.g. the World Bank, UN Food and Agriculture Organization, national departments of agriculture, the wastewater industry) liaise with each other. Proper resource governance can also ensure that waste along the production and consumption chain is minimized. For example, up to 80 per cent of global phosphate resources are wasted 'from mine to fork' through inefficient mining, fertilizer processing, excessive land application, and wasted food (Cordell, 2010).

Geopolitical scarcity refers to the concentration of resources in relatively few – and often politically sensitive – regions of the world (Cordell, 2010). The clearest example at the global level may be minerals such as rare earth elements (REEs): China currently accounts for about 95 per cent of global production, and attempts to diversify processing geographically have proceeded slowly and have faced substantial challenges.[5] Potash is another essential and non-substitutable component of fertilizers, of which about 90 per cent of current economic reserves are located in Canada, Russia, and Belarus. Geopolitical scarcity may manifest itself at smaller scales: for example, inter-basin management of key water resources, such as the Nile and Mekong rivers, within and across countries can exacerbate existing political tensions. In the past, geopolitical scarcity was at the forefront of investors' consciousness due to the power OPEC wielded over global oil markets, but in more recent decades it has receded as an issue of central concern. However, recent events have once again demonstrated the perils for companies of relying too heavily on specific geographies for resource supply: witness, for example, the effects felt from the Great Japan Earthquake and Fukushima nuclear disaster in Japan in 2011 by manufacturers worldwide who had grown overly dependent on a 'just-in-time' model of production.

Overall, Table 46.1 shows that in many cases scarcity is a social justice issue; governance is sorely lacking for many resources; and geopolitics may emerge as the greatest risk to supply as well as environmental governance. Such distinctions aside, we recognize atmospheric waste sinks as one of the most urgent and significant types of resource scarcity. Several recent studies published over the past few years demonstrate that the total cumulative amount of carbon dioxide released into the atmosphere determines the likely peak warming (Allen et al., 2009). Thus, in order to ensure that the peak remains within two degrees above pre-industrial temperature levels, a cumulative budget of between 0.75 and 1.5 trillion tonnes of carbon cannot be exceeded (Meinshausen et al., 2009, and Matthews et al., 2009, respectively). More recently, the Intergovernmental Panel on Climate Change has estimated the 'carbon budget' to be 1 trillion tonnes. By 2011, over half of this budget had been used. This also means that emissions rates within a single decade are of limited significance in and of themselves; they are important insofar as they contribute to cumulative warming (Allen, 2012). In this view, climate risks appear even more urgent, and adaptation measures take on greater importance as an area sorely in need of investment.

Water scarcity has also become an issue of great urgency. It is estimated that $23 trillion needs to be invested in water infrastructure worldwide by 2030, and much of this investment will have to be undertaken by the private sector (Water Resources Group, 2009. These contingent liabilities represent what is referred to as 'corporate water risk', which affects more than just utility companies: it applies to many sectors, including mining, food, chemical, and electronic industries (Money, 2014). It is particularly important for companies operating in emerging and developing countries, as these countries lack water infrastructure and have increasing bargaining power to make private foreign companies finance infrastructure from their own corporate resources. To be in a better position to evaluate corporate water risk, investors need to lobby for improvements in disclosure standards. In recent years, a number of initiatives such as the CDP's Water Disclosure Project and the Sustainability Accountability Standards Board have made important inroads into the problem of how to make the issue of water scarcity financially material. But however promising and increasingly popular these initiatives may be, it remains the case that on the whole, current accounting practices do not fully reflect either amount of water used by companies or the full costs of water withdrawal and disposal on local water supply.

Innovative solutions for investors

Corporate water risk illustrates the impact of resource scarcity on conventional financial instruments. However, sustainable investing requires not just a major revision of existing portfolios with regard to environmental risks, but, more important, a consideration for new financial instruments and vehicles and innovative ways of investment.

As one example, forest bonds are new financial instruments at the disposal of sustainable investors. Forest bonds are an example of a larger family of environmental asset–backed securities. They are important because sustainable forestry is crucial for many aspects of resource scarcity, including climate change mitigation, water, and biodiversity. They are a huge source of ecosystem services valued at trillions of USD annually. Despite recent advances in afforestation and reforestation, approximately 13 million hectares of forest per year are cleared globally for agriculture, mining, and logging (equal to the total area of England). To halve the rate of deforestation by 2020, global investment in sustainable forestry must increase to $30 billion annually. Forest bonds may be the fastest way to raise capital at the scale needed while spreading financial risks and environmental benefits across multiple time horizons. They can be issued by national governments and inter-governmental organizations and repaid using revenues from forest and non-forest-based sources (Cranford et al., 2011).

Sustainable investing also calls for entirely new investment vehicles, such as the International Green Fund (IGF). The IGF could help to scale up and coordinate investment in green technology to reach a critical mass of resources and effort to achieve a breakthrough in green technology development. At present, the centres of green technology development are scattered geographically across advanced economies in Western Europe, Japan, and North America (where they are needed least), while leading emerging market economies (where green technology is needed most) make their own investments mostly by trying to catch up with developments in advanced economies. From a global perspective this leads to fragmentation and inefficiencies (Bolton et al., 2011).

Another innovative way of coordinating investment in green technology is via investment networks, whereby investors cooperate with companies and governments in local, national, and international initiatives. A good example is the activity of Better Place,[6] headquartered in Palo Alto, California, which acts as a gateway to such innovative investment networks. Components of Better Place's strategy include not only careful supply chain management, but also the development of networks of battery switch and charging stations, investing in smart grid software, and engaging with international standard-setting bodies to develop best-practice global standards. Collaborators of Better Place include banks, venture capital and private equity firms, electric utilities, governments, automakers, and other businesses. It is an approach in which global knowledge must be combined with local, context-specific knowledge (Wójcik, 2011; Clark and Wójcik, 2007). Above all, then, resource scarcity calls for an active and collaborative approach to investment.

Emerging social realities

Indeed, we share the commonly held view that the separation of environmental degradation from social and macroeconomic realities is in many ways artificial, as these issues are interdependent. While social realities are often harder to quantify than structural issues such as climate change or environmental degradation, their salience for investors is equally relevant. In particular, sustainable investment must include a serious consideration of economic equity – a hot-button political issue of late on both sides of the Atlantic, and indeed around the world. Inequality is not only a moral issue – it is also a major obstacle to sustainability and economic growth, because unequal distribution of resources can lead to economic and political warfare between and within nations. When the causes and consequences of environmental damage are unevenly distributed, achieving consensus on how to address environmental challenges becomes extremely difficult. One stark example at the global level is the failure to reach a global climate agreement. Of course, inequality also poses challenges to sustainability at the national and sub-national level: issues such as energy poverty, deforestation, and inequitably shared water use all have their roots to at least some extent in socio-economic inequality.

Sustainable investors must ask themselves the question: What has been the impact of globalization on distribution and sustainability? While globalization has lowered the proportion of people living in absolute poverty in the last 40 years, income inequality has increased consistently between and within countries. In other words, globalization has opened up a pathway for economic growth and prosperity for some countries, but there remain losers – and research has shown that societies begin to lose their economic dynamism beyond certain levels of inequality. Mobility of goods, labour, and capital has also given rise to adverse environmental effects such as pollution, pandemics, and trade in hazardous wastes. Indeed, as Ian Goldin and Mike Mariathasan (2014) observe, the most serious threats to society raised by the spectre of globalization do not manifest in the form of risks in an individual system, including finance, health, infrastructure, energy, or the environment, but from our lack of capacity to understand and manage the interdependencies and complexities between these systems.

We have probably picked all the low-hanging fruits of globalization by basing our activities on resource-intensive production and consumption and by concentrating economic activity in places densely populated with educated people (Cowen, 2011). In other words, globalization will continue to increase consumption in developing regions at the expense of future generations if business continues as usual. Filling in the blind spots, such as large swathes of Africa, Latin America, and Central Asia, is going to be much more difficult. The credit boom in the US and in parts of Western Europe in the last decades has been very damaging from the perspective of distribution and sustainability. It has increased consumption where it had already been at its highest. This, in turn, makes rebalancing the global economy by increasing consumption in China and increasing exports from the US highly questionable in terms of environmental impact: it has been estimated that if China alone were to attain levels of per capita resource consumption comparable to that of America, global oil consumption would double; add India and it would triple (Diamond, 2008).

With all of these challenges, where can sustainable investors begin to look for opportunities? To begin with, we consider emerging economies as countries where long-term investment is crucial to improving sustainability worldwide. In other words, these regions would represent focal areas on a world map of investing risks and opportunities: this is where sustainable investing can make the most difference. Emerging economies face the choice between two stylized options. The short-term option is to borrow existing technologies and develop them at a lower cost for a mass market, domestically and internationally. The long-term option is to develop entirely new technologies, enabling both sustainable development and global market leadership. Where these countries stand at the moment, we cannot be sure. China on the one hand promises a massive green stimulus package at home, while on the other it pursues natural resource diplomacy abroad.

The concept and the reality of universal ownership, coupled with enhanced knowledge and understanding of natural resource scarcity, offers the promise of a transformation in investment practices, at least on the demand side of the industry. The supply side requires pioneering investment management and advisory firms that will embrace sustainable investment. As we suggest in the sections to follow, this would require these actors to embrace a revised view of fiduciary duty, wider risk management techniques, quality engagement activity, and appropriate resourcing of their own governance.

Fiduciary obligation and sustainable investing

While progress has been made on uncovering the salience of emerging environmental and social trends for investors, a significant challenge remains for the integration of these risks into decision-making and ownership practices. Research underlying this paper reveals a fear commonly held by asset owners: that sustainable investing (SI) could breach their fiduciary obligation. This fear is seemingly based on a perception that sustainable investing requires a financial sacrifice (see UNEP Finance Initiative, 2005). The fear is not surprising: legal decisions on fiduciary obligation sometimes appear to conflict (Woods, 2011); interpretative commentary provided by organizations such as the US Department of Labor is often unclear (Woods, 2011); and terminology in the field is confusing – few, if any, can navigate the differences between the overlapping and evolving concepts of sustainable, responsible, ethical, socially responsible, green, and clean investment (Woods and Urwin, 2010).[7]

Those who manage investments on behalf of others are bound by a number of fiduciary obligations (see generally Woods, 2011; Ellison, 2008; Richardson, 2008). Fiduciaries must put the interests of beneficiaries first when determining the investment strategy and avoid conflicts of interest (loyalty); invest like a prudent expert (in practice, for many asset owners, this obligation requires owners to appoint appropriate asset managers) (prudence); diversify according to modern portfolio theory (diversification);[8] and avoid favouring the interests of a particular beneficiary or class of beneficiaries over others (impartiality). The term 'fiduciary obligation' originates from trust law in common law jurisdictions such as the UK and the US. However, the concepts underlying the fiduciary obligations described above are generally accepted in all countries where agents invest on behalf of others.

Fiduciary obligation originates from trust law, a branch of law particular to common law countries. As such, the case law on fiduciary obligation is concentrated in the US, UK, Australia, and other common law countries. Countries that have a civil law, as is the case throughout continental Europe, often have fiduciary-like obligations based in statute or contract. They do not have a legacy of case law on fiduciary obligation that could be interpreted as preventing sustainable investing. Country-by-country data on the UN-backed Principles for Responsible Investment (PRI) shows that civil law countries have a greater number of PRI signatories (in terms of assets under management) than the UK and US combined. While many factors contribute to the uptake of sustainable or responsible investing processes, it seems reasonable to conclude that at least part of the greater uptake in civil law countries can be attributed to the absence of perceived legal obstacles. That said, investors from common law countries are increasingly signing on to the PRI. Of the 254 new signatories in 2012, 94 were from the US, Canada, UK, and Australia. Yet civil law countries continue to constitute the majority of finance committed to the PRI.

Unfortunately, many fiduciaries are currently failing to meet the challenges posed by deep changes to conditions within the global financial system. For example, asset owners and their agents have a fiduciary obligation to ensure, as far as possible that companies are run in the best interests of beneficiaries. Recent corporate governance failures highlight a breakdown of corporate accountability. Many things contribute to this breakdown: opacity in corporate reporting, costs associated with stronger corporate governance, legal obstacles to shareholder involvement, and lack of interest in long-term corporate performance. The consequences can be both systemic (e.g. only 60 per cent of potential shareholder votes were exercised in the UK in 2011) and extraordinary (Royal Bank of Scotland's acquisition of Algemene Bank Nederland AMRO Bank in 2007 occurred in the face of highly sceptical commentary; only around 5 per cent of shareholders opposed the acquisition, and it contributed to heavy losses for shareholders). As the scale and contagion of corporate failures increases, fiduciary obligation may require asset owners and managers to increase their oversight role in order to decrease the risk of corporate failure and the destruction of shareholder value.

Sustainable investing frameworks may help both asset owners and asset managers to meet their fiduciary obligations in today's changing economic, environmental, and political context. The integration of ESG risk assessment into the investment process provides a more comprehensive approach to due diligence. Structuring longer time horizons into the investment strategy helps to overcome the behavioural bias that individuals have toward shorter-term outcomes (see Clark et al., 2007, 2006), meaning that the interests of both younger and older beneficiaries are considered. A stronger commitment to corporate governance responsibilities, including voting proxies and engaging with companies in appropriate situations, provides an opportunity to enhance the interests of all beneficiaries. Finally, in contrast to many 'ethical investment' processes, sustainable investing does not involve the exclusion of particular asset classes or industries and therefore does not in itself limit the ability of investors to diversify their holdings.[9]

How could the interpretation of fiduciary obligation develop over time to encourage (or indeed require) a more sustainable approach to investing? There are three possible paths of evolution. Within each of these paths, there is a spectrum of scenarios. On what can be called the 'conventional' end of the spectrum, fiduciary obligation reflects the status quo. On the other end, fiduciary obligation requires a more sustainable approach to investment. The first set of scenarios describes what might occur if fiduciary obligation develops along a 'business as usual' path. The second and third are sparked by catalysts: legislative change and litigation.

The first path of development occurs in the absence of a catalyst. This means business as usual or incremental change. If fiduciary obligation continues to develop without the influence of an extraordinary event, there is a spectrum of ways it could evolve. On the conventional end, investors could become more short-term oriented as markets become more volatile. In this scenario, sustainable investing would become the exception. At the other end of the spectrum, more investors could gradually adopt sustainable investing processes, so that over many years, ESG integration, engagement, and longer investment horizons become the norm. The steady adoption of the PRI by mainstream investors suggests that the investment community is indeed becoming more open to the notion of sustainable investment. What remains to be seen, however, is the extent to which the adoption of the PRI leads to change in practice. Recent changes to the PRI reporting requirements introduced in the 2013–14 cycle may shed more light on this issue in the future. As courts, commentators, and legal practitioners tend to view 'prudence' as conforming to conventional investment practices (doing what other investors do) (see Woods, 2011), a business as usual scenario is likely to mean a very slow process of evolution.

A second path of development could follow the advent of legislative change. Academic studies have advocated legislative change or safe harbours as a means to overcome the uncertainty about the status of sustainable investment vis-à-vis fiduciary obligation (see Richardson, 2011; Woods, 2011; Woods and Urwin, 2010). In this set of scenarios, legislatures would make statutory changes to the concept of fiduciary obligation in order to clarify that fiduciaries should consider the financial impact of various ESG factors associated with a particular investment, and that fiduciaries may adopt longer-term time horizons.

There is a spectrum of ways that investors could respond to this sort of legislative change. On the one hand, it could mean that more investors adopt a sustainable investing approach, because it is completely clear that sustainable investing is consistent with meeting fiduciary obligations. In the absence of such legislation, the UK's Stewardship Code, while not mandating a more sustainable approach to investment, goes some way toward encouraging one. Legislative change or, in its absence, collective industry-based initiatives could spread the cost of corporate stewardship amongst investors and reduce the perceived free-rider problem. On the other hand, investors might choose to ignore the legislative provision, leading instead to the set of 'business as usual' scenarios described above. Moreover, any such provision is likely to be permissive, rather than mandatory. Regardless, a number of factors make this set of scenarios unlikely in the near future. First, creation of safe harbour does not necessarily result in change; it simply paves the way for it. Second, given the economic environment, it is a difficult time to propose legislative amendments that may be perceived as affecting pension fund benefits. Third, it would need wider political support beyond the NGO/sustainable investment community.

Finally, litigation could act as a catalyst for the development of fiduciary obligation. New case law could give further clarification to the parameters of fiduciary obligation in the context of sustainable investing. Litigation over the interpretation of various features of fiduciary obligation has had a large influence on perceptions of sustainable investment. There is a range of possible scenarios for litigation. Asset owners could sue managers for breach of fiduciary obligation where they believe that managers have failed to invest sustainably (where it is in the best interests of beneficiaries to do so). Asset owners appear to be increasingly ready to litigate in other contexts. For example, Unilever famously sued Merrill Lynch Investment Managers for damages over the alleged mismanagement of its pension fund in 2001. More recently, Dutch pension giant ABP launched a series of lawsuits against several asset management firms in 2010 and 2011 for misleading the fund in relation to the purchase of mortgage-backed securities that, according to APB, were far riskier than represented by the managers.

Looking forward, one significant challenge for investors may well be the imposition of liability for climate change impacts on companies and other asset holders that profit from the processes that cause climate change. As Allen (2012) argues, this can be considered an unknowable uncertainty: a possibility of which the probability is impossible to quantify. Perhaps in part for this reason investors' concerns about the issue of climate change normally focus on risks more likely to manifest over the coming decades: the potential impact of greenhouse gas emission controls on energy prices and the risk of stranded assets in carbon-intensive industries; on the impacts of projected climate change over the next few decades on investments in agriculture and the built environment; or on the impact of 'climate change mitigation'. Yet a dramatic change in carbon prices due to new scientific discoveries is unlikely given that the evolution of climate change science progresses only incrementally, and past predictions based on the assumption that most of the observed global-scale warming is caused by anthropogenic greenhouse gas emissions have been confirmed by observations (see, for example Allen et al., 2009).

By contrast, the science of climate change attribution has developed to the point where the possibility of identifying specific 'victims' of climate change and how they are being affected is no longer purely hypothetical. As a result, the issue of legal liability has been raised through test cases filed in US courts. If successful, these cases could focus the cost of climate change onto specific assets, with potentially substantial negative impact on their value. Yet whether these cases succeed, let alone set a precedent, depends on difficult-to-predict legal rather than scientific factors (Allen, 2011). Conceivably, courts could argue that oversight of greenhouse gas emissions is not within the remit of the judicial branch of government: this occurred, for example, in the case of *Connecticut vs. American Electric Power Company*, in which it was argued that Congressional designation of the US Environmental Protection Agency as the decision-maker on greenhouse gas regulation displaced any public nuisance claim (Allen, 2012).

Sustainable investing in the form presented in this chapter may help asset owners and asset managers to meet their fiduciary obligations in a context of changing environmental, economic, and political conditions. Thorough assessment of ESG risks increases the comprehensiveness of stock analysis, in line with the obligation of prudence. The adoption of longer investment time horizons helps investors to move away from the short-term decision-making that often prioritizes the interests of older beneficiaries over those of younger ones, in line with the obligation of impartiality. Finally, increased fulfilment of corporate stewardship responsibilities, through voting proxies and engaging where appropriate with investee companies to improve outcomes for shareholders, is ultimately in the best interests of beneficiaries. This, like improved ESG analysis and longer investment time horizons, helps asset owners and managers to fulfil their obligation of loyalty. The advantages of sustainable investing also exist in jurisdictions that do not have fiduciary obligations per se. Most important, sustainable investing requires a change of perspective on fiduciary obligation. Investors should ask not 'does my fiduciary obligation let me invest sustainably?', but rather 'am I investing sustainably enough to meet my obligations?' Legislation that provides favourable taxation policies and voting rights for long-term investors relative to short-term traders could complement changes to the interpretation of fiduciary duty, further contributing to advancing the sustainable investing agenda (see Richardson, 2009).

A long-term perspective on best practice fund governance

The above sections challenge us to re-conceptualize the immediate and obvious into data points that can be used to chart a way forward in anticipation of the future. A long-term perspective on resource scarcity, public attitudes and opinions, and climate change can transform how we think about the short term. By the same token, the long view reveals conventional issues, such as fiduciary duty, to have a history of changing interpretations with the prospect of more to come. At one level, pension fund trustees and those responsible for realizing the retirement objectives of beneficiaries have always looked to the long-term, stretching out beyond to 5 years to 25 years, even 50 years and more. But at another level, we all recognize the temptation to think and act in the short term (Kahneman, 2011). Too often, long-term objectives are left to unfold (hopefully) through the accumulation of short-term positions. Recent research has shown that this type of behaviour need not, in fact, take us anywhere near our long-term goals (Vayanos and Woolley, 2012).

Whereas some commentators seem to imagine that long-term investment is different in type or, indeed, requires a different behavioural template, compared to short-term investment, it seems obvious that to be an effective long-term investor requires an appreciation of the relationship between the short-term and the long-term. Adopting a long-term perspective does not make the short-term irrelevant. Rather, the challenge is to reconcile and manage the short-term with the long-term in ways that aid effective investment decision-making. This argument draws upon the work of Clark and Urwin (2010, 2008a) on best practice pension fund governance. In particular, it draws on their template of best practice, which assumes that which is inherited can be adapted to the new realities of global financial markets – increasing market volatility, the prospect of systemic risk, and the likelihood that 'fat-tail' events can trounce even the most sophisticated investment strategies.

Before explaining the relationship between short-term and long-term investment, it is important to identify three preconditions for bridging these temporal periods.

- Adaptive capacity: the potential of an institution to change its strategy in response to current, unanticipated events and future risks and opportunities. As Lo (2004) and others have recently remarked, financial markets evolve, they hardly ever go back to 'normal', and it is the 'fleet-of- foot' who are able to translate recognition of 'moments' and 'new trajectories' into market opportunity.
- Reflexivity: the willingness or capacity of a decision-maker to assess the success or otherwise of their strategies in the light of new information, and in anticipation of unfolding pathways (scenarios) that lie ahead. For many experts, reflexivity complements and deepens their skills and experience (Wagner 2002). The most successful institutions build into their decision-making the opportunities for understanding their own unintended contributions to outcomes and learning from mistakes as well as recognizing the payoffs to informed decision-making.
- Justified beliefs: the knowledge and understanding necessary to sustain the (explicit) beliefs that underpin investment strategy. At one level, beliefs simply justify or rationalize intuitive responses to market signals. At another level, however, beliefs need to be justified: data is crucial, assessing the underlying forces driving short-term and long-term market pricing is important, and testing competing suppositions against scenarios for the future is vital when framing long-term commitments.

Investment decision-making is often reactive, tends to reinforce past commitments, and is led by events rather than an analysis of underlying economic and financial processes. It also tends to condition herding behaviour because investment managers are often evaluated against common benchmarks. Therefore, managers have an incentive to ensure that their portfolios resemble these benchmarks closely (Rajan, 2006). More specifically, investment decision-making is typically based on 'certainties' like the commonplace assumption that equities outperform bonds over the long term. At one level, this is a truism justified by research on the performance of Western financial markets over the past 100 years (Dimson et al., 2002). At another level, however, it hides extended periods of financial crisis and market disjunction. Worse, it can be used to justify inertia and a lack of reflection (myopia) on the status of recent events against long-term trends (Clark, 2011). We have also observed that collective and individual decision-making is typically risk averse, avoiding future commitments where possible, as reflected in the premium attributed to liquidity (Clark et al., 2006). Yet some of the most successful institutions have, in recent years, exploited market agents' risk aversion to reap a premium on long-term commitment (witness the success of a number of Canadian pension fund institutions).

Pension fund governance is often under-resourced (Clark and Urwin, 2008a). As a consequence, many fund boards do not use the time available in effective and strategic ways, confusing their short-term reactions to market agents' under- and over-performance with informed reflection about the long-term viability of investment strategies. In some circumstances, fund boards and their sponsors turn a blind eye to the risks assumed by ambitious short-term return targets. We are not the only analysts to have noticed that during the global financial crisis and, more recently, over the euro crisis, under-resourced investment institutions and sponsors have sought safe-havens from further commitments to promised benefits through extended periods of 'recovery' based upon assumed higher rates of return. Risk assessments are rudimentary, reflection and reflexivity on the long-term plausibility of risk and return scenarios are superficial, and the beliefs justifying these decisions are, at best, simpleminded. We show that the size of an institution's governance budget is correlated with its capacity to assess risk and adapt accordingly over the long-term (Clark and Urwin, 2010).

A long-term perspective is more than the sum of short-term positions. It looks beyond market momentum (monthly), the rhythm of economic cycles (5 to 7 years), and technological innovation (10 to 25 years) to the transformation of whole societies and even global prospects. So, for example, population ageing is normally viewed in terms of whole generations (out to 2050). Similarly, climate change is viewed as a process whose consequences will unfold over the next 25, 50, and 100 years (and beyond). Both can be treated as irrelevant for current investment decision-making and planning for the future if we remain transfixed by current events and their resolution over the coming three to five years. We should remind ourselves that many pension funds, insurance companies, pension reserve schemes, and sovereign wealth funds have, either explicitly or implicitly, a duty to balance the interests of current generations with future generations. Intergenerational equity, the fiduciary duty of impartiality, is one way of conceptualizing in operational terms a commitment to long-term investment.

One of the lessons of the global financial crisis and the euro crisis is that the past is not the future (Lo, 2011). If institutions are to realize ambitious long-term target rates of return, one obvious way forward is to shift on an incremental basis asset allocation towards the emerging economies of the East and the South. For many institutions, large and small, scenario planning aided by investment managers and consultants has crystallized the need for incremental adaptation while pointing to the obvious costs and the (largely) negative risks associated with the status quo (home bias and reliance upon the nexus between the UK and Europe). If it takes a crisis to crystallize the way forward, it is a small step indeed towards incorporating resource scarcity and the map of climate change impacts into 5- and 10-year investment strategies. Indeed, the long-term economic futures of emerging markets could be seen through the lens of resource scarcity and climate change where, for example, the risks associated with climate-induced water scarcity intersect with economic growth potential.

Emerging markets, resource scarcity, and even the map of climate change have become mainstream topics for investment analysts and investment strategy. If we look beyond five years, reasonable estimates of their relative significance and likely impacts can be made just as probabilities can be assigned to likely possibilities. We understand the driving forces behind the growth of emerging markets and resource scarcity; likewise, we have very good estimates of the long-term pathway of climate change (measured in terms of CO_2 emissions etc.). Of course, there remain vigorous debates about the growth potentials of emerging markets and the dimensions of resource scarcity. There are those who contest climate change (although we find the science compelling). It is much harder to attribute probabilities to the growth potential of emerging markets and the relative importance of different kinds of resource scarcity when we look beyond economic cycles to long-term structural change (10 to 20 years out). Here, however, all is not lost. It is crucial that institutions invest in knowledge and understanding of the forces driving emerging markets and resource scarcity – adaptive learning can reap market advantage before others converge on accepted wisdom.

Whereas the forces driving climate change are well understood there remain many unknowns. Calibrating the geographical impact of climate change, thereby discriminating between regions of the earth on the basis of their likely environmental conditions over the next 20 to 50 to 100 years, remains a significant challenge. Furthermore, how governments might deal with these issues is also subject to considerable uncertainty. The impact and response to climate change are topics subject to great uncertainty, especially because there are likely to be significant interaction effects between these two issues. How should investors deal with these issues? There are two likely responses. As it is, investors closely monitor government policies and their consequences. Were there to be moves to introduce effective regional and global carbon markets, uncertainty would quickly morph into risk scenarios aimed at pricing the long-term value of the world's largest corporations that rely upon fossil fuels. Similarly, if scientists could bring to ground the impact of climate change (Allen, 2012), the growth potentials of whole countries could be dramatically revised.

These are not outrageous scenarios for the near future. But translating these prospects into investment opportunities requires investing in both knowledge and understanding of climate science as well as maintaining a connection with the emerging frontiers of research in the field. It seems inevitable that few institutions are willing to invest in the margins of climate science; many institutions are subject to close scrutiny of their budget allocations, treating the long-term as something that is tangible with immediate rewards. Further, many environmental risks like climate change represent un-situated risks; risks that we rarely observe directly in a tangible form, and which unfold gradually. We may realize them only when it is too late. The fact that two of the world's leading investment consultants have made concerted efforts to bring to market insights and information on these issues suggests that market intermediaries may play a major role in translating climate science into risk scenarios and prospective opportunities. In some regions of the world already identified as 'at risk' to adverse impacts of climate change, some investment institutions have sought to place themselves close to centres of technological innovation focused upon the amelioration of climate change. Perhaps there is a role for direct investment in technological futures, going beyond portfolio investment in known opportunities, known risks and rewards (Diebold et al., 2010). Yet this must be facilitated by appropriate funding mechanisms and regulatory support (Kaminker and Stewart, 2012).

What role should government play in promoting commitment to long-term investment? Some activists argue for policies that would require financial institutions to invest a portion of their assets in climate change related 'opportunities'. This type of policy would create as many problems as it solves – witness the perverse incentives that accompanied government rules on the allocation of assets to different asset classes. As a starting point, governments could begin by eliminating counterproductive tax breaks to energy companies. Governments could encourage institutions to hold investments longer (thereby encouraging a longer horizon over which risk is assessed) by changing tax policies and include a well-designed green stimulus. More important could be clarification of the meaning of fiduciary duty, thereby promoting an explicit balancing of interest between generations. Governments could apply the principles of intergenerational accounting to their own policies and to major banks and financial institutions.

But, most important, governments should ensure that markets have sufficient knowledge to adequately price the short-term and long-term environmental risks associated with different types of securities. Here, government can act in two different and complementary ways. Governments can set short-term and long-term CO_2 emission targets, starting with short-term voluntary compliance regimes relevant to large corporations and environment-heavy industries, which morph in the long-term into compulsory compliance.

This would have at least two benefits. First, it would signal to the market the direction of travel of government policy and the likely risks to be borne by affected companies and industries. Second, it would promote technological innovation and its associated investors and market intermediaries. Just as important, it could give greater salience to the services already offered by intermediaries such as the CDP, the Extractive Industries Transparency Initiative, and Trucost.[10] Whereas governments are wary of any regulatory burden that affects corporate competitiveness, this type of regime would promote long-term innovation on both the capital-raising side of the market and the capital-providing side of the market. In any event, governments must have the courage of their convictions and follow the emerging consensus amongst the public that the polluter 'must' pay. In other words, financial markets will take seriously corporate long-term environmental liabilities if there is evidence of government commitment to the proper pricing of those liabilities.

Conclusion

Investment managers have become fond of talking about the new realities emerging in capital markets. Over the past couple of decades, the investment industry has experienced the Asian financial crisis (1997), the Long-Term Capital Management debacle (1998), the dot-com bubble and bust (2000–3), the sub-prime bubble (2007–8), and, most recently, the euro crisis. But as we have shown, the industry is also experiencing reverberations from resource scarcity, environmental disasters, and growing inequality. Indeed, we are living in extraordinary times: Martin Wolf of the *Financial Times* has described the world as undergoing a shock and the shift; Paul Hawken of the Long New Foundation describes a New Great Transformation comparable in its epochal character with the Industrial Revolution two centuries ago. Recent events have revealed a failure of governance across many sectors and at multiples scales, but very little reform has been undertaken to date. The failure of the Copenhagen climate treaty, coupled with a shortage of funding post-2008, has sapped much of the energy from efforts to manage environmental change.

Yet we have also shown that at the same time the investment industry is exposed to new investment opportunities, such as low carbon technologies and water infrastructure. Scientific research is making it possible to establish new causal relationships between climate change and carbon emissions and extreme weather events such as tropical storms.

Aware that these broad-brush arguments are by now familiar to many, we have sketched out some practical frameworks through which investors may begin to deal with these new realities. Implementing them requires more than adjusting asset allocations and designing new portfolios. Long-term investing requires new perspectives on investment management that challenge the status quo of asset allocation on the basis of a traditional understanding of risk management. These new realities demand new investment vehicles and instruments to leverage economies of scope and scale and reach the critical mass required to transition to a more sustainable economy. But in doing so, investors must learn to shift management from focusing on the short-term to the long-term.

Internal governance is critical for managing the new dimensions of dynamic forms of risk and uncertainty across short-term and long-term investment perspectives, as it allows for adapting inherited structures to new market realities. It is important to recognize that adopting a long-term perspective does not render the short-term irrelevant, but rather requires bridging these perspectives. Achieving this goal requires governance that is adaptive to respond to future risks and opportunities; reflexive to learn from the past and adjust future trajectories; and based on justified beliefs that are supported by data and experience and are robust against various future scenarios.

This transition also requires moving beyond the fear that prevents investors from seeking out these new opportunities we identify. We demonstrate that it is possible to interpret fiduciary duty in ways that promote an explicit balance of interest between generations, while managing the underlying principal–agent problems it was originally intended to resolve. Common law has evolved in ways that reflect the context of present circumstances; similarly, it is possible to conceive of fiduciary duty as an evolving doctrine that is open to reinterpretation in the context of a changing environment.

In making plans for the future, we need a road map and set of tools by which those plans will be realized. Having agreed on our goals and objectives and having put in place the mechanisms or means by which we will realize those goals and objectives, we must carry forward ends and means in an iterative and adaptive fashion. In other words, the challenge facing us all is to suspend the 'automatic pilot' that typically governs our actions and institutions and take charge of realizing our plans for the future. In the meantime, there is good reason to believe that well-resourced institutions may reap a premium by managing their short-term temptation while focusing upon the knowledge and understanding necessary to anticipate new avenues of value and benefit.

Notes

1 See, for example, Porter, M. and Kramer, M. *Strategy & Society: The Link between Competitive Advantage and Corporate Social Responsibility*, 2006: 78–93; Porter, M. and Kramer, M. 'Creating Shared Value', *Harvard Business Review* Vol. 89 Issue 1/2, Jan/Feb 2011: 62–77.

2 Un-priced externalities refer to assets and liabilities that are financially material in the long-term, but not necessarily in the short-term. Pollution is an example. Un-priced externalities differ from extra-financial externalities, which refer to assets and liabilities that would not be priced in the short-term or long-term, due to their complexity. Poverty is an example of an extra-financial externality. Investors must take both forms of externalities seriously.

3 This issue was formalized in 1983 by economist Amartya Sen, who was subsequently awarded the Nobel Prize for his achievement.

4 China Water Risk, *Big Picture*, 2011, online, available HTTP: <http://chinawaterrisk.org/big-picture/>.

5 Witness, for example, conflicts over the attempt by Lynas Corporation, an Australian producer of rare earths, to open what would be the world's largest processing facility outside of China in Malaysia: local concerns about pollution led to strong opposition and legal action which delayed the opening of the refinery by five years. When the refinery did open in 2012, it was constrained by a temporary operating license, and did not receive a full operating license until September 2014.

6 *Better Place: Accelerating the Transition to Sustainable Transportation*, online, available HTTP: <http://www.betterplace.com>.

7 BlackRock intentionally does not distinguish between these investment strategies: "The terms 'corporate governance,' 'responsible investment', 'sustainability', 'ESG' (Environmental, Social and Governance), and 'SEE' (Social, Ethical and Environmental) are often used interchangeably. In our experience, companies seldom have sound practices on the SEE impacts of their business if they don't have sound governance. Therefore, we evaluate the SEE factors of a company's business through the lens of corporate governance" – Michelle Edkins, Global Head of CGRI.

8 Diversification as a process exploits the interaction of assets in a portfolio as a whole to eliminate idiosyncratic risks and has well-documented benefits for increasing expected returns while reducing risk. While modern portfolio theory is often used interchangeably with diversification, there are important differences between the theory, which postulates a trade-off between risk and return, and the practice of diversification, which requires increasingly sophisticated strategies beyond asset labels to consider risk factors underlying these assets.

9 Divestment and negative screening do not necessarily lead to loss of financial returns. Some studies suggest that as screening intensity increases, the diversification effect is offset because better managed and more stable companies are selected into the portfolio (e.g. Barnett and Salomon, 2006). Also, decreasing marginal diversification benefits (see Ang, 2012, mean-variance investing) suggest that ethical screening of a particular stock or industry has only negligible effects for a portfolio that is otherwise well diversified.

10 Carbon Disclosure Project (CDP), online, available HTTP: <https://www.cdproject.net>; Extractive Industry Transparency Initiative (EITI), available HTTP: <http://eiti.org/>; Trucost, available HTTP: <http://www.trucost.com/>.

References

Allen, M. R. (2011) 'The scientific basis for climate change liability', in Lord, R., Goldberk, S., Rajamani, L. and Brunnee, J. (eds.) *Climate change liability*, Cambridge: Cambridge University Press.

Allen, M. R. (2012) 'Climate change', in Clark, G. L., Urwin, R., Allen, M., Wójcik, D., Molinari, C. and McGill, S. (eds.) *Project Telos: Addressing the challenges of transformation through sustainable investing.* Report prepared for Project Telos (Towers Watson project on sustainable investing).

Allen, M. R., Stott, P. A., Mitchell, J.F.B, Schnur, R. and Delworth T. L. (2009) 'Quantifying the uncertainty in forecasts of anthropogenic climate change', *Nature* 407: 617–620.

Ang, A. (2012) 'Mean-variance investing', Columbia Business School Research Paper No. 12/49. Online. Available HTTP: <http://dx.doi.org/10.2139/ssrn.2131932>.

Barnett, M. L. and Salomon, R. M. (2006) 'Beyond dichotomy: The curvilinear relationship between social responsibility and financial performance', *Strategic Management Journal* 27(11): 1101–1122.

Barro, R. (2006) 'Rare disasters and asset markets in the twentieth century', *The Quarterly Journal of Economics* 121(3): 823–866.

Bolton, P., Guesnerie, R. and Samama, F. (2011) *Towards an international green fund*. Online. Available HTTP: <http://cgt.columbia.edu/papers/towards_an_international_green_fund/>.

Clark, G. L. (2011) 'Myopia and the global financial crisis: context-specific reasoning, market structure, and institutional governance', *Dialogues in Human Geography* 1: 4–25.

Clark, G. L. and Urwin, R. (2008a) 'Best-practice pension fund governance', *Journal of Asset Management* 9(1): 2–21.

Clark, G. L. and Urwin, R. (2010) 'Innovative models of pension fund governance in the context of the global financial crisis', *Pensions: An International Journal* 15(1): 62–77.

Clark, G. L. and Wójcik, D. (2007) *The geography of finance*, Oxford: Oxford University Press.

Clark, G. L., Caerlewy-Smith, E. and Marshall, J. C. (2006) 'Pension fund trustee competence: decision-making in problems relevant to investment practice', *Journal of Pension Economics & Finance* 5(1): 91–110.

Clark, G. L. Caerlewy-Smith, E. and Marshall, J. C. (2007) 'The consistency of UK pension fund trustee decision-making', *Journal of Pension Economics & Finance* 6(1): 67–86.

Cordell, D. (2010) 'The story of phosphorus: sustainability implications of global phosphorus scarcity for food security', PhD thesis, University of Technology, Sydney and Linköping, University, Sweden, Linköping Studies in Arts & Sciences No. 509.

Cowen, T. (2011) *The great stagnation: how America ate all the low-hanging fruit of modern history, got sick, and will (eventually) feel better*, New York: Dutton Group.

Cranford, M., Parker, C. and Trivedi, M. (2011) *Understanding forest bonds*, Oxford: Global Canopy Programme.

Diamond, J. (2008) *What's your consumption factor?, New York Times,* January 2.

Diebold, F. X., Doherty, N. A. and Herring, R. J. (eds.) (2010) *The known, the unknown, and the unknowable in financial risk management*, Princeton: Princeton University Press.

Dimson, E., Marsh, P. and Staunton, M. (2002) *Triumph of the optimists: 101 years of global investment returns*, Princeton, NJ: Princeton University Press.

Ellison, R. (2008) *Pension fund investment law*, New York: Tottel Publishing.

Goldin, I. and Mariathasan, M. (2014) *The butterfly defect*, Princeton: Princeton University Press.

Hawley, J.P. and Williams, A. T. (2000) The rise of fiduciary capitalism: how institutional investors can make corporate America more democratic, Philadelphia: University of Pennsylvania Press.

Kahneman, D. (2011) *Thinking fast and slow*, London: Allen Lane.

Kaminker, C. and Stewart, F. (2012) 'The role of institutional investors in financing clean energy', *OECD Working Papers on Finance, Insurance and Private Pensions*, No. 23, Paris: OECD Publishing.

Langbein, J. (1995) 'The contractarian basis of the law of trusts', *Yale Law Journal* 105(3): 625–675.

Lo, A. (2004) 'The adaptive markets hypothesis: market efficiency from an evolutional perspective', *Journal of Portfolio Management* 30: 15–29.

Lo, A. (2011) *Adaptive markets and the new world order*. Online. Available HTTP: <http://www.ssrn.com/abstract=1977721>.

Matthews, H. D., Gillet, N., Stott, P. and Zickfeld, K. (2009) 'The proportionality of global warming to cumulative carbon emissions', *Nature* 459: 829–832.

Meinshausen, M., Meinshausen, N., Hare, W., Raper, S.C.B., Frieler, K., Knutti, R., Frame, D. J. and Myles, R. A. (2009) 'Greenhouse-gas emission targets for limiting global warming to 2 °C', *Nature* 458: 1158–1162.

Money, A.L.N. (2014) 'Corporate water risk: a critique of prevailing best practice', *Journal of Management and Sustainability* 4(1): 42–59.

Rajan, R., (2006) 'Has finance made the world risker?', *European Financial Management* 12(4): 499–533.

Richardson, B. (2011) 'From fiduciary duties to fiduciary relationships for socially responsible investing: responding to the will of beneficiaries', *Journal of Sustainable Finance and Investment* 1(1): 5–19.

Richardson, B. J. (2008) *Socially responsible investment law: regulating the unseen polluters*, New York: Oxford University Press.

Richardson, B. J. (2009) 'Keeping ethical investment ethical: regulatory issues for investing for sustainability', *Journal of Business Ethics* 87(4): 555–572.

UNEP Finance Initiative (2005) *A legal framework for the integration of environmental, social and governance issues into institutional investment*. Report for the Asset Management Working Group of the UNEP Finance Initiative. Geneva. Online. Available HTTP: <http://www.unepfi.org/fileadmin/documents/freshfields_legal_resp_20051123.pdf>.

Urwin, R. (2011) 'Universal owners: opportunity beacons and leadership calls', *Rothman International Journal of Pension Management* 4(1): 26–33.

Vayanos, D. and Woolley, P. (2012) 'A theoretical analysis of momentum and value strategies', Working Paper, London School of Economics.

Wagner, R. K. (2002) 'Smart people doing dumb things', in Sternberg, R. J. (ed.) *Why smart people can be so stupid*, New Haven: Yale University Press: 42–63.

Water Resources Group (2009) 'Charting our water future', Online. Available HTTP: <http://www.mckinsey.com/client_service/sustainability/latest_thinking/charting_our_water_future>.

Wójcik, D. (2011) *The global stock market: issuers, investors and intermediaries in an uneven world*, Oxford: Oxford University Press.

Woods, C. (2011) 'Funding climate change: how pension fund fiduciary duty masks trustee inertia and short-termism', in Hawley, J., Kamath, S. and Williams, A. T. (eds.) *Institutional investors, risk/return tradeoffs, and corporate governance failures*, Philadelphia: University of Pennsylvania Press.

Woods, C. and Urwin, R. (2010) 'Putting sustainable investing into practice: a governance framework for pension funds', *Journal of Business Ethics* 92: 1–19.

47

Overcoming distractions on the road to increased levels of ESG integration

Cary Krosinsky

Introduction

Our goal when we originally set out to produce books on sustainable investing was to achieve three things. First, we aimed to help steer investment strategies towards more forward-looking, sophisticated approaches to our sustainability challenges, moving away from the more negative approaches that previously dominated early industry practices. To this day, many independent observers still believe that sustainable investing is exactly that – a negative approach to ESG challenges which any investor can apply simply by removing companies or sectors they don't like, regardless of the implications, financial or otherwise.

Fortunately, the field continues to evolve away from negativity. After five years of recovery from the Global Financial Crisis, we have seen in 2014 the responsible investment (RI) profession moving in exactly the more positive direction we long hoped for, and which is rewarding to see. However, much more is needed to tip the balance into the systemic positive dynamic we sought in our first edited book, *Sustainable Investing: The Art of Long Term Performance.*

Second, we aimed to look at investment practices in the field, as we did in our second edited book, *Evolutions in Sustainable Investing: Strategies, Funds and Thought Leadership*, and which came on the back of our paper presented at the PRI Academic Network conference at Carleton University in Ottawa in 2009, which was also incorporated into Tessa Hebb's *The Next Generation of Responsible Investing.* In this book, we provided 15 case studies of investor behavior, along with history, trends and regional perspectives, including visions of responsible investment in Asia that have since come to pass. Momentum behind our Ottawa premise that sustainable investing needs to be forward looking, opportunity directed and risk adjusted continues to drive evolving strategies, including through the development of better metrics, as was recently discussed at the annual gathering of Principles for Responsible Investment (PRI) signatories in Montreal in 2014.

The third aspect of what we set out to achieve might be best described as the professionalization of responsible investing. Practices have evolved, and will continue to do so. The existing data, while necessary, has proven to be insufficient, and we suggest that a number of unhelpful distractions have crept into the conversation.

If we are attempting as a field to achieve a necessary environmental and social evolution of both existing and new social businesses, and through good governance and better investment strategies, then the divestment from fossil fuel movement writ large, as well as the move to decarbonize portfolios with insufficient data and thought, are potentially distracting and unhelpful.

What investors can and should do would fall into the realms of:

- Using ESG as primary considerations in active and passive investment choices with all or a majority of their assets under management, and to explain if not, why not;
- To vote their proxies supporting thoughtful resolutions and engage with companies on the most pressing issues of the day;
- To have a culture that specifically seeks a positive environmental and social transition for all stakeholders, including shareholders, with intentionality, including as involves future asset allocation strategies;
- To have the capacity to execute on these strategies, and if not, to commit to training their professionals to fully understand the direction global society is taking and can take;
- To also commit to engaging with policymakers on what is needed to remove unnecessary obstacles to societal progress, such as old fiduciary interpretations, misaligned incentives and loopholes in disclosure and regulation which otherwise prevent or seriously inhibit investors from taking effective action.

Instead, we have a divestment movement standing on a stated 'moral high ground', yet one that is not mindful of the systemic nature of the problem of fossil fuels as fully embedded in commerce and society, nor of the limited time and energy students have to put into any cause beyond their studies.

The fossil-free divestment campaign

In November 2012, 350.org's 'Do the Math' tour did not get that much mainstream media notice, but has since become a catalyst for raising significant awareness about the 'unburnable carbon' question, and has brought some interesting energy to university campuses, where students can now start to take charge of their future. Kudos to 350.org for raising much-needed awareness of the problem we have been identifying within the Carbon Tracker Initiative, and to Bill McKibben for his landmark *Rolling Stone* piece on the subject, but I also have some concerns about aspects of the 350.org approach; more on that in a minute.

This Carbon Tracker Initiative (CTI), and where I'm one of the founding directors (and I write this as myself, not on behalf of CTI), has determined that we can burn only a small percentage of the remaining coal, oil and gas still in the ground and remain within a safe degree of global temperature increase. Solutions to this will not be easy, but it is essential to get more people aware that the implications of business as usual will likely be catastrophic. There are major consequences for investors if and when we try and deal with this question as well.

Hurricane Sandy, for example, was a clear, sharp sign of the sort of future we may have in store, with increasingly violent weather among other intensifying impacts causing ruin and chaos, both personal and financial. The financial crisis of 2008 is also worth mentioning as an example of free market capitalism run wild without adequate protections. Without intervention, the crisis likely would have brought the world's financial system to its knees. If, like me, you favor capitalism as an economic system, then we must find a way to factor in sustainability for that system to operate most efficiently. This would bring maximum benefit to all stakeholders, including those who hold equity portfolios.

We can no longer tolerate students emerging from leading academic institutions without this perspective. We need to start doing real future scenario work – hence my course at Columbia

University's Earth Institute, now entitled "Scenarios for A Sustainable World", and which has also since evolved into teaching at both Yale and at Columbia's Earth Institute with the Robert F. Kennedy Center for Justice and Human Rights.

Back to McKibben and his tour. Asking universities to divest from fossil fuels is an interesting angle to take to the subject. Public companies rely on a flow of capital, and cutting off a few endowments here and there might get some notice. But what about companies in the oil services sector, such as drillers and transporters: Are they not an issue? How about companies that use oil and gas to deliver or create their products and services, or companies where a majority of their footprint resides in the use of their products? Should we divest from them as well?

There's much we still don't know. What if we suggested owning oil and gas companies could make sense, but that investors should do practical, in-depth risk assessments and establish ratings schemes that take those risks into account, and allow portfolios to file their own integrated reports on risk as well as opportunity? Still unsolved as well, for example, is the true net environmental savings that best practice natural gas drilling could be versus that of oil or coal. Why haven't we done this work comprehensively yet? Until we do so, how can we know what's best?

It is time for practical, well-thought-out solutions that work for all stakeholders. And so it's a concern when 350.org originally pointed its website visitors wondering 'How can I divest my own money from fossil fuel companies?' to a link (no longer active) to all socially responsible mutual funds in the US – but with a caveat: "While not all of the funds there are fossil-fuel free, they are all moving that direction."

I did some research, and it turned out (perhaps obvious to most) that this claim was patently false. Almost none of the listed funds were divested from fossil fuels. I was happy then and still would be to share my research with anyone interested. Such funds were not at the time, nor are they now, largely moving in that direction, statements to that effect or otherwise.

And so we take out the megaphone, and suggest correctly that there is a problem that we all need to recognize yet refuse to see that no one person or company is at fault here. Instead, there is a severe systemic problem, one that requires really serious conversations, scenario analysis and consideration. Let's instead stop with the flag-waving and finger-pointing, roll up our sleeves and figure out what we really should be doing.[1]

In fact, creating a movement around divestment from fossil fuel is such a bad idea, so incapable of fixing climate change, so very ill conceived, that you would think the oil companies themselves came up with it. Who knows, maybe they did. That would seem to fly in the face of individuals such as Bill McKibben, seemingly quite sincere about their stated cause, but you just never know what truly motivates individuals these days.

Surely McKibben knows that divestment from oil has no real hope for fostering the changes we require, as is clearly evident if you spend any time studying the ownership patterns of both the publicly listed companies involved, as well as who holds the remaining reserves. Change comes from owning a problem that is systemic and fixing it with intentionality. One can buy a stock, or sell it once owned, and with climate change, divesting from fossil fuel is a copout from solving the problem. Divestment then is no different from high-frequency trading or hedge fund ownership – it comes without responsibility for any underlying problem that may exist.

What does the word 'divest' even mean? Dictionary.com tells us that it means "to strip of clothing, ornament, etc." as reflected in its example usage, "The wind divested the trees of their leaves."

However, with divesting from fossil fuels, selling the Carbon Underground 200 doesn't get rid of fossil fuel – it is still in the cars that auto manufacturers make, in the utilities that burn coal, in the trucks that transport goods and so on. So that definition fails to hold any water whatsoever.

Then we have a second possible definition – "to strip or deprive (someone or something), especially of property or rights; dispossess."

That doesn't work – 'divesting' or selling a stock doesn't make the underlying problem disappear – the fossil fuel will still exist, only now someone else will own it. The only rights dispossessed are your own – rights such as those inherent in ownership, as you will no longer be able to engage with the company. Even if some problems are potentially too severe to be solved by engagement, divestment doesn't come close to getting you there, and the fossil fuel keeps on being otherwise owned, produced and used. And you lose your voice with the company in question if you divest.

Should shareholders divest rather than asking for capital expenditure to be returned to shareholders instead of funding loss-making coal and oil and gas projects? Or to argue for the rights of local communities and people affected by companies in the extraction industries? Or to press companies to clean up their messes?

Okay, there is a third definition from Dictionary.com – "to rid of or free from", "He divested himself of all responsibility for the decision."

Now we are getting somewhere – divesting is to rid an owner of his or her responsibility for the decision. Exactly.

Instead, what is needed is investment in the sorts of solutions called for by the Climate Bonds Initiative, and as we are heralding in the *Journal of Environmental Investing*, and that is called for by CERES in the Clean Trillion report. Let's give universities the space to figure out what is best practice across a policy of 'Invest and Engage', such as demonstrated in the examples being set by the University of North Carolina, Yale University and the University of California system. Universities are uniquely positioned to figure out this tricky problem, and it should be their responsibility to help figure this out, and not cop out of the problem.

Climate change is a truly wicked problem. It is embedded in everything we buy, and there is a different story on this in every part of the world. The US–China bilateral agreement signed in the fall of 2014 was a major step forward in this regard, and is likely to create economic opportunity along the path to a badly needed energy transition. Now we must explore how to fund ways of leapfrogging the developing world to newer, cleaner sources of energy, especially as they didn't cause the climate conundrum in the first place. This bilateral approach is clearly a good idea if the American Enterprise Institute doesn't like it, and whose funding sources speak for themselves. I don't see such think tanks pushing back on divestment, as they are smart enough to know it's not a real issue.

Climate change can and will only be solved by owning the problem. We all own the problem. No one wanted global disaster from climate change. Let's solve it through smart, positive investment with incentives in the opportunities that can create community resilience and jobs.[2]

If a positive investment transition is needed, how will it be financed? What changes are needed within investment practice, and how will success be measured? What is the 'Value of Everything', and why is this important? Have those involved in the divestment movement studied the systemic nature of ownership to understand the potential their movement has or does not have? The Value of Everything is approximately $350 trillion, and this is a critically important fact to understand if we are to successfully respond to growing environmental and societal risks. The Value of Everything after all also represents the nature of the entrenched status quo, and there is a hidden cost to transitioning anything, which needs to be better understood. Why buy a new car in a tight economy where money is scarce and the future unsure, when it is cheaper to keep your current car going? Hence, people and businesses are understandably making what they have last as long as they can. Why buy the latest iPhone if your iPhone 5 is still working fine? This has an impact on the economy in general, and when people around the world get more financially cautious it makes new sales even more of an important focus in the developing world, where waves of Chinese citizens and others are getting a chance to experience middle-class lifestyles for the very first time.

ESG integration, if it is to be successful, needs to achieve three things – I'll call it a **three-point agenda**, and it includes:

1 A significant **energy transition** to avoid the worst effects of climate change.
2 The **rise of social business** to create badly needed local jobs and to revitalize communities.
3 An **evolution of the environmental and social impacts** of existing businesses into a more positive net impact state.

The challenge will be very much how to finance these transitions if economic conditions continue to make it less expensive to maintain what we already have and make do instead of making dramatic changes. So what does the Value of Everything look like? We understand the size of the fixed-income market (roughly $100 trillion) and public equity (about $70 trillion), but if we are to transition in the face of ongoing and evolving environmental and social challenges such as climate change, inequality, water shortages and resource constraints (The World Economic Forum's Global Risk Report is an essential resource here), the nature of assets needs to change. Our best current estimate shows that this $350 trillion of directly owned assets currently looks as shown in Figure 47.1.

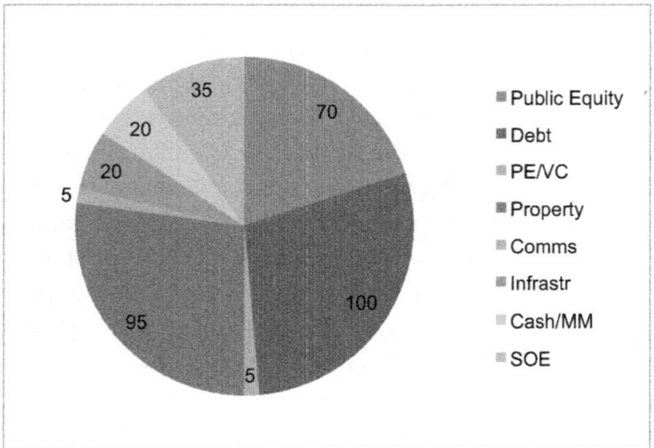

- Fixed Income = $100 trillion
- Global Real Estate (incl. value of people's homes) = $95 trillion
- Public Equity = $70 trillion
- State Owned Enterprises = $35 trillion
- Cash and other Personal Assets = $20 trillion
- Infrastructure = $20 trillion
- Commodities = $5 trillion
- Private Equity/Venture Capital = $5 trillion

Figure 47.1 The Value of Everything (US$350 trillion)

This makes global debt instruments the largest component of asset value at 29 per cent, property (commercial and residential) at 27 per cent, public equity at 20 per cent, all the way down to private equity and venture capital at 1 per cent. Why is this important? For example, CERES published its "Clean Trillion" report earlier this year, calling for $35 trillion of new investment in climate bonds and green infrastructure by 2050, or an average of $1 trillion per year between now and then, to help defray climate change impacts.

Where is this money going to come from? We need to understand the state of play of assets and investments that exist (detailed in Figure 47.1) as well as how entrenched or committed they are to see where this new funding can come from. Most of that $100 trillion of fixed income is already committed to existing loans and projects, so how can we scale this up to new greener instruments and investment vehicles remains a major challenge. Institutional investor commitments, such as those coming out of the 2014 Climate Week, certainly help but more is clearly needed.

Separately, for social businesses to truly flourish (whether via B corporations or via impact investing or similar, typically smaller companies which aim to provide an environmental, community and financial benefit simultaneously) they need to become a key part of the Value of Everything, at least at the 1 per cent level in order to get on the proverbial map of things. One per cent is roughly $3.5 trillion, and as the World Economic Forum reported last year, impact investing sits somewhere around $50 billion, roughly 1 per cent of the needed 1 per cent. This poses the question of how to scale impact-specific investments 100 times over. Easier said than done to be sure.

Lastly, we need the transformation of existing businesses along environmental and social dimensions, and what is really needed to make that happen is increased investor interest, hence the Value Driver Model, and the need to connect the average person with what their investments both fund and own.

Whatever we require, a better systemic understanding is necessary, both of what is and what may be truly possible, in order for there to be a chance of meeting the three-point agenda detailed above with any real chance of success.

Much work remains if we are to look back successfully, say 5, 10, even 20 years from now, at how this $350 trillion evolved in a more environmentally friendly and socially conscious manner. Or will the entrenched nature of the status quo get in the way of the changes that seem to be required? Will any of this happen via divestment from fossil fuel–producing companies? It seems very unlikely that this very large and expensive effort will lead to anything significant in the needed positive evolution of investment practices writ large. If the Value of Everything needs to change, and it does, it can only change effectively through ownership.[3]

The Montreal Carbon Pledge

Another concern arises from the efforts, announced in September 2014 in Montreal, to 'decarbonize portfolios'. The same issue we find in the fossil-free divestment campaign manifests itself here. With oil and gas having become fully embedded into all businesses, decarbonizing the economy through investment appears to be a very different question than what is available on the market today from fund providers.

Annual global carbon emissions continue to increase, and scientists are increasingly convinced we are approaching limits to how much more carbon we can burn as a society and stay within a safe degree of the future effects from what is expected to be a changing climate. Institutional investors at the same time now own a majority of public companies, mostly in a 'business as usual' capacity, in effect locking in the status quo.

Measuring and reducing the carbon footprints of equity portfolios and other assets emerges as a potentially important effort to encourage businesses to reduce their own carbon footprints through a resulting positive dynamic in a race for invested capital. Such carbon footprinting, however, can only achieve maximum effect through an optimization of performed techniques combined with an understanding of the strengths and weaknesses of the data. It is essential to pinpoint and not overlook the largest opportunities for decarbonization, which most current techniques do not accomplish.

Efforts to calculate the carbon footprint of equity and other portfolios trace back to Henderson Global Investors and Nick Robins working with Trucost on a report entitled "How Green is My Portfolio?" in 2005. Subsequent related efforts include the Sustainable City award-winning analysis of the carbon footprint of UK unit and investment trusts in 2006 by Cary Krosinsky and Trucost looking at the relative carbon intensity of portfolios comparatively for the first time. Green Century became the first US mutual fund to publish a carbon footprint, most recently heralding the fund as being "half the carbon of the S&P 500."

Fast forward to September 2014, and we have now a Montreal Carbon Pledge initiated by PRI, and a similar call from the United National Environment Programme (UNEP) to build a Portfolio Decarbonization Coalition seeking to "reduce the carbon in portfolios by hundreds of billions of dollars." This exciting initiative, in order to have maximum effect, needs to be optimized, for reasons we will start to explore in this piece, to ensure that:

a The largest opportunities for decarbonization are fully factored into these considerations and are not overlooked. Most carbon footprinting techniques currently overlook many of the largest categories of such opportunities.
b The strengths and weaknesses of present carbon footprinting and the parallel state of ecological economics data is fully understood.
c Pension funds and others signing up to the Pledge have the best chance to truly decarbonize the economy meaningfully through this practice.

The weaknesses in carbon footprinting techniques as presently practiced are that the largest opportunities to decarbonize are either missed or not prioritized. Ecological economics data-gathering techniques use the largely accepted and completed Greenhouse Gas (GHG) Protocol to either estimate or precisely measure the carbon dioxide and other greenhouse gas emissions of companies and their Scope 1 (operations), Scope 2 (purchased electricity) and Scope 3 (15 categories of indirect emissions) footprints.

Scope 1 and Scope 2 present the most robustly available data, even if not comprehensive (it is more so in some geographies than others) and not fully audited and verified. The state of reliability and completeness of Scope 1 and 2 data can be analyzed and understood by geography and by sector, which is important to understand vis-a-vis which portions of owned portfolios can be measured on their Scope 1 and 2 footprint. However, the larger weakness of carbon footprinting techniques involves Scope 3, especially the use of products, an area often ignored but that for many sectors provides the largest opportunity for decarbonization by far. A sample analysis of each sector shows the largest opportunity for decarbonization, as shown in the Ford Sustainability Report (2013–14), and whether current carbon footprinting practices reflect these understandings or not.[4]

For example, take Ford Motor Company, whose own reporting clearly demonstrates that fully 90 per cent of its carbon footprint comes from the use of its vehicles on the road. Carbon footprinting techniques that do not factor in use of products (and current footprinting techniques do not) miss the majority of the category of most concern. Other sectors show similar situations where the largest component of the carbon footprint of business is simply missed by currently practiced techniques. Financial services companies, for example, do not reflect the impact of their investments in their reporting on their carbon footprint. To properly reflect their footprints as per the GHG Protocol they need to include investments. Equity investments alone cause such organizations to have a very high footprint (see *Newsweek*'s Green Rankings for 2012), whereas carbon footprinting of portfolios without investments make financial services companies seem 'lighter' than average, and in fact many SRI funds prioritize and overweight this sector.

Let's take another sector, that of consumer goods. The largest opportunity for reduced carbon is in the energy use of their products. Again, this is not reflected in their carbon footprinting.

Consumer goods companies such as Procter & Gamble have found through a 'cradle to cradle' analysis that the heat generated while washing clothes is responsible for the largest component of their footprint by far, hence they prioritize cold wash clothes to have the largest positive impact possible. Yet, carbon footprinting techniques would not show this result, if not including use of products, which they do not.

Hence, there is an urgent need to develop a list of the largest opportunities to decarbonize by sector so that investment dollars can be prioritized by opportunity, which most present-day carbon footprinting does not currently consider. In fact, at a time when it is urgent to decarbonize the economy by all means possible, carbon footprinting misses the majority of the footprint of many sectors, either due to technique or lack of data. There would seem to be scope for important further research to determine by sector what the largest opportunities are to decarbonize, and perhaps as well what areas are less important to focus on.

The urgency to decarbonize per the largest priorities

Estimates show that we are increasingly emitting carbon dioxide at an annual rate now approximating 35 gigatonnes (Gt) or more every year, giving us possibly 20 to 30 years at most to begin seriously transitioning downward this annual emitted amount or face the likelihood of what the science tells us will result in climatic disaster. The CTI in conjunction with the Grantham Institute estimated in 2013 that we can burn an additional 900 Gt from 2013 through 2049 and have an 80 per cent chance of possibly avoiding such catastrophic damage.

A transition path can and should be designed indicating what portfolios can track and follow, what is decadal in nature and what takes annual emissions first from the 30–40 Gt/year range then down to 25 Gt/year through the 2020s, and then to 20 Gt in the 2030s and 10 Gt after that, giving time for other technologies to develop and mature along the way, keeping us within the range of safety.

There is an urgent need to annually decarbonize the economy looking to the largest categories of opportunity by sector in order to ensure that we have the best possible chance of staying on the transition path of maximum business efficiency. Current portfolio carbon footprinting techniques miss much of the footprint of two of the four major areas of commerce, those being transportation and property (which includes commercial buildings and residences).

Carbon footprinting using existing data is better at helping us understand industry, but it does little to inform us on which companies will be winners and losers, and why and when. Similarly, energy generation and agriculture – two rapidly evolving segments of the economy – arguably require a more granular look to understand who may emerge as winners in the new sustainability paradigm.

With institutional investors now owning over 70 per cent of public companies, their participation to truly decarbonize the economy is essential. Developing techniques to decarbonize by asset class, including equity, is now an essential component of success. We applaud UNEP and

PRI for taking this bold step towards building a coalition and asking asset owners to pledge to perform carbon footprinting on the back of the first efforts of the field. But it is essential for this effort to have the necessary effect on decarbonization that will ensure that these efforts are meaningful and positive for shareholders and society. Such clarity of technique and prioritization by opportunity category will help ensure that this effort creates the positive dynamic necessary to achieve its goals.[5]

Conclusion

We set out in our writings to add a degree of understanding and sophistication to practice, such that ESG considerations could start to have a chance of becoming fully embedded into all investment considerations, moving beyond a niche industry into a situation where corporate executives could see that they need to maximize their performance on these issues in a race for capital. Given the complexities and challenges that remain, the last, most recent emphasis of our work is in education. In partnership with the Robert F. Kennedy Center for Justice and Human Rights, the Earth Institute at Columbia University has built a sustainable investing program which takes an informative but open-minded and multidisciplinary approach to teaching this material. As a result, we have had senior decision-makers from pension funds and foundations participate with us in examining difficult questions with an aim to come up with new solutions. These questions include: What is our fiduciary duty in a modern global society? How can any investor really factor in human rights in investment considerations? What does the science tell us (directly from the most senior researchers at the Lamont Observatory of the Earth Institute)? How can systems thinking better inform practice? How can we really move the needle?

Such education programs are essential in a field that has evolved visibly since our first book and will continue to change. There is a reason that responsible investing has not coalesced as a profession. Unlike doctors and architects, who take regular training to keep their license to practice intact, responsible investing needs to constantly adapt to changing information and priorities and to challenge our own thinking as to what works and does not. Hence my own teaching at Yale, Columbia and beyond is becoming an exciting part of my own activities. Students are demanding this material in business schools and well beyond.

Teaching undergraduates at Yale has been particularly rewarding for me, given that these are among the brightest minds in the world, who are just starting to think about what they can do to advance their careers while making the world a better place. We have a clear opportunity to implement the positive energy of such students. But too many business school graduates at leading institutions still enter their careers ignoring the very factors that the World Economic Forum's Global Risk Report tell us are leading to growing financial concern, whether as relates to inequality, climate, human rights or through newer issues such as cybersecurity.

Among the goals we should establish for the field, we must all continually take stock of where we are. We exist in a world of imperfect and insufficient data, along with a lack of adequate capital deployed with ESG factors as a primary consideration, and part of this is a lack of training in business schools which continues to this very day. Our books concluded that our goal was to replace the financial system with something better, and with the legacy of the financial crisis remaining largely in place, we have a long, but critically important road ahead to achieve just that. At a minimum, we need to be honest about what the field has done successfully (engagement wins that prize for me) and not done as well. This includes not getting distracted by efforts such as divestment and portfolio decarbonization if such work does not help us make significant progress and ignores what's most important, namely making real societal progress that can be measured over time.

Success requires learning from what works, namely staying positive, and not being distracted by what does not and will not work. That said, I've never been more optimistic, after engaging with today's students, about the immediate potential we have to achieve both the financial and societal success we require.

Notes

1 http://socialinvesting.about.com/od/Sustainable-Investing/fl/Do-Your-Homework.htm
2 http://socialinvesting.about.com/od/Sustainable-Investing/fl/Do-Not-Divest-Sustainability-through-Ownership.htm
3 http://socialinvesting.about.com/od/Global-Considerations/fl/350-Trillion-Dollars.htm
4 http://corporate.ford.com/microsites/sustainability-report-2013–14/environment-climate-ghg.html
5 http://socialinvesting.about.com/od/Sustainability-Data-Rankings/fl/The-Montreal-Carbon-Pledge.htm

48

Reliable sustainability ratings

The influence of business models on information intermediaries

Robert G. Eccles, Jock Herron and George Serafeim

Introduction

Public policy initiatives to promote corporate sustainability[1] are contested on many fronts, but a strong case is emerging that firms that are operationally dedicated to sustainability tend to outperform firms less committed to sustainability (Eccles, Ioannou and Serafeim 2014). It is no coincidence, therefore, that a new generation of corporate reporting standards is emerging that will help investors and other key stakeholders including employees, customers, suppliers, communities and non-governmental organizations (NGOs) develop a more comprehensive understanding of corporate performance than GAAP financial reporting provides alone. As they have with traditional investment analysis, information intermediaries are playing an influential role in the development and dissemination of corporate sustainability reporting. While the market for sustainability information is still developing, broad-based, mainstream acceptance by diverse corporate stakeholders now seems assured. The question needs to be asked: What type of information intermediary business model is most likely to produce the least biased assessments?

A number of forward-thinking firms – including Natura Cosméticos, Novo Nordisk, Pfizer and Philips Electronics – have voluntarily initiated integrated reporting programs, and a number of information intermediaries – including Bloomberg and Thomson Reuters – have begun to actively disseminate and, in some cases, cumulatively assess corporate sustainability information. NGOs like US-based Ceres and the Global Reporting Initiative (GRI) are actively promoting sustainability reporting. For over a decade, Dow Jones and Sustainable Asset Management (SAM), a Swiss firm focused on sustainability investing, have produced a series of sustainability indices based on voluntary survey data from an invited pool of 2,500 of the largest companies in the world. Leading public accounting firms and the professional bodies representing the accounting profession are increasingly involved in both the policies and practices of sustainability reporting.

Momentum is gathering and the outlook is promising. In 2000, there were 624 companies that provided sustainability disclosures to the public, up from 26 in 1992. By 2010 the number had grown to 5,162 (Eccles, Serafeim and Andrews 2011). The creation in 2011 of the Sustainability Accounting Standards Board (SASB) – mirroring, as it does, the Financial Accounting Standards Board – provides a professional platform for specialists to set credible industry-specific standards for sustainability reporting that companies can use to codify and report consistent information.

Evidence of SASB's emerging stature is that Mary Schapiro, former head of the Securities and Exchange Commission (SEC), joined the board in 2014 and Michael Bloomberg became chairman of the board at the same time. Recalling the development of financial reporting and managerial accounting from the mid-nineteenth century through the Depression and the establishment of the SEC, we find historical precedence for the ambiguity currently being experienced in these early stages of establishing new corporate sustainability reporting standards. The centre of informational gravity is shifting in favour of higher-quality, more fully standardized sustainability reporting.

The purpose of this chapter is to examine some practical concerns about the influence the business model of an information intermediary can have on the quality, timeliness and even the integrity of the sustainability information they produce. Specifically, we will focus on two issues: the impact of 'who pays' for the information and which performance metrics should be included in assessing the sustainability performance of a company. The reason we are interested in these topics is because information intermediaries play an instrumental role in increasing the effectiveness of sustainability information. The more credible and relevant the information is, the more likely it is that stakeholders will use this information to make better decisions related to capital investments, supply-chain management (and partners), location choices, production processes, employee policies and customer priorities. When stakeholders use this information for decision-making, it can have material implications on corporate performance and capital allocation (Cheng, Ioannou, and Serafeim 2014).

In terms of consequences, one can ask 'What will happen if customers want to buy products from more sustainable rather than less sustainable companies; what if highly skilled employees prefer to work for those companies and what if investors prefer to hold their stock?' The most compelling answer is that the more sustainable companies are likely to outperform their less sustainable competitors. This creates strong incentives for companies to improve their sustainability performance. Preliminary empirical evidence indicates that this is, indeed, the case. According to one analysis, broadening the disclosure of sustainability information leads to a measurable improvement in sustainability performance (Ioannou and Serafeim 2011). Laws and regulations that mandate sustainability reporting promote more sustainable management practices that, in turn, boost the environmental and social performance of corporations.

Information intermediaries play an essential role in this causal chain. They generate, analyze and disseminate new information and regulate the flow of information from companies to product, labour and capital markets in ways that can be more easily digested by diverse end users. The relative value of information intermediation is even higher today in sustainability reporting than it is in traditional financial reporting, because the generally well-established standards in financial accounting do not yet exist in the sustainability domain. Positioning information intermediaries in a way that maximizes their effectiveness will make it more likely that corporations contribute toward a sustainable society without necessarily harming their economic performance.

After introducing the basic issues and motivations for improved sustainability reporting, we discuss the role of information intermediaries and the influence their business models can have on the reliability of the information they generate. We conclude with some concrete recommendations for improving the effectiveness of sustainability information intermediaries.

The importance of reliable sustainability information

Consider two firms that are in the exact same business. Firm A bribes customers, uses child labour, pollutes the environment by dumping toxic waste into rivers and cuts corners to save costs when it comes to product safety. Firm B, in contrast, has strict anticorruption systems in place, pays fair wages to adults, minimizes any environmental impact from its operations and follows strict product safety procedures. Based on these facts, it is not hard to imagine that Firm B is more likely to have a higher cost structure than Firm A. At the same time, it is clear that Firm B contributes more to the common good of society. However, if Firm B is unable to capture some value from these activities, in terms of cost savings, risk mitigation or revenue generation, then Firm B is creating a public good, but will likely be at a competitive disadvantage to Firm A.

There are two mechanisms to reward good behaviour by Firm B that directly contribute to its performance so the firm is not merely creating a public good. The first is through regulation. Imagine that governments impose penalties on companies that bribe, use child labour, pollute and compromise product safety. The positive activities of Firm B reduce the probability of paying those fines, resulting in probable cost savings relative to Firm A. Moreover, by not being involved in scandals, Firm B has a lower reputational risk than Firm A and is less likely to lose future revenues. If the benefits from lowering the expected costs from fines and reducing the likelihood of foregone revenues attributable to lower reputation risk are higher than the cost of implementing programs associated with good behaviour, then it is economically beneficial for companies to behave like Firm B.

The second mechanism, which can operate independently but which can also reinforce and complement the first, is if product, labour and capital markets take into account Firm A's and Firm B's actions. In other words, if Firm B can attract more customers to buy its products, hire and retain better employees and have a lower cost of capital, then Firm B will capture some value from the positive actions that it takes. Some of these effects seem to be evident already. Turban and Greening (1996) found that attracting high-quality human capital is more difficult and costly for companies like Firm A. Sen, Du and Bhattacharya (2015) showed that consumers have less loyalty to miscreant companies like Firm A, and are less likely to purchase products from them or advocate on their behalf. More recently, Cheng, Ioannou and Serafeim (2014) determined that companies like Firm A are more capital-constrained than companies like Firm B; for the same amount of financing they have a higher cost of capital or for the same cost of capital they have less access to financing.

In order for product, labour and capital markets to force companies like Firm A to internalize the negative externalities of their bad behaviour, access to credible and relevant information is essential. If customers, employees and investors have no way to distinguish between Firm A and Firm B, then Firm A will not be penalized and, conversely, Firm B will not be rewarded. This information asymmetry can be resolved by information intermediaries that help stakeholders distinguish between the operating practices of Firm A and Firm B. Traditional information intermediaries such as research analysts, credit rating agencies and newspapers are now complemented by new market entrants, some quite tech savvy and enabled by social media, that have accelerated and broadened the dissemination of information.

Information intermediaries

In considering the role that information plays in promoting sustainability, two reliable folk axioms come to mind. The first is the claim that 'knowledge is power', a broadly accepted premise that helps explain the steady growth in information services during the past several decades. The second axiom is the admonition that 'you get what you pay for', an intuitively accepted principle often ignored in practice – surprisingly so when it comes to information intermediaries. Here the particular issue is whether the user is actually paying for the information or whether the subject organization is paying for information about itself. In the former case, the information is not free, but we will argue that it is apt to be more reliable than in the latter case where the information is free to the user but at a potential cost of reliability. These two axioms are closely related. 'Who pays' has a large influence on 'how powerful' the information is in shaping behaviour.

Consistent with the first axiom, higher-quality sustainability information is an influential forcing mechanism that should promote more sustainable corporate behaviour for the long-term benefit of investors, employees and customers. Additionally, we believe – and corroborating evidence is emerging – that sustainably managed firms outperform competitors less committed to sustainability (Eccles, Ioannou and Serafeim 2014). While much work needs to be done to establish the details of what information should be made available by whom and for whom, sustainability advocates (including investors) generally accept that richer information is a key to promoting more sustainable business practices. When it comes to promoting sustainability, there seems to be little question that 'knowledge is power', with power being the ability to influence both decision-making itself – what is actually decided – and the context in which decisions are made – how decisions are actually made (Dahl 1957; Barach and Baratz 1962).

Our focus here is on the less examined issue of who pays for that information and what effect 'who pays' might have on its reliability, value and, by extension, 'power'. We take a market-oriented approach which assumes that more complete and independently generated information tends to facilitate better decision-making among the principal stakeholders in a public corporation, including shareholders, employees, customers, suppliers, host communities, NGOs and others who affect or are materially affected by corporate practice. We believe that information intermediaries with the most transparent business models – especially those in which the customer pays directly for the information provided – generate the most reliable, valuable and, importantly, the most 'powerful' information.

As the name suggests, information intermediaries are middlemen providing information to interested parties about the activities of another party, a set of parties or a market. This is a high-growth business with new entrants, new delivery platforms, more sophisticated analytical tools, greater demand and digestive capacity among users and heightened attentiveness from a broader range of interested parties. While conclusive estimates of the size of the market for business information are hard to establish, McKinsey & Company estimated that the global market for business-to-business information services was $200 billion in 2008, having grown at 6–8 per cent per year during the past decade, which was twice the growth rate of GDP (Benson-Armer and Hasker 2009). McKinsey projected continued annual growth of 5 per cent per annum with profit margins ranging between 20–30 per cent on average and higher for certain market leaders. A market research firm estimated that in 2010 the size of the market for financial and credit information was $42.8 billion (Mason 2011).

For our purposes, information intermediaries can be categorized as providing one of four services:

1 Data access: reformat and disseminate publicly available information in a more convenient and efficient way (e.g., *The Wall Street Journal* and much of Bloomberg and Thomson Reuters).
2 Data validation: monitor and independently validate corporate information according to certain agreed-upon industry standards using transparent auditing techniques with detailed, but summary information and a qualifying opinion made available to the public (e.g., Big Four auditing firms).
3 Data creation: construct unique data sets from public and/or private sources on a proprietary basis (e.g., Gallup polls, Cambridge Associates and elements of Bloomberg and Thomson Reuters).
4 Data assessment: make summary judgments about a particular party, a group or a market by evaluating public and/or private information and synthesizing it into a branded rating or relative ranking (e.g., bond rating agencies, *Consumer Reports* and LEED ratings).

As shown in Table 48.1, information intermediaries are active in very different domains, including finance, entertainment, automobiles, health care and consumer appliances. Within particular markets, business models vary significantly between intermediaries. This creates an opportunity to make an empirical comparison of how intermediaries perform under these different models, for example, the effect of 'who pays' on the information provided. Table 48.1 selectively gives a sense of the diverse types of information providers, the differences in their business

Table 48.1 Representative information intermediaries

Intermediary	*Information (primary focus)*	*Who Pays (potential conflicts of interest in BOLD)*
Data Access		
Bloomberg	Financial data	Subscribers
Reuters	Financial data	Subscribers
World Almanac	Statistical data	Purchasers
Data Validation		
Big Six auditors	Financial data on public companies	**Subject companies**
Bank regulators	Financial institutions' data	Taxpayers
Data Creation		
Cambridge Associates	Investment performance	Investors
A.C. Nielsen	Media usage	Subscribers
Gallup	Public opinion	Subscribers
Trip Advisor	Travel advice	**Advertisers**
Data Assessment		
Morningstar	Mutual fund performance	Investors
S&P	Credit quality	**Subject companies**
Moody's	Credit quality	**Subject companies**
Japan Credit Rating	Credit quality	**Subject companies**
Kroll	Credit quality	Investors
Egan Jones	Credit quality	Investors
Mikuni	Credit quality	Investors
AM Best	Insurance company credit quality	**Subject companies**
Sell-Side	Company and industry information	**Ambiguous**
MPAA	Film ratings	Film studios
Consumer Reports	Consumer products	Subscribers *and donors*
Energy Star	Energy efficiency of appliances	DoE *and* **companies**
Corporate Knights	"Clean capitalism" corporate ratings	Subscribers, investors and **companies**
Ethisphere	Corporate ethics	**Companies** and subscribers
Corporate Responsibility Magazine	Corporate responsibility rankings	**Companies** and subscribers
JD Power	Automobile performance	Subscribers
GoodGuide	Environmental, social and health performance	**Corporate advertisers** and purchasers of business intelligence
Fair Trade	Agriculture	**Companies** *and* donors
MSCI (ESG Indices)	Environmental, social and governance performance	Subscribers
Asset4/Thomson Reuters	Sustainability performance	Subscribers

models and the range of information tracked and assessments made, if any. Discussed later, there is an emerging group of information providers focused primarily on sustainability issues. Their business models deserve the same scrutiny given to established information intermediaries in the financial markets. The issue of 'who pays' generates the same tensions and potential conflicts of interest.

Structural bias in the business models of information intermediaries

Contrary to most introductory economics textbooks, information is expensive – often quite expensive – not free. Whether information is generated by a for-profit (e.g., Moody's) or a non-profit (e.g., *Consumer Reports*) intermediary, the intermediary needs to support its activities through some combination of fees, advertising, subscriptions, contributions and government mandate. The question of 'who pays' for the information, and how that might create conflicts of interest and, consequently, unintended biases in the information generated is an issue that is generally acknowledged but infrequently analyzed until something consequential goes wrong.

Several familiar examples highlight the risks of how the business model (e.g., 'who pays') of an information intermediary can distort the quality of the service provided. In investment banking, the sell-side conflict between a firm's analysts and its underwriters and relationship bankers makes an objective assessment of a company's prospects harder to make, because the fees generated are disproportionally and more clearly identified with the corporate client rather than the soft dollars earned from the investing client of the bank. A similar tension exists in rating the registered bonds of an issuer, because the issuer being evaluated generally pays the rating agency rather than the investors who may hold the securities. Specific examples of the conflict over 'who pays' include:

- As fallout from the so-called dot.com bust in 2000, the SEC charged Merrill Lynch investment analyst Henry Blodgett with civil fraud, because his published advice promoting certain Internet stocks differed so grossly from the views he expressed in his private e-mails. As penance, he later published *The Wall Street Self-Defense Manual* (Blodgett 2007).
- The collapse of Enron beginning in 2001 exposed the commercial conflicts an auditor faces when it has to evaluate controversial transactions designed to mask economic substance. Arthur Andersen consistently sided with the company by approving accounting treatments that hid losses and risks at Enron, which was paying its fees.
- The fact that Standard & Poor's (S&P) and Moody's rated WorldCom securities as 'investment grade' in April 2002, three months before the company filed for bankruptcy, and did the same for Enron in early November 2001, three weeks before it went bankrupt, significantly damaged the reputations of both rating agencies. Indeed, Enron exposed a range of interlocking failures by auditors, rating agencies, regulators and Wall Street analysts that made the company's accounting veil so hard to penetrate (Healy and Palepu 2003).
- The sub-prime mortgage crisis, exacerbated by the sharp increase of highly rated pools of sub-prime mortgages issued between 2004 and 2007, contributed to the global recession in 2008 (Joint Center for Housing Studies of Harvard University 2008) and highlighted, at least briefly, the generally ignored conflict of interest that rating agencies like S&P and Moody's have because their fees are paid by the company (or issuing entity) being rated as opposed to the investors and lenders for whom the ratings are developed.
- The conflict of interest over 'who pays' is not limited to the financial industry. In the medical profession, for example, steps have been taken to disclose potential conflicts of interest since

> the early 2000s and sporadically before that (Institute on Medicine as a Profession 2013), but the conflicts created by drug company subsidies that support medical research and payments to practicing doctors remain an issue. However, in medicine, far more than in finance, influential groups like the Institute of Medicine and journals like the *New England Journal of Medicine* have been actively promoting guidelines and practices that expose and protect against conflicts (Steinbrook 2009).

These examples are anecdotally useful, but the larger question is whether systemic biases can be detected. The empirical literature is not extensive, but as summarized below there are strong indications that a structural assessment bias is inherent in the business model of an information intermediary. 'Who pays' seems to influence the summary conclusions and the timing of when new opinions are made public by information intermediaries. Not surprisingly, the performance of a particularly influential type of information intermediary, the bond rating agency, has proven to be fertile territory for empirical analyses. This is because there is extensive data in two distinct and sophisticated markets – the United States and Japan – where the business models of competing rating agencies differ from each other. In both countries, there are examples of ratings firms paid by the issuer and ratings firms paid by investors. Consistent with the examples cited above and with the studies cited below, when the issuer pays there is a systematically positive bias in the ratings, but when the investor pays the ratings appear to be unbiased (Xia 2010).

In a study focused on the timeliness of corporate rating downgrades in the United States from late 1995 until 2002, Richard Johnson of the Kansas City Federal Reserve examined the timing differences between when S&P reduced the credit rating of a particular company and when another rating firm, Egan Jones Ratings (EJR), made a similar move on the same company (Johnson 2003). At the time, S&P, along with Moody's and Fitch, was one of three SEC-approved Nationally Recognized Statistical Rating Organizations (NRSROs). This designation officially sanctions their ratings for the purpose of legally determining whether a security registered with the SEC is 'investment grade' or not and, if so, eligible for a wide range of investors to hold in their portfolios. American firms need not pay to be rated, since both Moody's and S&P have a policy of rating all taxable securities registered by the SEC in the domestic market. However, some 98 per cent of American bond issuers pay fees to the major rating agencies anyway.

EJR is a non-NRSRO with a fundamentally different revenue model from S&P. Instead of being paid by issuers to rate their securities, EJR is paid by investors through a subscription service. For the period covered, Johnson determined that S&P consistently lagged yet eventually tracked EJR downgrades and upgrades by at least 10 weeks. A more recent study by Günter Strobl and Han Xia (2011) at the University of North Carolina used S&P and EJR data to examine the "severity of S&P's conflict of interest". They found it especially prevalent when an issuer changes senior management, when it is more dependent on short-term financing or when it has been proportionally less reliant on S&P than on another NRSROs like Moody's. All three situations identified by Strobl and Xia represent new business opportunities for S&P, a natural source of potential bias.

In a similar study comparing ratings made by Moody's, an NRSRO, with EJR, William Beaver and Mark Soliman of Stanford and Catherine Shakespeare of the University of Michigan (2006) observed that Moody's consistently lagged rating changes initiated by EJR. Defending Moody's and other NRSROs, they attributed this to the natural conservatism attending their 'contracting' role in determining which securities are eligible to be held by some of the largest investment pools in the country. They argue that rapid changes in credit ratings, especially downgrades, would limit the degrees of freedom available to both issuers and large investors who are bound by contractual obligations associated with a particular NRSRO's ratings. By contrast, they argue that

EJR, in its purely 'valuation' role, has fewer institutional constraints, and can, therefore, be more responsive when it comes to making ratings changes, because there are no immediate regulatory consequences to its decisions. If EJR, as a non-NRSRO, determines that a certain security is no longer investment grade, an investor that is limited by its charter to holding investment grade securities is not required to sell the securities, because the EJR rating has no official standing. Subscribing investors have discretion to use EJR ratings as they choose. The authors observe that this is "consistent with their [EJR's] role of providing information to investors". In their view, the NRSRO and the non-NRSRO are complements rather than substitutes, with each providing a different service for their respective client. A large holder of rated securities wants the unbiased 'valuation' assessment of an EJR, but would be understandably wary about being forced to make precipitous decisions based on the 'contractual' implications of a Moody's rating.

As noted, the conflict of interest issue is not unique to the United States. In Japan, a similar structure exists in which the government officially sanctions certain rating agencies while allowing others to operate independently. Three researchers, Nobuyoshi Yamori and Yoshiro Asai at Nagoya University and Narunto Nishigaki at Okayama University (2006) compared the credit rating decisions of the nationally sanctioned agencies with those of both Mikuni, an independent Japanese agency, and the two largest American agencies, all three of which rate companies for the benefit of foreign investors. The authors acknowledge that there is some political controversy over the relative harshness of the foreign rating agencies like S&P and Moody's, but the different assessments, and the relative timing of those assessments made by Mikuni, which is supported exclusively by investors, and those made by the officially sanctioned raters like Japan Credit Rating, are consistent with the results contrasting the timing and direction of assessments made by S&P and Moody's with those made by EJR. Mikuni is "well known as the strictest of Japanese firms" and, when evaluating the long-term credit banks in 2003, was considerably stricter than either S&P or Moody's.

Although we are focused here on evaluating corporate performance, it is worth reinforcing the point that issues concerning the quality and potential bias of information intermediaries are a general concern embracing a full range of social activity. In addition to observing that "empirical evidence is beginning to emerge on certifier bias and competition among credit rating agencies", David Dranove at Northwestern and Ginger Jin at the University of Maryland (2010) raise an additional concern that certifiers of other activities and institutions such as schools and hospitals may have similar biases. While 'for-profit' certifiers may have an incentive to favour their paying client, other certifiers, including government agencies, may have a different and less easy to detect set of influences shaping their assessments. As Dranove and Jin argue, 'gaming behavior' and 'inspector bias' in health care, education and finance warrant further research.

Sustainability reporting standards and user-based ratings

As noted earlier, a new generation of corporate reporting is emerging. In addition to financial data, information intermediaries are increasingly focused on a wider range of performance data with 'sustainability' as a broadly defined umbrella theme and a larger set of stakeholders as the intended audience. Representative examples include Thomson Reuter's Asset4 (index-based corporate sustainability performance), MSCI Analytics (environmental, social and governance performance assessment for institutional investors), Corporate Knights (ranking of leaders in corporate sustainability) and the Dow Jones Sustainability Index (tracking financial performance of companies against relative sustainability performance). A frequent criticism of firms that rate corporate sustainability performance is the limited consistency across different rating schemes. Examples include different rating providers assessing different performance metrics, raters assigning different weights to contributing factors when aggregating the metrics and raters simply having different assessments of particular performance metrics. While that is problematic, it is a natural phase in the evolution towards greater reporting standardization, not unlike the uneven but progressive development of GAAP reporting standards over the past 85 years.

We believe that two issues need to be addressed in order to improve the quality of sustainability ratings. The first is the development of measurement and reporting standards for the many dimensions of environmental, social and governance performance. The second is to recognize that the underlying nature and the perceived value of a particular rating will ultimately depend on the audience served and 'who pays' for the information provided.

A compelling case has been made that, compared to financial accounting standards, sustainability measurement and reporting standards need to be industry specific and based upon what environmental, social and governance (ESG) issues are most material (Lydenberg, Rogers and Wood 2010). Lydenberg et al. focus on investors, and they suggest a methodology for determining materiality. For the material issues in each sector, they recommend that appropriate metrics or Key Performance Indicators (KPI) be identified. The result would be 'apples-to-apples' performance comparisons of companies in a given sector. This is an important step – already underway – as it will make it easier for diverse stakeholders to evaluate, among other things, the relationship between sustainability and financial performance at the company level. But until stronger sustainability reporting standards are developed and more fully adopted, the reliability of sustainability reporting will be open to some question. The trend line, however, is promising.

In order for sustainability ratings to be more reliable and, consequently, more broadly accepted, we believe that information intermediaries need to provide ratings relevant to three key stakeholders: employees, customers and investors. Defining the key stakeholder for whom a particular rating is targeted will likely promote greater consensus on metrics across various intermediaries. If an information intermediary wants to influence customer choices, then product quality and safety needs to be more heavily weighted. If the intended consumers of a particular rating – or a rating sub-category – are employees, then workplace conditions and career development opportunities would be of primary importance. Finally, if investors are the target audience, then the impact of sustainability practices on future revenues, expenses, brand value and the cost of capital would be given the highest weight. This does not mean there are no universally relevant performance metrics. A firm's carbon footprint or the water consumed by a company might be of interest to diverse stakeholder groups that share a common concern about climate change or water scarcity, albeit from different perspectives.

Ratings should preferably incorporate a mix of KPIs that include inputs, outputs and impact. Inputs are the resources used by the company. In relative terms, they are the easiest to measure – although not in an absolute sense. For example, energy and water consumption are inputs, as are hours worked by employees and materials used. Inputs can be measured in both unitary (e.g., gallons of water) and monetary (e.g., price paid per gallon) terms. Outputs are products and consequences of the inputs and can be measured in both unitary (e.g., waste) and monetary (e.g., cost of waste) terms as well. One challenge is that there is no consensus pricing mechanism for measuring either the social costs or the social benefits of corporate externalities. Nevertheless, efforts can be made to estimate these externalities, as the footwear and apparel company Puma attempted to do in its 'Environmental Profit and Loss Account for the Year Ended 31 December 2010' (Puma 2010). The hardest KPIs to measure are the various marginal impacts – the uncompensated for externalities – that a company's operations have on society as a whole. An example would be the extent to which toxic wastewater from a company's plant degrades the natural environment and creates health risks for a surrounding community. The negative externalities of Firm A's behaviour are as hard to measure as the public good contributions of Firm B.

Establishing an appropriate business model

The final challenge of creating both reliable information and less biased performance ratings is to determine the appropriate business model for the information intermediary, in particular, establishing 'who pays'. Three basic models exist: (1) the subject company pays, (2) the information user pays (3) neither the company nor the user pays and the information is financed in another way, such as donations to a NGO, taxes or user fees in the case of a government provider or via advertising revenue in the case of a for-profit company. We favour the 'user pays' model. This is relatively easy to implement when the user is an investor, and examples exist such as ESG ratings provided by Bloomberg and Thomson Reuters that charge users a subscription fee for a broad range of data sets that include ESG ratings. An alternative to this would be a subscription service simply for the ESG ratings, but it is unlikely that such a narrow service would be commercially viable on a stand-alone basis unless it can easily be incorporated into the broader offerings of a Bloomberg or Thomson Reuters. Another type of 'user pays' model is one in which fees are collected indirectly by proxy, such as through a stock exchange or a regulatory body acting on behalf of investors. Some have suggested a 'pooling model' like this for financial audits as an alternative to the current 'company pays' model. However, the implementation complexity (how to identify the users? on what basis should the charge be set? how should it be collected? how to protect against regulatory capture) makes this logical solution difficult to institute.

As opposed to bond ratings, 'company pays' sustainability ratings are likely a non-starter. The credibility of the ratings would be contested, and there is no regulatory forcing mechanism as there is with publicly issued bonds to make a corporation willing to pay in the first place. There are a number of sustainability ratings that are free to both rated companies and investors, but these ratings seem to have modest influence with either audience.

Implementing a 'user pays' business model for consumers is problematic, too. In the Internet age with so much information available for free, consumers are reluctant to pay more than nominal fees for information. It is no surprise that *Consumer Reports* is a non-profit organization with a very low subscription price. An annual subscription costs only $30. GoodGuide, a venture-capital funded company that has developed a phone app for evaluating the health, environmental and social attributes of products, was faced with the dilemma over how to ensure unbiased ratings while still achieving profitability (Serafeim, Eccles and Clay 2012). A straight 'customer pays' model has to be profitable on a stand-alone basis for an information intermediary to adopt as a business model, and that may be an unrealistic hurdle for purely consumer-driven applications.

An 'investor pays' model, however, is more promising. In establishing successful business franchises, S&P and Moody's benefitted from the regulatory privilege extended to them by the SEC. Corporate issuers need ratings from an SEC-approved NRSRO such as S&P or Moody's in order for their bonds to be eligible for purchase by regulated investment companies. That's an advantage that sustainability-oriented information intermediaries will likely never have. However, as evidence continues to develop that sustainability performance is reliably correlated with investment performance, it is much more likely that investors would be willing to pay an information intermediary for high-quality corporate sustainability reports. In addition, fiduciary investors whose clients will only invest in high-sustainability companies may find that paying an information intermediary boosts their core business. Indeed, investors are often mistakenly treated as a homogenous pool of short run profit-maximizers, when, in fact, investors have very different time horizons and investment preferences.

Most challenging of all are ratings intended for employees. Like customers, they have a general expectation that relevant information will be made available for free, and are therefore more reluctant to pay even a nominal fee. Ratings information provided by the company will naturally be suspect since the company has a natural bias to provide the most positive information plausible.

In the case of both consumers and employees, a common alternative is free information generated by consumers and employees themselves. A number of online forums exist in which consumers can rate a company or its products and employees can do the same. This requires a nominal cost on the part of consumers and employees willing to take the time to share their opinions, and is a free good to consumers and employees who use this information for free even if they provide no input into the ratings. Successful examples include retail sites provided by Yelp and Trip Advisors. Such ratings are based on perceptions and opinions rather than underlying performance measurements. This does not completely invalidate their value, but it does mean that the user needs to determine for herself just how relevant the ratings are.

Another alternative would be for the state to generate sustainability ratings for consumers and employees, either directly or by paying another organization to do so. The perceived reliability of these ratings would depend on the legitimacy of the state, the degree of transparency regarding how these ratings were developed, the ability of citizens to audit or monitor the rating process and the perception that the process was not 'captured' in some way by the company being rated.

In the world of information intermediaries, including those focused on sustainability, there are no easy answers. Business models that produce reliable ratings are not necessarily commercially viable for a for-profit enterprise. Conversely, while a 'company pays' business model can be economically viable, legitimate questions can be raised about the objectivity of these ratings. Nevertheless, in order for investors, consumers and employees to have the information they need to reward more socially beneficial Firm B–type behaviour than Firm A–type misbehaviour, this is an issue that needs to be addressed.

The first step is to continue developing reliable sustainability measurements and reporting standards. The second step is for private entrepreneurs, social entrepreneurs and the state to experiment with different information intermediary business models to establish the most effective approach for generating unbiased sustainability data, standards, ratings and rankings. Common sense and the empirical research in other domains summarized above strongly indicate that the most reliable sustainability reporting will be conducted by independent information intermediaries who are paid, directly or indirectly, by the users of the information and not by their corporate subjects. As with publicly shared, financial accounting reports, the company will be an active partner in co-generating sustainability information, but it will do so according to externally agreed upon reporting standards that will likely have an audit trail to give users more confidence in the integrity of the data. The integrity of this collaboration is critically important. The reliability of sustainability ratings is fully contingent on the reporting corporation accepting that the data created is genuinely sovereign.

Note

1 'Sustainability' is defined as a corporate strategy, operations and governance structure and process that creates consistent and long-term economic, environmental and social value.

References

Barach, P. and Baratz, M., (1962) "The Two Faces of Power," *The American Political Science Review*, Volume 56, Issue 4, pp. 947–995.

Beaver, W., Shakespeare, C. and Soliman, M., (2006) "Differential Properties in the Ratings of Certified vs. Non-Certified Bond Rating Agencies" *Journal of Accounting and Economics*, Volume 42, Issue 3, pp. 303–334.

Benson-Armer, R. and Hasker, S. (2009) "B2B Information Services: The Opportunity for Strategic Growth," Working Paper, McKinsey & Company.
Blodgett, H. (2007) *The Wall Street Self-Defense Manual: A Consumer's Guide to Intelligent Investing*, Atlas Books.
Cheng, B., Ioannou, I. and Serafeim, G. (2014) "Corporate Social Responsibility and Access to Finance," *Strategic Management Journal*, Volume 35, Issue 1, pp. 1–23.
Dahl, R. (1957) "The Concept of Power," *Behavioral Science*, Volume 2, Issue 3, p. 201.
Dranove, D. and Jin, G. (2010) "Quality Disclosure and Certification: Theory and Practice," Working Paper 15644, National Bureau of Economic Research, January.
Eccles, R., Ioannou, I. and Serafeim, G. (2014) "The Impact of Corporate Sustainability on Organizational Processes and Performance," *Management Science*, forthcoming.
Eccles, R., Serafeim, G. and Andrews, P. (2011) "Mandatory Disclosure of Environmental, Social, and Governance in the European Union," HBS No.9–111–120, Harvard Business School Publishing.
Healy, P. and Palepu, K. (2003) "The Fall of Enron," *The Journal of Economic Perspectives*, Volume 17, Issue 2, pp. 3–26.
Institute of Medicine as a Profession, "Defining the Problem of Conflict of Interest – Conflicts of Interest among Physicians: Definition and Scope of the Problem," http://www.imapny.org/conflicts_of_interest/online-curriculum/1—defining-the-problem, accessed March 2013.
Ioannou, I. and Serafeim, G. (2011) "The Rise and Consequences of Corporate Sustainability Reporting," *European Business Review* (September–October).
Johnson, R. (2003) "An Examination of Rating Agencies' Actions Around the Investment-Grade Boundary," FRB of Kansas City Research Paper No. 03–01, Research Division, Federal Reserve Bank of Kansas City.
Joint Center for Housing Studies of Harvard University (2008) "Harvard University – The State of the Nation's Housing," p. 4.
Lydenberg, S., Rogers, J. and Wood, D. (2010) "From Transparency to Performance: Industry-Based Sustainability Reporting on Key Issues," http://hausercenter.org/iri/wp-content/uploads/2010/05/IRI_Transparency-to-Performance.pdf, accessed May 2012.
Mason, E. (2011) "The Market for Financial and Credit Information: 2010 Final Market Size and Share Report," *Outsell, Inc.*, http://www.outsellinc.com/store/products/1009, accessed June 2012.
Puma (2010) "Puma's Environmental Profit and Loss Account for the Year Ended 31 December 2010," http://about.puma.com/wp-content/themes/aboutPUMA_theme/financial-report/pdf/EPL080212final.pdf, accessed May 2012.
Sen, S., Du, S. and Bhattacharya, C. B. (2015) "Building Relationships through Corporate Responsibility," in D. J. MacInnis, W. Whan Park, and J. W. Priester, *Handbook of Brand Relationships*, Routledge.
Serafeim, G., Eccles, R. and Clay, T. (2012) "GoodGuide," HBS No. 9–112–031, Harvard Business School Publishing.
Steinbrook, R.M.D. (2009) "Controlling Conflict of Interest – Proposals from the Institute of Medicine," *The New England Journal of Medicine*, Volume 360, Issue 21, pp. 2160–2163.
Strobl, G. and Xia, H. (2011) "The Issuer-Pays Rating Model and Ratings Inflation: Evidence from Corporate Credit Ratings," Kenan-Flagler Business School, University of North Carolina at Chapel Hill.
Xia, H. (2010) "The Issuer-Pay Rating Model and Rating Inflation: Evidence from Corporate Credit Ratings," 7th Annual Conference on Corporate Finance at Washington University in St. Louis, PhD Session.
Yamori, N., Nishigaki, N. and Asai, Y. (2006) "Credit Ratings in the Japanese Bond Market," Discussion Paper 654, Institute of Social and Economic Research, Osaka University.

49

Reclaiming pension fund fiduciary duty fundamentals

James P. Hawley, Keith Johnson and Ed Waitzer

ORIGINALLY PUBLISHED AS JAMES HAWLEY, KEITH JOHNSON, AND ED WAITZER (2011) 'RECLAIMING FIDUCIARY DUTY BALANCE', ROTMAN INTERNATIONAL JOURNAL OF PENSION MANAGEMENT 4 (2): 4–16 (DOI:10.3138/RIJPM.4.2.4).

The dynamic nature of fiduciary duty

Fiduciary duty is grounded on a relatively stable set of legal principles that have survived for centuries. However, interpretation of fiduciary principles can be quite dynamic. We are again at an inflection point where our understanding and appreciation of fiduciary duty is evolving rapidly. In response to recent financial market, economic and asset management industry changes, fiduciaries are examining the continued appropriateness of norms and beliefs carried over from the twentieth century.

Trends of the past three decades have produced a concentration of capital managed by fiduciaries on a global basis, often against similar short-term and market-relative benchmarks. Increased market complexity has generated a longer and more conflicted chain of service providers that have growing influence over governing fiduciaries. Despite a series of unexpected market shocks, prevailing theories and practices have not been fully adjusted to reflect systemic and long-term risks that threaten to undermine the security of the pension (and other retirement savings) plan 'promise'.

These developments present a compelling case for evaluation of how fiduciary principles and practices might be better aligned to promote sustainable pension (and other retirement investment) success. Such a process is likely to be an extended journey of discovery rather than a single event of enlightenment. This chapter identifies recent changes and fundamental issues that should be examined in the quest to reclaim fiduciary duty fundamentals.

Changes in the market and risk environment

The extent of change since the mid-twentieth century in global financial markets, regulatory frameworks, economic theory, risk management and the role played by mandatory savings plans has been remarkable. For pension fiduciaries, the most important transformations have included:

- *Growth of pension funds* – Assets under the management of pension fiduciaries have grown from an insignificant part of economies to huge pools of capital. Total pension fund assets now exceed national GDP in each of the Netherlands, Switzerland and Iceland. Across all countries in the Organization for Economic Cooperation and Development (OECD), the average pension assets-to-GDP ratio in 2009 was 67 per cent. In the United Kingdom, it was 81 per cent; in Australia, 82 per cent.[1] Institutional investors collectively own 73 per cent of stock issued by companies in the Fortune 1000. Pension funds alone hold the largest ownership block, with almost 30 per cent.[2]

- *Expansion of service provider influence* – Innovation in the creation of financial instruments, products and services has produced a far more complex investment marketplace. Nearly every aspect of investment management now requires specialized expertise. This has generated a vast new industry of service providers upon which pension trustees rely.
- *Exposure to systemic and extra-financial risk* – Use of indexed investing has skyrocketed. Furthermore, Ibbotson reports that 75 per cent or more of a typical portfolio's returns now come from general market exposure (beta) rather than benchmark outperformance (alpha).[3] The recent financial crisis illustrates this phenomenon, which produced an unexpected global correlation of risks that lopped $5.4 trillion (20 per cent) off global pension assets in 2008 alone, accelerated the closure of defined benefit pension plans and ravaged retirement security for millions of plan participants.[4]
- *Focus on short-term returns* – The average holding period for shares listed on the New York Stock Exchange has gone from over five years in 1970 to less than a year today.[5] Mercer and the IRRC Institute report that nearly two-thirds of portfolio managers have higher annual portfolio turnover than claimed, some by as much as 200 per cent.[6] The CFA Centre for Financial Market Integrity and the Business Roundtable Institute for Corporate Ethics studied investor time horizons and concluded: "The obsession with short-term results by investors, asset management firms, and corporate managers collectively leads to the unintended consequences of destroying long-term value, decreasing market efficiency, reducing investment returns, and impeding efforts to strengthen corporate governance".[7] The World Economic Forum warns that short-termism is being fostered through adoption of regulatory frameworks that constrain the ability of investors with long-term liabilities to use long-term investment strategies.[8]
- *Evolving investment theory assumptions* – Modern portfolio theory (MPT) became accepted as the dominant approach for prudent investment and risk management practices toward the end of the twentieth century. It transformed the legal framework governing fiduciaries. However, recent developments in economics and behavioural finance have built a substantial critique of many assumptions underlying MPT and related academic theory.[9] An adjustment in prevailing investment theory is likely to follow, particularly in regard to the following:

    - *Understanding of risk* – MPT assumes that investment risk falls into four main types: market, credit, liquidity and operational. The rapid growth of financial instruments has led to underestimation and mispricing of risk, due primarily to market complexity and interactions among various risk types. Uncertainty (risk that is neither necessarily known nor calculable) has not been considered, though its effects have become evident.[10]
    - *View of markets* – MPT assumes that: (i) investors are rational; (ii) information is symmetric, cost free and immediately actionable; (iii) if markets are temporarily inefficient, they will revert to being efficient with the help of arbitrage; and (iv) returns are statistically stochastic and have been widely interpreted as following a normal bell curve distribution.[11] The growing dominance of large institutional investors using similar investment strategies and risk management techniques has produced returns that are increasingly linked. The resultant herding and cascading effects reflect the failure of MPT to take into account the effect of its own success and widespread adoption.

- *Beliefs about investors* – MPT also presumes that investors: (i) are risk averse, (ii) make decisions based on expected utility, (iii) have linear and consistent preferences and (iv) are price takers who cannot individually affect a security's price. MPT concludes that the overall risk of a portfolio depends on the risk of each asset in the portfolio, the proportion of the portfolio in that asset and the correlations among different portfolio assets. In critical instances, each of these assumptions (and conclusions) have not held.
- *Systemic risk* – From the original formulation of MPT, Sharpe introduced concepts of systemic and idiosyncratic risk, beta, diversification and the linear relationship between beta (a measure of portfolio risk) and expected return.[12] The critical point for contemporary risk management is the assumption that idiosyncratic (asset-specific) risk can be diversified away (including through leverage), increasing portfolio return and/or decreasing portfolio risk (beta). Unexamined was the impact of systemic risk, which Sharpe held as independent of idiosyncratic risk, and which he argued (correctly in our view) could not be diversified away. Systemic risk was seen as strictly exogenous.[13]

The ideological power of 'labelling' financial markets as 'efficient' (i.e., that they do not cause or amplify economic instability) or 'rational' has been undermined. This has implications for the application of fiduciary norms and merits the attention of institutional fiduciaries.[14]

The origins of fiduciary norms

Fiduciaries face the same challenges whether they oversee funds structured as trusts, mutual benefit societies, foundations, contractual pools of segregated assets or joint stock companies. While the following discussion tracks the evolution of fiduciary duty applicable to trusts in common law jurisdictions, the same fundamentals apply to civil law regimes and contractual pension schemes.[15]

Early roots

Fiduciary duty has its roots in Germanic, Roman and Islamic trust law.[16] The contemporary trust developed as a means to overcome feudal restrictions on the transfer of land and was imported to English common law from civil law structures.[17] The essential concept was that underlying assets were held in trust, under separate title from the designated beneficiaries, and managed by the trustee on behalf of designated beneficiaries.[18] Trustees initially had few powers or managerial responsibilities and, most often, were unpaid. The trustee's role has evolved dramatically over time.

Quantitative standards

Following the collapse of the 'South Sea Bubble' in the early 1700s, English courts of equity required trustees to restrict their investments to government debt and well-secured mortgages. This was the genesis of the 'legal list' approach, which restricted the range of permitted trustee investments.[19]

In the United States, *Harvard College v. Amory*[20] took a different approach. The court articulated an objective behavioural standard for trustee investment practice, focusing on conduct and imposing duties of care and loyalty, rather than prescribing permitted investments. While it admonished speculation, there was recognition that risk is inherent in investment decisions.

However, the flexibility of this approach was quickly circumscribed. For example, in *King v. Talbot*,[21] the court determined that it was imprudent for trustees to invest in corporate stock and limited them to investments in government bonds and mortgage-backed instruments. New York followed suit in 1889, enacting legislation that restricted trust investments to government bonds and mortgages, unless otherwise allowed by the trust creator. As recently as the 1970s, stock investments were widely viewed as imprudent for trust fiduciaries.[22]

Prudent person standard

Over time, the changing market environment made this restrictive approach impractical. Statutory expressions of a 'prudent person' rule for trustee investment began to supersede the legal list approach by the mid-twentieth century.[23] The need for trustees to effectively hedge against inflation and the superior performance of equities (and foreign securities) also led to the introduction of baskets for securities that fell outside of legal lists, to facilitate diversification. With growing acceptance of MPT in the 1970s and after, the abandonment of prescribed investment categories became common. The Employee Retirement Income Security Act (ERISA), adopted in 1974 to govern U.S. private pension funds, illustrates this legal paradigm shift from restricted trustee powers to one that confers broad managerial discretion on trustees, within the bounds of overarching fiduciary obligations. Most U.S. public pension plans also adopted similar standards.[24]

In addition, ERISA repealed the prior rule against delegation of investment responsibilities, in response to the growing complexity of managing financial assets and the need for trustees to rely upon delegation to professionals to discharge their obligations. This evolution was subsequently reflected in 1992 modifications of the Restatement (Third) of Trusts.[25]

Some variation of the prudent person rule has now been adopted in most common law and civil law countries with mature capital markets. It is generally effected by contract in civil law jurisdictions.

Prudent investor standard

One variation of the prudent person standard was the shift to a 'prudent investor' standard in the 1992 revisions of the Restatement of Trusts and the Uniform Prudent Investor Act of 1994, as well as the British Pensions Act in 1995. These changes reflected a recognition that, in accordance with MPT, prudence should be measured on an overall portfolio basis, rather than by discretely considering each particular investment. It also elevated the prudence standard by recognizing the fact that managing pension fund assets requires significant levels of professional expertise beyond that of the common person.

The Uniform Prudent Investor Act[26] was adopted to facilitate implementation of the standards for prudent trust investment advanced in the Restatement (Third). It made five major alterations in prudent investing: (i) focusing on the total portfolio, rather than individual investments, (ii) defining the fiduciary's central concern as the trade-off between risk and return, (iii) removing all categorical restrictions on types of investment, (iv) prescribing diversification as integral to prudent investing and (v) reversing the non-delegation rule with respect to investment and management functions. It also confirmed a 'prudent professional' standard, to clarify application of a higher standard of care when a trustee is an expert or professional with a higher level of skills (e.g., investment professionals).[27]

Fiduciary duty is a dynamic concept

This evolution of fiduciary duty demonstrates that fiduciary law is not a static concept, nor is it tied to a single investment theory. Rather, it is a flexible set of principles that have been subject to varying interpretations over time. When explaining rejection of prior interpretations of the fiduciary duty in the early 1990s, the Restatement of Trusts (Third) aptly observed:

> Trust investment law should reflect and accommodate current knowledge and concepts. It should avoid repeating the mistake of freezing its rules against future learning and developments.[28]

Fiduciary duty is a process-oriented standard which guides, rather than dictates, investment decisions. A generation of investment professionals has spent entire careers in a legal environment shaped by MPT. This has encouraged the view that fiduciary duty mandates a single investment approach. Absent a broadly accepted prescriptive alternative, there remains strong cognitive resistance to a dynamic understanding of the legal standards.

Pension fiduciary duty today

While the exact formulation of fiduciary duty varies between jurisdictions, the main concepts are relatively consistent.[29] Fiduciaries are generally required to discharge their duties:

(a) solely in the interest of participants and beneficiaries;
(b) for the exclusive purpose of providing benefits;
(c) impartially, taking into consideration differing interests of various participant and beneficiary groups;
(d) with the care, skill and prudence exercised by similar fiduciaries, including as to diversification of investments;
(e) incurring only costs that are appropriate and reasonable; and
(f) in accordance with governing law and documents.[30]

Duties (a) through (c) are often referred to as the 'duty of loyalty', while (d) is called the 'duty of prudence' or 'standard of care'. All must be grounded in the specific context – that is, the nature of the pension promise and success in delivering on it.[31]

Pension fiduciary standards are stricter than standards for corporate directors

Though often compared to corporate director statutory duties, pension fiduciaries are held to a higher standard of conduct that has different legal roots.[32] If a trustee's conduct is not excused as an honest and prudent act, she may be liable to the beneficiaries for the full benefit to which they were entitled.[33] The duty of loyalty owed by pension fiduciaries is to the actual human beneficiaries, as opposed to the legal entity. There is not the same ambiguity as may be inherent in corporate law, which imposes a duty to act in the best interests of the 'corporation'. Pension fiduciaries need not concern themselves with raising capital, and there are few market-based (or other) checks to discipline their conduct. Conversely, pension beneficiaries do not enjoy the liquidity of capital markets or the ability to oust trustees.

The governance remit of fund trustees is also different than that of corporate directors. The essence of private enterprise is risk-taking. In contrast, the history of fiduciary standards for the investment of pension fund assets is singular in its focus on the preservation of trust property by risk mitigation and cautious investment behaviour.[34]

Devolution of the pension fiduciary standard care

The standard of care (also known as the duty of prudence) encourages pension fiduciaries to adhere to practices followed by similar institutional investors.[35] However, with growth in pension assets over the past few decades and increased investor focus on short-term investing, herding can function like an economic wave generation machine.[36] Collectively, pension fund investors can *create market volatility and undermine sustainable wealth creation* when they invest with the same short-term bias and follow each other around the markets.

Excessive reliance on peer comparisons has also produced a shift to the use of relative performance metrics, rather than measuring performance on a risk-adjusted basis and against the best interests of beneficiaries. Perceived liability exposure increases for fiduciaries that are out of step with common practice (and results). Courts can easily compare performance to that of a similar portfolio or recognized index in order to evaluate prudence and assess damages. This often distracts fiduciaries from focusing on the interests of plan participants and is likely to distort efficient markets.[37]

The word 'prudence' derives from the Latin term for 'foresight' and means "acting with or showing care and thought for the future."[38] Peter Drucker argued this 35 years ago in 'The Unseen Revolution',[39] warning that pension funds would face the twin challenges (and opportunities) of becoming dominant owners as aging and longevity became key social, economic and political issues. In an epilogue to the 1995 edition (in which he noted that no book of his had been more on target or more totally ignored), Drucker argued in favour of a shift away from short-term thinking in favour of a focus on defining performance (and results) as "maximizing the wealth-producing capacity of the enterprise."[40] This, he argued, should define the role of institutional investors (and, more generally, managerial accountability).

The duty of impartiality

A recent Bank of England study found that "Investment choice, like other life choices, is being re-tuned to a shorter wave-length",[41] leading to irrational investment decisions, particularly in regard to long-duration projects which often yield the highest private (and social) returns. Their data suggests that, in the U.K. and U.S., 10-year-ahead cash flows are valued as if received 16 or more years ahead and little or no value is ascribed to cash flows more than 30 years ahead. This myopic discounting was found to be on the increase and to be distorting efficient capital allocation by diverting investment capital away from future growth, overlooking associated risks.

However, the duty of impartiality, which is part of the duty of loyalty, requires that fiduciaries balance short- and long-term considerations.[42] They must identify and impartially consider conflicting interests of different beneficiary groups, including those of current and future retirees.[43] While impartiality does not mandate uncompromising equality, it does apply across all trustee duties. It requires that "conduct in administering a trust cannot be influenced by a trustee's personal favouritism . . . nor is it permissible for a trustee to ignore the interests of some beneficiaries merely as a result of oversight or neglect."[44]

Most important, the duty of impartiality imposes 'procedural' duties. Not only must actual results reflect due regard for different beneficiaries' interests, but the "process of administration itself", including communication with beneficiaries, must be impartial.[45]

The duty of impartiality requires attention to long-term issues

For many plan participants, pension management results have become unfair, particularly from an inter-generational perspective.[46] While these outcomes may not present legal problems under the duty of prudence – common management approaches and poor results may be widely shared – the duty of impartiality presents a more clouded picture. In hindsight, at least, it is no surprise that widespread adherence to investment practices focused on producing short-term portfolio earnings at the expense of future capital growth comes with "consequences of destroying long-term value, decreasing market efficiency, reducing investment returns, and impeding efforts to strengthen corporate governance."[47]

The duty of impartiality assumes competence in respect of long-term value creation and risk mitigation. To be clear, the issue is not that a short-term outlook is wrong but, rather, that a deliberate balance should be struck between mission and risk-adjusted returns, including related opportunity costs. Fiduciaries must ensure that their decision-making processes balance allocation of capital between near-term needs and future wealth creation and consider the potential transfer of risks between participant generations. Intergenerational wealth maximization requires active consideration of a range of factors beyond narrow financial criteria.

Dilution of the duty of loyalty

Pension trustees have an overriding "duty to administer the trust solely in the interest of the beneficiaries" and are "prohibited from engaging in transactions that involve self-dealing or that otherwise involve or create a conflict between the trustee's fiduciary duties and personal interests."[48] Uncompromising rigidity of this rule is not just a formality (and applies to both defined benefit and defined contribution plans).[49]

> The courts have consistently held that this inflexibility is essential to its effective operation . . . First, the courts have acknowledged that it is difficult, if not impossible for a person to act impartially in a matter in which he has an interest . . . Secondly, the courts have realized that fiduciary relationships lend themselves to exploitation . . . Finally, the courts have made much of the fact that disloyal conduct is hard to detect.[50]

This focus on process and alignment of interests makes the duty of loyalty a demanding standard. "The fact that the [trustees] might have properly decided to choose the same course of action had they engaged in an unbiased and adequately informed process does not excuse how they went about reaching this course of action."[51]

Figure 49.1 provides a visual representation of the relative priority of the duty of care and duty of care. "When duties of loyalty and care collide, courts generally resolve the conflict in favour of the duty of loyalty representing minimum conduct to which the fiduciary must adhere."[52] Given primacy of the duty of loyalty, greater allocation of fiduciary time and resources to implementation of loyalty principles may be required.

Increasing financial market complexity along with resultant growth and influence of the advisory service supply chain have eroded the protections afforded to beneficiaries by the duty of loyalty. The US Government Accountability Office reports that pension consultant conflicts of interest appear to be associated with lower investment returns.[53] In response, the US Department of Labor has proposed new regulations under ERISA to bring within the definition of fiduciary certain consultants, advisors and appraisers, who "significantly influence the decisions of plan fiduciaries, and have a considerable impact on plan investments."[54]

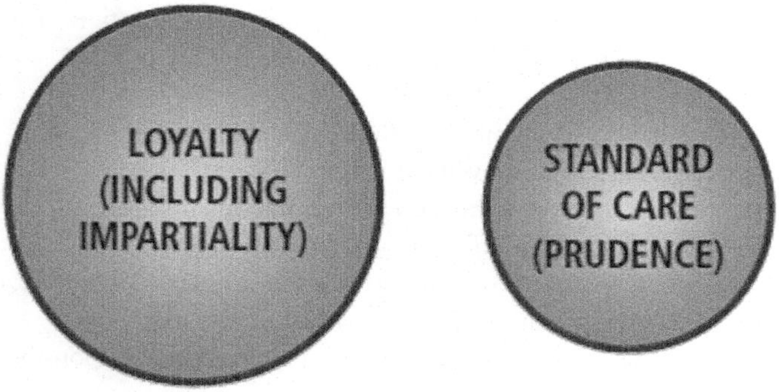

Figure 49.1 Relative priority on conflict of main fiduciary duties

A Create-Research survey of European pension fund executives and asset managers offers insight into the practical ramifications of these conflicts of interest, concluding that:

> There is a widespread perception in the pension world that the investment industry is perverse in one crucial sense: its food chain operates in reverse, with service providers at the top and clients at the bottom. Agents fare better than principals.[55]

By delegating duties to qualified experts, trustees in many jurisdictions can shift liability risk to the delegates. This can create perverse incentives for trustees to delegate responsibility, while the delegates try to avoid liability by providing advice but not making final decisions (or seeking indemnity).[56] The result can be a circular system where no one takes responsibility and the interests of agents trump those of pension beneficiaries. Nevertheless, the duty of loyalty assigns to governing fiduciaries the ultimate responsibility for oversight of supply-chain management conflicts of interest (which have widely become the norm in most commercial sectors).

Pension board governance practices

Implementation of the duty of loyalty presents particular challenges at the governing fiduciary level. Studies of pension fund governance practices have shown that good governance is associated with increased returns.[57] However, recent findings suggest that many pension funds do not have the governance capacity to adapt their practices for better success or to distinguish between (let alone act upon) the differences between short-term issues and long-term commitments.[58]

Ambachtsheer goes further in identifying key 'success driver' for tomorrow's pension funds:[59]

- aligned interests (conflict free);
- good governance (requisite skills and accountabilities);
- sensible investment beliefs (focusing on long-term wealth creation and effective risk management);
- right-scaled institutions (big enough to be internally competent and competitive); and
- competitive compensation (to attract the best).

Again, as the empirical support for the relevance of such factors becomes compelling, it is arguable that failure to consider them has fiduciary duty implications.

For example, recent research has identified good governance practices that are linked with pension fund success. They include:

- selection of governing board members with relevant skills and knowledge;
- development of a board self-improvement culture;
- clear understanding of the board's mission and its investment beliefs;
- sufficient fund size to allow cost effective management of assets;
- competitive staff compensation to permit acquisition of internal expertise;
- insulation from conflicting political or third party agendas; and
- clarity of board and staff roles about delegation of management responsibilities.[60]

While some of these factors can be beyond the control of influence of governing fiduciaries, most of them are not. Failure to consider material fiduciary governance success factors raises concerns about the alignment of process with beneficiary interests and compliance with the duty of loyalty.

Management of service provider conflicts

Similarly, governing fiduciaries have an obligation to ensure that procedures are in place to identify and manage conflicts of interest in their service provider chain. Regulatory initiatives are beginning to refocus on this duty, but regulation is no substitute for process and contract changes to improve management of conflicts. Attention to the development of an effective conflicts management program could include the following components:

- *Imposition of fiduciary liability throughout the supply chain* – While ERISA states that fiduciary liability attaches to anyone exercising discretion over plan assets, trustees have tended to view delegation as a shield (rather than a sword).[61] Even in jurisdictions where asset managers and consultants are not treated as fiduciaries, they could be contractually required to put beneficiaries' interests first through the use of selection process requirements.
- *Use of conflicts screening in selection of service providers* – The legal obligation to view conflicts of interest from beneficiaries' perspectives and focus on avoiding conflicts rather than monitoring them argues for selection of service providers without conflicts whenever practicable.[62]
- *Alignment of service provider interests with fund participants* – As noted above, contract mandates and fee structures could be more clearly aligned with the duty of impartiality to better incentivize service providers to achieve goals that serve the short-term and long-term interests of various beneficiary groups in a balanced manner.
- *Reporting to fund participants on management of conflicts* – Given the opacity of risks associated with conflicts of interest, transparency with respect to identification and management of conflicts is particularly important. This includes not only service provider conflicts of interest but also efforts to balance divergent interests of different beneficiary groups.
- *Monitoring of conflicts and enforcement of standards* – More attention could be paid to contractual mandates for reporting and ongoing oversight of areas where service providers are likely to have conflicts. For example, there may be situations where providers have competing interests that complicate compliance with the duty of impartiality, such as when a manager with a short-term strategy votes proxies on matters relating to systemic risk exposure over

the long-term or a manager votes proxies involving executive compensation matters at a company with which it also has a business relationship.

Precautionary risk management

Future value creation and management of risks for sustainable delivery of the pension promise depend on a range of interconnected social, environmental and economic factors which, until recently, were often viewed as too remote or speculative to take into account and report on. Contemporary interpretations of fiduciary duty have proven ill-suited to taking an integrated view of and actively managing them. The fact that they now present systemic risk issues, however, also recalls the precautionary principle – the duty to focus first on doing no harm and to impartially take account of the interests of beneficiaries to whom fiduciary obligations are owed when developing an investment approach.[63] Indeed, a trust fund beneficiary's "first claim is that the fiduciary must refrain from causing harm. . . . 'Do no harm' is the clarion call of every fiduciary."[64]

Loyalty to the interests of beneficiaries may require consideration of and response to their varying views on appropriate levels of risk exposure (including, perhaps, efforts to help inform such views). Ignoring the views of beneficiaries (or the interests of other key stakeholder groups) could have long-term ramifications on support for and sustainability of the pension promise. Attentiveness to and management of stakeholder expectations can be as important to sustainable success as investment management decisions.

These considerations (as well as the need to build governance capacity) suggest that trustees should be sensitizing themselves to the interests of beneficiaries (future and present), both directly (i.e., through efforts to consult and to inform) and by looking to evolving universal norms as a proxy therefore.[65] This, in turn, requires implementation of processes for engagement that identify and consider externalities associated with management practices.

Application of the duty of loyalty mandates that procedures be impartially aligned with participants' interests also has implications for resolving the tragedy of the commons paradox, wherein fiduciaries reject strategies expected to produce shared benefits while free riding on the efforts of others.[66] Fiduciaries cannot simply ignore the interests of a group of beneficiaries because most other fiduciaries are doing the same.

Likewise, in considering the interests of pension participants and beneficiaries, fiduciary responsibilities require that trustees measure and report on success in achieving the fundamental purpose of the pension trust – provision of an independent mechanism for securing the pension promise and actual performance in doing so.

Incorporating sustainability factors into the investment process

The assumption that risk can be managed solely or primarily through diversification was shown to be flawed by the recent economic crisis. For example, investors cannot avoid the risks associated with climate change by diversifying across asset classes; they must instead seek to diversify across sources of risk.[67] Yet legal uncertainty has led to a view within the investment supply chain that integration of long-term risks and opportunities into the investment process is someone else's problem.

Signatories to the UN-backed Principles for Responsible Investment (UN PRI) have now grown to over 1450 institutional owners with about US$ 46 trillion under management – a signal that they are beginning to recognize the connections between a commitment to incorporate environmental, social and governance (ESG) issues into their policies and practices and the fundamental fiduciary duties of loyalty and impartiality. ESG issues that might be of little concern to short-term traders can be material for long-term investors with obligations to manage assets impartially and in the interests of beneficiaries in order to deliver sustainable pension benefits over several generations.[68]

Urwin recently described the focus of 'universal owners' on investment strategies and ownership practices (including collective action to produce network benefits) that integrate ESG considerations.[69] Moreover, pension funds (along with other significant long-term investors) are uniquely positioned to benefit from investment opportunities that address unmet economic (and social) needs, rather than simply identifying and investing in existing assets. To do so, fiduciaries need to overcome the tendency to allocate capital based solely on historical practices and approach sustainable investing from a forward-looking risk management and value creation perspective.[70]

It is also increasingly apparent that regulatory leadership will be required to motivate long-term fiduciaries (and their service providers) to effectively integrate ESG criteria into their investment decision-making. Sustainable investing should be tethered to effective risk management and regulatory compliance. Incentives should be aligned – by mandating appropriate fiduciary, competencies, governance and reporting practices that are designed to deliver sustainable retirement income security. Part of the challenge (again) is to rediscover and operationalize fundamental fiduciary norms, as well as adapt them to an evolving global investment environment.[71]

Stewardship codes for institutional investors are now in place or being considered in Britain, Europe, Canada, Australia and elsewhere. South Africa has taken the lead in this regard, introducing, by regulation, a number of principles to be applied to investment institution fund assets. This includes a mandate that the investors: "Before making an investment into and while invested in an asset, consider any factor which may materially affect the sustainable long-term performance of the investment, including those of an environmental, social and governance character." The preamble to these regulations squarely frames the duty of prudence (and, by implication, impartiality) as including proper consideration of these issues.[72]

The way forward – development of key performance indicators

Business as usual is not likely to result in pension management practices that are designed to be unbiased and aligned solely with the interests of participants and beneficiaries, nor is it likely to provide suitable pension benefits on a sustainable and impartial basis. Yet that is the challenge today's fiduciaries face. We believe that plan sponsors, participants, beneficiaries, fiduciaries and their advisors could benefit from the development of key performance indicators to help guide pension management practices toward measurable success in meeting fundamental fiduciary goals. This chapter is intended to provoke an industry discussion focusing on that challenge.[73]

Table 49.1 contains an initial list of factors for consideration by fiduciaries in working toward the application of their fiduciary duties to contemporary challenges. We hope they provide a starting point for discussing how developments in knowledge and changes in the circumstances faced by pension funds affect fiduciary obligations and practices. Such discussions should help to inform the evolving understanding of fiduciary duties and, in turn, promote success in sustainable delivery of promised pension benefits.

Table 49.1 Reclaiming fiduciary duties: key governing fiduciary issues

Fiduciary Challenges	*Fiduciary Issues: Policies and Procedures*	*Fiduciary Issues: Oversight Responsibilities*
• Changing circumstances and knowledge base • Systemic and long-term risk exposures • Inter-generational equity and pension disparity • Unbalanced short-termism • Conflicts of interest • Pension governance quality • Implementation of 'do no harm' principle • Alignment of policies and procedures	• Allocate resources and time to understand challenges • Adopt enterprise risk management approach • Use beneficiary-aligned and impartial measures of success • Understand global best practices • Develop 'fit for purpose' governance capabilities • Ensure sustainable plan design • Expand reporting/ engagement to address loyalty and impartiality	• Acquire expertise to address fiduciary challenges • RFPs to address fiduciary challenges • Invest in research on long-term issues and fiduciary challenges • Foster collaboration on education and shared resource development • Measure success impartially on achieving beneficiary goals and interests • Identify and measure risks across all beneficiary groups • Align service provider contracts and fees with beneficiary interests • Manage ESG risks and opportunities for sustainability and impartiality

Notes

This chapter was made possible by a research funding grant from the Rotman International Centre for Pension Management. The authors would also like to thank participants in the Network for Sustainability Financial Markets for input on the development of this chapter, Mehdi Beyhaghi, who provided invaluable research on modern portfolio theory and risk management, and Steven Raphael, who assisted in the final editing. A version of this chapter appeared in the *Rotman International Journal of Pension Management* 4 (2), Fall 2011, and appears here with permission.

1 Organization of Economic Cooperation and Development (2010) *Pension Markets in Focus*, Issue 7. Online. Available HTTP: <http://stats.oecd.org/Index.aspx?DatasetCode=PNNI_NEW>.
2 The Conference Board (2010) *The 2010 Institutional Investment Report*, November.
3 Roger Ibbotson (2010) 'The Importance of Asset Allocation', *Financial Analysts Journal.*
4 Organization of Economic Cooperation and Development (2010) The Impact of the Financial Crisis on Defined Benefit Plans. In the UK, 73 per cent of defined benefit plans are now closed to new entrants.
5 The Conference Board (2003) Commission on Public Trust and Private Enterprise, Part 2 – Corporate Governance; New York Stock Exchange. Online. Available HTTP: <http://www.nyxdata/com/nysedata/asp/factbook>.
6 IRRC Institute and Mercer (2010) *Investment Horizons – Do Managers Do What They Say?*
7 CFA Centre for Financial Market Integrity and Business Roundtable Institute for Corporate Ethics (2006) *Breaking the Short-Term Cycle.* The long-term value destruction dynamic is illustrated in a study by Bhojraj, S., Hribar, P., Picconi, M. and McInnis, J. (2009) 'Making Sense of Cents: An Examination of Firms that Marginally Miss or Beat Analyst Forecasts', *The Journal of Finance*, where they found that companies which use reductions in R&D, advertising and other discretionary spending to narrowly beat Wall Street quarterly projections experience a short-term stock value increase but go on to underperform over the following three years.
8 World Economic Forum (2011) *The Future of Long-Term Investing*, p. 66.
9 See, for example, Montgomery, J. (2004) Economic Analaysis in ERISA Litigation over Fiduciary Duties, NERA Economic Consulting. Online. Available HTTP: <http://www.nera.com>. See also, Kahneman, D. and Tverskey, A. (1979) 'Prospect Theory: An Analysis of Decision under Risk', *Econometrica* 47 (2):

263–292; Devenow, A. and Welch, I. (1996) 'Rational Herding in Financial Economics', *European Economic Review* 40: 603–615.

10 Knight, F. (1921) *Risk, Uncertainty, and Profit*, Boston, MA: Hart, Schaffner & Marx with Houghton Mifflin Co.; Bookstaber, R. (2007) *A Demon of Our Own Design: Markets, Hedge Funds, and the Perils of Financial Innovation*, New York: Wiley.

11 See, for example, 'Non-normality of Market Returns', J. P. Morgan Asset Management. Online. Available HTTP: <www.jpmorgan.com/insight>; Taleb, N. (2007) *The Black Swan: The Impact of the Highly Improbable*, New York: Random House, pp. 20–150. A good example of this is the 'pack mentality' of hedge funds (correlations of returns) from 2004–2010; see Strasburg, J. and Pulliam. S. (2011) 'Pack Mentality Grips Hedge Funds', *The Wall Street Journal*, 14 January. Online. Available HTTP: <online.wsj.com/article> (accessed 14 January 2011).

12 Sharpe, W.F. (1964) 'Capital Asset Prices: A Theory of Market Equilibrium under Conditions of Risk', *Journal of Finance* 19 (3): 425–442.

13 The popularity of index funds had an unpredicted consequence, which illustrates the fallacy of composition problem, one manifestation of which is herding. As a result of increase in demand for stocks that are included in a market index, the price of these stocks has been moved to some extent independently from their fundamental values. The indexation paradox has led to undermining the efficacy of the risk metrics essential to calculating risk-adjusted returns since, paradoxically, a market index is no longer representative of a market. Rather it fluctuates due to the demand of index funds and portfolio managers that attempt to replicate the index. Therefore performance evaluation based on these indices (both alpha and beta) are subject to inefficiencies as these indices are not really an 'index' of the market.

14 Indeed, a 1935 Keynes' observation about the dangers of unrealistic economic assumptions is just as relevant today: "Too large a proportion of recent 'mathematical' economics are mere concoctions, as imprecise as the initial assumptions they rest on, which allow the author to lose sight of the complexities and interdependencies of the real world in a maze of pretentious and unhelpful symbols." Keynes, J. M., *The General Theory of Employment, Interest and Money,* Book 5, Ch. 21, sec. 3, p. 298.

15 Different forms of pension organizations, governing structures and legal regimes may require varying approaches to implementation of an evolving understanding of fiduciary duty. For example, changed regulations or stricter enforcement of existing laws might be appropriate in some civil law jurisdictions, while supervisory authorities or courts might adopt new interpretations of existing legal principles in some common law jurisdictions. Even under common law tradition, pension law is a unique combination of trust and contract principles that is effectively a specialized form of contract law. See Langbein, J. (1997) 'The Secret Life of the Trust: The Trust as an Instrument of Commerce', *Yale Law Journal* 107: 165–189. See also International Organisation of Pension Supervisors (2008) *Supervisory Oversight of Pension Fund Governance*, Working Paper No. 8 and Russell, G. (2002) *Prudent Person Rule Standard for the Investment of Pension Fund Assets,* OECD for a discussion of the fundamental pension fund governance issues that are common across various legal structures and jurisdictions.

16 Avini, A. (1996) 'The Origins of the Modern English Trust Revisited', *Tulane Law Review* 70: 1139.

17 Lupoi, M. (1999) 'The Civil Law Trust', *Vanderbilt Journal of Transnational Law* 32: 967.

18 Langbein, J. H. (1997) 'The Secret Life of the Trust: The Trust as an Instrument of Commerce', *Yale Law Journal* 107: 165.

19 Keeton, G. (1971) 'Modern Developments in the Law of Trusts' *Northern Ireland Legal Quarterly*, 46–62. Ironically, some recent regulatory reforms are moving toward a revival of constraints on permissible assets (and asset classes) in response to funds taking outsized risks to remedy their deficits. See, for example, David Norgrove, speech to National Association of Pension Funds Annual Trustee Conference (December 2010). Online. Available HTTP: <www.thepensionregulator.gov.uk/doc-library/david-norgrove-napf-annual-trustee-conference-speech.aspx>.

20 26 Mass. (9 Pick) 446 (1830).

21 40 N.Y. 76 (1869).

22 See Restatement of Trusts, Second, § 227, Comment f. (1959).

23 Friedman, L. M. (1964) 'The Dynastic Trust', *Yale Law Journal* 547: 554–572.

24 See, for example, the Uniform Management of Public Employee Retirement Systems Act (UMPERSA) (1997).

25 Restatement (Third) of Trusts, Section 171 (1992).

26 National Conference of Commissioners on Uniform State Laws, Uniform Prudent Investor Act, 7 B U.L.A. 18 (Supp. 1997).

27 See, for example, Nelson, A. J. (1993) 'The Prudent Person Rule: A Shield for the Professional Trustee', *Baylor Law Review* 45: 933; Stanley, B. J. (1984) 'A Standard for Trustees Stricter than the Prudent Man Standard: The Past and the Future,' *Oklahoma City University Law Review* 9: 485.

28 Restatement of Trusts, Third, § 227, Introduction (1992).

29 For a discussion of key fiduciary duty concepts across various jurisdictions, see Berry, C. (2011) *Protecting our Best Interests: Rediscovering Fiduciary Obligation*, Fairshare Educational Foundation – FairPensions.

30 National Conference of Commissioners on Uniform State Laws (1997) Uniform Management of Public Employee Retirement Systems Act and Restatement of Trusts, Third, § 227 (1992). Similar principles apply across common law countries (e.g., Canada, U.S., UK, Ireland, Australia) and civil law countries (e.g., Italy, Japan, the Netherlands). Galer, R. (2002) Prudent Person Rule Standard for the Investment of Pension Fund Assets, OECD.

31 While this paper does not focus on defined contribution pension plans, the same basic legal responsibilities of (including loyalty and impartiality) apply to selection and monitoring of investment options by the fiduciary, even though participants decide on allocation of their own savings between managers. *Howell v. Motorola,* 2011 WL 183066 (7th Cir. 1/21/11).

32 "[The] issues with respect to typical trusts . . . are materially different from those in the corporate-governance discussion, and trust beneficiaries ordinarily have available no close counterpart of the corporate shareholders' opportunities to sell their stock or to influence their company's behavior." Restatement of Trusts, Third, § 227, Comment c. (1992). For example, trust law generally precludes fiduciaries from doing self-interested transactions, though corporate directors can usually enter into related-party transactions with the company if disclosed and approved by disinterested directors as fair to the corporation. See Restatement of Trusts, Third, §78 and §144 of the Delaware General Corporation Law.

33 It is worth noting that courts have extended pension fiduciary liability. For example, in two related cases, the Ontario Divisional Court imposed a fiduciary liability on the (then) Pension Commission of Ontario for consenting to the withdrawal of surplus funds without giving notice to plan members. See *Re Reevie and Montreal Trust Co. of Canada* (1996), 53 O.R. (2d) 595 and *Re Collins and Pension Commission of Ontario* (1986) 56 O.R. (2d) 274.

34 Sitkoff, R. H. (2004) 'An Agency Costs Theory of Trust Law', *Cornell Law Review* 89: 621.

35 Galer, R. (2002) Prudent Person Rule Standard for the Investment of Pension Fund Assets, OECD. In the United States, pension funds subject to the Employee Retirement Security Income Act (ERISA) must be managed "with the care, skill, prudence, and diligence under the circumstances then prevailing that a prudent man acting in a like capacity and familiar with such matters would use in the conduct of an enterprise of a like character and with like aims" 29 USC §18.1104.

36 Johnson, K. and de Graaf, F. J. (2009) 'Modernizing Pension Fund Legal Standards for the Twenty-first Century', *Rotman International Journal of Pension Management* 2 (1).

37 Del Guercio, D. (1996) 'The Distorting Effect of the Prudent Man Laws on Institutional Equity Investments', *Journal of Financial Economics* 40. Thomas, A. and Tonks, I. (2001) 'Equity Performance of Segregated Pension Funds in the United Kingdom', *Journal of Asset Management* 4: 321.

38 Online. Available HTTP: <www.merriam-webster.com/dictionary/prudent>.

39 Drucker, P. F. (1976) The Unseen Revolution, New York: Harper & Row.

40 Drucker, P. F. (1996) The Pension Fund Revolution, New Brunswick (U.S.): Transaction Publishers. Drucker's focus on 'wealth-creating' investment traces its roots to Keynes, J. M. (1936) The General Theory of Employment, Interest and Money, New York: Harcourt, Brace and Company.

41 Haldane, A. and Davies, R. (2011) *The Short Long.* Online. Available HTTP: <http://www.bankofengland.co.uk/publications/speeches/2011/speech495.pdf>.

42 The U.S. Supreme Court, in *Varity v. Howe,* 516 U.S. 489 (1996), stated that "The common law of trusts [made applicable to ERISA§§ 404, 409] recognizes the need to preserve assets to satisfy future, as well as present, claims and requires a trustee to take impartial account of the interest of all beneficiaries."

43 Comment c to §79 (1) of the Restatement of Trusts, Third. In the UK, *Cowan v. Scargill,* [1984] All ER 750, turned on impartiality. See also *Withers v. Teachers' Retirement System*, 447 F. Supp. 12488 (S.D.N.Y. 1978) 1257–58. The CFA Institute's Code of Conduct for Members of a Pension Scheme Governing Body advises that an effective trustee will "consider the different types of beneficiaries relevant to each pension scheme" and "engage in a delicate balancing act of taking sufficient risk to generate long-term returns high enough to support real benefit increases for active participants who will become future beneficiaries while avoiding a level of risk that jeopardizes the safety of the payments to existing pensioners."

44 Restatement of Trusts, Third, § 79, Comment b. (1992). Similarly, article 5, paragraph 4 of the Dutch Pension and Savings Fund Act provides that "in performing their duties, the persons who determine or help determine the policy of a pension or savings fund shall act in accordance with the interests of the members, former members and other stakeholders involved in the fund." The legislative history of the act makes it clear that participants must be represented in a balanced way, with an eye for the possibly divergent interests of the various categories of stakeholder: members, dormant members, pensioners and other stakeholders. See Maatman, R. (2004) 'Dutch Pension Funds: Fiduciary Duties and Investing', *Law of Business and Finance* 7, Sec 6.5, Kluwer Legal Publishers.

45 Wakeman, A., Franklin, W. and Ascher, M. (2006) *Scott and Ascher on Trusts*, §17.15.

46 For example, more than 73 per cent of UK defined benefit plans are closed to new entrants. In 2009, only 49 per cent of the 200 largest U.S. companies had ongoing defined benefit plans, down from 61 per cent three years earlier. Yermo, J. and Severinson, C. (2010) *The Impact of the Financial Crisis on Defined Benefit Plans and the Need for Counter-Cyclical Funding Regulations*, OECD; see also, Mercer Consulting (2011) *Mercer's Retirement, Risk and Finance Perspective.*

47 See footnote 7, *supra*.

48 Restatement of Trusts, Third, § 78 and Comment b. (1992). In Europe, Article 18, Paragraph 1, of the EU Pensions Directive (Directive 2003/4 ED) provides that member states must observe the "solely in the interest rule" which requires that assets be invested in the interests of fund members and beneficiaries. In the event of a conflict with other stakeholders, their interests must prevail.

49 There has been a tendency to mistakenly conflate the obligation to manage trust assets in the interest of beneficiaries with the other aspects of the duty of loyalty that require assets be managed impartially and for the purpose of providing pension benefits. However, these different aspects of loyalty are distinct obligations. Pension management activities can be designed solely to produce pension benefits but still violate the duty of impartiality and not be in the interest of all beneficiaries. For example, pursuit of investment activities designed to produce short-term returns while generating long-term risks to pension sustainability may pass the 'sole purpose' test but fail the 'interest of beneficiaries' and 'impartiality' fiduciary duties.

50 Hallgring, R. (1966) 'The Uniform Trustees' Powers Act and the Basic Principles of Fiduciary Responsibility', *Washington Law Review* 41: 808–811.

51 *McNeil v Bennett*, 792 A.2d 190 (Del. Ch. 2001).

52 Laby, A. B. (2004) 'Resolving Conflicts of Duty in Fiduciary Relationships', *American University Law Review* 54: 75, at 78.

53 *Conflicts of Interest Can Affect Defined Benefit and Defined Contribution Plans*, GAO 09–503T (24 March 2009).

54 *Federal Register*, October 22, 2010 (Volume 75, Number 204).

55 Rajan, A. (2008) *DB & DC Plans: Strengthening Their Delivery*, Create-Research.

56 Sterk, S. E. (2009) 'Rethinking Trust Law Reform: How Prudent Is Modern Prudent Investor Doctrine?' *Cornell Law Review* 95: 851–904.

57 Ambachtsheer, K., Capelle, R. and Lum, H. (2008) 'The Pension Governance Deficit: Still with Us', *Rotman International Journal of Pension Management* 1 (1).

58 Clark, G. L. and Urwin, R. *supra* note 35.

59 Ambachtsheer, K. (2010) 'Building Tomorrow's Pension Fund Today: From Vision to Reality', *The Ambachtsheer Letter*, No. 297.

60 For more insight about the critical role of board leadership, see Clark, G. L. and Urwin, R. (2008a) 'Making Pension Boards Work: The Critical Role of Leadership', *Rotman International Journal of Pension Management* 1 (1): 38–45; Clark, G. L. and Urwin, R. (2008b) 'Best-Practices Pension Fund Governance', *Journal of Asset Management* 9 (1): 2–21.

61 ERISA s. 3(38). Viewing delegated responsibilities as carrying with them fiduciary obligations might also strengthen the view of such delegation as a fiduciary function.

62 "Viewed from the beneficiaries' perspective, especially that of remainder [long-term] beneficiaries, efforts to prevent or detect actual improprieties can be expected to be inefficient if not ineffective." Restatement of Trusts, Third, § 78, Comment b. (1992).

63 See, for example, CFSIEFF & ORS v. Fox & ORS [2005] EWHC 1312. Canadian courts have developed this concept, as well as the 'duty to consult', in the context of governments contemplating conduct that might adversely affect the rights of Aboriginal peoples. See, for example, Lawrence, S. and Macklem, P. (2000) 'From Consultation to Reconciliation: Aboriginal Rights and the Crown's Duty to Consult', *Canadian Bar Review* 79: 252.

64 Laby, *supra*, at p. 149.
65 See, for example, Richardson, B. J. (2010) 'From Fiduciary Duties to Fiduciary Relationships for Social Responsible Investment'.
66 'Free-riding' occurs when a shared resource or benefit is used without users paying the full cost of it. Over time, this typically leads to overconsumption or exhaustion of the resource or under-provision of it.
67 Mercer (2011) *Climate Change Scenarios – Implications for Strategic Asset Allocation*.
68 The duties to manage pension assets (a) solely in the interest of pension plan participants and beneficiaries, (b) for the exclusive purpose of providing benefits and (c) with impartiality, are separate components of the duty of loyalty. Sustainable investment practices recognize that an investment can be made for the purpose of generating income for benefits but still not meet fiduciary standards if it does not also qualify as impartial and in the interest of participants and beneficiaries.
69 Urwin, R. (2011) 'Pension Funds as Universal Owners: Opportunity Beckons and Leadership Calls', Rotman International Journal of Pension Management 4 (1): 26.
70 World Economic Forum (2011) *Accelerating the Transaction towards Sustainability Investing*.
71 See also, International Organization for Standardization (ISO) 26000, *Guidance on Social Responsibility* (London, British Standards Institution) which defines 'social responsibility' as responsibility of an organization for the impacts of its decisions and activities on society and the environment, through transparent and ethical behaviour that (i) contributes to sustainable development, including health and welfare of society; (ii) takes into account the expectations of stakeholders; (iii) is in compliance with international norms of behaviour; and (iv) is integrated throughout the organization and practiced in its relationships (ISO 26000, clause 2.18).
72 South Africa National Treasury, Pension Funds Act, 1956: Amendment of Regulation 28 of the Regulations made under Section 36, preamble and Section 1(b)(viii) February 23, 2011.
73 With support of a research funding grant from Rotman International Centre for Pension Management, the authors plan to hold fiduciary roundtables to explore development of key performance indicators and publish the findings in future articles.

References

Ambachtsheer, K. (2010) 'Building Tomorrow's Pension Fund Today: From Vision to Reality', *The Ambachtsheer Letter* 297.

Ambachtsheer, K., Capelle, R. and Lum, H. (2008) 'The Pension Governance Deficit: Still with Us', *Rotman International Journal of Pension Management* 1 (1): 14–21. Online. Available HTTP: <http://dx.doi.org/10.3138/rijpm.1.1.14>.

Avisheh, A. (1996) 'The Origins of the Modern English Trust Revisited', *Tulane Law Review* 70: 1139–1164.

Berry, C. (2011) *Protecting Our Best Interests: Rediscovering Fiduciary Obligation*, London: Fairshare Educational Foundation – FairPensions.

Bhojraj, S., Hribar, P., Picconi, M. and McInnis, J. (2009) 'Making Sense of Cents: An Examination of Firms That Marginally Miss or Beat Analyst Forecasts', *Journal of Finance* 64 (5): 2361–2388. Online. Available HTTP: <http://dx.doi.org/10.1111/j.1540–6261.2009.01503.x>.

Bookstaber, R. (2007) *A Demon of Our Own Design: Markets, Hedge Funds, and the Perils of Financial Innovation*, Hoboken, NJ: Wiley.

CFSIEFF & ORS v. Fox & ORS [2005] EWHC 1312.

Clark, G.L. and Urwin, R. (2008a) 'Making Pension Boards Work: The Critical Role of Leadership', *Rotman International Journal of Pension Management* 1 (1): 38–45. Online. Available HTTP: <http://dx.doi.org/10.3138/rijpm.1.1.38>.

Clark, G. L. and Urwin, R. (2008b) 'Best-Practices Pension Fund Governance', *Journal of Asset Management* 9 (1): 2–21. Online. Available HTTP: <http://dx.doi.org/10.1057/jam.2008.1>.

Conference Board Inc. (2003) *Commission on Public Trust and Private Enterprise Findings and Recommendations*, Part 2 – Corporate Governance. Online. Available HTTP: <http://www.conference- oard.org/pdf_free/SR-03–04.pdf>.

Cowan v. Scargill, [1984] All E.R. 750.

Del Guercio, D. (1996) 'The Distorting Effect of the Prudent Man Laws on Institutional Equity Investments', *Journal of Financial Economics* 40 (1): 31–62. Online. Available HTTP: <http://dx.doi.org/10.1016/0304–405X(95)00841–2>.

Devenow, A. and Welch, I. (1996) 'Rational Herding in Financial Economics', *European Economic Review* 40 (3–5): 603–615. Online. Available HTTP: <http://dx.doi.org/10.1016/0014–2921(95)00073–9>.

Drucker, P. (1976) *The Unseen Revolution: How Pension Fund Socialism Came to America*, New York: Heinemann.
Drucker, P. (1996) *The Pension Fund Revolution*, New Brunswick, NJ: Transaction Publishers.
Employee Retirement Security Income Act, 29 USC §18.1104.
EU Pensions Directive (2003) Directive 2003/4 ED.
Friedman, L. (1964) 'The Dynamic Trust', *Yale Law Journal* 73 (4): 547–592. Online. Available HTTP: <http://dx.doi.org/10.2307/794602>.
Galler, R. (2002) *Prudent Person Rule Standard for the Investment of Pension Fund Assets*, Paris: OECD Publishing.
Government Accountability Office (2009) Private Pensions: Conflicts of Interest Can Affect Defined Benefit and Defined Contribution Plans. Online. Available HTTP: <http://www.gao.gov/new.items/d09503t.pdf>.
Haldane, A. and Davies, R. (2011) 'The Short Long', *Proceedings of the 29th Societe Universitaire Européene de Recherches Financières Colloquium* (Brussels), May. Online. Available HTTP: <http://www.bis.org/review/r110511e.pdf>.
Hallgring, R. (1966) '"The Uniform Trustees" Powers Act and the Basic Principles of Fiduciary Responsibility', *Washington Law Review* 41: 808–811.
Harvard College v. Amory, 26 Mass. (9 Pick) 446 (1830).
Howell v. Motorola, 2011WL 183066 (7th Cir. 1/21/11).
Ibbotson, R. (2010) 'The Importance of Asset Allocation', *Financial Analysts Journal* 66 (2): 18–20. Online. Available HTTP: <http://dx.doi.org/10.2469/faj.v66.n2.4>.
International Organization of Pension Supervisors (2010) *Supervisory Oversight of Pension Fund Governance*, Working Paper no. 8. Online. Available HTTP: <http://www.oecd.org/finance/private-pensions/46260971.pdf>.
International Organization for Standardization (2010) *ISO 26000: Guidance on Social Responsibility*, International Organization for Standardization.
Johnson, K. L. and de Graaf, F. J. (2009) 'Modernizing Pension Fund Legal Standards for the Twenty-first Century', *Rotman International Journal of Pension Management* 2 (1): 44–51. Online. Available HTTP: <http://dx.doi.org/10.3138/rijpm.2.1.44>.
J. P. Morgan Asset Management (2009) *Non-normality of Market Returns*, New York: JPMorgan Chase & Co.
Kahneman, D. and Tversky, A. (1979) 'Prospect Theory: An Analysis of Decision under Risk', *Econometrica: Journal of the Econometric Society* 47 (2): 263–292. Online. Available HTTP: <http://dx.doi.org/10.2307/1914185>.
Keeton, G. (1971) *Modern Developments in the Law of Trusts,* Faculty of Law Queens University, Belfast, *Northern Ireland Legal Quarterly*: 46–62.
Keynes, J. M. (1936) *The General Theory of Employment, Interest, and Money*, New York: Harcourt, Brace.
King v. Talbot, 40 N.Y. 76 (1869).
Knight, F. (1921) *Risk, Uncertainty, and Profit*, Boston, MA: Hart, Schaffner & Marx/Houghton Mifflin.
Krehmeyer, D., Orsagh, M. and Schacht, K. (2006) *Breaking the Short-Term Cycle*, Charlottesville, VA: CFA Institute and the Business Roundtable Institute for Corporate Ethics.
Laby, A. (2004) 'Resolving Conflicts of Duty in Fiduciary Relationships', *American University Law Review* 54: 75–150.
Langbein, J. (1997) 'The Secret Life of the Trust: The Trust as an Instrument of Commerce', *Yale Law Journal* 107 (1): 165–189. Online. Available HTTP: <http://dx.doi.org/10.2307/797278>.
Lawrence, S. and Macklem, P. (2000) 'From Consultation to Reconciliation: Aboriginal Rights and the Crown's Duty to Consult', *Canadian Bar Review* 79: 252–279.
Lupoi, M. (1999) 'The Civil Law Trust', *Vanderbilt Journal of Transnational Law* 32: 967–988.
Maatman, R. (2004) *Dutch Pension Funds: Fiduciary Duties and Investing*, Dordrecht: Kluwer Law International.
McNeil v Bennett, 792 A.2d 190 (Del. Ch. 2001).
Mercer and the IRRC Institute (2010) *Investment Horizons – Do Managers Do What They Say?* Online. Available HTTP: <http://www.irrcinstitute.org/pdf/IRRCMercerInvestmentHorizonsReport_ Feb2010.pdf>.
Mercer Consulting (2011) *Climate Change Scenarios – Implications for Strategic Asset Allocation*. Online. Available HTTP: <http://www.ifc.org/ifcext/sustainability.nsf/AttachmentsByTitle/ p_ClimateChangeSurvey_report/$FILE/ClimateChangeSurvey_Report.pdf>.
Montgomery, J. (2011) *Economic Analysis in ERISA Litigation over Fiduciary Duties*, NERA Economic Consulting. Online. Available HTTP: <http://www.nera.com/nerafiles/ AAG_ERISA_Litigation_0310.pdf>.

National Conference of Commissioners on Uniform State Laws (1997a) *Uniform Management of Public Employee Retirement Systems Act*, 1997.

National Conference of Commissioners on Uniform State Laws (1997b) *Uniform Prudent Investor Act*, 7 B.U.L.A. 18 (Supp. 1997).

Nelson, J. A. (1993) 'The Prudent Person Rule: A Shield for the Professional Trustee', *Baylor Law Review* 45: 933–954.

Norgrove, D. (2010) Address at the NAPF Annual Trustee Conference, December. Online. Available HTTP: <http://www.thepensionsregulator.gov.uk/doc-library/david-norgrovenapf- annual-trustee-conference-speech.aspx>.

Organisation for Economic Co-operation and Development, Financial Affairs Division, Directorate for Financial and Enterprise Affairs (2010) 'Financial Performance of Pension Funds in Selected OECD and Non-OECD Countries', *Pension Markets in Focus* 7 (July). Online. Available HTTP: <http://www.oecd.org/dataoecd/46/46/45637367.pdf>.

Pension Funds Act (1956), South Africa.

Rajan, A. (2008) *DB & DC Plans: Strengthening Their Delivery*, London: CREATE-Research.

Re Collins and Pension Commission of Ontario (1986), 56 O.R. (2d) 274.

Re Reevie and Montreal Trust Co. of Canada (1996), 53 O.R. (2d) 595.

Restatement of Trusts, Second (1959).

Restatement of Trusts, Third (1992).

Richardson, B. (2010) 'From Fiduciary Duties to Fiduciary Relationships for Socially Responsible Investment', *Proceedings of the Principles of Responsible Investment Academic Conference*. Online. Available HTTP: <http://www.unpri.org/academic10/Paper_2_Benjamin_Richardson_From%20Fiduciary%20Duties%20to%20Fiduciary% 20Relationships%20for%20Socially%20Responsible%20Investment.pdf>.

Sharpe, W. (1964) 'Capital Asset Prices: A Theory of Market Equilibrium under Conditions of Risk', *Journal of Finance* 19 (3): 425–442. Online. Available HTTP: <http://dx.doi.org/10.2307/2977928>.

Sitkoff, R. (2004) 'An Agency Costs Theory of Trust Law', *Cornell Law Review* 89: 621–683.

Stanley, B. (1984) 'A Standard for Trustees Stricter Than the Prudent Man Standard: The Past and the Future', *Oklahoma City University Law Review. Oklahoma City University* 9: 485–504.

Sterk, S. (2009) 'Rethinking Trust Law Reform: How Prudent Is Modern Prudent Investor Doctrine?', *Cornell Law Review* 95: 851–904.

Strasburg, J. and Pulliam, S. (2011) 'Pack Mentality Grips Hedge Funds', *Wall Street Journal*, 14 January. Online. Available HTTP: <http://online.wsj.com/article/SB1000142405274870436150457555246223 3274 960.html>.

Taleb, N. (2007) *The Black Swan: The Impact of the Highly Improbable*, New York: Random House.

Thomas, A. and Tonks, I. (2001) 'Equity Performance of Segregated Pension Funds in the UK', *Journal of Asset Management* 1 (4): 321–343. Online. Available HTTP: <http://dx.doi.org/10.1057/palgrave.jam.2240025>.

Urwin, R. (2011) 'Pension Funds as Universal Owners: Opportunity Beckons and Leadership Calls', *Rotman International Journal of Pension Management* 4 (1): 26–33. Online. Available HTTP: <http://dx.doi.org/10.3138/rijpm.4.1.26>.

US Department of Labor (2010) 'Employee Benefits Security: Definition of the Term "Fiduciary"', *Federal Register* 75 (22 October): p. 204. Online. Available HTTP: <http://edocket.access.gpo.gov/2010/pdf/2010–26236.pdf>.

Varity v. Howe, 516 US 489 (1996).

Wakeman, A., Franklin, W. and Ascher, M. (2006) *Scott and Ascher on Trusts*, Frederick, MD: Aspen Law & Business.

Withers v. Teachers' Retirement System, 447 F. Supp. 12488 (S.D.N.Y. 1978) 1257.

World Economic Forum USA Inc. (2011) *Accelerating the Transition Toward Sustainable Investing*, New York: World Economic Forum USA Inc. Online. Available HTTP: <http://www3.weforum.org/docs/WEF_IV_AcceleratingSustainableInvesting>.

Yermo, J. and Severinson, C. (2010) *The Impact of the Financial Crisis on Defined Benefit Plans and the Need for Counter-Cyclical Funding Regulations*, OECD, Paris.

50
Governing fiduciary finance[1]

Benjamin J. Richardson

Introduction

The governance of socially responsible investing (SRI) has become in many jurisdictions inseparable from the fiduciary law context. This is because investment decisions are often made where the principal parties are in a fiduciary relationship. This contrasts to situations where individuals or organizations manage their own investments, without reliance on a trustee or other type of intermediary. When someone manages investments on behalf of others, as occurs with the trustee or fund manager of a pension plan, these intermediaries likely have fiduciary obligations to invest prudently in the best interests of the fund's beneficiaries. This legal framework may constrain or facilitate SRI, depending on the type of fund, its investment strategy and other variables

This chapter surveys the main legal responsibilities and procedures that govern fiduciary finance in order to understand its impact on SRI. In common law systems, as in the United Kingdom (UK) and the United States (US), many of these legal rules belong to the realm of 'trust law', which creates distinctive fiduciary-like responsibilities governing the management of institutional funds. Somewhat comparable legal duties for financial intermediaries have been codified in civil law systems, such as in Japan and Germany. This chapter considers only the fiduciary context to SRI in common law jurisdictions, and evaluates the general legal principles rather than dwelling on differences in their application to specific types of financial institutions such as pension plans, mutual funds or insurance companies.

The extent to which fiduciary law governs SRI has generated much debate and uncertainty. One Canadian study (Stratos, 2004, p. 12) suggests that "current interpretations of the fiduciary duties of pension fund managers may unnecessarily constrain their ability to address the full range of relevant corporate responsibility considerations related to prospective investments." Conversely, research commissioned by the United Nations Environment Program's Finance Initiative (UNEP-FI) suggests that SRI is not precluded or overly hampered by fiduciary duties when SRI addresses financially material considerations (Freshfields Bruckhaus Deringer, 2005). This quagmire partly reflects the underlying state of fiduciary law, which a Law Commission in the UK (Law Commission of England and Wales 1992, para. 2.4) once described as "highly complex, poorly delimited and in a state of flux." Curiously, however, the impact of fiduciary law on responsible investing has seldom attracted serious attention from governments; a rare example is the 2014 report of the English Law Commission (2014) on the fiduciary responsibility of investment intermediaries in the UK, but even here no recommendations were made on how to use fiduciary law to promote SRI.

It should be recognized that 'SRI' is a concept subject to diverse labels and interpretations, and these myriad understandings, in turn, have consequences for the legality of SRI. In recent years there has been a significant shift in the dominant understanding SRI, from being undertaken as an ethical imperative to a financial risk management strategy that over the long term promises to improve financial returns while underpinning sustainable development (Richardson 2008). Thus, how we define 'socially responsible' or 'ethical', and whether these notions have economic implications, influences our understanding of fiduciary law's impact in this area. They are contentious ideals full of complexity that mirrors the similarly passionate debates about the meaning of 'sustainable development' or 'sustainability' (Pezzoli, 1997). As those debates reveal, while some believe sustainability is achievable without major structural upheaval to capitalism (World Business Council for Sustainable Development, 2007), others, such as McKibben (2007) and Monbiot (2007), advocate more fundamental reforms to our economic and social systems. If SRI implies that financial fiduciaries should merely 'take into account' environmental and social issues that they perceive to be financially material to investment performance, as SRI is increasingly depicted in financial markets, such practices are generally lawful. Indeed, if trustees ignore such issues, and consequently incur avoidable financial losses, legal liabilities might arise.

More problematic is the situation where SRI infers radical changes such as ridding an investment portfolio of all companies involved in the tobacco or petroleum business. Taking the high road risks legal trouble, because it might seem legally unjustified for a fund to exclude a company plying a lawful business. If government regulators want to discourage such activities, presumably they should prohibit or control them directly, rather than expect social investors to fill the void as surrogate regulators. SRI historically catered to investors wanting to be in the vanguard of social change when governments had failed to act. The divestment campaign against South Africa's apartheid regime is the quintessential example. But without a financial rationale for such practices, there may be fiduciary law obstacles to them unless they reflect a fund's governing constitution or the beneficiaries provide a mandate.

The legal framework governing investing and SRI encompasses more than just fiduciary law. For investors in mutual funds, important legal rules in tort and contract law, as well as securities law, serve to protect investors from being misled or cheated. For instance, a fund that professes in its prospectus to invest ethically must adhere to such goals. Corporate governance can also affect the prospects for SRI, as it influences the opportunities for shareholders to exert influence within corporations such as by voting proxies, filing shareholder resolutions and seeking dialogue with corporate management. Securities law is also relevant to corporate activities, especially in governing how businesses must report their financial affairs, including disclosure of environmental and social impacts. Without such disclosures, investors may struggle to differentiate between corporate laggards and leaders in regard to sustainable development. At a more fundamental level, human rights and environmental regulation influence markets by setting baseline normative standards for all societal actors. Indeed, if the economy's externalities such as climate change were optimally controlled, there would be much less need for social investors to discipline the market.

Overall, the legal context of SRI is a complex and detailed subject, of which only a few issues can be meaningfully canvassed in this chapter. Taking a multi-jurisdictional approach, it focuses on the fiduciary and trust law duties that govern finance in the institutional sector, including consideration of judicial case law and academic commentary. The chapter also discusses some recent statutory reforms that affect fiduciary finance and SRI. The chapter does not consider the legal issues that arise in the retail sector that caters directly to individual investors, a subject that is covered in another of my publications (Richardson, 2013a). Other legal issues that may affect SRI, such as corporate governance, contract law and securities law, are also not examined.

General fiduciary law context of SRI

In broad terms, a 'fiduciary' means a person who holds a position of trust or confidence with respect to another, who ordinarily is in a position of some vulnerability. Hence, a fiduciary relationship is where someone in a position of trust has rights and powers that he or she is obliged to exercise for the benefit of another, who is usually referred to as his or her principal or beneficiary. The core function of fiduciary law is to control opportunism and self-interested behaviour in situations in which an actor has custody of the assets or affairs of another for a specific purpose (Conaglen, 2005; Flannigan, 2009). Other legal duties may occur in fiduciary relationships, depending on their context and purpose. Among various relationships that the law characterizes as fiduciary in nature are those between investors and fund custodians. In both common law and legislation, therefore, trustees, fund managers, advisors and certain other types of decision makers may be impressed with fiduciary status. There may be jurisdictional differences in the legal contours of such fiduciary finance relationships, with North American law tending to emphasize a positive duty to act in beneficiaries' best interests, while other common law nations, such as Britain and Australia, see fiduciary law as largely proscriptive and focusing on the avoidance of conflicts of interests. But international legal harmonization of investment management standards increasingly reflects a legislated preference for financial fiduciaries to have positive responsibilities.

Fiduciary obligations generally fall into two categories of relationships. Certain relationships such as doctor and patient or solicitor and client are considered fiduciary per se because of their inherent purpose. Alternatively, a fiduciary relationship can arise in an ad hoc manner depending on the specific fact situation. In investment management, it is common to find legislation prescribing specific categories of fiduciaries. In relation to pension funds, the US Employee Retirement Income Security Act (ERISA) of 1974 defines three types of fiduciaries: (i) those who exercise authority over the management or disposition of plan assets, (ii) providers of investment advice for a fee with respect to pension plan assets and (iii) administrators of a plan. Thus, ERISA defines 'fiduciary' not in terms of formal trusteeship, but in functional terms of control and authority over the pension plan assets. Yet it is important to recognize that not all fiduciary relationships and not all fiduciary obligations are alike, as they are influenced by specific circumstances.

Many of the fiduciary responsibilities and related legal standards this chapter discusses are part of 'trust law', and persons subject to such responsibilities are commonly known as 'trustees'. The duty of prudent investing is part of trust law. As one Australian court summarized the legal situation, "[t]he trust is a fiduciary relation, but not every fiduciary relation is a trust. The correct position is that trusts are a subclass of fiduciary relations" (*Visnic v. Sywak*, 2009, para. 47). The trust differs from other fiduciary relationships because of the presence of trust assets. Essentially, a trust is an entity in which property or money is held and managed on behalf of another (Hayton, 1999). The trust is an ingenious legal device of English law that divides the attributes of ownership between two persons: the right of management being in the trustee and the right of enjoyment in the beneficiary (Waters, 1967). Trusts are widely used as the legal structure for pension plans and mutual funds (O'Hagan, 2000). A trust may also be established to advance specific purposes, as in a charitable investment trust without an identifiable group of beneficiaries.

The parameters of fiduciary responsibility diverge somewhat in different financial institutions, a subject which requires more extensive discussion than possible in this chapter (Richardson, 2013b, pp. 153–225). Briefly, trust law is particularly applicable to pension plans, which have clearly defined beneficiaries. Likewise, investments by foundations are governed by trust principles.

Commercial banks do not owe their depositors a fiduciary duty in regard to how deposited funds are managed or disbursed, although they are often subject to detailed banking regulations and fiduciary duties that may arise when banks provide financial advice to clients. In most jurisdictions, insurance companies, which are major institutional investors, do not owe a fiduciary duty to insured policy-holders regarding their investment activities. But the senior officers and directors of insurance companies and banks owe a fiduciary duty to their company and sometimes its shareholders. Fiduciary standards in corporations, including banks and insurance companies, tend to differ from fiduciary standards in non-corporate entities, and they tend to be less stringent because of the defence offered by the business judgement rule. Although fiduciary principles also arise in mutual fund governance, contract law and securities regulation primarily serve to align investment decisions with the interests of fund members. Trustees of mutual funds, pension plans and other types of investment funds often delegate many of their decision-making powers to professional asset managers. Contrary to the common law prohibition on such delegations, legislation typically authorizes deputation of fund management so long as the fiduciary retains ultimate control and carefully supervises fund managers. The latter themselves may also incur fiduciary law obligations.

In sum, the principal fiduciary and trust law obligations are: (i) obey the trust deed, (ii) act in the best interests of the beneficiaries, (iii) treat all beneficiaries even-handedly and (iv) invest prudently with care and skill. These obligations are examined in the following sections. Trustees are potentially liable to beneficiaries for investment decisions that breach these duties (Ho, 1998). Trustees could be held liable for the consequences of improper disposal of investments, including losses in the value of the portfolio and transaction costs, as presumably offset by the value and earnings of the replacement assets. But measuring damages when fund managers or trustees fail to fulfill the ethical preferences of beneficiaries, when this is an avowed aim of an SRI fund, would be difficult to assess because there may be no measurable financial loss, only an 'ethical loss'. This chapter does not explore further the remedies available for these and other defective decisions by financial fiduciaries, but we should recognize that there are some material differences between the remedies available for breach of the fiduciary duty of loyalty and breach of the trust law duty of prudent investing (Richardson, 2013b, pp. 140–143).

Because the SRI movement has evolved in recent decades to give more emphasis to the financial materiality of social and environmental issues as a means to broaden its appeal to mainstream institutional investors, the situations in which SRI may be lawful have shifted. Presently, the legal framework governing fiduciary finance may allow SRI in essentially four situations:

1. When environmental, social, and corporate governance issues (i.e., ESG issues) are perceived by fiduciaries to be financially material to investment performance. This would help fulfill the duty of care to invest prudently. Both asset portfolio screening and corporate engagement should be acceptable methods of SRI, depending on the costs of engaging with companies and the extent to which the portfolio remains adequately diversified. Engagement per se does not reduce the diversity of an investment portfolio (unless as a result of unsuccessful engagement a recalcitrant firm is excluded), and active shareholding can be considered a fiduciary responsibility because the underlying shareholder rights are valuable assets to be safeguarded.
2. When two investments are equally suitable in financial terms, ethical considerations can be the 'tie breaker'. This is known as the 'tie-breaker' principle. It can, however, be difficult to apply given that investments tend to be managed on a portfolio basis that focuses on the overall risk-return profile of a pool of assets rather than through the comparison of two specific investment choices.
3. The trust deed may provide an explicit or implicit mandate for SRI. This might be the case for an endowment fund, which is structured to meet specific philanthropic goals. The investment

prospectus of an SRI mutual fund provides an equivalent function. Many financial institutions, however, function under the auspices of a legislative framework that limits the scope for trust deeds to have the impact they otherwise do in the case of a private or family trust.

4 Fiduciaries may practice SRI when beneficiaries consent. However, some financial institutions are subject to legislation that restricts administrators' latitude to act with regard to nonfinancial criteria, even when demanded by investors, and the likelihood of a consensus among beneficiary investors in a typical large financial institution is remote.

The next sections canvass in more detail the core fiduciary and trust law duties and how they may accommodate SRI.

Observe the governing instruments

Absent legislative directions to the contrary, a financial fiduciary must adhere to any specific legal instruments such as a trust deed or prospectus that governs the investment mandate of a specific fund. The trust deed is the legal document that creates the framework within which trustees must operate. It is drafted by the 'settlor' (such as the employer who sponsors a pension plan) and details the rights and powers of the trustees, benefits that accrue to beneficiaries, matters to be disclosed, record-keeping requirements and other procedures and standards. If the deed expressly requires the trustees to invest according to specific or social environmental criteria, they must heed those criteria unless there are other, overriding legal rules. It would surely be very unusual to find a trust fund established with an explicit purpose to engage in environmentally harmful investing or to harm the non-economic interests of beneficiaries. As Ron Davis (2009, p. 53) explains, "[i]t is much more likely that the trust agreement or declaration and the applicable legislation will be silent . . . Thus, the real issues are whether or not trustees are required to exercise the trust funds . . . to further the non-economic interests of the . . . beneficiaries." Even if the trust deed or equivalent instrument emphasizes only beneficiaries' economic interests, these interests may encompass ESG issues.

Although many charitable foundations lack an explicit ethical investment mission, an implication is that they should not invest contrary to their purpose (Parker, Mellows and Oakley, 1998). One example would be a foundation that promotes research into curing lung cancer; its trustees might agree that they should avoid investing in tobacco companies. Britain's Charity Commission (2001), which supervises UK charities pursuant to the Charities Act of 1993, has advised that a charity may choose investments that do not necessarily seek the best financial returns if it advances the organization's philanthropic mission. But it might be problematic for such a mission-based investor to dabble in other forms of SRI unrelated to its specific mandate.

While the trust deed is particularly determinative of fiduciary obligations in the context of a charitable foundation or a private trust established to manage family assets, it is less decisive for financial institutions that manage or sell investments to the general public. For employee pension funds, the trust deed is embedded within a legislative framework that elaborates rules on investment decision-making. Where legislation provides for the conferment of investment management powers on trustees, they must exercise their powers for that purpose. The US federal pension law, ERISA obliges fiduciaries to act, inter alia, solely in the interest of plan participants and beneficiaries and with the care, skill, prudence and diligence under the circumstances then prevailing of a prudent man acting in a like capacity (section 404). Also, the US Uniform Trust Code, which codifies as well as modifies some common law trust rules, has been adopted into legislation in approximately half the states (Cooper, 2008).

Where a trust has several stated purposes, such as to invest assets for financial return while fulfilling an ethical agenda, conflicts may arise. Litigation is illustrated by the English case of *Bishop of Oxford v. Church Commissioners for England* (1992). The bishop wanted the Commissioners to uphold Christian doctrine strictly, or at least his interpretation of it, even if this heightened financial risk for the Church's investment fund. Although the Commissioners had an SRI policy for managing the Church's assets, it applied only to the extent that it would not be financially injurious. The court explained the context as follows:

> It is axiomatic that charity trustees, in common with all other trustees, are concerned to further the purposes of the trust of which they have accepted the office of trustee. That is their duty. To enable them the better to discharge that duty, trustees have powers vested in them. Those powers must be exercised for the purpose for which they have been given: to further the purposes of the trust.
>
> *(Bishop of Oxford, 1992, p. 1244)*

The Church Commissioners' investment policy stated that "[w]hile financial responsibilities must remain of primary importance (given our position as trustees), as responsible investors . . . we do not invest in companies whose main business is armaments, gambling, alcohol, tobacco and newspapers" (*Bishop of Oxford*, 1992, p. 1249). The court took no issue with the goals behind the charity or the Commissioners' policy of negative screening, but it found that the declarations sought by the plaintiff would go beyond the legal obligations of the trustees, as

> [i]n most cases the best interests of the charity require that the trustees' choice of investments should be made solely on the basis of well-established investment criteria, having taken expert advice where appropriate and having due regard to such matters as the need to diversify, the need to balance income against capital growth, and the need to balance risk against return.
>
> *(Bishop of Oxford, 1992, p. 1246)*

The court felt that where the aims of the charity and the objects of investment would directly conflict the trustees must balance the extent of financial loss from offended supporters of the Church against the financial risks of SRI.

Loyalty to beneficiaries

Although the duty to obey the trust deed may itself ensure that fiduciaries act for beneficiaries, there is a separate, overarching legal duty to act only for beneficiaries (to ensure that a fiduciary does not act for its own self-interest or any third-party interests). In the US, authorities have expressed this duty as one of 'undivided loyalty' (*Meinhard v. Salmon,* 1928), requiring a trustee "to administer the trust solely in the interest of beneficiaries" (Serota and Brodie, 1995, p. 25). Various constituent elements of this duty have been developed over the years, including the obligation on trustees to avoid conflict of interests, the duty not to delegate responsibility and the duty to act impartially towards different beneficiaries. As noted above, in the case of a charitable trust, fidelity is owed to the purpose of the trust rather than any specific class of beneficiaries.

Fiduciary law does not prescribe what beneficiaries' interests are. Rather, their interests depend on the terms of the governing trust deed or the overall purpose and context of the fiduciary relationship. In investment institutions, the duty of loyalty is commonly interpreted as requiring the furtherance of the financial interests of beneficiaries and certainly at least not to profit at their expense. Depending on the context, scholars believe trustees may also consider non-financial criteria (Scott and Fratcher, 1988). If beneficiaries share a moral objection to a particular form of investment, they may benefit if their trust avoids that investment, possibly even at the cost of a lower financial return. In some cases, what appears to be purely an ethical issue for beneficiaries may over the long-term be highly financially material, such as a concern about climate change.

The duty of loyalty may also allow fiduciaries to make investments that provide incidental or collateral benefits to others (e.g., to a local community) so long as the beneficiaries are not adversely affected. ERISA has been interpreted by the US Department of Labor as "not preclud[ing] consideration of collateral benefits, such as those offered by a 'socially-responsible' fund" (Doyle, 1998, p. 2). In 2008, it issued further guidance specifically in relation to "economically targeted investment", and advised that only when two alternative investments "are of equal economic value to a plan", fiduciaries may "choose between the investment alternatives on the basis of a factor other than the economic interest of the plan" (US Department of Labor, 2008).

But there is vast difference between allowing a fiduciary to act beneficially for a third party and allowing that party to enforce rights against the fiduciary. Its interests are simply discretionary considerations for trustees. This limitation is illustrated by the unsuccessful lawsuit in *Associated Students of the University of Oregon v. Oregon Investment Council* (1987). The student organizations sought a judicial declaration that the Investment Council could not invest higher education endowment funds in corporations doing business in South Africa, Zimbabwe and Namibia. However, the substantive legal issues did not get to be heard. In denying the students standing to bring the case, the Court of Appeals of Oregon (1987, p. 150), stated "they do not allege any legally recognized injury, and neither agreement with plaintiffs' opposition to apartheid nor the desirability of encouraging students to become concerned with social and moral wrongs and to seek to right them can turn the alleged 'injuries' into legally recognized ones."

Standing, however, was not an issue in the seminal British case of *Cowan v. Scargill* (1985) that considered the parameters of the duty of loyalty to beneficiaries. The case stemmed from a disagreement between the trustees appointed jointly by the National Coal Board and the National Union of Mine Workers about the investment strategy for the workers' pension plan in question. Union trustees disapproved of any increase in foreign investment and, in particular, any investment in energy industries in competition with coal mining. The Coal Board trustees sued the union trustees claiming that they were in breach of fiduciary duties by insisting on the proposed restrictions. The presiding judge, Vice-Chancellor Robert Megarry, agreed with the National Coal Board trustees. Starting from the proposition that trustees must treat the interests of the beneficiaries as paramount, where the trust purpose is to provide financial benefits for the beneficiaries, he reasoned, the best interests of the beneficiaries normally mean their financial interests. If the actual or potential beneficiaries of a trust were only those individuals with strict views on moral or social matters, such as "condemning all forms of alcohol, tobacco and popular entertainment, as well as armaments" (*Cowan v. Scargill*, 1985, p. 288), Megarry conceded that investing in such problematic activities might not be for their 'benefit'.

Some investors have interpreted the *Cowan* case to mean that trustees must obtain the highest rate of return attainable and that trustees "and their fund managers and advisers [are precluded] from having regard to any considerations, other than the maximization of financial returns" (Freshfields Bruckhaus Deringer, 2005, p. 88). However, the Freshfields Report cites several persuasive reasons the *Cowan* ruling does not provide a good authority for the profit maximization argument. First, the case turns heavily on its facts, where the union trustees were trying to prop up an entire industry, namely the failing British coal industry, which was "clearly not in the interests of all the beneficiaries". Second, the judge had no previous authority upon which to rely, and the ruling is only that of an English lower court. Third, the mining union trustees' proposal sought a complete ban on certain investments rather than a more nuanced policy, and the proposal "bore little or no resemblance to a modern ESG investment policy" (Freshfields

Bruckhaus Deringer, 2005, p. 89). Nonetheless, these criticisms of the *Cowan* case do not detract from the fundamental legal status of a fiduciary's obligation to act in the interests of beneficiaries.

Not only must fiduciaries act loyally to beneficiaries, they must treat them equitably. This duty to act impartially is considered in the next section, and it is an important subset of the overarching duty of loyalty.

Treating beneficiaries impartially

Beneficiaries may not always have homogenous interests, and in such circumstances fiduciaries must treat them even-handedly. This duty of impartiality has important implications for SRI because if beneficiaries consent to trustees practicing SRI, presumably they must all consent. This duty of impartiality essentially obliges fiduciaries to identify and impartially balance any conflicting interests of different trust fund beneficiary groups. While rigid equality is not decreed, the duty of impartiality expects "conduct in administering a trust cannot be influenced by a trustee's personal favoritism . . . nor is it permissible for a trustee to ignore the interests of some beneficiaries merely as a result of oversight or neglect" (American Law Institute, 1992, s. 79, comment b).

Several important legal and practical issues arise with basing SRI on the will of beneficiaries. That fiduciary law may countenance SRI if it fulfils beneficiaries' wishes, as acknowledged by the seminal Freshfields Report (Freshfields Bruckhaus Deringer, 2005, p. 12), which advised that: "a decision-maker may integrate ESG considerations into an investment decision to give effect to the views of the beneficiaries in relation to matters beyond financial return." While this conclusion would seem a logical extension of the duty of loyalty, it is seemingly at odds with the passive role beneficiaries have traditionally assumed in fund governance as a matter of practice and legal precedent. A widespread assumption in financial markets is that investment management is a complex, specialist activity that few laypersons could competently undertake (Richardson, 2011a). On the other hand, the trend towards shifting investment risk to beneficiaries, as in pension plans offered to employees on a defined-contribution basis, presumptively justifies giving beneficiaries greater voice in fund governance.

Beneficiaries are legally entitled to be informed about the administration of the trust assets, but traditionally they have not enjoyed rights to be consulted or to instruct trustees. Trustees, unlike an agent subject to the control of his or her principal, are generally not legally obliged to consult with beneficiaries. They only need to act in their 'best interests', without necessarily being obliged to enquire what those best interests are. In Canada, the Ontario Law Reform Commission (1984, p. 74) observed that "[t]o allow beneficiaries to direct the ongoing administration of the trust confuses the role of trustee and beneficiary and is inconsistent with the trust concept. If the creator of a trust wishes the beneficiary to be actively involved in the administration of the trust, such person may always be appointed as trustee." But pension fund legislation and some insurance company legislation may require trustees or other financial managers at least to consult with beneficiaries, as discussed later in this chapter.

Trust law has recognized that beneficiaries may instruct trustees only in limited circumstances, such as when the trust in question is a small, intimate arrangement, as in a private family trust, and where all the beneficiaries are adults with full legal capacity. In *Cowan v. Scargill* (1985, p. 288), the judge gave one example of such a situation in relation to all members "condemning all forms of alcohol, tobacco and popular entertainment." But modern investment institutions hardly resemble such a situation, and many are subject to legislation that restricts the ability of trustees to heed any non-financial preferences expressed by beneficiaries. For instance, British Columbia's Pension Benefits Standards Act (1996, s. 44(1)) provides that: "pension plan investments . . . must be made . . . in the *best financial* interests of plan members, former members and other plan beneficiaries."

The duty of impartiality requires a trustee to treat beneficiaries even-handedly. In *Bishop of Oxford v. Church Commissioners for England* (1992, p. 1247), the court ruled: "trustees should not make investment decisions on the basis of preferring one view of whether on moral grounds an investment conflicts with the objects of the charity over another. This is so even when one view is more widely supported than the other." It remains legally unsettled whether there must be complete unanimity among beneficiaries or some lesser degree of congruence. Because of the assumed unlikelihood of any consensus of values amongst beneficiaries in a large institutional fund, trustees tend to retreat to the belief that beneficiaries' only common interest is the best financial return. Some legal commentators doubt both assumptions. One Canadian lawyer (Lane, 1986, p. 76) contends: "[u]nanimity is not the test. One cannot assume that beneficiaries would be unanimous about the question of maximizing raw dollar return. This is a false assumption. There will always be beneficiaries who disagree with investment decisions made by trustees." Furthermore, whether or not unanimity is legally required, courts have never obliged trustees to poll beneficiaries to ascertain their interests. Instead, courts tend to judge whether trustees have acted impartially and loyally by looking for evidence that they reasonably believed on the facts that they were acting in the beneficiaries' best interests.

Any legal mandate to respond to the will of beneficiaries faces various drawbacks and limitations. If beneficiaries can instruct trustees, and thereby influence investment decisions, trustees might be considered their agents and, consequently, beneficiaries might be liable as principals to third parties for any compensable losses. In Canada, beneficiary investors incurred liability in the case of *Trident Holdings Ltd. v. Danand Investments Ltd* (1988) in a situation where the trustees lacked discretionary powers and were considered effectively to be in an agency relationship with the beneficiaries.

A further dilemma is how to ascertain what beneficiaries want, and to reconcile any differences in their investment preferences. The likelihood of beneficiaries of a particular fund holding similar views on the desirability of SRI is far-fetched. Disagreements over social values are rife in modern society: disputes often arise over the environmental consequences of economic developments, which human rights deserve respect and a host of other ethical issues. Investors have similarly diverse values. Academic research on the psychological and socio-economic characteristics of individual social investors and their opinions on various ethical matters suggests that ethical deliberation must bridge some major differences of opinion (McLachlan and Gardner, 2004; Nilsson, 2008; Rosen, Sandler and Shani, 1991). Presumably, the heterogeneity of values among conventional investors is even greater than that among social investors. Not only may conflicts of interest exist among beneficiaries, the trustees of a fund may similarly disagree about investment priorities; such disagreements were pivotal to the *Cowan* litigation discussed above.

In the absence of an expressed consensus among beneficiaries, a fiduciary might look to broader societal values for guidance on any SRI position to take. The Freshfields Report (2005, p. 96) suggests that trustees could rely on well-established social customs as a proxy for the values of the beneficiaries, such as to exclude "investments that are linked to clear breaches of widely recognised norms, such as international conventions on human rights, labor conditions, tackling corruption and environmental protection." Social customs could be considered a proxy for beneficiaries' values, suggests Gifford (2004, p. 141), because "[g]iven the ubiquity of pension fund membership, especially in the developed world, it can also be argued that the interests of members of funds are broadly consistent with those of the society in which the members live." This approach is illustrated by the Norwegian Government Pension Fund – Global, a sovereign wealth fund whose legislated SRI mandate is based mainly on the norms found in international treaties that Norway has ratified (Richardson, 2011b). Numerous international treaties govern issues of interest to social investors, including environmental protection, human rights and labour standards. Some are widely ratified and thus putatively reflect a near-consensus of international opinion. But others are less helpful because of significant dissenting opinion or because their standards are too vague to provide concrete guidance for financial decision makers in contentious cases.

Although they do not appear to alter the underlying fiduciary norms, procedures that mandate consultation with beneficiaries or even appointment of their representatives to the governing boards of investment institutions may help convey beneficiaries' views. Australia's Superannuation Industry (Supervision) Act (1993) mandates 50 per cent beneficiary representation on trustee boards of funds that have at least five members. Being a representative of beneficiaries, however, does legally per se allow a trustee to consider him or herself an agent of the beneficiaries, acting only according to instructions given. Trustees remain obliged to respect the purpose of the fund and overriding statutory requirements, such as to invest prudently. Opportunities for participation by beneficiaries may also be found in mutual funds; many are structured around a corporate governance framework that gives shareholding investors rights to vote on strategic policy issues and to elect managing directors.

In the absence of any congruence of opinion among beneficiaries or social customs to guide SRI, a final option is to give beneficiaries more personal choice in making investments. Thus, one legislative approach in some countries has been to create segregated portfolios that give fund members some choice regarding their investments. This arrangement is possible in the US through the so-called '401(k)' retirement savings plans established for workers covered by ERISA; plan participants may choose among the options, and SRI funds can be offered. A similar approach has been adopted in Australia for employee pension funds, which are known as superannuation funds, pursuant to the Superannuation Legislation Amendment (Choice of Superannuation Funds) Act (2005). Such democratic reforms, however, do not necessarily make SRI more likely; investors may still choose to maximize their financial self-interest.

Investing prudently

Financial fiduciaries must invest prudently. In legal terms, this is known as the duty of care, which, along with the duty of loyalty, forms the core of the legal responsibilities governing fiduciary finance. The duty of care requires fiduciaries to exercise reasonable diligence, skill and caution that a person would exercise under similar circumstances. The traditional formulation of the 'prudent investor' standard, as this duty is often expressed, effectively precluded any investment that posed an unusual risk, as courts expected a trustee to assess and justify each investment individually (Ali and Yano, 2004). Under the influence of modern portfolio theory, this understanding of prudent investment has ceded to the view that optimal returns derive from a large, diversified portfolio that generally carries lower financial risks than the risk attaching to each investment taken in isolation (Haskell, 1990). Consequently, inclusion of investments selected for their social benefit might be easier to justify within a large portfolio than on a case-by-case basis.

The duty of prudent investment has sometimes been misunderstood as simply an obligation to maximize financial returns, an attitude that can pose a major barrier to SRI (Ransome and Sampford, 2011, pp. 125–126). Contemporary legal commentators continue to emphasize the overriding responsibility of trustees, particularly in the context of governing financial institutions, to "maximize the return to members" (Donald and Taylor, 2008, p. 49). Apart from legislative prescription, there is little legal precedent for such a duty. In the problematic *Cowan* case, Megarry (1985, p. 289) ruled, "[s]ubject to such matters, under a trust for the provision of financial benefits, the paramount duty of the trustees is to provide the *greatest* financial benefits for the present and future beneficiaries" (emphasis added). By contrast, the influential American *Third Restatement of the Law of Trusts*' (1992) modern prudent investor rule does not prescribe a duty to 'maximize returns' on an investment-by-investment or portfolio basis, but rather obliges fiduciaries to apply an overall investment strategy for a diversified portfolio that is rational and appropriate to the fund. Further, subsequent Anglo-American trusts case law departs from the *Cowan* ruling on this point. In *Martin v. Edinburgh District Council* (1988), involving a challenge to the Council trustees' decision to divest from South African-based assets owing to their ethical concerns about apartheid, Lord Murray added:

> I cannot conceive that trustees have an unqualified duty simply to invest trust funds in the most profitable investment available. To accept that without qualification would, in my view, involve substituting the discretion of financial advisers for the discretion of trustees.
>
> *(Martin v. Edinburgh District Council, 1988, p. 334)*

In particular, the duty of prudent investing may allow SRI when ethical considerations are a 'tie-breaker'. In the *Bishop of Oxford* case, discussed above, the judge ruled that trustees choosing between two investments of equal suitability according to conventional principles of prudent investment might account for the ethical considerations as the deciding factor. The court viewed the Church Commissioners' ethical investment policy as acceptable, but it would have been improper to have adopted a more restrictive policy burdened with greater financial risks.

An even more generous view of this tie-breaker principle was taken in the American case of *Board of Trustees of Employee Retirement System of the City of Baltimore v. City of Baltimore* (1989). The Maryland Court of Appeal examined the City of Baltimore's ordinances requiring its four municipal pension funds to divest from companies doing business in South Africa. The trustees of the funds argued that the ordinances unlawfully altered their common law duty of care by substantially reducing the universe of eligible investments. While the court agreed that the ordinances excluded a "not insignificant segment of the investment universe" (p. 103), it believed the reduced returns expected from the divestiture in South Africa would only amount to about 10 basis points each year, and that the measured way the divestments were to occur meant that they would not undermine the trustees' prudential duties. The court explained: "thus, if . . . social investment yields economically competitive returns at a comparable level of risk, the investment should not be deemed imprudent" (p. 107). It also found the ordinances acceptable so long as the cost of investing according to social responsibility precepts was de minimis. The court explained that a trustee's duty is not to maximize return on investments, but to secure a 'just' and 'reasonable' return, while avoiding undue risk.

As a practical consideration, the tie-breaker principle cannot be easily applied because trustees typically manage investments on a portfolio-wide basis rather than administering investments on a case-by-case basis. As Rosy Thornton (2008, p. 405) explains, in criticizing the tie-breaker standard as impractical, trustees "are not measuring one given asset against one given alternative, but (in the nature of modern portfolio investment) selecting a range of assets from amongst a very wide pool", and thus "trustees should be comparing not only the expected return and variance of the two assets themselves, but also the covariance between those assets and the rest of the holdings within the portfolio."

A further consequence of the duty of care is the importance of showing benefits *directly* accruing to beneficiaries, rather than simply attributing benefits circuitously, such as by virtue of their being members of society as a whole that benefits from an investment strategy. Thus, speculative and remote benefits to beneficiaries, such as improved sustainability of the economy, might not legally suffice. The universal investor thesis (see Hawley and Williams, 2000) aspires to create a new standard of prudent investment through the wider social and environmental 'returns' offered to beneficiaries, but it has yet to influence law-makers. In Cowan, one argument advanced to justify the SRI policy was that by restricting overseas investment and investment in energy sectors in competition with coal mining, important benefits would accrue to the British economy and thus the beneficiaries as members of that society. The court rebuffed that argument, explaining:

> the broad economic arguments of the defendants provide no justification for the restrictions that they wish to impose. Any possible benefits from imposing the restrictions that would accrue to the beneficiaries under the scheme (as distinct from the general public) are far too speculative and remote. Large though the fund is, I cannot see how the adoption of the restrictions can make any material impact on the national economy, or bring any appreciable benefit to the beneficiaries under the scheme.
>
> *(Cowan v. Scargill, 1985, p. 296)*

There are several further considerations in assessing compliance with the duty of care. The methods for practicing SRI also have some bearing on its legality. The SRI policy should be implemented without burdensome and costly administrative procedures. Some SRI funds carry higher expenses and charges due to the additional research required (Croome-Carther, 2007). The financial performance of SRI-focused funds has also been subject to much scrutiny, and some researchers believe that fund managers and trustees are likely to breach their fiduciary duties if they practice SRI, especially in economic downturns (Copp, Kremmer and Roca, 2010). Other research suggests that SRI can outperform the market (Kiernan, 2008) and that portfolio diversification has become easier because SRI funds are now available across a broad range of asset classes and economic sectors and there is a greater availability of SRI indexes that can be passively tracked by funds (US Social Investment Forum, 2006). SRI is likely to be most compatible with the duty of care when it is implemented through corporate engagement and shareholder activism, rather than strict exclusionary screening. In this way, funds can maintain reasonably diversified portfolios in accordance with the principles of modern portfolio theory. Depending on the size of the fund and the nature of the engagement process, it can be time-consuming and expensive to administer, and therefore might undermine compliance with fiduciary standards if undertaken extensively. But the increasing efforts of some investors to engage collaboratively, as exemplified by the Carbon Disclosure Project, should help lower the transaction costs of corporate engagement while increasing leverage over targeted firms.

A further consideration for understanding prudent investing is that global investors increasingly recognize the potential financial materiality of corporate social and environmental performance, and thus SRI has shifted somewhat from its ethical roots to an instrumental business consideration. The influential United Nations Environment Programme −Finance Initiative (UNEP-FI) (2006, p. 4) explained in its report, *Show Me the Money*, that: "[t]he first – and arguably for investors the most important reason to integrate [SRI] issues is, simply, to make more money." In another UNEP-FI publication (2004, p. 5), financial analysts are behooved to demonstrate "material links to business value; . . . [and] avoid moral arguments." This shift in thinking has implications for fiduciary responsibilities. As Woods (2011, p. 6) explains, "the fulfillment of the primary mandate [of fiduciaries to promote the best interests of the beneficiary] is likely to suffer if trustees ignore the long-term consequences of financing environmental degradation." Yaron (2001, p. 2), a Canadian lawyer, comments that: "there is significant legal and empirical support for viewing socially responsible investment practices as a requisite element of prudent and loyal trusteeship." Climate change has been identified as one example (Mercer Investment Consulting (2005, pp. 18–19). Thus, the evolving nature of SRI towards a special financial risk management strategy rather than an ethical imperative should improve the fiduciary law scope for SRI. However, such an approach to SRI is not necessarily an assurance for a more civilized and sustainable economy, as I have argued elsewhere (Richardson, 2013b).

Legislative reform

As already observed in this chapter, fiduciary and trust duties often manifest in a legislative rather than common law format, especially in the context of pension fund regulation. In most cases the statutes codify common law standards, but occasionally they modify those standards in ways that may hinder or facilitate SRI.

Particularly influential is the Uniform Trust Code, which has been adopted by many US states. One potentially adverse change for ethical investing engendered by the Code is its provisions that may prevent trust settlors from placing restrictions on investment decision-making that would override the preeminence given to the duty to act as a prudent investor. The assumption is that financial prudence dictates what is in beneficiaries' interests. Consequently, this standard could undermine a trust settlor's ability to safeguard his or her beneficiaries' non-monetary, ethical values through restraints on trust investments (Cooper, 2008). A few state jurisdictions in the US have gone further by attempting to ban SRI in some cases. For example, Nebraska's statutory duties of the Investment Council state that: "[n]o assets of the retirement systems . . . shall be invested or reinvested if the sole or primary investment objective is for economic development or social purposes or objectives" (Nebraska Revised Statutes, 2007, p. s. 72–1239.01). The effect of these provisions, however, may not be widespread, as some research points to growing interest in SRI among some US investors, particularly public sector pension plans (Hebb, 2008).

In a few countries a different legislative trend has been to acknowledge SRI as a legitimate investment practice without necessarily mandating that it be promoted. Typically, such regulation commonly involves informational and incentive-based policy mechanisms to stimulate, but not direct, SRI. Some governments have introduced green investment tax concessions (e.g., the Netherlands' 1996 Green Investment Directive), which aim to improve the cost–benefit equation in favour of sustainable development. Others have focused on getting financiers to report their SRI policies, proxy voting activities and environmental impacts of financial significance. These requirements may enable the assessment, verification and communication of performance and, in theory, thereby put pressure on environmental laggards to change or reward leaders through competitive market advantages. In 2000, for example, regulations in Britain came into effect modifying the Pensions Act's statement of investment principles requirement by requiring occupational pension fund trustees to disclose what role, if any, ESG criteria has in their investment decision-making (Occupational Pension Schemes [Investment, and Assignment, Forfeiture, Bankruptcy] Amendment Regulations, 1999). This reform inspired similar legislation in several other European Union states, Australia and New Zealand (Richardson, 2002). Many pension funds have responded to the disclosure regulation with vigour by adopting an SRI policy, although the quality of implementation of such policies has tended to be less satisfactory (UK Sustainable Investment and Finance Association, 2009, 2010). Reformers in North America focused on mutual funds, legislating requirements that they disclose their proxy voting policies and voting records when acting as shareholders (Canadian Securities Administrators, 2005; Securities and Exchange Commission, 2003). The latter North American reforms do not explicitly refer to SRI, but may facilitate it in the retail finance market through more transparent practices (Richardson, 2013a).

Unusually, a few jurisdictions have also modified fiduciary rules to give more latitude for SRI. In Canada, legislation in the province of Manitoba stipulates that unless the pension plan or trust instrument dictates otherwise, an investment decision partially motivated by non-financial criteria is permissible so long as trustees follow the duty of care (Trustee Act, 1995). A more pro-SRI reform was Ontario's 1990 South African Trust Investments Act. It absolved trustees from their fiduciary and other legal duties in "refusing to acquire a South African investment" or "disposing of a South African investment even if the value of the property for which the trustee is responsible decreases or fails to increase sufficiently as a result" (South African Trust Investments Act, 1990, s. 3(a)-(b)), so long as trustees had consulted with beneficiaries and had at least a majority's support. However, both the Manitoban and Ontarian (now repealed) provisions are couched in negative terms, indicating that a trustee will not breach fiduciary duties by considering non-financial factors, rather than creating a positive duty on trustees to invest in sustainable development or other positive ethical issues on the agenda of some SRI activists.

South Africa itself in its post-apartheid era has seemingly embraced SRI. The country's Pension Funds Act of 1956 was in 2012 modified by Regulation 28, which contains revised prudential investment guidelines for fund managers with specific reference to ESG criteria. Significantly, the legislation aims to exceed similar SRI-focused transparency reforms adopted in Europe and Oceania, as its section 2(c)(ix) obliges fiduciaries "at all times" in their investment decision-making to "consider any factor which may materially affect the sustainable long term performance of the asset including, but not limited to, those of an environmental, social and governance character." The South African investment community has described the reform as a "big game changer"; that is, turning the tide towards SRI (National Business Initiative, 2012, p. 2).

More ambitiously, explicit legal duties for such practices have been imposed on some public financial institutions (Richardson, 2011b). The first precedents were adopted in the 1980s by some US states and municipalities, which sought to restrict government pension funds from investing in apartheid South Africa (McCarroll, 1980–1981) or in strife-torn Northern Ireland (Conway, 2002). Since 2000, sovereign wealth funds of Sweden, Norway, New Zealand, and France have been subject to legislative direction to invest ethically, with obligations that are more comprehensive and ambitious than the American precedents (see, for example, Norway's Guidelines for Observation and Exclusion from the Government Pension Fund – Global's Investment Universe, 2010, s. 2(3)). None of these sovereign wealth funds (which encompass civil and common law jurisdictions) are in a strict fiduciary law relationship to their beneficiaries, but they are at least politically accountable in a quasi-fiduciary manner. A further possible limitation is that their legislative mandates frame SRI somewhat narrowly because of a focus on *avoiding* unethical investment rather than *positive* financing of sustainable development.

Conclusions

The legal framework governing SRI draws on a variety of sources, including securities regulation, companies law, contract law and fiduciary and trust law. The latter two are particularly important in controlling how institutional funds manage their assets on behalf of their beneficial owners. In most common law jurisdictions, these legal rules have been codified or modified by legislation, and their precise manifestation varies somewhat between pension funds, insurance companies, mutual funds and other types of financial institutions. The duty of prudence (care) has been interpreted as requiring trustees to assess investments not in isolation but by reference to their contribution to the whole investment portfolio, to create a diverse portfolio, and to take professional advice. The fiduciary duty of loyalty requires that fiduciaries advance the best interests of the beneficiaries and has been interpreted to ensure that they act honestly and exclusively for the beneficiaries, without consideration of third-party or social interests, except incidentally.

The extant case law suggests that courts and regulators have not provided a complete enunciation of all relevant considerations on the scope for SRI under fiduciary law. Presently, that law in the jurisdictions considered in this chapter may allow SRI in principally four situations: (i) when ESG issues are financially material to investment performance; (ii) where SRI option is a 'tie breaker' for investment options that are comparable in their financial prospects; (3) where the fund's governing instrument, such as the trust deed, provides a mandate for SRI, as in the case with charitable foundations; and (4) when beneficiaries consent to SRI. Though, as already explained in each case, often there are substantial practical difficulties to the application of these situations, such as the difficulty of comparing financial returns under the tie-breaker principle and the unlikelihood that all the beneficiaries in a large fund would agree to SRI. And while Anglo-American jurisprudence suggests some modest room for SRI, it is certainly hardly an encouraged or mandated investment practice.

Just as understandings of 'SRI' have evolved greatly in recent years, so, too, the law of fiduciary finance will likely continue to develop, especially as pressures grow to address the intertwined financial market and ecological crises that affect the global economy (Joly, 2011; Richardson, 2013b). Reforms in some jurisdictions, such as in Canada and Britain, are already revamping the fiduciary standards that apply at the level of ordinary business corporations in an effort to promote greater consideration of environmental and community interests as factors that can shape the prosperity of companies (Bone, 2009). Fiduciary standards that encourage long-term, sustainable investing might help reduce the harmful myopic and speculative tendencies of financial markets while channeling capital into environmentally beneficial and socially useful development.

On the other hand, the deeply embedded orthodoxy in the financial sector regarding how fiduciary responsibilities are construed will not easily be transformed. Because the fiduciary standard of prudent investment hinges substantially on adhering to the prevailing conventionality, a fund that wishes to take the initiative on SRI might be legally challenged merely because it is out of step with its conservative peers. Even the recent market shift in understanding of SRI as a pragmatic business case has struggled to gain dominance, partly because the business case for investing responsibly may not materialize for several decades, beyond the time frames that impatient financial fiduciaries are accustomed to. Thus, there is a significant collective inertia to SRI that might only be resolvable through additional legal intervention.

Note

1 This chapter draws partially on the author's other scholarship, including (Richardson, 2011a), (Richardson, 2012) and (Richardson, 2013b).

References

Ali, P., and Yano, K. (2004) *Eco-Finance*, The Hague: Kluwer Law.

American Law Institute (1992) *Restatement (3rd) of Trusts: Prudent Investor Rule*, Philadelphia: American Law Institute.

Associated Students of the University of Oregon v. Oregon Investment Council. (1987) 82 Or. App. 145, 728 P.2d 30.

Bishop of Oxford v. Church Commissioners for England. (1992) 1 WLR 1241.

Board of Trustees of Employee Retirement System of the City of Baltimore v. City of Baltimore. (1989) 317 Md. 72; 562 A.2d 720.

Bone, J. (2009) 'Corporate Environmental Responsibility in the Wake of the Supreme Court Decision of BCE Inc. and Bell Canada', *Windsor Review of Legal and Social Issues*, 27, May: 5–30.

Canadian Securities Administrators (2005) *National Instrument 81–106 Investment Fund Continuous Disclosure and Companion Policy 81–106CP*, Montreal: Canadian Securities Administrators.

Charity Commission (2001) *Guidance on Programme-Related Investment*, London: Charity Commission.

Conaglen, M. (2005) 'The Nature and Function of Fiduciary Loyalty', *Law Quarterly Review* 121: 452–480.

Conway, N.J. (2002) 'Investment Responsibility in Northern Ireland: The MacBride Principles of Fair Employment', *Loyola of Los Angeles International and Comparative Law Review* 24(1): 1–18.

Cooper, J. A. (2008) 'Empty Promises: Settlor's Intent, the Uniform Trust Code, and the Future of Trust Investment Law', *Boston University Law Review* 88(5): 1165–1216.

Copp, R., Kremmer, M. L. and Roca, E. (2010) 'Should Funds Invest in Socially Responsible Investments During Downturns?: Financial and Legal Implications of the Fund Manager's Dilemma', *Accounting Research Journal* 23(3): 254–266.

Cowan v. Scargill. (1985) Ch. 270.

Croome-Carther, S. (2007) 'Funds with Values', *Forbes.com*. Online. Available HTTP: <http://www.forbes.com/investoreducation/2007/11/14/sri-funds-domini-pf-education-in_sc_1114investopedia_inl.html> (accessed November 2014).

Davis, R. (2009) *Democratizing Pension Funds: Corporate Governance and Accountability*, Vancouver: UBC Press.

Donald, M.S. and Taylor. N. (2008) 'Does "Sustainable" Investing Compromise the Obligations Owed by Superannuation Trustees', *Australian Business Law Review* 36: 47–61.

Doyle, R.J. (1998) *Advisory Opinion*, Washington, DC: Pension and Welfare Benefits Administration, Office of Regulations and Interpretations.

Flannigan, R. (2009) 'The Core Nature of Fiduciary Accountability', *New Zealand Law Review* 3: 375–429.

Freshfields Bruckhaus Deringer. (2005) *A Legal Framework for the Integration of Environmental, Social and Governance Issues into Institutional Investment*, Geneva: UNEP-FI.

Gifford, J. (2004) 'Measuring the Social, Environmental and Ethical Performance of Pension Funds', *Journal of Australian Political Economy* 53, June: 139–160.

Guidelines for Observation and Exclusion from the Government Pension Fund Global's Investment Universe (2010) Norwegian Storting.

Haskell, P. G. (1990) 'The Prudent Person Rule for Trustee Investment and Modern Portfolio Theory', *North Carolina Law Review* 69(1): 87–112.

Hawley, J. and Williams, A. (2000) *The Rise of Fiduciary Capitalism: How Institutional Investors Can Make Corporate America More Democratic*, Philadelphia: University of Pennsylvania Press.

Hayton, D. (1999) 'English Fiduciary Standards and Trust Law', *Vanderbilt Journal of Transnational Law* 32(3): 555–612.

Hebb, T. (2008) *No Small Change: Pension Funds and Corporate Engagement*, Ithaca: Cornell University Press.

Ho, L. (1998) 'Attributing Losses to a Breach of Fiduciary Duty', *Trust Law International* 12(1): 66–76.

Joly, C. (2011) 'Reality and Potential of Responsible Investment', *Issues in Business Ethics* 31: 193–210.

Kiernan, M. (2008) *Investing in a Sustainable World: Why Green Is the New Color of Money on Wall Street*, New York: AMACOM.

Lane, P. (1986) 'Ethical Investment: Towards the Best Interest of Everyone', *The Advocate:* 171–182.

Law Commission of England and Wales (1992) *Fiduciary Duties and Regulatory Rules*, Consultation Paper No. 124, London: HMSO.

Law Commission (2014) *Fiduciary Duties of Investment Intermediaries*, LAW COM No. 350 UK Government.

Martin v. Edinburgh District Council (1988) S.L.T. 329.

McCarroll, P. (1980–1981) 'Socially Responsible Investment of Public Pension Funds: The South Africa Issue and State Law', *Review of Law and Social Change* 10(2): 407–434.

McKibben, B. (2007) *Deep Economy: The Wealth of Communities and the Durable Future*, New York: Henry Holt & Company.

McLachlan, J. and Gardner, J. (2004) 'A Comparison of Socially Responsible and Conventional Investors', *Journal of Business Ethics* 52(1): 11–25.

Meinhard v. Salmon (1928) 164 N.E. 545 (N.Y.).

Mercer Investment Consulting (MIC) (2005) *A Climate for Change: A Trustee's Guide to Understanding and Addressing Climate Risk*, Toronto: MIC.

Monbiot, G. (2007) *Heat: How to Stop the Planet from Burning*, New York: South End Press.

National Business Initiative. (2012) *Responsible Investment: Global Trends and Local Experience*, Johannesburg: National Business Initiative.

Nebraska Revised Statutes (2007) c. 72.

Nilsson, J. (2008) 'Investment with a Conscience', *Journal of Business Ethics* 83(2): 307–325.

Occupational Pension Schemes (Investment, and Assignment, Forfeiture, Bankruptcy) Amendment Regulations (1999) no. 1849.

O'Hagan, P. (2000) 'The Use of Trusts in Finance Structures', *Journal of International Tax, Trust and Corporate Planning* 8(2): 85–92.

Ontario Law Reform Commission (1984) *Report on the Law of Trusts*, Toronto: Ontario Law Reform Commission.

Parker, D. B., Mellows, A. R. and Oakley, A. J. (1998) *Parker and Mellows: The Modern Law of Trusts*, London: Sweet and Maxwell.

Pension Benefits Standards Act (1996) R.S.B.C., c. 352.

Pezzoli, K. (1997) 'Sustainable Development: A Transdisciplinary Overview of the Literature', *Journal of Environmental Planning and Management* 40(5): 549–574.

Ransome, W. and Sampford, C. (2011) *Ethics and Socially Responsible Investment: A Philosophical Approach*, Farnham, Surrey: Ashgate.
Richardson, B. J. (2002) 'Pensions Law Reform and Environmental Policy: A New Role for Institutional Investors?', *Journal of International Financial Markets: Law and Regulation* 3(5): 159–169.
Richardson, B. J. (2008) *Socially Responsible Investment Law: Regulating the Unseen Polluters,* New York: Oxford University Press.
Richardson, B. J. (2011a) 'Fiduciary Relationships for Socially Responsible Investing: A Multinational Perspective', *American Journal of Business Law* 48(3): 597–640.
Richardson, B. J. (2011b) 'Sovereign Wealth Funds and the Quest for Sustainability: Insights from Norway and New Zealand', *Nordic Journal of Commercial Law* Fall (2): 1–27.
Richardson, B. J. (2012) 'Fiduciary and Other Legal Duties', in Baker, K. and Nofsinger, J. R. (eds.) *Socially Responsible Finance and Investing*, New York: John Wiley & Sons: 69–87.
Richardson, B. J. (2013a) 'Fiduciary Responsibility in Retail Funds: Clarifying the Prospects for SRI', *Journal of Sustainable Finance and Investment* 3(1): 1–16.
Richardson, B. J. (2013b) *Fiduciary Law and Responsible Investing: In Nature's Trust*, London: Routledge.
Rosen, B., Sandler, D. and Shani, D. (1991) 'Social Issues and Socially Responsible Investment Behavior: A Preliminary Empirical Investigation', *Journal of Consumer Affairs* 25(2): 221–234.
Scott, A. W. and Fratcher, W. F. (1988) *The Law of Trusts*, 4th ed., New York: Little Brown and Company.
Securities and Exchange Commission (SEC). (2003) 'Disclosure of Proxy Voting Policies and Proxy Voting Records by Registered Management Investment Companies', Washington DC: SEC.
Serota, S. and Brodie, F. (1995) *ERISA Fiduciary Law*, Edison, NJ: BNA Books.
South African Trust Investments Act (1990) R.S.O. c. S.16
Stratos (2004) *Corporate Disclosure and Capital Markets*, Ottawa: National Roundtable on the Environment and Economy.
Superannuation Industry (Supervision) (SIS) Act (1993) (Cth).
Superannuation Legislation Amendment (Choice of Superannuation Funds) Act (2005) (Cth).
Thornton, R. (2008) 'Ethical Investments: A Case of Disjointed Thinking', *Cambridge Law Journal* 67: 396–422.
Trident Holdings Ltd. v. Danand Investments Ltd (1988) 49 D.L.R. (4th) 1.
Trustee Act (1995) S.M. c.14.
United Nations Environment Programme – Finance Initiative (UNEP-FI) (2004) *The Materiality of Social, Environmental and Corporate Governance Issues in Equity Pricing,* Geneva: UNEP-FI.
United Nations Environment Programme – Finance Initiative (UNEP-FI) (2006) *Show Me the Money: Linking Environmental, Social and Governance Issues to Company Value,* Geneva: UNEP-FI.
UK Sustainable Investment and Finance Association (UKSIF) (2009) *How the Pension Funds of the UK's Corporate Responsibility Leaders are Approaching Responsible Investment*, London: UKSIF.
UK Sustainable Investment and Finance Association (UKSIF) (2010) *Focused on the Future: 2000–2010 Celebrating Ten Years of Responsible Investment Disclosure by UK Occupational Pension Funds*, London: UKSIF.
US Department of Labor (2008) 'Supplemental Guidance Relating to Fiduciary Responsibility in Considering Economically Targeted Investments', 29 C.F.R. s. 2509.08–1, 73 *Federal Register* 61735, 17 October.
US Social Investment Forum (SIF) (2006) *2005 Report on Socially Responsible Investing Trends in the United States*, Washington, DC: SIF.
Visnic v. Sywak (2009) NSWCA 173.
Waters, D.W.M. (1967) 'The Nature of the Trust Beneficiary's Interest', *Canadian Bar Review* 45(2): 219–283.
Woods, C. (2011) 'Funding Climate Change: How Pension Fund Fiduciary Duty Masks Trustee Inertia and Short-Termism', in Hawley, J., Kamath, S. and Williams, A. T. (eds.) *Corporate Governance Failures: The Role of Institutional Investors in the Global Financial Crisis*, Philadelphia: University of Pennsylvania Press: 242–277.
World Business Council for Sustainable Development (WBCSD) (2007) *Catalyzing Change: A Short History of the WBCSD*, Geneva: WBCSD.
Yaron, G. (2001) *The Responsible Pension Trustee: Reinterpreting the Principles of Prudence and Loyalty in the Context of Socially Responsible Institutional Investing*, Vancouver: Canadian Shareholder Association for Research and Education.

51

Socially responsible screening in mutual funds

Jacquelyn Humphrey

Introduction

As you will have seen in earlier chapters of this book, responsible investment (RI) is by no means a new concept. Indeed Kinder and Domini (1997) trace the origin of responsible investment in the USA to as far back as the seventeenth century. The first RI fund was launched in 1923 (Plihon and Ponssard, 2002). Plihon and Ponssard (2002) document that the early responsible investors were motivated by a desire to exclude certain firms from their portfolios that engaged in businesses not aligned with their religious beliefs (see also Knoll, 2002; Derwall, Koedijk and Ter Horst, 2011). Thus was born the concept of negative screening. Stocks in these undesirable industries have subsequently been labelled 'sin stocks' and comprise stocks of firms involved in alcohol, tobacco, gambling, pornography and weapons production, among other issues. Today, there are still many RI products that use negative screening, although the available screens now also incorporate such issues as poor environmental behaviour, animal testing and human rights abuses, along with the traditional sin screens. Negative screening can also be performed at the country level. For example, during the apartheid regime many RI products did not invest in South Africa. More recently, with the ethnic cleansing in the Darfur region of the Sudan, a negative screen on Sudan has been imposed by a large number of RI products, as investors do not want to hold companies with involvement in that country. For example, in the USA, the US Social Investment Forum Foundation (2012) reported that a screen for Sudan was used by institutions that held over $1.63 trillion in assets.

RI products may also be positively screened. This is where firms involved in desirable activities are explicitly included into the portfolio. Examples of positive screens are progressive hiring policies, development of environmentally friendly technologies or involvement with community development. Most mutual funds that screen use a combination of positive and negative screening.

More recently, the best-of-sector, or best-in-class, methodology has emerged. Unlike negative or positive screening, this method involves comparing the firm to other firms within the same industry, regardless of the line of business the firm is in. The portfolio is formed by choosing firms that have the best environmental, social and/or governance records within their sector. This means that portfolios are diversified across industries. So, for example, a best-of-sector portfolio would include tobacco firms, but only those tobacco firms that were industry leaders in terms of their environmental, social and governance practices. While some have argued that the best-of-sector methodology is a more 'advanced' type of RI,[1] the reality remains that in many countries positive and negative screening is still the predominant way in which RI is operationalized.

Many RI products also engage in shareholder activism. Here, investors buy stocks in the firm and thereby become partial owners of the firm. They then use their ownership rights to engage with the company on matters of corporate responsibility. This can be achieved in a number of ways, including engaging in direct dialogue with the company's management, lodging shareholder resolutions or voting at the company's annual general meeting.

In this chapter we will take a closer look at screening: how it is implemented and the consequences, in terms of risk and return, of screening investment portfolios. While screening is implemented by a number of participants in the financial markets, such as money managers, wealthy individuals and institutional investors, we will focus on screening in RI (mutual) funds. This is because mutual funds make up a substantial portion of the RI market, as well as because much of the research into screening has specifically looked at its impact on RI funds. We will begin with a brief overview of how screening is implemented in different parts of the world. We will then move on to a discussion of the theories that have been advanced on the impact screening should have on portfolio risk and returns. The final section provides an overview of the research into the impact of screening on RI funds' risk and returns.

Screening around the world

It is interesting to note that the way in which RI portfolios are screened varies quite substantially from country to country. For illustrative purposes, Table 51.1 provides a list of the five most widely used screens utilized by RI funds in Australia, Europe and the USA.

A recent report into responsible investment in sub-Saharan Africa lists the following as the top five RI issues, as identified by general asset managers: corporate governance, infrastructure development, water scarcity/sanitation, HIV/AIDS and job creation (International Finance Corporation, 2011a). While the report did not specifically look at screening in RI funds, general asset managers' concerns are likely to be indicative of the type of issues that mutual fund holders in that region may be interested in.

It is clear, then, that there are differences in which issues are considered important, and therefore which screens are used by RI funds, in different regions. Indeed, closer examination reveals that there is considerable diversity in screening practices even between countries within the same region. For example, within Europe, in France the majority of SRI products use best-in-class methodology, whereas in the Netherlands almost no RI products use this methodology (EuroSIF, 2012).

Why are there such differences across countries in which issues are considered the most important? Plihon and Ponssard (2002) attribute the differences to variations in culture, legal

Table 51.1 Five most widely used screens by mutual funds in different regions

Australia	*Europe*	*USA*
Environment	Weapons and military	Sudan
Defence/weapons	Firearms	Tobacco
Tobacco	Tobacco	Alcohol
Labour relations	Human rights	Gambling
Gambling	Corporate governance	Defence/weapons

Sources: Humphrey and Lee (2011), Laurel (2011), Social Investment Forum Foundation (2012).

system and religion. For example, in a series of roundtables facilitated by the Association for Sustainable and Responsible Investment in Asia, the participants flagged differences in Western and Asian values as being important for the development of responsible investment in Asia (International Finance Corporation, 2011b). Further, the structure of the underlying market may greatly impact which issues responsible investors are concerned with. For example, the Australian market is dominated by mining companies, which is why most RI funds in Australia use environmental screening (Humphrey and Lee, 2011). Further, Capelle-Blancard and Monjon (2014) note that shareholder advocacy is confined to the US market. Consequently, there are numerous reasons why we should in fact expect differences in the way responsible investment is manifested in different regions around the globe.

The effect of screening on portfolios: the theoretical predictions

There is great debate about the effect screening will have on the returns and risks that investors can expect to receive from their RI investments. In this section we will outline the theoretical arguments that have emerged in the literature, and in the following section we will discuss the findings of the empirical studies that have investigated screening in RI funds.

Some have argued that positively screened or best-of-sector investments should outperform (provide a higher return than) other investments. These arguments rely on stakeholder theory, which sees a firm as being accountable to all of its stakeholders – employees, customers, suppliers, the community, etc. – and needing to manage its relationships with these stakeholders. It has been argued that responsible firms have good relationships with all their stakeholders and consequently will have fewer tensions with the society in which they operate. For example, firms that treat their employees well will be less likely to have their employees go on strike. Further, because the firm's employees are treated well, they are more productive. The argument is then that these are better companies and therefore will deliver higher returns.

However, this line of reasoning may be flawed. Specifically, in order for the argument to be correct, markets would need to be inefficient. That is, stock prices would not fully reflect information about companies. Let us take a closer look at the example of a company with good employee relations. Let us call the company with these policies GoodCo Ltd. We will accept the proposition that these employees perform better, which therefore makes GoodCo Ltd more profitable in the long run. This does not, however, necessarily result in long-run higher returns for GoodCo Ltd's stock. At the most basic level, a company's return is the difference in its stock price between two points in time. Stock price is determined by the expected future cash flows of the company. If it is known that GoodCo Ltd is going to be highly profitable and is expected to produce high cash flows going forward (in this case because of its hardworking employees), this fact should already be reflected in GoodCo Ltd's stock price. That is, the stock price will be high. However, recall that returns are calculated as the change in a company's stock price. If an investor, let's call her Tina, buys GoodCo Ltd's stock today, she will be buying it at a high price, which already reflects the market's anticipation of GoodCo Ltd's high future cash flows. We say that the profitability due to the good employee relations is already impounded into the stock price. If this is the case, then it will not be possible for Tina to receive higher returns for GoodCo Ltd.

The only way that good employee relations can improve returns would be if the market does not realize the link between good employee relations and higher cash flows. In this case, the market will incorrectly forecast GoodCo Ltd's future cash flows as lower than they should be and therefore GoodCo Ltd's stock will be underpriced today. That means that GoodCo Ltd's stock price is lower than it should be given what its future cash flows will be. So if Tina buys GoodCo Ltd's stock today, then she will be buying the stock 'cheap'. In the future, the market observes that GoodCo Ltd's cash flows are higher than was expected. This will cause the market to reassess GoodCo's future cash flows upwardly and GoodCo Ltd's stock price will increase. Since Tina bought the stock when it was underpriced, she can make a higher than expected return when the market finally works out that GoodCo Ltd's stock price should be higher than it initially thought.

Consequently, the only way that positive screening can result in higher returns is for the market to incorrectly value firms with good corporate responsibility practices and therefore undervalue their stocks (see Derwall, Koedijk and Ter Horst [2011] and Borgers, Derwall, Koedijk, and Ter Horst [2013] for further discussion of this issue). It is unlikely that this situation will exist in most (developed) markets; or at least it is unlikely to exist for long (Borgers et al., 2013). Further, looking back at the example of GoodCo Ltd, once the market realizes that higher than expected returns can be made, everyone will want to own GoodCo Ltd's stock, and the price will be pushed up, eliminating any opportunity to make an abnormally high return. That is not to say that it is necessarily impossible for investors to make higher than expected returns using positive screening. However, investors will have to identify when markets have incorrectly interpreted this information and buy the stocks before the market price adjusts to its correct level – which is no mean feat!

In terms of negative screening, it has been argued that this type of screening will decrease the returns on responsible investments (Fabozzi, Ma and Oliphant, 2008). In particular, it has been shown that sin stocks deliver higher returns than other stocks (Fabozzi et al., 2008; Hong and Kacperczyk, 2009). Therefore, if these stocks are excluded from the portfolio, then negatively screened portfolios' returns must be diminished. We will return to this point below.

The other factor that we need to think about when considering any investments is risk. One of the fundamental tenets of finance is that there should be a relation between the return on an investment and its (systematic) risk. This is because we assume that investors like returns, but do not like risk. Consequently, if an investment has a high risk, it should also offer a high return to compensate investors for taking on the increased risk. Therefore when we are considering responsible investment, it is not enough to just think about returns. We need to consider whether investing in this way will also impact on the type of risk the asset is likely to exhibit.

Risk is usually defined as the volatility of a company's cash flows (or stock price). The more volatile the cash flows, the higher the risk. Risk can be divided into systematic and idiosyncratic components. The systematic component of risk is the risk attributable to economy-wide events and impacts on all participants in the economy, albeit to varying degrees. An example of a systematic risk is inflation. Idiosyncratic risk is the risk attributable to firm-specific events. Examples of idiosyncratic risk would be consumers boycotting a product because of unethical behaviour or a fire in a warehouse destroying all of a manufacturer's inventory. These events are specific to a particular company, but do not affect the economy as a whole. Modern portfolio theory teaches that idiosyncratic risk can be practically eliminated by holding a portfolio comprising a large number of stocks. This is because positive and negative firm-specific events will cancel each other out, resulting in no net effect on the portfolio.

It has been argued that positive screening will reduce idiosyncratic risk. This is because companies in positively screened portfolios have good relationships with their employees, surrounding communities and other stakeholders. Consequently, these companies do not experience shocks to their cash flows caused by, for example, employee strikes or product boycotts. Fewer cash-flow shocks mean less cash-flow volatility, and therefore lower-risk investments.

On the other hand, drawing on modern portfolio theory, some authors have argued that because whole industries are excluded from negatively screened portfolios, adequate diversification cannot be achieved (see Bello, 2005; Lee, Humphrey, Benson and Ahn, 2010). This results in negatively screened portfolios having higher levels of idiosyncratic risk than unscreened portfolios. While this line of reasoning sounds compelling, in fact the number of true pure-play sin stocks is astonishingly small. For example, over the period January 1996 to December 2010, Humphrey and Tan (2014) found only 15 stocks in the S&P 500 that can be classified as alcohol, tobacco, gambling, firearms or defense/weapons. In terms of diversification, studies suggest that it does not in fact take that many stocks to be able to achieve adequate diversification: a portfolio of 50 well-chosen stocks should be enough (Campbell, Lettau, Malkiel and Xu, 2001). Consequently, eliminating sin stocks from a portfolio may have a negligible effect on the returns that can be expected, as well as the ability to diversify.

We will now turn to the research that has examined the impact of screening on returns and risk.

The research into screening

Much of the initial research into responsible investment focused on whether there was a return differential between RI and conventional products. The literature encompasses RI funds, stock portfolios and indexes. In this section we will focus on the research that has examined RI funds. There is now a quite large literature that has examined whether there is a difference in the returns of RI and conventional funds (interested readers should refer to Renneboog, Ter Horst and Zhang [2008a] and Margolis, Elfenbein and Walsh [2011] for overviews of the literature). Overall, it has been found that RI funds deliver neither a higher nor a lower risk-adjusted return than conventional funds.

More recently, however, researchers have acknowledged that not all RI funds are the same. From the second section of this chapter, we know that there are great differences in the screening processes used by funds in different geographic regions. A closer look at the funds themselves reveals that there is heterogeneity across RI funds even within the same country. These differences have caused researchers to question whether the kind of screens used matter for investment returns and risk.

The research into different types of screens can broadly be categorized into three approaches. In the first approach, researchers simply look at the impact the number of screens RI funds use has on returns and risk. The other approaches look at qualitative differences in the screens and investigate whether different types of screens have differing effects on risk and returns. These approaches either group screens into positive and negative, or examine specific screens (e.g., alcohol, environment, etc.). We will look at each of these approaches in turn. It is important to note that the studies examine different time periods and geographical locations and utilize differing methodologies – all of which may impact on the results. A summary is provided after each group of studies that synthesizes the main results.

The impact of the number of screens

Barnett and Salomon (2006) were the first to examine whether heterogeneity in screening practices impact RI fund returns. Their main tests look at screening intensity in RI funds in the USA; that is, whether funds' returns are impacted by the number of screens that the funds use. The authors do not find a linear relation between screening intensity and returns. However, they find a 'curvilinear' (U-shaped) relation between the number of screens and risk-adjusted performance. That is, as the number of screens increases, initially fund returns decrease, but then as more screens are added, returns start to increase again. Barnett and Salomon (2006) interpret their results as being compatible with both stakeholder theory and modern portfolio theory. Specifically, they argue that funds that only use a few screens are very similar to conventional funds, and there is therefore no reduction in returns because only a few stocks are excluded from their portfolios.

Funds that have a large number of screens also have good performance because they are very stringent about which stocks make it into the portfolio. Consequently, their portfolios comprise only the very best stocks. These stocks have good returns because they have excellent stakeholder relations (of course this interpretation may be critiqued using the logic we discussed in the earlier section about the link between corporate responsibility and stock returns). The authors argue that funds with a middle number of screens have poor performance because they screen too stringently to have diversified portfolios, but not stringently enough to hold only the very best firms. Barnett and Salomon (2006) only examine returns; they do not look at risk, the other side of the investment coin.

Lee et al. (2010) update Barnett and Salomon's (2006) study and investigate whether there is a relation between screening intensity and the returns and risks of US RI funds. These authors use a much wider spectrum of return measures than Barnett and Salomon (2006), who only use one definition of returns. Using most return variables, including one similar to that used by Barnett and Salomon (2006), Lee et al. (2010) also do not find a linear relation between returns and screening intensity. However, when they adjust returns for well-known sources of risk (size, book-to-market ratio and momentum factors), these authors find a negative relation between returns and screening intensity. Lee et al. (2010) do not find evidence of the curvilinear relation documented by Barnett and Salomon (2006). They do, however, find a curvilinear relation between screening intensity and total fund risk. However, contrary to the arguments based on market portfolio theory, this relation appears to mainly be driven by systematic, rather than idiosyncratic, risk.

Laurel (2011) investigates the impact of screening intensity on a sample of funds from 14 European countries. Using the same definition of risk-adjusted fund performance as Barnett and Salomon (2006), she does not find evidence of any relation, linear or curvilinear, between screening intensity and performance. Similar to Lee et al. (2010), however, she also finds a curvilinear relation between screening intensity and fund risk.

Humphrey and Lee (2011) find little evidence of a relation, either linear or curvilinear, between screening intensity and returns for Australian RI funds. However, these authors find a relation between screening intensity and fund risk. There is also a linear relation between the number of screens and systematic risk. This means that as the number of screens increases, the funds' systematic risks decrease. The authors suggest that this could be a deliberate strategy by Australian fund managers as they try to reduce their total risk by choosing lower beta stocks. The relationship between both total and idiosyncratic risk and number of screens appears to be curvilinear: Australian SRI funds that impose few or many screens are more likely to be unable to diversify well.

Capelle-Blancard and Monjon (2014) examine a sample of French RI funds and find a negative relation between the number of screens and performance. An interesting feature of the French RI landscape is that negative screening is not as widespread as in other jurisdictions: most French RI funds use best-of-sector screening. This means that the authors, rather than using number of screens as their variable of interest, form a dummy variable which equals one if the fund imposes one screen or zero otherwise (i.e., the fund uses the best-of-sector methodology). The coefficient on this dummy variable is negative, suggesting that French RI funds that screen experience a reduction in returns.

Summary

The first set of research into screening examines the link between the number of RI screens used by funds and returns and risk. Although the first study in the area found a curvilinear relation between number of RI screens and returns, later research in fact found little evidence of any relation between number of RI screens and returns. However, they did find evidence of a curvilinear relation between the number of RI screens and fund risk.

Types of screens

In the last section, we discussed the theories that have been advanced on the impact screening will have on RI funds' returns and risk. We will now turn to literature that has more closely examined the effect of different types of screens.

The theories we outlined suggest that positive screening should lead to higher returns and lower (idiosyncratic) risk, while negative screening should lead to lower returns and higher risk. There is actually surprisingly little empirical research to date that has specifically tested the link between positive or negative screening and fund returns and risk.

Humphrey and Lee (2011) examine a sample of Australian RI funds that use varying numbers of positive and negative screens. They do not find evidence of positive or negative screening having any impact on returns, in contrast to what has been argued in the literature. Similarly, Barnett and Salomon (2006) find the number of positive and number of negative screens to be insignificantly related to returns for US RI funds. In contrast, Goldreyer and Diltz (1999) find positive screening does increase the returns of US RI funds.

Jegourel and Maveyraud (2010) examine the number of negative screens used by a sample of European SRI funds and find that increasing numbers of negative SRI screens has a detrimental effect on fund performance. The authors do not investigate the impact of positive screening. Interestingly, they find that funds that use negative 'sectoral' screening (screening that excludes entire sectors; e.g., tobacco) underperform funds that use 'transversal' screening (screening that excludes specific firms within a sector; e.g., firms with human rights issues). This suggests that the impact of specific screens on performance may differ. We will investigate this further below.

In terms of risk, using a sample of Australian funds, Humphrey and Lee (2011) find exactly what is predicted by the literature. There is a negative relation between number of positive screens and total and idiosyncratic risk. In other words, positive screening does appear to reduce idiosyncratic risk. However, negative screening reduces RI funds' abilities to fully diversify. It must be noted that the Australian market is relatively small, with most fund managers having an investible universe of a maximum of 300 stocks. Further, the market is dominated by large resource (mining) firms, which tend to have a negative impact on the environment. As seen from Table 51.1, most Australian RI funds screen for environmental issues, which means a large proportion of the market will be screened out. This combination of factors means that the negative-screened Australian RI funds experiencing increased idiosyncratic risk is hardly surprising. The question, though, is whether this finding would be upheld in other markets that are not so concentrated in one particular industry. This would be an interesting study for future research. Unfortunately, the other studies did not examine whether there is a link between positive or negative screening and idiosyncratic risk.

We now turn to the question of whether particular screens have an impact on returns and risk. A summary of results from the literature is presented in Table 51.2. It should be noted that there is surprisingly little theoretical justification given in the literature for why one screen should impact returns or risk in a differing manner from another.

It is immediately clear from the table that the literature has examined differing sample periods and regions. Further, the way in which screens are categorized varies across the studies, making comparison difficult (where a study did not examine a particular screen, that cell is blank in the table). With these caveats in mind, the results can best be described as 'mixed', with the impact

Table 51.2 The impact of specific screens on mutual fund performance

This table provides a summary of the research into the relation between a particular RI screen and the return of RI funds: – denotes a negative relation, + a positive relation and 0 means there is no relation between returns and a particular RI screen.

Study	*Barnett and Salomon (2006)*	*Renneboog, Ter Horst and Zhang (2008b)*	*Capelle-Blancard and Monjon (2014)*	*Lee, Humphrey, Benson and Ahn (2010)*	*Laurel (2011)*	*Renneboog, Ter Horst and Zhang (2011)*	*Humphrey and Lee (2011)*
Country	USA	Europe, North America and the Asia-Pacific	France	USA	Europe	Global	Australia
Sample period	1972–2000	1991–2003	2004–2007	1989–2006	1980–2011	1992–2003	1996–2008
Environment	–	+		0	0	–***	–
Social		–			0	0	
Corporate governance			0		+*		
Sin and environmental			–				
Governance and social			0				
Ethical		0					
Labour relations	0			0			0
Equal employment	–			0			0
Community investment	0			0			0
Community relations	+	+					
Sin		0	0	0	–**	–****	0*****

* Financial crisis period only.

** 10-year performance only.

*** UK and USA only.

**** USA only.

***** Except alcohol, which is positive.

of a particular screen on returns varying across the studies. However, what is also apparent from the table is that the majority of the cells display a '0' value – indicating that there is no relation between that particular screen and the return of RI funds.

There is surprisingly little research that has looked at the impact of specific screens on fund risk. Similar to the return studies, the results are mixed. For the US market, Lee et al. (2010) find total risk is increased by gambling and community investment screens and reduced by screening for tobacco, weapons and human rights. They do not find a relation between risk and alcohol, environment, products and services or labour relations. In a European study, Laurel (2011) finds screening on environment, genetically modified organisms and nuclear energy decreases the risk of European RI funds, while excluding firearms from portfolios increases risk. Other screens do not appear to impact RI funds' risk.

Summary

In this section we reviewed studies that have examined whether the type of screening matters. First, we studied the impact of positive or negative screening on returns. While two studies did not find evidence of either type of screening impacting returns, a French study found negative screening decreased returns, and a US study found positive screening increased returns, in line with theoretical predictions. Only one study investigated risk, and found what would be anticipated by the theoretical literature: positive screening reduced idiosyncratic risk and negative screening increased idiosyncratic risk. However, this study was performed in a relatively small financial market where we might expect removing stocks from the investible universe to dampen the ability to fully diversify. More research is needed into the impact of positive and negative screening on RI fund risk. We also briefly outlined studies that examined whether particular screens have an impact on the risk and return of RI funds. There is little evidence of any particular screen impacting returns or risk in a consistent manner across the studies.

Conclusion

One strategy used by RI funds is to negatively or positively screen investment portfolios. Another is to select investments that have the best environmental, social or governance characteristics of firms in the industry in which they operate. RI funds may also attempt to influence companies through shareholder activism. As can be seen in earlier chapters, RI has developed in differing ways across regions of the world, and, indeed, even across countries within the same geographic region. While much of the early research into RI fund performance examined whether the returns and risk of RI funds differed from those of conventional funds, more recent research has recognized that even within the universe of RI funds there are substantial differences in how funds implement responsible investment. In this chapter we have taken a closer look at the screens used by RI funds.

We first discussed the theory behind how positive and negative screens could impact returns and risk. The literature has argued that positive screening may increase returns and decrease risk due to firms' good relationships with their stakeholders. In contrast, it has been argued that negative screening should decrease returns and increase risk as highly profitable sin stocks are excluded from the portfolio and fully diversified portfolios cannot be formed.

We next reviewed the empirical evidence that has tackled the question of the impact of screening on RI funds' returns and risk. Research has looked at (1) the number of RI screens, (2) positive and negative screening and (3) specific RI screens. The empirical studies have been performed in different countries and time periods, which perhaps is one contributing factor to the variation in findings across studies. What is clear, however, is that although there is a fair amount of research into the impact of RI screening on returns, there is still much work to be done in establishing whether there is a link between RI screening and risk.

Note

1 See, for example, Ethibel's definitions of responsible investment. Online. Available HTTP: <http://www.ethibel.be/subs_e/1_info/sub1_2.html> (accessed 17 September 2014).

References

Barnett, M. L. and Salomon, R. M. (2006) 'Beyond dichotomy: the curvilinear relationship between social responsibility and financial performance', *Strategic Management Journal* 27 (11): 1101–1122.

Bello (2005), 'Socially responsible investing and portfolio diversification', *Journal of Financial Service Research* 28 (1): 41–57.

Borgers, A., Derwall, J., Koedijk, K. and Ter Horst, J. (2013) 'Stakeholder relations and stock returns: on errors in investors' expectations and learning', *Journal of Empirical Finance* 22: 159–175.

Campbell, J. Y., Lettau, M., Malkiel, B. G. and Xu, Y. (2001) 'Have individual stocks become more volatile? An empirical exploration of idiosyncratic risk', *Journal of Finance* 56 (1): 1–43.

Capelle-Blancard, G. and Monjon, S. (2014) 'The performance of socially responsible funds: does the screening process matter?', *European Financial Management* 20 (3): 494–520.

Derwall, J., Koedijk, K. and Ter Horst, J. (2011) 'A tale of values-driven and profit-seeking social investors', *Journal of Banking and Finance* 35 (8): 2137–2147.

Eurosif (2012) *European SRI Study 2012*. Online. Available HTTP: <http://www.eurosif.org/publication/european-sri-study-2012/> (accessed 19 September 2014).

Fabozzi, F. J., Ma, K. C. and Oliphant, B. J. (2008) 'Sin stock returns', *Journal of Portfolio Management*, 35 (1): 82–94.

Goldreyer, E. F. and Diltz, J. D. (1999) 'The performance of socially responsible mutual funds: incorporating socio-political information in portfolio selection', *Managerial Finance* 25 (1): 23–36.

Hong, H. and Kacperczyk, M. (2009) 'The price of sin: the effects of social norms on markets', *Journal of Financial Economics* 93 (1): 15–36.

Humphrey, J. E. and Lee, D. D. (2011) 'Australian socially responsible funds: performance, risk and screening intensity', *Journal of Business Ethics* 102 (4): 519–535.

Humphrey, J. E. and Tan, D. T. (2014) 'Does it really hurt to be responsible?', *Journal of Business Ethics* 122 (3): 375–386.

International Finance Corporation (2011a) *Sustainable investment in sub-Saharan Africa*. Online. Available HTTP: <http://www1.ifc.org/wps/wcm/connect/topics_ext_content/ifc_external_corporate_site/ifc+sustainability/publications/publications_report_si-subsaharanafrica__wci__1319578679952> (accessed17 September 2014).

International Finance Corporation (2011b) *Sustainable investment in Asian emerging markets*. Online. Available HTTP: <http://www1.ifc.org/wps/wcm/connect/topics_ext_content/ifc_external_corporate_site/ifc+sustainability/publications/publications_report_siasianemergingmarkets__wci__1319579310962> (accessed 17 September 2014).

Jegourel, Y. and Maveyraud, S. (2010) 'A reassessment of the European SRI funds "underperformance": does the intensity of extra-financial negative screening matter?', *Economics Bulletin* 30 (1): 913–923.

Kinder, P. and Domini, A. (1997) 'Social screening: paradigms old and new', *Journal of Investing* 6 (4): 12–19.

Knoll, M. S. (2002) 'Ethical screening in modern financial markets: the conflicting claims underlying socially responsible investment', *Business Lawyer* 57: 681–726.

Laurel, D. (2011) 'Socially responsible investments in Europe: the effects of screening on risk and the clusters in the fund', Working paper, Politecnico di Milano.

Lee, D. D., Humphrey, J. E., Benson, K. L. and Ahn, J.Y.K. (2010) 'Socially responsible investment fund performance: the impact of screening intensity', *Accounting & Finance* 50 (2): 351–370.

Margolis, J. D., Elfenbein, H. and Walsh, P. (2011) 'Does it pay to be good . . . and does it matter? A meta-analysis of the relationship between corporate social and financial performance', Working Paper, Harvard University.

Plihon, D. and Ponssard, J. P. (2002) 'Les fonds ethiques', in Plihon, D. and Ponssard, J.P. (eds.) *La montée en puissance des fonds d'investissement: Quels enjeux pour les entreprises*, Paris: Documentation Française.

Renneboog, L., Ter Horst, J. R. and Zhang, C. (2008a) 'Socially responsible investments: institutional aspects, performance, and investor behavior', *Journal of Banking & Finance* 32 (9): 1723–1742.

Renneboog, L., Ter Horst, J. R. and Zhang, C. (2008b) 'The price of ethics and stakeholder governance: the performance of socially responsible mutual funds', *Journal of Corporate Finance* 14 (3): 302–322.

Renneboog, L., Ter Horst, J. R. and Zhang, C. (2011) 'Is ethical money financially smart?', *Journal of Financial Intermediation* 20 (4): 562–588

US Social Investment Forum Foundation (2012) *2012 Report on socially responsible investing trends in the United States*, Washington, DC: Social Investment Forum Foundation.

52

Beyond outreach

Corporate social responsibility and the financial performance of microfinance institutions

Andreas G. F. Hoepner, Guan Huang and Hong (Frank) Liu

Introduction

A key promise of microfinance is poverty alleviation combined with a notion of economic development and social responsibility. The underlying expectation is that good business can do well, as microfinance institutions can be profitable businesses and jointly play a meaningful part in the quest for poverty alleviation (Armendáriz and Morduch, 2007). This hypothesis is charming but also challenging. Is it really possible that an organization engages 100 per cent in two aims: profit and poverty alleviation? Or will any organization eventually have to accept a trade-off between profit or poverty alleviation?

Previous academic studies exploring this trade-off use standard financial performance measures (i.e. return on equity, financial self-sufficiency) as a proxy for financial success but face data unavailability issues when determining a suitable proxy for social success (i.e. Cull, Demirgüç-Kunt and Murdoch, 2007; Hermes, Lensink and Meesters, 2011). Hence, they usually employ the average size of a microfinance institution's loan as a measure of poverty. This measure, however, relates about as much to institutional policies and strategies as to the financial requests of clients, whereby even the financial demands of clients might be more related to a type of business opportunity than to poverty. In fact, it is possible that a client requests a smaller loan just because she already has small existing funds to support her business. An independent rating of the social responsibility and poverty alleviation capacities of microfinance institutions (MFIs) would appear clearly more suitable, and is the norm in studies of the relationship between social responsibility and financial performance elsewhere (Chatterjii and Levine, 2006; Hoepner and McMillan, 2009; Margolis and Walsh, 2003)

To the best of our knowledge, we are the first academics to have access to a set of independent social ratings of international microfinance institutions, provided to us by MicroFinanza Rating. Hence, we conduct the first academic analysis of the relationship between social ratings of MFIs and their financial performance. In particular, we hypothesize that the relationship is not linear, as MFIs can neither afford to invest all their resources into their social mission nor can they be seen to ignore social aspects entirely. Hence, we hypothesize the relationship to be parabolic, whereby we believe that external, competition-oriented corporate social performance (CSP) has a U-shaped relationship with corporate financial performance (CFP), while the relationship between financial performance measures and internal, employee motivation–oriented CSP indicators is more likely to approximate an inverted U-shape.

Our empirical results generally support these hypotheses, as we find the convex relationship between competition-driven CSP and CFP to be more pronounced among for-profit MFIs. In contrast, the concave relationship between motivation-oriented CSP and CFP appears to be a characteristics of non-profit MFIs. Our results imply that corporate social responsibility is a relevant driver of the financial success of MFIs. Hence, MFIs, their investors and policy makers appear well advised to devote more attention to MFIs' corporate social responsibility.

Background

In terms of current research which analyze the relationship between CSP and CFP of microfinance institutions, most of them are established on the framework of outreach. Schreiner (2002) defines outreach as the social benefits of microfinance for poor clients in terms to six aspects: worth to clients, cost to clients, depth, breadth, length and scope. Loan size has been widely used as proxy for depth of outreach.

Cull, Demirguc-Kunt and Morduch (2007) study the relation between outreach and CFP. They find the simple relationship between profitability and loan size to be insignificant in the base regressions. However, larger loan sizes are associated with lower average costs. Thus, they have provided evidence for a trade-off between sustainability and outreach. Through examining the trade-offs that arise in the choices of contracting mechanisms, level of commercialization, rigor of regulation and extent of competition, Cull et al. (2009) indicated that financial self-sustainability and serving the poor are compatible, while the profits of most MFIs are insufficient to seek purely commercial returns.

In contrast, Hermes, Lensink and Meesters (2011) used stochastic frontier analysis to examine the trade-offs between average loan size and cost-efficiency. They also find evidence that these two aspects are negatively related. Nevertheless, the finding of a trade-off relation between outreach and CFP in the present literatures is still subject to question, as previous studies assumed that the relation is linear and ignored the possibility of non-linearity, as presented by Barnett and Salomon (2006).

Furthermore, average loan size is not necessarily a good proxy for depth of outreach, as it relates about as much to institutional policies and strategies as to the financial requests of clients. In fact, it is possible that clients request smaller loans just because they already have small existing funds to support their businesses. Similarly, outreach itself is just one indicator of the social benefits that MFIs can generate for the poor. Outreach clearly does not represent every aspect contained in the CSP framework of the MFIs, in which other stakeholders, such as employees and communities, also have substantial influence. For instance, in Copestake's (2007) simple framework for analyzing social and financial performance, he recommends that MFIs should routinely monitor client exit and turnover and invest in the capacity to assess progress toward social goals from loyal clients.

Consequently, an independent rating of the social responsibility and poverty alleviation capacities of MFIs would appear clearly more suitable an indicator of CSP than outreach or even average loan size. Indeed, independent CSP ratings are the norm in studies of the relationship between social responsibility and financial performance elsewhere (Chatterjii and Levine, 2006; Hoepner and McMillan, 2009; Margolis and Walsh, 2003). While no academic study of the relationship between the financial performance of MFIs and their social ratings exist to date, the microfinance industry has launched a few professional studies. These studies do not use particularly robust statistical analysis and disclaim a commercial motivation, but their results suggest that social responsibility ratings might well be relevant for the financial characteristics of MFIs (i.e. Bédécarrats, Angora and Lapenu, 2009; Dewez and Perez, 2010; Gonzalez, 2010). Hence, we conduct, to the best of our knowledge, the first academic analysis of the relationship between social ratings of MFIs and their financial performance.

Theoretical debate

Following the the empirical literaure, the relationship function has at least three possible shapes: linear positive (Dewez and Perez, 2010), linear negative (Bédécarrats, Angora and Lapenu, 2009) and curvilinear/convex (Barnett and Salomon, 2006). Following Ullmann's (1985) and Mintzberg's (1983) theoretical views, a curvilinear/concave shape is also possible, which rewards firms for some degree of CSP but penalises those firms over-investing in CSP. In general, critics of CSP have pointed out that it is expensive and administratively burdensome for MFIs to engage in socially responsible practices such as improving the standards of customer protection, training employees and providing them carrier development. The extra costs associated with CSP directly impair the competitiveness of MFIs relative to those who do not engage in such practices. Hence, following the critics' view there should be a clear trade-off between CSP and CFP (Friedman, 1970; Jensen, 2002).

In contrast, stakeholder theorists inspired by Freeman (1984) argue that the financial performance of MFIs should be better off over time if their relationships with the myriad of groups that have some 'stakes' in the firms are well managed. In other words, CSP is not merely a cost but an investment in the welfare of stakeholders, which indirectly relates to the CFP. For instance, a favourable environment to work in can reduce hiring costs, increase empolyee retention rates and decrease legal costs when opening new branches (Waddock and Graves, 1997). Goodwill can buffer firms from unpredictable problems and provide them new opportunties not available to socially irresponsible competitors (Fombrun, Gardberg and Barnett, 2000; Godfrey, Merrill and Hansen, 2009). In general, advocates of CSP claim that effective stakeholder management can create competitive advantages and achieve superior long-run financial performance (Jones, 1995; Wicks, Berman and Jones, 1999).

This combination of conventional value maximization and stakeholder theory arguments implies that a strict linear relationship between CSP and CFP, either positive or negative, is doubtful, as the incremental utility of investments in social responsibility may vary considerably. In other words, since most of the arguments pro or contra a positive relationship between CSP and CFP among MFIs has itself a linear cost-benefit function, it is unlikely that the joint function of all relevant arguments is linear.

Furthermore, it is also unlikely that the function of CSP to CFP is equivalent for any type of CSP. While some CSP activities are directed at external stakeholders, such as clients, and hence experience direct competition, other CSP activities target internal stakeholders, such as employees, and might face a higher risk through quasi-corrupt overspending than through competition. Again other CSP activities are mainly focused on compliance processes and hence of predominantly risk management nature. Regarding these three different types, we consider competition related CSP to experience a parabolic relationship to CFP, as firms need to donimate the competition to gain returns. In contrast, however, we expect employee targeting CSP to experience a inverse parabolic relationship to CFP, as firms experience little competition here and some investment in motivation makes a lot of sense though the risk of over-investment in employee entertainment is also present. With respect to compliance focused CSP, we do not feel able to hyothesize the relationship.

The governance structures of MFIs may also exert significant influence on firms' CSP-CFP relationship. While a few MFIs have transformed into regulated and shareholder-based financial institutions, the majority remain driven by their social aims, especially those functioning as non-profit, non-governmental organizations (Armendáriz and Morduch, 2007). These MFIs usually have no shareholders and lack high-powered equity ownership incentives. Besides, there are few external controls on the management or the board of non-profit MFIs. The weaker governance and complex pursuits of both social performance and financial sustainability have direct influences on MFIs' risk profiles. MFI managers in non-sharesholder-based organizations have substantial discretionary decision freedom, such that CEO power should increase risk taking. In fact, Galema, Lensink and Mersland (2012) find that CEO power in NGOs may lead to declining financial performance regarding the drivers of greater performance variability. Consequently, we expect the inverse parabolic function between employee-focused CSP and CFP to be more pronounced for non-profit MFIs. In turn, however, we expect that the competition-driven parabolic relationship between CSP and CFP matters more to for-profit MFIs.

Research design

Data sample

Cross-sectional data on 87 MFIs from 35 countries were collected from MicroFinanza Rating,[1] a private, independent rating agency that specializes in microfinance and rural finance. The data set includes both financial performance and social rating data. To ensure a high reliability, MicroFinanza Rating conducts in-depth surveys of hundreds of MFI clients, consults the underlying loan books of each MFI and triangulates any data points wherever possible through cross checks of different data sources. The database contains one observation per institution, as in Cull et al. (2007), collected between 2007 and 2011. Independent social rating data is deemed to be superior to self-reported data (e.g. the MIX Market database). The highlighted benefits of social rating data include externality, credibility and accountability. MicroFinanza Rating measures the social performance of MFIs against international standards and demonstrates the social results of MFIs through an independent tool. Hence, it provides an objective judgment on the social performance of the institution.

Dependent variables

In reporting the overall financial performance of microfinance institutions, four major ratios have been widely used in the past decades: return on equity (ROE), return on assets (ROA), operational self-sufficiency (OSS) and financial self-sufficiency (FSS). ROE is the most traditional indicator used to measure the effect of shareholder profit maximization. By considering the impact of diverse capital structures, ROA measures not only the profit margin but also the efficiency of asset utilization. As the CSPs of the MFIs have very limited impacts on the divergent capital structures in the short term, using ROA to analyze the CSP-CFP relationships in the microfinance industry may induce misleading, or at least imprecise, results due to the impact of changing liabilities and equities. Therefore, ROE is more appropriate to assess external influences to the CFPs, while ROA is more suitable to compare the CFPs between different MFIs (Waterfield and Ramsing, 1998).

However, using only ROE as a measure of CFP is inadequate because of its failure to reflect the tremendous impact of received subsides (Yaron, 1992). ROE needs to be complemented by a measure that adjusts for the subsides, inflation, loan loss provision and exchange rate difference before use. Both, OSS and FSS indicate whether enough operating revenue has been earned to cover the MFIs' total costs. The only difference between them is that the cost of maintaining the value of equity relative to inflation and the cost of accessing commercial rate liabilities rather than concessional loans are adjusted by FSS, which is hence the more precise and realistic measure.

Consequently, we use return on equity (ROE) and the financial self-sufficiency ratio (FSS) as financial performance measures and dependent variables. ROE is after-tax profits divided by starting equity, which measures the returns produced on the owner's investment. The FSS indicates the MFI's ability to operate without ongoing subsidies. If the FSS is above 100 per cent, it indicates that the MFI has reached the breakeven point financially.

Social responsibility variables

We use six variables of MFIs' social responsibility: two have an external stakeholder focus, two have an internal stakeholder focus and two are compliance/process focused. The external stakeholder criteria are Social Responsibility towards Clients (CLIS) and Social Responsibility towards the Community and Environment (EVS). STAFF represents the MFI's Social Responsibility towards Staff. The other employee-focused CSP criteria is Social Mission, Governance and Strategy (SPM1). Finally, the two process/compliance-based criteria are Social Performance Tracking and Monitoring System (SPM2) and Human Resources Alignment to the Mission (SPM3).

Control variables

Yield is the ex post real gross interest rate realized on the portfolio. MFIs charge high interest rates to compensate for the high delinquency rates and the high administrative and personnel costs for dealing with a large number of small loans. By assuming that the poor are rate insensitive, MFIs can improve profitability (or achieve sustainability) by charging higher interest rates without reducing the poor's access to credit.[2] According to Cull et al. (2007), however, charging interest above a certain threshold could exacerbate the problem of adverse selection and moral hazard since only 'bad' borrowers are willing to borrow the loan with the high interest rate. Cull et al. (2007) also suggest that those MFIs charging high interest rates tend to make smaller loans, which is associated with higher labour costs. Overall they find an inverted U-relationship between real portfolio yield and financial sustainability (FSS and OSS) for individual-based lenders but not for the group lenders. Inconsistent with Cull et al.'s (2007) findings, Karlan and Zinman (2008) demonstrate that the loan demand sensitivity rises sharply at prices above the lender's standard rates and also that higher rates reduce repayment. In contrast, Dehejia et al. (2011) examine increases in the interest rate on MFI loans in the slums of Dhaka, Bangladesh, and find that when interest rates increased, interest income earned from most borrowers fell, but interest income earned from top (large scale) customers increased, generating overall profitability. Given the conflicting theory and empirical findings, we have no clear expectation on the impact of real portfolio yield on MFIs' financial sustainability.

Age represents how long the MFIs have been established. MFIs' performance is believed to be improved over time because of possible benefits from client relationship development, approval of lending methodologies, human capital and client information accumulation, establishment of international network and the resulting technology transfers, improvement of productivity and gaining reputation (Gonzalez-Vega et al., 1996). Opponents (Beard et al., 1991, 1997), however, argue that MFIs' operating costs may increase if MFIs reach beyond their initial target group and move into more isolated and rural markets and if MFIs have to address increasing default rates. Caudill et al. (2008) find that lower total subsidies are associated with greater cost reductions for MFIs over time and also that MFIs offering deposits tend to improve over time. We hence control for age of MFIs to examine whether MFIs improve their financial performance with the passage of time.

We also use two other variables, namely Operating Expense Ratio, or OER (operating expenses over average gross portfolio) and Risk Coverage Ratio, or RSCOV (accumulated reserve over portfolio at risk > 30 days) to control for the MFI's cost and reserve level. Intuitively, we expect a negative relationship between Operating Expense Ratio and financial profitability and a positive relationship between Risk Coverage Ratio and financial profitability.[3] In addition, we include regional dummy variables to control for the cultural differences across regions, in line with Cull et al. (2007). The regions include Latin America and the Caribbean, Eastern Europe and Central Asia, Sub-Saharan Africa, Asia (excludes Central Asia), and the Middle East and North Africa.[4]

Regression approach

The aim of the regression analysis is to understand the relationship between MFIs' social responsibility and profitability. We particularly consider this relationship from two perspectives. First, we consider the possible nonlinear relationship between social responsibility and CFP, which is found in Barnett and Salomon (2006). Second, we allow this relationship to vary by MFIs' profit/non-profit orientation. Specifically, we have four sets of regressions, as follows:

$$\delta_i = \beta_0 + \beta_1 X_i + \beta_2 S_i + \varepsilon_i \tag{52.1}$$

$$\delta_i = \beta_0 + \beta_1 X_i + \beta_2 profit \star S_i + \beta_3 nonprofit \star S_i + \varepsilon_i \tag{52.2}$$

$$\delta_i = \beta_0 + \beta_1 X_i + \beta_2 S_i + \beta_3 S_i^2 + \varepsilon_i \tag{52.3}$$

$$\delta_i = \beta_0 + \beta_1 X_i + \beta_2 profit \star S_i + \beta_3 profit \star S_i^2 + \beta_4 nonprofit \star S_i + \beta_5 nonprofit \star S_i^2 + \varepsilon_i \tag{52.4}$$

Where δ_i represents the financial profitability measures, which are ROE and the FSS for MFI *i*. *S* represents the social responsibility rating variables, which are SPM1, SPM2, SPM3, STAFF, CLIS and EVS. ε is the error term. Finally, *profit* represents the dummy variable if the MFI is profit oriented while *nonprofit* is the dummy if the MFI is non-profit oriented.

In Eq. 52.1, we test whether there is any linear relationship between the MFI's social responsibility and its profitability. In Eq. 52.2, we interact the social responsibility measure with *profit* and *nonprofit* dummies to test whether the linear relationship, if any, differs between profit and non-profit MFIs. In Eq. 52.3, we introduce the quadratic term of the social responsibility measure in addition to Eq. 52.1 to test whether there is any non-linear relationship between social responsibility and an MFI's profitability. Finally, in Eq 52.4, we test whether the non-linear relationship, if any, between social responsibility and profitability differs between profit and nonprofit MFIs. All the regressions are estimated with OLS with White-corrected standard errors.

Concluding discussion

We find no evidence of a linear relationship between any of the six CSP variables and any of the CFP variables. When we allow the linear relationship to differ between profit and non-profit MFIs, we still find no evidence of significant relationships. We do, however, find significant relationships when we allow the nonlinear relationship to differ between profit and non-profit MFIs as shown in Tables 52.1 and 52.2.

Table 52.1 Social responsibility ratings and ROE of MFIs

	SPM1		*SPM2*		*SPM3*		*STAFF*		*CLIS*		*EVS*	
Inage	3.266	3.569	3.384	4.043	2.226	−0.283	3.070	3.004	4.183	2.603	3.957	2.934
	(0.561)	(0.559)	(0.530)	(0.481)	(0.705)	(0.964)	(0.599)	(0.607)	(0.449)	(0.624)	(0.435)	(0.571)
RYLD	0.771***	0.696***	0.712***	0.719***	0.750***	0.754***	0.779***	0.783***	0.752***	0.760***	0.731***	0.838***
	(0.000)	(0.001)	(0.000)	(0.000)	(0.001)	(0.001)	(0.000)	(0.000)	(0.000)	(0.000)	(0.001)	(0.000)
OER	−0.905***	−0.871***	−0.757***	−0.769***	−0.973***	−0.978***	−0.963***	−0.965***	−0.885***	−0.918***	−0.882***	−0.986***
	(0.000)	(0.000)	(0.000)	(0.000)	(0.000)	(0.000)	(0.000)	(0.000)	(0.001)	(0.001)	(0.001)	(0.000)
RSCOVR	0.029**	0.027	0.036**	0.039*	0.021	0.011	0.031**	0.031**	0.037**	0.022	0.027**	0.033**
	(0.041)	(0.140)	(0.039)	(0.051)	(0.225)	(0.606)	(0.015)	(0.036)	(0.019)	(0.236)	(0.039)	(0.022)
Africa	−18.270*	−15.986*	−18.694	−17.712	−17.733*	−18.539*	−15.602	−15.630	−18.931*	−16.687*	−11.100	−16.737*
	(0.052)	(0.060)	(0.104)	(0.129)	(0.076)	(0.074)	(0.113)	(0.120)	(0.055)	(0.075)	(0.297)	(0.067)
Asia	6.406	7.048	10.209	8.894	5.012	10.006	7.929	8.267	4.811	9.164	8.674	7.522
	(0.431)	(0.381)	(0.206)	(0.305)	(0.574)	(0.326)	(0.290)	(0.310)	(0.499)	(0.288)	(0.403)	(0.432)
ECA	−5.296	−1.142	0.201	0.778	−7.643	−8.173	−5.045	−4.986	−2.039	1.183	1.310	−0.871
	(0.557)	(0.910)	(0.984)	(0.939)	(0.494)	(0.466)	(0.604)	(0.625)	(0.829)	(0.901)	(0.907)	(0.925)
LAC	−3.211	−0.134	−1.481	−1.925	−2.869	−0.500	−1.692	−1.540	−3.345	−1.843	2.873	−2.967
	(0.588)	(0.980)	(0.822)	(0.774)	(0.682)	(0.948)	(0.783)	(0.815)	(0.543)	(0.769)	(0.739)	(0.638)
profit	−5.636	150.569	−7.522	−30.902	−4.056	155.723	−4.437	−6.288	−5.408	466.917***	−5.596	153.637***
	(0.380)	(0.136)	(0.194)	(0.778)	(0.514)	(0.233)	(0.442)	(0.953)	(0.317)	(0.000)	(0.285)	(0.002)
Social	14.248		33.991		14.855		32.660		−49.693		−31.931	
	(0.636)		(0.209)		(0.556)		(0.101)		(0.344)		(0.176)	
Social square	−2.004		−6.086		−1.326		−4.499*		5.445		4.018	
	(0.601)		(0.107)		(0.686)		(0.085)		(0.407)		(0.217)	

(*Continued*)

Table 52.1 (Continued)

	SPM1		*SPM2*		*SPM3*		*STAFF*		*CLIS*		*EVS*	
profit* Social		−15.868		52.106		−52.010		32.907		**−213.184*** **		**−68.348*** **
		(0.713)		(0.423)		(0.327)		(0.560)		**(0.000)**		**(0.001)**
profit* Social square		1.632		−9.370		8.192		−4.446		**25.946*** **		**9.425*** **
		(0.778)		(0.395)		(0.267)		(0.546)		**(0.001)**		**(0.002)**
nonprofit* Social		**60.979* **		33.139		41.106		**33.154* **		31.148		29.626
		(0.058)		(0.310)		(0.266)		**(0.094)**		(0.388)		(0.149)
nonprofit* Social square		**−7.466* **		−5.830		−4.917		**−4.622* **		−4.963		−4.658*
		(0.072)		(0.191)		(0.300)		**(0.089)**		(0.274)		(0.095)
_cons	−22.803	−121.986*	−47.568	−49.566	−29.997	−69.687	−56.378	−56.356	105.449	−44.065	54.336	−42.757
	(0.706)	(0.076)	(0.293)	(0.388)	(0.563)	(0.352)	(0.106)	(0.105)	(0.326)	(0.529)	(0.202)	(0.264)
N	71	71	71	71	71	71	71	71	71	71	71	71
adj. R–sq	0.371	0.377	0.423	0.405	0.378	0.380	0.381	0.359	0.411	0.470	0.422	0.470
reflection	3.554484	4.083632	2.7926	2.842251	5.602651	4.179939	3.629754	3.586688	4.56285	3.137757	3.973816	3.179777
distribution	0.442852	0.551536	0.450895	0.463246	1.188605	0.595808	0.516952	0.524738	0.78321	0.232315	0.72732	0.397277

Notes: The table presents the empirical results for the relationship between an MFI's social responsibility rating and its ROE. We use OLS with White-corrected standard errors for estimation. SPM1, SPM2, SPM3, STAFF, CLIS, and EV represent the six social responsibility rating variables used in the regressions. 'profit*Social' indicates the interaction between the profit dummy and the social responsibility rating, 'profit*Social square' represents the interaction between the profit dummy and the square of the social responsibility rating, 'nonprofit*Social' represents the interaction between the nonprofit dummy and the social responsibility rating, while 'nonprofit*Social square' represents the interaction between the nonprofit dummy and the square of the social responsibility rating. 'Inflection' represents the inflection point where the U-shaped relationship between social responsibility ratings and financial profitability starts to reverse. P-values of the estimated coefficients are reported in brackets. Regional dummies are included in the model to control for the culture differences but are not reported in the table. *, **, and *** represent the 10, 5, and 1 per cent significance levels, respectively.

Table 52.2 Social responsibility ratings of FSS and MFIs

	SPM1		*SPM2*		*SPM3*		*STAFF*		*CLIS*		*EVS*	
Inage	7.743	8.001	7.917	6.324	7.746	6.154	7.882	7.798	9.830	7.662	9.885	5.758
	(0.301)	(0.286)	(0.306)	(0.389)	(0.269)	(0.411)	(0.334)	(0.346)	(0.252)	(0.386)	(0.217)	(0.362)
RYLD	0.952***	1.077***	0.992***	1.102***	0.831**	0.857**	0.902***	0.902***	0.922***	0.915***	0.911***	0.799***
	(0.007)	(0.005)	(0.005)	(0.003)	(0.013)	(0.014)	(0.009)	(0.010)	(0.007)	(0.006)	(0.006)	(0.006)
OER	–0.672***	–0.681***	–0.728***	–0.675***	–0.671***	–0.687***	–0.624***	–0.624***	–0.617***	–0.626***	–0.621***	–0.584***
	(0.000)	(0.001)	(0.001)	(0.003)	(0.000)	(0.001)	(0.002)	(0.002)	(0.002)	(0.001)	(0.001)	(0.002)
RSCOVR	0.041	0.040	0.038	0.017	0.039	0.032	0.059	0.059	0.064	0.039	0.064	0.051
	(0.292)	(0.305)	(0.367)	(0.698)	(0.316)	(0.425)	(0.196)	(0.210)	(0.190)	(0.480)	(0.154)	(0.174)
Africa	2.398	2.047	10.399	2.291	3.201	1.710	1.693	1.727	0.088	1.774	13.355	8.590
	(0.796)	(0.847)	(0.481)	(0.877)	(0.734)	(0.865)	(0.873)	(0.873)	(0.993)	(0.864)	(0.358)	(0.619)
Asia	27.777**	33.812**	26.987*	36.774**	23.102*	27.778*	17.347	16.761	16.868	25.287	25.395	44.033**
	(0.028)	(0.040)	(0.061)	(0.029)	(0.090)	(0.062)	(0.308)	(0.370)	(0.170)	(0.120)	(0.118)	(0.022)
ECA	22.968	19.489	27.253	26.631	21.469	19.229	20.674	20.647	23.561	27.514	33.520*	37.149
	(0.153)	(0.237)	(0.165)	(0.196)	(0.251)	(0.298)	(0.248)	(0.261)	(0.200)	(0.136)	(0.100)	(0.109)
LAC	6.132	4.761	8.244	9.248	5.497	5.530	1.915	1.969	1.549	4.224	13.290	15.214
	(0.318)	(0.427)	(0.336)	(0.288)	(0.466)	(0.474)	(0.836)	(0.833)	(0.842)	(0.626)	(0.184)	(0.293)
profit	–7.272	–208.063	–8.338	–281.115**	–5.146	–25.316	–8.571	17.444	–8.115	478.979***	–9.905	77.318
	(0.520)	(0.156)	(0.397)	(0.021)	(0.604)	(0.915)	(0.419)	(0.933)	(0.377)	(0.003)	(0.309)	(0.283)
Social	50.256		65.685		55.038		9.535		–53.236		–35.292*	
	(0.157)		(0.159)		(0.387)		(0.782)		(0.312)		(0.059)	
Social	–6.149		–9.963		–5.722		–0.719		6.124		4.340	
square	(0.182)		(0.161)		(0.478)		(0.886)		(0.402)		(0.118)	

(*Continued*)

Table 52.2 (Continued)

	SPM1		*SPM2*		*SPM3*		*STAFF*		*CLIS*		*EVS*	
profit* Social		96.056		**172.666****		38.223		−3.846		**−237.898*****		−90.765***
		(0.138)		**(0.037)**		(0.735)		(0.975)		**(0.001)**		(0.000)
profit* Social square		−11.137		**−24.939***		−2.223		1.065		**30.242*****		15.268***
		(0.204)		**(0.063)**		(0.877)		(0.951)		**(0.001)**		(0.000)
nonprofit* Social		0.779		14.931		44.134		10.118		24.100		−6.440
		(0.982)		(0.735)		(0.531)		(0.775)		(0.598)		(0.862)
nonprofit* Social square		−0.389		−3.215		−5.035		−0.780		−4.282		−0.498
		(0.927)		(0.632)		(0.574)		(0.881)		(0.505)		(0.920)
_cons	−42.547	57.782	−49.456	42.774	−65.254	−28.100	32.500	31.357	162.951	27.826	108.987***	84.528
	(0.603)	(0.463)	(0.598)	(0.630)	(0.636)	(0.851)	(0.611)	(0.633)	(0.106)	(0.725)	(0.001)	(0.137)
N	51	51	51	51	51	51	51	51	51	51	51	51
adj. R–sq	0.339	0.346	0.350	0.385	0.359	0.352	0.322	0.285	0.345	0.384	0.377	0.454
reflection	4.086773	1.001096	3.296561	2.322152	4.809365	4.382761	6.628558	6.486222	4.346684	2.813926	4.065599	−6.46841
distribution	0.613731	−0.59439	0.576259	0.333869	0.858069	0.680317	1.445374	1.460072	0.699099	0.104319	0.751474	−2.79749

Notes: The table presents the empirical results for the relationship between an MFI's social responsibility ratings and its FSS. We use OLS with White-corrected standard errors for estimation. SPM1, SPM2, SPM3, STAFF, CLIS and EV represent six social responsibility rating variables used in the regressions. 'profit*Social' indicates the interaction between the profit dummy and the social responsibility rating, 'profit*Social square' represents the interaction between the profit dummy and the square of the social responsibility rating, 'nonprofit*Social' represents the interaction between the nonprofit dummy and the social responsibility rating, while 'nonprofit*Social square' represents the interaction between the nonprofit dummy and the square of the social responsibility rating. 'Inflection' represents the inflection point where the U-shaped relationship between social responsibility ratings and financial profitability starts to reverse. P-values of the estimated coefficients are reported in brackets. Regional dummies are included in the model to control for the culture differences but are not reported in the table. *, **, and *** represent 10, 5 and 1 per cent significance levels, respectively.

In particular, we find a convex relationship between competition-driven CSP and CFP among for-profit MFIs. In contrast, a concave relationship between motivation-oriented CSP and CFP appears to be a characteristics of non-profit MFIs, while the process/compliance-oriented CSP variables remain insignificant throughout our regressions. Our results imply that corporate social responsibility is a relevant driver of the financial success of an MFI. Hence, MFIs, their investors and policy makers appear well advised to devote more attention to MFIs' corporate social responsibility.

Notes

1 MicroFinanza Rating (MFR) is qualified with the IADB/CGAP/EU by the Rating Initiative, licensed as a client protection certifier by the SMART campaign, received the best user review of all social performance raters from the Social Performance Taskforce and is also the first specialized rating agency to be recognized by a national regulatory authority (Superintendence of Banks and Insurance in Ecuador) and licensed to carry out credit ratings. For more information about MFR, please visit http://www.microfinanzarating.com.
2 See Armedariz de Aghion and Morduch (2010) for an overview.
3 We also control the effects of MFI size and capital structure by using a logarithm of total gross portfolio and debt-to-equity ratio; however, neither variable enters the regressions significantly. We hence exclude these two variables from the final regressions.
4 These regional dummy variables results are not reported in the tables to save space.

References

Armendáriz, B. and Morduch, J. (2007) *The economics of microfinance*, Cambridge: MIT Press.

Barnett, M. L., and Salomon, R. M. (2006) 'Beyond dichotomy: The curvilinear relationship between social responsibility and financial performance', *Strategic Management Journal* 27(11): 1101–1122.

Beard, T. R., Steven B. C. and Daniel M. G. (1991) 'Finite mixture estimation of multi-product cost functions', *Review of Economics and Statistics* 73: 654–664.

Beard, T. R., Steven B. C. and Daniel M. G. (1997) 'The diffusion of production processes in the U.S. banking industry: A finite mixture approach', *Journal of Banking and Finance*, 21: 721–740.

Bédécarrats, F., Angora, R. W. and Lapenu, C. (2009) 'Is social performance profitable? The relationship between social and financial performance in microfinance', *MicroBanking Bulletin* 19: 22–29.

Caudill, S. B., Gropper, D. M. and Hartarska, V. (2008) 'Which microfinance institutions are becoming more cost effective with time? Evidence from a mixture model', *Journal of Money, Credit and Banking*, 41(4): 651–672.

Chatterjii, A. K. and Levine, D. L. (2006) 'Breaking down the wall of codes: Evaluating non-financial performance measurement', *California Management Review* 48(2): 29–51.

Copestake, J. (2007) 'Mainstreaming microfinance: Social performance management or mission drift?', *World Development* 35(10): 1721–1738.

Cull, R., Demirgüç-Kunt, A. and Murdoch, J. (2007) 'Financial performance and outreach: A global analysis of leading microbanks', *Economic Journal* 117(517): F107-F133.

Cull, R., Demirgüç-Kunt, A. and Morduch, J. (2009) 'Microfinance tradeoffs: Regulation, competition, and financing', World Bank Policy Research Working Paper.

Dehejia, R., Montgomery, H. and Morduch, J. (2011) 'Do interest rates matter? Credit demand in the Dhaka slums', *Journal of Development Economics*, forthcoming.

Dewez, D. and Perez, L. (2010) 'Inconfin's experience in assessing MFIs' social performance'. White Paper, Incofin.

Fombrun, C. J., Gardberg, N. A. and Barnett, M. L. (2000) 'Opportunity platforms and safety nets: Corporate citizenship and reputational risk', *Business and Society Review* 105(1): 85–106.

Freeman, R. E. (1984) *Strategic management: A stakeholder approach*, Boston, MA: Pitman.

Friedman, M. (1970) 'The social responsibility of business is to increase its profits', *New York Times Magazine* 13: 32–33.

Galema, R., Lensink, R. and Mersland, R. (2012) 'Do powerful CEOs determine microfinance performance?', *Journal of Management Studies* 49(4): 718–742.

Godfrey, P. C., Merrill, C. B. and Hansen, J. M. (2009) 'The relationship between corporate social responsibility and shareholder value: An empirical test of the risk management hypothesis', *Strategic Management Journal* 30(4): 425–445.

Gonzalez, A. (2010) *Microfinance synergies and trade-offs: Social versus financial performance outcomes in 2008.* MIX data brief 7.

Gonzalez-Vega, C., Schreiner, M., Meyer, R. L., Rodriguez, J. and Navajas, S. (1996) 'BANCOSOL: The Challenge of Growth for Microfinance Organizations', *Rural Finance Program, Department of Agricultural Economics,* The Ohio State University, Economics and Sociology, Occasional Paper, No. 2332.

Hermes, N., Lensink, R. and Meesters, A., 2011, "Outreach and efficiency of microfinance institutions', *World Development* 39(6): 938–948.

Hoepner, A. G. F. and Mcmillan, D. G. (2009) 'Research on "responsible investment": An influential literature analysis comprising a rating, characterisation, categorisation & investigation', Working Paper, School of Management, University of St. Andrews. Online. Available HTTP: <http://papers.ssrn.com/sol3/papers.cfm?abstract_id=1454793>.

Jensen, M. C. (2002) 'Value maximization, stakeholder theory, and the corporate objective function', *Business Ethics Quarterly* 12(2): 235–256.

Jones, T. M. (1995) 'Instrumental stakeholder theory: A synthesis of ethics and economics', *Academy of Management Review* 20(2): 404–437.

Karlan, D. S., and Zinman, J., (2008). 'Credit elasicities in less-developed economies: Implications for microfinance', *American Economic Review* 98(3): 1040–1068.

Margolis, J. D. and Walsh, J. P. (2003) 'Misery loves companies: Rethinking social initiatives by business', *Administrative Science Quarterly* 48(2): 268–305.

Mintzberg, H. (1983) 'The case for corporate social responsibility', *Journal of Business Strategy* 4(2): 3–15.

Schreiner, M. (2002) 'Aspects of outreach: A framework for discussion of the social benefits of microfinance', *Journal of International Development* 14(5): 591–603.

Ullmann, A. A. (1985) 'Data in search of a theory: A critical examination of the relationships among social performance, social disclosure, and economic performance of U.S. firms', *Academy of Management Review* 10(3): 540–557.

Waddock, S. A. and Graves, S. B. (1997) 'The corporate social performance', *Strategic Management Journal* 8(4): 303–319.

Waterfield, C. and Ramsing, N. (1998) *Management information systems for microfinance institutions. A handbook,* Consultative Group to Assist the Poorest, Deloitte Touche Tohmatsu International, MEDA Trade & Consulting, Shorebank Advisory Services.

Wicks, A.C., Berman, S.L. and Jones, T.M. (1999) 'The structure of optimal trust: Moral and strategic implications', *Academy of Management Review* 24(1): 99–116.

Yaron, J. (1992) *Assessing development finance institutions, a public interest analysis.* World Bank discussion papers ; no. WDP 174. Washington, DC : The World Bank. http://documents.worldbank.org/curated/en/1992/08/440435/assessing-development-finance-institutions-public-interest-analysis

53

Financial markets' inefficiencies and long-term investments

Sébastien Pouget

Introduction

This chapter deals with the sources and regulation of financial markets' short-termism. One of the major goals is to show how an integrated multidisciplinary framework might be useful to understand how inefficiencies arise in financial markets and how long-term investments, when they are desirable, may be promoted. This chapter is thus neither a literature review nor an original research report. Instead, it offers various research avenues that may fruitfully inform the debate on how to design efficient incentive schemes in the long-term asset management industry.

Financial markets enable people and institutions to invest capital in the most promising projects, to share risk and to smooth income over time. Their social usefulness heavily relies on their ability to incorporate information on future economic prospects. Yet, as shown by the Great Financial Crisis of 2007–9, asset prices may not reflect the fundamental value of financial assets – that is, the expected present value of their future cash flows. Inefficiencies can arise due to investors' irrational behaviour, speculative bubbles, information asymmetries or moral hazard. This chapter relies on insights and methods from economics, psychology and history to study such inefficiencies. To do so, it mobilizes recent advances in microeconomic theory – in particular in behavioural game theory – that enable the design of novel economic experiments and empirical interpretations.

Financial markets' inefficiencies weaken the incentives of economic agents to incorporate long-term information into their decision-making processes (Shleifer and Vishny, 1990); they thus lead to short-termism. Such short-termism may, in turn, have harmful macroeconomic consequences, leading to frequent and large financial crises and inappropriate pollution and accident prevention policies. Several institutions, most recently the Group of Thirty currently chaired by Jean-Claude Trichet (Group of Thirty, 2013), have underlined the pressure towards a short-term focus and its potential detrimental influence for long-term growth.

A better understanding of the micro-level mechanisms that lead to short-termism will provide new directions to promote long-term investments. These directions include designing financial products that improve the quality of investors' decision-making, proposing regulatory interventions that lengthen investors' horizons and improving incentives along the investment chain from asset owners to asset managers to corporate executives. Applying formal economic thinking to analyze the history of businesses over the very long run, focusing on businesses that succeeded and those that failed, may also prove useful to uncover what institutional and contractual arrangements are most conducive to long-term economic growth (Hoffman, Postel-Vinay and Rosenthal, 1992).

This is a timely topic. Financial markets have witnessed several calls for curbing short-termism. The investment management industry is characterized by several delegation relationships in which asymmetric information and moral hazard issues open the possibility of large rents to be extracted away from productive activities. Several panels of professionals and academics have enumerated the methods that may serve to mitigate short-termism in financial markets (see, for example, CFA [2006], 'Breaking the Short-Term Cycle'; Aspen Institute [2009], 'Overcoming Short-Termism'; and Kay Review [2012], 'UK Equity Markets and Long-Term Decision Making'). These dispositions revolve around aligning the interests of asset owners and asset managers. But absent in these analyses is a profound understanding of the sources of short-termism as they relate to financial markets' inefficiencies, and they may thus remain unheeded.

We begin with a focus on the microeconomic sources of financial markets' inefficiencies. A first source of inefficiency is the tendency of markets to enter into speculative bubbles. Various historical episodes point to their prevalence: dot-com, South Sea, and Mississippi are names often associated with speculative bubbles. Housing bubbles have played a major role in triggering sovereign crises and recessions (Reinhart and Rogoff, 2009). However, it is very difficult to offer a clear empirical identification of such phenomena because it is often possible to come up with alternative explanations for price run-ups and crashes, explanations stemming from changes in preferences to changes in expectations. The first section in this chapter uses on a new conceptual framework whereby speculative bubbles may arise at equilibrium even if the asset cash flows are common knowledge and if there is a finite number of trading opportunities (Moinas and Pouget, 2013). This is possible when no investor is ever sure to be last in the market sequence. This idea is inspired by clock games, as analyzed by Allen and Gorton (1993) and Abreu and Brunnermeier (2003), and shows that the conditions for a bubble to arise are less restrictive than what was previously believed. This framework is amenable to both experimental and empirical analysis and is useful to understand how to prevent the formation of speculative bubbles.

A second source of inefficiencies in financial markets derives from investors' psychology. Various pieces of empirical evidence suggest that cognitive biases and nonstandard preferences influence financial markets' outcomes. Psychological dispositions affect individual behaviour and thus the allocation of assets in the economy (Biais et al., 2005). In addition, they can also be expected to affect prices and real activity because of limits to arbitrage that prevent rational investors from eliminating mispricings (see Mitchell, Pedersen and Pulvino [2007] on slow moving capital in financial markets). The second section of this chapter thus discusses the psychology of investing by presenting the most recent empirical studies on the topic. Among other things, it deals with one of the major cognitive biases documented in the psychology literature: confirmation bias. This bias induces investors to selectively search and process information in an attempt to reinforce prior beliefs. This project investigates how confirmation bias induces mispricing and predictability in price changes and in volume patterns. Confirmation bias also impedes proper aggregation of information into prices and thus dampens the informational efficiency of financial markets.

A number of scholars have pointed out that irrational behaviour in financial markets as well as speculative bubbles may have a detrimental effect on real activity, in particular through the emergence of short-termism at the corporate level (Bolton, Scheinkman and Xiong, 2006). The existence of asymmetric information and moral hazard in the investment management industry also favours the emergence of short-termism (Guembel, 2005). In this context, it becomes of acute importance to understand how one can promote long-term investments, when desirable. The third section of this chapter draws attention to the lessons from the past by focusing on an exceptional episode in the history of capitalism, namely the birth, in Toulouse during the Middle

Ages, of stockholding companies, including some that are still currently operating. This section discusses how hundreds of years of corporate history could shed some light on the evolution of capitalism. How was the value of capital affected by disasters such as wars, plague, or drought? How did investment returns behave over the very long run? Was there an equity premium puzzle? How did governance develop over time to solve operational and strategic issues? The Bazacle company offers the opportunity to document the birth and evolution of annual shareholder meetings, boards of directors and shareholder-oriented accounting systems. How did long-term investors participate in the governance of the company to build a sustainable business? Some records show that an ecclesiastic institution remained a shareholder of the firm for over 350 years and actively monitored the firm by nominating representatives to the board of directors. We also have records of companies that failed. Overall, this rich and unique piece of economic history, as well as others that are still to be discovered, might prove useful to identify the institutional and contractual arrangements that enable business ventures to survive through the centuries.

Finally, this chapter underlines the importance of analyzing in detail the delegation relationships that exist at various levels of the investment management industry from asset owners (banks, insurance companies, pension funds, mutual funds, etc.) to asset managers and then to corporate executives. These delegation relationships are subject to asymmetric information and moral hazard. Moreover, the design of incentive contracts is complicated by the presence of financial market inefficiencies. As noted in Benabou and Tirole (2010), delegation relationships in the asset management industry may induce a short-term bias for fund managers and corporate executives. The fourth section of this chapter proposes a framework to analyze incentives for long-term management. It first develops a conceptual analysis to assess the usefulness of using short-term market-based compensation and to propose adequate ways of designing management mandates, including performance benchmarks and termination terms. This section highlights a new source of short-termism associated with the presence of successive asset managers collecting information on future asset cash flows. This section also provides new directions on how to favour long sight in economic decision-making.

Existing literature

The sections in this chapter build on various strands of literature. A first strand of literature has analyzed the conditions under which speculative bubbles could arise at equilibrium. The basic conclusion has been that, absent asymmetric information on assets' cash flows, infinite trading opportunities were needed for rational bubbles to arise. Such infinite trading opportunities may derive from infinite horizon models (see, for example, Tirole [1985] for deterministic bubbles, Blanchard [1979] and Weil [1987] for stochastic bubbles, Abreu and Brunnermeier [2003] and Doblas-Madrid [2012] for clock games) and from continuous trading models (see Allen and Gorton, 1993). In the framework used in this chapter, rational bubbles can also arise with a finite number of trading opportunities if and only if no investor is ever sure to be last in the market sequence. This condition is, for example, satisfied in the envelope puzzle environment set up by Geanakoplos (1992). The main contribution of this framework is to be simple enough to allow for a game-theoretic analysis and to enable us to analyze the impact of investors' cognitive limitations on bubble formation via the use of behavioural game theory models.

Second, the literature on behavioural finance models based on cognitive biases offers many insights about the time-series properties of asset prices, in particular about the momentum effect documented by Jegadeesh and Titman (1993) for the US stock market and more recently by Asness, Moskowitz and Pedersen (2012) for a variety of international asset classes. The momentum effect refers to the fact that assets whose prices increased (or decreased) in the past are expected to go up (or down) in the future. In Barberis, Shleifer and Vishny (1998), conservatism induces investors to underreact to isolated news, and representativeness heuristic induces them to overreact to a series of news. When associated with limited learning capabilities, these two effects generate excessive price continuation. In Rabin and Vayanos (2010), investors are subject to the gambler's fallacy and expect outcomes in random series to exhibit systematic reversals. Rabin and Vayanos (2010) show that the gambler's fallacy can lead to the hot-hand fallacy: when investment performance can be due to luck or skill, investors over infer that their asset manager is good after observing a streak of above average performance. Thus, the gambler's fallacy coupled with delegated portfolio management can also explain momentum. Pouget, Sauvagnat and Villeneuve (2014) complement this literature by focusing on confirmation bias (see the seminal papers in psychology by Lord, Ross and Lepper [1979] and Darley and Gross [1983]), which was first introduced in economics by Rabin and Schrag (1999) but that has not been studied in the context of financial markets. First results show that this bias can explain not only momentum but also a variety of other phenomena, including long-term reversals. Moreover, empirical evidence suggests confirmation bias being at work in financial markets.

The analyses in this chapter are also related to the literature on the history of capitalism. Scholars have dated the early history of modern corporations to the advent of the Dutch East India Company in the early seventeenth century (Gelderblom, de Jong and Jonker, 2012). However, as argued in Sicard (1953) and in Goetzmann and Pouget (2011), shareholder corporations already existed more than two centuries earlier in the Toulouse region. Indeed, the Bazacle company, as well as other milling companies, operated on the Garonne river banks from the Middle Ages onwards with limited liability for shareholders, freely transferable shares and a clear corporate governance. The Bazacle company thus provides a unique opportunity to complement studies in economic history that document the long-run valuation of firms (Siegel, 1992; Jorion and Goetzmann, 1999; Dimson, Marsh and Staunton, 2002; Jorion 2003; Le Bris and Hautcoeur, 2010) and the evolution of corporate governance (North, 1990; Hansmann, Kraakman and Squire, 2006).

Finally, this chapter builds on a fourth strand of literature that studies market-based incentive provisions. Holmström and Tirole (1993) show how information useful for providing managerial incentives can be extracted from short-term financial market prices. This is due to the fact that these prices partly reveal informed investors' knowledge concerning firms' cash flows far down into the future. Faure-Grimaud and Gromb (2004) also recognize the role stock prices can play to provide incentives to a large shareholder who can affect firms' future cash flow. Stock market efficiency pushes the large shareholder to make an effort to enhance a firm's profitability so that he can resell his stake at a higher price in case of a liquidity shock. In both of these analyses, financial markets' informational efficiency is crucial to give managers the appropriate incentives. Investors' psychological biases and their tendency to enter into speculative bubbles reduce the level of efficiency of financial markets and thus impede the incentive role of prices (e.g., Chirinko and Schaller, 2001; Polk and Sapienza, 2009). Even worse, as shown by Bolton, Scheinkman and Xiong (2006), shareholders might have an incentive to offer managerial compensation contracts based on short-term stock prices to induce managers to choose the projects that are the most likely to generate a speculative bubble. This boost to short-term financial market prices operates at the expense of the long-term value of the firm.

The present chapter complements this literature by moving one level up in the investment chain. How should long-term asset owners design asset managers' incentive contracts? What are the current practices in the investment management industry? From a theoretical perspective, Casamatta and Pouget (2014) show how short-term bonuses and long-term compensation should be structured and study the cases in which delegation of asset management may create another layer of short-termism in the investment chain by preventing long-term information from being collected. This result complements the growing literature on delegated asset management (Admati and Pfleiderer, 1997; Palomino and Prat, 2003; Dasgupta and Prat, 2008; Kaniel and Kondor, 2013). For example, it provides an explanation for short-termism that is complementary to the theory of momentum and reversal, offered by Vayanos and Woolley (2013), in which fund flows are slow to react to news and impact asset prices in a predictable way.

Speculative bubbles

Economists have long recognized speculative bubbles as a major potential source of inefficiency in capital markets. For example, the recent subprime crisis linked to a bubble on structured products sheds some doubt as to whether financial markets are always able to allocate capital to its most productive use (see Camerer [1989] and Brunnermeier [2009] for surveys on bubbles).

To overcome the bubble identification problem, economists have relied on the experimental methodology: in the laboratory, researchers induce fundamental values and can compare them to asset prices. Starting with Smith, Suchanek and Williams (1988), many researchers document the existence of speculative bubbles in experimental financial markets, thus echoing the suspicion that bubbles may occur in actual financial markets.

Understanding the formation of bubbles in the type of experimental setting described by Smith, Suchanek and Williams (1988) is difficult for at least two reasons. On the one hand, their experiment features a continuous double-auction market within which complex functioning is difficult to study. This raises the issue of the characterization of subjects' optimal behaviour on and external to the equilibrium path. On the other hand, it is in general not possible to control or observe subjects' beliefs concerning the available reselling opportunities. This makes it challenging to interpret experimental observations, and in particular whether the decision to speculate is rational or not.

Moinas and Pouget (2013) propose a framework that overcomes these limitations. We design a bubble game that involves sequential trading of an asset commonly known to be valueless. Because no investor is ever sure to be last in the market sequence, the game allows for a bubble at the Nash equilibrium when there is no cap on the maximum price. We ran experiments both with and without a price cap. Structural estimation of behavioural game theory models, derived from Camerer, Palfrey and Rogers' (2009) 'Heterogeneous Quantal Response Equilibrium' and Jehiel's (2005) 'Analogy-Based Expectation Equilibrium', suggests that noisy best responses and analogy-based expectations are important drivers of speculation.

In order to deepen our understanding of bubble formation in financial markets, we propose to study whether investors may learn to avoid participating in speculative bubbles. This question is the object of a long-standing debate in the financial economics literature. Smith, Suchanek and Williams (1988) show that bubbles are less likely, but do not disappear, with experimental subjects' experience. King, Smith, Williams and Van Boening (1993) confirmed this result. Dufwenberg, Lindqvist and Moore (2005) further show that bubbles also diminish when only part of the subjects are experienced. On the contrary, using an alternative experimental design, Moinas and Pouget (2013) show that when the price cap is high enough subjects' propensity to speculate does not decrease after several rounds of play.

To shed some light on this debate, Hong, Moinas and Pouget (2013) propose a formal analysis of learning in speculative situations. We capture investors' learning process using Camerer and Ho's (1999) experience-weighted attraction model. This adaptive learning model is general in the sense that it nests belief-based learning and reinforcement learning. A crucial parameter in this model is the imagination parameter. When it is equal to zero, agents only reinforce chosen actions, as is the case in reinforcement learning. When the imagination parameter is greater than zero, agents also reinforce actions that were not actually chosen, as it is implicitly assumed in belief-based learning. Using Camerer and Ho's (1999) model is useful because it enables us to study whether adaptive investors' speculative behaviour depends on the type of learning process they use. To obtain our result, we use analytical derivations as well as agent-based simulations. A typical simulation includes 1,000 independent trials that each feature 1,000 successive runs. Investors' attraction towards the various actions (which depend on past payoffs) are transformed into choice probabilities via a logistic function with a given payoff responsiveness parameter. When this parameter is zero, players choose each action with the same probability; when it is infinite, players choose with probability the action with the highest attraction, in which case players choose the best responses. We consider a situation in which the bubble cannot grow above a given price, due, for example, to a limit on the amount of wealth in the economy. We are thus considering the case of irrational bubbles (Tirole, 1982).

Preliminary results show that, in the long run, the market does not display any bubble. This is to be expected given that the no-bubble equilibrium is unique and dominance solvable. However, we show that learning initially boosts investors' propensity to speculate. In the short run, more experienced investors thus pop on more bubbles. Moreover, we show that this effect is stronger when investors are more sophisticated (i.e. when they have a higher degree of imagination) and when the price cap is higher. We plan to extend our analysis in several directions to feature endogenous transaction prices and limited liability and to study the impact of market transparency. This last issue is of particular importance since both US regulators (with the Dodd-Frank Act) and European regulators (with the revision of the Markets in Financial Instrument Directive) are attempting to increase the level of transparency in financial markets. Market transparency may have a beneficial impact by reducing the length and amount of bubbles.

Potential useful avenues for future research include empirical analyses on naturally occurring data. For example, despite the difficulty to empirically identify speculative bubbles in the field, Xiong and Yu (2011) discover an important exception. They empirically study the Chinese warrant market from 2005 to 2008 and uncover cases in which option prices were higher than their maximal potential payoff. Such clear empirical indication of a bubble offers the opportunity to structurally estimate models of irrational bubbles and test whether noisy best responses and analogic reasoning are important drivers of speculation in the field as they are in the lab. To the extent that bubbles dampen the incentives of asset managers to focus on long-term fundamentals of the companies they invest in, a better understanding of bubble formation appears crucial to achieve sustainable growth. Guenster, Kole and Jacobsen (2012) identify bubbles in industry returns thanks to an econometric methodology that detects structural breaks in time-series data without relying on forward-looking information. Their analysis shows that investors could have detected many bubbles in the last 90 years of stock market history in the US. It also suggests that riding bubbles would have been profitable for investors.

Psychology of investing

Information processing is a major aspect of investing in financial markets. Investors need to pay attention to financial news and to learn about the fundamental characteristics of the assets that are traded. They also need to forecast what other investors will think about these fundamentals in order to better estimate future asset prices. Economic theory traditionally assumes that investors have perfect information perception and processing capabilities; that is, investors have unlimited and unbiased cognition. In contrast, the psychological literature on judgment and decision-making suggests that some individuals are prone to cognitive biases and make systematic mistakes when processing information (see, for example, Kahneman, Slovic and Tversky [1982] and Gilovich, Griffin and Kahneman [2002]).

This section focuses on the impact of confirmation bias in financial markets. Nickerson (1998) defines confirmation bias as "the seeking or interpreting of evidence in ways that are partial to existing beliefs" (p. 175). We focus on confirmation bias because Jonathan Evans (1989) indicates that "confirmation bias is perhaps the best known and most widely accepted notion of inferential error to come out of the literature on human reasoning" (p. 41). Hart et al. (2009) recently established quantitatively the prevalence of confirmation bias thanks to a meta-analysis that aggregates studies on almost 8,000 individuals.

Behavioural economics has analyzed the financial impact of various psychological biases. Kyle and Wang (1997), Odean (1998), Barber and Odean (2000, 2001), Scheinkman and Xiong (2003) and Dumas, Kurshev and Uppal (2009) study overconfidence. Daniel, Hirshleifer and Subrahmanyam (1998) and Gervais and Odean (2001) study self-attribution bias; Rabin and Vayanos (2010), the gambler's fallacy; and Barberis, Shleifer and Vishny (1998), representativeness and conservatism. The actual impact of psychological biases on market prices has been documented by several researchers: for example, Hwang (2011) identifies mispricing in country closed-end funds due to countries' popularity. Coval and Shumway (2005) analyze mispricing in futures markets due to loss aversion. However, the consequences of confirmation bias for financial markets' outcomes have not been studied before.

Pouget, Sauvagnat and Villeneuve (2014) propose a formal model of confirmation bias. In line with the evidence offered by psychologists (e.g. Bodenhausen, 1988), an investor prone to confirmation bias amplifies information that is consistent with his or her prior views, or dampens inconsistent information. In our framework, this bias creates differences of opinion between rational arbitrageurs and biased investors over the interpretation of public information. These differences of opinion in turn motivate trading. Arbitrageurs with a long-term orientation take opposite positions with respect to biased investors and thus have a stabilizing impact on prices. Transaction costs, however, limit the effectiveness of arbitrage strategies, causing the views of both arbitrageurs and biased investors to be incorporated into asset prices.

Our preliminary theoretical results have implications for asset pricing and short-term quantitative investment strategies. First, our model shows that momentum can be explained by confirmation bias. This is because when they have an opinion, investors can be expected to be biased in their future information perception. In our framework, the presence of investors prone to confirmation bias also creates bubbles and crashes and induces long-term reversals, excess price volatility and volume.

These asset pricing patterns are in line with the results of various empirical studies. At quarterly, semi-annual and yearly horizons, Jegadeesh and Titman (1993) document a momentum effect wherein US stocks that have performed well in the past have better current performance than those that performed poorly. Rouwenhorst (1998) confirms this result in an international context, including Europe. DeBondt and Thaler (1985) and Fama and French (1988) document a reversal effect: at a three- or five-year horizon, past losers tend to outperform past winners. Starting with Leroy and Porter (1981) and Shiller (1981), several contributions report that asset prices are excessively volatile.

Finally, DeBondt and Thaler (1995) indicate that "the high trading volume on organized exchanges is perhaps the single most embarrassing fact to the standard finance paradigm" (p. 392). The present section offers a parsimonious model based on investors' misperception of public information that is consistent with these stylized facts.

To analyze the impact of confirmation bias on arbitrageurs' strategy, we differentiate between arbitrageurs with long- and short-term horizons. We show that long-term arbitrageurs have an incentive to fight against the mispricing to fully exploit the reversal effect. In practice, value investors such as Warren Buffet are known to implement such a contrarian strategy. Conversely, we find that arbitrageurs with a short-term horizon have an incentive to 'ride' bubbles and crashes despite knowledge of respective over- and under-valuations. This is because short-term arbitrageurs correctly anticipate that mispricings tend to worsen when biased investors have formed an opinion. This is consistent with hedge funds' behaviour during the technology bubble, as described by Brunnermeier and Nagel (2004), or with Hoare's (a London-based bank) trading behaviour during the 1720s South Sea bubble, as reported by Temin and Voth (2004).

To gather more information on the psychology of investing, we are currently working with two psychologists, Marco Heimann and Jean-François Bonnefon, to study how individual preferences and cognitive characteristics impact investment decisions. The objective is to discover what psychological dispositions favor long-term investments in an effort to better design long-term investment products and to enhance communication regarding these products. Several dimensions seem relevant to have a full picture of the psychological factors involved in long-term investments, including risk aversion, present bias, moral values towards long-term aspects such as environmental (pollution, climate change, etc.) and social issues (inequality, forced labour, etc.) and altruism and image concerns as they relate to future generations' welfare. Risk aversion can be measured via the methodology of Holt and Laury (2002). Present bias has been introduced in economics by Laibson (1997) and Harris and Laibson (2012), and can be measured by items inspired by McClure, Laibson, Lowenstein and Cohen (2004). Andreoni (1989) and Benabou and Tirole (2006), among others, study the economics of altruism and image. These constructs can be for example measured thanks to the scale developed by Snyder and Gangestad (1986). Finally, moral values are measured thanks to moral dilemmas (Foot, 1967).

In this project, we propose a large-scale empirical study on hundreds of individual investors affiliated with several French banking and insurance networks. Some of these individuals have invested in socially responsible investment (SRI) products, which we consider to be the funds with the most long-term orientation. According to Eurosif, SRI currently represents 17 per cent of the assets under management in Europe. SRI invests in firms that go beyond their legal obligations and internalize part of the externalities they exert on the environment and society. Most of the externalities are in fact related to the long-term impact of economic activities such as pollution emissions and employees' health deterioration. The study will be implemented via a web-based questionnaire and investment game. Investors will be contacted via email and invited to fill in a questionnaire. This questionnaire includes items to measure various psychological dispositions as well as the investment game designed to observe an actual investment choice.

The investment game is set up as follows. Each participant indicates how he or she would allocate 5,000 euros across different SRI and traditional investment funds. One participant in the study will randomly be selected to actually receive the 5,000 euros on an investment account. The 5,000 euros will be allocated as indicated in the investor's answer to the investment game (with a commitment not to change the allocation within one year). Such an investment game offers a realistic and simple environment that provides participants with incentives to think about the task at hand. A deeper understanding of the psychology of investing will prove useful to design financial products and markets that promote efficient long-term investment decisions (Pouget, 2007).

Six centuries of corporate history

Toulouse is the birthplace of the longest-lived firm, the Bazacle mill company. This company was formally incorporated in 1372 via a merger of lesser firms that had operated water mills in Toulouse at least since the eleventh century. This company never disappeared: it turned from milling to hydroelectricity in 1888, traded on the Paris Bourse thereafter, and was nationalized in 1946 as part of EDF, Electricité de France. EDF was introduced on the Paris Bourse in 2005 marking, in a sense, the return of the Bazacle company to the stock exchange. On the riverbanks of the Garonne River, business and electricity generation are still going on at the very same place that saw the birth of the Bazacle company more than 600 years ago.

What is fascinating for economists, in addition to its longevity, is the fact that the Bazacle company features, from 1372 onward (and probably before), freely transferable shares, limited liability for shareholders, regular pro-rata dividend distributions and a corporate governance with annual shareholder meetings and a rotating board of directors. Sicard (1953) analyzes the emergence of this early stockholding company in the Middle Age feudal environment. However, the long history of the company has not been studied to date, and more than 80 linear meters of documents are waiting in the archives to be read and analyzed.

In Le Bris, Goetzmann, and Pouget (2014), we collect dividends and stock prices from 1372 to 1946. We use this long history to measure and analyze the realized return to equity investment and to test various capital asset pricing hypotheses. In particular, we examine how prices react to the dividend process, whether there is an equity premium puzzle and whether dividend yields forecast price and dividend innovations.

The length of the time series and the nature of the dividend process offer several methodological advantages. We are able to perform predictive regressions with nonoverlapping data and to mitigate concerns that investors lack sufficient history to forecast future dividends. Because the firm did not retain earnings, the dividend-smoothing critique is not applicable. Finally, the long history of the Bazacle company gives us insight into how rare events such as severe shocks to GDP and natural disasters affected security prices, returns and expectations (Rietz, 1988; Barro, 2006; Ghosh and Julliard, 2012).

In preliminary analyses, we find that, over the period of 417 years for which we have an almost complete set of dividend and price information, the mean and median dividend yields were 5.6 per cent and 5.2 per cent, with the interquartile range being 3.5 per cent to 7 per cent. Analysis of the time-series properties of the yields indicates that they predict future price changes over long horizons, consistent with previously obtained results (see, for example, Campbell and Shiller, 1988). Yields also have some power to predict future dividend growth, consistent with findings that rely on more sophisticated econometric methods applied to recent data (cf. van Binsbergen and Koijen, 2010). Treating prices and dividends separately we regress prices on dividends, past and future, and show that prices adjust to past dividend trends (which are highly persistent) and also reflect future innovations in dividends. This suggests that shareholders used information included in past dividends to value the shares. Moreover, this evidence is consistent with shareholders being able to predict future dividends beyond what is possible by looking only at past dividend trends, and then using these predictions to value assets. Thus, there is evidence that the value of the earliest known corporation may reflect rational expectations about long-term future cash flows.

We also use this very long time series to explore the link between the value of the Bazacle company and the general macroeconomic conditions by estimating the consumption-based capital asset pricing model and the equity premium. We are able to use data from the subperiod 1532 to 1815 during which dividend payments were made in the main consumption good of the time, namely wheat. We find that dividend volatility is high enough to warrant the significant equity premium we observe for Bazacle shares. However in the time series, various proxies for aggregate consumption, such as the wheat price or the wheat-rye price ratio, are not strongly positively correlated with returns. Only the volatility of monthly grain prices, a proxy for general uncertainty, is correlated with the risk correction. This indicates that Bazacle shareholders priced macroeconomic risk. Additional data on other sources of consumption would be useful to check the robustness of our results.

Sicard (1953) provides a detailed study of the Bazacle mills company up to 1472. Our contribution is the collection of data for the company over the period following 1472. To do this, we rely on corporate records kept in the Toulouse city municipal and departmental archives. These archives contain information on transaction prices, revenues, expenses, dividends, shareholder meetings and lawsuit records. They are also the principal basis for our understanding of corporate operations up to modern times. The archives also include records from companies that did not survive after the Middle Ages, such as the Daurade Mills. This offers a unique opportunity to identify the features that were crucial in enabling companies to survive through the ages.

Looking into the history of finance, in addition to enhancing our understanding of financial assets' valuation over the long run, may shed some light on the evolution of corporate governance and the relationship between shareholders and other stakeholders, such as employees. For example, it might be useful to better understand the investment logic of long-term investors. In particular, the Chapître Saint Etienne, an ecclesiastic institution, was one of the largest shareholders of the Bazacle company, with up to 10 per cent of the shares, and it held its position from at least 1441 until the French Revolution, during which it was expropriated. Some documents that we have seen suggest that this long-term shareholder fought in court against the Bazacle company in order to be granted the right to nominate a representative on the board of directors every year. This constitutes an attempt to influence the governance of the Bazacle company that is very much in line with the current evolution of institutional investors.

Finally, many documents from the Middle Ages onwards have been conserved and offer the opportunity to understand the logic of accounting, financial reporting and monitoring. A preliminary inspection of the oldest accounting register available, dating back from 1469, shows that the first item in the accounting books was the amount of capital that shareholders had to invest annually in the firm in order to cover exceptional expenses. This is an indication of the fact that the accounting books were maintained with shareholders' interest as a guiding principle.

Overall, gathering data on business and finance over a long time period may prove useful to enhance our understanding of the institutional and contractual features that guarantee a sustainable development for corporations as well as other organizations.

Incentives for long-term investments

Do short-term financial market movements, spurred by speculative bubbles and irrational behaviours, prevent fund managers from taking into account the long-term value of assets? How should long-term investors design delegation contracts so that asset managers have an incentive to hold on to valuable long-term assets? What type of performance benchmarks and compensation should be used in order to lengthen the investment horizon of managers and traders? Is regulation needed to foster long-term investments? If so, how should it guide delegation mandates?

This section explores these issues and investigates the link between the time structure of fund managers' mandates and market efficiency. Short-termism in financial markets is hard to reconcile with finance theory because of market efficiency: if short-term prices incorporate all available information about the future, the fact that agents' compensation is based on short-term prices cannot induce a short-term bias. However, several scholars have shown that long-term information might not be reflected into asset prices. If investors are impatient, Dow and Gorton (1994) show that they may fail to acquire long-term information unless they think other investors will focus on the same information. In Froot, Scharfstein and Stein (1992), short-term investors herd on the same (potentially useless) information because they care only about short-term prices. Holden and Subrahmanyam (1996) argue that risk averse investors do not like to hold positions for a long time when prices are volatile. Vives (1995) further indicates that the rate of information arrival matters when traders have short horizons. In all of these papers, investors have an exogenous limited horizon or are risk averse and cannot contract with risk-neutral agents. Having in mind the situation faced by long-term investors such as pension funds, insurance companies or sovereign funds, Casamatta and Pouget (2012) take a different route, and assume that investors have a long-term orientation and are risk neutral. This allows us to study explicitly the delegation problem with risk averse fund managers. We then investigate how fund managers' compensation contracts can be designed to induce long-term information acquisition.

It is common in the financial industry to believe that relying on short-term performance makes it harder to implement a long-term strategy. For instance, Guyatt (2012) reports the arguments of an SRI fund manager who indicates that "The big difficulty is that a lot of the reputational issues and environmental issues play out over a very long period of time" (p. 168). Likewise, some hedge funds, in an attempt to convince investors that they will generate long-term value, are starting to pay annual bonuses over several years. This is, for example, the case of Brevan Howard Asset Management, a large European fund company. The objective of Casamatta and Pouget (2012) is to explore the link between short-termism and short-term based compensation in the asset management industry.

We consider the problem faced by long-term investors who have to delegate the management of their money to professional fund managers. Investors can earn profits if fund managers collect long-term information. However, information acquisition is subject to moral hazard, in the sense that fund managers have to exert an unobservable effort to increase the level of precision of their information. In this context, we determine the optimal compensation package offered by investors to their fund managers. Consistent with long-run objectives, asset owners compensate asset managers after investments have paid off in order to ensure that managers do not take excessive risks. Compensation also relies on short-term market prices in order to shorten the duration of managers' consumption, which is useful if asset managers are risk averse or impatient. We also investigate to what extent the delegation of fund management prevents long-term information acquisition. The contribution of this work is twofold. First, it highlights a new source of short-termism due to a negative feedback effect between market efficiency and agency costs: short-term compensation can only be useful if future asset managers collect information but future managers only do so if information has not yet been incorporated into prices. If long-term asset managers' information is revealed by prices when they invest, asset owners might not be able to use future short-term prices to compensate asset managers. Incentives to collect information might become too costly and, as result, long-term information might not be collected. Second, we show how the optimal mix of short-term and long-term compensations depends on the precision of information.

The European Union Capital Requirements Directive (CRD III) introduces explicit limits to bankers' bonuses and invites funds to make bonuses dependent on performance. In Casamatta and Pouget (2012), we aim at providing the conceptual basis and guidance to evaluate and adjust such regulations.

Several contributions in the literature also study how frictions in financial markets can prevent investors from trading on long-term information. Impatient investors may decline to acquire long-term information because they are not sure that a future trader will be present when they have to liquidate their position (Dow and Gorton, 1994). Short-term traders may herd on the same (potentially useless) information because they care only about short-term prices (Froot, Scharfstein and Stein, 1992). Arbitrage with long-run prospects might be more costly than arbitrage with short-run ones (Shleifer and Vishny, 1990). Risk-averse investors may not like to hold positions for a long time when prices are volatile (Holden and Subrahmanyam, 1996). Finally, investors might have an interest in inducing their fund managers to trade on short-term information, even if it is less profitable, because it provides them with a more precise signal on fund managers' ability (Guembel, 2005).

Incentives for long-term management should not focus only on the delegation between asset owners (who we have called investors up to now) and asset managers. In fact, the investment management industry displays a long cascade of delegation relationships. At the top of the investment management industry are the individual investors, those who invest in pension funds and mutual funds or invest through bank savings accounts and insurance contracts. Individual investors are delegating most of their investment decisions to these asset owners. Asset owners then delegate asset management to in-house managers or external funds. These asset managers then delegate the decision on how to allocate capital across productive projects to corporate executives. Corporate executive can thus be viewed as the bottom of the investment management industry.

As shown by von Thadden (1995), a number of contractual frictions between investors and firms (e.g. asymmetric information regarding the quality of firms' project or investors' commitment issues) can induce short-termism at the corporate level. This chain of delegation of investment decisions is plagued with moral hazard issues. Studying incentive provisions at the various levels of the chain is important to have a better understanding of how to reform the system in order to promote long-term investments when they are desirable. As discussed by Benabou and Tirole (2010), short-term-oriented compensation schemes and managerial career concerns may prompt corporate strategies that are not in the best interest of long-term shareholders. These shareholders will likely speak up to reduce corporate short-termism. It would be interesting to test this idea by documenting the type of engagement, dialogue and activism long-term asset owners develop with corporations. Bauer, Moers and Viehs (2015) and Dimson, Karakas and Li (2012) offer empirical evidence on these issues. Bauer et al. (2015) study the determinants of shareholder proposal withdrawals. They interpret such withdrawals as successful engagements because corporate managers prefer to negotiate rather to let a proposal go for a vote at the general assembly of shareholders in an attempt not to risk losing their reputation. Interestingly, Bauer et al. (2015) indicate that proposals on sustainable development such as environmental and social issues are more likely to be withdrawn than governance proposals. Dimson et al. (2012) investigate activism on environmental and social issues by a large long-term institutional investor. Their results indicate that engagement by itself raises the market value of target corporations. Moreover, they suggest that successful engagement is associated with a 3 per cent annual abnormal return. This is in line with the theoretical results of Gollier and Pouget (2014) who show that a large shareholder with a long-term horizon and a credible pro-social orientation can be successful at both improving corporate social responsibility and generating abnormal returns. As underlined by Hebb (2008), engagement constitutes a significant opportunity for pension funds to enhance the returns (be them financial or social) that they offer to their beneficiaries.

Various institutional arrangements or practices in the asset management industry suggest that short-termism might be an issue: turnover is pretty high, asset managers' bonuses are paid on an annual basis, performance is monitored on a quarterly basis and managers can lose mandates after a few years of underperformance, asset management performance benchmarks rely on standard market indices and corporations are focusing on meeting short-term earnings expectations (see, for example, Luber, 2012). However, it is not straightforward to actually provide empirical evidence on the real impact of short-termism. Current evidence on this issue is mixed. On the one hand, realized risk-free rates seem much smaller than what one would predict using standard asset pricing models, a situation named the 'risk-free rate puzzle' (Weil, 1989). On the other hand, other papers argue that realized rates of return on risky assets are too high (Mehra and Prescott, 1985). This indicates a higher (respectively lower) preference for long-term riskless (respectively risky) outcomes by financial markets than what one would expect from standard models. Moreover, some asset-pricing tests of short-termism suggest that stock markets undervalue distant future cash flows (see, for example, Miles, 1993, and Haldane and Davies, 2011). It would be very interesting to build on these empirical studies, for example, by using more general asset pricing models.

The impact of short-termism on corporate behaviour has also been investigated. Bushee (1998) shows that firms held by investors with shorter horizons are more likely to reduce their

R&D expenditures to compensate for declines in earnings. Gaspard, Massa and Matos (2005) indicate that firms held by shorter-term investors display a lower abnormal performance after acquisitions. This indicates that such short-term-oriented investors exert less monitoring on managers who can therefore indulge into value-reducing activities. Barrot (2012) focuses on venture capital funds and shows that funds with a longer horizon hold more innovative firms. Finally, Xu (2013) shows that firms managed by executives with shorter-term employment contracts are more likely to have lower capital expenditures and R&D expenses.

Concluding remarks

This chapter has outlined a broad research agenda that aims at building an integrated multidisciplinary framework to study financial markets' inefficiencies and short-termism based on formal theory and empirical evidence. This would prove useful to inform investment management regulation and promote long-term investments, when desirable. Given the various contributions discussed in the present chapter, we believe that the most promising venues for future research are: (i) empirically assessing the frequency and severity of speculative episodes in financial markets, (ii) econometrically investigating what are the most important and distortive psychological forces in financial markets, (iii) understanding historically the very-long term performance of financial investments, (iv) theoretically studying how best to design incentives within the asset management industry and (v) empirically identifying the real impact of short-termism.

References

Abreu, D. and Brunnermeier, M. (2003) 'Bubbles and Crashes', *Econometrica* 71: 173–204.

Admati, A. and Pfleiderer, P. (1997) 'Does It All Add Up? Benchmarks and the Compensation of Active Portfolio Managers', *Journal of Business* 70: 323–350.

Allen, F. and Gorton, G. (1993) 'Churning Bubbles', *Review of Economic Studies* 60: 813–836.

Andreoni, J. (1989) 'Giving with Impure Altruism: Applications to Charity and Ricardian Equivalence', *Journal of Political Economy* 97: 1447–1458.

Aspen Institute (2009) 'Overcoming Short-Termism', Report.

Asness, C., Moskowitz, T. and Pedersen, L. (2012) 'Value and Momentum Everywhere', *Journal of Finance* 68: 929–985.

Barber, B. and Odean, T. (2000) 'Trading Is Hazardous to Your Wealth: The Common Stock Investment Performance of Individual Investors', *Journal of Finance* 55: 773–806.

Barber, B. and Odean, T. (2001) 'Boys Will Be Boys: Gender, Overconfidence, and Common Stock Investment', *Quarterly Journal of Economics* 116: 261–292.

Barberis, N., Shleifer, A. and Vishny, R. (1998) 'A Model of Investor Sentiment', *Journal of Financial Economics* 49: 307–343.

Barro, R. (2006) 'Rare Disasters and Asset Markets in the Twentieth Century', *Quarterly Journal of Economics* 121: 823–866.

Barrot J.-N. (2012), 'Investor Horizon and the Life Cycle of Innovative Firms: Evidence from Venture Capital', Working Paper.

Bauer R., Moers F. and Viehs M. (2015), 'Who Withdraws Shareholder Proposals and Does It Matter? An Analysis of Sponsor Identity and Pay Practices', forthcoming *Corporate Governance: An International Review*

Benabou, R. and Tirole, J. (2006) 'Incentives and Prosocial Behavior', *American Economic Review* 96: 1652–1678.

Benabou, R. and Tirole, J. (2010) 'Individual and Corporate Social Responsibility', *Economica* 77: 1–19.

Biais, B., Hilton, D., Mazurier, K. and Pouget, S. (2005) 'Judgmental Overconfidence, Self-Monitoring, and Performance in an Experimental Financial Market', *Review of Economic Studies* 72: 287–312.

Blanchard, O. (1979) 'Speculative Bubbles, Crashes, and Rational Expectations', *Economic Letters* 3: 387–389.

Bodenhausen, G. (1988) 'Stereotypic Biases in Social Decision Making and Memory: Testing Process Models of Stereotype Use', *Journal of Personality and Social Psychology* 55: 726–737.

Bolton, P., Scheinkman, J. and Xiong, W. (2006) 'Executive Compensation and Short-Termist Behavior in Speculative Markets', *Review of Economic Studies* 73: 577–610.

Brunnermeier, M. K. (2009) 'Bubbles', in Durlauf, S. and Blume, L. (eds.), *The New Palgrave Dictionary of Economics*, 2nd ed., Kings Cross: Palgrave MacMillan.
Brunnermeier, M. and Nagel, S. (2004) 'Hedge Funds and the Technology Bubble', *Journal of Finance* 59: 2013–2040.
Bushee B. (1998), 'The Influence of Institutional Investors on Myopic R&D Investment Behavior', *The Accounting Review* 73: 305–333.
Camerer, C. (1989) 'Bubbles and Fads in Asset Prices: A Review of Theory and Evidence', *Journal of Economic Surveys* 3: 3–41.
Camerer, C., and Ho, T. H. (1999) 'Experience-weighted Attraction Learning in Normal Form Games', *Econometrica* 67: 827–874.
Camerer, C., Palfrey, T. and Rogers, B. (2009) 'Heterogeneous Quantal Response Equilibrium and Cognitive Hierarchies', *Journal of Economic Theory* 144: 1440–1467.
Campbell, J. and Shiller, R. (1988) 'The Dividend-Price Ratio and Expectations of Future Dividends and Discount Factor', *Review of Financial Studies* 1: 195–228.
Casamatta, C. and Pouget, S. (2014) 'Fund Managers' Contracts and Financial Markets' Short-Termism', Working Paper.
CFA (2006) 'Breaking the Short-Term Cycle', Report.
Chirinko, R. and Schaller, H. (2001) 'Business Fixed Investment and "Bubbles": The Japanese Case', *American Economic Review* 91: 663–680.
Coval, J. and Shumway, T. (2005) 'Do Behavioral Biases Affect Prices?', *Journal of Finance* 60: 1–34.
Daniel, K., Hirshleifer, D. and Subrahmanyam, A. (1998) 'Investor Psychology and Security Market Under – and Overreactions', *Journal of Finance* 53: 1839–1885.
Darley, J. and Gross, P. (1983) 'A Hypothesis-Confirming Bias in Labeling Effects', *Journal of Personality and Social Psychology* 44: 20–33.
Dasgupta, A. and Prat, A. (2008) 'Information Aggregation in Financial Markets with Career Concerns', *Journal of Economic Theory* 143: 83–113.
DeBondt, W. and Thaler, R. (1985) 'Does the Stock Market Overreact?', *Journal of Finance* 40: 793–805.
Dimson E., Karakas O. and Li X. (2012), 'Active Ownership', Working Paper.
Dimson, E., Marsh, P. and Staunton, M. (2002) *Triumph of the Optimists: 101 Years of Global Investment Returns*, Princeton: Princeton University Press.
Doblas-Madrid, A. (2012) 'A Robust Model of Bubbles with Multidimensional Uncertainty', *Econometrica* 80: 1845–1893.
Dow, J. and Gorton, G. (1994) 'Arbitrage Chains', *Journal of Finance* 49: 819–849.
Dufwenberg, M., Lindqvist, T. and Moore, E. (2005) 'Bubbles and Experience: An Experiment', *American Economic Review* 95: 1731–1737.
Dumas, B., Kurshev, A. and Uppal, R. (2009) 'Equilibrium Portfolio Strategies in the Presence of Sentiment Risk and Excess Volatility', *Journal of Finance* 64: 579–629.
Evans, J. (1989) *Bias in Human Reasoning: Causes and Consequences*, Mahwah, NJ: Erlbaum Associates.
Fama, E. and French, K. (1988) 'Permanent and Temporary Components of Stock Prices', *Journal of Political Economy* 96: 246–273.
Faure-Grimaud, A. and Gromb, D. (2004) 'Public Trading and Private Incentives', *Review of Financial Studies.*
Foot, P. (1967) 'The Problem of Abortion and the Doctrine of the Double Effect', *Oxford Review* 5: 5–15.
Froot, K., Scharfstein, D. and Stein, J. (1992) 'Herd on the Street: Informational Inefficiencies in a Market with Short-Term Speculation', *Journal of Finance* 47: 1461–1484.
Gaspard J. M., Massa M. and Matos P. (2005), 'Shareholder Investment Horizons and the Market for Corporate Control', *Journal of Financial Economics* 76: 135–165.
Geanakoplos, J. (1992) 'Common Knowledge', *Journal of Economic Perspectives* 6: 52–83.
Gelderblom, O., de Jong, A. and Jonker, J. (2012) 'The Formative Years of the Modern Corporation: The Dutch East India Company VOC, 1602–1623', Working Paper.
Gervais, S. and Odean, T. (2001) 'Learning to be Overconfident', *Review of Financial Studies* 14.
Ghosh, A. and Julliard, C. (2012) 'Can Rare Events Explain the Equity Premium Puzzle?', *The Review of Financial Studies*, forthcoming.
Gilovich, T., Griffin, D. and Kahneman, D. (2002) *Heuristics and Biases: The Psychology of Intuitive Judgment*, New York: Cambridge University Press.
Goetzmann, W. and Pouget, S. (2011) 'A Shareholder Lawsuit in Fourteenth-Century Toulouse', in Koppell J.G.S. (ed.), *Origins of Shareholder Advocacy*, Kings Cross: Palgrave-MacMillan.
Group of Thirty (2013) *Long Term Finance and Economic Growth*, Report, Washington D.C.

Gollier, C. and Pouget, S. (2014) 'The Washing Machine: Investment Strategies and Corporate Behaviour with Socially Responsible Investors', Working Paper.

Guembel, A. (2005) 'Trading on Short-Term Information', *Journal of Institutional and Theoretical Economics* 161: 428–452.

Guenster, N., Kole, E., and Jacobsen, B. (2012), 'Riding Bubbles', Working Paper.

Guyatt, D. (2012) 'Corporate social responsibility: the case of long term and responsible investment', in Lewis A. (ed.), *The Cambridge Handbook of Psychology and Economic Behaviour*, Cambridge University Press.

Haldane, A. and Davies, R. (2011), 'The short long', speech to 29th Société Universitaire Européene de Recherches Financières Colloquium: New Paradigms in Money and Finance?, May.

Hansmann, H., Kraakman, R. and Squire, R. (2006) 'Law and the Rise of the Firm', Working Paper.

Harris, C. and Laibson, D. (2012) 'Instantaneous Gratification', *Quarterly Journal of Economics*, forthcoming.

Hart, W., Albarracin, D., Eagly, A., Brechan, I., Lindberg, M. and Merrill, L. (2009) 'Feeling Validated versus Being Correct: A Meta-Analysis of Selective Exposure to Information', *Psychological Bulletin* 135: 555–588.

Hebb, T. (2008) *No Small Change: Pension Fund Corporate Engagement*, Ithaca: Cornell University Press.

Hoffman, P., Postel-Vinay, G. and Rosenthal, J. L. (1992) 'Private Credit Markets in Paris, 1690–1840', *Journal of Economic History* 52: 293–306.

Holden, C. and Subrahmanyam, A. (1996) 'Risk Aversion, Liquidity, and Endogenous Short Horizons', *Review of Financial Studies* 9: 691–722.

Holmström, B. and Tirole, J. (1993) 'Market Liquidity and Performance Measurement', *Journal of Political Economy* 101: 678–709.

Holt, C. and Laury, S. (2002) 'Risk Aversion and Incentive Effects', *American Economic Review* 92: 1644–1655.

Hwang, B. H. (2011) 'Country-Specific Sentiment and Security Prices', *Journal of Financial Economics* 100: 382–401.

Jegadeesh, N. and Titman, S. (1993) 'Returns to Buying Winners and Selling Losers: Implications for Stock Market Efficiency', *Journal of Finance* 48: 65–91.

Jehiel, P. (2005) 'Analogy-Based Expectation Equilibrium', *Journal of Economic Theory* 123: 81–104.

Jorion, P. (2003) 'The Long-Term Risks of Global Stock Markets', *Financial Management.*

Jorion, P. and Goetzmann, W. (1999) 'Global Stock Market in the 20th Century', *Journal of Finance* 54: 953–980.

Kahneman, D., Slovic P. and Tversky, A. (eds.) (1982) *Judgment under Uncertainty: Heuristics and Biases*, Cambridge: Cambridge University Press.

Kaniel, R. and Kondor, P. (2013) 'The Delegated Lucas-Tree', *Review of Financial Studies*, forthcoming.

Kay Review (2012) 'UK Equity Markets and Long-Term Decision Making', Report.

King, R., Smith, V., Williams, A. and Van Boening, M. (1993) 'The Robustness of Bubbles and Crashes in Experimental Stock Markets', in Day, R. H. and Chen, P. (eds.), *Nonlinear Dynamics and Evolutionary Economics*, New York: Oxford University Press, 183–200.

Kyle, A. and Wang, A. (1997) 'Speculation Duopoly with Agreement to Disagree: Can Overconfidence Survive the Market Test?', *Journal of Finance* 52: 2073–2090.

Laibson, D. (1997) 'Golden Eggs and Hyperbolic Discounting', *Quarterly Journal of Economics* 62.

Le Bris, D., Goetzmann, W. and Pouget, S. (2014) 'Testing Asset Pricing Theory on Six Hundred Years of Stock Returns: Prices and Dividends for the Bazacle Company from 1372 to 1946', Working Paper.

Le Bris, D. and Hautcœur, P. C. (2010) 'A Challenge to Triumphant Optimists? A Blue Chips Index for the Paris Stock Exchange, 1854–2007', *Financial History Review* 17: 141–183.

Lee, C. and Swaminathan, B. (2000) 'Price Momentum and Trading Volume', *Journal of Finance* 55.

Leroy, S. and Porter, R. (1981) 'The Present-Value Relation: Tests Based on Implied Variance Bounds', *Econometrica* 49: 555–574.

Lord, C., Ross, L. and Lepper, M. (1979) 'Biased Assimilation and Attitude Polarization: The Effects of Prior Theories on Subsequently Considered Evidence', *Journal of Personality and Social Psychology* 37: 2098–2109.

Lubber, M. (2012) 'Ending Quarterly Capitalism', *Forbes*, 2 December.

McClure, S., Laibson, D., Loewenstein G. and Cohen J. (2004) 'Separate Neural Systems Value Immediate and Delayed Monetary Rewards', *Science* 306: 503–507.

Mehra R. and Prescott T. (1985), 'The Equity Premium: A Puzzle', *Journal of Monetary Economics* 15: 145–161.

Miles D. (1993), 'Test for Short Termism in the UK Stock Market, *The Economic Journal* 103: 1379–1396.

Mitchell, M., Pedersen, L. and Pulvino, T. (2007) 'Slow Moving Capital', *American Economic Review P&P* 97: 215–220.

Moinas, S. and Pouget, S. (2013) 'The Bubble Game: An Experimental Investigation of Speculation', *Econometrica*, forthcoming.
Nickerson, R. (1998) 'Confirmation Bias: A Ubiquitous Phenomenon in Many Guises', *Review of General Psychology* 2.
North, D. (1990) *Institutions, Institutional Change, and Economic Performance*, Cambridge: Cambridge University Press.
Odean, T. (1998) 'Volume, Volatility, Price, and Profits When All Traders Are Above Average', *Journal of Finance* 53: 1887–1934.
Ostling, R, Wang, J. T., Chou, E. and Camerer, C. (2011) 'Testing Game Theory in the Field: Swedish LUPI Lottery Games', *American Economic Journal: Microeconomics* 3: 1–33.
Palomino, F. and Prat, A. (2003) 'Risk Taking and Optimal Contracts for Money Managers', *Rand Journal of Economics* 34: 113–137.
Plous, S. (1991) 'Biases in the Assimilation of Technological Breakdowns: Do Accidents Make Us Safer?', *Journal of Applied Social Psychology* 21: 1058–1082.
Polk, C. and Sapienza, P. (2009) 'The Stock Market and Corporate Investment: A Test of Catering Theory', *Review of Financial Studies* 22: 187–217.
Pouget, S. (2007) 'Adaptive Learning and the Design of Financial Markets', *Journal of Finance* 62.
Pouget, S., Sauvagnat, J. and Villeneuve, S. (2014) 'A Mind Is a Terrible Thing to Change: Confirmatory Bias in Financial Markets', Working Paper.
Rabin, M. and Schrag, J. (1999) 'First Impressions Matter: A Model of Confirmatory Bias', *Quarterly Journal of Economics* 114: 37–82.
Rabin, M. and Vayanos, D. (2010) 'The Gambler's and Hot-Hand Fallacies: Theory and Applications', *Review of Economic Studies* 77: 730–778.
Reinhart, C. and Rogoff, K. (2009) 'The Aftermath of Financial Crises', *American Economic Review* 99: 466–472.
Rietz, T. (1988) 'The Equity Risk Premium: A Solution', *Journal of Monetary Economics* 22: 117–131.
Rouwenhorst, G. (1998) 'International Momentum Strategies', *Journal of Finance* 53: 267–284.
Scheinkman, J. and Xiong, W. (2003) 'Overconfidence and Speculative Bubbles', *Journal of Political Economy* 111: 1183–1219.
Shiller, R. (1981) 'The Use of Volatility Measures in Assessing Market Efficiency', *The Journal of Finance* 36: 291–304.
Shleifer, A. and Vishny, R. (1990) 'Equilibrium Short Horizons of Investors and Firms', *American Economic Review* 80: 148–153.
Sicard, G. (1953) *Aux origines des sociétés anonymes – Les moulins de Toulouse au Moyen Age*, Paris: Armand Colin.
Siegel J. (1992) 'The Equity Premium: Stock and Bond Returns since 1802', *Financial Analysts Journal* 48: 28–38.
Smith, V., Suchanek, G. and Williams, A. (1988) 'Bubbles, Crashes, and Endogenous Expectations in Experimental Spot Asset Markets', *Econometrica* 56: 1119–1151.
Snyder, M. and Gangestad, S. (1986) 'On the Nature of Self-Monitoring: Matters of Assessment, Matters of Validity', *Journal of Personality and Social Psychology* 51: 125–139.
Temin, P. and Voth, H.J. (2004) 'Riding the South Sea Bubble', *American Economic Review* 94.
Tirole, J. (1982) 'On the Possibility of Speculation under Rational Expectations', *Econometrica*, 50: 1163–1181.
Tirole, J. (1985) 'Asset Bubbles and Overlapping Generations', *Econometrica* 53: 1499–1528.
van Binsbergen, J. and Koijen, R. (2010) 'Predictive Regressions: A Present-Value Approach', *Journal of Finance* 65: 1439–1471.
Vayanos, D. and Woolley, P. (2013) 'An Institutional Theory of Momentum and Reversal', *Review of Financial Studies*, forthcoming.
Vives, X. (1995) 'The Speed of Information Revelation in a Financial Market Mechanism', *Journal of Economic Theory* 67: 178–204.
von Thadden, E. L. (1995) 'Long-Term Contracts, Short-Term Investment and Monitoring', *Review of Economic Studies* 62: 557–575.
Weil, P. (1987) 'Confidence and the Real Value of Money in an Overlapping Generations Economy', *Quarterly Journal of Economics* 102: 1–22.
Weil, P. (1989) 'The equity premium puzzle and the risk-free rate puzzle', *Journal of Monetary Economics* 24: 401–421.
Xiong, W. and Yu, J. (2011) 'The Chinese Warrants Bubble', *American Economic Review* 101: 2723–2753.
Xu, M. (2013) 'The Costs and benefits of Long-Term CEO Contracts', Working Paper.

54

What matters to SRI investors?[1]

Peer Osthoff

Introduction

Interest in socially responsible investments (SRI) is steadily increasing. The Social Investment Forum reports that about one out of nine dollars under professional management in the US is invested according to socially responsible investment criteria.[2] In accordance with the growth of the SRI market the number of SRI studies has also increased. Most SRI studies focus on the performance of SRI mutual funds. Generally, these studies indicate that the performance of SRI mutual funds is comparable to the performance of their conventional counterparts.[3] However, all these studies neglect the question of to what extent SRI investors actually care about performance.

The large body of literature on the investment decisions of conventional mutual fund investors shows that conventional investors chase past top performing funds, but do not sell poor performing funds to the same extent.[4] They document an asymmetric and convex performance flow relationship for conventional funds. While it is assumed in the traditional finance literature that conventional investors are risk-reward optimizers, SRI investors pursue, by definition, not only financial goals, but also non-financial goals.[5] This raises the question of whether SRI investors behave differently from conventional investors.

In this paper I analyze the flows into SRI funds to address the following three main questions: (i) Do SRI investors care about performance? In particular, does their performance sensitivity differ from that of conventional investors, and does that performance sensitivity depend on the degree of maturity of the SRI market? (ii) Do SRI investors care about the actual ethical standards of their investments, or do they just care about the label 'SRI'? (iii) Are SRI investors more likely to reinvest in the same fund than conventional investors because of higher search costs?

To explore these issues, I study the inflows of SRI and conventional mutual funds in the US for the time period from 1993 to 2004.

I first analyze the performance sensitivity of SRI investors in order to compare it to that of conventional investors. One might suspect that SRI investors care less about performance in their investment decisions, paying more attention to social and environmental issues. However, if SRI investors can identify substitutes among the funds in the SRI segment regarding their social and environmental aspects, they will choose the funds with the highest performance; thus, their reaction is performance sensitive. Whether SRI investors are performance sensitive or not therefore depends on the number of alternatives available in the SRI fund segment. Over the sample period I investigated, the number of SRI funds grew rapidly (see Table 54.1). I hypothesize that with the increasing number of SRI funds, the performance sensitivity of SRI investors has also increased due to the availability of high-performing alternatives. A second argument which supports the assumption of an increasing performance sensitivity over time is that the SRI pioneers cared less about performance than current SRI investors.

Second, I analyze whether SRI investors care about the actual ethical standards of the SRI funds or whether they are simply satisfied with the funds being labelled as SRI funds. I am the first to examine this question. To measure the ethical standards of the funds, I combine the portfolio holdings information of the funds with ethical stock ratings data. By definition, SRI investors are supposed to derive utility from the social and environmental aspects of their investments. I therefore expect that investors in the SRI fund market care about ethical standards. I further anticipate that their sensitivity to ethical standards increases over time as a result of a growing market within which they can choose funds which best satisfy their needs.

Third, I analyze whether SRI investors are more likely to reinvest in the same fund than conventional investors. SRI investors face search costs if they want to identify an SRI fund fitting their personal values and their financial goals. Contrary to the SRI investors, conventional investors have only to align their funds with their financial goals; their search costs are as a result presumably lower than for SRI investors. Higher search costs induce SRI investors to reinvest in the same fund in the future. The search costs argument leads to a higher autocorrelation in fund flows for the SRI funds.

I find the following main results: (i) over the whole sample period SRI investors seem to chase past top performing funds, but not to sell poor performing funds to the same extent. This behaviour is similar to that of conventional investors and in line with the results of Bollen (2007) and Renneboog et al. (2006).[6] However, along with the fast development of the SRI fund market, the performance sensitivity of SRI investors has increased over time. SRI investors chase past top performing funds to a greater extent in the second half of the sample period than in the first. This result colludes with the assumption that with an increasing number of SRI funds, the number of alternatives grows, and thus SRI investors become more performance sensitive. This finding is also consistent with the conjecture that the SRI pioneers in the early stages of the SRI market cared less about performance and that today they are outnumbered by mainstream SRI investors who value performance. Current SRI investors chase past top performing funds at least as much as conventional investors do. (ii) Consistent with my hypothesis I find that SRI investors care about the actual ethical standards of the mutual funds. They are not satisfied with the funds being labelled as SRI funds. They prefer funds with high ethical standards regarding the positive rating which consists of the criteria community, diversity, employee relations, environment, human rights, and product. The sensitivity to ethical standards regarding the positive rating increases over time. This finding is in line with the expectation that in the fast-growing SRI market investors choose that fund which satisfies their needs best. Furthermore, I find that SRI investors especially prefer funds with high environmental standards. The interest in environmental standards is probably sparked by the frequent reports about environmental issues such as global warming or alternative energy solutions in the public press. (iii) I document a higher positive autocorrelation in flows for the SRI mutual funds than for the conventional funds. This is in line with the conjecture that SRI investors face higher search costs than conventional investors and thus are more likely to reinvest in the same fund they already own.

Overall, I conclude that nowadays SRI investors invest disproportionately more in funds with past top performance – similar to conventional investors – but additionally pay attention to the actual ethical standards of their investments.

The remainder of the paper proceeds as follows. The data and the design of the study are described in the second section; the empirical results are reported in the third section. The fourth section concludes by reiterating the results of the study and their significance.

Methodology

Data

To study how SRI investors react to past performance and ethical standards when investing in SRI funds and to compare their investment behaviour to that of conventional investors, I combine the information of five different databases: the CRSP Survivor-Bias Free US Mutual Fund database, the KLD Stats database, the Thomson Financial Mutual Fund Holdings database, the CRSP US Stock database, and the Morningstar Principia database. For my sample of US equity funds in the period from 1992 to 2004, I retrieve information about the fund characteristics such as size, loads, returns, turnover, age, and expense ratio from the CRSP Survivor-Bias Free US Mutual Fund database.

There exists no direct measure for the ethical standards of mutual funds. To obtain ethical rankings for mutual funds, I combine the portfolio holdings of the funds with ethical stock ratings data. The procedure I use is similar to the one used by Kempf and Osthoff (2008). In a first step, I prepare the ethical stock ratings data retrieved from the KLD Stats Database. This database is free of survivorship bias and covers annual ratings for all S&P 500 and Domini 400 Social Index (DSI 400) stocks over the period from 1992 to 2004. KLD has extended its stock coverage through time. From 2001 to 2002 ethical ratings are provided for all stocks of the Russell 1000 and from 2003 onwards for all stocks of the Russell 3000. KLD evaluates the stocks using multiple criteria, which can be classified in two broad categories: qualitative and exclusionary criteria.[7] The qualitative criteria are community, diversity, employee relations, environment, human rights, and product.[8] By following the positive screening approach investors use these criteria to evaluate the ethical standards of companies and then select the companies with the highest ethical standards. Each qualitative criterion consists of several sub-criteria for which KLD provides a binary score. To calculate a single rating for each qualitative criterion, I average all binary scores, as done by Kempf and Osthoff (2007). Then I average all these qualitative ratings to obtain a positive overall rating (hereafter referred to as a 'positive rating') between zero and one. The higher the rating, the higher the social responsibility of the company. The exclusionary criteria, which are used for the negative screening, are alcohol, tobacco, gambling, military, and nuclear power. Investors following a negative screening policy avoid companies involved in these controversial business areas. To obtain a negative overall rating (hereafter referred to as a 'negative rating'), I assign a one to a company if it is not involved in any of these controversial business areas and a zero if the company is involved in at least one controversial business area. Since I use ethical ratings of US stocks to evaluate the ethical standards of the mutual funds, I exclude from my sample all international, bond, and money market funds.

In a second step, I prepare the mutual fund holdings data. The holdings data for the period from 1992 to 2003 is retrieved from the Thomson Financial Mutual Fund Holdings database, which is free of survivorship bias (see Wermers (2000), and the holdings data for 2004 is retrieved from the CRSP Survivor-Bias Free US Mutual Fund database. To obtain a complete record of the stock holdings for each fund along with other fund characteristics such as size, loads, returns, turnover, age, and expense ratio over my sample period, I merge these two databases. The two databases are matched by fund ticker and fund name information.[9] Although in the CRSP Survivor-Bias Free US Mutual Fund database multiple share classes are listed as different funds, they are based on the same set of holdings. I aggregate different share classes of the same fund by weighting the respective fund characteristic with the previous year's total net assets under management of that share class. For some fund characteristics a different aggregation method is used. The age of a fund is the age of the oldest share class; the total net assets of a fund are the sum of total net assets of all share classes. The procedure is similar to the one used by Wermers (2000). Finally, I retrieve the prices for the stocks held by the funds from the CRSP US Stock database. The database covers all stocks traded at the American Stock Exchange (AMEX), the New York Stock Exchange (NYSE), and NASDAQ.

In a third step, I now combine the mutual fund holdings with the stock ratings data to obtain an ethical ranking of the funds. For each fund I calculate normalized portfolio weights for the rated stock positions at the end of the year. I include only fund observations in my sample where the percentage of all stocks is at least 50 per cent. Then, I sum these portfolio weights for the rated stocks multiplied by the ethical stock ratings. This weighted sum is the aggregated ethical rating for a mutual fund. Thereby, I implicitly assume that the rated stocks behave like the stocks not rated. The average percentage of the rated stocks for the SRI funds in my sample is 79 per cent, and 70 per cent for the conventional funds. Based on the aggregated ratings I assign fractional ranks in each year ranging from zero to one for both the group of SRI funds and the group of conventional funds. The higher the ranking of a fund, the higher the ethical standards of that fund. $Pos_{i,t}$ denotes the ethical rank based on the positive rating for fund i in year t; $Neg_{i,t}$ denotes the ethical rank based on the negative rating. Kempf and Osthoff (2008) show that SRI funds indeed hold stocks with higher ethical ratings than their conventional counterparts.[10]

Since I have no direct measure on net-inflows for mutual funds, I have to calculate a synthetic measure. I employ the standard procedure in the literature (see, for example, Chevalier and Ellison, 1997, or Sirri and Tufano, 1998) to construct a measure on the net-inflows of fund i in year t:[11]

$$FLOW_{i,t} = \frac{TNA_{i,t} - TNA_{i,t-1}}{TNA_{i,t-1}} - R_{i,t} \quad (1)$$

$TNA_{i,t}$ is defined as the total net assets under management of fund i in year t. $R_{i,t}$ denotes the total return of fund i in year t. Consequently, $FLOW_{i,t}$ reflects the percentage growth of fund i minus the internal growth in year t. It is assumed that flows occur at the end of the year and that dividends and distributions are reinvested in the same fund. I exclude fund year observations from my sample where funds grew more than 1,000 per cent, because a higher growth rate is probably due to data errors.[12]

To obtain a list of SRI mutual funds, I retrieve the SRI mutual funds from the Morningstar Principia database for the time period from 1996 to 2005 on an annual frequency. I backdate the list of SRI funds from 1992 until 1996, because no Morningstar data is available prior to 1996. In my sample I have 49 different SRI funds and 2,643 different conventional funds which comply with this restriction. Table 54.1 reports descriptive statistics on the SRI funds (Panel A) and on the conventional funds (Panel B) in my sample.

The number of funds is increasing over time for both groups of funds. The number of funds in the young SRI market grew especially rapidly. While the number of conventional funds quintupled, the number of SRI funds increased 10-fold. Figure 54.1(a) presents the development of the total assets under management for the SRI and conventional funds over time. Whereas the total assets of the conventional funds grew faster in the first part of my sample period, the total assets of the SRI funds grew constantly faster in the second part of my sample period. These results are confirmed by Figure 54.1(b) which shows the percentage growth of the SRI and

Table 54.1 Summary statistics

Panel A: SRI Funds							
Year	*No. of funds*	*Growth*	*Size*	*Age*	*Expense Ratio*	*Loads*	*Turnover*
1992	4	35.02	331.70	13.50	1.09	2.38	0.27
1993	4	-5.78	310.02	14.50	1.11	1.19	0.43
1994	8	-1.86	161.45	11.13	1.20	1.03	0.44
1995	11	7.54	194.37	10.45	1.43	1.58	0.46
1996	12	2.03	200.66	10.92	1.43	1.47	0.60
1997	21	17.46	166.88	7.90	1.44	1.08	0.76
1998	24	21.19	230.42	8.38	1.39	0.94	0.72
1999	26	30.97	327.74	9.27	1.40	1.06	0.69
2000	31	21.14	302.82	9.13	1.43	1.27	0.64
2001	33	16.07	269.29	9.39	1.37	1.41	0.64
2002	35	11.06	248.05	10.09	1.49	1.52	0.67
2003	39	16.11	362.67	10.56	1.45	1.83	0.70
2004	42	22.76	440.99	11.02	1.44	2.11	0.71
Total	290	17.40	295.11	9.92	1.41	1.48	0.66
Panel B: Conventional Funds							
Year	*No. of funds*	*Growth*	*Size*	*Age*	*Expense Ratio*	*Loads*	*Turnover*
1992	386	25.49	810.69	21.79	1.19	3.44	0.65
1993	404	21.55	1022.38	22.72	1.18	3.25	0.71
1994	736	11.16	733.43	17.08	1.26	2.51	0.76
1995	884	21.17	948.83	15.68	1.27	2.30	0.79
1996	1062	21.02	1153.37	14.82	1.25	2.15	0.82
1997	1180	24.84	1416.77	14.41	1.22	2.08	0.82
1998	1264	11.21	1697.14	14.48	1.22	2.02	0.87
1999	1376	9.11	2039.66	14.55	1.22	1.99	0.86
2000	1550	12.78	1752.69	13.89	1.24	1.98	0.91
2001	1659	13.72	1464.36	13.79	1.29	1.98	1.01
2002	1748	6.64	1093.29	14.15	1.33	1.95	0.95
2003	1789	13.90	1470.38	14.58	1.37	2.12	0.91
2004	1892	9.15	1625.11	14.73	1.38	2.36	0.88
Total	15930	13.82	1425.94	14.95	1.28	2.17	0.87

Notes: This table reports summary statistics for the SRI funds (Panel A) and for the conventional funds (Panel B) over the time period from 1992 to 2004. Year by year it presents the number of funds, average net-growth (in percentage), average size (in million US dollars), average age (in years), average expenses (percentage of assets invested), average loads (percentage total of all maximum front, deferred, and redemption fees), and average turnover (minimum of aggregate purchases of securities or aggregate sales of securities, divided by the average total net assets of the fund).

conventional fund market minus the internal growth over time. The average net-growth for the SRI funds with about 17 per cent per annum is slightly higher than for conventional funds with about 14 per cent per annum. The average SRI fund is smaller in size and younger than the average conventional fund. Furthermore, the average SRI fund has higher expense ratios than

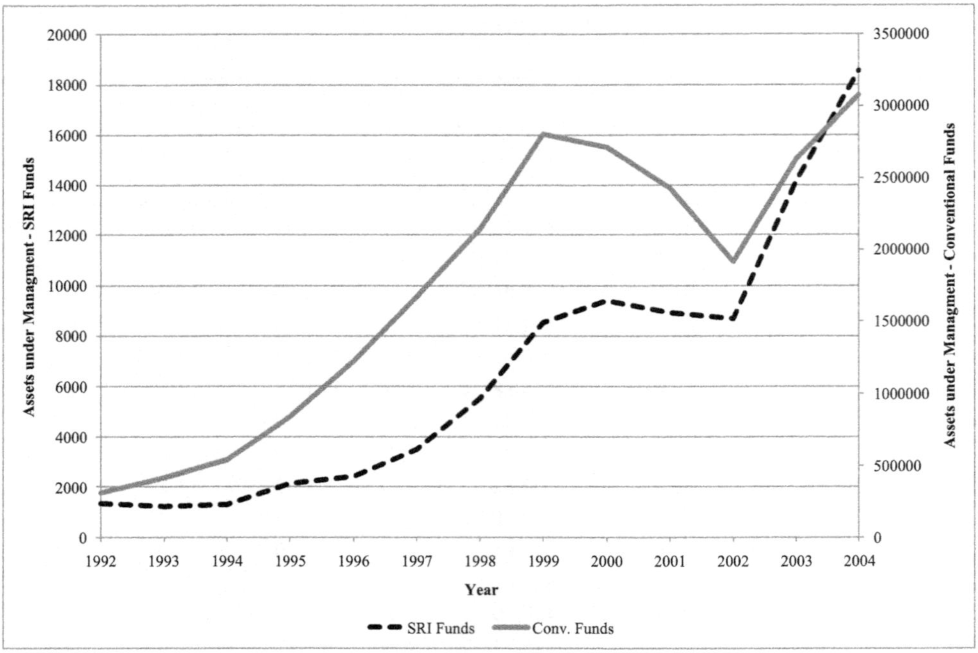

(a) Total Assets Under Management of SRI and Conventional Funds

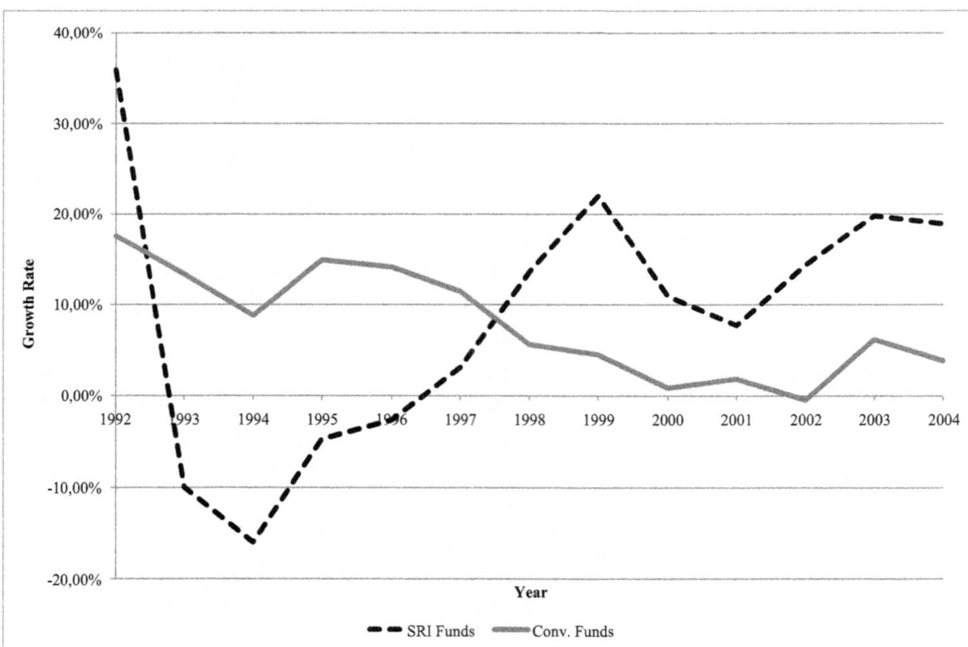

(b) Growth Rates of SRI and Conventional Funds

Figure 54.1 Development of the SRI mutual fund market

Notes: Panel (a) shows the development of the total assets under management (in million US dollars) for SRI funds and conventional funds over time. Panel (b) shows the development of the growth rates of SRI funds and conventional funds over time.

the average conventional fund, although the loads are lower. The lower turnover rate for the SRI funds indicates that they trade less than their conventional counterparts.

Model

To compare the performance sensitivity of SRI investors to the performance sensitivity of conventional investors, I investigate how past fund performance influences the net-inflows in SRI and conventional funds. In the literature ordinal performance measures (ranks) are often used instead of cardinal measures to analyze the impact of performance on net-inflows.[13] Studies comparing ordinal and cardinal measures have shown that ordinal measures explain fund flows much better than cardinal measures (see Patel et al., 1994, and Navone, 2003). The survey studies of Capon et al. (1994) and Capon et al. (1996) confirm this result. Therefore, I calculate performance ranks, $PerfRank_{i,t}$, within segments based on raw returns. The procedure to construct the performance ranks is similar to the one used by Sirri and Tufano (1998). I sort the funds in every segment according to their realized returns. The segments I use are 'Socially Responsible', 'Small Company Growth', 'Other Aggressive Growth', 'Growth', 'Income', 'Growth and Income', 'Balanced', and 'Sector Funds'.[14] I then assign fractional ranks to the funds in each segment, which I normalize between zero and one. The fund with the highest return gets assigned rank one.

Previous studies document a convex relationship between the fund flows and performance.[15] To study the convex relation, I adopt the approach of Sirri and Tufano (1998) and employ a piecewise linear regression. I estimate three slope coefficients based on the fractional performance ranks: one for the bottom quintile, one for the three middle quintiles, and one for the top quintile. I estimate the complete model using a pooled regression with White's (1980) correction for heteroscedasticity. It reads:[16]

$$\begin{aligned} FLOW_{i,t} &= \alpha_1 Low_{i,t-1} + \alpha_2 Mid_{i,t-1} + \alpha_3 Top_{i,t-1} \\ &+ \alpha_4 SR_{i,t-1} Low_{i,t-1} + \alpha_5 SR_{i,t-1} Mid_{i,t-1} + \alpha_6 SR_{i,t-1} Top_{i,t-1} \\ &+ \alpha_7 FLOW_{i,t-1} + \alpha_8 SR_{i,t-1} FLOW_{i,t-1} \\ &+ \sum_{j=1}^{6} \beta_j v^j_{i,t-1} + \sum_{k=1}^{96} \zeta_k TS_k + \varepsilon_{i,t}, \end{aligned} \tag{2}$$

where:

$$\begin{aligned} Low_{i,t-1} &= \min\left(PerfRank_{i,t-1}, 0.2\right) \\ Mid_{i,t-1} &= \min\left(PerfRank_{i,t-1} - Low_{i,t-1}, 0.6\right) \\ Top_{i,t-1} &= PerfRank_{i,t-1} - \left(Low_{i,t-1} + Mid_{i,t-1}\right). \end{aligned}$$

The dependent variable, $FLOW_{i,t}$, reflects the net-growth of a fund i in year t, as described in Model 2. I use an annual frequency to examine the determinants of fund flows. I include all independent variables as lagged variables, because investors can only base their investment decision on the information available at the beginning of the year.

The fractional performance ranks, $PerfRank_{i,t-1}$, are decomposed into three groupings: $Low_{i,t-1}$, $Mid_{i,t-1}$, and $Top_{i,t-1}$. The coefficients on these three groupings represent the slope of the performance flow relationship in the respective quintile(s). To study potential differences regarding performance between SRI and conventional funds, I interact the performance variables with the

$SR_{i,t-1}$ dummy. $SR_{i,t-1}$ takes on the value one for a SRI fund and zero for a conventional fund. For example, the coefficient α_6 is the additional increase in fund flows for the top performing SRI funds, compared to the estimated slope coefficient α_3 for the conventional funds.

I also control for the net-inflows of the fund in the previous year, $FLOW_{i,t-1}$. Sirri and Tufano (1998) and Zeckhauser et al. (1991) find a positive impact of the previous fund flows on the subsequent fund flows. One reason for the positive autocorrelation in flows could be that I do not control for specific fund characteristics which have an influence on flows and are constant over time. Another reason might be that investors suffer from a status-quo bias. This bias predicts that investors repeatedly facing the same investment situation tend to decide in favour of the same alternative regardless of whether this decision is optimal because of changed conditions. This behaviour leads to positive autocorrelation in flows.[17] For SRI funds one may expect an even higher positive autocorrelation in flows because of search costs. SRI investors have to put more time and effort into finding the SRI fund which suits to their personal values, and thus are likely to reinvest in this fund when facing future investment decisions. For this reason I interact the past net-inflows with the $SR_{i,t-1}$ dummy.

$v^j_{i,t-1}$ is a vector consisting of the following control variables: *risk* ($Risk_{i,t-1}$), *size* ($Size_{i,t-1}$), *age* ($Age_{i,t-1}$), *total loads* ($Loads_{i,t-1}$), *expense ratio* ($ExpRatio_{i,t-1}$), and *turnover ratio* ($Turnover_{i,t-1}$). Previous studies have shown an impact of these variables on fund flows. I control for the risk of a fund, $Risk_{i,t-1}$, measured by the annualized standard deviation of the monthly returns. Barber et al. (2005), Ippolito (1992), and Sirri and Tufano (1998) find a marginal negative impact of risk on fund flows.

Chevalier and Ellison (1997) and Sirri and Tufano (1998) find a negative impact of fund size, $Size_{i,t-1}$, on fund flows. I include the logarithm of the size of a fund, because large funds are likely to grow slower than small funds. This approach is in line with the literature.

Furthermore, I control for the age of a fund, $Age_{i,t-1}$. Consistent with the literature I consider the logarithm of age. Bergstresser and Poterba (2002) and Guercio and Tkac (2002) identify a negative impact of age on fund flows.

The fees of a fund are a further factor which influences the fund flows. Sirri and Tufano (1998) assume a holding period of seven years for a fund and take the sum of the expense ratio plus one seventh of the total loads. They find a negative influence for this constructed fee measure on fund flows. Bergstresser and Poterba (2002) and Ruenzi (2005) consider separately the expense ratio and the total loads of a fund. They report a negative impact for the expense ratio and a positive impact for the total loads. This could be due to the fact that loads are often used for marketing efforts, but expenses negatively affect performance. I follow their approach and control for the total loads, $Loads_{i,t-1}$, and the expense ratio, $ExpRatio_{i,t-1}$.

To investigate whether investors mind how much a fund trades, I include the turnover, $Turnover_{i,t-1}$. While Bergstresser and Poterba (2002) document no significant influence of the turnover on fund flow, Kempf and Ruenzi (2006) find a positive influence.

Finally, I include time-segment interaction dummies as done by Guercio and Tkac (2002) – one for each combination of year and segment. The time component captures differing average flows over the sample years. The segment component captures differing demands across the segments. Thus, the combination of these components adjusts for both potential effects, differing demand over segments and over time. Table 54.1 shows that the growth of SRI mutual funds differs from the growth of conventional mutual funds over time.

In addition to the piecewise linear regression as described in Model 2, I also implement an alternative model to consider the convex relationship between the fund flows and performance. I apply the approach of Barber et al. (2005) and estimate a quadratic relationship between the performance ranks and fund flows by adding a linear term and a quadratic term for the performance ranks as explanatory variables. This alternative model reads:

$$
\begin{aligned}
FLOW_{i,t} &= \alpha_1 PerfRank_{i,t-1} + \alpha_2 PerfRank^2_{i,t-1} \\
&+ \alpha_3 SR_{i,t-1} PerfRank_{i,t-1} + \alpha_4 SR_{i,t-1} PerfRank^2_{i,t-1} \\
&+ \alpha_5 FLOW_{i,t-1} + \alpha_6 SR_{i,t-1} FLOW_{i,t-1} \\
&+ \sum_{j=1}^{6} \beta_j v^j_{i,t-1} + \sum_{k=1}^{96} \zeta_k TS_k + \varepsilon_{i,t}.
\end{aligned} \tag{3}
$$

The performance flow relationship is convex if the coefficient of the squared performance rank is positive.

Empirical results

In a first step I study whether the performance sensitivity of SRI investors differs from conventional investors and whether it changes over time (see section "investor behaviour regarding performance"). I subequently investigate whether SRI investors care about the actual ethical standards of the SRI funds (see section "investor behaviour regarding ethical standards").

Investor behaviour regarding performance

To compare the reaction regarding past performance of SRI investors to that of conventional investors, I estimate Models 2 and 3 using a pooled regression with White's (1980) correction for heteroscedasticity. The results are reported in Table 54.2.

Table 54.2 Impact of the performance on net-inflows

$Low_{i,t-1}$	0.3080***	
$Mid_{i,t-1}$	0.4186***	
$Top_{i,t-1}$	1.6786***	
$SR_{i,t-1}Low_{i,t-1}$	–0.3658	
$SR_{i,t-1}Mid_{i,t-1}$	–0.1180	
$SR_{i,t-1}Top_{i,t-1}$	0.8088	
$PerfRank_{i,t-1}$		0.0069
$PerfRank^2_{i,t-1}$		0.5314***
$SR_{i,t-1}PerfRank_{i,t-1}$		–0.5721**
$SR_{i,t-1}PerfRank^2_{i,t-1}$		0.5445
$FLOW_{i,t-1}$	0.1471***	0.1500***
$SR_{i,t-1}FLOW_{i,t-1}$	0.1834***	0.1955***
$Risk_{i,t-1}$	–0.0381	–0.0617
$Size_{i,t-1}$	–0.0435***	–0.0436***
$Age_{i,t-1}$	–0.0582***	–0.0578***
$Loads_{i,t-1}$	1.3776***	1.3777***
$ExpRatio_{i,t-1}$	–2.9725**	–2.9881**
$Turnover_{i,t-1}$	0.0168	0.0172
Adj. R^2	13.30%	13.16%

Notes: Estimation results are based on Model 2 (Column 1) and 2 (Column 2). The dependent variable, $FLOW_{i,t}$, reflects the percentage growth of fund *i* minus the internal growth in year *t*. The explanatory variables are contained in Column 1. The last line contains the adjusted R^2. The total number of observations is 15,732; 15,447 observations apply to the conventional funds and 285 observations apply to the SRI funds. ***, **, and * indicate significance at the 1, 5, and 10 per cent levels, respectively.

I find that all estimated slope coefficients are significantly positive in Column 2 for the conventional funds. The slope coefficient of the top performance quintile is about four times as large as the slope coefficient of the three middle quintiles and even larger in comparison to the slope coefficient of the low quintile. Thus, the conventional investors respond differently to high and low performance. They disproportionately invest in the last year's top performing funds, but they do not punish poor performing funds to the same extent. The results confirm the earlier finding in the literature (see, for example, Chevalier and Ellison, 1997, and Sirri and Tufano, 1998) that the performance flow relationship is asymmetric and convex. Goetzmann and Peles (1997) explain the absence of significant outflows of the poor performing funds by cognitive dissonance. Investors stick to the poor performing funds, because otherwise they would have to admit to themselves that they came to the wrong investment decision before.

I find a similar result for the SRI investors. They also disproportionately chase past top performing funds. All slope coefficients for the SRI funds do not significantly differ from the slope coefficients for the conventional funds.[18] Each estimated slope coefficient for the SRI funds is composed of that for the conventional funds plus the estimated additional impact for the SRI funds. For example, the estimated slope coefficient in the top performing quintile for the SRI funds is about 2.49. An increase of 10 percentiles in the top performing quintile for the SRI funds, for example, from 0.85 to 0.95, boosts asset growth by about 25 per cent per annum, all else equal. The result that SRI investors chase past top performing funds is in line with the findings of Bollen (2007) and Renneboog et al. (2006). The estimated performance flow relationship of Model 2 can be seen graphically in Figure 54.2. This figure presents the convexity of the performance flow relationship for the conventional and SRI funds.

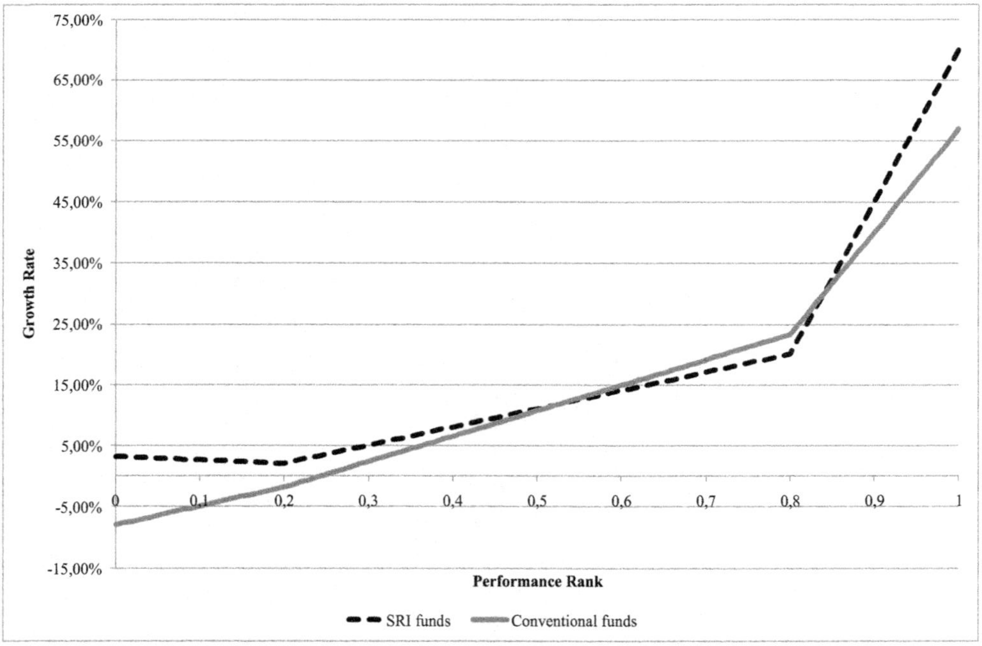

Figure 54.2 Performance flow relationship

Notes: The figure presents the performance flow relationship for SRI funds and conventional funds. It is based on the estimated slope coefficients from Model 2 for the time period from 1993 to 2004.

The results concerning the performance flow relationship in Column 3 support the finding that the relation is convex for the conventional funds. The relation for the SRI funds is also convex. The significantly lower coefficient of the linear SRI performance term in conjunction with the not significant higher quadratic term indicates that SRI investors invest slightly more in low performing funds, but still disproportionately invest more in top performing funds. Overall, the results of Columns 2 and 3 suggest that SRI investors chase past top performing funds the same way conventional investors do.

For the further determinants of the net-inflows into mutual funds, I find similar results for both models. Therefore, I describe in the following only the results of Column 2. The estimated coefficient of the lagged flow, $FLOW_{i,t-1}$, is positive and significant. This finding is consistent with the status-quo bias behaviour of mutual fund investors. Previous studies such as Gruber (1996), Patel et al. (1994), and Fant and O'Neal (2000) also document a strong positive impact of the lagged flow on the subsequent flow; the additional impact for the SRI funds is significantly higher. The total impact for the conventional funds is only about 15 per cent per annum, whereas that of the SRI funds is about 33 per cent per annum, all else equal. The high positive significant coefficient on the lagged flows for SRI funds is in line with my conjecture that SRI investors face higher search costs than conventional investors. SRI investors have to put more time and effort in identifying the SRI funds which fit their personal values and then are more likely to reinvest in those funds in the future.

The relation between the control variables and net-inflows of mutual funds is in line with previous findings in the literature. The *fund risk*, measured by the standard deviation of monthly returns, has no significant impact on net-inflows. Investors seem not to care about the risk of the funds. The coefficient of the *size* and *age* of a fund is significantly negative. This result indicates that large (old) mutual funds receive less inflow than smaller (younger) mutual funds. While the total loads have a significant and positive impact on subsequent net-inflows, the *expense ratio* has significant and negative impact on subsequent net-inflows. The estimated coefficient on the fund *turnover* indicates whether investors care about the trading activity of the funds. I find no significant impact for the funds. The adjusted R^2 for Model 2 is 13.30 per cent and 13.16 per cent for Model 3. The time-segment interaction dummies not reported in the table are mostly significant.

To examine whether the performance sensitivity of SRI investors depends on the development of the SRI fund market, I split the sample into a first sub-period from 1993 to 1998 and a second sub-period from 1999 to 2004. Table 54.3 summarizes the estimates of Model 2 and Model 3 sub-samples. The performance flow relationship of the conventional funds is positive and convex in both sub-periods. In contrast to this finding, the performance flow relationship for the SRI funds changes over time. While in the first sub-period the performance flow relationship for the SRI funds is not so pronounced, the relationship in the second sub-period is even more convex than for conventional funds. The additional impact in the first sub-period is significantly negative for the middle and top quintiles. In the second sub-period the estimated SRI coefficient on the top quintile is significantly positive. The results for the quadratic specification of the performance rank are similar. Overall, SRI investors chase top performing funds to a larger extent in the sub-period from 1999 to 2004 than from 1993 to 1998. This result is consistent with the hypothesis that along with the fast-growing SRI market, the performance sensitivity increased. This can be attributed to the fact that with an increasing number of SRI funds the number of alternatives grew and thus SRI investors became more performance sensitive over the years. Another explanation for this finding is that SRI early adopters cared less about performance than the mainstream SRI investors today. The SRI early adopters may have derived more utility from the social and environmental aspects of their funds. Since the SRI market has grown from a tiny niche to a respectable market segment, SRI investors nowadays seem to chase past top performing funds

Table 54.3 Impact of the performance on net-inflows for sub-samples

	1993–1998		1999–2004	
$Low_{i,t-1}$	0.4234***		0.2110	
$Mid_{i,t-1}$	0.5182***		0.3620***	
$Top_{i,t-1}$	2.1187***		1.4303***	
$SR_{i,t-1}Low_{i,t-1}$	0.1719		–0.5250	
$SR_{i,t-1}Mid_{i,t-1}$	–0.3884***		–0.0222	
$SR_{i,t-1}Top_{i,t-1}$	-1.0453*		2.0008*	
$PerfRank_{i,t-1}$		0.0107		–0.0094
$PerfRank^2_{i,t-1}$		0.6667***		0.4661***
$SR_{i,t-1}PerfRank_{i,t-1}$		0.1686		–0.9383**
$SR_{i,t-1}PerfRank^2_{i,t-1}$		–0.5364*		1.0836**
$FLOW_{i,t-1}$	0.1429***	0.1457***	0.1494***	0.1521***
$SR_{i,t-1}FLOW_{i,t-1}$	0.1600**	0.1597**	0.1377	0.1611*
$Risk_{i,t-1}$	0.4120	0.4708	–0.3242	–0.3446
$Size_{i,t-1}$	–0.0484***	–0.0484***	–0.0415***	–0.0416***
$Age_{i,t-1}$	–0.0537***	–0.0525***	–0.0613***	–0.0612***
$Loads_{i,t-1}$	1.7748***	1.7778***	1.1142***	1.1107***
$ExpRatio_{i,t-1}$	-5.2642***	-5.0941***	-2.0001	-2.0379
$Turnover_{i,t-1}$	0.0045	0.0047	0.0240	0.0244
Adj. R^2	16.36%	16.14%	11.60%	11.50%

Notes: Estimation results are based on Model 2 and 3 for two sub-periods: 1993–1998 (Columns 2–3) and 1999–2004 (Columns 4–5). The dependent variable, $FLOW_{i,t}$, reflects the percentage growth of fund *i* minus the internal growth in year *t*. The explanatory variables are contained in Column 1. The last line contains the adjusted R^2. The total number of observations is 5,552 (10,180) for the period 1993–1998 (1999–2004); 5,473 (9,974) observations apply to the conventional funds and 79 (206) observations apply to the SRI funds. ***, **, and * indicate significance at the 1, 5, and 10 per cent levels, respectively.

even more than conventional investors. This finding may result from mainstream SRI investors being more alert to an inferior performance due to ethical investment restrictions and thus trying to counteract it by the selection of top performers. SRI fund managers have to perform well to attract additional inflows.

The autocorrelation in fund flows remains significantly positive for the conventional funds in both sub-periods. As for the whole sample, the SRI funds exhibit an even stronger autocorrelation in flows in both sub-periods indicating that SRI investors have higher search costs and therefore reinvest more in the same funds. Only for the piecewise linear specification in the second sub-period (Column 4) is the estimate marginally not significant. The results regarding the control variables remain qualitatively unchanged. Only for the second sub-period do I find that the influence of the expense ratios on flows is no longer significantly negative. Today, investors seem to care less about the expenses of their funds.

Investor behaviour regarding ethical standards

To investigate whether SRI investors care about the actual ethical standards of the SRI funds, I augment Models 2 and 3 by including the positive rating, $Pos_{i,t-1}$, and the negative rating, $Neg_{i,t-1}$. The construction of these ratings is described in the data section. Table 54.4 reports the results of the extended models.

Table 54.4 Impact of the positive and negative rating on net-inflows

$Low_{i,t-1}$	0.2993***	
$Mid_{i,t-1}$	0.4190***	
$Top_{i,t-1}$	1.6893***	
$SR_{i,t-1}Low_{i,t-1}$	–0.4637	
$SR_{i,t-1}Mid_{i,t-1}$	–0.1023	
$SR_{i,t-1}Top_{i,t-1}$	0.8471	
$PerfRank_{i,t-1}$		–0.0008
$PerfRank^2_{i,t-1}$		0.5396***
$SR_{i,t-1}PerfRank_{i,t-1}$		–0.6225**
$SR_{i,t-1}PerfRank^2_{i,t-1}$		0.6003*
$Pos_{i,t-1}$	0.0240	0.0248
$Neg_{i,t-1}$	–0.0208	–0.0188
$SR_{i,t-1}Pos_{i,t-1}$	0.1997**	0.2004**
$SR_{i,t-1}Neg_{i,t-1}$	–0.0752	–0.0859
$FLOW_{i,t-1}$	0.1469***	0.1498***
$SR_{i,t-1}FLOW_{i,t-1}$	0.1779***	0.1902***
$Risk_{i,t-1}$	–0.0412	–0.0692
$Size_{i,t-1}$	–0.0436***	–0.0437***
$Age_{i,t-1}$	–0.0583***	–0.0578***
$Loads_{i,t-1}$	1.3703***	1.3714***
$ExpRatio_{i,t-1}$	–2.9068**	–2.9258**
$Turnover_{i,t-1}$	0.0170	0.0175
Adj. R^2	13.31%	13.16%

Notes: Estimation results are based on Model 2 (Column 2) and 3 (Column 3) extended by the positive rating and the negative rating as additional explanatory variables. The dependent variable, $FLOW_{i,t}$ reflects the percentage growth of fund *i* minus the internal growth in year *t*. The explanatory variables are contained in Column 1. The last line contains the adjusted R^2. The total number of observations is 15,732; 15,447 observations apply to the conventional funds and 285 observations apply to the SRI funds. ***, **, and * indicate significance at the 1, 5, and 10 per cent levels, respectively.

I find neither any significant impact of the positive rating nor of the negative rating for the conventional funds in both models. As expected, conventional investors seem not to care about the ethical standards of their funds. However, I find evidence that, consistent with my conjecture, SRI investors care about the ethical standards; that is, how the SRI funds actually invest. The coefficient of the positive rating is significantly positive. An increase from the lowest rank to the highest rank regarding the positive rating is associated with an increase in net-inflows from about 23 per cent per annum, all else equal. In contrast to the positive rating, the negative rating has no significant effect on the inflows of SRI funds. The negative screening approach seems not to be popular among SRI investors. Overall, these findings suggest that SRI investors prefer funds with high ethical standards regarding the positive rating and that they do look behind the label 'SRI fund'.

The performance flow relationship is similar to the one reported in Table 54.2 earlier. For the quadratic performance term in Column 3 I now find a marginally significant positive impact, suggesting that SRI investors react even more strongly to top performing funds. However, the result is not confirmed by the piecewise linear specification (Column 2). The estimates of the lagged flow and the control variables remain qualitatively unchanged.

Table 54.5 Impact of the positive and negative rating on net-inflows for sub-samples

	1993–1998		*1999–2004*	
$Low_{i,t-1}$	0.4167***		0.2055	
$Mid_{i,t-1}$	0.5167***		0.3633***	
$Top_{i,t-1}$	2.1259***		1.4395***	
$SR_{i,t-1}Low_{i,t-1}$	0.5419		–0.9916**	
$SR_{i,t-1}Mid_{i,t-1}$	–0.4205***		0.0273	
$SR_{i,t-1}Top_{i,t-1}$	–1.1474**		2.1072*	
$PerfRank_{i,t-1}$		0.0049		–0.0146
$PerfRank^2_{i,t-1}$		0.6714***		0.4728***
$SR_{i,t-1}PerfRank_{i,t-1}$		0.3593		–1.1626***
$SR_{i,t-1}PerfRank^2_{i,t-1}$		–0.7186**		1.3069***
$Pos_{i,t-1}$	0.0116	0.0122	0.0186	0.0192
$Neg_{i,t-1}$	–0.0198	–0.0164	–0.0129	–0.0117
$SR_{i,t-1}Pos_{i,t-1}$	0.1685*	0.1505	0.2971**	0.3014**
$SR_{i,t-1}Neg_{i,t-1}$	0.0047	0.0034	–0.1278	–0.1404
$FLOW_{i,t-1}$	0.1427***	0.1456***	0.1492***	0.1520***
$SR_{i,t-1}FLOW_{i,t-1}$	0.1413**	0.1402**	0.1388	0.1611*
$Risk_{i,t-1}$	0.4118	0.4631	–0.3273	–0.3502
$Size_{i,t-1}$	–0.0484***	–0.0485***	–0.0416***	–0.0417***
$Age_{i,t-1}$	–0.0539***	–0.0526***	–0.0614***	–0.0613***
$Loads_{i,t-1}$	1.7667***	1.7715***	1.1082***	1.1048***
$ExpRatio_{i,t-1}$	–5.1578***	–5.0012**	–1.9496	–1.9870
$Turnover_{i,t-1}$	0.0045	0.0048	0.0243	0.0247
Adj. R^2	16.31%	16.09%	11.61%	11.51%

Notes: Estimation results are based on Model 2 and 3 extended by the positive rating and the negative rating as additional explanatory variables for two sub-periods: 1993–1998 (Columns 2–3) and 1999–2004 (Columns 4–5). The dependent variable, $FLOW_{i,t}$, reflects the percentage growth of fund *i* minus the internal growth in year *t*. The explanatory variables are contained in Column 1. The last line contains the adjusted R^2. The total number of observations is 5,552 (10,180) for the period 1993–1998 (1999–2004); 5,473 (9,974) observations apply to the conventional funds and 79 (206) observations apply to the SRI funds. ***, **, and * indicate significance at the 1, 5, and 10 per cent levels, respectively.

To examine whether the investment behaviour of SRI investors regarding the ethical standards has changed over time, I split the sample as before into a first sub-period from 1993 to 1998 and a second sub-period from 1999 to 2004. Table 54.5 summarizes the results.

I find no significant relation between fund flows and the positive and negative rating for the conventional funds in both sub-periods. In the first sub-period the estimates of the additional impact on SRI funds of the positive rating are marginally significant in Column 2, but not in Column 3. Therefore, I find only weak evidence that SRI investors care about the positive rating in the first sub-period. However, in second sub-period I find that SRI investors care about the positive rating – the estimates are significant and almost double compared to the first sub-period. For the negative rating I find no significant influence on the flows, as for the whole sample period. Overall, today's SRI investors seem to care more about the actual ethical standards of their funds. The performance flow relationship remains similar to that of Table 54.3. Only the estimate on the additional impact for the low performance quintile is now significantly negative, indicating that SRI funds with a low performance get inflows. This could be because some SRI investors do not find any alternatives for these funds. The estimates of the lagged flows and the control variables remain qualitatively unchanged.

The positive and negative rating studied earlier consist of several criteria. To investigate whether the single criteria have an influence on fund net-inflows, I replace the positive rating with the ethical rankings of the criteria – community, diversity, employee relations, human rights, and product. The negative rating is replaced with ethical rankings of the criteria alcohol, gambling, military, nuclear, and tobacco. Table 54.6 reports the results.

Table 54.6 Impact of single qualitative and exclusionary criteria on net-inflows

$Low_{i,t-1}$	0.2879**	
$Mid_{i,t-1}$	0.4179***	
$Top_{i,t-1}$	1.7065***	
$SR_{i,t-1}Low_{i,t-1}$	–0.3690	
$SR_{i,t-1}Mid_{i,t-1}$	–0.1354	
$SR_{i,t-1}Top_{i,t-1}$	0.6990	
$PerfRank_{i,t-1}$		–0.0124
$PerfRank^2_{i,t-1}$		0.5510***
$SR_{i,t-1}PerfRank_{i,t-1}$		–0.5944**
$SR_{i,t-1}PerfRank^2_{i,t-1}$		0.5383
$Community_{i,t-1}$	–0.0546	–0.0538
$Diversity_{i,t-1}$	0.0593	0.0582
$EmployeeRelations_{i,t-1}$	–0.0062	–0.0054
$Environment_{i,t-1}$	–0.0132	–0.0117
$HumanRights_{i,t-1}$	–0.0237	–0.0263
$Product_{i,t-1}$	–0.0315	–0.0308
$Alcohol_{i,t-1}$	–0.0037	–0.0056
$Gambling_{i,t-1}$	–0.0229	–0.0205
$Military_{i,t-1}$	–0.0077	–0.0049
$Nuclear_{i,t-1}$	0.0415	0.0411
$Tobacco_{i,t-1}$	–0.0420	–0.0412
$SR_{i,t-1}Community_{i,t-1}$	0.0453	0.0351
$SR_{i,t-1}Diversity_{i,t-1}$	0.1774	0.1745
$SR_{i,t-1}EmployeeRelations_{i,t-1}$	–0.0855	–0.0827
$SR_{i,t-1}Environment_{i,t-1}$	0.3201***	0.3256***
$SR_{i,t-1}HumanRights_{i,t-1}$	0.0854	0.0961
$SR_{i,t-1}Product_{i,t-1}$	0.0480	0.0311
$SR_{i,t-1}Alcohol_{i,t-1}$	0.1499	0.1422
$SR_{i,t-1}Gambling_{i,t-1}$	–0.1411	–0.1714
$SR_{i,t-1}Military_{i,t-1}$	–0.1175	–0.1271
$SR_{i,t-1}Nuclear_{i,t-1}$	–0.0563	–0.0601
$SR_{i,t-1}Tobacco_{i,t-1}$	0.0157	0.0542
Adj. R^2	13.32%	13.17%

Notes: Estimation results are based on Model 2 (Column 2) and 3 (Column 3) extended by single qualitative and exclusionary criteria as additional explanatory variables. The dependent variable, $FLOW_{i,t}$, reflects the percentage growth of fund *i* minus the internal growth in year *t*. The explanatory variables are contained in Column 1. The last line contains the adjusted R^2. The total number of observations is 15,732; 15,447 observations apply to the conventional funds and 285 observations apply to the SRI funds. ***, **, and * indicate significance at the 1, 5, and 10 per cent levels, respectively.

There exists no significant influence of a single criterion on flows for the conventional funds. The flows of SRI funds are also not significantly influenced by most single criteria. However, the criterion environment has a significantly positive impact on flows in both models. SRI investors prefer to buy funds with high actual environmental standards. The interest in environmental issues such as global warming or efficient use of energy is probably aroused by the frequent reports in the public press. The performance flow relationship is similar to the one reported before. SRI investors chase past winners. The estimates for the lagged flow and control variables are not reported in Table 54.6. The results remain qualitatively unchanged.

Conclusion

By definition SRI investors pursue not only financial goals, but non-financial goals as well. In this paper I compare the performance sensitivity of SRI investors' investment decisions to that of conventional investors' investment decisions. In addition to the performance sensitivity I analyze whether SRI investors consider the actual ethical standards of their investments. To explore these issues, I investigate the flows into SRI and conventional mutual funds. My sample consists of US equity mutual funds in the period from 1993 to 2004.

I find that along with the fast development of the SRI fund market the performance sensitivity among SRI investors increased. While SRI investors in the early stages of the market cared less about performance, they today chase past top performing funds. This result is in line with the conjecture that SRI investors today have more alternatives in the segment of SRI funds because of the increasing number and thus choose the funds with a top performance among the alternatives. The finding is also consistent with the assumption that in the beginning SRI pioneers dominated the market and cared less about performance than the mainstream SRI investors today. Furthermore, I am the first to analyze whether SRI investors care about the actual ethical standards of their mutual funds. To measure the ethical standards of a fund, I combine the portfolio holdings information with ethical stock ratings data. I find that SRI investors, in contrast to conventional investors, care about the actual ethical standards regarding the positive rating and especially about the criterion environment; they do not just care about the label 'SRI fund'. The frequent reports about environmental issues in the public press may lead to the consideration of environmental standards when facing an investment situation. Along with the development of the SRI market, the sensitivity to the ethical standards regarding the positive rating has increased over time. In addition to these results I find evidence that SRI investors have higher search costs than conventional investors when selecting a fund and thus are more likely to reinvest in the same funds in the future. SRI investors have to identify not only a fund fitting their financial goals, but also their personal values.

Overall, my findings suggest that SRI investors are different from conventional investors. SRI investors today chase not only past top performing funds, but also care about the ethical standards of their investments. A line for future research may be to study how different characteristics and attitudes of SRI investors affect their investment decisions.

Notes

1 I wish to thank Knut Griese, Alexander Kempf, Christoph Memmel, Alexander Pütz, and Stefan Ruenzi for helpful comments on this paper. This work has been conducted during my time as research assistant at the University of Cologne. An earlier version has been published in Osthoff (2008), PhD.

2 See Social Investment Forum (2008).

3 See, for example, Hamilton et al. (1993), Mallin et al. (1995), Gregory et al. (1997), Sauer (1997), Statman (2000), Bauer et al. (2005), Bauer et al. (2006), Bello (2005), Kreander et al. (2005), Gregory and

Whittaker (2007), and Kempf and Osthoff (2008). Schroeder (2007) studies the performance of indices and finds no significant difference between SRI and conventional indices. Derwall et al. (2005) and Kempf and Osthoff (2007) study the performance of synthetic stock portfolios based on SRI ratings and even document an outperformance of these synthetic portfolios.

4 See, for example, Ippolito (1992), Chevalier and Ellison (1997), and Sirri and Tufano (1998).

5 See, for example, Beal et al. (2005).

6 Bollen (2007) examines the performance flow relationship of SRI mutual funds in the US. Renneboog et al. (2006) investigate the determinants of SRI mutual fund flows around the world. Louche and Lydenberg (2006) and Scholtens and Dam (2007) point out that there exist cultural differences concerning social responsibility.

7 For more detailed information about the KLD Stats database and the criteria used, see online, available HTTP: <http://www.kld.com/research/stats/indicators.html.>.

8 KLD also provides a criterion "Corporate Governance" which is not used in this study. This criterion differs in many respects from the corporate governance issues used by Gompers et al. (2003) for their corporate governance index.

9 For further details of the matching procedure, please see Gaspar et al. (2006).

10 In unreported results I confirm the finding of Kempf and Osthoff (2008).

11 Ber and Ruenzi (2007) show that the synthetic measure is a good approximation for actual fund flows.

12 Bergstresser and Poterba (2002) also exclude fund observations with a growth rate above 1,000 per cent.

13 Examples for studies using ordinal measures are: Patel et al. (1994), Sirri and Tufano (1998), Fant and O'Neal (2000), and Bergstresser et al. (2006). Studies using cardinal measures are, for example, Ippolito (1992) and Lynch and Musto (2003).

14 CRSP does not provide general investment objectives for the whole time period. Therefore, I use the classifications by Wiesenberger (OBJ), ICDI (ICDI_OBJ), and Strategic Insight (SI_OBJ) to obtain uniform investment objectives. The procedure is similar to the one used by Pastor and Stambaugh (2002).

15 See, for example, Sirri and Tufano (1998), Chevalier and Ellison (1997), and Ippolito (1992).

16 Guercio and Tkac (2002) also use a pooled regression with White's (1980) correction for heteroscedasticity.

17 For a detailed description of the status-quo bias, see also Kempf and Ruenzi (2006).

18 I also investigated the performance flow relationship separately for the SRI funds. I find that the coefficients for the three middle quintiles and the top quintile are significantly positive; the coefficient on the low quintile is not significant.

References

Barber, B. M., Odean, T. and Zheng, L. (2005) 'Out of sight, out of mind: The effects of expenses on mutual fund flows', *Journal of Business* 78(6): 2095–2119. Online. Available doi:<10.1086/497042>.

Bauer, R., Koedijk, K. and Otten, R. (2005) 'International evidence on ethical mutual fund performance and investment style', *Journal of Banking and Finance* 29(7): 1751–1767. Online. Available doi:<10.1016/j.jbankfin.2004.06.035>.

Bauer, R., Otten, R. and Rad, A. (2006) 'Ethical investing in Australia: Is there a financial penalty?', *Pacific Basin Finance Journal* 14(1): 33–48. Online. Available doi:<10.1016/j.pacfin.2004.12.004>.

Beal, D. J., Goyen, M. and Phillips, P. (2005) 'Why do we invest ethically?', *Journal of Investing* 14(3): 66–77. Online. Available doi:<10.3905/joi.2005.580551>.

Bello, Z. Y. (2005) 'Socially responsible investing and portfolio diversification', *Journal of Financial Research* 28(1): 41–57. Online. Available doi:<10.1111/j.1475–6803.2005.00113.x>.

Ber, S. and Ruenzi, S. (2007) 'On the usability of synthetic mutual fund flow measures', Working Paper.

Bergstresser, D. B., Chalmers, J. M. and Tufano, P. (2006) 'Assessing the costs and benefits of brokers in the mutual fund industry', *Review of Financial Studies* 22(10): 4129–4156. Online. Available doi:<10.1093/rfs/hhp022>.

Bergstresser, D. B. and Poterba, J. (2002) 'Do after-tax returns affect mutual fund inflows?', *Journal of Financial Economics* 63(3): 381–414. Online. Available doi:<10.1016/S0304–405X(02)00066–1>.

Bollen, N.P.B. (2007) 'Mutual fund attributes and investor behavior', *Journal of Financial and Quantitative Analysis* 42(3): 683–708. Online. Available doi:<10.1017/S0022109000004142>.

Capon, N., Fitzsimons, G. J. and Prince, R. A. (1996) 'An individual level analysis of the mutual fund investment decision', *Journal of Financial Services Research* 10(1): 59–82. Online. Available doi:<10.1007/BF00120146>.

Capon, N., Fitzsimons, G. J. and Weingarten, R. (1994) 'Affluent investors and mutual fund purchases', *International Journal of Bank Marketing* 12(3): 17–25. Online. Available doi:<10.1108/02652329410055178>.

Chevalier, J. and Ellison, G. (1997) 'Risk taking by mutual funds as a response to incentives', *Journal of Political Economy* 105(6): 1167–1200. Online. Available doi:<10.1086/516389>.

Del Guercio, D. and Tkac, P. A. (2002) 'The determinants of the flow of funds of managed portfolios: Mutual funds versus pension funds', *Journal of Financial and Quantitiative Analysis* 37(4): 523–558. Online. Available doi:<10.2307/3595011>.

Derwall, J., Günster, N., Bauer, R. and Koedijk, K. (2005) 'The ecoefficiency premium puzzle', *Financial Analysts Journal* 61(2): 51–63. Online. Available doi:<10.2469/faj.v61.n2.2716>.

Fant, L. and O'Neal, E. S. (2000) 'Temporal changes in the determinants of mutual fund flows', *Journal of Financial Research* 23(3): 353–371.

Gaspar, J. M., Massa, M. and Matos, P. (2006) 'Favoritism in mutual fund families? Evidence on strategic cross-fund subsidization', *Journal of Finance* 61(1): 73–104. Online. Available doi:<10.1111/j.1540–6261.2006.00830.x>

Goetzmann, W. N. and Peles, N. (1997) 'Cognitive dissonance and mutual fund investors', *Journal of Financial Research* 20(2): 145–158.

Gompers, P., Ishii, J. and Metrick, A. (2003) 'Corporate governance and equity prices', *Quarterly Journal of Economics* 118(1): 107–155. Online. Available doi:<10.1162/00335530360535162>.

Gregory, A., Matatko, J. and Luther, R. (1997) 'Ethical unit trust financial performance: Small company effects and fund size effects', *Journal of Business Finance and Accounting* 24(5): 705–724. Online. Available doi:<10.1111/1468–5957.00130>.

Gregory, A. and Whittaker, J. (2007) 'Performance and performance persistence of ethical unit trusts in the UK', *Journal of Business Finance and Accounting* 34(7/8): 1327–1344. Online. Available doi:<10.1111/j.1468–5957.2007.02006.x>.

Gruber, M. J. (1996) 'Another puzzle: The growth in actively managed mutual funds', *The Journal of Finance* 51(3): 783–810.

Hamilton, S., Jo, H. and Statman, M. (1993) 'Doing well while doing good? The investment performance of socially responsible mutual funds', *Financial Analysts Journal* 49(6): 62–66. Online. Available doi:<10.2469/faj.v49.n6.62>.

Ippolito, R. A. (1992) 'Consumer reaction to measures of poor quality: Evidence from the mutual fund industry', *Journal of Law & Economics* 35(1): 45–70. Online. Available doi:<10.1086/467244>.

Kempf, A. and Osthoff, P. (2007) 'The effect of socially responsible investing on portfolio performance', *European Financial Management* 13(5): 908–922. Online. Available doi:<10.1111/j.1468–036X.2007.00402.x>.

Kempf, A. and Osthoff, P. (2008) 'SRI funds: Nomen est omen', *Journal of Business Finance and Accounting* 35(9/10): 1276–1294. Online. Available doi:<10.1111/j.1468–5957.2008.02107.x>.

Kempf, A. and Ruenzi, S. (2006) 'Status quo bias and the number of alternatives: An empirical illustration from the mutual fund industry', *Journal of Behavioral Finance* 7(4): 204–213. Online. Available doi:<10.1207/s15427579jpfm0704\3>.

Kreander, N., Gray, R., Power, D. and Sinclair, C. (2005) 'Evaluating the performance of ethical and non-ethical funds: A matched pair analysis', *Journal of Business Finance and Accounting* 32(7/8): 1465–1493. Online. Available doi:<10.1111/j.0306–686X.2005.00636.x>.

Louche, C. and Lydenberg, S. (2006) 'Socially responsible investment: Differences between Europe and the United States', Working Paper.

Lynch, A. W. and Musto, D. K. (2003) 'How investors interpret past fund returns', *Journal of Finance* 58(5): 2033–2058. Online. Available doi:<10.1111/1540–6261.00596>.

Mallin, C. A., Saadouni, B. and Briston, R. J. (1995) 'The financial performance of ethical investment funds', *Journal of Business Finance and Accounting* 22(4): 483–496. Online. Available doi:<10.1111/j.1468–5957.1995.tb00373.x>.

Navone, M. A. (2003) 'Mutual fund competition with misspecified investment objectives', Working Paper.

Osthoff, P. (2008) *Socially Responsible Investment*, PhD Dissertation, Berlin, Germany: Logos Verlag.

Pastor, L. and Stambaugh, R. F. (2002) 'Mutual fund performance and seemingly unrelated assets', *Journal of Financial Economics* 63(3): 315–349. Online. Available doi:<10.1016/S0304–405X(02)00064–8>.

Patel, J., Zeckhauser, R. J. and Hendricks, D. (1994) 'Investment flows and performance: Evidence from mutual funds, cross-border investments and new issues', in Sato, R., Levich, R. M. and Ramachandran, R. V. (eds.), *Japan, Europe and International Financial Markets: Analytical and Empirical Perspectives*, Cambridge, UK: Cambridge University Press, 51–72.

Renneboog, L., Ter Horst, J. and Zhang, C. (2006) 'Is ethical money financially smart?', Working Paper.

Ruenzi, S. (2005) 'Mutual fund growth in standard and specialist market segments', *Financial Market and Portfolio Management* 19(2): 153–167. Online. Available doi:<10.1007/s11408–005–3383–3>.

Sauer, D.A. (1997) 'The impact of social-responsibility screens on investment performance: Evidence from the Domini 400 Social Index and Domini Equity Mutual Fund', *Review of Financial Economics* 6(2): 137–149. Online. Available doi:<10.1016/S1058–3300(97)90002–1>.

Scholtens, B. and Dam, L. (2007) 'Cultural values and international differences in business ethics', *Journal of Business Ethics* 75(3): 273–284. Online. Available doi:<10.1007/s10551–006–9252–9>.

Schröder, M. (2007) 'Is there a difference? The performance characteristics of SRI equity indices', *Journal of Business Finance and Accounting* 34(1/2): 331–48. Online. Available doi:<10.1111/j.1468–5957.2006.00647.x>

Sirri, E. R. and Tufano, P. (1998) 'Costly search and mutual fund flows', *Journal of Finance* 53(5): 1589–1622. Online. Available doi:<10.1111/0022–1082.00066>.

Social Investment Forum (2008) *2007 Report on Socially Responsible Investing Trends in the United States*, SIF Industry Research Program, Executive Summary. Online. Available HTTP: <http://www.socialinvest.org/>.

Statman, M. (2000) 'Socially responsible mutual funds', *Financial Analysts Journal* 56(3): 30–39. Online. Available doi:<10.2469/faj.v56.n3.2358>.

Wermers, R. (2000) 'Mutual fund performance: An empirical decomposition into stock-picking talent, style, transactions costs, and expenses', *Journal of Finance* 55(4): 1655–1695. Online. Available doi:<10.1111/0022–1082.00263>.

White, H. (1980) 'A heteroskedastic-consistent covariance matrix estimator and a direct test of heteroskedasticity', *Econometrica* 48(4): 817–838. Online. Available doi:<10.2307/1912934>.

Zeckhauser, R., Patel, J. and Hendricks, D. (1991) 'Nonrational actors and financial market behavior', *Theory and Decision* 31(2): 257–287. Online. Available doi:<10.1007/BF00132995>.

Index

Note: *Italicized* page numbers indicate tables and figures.

Abe, Shinzo 217
aboriginal funds, Canada 74
Abu Dhabi Sustainability Group 458
Access Bank (Nigeria) 123
active ownership: Australia 153, 162; Denmark 319; government-sponsored investment funds (GSIFs) 444; Hong Kong 187–8, 195; Norway 349, 351; pension funds 566; responsible investment and 5, 436, 438, 441, 494–5, 503–4, 668
adaptive capacity 603
Aegon-Industrial Fund Management Co., Ltd. 169
Affinity Credit Union 76, 79
Africa, responsible investment 11, 116, 367
African Sustainable Investment Forum (AfricaSIF) 11, 107
Agency for Strategic Initiatives (Russia) 227
agent-centered hypothesis 450–1
Ageon 304–5
AktieAnsvar Aktiefond 314
alternative investments 22, 62
Altshuler Shaham 143
American International Assurance Trustee (AIA) 186
Amnesty Business Group 340
Amundi Asset Management 264, 271
Anbima 93
annual general meeting (Nigeria) 121
Aon Hewitt 521, 523
AP Funds (Sweden) 444, 447
APG 302
Arab Institute of Business Managers 134
Arbejdsmarkedets Tillægspensions (ATP) 318
Arese 266
Argentina: carbon emissions 89; impact investing 89; overview 417–18; responsible investment 89, 419–21
Arigato Asset Management 216
ARISTA 3.0 295–6
Arthur Andersen 625
Arvopaperimarkkinayhdistys 332
Asia: assets under management (AUM) 150; responsible investment 11, 56, 175; working conditions 162; *see also individual countries*
ASN Bank 303–4
Asset4 ESG-Thomson Reuters 627; Italy 248–9, *249*
asset managers: asset allocation 587; benchmarks 512–13; capital preservation 512; client guidance 511; corporate governance 600; delegation relationships 699–700; ESG integration 514–17; fiduciary obligations 510–11, 599–600; incentive contracts 692; integrated reporting 518; investment policies 515; investment strategies 511; long-term results 511–13; public authorities and 517–18; purpose of 510; religious investors 513–14; responsible investment 510–19; shareholding structure 511; social factors 558
asset owners: collaborative engagement 525–6; defined 437; delegation relationships 699–700; engagement 435–6, 442; investment consultants 520–1, 524–5; investment managers 440, 510; positive impact of 441; social factors 558; social responsibility 436–8; *see also* institutional investors
Assicurazioni Generali 245
Assiniboine Credit Union 76, 79
Association for Responsible Investment Services (ARISE) 293
Association for Savings and Investment South Africa (ASISA) 105
Association for Sustainable and Responsible Investment in Asia 175
Association Francaise de Gestion (AFG) 267
Association of Chartered Certified Accountants (ACCA) 361
Audit Analytics 571
Audit Integrity 566, 571
Australasian Centre for Corporate Responsibility 153

Australia: assets under management (AUM) 151; broad responsible investment 151; carbon emissions 156, 161; carbon pricing 155–6, 162; climate change 162; coal industry 161–2, 164; core responsible investment 150–1; demographics 150; environmental issues 153–62; ESG factors 162–3; extractive industries 164; fiduciary obligations 21; government regulation 155–60; institutional shareholder advocacy 153–4; market environment 151; non-governmental organizations (NGOs) 163; overview 149–50, 377; path dependence 55; policy environment 154; proxy voting 154; responsible investment 11, 53, 149–64, 368, 377–9, 584; shareholder advocacy 153–4; superannuation contributions 151–2, *152*, 153, 164
Australia Council of Superannuation Investors 159
Australian Carbon Credit Units 156
Australian Corporate Law Economic Reform Program (Audit Reform and Corporate Disclosure 158
Australian Corporations Act 158
Australian Council of Superannuation Investors 154
Australian Ethical Investment 150, 153
Australian Renewable Energy Agency 157
Australian Securities Exchange 158
Austria: banking 277–8; eco-label 278; government regulation 278; institutional investors 279; overview 276–7, 374–5; pension funds 279; responsible investment 276–8, *278*, 279, 375–7
Austrian Society for Environment and Technology (ÖGUT) 278
Avaron Asset Management 235
Avon letter 63, 566
AXA IM 511

Baltcap 235
Banco de España 259
Bank of Israel 140
Bank of Russia 228, 230
Bank Sarasin 511
Banque Centrale de Tunisie 131
Barclays Capital 531
Baring Private Equity Asia 191
Barrick Gold 496–7, 501–3
Bazacle mill company 696–8
BBVA Bancomer (Mexico) 82
B corporations 30
Belgian Asset Managers Association (BEAMA) 288, 292–3
Belgian Sustainable and Socially Responsible Investment Forum (BELSIF) 293
Belgium: accountability 295–6; asset classes 296; assets under management (AUM) 289; codes of conduct 292–3; consumer protection 293; disclosure law 292; institutional investors 291; market profile *290*; overview 287–8, 380; pension funds 292, 366; policy environment 292; political initiatives 296; prohibition laws 292; responsible investment 287–91, 293–5, *295*, 296, 298–9, 366–7, 380–1; responsible savings 287, 289–91, *291*; screening 294; undertakings for collective investments 289–90
BELSIF Matrix 294
best-in-class investing 667–9
Better Place (Palo Alto, Ca.) 597
big data, corporate behavior and 442
BlackRock 17, 20, 22, 511
Bloomberg 53, 620, 629
blue washing 371
BM&FBOVESPA 86–7, 89, 91, 93
BNP Paribas 290, 294
boards of directors 567–9
Bogle, John 527
Bolivia: overview 417–18; responsible investment 419–21
Bombay Stock Exchange 531
bond rating agencies 626–7
Botha, Theo 103
Botswana, responsible investment 367
BP Deepwater Horizon explosion 534, 557
Brazil: carbon emissions 89, 94; collaborative engagement 90–1; corporate governance 94; corporate governance indices 88; ESG factors 90; fixed-income funds 88; impact investing 89; overview 417–18; pension funds 90–1, 94; responsible investment 86–95, 419–21; RI legislation 92; shareholder advocacy 93; slave labour 90–1
Brazilian Association of Pension Funds 91
Brazilian Central Bank 92
Brazilian Institute of Corporate Governance 93
Brazilian National Monetary Council 92
Brazilian Securities and Exchange Commission 88
British Pensions Act (1995) 635
Broad-Based Black Economic Empowerment (BBBEE) 103
Brundtland Report (UN) 514, 545
bubble identification problem 693–4
Buenos Aires Stock Exchange 89, 91
Bulgaria, responsible investment 233
businesses: carbon footprints 616–17; customer loyalty 622; government regulation 622; sustainability reporting 620–1
Business Reporting Leaders Forum (Australia) 160

Caisse des Dépôts and Consignations 262, 264, 266
Caisses d'Epargne 266
Cajas de Ahorro 259
CalPers (California Public Employees' Retirement System) 22; Japanese companies 213; responsible investment 121, 444, 447; shareholder engagement 65; stakeholders and 28, 442

Calvert Group 478
Canada: assets under management (AUM) *73*; Community Loan Funds 77; corporate engagement 496–504; credit unions 72, 74–6, 79; equity markets 19; ESG rating agencies 75; extractive industries 78; fiduciary obligations 21; impact finance 79; impact investing 72–3; institutional finance 72; market capitalization 71, *71*; mutual retail funds 73; overview 70–1, 382; path dependence 55; pension funds 73–5; responsible investment 11, 19, 70–2, *72*, 73–9, 383–4, 584; socially responsible lending 72
Canadian Coalition for Good Governance 500
Canadian Securities Administrators (CSA) 74
Canadian Social Investment Organization 70, 72
Canadian Task Force on Social Finance 77, 79
capital: equitable access to 477; positive impact of 441; social impact of 474–5
capitalism 692
Carbon Development Mechanism (CDM) 89
Carbon Disclosure Project 5, 496
Carbon Efficient Index (ICO2) 89
carbon emissions: annual 615; Argentina 89; Australia 156, 161; Brazil 89, 94; South Africa 109, 111
Carbon Farming Initiative (Australia) 156
carbon footprinting techniques 616–17
carbon pricing: attribution 601; Australia 155–6, 162; changes in 601; liability risk 602
Carbon Tracker Initiative (CTI) 611, 617
CCB Socially Responsible Investments Fund (China) 167, 169
CCB Social Responsibility Open Index ETF (China) 167
CDP 605
Center for Financial Research and Accounting 571
Center for Sustainable Investment Education 67
Central Bank of Nigeria 117, 122
Centre for Impact Investing (Canada) 78–9
Centre for Sustainability Studies (CES) 87
CEO performance goals 569
Ceres 620
CERES Principles 5, 613, 615
CFP *see* corporate financial performance (CFP)
Chile: corporate governance 94; overview 417–18; responsible investment 419–21
Chilean Santiago Stock Exchange 86
China: assets under management (AUM) 167, 169; banking 175, 177; corporate governance 176; environmental issues 175; ESG disclosure 175–6; ESG factors 167, 169; ESG-themed indices *171*; GDP growth 167; global initiatives 172; government policies 172, *173*, 174, *174*, 176–7; government regulation 174; green banks 175; green policies 172; institutional supports 169; non-governmental organizations (NGOs) 175; overview 167, 384–6; pension funds 177; private equity 189; public funds 169; responsible investment 166–7, *168*, 169–78, 386–7; responsible investment timeline *170*; state-owned enterprises 177; stock exchanges 167, 174–5, 177
China Merchants Bank and Industrial 175
China Securities Depository and Clearing Corporation (ChinaClear) 182
China SIF 176
China State Environmental Protection Administration 174
China Universal Socially Responsible Investments Fund 167
Church of Scotland 358
Church of Sweden 314, 338, 341
CIBanco 83
CIES (inter-union committee for employee saving) 266, 271
Citizens United v. Federal Election Commission 66
Clean Energy Finance Corporation (Australia) 157
Clean Energy Regulator (Australia) 157
Cleantech Global Innovation Index 143
cleantech start-ups, Israel 143
Clearinghouse on Alternative Investment 477
Climate Advocacy Fund (Australia) 153
Climate Bonds Initiative 613
climate change: assessment of 547; Australia 162; carbon budget 596; decarbonizing 617; Denmark 323–4; ESG factors 22; Finland 332; impact of 604–5; international efforts 596; liability risk 601; mitigation 601; owning the problem 613; research 595; social cost of 18; socially constructed importance 549, *549*; United Kingdom 361
Climate Change Authority (Australia) 157
Club Investlife (Japan) 216
coal industry, Australia 161–2, 164
Coca-Cola Company 479
Code for Responsible and Sustainable Investing in Zimbabwe (CRESIZ) 367
Code for Responsible Investing in South Africa (CRISA) 56, 99, 106–7, 367
codes of conduct 5
Código Olivencia (Spain) 257–8
collaborative engagement 438
collateral benefits 559
Colombia: overview 417–18; responsible investment 419–21
Colombian Fondo de Capital Privado Inversor 89
Colombian Securities Exchange 92
Colombia Stock Exchange 86–7
Comision Nacional Bancaria y de Valores (Mexico) 81
Commercial Bank of China 175
Commons Asset Management 216
community engagement 501–3

Community Futures Development Corporations 77
Community Growth Equity Fund (South Africa) 102
Community Growth Funds (South Africa) 108
Community Growth Management Company (COMANCO) 108
community investment 477
Community Loan Funds 77
Companies Ordinance (Hong Kong) 183
Confederation of Tunisian Citizen Entreprises 134
confirmation bias 694–6
Conseil du Marché Financier (Tunisia) 131
consumer goods, carbon footprints 617
consumers: female 487; socially responsible behavior 487–8; SRI mutual funds 486–7; sustainability ratings 629–30
Copula Capital Advisors 233
CoreRating 266
corporate disclosure 64–5
corporate engagement: active ownership 496; Canada 496–504; defined 494; divestiture 495; ESG factors 494; institutional investors 494, 496; monitoring 495; principal-agent problem 495; shareholder activism 495; successful 503–5
corporate financial performance (CFP): competition-driven 678; microfinance institutions 677–8; motivation-oriented 678; relationship with corporate social performance 678–82, 687
corporate governance: boards of directors 567–9; CEO pay 569; CEO performance goals 569; defined 565; development of 565–6; failures in 600; financial reporting 570–1; history of 696–8; ownership and control 569–70; ratings methodologies 567–72; research 566; responsible investment 651; short-termism 700
corporate governance codes 93
corporate governance indices, Brazil 88
Corporate Governance Trade Index (Brazil) 88
corporate history 696–8
Corporate Knights 627
The Corporate Library 566, 571
corporate performance: accountability 600; government regulation 478; information intermediaries 627; reporting standards 620; shareholder advocacy 213, 444, 621; social factors 554, 556–7, 561
corporate reporting: corporate governance failures 600; ESG disclosure 110, 153; information intermediaries 627; integrated reporting 362; standards 620, 627
corporate reputation 594
corporate social performance (CSP): competition-driven 678; cost of debt 26; environmental issues 26; equity financing 25–6; governance issues 26; microfinance institutions 677–8; motivation-oriented 678; relationship with corporate financial performance 677, 679–82, 687; social issues 26
corporate social responsibility (CSR) 21, 25, 30; China 169; corporate engagement 481, *481*, 482; Denmark 317–24, 366; Europe 56; expectations for 593–4; industrial markets 243; insider-initiated corporate philanthropy 590; Italy 244; long-term results 590; Mexico 83; public relations aspects of 30; religious investors 479–80; stakeholder philanthropy 590; standards of practice 559–61; Tunisia 135
Corporate Sustainability Index (ISE) 87
corporate sustainability reporting standards 620–3
corporate water risk 596–7
Council for Institutional Investors 566
Council of Ethics (Norway) 351
Council on Social Responsibility (Denmark) 323
Country Code (Código País) 93
credit unions: Canada 72, 74–6, 79; Japan 207; Mexico 82
Cricket saving (Belgium) 290
CRISA *see* Code for Responsible Investing in South Africa (CRISA)
Croatia, corporate social responsibility (CSR) 234
CRSP Survivor-Bias Free US Mutual Fund 707–8
CSP *see* corporate social performance (CSP)
CSR-in Action 123
CSR Manager Network Italy (CSRMNI) 244
CTI *see* Carbon Tracker Initiative (CTI)

Daiwa Securities 210
Danish Agency for Commerce and Companies/ Danish Business Authority 322
Danish Financial Statements Act 320–1
Danish Sustainable Investment Forum (Dansif) 318–19
Danske Bank 318
data: assessment 623; creation 623; validation 623
DB Climate Change Advisory 25
decarbonizing 615–18
defined-benefit pension funds 16–17
deforestation: forest bonds 597; South America 94
delegation relationships 691, 699–700
Deloitte 92
Denmark: auditing of reports 322; climate change reporting 323–4; corporate social responsibility (CSR) 317–24, 366; EU requirements 319, 324; human rights reporting 323–4; institutional investors 318–19, 324; overview 317, 387–8; reporting requirement 318–23; responsible investment 314, 317–24, 388–9; small and medium sized enterprises 317; *see also* Scandinavia
Desjardins Group 76, 79

Deutsche Bank Group 26
Dexia AM 294
Disney Consumer Products Sustainable Business Practices 479
divestment campaigns 6; fossil fuel 611–13, 615; South Africa 21, 100; systemic problems 612–13
Dodd-Frank Wall Street Reform and Consumer Protection Act 64–6
Domini 400 Social Index 528
Dow, Charles 527
Dow Jones Industrial Average index 527
Dow Jones Sustainability Index 314, 529, 620, 627
Dow Jones Transportation Average 527
Dutch Association of Investors for Sustainable Development (VBDO) 302–5, 307–8, 310
Dutch Central Bank 301, 306
Dutch Corporate Governance Code 305–6
Dutch Fund and Asset Management Organization (DUFAS) 307–9
Dutch Pension Fund for Public Employees (APB) 121
Dutch Platform for Inclusive Finance (NpM) 309
duty of care *see* duty of prudence
duty of impartiality 637–8, 657–8
duty of loyalty 638, 641, 655–7
duty of prudence 27, 636–7, 659–61

Earth Institute (Columbia University) 612, 618
Earthrate 332
Eastern Europe: corporate governance 233; financial markets 234; overview 233–4; pension funds 234; responsible investment 11, 233–41, 366; stock exchanges 234
economic risks 368–9
Edinburgh University Students Association 464
efficient market hypothesis 4
Egan Jones Ratings (EJR) 626
Eiris 266, 530
Electricité de France 696
Element Earth Equity Fund (South Africa) 102
Element Investment Managers 102–3
emerging markets: long-term investment 598; responsible investment 56, 598
Emerging Markets Disclosure Program 90
Employee Retirement Income Security Act (ERISA) 63–4, 566, 635, 652
employer-sponsored retirement plans: Hong Kong 185; United States 59
Energy Efficiency Index 531
Energy Efficiency Opportunities Program (Australia) 157
England *see* United Kingdom
Enhanced Self-Reliance (ESR) Programme 191
Enron 486, 565, 570, 625
environment *see* natural environment
environmental, social and governance (ESG) factors *see* ESG factors
environmental asset-backed securities 597
environmental pressure groups 545
Environment Canada 73
Equador: overview 417–18; responsible investment 419–21
Equator Principles 105, 172
Equitas Ventures (Argentina) 89
equity financing, costs 25–6
equity investments: carbon footprints 616–17; decarbonizing 611, 615–16
equity pricing, ESG factors 27, 435
ESG factors: alpha 8, 26; assets under management (AUM) 24; decision-making and 3–4; duplication of effort 370; emergence of 22; equity pricing 435; fiduciary obligations 63–4; financial performance 4; governance issues 565–71; government regulation 56; growth of 24–5; importance of 19; institutional investors 7, 61, 585; materiality reporting 23–4; money managers 61–2; opportunities/losses 369; rating agencies 75; rating market 27; reputational risk 368–9; research 571–2; risk management 5; social factors 553–62; social media 370; university endowments 370
ESG integration 437; energy transition 614; evolution of environmental/social impacts 614; rise of social business 614
ESG Research Australia 160
Estonia: corporate governance 237; corporate social responsibility (CSR) 234; market environment 236; overview 235, 389–90; pension funds 235–6; responsible investment 233, 235–7, 390–1; stock exchanges 236–7
Estonian Financial Supervision Authority 236
Etablissement de la Retraite Additionnelle pour la Fonction Publique (ERAFP) 265
Ethical Council (Sweden) 340
ethical/SRI investment 21; history of 21–2, 55
Eumedion 308
euro crisis: incremental adaptation 604; recovery periods 603
EURO iSTOXX 50 SD-KPI Index 531–2
Europe: corporate social responsibility 56; discretionary mandates 587; government pension system 55; pension funds 121; responsible investment 53, 583–4; RI strategies *586*
European Emissions Trading Scheme 545
European Union: Central European countries 234; Eastern European countries 234; materiality reporting 24; responsible investment 11, 25
European Union Capital Requirements Directive (CRD III) 699
Eurosif 20, 327, 337, 348, 485, 583–4
exclusionary screens 558
executive compensation practices 496–500, 569

extractive industries: Australia 164; Canada 78; government payments 64; mineral sourcing 65; mine safety 65; Nigeria 115
Extractive Industries Transparency Initiative (EITI) 5, 115, 605

FairFin 293
fair trade 89, *299*, 480, 491, *624*
faith-based investors *see* religious investors
Fat Cat Initiative (Switzerland) 283
Federal Plan for Sustainable Development 2004–2008 (Belgium) 292
fiduciaries: duties of 636–40, 655–7, 659–61, 663; ESG factors 601, 642, 651; fiduciary law 652–4; institutional 27, 634; pension 366, 632–3, 636–7; proxy voting 63; risk adjustment 28; risk management 641; shareholder engagement 65, 482; trust 635; types of 652; *see also* fiduciary obligations
fiduciary law: beneficiaries 655, 657–8; common law countries 650; defined 652; responsible investment 650–1
fiduciary obligations 9; common law countries 21, 27–8; conflicts of interest 638–40; corporate governance failures 600; corporate stewardship responsibilities 602; duty of impartiality 637–8, 657–8; duty of loyalty 636, 638, 641, 655–7; duty of prudence 636–7, 659–61; ESG factors 63–4; key issues *643*; legislative change 600–1; legislative reform 662–3; litigation 601–2; pension funds 632–41; principles of 634–6; priority of *639*; prudent investor standard 635; prudent person standard 635; responsible investment 27–8, 599–602, 641–2, 653–4, 658–64; risk management 641; service provider chain 640; tie-breaker principle 660; trust law 652–5, 657–8
financial cooperative movement 74
financial markets: cognitive biases 691–2, 694–6; confirmation bias 694–6; inefficiencies 690–1, 693; information processing 694; investor psychology 690, 694–6; long-term investment 689–90, 698–9; short-termism 689–90, 692, 698–701; speculative bubbles 690–1, 693–4
financial reporting 570–1
financial risk 9
Financial Services Agency (Japan) 217
Financial System Inquiry (Australia) 154–5
Finland: asset classes 332; climate change 332; corporate governance 332–3; equity markets 328; exclusion strategy 331–3; government ownership 333; institutional investors 330; investment strategies *331*; market value of companies *329*; norm-based screening 332; overview 328, 392; pension funds 329–30, 333; responsible investment 327–33, 366, 392–4; screening 331; stock exchanges 328; well-being indicators 330
Finland Chamber of Commerce 332–3
Finland Sustainable Investment Forum (FINSIF) 327, 330–2
Finnish Pension Alliance (TELA) 331, 333
FINSIF *see* Finland Sustainable Investment Forum (FINSIF)
First Eastern Investment Group 191
Fitch 626
fixed-income indexes 528
le Fond de Reserve des Retraites 264
Fondo Educa (Mexico) 82
Fonds de Réserve des Retraites (FRR) 265
Ford Motor Company 479, 616
forest bonds 597
Forum ETHIBEL 293
Forum for Socially Responsible Investment 20
Forum for Sustainable and Responsible Investment 20
Forum Nachhaltige Geldanlagen (FNG) 279, 281–2, 284
forward-looking adjustments 23
fossil-free divestment campaign 611–13, 615
France: asset classes 269–70, *270*; assets under management (AUM) *263*, 264; calculative framing 266, 271, 274–5; corporate governance 268; corporate social responsibility (CSR) 262; employee savings plans (ESPs) 265; ESG factors 263; ESG integration 268–9; ESG rating agencies 266–7; ethical funds 262, 264; financial regulation authority (AMF) 266; government pension system 55; impact investing 269; institutional investors 269, *269*, 271; investment vehicles *263*; overview 262, 395; pension funds 265, 366; political framing 264–5, 270, 274–5; responsible investment 53, 262–72, 366, 395–6; retail investors 271; screening 267–8; themed investment 268
Free and Prior and Informed Consent (FPIC) 560
French Social Investment Forum (FIR) 267
FRR *see* Fonds de Réserve des Retraites (FRR)
FTSE4Good indexes 529–31
FTSE All World Index 144
FTSE ECPI Italia SRI Indexes 246–7
FTSE ECPI Italia SRI Leader Index 247
FTSE Italia All-Share Index 246, 249
FTSE/JSE SRI index 109
Futuregrowth Albaraka Equity Fund 102
Futuregrowth Asset Management (South Africa) 101
Future of Financial Advice (FoFA) reforms (Australia) 155

Generation Investment Management (UK) 511–12
Germany: banking 277; environmental issues 280; ESG factors 279; government pension system 55; Green Party 277; institutional investors 280–1; investment market 280; overview

276–7, 374–5; pension funds 281; responsible investment 276, 279–82, 375–7
Glass Lewis & Co. 566
Glass-Steagall Act of 1934 477
Global Alliance for Banking on Values 76, 79
Global Carbon Index 531
Global Climate Index 531
Global Compact 100 Index 531
Global Compact Network Italy (GCNI) 248
global consumption 598
Global Financial Crisis of 2008 4–5, 7; financial assets 689; financial risk 18; impact on responsible investment 18–19, 25, 512; impact on world's financial system 611; incremental adaptation 604; recovery periods 603; sub-prime mortgage crisis 625
Global Impact Investing Rating System 308
Global Initiative for Sustainability Ratings (GISR) 296
globalization 598
Global Reporting Initiative 90, 123, 620
Global Risk Report (World Economic Forum) 614, 618
Global Sullivan Principles of Corporate Social Responsibility 5
GMI Ratings 566, 571
Goldman Sachs 22
GovernanceMetrics International 566, 571
governance ratings systems: boards of directors 567–9; CEO pay 569; CEO performance goals 569; ESG factors 571–2; financial reporting 570–1; ownership and control 569–70
Government Employees Pension Fund (GEPF) 108
Government Pension Act of 2005 (Norway) 351
Government Pension Investment Fund (Japan) 212
government-sponsored investment funds (GSIFs): agent-centered explanations 445, 447–8, 450; agent-centered hypothesis 450–1, 456; empirical analysis 445, 448–9, 451, 457–8; ESG factors 444; in the global economy 446–7; institutional investors 444, 447; pension funds 444, 446–7, 450; responsible investment 444–58; shareholder engagement 444; small populations 451–2; sovereign wealth funds (SWFs) 444, 446–7, 450; structural factors for RI 445, 448–9; structure-related hypothesis 450
Gramm-Leach-Bliley Act of 1999 (GLBA) 477
Grantham Institute 617
Great Britain *see* United Kingdom
green banks, Mexico 83, *84*
Green Economy Indexes 531
The Green Fund (Hong Kong) 186
Green Funds Scheme 305
Greenhouse Gas (GHG) Protocol 616
green technology: development of 597; investment networks 597
green washing 30, 371, 518
Grønt Norge 348
Group of Thirty 689
Gunns Ltd. 435–6

Haitong Socially Responsible Investment (SRI) Asia Fund 185
Hang Seng Corporate Sustainability Index Series 185
hedge funds: academic research *38–40*; aggregated research *41–2*
Herfindahl index 328, *330*
Het Aandere Beleggingsfonds 301
Histadrut Employees Union 139
HIV/AIDS, South Africa 100, 109
Hong Kong: active ownership 187–8; asset classes 189, 195; assets under management (AUM) 185–6; corporate governance 184, 188, 194; ESG disclosure 183, 187, 189; ESG factors 194; government regulation 183, 187; Hong Kong Baptist University 187; Hong Kong Exchanges and Clearing Limited 182; Hong Kong Institute of Investors 188; Hong Kong Monetary Authority 188; Hong Kong Securities and Futures Commission 184; Hong Kong Social Enterprise Challenge 192; Hong Kong Social Enterprise Forum 193; Hong Kong Stock Exchange 177, 182–3; Hong Kong University of Science and Technology 192; impact investing 191–5; infrastructure investment 190–1; institutional investors 195; key players 194, *196*–7; Lehman mini-bonds 188; mandatory provident fund market share 205; market structure 189; overview 182, 396–7; pension funds 185–7, 189, 194, 206; private equity 189–91, 195; related-party transactions 183; responsible investment 166, 175, 182–95, 397–8; responsible investment funds 200–5; retail fund market 184–5; shareholder advocacy 188; social enterprises 191, 193; stock exchanges 177, 182–3
HSBC Brazil Asset Management 90
HSBC Low Carbon Pioneer Fund 169
Human Rights Impact Assessments (HRIAs) 502
human rights reporting: Denmark 323–4; extractive industries 501–3
Hungary, corporate social responsibility (CSR) 234

ICCR *see* Interfaith Center on Corporate Responsibility (ICCR)
idiosyncratic risk 670
impact finance 79
impact investing 22; aboriginal funds 74; asset managers 514; assets under management (AUM) *74*; Brazil 89; Canada 70, 72–4; ESG factors 72; financial cooperative movement 74; France 269;

Hong Kong 191–5; Japan 210; Netherlands 304–5; social goals 558; South Africa 102; South America 88–9
Impax 512
income inequality 598
index investing 527–33, 633
India: fiduciary obligations 21; shareholder advocacy 188
Índice de Buen Gobierno Corporativo (IBGC) 88
Industrial Social Responsibility Securities Investment Fund (China) 167, 169
Industrifonden 341
information intermediaries: business models 620–30; data access 623; data assessment 623; data creation 623; data validation 623; structural bias 620–1, 625–7; types of 624, *624*
infrastructure investment: Hong Kong 190–1; social infrastructure 190; transport 190; utilities 190
Institute of Retirement Funds (South Africa) 104
institutional finance 72
institutional investors: asset classes 19; assets 17; Austria 279; Belgium 291; Canada 73; coalition building 6; corporate engagement 494, 496; corporate governance 566; decarbonizing 617; defined-benefit pension funds 16–17; Denmark 318–19, 324; diversified investment portfolios 17–18; divestment campaigns 6; ESG factors 7, 61, 585; fiduciary obligations 21; financial performance 359; financial risk 9; Finland 330; France 269, 271; free-rider problem 6, 9; Germany 280–1; growth of 16–17; Hong Kong 195; long-term results 4–5, 7, 17–18; mutual funds 16–17; Netherlands 302–3, 305–8; OECD countries 16–17; pension funds 4, 280, 444, 585; proxy voting 566; shareholder advocacy 61; stewardship codes 642; Switzerland 283–4; United Kingdom 358–9; United States 61; *see also* asset owners
Institutional Investors on Climate Risk 6
Institutional Shareholder Services (ISS) 566
Instituto Argentino para el Gobierno de las Organizaciones 93
insurance industry, Nigeria 121
Integrated Latin American Market (MILA) 87
integrated reporting 24, 518
Inter-American Development Bank 83
Interfaith Center on Corporate Responsibility (ICCR) 475–82
Intergovernmental Panel on Climate Change 596
International Finance Corporation (IFC) 87
International Finance Facility for Immunization (Japan) 210
International Financial Reporting Standards (IFRS) 234
International Green Fund (IGF) 597
International Labour Organization (ILO) 352
INVERCO *see* Spanish Association of Collective Investment Schemes and Pension Funds
investment analysis: climate change impacts 159; ESG factors 7, 25, 58–60, 64, 66, 101, 160, 307, 365, 438, 553; government regulation 365; responsible investment 58, 580, 620; social factors 554, 556, 560
investment consultants: core consultants 525; in-house expertise 524–5; outside specialist consultants 524; project contracts 521; responsible investment 520–6; retainer contracts 521
investment industry: conflicts of interest 625–6; investment decisions 603; investment horizons 439; environmental risk 595–7; financial crises 606; new opportunities 606
investment management industry: assets under management (AUM) 59–60; delegation relationships 691; ESG factors 59–60, 62; pension funds 59, 633; responsible investment 440; RI assets 59–60; short-termism 700–1; United States 58–60
investment portfolios: diversified 17–18; long-term trends 18; negative screening 21; positive screening 22
investment practice: ethical 55; exclusion strategy 558; mainstream 34; responsible investment 34–5
investment risk 670
investment styles 29–30
Investor Group on Climate Change (Australia) 159–60
Investor Protection Association (IPA) (Russia) 225, 231
investor transparency 438
Iran-related investing criteria 61
Israel: banking 142; cleantech start-ups 143; community funds 143; corporate governance 139–40; environmental issues 141–2; ethical funds 143; financial regulations 140–2; green funds 143; institutional investors 142; investment market 139; kosher funds 139, 142–3; overview 138–9, 399; pension funds 139; responsible investment 138–9, 142–6, 399–400; socially responsible investment (SRI) 145; venture capital 143
Israel Securities Authority 141
ISS 571
Italian Bank Association (ABI) 244
Italy: assets under management (AUM) 244–6; corporate citizenship 248; corporate social responsibility (CSR) 244; financial performance 248–9, *250*, 251; overview 245, 401; pension funds 244, 246; responsible investment 243–9, 251, 401–2
Itaú-Unibanco 90

Jantzi Research Inc. 75
Japan: assets under management (AUM) 207, 209, 212; business incubation 207, 209; corporate disclosure 216; corporate governance 214; credit unions 207; economic growth 208, 217–18; environmental issues 207, 213–14, 217; ESG disclosure 215, 218–19; ESG factors 213–14; gender diversity 218; government regulation 218–19; impact investing 210; institutional investors 214; key players 215–16; legal environment 216; long-term asset managers 207; long-term investment funds 210, 211*t*, 216, *219*; overview 208, 403; pension funds 212, 218; policy environment 216–18; responsible investment 207–19, 368, 403–4, 584; responsible investment concepts *209*; retail investors 214, *215*; shareholder advocacy 213; social contribution bonds 210, 213; social issues 214; stock exchanges 218; vaccine bonds 210
Japan Credit Rating 627
Japanese Pension Fund Association 212
Japanese Social Investment Forum 208
Japan Exchange Group 218
Japan Trade Union Confederation (Rengo) 215–16
Jiuding Capital 172
Johannesburg Stock Exchange (JSE) 99, 109, 529
JPX-Nikkei Index 400 218
justified beliefs 603

Kamakura Asset Management 216
KBC Asset Management 294
KBC Ecofund 289
Key Performance Indicators (KPI) 23, 628
KLD Research & Analytics 582
KLD Stats Database 707
Kommunal Landspensjonskasse Gjensidig Forsikringsselskap (KLP) 352
Kyoto Protocol 595

Latin America: corporate governance 93–4; pension funds 90; responsible investment 83, 85, 87, 90
Latin American Sustainable Finance Forum 90–1
Latin American Sustainable Investment Forum (LatinSIF) 92
Latvia, corporate social responsibility (CSR) 234
Lehman mini-bonds 188
license to operate 18
Lima Stock Exchange 88, 91, 93
Limestone Fund Management 235, 237
Loi sur les Nouvelles Régulations Economiques (NRE) (France) 265
long-term investment 439–40; adaptive capacity 603; climate change 602; environmental risk 605–6; ESG factors 4–5, 7–8; government policies 605–6; incentives for 698–700; institutional investors 17–18; justified beliefs 603; pension funds 602; reflexivity 603; resource scarcity 602; socially responsible investment (SRI) 696; transformation 604
Lotus Capital 118–19, 122
Lunar Capital Management 172

Maala CSR Index 144
Macau, responsible investment 166
MacBride Principles on Fair Employment 479
McKibben, Bill 611–12
market capitalization, Canada 71, *71*
market movement 22–3
materiality 22; defined 23; ESG factors 23–4; forward-looking adjustments 23; risk analysis 23
materiality reporting 23–4
MeesPierson 309
Meitav Green Energy 143
Mennonite Economic Development Associates (MEDA) 79
Mercer LLC 73, 75, 87, 437, 521–2
Meritas Mutual Funds 497
Merkur 318
Merrill Lynch 531, 625
Mexican Stock Exchange (MSE) 82
Mexico: credit unions 82; green banks 83, *84*; overview 81, 405; pension funds 81–2; responsible investment 81–3, *84*, 85, 405–6
Microfinance Institution (Tunisia) 131
microfinance institutions: corporate social performance (CSP) 678–9; financial performance 677, 679–80; governance structure 680; loan size 678; outreach 678; poverty alleviation 677–8; research design 680–2; social responsibility 677–9, 681, *683–6*, 687
MicroFinanza Rating 677, 680
micro lending 477
Middle East and North Africa (MENA): ESG factors 134; government regulation 128
Mikuni 627
Miljøinvest 348
Ministry of Environmental Protection (China) 172, 174
Ministry of Finance (Tunisia) 131
Minow, Nell 566
Mira & Forum Ethibel 288
Mira Report 289
Modern Company Law Review 360
modern portfolio theory 4, 633, 670–2
money managers: alternative investments 62; ESG factors 61–2; *see also* asset managers
Monks, Robert 439, 561, 566
Montreal Carbon Pledge 616
Montreal Protocol 596
Moody's 625–7, 629
MORE Tithe Bonds 143
Moscow Interbank Currency Exchange (MICEX) 230

Moscow International Finance Centre (MIFC) Taskforce 228–9
Moscow Stock Exchange (MOEX) 230
MSCI 53, 176, 528, 531, 566, 571
MSCI Analytics 627
MSCI equity indexes 529
MSCI ESG Research 266
MSCI KLD 400 Social Index 528
MSE Sustainability Index 81–3, 85
mutual funds 16–17; holdings data 707; indexed stock products 527–8; legal environment 651; responsible investment 485–7, 667; screening 668
mutual retail funds, Canada 73
Myners Report 360

Namibia, responsible investment 367
Nasdaq/OMX 531
Nasdaq omx Helsinki 332
National Greenhouse Energy Reporting Act (Australia) 156
National Institute for Statistics (ISTAT) (Italy) 244
National Insurance Commission (Nigeria) 121
Nationally Recognized Statistical Rating Organizations (NRSROs) 626
National Pension Funds Regulator (CONSAR) 82
National Pension Scheme (South Korea) 189
National Social Security Fund of China 177
natural environment: environmental issues 543; environmental pressure groups 545; globalization 598; public awareness 547–8, *548*, 549, *549*; research 595; resource scarcity 595–7; responsible investment 545–51; salient stakeholders 544–5; socially constructed importance 548–9; social realities and 598; stakeholder theory 543–4, *544*; value-relevance 549–50
NEI *see* Northwest & Ethical Investment (NEI) Funds
Neste Oil 333
Netherlands: banking 303; corporate governance 304–6; ESG integration 304; exclusion strategy 303; fiduciary obligations 305, 307; fiscal incentives 305; foundations and charities 302–3; government regulation 305, 309–10; impact investing 304–5; institutional investors 302–3, 305–8; overview 300–1, 406–7; pension funds 301–7, 366; policy environment 305, 309; positive selection 304; private sector-led initiatives 307; public/private collaboration 300, 309–10; responsible investment 264, 300–10, 366, 407–9; shareholder advocacy 306
Netherlands Authority for Financial Markets 306
Netwerk Vlaanderen 290
New Europe Socially Responsible Fund (Estonia) 237
Newton IM 511
New Zealand: ESG risks 190; legislative reform 662; responsible investment 150, 159, 457, 584, 663
Nigeria: asset classes 119, *119–20*; assets under management (AUM) *117*; corporate governance 121–2; ethical funds *117*, 118, *118*, 119, 122; insurance industry 121; negative screening 118–19; oil industry 115; overview 115–16, 409–10; pension funds 120, *120*, 121; policy environment 122; responsible investment 115–24, 410–11; shareholder advocacy 121; sustainable banking 117, 122–3; sustainable reporting 122
Nigerian Sovereign Investment Authority 121
Nikkei 218
90 Stock Composite Price Index 527
non-governmental organizations (NGOs): Australia 163; China 175; media campaigns 594; microfinance 131; responsible investment 123; sustainability reporting 620
Nordic countries *see* Denmark; Finland; Norway; Sweden
Norges Bank Investment Management (NBIM) 349–50
North American Free Trade Agreement Act of 1993 478
Northern Ireland *see* United Kingdom
Northern Star 235
Northwest & Ethical Investment (NEI) Funds: engagement with Barrick Gold 496–7, 501–3; interviewees 508–9
Norway: asset classes 348–50, *350*; assets under management (AUM) 315; exclusion strategy 349, 351; GDP sectors *347*; key players 352–3; market evolution strategies *349*; norm-based screening 348; oil and gas industry 347–8, 350; overview 345–7, 411; pension funds 350–1; responsible investment 314, 345, 348–53, 365–6, 411–12; *see also* Scandinavia
Norwegian Government Pension Fund – Global 17, 315, 345, 347–8, 350, 352–3, 444
Norwegian Sustainable Value Creation Initiative 341–2
Novethic 262–4, 266–7, 269, 271
NpM *see* Dutch Platform for Inclusive Finance (NpM)

Oceania, responsible investment 53
Oddo AM 511
ODIN Fund Management 352–3
OECD: corporate governance standards 229; institutional investors 16–17; Israel 138; Japan 208, 212; Spain 254
oil industry: Mexico 81; Nigeria 115; Norway 347–8, 350
oil-sands 78
Old Mutual Albaraka Equity Fund 102

Old Mutual Group South Africa 108
outside specialist consultants 524

Pan Arab region, responsible investment 134
Paris Stock Exchange 264
Partners for Financial Stability (PFS) Program 234
path dependence 55
pay disparity 64, 66
Pension Fund Administrators (Mexico) 82
Pension Fund of the Russian Federation 229
pension funds 4; annuities 59; assets under management (AUM) 444; Austria 279; Belgium 292, 366; Brazil 90–1, 94; Canada 74–5; China 177; employer-sponsored plans 59, 185; ESG factors 25; Estonia 235–6; Europe 121, 234; fiduciary obligations 63–4, 446, 448, 632–41; Finland 329–30, 333; France 265, 366; Germany 280–1; governance practices 639–40; growth of 632–3; Hong Kong 185–7, 189, 194; individual retirement accounts (IRAs) 59; institutional investors 444, 585; investment risk 633; investors 634; Israel 139; Italy 244, 246; Japan 212, 218; Latin America 90; long-term investment 638; Mexico 81–2; Netherlands 301–7, 366; Nigeria 120, *120*, 121; Norway 350–1; Poland 234, 239; responsible investment 53, 437–8, 447, 662–3; risk analysis 603–4; Russia 228–9; short-term investment 633, 637; South Africa 104, 108; South America 368; sovereign 448; Spain 255–7; Sweden 338–9, 341, 366; systemic risk 634; time horizons 439, 448; United Kingdom 358–61, 366; United States 59, 61, 121; view of markets 633
Pension Funds Act (South Africa) 56, 99, 106, 663
Pension Governance Code (Netherlands) 306
Pension Reform Act of 2004 (Nigeria) 120
People's Bank of China 175
Petoro 348
PFZW (Pensioenfonds Zorg en Welzijn) 303
PGGM 305, 309
Poland: corporate governance 240; gender diversity 240; market environment 239; overview 237–8, 389–90; pension funds 234, 239; responsible investment 233, 238–41, 390–1; stock exchanges 238–9
Porter, Michael 559, 594
Portfolio Decarbonization Coalition 616
positive investment transitions 613
Premium Reserve System (Sweden) 338–40, 342
PREVI 90
PRI Academic Network *see* Principles for Responsible Investment Academic Network (PRI AN)
PricewaterhouseCoopers 588
PRI Engagement Working Group 90
principal-agent problem 4, 495
Principal Officers Association of South Africa 104
Principles for Responsible Investment (PRI) 3, 594; asset managers 511–12, 518–19; assets under management (AUM) 24, 53, 74, 371; Australia 150, 163; Austria 279; Belgium 294; Brazil 90, 92; China 172; civil law countries 599; common law countries 599; corporate engagement 496, 532; country tables 374–431; definition of responsible investment 553; Denmark 318, 321–3; development of 6–8, 435–9, 518; ESG factors 562; Estonia 233, 235; Finland 327, 330–2; France 262, 264, 268; Germany 281; growth of 364–71, 641; Hong Kong 189; investment consultants 521–3; long-term results 439–40; mainstreaming RI 19–20; Montreal Carbon Pledge 616; Netherlands 264, 308; New Zealand 150, 159; Nigeria 115, 123; Norway 345, 348; Poland 233; public commitment 440–1; reporting requirement 371; research in RI 35; Russia 225; Scandinavia 314, *314*; South Africa 107, *107*, 108–9; South America 86, 92; South Korea 189; Sweden 336, 340; Switzerland 283; United Arab Emirates (UAE) 134; United Kingdom 264, 359; United States 61; University of Edinburgh 462, 464
Principles for Responsible Investment Academic Network (PRI AN) 35, 516
Principles of Good Corporate Governance (Peru) 93
private equity: academic research *38–40*; aggregated research *41–2*; China 189; Hong Kong 189–91; investor concern 588; risk management 588; South Africa 105
product disclosure statements (Australia) 159
Proposal for Pension Fund Disclosure Directive 57
proxy voting 63, 566, 611
prudent investor standard 635
prudent person standard 635
public fiduciary 28
Public Investment Corporation Limited (South Africa) 108

reflexivity 603
RegCharles Finance and Capital Ltd. 123
related-party transactions, Hong Kong 183
religious investors: anti-apartheid resolution 476; Christian 474; community investment 477; environmental issues 478; equitable access to capital 477; globalization 478; Jewish 474; Muslim 474; responsible investment 474–83; shareholder advocacy 475, 479–82; shareholder resolutions 476; social issues 478; Sullivan Principles 476
Renewable Energy Law (China) 174
Renewable Energy Target (Australia) 156–7
reputational risk 368–9
research: academic 575, *576*, 577, *577*, 578–82, 591; government funding 36, 45; growth of

41, 45; journal quality 37–8; keywords *580*, 581; KLD ratings 582; methodologies 578–82; multidisciplinary 580–1, *581*; output quality 37, 39–40, 43; output quantity 37–9, 43, *44–5*; publications and 578, *578*, 579–80, 582; responsibility issues 35–46, 582; theoretical framework 589, 591
Research Institute of Economy, Trade and Industry (Japan) 213
Réseau Financité (RFA) 288, 290, 293
resource scarcity: corporate water risk 596–7; geopolitical *595*, 596; non-physical factors 595, *595*; resource governance *595*, 596; social justice 596; socio-economic *595*; universal ownership 599
responsibilization 536
responsible investment: adaptation of 618; adoption of 4–5, 452–8; agent-centered 447–8, 450–1, 456; aggregated research *41–2*, *45*; arguments for 29; best-in-class 667–9; business practices 583–9; challenges of 8–10, 56; defined 3, 20–1; environmental issues 545–50, *550*, 551; ESG factors 25, 438, 553–4, 585, 611, 614, 642; fiduciary obligations 9, 27–8, 63–4, 599–602, 650–1, 653–4, 658–64; financial performance 620–3, 671–2, 674; formalization of 514; forums for 60; goals of 534; government regulation 55–7, 365; growth of 30, 34–5, 66–7, 441, 575, 584, *584*; history of 19; information intermediaries 623; international standards 370, 372–3; investment styles 29–30; legal environment 651; long-term results 8, 27; mainstreaming 546–7; non-governmental organizations (NGOs) 123; policy environment 662–3; positive transitions 613–15; professionalization of 610; religious investors 474–83, 513–14; reporting requirement 370–1; research 35–46, 575–82, 589–91; responsibilization 536; retail investors 485–6; risk management 641; screening 667–75; shareholder advocacy 475–6, 514, 585, 668; shareholder engagement 5–6, 533; small populations 451–2; social factors 9–10, 553–62; SRI mutual funds 485–90; standards of practice 559–61; structural factors 448–9; supply/demand for advice 523–4; systemic risk monitoring 9; theoretical framework 4; types of 584–5; universal ownership 561, 642; voice and accountability indicators 456; worldwide implementation 53, *54*, 55; *see also* sustainable and responsible investing (SRI); *individual countries*
Responsible Investment Association (RIA) 75–6
Responsible Investment Association Australasia 149–50, 159
responsible investment indexes: benchmarks 528; best-in-class 529–30; contributions of 532, 534; criticism of 532–4; decision-making tools 528; development of 527–8; equities indexes 528; growth of 528–9; market definition 528; theme-based 531–2; values-based 530–1
responsible investment research: challenges of 536–9; ethics of responsibility 541; interdisciplinarity 540; legitimacy 538–41; publications and 537–41; systemic perspective 539
Restatement of Trusts and the Uniform Prudent Investor Act of 1994 635
retail investors *see* socially responsible retail investors
retirement funds *see* pension funds
RI *see* responsible investment
RisCura 109
risk adjustment 28
risk analysis 23
RobecoSAM 529–30
Robeco TEDA Sustainable Private Equity Fund 191
Robert F. Kennedy Center for Justice and Human Rights 612, 618
Rousseau, Jean-Jacques 451
Russell 3000 707
Russia: company ownership structure 226; corporate governance 229–30; corruption 226–7; ESG factors 227, 230–1; financial markets 228, 231; governance issues 226–7; government regulation 227–8; investment environment 226–8; overview 225–6, 413; pension funds 228–9; responsible investment 225, 367, 413–14; social issues 227; stock exchanges 230
Russian Corporate Governance Code 227, 229
Russian Direct Investment Fund (RDIF) 227
Russian Trading System (RTS) 230

Saison Asset Management 216
SAM *see* Sustainable Asset Management (SAM)
SARONA 79
Savings and Investment Plan for Cultural Organisations (Netherlands) 305
Sawakami Fund 216
Say on Pay campaign 496–500
Scandinavia: asset classes 315; assets under management (AUM) 314, *314*, 315; corporate social responsibility (CSR) 313; environmental issues 314; ESG integration 313; government pension system 55; overview 313; responsible investment 313–15, 365; social welfare models 313; structural factors for RI 449
Scandinavian model 315
Scotland *see* United Kingdom
screening: best-in-class 667–9; effect on portfolios 669–70, 673, 675, *675*; idiosyncratic risk 670; intensity of 671–3; mutual funds 668, *675*; negative 667, 670–1, 673; positive 667, 670, 673; risk and 670–2, 675; types of *668*, 669, 673

SEC *see* U.S. Securities and Exchange Commission (SEC)
Securities Analysts Association of Japan 214
Securities and Futures Commission (Hong Kong) 188
securities law 651
Senior Citizen Home Safety Association (Hong Kong) 192
Shanghai-Hong Kong Stock Connect 182
Shanghai Stock Exchange 167, 174, 182
SHARE *see* Shareholder Association for Research and Education (SHARE)
ShareAction 442
Shareholder Association for Research and Education (SHARE): engagement with Say on Pay 496–500; interviewees 508
shareholder proposal rule 62–3
shareholders: active ownership 438, 495, 503–4, 668; director nominations 64; divestiture 495; divestment campaigns 6; engagement 65, 370; institutional investors 4, 16, 61, 566; legitimacy 503–5; money managers 62; passive engagement 5–6; power 503–4; private active engagement 6; proxy voting 5–6, 63, 93, 566; public active engagement 6; resolutions 62, 66, 436, 480–2; saliency 503; stock market efficiencies 692
shareholder value 589–90
Shenzhen Stock Exchange 167, 174
Sherman, Howard 566
short-term investment: adaptive capacity 603; environmental risk 605; justified beliefs 603; reflexivity 603; results 5
social and environmental accounting: academic research *38–40*; aggregated research *41–2*
social contribution bonds 210, 213
social factors: asset managers 558; asset owners 558; collateral benefits 559; corporate engagement 562; corporate social responsibility 559–61; defining 554–5; impact investing 558; inequality of wealth and income 561–2; integrating 556–7; risk indicators 557; stakeholders 555–6; targeted investment 559; universal ownership 561–2; workforce relations 556–7
social infrastructure 190
Social Innovation Generation 77
Social Investment Forum 85, 705
Social Investment Forum Japan 215
Social Investment Forum Spain 259
Social Investment Organization (Canada) 73
socially responsible investment (SRI) 7, 19–20; asset allocation 587, *587*; assets under management (AUM) *710*; broad 585; composition of market centers 583, *583*, 584; core 584; engagement 585; ESG factors 70; fiduciary obligations 650; growth of 584, *584*, 589, 706, *710*; history of 21–2; impact investing 70, 72–3; influence on RI 55; integration 585; long-term investment 696; national markets 583; private equity 588; research design 707–9, 711–16; research studies 705; screening 70, 72; shareholder engagement 70, 436–7; simple exclusions 585; socially responsible lending 72; strategies *586*; summary statistics *709*; sustainability-themed investing 70; theoretical framework 589; *see also* responsible investment
socially responsible investors: ethical standards 705–7, 716–17, *717*, 718, *718*, 719, *719*, 720; performance sensitivity 705–7, 711–16, 720; re-investment 705–6; research design 707–8
socially responsible lending 72
socially responsible mutual fund investment *see* SRI mutual funds
socially responsible retail investors 485–6, 490; *see also* SRI mutual funds
social marketing: academic research *38–40*; aggregated research *41–2*
social media: ESG factors 169, 370; information intermediaries 622; responsible investment campaigns 270, 365, 369
Social Security (U.S.) 59
Social Ventures Hong Kong 193
South Africa: carbon emissions 109, 111; corporate governance 99, 110; demographics *100*; divestment campaigns 21, 100; environmental issues 109, 111; ESG factors 110, *110*, 111, 370; ESG legal provisions 106, *106*; financial markets 104–5, *105*; foreign investment 101; governance issues 109–10; government regulation 56; HIV/AIDS 100, 109; impact investing 102; materiality reporting 23; overview 99–100, 414–15; pension funds 104, 108; policy environment 106–7; private equity 105; responsible investment 11, 56, 99–102, 104, *104*, 105–11, 367, 370, 415–17; responsible investment terms *101*; shareholder advocacy 103; social issues 109; venture capital 105
South African Venture Capital and Private Equity Association 105
South America: corporate governance 93–4; deforestation 94; impact investing 88–9; overview 86–7, 417–18; pension funds 368; responsible investment 11, 86–95, *102*, 103, *103*, 367–8, 419–21; social issues 94–5
South Korea: market structure 189; shareholder advocacy 188
sovereign pension funds 448
sovereign wealth funds (SWFs): assets under management (AUM) 17, 444; defined 446; in the global economy 446–7; institutional investors 16, 19; Norwegian 17, 315, 345, 348, 350; responsible investment 448, 457–8
Spain: corporate governance 258; corporate social responsibility (CSR) 258–9; environmental issues 255; ESG factors 259–60; governance issues 255,

260; Law 26/2003 257–8; market environment 256; overview 254–5, 422; pension funds 255–7; policy environment 257; responsible investment 254–5, 258–60, 422–3; screening 255
Spainsif 259
Spanish Association of Collective Investment Schemes and Pension Funds (INVERCO) 256
Spanish Confederation of Saving Banks (CECA) 259
Special Corporate Governance Stock Index – Novo Mercado 88
Special Tag Along Stock Index (ITAG) 88
speculative bubbles 690–1, 693–4
SRI mutual funds: decision-making tools 490–1; financial performance 490; growth of 485–6; investor characteristics 487–8; motivations for 488, *489*; positive impact of 489; social impact of 491; transparency 487
stakeholders: corporate strategy 496; public statements 28; saliency 496; types of 544–5
stakeholder theory: microfinance institutions 679; natural environment and 543–4; screening intensity 671
Stanbic IBTC Ethical Fund 117–19, 122
Standard & Poor's 500 Stock Index 527
Standard & Poor's ESG indexes 529, 531
Standard & Poor's Financial Services LLC 625–7, 629
Standard & Poor's Global Water Index 531
standards of practice 559–61
State Council on Corporate Social Responsibility (Spain) 258
State Environmental Protection Administration (China) 175
State's Direct Financial Interest (SDFI) 348
State Street Global Advisors 22, 511
Stewardship Code (UK) 601
Stora Enso 333
Storebrand 348, 352
Storebrand Principle Global Fund 348, 352
STOXX 531
stranded assets 18
Strategy for a Sustainable Economy (Spain) 258
structure-related hypothesis 450
Sudan-related investing criteria 61–2
Sullivan, Leon 560
Sullivan Principles 21, 476, 560
superannuation contributions, Australia 151–2, *152*, 153
sustainability: corporate reporting 620, 622–3, 627–8; information intermediaries 623–8; responsibility and 537
Sustainability Accounting Standards Board (SASB) 23, 620
sustainability ratings 628; business models 629–30; performance metrics 621, 628–9; state sponsored 630
sustainable and responsible investing (SRI) 59–60; *see also* responsible investment
Sustainable Asset Management (SAM) 512, 620
sustainable banking: Mexico *84*; Nigeria 117, 122–4
sustainable companies: corporate reporting 620–2; customer loyalty 622; financial performance 620–3; government regulation 622; information about 622–3
Sustainable Development Capital 191
sustainable finance 20
sustainable investment *see* responsible investment
Sustainable Stock Exchanges initiative 529
Sustainalytics 75, 92, 266, 309, 502–3, 566
Swaziland, responsible investment 367
Sweden: asset classes 338, *339*; assets under management (AUM) 337; corporate social responsibility (CSR) 341; demographics *336*; ESG factors 341–2; exclusion strategy 337, 342; investment strategies *337*, *338*; negative screening 338; norm-based screening 338–9; overview 336, 424; pension funds 338–9, 341, 366; policy environment 340; responsible investment 314, 336–42, 366, 424–5; shareholder advocacy 339–40; trade unions 340; *see also* Scandinavia
Swedish Sustainable Value Creation Initiative 341–2
Swesif 337, 339, 341
Switzerland: asset managers 284; assets under management (AUM) 282; banking 277, 283; institutional investors 283–4; overview 276–7, 374–5; responsible investment 276, 282, *282*, 283–4, 375–7; shareholder advocacy 283
Sycomore (France) 511
SynTao 172, 176
systemic risk 670, 672; monitoring 9, 18–19

Tallinn Stock Exchange 236–7
targeted investment 559
Tel Aviv Stock Exchange 144
TeliaSonera 333
TFI SKOK SA (Poland) 238–9
Thomson Financial Mutual Fund Holdings 707
Thomson Reuters 620, 629
350.org 611–12
TIAA-CREF 22, 478
tie-breaker principle 660
time horizons 439
Tokyo Stock Exchange 217–18
Toronto Stock Exchange (TSX 60) 71
Towers Watson 521–2
trade unions: Austria 279; ethical/SRI investment 307; Finland 330–1, *393*; France 264–7, 270, 272, *274*; Netherlands 307; South Africa 108; Spain 259; Sweden 340, *424*
Trichet, Jean-Claude 689
Triodos Bank 301, 303–4, 308–9, 512
Trucost 605

trust law 652–3, 657–8
Tunisia: assets under management (AUM) 125; corporate governance 128, 131; corporate social responsibility (CSR) 135; environmental issues 132, 135; ESG factors 132, *133*; governance issues 134; institutional investors 134–5; microfinance 131–3; mutual funds 127–8, *129–30*; national solidarity fund 131; overview 126, 425–6; private equity 128; responsible investment 125–8, *128*, 131–5, 426–8; stock market 126–7, *127*
Tunisian General Labour Union 134
Tunisian Solidarity Bank 131
Tunisian Stock Exchange 131
Tunisian Union for Industry, Commerce and Handicrafts 134

UBS Eco-Performance Fund (Hong Kong) 185
UK Corporate Governance Code 360
UKSIF 361
UK Social Investment Forum (UKSIF) 357
UK Stewardship Code 360
UN Declaration of Human Rights 5
UN Development Program (UNDP) 234
UN Environment Programme Finance Initiative (UNEP FI) 6, 90, 172, 435, 437, 616, 650, 661
UNEP FI *see* UN Environment Programme Finance Initiative
UN Global Compact (UNGC) 5–6, 172, 234, 248, 302, 321–3, 352, 435, 437, 501, 531, 560
UN Guiding Principles on Business and Human Rights 560
Uniform Prudent Investor Act 635
Uniform Trust Code 662
United Arab Emirates (UAE), responsible investment 134
United Kingdom: assets under management (AUM) 359; best-in-sector approach 360; climate change reporting 361; corporate governance 357–9; engagement 357–8, 362; equity markets 19; ethical investment 356–7; fiduciary obligations 21; institutional investors 16, 358–9; integrated reporting 362; materiality reporting 24; overview 355–6, 428; path dependence 55; pension funds 358–61, 366; private social and environmental reporting 360–2; responsible investment 11, 19–20, 53, 264, 355–62, 366, 428–9
United States: equity markets 19; fiduciary obligations 21; institutional investors 16; investment management industry 58–9; overview 58, 429–30; path dependence 55; pension funds 58–9, 61, 121; policy environment 62; responsible investment 11, 19–20, 53, 58–67, 430–1, 585; retail investors 587; RI strategies *586*; shareholder resolutions 62
unit trusts *see* mutual funds
Unity Incorporation 108
universal ownership theory 4, 439, 445, 448, 450, 561–2, 599, 642
Universities Superannuation Scheme 436
University of Edinburgh: Department for Social Responsibility and Sustainability 463, 465, 473; divestment campaigns 462; divestment decisions 470; endowment funds 462–4, 469; ethical investment 464–5; institutional assessment of investment approach 465–73; investment decisions 463–5; investment view approach 471, *471*, 472; principles to inform decision making 467–8, *468*; shareholder activism 464; socially responsible investment (SRI) 465; Socially Responsible Investment Policy 464; social responsibility 462–4; stakeholders 466–7, *467*, 468–73; strategic investment options 469, *469*, 470; transparency and reporting 472; values and investment decisions 470–1
University of Edinburgh Development Trust 463
University of Hong Kong 192
U.S. Department of Labor 63, 566
U.S. Securities and Exchange Commission (SEC) 3, 20, 58, 65
US Social Investment Forum 583, 585
U.S. Supreme Court 21

vaccine bonds 210
Value of Everything 613–14, *614*, 615
VanCity 76, 79
Vanguard Group 527–8
VBDO *see* Dutch Association of Investors for Sustainable Development (VBDO)
venture capital: Israel 143; South Africa 105
Vestar Capital Partners 566
Vigeo Ratings 264, 266
VMS Luxinter Ethifond 289
Vnesheconombank 229, 231

Walden Asset Management 512
Wales *see* United Kingdom
Warsaw Institute of Banking 239
Warsaw Stock Exchange 234, 238–9, 241
water scarcity 596–7
Wellington 22
Wesley, John 474
Wilderness Society (Australia) 435–6, 442
workforce issues: diversity 556; health and human safety 557, 560; working conditions 557, 560
World Business Council for Sustainable Development (WBCSD) 545
WorldCom 570, 625

Xingye Green Investment Fund 169

Zambia, responsible investment 367
Zenith Ethical Fund 119